A HISTORY OF THE CRUSADES

Kenneth M. Setton, GENERAL EDITOR

A HISTORY OF THE CRUSADES

Kenneth M. Setton, GENERAL EDITOR

I The First Hundred Years

II The Later Crusades, 1189–1311

III The Fourteenth and Fifteenth Centuries

IV Civilization and Institutions

V Influence and Consequences, with Genealogies and Bibliography

VI An Atlas and Gazetteer of the Crusades

Volume II

THE LATER CRUSADES

1189-1311

The Four Tetrarchs, Venice

A HISTORY OF THE CRUSADES

KENNETH M. SETTON
GENERAL EDITOR

Volume II

THE LATER CRUSADES, 1189-1311

EDITED BY
ROBERT LEE WOLFF
AND
HARRY W. HAZARD

THE UNIVERSITY OF WISCONSIN PRESS
Madison, Milwaukee, and London, 1969

Published by
The University of Wisconsin Press
Box 1379, Madison, Wisconsin 53701

The University of Wisconsin Press, Ltd.
27–29 Whitfield Street, London, W.1

First Edition, 1962, University of Pennsylvania Press

Printed in the United States of America
Library of Congress Catalog Card Number 68–9837

Mirabile in oculis nostris

CONTENTS

Foreword xiii

Foreword to the Second Edition xv

Preface xvii

A Note on Transliteration and Nomenclature xix

Abbreviations xxiii

I The Norman Kingdom of Sicily and the Crusades 3
Helene Wieruszowski, The City College of New York

II The Third Crusade: Richard the Lionhearted and Philip Augustus 45
Sidney Painter† (The Johns Hopkins University)

III The Crusades of Frederick Barbarossa and Henry VI 87
Edgar N. Johnson, The University of Massachusetts

IV Byzantium and the Crusades, 1081–1204 123
Joan M. Hussey, Royal Holloway College, University of London

V The Fourth Crusade 153
Edgar H. McNeal† (The Ohio State University) and
Robert Lee Wolff, Harvard University

VI The Latin Empire of Constantinople, 1204–1261 187
Robert Lee Wolff, Harvard University

VII The Frankish States in Greece, 1204–1311 235
Jean Longnon, Bibliothèque de l'Institut de France

VIII The Albigensian Crusade 277
Austin P. Evans† (Columbia University)

IX The Children's Crusade 325
Norman P. Zacour, University of Toronto

X The Political Crusades of the Thirteenth Century 343
Joseph R. Strayer, Princeton University

XI The Fifth Crusade 377
Thomas C. Van Cleve, Bowdoin College

XII The Crusade of Frederick II 429
Thomas C. Van Cleve, Bowdoin College

XIII The Crusade of Theobald of Champagne and Richard of Cornwall, 1239–1241 463
Sidney Painter† (The Johns Hopkins University)

XIV The Crusades of Louis IX 487
Joseph R. Strayer, Princeton University

XV The Crusader States, 1192–1243 522
Mary Nickerson Hardwicke, Downey, California

XVI The Crusader States, 1243–1291 557
Sir Steven Runciman, London, England

XVII The Kingdom of Cyprus, 1191–1291 599
Elizabeth Chapin Furber, Philadelphia, Pennsylvania

XVIII The Kingdom of Cilician Armenia 630
Sirarpie Der Nersessian, Dumbarton Oaks, Washington, D.C.

XIX The Turks in Iran and Anatolia before the Mongol Invasions 661
Claude Cahen, University of Strasbourg

XX The Aiyūbids 693
Sir Hamilton A. R. Gibb, Harvard University

XXI The Mongols and the Near East 715
Claude Cahen, University of Strasbourg

XXII The Mamluk Sultans to 1293 735
Mustafa M. Ziada, University of Cairo

Important Dates and Events 759

Gazetteer and Note on Maps 763

Index 812

ILLUSTRATIONS

The Four Tetrarchs, from St. Mark's Square, Venice (Hirmer Fotoarchiv München) *frontispiece*

Frederick Barbarossa as a Crusader. Vatican MS Cat. 2002, f. 1 *page* 275

John II Comnenus and His Wife Irene. Mosaic Portraits from Hagia Sophia, South Gallery (The Byzantine Institute) *page* 521

The Battle of Hattin, from Matthew Paris, *Chronica Majora*. Corpus Christi College, Cambridge, MS 26, f. 279 (Courtauld Institute) *facing page* 606

Frankish Prisoners Freed from the Saracens, from Matthew Paris, *Chronica Majora*. Corpus Christi College, Cambridge, MS 16, f. 148 (Courtauld Institute) *facing page* 606

MAPS

facing page

1 Central Europe and the Mediterranean 3
2 Western Europe and the Mediterranean 42
3 The Latin States in 1189 45
4 The Near East during the Third Crusade, 1189–1192 87
5 The Crusade of 1197 122
6 The Straits and the Aegean 123
7 The Balkans under the Angeli, 1185–1204 153
8 The Balkans in 1216, at the Death of the Latin Emperor Henry 187
9 The Balkans in 1237, at the Death of John of Brienne 226
10 The Balkans in 1291, at the Fall of Acre 227
11 Frankish Greece 235
12 Languedoc and Central France 277
13 The Near East 377
14 The Fifth Crusade, 1218–1221 487
15 The Crusade of Louis IX, 1249–1250 487
16 Palestine 518
17 Northern Syria 521
18 The Latin States, 1192–1243 554
19 The Latin States, 1243–1291 557
20 Cyprus 607
21 Persia and Adjacent Regions 661
22 The Mongols in the Near East (to 1291) 732
23 The Mamluks in the Near East (to 1291) 735

FOREWORD

In a letter addressed to the Catholic clergy in the east on November 13, 1204, pope Innocent III wrote that the transfer of imperial power in Constantinople from the Greeks to the Latins was "the Lord's doing, and it is marvelous in our eyes."[1] His words are those of the psalmist (117:23), and well depict the wonder then felt in Christendom at the astonishing success of the Fourth Crusade. Considering the difficulties and delays we have encountered in getting out the present volume, the editors may well apply Innocent's sentiment to the conclusion of their own work. But we have other debts than those of a celestial nature. Professor Norman P. Zacour of Franklin and Marshall College has given us invaluable assistance in various ways in addition to translating Professor Cahen's two chapters (XIX and XXI) from French into English. We are much indebted to Dr. Elizabeth Chapin Furber, who very kindly translated M. Longnon's chapter (VII), also from French, besides undertaking for us a chapter (XVII), which the late Professor John L. LaMonte had been scheduled to write, on the history of his beloved Cyprus. Miss Margaret C. Nolan of the library staff of the University of Pennsylvania has kept the voluminous files relating to this *History of the Crusades*, done much typing, and read the galley proofs with imperturbable patience. More than a word of thanks is due Mr. Thomas Yoseloff, director of the University Press, who has cheerfully had type reset, and other things redone, to help us make this as good a volume as possible.

Death has unfortunately carried off two of our contributors, Professors Edgar H. McNeal and Sidney Painter, during the years we have been at work on this volume. The former never saw in print the chapter on which he collaborated. Professor Painter had the opportunity to correct his proofs.

If I may be permitted a personal note in this Foreword, it must be to thank my old friend and colleague, Professor Robert Lee Wolff, who first attacked the mountain of typescript with which we began this volume. He effected in remarkable fashion a reduction of the whole to manageable size. No less recognition is due Dr.

[1] Innocent III, *Epp.*, an. VII, no. 154 (*PL*, CCXV, col. 456A): ". . . a Domino factum est istud, et est mirabile in oculis nostris."

Harry W. Hazard, whose more than human ability to handle detail never fails to inspire me with awe for his skill as an editor. To him we owe also the maps, the gazetteer, and the index. For myself, I have done what I could to improve the work. Professor Wolff and Dr. Hazard would join me, however, in paying chief tribute to our contributors, whose generosity and forgiveness of our sins have been an education in themselves. It is not easy to receive your manuscript back from a board of editors reduced in size (with alien material added, because otherwise it would not appear in the volume), and be told that this is the way the editors want to publish it. Certain of our contributors will understand our deep appreciation of their courtesy and forbearance. We have lost two or three contributors along the way for one reason or another, but to the stalwart crusaders in this volume who have helped us to march closer to the final goal, we would render a salute with full panoply of arms.

The general structure of our projected *History* has been outlined briefly in the Foreword to the first volume. There remain three volumes to come, and there will be further delay in getting them out. But we will get them out, for the editors will persist regardless of the obstacles.

KENNETH M. SETTON

[*University of Pennsylvania, 1962*]

FOREWORD TO THE SECOND EDITION

There is a universal assumption that an historical work should have a foreword as well as an index. The need for the latter is abundantly clear, and I yield again to the categorical imperative in supplying a foreword to the second edition of Volumes I and II. In fact I am very glad of the opportunity to express my gratitude to President Fred Harvey Harrington of the University of Wisconsin for his willingness to take over the *History of the Crusades* from the University of Pennsylvania, which published the first edition of these volumes. The University of Wisconsin Press will publish the remainder of the work.

Republication of the present two volumes has made possible the complete redoing of the maps by the University of Wisconsin Cartographic Laboratory under the direction of Professor Randall D. Sale, whose labors have been lightened by the continued cooperation of Dr. Harry W. Hazard, my fellow crusader for many years. Moreover we now plan to add as a sixth volume to this work *An Atlas and Gazetteer of the Crusades*, to be done by Dr. Hazard and Professor Sale.

The conscientious efforts of Mr. Thompson Webb, Jr., director of the University of Wisconsin Press, and his vigilant staff have made the production of the second edition a painless process, painless at least for me if not for them. I want them to know how grateful I am. Special acknowledgment must be made of the help of Professor C. Julian Bishko of the University of Virginia, who revised the first part of Volume I, Chapter II, on the Spanish *reconquista* before 1095.

We have been able to correct a few slips in these volumes, typographical and otherwise, as well as to augment the gazetteers which accompany the maps. The Wisconsin Press has also effected other improvements of style and format.

KENNETH M. SETTON

The Institute for Advanced Study
Princeton, New Jersey
July 2, 1968

PREFACE

The second volume of this work now lies before us at last. As the editors of volume I promised and warned, the narrative continues the account there set forth. It begins essentially with the critical events of 1189, and carries on through the tumultuous decades of the thirteenth century to various suitable stopping points a hundred years or so beyond the start. Only occasionally — as in the first chapter, on the Normans, the fourth, on Byzantium, and the eighteenth, on Armenia — will the reader find any considerable retrospect into the earlier twelfth century, and this the authors always undertake with an eye to the events of the late twelfth or thirteenth. In these cases we try to pick up at their point of origin threads which, in the course of time, wove themselves into the later fabric of events.

Once the operations of Richard the Lionhearted and Philip Augustus have been completed, and those of Frederick Barbarossa and Henry VI brought to their abortive ends, we focus our attention upon the Byzantine empire, against which Henry, like so many of his Norman predecessors, had planned to sail. With the tragic and controversial Fourth Crusade, the whole crusading enterprise changes its complexion, as Christians overturn a Christian empire, and found new states upon its dismembered territories — a development that not only effectively destroys the hope of Christian unity against the Moslems and sets Greek against Latin, but also divides the efforts of the western Europeans themselves, who must now protect and support, defend and reinforce both their establishments in the Levant and those in lands formerly Byzantine. This dispersal of effort and frittering away of resources is further enhanced as the popes of the thirteenth century begin to use the crusade first as an instrument against the Albigensian heretics in their own western European world, and then as a weapon in their private political quarrels.

Yet the efforts against the Moslems continue, of course, and once we have chronicled these various thirteenth-century perversions of the crusading undertaking, we move east once more for the operations of Pelagius and John of Brienne in Egypt, for the spectacular diplomatic triumphs of Frederick II (their lustre dimmed by the hostility of the papacy), for the peculiar performance of the westerners in the years 1239–1241, and for the mighty but ineffectual efforts of Louis IX, perhaps the only real crusader that ever existed, and certainly the last. We close the volume with a series of eight chapters considering all these events from the point of view of the easterners themselves and in connection with their own domestic history: first of the Christians now domiciled in the crusader states and on Cyprus, and of the Armenians of Cilicia, and then of the Moslems: Turks, Aiyūbids, Mongols, and Mamluks.

The brave reader who sits down and reads the book straight through will sometimes encounter the same military operation or diplomatic negotiation discussed twice or even oftener. Let him remember that the editors and authors planned it that way: in part because we have striven to see around events where possible, by treating them from all the points of view made identifiable by the sources. Our hypothetical consecutive reader at times may feel, as the editors have felt, often to their anguish, that he is confronted by an almost intolerable dose of marching and countermarching. As he swallows it, let him consider that this is what chiefly interested the medieval writers on whose accounts scholars must so largely depend.

But behind the dust clouds raised by the trampling hooves, let the thoughtful reader notice the flashes by whose light we gain insight into the motives and character of human beings: the giants, like Innocent III or Frederick II or St. Louis, often glimpsed in unfamiliar aspects of their careers; the lesser-known but often arrestingly attractive or repulsive figures, like the Sicilian admiral George of Antioch, the Latin emperor Henry of Constantinople, John of Brienne, Baybars; or even, in rare cases, the *menus gens*. Explicitly in the chapter on the Children's Crusade, and implicitly in many other places, the reader will find himself looking at the evidence for the pathology of religious emotion; if he reflects on these data he may discover that he is leaving the Middle Ages altogether and considering later chiliastic movements, the delusions of crowds, or even the essential nature of human piety. He can single out the few moments of heroism or disinterested nobility that contrast the more sharply with the long chronicle of greed, stupidity, treachery, duplicity, and incompetence. He can ponder the lasting effects of the actions here described — not least perhaps those of the permanent breach between western and Orthodox Christians. And if he does indeed avail himself of these privileges, we hope he may come to regard our shortcomings with a tolerant eye.

ROBERT LEE WOLFF

[*Harvard University, 1962*]

A NOTE ON TRANSLITERATION AND NOMENCLATURE

One of the obvious problems to be solved by the editors of such a work as this, intended both for general readers and for scholars in many different disciplines, is how to render the names of persons and places, and a few other terms, originating in languages and scripts unfamiliar to the English-speaking reader and, indeed, to most readers whose native languages are European. In the present volume, and presumably in the entire work, these comprise principally Arabic, Turkish, Persian, and Armenian, none of which was normally written in our Latin alphabet until its adoption by Turkey in 1928. The analogous problem of Byzantine Greek names and terms has been handled by using the familiar Latin equivalents, Anglicized Greek, or, occasionally, Greek type, as has seemed appropriate in each instance, but a broader approach is desirable for the other languages under consideration.

The somewhat contradictory criteria applied are ease of recognition and readability on the one hand, and scientific accuracy and consistency on the other. It has proved possible to reconcile these, and to standardize the great variety of forms in which identical names have been submitted to us by different contributors, through constant consultation with specialists in each language, research in the sources, and adherence to systems conforming to the requirements of each language.

Of these Arabic presents the fewest difficulties, since the script in which it is written is admirably suited to the classical language. The basic system used, with minor variants, by all English-speaking scholars was restudied and found entirely satisfactory, with the slight modifications noted. The chief alternative system, in which every Arabic consonant is represented by a single Latin character (t̲ for th, ḫ for kh, d̲ for dh, š for sh, ġ for gh) was rejected for several reasons, needless proliferation of diacritical marks to bother the eye and multiply occasions for error, absence of strong countervailing arguments, and, most decisively, the natural tendency of non-specialists to adopt these spellings but omit the diacritical marks. The use of single letters in this manner leads to undesirable results, but the spellings adopted for the present work may be thus treated with confidence by any writer not requiring the discriminations which the remaining diacritical marks indicate.

The letters used for Arabic consonants, in the order of the Arabic alphabet, are these: ', b, t, th, j, ḥ, kh, d, dh, r, z, s, sh, ṣ, ḍ, ṭ, ẓ, ', gh, f, q, k, l, m, n, h, w, y. The vowels are a, i, u, lengthened as ā, ī, ū, with the *alif bi-ṣūrati-l-yā'* distinguished as â; initial ' is omitted, but terminal macrons are retained. Diphthongs are *au* and *ai*, not *aw* and *ay*, as being both philologically preferable and visually less misleading. The same considerations lead to the omission of *l* of *al-* before a duplicated consonant (Nūr-ad-Dīn rather than Nūr-al-Dīn). As in this example, hyphens are used to link words composing a single name (as also 'Abd-Allāh), with weak initial vowels elided (as Abū-l-Ḥasan). Normally *al-* (meaning "the") is not capitalized; *ibn-* is not when it means literally "son of", but is otherwise (as Ibn-Khaldūn).

Some readers may be disconcerted to find the prophet called "Mohammed" and his followers "Moslems", but this can readily be justified. These spellings are valid English proper names, derived from Arabic originals which would be correctly transliterated "Muḥammad" and "Muslimūn" or "Muslimīn". The best criterion for deciding whether to use the Anglicized spellings or the accurate transliterations is the treatment accorded the third of this cluster of names, that of the religion "Islam". Where this is transliterated "Islām", with a macron over the *a*, it should be accompanied by "Muslim" and "Muḥammad", but where the macron is omitted consistency and common sense require "Moslem" and "Mohammed", and it is the latter triad which have been considered appropriate in this work. All namesakes of the prophet, however, have had their names duly transliterated "Muḥammad", to correspond with names of other Arabs who are not individually so familiar to westerners as to be better recognized in Anglicized forms.

All names of other Arabs, and of non-Arabs with Arabic names, have been systematically transliterated, with the single exception of Ṣalāḥ-ad-Dīn, whom it would have been pedantic to call that rather than Saladin. For places held, in the crusading era or now, by Arabs the Arabic names appear either in the text or in the gazetteer, where some additional ones are also included to broaden the usefulness of this feature.

Large numbers of names of persons and groups, however, customarily found in Arabicized spellings because they were written in Arabic script, have been restored to their underlying identity whenever this is ascertainable. For example, Arabic "Saljūq" misrepresents four of the six component phonemes: *s* is correct, *a* replaces Turkish *e*, for which Arabic script provides no equivalent, *l* is correct, *j* replaces the non-Arabic *ch*, *ū* substitutes a non-Turkish long *u* for the original *ü*, and *q* as distinguished from *k* is non-existent in Turkish; this quadruple rectification yields "Selchük" as the name of the eponymous leader, and "Selchükid" — on the model of 'Abbāsid and Timurid — for the dynasty and the people.

It might be thought that as Turkish is now written in a well conceived modified Latin alphabet, there would be no reason to alter this, and this presumption is substantially valid. For the same reasons as apply to Arabic, *ch* has been preferred above *ç*, *sh* above *ş*, and *gh* above *ğ*, with *kh* in a few instances given as a preferred alternate of *h*, from which it is not distinguished in modern Turkish. No long vowels have been indicated, as being functionless survivals. Two other changes have been made in the interest of the English-speaking reader, and should be remembered by those using map sheets and standard reference works: *c* (pronounced dj) has been changed to *j*, so that one is not visually led to imagine that the Turkish name for the Tigris — Dijle/Dicle — rhymes with "tickle", and what the eminent lexicographer H. C. Hony terms "that abomination the undotted ı" has, after the model of *The Encyclopaedia of Islām*, been written i̊.

Spellings, modified as above indicated, have usually been founded on those of the Turkish edition, *İslâm Ansiklopedisi*, hampered by occasional inconsistencies within that work. All names of Turks appear thus emended, and Turkish equivalents of almost all places within or near modern Turkey appear in the gazetteer.

In addition to *kh*, Middle Turkish utilized a few other phonemes not common in modern Turkish: *zh* (modern *j*), *dh*, *ng*, and *ä* (modern *e*); the first three of these will be used as needed, while the last-mentioned may be assumed to underlie every medieval Turkish name now spelled with *e*. Plaintive eyebrows may be raised at our exclusion of *q*, but this was in Middle Turkish only the alternate spelling used when the sound *k* was combined with back instead of front vowels, and its elimination by the Turks is commendable.

Persian names have been transliterated like Arabic with certain modifications, chiefly use of the additional vowels *e* and *o* and replacing *ḍ* and *dh* with *ẓ̧* and *z̲*, so that Arabic "Ādharbaijān" becomes Persian "Āz̲erbaijān", more accurate as well as more recognizable. Omission of the definite article from personal names was considered but eventually disapproved.

Armenian presented great difficulties: the absence of an authoritative reference source for spelling names, the lack of agreement on transliteration, and the sound-shift by which classical and eastern Armenian *b*, *d*, *g* became western Armenian *p*, *t*, *k* and — incredible as it may seem to the unwary — *vice versa*; similar reciprocal interchanges involved *ts* and *dz*, and *ch* and *j*. The following alphabet represents western Armenian letters, with eastern variants in parentheses: a, p (b), k (g), t (d), e, z, ē, i̊, ṭ, zh, i, l, kh, dz (ts), g (k), h, ts (dz), gh, j (ch), m, y, n, sh, o, c̮h, b (p), ch (j), ṛ, s, ṿ, d (t), r, t̮s, u or v, ṗ, ḳ, ō, f. Many spellings are based on the Armenian texts in the *Recueil des historiens des croisades*.

In standardizing names of groups, the correct root forms in the respective languages have been hopefully identified, with the ending "-id" for dynasties and their peoples but "-ite" for sects, and with plural either identical with singular (as Kirghiz) or plus "-s" (Khazars) or "-es" (Uzes). In cases where this sounded hopelessly awkward, it was abandoned (Muwaḥḥids, not Muwaḥḥidids or Muwaḥḥidites and certainly not Almohads, which is, however, cross-referenced).

The use of place names is explained in the note preceding the gazetteer, but may be summarized by saying that in general the most familiar correct form is used in the text and maps, normally an English version of the name by which the place was known to Europeans during the crusades. Variant forms are given and identified in the gazetteer.

Despite conscientious efforts to perfect the nomenclature, errors will probably be detected by specialists; they are to be blamed on me and not on individual contributors or editorial colleagues, for I have been accorded a free hand. Justifiable suggestions for improvements will be welcomed, and used to bring succeeding volumes nearer that elusive goal, impeccability in nomenclature.

Harry W. Hazard

[*Princeton, New Jersey, 1962*]

Reprinted from Volume I, with minor modifications.

ABBREVIATIONS

AHR *American Historical Review*, I (1895) and ff.

BAS Michele Amari, *Biblioteca arabo-sicula*, versione italiana, 2 vols., Turin and Rome, 1880–1881.

CSHB *Corpus scriptorum historiae byzantinae*, eds. B. G. Niebuhr, Imm. Bekker, and others, 50 vols., Bonn, 1828–1897.

FSI *Fonti per la storia d'Italia*, 91 vols., Rome, 1887–1946 (?).

Hist. Zeitschr. *Historische Zeitschrift*, I (1859) and ff.

MGH *Monumenta Germaniae historica*, eds. G. H. Pertz, T. Mommsen, and others, Reichsinstitut für ältere deutsche Geschichtskunde, Hanover, 1826 and ff. [*SS* = *Scriptores*, etc.].

MGH, SSRG *Monumenta Germaniae historica . . . Scriptores rerum germanicarum*, new series, 10 vols., 1922 and ff.

PG *Patrologiae graecae cursus completus . . .*, ed. J.-P. Migne, 161 vols., Paris, 1857 and ff.

PL *Patrologiae latinae cursus completus . . .*, ed. J.-P. Migne, 221 vols., Paris, 1844 and ff.

RHC *Recueil des historiens des croisades*, Académie des inscriptions et belles-lettres, Paris, 16 vols. in fol., 1841–1906:

- *Arm.* *Documents arméniens*, 2 vols., 1869–1906.
- *Grecs* *Historiens grecs*, 2 vols., 1875–1881.
- *Lois* *Assises de Jérusalem*, 2 vols., 1841–1843.
- *Occ.* *Historiens occidentaux*, 5 vols., 1841–1895.
- *Or.* *Historiens orientaux: Arabes*, 5 vols., 1872–1906.

RHGF *Recueil des historiens des Gaules et de la France*, ed. Martin Bouquet [1685–1754] and others, 24 vols. in fol., Paris, 1738–1904.

RISS *Rerum italicarum scriptores . . .*, ed. L. A. Muratori [1672–1750], 25 vols. in 28, Milan, 1723–1751; new edition by G. Carducci and V. Fiorini, Città di Castello, 1900 and ff.

ROL *Revue de l'Orient Latin*, 12 vols., Paris, 1893–1911.

Rolls Series *Rerum britanicarum medii aevi scriptores: The Chronicles and Memorials of Great Britain and Ireland during the Middle Ages*, 244 vols., London, 1858–1896.

Volume II

THE LATER CRUSADES

1189-1311

1. Central Europe and the Mediterranean (*Map by the University of Wisconsin Cartographic Laboratory*)

I

THE NORMAN KINGDOM OF SICILY AND THE CRUSADES

There was much in the geography, resources, and traditions of the Norman kingdom of Sicily in the twelfth century to recommend it as a valuable bulwark of the crusades. Armies bound for Constantinople could use its Adriatic ports for the passage to Durazzo (Dyrrachium) or Avlona, whence they could take the Via Egnatia to

On the sources for the history of the Normans in Italy, see F. Chalandon, *Histoire de la domination normande en Italie et en Sicile* (2 vols., Paris, 1907), I, introduction. A more recent survey may be found in P. Kehr, *Italia Pontificia*, VIII (Berlin, 1935), 1–5. The following are the most important general accounts of southern Italy in the Norman period: Falco of Benevento, *Chronicon de rebus aetate sua gestis* (ed. G. Del Re, *Cronisti e scrittori*, I [Naples, 1845], 161–252; for other editions, see Chalandon, *Domination normande*, I, xli–xlvi; on Falco, the only native historian with an outright hostility to the Norman dynasty, see E. Gervasio, "Falcone Beneventano e la sua cronica," *Bolletino dell' Istituto Storico Italiano*, LIV [1939], 1–128); Alexander of Telese, *De rebus gestis Rogerii Siciliae regis* (ed. G. Del Re, *Cronisti e scrittori*, I, 85–146); Hugo Falcandus, *Liber de regno Siciliae* (ed. G. B. Siragusa, *FSI*, XXII [Rome, 1897]; on Falco of Benevento, Alexander of Telese, and Hugo Falcandus, see A. Pagano, *Studi di letteratura latina medievale* [Nicotera, 1931]; and on the possibility that Hugo was the admiral Eugenius, see E. Jamison, *Admiral Eugenius of Sicily . . . and the Authorship of . . . "Historia Hugonis Falcandi Siculi"* [London, 1957], pp. 233–277; but compare review by Lynn White, Jr., in *AHR*, LXIII [1957–1958], 645–647); Romuald Guarna of Salerno, *Chronicon* (ed. C. A. Garufi, *RISS*, VII, 1914–1935); and Peter of Eboli, *De rebus Siculis carmen* (ed. E. Rota, *RISS*, XXXI, 1904). Of the annalistic works written in southern Italy, the most important are: *Annales Cavenses* and *Annales Beneventani* (*MGH, SS.*, III); Lupus Protospatarius Barensis, *Rerum gestarum breve chronicon* (*MGH, SS.*, V); *Petri Diaconi chronica monasterii Casinensis* (*MGH, SS.*, VII); *Annales Casinenses* and *Annales Ceccanenses* (*MGH, SS.*, XIX). Other sources will be cited below. The Arabic sources relating to Sicily are collected and translated by M. Amari, *Biblioteca arabo-sicula* (2 vols., Turin and Rome, 1880–1881), hereafter referred to as *BAS*.

Works of comprehensive character, or dealing with background problems for the whole period covered in this chapter, are: M. Amari, *Storia dei musulmani di Sicilia* (2nd ed. revised by the author and ed. by C. A. Nallino, 3 vols., Catania, 1933–1939); Chalandon, *Domination normande*; C. H. Haskins, *The Normans in European History* (Boston, 1915), chaps. VII, VIII; *idem*, "England and Sicily in the Twelfth Century," *English Historical Review*, XXVI (1911), 433–447, 641–665; W. Cohn, *Das Zeitalter der Normannen in Sizilien* (Bonn and Leipzig, 1920); J. B. Villars, *Les Normands en Méditerranée* (Paris, 1951); *idem*, "I Normanni dalle origini," *Archivio storico siciliano*, ser. 3, IV (1950–1951), 399–413; K. A. Kehr, "Die Belehnungen der süditalienischen Normannenfürsten durch die Päpste (1059–1192)," *Abhandlungen der preussischen Akademie der Wissenschaften*, Phil.-hist. Kl. (1934), no. 1; *Il Regno normanno* (Conferenze tenute in Palermo per l'VIII centenario dell' incoronazione di Ruggero a Re di Sicilia, Messina and Milan, 1932); C. Cahen, *Le Régime*

Thessalonica and Constantinople.[1] From the ports of the east coast of Sicily, crusaders could reach Syria and Palestine by the shortest route. And since the northern tip of Tunisia was less than a hundred miles distant from its southwestern corner, the kingdom might even take up the fight against Islam in Africa. Furthermore, Sicily was rich in resources: the soil was fruitful, and the proceeds of commerce and industry large. Its kings, should they care to do so, could

féodal de l'Italie normande (Paris, 1940); E. Besta, *Il Diritto pubblico nell' Italia meridionale* (Padua, 1939); H. Niese, *Die Gesetzgebung der normannischen Dynastie im 'Regnum Siciliae'* (Halle, 1910); E. Jamison, *The Norman Administration of Apulia and Capua, more especially under Roger II and William I, 1127–1166* (Papers of the British School at Rome, VI, Rome, 1913); F. Ciccaglione, "La Vita economica siciliana nel periodo normanno-suevo, "*Archivio storico per la Sicilia orientale,* X (1913), 321–345; G. Coniglio, "Amalfi e il commercio Amalfitano," *Nuova rivista storica,* XXVIII–XXIX (1944–1945), 100–114; A. de Stefano, "La Cultura in Sicilia nel periodo normanno," in *Il Regno normanno*, pp. 127–194; F. Giunta, *Bizantini e bizantinismo nell' Sicilia normanna* (Palermo, 1950); and L. T. White, *Latin Monasticism in Norman Sicily* (Cambridge, Mass., 1938). Various aspects of the history of the kingdom of Sicily are presented in the voluminous *Atti del Convegno internazionale di studi ruggeriani* (VIII Centenario della morte di Ruggero II, 2 vols., Palermo, 1955), and in *Studi medievali in onore di A. de Stefano* (Palermo, 1956).

Among works on king Roger II, founder of the dynasty, the only one of independent scholarly value is E. Caspar, *Roger II. (1101–1154) und die Gründung der normannisch-sizilischen Monarchie* (Innsbruck, 1904). While Caspar's mastery of the sources is unsurpassed, his interpretation suffers from an overemphasis on power politics, typical of the German scholars of his generation. An appendix of *Regesten* is added to the work (pp. 481–580), which has been supplemented by P. Colluri, "Appendice al regesto dei diplomi di re Ruggero compilato da E. Caspar," *Atti del Convegno di studi ruggeriani,* II, 545–626. E. Curtis, *Roger of Sicily and the Normans in Lower Italy* (New York, 1912) is richly documented but not always reliable. On Roger see also E. Pontieri, "I Normanni e la fondazione del regno di Sicilia," and P. S. Leicht, "Lo Stato normanno " (both in *Il Regno normanno,* pp. 1–52); Pontieri's study has been republished in his *Tra i Normanni nell' Italia meridionale* (Naples, 1948). C. A. Garufi, "Ruggiero II e la fondazione della monarchia di Sicilia," *Archivio storico siciliano,* LII (1932), 1–33, is valuable mainly because of its bibliography. See also W. Holtzmann, "Il Regno di Ruggero II e gli inizi di un sistema di stati europei," *Atti del Convegno di studi ruggeriani,* I, 29–45. For the reign of William I, see G. B. Siragusa, *Il Regno di Guglielmo I in Sicilia* (Palermo, 1929). The only existing monograph on William II, by I. La Lumia, *Storia della Sicilia sotto Guglielmo il Buono* (Florence, 1867), needs revision.

On the Mediterranean policy of the Norman kings, see F. Cerone, *L'Opera politica e militare di Ruggiero II in Africa ed in Oriente* (Catania, 1913); A. Cartellieri, *Der Vorrang des Papsttums zur Zeit der ersten Kreuzzüge* (Munich, 1941); and the works of G. M. Monti, *Il Mezzogiorno d'Italia nel medioevo* (Bari, 1930), *L'Italia e le crociate in Terra Santa* (Naples, 1940), and *La Espansione mediterranea del mezzogiorno d'Italia e della Sicilia* (Bologna, 1942). Of these, the last is the most important. Monti's views are stimulating but his references to sources are not always accurate. See also R. Cessi, "Il Problema adriatico al tempo di Ruggero II," *Atti del Convegno di studi ruggeriani,* I, 53–72; O. Vehse, "Die Normannen im Mittelmeer," *Die Welt als Geschichte,* V (1939), 25–58, 233–276; and H. Hochholzer, "Sizilien als Beispiel der mittelmeerischen Kulturschichtung," *Hist. Zeitschr.*, CLV (1937), 1–27.

On the Sicilian navy, see C. Manfroni, *Storia della marina italiana dalle invasioni barbariche al trattato di Ninfeo* (Leghorn, 1899), and W. Cohn, *Die Geschichte der normannisch-sicilischen Flotte unter der Regierung Rogers I. und Rogers II.* (Breslau, 1910).

[1] See H. Hagenmeyer's notes to *Anonymi gesta Francorum* (Heidelberg, 1890), pp. 135–137. On the geographical conditions, see S. Runciman, *A History of the Crusades* (3 vols., Cambridge, 1951–1954), II, 251; Villars, *Les Normands en Méditerranée*, pp. 191–192; A. v. Hofmann, *Das Land Italien und seine Geschichte* (Stuttgart and Berlin, 1921), chs. XIII, XIV; Vehse, "Die Normannen im Mittelmeer," *Die Welt als Geschichte*, V, 151 ff.; and Hochholzer, "Sizilien als Beispiel der mittelmeerischen Kulturschichtung," *Hist. Zeitschr.*, CLV, 7 ff.

place at the disposal of crusaders a large navy and merchant marine, and could provide markets, equip expeditions with money and grain, and keep the armies and colonies in the east supplied with materials and men. The cosmopolitan population of Sicily, with its Greek and oriental elements, had much to contribute to the knowledge and understanding of the religions, languages, and customs of the east, and in general could serve as a bridge between east and west. And yet, the promise inherent in all this was only partly fulfilled. The Second Crusade would come and go without Roger II, the first king of Sicily, and the contributions of his grandson William II to the Third Crusade would be canceled out by his death in 1189.

Not that Sicily lacked a strong crusading heritage. Six members of the house of Hauteville had gone on the First Crusade. Two of them, Bohemond, son of Robert Guiscard, and his nephew Tancred, had written brilliant pages in its history and in that of "Outremer". For a time, Bohemond's leadership in the First Crusade was unrivaled. When he returned to Europe in 1104 to seek help for the principality of Antioch, he was hailed in Italy and France as the hero of the Crusade, and great contingents of Christian knights enlisted in the expedition which he planned to lead through Greece to assault Constantinople. Roger II, then in his early teens and still under the regency of his mother Adelaide, watched this new "crusade" get under way. Admittedly, Bohemond's saga came to an abrupt end with his surrender to emperor Alexius I Comnenus. Yet he may well have impressed his young cousin as a model of shrewdness and bravery.

Bohemond's actions directed the eyes of the Norman princes of Sicily toward the conquest of the Byzantine empire. Within a quarter-century, in the campaigns of Robert Guiscard and Bohemond's attack in 1107–1108, the Normans twice had bid for Constantinople, and twice had failed. The Byzantine emperors, of course, had never even recognized Norman rule over Apulia, much less tolerated any Norman expansion into the eastern Mediterranean. They suspected Norman aims, and plotted against them in Italy and Antioch alike. Thus the ambition to seize Constantinople itself, inherited from Guiscard and Bohemond, involved great danger, despite the fact that the project of a "crusade" against the Byzantines appealed to many western Europeans and sometimes received the approval of the pope.[2]

[2] On Bohemond's last war with the Byzantine empire, see volume I of this work, chapter XII, pp. 390–391 (bibliography in note 30); also Monti, *La Espansione mediterranea*, pp. 58–60.

On the other hand, the political tradition that Roger II inherited from his father, count Roger I of Sicily, was quite different from that of the Apulian and Antiochene members of his house. To be sure, contemporaries looked on Roger I as a true crusader. Pope Urban II may have invited him to participate in the First Crusade in 1089 at Troina.[3] But the count could not afford to strain the loyalty of his Saracen subjects by sharing in such a great Christian enterprise against Islam. Besides, he had more immediate and pressing cares. He was primarily concerned to heal the scars of war in Sicily, to repopulate the island and revive its economy. In at least one case we know of, he even persuaded some pilgrims, passing through Sicily on their way to Palestine, to stay and settle on land that he granted them.[4] When the First Crusade was getting under way, count Roger was busy helping his nephew duke Roger Borsa, who had succeeded his father Robert Guiscard, to quell the rebellions of his Apulian vassals and cities. It was during one of these joint actions, at the siege of Amalfi in 1096, that the Norman princes, Bohemond among them, first encountered crusaders. Bohemond and many another young man in their armies took the cross. Deserted by the majority of their knights, the two Rogers "sadly" lifted the siege and returned to their respective lands. There was no doubt about their unwillingness to participate in any common enterprise against the "infidels". Indeed, count Roger of Sicily did not even believe in the religious ideal of the crusades.[5]

[3] K. Erdmann, *Die Entstehung des Kreuzzugsgedankens* (Stuttgart, 1935), pp. 296 ff. Erdmann believes that at the meeting of Troina Urban proposed that Roger accompany him to Constantinople and participate in the war against the Turks. On Urban's negotiations with Constantinople, see volume I of the present work, chapter VII, p. 226.

[4] The document is printed in K. A. Kehr, *Die Urkunden der normannisch-sicilischen Könige*, no. 2 (1085?), p. 410. See Caspar, *Roger II*, p. 13. It is believed that Roger I started the policy of settling "Lombards" (Italians) on the island. It was continued throughout the twelfth and part of the thirteenth centuries. See Chalandon, *Domination normande*, I, 349, and Amari, *Storia dei musulmani di Sicilia*, III, 223–231.

[5] For the scene at Amalfi, see G. Malaterra, *De rebus gestis Rogerii Calabriae et Siciliae comitis et Roberti Guiscardi ducis*, IV, 24 (ed. E. Pontieri, *RISS*, V, 1927), p. 102; also *Anonymi gesta Francorum*, IV (ed. Hagenmeyer), p. 152: "Coepit tunc ad eum [Bohemundum] vehementer concurrere maxima pars militum, qui erant in obsidione illa adeo ut Rogerius comes pene solus remanserit reversusque Siciliam dolebat et maerebat quandoque gentem amittere suam." In this version, Roger Borsa is not mentioned; see Caspar, *Roger II*, p. 14, and E. Pontieri, "I Normanni dell' Italia meridionale e la prima crociata," *Archivio storico italiano*, CXIV (1956), 1 ff. Ibn-al-Athīr tells us that count Roger rejected a crusading proposal on the grounds that this would ruin his trade with the Moslems of Africa: *Al-kāmil fī-t-ta'rikh . . . [Perfection in History . . .]* (Amari, *BAS*, 1), pp. 450–452; cf. Amari, *Storia dei musulmani*, III, 192–193. Giunta (*Medioevo mediterraneo*, p. 88) points out that the crusade had no part in Sicilian tradition; much later, when Henry VI planned his crusade, it was purely a German venture, looked upon by the Sicilians only as a means of their being exploited. Compare Cerone, *L'Opera . . . di Ruggiero II in Africa ed in Oriente*, p. 10.

If the old count's attitude had prevailed after his death in 1101, his widow Adelaide would not have fallen into the trap when in 1113 wily politicians invited her to marry king Baldwin I of Jerusalem.[6] No one seems to have warned her that the whole purpose of the project was to acquire her immense dowry, and eventually the wealth of her son, in order to put the poverty-stricken kingdom on a sounder financial footing. Three years later, when Adelaide's dowry was exhausted and the marriage had proved barren, she was repudiated on the pretext that Baldwin's previous divorce, and therefore his marriage with Adelaide, had been illegal. Baldwin's vassals did not wish Jerusalem to become a dependency of the county of Sicily or to be ruled by an absentee prince. The queen returned to Sicily humiliated, and died shortly thereafter. Her son Roger II, who according to the marriage contract should have inherited Jerusalem, naturally conceived an "eternal hatred" of the kingdom and its people.

The failure to acquire Jerusalem was more than compensated for elsewhere: in Africa eventually, but more immediately on the Italian mainland. In August 1127 duke William of Apulia, son of Roger Borsa and last male successor of Robert Guiscard in the direct line, died, whereupon Roger II crossed the strait of Messina with an army and marched on Apulia to claim it as his "heritage". In one victorious battle after another he forced pope Honorius II and the barons and cities of Apulia and Calabria to submit and to recognize him. Soon the contested papal election of 1130 gave Roger a splendid opportunity. One of the two competing popes, the schismatic Pierleone, Anacletus II, turned to Roger for assistance against his rival, Innocent II, who was supported by Bernard of Clairvaux and, through Bernard's influence, by the kings and most of the princes and churches of the west. In return for a pledge of support, Anacletus granted Roger in hereditary right the title and dignity of king of Sicily and of Calabria and Apulia (often summed up as "Italy"). On Christmas day 1130, in the presence of the magnates of his lands and with the pomp befitting a ruler of Sicily, Roger was crowned by a representative of Anacletus in the cathedral of Palermo, the city "which in the days of old had been

[6] William of Tyre, *Historia*, XI, 29 (*RHC, Occ.*, I), pp. 505–506. For the sources on Adelaide's marriage, see H. Hagenmeyer's notes to Fulcher of Chartres, *Historia Hierosolymitana* (Heidelberg, 1913), pp. 576–577. Compare R. Röhricht, *Geschichte des Königreichs Jerusalem* (Innsbruck, 1898), pp. 103, 113, 118; Runciman, *Crusades*, II, 102–105; and volume I of the present work, chapter XII, pp. 406–407; also E. Pontieri, "La Madre di re Ruggero, Adelaide del Vasto, contessa di Sicilia, regina di Gerusalemme," *Atti del Convegno di studi ruggeriani*, II, 422–432.

the seat of kings." [7] Although the title was later changed to emphasize the original divisions of Norman Italy, and the papal right to the investiture of each of them (*regnum Siciliae*, *ducatus Apuliae*, *et principatus Capuae*), Christmas day of 1130 foreshadows the later kingdom of the Two Sicilies.

In the decade following, Roger had to fight against all the powers that saw themselves threatened by the rise of a great new territorial state in the heart of the Mediterranean: the pope, the German and Byzantine emperors, and the three maritime republics of northern Italy—Venice, Genoa, and Pisa.[8] Fortunately for Roger, coöperation among his enemies was seriously hampered by con-

[7] For Anacletus's bull of September 27, 1130, see Jaffé-Löwenfeld, *Regesta pontificum Romanorum*, no. 8411; Caspar, *Roger II*, Regesten, no. 65. The full grant includes the honor of Naples and military help from the population of Benevento. On Roger's obligations, see Jaffé-Löwenfeld, no. 8413. On the coronation, see Caspar, *Roger II*, pp. 96 f., and Chalandon, *Domination normande*, II, 7 ff. The fact that the house of Hauteville owed the royal title originally to a deal with the papacy, and with a schismatic pope at that, was glossed over by later south Italian historians. Only Falco of Benevento mentions the negotiations with Anacletus: see his *Chronicon*, ad ann. 1129 (*Cronisti e scrittori*, I, 201). Another difficulty was the Moslem tradition implicit in the choice of Palermo as capital. Compare the somewhat obscure statement by Alexander of Telese, *De rebus gestis Rogerii*, II, 1 (*Cronisti e scrittori*, I, 101–102) about Palermo "quae olim sub priscis temporibus, super hanc ipsam provinciam Reges nonnullos habuisse traditur quae postea, pluribus evolutis annis, occulto Dei disponente judicio nunc usque sine Regibus mansit." To make the title appear more legitimate, stories about a second coronation were invented, among them that of Roger's coronation by Louis VII of France upon his return from the Second Crusade, which is accepted by Virginia Berry (volume I of the present work, chapter XV, p. 511). It is found in one of the many interpolations in Romuald Guarna of Salerno's *Chronicon* (*RISS*, VII), p. 218.

[8] The main sources for Roger's foreign policy before and during the Second Crusade are: Otto of Freising, *Chronicon* (ed. A. Hofmeister, Hanover, 1912); *Gesta Friderici I* (ed. G. Waitz, Hanover, 1912); John of Salisbury, *Historia pontificalis* (ed. R. L. Poole, Oxford, 1927); *Annalista Saxo* and *Sigeberti continuatio Praemonstratensis* (*MGH, SS.*, VI); *Canonici Wisegradensis continuatio Cosmae chronicae Bohemorum* (*MGH, SS.*, IX); *Annales Magdeburgenses*, *Annales Herbipolenses*, and *Annales Palidenses* (*MGH, SS.*, XVI); *Annales Erphesfurdenses* (ed. O. Holder-Egger, Hanover, 1899); *Historia Welforum Weingartensis* (ed. E. König in *Schwäbische Chroniken der Stauferzeit*, I [1937]; and *MGH, SS.*, XXI); *Sancti Bernardi epistolae* (*PL*, CLXXXII); *Petri abbatis Cluniacensis epistolae* (*PL*, CLXXXIX); William of Tyre, *Historia* (*RHC, Occ.*, I); Odo of Deuil, *De profectione Ludovici VII in orientem* (ed. and trans. V. G. Berry, New York, 1948); Romuald Guarna of Salerno, *Chronicon* (*RISS*, VII); *Historia ducum Veneticorum* (*MGH, SS.*, XIV); Andrea Dandolo, *Chronicon* (ed. E. Pastorello, *RISS*, XII, 1938 ff.); G. L. Tafel and G. M. Thomas, *Urkunden zur älteren Handels- und Staatsgeschichte der Republik Venedig* (*Fontes rerum Austriacarum*, Vienna, 1856–1857); and *Annales Cavenses* (*MGH, SS.*, III). Greek sources include John Cinnamus, *Epitome rerum ab Ioanne et Alexio Comnenis gestarum* (*CSHB*, Bonn, 1836), and Nicetas Choniates, *Historia* (*CSHB*, Bonn, 1835).

For secondary works, see Chalandon, *Domination normande*, II, chaps. I–IV; Caspar, *Roger II*, pp. 1–236, 328–394; W. Bernhardi, *Lothar von Supplinburg* (Leipzig, 1879), and *Konrad III.* (Leipzig, 1883); H. Bloch, "The Schism of Anacletus II and the Grandfeuil Forgeries of Peter the Deacon," *Traditio*, VIII (1952), 159–265; E. Vacandard, *Vie de Saint Bernard, abbé de Clairvaux* (2 vols., Paris, 1895); *idem*, "Saint Bernard et la seconde croisade," *Revue des questions historiques*, XXXVIII (1885), 398–457; E. Caspar, "Bernard von Clairvaux," *Meister der Politik* (3 vols., Stuttgart and Berlin, 1922–1923), III, 181–220; W. Williams, *Saint Bernard of Clairvaux* (Westminster, Md., 1952); E. Willems, "Cîteaux et la

flicting German, papal, and Byzantine claims to Apulia, and by the latent antagonism between Genoa and Pisa. It is more than likely that the failure of the Byzantines to support either the invading armies of the German emperor Lothair II or the simultaneous rebellion of the Apulian barons in 1137 saved the kingdom of Sicily from destruction. By July 1139 Roger had not only recovered all his Italian possessions lost in the course of the war, but had also defeated a papal army and extracted recognition of his kingdom and kingship from pope Innocent II by the peace of Mignano.[9] Bernard of Clairvaux, who had been the architect of the anti-Sicilian coalition, also made his peace with Roger. It was to be along lines laid down by Bernard, however, that the Byzantines and the refugee Apulian barons would plan a new political encirclement of the Sicilian king in the years 1140–1146, the period immediately preceding the Second Crusade.

In spite of his struggle to hold the Italian mainland, Roger had not allowed his Mediterranean objectives to slip from sight. At Merseburg in 1135, when the great coalition against Sicily was born, Venetian and Byzantine ambassadors complained to Lothair that the "count of Sicily" had attacked the coast of Greece, that Sicilian ships were preying on Venetian merchantmen and had despoiled them of goods worth 40,000 talents, and that Roger "was conquering . . . Africa, which is known to be the third part of the world."[10] Even more alarming, Roger had been trying to secure for himself the principality of Antioch, which had lost its ruler in

seconde croisade," *Revue d'histoire ecclésiastique,* XLIX (1954), 116–151; R. Grousset, *Histoire des croisades et du royaume franc de Jérusalem* (3 vols., Paris, 1934–1936), II; B. Kugler, *Studien zur Geschichte des zweiten Kreuzzuges* (Stuttgart, 1866); G. Constable, "The Second Crusade as Seen by Contemporaries," *Traditio,* IX (1953), 213–279; H. Gleber, *Papst Eugen III. (1145–1153) unter besonderer Berücksichtigung seiner politischen Tätigkeit* (Jena, 1936); C. Cahen, *La Syrie du nord à l'époque des croisades* (Paris, 1940); F. Chalandon, *Les Comnène: Études sur l'empire byzantin au XIe et au XIIe siècles* (2 vols., Paris, 1900–1912); and M. Mathieu, "La Sicile normande dans la poésie byzantine," *Bolletino del Centro di studi filologici e linguistici siciliani,* II (1954), 1–28. P. Lamma, *Comneni e Staufer: Ricerche sui rapporti fra Bisanzio e l' Occidente nel secolo XII,* I (Rome, 1955), is important because of extensive quotations from sources not easily available, such as the *epistolarium* of Wibald of Stavelot. The work sums up the results of recent studies by P. Rassow, "Zum byzantinisch-normannischen Krieg, 1147–1149," *Mitteilungen des Instituts für österreichische Geschichtsforschung,* LXII (1954), 213–218, and K. Heilig, *Ostrom und das deutsche Reich* (Stuttgart, 1951).

[9] Innocent II invested Roger and his two sons, as, respectively, king of Sicily, duke of Apulia, and prince of Capua, the titles corresponding to the original divisions of Norman Italy. Roger received suzerainty as *rex* over all areas, but the pope reserved the right to invest separately the lord of each of the three portions. See Jaffé-Löwenfeld, *Regesta pontificum Romanorum,* nos. 8042–8043; Caspar, *Roger II,* pp. 229–230, and Regesten, no. 124; K. A. Kehr, *Urkunden,* pp. 253–254; and Chalandon, *Domination normande,* II, 91.

[10] *Annales Erphesfurdenses,* ad ann. 1135 (ed. Holder-Egger), p. 42; cf. Bernhardi, *Lothar von Supplinburg,* p. 575, notes 33, 34.

1130 when Bohemond II was killed in battle against the Turks, and to which the Byzantines had never relinquished their claim.

If female succession was invalid, then Roger's right to the throne of Antioch as the cousin of Bohemond's father and thus the nearest male relative was presumably incontestable. But in 1135 king Fulk of Jerusalem, at the request of the Latin barons of Antioch, had chosen Raymond of Poitiers as Bohemond's successor and as husband for the heiress Constance. Although Fulk took care to shroud in secrecy the voyage of his messengers to England, where Raymond was living at the time, Roger, who had friends among the English barons, heard the news, and ordered a watch kept for Raymond in all the Adriatic embarkation ports. But Raymond, traveling in disguise, escaped Roger's spies and arrived safely at St. Simeon, the port nearest Antioch. In 1138 Roger tried to exploit a conflict between Raymond and Ralph, the Latin patriarch of Antioch. After a sojourn in Italy, where he was twice exposed to Roger's arguments and bribes, and twice succumbed, the patriarch was deposed, and Raymond, who rightly suspected him of being privy to a Norman conspiracy, threw him into prison, where he died in 1139.[11]

But the Byzantine emperor, John II Comnenus, now had sufficient proof of Roger's dangerous aspirations. John himself hoped to secure Antioch for his youngest son Manuel, and to convert it into a center of armed resistance to the Turks. A new offensive in the east could succeed, however, only if his Sicilian neighbor was kept in check. Therefore, he decided to build a new coalition starting with the German king Conrad III, whose rival, Welf of Bavaria, was receiving subsidies from Roger. It was under favorable conditions that John's ambassadors arrived in Germany in 1140 and began negotiations with the king "to renew the ties of an alliance between the two empires of the west and the east because of the arrogance of Roger of Sicily." Conrad agreed to cement the alliance by a marriage between his sister-in-law, Bertha of Sulzbach, and John's son Manuel.[12] Conrad also asked the doge of Venice, Peter of Pola, to mediate questions at issue between himself and the basileus, and received a Venetian pledge of naval assistance in the coming war. The coalition was taking shape when suddenly, on

[11] William of Tyre, XIV, XV (*RHC, Occ.*, I), pp. 618, 619, 635, 678, 679. On the background, see Grousset, *Histoire des croisades*, II, chap. VIII; Runciman, *Crusades*, II, chap. II; Cahen, *Syrie du nord*, pp. 357, 488–489, 502–503; Chalandon, *Domination normande*, II, 124–125; and volume I of the present work, chapter XIII, pp. 434–446. Roger also claimed he was entitled to Antioch because he had conquered Bohemond's Italian fiefs ceded to duke William. See Caspar, *Roger II*, pp. 65, 70, 79, 166.

[12] Otto of Freising, *Gesta Friderici I* (ed. Waitz), pp. 24, 25.

April 12, 1143, the emperor John died. Manuel, designated as his father's successor, had to fight a rival for the throne, and the negotiations for his marriage came to a temporary standstill.

Roger skillfully exploited this opportunity, by trying to win over the Byzantines. He too had a marriage to propose, between duke Roger, his eldest son, and a Byzantine princess. For a moment it seemed that the curious project might succeed. Angered by alleged associations between his rival to the Byzantine throne and the Norman refugees at Conrad's court, Manuel sent one of his courtiers, Basil Xeros, to Sicily to negotiate a pact with Roger. According to the historian Cinnamus, Basil accepted Sicilian money to write into the pact provisions detrimental to the interests of the Byzantine emperor — conceivably recognition of Roger's claim to Antioch, or some other territory claimed by Byzantium. At any rate, upon seeing the text Manuel threw into prison the Norman ambassadors who had come to Constantinople for ratification (Basil had died on the return trip) and broke off relations with Sicily, insults which Roger never forgave.

Manuel then resumed negotiations with Conrad, and in January 1146 he married Bertha of Sulzbach at Constantinople in the presence of Conrad's ambassadors. She became the empress Irene. At the same time, the political alliance against "the invader of two empires" was ratified. As a further step, Conrad sent his half-brother Otto, bishop of Freising, to Rome to notify pope Eugenius III of the new alliance and to announce Conrad's own early arrival in Italy. Suddenly, however, fortune began to favor the kingdom of Sicily. At Viterbo in November 1145 pope Eugenius received the news of Zengi's capture of Edessa. He decided to preach a new crusade.

No sooner was the new crusading movement announced than an anti-Byzantine faction raised its head in France and looked to Roger of Sicily for leadership. As early as 1140, in the face of the German-Byzantine threat, Roger had turned a hopeful eye toward France. Many ties of family relationships, tradition, and natural affinity bound the Italian Hautevilles to their country of origin and its royal house. As later events were to show, Roger had gained friends among those French leaders who believed that the great stumbling block to the success of the Franks in the east was the Byzantine empire.[13] Although it is doubtful that this idea had

[13] On the Sicilian-French rapprochements see Caspar, *Roger II*, pp. 365–370, and Chalandon, *Domination normande*, II, 106–107. Roger won the friendship of Bernard of Clairvaux by allowing Cistercian monks to settle in Sicily. See *Bernardi epistolae*, nos. 207, 208, 209, 447 (*PL*, CLXXXII). The letters must be dated after the peace of Mignano, 1139, when Bernard

much influence on the king of France, Louis VII certainly believed that Roger would be a useful ally in the crusade. After the assembly of Vézelay on March 31, 1146, Louis began negotiations with the rulers of the countries through which his armies might pass on their way to Asia Minor or to Syria. Among others, he approached Roger. The king of Sicily, seizing the occasion, sent to France ambassadors who "pledged the full support of his kingdom as to food supplies and transportation by water and every other need, and also promised that he or his son would go along on the journey."

Whether Louis accepted the offer or not, the crusade was a god-send for Roger. If Conrad were to invade southern Italy, as pope Eugenius expected him to do, he could not rely on Manuel, who would need his forces to keep the Latin crusaders in check once they had entered imperial territory. If Louis should accept, prospects would be brighter still. Roger could then move onto the stage of European politics as ally and comrade-in-arms of the king of France, and could use his influence to prevent the French from becoming the allies of the Byzantines. Finally, if Roger, or one of his sons, should join the crusade, he would be entitled to a share of the spoils. Most historians believe he had his eye on Antioch; but the crusade, it must be remembered, was launched to bring aid to Raymond of Antioch, who was the uncle of Louis's queen, Eleanor of Aquitaine. To avoid a conflict with the French royal family, Roger may well have dropped for the time his claim to Antioch, or may have thought of trading this claim for the kingdom of Jerusalem or even for a free hand against Constantinople.

Since Roger's ambassadors had received orders to stay in France until final decisions should be reached by an assembly being held at Étampes at the beginning of 1147, they had ample time to establish contact with the anti-Byzantine party, especially with its leader, Godfrey, bishop of Langres, and to use Sicilian money to gain more partisans. But with the enlistment in the crusade of Conrad of Germany, Roger's enemy and Manuel's friend and relative, and the subsequent decision of the assembly of Étampes to take the overland route to Constantinople, Roger withdrew from

found it expedient, for the benefit of the Cistercian order, to make his peace with the man whom he had castigated as the "tyrant of Sicily". See Vacandard, *Vie de Saint Bernard*, II, 60 ff. On the Cistercians in Sicily, see White, *Latin Monasticism in Norman Sicily*, pp. 163–165, and E. D. Theseider, "Su gli inizi dello stanziamento cisterciense nel regno di Sicilia," *Studi medievali in onore di A. de Stefano*, pp. 207–209. Peter of Cluny, on the other hand, claimed to have always been on Roger's side. See *Petri Venerabilis epistolarum libri sex*, III, 3 (*PL*, CLXXXIX), cols. 280–281; Caspar, *Roger II*, Regesten, no. 125.

the crusade completely, and showed no further interest in the well-being of its members.[14]

Nevertheless, the assumed French-Sicilian friendship seriously hampered coöperation between the Byzantines and the French, once the crusaders had entered Greek territory, a matter of some advantage to Roger of Sicily. The emperor's preoccupation with the reception of the crusaders left the Greek islands and the coasts of the Adriatic unprotected and open to Sicilian attack,[15] and Roger was not slow to seize his opportunity. A plan to assault Constantinople may well have underlain his desire to route the Second Crusade through his kingdom, but without the support of the crusaders this plan, if it existed, was abandoned for more limited objectives. The fleet he dispatched in the fall of 1147 was very powerful, consisting of many biremes and triremes manned and equipped in Apulia, Calabria, and Sicily, carrying a sizeable land force, and commanded by energetic and experienced leaders. This force took Corfu, Cephalonia, and other islands in the Ionian Sea, almost without having to fight. Then, skirting the west and south coasts of the Morea (Peloponnesus), the fleet entered the Gulf of Laconia, passed Cape Malea, and proceeded north to the great fortress of Monemvasia, which was besieged in the face of stout resistance from the inhabitants.

Suddenly, however, the siege was lifted, and the fleet returned by the same course. The ships entered the Gulf of Corinth and landed near Salona (the ancient Amphissa), whence soldiers and sailors, organized as a land force, penetrated into Acarnania, Boeotia, and even the island of Euboea (Negroponte), systematically ravaging and looting these flourishing regions and cities "famous for their ancient nobility". The city of Thebes was captured, and the inhabitants were forced to make detailed declarations of their estates so that everything movable could be carried away. Among the prisoners were "women skilled in weaving fine silk cloth". These silk workers from Thebes, along with others captured in Corinth and apparently Athens too, were settled at Palermo to teach their craft to the Sicilians.[16] Athens seems to have been sacked as well as Corinth, which Nicetas describes as "the rich city on the

[14] Odo of Deuil, *De profectione*, I (ed. Berry), pp. 6–14. For details, see Mrs. Berry's account in volume I of the present work, pp. 469–470.

[15] See emperor Manuel's own statement in a chrysobull for the Venetians of March 1148, in Tafel and Thomas, *Urkunden zur älteren Handels- und Staatsgeschichte der Republik Venedig*, I, 109–110.

[16] Nicetas, *Historia*; *De Manuele Comneno*, II, 1 (*CSHB*), p. 99. Compare Otto of Freising, *Gesta Friderici I* (ed. Waitz), p. 43: "Inde ad interiora Graeciae progressi Corinthum, Thebas, Athenas antiqua nobilitate celebres expugnant . . . opifices etiam qui sericos pannos texere solent ob ignominiam imperatoris illius suique principis gloriam captivos deducunt. Quos

isthmus famous for its two very convenient ports that handled the export and trans-shipment of goods from Asia and Italy." Both the city and Acrocorinth were taken. From all these places the Normans carried off such enormous booty of gold and silver and silk textiles that on its way home the fleet gave the impression of a "flotilla of freighters rather than of men-of-war". On the return trip, the Normans heavily fortified Corfu and other islands, for Roger was determined to hold on to his new Adriatic conquests.

In addition to material damage, the Byzantine empire suffered a serious loss of prestige. One of its basic weaknesses, the apathy of the civilian population and their lack of fighting spirit, was disclosed to the world. The emperor felt obliged to avenge this disgrace, reconquer Corfu and the other Adriatic islands, and carry the war to the "dragon of the west, the New Amalech". In March 1148 Manuel concluded a treaty with the Venetians, who saw their trade in the Adriatic seriously threatened by the new occupants of Corfu. For various reasons the great counter-offensive had to be postponed, and it was only in the late fall that the siege of Corfu was finally begun. In the early summer of 1149 Roger again dispatched a fleet, comprising sixty ships under George of Antioch, to raid the coasts of Greece. No doubt he hoped Manuel would lift the siege of Corfu to come to the rescue of his European provinces. Manuel only sent one of his commanders, however, with a naval detachment which twice inflicted heavy losses on George's fleet. Roger's ships carried out a dashing raid on Constantinople itself, in the course of which George's men shot burning arrows into the palace of Blachernae and ravaged the imperial orchards.[17] Moreover a stroke of

Rogerius in Palermo Siciliae metropoli collocans, artem illam texendi suos edocere precepit. . . ." The *Annales Cavenses* (ad ann. 1147) speak of many Jews' being deported from Thebes, Corinth, and the Ionian islands to Sicily. As many of the goldsmiths and manufacturers of silk and purple garments in the Byzantine empire were Jews, this notice would seem to add to our knowledge of Roger's religious as well as his economic policy. See R. S. Lopez, "Silk Industry in the Byzantine Empire," *Speculum*, XX (1945), 24. Although only western sources (such as Otto of Freising) mention the Norman pillage of Athens, which has led some historians to omit Athens from the list of places captured by Roger's forces, the American excavations in the Athenian Agora have recently revealed some evidence that seems to confirm the western tradition that Athens was captured along with Thebes and Corinth, on which see K. M. Setton, "The Archaeology of Medieval Athens," *Essays in Medieval Life and Thought, Presented in Honor of Austin Patterson Evans* (New York, 1955), p. 251.

[17] Ibn-al-Athīr, *Al-kāmil* (Amari, *BAS*, I), pp. 476–477; Andrea Dandolo (*RISS*, XII), p. 282; and *Sigeberti continuatio Praemonstratensis* (*MGH, SS.*, VI), p. 454, Nicetas, *Historia; De Manuele Comneno*, III, 8 (*CSHB*), p. 135, places this story in the reign of William I. See the discussion of this question in Siragusa, *Regno di Guglielmo I*, p. 72, note 2, and in Caspar, *Roger II*, p. 394, note 1. Recently available Byzantine sources prove beyond doubt that these events occurred in Roger's reign. See Mathieu, "La Sicile normande dans la poésie byzantine," *Bolletino del Centro di studi filologici e linguistici siciliani*, II, 1–28, and Rassow, "Zum byzantinisch-normannischen Krieg, 1147–1149," *Mitteilungen des Instituts für Österreichische Geschichtsforschung*, LXII (1954), 213–218.

fortune, or perhaps their own watchfulness, enabled the Normans to rescue from the Byzantines king Louis and queen Eleanor of France, now returning from Palestine, and to send them safely to a Calabrian port.[18] Shortly afterwards, however, the Byzantines reconquered the Ionian islands earlier seized by the Normans, but two Byzantine attempts on Apulia itself in the late fall of 1149 were thwarted by heavy storms. A war with the Serbs, perhaps instigated by Roger himself, put a stop to further Byzantine attacks.

The Sicilian-Byzantine war outlasted the Second Crusade. Manuel and Roger continued to build coalitions designed to destroy each other. Both turned to advantage the tragic circumstances that marked the return of Louis VII and Conrad III from the scenes of their defeats. Facing embarrassing criticism and accusations, Louis and Conrad hoped to retrieve their honor and to acquire fame in new enterprises. Thus, upon his arrival at the imperial court — in a Byzantine ship in order to escape Roger's spies — Conrad agreed to conclude a treaty of alliance with Manuel on terms which included, among others, the renunciation of German claims to Apulia. In the event that the allies won Apulia, Conrad would grant it as a dowry to his sister-in-law Bertha, empress under the name of Irene.[19]

Meanwhile, at Potenza late in August 1149, Louis met Roger, who was only too eager to establish a close relationship with him.[20] Just what the two kings said to each other we do not know, but there can be no doubt that they were concerned with forming an offensive and defensive alliance against Manuel. After the interview, Sicilian barons escorted Louis and Eleanor to Rome, where Louis was expected to strengthen earlier agreements made between Roger and the pope. Eugenius had adopted the views of many returning crusaders, who blamed their failure on Manuel and the "heretic Greeks". For the moment at least, the pope was willing to endorse any plan that would distract the attention of western Christendom from what even the king of France admitted to be

18 The Greek and Latin sources give a confused and contradictory picture of the circumstances surrounding the capture and release of the king and queen; however, see Kugler, *Studien zur Geschichte des zweiten Kreuzzuges*, pp. 209–210, and Caspar, *Roger II*, pp. 392–393.

19 On the treaty and its importance for the anti-Byzantine policy of Frederick Barbarossa, see P. Rassow, *Honor imperii* (Munich and Berlin, 1940), pp. 26–44, and Lamma, *Comneni e Staufer*, I, 89–93.

20 See Louis's letter to Suger, in which he mentions the "devoted and reverent reception" Roger gave him and Eleanor, *Epistolae Sugerii*, LXXXI (*RHGF*, XV), p. 514; John of Salisbury, *Historia pontificalis*, 28. The importance that Roger attached to this meeting with Louis gave rise to the legend that Louis crowned Roger king. See Caspar, *Roger II*, p. 405, and above, note 7.

"the faults and sins" of the Latins. Louis returned to France, assured of the pope's consent to any action which might help western Christendom retrieve its honor and avenge itself upon the Greeks.[21]

But the new "crusade" was still-born. The French assembly which met at Laon in March 1150 found the barons, and the king himself, reluctant to embark on any new adventure. Feeling that the authority and prestige of the church were at stake if, as seemed almost certain, the crusade should result in a new catastrophe, pope Eugenius began to withdraw his support. So did Louis VII, who despaired of seeing Conrad and Roger reconciled, and could not risk a venture which invited German reprisal. The dreams of Roger of Sicily dissolved. As at the start of the Second Crusade, so again he found himself abandoned by the French and threatened by a new coalition of all his enemies.

Meanwhile, however, Roger could stand before an admiring Europe as a conqueror in Moslem Africa. Peter of Cluny praised his impressive victories as "the increase of the church of God by land which had belonged to the enemies of God, that is the Saracens."[22] Contemporaries looked on Roger's colonial outposts in Africa, along with the Christian advances in Spain and Portugal, as the only territorial gains made during the time of the Second Crusade, and as in some measure a compensation for its failure. Yet in Roger's African venture, crusading zeal and motives, although not wholly absent, played a lesser role than did Sicilian political traditions, economic needs, and military interests.

The region of Africa which came into the Norman orbit was the old Roman province of Africa proconsularis, together with a part of Roman Numidia, roughly covering the northern and central

[21] Constable, "The Second Crusade," *Traditio*, IX, 272–273, stresses that, in contrast to France, public opinion in Germany was not unfavorable to the Byzantine emperor, and that discussions of the failure of the Second Crusade contain no mention of Greek "treachery". For the aftermath of the Second Crusade, the letters of the principals are the most important source: *Epistolae Ludovici VII, Eugenii III papae, Bernardi, Sugerii, Petri abbatis Cluniacensis* (*PL*, CLXXXIX; *RHGF*, XV; A. Duchesne, *Historiae Francorum scriptores*, IV [Paris, 1641]). Suger's letters, together with the important *Guilelmi vita Sugerii*, may be consulted in A. Lecoy de la Marche (ed.), *Oeuvres complètes de Suger* (Paris, 1867). Letters of king Conrad and some prominent Germans are found in *Wibaldi epistolae* (ed. P. Jaffé, *Bibliotheca rerum Germanicarum*, 6 vols., Berlin, 1864–1873), I. See also *Sigeberti continuatio Praemonstratensis*, ad ann. 1150 (*MGH, SS.*, VI), p. 455. In addition to works cited elsewhere in this chapter, the following studies are of importance: A. Luchaire, *Louis VII, Philippe-Auguste, Louis VIII* (Paris, 1901); A. Cartellieri, *Abt Suger von Saint-Denis, 1081–1151* (Berlin, 1898); R. Hirsch, *Studien zur Geschichte König Ludwigs VII. von Frankreich* (Leipzig, 1892); and Lamma, *Comneni e Staufer*, 99–115.

[22] *Petri Venerabilis epistolarum libri sex*, VI, 16 (*PL*, CLXXXIX), col. 424.

parts of modern Tunisia, and known to Arab geographers as Ifrīqiyah (Arabic corruption of Latin "Africa").[23] The conquest of Berber North Africa by the Arabs in the seventh century had aroused a desperate resistance, and the spread of Islam, which came to the mass of the rural population in the form of Khārijite sectarianism based on the principle of religious equality, only widened the gap between them and their new rulers, the Sunnite nobility (*jund*). Yet under the 'Abbāsid caliphs at Baghdad, Tunisia, soon separated from western Barbary, flourished as it never had since the great days of the Roman empire. The Aghlabids, who ruled it in the name of the caliphs, eventually conquered Sicily and Malta and made their state a prominent Mediterranean sea power. Throughout the ninth century Tunisia enjoyed unprecedented economic prosperity, and its capital Kairawan, with its famous mosque, became one of the most important religious and cultural centers of Islam.

The rise of the Shī'ite caliphate of the Fāṭimids put an end to the rule of the Aghlabids of Kairawan in 909. The new masters imposed on Barbary their Shī'ite religion along with an utterly oppressive system of financial exploitation. When the fourth Fāṭimid caliph, al-Mu'izz, moved to Cairo in 972, he entrusted Tunisia and part of Algeria to the house of the Berber chieftain Zīrī, who soon lost the Algerian province to their Ḥammādid cousins, but continued ruling Tunisia in the name of the caliphs at Cairo. The Zīrids found it increasingly difficult to reconcile their loyalty toward their overlords with the sentiments of their people, who hated the Shī'ites. When, therefore, the power of the caliphs in Cairo began to weaken, the Zīrid emir al-Mu'izz followed the example of the Ḥammādids and in 1048 publicly declared the 'Abbāsid caliph at Baghdad his suzerain. This fateful step was

[23] In addition to the works of Amari, Chalandon, Caspar, W. Cohn, Monti, Cerone, and Cartellieri, already cited, the following may be referred to for the background and history of the conquest of Tunisia: C. Brockelmann, *Geschichte der islamischen Völker und Staaten* (Munich and Berlin, 1943); P. K. Hitti, *History of the Arabs*, 6th ed. (London, 1956); G. Marçais, *La Berbérie musulmane et l'orient au moyen-âge* (Paris, 1946); J. Mesnage, *Le Christianisme en Afrique: Déclin et extinction* (Algiers and Paris, 1915); H. W. Hazard, *The Numismatic History of Late Medieval North Africa* (New York, 1952); and articles by Marçais, Yver, and others on Berbers, Zīrids, Hilāl, Aghlabides, Ifrīḳiya, al-Mahdīya, Tunis, Tripoli, Sfax, etc. in *The Encyclopaedia of Islām*. See also the chapter on North Africa in volume III of the present work (in preparation).

On Sicilian rule in Africa, see A. Solmi, "La Politica mediterranea del regno normanno-suevo," in *Il Regno normanno*, pp. 71–93; G. La Mantia, "La Sicilia ed il suo dominio nell' Africa settentrionale dal secolo XI al XVI," *Archivio storico siciliano*, n.s., XLIV (1922), 154 ff.; and F. Giunta, "Sicilia e Tunisia nei secoli XIV e XV," in Giunta, *Medioevo mediterraneo*, pp. 137–190. On the Swabian period, see Giunta, "Enrico VI e l'impero d'oriente," *ibid.*, pp. 53–118. For a description of African cities, see MacG. de Slane, "Ibn Haucal, Déscription de l'Afrique," *Journal asiatique*, ser. 3, III (1842), 160 ff.

tantamount to open denunciation of Fāṭimid suzerainty over Tunisia. The mosque of Kairawan was restored to Sunnite Islam and the name of the 'Abbāsid caliph al-Qā'im replaced that of the Fāṭimid in the Friday prayer.

To punish this disloyalty, the Fāṭimid caliph al-Mustanṣir persuaded the wild beduin tribes of the Banū-Hilāl, Banū-Sulaim, and others to invade Tunisia in 1052. The whole of this rich and prosperous land between Kairawan and Cape Bon was overrun and laid waste. Along with the fields, orchards, and hamlets, all the unfortified cities fell to the new wave of Arabs. Kairawan, one of the holy cities of Islam, survived because it was fortified at the last moment. But life became increasingly difficult and, after a few years, the Zīrids moved their capital to the sea-fortress of Mahdia. The caravan trade, once the glory of Tunisia, was completely ruined. One after another the cities broke away from the Zīrids and set up their own dynasties, Arab or Berber. Mahdia alone was all that survived of the once strong state.

The Zīrids tried to retrieve their fortunes by turning to the sea. Utilizing Mahdia as a great naval base and arsenal, they sent out expeditions to Sicily and attacked Italian shipping. In response to this piracy, the Italian maritime cities assaulted and ravaged Mahdia in 1087. But even before this, count Roger I of Sicily had taken the first step toward Norman interference in Tunisia. The Zīrid Tamīm (1062–1108), son of al-Mu'izz, had promised to cease molesting Sicily, and in return count Roger had promised the shipment of grain to Mahdia. This treaty, concluded about 1075, while restricting manifestations of Norman hostility for the time being, had given Sicily protection against Zīrid attack and secured permanent markets for Sicilian grain, of lasting benefit to the Sicilian economy and Roger's treasury.[24]

Under cover of this agreement, which his mother Adelaide and he continued with Tamīm's son and successor Yaḥyâ (1108–1116), count Roger II pursued a more aggressive policy. For one thing, he wanted to make good his failure to acquire the kingdom of Jerusalem.[25]

[24] Malaterra, *De rebus gestis Rogerii*, IV, 3 (*RISS*, V), pp. 86–87. On the treaty, see L. de Mas Latrie, *Traités de paix et de commerce* (Paris, 1866), introduction, pp. 29, 33, and Amari, *Storia dei musulmani*, III, 170.

[25] On the struggle between Roger II and the Zīrid emirs of Mahdia hardly any other than Arabic sources are available. Since Roger's early attempts on North Africa were failures, Sicilian chroniclers make no mention of them. The later conquests are only summarily listed in some Italian and French chronicles (see below, note 32). The Arabic sources, though all of a later date, derive their information from good contemporary reports, and in part from official documents. See Amari, *Storia dei musulmani*, III, 387, note 2, and *passim*, and Chalandon, *Domination normande*, I, introduction. The most important of these Arab works are:

Roger II was young, ambitious, and eager to make a name for himself. He had inherited a territory better organized than any other in contemporary western Europe, a well stocked treasury, and the loyalty of his subjects including Moslems and Greeks. He felt a genuine affinity for the Moslem way of life and of thought, all the more so after the residence of the counts was moved to Palermo, a cosmopolitan city of predominantly eastern character. He was also influenced by George of Antioch, a Syrian Christian who had held high office in Mahdia under Tamīm, but had fled from Yaḥyâ and obtained asylum in Sicily. First tax-collector (*strategos*) in a provincial district, then diplomat on a mission to Egypt, George rose to the important post of naval commander and assistant to the "admiral" of the Sicilian navy.[26] His experience in African affairs, his knowledge of the land and people, and his command of Arabic recommended him to Roger II as an ideal commander in a war with the Zīrids.

If Roger had listened to the "elder statesmen", who favored the moderate policies of his father, rather than to George, perhaps he would have concluded that war in Africa entailed too great economic risks. By 1117 he was already employing several agents in Mahdia entrusted with the handling of large amounts of money, probably payment for Sicilian grain. Export duties paid by the merchants, Sicilian and other, to the Sicilian exchequer would be lost, together with the profitable African market. Roger decided to accept the risk. Early in his reign he seems to have made an alliance with the Ḥammādids of Bougie in eastern Algeria, the traditional enemies of

Ibn-al-Athīr, *Al-kāmil* (Amari, *BAS*, I), pp. 353–507; Ibn-'Idhārī, *Kitāb al-bayān al-mughrib fī akhbār mulūk al-Andalus wa-l-Maghrib* [. . . *Reports of the Kings of Andalusia and North Africa*] (Amari, *BAS*, II), pp. 1–40; Ibn-abī-Dīnār, *Kitāb al-mu'nis fī akhbār Ifrīqiyah wa-Tūnis* [. . . *Reports of Africa and Tunis*] (Amari, *BAS*, II), pp. 273–297; at-Tijānī, *Riḥlah* [*Voyage*] (Amari, *BAS*, II), pp. 41–81; and Ibn-Khaldūn, *Kitāb al-'ibar* (Amari, *BAS*, II), pp. 163–243. For the interpretation and chronology of events, see Chalandon, *Domination normande*, I, 367 ff., II, chaps. I, II, IV; Caspar, *Roger II*, pp. 43–47, 163–164, 415–423; Amari, *Storia dei musulmani*, III, book VI; and Marçais, *La Berbérie musulmane*, pp. 215–225.

[26] "Admiral" is derived from the Arabic *amīr* (emir) through the Greek genitive ἀμηράδος; hence the Latin *ammiratus*, *admiratus*, or *ammiralius*. The office, as it is first referred to under the regency of Adelaide (1110), was originally derived from that of the (Fāṭimid) emir of Palermo who, after the city fell to the Normans, was replaced by a Christian "emir", whose main function became the supervision of the Saracen communities in Palermo and other places. Since the navy was built up with the help of Saracen contributions of ships, materials, and money, and was, in part, manned by Saracen sailors and marines, the Norman "emir" was put in charge of the navy. The importance of the navy under the second count of Sicily is emphasized by the fact that the admiral was now entrusted with the functions of a first minister in the civil government of Sicily. See the brilliant reconstruction of this development by Amari, *Storia dei musulmani*, III, 357 ff. On George of Antioch, see *ibid.*; Caspar, *Roger II*, pp. 41 ff., and 300 ff.; and W. Cohn, *Die Geschichte der normannisch-sicilischen Flotte unter der Regierung Rogers I. und Rogers II.*, pp. 14 ff.

the Zīrids,[27] and while he renewed the earlier agreement with Yaḥyâ's son and successor 'Alī (1116–1121), he seems to have supported the efforts of Rāfi', the governor of Gabes and a chieftain of the Banū-Hilāl, to break with the emir. In 1117–1118 an occasion for direct interference arose when the energetic 'Alī forbade Rāfi' to launch a merchant ship from the port of Gabes on the ground that "no inhabitant of Ifrīqiyah was permitted to compete with him in dispatching merchant ships." Roger may well have felt inclined to challenge so sweeping a claim. Rāfi' turned to him for help, and he sent twenty-four galleys to Gabes, but the captain of this force had the good sense to retire to Sicily when the Zīrid fleet put out from Mahdia to meet him. Relations soon reached the breaking-point. The emir confiscated Roger's money deposited in Mahdia and threw his agents into prison. On Roger's angry complaints he later released both, but he did not respond to Roger's request for "renewal of the treaties and for confirmation of the alliance". When Roger insisted, in letters "full of arrogant words and threats and written in a form that ran counter to decent usages", 'Alī dismissed the Norman ambassadors without answer and prepared for war.

The conditions under which the war broke out tend to obscure somewhat the true reasons and initial accidents that had led to it. For one thing, the Zīrid 'Alī — and after his death the government of his young son al-Ḥasan (1121–1148) — felt too weak to face the Sicilian antagonist alone, and called in the help of the Murābiṭ (Almoravid) sultan of Morocco, 'Alī ibn-Yūsuf. 'Alī promptly sent his governor of the Baleares, the fiery and capable sea-captain Muḥammad ibn-Maimūn, to raid the coast of Calabria. Ibn-Maimūn's men plundered Nicotera and perpetrated on the civilian population there all the horrors habitually accompanying this type of warfare. Roger, who was count of Calabria as well as of Sicily, seems to have worked on the indignation of his Christian subjects to arouse enthusiasm for an expedition against the Zīrids, whom he represented as responsible for these misdeeds. The emir in turn proclaimed a holy war against Roger, hoping thus to submerge the latent antagonism between Berbers and Arabs in a common struggle against the Christians. In this he was not disappointed.

In June 1123, a year after the raid on Nicotera, a Sicilian fleet of about three hundred vessels (galleys and transports conveying 30,000

[27] The fact is known from an incident which caused Roger II to threaten the Ḥammādid emir al-'Azīz with the withdrawal of his "friendship". See *Petri Diaconi chronicon*, IV, 50 (*MGH, SS.*, VII), p. 786; Caspar, *Roger II*, p. 41.

men and 1,000 horses), under the command of the admiral Christodoulus and his assistant George of Antioch, landed on the small island of Ahasi off the coast of Mahdia. They found unorganized but formidable and enthusiastic forces ready to repel them. The unity and determination of Berber and Arab led to the defeat of the Normans after they had occupied the little island and the mainland fortress of Dimas for only four days. True, the Norman navy was not yet fully integrated; sea and land forces did not work well together; the marines especially failed to carry out landing operations under enemy attack. Roger's force seems to have lacked enthusiasm and fighting spirit, while the enemy, on the defensive against Christian invaders, "knew what they were fighting for", and of course represented their victory as a triumph of Islam over Christianity. Christian chroniclers do not even mention the expedition of 1123, and their silence is eloquent evidence of the dismay that prevailed at the court of Palermo.[28]

The war dragged on for several years, the initiative now with the Moslems. But in July 1127 Roger reconquered the Mediterranean islands of Malta, Gozo, and Pantelleria, lost by the Normans soon after his father's death, a success that proved its importance at a later stage in his African exploits. On the other hand, he could neither prevent nor avenge the terrible raids carried out in the same month against Patti and Syracuse. Most Christian sources attribute these raids to the Balearic corsair captain Ibn-Maimūn, but William of Tyre, usually well informed about events in southern Italy, says that the raids against Patti and "the noble and ancient city of Syracuse" had been launched from the African coast and had been touched off by the sudden appearance of Sicilian raiders there.[29]

Whatever the truth of the matter, Roger was unable to cope with the situation. In 1128 he responded, however, to the request of count Raymond Berengar III of Barcelona for help against the Moors of Spain, promising to send in the summer of that year fifty galleys and an army "in servitium Dei".[30] The plan never materialized, probably because of the war against the pope and the Apulian barons. But he prepared for his future role as lord of the African sea by concluding a treaty with Savona, a client city of Genoa, containing

[28] Al-Ḥasan's official report is included in at-Tijānī, *Riḥlah* (Amari, *BAS*, II), pp. 71 ff. All the Arab authors drew from it. A passage from a poem by Ibn-Ḥamdīs in praise of al-Ḥasan's victories may be found in Amari, *BAS*, II, 400. See Caspar, *Roger II*, p. 49.

[29] William of Tyre, XIII, 22 (*RHC, Occ.*, I), pp. 590–591. For other sources, see Amari, *Storia dei musulmani*, III, 384–385, note 5.

[30] Caspar, *Roger II*, Regesten, no. 53. On the content of the documents containing the treaties, see *ibid.*, pp. 50–51, 70–78; also Amari, *Storia dei musulmani*, III, 396–398, and Cohn, *Geschichte der . . . Flotte*, pp. 23 ff.

guarantees against Savonese piracy and the promise of one Savonese galley to help police the sea from Savona to Sicily and from "Nubia" (Numidia) to Tripoli.[31]

Until the peace of Mignano in 1139, when his hold on the Italian mainland was finally made secure, Roger could interfere in Mahdia actively only in 1134–1135 during a short lull in Europe. Meanwhile, however, he spun the net of intrigue in which he eventually trapped his victim. He used "peaceful" infiltration, political and economic blackmail, and intimidation, as well as force. In 1134 Roger heeded the call of al-Ḥasan for help against Yaḥyâ, the emir of Bougie, who was besieging Mahdia. Roger's navy helped to relieve Mahdia. Although al-Ḥasan would not allow the Sicilians to destroy his rival, he was keenly aware of his need for Roger's friendship, and accepted his hard terms for a defensive and offensive alliance.

In 1135 Roger sent a strong force that included Frankish knights and Moslems from Sicily to the Gulf of Gabes in order to take the island of Jerba. It was his first conquest in this region, and proved an excellent base for future operations. The conquerors mistreated the population, described as consisting of criminals and freebooters who "had never before obeyed the rule of a sultan". Those who survived the first onslaught were reduced to servitude, and the island was subjected to the rule of an official (Arabic, *'āmil*) appointed by Roger. The intervention at Mahdia and the conquest of Jerba, though not followed by new military aggressions for several years to come, caused considerable stir among Roger's enemies. Arab observers predicted the doom of the "province of Mahdia" and, as we saw above, Roger's successes gave the Byzantine and Venetian ambassadors at Merseburg grounds for apprehension.

In 1141–1142, with famine and plague harassing the people of Tunisia, Roger demanded that his agents be paid what the emir owed them. When al-Ḥasan declared his insolvency, Roger sent twenty-five ships under the command of George of Antioch, who confiscated Egyptian ships anchored in the harbor of Mahdia and a ship belonging to al-Ḥasan, about to sail for Cairo with gifts for the caliph al-Ḥāfiz. Next, Roger forced new agreements upon al-Ḥasan, attaching so many conditions that, as one Arab author puts it, al-Ḥasan was in the position of Roger's 'amil. Roger

[31] Caspar, *Roger II*, Regesten, no. 54. The treaty is printed in G. Filippi, "Patto di pace tra Ruggiero II normanno e la città di Savona," *Archivio storico napoletano*, XIV (1889), 750–757. On its content, see Caspar, *Roger II*, pp. 77–78, and Cohn, *Geschichte der . . . Flotte*, pp. 23 ff. The printed text has Nubia, but this must be an error for Numidia.

probably demanded as guarantee the proceeds from customs duties collected in the ports of Mahdia and Susa. He also secured the right to conquer any places that might revolt against the Zīrids.

From 1143 on, no year went by without a Norman attack on the African coast. In June 1143 a Sicilian fleet attempted to take the city of Tripoli, which was ruled by the Arab house of the Banū-Maṭrūḥ. The attack failed because the Arab tribes of the neighborhood made common cause with the inhabitants and forced the "Franks" to sail for home. In the main, however, the attacks hit points along the coasts from Bougie to Mahdia, being launched each summer during the years 1143–1146 and probably with some regularity each year thereafter, and do not fit into any strategic pattern. They seem to have been intended to frighten the inhabitants or to reconnoiter and test the strength of possible naval resistance. The Normans must soon have found that the Zīrid navy, once formidable, had dwindled away. The Zīrid state was poverty-stricken and unable to maintain ships or to employ the services of corsairs on any large scale. Whatever barges were left were used in the grain traffic with Egypt and Sicily. Clearly the control of the sea had passed to Sicily. But Roger needed African bases, and in the summer of 1146 a Sicilian fleet of two hundred ships under the command of George of Antioch again appeared before Tripoli. A few days before their arrival, the government of the Banū-Maṭrūḥ had been overthrown by a Murābiṭ chieftain returning to Morocco after a pilgrimage to Mecca. The turmoil that followed weakened resistance, and the city fell to the Normans within three days. After several days of plundering, George declared an amnesty and immediately began to fortify and reorganize the place.

The capture of Tripoli by the Sicilians made a great impression on Christians and Moslems alike. For the time being, Roger did not follow up his great victory with an attack on Mahdia as might have been expected. The Second Crusade, and his efforts in connection with it, may have had something to do with the delay. But in 1147 famine in North Africa had reached a stage beyond endurance. Some Arab historians report cases of cannibalism committed in desperation. There was an exodus from Tunisia to Sicily of nobles and wealthy citizens, some of whom urged Roger to take over Tunisia entirely. Many who did not emigrate were ready to surrender the cities to him. They pointed to the tempting example of Tripoli: after its occupation by the Normans it had made a remarkable recovery. Naturally, Roger and George of Antioch welcomed this mood. Ibn-'Idhārī emphasizes George's role:

"This accursed one," he writes, "knew the weak points in the situation of Mahdia."

Among the African chiefs who saw in Roger of Sicily the future master of Tunisia was a certain Yūsuf, a former slave who governed the city of Gabes in the name of Muḥammad, the youngest son of the late Rāfi', the same who had called upon Roger to interfere in African affairs some thirty years previously. Yūsuf offered Gabes to Roger, and received from him the diploma and insignia of a governor, to rule Gabes thenceforth as a Sicilian protectorate. But al-Ḥasan, as suzerain of Gabes and protector of the eldest son and rightful heir of Rāfi', occupied Gabes with the help of the local inhabitants, who executed Yūsuf in an obscene lynching. Since at the time, in the late fall of 1147, the bulk of Roger's navy was engaged in large-scale operations in Greek waters, Roger could send only a few ships, which were unable to take Gabes. This setback hastened his decision to end the diplomatic game and to destroy the Zīrids with an all-out military attack. Probably the relatives of Yūsuf, who took refuge at his court, urged him to punish al-Ḥasan, and gave information valuable for an invasion. As soon as the Sicilian navy had completed its assignment on the Greek coast, by strengthening and fortifying Corfu, and Roger had made sure that the Byzantines were engaged in a war in the north of Greece, he began to prepare this expedition to Mahdia for the early summer of 1148.

Tunisia was by now so exhausted and impoverished that strong resistance was no longer to be expected. Nevertheless, Roger lulled al-Ḥasan into thinking that he was still honoring the two-year treaty concluded in 1146. Even after the incident of Gabes he received al-Ḥasan's ambassador in Palermo. When all was ready, George of Antioch assembled at Pantelleria the fleet of 250 ships which were to carry a strong army and siege machines, and then sent a fake message by carrier pigeon to al-Ḥasan to deceive him into the belief that the fleet was headed for Constantinople. In the early morning of June 22, the inhabitants of Mahdia saw a dark cloud of Sicilian ships coming over the horizon, their oarsmen making for the harbor against adverse winds. The emir realized that their arrival meant the end of his dynasty. Before the Sicilian fleet could land, al-Ḥasan, accompanied by his family and court and followed by many citizens, left the royal palace which had served the Zīrids as a residence for nearly a hundred years. In the late afternoon of June 22, George of Antioch and his army entered the fortress without the loss of a single man.

Once order had been restored in the capital, George sent detachments to conquer other cities along the North African coast. By the end of July, within a month after the landing in Mahdia, all the cities and minor castles along the littoral had been taken, among them the great ports and trade centers of Gabes, Susa, and, despite considerable resistance, Sfax. An attack on Kelibia, probably with Tunis the ultimate objective, was stopped by the determined resistance of the Arabs. It is probable that Tunis, ruled by members of the Arab house of the Banū-Khurasān, voluntarily submitted to the overlordship of the Sicilian king. Ibn-al-Athīr describes the territory in Africa now ruled by Roger II as extending from Tripoli to Cape Bon and from the desert to Kairawan. Apparently Roger had not planned to extend his conquests farther west into the territory of the Ḥammādids, whose position was stronger than that of the Zīrids. He could not spare additional men for further conquest or for garrison service. The emperor Manuel was preparing feverishly for the reconquest of Corfu and for an invasion of the Italian mainland. Had it not been for the war between "the prince of Sicily and the king of the Romans in Constantinople," says Ibn-al-Athīr, Roger would have conquered "all Africa".

Christians in the age of the crusades could not but hail Roger's African conquests as a great Christian victory in the Mediterranean. In a short obituary for Roger a French chronicler praised them as outstanding triumphs over the Saracens, and along with another annalist places Roger's campaign with the crusading events in the east. On the other hand, the two court historians of the Norman dynasty of Sicily, archbishop Romuald Guarna of Salerno and Hugo Falcandus, do not impute religious motives to Roger. Both speak of Roger's desire for territorial aggrandizement, and Romuald emphasizes the king's ambition (*cor magnificum*) and his lust for power (*dominandi animus*) which was not satisfied with the rule of Sicily and Apulia.[32] Nor do Arab historians interpret as an expression of religious zeal Roger's "cruelty" in exploiting the calamities

[32] Roger's obituary is in *Sigeberti continuatio Praemonstratensis*, ad ann. 1154 (*MGH, SS.*, VI), p. 455; "Princeps utilis et strenuus et actibus clarus Rogerius rex Siciliae post insignes de Saracenis victorias et terras eorum occupatas obit. . . ." His African campaign is associated, in the context, with the Second Crusade in the same chronicle (p. 454) and in Robert of Torigny's *Chronicon* (*ibid.*, p. 503). See also *Annales Casinenses* (*MGH, SS.*, XIX), p. 310; Andrea Dandolo, *Chronicon*, ad ann. 1147–1148 (*RISS*, XII), p. 243; Romuald Guarna of Salerno, *Chronicon* (*RISS*, VII), p. 227; and Hugo Falcandus, *Liber de regno Siciliae* (*FSI*, XXII), pp. 5–6. All Latin sources except Robert of Torigny mention the capture of Mahdia, which they call Africa (Affrica or Africax), but only Romuald Guarna mentions all the important cities: "Africa" (Mahdia), Susa, Bona, Gabes, Sfax, and Tripoli. Robert of Torigny speaks of the capture of "Tonita" (Tunis), for which there is otherwise only indirect evidence. See Cerone, *L'Opera . . . di Ruggiero II in Africa ed in Oriente*, pp. 63 ff., and Constable, "Second Crusade," *Traditio*, IX, 235–237.

of Tunisia. They knew well enough that Roger's African policy, from the very beginning, was dictated by the financial and commercial interests of his kingdom, and it is to their understanding of the underlying economic factors that we owe our knowledge of Roger's methods.

Exciting opportunities now existed for the expansion of Sicilian trade into the southern and eastern Mediterranean. Their realization depended, however, upon the degree to which the king could integrate his new "colonies" into his kingdom and revive their economy. The organization of the African outposts was entrusted to George of Antioch, who acted as Roger's viceroy, and whom the Arabs called his vizir (*wazīr*). George refrained from extending the conquest to the African hinterland. Instead, he devoted himself to restoring order, according to a plan probably worked out with the king prior to the conquest of Tripoli in 1146, and tested in this city after its occupation. In each occupied city the Sicilians garrisoned the citadel under a captain who was responsible for defense and internal security. Civil administration, on the other hand, was entrusted to an 'amil chosen by the Sicilian government from among the native nobility. To assure this official's loyalty the Sicilians took a hostage, usually a close relative, off to Palermo. Under the 'amils, local magistrates (Arabic singular, *qāḍī*) served as judges; they were appointed by the Sicilian government with a view to pleasing the people. The population had to pay a special head tax, the *jizyah*, but no other services or tributes. As regards the collection of the customary taxes, such as the land tax and excise taxes formerly paid to the emir and the local shaikhs, Roger's representatives "employed persuasion rather than force". Ibn-abī-Dīnār mentions this as one, but not the only, example of treatment which he calls just and humane, and which reconciled Roger's new Moslem subjects to his government. In accord with the traditional policy toward the Saracens in Sicily, George of Antioch granted, and Roger later solemnly confirmed, complete religious toleration.

With their religion and their customs unchanged, and with co-nationals as their immediate governors, the Berbers of Tunisia found conditions little altered, except that their economic life was improving and even showing signs of a new prosperity. Shortly after the conquest George of Antioch restored Mahdia and its commercial suburb Zawila. He lent money to merchants and supported the poor. As in Tripoli two years earlier, Italian and Sicilian merchants and wares began to pour into the new colonies. Roger actively encouraged emigration from his kingdom to "the land of Tripoli", and it is said that Sicilians and Italians repopulated Tripoli, which began to prosper. It is likely that Roger applied the same policy of colonization to his conquests of 1148. By proclamation he made it known throughout Tunisia that he would give special favors to those who would voluntarily submit to his rule. In response to this appeal caravans arriving under their chiefs in Sfax shortly after the conquest of the city swore allegiance to him. To revive the trade with Egypt, Roger concluded a treaty with al-Ḥāfiz, the Fāṭimid caliph in "Babylon" (Cairo).[33] We do not know the contents of this treaty, but it is safe to assume that it guaranteed to Sicilian merchants the same rights and privileges formerly enjoyed by those of the emir of Mahdia.

As in Sicily, the new *rex Africae*, as Roger liked to style himself, tried to curry favor with his new subjects by occasionally using the Arabic language and thus showing that he was the protector of Moslems as well as the protected of God.[34] He chose the inscriptions on his coins to make it known that he would rule Tunisia in the fashion of a Moslem emir.[35] This squares with his apparent reluctance to pay more than superficial attention to the problems of the Christian faith and church in Tunisia. When, however, bishop Cosmas of Mahdia stopped at Palermo on his return from Rome, where he had been confirmed in his see by pope Eugenius III, Roger allowed him to go back to Mahdia "as a freeman".[36] But if

[33] Romuald Guarna of Salerno, *Chronicon*, ad ann. 1148 (*RISS*, XII), p. 227. On the treaty with Egypt, see Siragusa, *Il Regno di Guglielmo I*, p. 47.

[34] An old tradition has it that after the conquest of the African cities Roger had his sword inscribed with the verse: "Apulus et Calaber, Siculus michi servit et Afer." The earliest reference to it is in Dandolo, *Chronicon* (*RISS*, XII), p. 243. It has a certain similarity to two verses in Peter of Eboli's *De rebus Siculus carmen*, vv. 1323–1324 (*RISS*, XXXI), p. 243. See Amari, *Storia dei musulmani*, III, 562, note 2, and La Mantia, "La Sicilia ed il suo dominio nell' Africa," *Archivio storico siciliano*, n.s., XLIV, 167. On the use of the title *rex Africae*, see K. A. Kehr, *Urkunden*, p. 246, note 3.

[35] Like the 'Abbāsid and Fāṭimid caliphs, the Norman kings used devices with pious invocations, for instance in Sicilian documents where they might replace the personal signature of the kings. They also appear on Sicilian coins. As regards the language, Arabic was used in Sicily in conjunction with either Greek or Latin, while from the two coins known to have been struck in an African mint (Mahdia) for Roger II and William I respectively, it would appear that the African mints used Arabic alone. See Amari, *Storia dei musulmani*, III, 456–459, 493; La Mantia, "La Sicilia ed il suo dominio nell' Africa," *Archivio storico siciliano*, n.s., XLIV, 167 (with bibliography); and H. H. Abdul Wahab, "Deux dinars normands de Mahdia," *Revue tunisienne*, n.s., I (1930), 215–219.

[36] There were only five or six sees that had survived the Arabization of Tunisia. Two bishops of Mahdia, between 1087 and 1148, died in Palermo, which suggests that Christians were not well treated by the Zīrid emirs. In addition to the cathedral churches that served the religious needs of the "Afāriqah" (African Christians), several other churches are mentioned in the sources, some of which might have belonged to merchant colonies of Pisans, Genoese, or Amalfitans in their "extraterritorial" quarters. Besides Mahdia, there were Christian communities in Bougie, Kairawan, Bona (Hippo), Carthage, and Gabes. On the controversial question of the survival of Christianity in North Africa, see J. Mesnage, *Le Christianisme en Afrique: Déclin et extinction*, pp. 219–225, and Amari, *Storia dei musulmani*, III, 376, 424.

Roger had made any significant contribution to the cause of Christianity in North Africa, no doubt historians would have noted the fact. Very likely he did not desire to change the overwhelmingly Moslem character of his new province. When, after the capture of Tripoli in 1146, he encouraged emigration thither from Sicily, it would seem that his appeal was addressed primarily to Sicilian Moslems, whose situation on the island had deteriorated, owing to the influx of Italians. The royal policy of toleration was not acceptable to the Christian hierarchy of the kingdom, and Roger must have welcomed the occasion to ease the tension in Sicily by encouraging the emigration of Sicilian Saracens. This policy can be regarded as the first step in the direction of building the cosmopolitan state of Roger's dreams, with a high degree of material welfare and a comprehensive civilization.

Roger's farsighted plans were not given time to mature. In the last years of his life he himself saw the chances for a permanent integration of the African outposts into the kingdom of Sicily diminishing rapidly. The most serious threat to the new Sicilian holdings came from the rise, in the mountains of Morocco, of the great new religious movement of the Muwaḥḥids (Almohads). 'Abd-al-Mu'min, first successor to the religious founder of the sect, organized the growing number of sectarians into an army which he led first against the Murābiṭs of Spain and then against Morocco. After sweeping victories that gave these western strongholds of Islam into his hands, he turned eastward and, in 1152, entered Algeria in force, conquering the entire state of the Ḥammādids of Bougie with the exception of Bona. The last scions of the house sought refuge at Palermo. Roger, who once before had attempted to gain a foothold in Algeria, and whose corsairs, year after year, had attacked the islands off the Algerian coasts, now decided to make common cause with the Ḥammādids and with a number of local Arab shaikhs. In exchange for hostages, Roger promised to send 5,000 horsemen to help them fight off the half-savage hordes of Berbers from the west. But then, as before and after, the Arabs refused to fight fellow-Moslems side by side with "infidels". Trusting in their great numbers, the Arabs went into the decisive battle as into a holy war, with an enthusiasm that was intensified by the presence of their wives and children whom they had taken along to witness their triumph. 'Abd-al-Mu'min crushed them at Setif on April 28, 1153.

Tunisia now lay open to the invader. In a desperate attempt to stem the tide, Roger sent a fleet against Bona under the command of

Philip of Mahdia, who had succeeded the recently deceased George of Antioch as admiral. With the help of Arab auxiliaries, Philip laid siege to the strong coastal fortress, which he conquered in the fall of 1153. This victory was the last feat of arms accomplished in the reign of Roger II.

William I, Roger's youngest and only surviving son, succeeded him as second king of Sicily (1154–1166). But he did not inherit his father's industry or interest in the details of government. In June 1154 he appointed Maio of Bari, a commoner who had worked his way up to the highest position in the royal chancery under Roger II, "admiral of the admirals". From the beginning of the new regime the feudal barons, who had chafed under Roger's iron grip and waited only for his death to do away with royal absolutism, were determined to overthrow the commoner who monopolized royal favor and power. They were ready to join hands with any foreign enemy of the kingdom who would engage the king in war, and they had not long to wait for the occasion. As if overnight, all the hostile forces that had threatened the kingdom under Roger, but had been checked by his diplomacy and good luck, were loosed upon his son. What saved the kingdom was the fact that the dreaded coalition between the Byzantine and the German emperors, who at first planned to ally against "the usurper of two empires", never came off. Yet to its very end the Norman kingdom of Sicily never came closer to complete collapse than in the fall and winter of 1155–1156. The Byzantines held the Adriatic coast from Vieste to Brindisi. A papal army was advancing on Benevento. Apulia was aflame with revolts of the cities and barons, which spread to Sicily where rebellion had never before gained a foothold. But the emergency shook William out of his usual lethargy, and showed his remarkable talents. The Byzantines were soon driven out, never to wage war on Italian soil again, and the royal power was restored. In the spring of 1157 the king was able to take the offensive, to launch a great naval expedition against the Greek island of Euboea, and even to plan a raid on Constantinople itself.

The king's victories were matched by Maio's diplomatic successes. He concluded the peace of Benevento with pope Hadrian IV in June 1156, and in the spring of 1158 extended it to include the Byzantine emperor. Yet, despite the final triumph of Sicilian arms and diplomacy, the great crisis of 1155–1157 had dismal consequences. It cost the kingdom its leading position in the Mediterranean and its colonies in Africa.

In April 1154 war had broken out with the Fāṭimids of Egypt, who had violated their old agreement with Roger by entering into commercial relations with the republic of Pisa.[37] William sent a fleet of sixty vessels to the Egyptian coast for a surprise attack on Tinnis, Damietta, Rosetta, and Alexandria. The enterprise as such was successful. An enormous haul of gold and silver and other treasure was carried home, and the fleet showed its worth by inflicting heavy losses on a numerically superior Byzantine force which tried to block its way. But the Egyptians soon retaliated at the same time that the Muwaḥḥids, from their newly conquered ports in Algeria, were sending out corsairs to raid the Italian and Sicilian coasts. Again, in a clash with one of these corsair flotillas returning from a looting raid on Pozzuoli, the Sicilian fleet was victorious.

But 'Abd-al-Mu'min was not discouraged. He spread the rumor that he was preparing an "invasion of Sicily, Apulia, and Rome", meanwhile getting ready to conquer Tunisia. The moment was well chosen. Weakened by revolts and at war with the Byzantines, the government at Palermo was able neither to send needed reinforcements to Africa nor to keep the military governors in the African cities under close control. Ibn-Khaldūn reports that the Norman commanders began to exploit and ill-treat the natives. The 'amils, who had been picked by king Roger from among the local shaikhs and whose loyalty had — it was hoped — been guaranteed by hostages taken to Palermo, were well informed about the troubles facing king William and Maio. They felt that the time had come to shake off the yoke of the "infidel" and to rally round the Muwaḥḥid ruler, whose political and religious cause had been so visibly blessed by God. Their fight for political independence was to become part of the holy war for the rightful *imām* and for his new religion. The Muwaḥḥid ruler, for his part, exploited to the full the unrest in the cities, weaving intrigues and winning partisans who agitated for his cause.

By the spring of 1159 all Roger's conquests from Tunis to Tripoli had shaken off Sicilian rule except for the great capital and naval base of Mahdia. After their successful revolt, the governor and

[37] Siragusa, *Il Regno di Guglielmo I*, p. 46, note 2. For Pisan relations with the Fāṭimids of Cairo and the Norman kingdom of Sicily, see Schaube, *Handelsgeschichte der romanischen Völker*, pp. 149 and 461 ff., and M. Amari, *Diplomi arabi del R. archivio fiorentino* (Florence, 1863), introduction, p. lxxix. On Norman relations with Egypt, see M. Canard, "Une Lettre du Calife Fatimite al-Hafiz (524–544/1130–1149) à Roger II," *Atti del Convegno internazionale di studi ruggeriani*, I, 125–146. The sources for the war with Egypt and the Muwaḥḥids are: Ibn-al-Athīr, *Al-kāmil* (Amari, *BAS*, I), p. 480; al-Maqrīzī, *Kitāb al-mawā'iz* . . . (Amari, *BAS*, II), pp. 591 ff.; *Sigeberti continuatio Praemonstratensis* (*MGH, SS.*, VI), p. 455; and Amari, *Diplomi arabi*.

people of Sfax had hoped to take Mahdia by surprise. They only succeeded, however, in penetrating into the commercial suburb of Zawila, because there the number of Christian residents was small. Their attempt to take the fortress itself was thwarted. The Sicilian government, it would appear, made great efforts to hold this important maritime center against heavy odds. Having just driven the Byzantines from Apulia, king William and Maio sent twenty galleys with men, arms, and supplies to Mahdia. With their help the Norman garrison took the offensive, reconquered Zawila, and even extended Norman rule as far as Cape Bon. William organized Zawila as a center for fugitive Christians, those who had fled from Algeria after its conquest by 'Abd-al-Mu'min and those ousted from the rebellious cities of Tunisia. According to Robert of Torigny, he even established an archbishop there, but if so, this arrangement was of short duration. Early in 1159 the Muwaḥḥid caliph 'Abd-al-Mu'min led a well trained and well equipped army of 100,000 into Tunisia, and received the surrender of Sfax, Tripoli, and other cities from Roger's former 'amils, whom he confirmed in their offices. Then, seeing that he could not take Mahdia by assault, he drew a tight blockade around the town with his army and navy. About six months later, in January or February 1160, he forced the Sicilian garrison to surrender. Tunisia was restored to the Moslems.[38]

Contemporaries were quick to accuse Maio of deliberately abandoning the garrison of Mahdia to its fate and of betraying the cause of Christendom. They charged him, among much else, with advising the king to give up Mahdia and the other African outposts in order to free the treasury from a "useless and costly burden". This and other practical considerations may indeed have played a part. The relief of Mahdia would not inevitably have led to the reconquest of the African coast. There were too many hazards involved in an all-out war with 'Abd-al-Mu'min, especially at a time when Sicily was threatened by an invasion from the north led

[38] On the loss of the African cities, see the sources listed above, notes 25 and 32. Of the Latin writers, Hugo Falcandus is the most important, but his account of the fall of Mahdia and the revolution in the kingdom that followed is distorted by his bias against Maio. On Maio's responsibility for the loss of Mahdia see also *Chronica Ferrarensis* (ed. A. Gaudenzi, *Monumenta historica ed. dalla Società napoletana di storia patria*, ser. I, Naples, 1888), p. 29. On the events, compare Chalandon, *Domination normande*, II, 236–244, and Amari, *Storia dei musulmani*, III, 474–502. For the reconquest of Zawila ("Sibilla") and the alleged establishment of an archbishop there, see Robert of Torigny (*MGH, SS.*, VI), p. 506; note also Amari, *Storia dei musulmani*, III, 483–484. After the fall of Mahdia, bishop Cosmas of Mahdia took refuge in Palermo. He was buried in the cathedral, where an inventory of his treasures and books is still preserved. See La Mantia, "La Sicilia ed il suo dominio nell' Africa," *Archivio storico siciliano*, n.s., XLIV, 168, note 1.

by Frederick Barbarossa. But such political realism could only be misunderstood by "honor"-conscious Norman knights and zealous priests. It is certain that the fall of Mahdia added to Maio's unpopularity and helped to rekindle the flames of rebellion against the king, who was now believed to be the helpless victim of his minister. Nevertheless, the immediate antecedents of the rebellion that broke out in March 1161, a little more than a year after the fall of Mahdia, are obscure. We know only that during the summer of 1160 Maio had the Moslems of Palermo disarmed, perhaps in the hope of silencing his critics. The rebels, however, assassinated him, imprisoned the king in his palace, and then turned on the Moslems of Palermo, the court eunuchs, the officials, the tax-collectors, and the merchants, slaughtering a considerable number. When later, after a successful counter-revolution, Moslem officials and courtiers made their comeback, they took a terrible revenge upon the Christians who had participated in the rebellion.

With the exception of occasional raids, neither William I nor his son William II (1166–1189) resumed Roger's policy of conquest and occupation in North Africa. The Berber rebellions which had led to the loss of the cities in the 1150's were sufficient warning of the risks involved. In William II's time the Muwaḥḥid ruler himself, Yūsuf ibn-'Abd-al-Mu'min, had to struggle against revolts staged by the tribes and princes of the same Berbers of Tunisia who had once hailed the coming of the new caliph with so much enthusiasm. William II was inclined to open negotiations with the Muwaḥḥid. Sicilian interests urgently required an end of the hostilities that exposed the Italian coasts to African corsairs and closed the African markets to Sicilian grain. Plagued by anarchy and famine, Tunisia also needed peace. Therefore, when William's ambassadors arrived in Mahdia in 1180, the African ruler was ready to make concessions. We have contradictory reports about the terms of the peace ratified in Palermo the same year, but it is certain that they dealt primarily with economic questions. Yūsuf agreed to pay a yearly sum to the Sicilian treasury. This did not involve any political dependence, but was the price of protection for Moslem merchants buying wheat and other commodities in Sicily for the suffering people of their homeland. The Sicilians also probably received the privilege of establishing warehouses in African cities. Both sides kept the agreements even beyond the stipulated ten years. Even William's frequent interference in the political affairs of the Balearic islands, where he occasionally supported the anti-Muwaḥḥid, pro-Murābiṭ faction, did not disturb the commercial agreements, including the financial obligations that they entailed for the *rex Marroc et Africae*, later for the "king" of Tunisia. They became a part of the Sicilian political heritage and an important source of income for the Sicilian treasury under the dynasties succeeding the Norman house. As late as the fifteenth century the Aragonese ruler of the "Two Sicilies" would base a claim upon them.[39]

Outside North Africa, however, William II reversed his father's policy of caution and revived his grandfather's policy of aggressive expansion in the eastern Mediterranean. Like Roger, he was ready to profit from a new crusading movement; but unlike Roger, who never aspired to the reputation of a crusader in the strict sense of the word, William tried to achieve his goal by assuming the protection of the Christians in the east and proclaiming an uncompromising attitude of hostility toward the enemies of his faith. He was allowed to do so by the general conditions of his kingdom at the time he took over the reins of government from his mother in 1171.

Relations with the papacy were good, and the treaty of Venice in 1177 brought a fifteen-year truce with Barbarossa. Internally, the kingdom was at peace, and the authority of the crown unquestioned. At the congress of Venice William's "orators" boasted that he had never waged war against Christian princes; that he was the only one who had directed all his efforts toward the defense of the Holy Sepulcher; that, without sparing his treasury, year by year he had dispatched his ships and knights to fight the infidel and make the sea safe for Christian pilgrims going to the Holy Land.[40] Meanwhile this champion of Christendom and the crusade lived like an oriental despot, complete with harem, eunuchs, and slaves, most of them ostensibly Christian converts, but in fact Moslems allowed to

[39] Mas Latrie, *Traités de paix*, pp. 51, 162–163; Amari, *Storia dei musulmani*, III, 524–527, 643; and Giunta, *Medioevo mediterraneo*, pp. 142 ff. The first evidence for the prolongation of the treaty beyond ten years is found in the *Chronica regia Coloniensis*, ad ann. 1195 (ed, G. Waitz, Hanover, 1880): "Rex Affricae 25 summarios auro et lapide precioso multisque donis oneratos imperatori [Henrico VI] mittit." For the older literature on the question of the nature of the treaty, see La Mantia, "La Sicilia e il suo dominio nell' Africa," *Archivio storico siciliano*, n.s., XLIV, 168, note 2.

[40] The two speeches that play on this theme are an address delivered before the assembly at Venice by Romuald Guarna of Salerno, head of the Sicilian delegation, and an official reply by a representative of Frederick Barbarossa. See Romuald Guarna of Salerno (*RISS*, VII), pp. 290–291. Cf. the obituaries of William II in Richard of London, *Itinerarium peregrinorum* (ed. W. Stubbs, Rolls Series, XXXVIII), p. 33, and *Sigeberti continuatio Aquacinctina* (*MGH, SS.*, VI), p. 425. On William's attitude and policy toward the Saracens the most important source is Ibn-Jubair, *Riḥlah* [*Voyage*] (Amari, *BAS*, I), pp. 137 ff. See La Lumia, *Storia della Sicilia*, pp. 179–192; Chalandon, *Domination normande*, II, 428–430; and Amari, *Storia dei musulmani*, III, 514. Amari remarks that William took the crusade too seriously for the good of his kingdom, yet never considered sacrificing his personal comfort for the risks of war.

practice their religion under the king's very eyes. Indeed, under William's regime the Moslems of Sicily enjoyed the blessings of an official policy of toleration. Like his predecessors William employed Sicilian Saracens in his army and navy and did not hestitate to lead them against Christian princes. Also the world must have wondered why this fervent advocate of the crusade never went in person on any of his many expeditions. In fact, he was the only scion of the house of Hauteville who all his life avoided the dangers and strains of war. Yet the world was impressed by his readiness to send knights and marines overseas to die in Egypt and Syria. William's decisions, though essentially the results of an untutored ambition, were taken as signs of Christian devotion and a true crusading spirit. He wasted his resources and manpower with little benefit to his kingdom, but he earned the reputation of being a "protector and defender of the Christians of Outremer".

An occasion for serious intervention in the Levant was not long in coming. The news of the defeat of the Byzantine and Frankish forces at Damietta in 1169 seems to have made a great impression on William. It appears that he began to prepare for an expedition against Egypt shortly after 1171.[41] The situation in Egypt would not have seemed beyond repair; the Byzantine-Frankish alliance stood the test of common defeat; king Amalric of Jerusalem held the friendship of the Assassins; and most important, Saladin's position was growing increasingly difficult. His relations with Nūr-ad-Dīn were strained to the breaking-point, and, after he declared the Sunnite religion of the caliphs at Baghdad to be the orthodox creed for all Egypt, his Shī'ite opponents were seeking to encompass his overthrow. In 1173 some of the Shī'ite nobles began negotiations with the kings of Jerusalem and Sicily for common action against Saladin. An embassy which Amalric sent to the west

[41] There may have been a Sicilian expedition to Egypt as early as 1169, when Amalric sent an appeal for help in the reconquest of Damietta. It is generally assumed by historians that there was no response, but Ibn-al-Athīr says that "the Franks of Sicily, of Spain, and other countries sent money, men, and arms" to their harassed brethren in the east. On the Sicilian expeditions (alleged or real) to Damietta and Alexandria in 1169 and 1174 and the corsair war with Egypt in 1175–1178, see Abū-Shāmah, *Kitāb ar-rauḍatain* [*Book of the Two Gardens*] (Amari, *BAS*, I), pp. 536–541; Ibn-al-Athīr, *Al-kāmil* (Amari, *BAS*, I), pp. 491–499 (also in *RHC, Or.*, I, 599–602, 611–614); and al-Maqrīzī, *Al-mawā'iẓ* (Amari, *BAS*, II), pp. 591–593. For other Arabic sources, see Amari, *Storia dei musulmani*, III, 515, note 1, 516, note 2. Latin sources include William of Tyre, XXI, 3 (*RHC, Occ.*, I), pp. 1007–1008; *Annales Pisani*, ad ann. 1175, and *Annales Casinenses*, ad ann. 1174 (*MGH, SS.*, XIX), pp. 266, 312. Compare Chalandon, *Domination normande*, II, 394–398; Amari, *Storia dei musulmani*, III, 515–524 (with a chronology of the expedition to Alexandria); and Grousset, *Histoire des croisades*, II, 594–596, 617–619. Al-Maqrīzī speaks of a major naval force sent to Damietta, which is contradicted by Saladin's own official report on William's expedition to Alexandria, described as the first that the king launched. See Chalandon, *Domination normande*, II, 394–395.

to renew his urgent appeals for help probably met William at Palermo and discussed with him a plan for common action. After the landing of a Christian force near the Delta, and in the event Saladin should march his army to the coast to fight them off, the Shī'ite nobility would arouse the populace of Cairo and Fustat and restore the Fāṭimids to the throne. Should Saladin remain in the city with only minor forces, the Fāṭimid partisans would arrest him, and the Sicilian fleet would lay siege to Alexandria while an army under Amalric closed in on the city by land.

William now feverishly prepared his navy and army for the early summer of 1174, when the expedition was to get under way. But while these preparations were going on, and while the secrecy surrounding them kept William's potential enemies in suspense, everything went wrong in the east. Saladin learned of the Shī'ite conspiracy, and in April 1174 arrested the ring-leaders and executed them. Neither William of Sicily nor Amalric of Jerusalem learned of this, and therefore could not know that their attack would receive no assistance from a Shī'ite revolt. Then Amalric died on July 11, 1174, just about the time when the Sicilian fleet was to sail for Alexandria. When the expedition reached Alexandria on July 28, the commanders were probably still unaware that, as a result, they would get no assistance from a Frankish army. Consequently the Sicilians were at a considerable disadvantage. Despite the size of their force — even the most conservative sources assert that it consisted of two hundred galleys carrying 30,000 men, including a thousand knights and five hundred Saracen cavalry (the so-called Turcopoles), and more than eighty freighters for horses, equipment, supplies, and war machines — it did not suffice to make the siege of a city as large as Alexandria effective. Another serious setback came right at the outset when the Alexandrians, though taken by surprise, managed to block the entrance to the harbor by sinking all the ships anchored there.

The Sicilian attempt to take the city was thwarted even before Saladin could get there with a relieving force. Saracen reinforcements from the countryside kept pouring into the city, and on July 31 the inhabitants made a sortie during which they succeeded in burning the formidable siege engines placed against their walls. On the night of August 1 they surprised the besiegers' camp, looted and slaughtered, and terrified the Normans, who fled for the ships with their attackers in hot pursuit. The commanders decided to avoid the major disaster which threatened should they clash with Saladin himself, and sailed for home the next morning with the sad remnants of what, only three days before, had been the proud army of the king of Sicily. Only a small force of three hundred knights, entrenched on a hill near the city, continued the fight, until the very last of them was either killed or taken.

William was not discouraged. He sent two expeditions in 1175–1176 to attack the commercial center of Tinnis near the Nile delta. These were mere raids for plunder, however, with hardly forty ships involved in either action. William also launched three expeditions against the Balearic islands between 1180 and 1186, aimed at eliminating the constant threat to Sicilian and Italian commerce from corsairs through the conquest of Majorca (Mallorca), the largest of the islands.[42] None of these expeditions achieved its goal, and the forces engaged in the third cannot have been very substantial, for by this time Sicily was caught up in a major war with the Byzantines.

The troubles that followed the death of the emperor Manuel in 1180 provided William with an opportunity to intervene in Byzantine affairs. The usurpation of the Byzantine throne by Andronicus Comnenus precipitated rebellions in many parts of the empire. Several of the nobles whose power Andronicus was trying to curb fled to Italy to seek help from William and others. Among them was one of the pretenders to the Byzantine throne, Alexius Comnenus, nephew of the late emperor Manuel. Alexius urged William to conquer the Byzantine empire on his behalf. Because of the final failure of the great plan, historians have reproached William with wanton waste of manpower and material, and with lack of political foresight. But Chalandon convincingly points out that the enterprise was not only politically sound but also promising of success, and that, in fact, William came very close to "consummating triumphantly the heroic epic of his house which the sons of Tancred of Hauteville had started in Italy."

The land phase of the war with the Byzantines began in June 1185 with the taking of Durazzo, reached its climax in August with a spectacular success, the sack of Thessalonica, and ended in September with the no less spectacular defeat of the Sicilian army at the Strymon river.[43] The Sicilian navy, on the other hand, under the

[42] On the historical background, see the article on the Balearic Islands in *The Encyclopaedia of Islām*. On William's expeditions to the Baleares, see Chalandon, *Domination normande*, II, 398, and Amari, *Storia dei musulmani*, III, 527–530. The sources are contradictory and vague.

[43] The most important source for the expedition against Constantinople that led to the sack of Thessalonica is Eustathius of Thessalonica, *De capta Thessalonica liber* (*CSHB*, Bonn, 1842). See also Nicetas Choniates, *Historia*; *De Andronico Comneno*, I (*CSHB*), pp. 386–401. For the

command of Tancred, count of Lecce and future king of Sicily, was never defeated. It cruised in the neighborhood of Constantinople for seventeen days waiting for the army to arrive to lay siege to the city. Afterwards it withdrew in good order to Sicily, ravaging islands and the Greek coast on the way. The war continued relentlessly. To avenge the defeat on the Strymon, William sent a fleet under the command of the sea-captain Margarit of Brindisi to Cyprus to assist the governor of the island, Isaac Comnenus, who had now proclaimed himself emperor. This episode began the career of Margarit, later admiral and count of Malta, nicknamed king, or even god (Neptunus), of the sea.[44] When a Byzantine fleet put into Cyprus, where it discharged an army, Margarit destroyed a large part of it while Isaac Comnenus defeated the army and turned the captured Byzantine generals over to Margarit for confinement in Sicily. Shortly thereafter, Margarit inflicted another defeat on a Byzantine fleet en route to Palestine to support Saladin.

The Norman attack on the Byzantine empire had no little influence on the situation in the east. For one thing, it strengthened Saladin's position on the eve of his conquest of Jerusalem. Up to this moment the alliance between the Latins of Jerusalem and the Byzantines had proved one of the bulwarks of the Christian position in the east, withstanding even the test of the common defeat at Damietta in 1169. But, in fear of a Sicilian (or even a combined German-Sicilian) attack, Andronicus had accepted Saladin's overtures and concluded a treaty which was later confirmed by Isaac II Angelus. The Kurdish leader maintained good relations with both Isaac Angelus in Constantinople and Isaac Comnenus in Cyprus. On the other hand, while the attack on the Greek empire had brought the Sicilian king no gain, and probably a serious loss of prestige, it considerably weakened the empire on the Bosporus and showed the way to the conquest of 1203–1204.

The Sicilian assault had clearly revealed the military weakness of Byzantium. Not since Guiscard's time had the Normans come nearer their goal, and if they had followed up their victory at Thessalonica by marching immediately on the capital, instead of

history of the siege, Nicetas copied Eustathius. Other sources include Ibn-Jubair, *Riḥlah* (Amari, *BAS*, I); *Annales Ceccanenses* (*MGH, SS.*, XIX), p. 287; and *Estoire d'Eracles*, XXIV, 5, 6 (*RHC, Occ.*, II), pp. 112–113. Compare G. Spata, *I Siciliani a Salonica* (Palermo, 1892), which includes an Italian translation of Eustathius, and Chalandon, *Domination normande*, II, 400–415. On Byzantium under the Comneni, see below, chapter IV, pp. 123–146.

[44] Nicetas Choniates, *Historia*; *De Isaacio Angelo*, I (*CSHB*), pp. 474 ff., 484. See Chalandon, *Domination normande*, II, 415; Röhricht, *Geschichte des Königreichs Jerusalem*, p. 494, note; and G. Hill, *History of Cyprus* (4 vols., Cambridge, 1948–1952), II, 312–314.

allowing their forces to disperse and loot, and if complete coöperation between navy and army could have been achieved, they might well have conquered Constantinople. It remained for the Venetians, however, watchful neutrals during the Sicilian-Byzantine war, to draw the appropriate conclusions, and only nineteen years later to put them into effect.

In 1187, when Jerusalem fell to Saladin, an urgent appeal went out for help to hold Tyre, Tripoli, and Antioch. The archbishop of Tyre, Joscius, told William at Palermo of the courageous stand made by the Christians in Tyre under the energetic leadership of Conrad of Montferrat. He probably reproached the king for his un-Christian attitude in imposing an embargo on ships in Sicilian ports early in 1185 which, he claimed, had kept pilgrims from getting to Palestine in time to fight. He also chided William for having pressed pilgrims into his army to fight Christians in the Byzantine empire. William admitted his sins, and in a great display of repentance and mourning he donned a hair-shirt and secluded himself for four days. Then he promised the archbishop that he would appease God by helping the Christians in the east. After all, here was a new occasion to assert himself as the protector of Outremer and to blot out the disgrace of the defeat of 1174. He hastily made his peace with Isaac Angelus and called Margarit home from the eastern theater of war.

Without waiting for the organization of a new crusade, William sent Margarit with some fifty or sixty vessels and two hundred knights to Tyre, where Conrad of Montferrat assigned him the task of defending Tripoli and other places of northern Syria against Saladin who, at the time (the early summer of 1188), was moving his army from Damascus for the conquest of the Syrian cities still held by the Franks.[45] Margarit succeeded in reorganizing and strengthening the defenses of Tripoli so efficiently as to discourage Saladin from besieging it. But the admiral was unable to prevent

[45] On William's contributions to the Third Crusade, see *Estoire d'Eracles*, XXIV, 5, 7, 11 (*RHC, Occ.*, II), pp. 111–113, 114–115, 119, 120; 'Imād-ad-Dīn al-Iṣfahānī, *Al-fatḥ al-qussī* (Amari, *BAS*, I), pp. 339–344; Ibn-al-Athīr, *Al-kāmil* (Amari, *BAS*, I), pp. 499–501; Abū-Shāmah, *Ar-rauḍatain* (Amari, *BAS*, I), pp. 541–543; *Gesta regis Henrici secundi* . . . (ed. W. Stubbs, 2 vols., Rolls Series, XLIX), II, 54, 132–133; Richard of London, *Itinerarium* (ed. W. Stubbs, 2 vols., Rolls Series, XXXVIII), I, 27 ff.; Robert of Auxerre, *Chronica* (*MGH, SS.*, XXVI), p. 253; *Breve chronicon de rebus Siculus* (ed. J. L. A. Huillard-Bréholles, *Historia diplomatica Friderici II*, I, part II), pp. 890–891; *Ottoboni annales Januenses* (*MGH, SS.*, VIII), p. 102; Sicard of Cremona, *Chronicon*, ad ann. 1188, and *Bernardi Thesaurarii chronicon*, 169, 170 (both in *RISS*, VII); and Francesco Pipino, *Chronicon*, I, 41 (*RISS*, IX). See La Lumia, *Storia della Sicilia*, pp. 333–336; Chalandon, *Domination normande*, II, 416–417; Amari, *Storia dei musulmani*, III, 532–540; Röhricht, *Königreich Jerusalem*, pp. 474, 490; Runciman, *Crusades*, II, 470; III, 4–9; Monti, *Espansione mediterranea*, p. 163; and volume I of the present work, chapter XVIII, p. 588, and chapter XIX, p. 618.

Saladin's victorious march northward along the coast and his conquest of Tortosa, Maraclea, and Jabala. Arabic historians report that after all his attempts had been frustrated, Margarit approached Saladin with the proposal of an alliance, on condition that Saladin leave the Christian cities alone and guarantee them their land and safety; in return he would receive their help in the conquest of neighboring territories held by Nūr-ad-Dīn's heirs, the atabegs of northern Syria. Should Saladin reject the pact, Margarit threatened an invasion of the east by such forces of western Christendom as to make Saladin's resistance hopeless. As a matter of course, Saladin refused. Apparently the Christians knew that Saladin hoped to dominate the north of Syria, were aware of his rivalry with the heirs of Nūr-ad-Dīn, and tried to exploit this situation. At any rate, it seems that it was through this interview that Saladin was first informed about a new crusade being prepared in the west.[46]

During the following summer Margarit received reinforcements from Sicily. He must have realized that he could not attack Saladin's coastal cities and castles directly. Instead, he turned to harassing and chasing the enemy like the corsair he may have been in his early days. Operating back and forth between Tyre and Tripoli and also along the coast near Antioch, he dealt telling blows at the Saracen freebooters and warships, keeping the lifeline for Christian ships carrying supplies, arms, and later an ever growing number of crusaders to the harassed Christians in their Syrian strongholds. It is to these activities that an English writer refers when gratefully crediting Margarit with having supported Antioch, defended Tripoli, and saved Tyre.[47] The admiral's activities in Syria came to an end late in the fall of 1189. On November 18 king William of Sicily died, and Margarit was probably recalled by Tancred, William's temporary successor, who badly needed armed support

[46] See 'Imād-ad-Dīn, *Al-fatḥ al-qussī* (Amari, *BAS,* I), pp. 343–344; Abū-Shāmah, *Ar-rauḍatain* (Amari, *BAS,* I), pp. 543–544, and Ibn-al-Athīr, *Al-kāmil* (Amari, *BAS,* I), pp. 499–501. The west was informed of Saladin's ambition to subjugate the atabegs of northern Syria. An alliance with the new sultan of Egypt seemed within the range of political possibilities. Saladin himself made a similar offer; see *Gesta regis Henrici II* (Rolls Series, XLIX), II, 175–176, 180. Amari (*Storia dei musulmani,* III, 539, note 1) believes that Saladin made this offer after a defeat suffered at the hands of Margarit (before 1190).

[47] Richard of London, *Itinerarium* (Rolls Series, XXXVIII), I, 27: ". . . quis dubitat quod Antiochia retenta, quod Tripolis defensa, quod Tyrus servata . . ." On the reaction of the Arab historians who refer to Margarit's tactics as purposeless blundering, see Amari, *Storia dei musulmani,* III, 534. On Margarit's activities at Acre, see *Gesta regis Henrici II* (Rolls Series, XLIX), II, 54, and Robert of Auxerre (*MGH, SS.,* XXVI), p. 253. Compare Amari, *Storia dei musulmani,* III, 539–540. Margarit's adventures were glorified as "fes per mer" by the troubadour Raymond Vidal, cited by Chalandon, *Domination normande,* II, 417, note 4. On Margarit's identity and career, see C. A. Garufi, "Margarito di Brindisi, conte di Malta e amiraglio di Sicilia," *Miscellanea . . . Salinas* (Palermo, 1907), pp. 273–282.

in his struggle for the throne.[48] Fortunately for the Christians in the east, more and more crusaders, mostly from northern Europe, kept arriving at Acre and filled the gap left by the departure of the Sicilian ships.

King William must have been greatly satisfied with the news of Margarit's successes, which reflected credit on himself. He intended that these should be only the harbinger of greater things to come. Knowing that archbishop Joscius of Tyre intended to win the kings of France and England for a new crusade, William approached them himself and laid before them a plan for common action, according to which Sicily would be the meeting-place of the crusading armies from the west. The king offered the use of his harbors, his navy, and other facilities and resources of his kingdom. Jointly with the English and French, the Sicilians would cross the seas and wage war against Saladin. The plan was the same as that suggested by Roger II to Louis VII of France on the eve of the Second Crusade and rejected by the assembly at Étampes in February 1147. This time it must have been accepted by the western princes immediately, for in his interview with Saladin in July or August of 1188 Margarit was already threatening a joint crusade of the kings of Christendom. Whether William would have participated in person had he lived must remain uncertain.[49] More likely he would have named Margarit or count Tancred of Lecce as his representative.

When William felt his death near, he bequeathed a handsome legacy to Henry II of England, his father-in-law. Part of it consisted of a large amount of grain, wine, and money, and of a hundred armed galleys with equipment and supplies to last for two years.[50] Obviously the legacy was intended to fulfil William's crusading

[48] It is certain that Margarit was in Messina in October 1190, for he participated in the negotiations between Tancred's representatives and the kings of England and France. His siding with Tancred aroused the suspicion of the English, and he had to leave Messina. Richard confiscated his property in the city along with that of other suspect magnates. See *Gesta regis Henrici II* (Rolls Series, XLIX), II, 128, 138; compare Chalandon, *Domination normande*, II, 438–439.

[49] See *Estoire d'Eracles*, XXIV, 7 (*RHC, Occ.*, II), pp. 114–115. Among the authors who mention William's contributions to the struggle against Saladin only Francesco Pipino, who wrote much later, assumes as a matter of course that William, had he lived, would have gone on the crusade. Some of the more recent Sicilian historians credit the story of William's participation in Margarit's expedition to Tripoli and Tyre in 1188, but they do not quote any contemporary evidence. See La Lumia, *Storia della Sicilia*, pp. 624–625.

[50] And in addition, many precious objects such as a gold table mounted on two gold tripods, a silk tent in which two hundred knights could dine together, and silver cups and dishes. It is doubtful that this legacy to Henry II, as described in the *Gesta regis Henrici II* (Rolls Series, XLIX), II, 132–133, formed part of a general testament. According to the *Annales Casinenses*, ad ann. 1189 (*MGH, SS.*, XIX), p. 314, William died "sine liberis et testamento".

obligations even after his death. It probably reflects his proposed contributions had he lived to see the crusade launched.

Whether full participation of Sicilians in the Third Crusade would have changed the military and political situation in the Near East in favor of the Latin Christians of Outremer nobody can tell. It might well have brought the kingdom of Sicily economic and political advantages, and a position that could have served as a springboard for the conquest of Constantinople. From this point of view William's death was a tragic misfortune for the kingdom. When conditions which two kings of Sicily had long tried to bring about were finally present, there was no one who could benefit from them.

Tancred of Lecce had been elected and crowned king by a national party headed by Matthew of Salerno,[51] but he was hardly able to establish his authority against those who saw in the new German emperor Henry VI, husband of Roger II's daughter Constance, the legitimate heir endorsed by the late king. Therefore, when the kings of France and England successively landed in Sicily in September 1190, Tancred, who feared an invasion of Apulia by Henry's armies and new rebellions by his vassals, could think neither of participating in the crusade nor even of making a substantial contribution to it. The very legacy bequeathed by William to Henry II added to Tancred's embarrassment. It was this legacy, and the dowry for his sister Joan, king William's queen, that gave Richard the Lionhearted a pretext for entering Sicily as an enemy and occupying Messina.[52] These incidents gave rise to rumors of an English plan to conquer the whole island. It all ended with an agreement in the negotiation of which king Philip Augustus of France played a somewhat ambiguous role. Tancred paid off the obligations both to the dowager queen and to the greedy English king. Fifteen galleys and four transports, which Richard received as a gift from king Tancred shortly before he embarked for Acre, were all that was left of the great project nurtured by the last legitimate Norman king of Sicily.

When in 1194, after the death of Tancred and the defeat of his partisans, Henry VI ascended the throne of the Hautevilles in Palermo, the Norman tradition was once more revived. Henry's somewhat vague imperial dream "to subjugate all lands" now took on the concrete and distinctive traits of the Norman-Sicilian

[51] Often erroneously termed "of Ajello" (Aiello), apparently because his son Richard became count of Ajello. See Jamison, *Admiral Eugenius of Sicily*, p. 94, n. 1.

[52] See below, chapter II, pp. 58–61.

program of Mediterranean expansion in three directions, towards North Africa, Constantinople, and the Near East. As regards North Africa, Henry fell heir to the agreement between William II and the "king of Africa" (emir of Tunis), received the tribute, and continued in good commercial relations with him. To settle his account, both inherited and personal, with the emperor in Constantinople, Henry wrested from the weak Alexius III Angelus the concession of a high annual tribute. Finally, for his ambitious plans in the Near East he proclaimed, prepared, and launched a crusade, the first German expedition to start from Italian bases.[53] The crusade began under good auspices, for even before it got under way, king Leon II of Cilician Armenia and king Aimery of Cyprus (the later titular king of Jerusalem) asked to receive their crowns and lands at the hands of Henry or his representative. But death cut short all these hopes, and it was Henry's son Frederick II who was destined to be the first king of Sicily to wear the crown of Jerusalem, although by then not much more than prestige would be attached to it.[54] The traditional Norman-Sicilian policy would inspire and direct later kings of Sicily, the Hohenstaufen Manfred and the Angevin Charles. But the great days of Sicilian prominence in the politics and commerce of the Mediterranean had come to an end with the death of William II.

[53] See below, chapter III, pp. 116–122.
[54] See below, chapter XII, pp. 442–462.

2. Western Europe and the Mediterranean (*Map by the University of Wisconsin Cartographic Laboratory*)

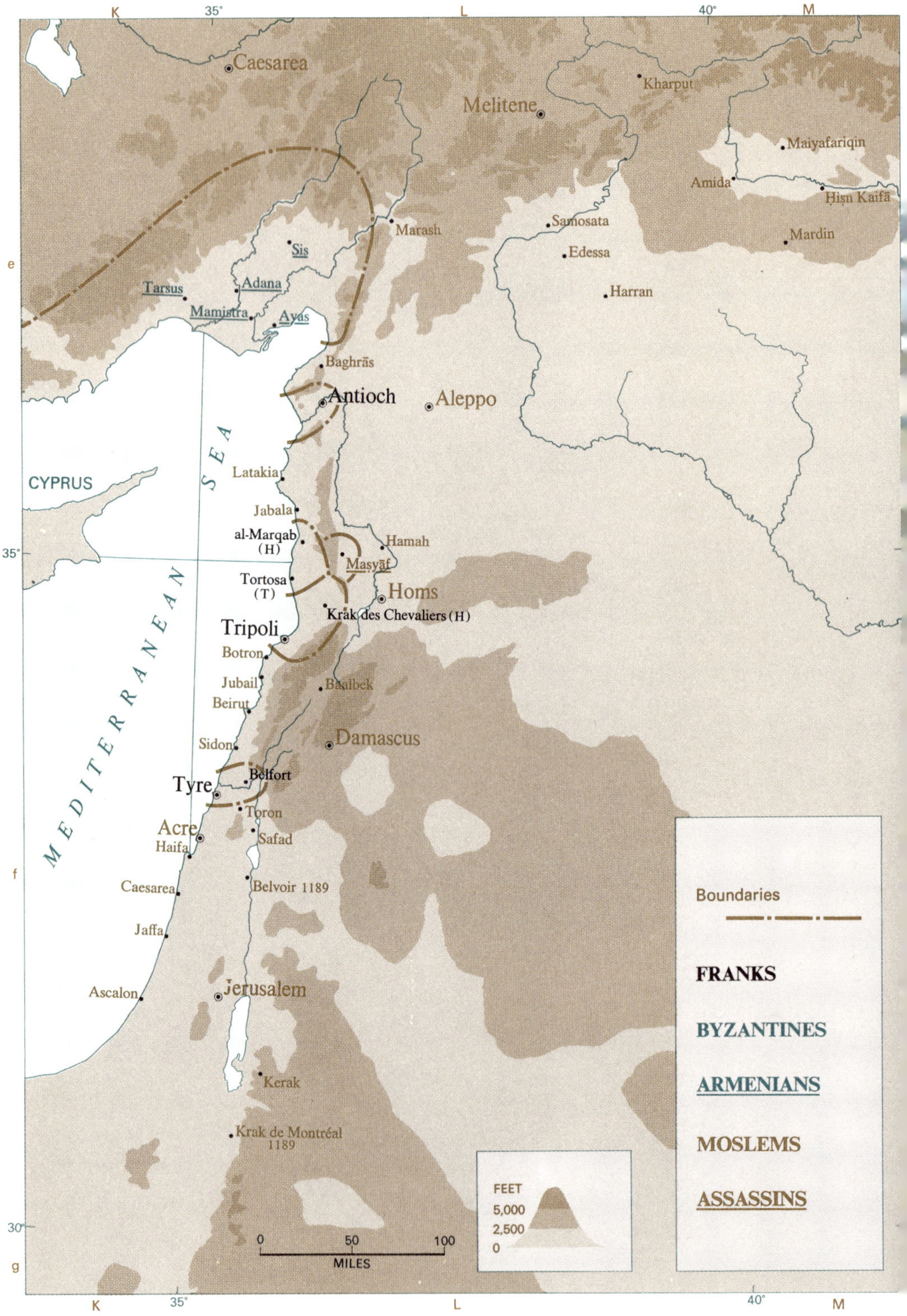

3. The Latin States in 1189 (*Map by the University of Wisconsin Cartographic Laboratory*)

II

THE THIRD CRUSADE: RICHARD THE LIONHEARTED AND PHILIP AUGUSTUS

On July 4, 1187, the levies of the kingdom of Jerusalem, reinforced by members of the military orders, contingents from the county of Tripoli, and itinerant crusaders, were routed at Hattin near Tiberias by Saladin, sultan of Egypt, Damascus, and Aleppo. Guy of Lusignan, king of Jerusalem; his brother Aimery, constable of the kingdom; the masters of the Temple and the Hospital;

The fullest account of the crusade of Richard I (the Lionhearted) of England and Philip II (Augustus) of France is the *Estoire de la guerre sainte*. This work has been translated by Merton Jerome Hubert as *The Crusade of Richard Lion-heart* (New York, 1941). John L. La Monte provided extensive notes which in general give the testimony of the other sources on most questions of importance. This book also contains an excellent bibliography of both source materials and modern works on this crusade. It will be cited as *Estoire*. Lionel Landon, *The Itinerary of King Richard I* (Pipe Roll Society, London, 1935), gives a day by day account of Richard's activities with citations of the relevant sources. The *Itinerarium peregrinorum et gesta regis Ricardi* (ed. William Stubbs in *Chronicles and Memorials of the Reign of Richard I*, 2 vols., Rolls Series, XXXVIII) is drawn from the same source as the *Estoire* and differs little from it. It is cited as *Itinerarium*. Two other valuable and very closely related chronicles are the *Gesta regis Henrici II*, ascribed to abbot Benedict of Peterborough and edited by William Stubbs (2 vols., Rolls Series, XLIX), and Roger of "Hoveden" (Howden), *Chronica* (ed. William Stubbs, 4 vols., Rolls Series, LI). These are cited as *Gesta* and Hoveden. Other useful English chronicles are Richard of Devizes, *De rebus gestis Ricardi primi* (ed. Richard Howlett, in *Chronicles of the Reigns of Stephen, Henry II, and Richard I*, vol. III, Rolls Series, LXXXII), and Ralph de Diceto (of "Dicetum", not identified), *Opera historica* (ed. William Stubbs, 2 vols., Rolls Series, LXVIII). These are cited as Devizes and Diceto. The French side of the crusade is much more meagerly presented. The only reasonably full French account is in Rigord, *Gesta Philippi Augusti* (ed. H. F. Delaborde, *Oeuvres de Rigord et de Guillaume le Breton*, Société de l'histoire de France, Paris, 1885), I. There are two other closely related chronicles in French, but they represent the point of view of the Syrian and Palestinian baronage. These are the *Chronique d'Ernoul et de Bernard le Trésorier* (ed. L. de Mas Latrie, Société de l'histoire de France, Paris, 1871) and *Le Livre d'Eracles Empereur* (*RHC, Occ.*, II). Of a number of Moslem works which bear on this crusade the most valuable is Bahā'-ad-Dīn's biography of Saladin (*RHC, Or.*, III), which is cited in the translation by C. W. Wilson for the Palestine Pilgrim's Text Society (London, 1896). Very extensive use has also been made of a manuscript entitled "Saladin in the Third Crusade" by Sir Hamilton A. R. Gibb, who has very generously made it available to the author of this chapter.

The two basic secondary works on this crusade are Kate Norgate, *Richard the Lion Heart* (London, 1924), and the second volume of Alexander Cartellieri, *Philipp II. August* (Leipzig, 1906). For the military history Charles Oman, *A History of the Art of War in the Middle Ages* (Boston, 1923) and Ferdinand Lot, *L'Art militaire et les armées au moyen-âge* (Paris, 1946) are very useful.

William III, marquis of Montferrat; Roger de Mowbray, lord of Thirsk in Yorkshire; and many another baron, knight, and sergeant were captured. Large numbers of Christians were slain in the battle, and Saladin slaughtered all the rank and file of the Temple and Hospital who fell into his hands. The True Cross, borne in the midst of the host by a succession of prelates, came into the possession of the "infidels". In mustering his army to meet Saladin's invasion king Guy had drained his fortresses of their garrisons. Except for Raymond III, count of Tripoli, Reginald, lord of Sidon, and Balian of Ibelin, who had escaped from the field of Hattin, the realm of Jerusalem was leaderless.[1] Acre fell almost at once, and Saladin soon conquered most of the other towns and castles. By the end of 1187 the only important towns still holding out were Tyre, Tripoli, and Antioch.

Tyre was saved by a stroke of chance — the fortuitous arrival of an able, vigorous soldier of high rank. Conrad of Montferrat, eldest surviving son of marquis William, and uncle of the young king Baldwin V of Jerusalem, had started for the Holy Land in 1185. Conrad had stopped in Constantinople and entered the service of emperor Isaac II Angelus. When he learned of the threatened invasion of the kingdom of Jerusalem, he obtained the emperor's leave to go to Palestine. The ship bearing him and his small band arrived at Acre after its capture by Saladin. Fortunately for the Franks Conrad discovered the state of affairs before he landed, and promptly sailed up the coast to Tyre. He found that city about to surrender. The commander of the town, lacking both garrison and supplies, had agreed with Saladin on terms of capitulation. But the citizens took heart from Conrad's arrival, delivered the city to him, and prepared to defend it under his leadership.[2] Tyre became the refuge for the inhabitants of the places captured by Saladin during the following months, for the sultan's conquest of the kingdom of Jerusalem was no orgy of bloodshed. Although Saladin was fully capable of savage cruelty, he preferred to be merciful — especially when mercy paid. The towns of the kingdom were leaderless and had almost no soldiers, but they were strongly fortified. The inhabitants were discouraged by the loss of the leaders and troops, and were willing to surrender in exchange for their lives. Saladin's troops were horsemen who felt at home only in the open field and had no taste for attacking fortifications. Hence it was good policy

[1] Bahā'-ad-Dīn, pp. 113–114; *Eracles*, pp. 65–67; *Gesta*, II, 12, 22. For details see volume I of the present work: chapters XVIII and XIX, map 14, and the supplementary list of towns and fortresses in the gazetteer.

[2] *Eracles*, pp. 15–16, 73–76; Bernard le Trésorier, pp. 179–182. Baldwin V died in 1186.

for the sultan to buy the towns by allowing the inhabitants to go free. Every such displaced person made the food problem more serious in the remaining Christian strongholds.

Conrad, the officials of the Temple and Hospital who had not been captured at Hattin, and the prelates of the kingdom promptly sent appeals for aid to the princes and lords of western Europe. According to a Moslem writer, Conrad sought to arouse crusading enthusiasm by circulating a picture of a Turkish horseman allowing his mount to urinate on the Holy Sepulcher.[3] At some time during the autumn of 1187 Conrad reinforced his letters by dispatching to the west Joscius, archbishop of Tyre, the successor to William, the historian. The archbishop's first stop was Sicily, where he found a sympathetic listener in king William II. Had it not been for king William, the slow-moving monarchs of the west might well have found no kingdom of Jerusalem to succor. In the spring and summer of 1188 a Sicilian fleet commanded by the famous admiral Margarit saved Tripoli from capture and reinforced and provisioned Antioch and Tyre.[4] Had William II survived, the Sicilian forces would probably have played an important part in the Third Crusade, but he died in 1189, and a disputed succession kept Sicilian energies fully occupied until 1194.

On January 22, 1189, archbishop Joscius found Henry II of England, Philip II Augustus of France, Philip of Alsace, count of Flanders, and many lords and prelates of the two realms engaged in a conference on the Norman frontier. So eloquent was his appeal for aid for the Holy Land that both kings, the count of Flanders, and many other lords took the cross, and agreed to begin preparations for a crusade. The French were to wear red crosses, the English white crosses, and the Flemish green crosses. King Henry soon proceeded to Le Mans, where he ordered the levying of the "Saladin tithe", a tax of a tenth on everyone's income and movable property, to raise money for the crusade. While archbishop Baldwin of Canterbury and other prelates preached the crusade, Henry vigorously collected the tax throughout his lands. Henry also dispatched letters to the Holy Roman emperor, Frederick I Barbarossa, to king Bela III of Hungary, and to the Byzantine emperor, Isaac Angelus, announcing that he intended to go to the relief of the kingdom of Jerusalem and asking free passage through their realms.[5] But while Henry was industriously preparing for his

[3] Bahā'-ad-Dīn, p. 207; Diceto, II, 60–62.

[4] *Eracles*, pp. 111–112, 114, 119–120; Bernard le Trésorier, pp. 244, 247, 251; *Itinerarium*, p. 27. On the Sicilian admiral Margarit, see above, chapter I, pp. 37–40.

[5] *Gesta*, II, 29–32; Diceto, II, 51–54.

pious journey, his eldest surviving son, Richard, count of Poitou, became embroiled in a fierce war with his vassals and his neighbor, count Raymond V of Toulouse. The Poitevin rebels were quickly crushed and their leader, Geoffrey of Lusignan, departed for Palestine to join his brothers Guy and Aimery, but the conflict with Toulouse soon involved king Philip.[6] Hence after a very brief respite war raged once more along the Angevin frontiers.

No one who understood the political situation in northwestern Europe in 1188 could have had much hope of any long-term agreement between the kings of France and England. Philip Augustus was determined to develop the power of the French crown. The greatest menace to that power was the Plantagenet lord of England, Ireland, Normandy, Maine, Anjou, Touraine, and Aquitaine. With the king of England in possession of the maritime districts of France from Boulogne to the Pyrenees, the French monarchy was in grave danger. King Louis VII of France had combatted his mighty rival by both arms and intrigue, and Philip carried on his father's policy. This basic hostility between the French king and his vassal took various forms at different times. In 1188 the immediate issue was Philip's sister Alice and her marriage portion. The Norman Vexin with its great fortress of Gisors had long been a bone of contention between the two monarchs. In an attempt to settle this issue Alice had been affianced to Richard, and the Vexin assigned to her as a marriage portion. Until the wedding took place, both Alice and the Vexin were to be in Henry's custody. In 1188 Philip was insisting that Richard marry Alice, and Richard was showing no inclination to do so. The men of the day believed that Richard's unwillingness stemmed from his belief that his father had seduced Alice, an act which would have been unlikely to disturb Henry's conscience. As Henry wanted to keep the Vexin in his own hands instead of turning it over to his turbulent son, he made no effort to hasten Richard's marriage.

Had Alice been the only issue, Henry and Richard could cheerfully have waged war on Philip. But Henry had never been sympathetic to Richard and preferred his youngest son, John. He was contemplating giving John a large part of his vast domains. Naturally Richard was opposed to this idea. When Richard's disinclination to marry Alice was uppermost in his mind, he was on good terms with his father, but when his fear of John was dominant, he was inclined to negotiate with king Philip. Philip lost no opportunity to take advantage of the difficulties between Henry and Richard.

[6] *Gesta*, II, 34–36; Diceto, II, 54–55.

In November 1188 he demanded that Henry require all his vassals to do homage to Richard as his heir. When Henry refused, Richard did homage to Philip for the fiefs held in France by the house of Anjou. Late in May 1189 Philip and Richard demanded that John take the cross. Henry's refusal to agree to this sent Richard into open rebellion. On July 6, 1189, Henry died at Chinon. On July 22 Richard had a conference with Philip and renewed his promise to marry Alice — a promise he clearly had no intention of keeping. On September 3 Richard was solemnly crowned king of England.

In November 1189 king Philip sent Rotrou, count of Perche, to England to inform Richard that he and his barons had agreed to meet at Vézelay on April 1 to set out on the crusade. Richard had taken the cross earlier than had his father and Philip. He delighted in war in all its forms and was an enthusiast for adventure. Hence he willingly accepted Philip's challenge. At a council held in London the count of Perche swore that Philip would keep the rendezvous, and William de Mandeville, earl of Essex and count of Aumale, swore that Richard would join him. On December 30 the two kings met at Nonancourt to complete their arrangements. In a formal document they announced their intention to go on the crusade. Philip promised to treat Richard as his friend and vassal, while Richard was to behave toward Philip as to his lord and friend. All crusaders in the two realms were to join the host unless specifically excused. The property of all crusaders was to be safeguarded. Peace was to reign between the two kingdoms, and the governors of each were to aid the other in case of need. On March 30, 1190, the kings confirmed this agreement but postponed the meeting at Vézelay until July 1.[7]

While the kings of France and England fought, conferred, prepared, and delayed, the effort to restore the kingdom of Jerusalem that is usually known as the Third Crusade gained momentum. The emperor Frederick Barbarossa marched from Regensburg (Ratisbon) on May 11, 1189, with a strong army of mounted men and headed east through Hungary. After successfully crossing Asia Minor, the emperor was drowned in the "Saleph" river, (Calycadnus) on June 10, 1190. Some ten days later, his army reached Antioch under the command of his son Frederick, duke of Swabia. But the comforts of Antioch were too much for the troops exhausted by long marches and bitter battles. Some died there and most of the rest went home. When Frederick of Swabia advanced

[7] *Gesta*, II, 92–93, 104–105; Diceto, II, 50, 73–74; Hoveden, III, 19, 30–31.

into the kingdom of Jerusalem, he had only some three hundred knights.[8]

During May 1189 a series of crusading fleets left the ports of northwestern Europe. They bore Danes, Frisians, North Germans, Flemings, English, Bretons, and men of northern France. There is little definite information about these fleets or their commanders. The Frisians and North Germans were led by Otto, count of Guelders, and Henry, count of Altenburg. The Flemings were under the command of a famous warrior, James of Avesnes. If one may assume that all the barons who arrived in Palestine in September 1189 came in these fleets, their leaders included William de Ferrers, earl of Derby; Louis, landgrave of Thuringia; count John of Sées; count Henry of Bar; the viscounts of Turenne and Châtelerault; Guy of Dampierre; Robert, count of Dreux; his brother Philip, bishop of Beauvais; Erard, count of Brienne; and his brother Andrew, lord of Ramerupt. It is, however, quite possible that some of these lords went by other routes. One of these fleets sailed from Dartmouth on May 18, and halted in Portugal to aid king Sancho I against his Moslem foes. On September 6 its men captured the town of Silves, turned it over to the Portuguese, and then proceeded on their way to Palestine.[9]

When these fleets reached the Holy Land, they found that the forces of the kingdom of Jerusalem had already begun an offensive campaign. Early in September 1187, Saladin had found Ascalon too strong to take by storm, and to avoid a long siege he had offered to exchange king Guy for the city. Ascalon surrendered on September 4, but Saladin was in no hurry to keep his promise. It was not until the spring of 1188 that Guy, his brother Aimery, and the master of the Temple were freed. Before he released the king, Saladin exacted from him a promise that he would not again bear arms against him. Guy seems to have taken this promise seriously. For over a year he stayed quietly in Antioch and Tripoli while Saladin reduced several of the castles that still held out against him. Then in the summer of 1189 he decided to move toward the recovery of his kingdom. It is not clear whether he simply ignored his promise to Saladin or obtained a release in some way. No Christian prelate would have hesitated to absolve him from such an oath. One

[8] Bahā'-ad-Dīn, pp. 207–208, 213; *Eracles*, p. 141; *Gesta*, II, 142; Arnold of Lübeck, *Chronica Slavorum* (*MGH, SS.*, XXI), p. 175. The crusade of Frederick Barbarossa is dealt with in chapter III of this volume.

[9] *Gesta*, II, 89–90, 94; Diceto, II, 65–66; *Eracles*, pp. 127–128; *Estoire*, pp. 137, 139–140, 146; *Itinerarium*, pp. 62, 64–65, 67–68, 74; Arnold of Lübeck, *Chronica Slavorum* (*MGH, SS.*, XXI), p. 177.

source suggests that Saladin released him for fear that his inability to lead the armies of the kingdom would lead to his replacement by a more effective monarch. Guy of Lusignan was a brave soldier, but he was a most incompetent general and an ineffective king.

At any rate Guy mustered a small army and marched to Tyre. When he demanded admission to this city, Conrad of Montferrat refused to open the gates. According to one source, Conrad said that he had saved Tyre and it was his. Another authority states that Conrad declared himself a mere lieutenant of the monarchs of the west and unable to act without their orders. Whatever his arguments may have been, Conrad clearly refused to recognize Guy's royal rights in Tyre. He did, however, form an alliance with him against Saladin. Towards the end of August, probably on the 27th, king Guy and his troops occupied a hill near Acre, while the Pisan squadron that had escorted him down the coast blockaded the port.[10] In the Middle Ages all that was required for a "siege" was a force camped near a hostile fortress. Hence contemporaries called this the beginning of the siege of Acre. Actually it was nearly a year before the crusading army could make a serious pretense of blockading the city on the landward side.

Saladin was lying with a small force before the great fortress of Belfort when he learned of Guy's march toward Acre. The sultan wanted to cut across country to intercept the king, but his emirs insisted on the longer and easier route by the main roads. Hence Guy was in position when Saladin arrived. As the sultan did not have enough troops to attack the royal army in a position of its own choosing, he was obliged to await the arrival of the vassal lords whom he had summoned from the east. It was at this point that the crusading fleets which had left Europe in May began to arrive. Guy's little body of knights was reinforced by the followers of James of Avesnes, count Otto of Guelders, earl William de Ferrers, Guy of Dampierre, the counts of Dreux and Brienne, and other barons. But far more important than the feudal contingents was the magnificent north European infantry, Danes, Frisians, and Saxons. They were the men who made it possible for Guy to continue operations in the face of Saladin's host. The Turks were mounted archers used to fighting in broad, open fields. They could not withstand a charge by the heavy feudal cavalry, but they could usually avoid it by rapid maneuvering. Their tactics were to sweep

[10] *Itinerarium*, pp. 20, 25–26, 61–62; *Estoire*, pp. 127–128, 130–134; Bahā'-ad-Dīn, pp. 143–144; Bernard le Trésorier, pp. 184–185, 252–253, 256–257; *Eracles*, pp. 78–79, 120–121, 124–125, 131.

up close to the knights, discharge a rain of arrows, and retire before the knights could reach them. If the knights pursued them and became scattered, the Turks could cut to pieces isolated parties. But the Turkish cavalry had no taste for attacking massed infantry. The crossbows of the crusaders outranged their bows, and the solid line of spears formed an almost impossible obstacle to a cavalry charge.[11]

As soon as his reinforcements arrived, Saladin moved into position near the crusaders' camp. The last two weeks of September 1189 saw a number of sharp skirmishes. One day Saladin brushed away a thin screen of knights to reinforce and reprovision Acre. But he could not persuade his troops to attempt an attack on the crusading infantry defending the camp. Nevertheless, Guy's position was extremely unpleasant. He was bottled up in his camp and continually harassed by the Turkish cavalry. Late in September Conrad of Montferrat arrived with the Syrian barons who had been with him in Tyre. This addition to his forces encouraged Guy to take the offensive. On October 4 the crusader cavalry emerged from their camp and charged the Turkish line. They easily routed their foes, but they themselves became scattered in the pursuit and were completely unable to withstand a Turkish counterattack. The crusaders were thrown back on their camp in disorder. Many knights were slain including Andrew of Brienne, lord of Ramerupt. Meanwhile the garrison of Acre had made a sortie against the crusaders' rear. King Guy had foreseen this possibility and had left a force to watch Acre under that most turbulent and war-hardened of Poitevin barons, his brother Geoffrey of Lusignan, who repulsed the sortie successfully. Once more Saladin's troops showed no inclination to press home their advantage by attacking the infantry. Saladin had won a victory, but discouragement at its indecisiveness combined with the fearful stench from the bodies of those slain in the battle made him retire a dozen or so miles to a hill called al-Kharrūbah where he went into winter quarters.[12]

Winter was a time of great hardship for the crusaders lying before Acre, because during that season they could not control the seas, and hence lacked reinforcements and supplies. The kingdom of Jerusalem had always relied heavily on Italian naval forces, and after the battle of Hattin the Christians clinging to the coast of Syria and Palestine were almost entirely dependent on them. We have seen how a Sicilian fleet saved Tripoli, Tyre, and Antioch in

[11] Gibb MS., referred to above, in bibliographical note.
[12] Gibb MS.; Diceto, II, 70–71; *Estoire*, pp. 141–143.

the summer of 1188. Although the Sicilians did not appear again, each spring saw the arrival of Genoese, Pisan, and Venetian squadrons. A Pisan fleet covered king Guy's march to Acre in August 1189. These great fleets brought supplies, and their crews were excellent soldiers. During the winter the crusaders had to rely on such vessels as they kept in their own ports, and as a result during that season the Egyptian navy was usually in command of the sea. In this winter of 1189–1190 a fleet from Egypt provisioned and reinforced the garrison of Acre while the crusaders suffered severely from shortage of supplies, but in the spring the Italian ships once again assumed command of the seas. While a determined effort on the part of the Egyptians could usually get a few ships into Acre, in general during the summer it was effectively blockaded on the sea side.

Although Richard and Philip Augustus had postponed the commencement of their crusade from April to July, the most powerful baron of France started at the earlier date. Henry, count of Champagne and count-palatine of Troyes, was master of a large and rich feudal state. As his mother Mary was half-sister to both Richard and Philip, he was the nephew of both kings. He was accompanied by two of his uncles, Theobald, count of Blois, and Stephen, count of Sancerre, together with count Ralph of Clermont, count William of Chalon, count John of Ponthieu, and a number of important barons. According to the *Eracles*, he took with him king Philip's train of siege engines. This formidable force arrived at Acre near the end of July 1190. As Saladin had already sent part of his forces to watch the movements of Frederick of Swabia, count Henry's arrival forced him to withdraw his main army from the vicinity of Acre.[13]

A monarch preparing to go on a crusade was faced with both financial and political problems. He had to raise enough money to finance his expedition, and he wanted to secure the safety of his kingdom until his return. The political difficulties faced by Richard were unusually great, and his attempts to solve them were notably incompetent. The king was unmarried, and his heir would be either his brother John or his nephew Arthur. Norman feudal custom favored the uncle against the nephew. English law was not clear, but leaned the other way. John was a grown man, while

[13] Bahā'-ad-Dīn, pp. 197, 201; *Eracles*, p. 150; *Itinerarium*, pp. 92–93; *Estoire*, pp. 158–159. For a full account of the crusading activities of count Henry see M. H. d'Arbois de Jubainville, *Histoire des ducs et des comtes de Champagne* (Paris, 1865), IV.

Arthur was a young boy. Naturally John would try to do all he could to place himself in a strong position in case Richard failed to return. Richard gave John extensive lands in England in addition to the great earldom of Gloucester that he had just obtained by marriage. John received two great honors, Lancaster and Tickhill, and complete control over the counties of Dorset, Somerset, Devon, and Cornwall.

But Richard gave his brother no place in the government of the rest of the realm. This was placed in the hands of two justiciars. One of these, Hugh de Puiset,[14] bishop of Durham, was a man of noble birth, haughty, turbulent, and grasping. The other, William Longchamp, bishop of Ely, was of lowly origin, arrogant, arbitrary, and stubborn. The two men hated each other cordially. These three men — John, Hugh de Puiset, and William Longchamp — quarreled enthusiastically throughout Richard's absence. The news of their disputes worried him continuously. While in Sicily he tried to improve the situation by sending to England Walter of Coutances, archbishop of Rouen, with a commission empowering him to take over the government if he saw fit. At the same time Richard made the English situation worse by solemnly declaring Arthur his heir, and hence driving John to desperate measures. John's attempts to strengthen his position in anticipation of his brother's possible death on the crusade seriously impeded the success of the expedition by hastening, at least to some extent, Richard's return to the west.

King Philip's political problems were much simpler. He was a widower with an infant son. He entrusted the regency to his mother Adela and her brother William, archbishop of Rheims. The only serious menaces to this regency were the great vassals of the crown and the two Capetian lords who would be heirs to the throne if Philip's young son Louis died. Richard, duke of Normandy and Aquitaine, Philip, count of Flanders, Henry, count of Champagne, and Hugh, duke of Burgundy, went on the crusade, leaving only one peer of France at home — the comparatively harmless count Raymond of Toulouse. The head of the senior cadet line of the Capetians, Robert, count of Dreux, was at Acre before Philip left home. The king took with him the head of the junior branch, Peter of Courtenay, count of Nevers. Thus north of Toulouse, there was no baron left in France powerful enough to give any trouble. Yet, as we shall see, it seems likely that it was primarily the political situation at home that cut short Philip's stay in Palestine.

[14] On bishop Hugh, cf. the recent study by G. V. Scammell, *Hugh du Puiset, Bishop of Durham* (New York, 1956).

No medieval monarch could leave his kingdom with a really free mind unless, like Frederick Barbarossa, he left behind a son and heir of full age able to rule the realm.

According to Roger of Hoveden, Richard found 100,000 marks in his father's treasury. The *Itinerarium* states that in 1188 Henry II gave the Templars and Hospitallers 30,000 marks which they spent on the defense of Tyre. These figures do not seem unreasonable. In 1207 king John would collect about 90,000 marks from a tax of a thirteenth on the income and movables of the laity alone. As the Saladin tithe was a levy of one tenth on both clerics and laymen, it probably yielded a substantially larger sum. As soon as he came to the throne, Richard proceeded to build up his financial reserves. He exacted large sums for reliefs and fines. Several of his father's servants paid considerable sums for his good-will, and generous fines were offered for lands, castles, and offices.[15] But it seems unlikely that Richard actually collected very much extra money before he left. In general he must have relied on what Henry had accumulated.

There is little information about the costs of the crusade. Richard spent some £5,000 in acquiring thirty-three ships and giving their crews a year's pay. The chroniclers estimate the fleet that finally sailed at about 100 ships. We have no way of knowing whether we have here the cost of one third of the king's fleet or whether Richard's barons paid for the other ships. The king was not in a penurious mood, for he authorized the expenditure of some £2,800 for improving the fortifications of the Tower of London.[16] Richard liked to be able to spend with a free hand, and we shall find him using every opportunity to replenish his treasury as he journeyed toward Palestine.

Almost nothing is known about the financial affairs of king Philip, but he was undoubtedly poorer than his rival. A guess based on later evidence would place Philip's annual revenue at about half of what Richard drew from England alone. The *Gesta regis Henrici II* states that Richard at his accession promised Philip 24,000 marks, and if this was actually paid, it must have formed an important part of the French king's war chest. In addition, a tax similar to the Saladin tithe was levied in France, but it seems unlikely that Philip himself could have received the yield outside his demesne. Such great lords as Philip of Flanders, Henry of Cham-

[15] Hoveden, III, 8; Devizes, pp. 384–388.

[16] Hoveden, III, 46; *Gesta*, II, 120; Devizes, p. 394; *Estoire*, p. 42; *Pipe Roll 2 Richard I* (Pipe Roll Society, London, 1925), pp. 4, 8–9.

pagne, and Hugh of Burgundy had their own expeditions to finance. As to Philip's expenses we have only one useful figure — he paid the Genoese 5,850 marks to transport his army and to supply food for men and horses for eight months.[17] Unfortunately the contract does not specify what kind of marks were meant — the mark of Paris was worth about one third as much as a mark sterling. The chroniclers indicate fairly clearly that throughout his crusade Philip was less well supplied with funds than was Richard.

King Richard spent May and early June of 1190 in a rapid survey of his duchy of Aquitaine. On June 18 he arrived at his castle of Chinon for a week's stay. While there he appointed the commanders of his fleet and issued ordinances for its government. The commanders were Gerard, archbishop of Auch; Bernard, bishop of Bayonne; Robert of Sablé, the most powerful baron of Anjou; William of Fors, a Poitevin lord; and an English knight, Richard de Camville. The ordinances provided punishments for offences committed aboard the fleet. Thus if one man killed another, he was to be tied to the corpse and thrown into the sea. Richard de Camville was at Chinon when these decrees were issued. It seems probable that he and Robert of Sablé took ship soon after. William of Fors was still with Richard at Vézelay on July 3. It is quite possible that the archbishop of Auch and the bishop of Bayonne had already started. Certainly an English fleet had sailed in April, and had followed the well established custom of stopping in Portugal to strike a few blows at the Moslems there. In late June or early July Richard de Camville and Robert of Sablé joined the advance squadron at Lisbon with 63 ships. When king Richard issued his severe, almost savage, ordinances for governing his fleet, he judged the nature of his seamen only too well. The sailors invaded Lisbon, raping and plundering at will, and their two commanders had considerable trouble reducing them to order. They finally sailed from Lisbon on July 24. At the mouth of the Tagus river they met William of Fors with 33 ships, and the whole fleet proceeded on its voyage.[18]

On June 24, 1190, king Richard went from Chinon to Tours, where he stayed until the 27th. At Tours he solemnly received the scrip and staff of a pilgrim from the hands of archbishop Bartholomew. From Tours he rode eastward up the valley of the Cher, crossed the Loire at Sancerre, and arrived in Vézelay on July 2.[19]

[17] *Gesta,* II, 74; Rigord, p. 88; Lot, *L'Art militaire,* I, 158, n. 2.

[18] *Gesta,* II, 110–111, 115–120; Hoveden, III, 33–36, 42–46; Landon, *Itinerary,* pp. 33–34, 36.

[19] *Ibid.*; Hoveden, III, 36–37.

Meanwhile king Philip had received the insignia of a pilgrim from his uncle William, archbishop of Rheims, in the abbey church of St. Denis on June 24. He was also given the standard of the Capetian house, the oriflamme, which he was entitled to bear as the advocate of the great abbey.[20] Philip then proceeded to Vézelay and the two kings set out on their crusade on July 4. They travelled together as far as Lyons. From there Philip headed for Genoa, while Richard marched down the Rhone valley toward Marseilles, which he reached on July 31.

As the reader thinks of Richard and Philip Augustus leading their crusading forces from Vézelay to Lyons, what sort of picture should take shape in his mind? Should he imagine serried ranks of soldiers flowing along the roads or a few small bands of armed men? Should he think in terms of hundreds, thousands, or tens of thousands? The only truthful answer the historian can give is that he does not know. The bane of all scholars who attempt to deal with the military history of the Middle Ages is the impossibility of giving any reliable estimates of numbers. When a medieval writer had to guess at a number, he did so with lavish generosity. When he was an eye-witness, he made his estimates with dashing casualness. The figures given by contemporary writers are usually magnificently improbable round numbers. Their complete unreliability is shown most clearly on the few occasions when precise numbers are given. They are always extremely low compared to the more usual rounded figures. Ferdinand Lot has made an attempt to estimate the size of important medieval armies by using a wide range of methods, but the results, while more probable than the figures presented by the chroniclers, are far from convincing. In this chapter the practice will be to mention a number occasionally when it seems probable but in general to refrain from numerical estimates. In this particular case, the march across France of Richard and Philip, we have some fairly good evidence. Philip contracted with the Genoese for the passage of 650 knights and 1,300 squires. Lot states that there were probably three or four times that many infantry "according to the custom of the time". We cannot, however, find any actual evidence that Philip had infantry with him. As Lot himself declares that the emperor Frederick's crusading host was composed entirely of mounted men, it seems reasonable to suppose that Philip's was too. Lot estimates Richard's force at 800 from the number of ships he is said to have hired at Marseilles, but we see no reason to rely on the chronicler's statement about the

[20] Rigord, p. 99.

ships, and we may well entertain some doubt as to how many men Richard's ships could carry. Certainly if Richard led 800 men, it was a strangely composed army. He had with him five prelates, the archbishops of Canterbury and Rouen and the bishops of Bath, Salisbury, and Évreux, two barons of some position, Andrew of Chauvigny and Garin fitz Gerald, three minor barons, and some dozen important knights.[21] The bulk of the English army was aboard the fleet and Richard's escort was clearly little more than his *mesnie*. Hence the estimate of 800 men seems rather high.

King Richard expected to meet his fleet, or at least the advance squadrons of it, at Marseilles. It is inconceivable that the king could have thought that William of Fors, who had been with him at Vézelay on July 3, could have reached the coast, boarded his ship, and brought his squadron to Marseilles by July 31; but the ships that had sailed in April would have been there had they not dallied in Portugal. After waiting some days, Richard hired other ships and sailed from Marseilles sometime between August 7 and 9. On the 13th he reached Genoa, where he found Philip Augustus sick. The English king then proceeded down the Italian coast. It was a leisurely journey. Occasionally he would land to explore the countryside. Sometimes he would travel by land and rejoin his ships farther down the coast. At the mouth of the Tiber he had a conference with Octavian, cardinal-bishop of Ostia, at which the king apparently expressed rather freely his low opinion of the reigning pope, Clement III. He spent ten days in Naples and five more in Salerno. While at the latter place he received the advice of the doctors of that famous medical center about the best methods for preserving his health. He also received word that his fleet, which had arrived at Marseilles on August 22 and left on August 30, was approaching Messina in Sicily. The English fleet reached Messina on September 14 and Philip arrived from Genoa two days later. Richard himself camped outside Messina on September 22 and entered the town the next day.[22]

King Richard did not regard his visit to Sicily as a mere halt to provision his fleet. He had family business to transact, and he hoped that its successful completion would materially increase his resources for the crusade. When king William II of Sicily had died in 1189, Tancred, count of Lecce, had seized the throne. William's widow Joan was Richard's sister, and the English king intended to collect

[21] Landon, *Itinerary*, pp. 37–38; Lot, *L'Art militaire*, I, 158–162.
[22] *Gesta*, II, 112–115, 124–125.

her dowry, as well as the legacy which William had left his father Henry II. Tancred was in a difficult political position. His right to the kingdom was disputed by the Hohenstaufen heir, Henry VI, who had married his aunt Constance. In the autumn of 1190 Henry, now Holy Roman emperor, was consolidating his position in central Italy in preparation for a campaign against Tancred. The Capetian kings were traditional friends of the house of Hohenstaufen, and the Plantagenets were their traditional enemies. Hence one might argue that Tancred should quickly have tried to form an alliance with Richard. But Tancred had no great desire to pay Joan's dowry, and England was a long way off and could be of little actual aid to him. An alliance with Philip Augustus might simultaneously save the dowry and procure an effective friend against Henry VI. Tancred approached king Philip with an offer of a marriage between their children.[23] Philip, however, had no intention of offending Henry VI, especially at a time when he was leaving his kingdom, perhaps forever. He declined the offer. This left Tancred no alternative but to come to terms with Richard.

While Tancred was considering what course he should follow, Richard in his usual high-handed manner was preparing for a long stay in Sicily. About a week after his arrival at Messina he recrossed the straits and seized the Calabrian town of Bagnara. There he placed his sister Joan in the care of an adequate garrison. His next step was to take possession of a monastery, apparently on an island in the strait of Messina, as a warehouse for his supplies. Richard also built a wooden castle which he named "Mategriffons" ("to stop the Greeks") outside the walls of Messina to serve as his own headquarters. Meanwhile, as one might have expected, the English troops and sailors had quarreled with the citizens of Messina and riots had ensued. On October 4 a conference to settle the relations between the army and the town was broken up by further riots. Richard's easily exhausted patience gave way. He took the city by storm, and his troops sacked it thoroughly.[24]

The capture of Messina probably hastened Tancred's desire to make terms with Richard. He agreed to pay 40,000 ounces of gold — 20,000 for Joan's dowry and 20,000 as the marriage portion of his daughter, who was to marry young Arthur of Brittany, Richard's acknowledged heir. Richard promised to aid Tancred against any foe who attacked him while the English king was in

[23] Rigord, p. 106. For the crusading plans and legacy of William II, see above, chapter I, pp. 38–41.

[24] *Gesta*, II, 127–129, 138; *Estoire*, pp. 52–60; Diceto, II, 85; Devizes, pp. 396–402.

Sicily. After the conclusion of the treaty, the English returned the plunder taken from Messina.[25]

The relations between Richard and Philip Augustus during their stay in Sicily were rather better than one would have expected, and both monarchs showed unusual forbearance. When the people of Messina attacked the English, the French refused to aid their crusading allies; yet once the city was captured Philip insisted that his standard should fly beside Richard's on its walls. Richard was annoyed, but gave way. A few days later the two kings combined to issue regulations governing the crusading armies. If a man died on the crusade, he could dispose of half the property he had with him by will, so long as he did not leave it to legatees at home, but to fellow-crusaders or to religious foundations in Palestine. The other half was placed in the hands of a committee of prelates and barons for the benefit of the crusade as a whole. No one in the army except knights and clerics was to gamble, and they were forbidden to lose more than 20 shillings in 24 hours. The kings could gamble as much as they pleased, and the servants in their courts could do so if they kept within the 20-shilling limit. No sailor or ordinary soldier was to change masters without permission. Speculation in food was forbidden and mercantile profits were limited to ten per cent. The prices of bread and wine were regulated. Finally, a penny sterling was declared to be worth 4 pennies Angevin.[26]

The treaty between Richard and Tancred brought up a question that was to be a frequent cause of friction between the two crusading monarchs. Before they had left Vézelay, the two kings had agreed to share all conquests equally, and apparently Philip demanded half the money Richard obtained from Tancred. As it is difficult to see how Philip could reasonably regard this as spoils of conquest, the compromise by which Richard gave Philip one third seems a decided tribute to Richard's generosity and desire for peace. It is likely that it was this windfall which enabled Philip to make generous gifts of money to his noble followers at Christmas — 1,000 marks to the duke of Burgundy, 600 to the count of Nevers, and lesser sums to many others. Soon it was Philip who needed patience. In a mock tourney fought with reeds Richard fell into a silly quarrel with a Poitevin knight, William of Les Barres. Actually it was probably a flaring up of ancient grievances. William was the most noted French warrior of his day and one of Philip's most trusted captains. He had commanded French forces raiding

[25] *Gesta*, II, 133–136; *Itinerarium*, pp. 169–170; Rigord, pp. 106–107; Devizes, p. 401.
[26] *Estoire*, p. 60; *Gesta*, II, 129–132.

Richard's lands in 1188–1189. Richard insisted that William leave the crusading host, and only long, patient negotiation by Philip and his nobles persuaded him to relent.[27]

Early in 1191 a new cloud appeared to darken the relations between the two kings. Although Richard was still officially affianced to Alice of France, he had entrusted his mother Eleanor with the task of finding him another bride. She had persuaded king Sancho VI of Navarre to give Richard his daughter Berengaria. Early in January Eleanor and Berengaria reached northern Italy on their way to Messina. Apparently they were escorted by a belated French crusader, Philip of Alsace, count of Flanders. The approach of Berengaria made the problem of Alice acute. Late in February Philip of Flanders left his fair companions at Naples and proceeded by ship to Messina. This old and experienced politician seems to have brought the two kings together to clear up the points in dispute between them. As the French and English versions of the treaty concluded differ decidedly, we shall probably never know just what the agreement was, but it is clear that Philip released Richard from his promise to marry Alice, Richard promised Philip 10,000 marks payable in Normandy, and various territorial settlements were made. On March 30 Philip sailed from Messina on his way to Acre.[28]

Queen Eleanor was as unhurried a tourist as her son, and it was the end of March before she reached Reggio in Calabria. There Richard met his mother and fiancée and escorted them to Messina. As early as February the king had been disturbed by reports of the quarrels among the rulers of England and had decided to send home Walter of Coutances, archbishop of Rouen. Early in April the archbishop and the aged queen departed for England. Berengaria was placed in the care of queen Joan of Sicily, who was to accompany her brother to Palestine. On April 10, 1191, Richard's fleet sailed from Messina.

According to the contemporary chronicles, Richard's fleet as it sailed from Messina consisted of about 180 ships and 39 galleys ranged in eight divisions. The first line was composed of three very large ships, one of which carried Joan and Berengaria and the other two the royal treasure. Then followed six lines of ships.

[27] *Estoire*, p. 68; *Gesta*, II, 155–156; Rigord, pp. 106–107; *Itinerarium*, p. 169. The *Itinerarium* seems to say that Richard gave Philip half the money, but it is difficult to reject Rigord's clear statement.

[28] *Gesta*, II, 157, 160–161, 236; *Itinerarium*, pp. 175–176; Thomas Rymer, *Foedera* (Record Commission, London, 1816), I, part I, 54.

The last division was made up of the galleys under the king's personal command. The divisions were ordered to stay near enough so that a trumpet blast could be heard from one to another, and the ships in the divisions were to keep within calling distance of one another. At night Richard placed a great lantern on his galley to guide stragglers. Unfortunately the weather disrupted these careful arrangements. A severe storm struck the fleet, and many ships, including the one carrying the royal ladies, got detached from the main body. On April 17 Richard arrived at Crete, leaving the next day. Rhodes was apparently more attractive or, as one chronicler states, Richard was not feeling well. He reached that island on April 22 and did not leave until May 1.[29]

A week before Richard left Rhodes, some of the ships which had strayed from the fleet during the storm were driven to the coast of Cyprus. Among these were the three great leaders of the fleet bearing the royal ladies and the treasure. Two or three ships, probably including at least one of the treasure ships, were wrecked near the port of Limassol. The vessel carrying Joan and Berengaria cast anchor outside the port. Many of the men on the wrecked ships were drowned, including the keeper of the Great Seal of England, whose body was later found with the seal on it. Others succeeded in making their way to the shore. They were robbed of all their possessions by the Cypriotes, and some were imprisoned. Others seem to have seized a fort of some sort and defended it against their foes. Stephen of Turnham, who was probably the commander of the ladies' escort, tried to supply these men, but was prevented from doing so by Cypriote troops.[30]

The ruler of Cyprus, who called himself Byzantine emperor, was Isaac Comnenus. In 1184, even before Isaac Angelus had overthrown Andronicus Comnenus at Constantinople (1185) and seized the imperial throne, Isaac Comnenus, with the aid of his brother-in-law, the great Sicilian admiral Margarit, had seized Cyprus; he naturally refused to recognize the Angeli. The English chroniclers call Isaac Comnenus a thorough villain, who refused to send supplies to the Christians in Palestine, robbed and murdered all pilgrims who came to his shores, and oppressed the people of Cyprus. As Isaac seems to have been friendly with the group of Syrian barons headed by Conrad of Montferrat, some of this may represent enthusiastic political libel. It is, however, clear that the Cypriotes

[29] Devizes, pp. 422–423; Diceto, II, 86, 91; *Gesta*, II, 162; *Estoire*, pp. 74–80; *Itinerarium*, pp. 177–182.

[30] *Itinerarium*, pp. 184–186; *Estoire*, pp. 83–84; *Eracles*, pp. 159, 162–163; Bernard le Trésorier, p. 270; Devizes, p. 423.

had no deep affection for their ruler, and that he plundered Richard's men who were cast on his shore. Isaac tried to persuade Joan and Berengaria to land, but they discreetly declined to do so and stayed outside the port. They were rescued from this rather uncomfortable position on May 6 by the arrival of Richard.[31]

The English king promptly demanded that Isaac Comnenus release his prisoners and return all the booty taken from the men and their wrecked ships. When Isaac refused, Richard led his galleys and smaller ships into the port, beached them, and landed with his troops. Although Isaac had drawn up an army on the shore, the Cypriotes, perhaps because of lack of enthusiasm for their cause, offered little resistance to the English, and soon fled. As the English were on foot and did not know the country, they made little effort to pursue their foes. But Richard quickly disembarked some horses, and early the next morning attacked Isaac's camp some distance inland. Again Isaac and his men fled, leaving a great deal of booty and, more important still, good war-horses in Richard's hands.

On May 11 three galleys arrived at Limassol bearing Guy of Lusignan, king of Jerusalem; his brother Geoffrey; his ex-brother-in-law Humphrey of Toron; Bohemond III, prince of Antioch; and Bohemond's son Raymond. This was essentially a political delegation. The king of Jerusalem and his supporters wanted to persuade Richard, before he reached Palestine, to favor their cause in a quarrel over the crown of Jerusalem, which, as we shall see, was now raging between the Lusignans and Conrad of Montferrat. The two Lusignan brothers, who had each in his turn been driven from Poitou for an act of violence against the agents of their lord, might well feel some apprehension concerning Richard's attitude toward them. But he received them with enthusiasm and gave them rich gifts. Presumably he had already heard that his rival Philip, who had reached Acre on April 20, had espoused the cause of Conrad of Montferrat against the Lusignans.

The next day Richard took the step that he had been avoiding for so long. Nicholas, the royal chaplain, married him to Berengaria of Navarre, and she was solemnly crowned queen by John, bishop of Évreux. Thus the neglected fiancée became a neglected wife and started her long and unenviable career as queen and dowager queen of England. She and the priest who married her were to end their days in Le Mans — Berengaria as countess and Nicholas as bishop — under the firm rule of Philip Augustus.

[31] *Itinerarium*, p. 183; *Estoire*, p. 82.

Isaac Comnenus soon decided to come to terms with Richard. At a meeting near Limassol he did homage to the English king, promised to pay him a large sum of money, and agreed to lead a body of troops to Palestine. But towards evening Isaac thought better of his bargain and fled into the interior of Cyprus. Richard then divided his galleys into two squadrons. One of these under Robert of Turnham was to sweep the coasts of Cyprus to the west to seize all Isaac's ships and ports. He himself with the other squadron sailed east to Famagusta. The land forces under the command of king Guy followed along the coast. From Famagusta Richard and Guy went to Nicosia, where Richard rested while Guy reduced Isaac's fortresses. Actually there was no serious resistance. Famagusta, Nicosia, and the castles surrendered when called upon to do so. In one castle king Guy captured Isaac's daughter, who was placed in the care of Joan and Berengaria. At last, deserted by all, Isaac surrendered, asking only that he be not put in irons. Richard kindly ordered that he be given silver fetters and sent him off to prison in Tripoli in the care of his chamberlain, Ralph fitz Godfrey.

The conquest of Cyprus was a very profitable venture. In addition to the booty taken in battle and Isaac's treasures, Richard levied a heavy tax on the island. The English chroniclers state that he took one half the movable property of every inhabitant. But more important was the fact that Cyprus was extremely fertile, and lay not far from the coast of Palestine. Throughout the crusade it was a valuable source of supplies. Richard left a small garrison on the island under the command of two hardy warriors, Richard de Camville and Robert of Turnham, and on June 5, 1191, set sail for Acre.[32]

When king Richard had left Marseilles for his leisurely journey down the Italian coast, a group of his subjects had taken ship for a direct journey to Palestine. This party was headed by two elderly men who had played an important part in the reign of Henry II and who were looked on with suspicion by his successor — Baldwin, archbishop of Canterbury, and Ranulf de Glanville, who had been Henry II's justiciar. With them went Ranulf's nephew and protegé, Hubert Walter, bishop of Salisbury, who was already well liked by Richard and was to become one of his prime favorites. The party

[32] *Estoire*, pp. 85–107; *Itinerarium*, pp. 187–204; *Gesta*, II, 163–168; Diceto, II, 91–92; Devizes, pp. 424–425; *Eracles*, pp. 163–169; Bernard le Trésorier, pp. 271–273. Cf. Sir George Hill, *A History of Cyprus*, II (1948), 31 ff.

also included three Norman barons and two from the north of England. This band of crusaders had arrived at Tyre on September 16 and at Acre on October 12, 1190.[33]

Ralph de Diceto gives us a panorama of the army besieging Acre shortly after the arrival of archbishop Baldwin. By that time the host was large enough to blockade the city completely. Each end of the line where it rested on the sea was held by men from the fleets — the Genoese on the north and the Pisans on the south. Next to the Genoese came the knights of the Hospital, and thereafter Conrad of Montferrat, a number of French bands each commanded by its own lord, the English under bishop Hubert of Salisbury, the Flemings under the seneschal of Flanders, king Guy with his brothers Aimery and Geoffrey, and the barons of the kingdom of Jerusalem who followed his banner. South of Guy's forces were the knights of the Temple and the band of James of Avesnes. Between them and the Pisans on the coast were the Danes, Frisians, and Germans under duke Frederick of Swabia, landgrave Louis of Thuringia, and count Otto of Guelders.[34] This was a formidable force, but it was less an army than a conglomeration of armed bands. Conrad of Montferrat was important because of his warlike vigor and his popularity with the Palestinian baronage, Guy because of his royal title, Henry of Champagne because of his great feudal power, which made him overlord of many of the French captains, and Frederick of Swabia because of his royal birth, but no one man stood forth as a dominant and effective leader. The army had plenty of generals but no commander-in-chief, while in Sicily there waited not one commander-in-chief but two.

On October 21 the chaplain of archbishop Baldwin wrote to the chapter of Canterbury. The army was thoroughly wicked and indulged in all vices. The princes were jealous of one another and quarreled continually. The lesser men were desperately impoverished. Many men had been lost in battle and many more had died; indeed several nobles mentioned in the panorama sketched by Ralph de Diceto were dead. It is doubtful whether the good monks of Christ Church, Canterbury, realized the overwhelming significance of one death reported by the chaplain — that of Sibyl, queen of Jerusalem, elder daughter of king Amalric and wife of Guy of Lusignan. In fact death had taken not only king Guy's wife, but also his two daughters by her.[35]

[33] Diceto, II, 84; *Itinerarium,* p. 93; Hoveden, III, 42.

[34] Diceto, II, 79–80.

[35] *Epistolae Cantuariensis* (ed. William Stubbs, in *Chronicles and Memorials of the Reign of Richard I,* Rolls Series, XXXVIII) II, 328–329.

The death of queen Sibyl made Guy of Lusignan's position extremely uncomfortable. Even before this Conrad of Montferrat had refused either to recognize Guy's rights in Tyre or to obey him as king, and the majority of the barons of the kingdom had followed Conrad's leadership. Now, Guy's only claim to the throne was that he had been crowned and anointed, and had done nothing to deserve deposition.

The heir by blood of queen Sibyl was her sister Isabel, who was, however, married to a man thoroughly despised by the barons, Humphrey of Toron, handsome, gay, gentle, and amiable — qualities most unsuitable in a king of Jerusalem. To Conrad of Montferrat the solution seemed simple and obvious. The marriage of Isabel and Humphrey should be annulled, and he should marry the lady. Isabel's mother, Maria Comnena, was the wife of Balian of Ibelin, one of Conrad's strongest supporters, and she had never liked Humphrey of Toron. Thus her mother and the barons put all the pressure they could on Isabel to accept Conrad's suggestion. Unfortunately for all concerned, the very qualities that made Humphrey an unpromising candidate for the crown made him a pleasant husband, and Isabel loved him. Only when the gentle Humphrey had been driven off by his fierce foes was Maria able to prevail over her daughter. Two prelates, archbishop Ubald of Pisa, who was the papal legate, and Philip of Dreux, bishop of Beauvais, were glad to aid. Maria calmly swore that Isabel had been forced to marry Humphrey against her will, and the marriage was solemnly annulled. Only one stumbling block remained. Archbishop Baldwin of Canterbury was a stern old prelate with a rigid sense of propriety. His unpopularity with king Richard stemmed from his fruitless prohibition of the marriage of the king's brother John to Isabel, countess of Gloucester. Now he firmly forbade the marriage of Conrad and Isabel of Jerusalem. But Baldwin was old and worn. He died on November 19, 1190, and five days later Conrad and Isabel were married. As far as Conrad was concerned, he was king of Jerusalem.[36]

When Philip Augustus reached Acre on April 20, 1191, he promptly aligned himself with the party supporting Conrad. The reasons for this decision are obvious. Conrad was the husband of the heiress to the kingdom of Jerusalem. He was a vigorous soldier and effective ruler who had the support of the majority of the barons of the kingdom. In taking his part, Philip was clearly

[36] *Eracles,* pp. 151–154; Bernard le Trésorier, p. 267; *Estoire,* pp. 177–179; *Gesta,* II, 141–142.

following the sensible course. Philip's decision explains Guy's trip to Cyprus to meet Richard. With Philip committed to one side of the controversy, even an old foe of the Plantagenet house had hopes that he might persuade Richard to take the other.

The arrival of Philip Augustus before Acre gave the crusading army, for the time being at least, a single commander. Although the French king probably did not bring a very large force, his presence increased the enthusiasm and coördination with which the besiegers pressed their attacks. While masses of crossbowmen made it almost impossible for the garrison to man the walls, artillerymen pounded the fortifications with mangonels and rams housed in "cats", while other troops mined under them. Great towers were built from which missiles could be rained on the walls. The garrison resisted vigorously, and burned many of the towers and engines, but they were in desperate straits. Apparently Saladin had taken advantage of a temporary naval supremacy in the waters of Acre in late January and early February to attempt to replace the exhausted garrison with fresh troops. This process had been interrupted before its completion by the arrival of an Italian squadron, with the result that the new garrison was much smaller than the previous one. Moreover, Saladin himself was extremely short of troops. His nephew Taqī-ad-Dīn, al-Muẓaffar 'Umar, lord of the region about Hamah in Syria, had started a private war of aggrandizement against his neighbors, and the emirs of the region had hastened home to protect their own lands. Hence at a crucial time Saladin was left with only his household troops and a few contingents from Damascus and Egypt. If Philip had launched a series of major assaults, he could probably have taken Acre before Richard arrived, but he declined to do this.[37]

King Richard sailed from Cyprus, as we have noted, on June 5, 1191. The next day he landed at Tyre, but the lieutenant of Conrad of Montferrat refused to admit him to the city, and he camped outside the walls. A day or two later the king and his galleys reached Acre, to be followed in a few days by the rest of his fleet. On his journey Richard and his galley's met a great enemy ship laden with reinforcements and supplies for the garrison of Acre. The accounts of this affair differ widely. The estimates of the troops aboard range from 650 to 1,300, with the first figure the more likely. Some accounts have it that the English galleys sank the ship by ramming it, while others insist the crew sank it to avoid

[37] Gibb MS.; *Eracles*, pp. 156–157; Bahā'-ad-Dīn, pp. 233–234, 240; Rigord, p. 108.

capture. At any rate the ship was destroyed, and its loss was a serious blow to the morale of the garrison of Acre.[38]

No sooner had Richard reached Acre than both he and Philip fell sick. They were not, however, too sick to quarrel. King Philip promptly demanded that, in accordance with their agreement to share all acquisitions made during the crusade, Richard should give him half of Cyprus. Since count Philip of Flanders had just been killed at Acre (June 1), and his great fief had come into Philip's custody, Richard replied by demanding half of Flanders. These were simply unamiable pleasantries. Richard's behavior was not far from outrageous. Count Henry of Champagne had run out of funds, asked Philip for a loan, and received the answer that he could have the money as a mortgage on Champagne; Richard gave him the funds he needed. As count Henry was Richard's nephew as well as Philip's, this may have been pure generosity to a relative. But when Richard offered to pay four bezants a month to all knights who would serve him, in contrast to the three paid by Philip, he was clearly bent on humiliating the French king. Then Richard immediately demonstrated his support of Guy of Lusignan. When the Pisans and Genoese sought to do him homage as a leader of the host, he rebuffed the Genoese because they had supported Conrad. In mid-June king Guy carried before the kings a formal complaint against Conrad as a contumacious vassal, and Geoffrey of Lusignan challenged Conrad to battle. Conrad retired to Tyre in anger. It is hard to believe that Guy took this step without Richard's approval.[39]

About the time of Richard's arrival, Saladin had brought his army close to Acre, so that he could give all possible aid to the garrison. He arranged that, when the crusaders launched a serious attack on the walls, the garrison would beat their drums to notify the Turkish troops, who would then assault the besiegers from the rear. King Philip was the first of the crusading kings to recover his strength, and about July 1 he launched an attack on the city, while Geoffrey of Lusignan held off Saladin's troops. On July 3 Philip's miners succeeded in bringing down a section of the city wall, and the king ordered an attack, but the defenders held firm and the besiegers were repulsed with the loss of Aubrey Clement, marshal of France. During this attack on the breach Saladin hurled his cavalry against the crusader's camp. As the camp was well fortified with a deep trench, and firmly held by the crusading infantry, the

[38] Hoveden, III, 112; Diceto, II, 93–94; Devizes, p. 425; *Itinerarium*, pp. 204–210; *Estoire*, pp. 108–114; Bahā'-ad-Dīn, pp. 249–250; *Eracles*, p. 170.

[39] *Itinerarium*, pp. 212, 214–215; Devizes, p. 426; *Gesta*, II, 170–171; Bahā'-ad-Dīn, p. 254; *Estoire*, pp. 193–196.

Turkish attack was repulsed. Once more Saladin discovered that his horsemen could not break a line of infantry, especially when it was protected by a ditch. The next day he withdrew his troops and proceeded to ravage the neighboring countryside so that it could not supply the crusaders after their capture of Acre. On July 6 Richard was well enough to be carried out to direct an attack on the walls by his troops. Each day the crusaders assaulted the walls, and each day they were repulsed, but the garrison of Acre grew steadily weaker from losses and simple exhaustion. On July 11 the garrison repulsed a great assault by the English and Pisans. The next day they asked for terms of surrender.[40]

The contemporary writers agree on the chief items in the terms offered the garrison of Acre, but, as usual, vary widely on the exact figures involved. The lives of the garrison were to be spared. The True Cross was to be returned to the Christians, and a large number of Christian prisoners were to be released. The statements about the number of prisoners to be freed are irreconcilable — the most reliable source seems to be Richard's own statement that he was to receive 1,500. The sultan was to pay a heavy ransom, probably 200,000 dinars, for the garrison. The troops in Acre were to give hostages to guarantee the carrying out of this agreement.[41]

In accordance with their agreement to share all conquests, Philip and Richard divided Acre between them. Philip took the castle for his residence while Richard reserved for himself the house of the Templars. Each appointed his own commander for his part of the city — Dreux of Mello for Philip and Hugh of Gournay for Richard. The nobles and knights of the crusading host occupied the houses of the city. This led to immediate difficulties. The Christian citizens of Acre who had been expelled by Saladin demanded their property. It was finally agreed that the citizens should have possession of their houses, but must lodge the crusaders as guests. Another important task was the purification of the churches of Acre, which had been defiled by being in the possession of the "infidel". This was carried out on July 16 by the papal legate with the assistance of the prelates of the host.[42]

After the fall of Acre king Philip had but one burning desire — to go home as quickly as possible. In order to understand this wish

[40] Bahā'-ad-Dīn, pp. 251–266; Gibb MS.; *Eracles*, p. 172; Rigord, pp. 109, 115; *Gesta*, II, 173–174; *Estoire*, pp. 194–216; *Itinerarium*, pp. 220–232.

[41] *Ibid.*; *Estoire*, p. 217; Hoveden, III, 131; Devizes, p. 427; Bahā'-ad-Dīn, p. 266; Diceto, II, 94; *Eracles*, p. 173; *Gesta*, II, 178–179.

[42] *Gesta*, pp. 179–181; *Eracles*, pp. 175–176; Bernard le Trésorier, pp. 274–275.

we need not believe the wild tales of contemporary writers, such as the story that count Philip of Flanders on his deathbed told the king that a group of crusaders planned to murder him, or that when king Philip was extremely sick, Richard tried to shock him to death with a false report of the death of his son Louis. Prince Louis was in fact desperately ill, and the reports of his condition may possibly have reached Philip. Then the death of count Philip of Flanders had created a situation that could easily be too difficult for a regency. The count had no children and his heir was his sister Margaret, the wife of count Baldwin of Hainault. Isabel, Philip's first queen, had been a daughter of Baldwin, and he had been promised Artois after count Philip's death. While as a matter of fact the regents of France had no great difficulty in seizing Artois in the name of prince Louis, Philip may well have feared that Baldwin would repudiate the earlier agreement and seize all Flanders. But not even these fairly serious political considerations are needed to explain Philip's desire to quit the crusade.

He had been very sick and was far from completely recovered. He was, moreover, a proud young monarch with a jealous sense of the respect that was due to the king of France. Yet his vassal, Richard of England, outshone him and humiliated him. Richard had more money and more troops. He was ten years older than Philip, and was widely famed as a warrior. Richard was arrogant, high-handed, and hot-tempered. In a military expedition from Acre to Jerusalem, Philip could not hope to compete with Richard for military glory, and he would have to suffer from his rival's bumptiousness. One can hardly blame the French king for wanting to depart. Richard seems to have opposed the plan but not very vigorously. He could clearly have more fun without Philip to hamper him, and the French troops were to remain under the duke of Burgundy. Philip cheerfully swore that he would respect Richard's lands while he was on the crusade. While it is possible that Philip was plotting an attack on Normandy before Richard got home, it is probable that he was sincere at the moment and later yielded to temptation.[43]

Before Philip departed, he and Richard made an honest attempt to settle the affairs of the kingdom of Jerusalem. Conrad of Montferrat, who had been styling himself "king-elect of Jerusalem" since May, was persuaded to return to Acre to plead his cause against

[43] *Eracles*, pp. 179–180; Bernard le Trésorier, p. 277; *Gesta*, II, 184–185; *Estoire*, pp. 220–221. The question of Louis's illness is a curious one. Rigord says that the prince fell sick July 23. If this date is correct, Philip could not have heard about it before he left Acre on July 31. Devizes, p. 429, states that Philip's entourage forged letters saying Louis was sick.

king Guy before the two monarchs and the barons of the host. Both claimants swore to accept the decision of the assembly. It was decided that Guy was to hold the royal title for life but without any right to transmit it to his heirs. Conrad should hold Tyre, Sidon, and Beirut as a fief and he or his heir should succeed Guy as king. The revenues of the kingdom should be divided equally between Conrad and Guy. Geoffrey of Lusignan was to become count of Jaffa (Joppa), and hold Jaffa and Ascalon as a hereditary fief. Thus Guy kept the royal dignity, but the only demesne of any importance left to him that was actually in Christian hands was Acre, and this possession became of dubious value when a few days later king Philip handed over his half of the city to Conrad, along with his share of the hostages. Conrad showed his continued lack of enthusiasm for his crusading comrades by returning to Tyre with the hostages. On July 31, 1191, king Philip sailed for Tyre on his way home.[44]

Richard's first concerns after Philip's departure were to repair the fortifications of Acre, and enforce the agreement that had led to its surrender. He immediately put men to work on the walls and towers of the city and sent messengers to Saladin to inform him when he expected the first instalments of prisoners and money due under the truce. But before he could carry out his part of the agreement, Richard had to have at his disposal Philip's share of the hostages, whom Conrad had taken to Tyre. Bishop Hubert of Salisbury and count Robert of Dreux were sent to Tyre to direct Conrad to bring the hostages to Acre. Conrad refused to obey, and only when the French commander, duke Hugh of Burgundy, went to Tyre did he give up the hostages. Meanwhile envoys of Richard and Saladin had been carrying on negotiations, but we can get no clear picture of the details. Apparently at least one Christian mission visited the sultan's prisons at Damascus.[45]

When the time came for the payment of the first instalment, something went wrong, but it is impossible to discover just what happened. The Christian writers state simply that Saladin failed to keep his promises. While the Moslem sources differ in detail, their stories are essentially the same. When the first payment came due, Saladin was thought to have on hand the True Cross, 100,000 dinars, and 1,600 prisoners, but he did not have certain captives

[44] R. Röhricht, *Regesta regni Hierosolymitani* (Osnabrück, 1893), no. 705; *Gesta*, II, 183–184; *Estoire*, pp. 210–211; *Itinerarium*, pp. 235–236.

[45] *Itinerarium*, pp. 240–242; *Estoire*, pp. 223–226; *Gesta*, II, 186–187; Bahā'-ad-Dīn, p. 271; *Eracles*, p. 177.

who had been specifically named in one of the agreements. He offered to turn all these over to Richard and give hostages for completing the transfers if the king would free his hostages from the garrison of Acre. Or Richard could take the Cross, money, and prisoners, and give hostages to guarantee that he would free the hostages from Acre. Richard's envoys insisted that the instalment be delivered, and their word accepted for the freeing of the hostages.

When Saladin refused, Richard lost his temper. He selected a few of the hostages who were important enough to be worth large ransoms. The rest he and the duke of Burgundy led outside the city and slaughtered in sight of Saladin's host. The Moslem writers believed that this had been the king's intention from the beginning — and Christian references to the murder as vengeance for the crusaders slain before Acre would seem to support their view, but this seems improbable. It is more likely that there was mutual distrust and misunderstanding between Richard and Saladin about the exact arrangements. Richard was by nature arrogant, impulsive, and impatient. He wanted to clear up the business so he could start his campaign. Hence he took what seemed the simplest course. No Christian king would worry much about the lives of two or three thousand Moslems. As to the Christian prisoners left in Saladin's hands, one is forced to conclude that Richard was convinced that few if any were men of importance. A chivalric king would worry little more about low-born Christian sergeants than about Moslems.[46]

As king Richard waited at Acre, he must have considered the general strategic situation very carefully. He knew that, if his crusaders were adequately supplied with food and water and intelligently led, they could defeat any army Saladin was likely to muster. Apparently the sultan's best course was to use his large reserves of manpower to wear down the Christian army by continuous attacks in the field and by determined defense of all fortresses. Richard probably realized, however, that this policy was actually impossible. Saladin's troops could not be persuaded to sacrifice themselves in fierce assaults on the crusading host in the hope that it would mean victory for their successors. The fall of Acre had completely discouraged the Moslem garrisons. In the purely military sense, Saladin's one hope lay in a crushing defeat of his foes before his own men lost all their spirit. Richard's chief problem was to keep his troops supplied. The sultan had already ravaged

[46] *Eracles*, p. 178; Bernard le Trésorier, p. 276; Bahā'-ad-Dīn, pp. 272–273; Diceto, II, 94; Devizes, p. 428; *Gesta*, II, 188–189; *Estoire*, pp. 226–228; *Itinerarium*, p. 243.

the countryside extensively, and his light horsemen could easily complete the task. The crusading army would have to depend on its fleet for supplies. If it advanced inland, the army's communications would have to be strongly defended. These considerations left Richard no choice as to his immediate course. An attempt to march direct from Acre to Jerusalem would take the army through very difficult country, the hills of Ephraim, and give it an impossibly long line of communications. The only practicable base for a march on Jerusalem was the port of Jaffa. Hence on August 22 king Richard led his host from Acre and started the journey down the coast.

Few captains in history have been as difficult to understand as Richard the Lionhearted. As a soldier he was little short of mad, incredibly reckless and foolhardy, but as a commander he was intelligent, cautious, and calculating. He would risk his own life with complete nonchalance, but nothing could persuade him to endanger his troops more than was absolutely necessary. His march along the coast was carefully planned. The army was organized in divisions, each of which consisted of both cavalry and infantry. On the inland side of each division marched the infantry — the archers and crossbowmen on the outside with the spearmen beside them ready to form a solid wall of spears if the enemy charged. To the seaward of the infantry rode the cavalry, and along the coast itself moved the baggage train. The daily marches were short, so that the infantry would not become exhausted. At each spot on the coast where ships could be brought up to the shore, Richard rested and supplied his army.[47]

When the crusading army marched south from Acre, Saladin broke up his camp and followed. Keeping his main force concentrated some distance from his enemies, he sent bands of skirmishers to harass their march. The Turks would dash up to the crusaders, rain arrows on them, and ride away. In doing this, they suffered losses from the bolts of the crossbowmen. The armor of the crusading infantry protected them from the Turkish arrows, but the cavalry lost many horses. Saladin hoped that Richard would lose his head and order his cavalry to drive off the skirmishers. If they did this and became scattered, they would be easy prey for Saladin's main squadrons. But the English king kept his army in formation, and only permitted small detached bands of horsemen to attack the skirmishers. Early in the march the Turks had one small success. Two of the crusading divisions got separated far enough so that

[47] *Gesta*, II, 190; *Itinerarium*, p. 244; Bahā'-ad-Dīn, p. 282.

the enemy could break through, but Richard himself rushed to the scene, drove off the Turks, and closed up the line. The only Christian losses were a few infantry and some baggage animals. In this combat William of Les Barres performed so well that Richard abandoned his hostility to him.[48]

Saladin soon lost hope of being able to tempt the crusaders to break their ranks, and decided that he would have to fight a pitched battle. For several days he and his commanders scouted the countryside in search of a suitable place. They finally chose a section of the route just north of the town of Arsuf. There a forest, lying to the east of the crusaders' route, would shelter the main Turkish host until it was ready to attack. Apparently Saladin planned to throw the main weight of his assault against the rear-guard, in the hope of slowing it up enough to create a gap between it and the advanced troops. This might well cause the confusion needed to make possible a successful charge by the Turkish cavalry.

King Richard was fully aware that the pass between the forest of Arsuf and the sea was a likely spot for a Turkish attack, and as he approached it he arrayed his troops with particular care. The Templars formed the vanguard. Behind them came Richard's own troops, Bretons, Angevins, Poitevins, Normans, and English. Apparently king Guy commanded the Poitevins as well as the local barons of his party. Then came the French contingents. The Hospitallers formed the rear-guard. Count Henry of Champagne was entrusted with the task of watching the edge of the forest to give warning of a Turkish attack. Richard and duke Hugh of Burgundy as generals in command rode up and down the line to see that the divisions kept close together.[49]

On the night of September 5, Richard camped between the sea and a marsh that covered him from attack. On the morning of the 6th the army set out for Arsuf. Soon its flank and rear were beset by Turkish skirmishers, and Saladin's main force could be seen issuing from the woods and forming behind the skirmish line. Before long, the crusaders' rear-guard was under full attack. The crossbowmen took heavy toll of their foes, but they found it difficult to withstand the rain of Turkish arrows, and the Hospitallers began to lose their horses at an alarming rate. They requested permission to charge the enemy cavalry. But king Richard did not want merely to repulse the attack — he hoped for a decisive victory. If he could get the entire Turkish host closely engaged, a

[48] Bahā'-ad-Dīn, p. 275; *Itinerarium*, pp. 250–251; *Estoire*, pp. 236–239.
[49] *Itinerarium*, pp. 260–261; *Estoire*, pp. 250–251.

cavalry charge could crush it. Hence he ordered the Hospitallers to wait until he gave the order for a general assault. The Hospitallers were soon goaded beyond endurance, however, and shortly before Richard was ready to give the signal for a cavalry charge, they passed through their infantry and rode at the Moslems. This left Richard and Hugh of Burgundy no choice, and they ordered a general attack. The cavalry squadrons rode through the infantry, and charged all along the line. The Turkish horse could not withstand the heavily armed knights. In the rear, where they had been closely engaged, their losses were very heavy. The French also slew many of their foes. The troops of Richard's command and the Templars barely made contact with the rapidly retreating Turks.

Saladin still had a chance for victory. At the battle of Acre the crusaders had routed the Turks, had scattered in the pursuit, and had been cut to pieces when the enemy rallied. Richard, however, had no intention of being caught in that trap. When his cavalry lost contact with the enemy, he halted and reformed his line so that the inevitable Turkish rally met another orderly charge. This process was repeated once more before the Turks finally retired into the forest of Arsuf. The battle was a decided victory for Richard. The enemy had suffered severely while his own losses had been comparatively light. The only crusader of importance to fall was the heroic James of Avesnes, who had probably pressed the pursuit with more enthusiasm than sense.[50] But more important than the actual Turkish losses was the effect on their morale. Saladin's troops became convinced that they could not win in the open field, and lost all interest in attempting pitched battles. The battle of Arsuf was the last Turkish attempt to destroy king Richard's host.

Three days after the battle of Arsuf, the crusading army arrived at Jaffa. As Saladin had destroyed the fortifications of the town, the first task of the crusaders was to restore them. Meanwhile king Richard considered his future course. There were several possibilities, of which the most obvious was to march on Jerusalem as soon as he had established a firm base at Jaffa. But Richard was too much of a realist to regard this plan with any great optimism. Although he could undoubtedly lead his army to Jerusalem and lay siege to it, there was grave doubt as to whether he had enough men to keep his supply line secure. And if his communications were cut, he might well have difficulty extricating his army even if he captured

[50] *Estoire*, pp. 252–266; Hoveden, III, 131; *Itinerarium*, pp. 262–275; Bahā'-ad-Dīn, pp. 290–293; *Eracles*, p. 185.

Jerusalem. However much Jerusalem might be the goal of every enthusiastic crusader, its practical value to the kingdom of Jerusalem was doubtful. If it was to be held against Saladin, the holy city required a strong garrison and a safe route to the sea. The latter could be secured only by garrisoning the castles that lay between Jerusalem and Jaffa. Once they had visited the shrines of the holy city, the crusaders would go home, and the forces of the kingdom would have to hold the conquests. But the kingdom lacked a force adequate for such a purpose. If Richard did not realize this of his own accord, it was certainly pointed out to him by the barons of the kingdom.

A rather more tempting idea was to conclude a peace or a truce with Saladin. Jerusalem or at least access to it by pilgrims might be obtained in this way and the kingdom given time to recover its strength. This possibility appealed to Richard for reasons having nothing to do with the situation in Palestine. He was worried about affairs at home. The idea of having Philip Augustus in Paris while he was in Palestine could not fail to disturb an Angevin prince.

Furthermore, there was a military move that was comparatively safe and easy and would profit the kingdom of Jerusalem more than the recovery of its capital. Far down the coast stood the great fortress of Ascalon. This place and some lesser strongholds near it were of immense strategic importance. Saladin was primarily sultan of Egypt and drew most of his strength from that country. Ascalon was the key to the land route between Egypt and Saladin's Asiatic lands. A strong Christian garrison there could make communications with Egypt extremely difficult.

The possibilities open to Richard were perfectly obvious to Saladin. Immediately after the battle of Arsuf he called a council to decide what he should do. The sultan wanted to place strong garrisons in Jerusalem and Ascalon, strengthen their fortifications as much as possible, and await Richard's next move. But his emirs insisted that he lacked troops enough to hold both places and must concentrate on the defense of one of them. He chose to defend Jerusalem, but decided to dismantle Ascalon so that Richard could not use it. On the same day that Richard entered Jaffa, Saladin reached Ascalon and began the destruction of its fortifications. Not until the last week of September did he rejoin the covering force that had been left to watch the crusading host at Jaffa.[51]

During October 1191 king Richard made preliminary moves toward all three objectives. Without indicating whether his aim

[51] Bahā'-ad-Dīn, pp. 295–300; Gibb MS.

was Jerusalem or Ascalon, he concentrated all the forces he could muster at Jaffa. Many crusaders had quietly wandered back to the fleshpots of Acre. Early in October king Guy was sent to bring them back to the host. When he failed, Richard himself went to Acre. He was more successful, and brought some of them back to Jaffa. He also moved Berengaria and Joan from Acre to Jaffa. As soon as Richard returned from Acre, he entered into active negotiations with Saladin. Apparently he started with a proposition he had made earlier, and one that there was little or no chance that Saladin would accept, the cession to the Christians of all territory west of the Jordan. Then, if we are to believe Bahā'-ad-Dīn, Richard advanced a most extraordinary proposal. Queen Joan was to marry Saladin's brother, al-'Ādil Saif-ad-Dīn ("Saphadin"), and they were to rule all the land west of the Jordan, the True Cross was to be returned, and all prisoners were to be freed. Saladin did not take this proposition seriously, but authorized his brother to continue negotiations. Soon Richard said that Joan refused to accept the idea, but might be persuaded if her future husband turned Christian.[52] While it seems almost certain that these negotiations took place, it is difficult to believe that anyone took them very seriously. Yet it is equally difficult to see why Richard should make such a proposition if he had no intention of carrying it out. The only reasonable explanation seems to be that the king was caught for a while in a fog of romantic optimism.

In the last days of October Richard moved his army to the vicinity of Yāzūr a few miles southeast of Jaffa. There he restored two castles which Saladin had dismantled and which were needed to protect the road to Jerusalem. On November 15 he marched farther southeast along the same road to a place near Ramla, where he remained until December 23, when he moved on to Latrun. This placed the crusading host a little more than halfway along the route from Jaffa to Jerusalem. During these operations there were no major engagements. As the crusaders advanced, Saladin withdrew his main forces. There were many pleasant skirmishes in which the dashing English king and his knights could earn military renown. Sometimes a crusading scouting party on the flanks or in front of the host would meet a detachment of Turks. Other encounters were apparently Turkish attempts to interfere with Richard's supply line to Jaffa. These skirmishes did nothing to alter the conviction of the Turkish emirs that they did not want to fight pitched battles with the crusaders. They must also have

[52] Bahā'-ad-Dīn, pp. 307–313; *Estoire*, pp. 277–291.

strengthened Richard's realization that the Turkish army was still in existence and that a siege of Jerusalem would be a most hazardous venture.[53]

While his army was making this very leisurely progress along the road to Jerusalem, Richard continued to negotiate with Saladin concerning the proposed marriage of Joan to the sultan's brother. By November 9 he announced that the marriage would require papal approval and that he was seeking it. This effectively stalled the negotiations without actually closing them. Meanwhile Saladin had been in communication with Conrad of Montferrat, who offered to enter into an alliance with Saladin. The sultan was willing if Conrad would agree to enter the field against the crusaders, but the lord of Tyre was hesitant about going as far as that. Saladin believed that in alliance with Conrad he could drive Richard and his crusaders from the land. This prospect did not, however, fill his emirs with enthusiasm. They wanted peace, and a treaty with Richard would bring it. Hence Saladin continued his negotiations with both factions.[54]

Early in January 1192 Richard held a council to decide on the best course to pursue. This body came to the conclusion which the king had probably reached some time before — that the wisest plan was to rebuild the demolished fortifications of Ascalon. This would maintain the pressure on Saladin by threatening his communications with Egypt, and yet keep the army in close touch with its fleet. The decision not to lay siege to Jerusalem was immensely unpopular with enthusiastic crusaders. Every contemporary writer felt called upon to throw the blame for it on whatever group or leader he disliked. Hugh of Burgundy and his French followers, the barons of the kingdom, and Richard all stand accused of lack of crusading zeal. Actually it seems unlikely that any of the leaders except possibly Hugh wanted to attack Jerusalem. They realized the hazardous nature of the enterprise and the improbability that the city could be long held even if it were taken. Hugh, however, may have argued for laying siege to Jerusalem. Certainly he refused to join the march to Ascalon. This resulted in a division among the French crusaders. While Hugh and a majority of his followers retired to Jaffa and its vicinity and some went back to Acre, count Henry of Champagne accompanied his uncle Richard to Ascalon.[55]

On January 20 the crusading army reached Ascalon, and set

[53] *Estoire*, pp. 280–300; *Itinerarium*, pp. 285–295, 297–304.

[54] Bahā'-ad-Dīn, pp. 302–303, 317–318, 323–325.

[55] *Itinerarium*, pp. 305–306, 308–309, 311; *Estoire*, pp. 300–301, 302–303, 305; Hoveden, III, 179; Bernard le Trésorier, pp. 278–279; *Eracles*, p. 186.

about the enormous task of restoring its extensive fortifications. The host was to remain at Ascalon until early June. For a considerable part of this time it consisted only of Richard's own troops and those of count Henry. Late in January or early in February duke Hugh and his French forces joined the army at Ascalon. The duke, extremely short of funds, soon quarreled with Richard, who declined to help him. Hugh retired to Acre before the end of February, but a number of other French barons stayed at Ascalon until Easter. Despite several invitations Conrad of Montferrat absolutely refused to bring his forces to Ascalon. During the army's stay at Ascalon, military activities were confined to a few raids against Saladin's line of communications to Egypt. On one occasion Richard led a party to Darum, where he found a convoy of Christian prisoners bound for Egypt. Most of the Turkish escort escaped into the castle, but Richard rescued the captives. Other raids captured supplies and prisoners in the same region.[56]

On April 15 an English cleric, Robert, prior of Hereford, arrived at Ascalon with letters for king Richard from his trusted servant William Longchamp, bishop of Ely. William had become involved in a violent quarrel with the king's brother John and with his bastard half-brother Geoffrey, archbishop of York. When Walter of Coutances, archbishop of Rouen, had left the crusading host in Sicily to return to England, he had carried with him royal letters authorizing him to take over the government of the realm if such a move seemed necessary. In the hope of restoring peace in England, archbishop Walter had exercised these powers, deposed William Longchamp from the justiciarship, and assumed that office himself. While the account given in Longchamp's letters may well have been a highly colored one, Richard cannot have been unduly disturbed by the news. He had foreseen what had arisen; the man he had sent to handle it was firmly in control. What probably worried the king more was what the messenger told him of the activities of Philip Augustus. Philip had appeared at the Norman frontier with his private version of the treaty of Messina. When the seneschal of Normandy refused to honor it, the French king had entered into negotiations with prince John. At any rate the prior of Hereford's report convinced Richard that he should not long delay his return to England.

King Richard fully realized that the first step required to pave the way for his own departure was to establish an effective government in the kingdom of Jerusalem. The compromise of the previous year had not worked. Conrad of Montferrat had held aloof from the

[56] *Estoire*, pp. 308–320; *Itinerarium*, pp. 314–320, 327.

crusade and had been attempting to negotiate a treaty with Saladin, and the chief barons of the kingdom had continued to support him. On April 16 Richard called a council of the prelates and barons of his host and asked them who should be king. Without hesitation they chose Conrad. Richard then displayed the good sense and magnanimity of which he was capable. He accepted the decision, and dispatched count Henry of Champagne to inform Conrad of his election. Count Henry went to Tyre to perform his errand, and went on to Acre. In Tyre preparations were under way for Conrad's coronation.[57] But it was not to be.

Isabel, marchioness of Montferrat and heiress to the kingdom of Jerusalem, liked to dally in her bath. On April 28, 1192, she was unusually slow, and Conrad, who was very hungry, got tired of waiting for his dinner. He went to the house of Philip of Dreux, bishop of Beauvais, to see if he could dine there. When he found that the prelate had already dined, Conrad started home. As he walked along a narrow street, two men approached him and one of them held out a letter is if he intended to give it to the marquis. As Conrad reached for the letter, both men plunged knives into him. The assassins were quickly seized and slain. Conrad lived long enough to receive the last rites of the church, and to command his wife to deliver Tyre to no one except Richard or a duly chosen king of Jerusalem.[58]

All the contemporary writers agree that the murderers were followers of Rāshid-ad-Dīn Sinān, master of the sect known as the Assassins. But there was a wide variation in the views as to the motives of the Assassin chieftain. Philip of Dreux and his fellow Frenchmen maintained that Richard had arranged the assassination, and informed king Philip of their belief. According to Rigord, Philip sent messengers to ask Sinān if the story was true, and received assurances that it was not. As a matter of fact, Philip must have known Richard well enough to realize that such an act would be impossible for him. The English king might kill a man in a burst of rage, but he would never plan a murder. Nevertheless the English writers were so troubled by the tale that they felt it necessary to invent a letter from Sinān guaranteeing the king's innocence. A Moslem source asserts that Saladin offered Sinān a large sum to procure the murder of both Richard and Conrad or either one. As Conrad was easier to get at, he was the victim. Far more believable is the story told by the chroniclers who represented the views of the

[57] *Itinerarium*, pp. 334–338; *Estoire*, pp. 328–334.

[58] *Estoire*, pp. 334–335; *Itinerarium*, pp. 338–340; Hoveden, III, 181; Bahā'-ad-Dīn, pp. 332–333; Bernard le Trésorier, pp. 289–290; *Eracles*, p. 193. For a different version of this killing, see volume I of the present work, chapter IV, pp. 125–127.

local barons. According to them, Conrad had seized a richly laden ship belonging to the Assassins and had refused to give up the valuable cargo.[59]

When count Henry of Champagne, who was still at Acre, learned of Conrad's death, he immediately set out for Tyre. Meanwhile the duke of Burgundy had demanded that the marchioness deliver the city to him as king Philip's lieutenant, but she had resolutely refused. Although she was heiress to the kingdom, Tyre was her one concrete asset. The arrival of count Henry offered a simple solution. Here was a gay young bachelor, a competent captain, and the mightiest feudal prince of France. The barons loudly acclaimed him as their new king, and the lady offered her hand. Count Henry was willing to accept the double honor, but he dared not act without Richard's assent. Needless to say, this was easily obtained. Henry of Champagne, Richard's nephew, had been inclined to follow his leadership in the crusade. One writer states that Richard advised his nephew not to marry the lady. A possible reason for this attitude would be the fact that, if Henry were elected without marrying the heiress, his right to the throne could not be made dependent on her, and he could avoid the situation which Guy of Lusignan had faced when his wife Sibyl died. It seems unlikely that Richard was disturbed by the thought of the dubious separation of Isabel from Humphrey of Toron. But as a practical matter, if Henry wanted to be accepted as king, he had to marry the heiress of the land. The wedding was promptly celebrated, and Richard gave Henry the cities that were in Christian hands.[60]

Although there is no doubt that Henry of Champagne was the effective ruler of the kingdom of Jerusalem from the time of his marriage in 1192 to his death in 1197, his exact legal status is not entirely clear. He seems never to have assumed the royal title and ordinarily called himself simply count-palatine of Troyes. Until 1194, this restraint might be accounted for by the fact that Guy of Lusignan, the crowned and anointed king, was still alive. In May 1192 Guy had become lord of Cyprus. Richard had sold the island to the Templars, but they had found it too hard to rule and had regretted their purchase. Guy obtained Richard's permission to buy it from

[59] *Eracles*, pp. 192, 194; Bernard le Trésorier, pp. 288–289, 290; *Estoire*, p. 338; *Itinerarium*, pp. 341–342; Devizes, pp. 449–450; Diceto, II, 127; Rigord, pp. 120–121. On the Assassins, see volume I of the present work, chapter IV.

[60] *Estoire*, pp. 339–345; *Itinerarium*, pp. 342–343, 346–349; Bernard le Trésorier, p. 291; *Eracles*, pp. 194–195; Hoveden, III, 181; Diceto, II, 104. La Monte, however, conjectures (*Estoire*, p. 342, note) that "Richard's opposition to the marriage may well have been due to the fact . . . that [Isabel] was at the moment pregnant with a child by Conrad."

them. Guy offered fiefs in Cyprus to those whose lands in Palestine had been conquered by Saladin, and built up a governing feudal class in the island. At his death in 1194, he was succeeded by his brother Aimery, who obtained the title king of Cyprus from emperor Henry VI. When Henry of Champagne died in 1197, Aimery of Lusignan married Isabel, and assumed the title king of Jerusalem and Cyprus.[61]

When Richard heard that Henry of Champagne had married Isabel, he ordered him to bring all the troops in Tyre and Acre to join the host at Ascalon. Without waiting for their arrival, the king led his own forces south to attack Darum, and on May 22 he took the fortress by storm. The next day Henry and the duke of Burgundy arrived, and Richard gave the captured place to the new lord of Jerusalem. For the rest of the month the army moved about the countryside behind Ascalon. On May 29 another messenger, John of Alençon, archdeacon of Lisieux, arrived from England. He carried further news of John's negotiations with king Philip. Richard then called a council of his captains, and discovered that there was a strong general demand for an attack on Jerusalem. He finally agreed to stay in Palestine until Easter 1193 and to attack Jerusalem if it seemed feasible. On June 7, the host marched north from Ascalon, and four days later reached Bait Nūbā, some thirteen miles from Jerusalem. Meanwhile Henry was sent to Acre to round up the crusaders who were still immersed in its fleshpots.[62]

On June 20, a spy brought word to Richard's camp that a great caravan laden with supplies for Saladin's army was en route from Egypt to Jerusalem, and he decided to attempt to intercept it. With a mixed force of French and English crusaders Richard marched south through the back country, and found the caravan and its escort camped at a watering place about half way between Darum and the Dead Sea. Taken by surprise, the caravan was easily captured. According to Bahā'-ad-Dīn the crusaders took 3,000 camels, 3,000 horses, 500 prisoners, and a large amount of supplies. By June 29 Richard was back at Bait Nūbā with his booty.[63]

While the crusading army was camped at Bait Nūbā, the Turks made a number of attacks on its supply line to Jaffa. If Richard had had any real intention of besieging Jerusalem, these blows at his

[61] *Estoire*, pp. 345–346; Bernard le Trésorier, p. 286; Hoveden, III, 181; *Eracles*, pp. 189–190, 191; Röhricht, *Regesta*, pp. 189–194. On the acquisition of Cyprus by Guy of Lusignan, see Hill, *History of Cyprus*, II, 36–38, and below, chapter XVII, pp. 599–603. On the kingdom of Jerusalem under Henry and Aimery, see below, chapter XV, pp. 522–532.

[62] Hoveden, III, 181–182; Diceto, II, 104; *Estoire*, pp. 346–366; *Itinerarium*, pp. 352–356, 358–359, 364–368; Bahā'-ad-Dīn, pp. 337–347.

[63] Hoveden, III, 182; Diceto, II, 104; Bernard le Trésorier, p. 283; *Estoire*, pp. 381–391; *Itinerarium*, pp. 383–391.

communications convinced him that it was not feasible. Apparently the king proposed a new alternative, one that was to be used by later crusades — an expedition against Egypt. But the duke of Burgundy and his French followers were completely disgusted with Richard's caution and refused further coöperation. Disappointed, discouraged, and torn by feuds the army retired to Ramla. Most of the French immediately went to Jaffa and on to Acre. Richard with a small detachment rode south to Darum, razed its fortifications, strengthened those of Ascalon, and then rejoined his army. On July 26 he led the remnants of the host into Acre.[64]

During the spring and summer of 1192 Richard's negotiations with Saladin had never ceased completely. When in mid-June the king realized that there was no hope whatever that he could take Jerusalem, he pressed more seriously his offers for peace or a truce. Although Saladin was fully aware both of Richard's desire to go home and of the dissension in the crusading army, his own situation was such that he could not afford to ignore these offers. His people and troops were desperately tired of the war. The capture of the caravan from Egypt broke the spirit of the men he trusted most, his mamluks (Arabic singular, *mamlūk*, slave). Only the iron determination of Saladin kept the army together, and by early July the troops were in a mutinous mood. By the time Richard retired from Bait Nūbā only one question blocked the reaching of an accord. Saladin insisted that Ascalon, the threat to his communications with Egypt, should be dismantled, but Richard absolutely refused to agree to this.[65]

When Saladin learned that the crusading host had withdrawn to Acre, he decided on a quick stroke that would strengthen his position in future negotiations. On July 27 he pushed his unenthusiastic forces against Jaffa. When the crusaders had occupied the city in the previous autumn, they had hastily and imperfectly repaired the east gate and the adjoining walls. While Saladin's miners dug under this weak spot in the fortifications, his siege engines battered it with great stones. The garrison of Jaffa defended the city vigorously, returning the fire of the siege engines and digging counter-mines. When a breach was finally made, they filled it with a solid wall of spears and shields. Saladin's troops fought half-heartedly, and only the thought of the booty in the city kept them at the assault. Finally on Friday, July 30, the garrison asked for terms. Saladin agreed to accept a money ransom to allow the

[64] *Estoire*, pp. 367–376, 377–381, 391–397; *Itinerarium*, pp. 370–376, 379–382, 394, 396–399; Hoveden, III, 182–183.

[65] Gibb MS.; Bahā'-ad-Dīn, pp. 353–360; *Estoire*, p. 396; *Itinerarium*, pp. 398–399.

Christians in the city to leave with their goods. But he could not control his troops, who had at last broken into the town. The garrison retired to the citadel while the Turks and Kurds pillaged. The disgusted sultan ordered his mamluks to stand at the city gates and take the booty away from the plunderers.

Word of the attack on Jaffa reached Richard at Acre on July 29. He immediately ordered Henry of Champagne to start south with the army while with a picked force of knights and crossbowmen he boarded a squadron of galleys to go by sea. When the king arrived at Jaffa, the Moslems were in full possession of the city, and their banners were flying from the walls. The garrison had just begun to file out of the citadel to surrender. But when they saw Richard's galleys, they took up their arms once more, and one of their number jumped from the walls down to the beach and swam out to the galleys to inform Richard that the citadel was still holding out. This was the sort of situation that delighted Richard. Bringing his galleys as near as possible to the shore, he and his men waded to the land and attacked the enemy on the beach. Supported by a sally from the citadel, the crusaders quickly drove the dispirited enemy from the city, slaying large numbers in the process.

Richard immediately set about repairing the walls of Jaffa. As the stench of dead bodies made the city extremely unpleasant, he and his tiny force camped outside the walls. Except for Henry of Champagne and a few followers who had come to Jaffa by sea after the army had been stopped at Caesarea by the Moslem host, the king had only the troops who had accompanied him in the galleys — perhaps fifty knights and a few hundred crossbowmen. As the knights had no horses, they could only fight as spearmen or bowmen. When Saladin learned of this situation, he decided upon an attempt to capture Richard and his men by a surprise attack. After dark on August 4 the squadrons of Moslem horse moved against the camp. But their movement had been noticed, and Richard warned. He drew up his little troop in battle array. Between each two dismounted knights or sergeants stood a crossbowman. When Saladin's troops saw once more the solid line of crusaders, they lost all interest in battle. The mamluks made a few assaults and suffered heavily from the crossbow bolts. The rest of the troops simply refused to attack, and reminded Saladin that he had despoiled them of the booty found in Jaffa.[66]

[66] Gibb MS.; Bahā'-ad-Dīn, pp. 361–371; Hoveden, III, 183–184; Diceto, II, 104–105; Bernard le Trésorier, pp. 280–282; *Eracles*, pp. 196–197; *Estoire*, pp. 399–424; *Itinerarium*, pp. 400–420.

Soon after this little victory, Richard fell desperately ill. At about the same time duke Hugh of Burgundy died at Acre. Although the news of the duke's death is said to have cheered Richard so much that he began to recover, he realized that the crusade had spent its force. On September 2, a truce for three years was signed by the representatives of the king and the sultan. The Christians were to hold a narrow strip along the coast from Tyre to Jaffa. Ascalon was to have its fortifications demolished before it was turned over to the sultan. Both Christians and Moslems were to have free passage through the whole of Palestine. If the prince of Antioch and the count of Tripoli desired, they were to be included in the treaty. Once peace was concluded, Richard moved north along the coast to nurse his health in some more salubrious spot than death-ridden Jaffa. In order to prevent the French crusaders from using the truce to visit Jerusalem, the king arranged with Saladin to permit the passage only of pilgrims bearing his pass. A number of English pilgrims headed by bishop Hubert of Salisbury made visits to the holy city and its shrines. On October 9, 1192, king Richard set sail from Acre. The Third Crusade was ended.[67]

In considering the accomplishments of the Third Crusade, it is necessary to distinguish between the crusade as a whole and the expedition led by Richard and Philip Augustus. Without the aid of the crusaders who had arrived in the autumn of 1189 Guy of Lusignan's attack on Acre would have been a futile gesture, and it was probably the coming of count Henry of Champagne that made the eventual capture of the city certain. It seems fairly clear that Acre would have fallen without the aid of the French and English kings. In all probability, however, the conquest of the coastal region from Acre to Jaffa could not have been accomplished without the troops of Richard and the duke of Burgundy. In short, the Third Crusade reëstablished the kingdom of Jerusalem as a political and military power. Actually it did more — it protected the remnants of the kingdom from Saladin while he was at the height of his power. Before the truce was over, the great sultan was dead, and his heirs were squabbling over his inheritance. Thus the mere presence of Richard and his host through 1191 and 1192 may well have prevented Saladin from reaping the full fruits of his victory at Hattin.

[67] Hoveden, III, 184–185; Diceto, II, 104–105; Bernard le Trésorier, pp. 292–293; *Eracles*, pp. 198–199; *Itinerarium*, pp. 425–440; *Estoire*, pp. 426–443; Devizes, pp. 444, 449.

4. The Near East during the Third Crusade, 1189–1192 (*Map by the University of Wisconsin Cartographic Laboratory*)

III
THE CRUSADES OF FREDERICK BARBAROSSA AND HENRY VI

Saladin's reconquest of Syria and Palestine found the Christian world still unable to coöperate. For over a century it had been officially divided into western Roman Catholic and eastern Greek Orthodox halves which increasingly looked upon each other with deep suspicion and distrust, and even with actual hatred. Had these two divisions of the Christian world concerted their efforts, after

The Latin sources for the history of Frederick Barbarossa's crusade — the so-called Ansbert's *Historia de expeditione Friderici imperatoris, Historia peregrinorum, Epistola de morte Friderici imperatoris,* and *Narratio itineris navalis ad Terram Sanctam* — have been edited with an important introduction by Anton Chroust in the *MGH, SS.*, n.s., V (Berlin, 1928). In this introduction, as well as in his monograph *Tageno, Ansbert, und die Historia peregrinorum* (Graz, 1892), Chroust discusses the interdependence among the *Historia* of "Ansbert", the chronicle of Magnus of Reichersberg (*MGH, SS.*, XVII, 476–528), and what is supposed to have been a diary of the crusade written by Tageno, a member of the cathedral chapter of Passau. Supplementary details of the crusade are to be found in the chronicle of the Slavs by Arnold of Lübeck (*MGH, SS.*, XXI) and the chronicle of Otto of St. Blaise (*Scriptores . . . in usum scholarum*, ed A. Hofmeister, 1912), among others. Pertinent quotations from the most valuable of these sources, "Ansbert", have been incorporated in this chapter; the translation used, with occasional modifications, is an unpublished one by Chester E. Wilcox, to be found in typescript in the library of the University of Nebraska. Identification of persons and places rests largely on Chroust's excellent notes.

The chief Greek sources for the crusade is the history of Nicetas Choniates (*CSHB*, Bonn, 1835; also *RHC, Grecs*, I, 319–337). Other materials useful in writing the part of this chapter concerning Barbarossa include: Steven Runciman, *A History of the Crusades*, III (Cambridge, 1954), 10–17; A. A. Vasiliev, *History of the Byzantine Empire* (Madison, 1952); A. L. Poole in chapters XII and XIV of the *Cambridge Medieval History*, V (1926); Z. N. Brooke, *History of Europe from 911 to 1198* (London, 1938); Louis Bréhier, *L'Église et l'orient au moyen-âge: Les Croisades* (Paris, 1928); René Grousset, *Histoire des croisades et du royaume franc de Jérusalem*, III (Paris, 1936); Karl Fischer, *Geschichte des Kreuzzugs Kaiser Friedrichs I.* (Leipzig, 1870); W. von Giesebrecht (ed. and continued by Bernhard von Simson), *Geschichte der deutschen Kaiserzeit*, VI: *Die letzten Zeiten Kaiser Friedrichs des Rotbarts* (Berlin, 1895); Hans Prutz, *Kaiser Friedrich I.*, III: *1177–1190* (Danzig, 1874); S. O. Riezler, "Der Kreuzzug Friedrichs I.," *Forschungen zur deutschen Geschichte*, X (1870), 1–149; and two articles by Karl Zimmert in the *Byzantinische Zeitschrift*: "Der Friede zu Adrianopel (Februar 1190)," XI (1902), 302–320, and "Der deutsch-byzantinische Konflict vom Juli 1189 bis Februar 1190," XII (1903), 42–77.

For Henry VI's crusade: J. Haller, "Kaiser Heinrich VI.," *Hist. Zeitschr.*, CXIII (ser. 3, XVII; 1914), 473–504; W. Leonhardt, *Der Kreuzzugsplan Kaiser Heinrichs VI.* (Leipzig, 1913); Th. Toeche, *Kaiser Heinrich VI.* (Leipzig, 1867); and E. Traub, *Der Kreuzzugsplan Kaiser Heinrich's VI. in Zusammenhang mit der Politik der Jahren 1195–97* (Jena, 1910).

Saladin's conquests, to meet the Moslem challenge as they had done before, it is more than likely that the kingdom of Jerusalem could have been easily reëstablished. Yet such an easy disposition of what was regarded as the Moslem peril was impossible for this age. Not only was there no attempt to come to any agreement of this kind, but Isaac II Angelus, the feeble, tricky, and irresponsible occupant of the tottering eastern throne, by an alliance with Saladin among other things, prodded the aggressive princes of the west to think of the destruction of the Byzantine state. The chief result of the German participation in the Third Crusade was thus the overthrow of the Byzantine empire by the Fourth. The latter was, to be sure, the work of Venetians and Frenchmen, but the experience of the Germans under Frederick Barbarossa and Henry VI had demonstrated the possibility of removing the Byzantine obstacle to western designs.

Nor was western Christendom, any more than Christendom as a whole, prepared at this moment of crisis to act in concord. Any crusade undertaken by the Germans had to fit into Hohenstaufen plans to strengthen and enlarge the empire. The emperors found in the papacy, which was a constant promoter of the crusade to the east, a steady opponent of their imperial plans. The papacy did, indeed, succeed in limiting Barbarossa's Italian ambitions, but it was unable to prevent Henry VI's acquisition of the Norman kingdom of southern Italy and Sicily. Both men undertook to lead crusades partly in the hope of softening papal opposition to their domestic policies. The popes, however reluctant to support any project calculated to increase the material resources of the Hohenstaufens, could not withhold official approval from a movement so likely to enhance their own spiritual power. Except, however, for initial support in arousing enthusiasm for the proposed crusades, they left the monarchs free to organize and manage them as they saw fit. These crusades may accordingly be considered imperial in character, aimed at justifying the predominance of the German empire in Europe by solving the Moslem problem. They did nothing to allay the long struggle between the western church and the empire. On the contrary, by transferring leadership to the latter and emphasizing the secular aspects of the crusading movement, they heightened the tension.

The political organization of central and western Europe prevented close coöperation among the monarchs. The kings of France and England were at odds over the Angevin empire, and neither could leave on a crusade while the other was determined to continue the struggle, or stay long in the east while the other was at home. Nor was the Saxon Henry the Lion a person to leave unwatched in Germany while the emperor went off on a holy mission. Thus no serious efforts were made by the three monarchs to work out concerted plans. There can be little doubt, moreover, that the English and French monarchs resented the assumption of crusading leadership by Frederick. What might have been a successful recapture of the holy places by a combined west operating as a unit was thwarted by those animosities, imperial and papal, monarchical and feudal, which, in however modified form, continued to hamper western unity.

When the news of Saladin's offensive began to filter into Italy, Germany, France, and England, the papacy undertook to direct and stimulate the emotions aroused. Gregory VIII sent Henry, cardinal-bishop of Albano, with papal letters, despite his ignorance of French and German, into France and the Rhinelands. That the Lord would have permitted his church to suffer so horribly at the hands of infidel enemies could be explained, in papal eyes, only by the overpowering sins of the faithful. A successful crusade therefore could be undertaken only by those who had corrected their "sins by voluntary chastisement" and turned "through penitence and works of piety to the Lord. . . . To those who with contrite heart and humbled spirit undertake the labor of this journey, and depart in sorrow for their sins and in the true faith, we promise full pardon for their offenses and eternal life." A pilgrimage to be made by penitents was to avoid all show. Let them not go "in expensive clothes or with dogs or birds or other things which seem rather to supply delight and wantonness than to serve necessary uses. Let them go rather with modest equipment and dress, in which they seem to be doing penance rather than to be striving after vain glory."[1] The cardinal himself in summoning the German lay and ecclesiastical nobility to attend Barbarossa's "court of Christ" (*curia Christi*) at Mainz on March 27, 1188, reiterated the papal injunctions. "We think that all of you, after all idleness, all curiosity, and temporal glory have been put aside, should be enjoined to try to be present at the court of Jesus Christ with becoming seriousness and modesty. Let all be so inflamed by the fire of love and obedience to exalt the Christian name, that dress and deportment confess the faith which our tongue professes."[2]

[1] This letter is given in Ansbert's *Historia de expeditione Friderici imperatoris* (ed. Anton Chroust, *MGH, SS.*, n.s., V) pp. 6–10. (All the references to Ansbert which follow are to this edition.)

[2] *Ibid.*, pp. 12–13.

By this time the German aristocracy had been somewhat aroused. The response to the preaching of the cardinal-legate's representatives at the diet of Strassburg in December of the previous year had not been notable until supplemented by bishop Henry of Strassburg's more adequate rhetoric. Meanwhile, moreover, the "elegant eloquence" of bishop Godfrey of Würzburg had led to a numerous response when the pressure of public opinion had reached the point where "no one in all Germany . . . was considered of any manly steadfastness at all, who was seen without the saving sign, and who would not join the comradeship of the crusaders."[3]

The movement had been promoted from the first by Barbarossa. It is not likely that the old emperor (he was now close to seventy) had much more in mind than to bring his long and arduous career to a heroic climax, "the good consummation of his virtues", as the chronicler puts it. He, no less than others, knew that he might pay with his life. He had been with Conrad III on the first attempt of the Germans to make their mark in the east. The opportunity now presented itself to redeem that disaster and to complement the successes of the empire in Italy, however limited, with a supreme effort on behalf of western Christendom. No matter how annoyed he may have been over the attempts of Manuel, the late Byzantine emperor, to thwart his Italian ambitions, these had come to naught and were now past. The predicament in which the Byzantine empire found itself at the moment might be tempting to one politically over-ambitious. But to Frederick it meant only that, if properly utilized, the German pilgrimage to the east could be facilitated. There is accordingly no good reason to disagree with the admiring estimate of the official reporter of his crusade. "Neither the weakening limbs of venerable old age, nor the long toils of veteran military service . . . nor the abundance of riches or pleasures, nor the great affairs of state, . . . nor his fondness for his dearest sons could deter him from the long and hard road of holy pilgrimage. A glorious old man, by his own example he inspired all the young men to fight for Christ."

With tears of joy Frederick took the cross at "Christ's court" amidst a weeping multitude. Thousands upon thousands followed him in this — perhaps as many as thirteen thousand in all. The date of departure from Germany was set for April 23, 1189, St. George's day. It was necessary, meanwhile, to pacify Germany and prepare diplomatically for the march. The stubborn archbishop Philip of Cologne had made his peace at Mainz. Henry the Lion, given the

[3] Ansbert, p. 15, lines 7–10.

alternative of going along at the emperor's expense or going into exile for three years, chose the latter and went to England. Cardinal Conrad, the archbishop of Mainz, went to negotiate with king Bela III of Hungary for passage through that country. It is likely that letters were sent to the "grand župan" (ruler) of Serbia, Stephen Nemanya, and his brothers. An embassy set off to arrange with Isaac Angelus for passage through Byzantine territory. Godfrey of Wiesenbach was sent to Kilij Arslan II, the Selchükid sultan at Iconium (Konya), and Henry of Dietz was dispatched to Saladin himself, threatening war within a year if the holy places were not surrendered. Despite all the difficulties involved in the land route, difficulties which the emperor himself had experienced, he must have felt that it would be simpler to remove them by negotiation than to arrange for the transport by sea of a large German army that might find no Christian port at which to land.

Saladin scornfully rejected the emperor's ultimatum, and set about arranging an alliance with the Byzantine emperor that would harass the German progress through Greek lands. Other embassies came to Germany to meet Frederick at the diet at Nuremberg in late December 1188. The Serbian embassy announced that Nish would be put in readiness for his arrival. The news of the prospective invasion of the east by a powerful Germany army had made a deep impression. The large embassy of Kilij Arslan, one thousand men and five hundred horse according to some German reports, promised the emperor that no obstacles would be put in the way of his march through Selchükid territory in Asia Minor. The Byzantine embassy, led by the chancellor John Ducas, was more cautious and frank. To Frederick it was explained that Isaac, "from the time when the idea of an expedition to Jerusalem had become generally known," had suspected that "not only the emperor but also the king of France would lead a hostile invasion into his realm."[4] Unless Barbarossa could remove these fears, it would be necessary for Byzantium to refuse to allow the Germans to go through the passes of Bulgaria and indeed "in all ways" to oppose them.

This appeared reasonable to Frederick, and three distinguished German princes, bishop Godfrey of Würzburg, the emperor's son Frederick, duke of Swabia, and Leopold of Babenberg, duke of Austria, swore before the Greeks to the pacific intentions of the German crusaders. Thereupon the Greek envoys, "vowed by the

[4] *Ibid.*, p. 15, lines 24–28. For Byzantium under Isaac II Angelus, see below, chapter IV, pp. 146–149.

holy gospels, on behalf of their lord the king and of all the princes of Greece, true and steadfast friendship for the lord emperor and the whole army of Christ." It was agreed that the Greeks would give the crusaders guides through Byzantine territory, furnish them with food and supplies at regular markets, and provide transportation across the straits to Asia Minor. To impress the Greek envoys the more, the three German princes "vowed again that as long as the Greeks kept the agreement to which they had sworn, the entrance of our men into their land would be peaceful and quiet." To supervise the preparations for the reception of the crusading army, a German embassy was sent ahead to Constantinople consisting of the bishop Hermann of Münster, count Rupert of Nassau, his kinsman count Walram, Henry of Dietz, and the imperial chamberlain, Markward of Neuenburg. Knowing what happened to these promises and to these envoys, Ansbert cannot help but remark of the Greeks at this point in his chronicle, "They lied . . . nothing they vowed did they afterwards perform. . . . Neither the prudent emperor nor the simple and faithful legates knew 'that they were being sent as sheep in the midst of wolves'."[5]

On St. George's day, April 23, 1189, the crusaders gathered for a diet at Regensburg (Ratisbon) at which final arrangements were made. On the 11th of May the German army, said to have been some one hundred thousand strong and with a core of twenty thousand knights, set out on their crusade with purses bulging with money, the emperor and a small number by boat, and the rest along the banks of the Danube. In this stately procession were the leaders of the German church and the German aristocracy. Headed by the two Fredericks, father and son, there came from the church the bishops of Liége, Würzburg, Passau, Regensburg, Basel, Meissen, and Osnabrück, to whom were added later the archbishop of Tarentaise and the bishop of Toul. The only abbot to come was Isenric of Admont. The leaders among the aristocracy were Berthold, the duke of Dalmatia and Meran (Croatia) and margrave of Istria, the margraves of Vohburg and Baden, count Florent III of Holland and the counts of Sayn, Sponheim, Cuyk, Wied, Berg, Saarbrücken, Abenberg, and Henneberg. From Swabia came the counts of Öttingen, Kyburg, Dillingen, Nimburg, and Vöhringen; from Bavaria, the counts of Dollnstein, Liebenau, Dornberg, and Falkenstein; from Saxony, count Adolf of Schaumburg and Holstein, and the counts of Oldenburg, Hallermund, and Wöltin-

[5] Ansbert, p. 16, lines 12–14, 25–27.

gerode. The burggrave of Magdeburg was there, and Frederick of Berg, the advocate (*Vogt*) of Passau and of the monastery of Melk. Burghers of Metz joined later with the many "ministerials and other chosen knights" to form this *terribilis et ordinata acies*. There were backsliders of course who did not keep their vows, or who went later. From the German point of view Philip of France and Henry of England were the chief of these, but they numbered also count Philip of Flanders, dukes Conrad Otto of Bohemia and Moravia, Godfrey of Lower Lorraine, and Henry of Limburg, the bishops of Speyer and Cambrai, and several counts, among others. There were some who chose to go by sea rather than land, preferring the "short voyage which reduced the element of fear from hostile pagans" and "lazily" awaiting "the arrival of our forces in one of the cities left to the Christians".

The spirit of this army as it got on its way was tough. In the course of the march it was purged of unwelcome elements and given a fairly tight organization. When the inhabitants of Mauthausen, "with novel and haughty pride, demanded an unaccustomed toll of the passing pilgrims of Christ, even though crusaders," the emperor set fire to their village. At Vienna some five hundred prostitutes, thieves, and wastrels were sent back to Germany. At the first major halt of the whole army near Pressburg (Bratislava) it became evident that some body of regulations would have to be set up to restrain "so great a multitude of sometimes licentious and insolent knights and servingmen". These regulations, drawn up in council, were sworn to by the whole army, and judges appointed to enforce them. The hands of some bullies were cut off and the heads of some thieves rolled.

At Nish the army was divided into four divisions "so that whenever the enemy should attack, they would not find Christ's knights unprepared and in disorder." The first division was composed of the troops of duke Frederick of Swabia, bishop Conrad of Regensburg, margraves Berthold of Vohburg and Hermann of Baden, and five Swabian and four Bavarian counts. Its standard-bearer was count Berthold of Nimburg. The second was the Bohemian and Hungarian division, each group with its own standard-bearer. The third division was composed of the troops of duke Berthold of Dalmatia and of the bishops of Würzburg, Liége, Passau, Münster, Basel, and Osnabrück; the duke himself bore the banner. The fourth was the imperial division drawn from the emperor's own men and including the archbishop of Tarentaise, the bishop of Meissen, count Florent of Holland, and some sixteen remaining counts. Count Rupert of Nassau was made their standard-bearer *in absentia*. A fifth division was formed at Philippopolis of foot-soldiers and the sturdier serving-men. Here, too, the army was given a tighter judicial organization. The emperor divided the army into units of fifty, for each of which was appointed a judge for civil and military cases, with reservation only of the jurisdiction of the imperial marshal. Frederick also chose here a council of sixty men (later reduced to sixteen) to advise him in military matters.

The five weeks' march through Hungary was calculated to inspire in the hearts of the crusaders great hopes for an easy, pleasant journey all the way to their goal. It was to impress them also with the proper way in which foreign monarchs should receive the German "army of the Lord". Bela III had sent forward his ambassadors to greet the crusaders at Pressburg, and on June 4 he, together with his queen, received Frederick personally in the neighborhood of Gran (Esztergom). Queen Margaret presented the emperor with a magnificent and roomy tent. The king entertained him for two days "on his rather extensive private hunting preserve situated on an island in the Danube". The expedition was provided with ships, wagons laden with supplies, and three camels. It was quartered in luxuriant pasture. In Gran itself houses stuffed with provisions were set aside for the poor pilgrims. Bela had commanded the towns and bishoprics to receive the emperor with great ceremony. When, in comparison with what they had to endure elsewhere, the crusaders thought back on the passage through Hungary, these seemed halcyon weeks. "We passed through . . . in the greatest tranquillity and with the air smiling upon us with much more than usual mildness and agreeableness. Indeed, the gnats, gadflies, insects, and snakes, which seriously disturb those making a journey on horses in the summertime in Hungary, not only did not hurt us or the animals, but were rarely even seen by us."[6] The only unpleasant thing the Germans resented about their Hungarian experience was the extremely unfavorable rate of exchange.

A shocking contrast came with the entrance into Byzantine territory at Branits on July 2. No better short account of the incidents of the subsequent march through Bulgarian territory to Philippopolis (Plovdiv), and no better commentary upon the German reaction to these, can be had than in the letter which Frederick sent back on November 16 to his son Henry VI: "As soon as we reached the borders of our imperial brother, the emperor

[6] Ansbert, p. 27, lines 2–7.

of Constantinople," Frederick wrote, "we suffered no small loss in robbery of goods and killing of our men; and this is known without doubt to have been instigated by the emperor himself. Certain bandits and bowmen, lurking in the thorn thickets near the public highway, continued to surprise and harass with poisoned arrows a great many of our men who were unarmed and proceeding incautiously. . . . They were [however] completely surrounded by our *balistarii* and knights and . . . paid the just penalty for their deserts; in one day and on one gallows thirty-two of them, suspended like wolves, shamefully ended their lives. Nonetheless the remaining criminals followed at our side and molested us with nocturnal theft . . . through all of the Bulgarian forests. Yet our army in turn dreadfully tortured great numbers of them with various kinds of torments.

"The . . . emperor of Constantinople [moreover] did not hesitate not only to break every vow he is known to have made on his own life and soul, through his chancellor, at Nuremberg, but also under threat of punishment to take from us the opportunity to exchange money and to buy and sell. He also ordered the defiles of the roads to be blocked by cutting down trees and rolling huge rocks in the way, and commanded certain ancient passes, the fortifications of which had been ruined with age . . . to be fortified with war-towers and bulwarks, in order, contrary to the honor of God and of the holy, living cross, to destroy us and all Christians. We, however, relying on the help of heaven, set fire to the Greeks' machines, and reduced their wood and stones to coals and ashes. And so, by the grace of God, we went through all the passes victoriously and, stuffed with all good things, arrived at the plain of Circuiz [Pazarjik?]. We thus spent six weeks in a rather toilsome traverse of Bulgaria.

"Setting out thence again, we occupied Philippopolis, . . . a place very well defended by natural site and the hand of man and very rich, but utterly deserted. And behold, on the following day, we received letters from the emperor of Constantinople that, written with great pomp, sang equally of threats, flattery, and craft. At that time, moreover, we were first fully informed of the captivity of our legates, namely of the bishop of Münster, count Rupert, and Markward the chamberlain, whom the . . . emperor, while we were still in Hungary, . . . ordered to be taken. Unmindful of his reputation, and contrary to the law of all nations regarding legates, he had them shamefully stripped and thrown into prison. When they heard such reports the whole army of the cross became enraged, and took, shortly, to the uninterrupted ravaging and occupation of cities, castles, and villages until [finally] the emperor . . . indicated to us by the tenor of his letters that the ambassadors . . . would return to us with great honor. In the end, however, after many embassies and diplomatic evasions, he craftily maintained the guile he had long since conceived against Our Benevolence, by prolonging our passage until the harshness of winter. In this spirit, when he returned our envoys . . . as if he had done a good turn, he kept more than two thousand marks of their money and went on promising a safe passage, an abundance of boats, a good market, and the usual money-exchange. As the familiar proverb says, however, 'the burnt child dreads the fire', we have no further faith in Greek vows and pretensions, and so have decided to winter in Philippopolis. . . . The duke of Swabia, the brother of Your Sublimity, is going to stay with a great part of the army in . . . Berrhoea [Stara Zagora] . . . until the mildness of spring destroys the harsh winter air.

"Since then we cannot cross the Arm of St. George unless we get from the emperor . . . very select . . . hostages and unless we subject all Romania [the Byzantine empire] to our rule, we strongly urge and request Your Prudent Royal Nobility to send suitable envoys . . . to Genoa, Venice, Ancona, and Pisa, and to other places, for a squadron of galleys and smaller vessels, in order that, meeting us at Constantinople around the middle of March, they may besiege the city by sea and we by land. We advise Your Royal Discretion, furthermore, . . . to collect immediately all the outstanding money which is owed us in different places, and have it deposited in the house of Bernard, our Venetian agent. In this way . . . let it be transferred to Tyre, since you know it will be very necessary to us on account of the unexpected delay we are about to endure. . . .

"We affectionately request Your Royal Benevolence . . . to get monks with never-failing vigilance to pour forth prayer to God for us. We . . . advise you also to take heed that the royal hand lay hold of judgment, and the zeal of the royal dignity glow against criminals, for especially by this service will you secure the grace of God and the favor of the people. Do not neglect, moreover, to write the lord pope to send some monks to the various provinces to exhort the people of God against the enemies of the cross, and especially against the Greeks. For in the presence of our envoys, the bishop of Münster and his colleagues, the patriarch of Constantinople publicly proclaimed [in the church of Hagia Sophia], that any

Greek who killed one hundred pilgrims, even if he were charged with murdering ten Greeks, would secure a pardon. . . . We have already spent twelve weeks at Philippopolis. From Philippopolis to Constantinople no inhabitant of city or fort is to be found."[7]

From this letter it is obvious that the march through Bulgaria and Thrace succeeded in so building up German fury against the Greeks that Frederick planned the capture of Constantinople, and, to promote it in the west, asked for a papal campaign of hatred against Byzantium. If one accepts Frederick's account at its face value the responsibility for this wholly unnecessary exacerbation of German sentiment must be put upon the feeble judgment and puerile diplomatic machinations of a cagey emperor, Isaac Angelus, who, without material means to retrieve the fortunes of a contracting empire, thought to frighten the Germans into making profitable concessions in the east by harassing their march and allying himself with the supreme enemy of western Christendom, Saladin himself. It is, however, conceivable that some, at least, of the attacks upon the crusader forces came from Balkan brigands. The writ of Constantinople no longer ran unchallenged in this area; witness the major rebellion of Vlachs and Bulgars that had exploded only three years before, and was still unquelled. It may have been impossible for Isaac to carry out the provisions of the treaty which his chancellor had made with Frederick at Nuremberg — to supply guides, provisions, and transportation across the straits. Had he done so, however, he might have delivered his potential western enemies into the hands of the Selchükid Turks with dispatch.

Barbarossa had no aggressive intentions against Byzantium, as Isaac had every reason to know from his conduct. Indeed the German emperor, bent upon a crusade to the east and not upon a hazardous political adventure, went out of his way, in the face of what appeared to be outrageous provocation and at great cost to the crusading army, to deal coolly with the impossible demands of his imperial colleague. Even if Isaac's fear of German aggression had been well founded, it was madness to stimulate rather than attempt to divert it, at a moment when Frederick was in direct touch with the Serbian and Bulgarian rebels. No Byzantine army could resist the German army if the petty diplomatic trickery of a despot failed to scare the untutored western barbarians into submission. It was irresponsible and callous to turn his subjects over to plunder and finally to an occupation. Indeed in provoking his own people, and in arousing the hatred and contempt of the German empire, and,

[7] This letter is in Ansbert, pp. 40–43.

moreover, in offending the aroused crusading spirit of the west, Isaac was preparing, in ways it is difficult to measure, doom for his state.

The succession of incidents which raised the German fury to a pitch was as follows. As soon as crusaders had entered Byzantine territory at Branits on July 2, without any formal welcome from Constantinople, the Byzantine governor "diverted us from . . . the public highway and . . . by command of his lord the emperor of Greece . . . blocked the rocky and non-public road to which he had led us". The "little double-dealing" Greeks were not able to prevent the opening of this road. As the army advanced through the Bulgarian forest on July 11 they encountered the ambushes of "puny Greeks, Bulgars, Serbs, and half-civilized Vlachs. . . . Many of them, when seized, confessed that they had been forced to do these things by order of the duke of Branits, and chiefly because of an edict of the Greek emperor. . . . Day after day occurred the rout and murder of foragers, and robbery by bandits who made sallies from the Greek side and incessantly stole horses and pillaged the carts which were proceeding without military escort."[8]

Without preparing carefully for the arrival of the German army except for an edict, unenforced, indicating that it was to be provided with facilities to purchase supplies and exchange money, Isaac had gone off to Philadelphia (Alashehir) to deal with the rebel Theodore Mancaphas. The German embassy to Constantinople was thus obliged to wait outside the city until he returned. When he did return and learned, as he had every reason to expect, of the arrival of Germans in Byzantine territory, he ordered his chancellor and other officials to act as guides for the German army. His arrest and imprisonment of the German embassy late in June gave him hostages to guarantee the behavior of the crusading army. Under these circumstances his subordinates drew their own conclusions, and Isaac himself was apparently content to let matters take their course. A homeward-bound Hungarian envoy explained to Frederick that Isaac had had to go to Philadelphia and that, accordingly, he should not "wonder over the fact that he had not yet been greeted or honored by any envoys." At the same time an envoy of that Greek chancellor who should have been conducting Frederick's army on its way asserted that Isaac was "much surprised that Frederick had not yet notified him by accredited envoys of his approach and that of the army, so that he might have greeted him

[8] Ansbert, pp. 27–28.

and the army more carefully by a splendid reception of his own men and the preparation of a good market." Ambassadors would be awaiting him in Sofia. Instead Frederick was greeted at Nish by an embassy from Alexius, a cousin of Isaac's, who blamed the Greek treatment of the Germans upon the duke of Branits, who "had been much at fault in not guiding them reliably, and in not rendering . . . the service . . . agreed upon." Henceforward "adequate guides and a market all through Greece" would be furnished provided that Frederick and his army "entered peacefully". Frederick was warned that at Sofia he would find a Greek army guarding the passes into Thrace, not against the Germans but against the counts of Serbia, the invaders of Byzantine territory. "Hence no suspicion of warlike intent should be harbored against him [Isaac] or the Greeks." "In all, however, that he [Alexius] or the chancellor of the emperor of Constantinople said, they mouthed one thing and meant another."

Meanwhile at Nish on July 27 Frederick and the leaders of the army received Stephen Nemanya, the "grand župan" of Serbia, and the leader of the Serbs' rebellion against Byzantium, together with his two brothers. The Serb leaders were determined to take full advantage of Frederick's passage to make secure their rebellion. They loaded him and the leaders of the army closest to him with a wide variety of gifts: wine, grain, sheep, cattle, "a tame boar, and three live stags, likewise tame". The Serb counts offered an alliance to Frederick "to help the present expedition, and in particular against the emperor of Greece, should he happen to resist the army of Christ." They were willing moreover to become the vassals of Frederick for the Byzantine territory they had recently conquered and "to receive that very land . . . from the hand of the emperor of the Romans himself".[9] This must have been an altogether pleasant prospect for Frederick and his crusading chiefs at a moment when it seemed likely that Byzantine opposition might obstruct their march.

Yet the Hohenstaufen emperor was not ready at the moment to ally himself with rebels and thus force the hand of Isaac. He did "not want," the chronicler says, "by means of a war against someone else, to alter or abandon the proposed march against the invaders of the Holy Sepulcher." Nor did he, of course, wish to preclude a possible use of the Serbs for the future. He replied therefore "to those counts in a kindly manner. He said that for the love of Christ he had undertaken a toilsome pilgrimage against the oppressors of

[9] *Ibid.*, p. 30, lines 7–27.

the land of Jerusalem, and that he was not, out of pride, or any ambition, designing evil against any Christian king whatever, including the king of Greece. This, however, was only on the condition that he [Isaac] supply for the army trustworthy guidance and an adequate market, as he had repeatedly promised. Should this not be the case . . . he was prepared to fight against false Christians who waylay the pilgrims of Christ, as well as against pagans, and would make his way with his men by the sword."[10] Frederick could count if need be upon the support, not only of the Serbs, but also of their rebel allies against Byzantium, the Bulgars and Vlachs led by Asen and his brother Peter, who likewise "with letters and envoys, influenced his majesty in his favor by proper deference and the promise of loyal aid against his enemies."

The march from Nish to Sofia, where the army arrived on August 13, was a repetition of the one from Branits to Nish. Greek hostility had already increased the retaliatory German pillage of the countryside to such an extent that, at Nish, Frederick had had to take steps to halt it. But the army, newly organized in its four divisions, continued to be harassed "through the rough and wild paths of the forests" by "ambushes and raids of enemy Greeks and Vlachs, instigated, as is known, by Isaac, the emperor of the Greeks." The column of duke Berthold was attacked by "the bandits. . . . They immediately engaged them like men, and cut down more than forty in a great slaughter. We saw twenty-four of them, who had been tied to the tails of horses and brought back to camp, hung on one gibbet, like wolves, head downwards." Frederick of Berg, the advocate, became expert in shooting snipers out of the trees. "He then fastened [them] to the [trees] more firmly than [they] had hitherto clung to [them], but with a noose." Young Frederick, the emperor's son, "executed by disgraceful hanging" a great many of the Bulgarian bandits he had taken. German knights were stimulated to heroic feats by such opportunities. "It happened that a certain knight who was so sick that he had been carried in a litter for a long time, found when the bandits broke out, that his spirit was renewed. . . . He boldly sprang from his bed, and, fighting manfully, gave one of them to the edge of the sword and turned the rest to flight; yet as soon as they scattered in flight his pain returned and again he lay down on his bed." But despite the German resistance, "the culprits . . . followed beside us over the mountain-slopes and plagued us by nocturnal pillage, through the whole of the Bulgarian forest." When, moreover, the

[10] Ansbert, pp. 30–31.

army arrived at Sofia, it was found "empty and destitute of every satisfaction for human wants. The tricks and perjury of the Greek emperor and his men then began to be clearly evident. The perjured emperor had ordered the market and money-exchange, which had been promised under oath, withdrawn, under threat of punishment. In addition, there were no signs of the meeting which not only John [Ducas], his chancellor, but also . . . Alexius, had, a short time ago, promised to the lord emperor. . . . By order of the emperor . . . in order to slaughter the pilgrims of Christ and to dishonor God, [they] had, by renewing its war-towers and defenses, strengthened the ancient pass of St. Basil."[11]

With the threat of force Frederick obliged the Byzantine army to withdraw from before the last Bulgarian pass, "blocked up by treacherous Greek craft", leading into the Maritsa valley. "On 20 August, after burning the machines of the Greeks, we issued from those manifold and detestable defiles." On August 24 they approached Philippopolis, "empty and abandoned by the Greeks for fear of us". On the following day Frederick "received letters from the Greek emperor Isaac, full of pride and arrogance and absolutely refusing us passage. . . ." At the same time Frederick learned of the arrest of his envoys in Constantinople. "For the emperor Isaac — in a new and unprecedented crime, one contrary to the law and usage of all nations, not only of those which fight for the Christian religion, but even of barbarian ones — had delivered those sent to him for the sake of peace and friendship to prison, after stripping them of effects and goods and insulting them in various ways. He did this to the dishonor of the army of the holy cross and of all Christianity, since he desired to offer this favor to his friend and confederate Saladin . . . the enemy of the cross and of all Christians. The whole army was enraged because of this and thenceforward freely pillaged the property of Greeks and ruined what was left."[12] On August 26 Philippopolis was occupied.

In a letter of August 25 Isaac had refused passage across the Dardanelles until Frederick sent hostages to Constantinople and promised to surrender to Byzantium one half of whatever conquests should be made in Syria. The German emperor, however, had no intention of dealing further with the Greeks until his arrested ambassadors were returned. He now regarded himself as freed from the obligations of the agreement made at Nuremberg. The only way in which Isaac's hand could be forced, Frederick decided, was by war and plunder, and immediately after their entrance into

[11] *Ibid.*, pp. 35–37. [12] *Ibid.*, pp. 38–39.

Philippopolis, the German army began to occupy the surrounding territory. "We gathered the grape-harvest of that country, pressing out the grapes; we took fruits from artificial caves, and everyone stored up enough for the quarters to which he had been assigned." The emperor indeed "would have occupied all Macedonia if the cause of the Crucified . . . had not held him back." For the time being, duke Frederick of Swabia, after defeating a Byzantine army stationed near Philippopolis, was permitted, "according to the plan determined on by the emperor and the princes," together with duke Berthold of Dalmatia and the greater part of the army "to assault the exceedingly rich city called Berrhoea." It was easily taken. "When our men were in possession of the city they found grain and barley, meal, wine, cattle, and sheep in great abundance and gathered a supply of various garments." The imperial marshal, Henry of Kalden, took "Scribention" (Sopot?). The marshal of the bishop of Passau took "Brandoveus" (Voden). "The strong city called Pernis [Petrich] surrendered unconditionally. . . . Thus in a short time the army of Christ and of the holy cross secured the three above-mentioned cities and about ten castles."[13]

The negotiations between Frederick and Stephen Nemanya, and the Vlach brothers Asen and Peter, together with the actual occupation of Byzantine territory by the German army, at length made an impression upon emperor Isaac. It was not until late October, however, that he decided to release the German ambassadors, and proceed with further negotiations concerning the advance of the German army. The delay only served to intensify German suspicions. It seemed to them obviously deliberate, and meant, in the interest of Saladin, to postpone the German crossing of the straits "until hard winter was upon them". It was calculated, they believed, to provide time for Isaac to prepare plans for the destruction of the German army as it crossed the Dardanelles. For the Germans had heard that Isaac, "thinking us ignorant and unsuspecting", had prepared his Turks and Kumans "to lay three ambushes for us as we crossed the straits". The army was first to be divided for the crossing on the specious plea that the lack of boats made this necessary. "When a part of the army had crossed, attacks were to be made from both the European and Asiatic sides," and finally "while rowing on the sea it was to be surrounded by the galleys of these same enemies and given to slaughter."[14]

The return of the ambassadors on October 28, accompanied by an impressive Byzantine mission, did nothing at all to allay these

[13] Ansbert, pp. 44–45. [14] *Ibid.*, p. 48, lines 8–15.

suspicions. It only strengthened the position of those in the army who were anxious to continue the war, to attack Constantinople itself, and to be done once and for all with the infuriating tactics of hypocritical Greeks. The German envoys were received with tears of joy by the whole German army. "Even the emperor could not restrain himself from tears." On the following day they were permitted to tell "to the assembled princes, clergy, and knights, the pitifully sad story of how they were shamefully taken prisoner, robbed, starved, mocked, and insulted in various ways." Isaac had had the effrontery to give their stallions to the envoys of Saladin, then in Constantinople. Nicetas, patriarch of Constantinople, "that pseudo-apostle", had called the crusaders "dogs" in one of his sermons, and had made the inflammatory offer of absolution for their wholesale murder, as later reported by Frederick to Henry in the letter already quoted.[15]

The Byzantine embassy, deliberately snubbed by the Germans, had been kept from coming to any agreement by its instructions to raise the question of protocol. The Germans, indeed, after all that had happened could not believe their ears when the Byzantine chancellor, the head of the delegation, began to read the letter of Isaac demanding further German hostages, and, in order to facilitate a speedy continuance of the German march, promising the "provision of a market and the passage of the Hellespont [Dardanelles] between the cities of Abydus and Sestus". "For that contemptible Greek, with his usual pride, lyingly proclaimed himself to be the 'emperor of the Romans', and our most serene august lord himself to be not emperor of the Romans but only 'king of Alamannia' [Germany]." This was too much even for Frederick. He sprang to his feet and instructed the Byzantine envoys in the western view of the history of the Roman empire. "It is greatly to be wondered at," he said, "why my brother, your lord and emperor . . . should usurp this futile and undeserved title, and should glory foolishly in an honor which is, by all odds, not his, for clearly he understands that I am 'Frederick the ever-august emperor of the Romans' both in name and in fact." He then spoke his mind upon how Isaac had "robbed my faithful envoys, noblemen, Christ's pilgrims and crusaders, of their property, taken them prisoner and jailed them, tormented them with hunger, and insulted them in various ways. . . . Unless," he concluded, "he restores what he took from my envoys, and makes suitable satisfaction for the injury he put upon them without cause, and unless in his letter

[15] *Ibid.*, pp. 48–49.

he salutes me with due respect by the name of Roman emperor, and unless, by means of very select hostages, he guarantees me a fair market and money-exchange, and a secure passage over the sea which is called the Arm of St. George, he may henceforth by no means presume to send me either envoys or letters. Let him know that I, in reliance upon divine love, will unhesitatingly cut my way through with the sword."[16]

In subsequent correspondence the matter of title was satisfactorily settled. In a following letter Isaac got to the point of calling Frederick "the most excellent emperor of Alamannia", and finally in a third "the most noble emperor of ancient Rome", but the new demands of Frederick for very select hostages to guarantee for the future the fulfilment of the agreement of Nuremberg enraged him with the knowledge that the surrender of the German envoys had brought him nothing in return.

Meanwhile, in the absence of a settlement, the German army decided to set up winter quarters in Adrianople, and to continue the war against the Byzantines by an occupation of Thrace up to the very walls of Constantinople. Indeed, in the weeks preceding his letter home (November 16) Frederick surrendered to the demands of the war party in the army, led by duke Berthold of Dalmatia, demanding an attack on Constantinople. Yet he seemed to think that Isaac might come to his senses and make possible, for the spring of 1190, a passage of the straits. Frederick was certainly well aware of the difficulties of an attack upon Constantinople. The death of William II of Norman Italy and Sicily, as we saw in an earlier chapter, would make it unlikely that help could come from that quarter for a long time. Venice, an ally of Isaac, could be counted on for nothing more than neutrality. The rivalry between Genoa and Pisa could hardly be quieted by a projected attack on Constantinople by the Germans. It was not to be expected that the papacy would launch a campaign against the Byzantines in the west, merely because Barbarossa and Henry VI wanted it. And if, despite these difficulties, it should come to an attack upon Constantinople, and this was to be successful, it would be difficult to prevent the crusade from stopping here. Frederick preferred to get on with the crusade. An attack on Constantinople, for him at least, was a last resort after all else had failed.

Leaving the bishops of Liége, Passau, Münster, and Toul and the archbishop of Tarentaise behind to hold Philippopolis, the main

[16] Ansbert, pp. 49–50.

army left for Adrianople on November 5, and occupied the abandoned city on November 22. Meanwhile bishop Conrad of Regensburg took Probaton and "was quick to gather there for himself and for his companions an abundance of all necessities." On November 24 duke Frederick of Swabia took Demotica, "a very well fortified city. . . . All those, however, [except small children and women] who were found in the town were butchered by the sword to a number reckoned at more than one thousand five hundred. . . . Certain of our knights recognized in the loot from the city the three horses which robbers had forcefully taken from them in Bulgaria."[17] Indeed, on his roundabout way from Philippopolis to Adrianople, the duke had "made a steady progress through Macedonia and took the city of Culos [Chelebiköy] with two others whose names are not remembered." Boldly going on from there, he reached the sea "and attacked the rich city called Menas [Enos]. When the citizens escaped from it in boats, he took . . . fabulous booty." Subsequently the duke attacked from Adrianople Arcadiopolis, and "found it as empty of warriors as of the necessities of life. Some of our men nevertheless found wine and grain there which they carried back to their fellows." More or less constant fighting with Byzantine forces took place until the territory to the very walls of Constantinople was occupied. Dense forest areas had to be cleared. Regular engagements with Isaac's Vlach and Kuman mercenaries were carried out. "Bohemians [better trained for war and pillage than the others] came together with some others from the army who were seeking necessary provisions for themselves, to a certain seacoast city. There they seized more than enough horses and mules, wine, and grain, and all sorts of desirable things." From an "almost inaccessible swamp, to which a not inconsiderable crowd of the enemy had fled with all their possessions," they carried a notable booty. A column of the bishop of Würzburg and of the counts of Salm, Wied, and Sponheim "captured two cities in the direction of Vlach territory. . . . A third was taken by assault — more than five thousand were killed in a great massacre. One of these cities was given to the flames. . . . The second column, of the count of Abenberg and the advocate Frederick of Berg, always a very dangerous one, . . . turned southwards, inflicted a pitiable slaughter upon the enemy, and brought back abundant booty."

The troops of the bishops at Philippopolis were also active in the neighborhood, and they were joined by the twelve hundred men

[17] *Ibid.*, pp. 53–54.

who, together with duke Berthold, count Florent of Holland, and Frederick of Berg, were sent from Adrianople on December 7 to bring the garrison at Philippopolis to Adrianople. Duke Berthold had to rescue the troops of bishop Dietpold of Passau at "Bacon" (Batkun). The advocate "invaded a rich region called Vlachia, not far distant from Thessalonica. Here he killed a few rebels and found a greater store of supplies than his men could carry back. . . . The bishop of Passau and the duke of Dalmatia followed with an armed band, subdued the land, and loaded their men with pillage taken from the enemy."

The incidents of battle kept the German animosity toward the Byzantines at white heat and stimulated their plundering zeal. In the course of the slaughter at Demotica, and of the capture of the castle of "Nikiz" (at Hafsa), the Germans were convinced that the Byzantines were attempting to undo them with poisoned wine and that, at least in the neighborhood of Nikiz, "which with all the surrounding region is known to serve the emperor at Constantinople in the making of toxics and poisons", this was done upon imperial orders. The strong constitutions of the Germans preserved them from this treachery. "That same wine" which, when forced down the throat of the recalcitrant Greek, caused him to turn pale, foam at the mouth, and wildly roll his eyes, "hardly so much as intoxicated some of our men. . . . Lo, in the ten plagues of Egypt the waters of Egypt became thick blood for the Egyptians, but clear waters for the Hebrews. And now, by no less of a miracle, the wine of the Greeks, steeped in poison and prepared for the destruction of our men, was deadly for the Greeks, but a healthy drink for our men. Our men now knew that from the time they entered Bulgaria, poison had very often been prepared for us."[18] Nor were the Germans able to take with equanimity the taunting posters which Byzantine artists had painted in churches and public buildings. "When they visited in force the region called Graditz, they found in the pictures of churches and other buildings, Greeks astride the necks of pilgrims, and, as if they were enemies, restraining them with bridles. Our men, enraged at this, set the churches and other buildings on fire, killed very many people with their swords, devastated that whole land, and took huge amounts of booty."[19] Indeed because "the excitement of our people toward the Greeks was fanned to a higher pitch day by day", the pillaging increased. In fact, "the entire army was swamped with the booty of these enemy Greeks. . . . Greed ruled at that time in the hearts of many as a result of the

[18] Ansbert, pp. 54–55. [19] *Ibid.*, p. 56, lines 14–19.

excess of pillage and murder." Obviously, there was some cause for Byzantine fear of the German advance toward Constantinople.

At Philippopolis and Adrianople, "under cover of the freedom necessary to bring together provisions, there crept into almost everybody the general abuse of pillaging more than the necessary things."[20] The prolonged stay at Philippopolis and Adrianople further relaxed the discipline of the army. "Many lacked that good faith and harmony which formerly flourished in the army of Christ", and steps had to be taken to correct the excessive fraternization with native women. "For, to be specific, they publicly stripped both the men and the women, tied their hands behind their backs, tied a rope about their loins, and led them around through the whole city. . . . They finally in the very cold of winter immersed them several times in the river which flows by, and dismissed them with proper scoffing and mockery."[21] When the Germans left Philippopolis for Adrianople, "to show their hatred of the Greeks, they utterly destroyed that city by fire. Some of them, moreover, on the march forward turned aside to the city of Berrhoea, and after collecting all the booty they wanted, gave it to the avenging flames."

While at Adrianople Frederick attempted through duke Berthold to renew diplomatic contact with Stephen Nemanya, "about sending an army to help us if perchance war should be declared against Constantinople". When the duke finally arrived in Adrianople on January 21, 1190, he presented to Frederick an embassy of the "grand župan", and was charged with carrying the negotiations with the Serbs to completion. Meanwhile, too, the Vlach Peter "urgently requested Frederick to make him emperor . . . and to place on his head the imperial crown of the kingdom of Greece. He steadfastly asserted that, at the beginning of spring, he would send forty thousand Vlachs and Kumans . . . against Constantinople. The emperor preferred to hold their offer in reserve while maintaining Peter's good will."[22] These negotiations and the continuance of the war led to the further exchange of envoys between Frederick and Isaac Angelus on the basis of the agreement at Nuremberg, and the furnishing of select hostages by the Byzantines, for "the Greek emperor saw his land and cities unable to resist, and furthermore laid waste by our men." By December 24 negotiations had proceeded to the point where definite terms were being discussed. But at the last moment, the Byzantine envoys, with what the Germans regarded as "their usual shifting and inconstancy, shrank from the promised conditions and rejected the terms of certain

20 *Ibid.*, pp. 59–60. 21 *Ibid.*, p. 60, lines 12–20. 22 *Ibid.*, p. 58, lines 12–20.

articles." The negotiations were broken off immediately, and "the envoys of the Greek emperor were sent back home with a threat of further war. Thereafter the indignation of our men toward the Greeks boiled up more and more."

Isaac thereafter again capitulated, and on January 21, 1190, his embassy arrived in Adrianople ready to carry out the terms of Nuremberg, and "to give most noble hostages to show his good faith in this promise, and to assure its performance." Frederick sent back with this legation to Constantinople "count Berthold of Tuscany, Markward of Anweiler, the lord high steward, and Markward of Neuenburg, the chamberlain . . . to investigate carefully the truth of the promises, and if they found them assuredly true, to act as plenipotentiaries in negotiating conditions of peace."[23] On February 14 these German and Byzantine envoys returned to Adrianople with the specific terms of a treaty of peace, whose chief provisions were: (1) Isaac renounced all claims to indemnity for the losses suffered from the crusading army in Macedonia and Thrace. (2) "For the crossing, either at Gallipoli or between Sestus and Abydus, he shall furnish enough ships to transport the glorious army of Christ . . ."; Frederick in turn promised to do no further damage in any part of the Byzantine empire, and not to prevent any ships from going on to Constantinople. (3) During the crossing all Byzantine galleys "stationed between Abydus and Constantinople" were to remain "motionless on the beaches". (4) The Byzantine army was to keep a "four days' march away from the army of Christ and of the emperor of the Romans, for as long as the latter shall be in the land of the former". (5) "In order that he may rest his expedition" Frederick was to be given "two cities near the shore, here and on the other side". (6) "To assure the good faith of these promises, Isaac . . . shall give the lord emperor eighteen very select hostages of royal blood, and of the rank of duke" (the more important of these are named). (7) In case provisions were not supplied the army, it was to be free to act on its own behalf except that no land is to be transferred "to any heathen ruler". (8) "The emperor of Constantinople was to be indulgent with all the Greeks, Armenians, and Latins who have followed and served the most serene emperor of the Romans". (9) Exchange rates for money were fixed. (10) Markets were to be provided the German army: "The inhabitants shall sell to it at as fair a price as they would be bound to sell to Isaac". (11) "The emperor of Constantinople shall act as the lord emperor of the

[23] Ansbert, p. 61, lines 3–10.

Romans shall advise with respect to the possessions which the bishop of Münster, count Rupert, and their companions lost at Constantinople". (12) All Latins, whether pilgrims or merchants, "captured on land or sea from the time hostilities began", were to be released. The treaty was to be ratified by five hundred distinguished Greeks in Hagia Sophia, in the presence of the patriarch, who was to sign the treaty himself. On the German side it was to be guaranteed by the oaths of five hundred knights.[24]

On these moderate terms did Isaac prevent an attack upon his capital, and Frederick hasten the march of his crusaders. To the German chronicler the treaty is a diplomatic victory for Frederick. "This emperor [Isaac] who foolishly boasted that all Christ's pilgrims were caught in his net, and . . . by lying and empty excuses utterly refused passage to the army of the living cross, now, after his land had been monstrously devastated and his forces horribly massacred, put aside his usual pride. . . . Wishing to take thought for the only part of Bulgaria left him, and then for Constantinople, he sought peace. For the whole army of Christ longed to take Constantinople by storm. . . . The most pious emperor of the Romans, however unwillingly, . . . had . . . made ready ships and galleys from Italy, Apulia, and the maritime provinces. He had also in readiness an army of more than sixty thousand Serb and Vlach auxiliaries."[25]

There was now no reason why the German army should not get on its way. After Frederick had refused to intervene in the conflict between Constantinople and Peter's Vlachs, the army moved southward from Adrianople on March 1, headed by duke Frederick and his Swabians and Bavarians. On March 21 they arrived at Gallipoli. Here was found a Venetian ship which had, despite warning, sought to escape the demands of Frederick and his army by sailing on to Constantinople, "as if to seek greater gain there". But a storm had driven them back to Gallipoli where they were obliged to sell their wares to the crusaders. In response to his previous orders to the regent Henry in Germany, there appeared also "envoys of the Pisans . . . greeting the lord emperor with a due profession of subjection and fealty, and earnestly inquiring how he and the army were." What was more to the point, they offered him "ships and galleys with which to besiege Constantinople."[26] From the 22nd to

[24] The terms of the treaty are given by Ansbert, pp. 64–66. For this whole affair as it appeared to the Byzantines, see below, chapter IV, pp. 147–148.

[25] Ansbert, p. 68, lines 27–34.

[26] *Ibid.*, p. 71, lines 13–17.

the 24th, duke Frederick crossed with his division. Rain on Easter Sunday, the 25th, made it possible for the army to attend religious services rather than to "labor exclusively in the work of crossing the straits". On the following three days the rest of the army crossed, "in joy and exultation". Barbarossa himself crossed on the 28th, "with the last of his troops, screened by five war-galleys and by other vessels, while the Greeks sounded their trumpets on the sea and on the shore. . . . We were now translated from the west into the east . . . from Europe into Asia."

In spite of the treaty of Adrianople, the march through mountainous Byzantine territory in Asia Minor to the Selchükid border was not altogether peaceful. Once again, this seemed pure treachery to the crusaders. Once again, it is possible that they failed to realize the feebleness of the Byzantine central government, and the conditions of near-anarchy prevailing in Asia Minor, as in the Balkans. "With their accustomed treachery the Greeks violated the peace pact, and day after day harassed the more careless of our men, killed some who were not armed, and stole the goods of those who were killed."[27] Bad feeling between Byzantines and Latins at Philadelphia almost led to the destruction of the city by the Latins, who found no provisions and supplies awaiting them. They had "hoped for good merchandise from the governor and citizens of Philadelphia", but "those citizens, from a certain rash scorn, not only did not supply the promised provisions and merchandise, but certain more imprudent ones even ventured to bait our men with haughty words" and isolated skirmishes arose.[28] The brawls were settled by negotiation between Frederick and the governor of the city, who reminded the emperor "that all Christians ought to be moved with mercy for the aforementioned city, seeing that it, old and alone, had till now resisted the neighboring Turks and other peoples, and thus was guarding the cultivation and honor of Christian doctrine. . . . On that account, he said, we should all incur greater fault for destroying this city than for destroying Philippopolis and Adrianople." The army left Philadelphia on April 22 with citizens of Philadelphia attacking its rear, and on the following day "the Turks attacked the extreme van of the lord emperor's army". On the 25th "we passed the ruined city of Hierapolis. . . . Through a very pleasant valley, rich with licorice, cardamon, myrtle, figs, and other species of plants, we entered the territory of the Turks."

The Selchükids no less than the Byzantines were prepared to

[27] Ansbert, p. 72, lines 17–19. [28] *Ibid.*, p. 73, lines 14–20.

make the most of the passage of these westerners through their land. Godfrey of Wiesenbach had appeared with an embassy from Kilij Arslan before the Germans had left Adrianople, and through this embassy the sultan had promised "the very best market throughout his land." In fact, however, the old sultan had already divided his domain among his sons, the eldest of whom, Qutb-ad-Dīn Malik-Shāh, had imprisoned his father and seized Iconium.[29] Qutb-ad-Dīn had also sent an envoy to Adrianople bearing letters in which he "likewise asserted steadfastly that he would follow him [Frederick] with devotion and loyal obedience." The Germans subsequently concluded that this envoy "sang so guilefully in order to hurt and deceive the most faithful emperor and overthrow the innocent Christian army, and the Lord's Christian people, who were in exile for the love of His passion."

The march across the mountainous terrain to Iconium (April 28–May 18) was the most difficult, costly, and trying of the whole journey. Often without food and drink for men and horses, subject to constant flank attacks from the fleet Turkish cavalry, traversing hazardous and unknown territory, the army straggled before the capital city after having suffered tremendous losses in men and beasts. Avoiding the pass of Myriokephalon, where a large Turkish army had gathered, the pilgrims were caught on a "very rough and lofty mountain that only mountain-goats could traverse" and suffered from ambush and falling stones. On May 6 they lost their minnesinger, Frederick of Hausen, the "special comfort of the army."[30] On the 7th near Philomelium (Akshehir), the dukes of Swabia and Dalmatia inflicted a serious defeat upon the enemy that cost the Turks, it was said, 4,174 men. By the 8th, the dearth of supplies had grown so great that prices had risen to a forbidding height, and the "flesh of horses and mules was bought as a delicacy". Desertions to the enemy also began. "Some of the foot-soldiers, who were exhausted by labor, by hunger and sickness, and about to die, when they could not by any means keep up with the army", cast "themselves down to the ground in the form of a cross", and "awaited imminent death in the name of the Lord. These, when we were not far off, were made Christ's martyrs by being beheaded by the enemy who were following us." On Pentecost (May 13) "the Lord spared us from attacks of the evil Turks. Banquets of the festival consisted of cooked hides of cattle and horses, though the richer ones had horse meat. . . . Small quantities of meal, if there

[29] For details on Selchükid affairs, see below, chapter XIX, pp. 680–681.

[30] Ansbert, p. 79, lines 4–5: "speciale solatium exercitus".

was any in the army, were guarded like gold and hidden away." On the following day, "with the help of St. George", Frederick himself met and routed the main Turkish army. The "great king was knocked from his horse by a knight, and one of his barons had his right arm, together with the sleeve of the corselet, cut off by the blow of a sword." To one Turkish emir this was the victory of "seven thousand white-clad horsemen sitting on white horses . . . who very roughly cut us all down with the lances they carried." On the eve of that day they "pitched camp, though without water or grass. As a result uncounted numbers of beasts of burden perished", and "the men too were dry with excessive thirst. . . . On the next morning, like wanderers about to die, we went on wretchedly, with some drinking their own urine, some the blood of horses, others chewing horse manure for the moisture, many chewing a cud of tufts of grass."[31]

For the attack on Iconium, which the Germans felt they must take to secure their march, they rallied themselves, after Frederick had rejected an offer of the Turks to allow them to pass and to supply them with provisions for "three hundred pounds of gold and the land of the Armenians". "Rather than making a royal highway with gold and silver," Frederick had said, "with the help of our Lord Jesus Christ, whose knights we are, the road will have to be opened with iron."[32] On the 17th the German army camped in the "garden and pleasure ground of the sultan" outside the city limits. On the following morning the army was divided into two groups, one under the duke of Swabia and the other under the emperor. The former was to attack Iconium while Barbarossa remained outside the city.[33]

In view of the condition of the German army the assault proceeded with unusual ease. On the way to the city the advancing troops of duke Frederick met the German envoy to the Turks, Godfrey of Wiesenbach, and were told that "God has given this city and the land into your hands." The old sultan, who with his army had fled the first sight of the German troops, took refuge in the fortress which rose above the city and into which "almost all the citizens of the city, both rich and poor, withdrew, carrying with them an infinite store of gold and silver and a great abundance of provisions." Duke Frederick took the first gate of the city by assault, beat down the Turkish resistance, and advanced to the

[31] Ansbert, pp. 80–83.

[32] *Ibid.*, p. 83, lines 20–22.

[33] The account of the siege is given in Ansbert, pp. 84–86.

walls of the fortress. There was a general massacre of those found in the city ("he took the city and killed the citizens").

Meanwhile, unaware of his son's victory, the emperor Frederick and his troops outside the city were surrounded by Turkish contingents. The situation at first appeared hopeless. The clergy "offering themselves as a living sacrifice to the high priest . . . put their stoles about their necks." Frederick himself, "that glorious emperor of the Romans . . . whose like the whole world could not find", stood in the midst of the troops knowing full well that their doom was impending. He is reported to have said to them with grave concern that he would gladly lose his own head if only they "could come as a whole to Antioch", and to have urged them: "But why do we tarry, of what are we afraid? Christ reigns. Christ conquers. Christ commands," and "leading his men like a lion was first to spring upon the enemy", and "so put them to flight that not one of them raised his hand against him. . . . If the weakness of the knights, who languished from hunger, had not stood in the way, the fortress itself would have been taken by storm that night. The knights, however, had labored for about fourteen days under unbelievable and unheard-of want and hunger." Thereupon Frederick and his troops joined his son and the troops in the city. "There the madness of our stomachs was somewhat soothed by spoils of the enemy." There was not only wheat and barley, but also gold and silver, jewels, and purple cloth to a reckoning of more than one hundred thousand marks. There was also the satisfaction of capturing the dowry of Saladin's niece in the sultan's palace.[34]

Frederick was as anxious to get beyond Iconium as he had been to get beyond Adrianople. Proposals of peace from Kilij Arslan and his son were quickly entertained, and it was arranged upon the reception of twenty distinguished Turkish hostages and the provision of adequate supplies. The Germans left Iconium on the 23rd, pitched camp near the garden and pleasure-ground of the sultan, and spent three days supplying themselves at the market set up there, purchasing some six thousand horses and mules, bread and meat, butter and cheeses. By the 26th they were on their way again, and only the threat to execute the hostages kept the army from being harassed again by "wild Turks". On May 30 they arrived at Laranda (Karaman), "a beautiful city which divides Cilicia, that is, Armenia, from Lycaonia".[35]

[34] Ansbert, p. 86, lines 26–30. Saladin's niece, daughter of al-'Ādil, was believed by the crusaders and chroniclers to be his daughter. She was the wife of Kai-Qobād (I).

[35] *Ibid.*, p. 88, lines 26–27.

The German army was in Christian territory at last. The chief obstacles to their arriving at their goal had now been surmounted. When Ansbert compares his meager account of the journey through Anatolia with what more gifted authors might have written, he excuses himself with the thought that even they would have been unequal to it. "For I think that if faced with an adequate and full description of such great labor, the famous Homer, or the eloquent Lucan, or the bard of Mantua himself, would as if speechless have placed a finger on his mouth." Here they were greeted by friendly local princes and envoys of the Ṛoupenid prince of Armenia, Leon II.

Yet the bitterest disappointment still faced them. The mountainous approach across the Taurus range to the valley of the "Saleph" river (Calycadnus) was very difficult, and to avoid it Frederick, following the advice of local guides, sought a more circuitous and also difficult route. He arrived at the stream while the main army was still straggling over the mountain passes "in the summer sun and the boiling heat. . . . He tried," Ansbert says, "to swim the channel of the Saleph river, a very rapid one," in order to cool himself off and "to detour the jagged mountains. . . . In spite of everyone's attempt to dissuade him, he entered the water, and, submerged in a whirlpool, he who had often avoided great dangers miserably perished." When "other nobles near him hastened to help him, . . . they were too late. . . . They then took him out and brought him to the bank. Everyone was upset by his death and struck with such violent grief that . . . some ended their lives with him, but others in despair and, as it were, seeing that God had no care of them, renounced the Christian faith and went over to the heathen. The death of such a prince warranted the lamentation and immoderate grief which took possession of everyone's heart."[36]

The death of the emperor (June 10, 1190) turned the German crusade into something like a funeral procession, breaking its spirit and its unity. A western army, the news of whose approach had terrified Saladin and which, together with powerful English and French armies, was calculated to break his power, was now rendered progressively impotent. From the day it had set out from Regensburg until after the victory at Iconium it had lost something like sixty thousand men. If duke Frederick, its newly elected leader,

[36] The account of Frederick's drowning is in Ansbert, pp. 91, lines 20–36, and 92, lines 1–9.

could have preserved the morale and unity of those who were left, it still might have made its mark upon the east. As it was, a few left immediately for home from Cilician ports. The rest of the army divided into three groups, one going from Tarsus to Tripoli by sea, a second with duke Frederick to Antioch by sea, and a third overland to Antioch. Frederick reached Antioch on June 21 and was joined by the land force, which had lost many men. Here "after such great labors, lack of food, and torments of hunger, they wanted to rest and recoup themselves", when plague struck them. It carried away bishops Godfrey of Würzburg and Martin of Meissen, margrave Hermann of Baden, burggrave Burkhard of Magdeburg, counts Florent of Holland, Poppo of Henneberg, and Wilbrand of Hallermund, and the advocate Frederick of Berg. Duke Frederick, tempted by a career of conquest in northern Syria, did not start for Acre until late August. He moved first down the coast to Tripoli, and from Tripoli to Tyre, where count Adolf of Holstein took ship for Germany to defend his lands against Henry the Lion. Early in October Frederick arrived at Acre.

In September some Germans who had preferred the sea route from the west arrived at Acre — Frisians and Flemings under James of Avesnes and a group of Saxon nobles including counts Otto of Guelders and Henry of Altenburg. The fleet of sixty ships which had left Cologne in February 1189, and had gathered up Netherlanders and English on the way, had been stranded in Portugal fighting for its king. Landgrave Louis of Thuringia, sailing from Brindisi to Tyre, had also reached Acre, but left for home, critically ill, in October and died en route.

Frederick's troops, decimated further by Moslem attack on the way from Antioch to Tripoli, and depleted by shipwreck, were unable to exert any great effort before Acre. Death and disease still further reduced German manpower to a pitiful remnant of what had been its strength even after Iconium. "One . . . could believe that human affairs had at that time come to an end. . . . Unprecedented destruction and pestilence laid everybody low, without exception, so that they who did not die at Antioch, when they sought a postponement of their death and sailed in their sickness to Acre, died there; and those who, though sick, stayed to besiege that city, were taken with a like death." Bishop Dietpold of Passau went in November, together with his canons and clerics. Duke Frederick of Swabia died on January 20, 1191, and was buried in the cemetery of the German Hospital, a foundation of burghers from Bremen and Lübeck which the duke had maintained and which was soon to become the home of the Teutonic Knights. "Since the deaths of the other princes occurred so thick and fast, and fatal day piled upon fatal day, we could by no means note their dates."[37]

After Frederick's death the remaining Germans put themselves under Conrad of Montferrat, and by the time of duke Leopold of Austria's arrival in the spring of 1191 had for the most part embarked for Germany. With the arrival of the French and English armies under Philip and Richard, Leopold's part in the siege of Acre was but a small one. Only a few Germans were present to witness the fall of the city.[38] Leopold himself set out for home in November or December 1191, smarting under the treatment he and the Germans had received from Richard, and quite ready to coöperate with Richard's enemies, Henry VI and Philip Augustus, in taking full advantage of Richard's capture after his forced landing on the Istrian coast.

As a young man of twenty-three Henry VI had been entrusted with the governance of the empire while Frederick Barbarossa went off on the crusade that ended in his death. He was thus intimately acquainted with the hopes that had led his aged father to undertake such a hazardous mission, and with the ambitions that had lured the German aristocracy, lay and ecclesiastical, to follow him in such great numbers. He had been kept informed of the progress of the march to the Dardanelles, and had been made responsible for the execution in the west of Frederick's plans to organize a crusade against the Byzantine empire in case Isaac Angelus persisted in his efforts to block the advance of the German army. He must have shared the angry resentment of his father, and may even have attributed to the eastern emperor the ultimate responsibility for Barbarossa's death. This resentment was kept burning by the individual reports of those who managed to survive the expedition.

Henry knew also of the precarious position of the Byzantine state, of the readiness of Serbs and Bulgars to attack it from the European side, and of its inability to deal with those Selchükids of Iconium whom even an enfeebled and decimated German army had managed to dispose of with comparative ease. If the huge effort of his father's campaign were not to be wholly in vain, it would have to be repeated and the mistakes previously made avoided. Of the desire of the German aristocracy for a speedy renewal of the effort

[37] The events after Frederick's death are narrated by Ansbert, pp. 92–93, and in *Chronicon Magni presbiteri*, ad ann. 1190–1191 (*MGH, SS.*, XVII), pp. 516–518.

[38] For the siege of Acre, see above, chapter II, pp. 53, 65–69.

he was well aware. The civil wars between Saladin's sons and their uncle al-'Ādil Saif-ad-Dīn ("Saphadin"), the sultan of Egypt, were an added inducement.[39] Whether the campaign would be a war of revenge against the Byzantine state depended, first, upon the conduct of the eastern emperor with respect to this second German effort, and second, upon circumstances within the empire at home. Constantinople had reason to be more fearful of a crusade led by Henry VI than of those led by Conrad III or Barbarossa. And the young Henry knew from the history of the negotiations between his father and Isaac that it was only necessary to be firm to get what he wanted. In any case the Hohenstaufen plans for the integration of Italy and Germany into a strong central European state must not be upset by attempting the impossible in either the Byzantine or the Moslem east. In this respect there is no reason to suppose that Henry was any less wise than his father.

When the news of Barbarossa's death reached him, Henry was already faced with the problem of conquering his wife Constance's inheritance, the Norman kingdom of southern Italy and Sicily. His first effort failed before Naples. By 1195 his second effort, financed by Richard's ransom, had succeeded. Meanwhile the birth of a son at Iesi opened to him the prospect of transforming the German empire into a hereditary monarchy similar to the monarchies of the west. In exchange for papal support of this important step Henry was ready to offer his personal leadership of a crusade. These plans, however, were thwarted by the opposition of archbishop Adolf of Cologne, and the ultimate refusal of the papacy to consider the coronation of his son Frederick. Henry knew only too well how difficult it would be to reconcile the inhabitants of the Norman kingdom to their new German master, or to render the papacy content with German possession of a kingdom which had long been a papal fief. Now that the truce in the east with Saladin had expired, a successful crusade might accomplish many desirable ends, even without Henry's personal direction. It would strengthen the position of the emperor among the German nobility, lay and ecclesiastical. It would enhance the dignity of the empire in Europe. It might restore the relations of papacy and empire to some kind of harmony, and this might, in turn, facilitate the pacification of the newly acquired Norman kingdom of Sicily. Thus, if carefully prepared and managed, the resumption of his father's effort to restore the kingdom of Jerusalem would almost certainly contribute to the solidification of the German empire.

[39] On Aiyūbid affairs, see below, chapter XX, pp. 693–695.

Postponing any announcement of his personal leadership of the crusade until it was clear that circumstances would permit of his going, Henry received the cross privately from bishop John of Sutri in Easter week of 1195. This was followed in the diet at Bari on Easter day with a public imperial summons to the crusade. At about the same time Henry announced his own special contribution to the expedition. He was ready to supply a force of three thousand paid mounted troops, half knights and half squires, for the duration of a year. This meant that to the German knights who followed their lords from beyond the Alps would be given a hard central core of mercenary troops under imperial officers. In June Henry left for Germany to promote the recruitment of the German nobility. There soon followed papal legates to inaugurate the preaching of the crusade. By early August pope Celestine III called upon the German clergy to preach the new crusade. Yet Henry's own illness postponed the organization of the movement, and it was, accordingly, not until the fall and early winter that the growing enthusiasm could be organized in formal meetings of the princes.

Before leaving Italy for Germany Henry had made his first démarche upon Constantinople preliminary to the organization of the crusading army. It was quite evidently meant to forestall any Byzantine attempts to interfere with the organization of the crusade, and to inform Isaac moreover that the Byzantine empire was expected to contribute to rather than obstruct the expedition. As the new king of the former Norman kingdom of southern Italy and Sicily, Henry demanded the "return" of the Balkan territory which king William II had formerly conquered, from Durazzo (Dyrrachium) to Thessalonica.[40] He demanded compensation for damages suffered by his father while in Byzantine territory en route to Palestine. He asked, moreover, that a Byzantine fleet support his own crusade to Palestine. Before negotiations over these demands could be completed, the incompetent Isaac had been deposed and blinded by his brother Alexius III (April 8, 1195).[41]

Possibilities for further pressure upon the Byzantine empire, for further support of the new crusade, and for an extension of German political influence in the eastern Mediterranean became evident at the diet of Gelnhausen in October 1195, when envoys of Aimery of Lusignan, the new ruler of Cyprus, arrived, offering to do homage to Henry and hold Cyprus as a fief, and requesting that Henry crown him king. Henry accepted homage from one of the

[40] See above, chapter I, pp. 36–37.

[41] On Alexius III, see below, chapter IV, pp. 148–150.

envoys, and promised to crown Aimery personally at a subsequent date. Meanwhile he entrusted the archbishops of Trani and Brindisi with the mission of taking to Aimery on his behalf the symbol of investiture, a golden scepter. A similar request from Leon II of Cilician Armenia must have revealed to Henry again the great impression his impending arrival in the east was making there. He may well have thought of renewing the ties which his father had maintained with the new Serbian and Bulgarian dynasties. The precarious position in which this encirclement would put the Byzantine emperor must have been clear to him. A successful crusade would sink a large German anchor in Syria and Palestine.

Henry maintained the pressure upon Constantinople by demanding from Alexius III Angelus tribute sufficient to pay for the mercenary troops he had promised to contribute to the crusading army. The original sum demanded (five thousand gold pounds) was reduced after negotiation to one thousand six hundred talents, and Alexius was obliged to institute a very unpopular special tax, the "Alamanikon" (Ἀλαμανικόν) or "German levy", to meet the demand. From this levy Constantinople escaped only at the death of the German emperor. Even before this, Henry had arranged for the marriage of Irene, the daughter of the blinded Isaac, to his brother Philip of Swabia (May 25, 1197). She was the widow of Roger, the son of Tancred of Lecce, who had been the last Norman king of the Italian south.[42] Henry had found her in Palermo after his ruthless crushing of the 1194 revolt. It was rumored in the west that Isaac had agreed to accept the pair as his heirs to the Byzantine throne. In any case, the man who was browbeating Alexius III into support of a western crusading venture had now, like Robert Guiscard and William II before him, acquired a Byzantine pretender, and could pose as the defender of the rights of Isaac's children. The setting was thus prepared for the later intervention of Philip of Swabia in the counsels of the leaders of the Fourth Crusade.[43]

Meanwhile, at the diet of Gelnhausen (October 1195), and in December at Worms, German princes had been enrolling for the crusade. At Worms, Henry sat for hours in the cathedral together with the papal legate receiving crusading oaths. At the diet of Würzburg (March 1196), the German arrangements were completed. The date of departure from Germany was set finally, after Henry's return to Italy, for Christmas 1196. The large and impressive band of German princes, more than the equal of those who

[42] On Tancred, see above, chapter I, pp. 39–41.
[43] On Philip of Swabia and the Fourth Crusade, see below, chapter V, pp. 166–173.

responded to Barbarossa's call, was led by Conrad of Wittelsbach, archbishop of Mainz; archbishop Hartwig of Bremen; the chancellor of the empire, Conrad of Querfurt, newly elected bishop of Hildesheim; and the bishops of Halberstadt, Verden, Naumburg and Zeitz, Münster (who later backed out), Regensburg, Passau, Prague, and Toul. Among the leading laymen who went were duke Henry of Brabant, the count-palatine of the Rhine, Henry of Brunswick, duke Frederick of Austria, duke Berthold of Dalmatia, duke Ulrich of Carinthia, landgrave Hermann of Thuringia, the margraves of Landsberg and Meissen, and many counts. Led by the archbishop of Mainz, the majority managed to leave near the appointed time for the carefully prepared harbors of southern Italy and Sicily. To the Italians they seemed like ravaging wolves descending upon the countryside, about to join with an imperial mercenary army which could hardly be said to be fighting for a heavenly cause.

They began to arrive in southern Italy just as a serious revolt against Henry's hard regime in the south was gathering momentum. Some thought they had been called south to quell the unrest, and indeed some did help to quell it. But though Henry abandoned all thought of leading the crusade personally, he did not allow his critical political position to interfere with its progress. From March 1197 onwards, ships laden with German crusaders were leaving southern ports. By August the contingent from the Rhinelands and Saxony led by Henry of Brunswick and the archbishop of Bremen arrived in Messina with forty-four ships, after having stopped in Norway, England, and Portugal. These, together with those German princes and imperial troops who had not yet sailed, left Messina for Acre in early September under the command of the imperial chancellor Conrad of Querfurt and Henry of Kalden. Arnold of Lübeck estimates their number at sixty thousand, including four hundred burghers from Lübeck. Henry's fifteen hundred knights with their attendants, and his fifteen hundred squires formed a nucleus of six thousand men. On September 22 the main German fleet arrived in Acre. A part of the fleet under the chancellor stopped at Cyprus to crown Aimery of Lusignan and receive his homage.[44]

On September 28, 1197, one of Henry's frequent fevers caused his death at Messina. Vague rumors of the emperor's death reached the German army in Beirut, and it was confirmed as they were besieging a Turkish stronghold at Toron outside of Tyre. The

[44] On Cyprus under the Lusignan kings, see below, chapter XVII.

German arrival in Acre had been none too well received by the French, who thought at one moment of driving the Germans out of the city because of their violent occupation of the houses of Acre citizens. When once the Germans had accomplished their opening skirmishes and plundering raids upon the Moslems, they united under duke Henry of Brabant for a campaign based on Tyre, designed to bring the Syrian coast into Christian hands, to clear out a nest of pirates from Beirut, and to link the kingdom with the county of Tripoli.[45] After occupying abandoned and destroyed Sidon, the Germans on the 24th of October advanced upon Beirut, which too had been abandoned and largely destroyed. They utilized the stay at Beirut to promote the candidacy of the German vassal, king Aimery of Cyprus, for the crown of Jerusalem. Their success was a decisive recognition of German strength in the east. As they moved away from the coast to clear the interior, they were blocked for months before the stronghold of Toron.

Confirmation of the news of Henry VI's death led immediately to the defection of the imperial chancellor, Conrad of Querfurt, and before the end of the summer of 1198 most of the principal German nobles had left for home to protect their interests in the raging civil war. Indeed, on July 1, 1198, a truce was made with al-'Ādil, who abandoned Beirut to the kingdom. The archbishop of Mainz, before his departure early in 1198, crowned prince Leon II as the first Ṛoupenid king of Armenia.[46]

The German participation in these crusades ended in the double anticlimax of the deaths of the two leaders, Frederick Barbarossa on June 10, 1190, and Henry VI on September 28, 1197. The whole strenuous effort to retrieve the dismal failure of Conrad III on the Second Crusade[47] ended in frustration and tragic disaster. This setback at a time when it seemed that the Holy Roman Empire of the German Nation was to be raised to its height served to remind the German aristocracy of the real crusade it had left behind when it marched to the east: the crusade against the trans-Elbean Slavs. Early efforts to subject and Christianize these peoples had culminated in the abortive and absurd Slavic crusade of 1147. Since that time such men as Adolf of Holstein and Henry the Lion had made notable progress in bringing the area under control. Beyond it lay the homes of the primitive, pagan Prussians, Lithuanians, Livs,

[45] On the situation in the Latin states at this time see below, chapter XV, pp. 528–530.
[46] On the kingdom of Cilician Armenia see below, chapter XVIII, pp. 645–659.
[47] On the Second Crusade see volume I of this work, chapter XV.

Letts, and Estonians, and the schismatic Russians. Here was a more practicable prospect than any offered by the Near East. Out of the needs of those Germans who managed to get to Palestine arose the institution which was to incorporate the frustrated energies of the German aristocracy and merchants — the Teutonic Knights.[48] It is thus that the German failures in the eastern Mediterranean prepared not only for the destruction of the Byzantine empire, but also for the building of a new German colonial empire on the Baltic.

[48] On German crusades against the Baltic pagans, see the chapter in volume III of this work (in preparation).

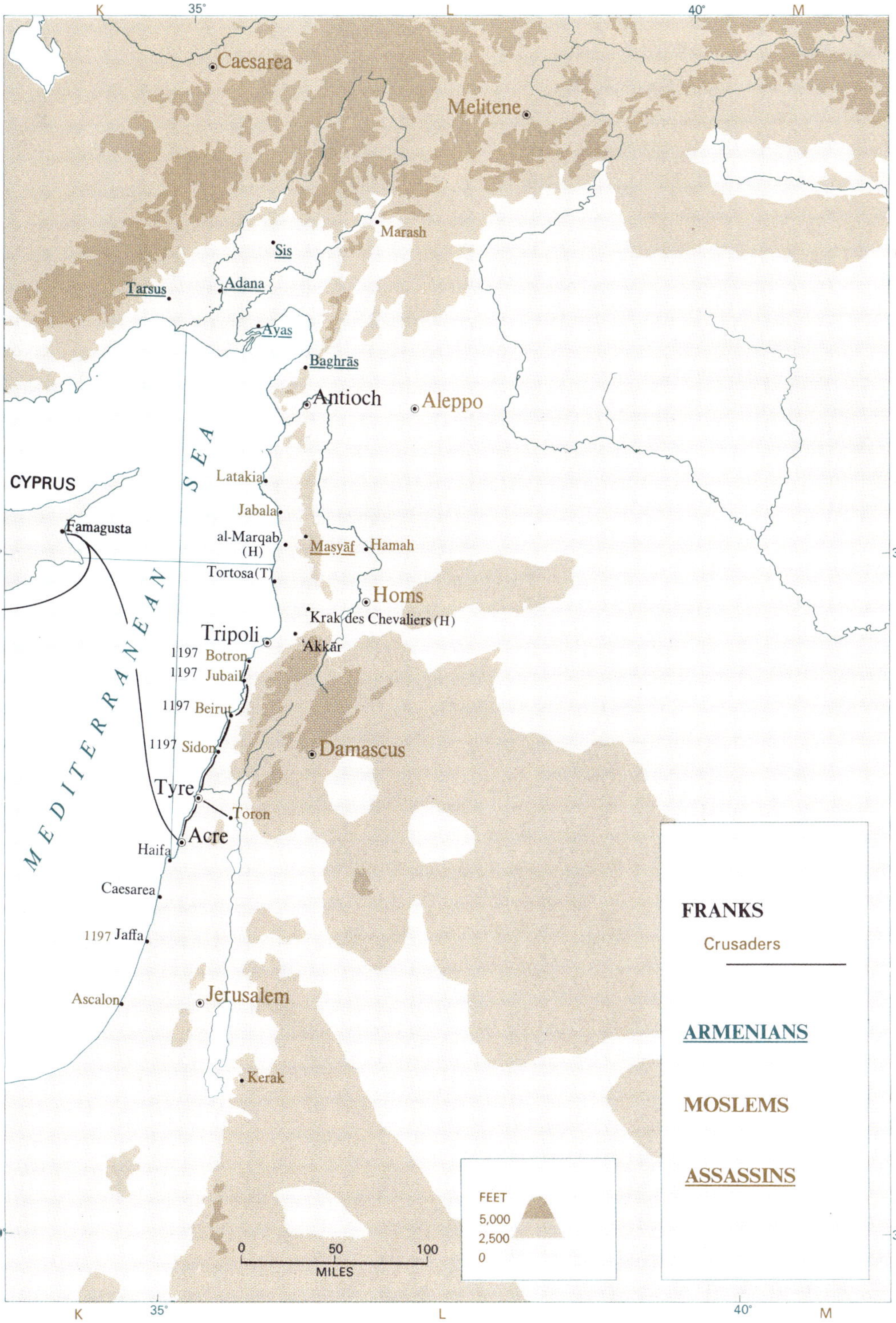

5. The Crusade of 1197 (*Map by the University of Wisconsin Cartographic Laboratory*)

6. The Straits and the Aegean (*Map by the University of Wisconsin Cartographic Laboratory*)

IV

BYZANTIUM AND THE CRUSADES, 1081–1204

The middle part of the eleventh century was a watershed in the history of the Byzantine empire. It is only necessary to compare the successful expansion of the frontier under Basil II and his determined onslaught on the aristocracy with the straitened circumstances of Alexius I Comnenus and the steady growth in the power

The main Greek historical sources are: Anna Comnena, *Alexiad* (the best edition is by A. Reifferscheid, 2 vols., Leipzig, 1884; there are also *CSHB*, 2 vols., Bonn, 1839, 1872, and ed. B. Leib, 3 vols., Paris, 1937–1945, with translation; English translation by E. Dawes, London, 1928); John Zonaras, *Epitome historiarum* (3 vols., *CSHB*, 1841–1897; ed. L. Dindorf, 6 vols., Leipzig, 1868–1875); John Cinnamus, *Historia* (*CSHB*, Bonn, 1836); Nicetas Choniates (wrongly called Acominatus), *Historia* (*CSHB*, Bonn, 1835). These texts are also in Migne, *Patrologia graeca*. The rise of the Comnenian house is also dealt with by the historians of the period before 1081, for which see volume I of the present work, chapter VI. There are several world chronicles of little value—Michael Glycas (*CSHB*, Bonn, 1836); Constantine Manasses (*CSHB*, Bonn, 1836); Joel (*CSHB*, Bonn, 1836); and Ephraem (*CSHB*, Bonn, 1840). The capture of Thessalonica in 1185 is described by Eustathius, metropolitan of Thessalonica (*CSHB*, Bonn, 1842, after Leo Grammaticus; German translation by H. Hunger in *Byzantinische Geschichtsschreiber*, ed. E. Ivanka, vol. III, Vienna, 1955).

The most important of the numerous occasional pieces, letters, and poems are: Theophylact of Ochrida, *Epistolae* (*PG*, vol. 126); Theodore Prodromus, *Scripta* (*PG*, vol. 133, and various critical editions scattered in periodicals; see details in G. Moravcsik, *Byzantinoturcica*, 2 vols., rev. ed., Budapest, 1958, pp. 522 ff.); Eustathius of Thessalonica, *Opuscula* (ed. G. L. F. Tafel, Frankfurt, 1832), and *PG*, vols, 135–136; Nicetas Choniates, ed. K. Sathas, *Μεσαιωνικὴ Βιβλ.*, I (1872), and ed. E. Miller, in *RHC*, *Grecs*, II; Michael Choniates, *Opera* (ed. Sp. P. Lampros, 2 vols., Athens, 1879–1880), and in G. Stadtmüller, *Michael Choniates Metropolit von Athen* (*Or. Christ. Analecta*, XXXIII, Rome, 1934).

Documents, secular and ecclesiastical, are cited in F. Dölger, *Regesten der Kaiserurkunden des oströmischen Reiches*, part II: *1025–1204* (Munich, 1925), and in V. Grumel, *Les Actes du patriarcat de Constantinople*, I, fasc. 3: *Les Regestes de 1043 à 1206* (1947). Reference should also be made to F. Dölger, *Byzantinische Diplomatik* (Ettal, 1956), and to G. Moravcsik, *op. cit.*, which is an indispensable bibliographical guide to the Greek sources.

Reference to Latin and oriental sources will be found in the relevant chapters in this volume. Brief references to the more important Slavic sources may be found in G. Ostrogorsky, *History of the Byzantine State* (Oxford, 1956), *passim*, which gives the best short survey both of the sources and of the historical background, with bibliography to the end of 1954.

The most substantial secondary authority is still F. Chalandon, *Essai sur le regne d'Alexis I Comnène (1081–1118)* (Paris, 1900); *Les Comnène: Jean II Comnène (1118–1143) et Manuel Comnène (1143–1180)* (Paris, 1912); and *Histoire de la domination normande en Italie et en Sicile* (2 vols., Paris, 1907); Chalandon's work sometimes needs to be modified in the light of recent research, often scattered in periodicals. Other studies on political aspects are: H. v. Kap-Herr, *Die abendländische Politik Kaiser Manuels mit besonderer Rücksicht auf Deutschland* (Strassburg, 1881); F. Cognasso, "Partiti politici e lotte dinastiche in Bisanzio alla morte di Manuele Comneno," *Memorie della R. Accademia della Scienze di Torino*, ser. 2, LXII,

of the great military families. The period of transition was characterized by a bitter struggle between the civil and military parties. The accession of Alexius Comnenus in 1081 marked the end of a half century which had seen a swift succession of inefficient or ill-fated rulers. He, his son, and his grandson among them ruled for almost a hundred years. But even their statesmanship could only check the ring of hostile powers, and at home they often had to accept, and use, precisely those elements which some of their greatest predecessors had been most anxious to curb. Indeed, from the end of the eleventh century and throughout its precarious existence in the later Middle Ages, the two decisive factors which molded the history of the empire were the predominance of the military aristocracy, to which the Comneni belonged, and the steady growth of feudal and separatist elements. The inevitable corollary was the impossibility of restoring the systems of government and defense which had been the twin pillars of the middle Byzantine empire. Effective central administration and the farmer-soldier as the mainstay of the armed forces virtually vanished with the death in 1025 of the greatest Macedonian emperor, Basil II. After the follies of the civil party, it was left to rulers drawn from a wealthy landed family to use what resources were available, and it was only by reason of Comnenian statesmanship that the empire, during most of the twelfth century at any rate, was able to hold its own among the rising Slav and Latin powers and to check the various Moslem potentates.

The way in which the young but astute Alexius Comnenus came to the throne in 1081 has already been traced.[1] With the help of his own native wits and the support of his family, including his

1912), and *idem*, "Un imperatore bizantino della decadenza: Isacco II Angelo," in *Bessarione*' XIX (1915), 29–60; W. Ohnsorge, "Ein Beitrag zur Geschichte Manuels I. von Byzanz," *Brackmann Festschrift* (1931).

On social, intellectual, and ecclesiastical life see: C. Diehl, *La Société byzantine à l'époque des Comnènes* (Paris, 1919); J. M. Hussey, *Church and Learning in the Byzantine Empire 867–1185* (Oxford, 1937); L. Oeconomos, *La Vie religieuse dans l'empire byzantin au temps des Comnènes et des Anges* (Paris, 1918); P. E. Stephanou, *Jean Italos, philosophe et humaniste* (Rome, 1949); D. Obolensky, *The Bogomils* (Cambridge, 1948); and P. Joannou, *Christliche Metaphysik*, I (Ettal, 1956).

On the administrative and economic side, fresh ground has been broken by the brilliant work of G. Ostrogorsky, *Pour la féodalité byzantine* (Brussels, 1954), and *Quelques problèmes d'histoire de la paysannerie byzantine* (Brussels, 1956). See also P. Charanis, "The Monastic Properties and the State in the Byzantine Empire," *Dumbarton Oaks Papers*, IV (1948), 51–118, and E. Stein, "Untersuchungen zur spätbyzantinischen Verfassungs- und Wirtschaftsgeschichte" in *Mitteilungen zur osmanischen Geschichte*, II (1923–1925), 1–62. An indispensable study for diplomatic relations, particularly during the years 1143–1185, is P. Lamma, *Comneni e Staufer: ricerche sui rapporti fra Bisanzio e l'occidente nel secolo XII* (Studi storici, fasc. 14–18 and 22–25, 2 vols., Rome, 1955–1957).

[1] See volume I of this work, chapter VI.

redoubtable mother Anna Dalassena, he weathered "the stormy waters of government" which threatened him. But the first ten years of his reign revealed difficulties which were to recur throughout the twelfth century. At home the treasury was short of money, while recruitment for the navy and army slackened seriously. Abroad Alexius' authority was challenged on all sides, for he was ringed by enemies in Asia Minor, in the Balkans and beyond, and in Italy. Much of Anatolia was in the hands of the Selchükid Turks, and the empire was thus deprived of an important source of man-power and wealth. The native recruitment of its army and of its navy suffered accordingly, and, further, its trade, as well as its defense, was adversely affected by the decline of its maritime strength, at a time when the Italian powers were developing apace.

It was indeed from the west, from the Normans and later the growing Italian maritime cities, that Alexius' most dangerous foes were to come. In the months immediately succeeding his coronation, imperial defense and imperial diplomacy were concentrated against the Norman Robert Guiscard, whose flagrant and persistent attacks on Byzantine territory bore out Anna Comnena's belief that he "desired to become Roman emperor".[2] Between Alexius' accession in April 1081 and the arrival of the First Crusade in 1096, the Comnenian came to terms with the Selchükid ruler of Rūm, Sulaimān, thus temporarily stabilizing the position in Anatolia. He made various diplomatic moves in the west, seeking help against Guiscard. He enlisted the naval support of Venice and obtained mercenaries from Sulaimān. He kept a wary eye on the Balkans and fomented revolts in the Norman lands in Italy. Though Guiscard's unexpected death in 1085 was opportune for Alexius and was followed by Norman withdrawal from Greek territory, it entailed no more than a truce in the duel between Constantinople and the Latins; in the immediate future Bohemond, the son of Guiscard, was to carry on his father's aggressive and ambitious policy.

This early period of Alexius' reign revealed certain important factors which no Byzantine ruler could afford to neglect. In particular, the various minor principalities in the Balkans were potential enemies whose defection might turn the balance; overwhelming disaster might threaten from the roving Pecheneg or Kuman tribes beyond the Danube; maritime help was required, even at the cost of ever-increasing trading privileges, thus piling up economic problems and the ill-will of the native Greeks towards the Italian cities, first Venice, and then Pisa and Genoa. In the east, the

[2] Anna Comnena, *Alexiad*, I, xii, 5 (ed. Leib, I, 44).

diplomatic situation at this time was perhaps more favorable than in the west or in the Balkans. The death of Sulaimān of Rūm, the partition of the sultanate, and the mutual hostility of the emirs had considerably eased the position and, as always, the precarious balancing of forces in the Moslem world gave scope of which Byzantine diplomacy was quick to take advantage.

This situation had been exploited to the full by the resourceful Alexius. It was, however, radically changed by the coming of the western crusaders, for Greek and Latin aims were marked by fundamental differences. It is unlikely that Alexius invited the crusade by appealing to Urban II[3]; the Byzantine need was for mercenaries or auxiliaries under imperial control to be employed as required, whether in the Balkans or in Asia Minor. Latin concentration on Syria, and particularly Palestine, the natural goal of the devout crusader, and the refusal of the westerners to put the needs of Byzantine foreign policy before their own individual ambitions inevitably led to mounting hostility between eastern and western Christendom during the twelfth century.

The advent of the Latin crusaders and their establishment in the eastern Mediterranean may have influenced, but did not dominate, Alexius' policy at home and abroad. The more detailed account of the first few crusades[4] has already demonstrated Comnenian adaptability and clearsighted recognition of the real danger, never far below the surface, of a western attack on Constantinople itself. Alexius' exaction of homage and fealty, and of an oath to restore former Byzantine territory, and his genuine coöperation with western military leaders, particularly in providing essential supplies and guides, show his understanding of the feudal tie and its obligations, and his determination to control and direct the adventure. He reaped his reward in western Asia Minor, where land was regained, but with the capture of Antioch in 1098 and the astute maneuvering of his enemy, the Norman Bohemond, he received his first real check. Antioch, though uncontestably Byzantine and recently in imperial hands, became the center of a virtually independent principality ruled by Guiscard's son. The kingdom of Jerusalem and the county of Edessa were farther off, and for various reasons not of such immediate concern to Constantinople.

During the years 1096–1108 Alexius had to reckon with open Norman aggression directed from both Antioch and Italy, and with

[3] See G. Ostrogorsky, *History of the Byzantine State*, p. 321; a different view is to be found in volume I of this work, p. 219.

[4] See volume I, chapters VIII–X, XIV.

an insidious propaganda campaign against Byzantium in the west, of which Bohemond was almost certainly one of the main instigators. Fickle, malicious, courageous, tenacious, Bohemond in Syria quarreled with his fellow crusaders and with the emperor, and was worsted by the Turks. He was forced to return to Italy to seek help; there he spread the story that the crusaders had been betrayed by the Byzantines, and even suggested the conquest of Constantinople, a feat at which he himself aimed in his renewed attack on Greece in 1107, when he landed at Avlona. But he had no more success than his father, and was defeated by Alexius. By the treaty of Devol (Deabolis; 1108) Bohemond had to recognize the overlordship of Alexius and his son John, and to promise to hold Antioch as a fief and to give military service to the emperor. He also swore that "there shall never be a patriarch of our race, but he shall be one whom your Majesties shall appoint from among the servants of the great church of Constantinople",[5] for the appointment of a Latin patriarch (Bernard of Valence) to the ancient see of Antioch had caused great offense in Byzantium. Tancred, who was at the time acting for his uncle in the principality, refused to implement this treaty, and Antioch long continued to be a center of opposition to Constantinople. But Alexius had at least checked Bohemond and guarded his western approaches.

The defeat of Bohemond indicated the steady increase of Alexius' strength. His prestige grew commensurately. He held the balance between the Serbian principalities of Zeta and Rascia in the Balkans; in 1104 he married his son and heir John to a Hungarian princess, thus recognizing the increasing importance of Hungary in Balkan and Adriatic politics; he organized campaigns against the Selchükids in Anatolia. Although he excelled at playing off one power against another, his weapons were not only diplomatic ones. Indeed diplomacy alone would not suffice to build up the military and naval strength of the empire, and imperial attention and astuteness were therefore also constantly directed towards the improvement of internal affairs.

Amid fundamental changes which distinguish the Comnenian from earlier periods, the old Byzantine conception of the imperial office still remained unchallenged, as the *Alexiad* demonstrates. At home Alexius was a vigorous administrator and a keen churchman, aware of his responsibilities in both secular and spiritual spheres. His support of orthodoxy and of the church was unwavering. In acute financial difficulties in the early years of his reign, he had

[5] Anna Comnena, *Alexiad*, XIII, xii, 20 (ed. Leib, III, 134).

incurred ecclesiastical displeasure by pawning certain church treasures. Differences over property did not, however, sour his good relations with the church. Alexius led the campaigns against heresy, chiefly Bogomilism, already entrenched in the Balkans and now creeping into the capital itself. It is even possible that the emperor's mother Anna Dalassena became tainted with heresy.[6] Though armed with military force as well as powerful theological arguments, even Alexius could not root out the insidious dualist heresy which exploited national feeling in Bulgaria against the imperial conquerors and their churchmen, and various forms of dualism lingered on in the Balkans long after 1204. Alexius was more successful with the theological aberrations of intellectuals, and the philosopher and scholar John Italus, for instance, was made to recant his "errors" from the pulpit of Hagia Sophia.[6a]

Monasticism received full imperial support. Alexius regulated life on Mt. Athos, and encouraged reform and new foundations on and around Patmos, and elsewhere. His wife, the empress Irene, did likewise; the regulations for her house in Constantinople reveal everyday life in an ordinary nunnery, as well as the foundress's practical nature. The careful detail found in monastic charters, or ecclesiastical reports, or recorded in the *Alexiad*, admirably illustrate the imperial sense of values. However precarious the foreign situation, however imminent the threat of invasion or treachery, no Byzantine emperor could afford to neglect what was universally regarded as one of his most important responsibilities.

Alexius' main administrative concern was with problems of finance and defense. Both had been inefficiently dealt with by his more immediate predecessors. Though he did not introduce radical changes in policy — the taxes for instance continued to be farmed out, thus increasing the taxpayers' burden — he did to some extent attempt to check the debasement and inflation which had been chronic from the mid-eleventh century onwards.[7] He ruled that a nomisma should have the value of four silver coins (miliaresia), only a third of its original value, thus effecting a devaluation the impact of which extended to the poorest classes. The population was also

[6] See S. Runciman, "The End of Anna Dalassena," *Mélanges Henri Grégoire*, I (Brussels, 1949), 517–524.

[6a] On possible political implications of John Italus' trial, see Joannou, *Christliche Metaphysik*, I, 26–29.

[7] See P. Grierson, "The Debasement of the Bezant in the Eleventh Century," *Byzantinische Zeitschrift*, XLVII (1954), 386, "It was left for Alexius I Comnenus to restore a 'hyper-pure' gold nomisma and to build up out of the debased nomismata a system of fractional coinage whose intricacies we still only very imperfectly understand." On this controversial and difficult subject see also Ostrogorsky, *Byzantine State*, pp. 327–328.

burdened with obligatory labor services and billeting. By these acts Alexius contrived to extract for the treasury the maximum revenue, and the government found some relief from its financial straits and could build up its military and naval defenses.

The mainstay of the Byzantine army in Alexius' day was no longer the native soldier-farmer with his small heritable military holding, though the Comneni did from time to time settle prisoners of war on the land in this way. Cecaumenus's continuator, who wrote at the beginning of Alexius' reign, speaks at length on military matters. It is noticeable that he says a good deal about mercenaries, who had become a particularly vital element in the Byzantine army in the eleventh century, and on whom Alexius had at first largely to rely. He also drew on levies, particularly of light-armed infantry, from the great secular and ecclesiastical estates. Of particular importance for the future was the device of granting an estate for a specific time in return for military service. The first known grant in *pronoia* is found in the mid-eleventh century, but it is not until Alexius' reign that a military obligation can be traced. The grantee, or *pronoiar*, became known as a rule as the "soldier" (*stratiotes*). Equipped and mounted and accompanied by his contingent of troops, he was of a different social class from the small farming militia. As long as the estate was held by him in pronoia he enjoyed its revenues, and the taxes and dues of the peasant tenants (*paroikoi*) were now collected by him. This financial aspect constituted one of the main attractions of the grant, which at this time was usually made for life while title and disposition remained with the state.

Alexius also made use of the *charistikion*, a device by which monastic property was handed over, in the past usually by ecclesiastical authorities, to the care of a private person. In this way the property was developed, the monastic community was guaranteed an income sufficient for their needs, and any excess went to the *charistikarios*. Alexius found this a convenient way of rewarding individuals and the practice increased during his reign, though the grant remained, as before, without specific conditions. As a method for promoting a more economic development of monastic lands it was sometimes defended by churchmen, but was also sometimes condemned, for it was obviously open to abuse.

The establishment of the Comnenian dynasty in 1081 had marked the triumph of the great military families after their long struggle with the civil aristocracy in the eleventh century. Alexius, true to his upbringing and party, chose to build on those elements which the strongest rulers of the middle Byzantine period had tried to check. He was as statesmanlike and as capable an emperor as Romanus Lecapenus or Basil II, but he was sufficiently realistic to accept the fact that in changing circumstances he could only recognize and use the landed families. Such a development at a time when Latin feudal states were established in the east, when western crusaders thronged to and fro through the empire, and when the Byzantine court was so often linked by marriage and friendship to Frankish families, has sometimes given rise to the view that it owed much to western feudalism. Recent research has shown, however, that Byzantine feudalism was in many ways the product of its own internal forces and was not a Frankish import,[8] though naturally the influx of Latin crusaders familiarized the Byzantines with many of the customs of western feudalism.

Thus Alexius' domestic and foreign policy was characterized by the growing ascendancy of the military aristocracy. The success with which he maintained Byzantine prestige abroad in the face of major threats on all fronts, particularly from the Normans, and upheld the imperial tradition in church and state, should not blind the historian to those fundamental changes at work within the polity which were ultimately to undermine the imperial authority and to strengthen local and separatist elements.

In essentials the situation remained unaltered throughout the reigns of Alexius' son John II (1118–1143) and his grandson Manuel I (1143–1180). Thus to some extent the policies of John and Manuel were predetermined for them. The main concern of the Comnenian house was the problem of finding some *modus vivendi* with the Normans of Sicily, and then, after the failure of direct male heirs in the Norman house, with the German emperors, Frederick Barbarossa and his son Henry VI, who married the heiress of the Sicilian kingdom and planned the conquest of Constantinople. Generally speaking, the policies of John and Manuel Comnenus were distinguished by variations in emphasis and orientation rather than by fundamental differences. John concentrated more on the east, but was unexpectedly cut short in the midst of his career; Manuel had a more original western policy and a longer reign, but was inevitably alive to eastern problems, if only because Mediterranean politics were now an inescapable factor in European diplomacy. Indeed, events during the sixty-odd years

[8] See G. Ostrogorsky, *Pour l'histoire de la féodalité byzantine* (Brussels, 1954); cf. A. A. Vasiliev, *History of the Byzantine Empire* (Madison, 1952), pp. 563 ff. (on Byzantine feudalism).

covered by the reigns of these two impressive rulers highlight the startling changes introduced by the crusading movements and by the steady development of western states and Balkan powers.

John Comnenus was the finest of the three Comneni, though his fame has perhaps suffered from lack of any particular contemporary historian of his own. He was a mild and moderate man in his personal life, but an austere disciplinarian in military matters, and his principles and statesmanship continued the best traditions of his house and enabled him to maintain the imperial position. There is a comparative dearth of material for reconstructing the domestic policy of his twenty-five years. John found time to interest himself in the trial of heretics, and, with his wife, the Hungarian Piriska ("Irene"), to promote hospitals and social welfare through a splendid monastic foundation. His agrarian policy was that of his father and was dictated by military needs: he settled prisoners of war (such as the Pechenegs and Serbs) on small farms in return for military service, and continued to grant lands in pronoia for the same reason. For the most part he was a military emperor, who used both diplomacy and force in his successful exploitation of the advantages secured by his father.

John thought in terms of allies and recognition in the west and in the Balkans, and of an offensive in the east. In the Balkans two factors were of importance — the rise to power of the Serb principality of Rascia and the growing encroachment of Hungary south of the Danube. Where he could not hope for direct control — in Hungary, in Rascia, and in Zeta — John intervened in disputed elections. Although Rascia, as also Bosnia, was drawn into the orbit of Hungarian influence — the ruler (župan) of Rascia had married his daughter Helena to Bela the Blind, king of Hungary (1131–1141) — Constantinople on the whole outweighed the Magyars, especially when it came to war, and in 1128 forced Hungary to make peace. Further, after 1131 Byzantium was helped by the understanding between Bela II of Hungary and the pro-Byzantine Conrad III of Germany, and no doubt by Hungary's realization that its Dalmatian ambitions would inevitably antagonize Venice, in which case it might be advisable to have an ally in its powerful Byzantine neighbor.

Byzantium for its part was not averse to reducing the power of Venice, which had been extended in Dalmatia during the later years of Alexius' reign. Venice had applied to John on his accession for a renewal of the trading privileges in the empire which had brought it great wealth, though also great unpopularity. John's attempt to reduce Venetian influence resulted in attacks on Byzantine territory, particularly the islands, during the years 1122–1126. Finally he judged it expedient to make peace and in 1126 renewed the privileges granted by his father. He had to recognize that Venetian enmity would damage his position in Italy. He did, however, attempt to establish good relations with Venice's rivals, Pisa and Genoa. Pisa, which was being approached by Roger II of Sicily, was courted by a Byzantine embassy in 1136, followed by the confirmation of the trading privileges which had been granted it by Alexius Comnenus. The Genoese, who were to play so important a role in the later empire, also wished for a share in imperial trade, and they appear to have been in Constantinople in 1142 for purposes of negotiation.

At the opening of John's reign affairs in Germany and Italy were not unfavorable to him. Emperor Henry V of Germany and pope Gelasius II were at loggerheads and Apulia was rent by feuds. But when Roger II united the Norman lands in southern Italy and Sicily in 1127 and was crowned king in 1130, danger threatened. John sought to counter this by a rapprochement with the German rulers, first Lothair II, who followed Henry in 1125, and then his successor, Conrad III. Throughout he also kept in touch with the popes, who were precariously placed between the Normans and the Germans; he approached first Calixtus II in 1124, and then Honorius II in 1126,[8a] with the prospect of ecclesiastical reunion. In particular, he suggested an understanding whereby the pope would have the spiritual, and the "Roman" (Byzantine) emperor the secular, supremacy, though the actual wording of this famous letter is so vague as to defy precise elucidation (which was perhaps what was intended).

With his position to some extent safeguarded by his network of alliances in the west, John in 1136 judged it opportune to attempt the extension of his authority in the east by striking at both Moslem and Christian powers. His goal was full control of Antioch and the implementation of the treaty of Devol which his father had made with Bohemond in 1108. Apart from constant vigilance towards his Selchükid neighbors at Iconium (Konya), John's more particular concern in Anatolia at this time was the rising power of the Dānishmendids, who had in 1125 captured Melitene. They had penetrated into Cilicia, compelling the Ṛoupenids to pay tribute, and

[8a] Some scholars suggest the years 1139 and 1141 in Innocent II's pontificate. See Lamma, *Comneni e Staufer*, I, 28.

moving still further south had defeated the Normans of Antioch, killing Bohemond II in 1130. It was therefore necessary for John Comnenus to safeguard his own frontiers in Paphlagonia and to check the Dānishmendids as a preliminary to the advance south which he himself was planning, and with this in view, during the years 1132–1134 he undertook campaigns in the neighborhood of Kastamonu against the emir Gümüshtigin Ghāzī. John's position was eased by the death of the powerful Gümüshtigin Ghāzī about 1134. Towards the end of 1136 he advanced against the Christian Armenians who had settled in the Taurus and Anti-Taurus districts and took the offensive against the Ṛoupenids of Lesser Armenia, the principality which stood between his domains and the crusading kingdoms. Its ruler Leon I fled to the mountains in 1137 but was captured in the following year and sent to Constantinople. John was thus able to turn his full attention to Antioch.

His intervention was opportune for various reasons. In both Jerusalem and Antioch the throne had passed in 1131 to the female line; problems of succession were already threatening to weaken the Latin principalities. In Antioch at any rate there was a pro-Byzantine party who realized the wisdom of a firm alliance with Constantinople, all the more so since in the north Zengi, the regent (*atabeg*) of Mosul, was daily growing in power. By August 1137 John had reached Antioch, and Raymond of Poitiers, the husband of the Norman princess Constance, was compelled to swear allegiance. A year later John made a solemn entrance into the city. Even so, the Byzantine, and indeed the Christian, cause was weakened by lack of Latin support. It was largely for this reason that John had been unable to make any real headway against the Moslems in northern Syria earlier in 1138, and later in the year he judged it wiser to leave Antioch, where riots were being stirred up against the Greeks.

Afraid of papal and Sicilian activities in the west, as well as the Dānishmendids in Anatolia, John returned to Constantinople in 1138. Here he renewed his links with Germany and negotiated a marriage between Bertha of Sulzbach, the sister-in-law of Conrad III, now undisputed king, and his son Manuel. After further campaigns against the Dānishmendids, he again turned his attention towards Antioch. Cinnamus suggests that John, who had every reason to distrust the Latins, now intended to create a frontier principality, consisting of Adalia, Antioch, and Cyprus, for his son Manuel,[9] or he may possibly have had in mind the revival of the old

[9] John Cinnamus, *Historia*, I, 10 (*CSHB*, p. 23).

duchy of Antioch,[10] only on a wider basis. Byzantine intentions were bitterly resented by an influential party among the Latin knights and clergy in Antioch. Both laity and clergy clearly had everything to lose if John's demand in 1142 for the surrender of the entire city was met. Therefore the prince of Antioch repudiated the agreement of 1137, ostensibly on the ground that he could not dispose of his wife's inheritance. John clearly intended to force the issue. He wintered near Mamistra (1142–1143), and from a letter he wrote to king Fulk of Jerusalem, we may surmise that he hoped to extend his authority southwards as soon as he had taken control in Antioch. But in the spring of 1143 he died of a septic wound.

Thus Christian feuds and John's untimely death prevented any effective drive against the Moslems, and in the next year Zengi captured Edessa, thus provoking the ill-fated Second Crusade.

Before he died John had had his youngest son Manuel, who was with him in Cilicia, acclaimed emperor. Manuel Comnenus was exceedingly tall, with a complexion so dark that his enemies taunted him with being like a negro. He possessed great physical strength and endurance and could hold his own with the best of the western knights (though it seemed odd to his subjects that he should even wish to do so). He had charm of manner and was a gracious host; he had too the family taste for letters and had read widely, though his mind was vivacious and lively rather than profound or deeply intellectual, and, as the discerning Cinnamus remarked, he tried to make up for inadequacies in logic and dialectic by being exceedingly quick witted.[11] Both Greek and Latin contemporary writers testify to his medical knowledge, which he did not hesitate to use, as for instance when he set Baldwin's arm when it was broken on a hunting expedition.

Manuel was removed by two generations from the days of the First Crusade, and he got on with westerners in a way which would have seemed unbecoming to his grandfather Alexius, still more to his earlier predecessors. His mother was a Hungarian, his first wife the German Bertha of Sulzbach (renamed Irene by the Greeks), his second the Norman princess Maria of Antioch. His little son Alexius was betrothed to a daughter of the French Louis VII. Half a century had witnessed great changes in the eastern Mediter-

[10] Cf. Chalandon, *Les Comnène*, pp. 184–185. For an adverse judgment on John's accomplishments, see volume I, chapter XIII, pp. 445–446.

[11] John Cinnamus, *Historia*, VI, 2 (*CSHB*, p. 253).

ranean, and political and economic circumstances, as well as imperial marriages and friendships, had brought an influx of Latins into all parts of the Byzantine empire, thus sowing seeds of future trouble. It has even been suggested that Manuel sought to renew the internal vigor of Byzantium by deliberately introducing Latin elements into the empire.[12] At the same time he was essentially Byzantine: he would concede nothing to the west insofar as his imperial position was concerned, for like any true medieval "Roman" emperor he regarded himself as the heir of a long line stretching back to Caesar Augustus.

Manuel's outlook and needs determined his policy at home and abroad. He had to establish his somewhat unexpected succession to the throne and secure allies among the western powers. And he even went a step further by aiming at active rehabilitation of Byzantine authority in the west. His ceaseless diplomatic moves, like those of other powers interested in the Mediterranean, were characterized by a fluidity, a readiness to consider offers from any quarter, a reluctance to close any door, which created a constantly shifting situation, though the main trends are clearly discernible.[13]

Like Alexius and John, Manuel knew that his interests conflicted with those of Sicily. At the very start of his reign in 1143 he was apparently willing to consider a rapprochement with Roger II, who had asked for a Greek princess to wed his son, but this plan fell through. The first major phase of Manuel's Italian policy was primarily one of military intervention, and concluded with his defeat in Sicily in 1158; after this he changed his methods somewhat, confining himself on the whole to diplomatic weapons. Throughout he sought to continue his father's alliance with the German ruler, Conrad III, who shared his hostility to Roger. In 1147 the Second Crusade forced a temporary suspension of their plans. Conrad had taken the cross and was moving east, leaving his ally Manuel isolated in the west and exposed to attack, as well as faced with the passage of crusading armies through his lands. Roger of Sicily, now hostile to Manuel, was trying to rouse the French king, Louis VII, and was himself plotting against the Byzantine emperor. Manuel was able to take little part in the disastrous expedition[14]: he was engaged with Roger, who had attacked Corfu and the Morea (1147) at a time when Manuel might reasonably be supposed to have concentrated his forces in the east to aid the

[12] See Lamma, *Comneni e Staufer*, passim.

[13] This lack of any fixed political system is one of the main themes of Lamma, *Comneni e Staufer*.

[14] See volume I, chapter XIV; on Roger's moves, see above, chapter I, pp. 11–15.

crusaders. Manuel had to safeguard his eastern borders by making a treaty with Mas'ūd, the Selchükid ruler at Iconium, and by getting Venetian help against the Normans at the cost of still further trading privileges. The Normans were driven out, but they took with them an enormous booty and a number of captured Greek silk weavers. At the same time Manuel reinforced his alliance with Conrad when the latter journeyed through the Byzantine empire on his return from the Second Crusade.

By the treaty of Thessalonica (1148) it was evidently agreed that Manuel had some claim on Italian territory. The text itself has not survived, but the account of Cinnamus states that the emperor reminded Conrad of what he had previously undertaken to do, "to restore to Irene [his kinswoman Bertha of Sulzbach] her dowry, Italy ['Ιταλία]".[15] However the word "Italia" may be interpreted — and it has been suggested that it might mean the whole of Italy — it would certainly include the southern Italian lands of Apulia and Calabria. A joint expedition proposed against Roger did not materialize. Manuel's preparations were held up by a Serbian revolt fostered by Hungary and by Venetian intrigues; Conrad was hampered by Welf troubles fomented by Roger, who had by now gained papal recognition and had signed a truce with Eugenius III. But fortunately for Manuel any active western league against Byzantium foundered on the papal fear of increasing Roger's power and the steady pro-Byzantine policy of Conrad. Both Conrad and Manuel were planning an expedition in Italy for 1152, when Conrad died in the February of that year.

The new German ruler, Frederick Barbarossa, managed to come to an understanding with the pope (1153) whereby both agreed that no land in Italy was to be ceded to Manuel, "the king [*rex*] of the Greeks". Undeterred, Manuel still hoped to win Barbarossa over and to continue his western offensive by means of both diplomacy and force. When it suited his plans, the German emperor was, indeed, willing to negotiate with Manuel; there were a number of diplomatic approaches between the two courts, and Frederick even considered taking a Byzantine wife. On Roger's death in 1154 Manuel took advantage of opposition to William I of Sicily, and, without German assistance, he launched his attack. His forces and those of his allies at first gained ground. Frederick I, newly crowned in 1155, evidently wished to assist Manuel, or at least to have some share in the project, but he could not get the support of his vassals and had to go north, not returning to Italy

[15] John Cinnamus, *Historia,* II, 19 (*CSHB,* p. 87); Dölger, *Regesten,* no. 1374.

until 1158. Manuel's successes in Apulia aroused the hostility of Venice, and William grew in strength. The Greeks were trapped and badly defeated at Brindisi. Pope Hadrian IV, who had been wooed by Manuel, had judged it expedient to come to terms with William in June 1156. In Germany Frederick was cooling off, and a Byzantine embassy to his court in 1157 had no success. In 1158 Manuel had to sign a thirty years' truce with William, and he evacuated his troops from Italy.

By now Manuel must have realized the difficulties caused by Frederick's imperial ambitions, and perhaps also the hazardous nature of military action in a country where, in spite of lavish expenditure of money, he could count on no secure base and no sure ally. He did not abandon his western policy, but henceforth he concentrated on diplomacy which, if more cautious than formerly, yet still showed his resourcefulness and determination. The flow of embassies and correspondence between Constantinople and the western powers was unceasing. Manuel tried to utilize the rift between the papacy and Barbarossa, negotiating first with Hadrian and then with his successor Alexander III. From 1159 to October 1177 there were cordial relations between Alexander and Manuel and discussion of the terms on which the Byzantine emperor might receive the imperial crown from the pope. Manuel offered financial aid and ecclesiastical reunion. At this time Alexander feared Barbarossa, who was supporting an anti-pope; hence his negotiations with Constantinople, Sicily, and France. But with the formation of the Lombard League, the pope became less dependent on Manuel, and after the treaty of Venice (1177) and the defeat of Manuel at Myriokephalon, any real hope for a Byzantino-papal understanding faded out.

From the outset Manuel had responded to pope Alexander III's overtures, and had also hoped for the support of Louis VII in a concerted attack against Frederick in 1163, which however came to nothing. He then turned to the project of a marriage alliance with Sicily. William I had died in May 1166 and his heir was a boy of thirteen, William II. According to Romuald Guarna of Salerno, Manuel proposed that the Norman should marry his daughter Maria, who was then his heiress (his son Alexius was not born until 1169). She was already betrothed to Bela (III) of Hungary, but apparently Manuel was prepared to throw over this arrangement and its advantages, possibly as a counter-move to Frederick Barbarossa's fourth expedition to Italy in that year (1166), and perhaps with the hope of being himself crowned by the pope as sole emperor should the kingdom of Sicily be united to the Byzantine empire. But the marriage proposal came to nothing, possibly because the news of Maria's betrothal to Bela had become known, though no specific explanation is given, only the cryptic phrase "for various reasons". Later on, after 1170, a second attempt was made, and negotiations were so far carried through that the young William II went to Taranto to meet a bride who never came. It was a humiliating experience for the Norman, all the more so if he realized that Manuel may have changed his plans because he thought that there might be a possibility of marrying Maria to the heir of Frederick I.

Throughout the second phase of Manuel's western policy (1158–1180) he was also involved in constant negotiation with the various Italian cities, particularly Venice, Pisa, and Genoa. Venice had always had substantial commercial interests in the east; the rapid rise of Pisa and Genoa now introduced rivals and provided Constantinople with alternative allies, particularly in the Genoese. Support could be bought only by trading concessions, as Alexius and John Comnenus had found; further, it was impossible to satisfy one party without arousing the dangerous hostility of others, and in any case the privileged position of foreign merchants within the empire was bitterly resented by the Greeks themselves. Hence the mounting tension in Manuel's reign, and a radical change in relations which was one of the underlying causes of the Fourth Crusade. Common distrust, first of Roger II, and then of Barbarossa, had for a time united Venice and Constantinople. But Venetian suspicion had been aroused by Byzantine activities in Italy, and partially successful designs on Dalmatia, as well as by the concessions granted to their Italian rivals; treaties were made with Genoa in 1169 and with Pisa in 1170.[16] Venetians within the empire had long been hated for their arrogance and envied for their wealth. In 1162 they had taken part in an attack on the Genoese in Constantinople which had annoyed Manuel, who was at that time trying to win Genoese support. He himself may still have resented the Venetian parody of him at the time of Corfu's recapture from the Normans in 1148, when the Venetians had a mock Byzantine ceremony in which the part of the emperor was played by a huge negro. And it is suggested by a Venetian source that his anger had been aroused by his failure to receive the active support of Venice against the Normans, whose ruler he had alienated by withholding the promised Byzantine bride. Thus the accumu-

[16] Dölger, *Regesten*, nos. 1488, 1497, 1498, 1499.

lated resentment of the native Greek populace coincided with reasons of policy which may have contributed to the carefully planned attack.

On March 12, 1171, all Venetians in the empire were arrested and their goods confiscated. The doge, Vitale Michiele, had to send a fleet to attack Dalmatia and the Greek islands, though he was favorably disposed toward Byzantium and wanted to maintain diplomatic relations. Manuel now realized the danger of an alliance between Venice and Sicily, and began negotiations with Venice. Nicetas Choniates says that he restored Venetian privileges and paid them compensation and made peace,[17] but Venetian sources suggest that the treaty was probably not concluded or relations restored until the following reign, that of Andronicus I.[18] Even then Venetian resentment remained.

In the Balkans and Hungary Manuel scored successes. Rascia, inclined to be independent and open to approach from Latin powers, such as Sicily, had put up irritating opposition, particularly under Stephen Nemanya, who became "župan" in either 1166 or 1167. Stephen approached Hungary and Germany, and tried to stir up trouble in Dalmatia, where Manuel had restored imperial control in 1166. He was finally subdued in 1172 and had to play a humiliating part in Manuel's triumphal entry into Constantinople.

In Hungary, as elsewhere, Manuel took his father's policy a step further. He not only intervened to his own advantage in disputed successions, but went so far as to have in mind the acquisition of the whole country. He proposed a novel solution to end the long hostility between Hungary and Constantinople. After endless diplomacy, he agreed to recognize Stephen III as king in return for his brother and heir Bela as hostage. Bela was to have Hungary's Croatian and Dalmatian lands as appanage, and was to marry Manuel's heiress Maria. The treaty of 1164 was executed only after further fighting, but by 1167 Manuel had Dalmatia, Croatia, Bosnia, and Sirmium. He planned to make Bela his heir, and gave him the name of Alexius and the title of despot. He thus hoped to secure Hungary and incorporate it into the empire, a plan similar to that which he entertained from time to time with regard to Sicily.

The situation changed with the birth of his son in 1169. The betrothal of Bela and Maria was dissolved, and Bela was reduced to the rank of a caesar and married to Agnes of Châtillon, the daughter

[17] Nicetas Choniates, *Historia*; *De Manuele Comneno*, V, 9 (*CSHB*, p. 225).
[18] Cf. Ostrogorsky, *Byzantine State*, p. 346.

of Constance of Antioch. With Greek support, Bela succeeded to the Hungarian throne in 1173, and as long as Manuel lived he was loyal to Byzantium, making no attempt to regain lost territory until after 1180. Manuel had thus gained some measure of security in the Balkans and in the north, as well as considerable territory.

In the east, before he was really hampered by Frederick Barbarossa, Manuel successfully developed his father's policy.[19] He asserted his suzerainty, first over the Armenian prince Ṭoros II in Cilicia in 1158, and then over Reginald of Antioch in 1159, where the crowning symbol of his victory was to be the restoration of a Greek, Athanasius, to the ancient patriarchate in 1165. He was on particularly friendly terms with Baldwin III of Jerusalem, and anxious to prevent the encirclement of the crusading principalities by a single Moslem power. Manuel may have foreseen that any drastic reduction of crusading prestige and territory might turn the Latins towards his own lands. But neither his overtures to the ruler of Aleppo, Nūr-ad-Dīn, nor his expeditions with Amalric of Jerusalem against Egypt, could stay the rise of Saladin. Moreover the death of Nūr-ad-Dīn in 1174 affected the political situation in Anatolia, as well as in Syria and Egypt.

Manuel's position in Anatolia had to some extent been safeguarded by the tension between the rival Moslem powers, the Selchükids at Iconium and the Dānishmendids. The eastern ambitions of the former had been kept in check by Nūr-ad-Dīn's support of the Dānishmendids. Now dissident Moslem elements looked to Constantinople for help. Manuel, aware of the Selchükid sultan's quiet consolidation of his position, turned to his own frontier defenses on the marches of Iconium. He refused the overtures of Kilij Arslan II and led an expedition against him in 1176. Showing marked lack of generalship he allowed himself to be trapped in the pass of Myriokephalon, and was prevented from headlong flight only by the firm refusal of his officers to countenance this. What might well have been a wholesale massacre was checked by Kilij Arslan, who again offered terms. Manuel's prestige and that of the Christians in Syria was shaken by this defeat, though his generals still carried on intermittent warfare against Moslem penetration into the Maeander valley. Manuel himself may have felt that his earlier policy towards Iconium, in particular the treaty of 1161,[20] had been mistaken and perhaps opportunist. He had obtained an

[19] See volume I, chapter XVII, and below, chapter XIX.
[20] Dölger, *Regesten*, no. 1444.

ally, but only at the cost of permitting the steady growth of a Moslem principality on his very borders. Nicetas Choniates says that the sultan of Rūm observed that the worse the "Romans" were treated, the more splendid were the presents which their emperor gave.[21]

It might be pointed out that the difficulties with Iconium had been fomented by Frederick Barbarossa, at heart an enemy of the empire, who revealed his real plans in a letter to Manuel after Myriokephalon in which he announced himself as the heir of the Roman emperors with authority over the "rex Grecorum" and the "regnum Greciae".

The rise of Frederick Barbarossa and the dramatic humiliation of Myriokephalon should not be allowed to obscure Manuel's achievements and his statesmanship. His diplomacy was marked by a bold attempt to adapt a traditional policy to changing circumstances. His conception of imperial authority might have been held by any Byzantine ruler, but its execution had certain original features, such as his project for uniting the thrones of Hungary and Constantinople in the person of his prospective son-in-law Bela-Alexius, or of Sicily and Constantinople by a marriage alliance with William II (and possibly, earlier, with Roger II), demonstrating by this latter move a flexibility of outlook with regard to the Norman problem. The main threat to the empire was from the western, rather than the Moslem, powers. Manuel did at least succeed in postponing during his lifetime a fresh crusade, which would perhaps have struck its first blow at Constantinople, as in 1204, and if successful in the east would in any case have weakened Byzantine influence there. Almost his last move, the marriage of his son Alexius to Agnes of France, was an attempt to stay the hand of Louis VII, who, with pope Alexander III, was contemplating a new crusade. To condemn Manuel for not having concentrated exclusively on strengthening his position in Anatolia and Syria would be completely to misunderstand the practical needs of Byzantium.

The internal life of the empire at this time shows no marked break with the days of the earlier Comneni. Its main features were concentration on needs of defense, the steady growth in the use of grants in pronoia and of the power of the landowner, and the continuity of the normal activities of a cultured society. As under John Comnenus, the army was well organized and well disciplined. Recruitment presented serious problems. Manuel tried to increase

[21] Nicetas Choniates, *Historia*; *De Manuele Comneno*, III, 9 (*CSHB*, p. 163).

the free population by liberating those who had become enslaved and by settling prisoners of war within the empire. A good many troops were provided by the system of grants in pronoia. Mercenaries were an important element, whether hired on a purely temporary basis, or provided by the various enrolled corps, or furnished by vassals or allies, such as the Serbs or the Selchükids. Nicetas Choniates says that the navy was somewhat diminished by Manuel's policy of allowing the islands and littoral to pay ship-money in lieu of maritime service and duties,[22] but even so, Byzantium was in a stronger position than in Alexius' day, when it had to rely almost exclusively on Venetian maritime assistance.

Foreign policy, however directed, had always been an expensive item in the Byzantine budget. But though burdens fell heavily on the poorer classes, Byzantium was by no means impoverished. In spite of the territorial contraction of the eleventh century and loss of customs revenue by reason of privileges granted to foreign merchants, there were still strong reserves, and lucrative trade was carried on in the great commercial centers of the empire, such as Thessalonica and Constantinople. The riches of Byzantium were the surprise and envy of all visitors; Benjamin of Tudela reports that the Greeks went about looking like princes.[23]

The fundamental difference between this period and that of the middle Byzantine state was however the gradual weakening of the central authority, particularly by reason of grants made to individuals. This was not so acute in Manuel's day as after 1204, but even under him the use of the pronoia had become an established feature of Byzantine administration. The strictly limited and non-heritable character of the grant was in the course of time to be gradually modified, so that the property became more like the western fief handed down from father to son. The grant carried with it the right to collect taxes from the tenants (paroikoi) on the estate, as well as any other duties owed. This system had become so accepted a part of the Byzantine social structure that by the end of the twelfth century it seemed quite normal to speak of all land as being either heritable or in pronoia. It was used of other than landed wealth, and was not reserved for Greeks alone. When Nicetas Choniates spoke of some of the pronoiars as being "half barbarian", he may have been thinking of the steppe peoples settled in the Balkans whose wealth was not in land but in herds and flocks, or

[22] Nicetas Choniates, *Historia; Manuele Comneno*, I, 3 (*CSHB*, p. 75).

[23] Benjamin of Tudela, *Reisebeschreibungen* (ed. L. Grünhut and M. N. Adler, 2 vols., Jerusalem and Frankfurt a. M., 1903–1904), II, 17–18.

even of the Latin knights, such as Renier of Montferrat, to whom Manuel granted what his brother Boniface refers to as "a feudum".[24]

Manuel's reign saw a marked strengthening of the feudal element. Though not hostile to monasticism or the church, Manuel furthered the interests of secular landlords at the expense of ecclesiastical estates when in 1158 he forbade monasteries to add to their land or to the number of their paroikoi, and did not permit alienation of property except to the senatorial and the military (i.e. the pronoiar) classes. Nicetas Choniates remarked on the liberality with which he assigned paroikoi to the pronoiars. But at the same time Manuel did attempt to control the movement of labor and the financial rights of the exchequer. So in confirming the claim to an estate, the imperial charter would give the number of its paroikoi, and new paroikoi could be acquired only if they were without obligations to the fisc, and then only up to a permitted number. The struggle to retain control over the state paroikoi (*demosiakoi*), which is evident as early as the tenth century, was not abandoned by the Comneni, though in the end, as the Palaeologian period was to show, feudal and separatist forces were to triumph at the expense of the central authority.

Manuel's activities at home included administrative and ecclesiastical reform. His chrysobulls and rulings deal with subjects ranging from the reorganization of the secular courts in order to expedite justice to decisions on points of ecclesiastical discipline and ownership of church property.[25] For instance, he forbade bishops to linger long in the capital and charged the civil authorities with the responsibility of seeing that they returned to their dioceses. He and his family were generous patrons of monasticism, but like others before him, he made it clear that the proper home of the monk was in the remote countryside and not in the crowded city.

Manuel took a lively and characteristic part in the theological discussions and problems of his day. Disputes over the nature of the sacrifice of the mass, or of the Trinity, divided Byzantine circles, and Manuel's views were not always those of orthodoxy. He evidently fancied his powers of persuasion, and almost abused his imperial position in his attempt to win supporters over to his point of view. Both inclination and political considerations fostered a certain flexibility in Manuel's outlook. He was for instance

[24] Nicetas Choniates, *Historia*; *De Manuele Comneno*, VII, 4 (*CSHB*, p. 273): see Ostrogorsky, *Pour l'histoire de la féodalité byzantine*, pp. 28–31 and p. 53.

[25] See Dölger, *Regesten*, *passim*.

anxious for a rapprochement between the Orthodox and dissident churches, and embassies went backwards and forwards between Constantinople and Armenia. They were fruitless, for in both churches a solid block of conservative opinion prevented any form of compromise. By his tolerant attitude towards Moslems, Manuel roused vigorous and open protest. His suggestion that his visitor, the sultan of Iconium, should accompany him in the procession to Hagia Sophia was regarded as wholly unsuitable. His view that the abjuration exacted from Moslems could be worded in a more acceptable form did however prevail, and instead of anathematizing the God of Mohammed the convert was required only to condemn Mohammed, his doctrine, and his successors. It is not surprising that Manuel's contemporaries did not always find his views on theological matters acceptable, and it was even considered after his death that he ought to be condemned as a heretic.[26] No taint of this kind could however cling in respect of his policy towards the various forms of the Bogomil, Massalian, and Paulician heresies which persisted within and without the empire. In Constantinople in 1143 two bishops, and then a monk Niphon, were condemned as Bogomils. They had all worked in Anatolia, and evidently the sect was particularly prevalent in Cappadocia. It was also strong in the Balkans, especially Macedonia and Bulgaria.[27] Manuel could do comparatively little to purge these heretical movements. They gained added strength from underlying Slav antagonism to Byzantine, and later Frankish, rule, and were an important factor in adding to the complexity of the situation in the Balkans at the time of the Fourth Crusade.

During the years 1081–1180 the Comnenian house had given the empire three outstanding rulers whose statesmanship and personality blinded contemporaries and later historians to the fundamental nature of the changes at work in Byzantine society and in neighboring polities. Manuel left a minor heir, Alexius II, whose mother was the Latin Maria of Antioch. Hatred of the strong Latin element in the empire had already been shown during Manuel's reign, though directed in 1171 against the Venetian traders. Political circumstances, marriage alliances, Manuel's personal friendships, all helped to bring a flood of westerners into the empire, and long-pent-up hatred against "the accursed Latins"

[26] John Cinnamus, *Historia*, VI, 2 (*CSHB*, pp. 251 ff.), and Nicetas Choniates, *Historia; De Manuele Comneno*, VII, 5 (*CSHB*, pp. 274 ff.); cf. Chalandon, *Les Comnène*, pp. 644 ff.

[27] See D. Obolensky, *The Bogomils*, pp. 219 ff., and V. Grumel, *Les Actes des patriarches*, I, fasc. 3 (especially on chronology).

broke out in May 1182, when the people of Constantinople made an indiscriminate attack on all foreigners in the city.

At this point Manuel's cousin Andronicus Comnenus was already preparing to take control. An element of instability and restlessness in his character and an underlying antagonism toward Manuel had prevented him from giving service to the empire or settling on his estates; wandering from court to court, Moslem and Christian alike, he had toured the Near East for a number of years, living on his personality and charm. Now he returned to seize his opportunity and to show that he had views of his own on the nature of imperial rule. The reaction against Maria of Antioch and the Latin elements served his purpose. In May 1182 he was accepted by the city, and in September 1183 was crowned co-emperor with Alexius II. So far this was normal procedure, but Andronicus had an impetuous, violent streak in his make-up. Autocratic and dominating, impatient and impulsive, he could not refrain from the elimination, first of Maria, and then of Alexius, though not of Alexius' widow, the little French princess Agnes ("Anna"), whom he married.

Andronicus instituted a vigorous campaign against administrative corruption and the power of the aristocracy. He tried to protect the lower classes against the extortions of tax collectors, government officials, and landlords, so that those who had rendered unto Caesar what was Caesar's could sleep at ease in the shade of their trees.[28] Thus good salaries were to be paid, suitable men were to be appointed, and the sale of offices was prohibited. For various reasons Andronicus was biased against the aristocracy. Their power and their privileges were incompatible with his conception of imperial autocracy and the well-being of his subjects. The bulls of 1158 and 1170[29] which permitted alienation of imperial grants of land only to the senatorial or military class were revoked in December 1182 in the early months of Andronicus's regency.[30] His anti-Latin bias might have gained some support from the aristocracy, but it was more than outweighed by his open hostility to their own privileged position. The widespread practice of grants, whether in pronoia, or of charistikion, had gone too far to be successfully challenged.

There was strong opposition to Andronicus, who met conspiracy and risings with violence and executions. As external

[28] See Nicetas Choniates, *Historia*; *De Manuele Comneno*, VII, 2 (*CSHB*, pp. 265–268).

[29] Dölger, *Regesten*, nos. 1333 and 1398, but on the dating see Ostrogorsky, *Byzantine State*, p. 348, note 6.

[30] Dölger, *Regesten*, no. 1553.

troubles once more threatened, the reaction in his favor rapidly turned to hostility. He lost the support of the military families on whom the empire now depended, and he had no effective weapon with which to ward off attacks from without and revolts from within. Hungary took the offensive and regained Dalmatia and parts of Croatia and Sirmium; Stephen Nemanya shook off his allegiance; in 1185 the Normans of Sicily took Corfu and other islands and advanced to capture Thessalonica. Centrifugal tendencies within the empire were evidenced by Isaac Comnenus, who proclaimed himself independent ruler of Cyprus. Andronicus had tried to stave off western attack by approaching the papacy and by allying with Venice and with Saladin. But news of the dramatic fall and sack of Thessalonica and fear of suffering a similar fate led the people of Constantinople to dethrone and kill Andronicus, the last emperor of the Comnenian house.

The rulers of the dynasty of the Angeli had not the character or qualities of the Comneni. Their policy represented a compromise: it was aristocratic, but not pro-Latin. The difficulties of the empire during the years 1185–1204 were aggravated, but not caused, by the ineffectiveness of the Angeli. Internally the old abuses in the administration reappeared — the sale of offices, the extortions of the tax collector, the oppression and predominance of the landowner. The themes had increased in number despite loss of territory[31]; the provincial governor was overshadowed by the local magnate, thus heralding one of the distinctive features of Byzantium in the Palaeologian age.

Had Isaac II been a statesman of the caliber of John Comnenus he would still have been tried to the utmost. As it was he showed that he was not a mere nonentity. He had to deal first with Norman aggression and then with Hohenstaufen hostility and the Third Crusade. The most pressing problem, once the Normans had been driven from Thessalonica and Durazzo and their fleet recalled from the Sea of Marmara, was in the Balkans, where the discontented Bulgarian provinces were ripe for rebellion and every small Slav principality was easy prey for western mischief-makers. Bulgaria had never wholly acquiesced in its incorporation in the empire in 1018. Religious and political discontent simmered throughout the eleventh and twelfth centuries and came to the surface in the troubled days following the death of Manuel Comnenus. The situation was successfully exploited by two local magnates, Peter

[31] Dölger, *Regesten*, no. 1647.

and Asen, who successfully reëstablished an independent kingdom and called themselves the *imperatores* (tsars) of the whole of Bulgaria and Vlachia. Fierce controversy has raged around the question of their own ethnic origins, whether Bulgar, Vlach, or Kuman, for in the foundation of the Second Bulgarian empire all three racial groups took part,[32] and the Kumans, for instance, were an important element in the new kingdom. Isaac had already tried to win the support of Hungary by the treaty of 1185 and by his marriage to the Hungarian princess Margaret. He now struggled against centrifugal forces in the Balkans, and after the treachery of his general Alexius Branas, himself led military expeditions during 1186–1187. But he had to accept the situation, and in 1186 Asen was crowned tsar by Basil, the newly established archbishop of Tirnovo. Stephen Nemanya of Rascia made himself "grand župan" of Serbia in 1186, and continued to build up his power at Byzantine expense; he supported the Bulgarian rebels. Imperial authority in the Balkans was therefore being constantly undermined, a situation which the western leaders of the Third Crusade were quick to exploit.

Thus weakened by civil war and campaigns in the Balkans, and without strong military leadership, Byzantium was in no position to control the new crusade or to counter Hohenstaufen ambitions.[33] With the continual deterioration of the crusading position in Syria and Palestine and the comparative failure of the Third Crusade, attention was more and more focussed on the Byzantine empire. Political hostility, keen commercial rivalries, and even the schism between the two churches created a situation in which a concerted western attack on the empire seemed only a question of time. The Third Crusade was a convenient cloak for the ambitions of Frederick Barbarossa, whose son was betrothed to the heiress of the Sicilian kingdom. Frederick traveled through Hungary and the Balkans. He had in 1188 negotiated with Byzantium on the subject of his passage through its territory,[34] but he was also in touch with the sultan at Iconium, and was regarded by both Serbia and Bulgaria as a desirable ally, particularly in view of the understanding between Hungary and Constantinople. Both the "grand župan" and the Bulgarian tsar were willing to submit to Frederick and to attack Constantinople.

Isaac could hardly afford to support the Latin crusading cause,

[32] Cf. Ostrogorsky, *Byzantine State*, p. 358, note 4, and see in general R. L. Wolff, "The Second Bulgarian Empire: Its Origin and History to 1204," *Speculum*, XXIV (1949), 167–206.

[33] See above, chapters II and III, for details of the Third Crusade.

[34] Dölger, *Regesten*, no. 1581; cf. above, chapter III, pp. 90–91.

and in the early summer of 1189 he renewed the treaty which Andronicus had made with Saladin, probably in 1185. Frederick prepared to take the offensive against Isaac, who had no diplomatic finesse and mishandled the situation. Philippopolis and Adrianople were occupied by the Germans, who then approached Constantinople. Frederick had already written to his son Henry telling him to bring a fleet to attack the city by sea. Constantinople awaited its fate, fearing that, like Thessalonica, it would be captured and looted. Isaac had no option but to accept Frederick's terms, and in February 1190 he agreed to the treaty of Adrianople, which granted the Germans transport and shipping and Byzantine hostages. Thus Barbarossa had very nearly anticipated events of 1204; he had certainly demonstrated the weakness of the Byzantine government. Meanwhile he crossed into Asia Minor and shortly afterwards his untimely death removed a dangerous enemy.

His western fellows in the Third Crusade, Richard the Lion-hearted of England and Philip Augustus of France, reached the Holy Land, but achieved little for the Christian cause there. But an event of significance for eastern Mediterranean politics in the later Middle Ages was Richard's conquest of the strategic island of Cyprus, then under the independent control of the Byzantine, Isaac Comnenus. From Richard it passed first to the Templars, and then in 1192 to Guy of Lusignan and his dynasty.

Temporarily freed from the German danger, Isaac hastened to retrieve the position in the Balkans. In the autumn of 1190 he defeated the Serbs and came to terms with Stephen Nemanya. The "grand župan" was allowed to retain certain of his conquests and was given the title of sebastocrator and the emperor's niece Eudocia as wife for his son Stephen. Though Isaac could not subdue the Serbian ruler as Manuel had done, in true Byzantine fashion he did at least try to retain him in the hierarchy of princes under the "Roman" basileus. Bulgaria proved more difficult to tame and Byzantine expeditions were defeated. Isaac was undertaking a fresh campaign with Hungarian help when his brother Alexius III deposed and blinded him, and ascended the throne on April 8, 1195.

Isaac has been, perhaps unfairly, denounced as "utterly ineffectual".[35] Faced with contemporaries of the caliber of Frederick Barbarossa, Henry VI, Stephen Nemanya, Peter and Asen, and Saladin, he could not hope to hold his own. But unwise and impetuous and shortsighted as he was, particularly in his internal policy, his military expeditions and his diplomatic activity do at least show

[35] Runciman, *Crusades,* II, 429.

him attempting to retrieve Byzantine prestige in the Balkans with Hungarian assistance, or trying to safeguard Byzantine interests in the east by coming to an understanding with Saladin. Indeed Isaac's negotiations with Saladin reveal the essential rift between the Latins and Greeks and the futility of hoping for any measure of unity in the Christian ranks.

Isaac's successor, Alexius III Angelus, ruled from April 8, 1195, to July 17–18, 1203. His weakness and greed lost the empire what little prestige it still enjoyed, and played directly into the hands of the western and Balkan powers. Already in 1195 Barbarossa's son the German emperor Henry VI, now ruler of Sicily, had demanded from Isaac II the cession of the Greek territory occupied by the Normans under William II of Sicily. The marriage of his brother Philip of Swabia to Irene, the daughter of the deposed Isaac II, provided Henry with a fresh weapon which he did not hesitate to use in his bold policy of attack. Henry planned a new crusade to conquer Constantinople and the empire before passing on to Syria and Palestine. Alexius in his fear tried to meet Henry's demands for heavy tribute, by levying what was known as the "German" tax, though this would doubtless have afforded only a temporary breathing space. Henry, in spite of papal opposition, continued to strengthen his position and was recognized by the rulers of Cyprus and of Cilician Armenia. The danger was averted only by his unexpected death in 1197.

Meanwhile Byzantine weakness had been further exposed by the advances made by Serbia and Bulgaria, both of which now judged it expedient to turn to Rome and to Hungary rather than to Constantinople. In both countries Constantinople had opportunities to extend its influence, but failed to do so. Stephen of Serbia, who was married to Alexius III's daughter Eudocia, in vain sought Byzantine help against his brother Vukan, who succeeded in temporarily gaining control of the government in 1202 with papal and Hungarian help, though only at the price of acknowledging Rome's supremacy and Hungary's suzerainty. The "ban" (ruler) of Bosnia, Kulin, strengthened his position by similar action. In Bulgaria civil war had broken out, and the throne was gained by Ioannitsa (Kaloyan), who had lived in Constantinople as a hostage. But even he, significantly, looked to Rome and not to Byzantium, and in 1204 he was crowned king by the Bulgarian archbishop Basil, who had just been consecrated primate by Innocent III's legate, cardinal Leo.

It needed only Venetian ambition to give direction to the hostile forces waiting to take advantage of Byzantine difficulties. The dismemberment of the empire would ensure the maritime supremacy of Venice, which in the course of the twelfth century had from time to time been threatened by Byzantine imperial policy and by the antagonism of the Greek people. The Fourth Crusade could have presented no surprise in western diplomatic circles. In fact, the internal condition of the empire did in several respects favor such an attack. In the past scholars have stressed the weakness of the dynasty of the Angeli and the hostility and greed of Byzantium's Latin enemies. But in reality a prime cause in determining the course of events was the fundamental change in the character of the empire from the eleventh century onwards. This was largely due to separatist and centrifugal forces which were continually undermining the central authority; such forces were enormously accelerated by the method of land holding based on grants in pronoia which bore a marked similarity to the western feudal system.

Thus weakened, the empire was no match for its western enemies. When Alexius III considered the strength of the crusading host, actually bent on restoring his imprisoned and blinded brother to his throne, he fled with what portable funds he could lay hands on. Nicetas Choniates, who disliked him, said that he was too cowardly to attempt any defense of the city as his son-in-law Theodore Lascaris wished.[36] And so Isaac II was again placed on the throne with his son Alexius IV as co-emperor. But it was an impossible position for the unfortunate Angeli: the hovering Latins continually pressed them for funds which they could not easily raise, while the populace resented and feared the influence of the westerners. Both Greek and Latin sources tell of continual tension and of constant clashes and skirmishes which came to a climax on January 1, 1204, with the Greek attempt to send fire-ships against the Venetian fleet. "This, then, was the way in which Alexius repaid us for all that we had done for him," wrote Villehardouin.[37] The Greeks, for their part, reproached Alexius IV for his failure to control the crusaders; terrified of his own people, the young emperor even thought of admitting the French and Italians into the palace of the Blachernae for his own defense. At this, Alexius Ducas "Mourtzouphlus", another son-in-law of Alexius III, promptly seized the throne in late January 1204. He had Isaac and Alexius IV im-

[36] Nicetas Choniates, *Historia* (*CSHB*), p. 720.

[37] Geoffrey of Villehardouin, *La Conquête de Constantinople*, chap. 220.

prisoned and was himself proclaimed as Alexius V. Isaac died shortly afterwards and Alexius IV was probably strangled.

Alexius IV, understandably enough, had been favorably disposed towards the Latins. Alexius V, on the other hand, did at least attempt to keep them in check, and he set about fortifying the city against the inevitable attack. The very severity of his discipline made enemies. The Latins were by no means at one among themselves, but expediency and ambition determined Boniface and the other leaders to support the intentions of the doge. The empire was partitioned in advance (March 1204) and the city taken by assault on April 13.[38] Mourtzouphlus' troops fought with determination to stave off the repeated attacks made from the crusading ships in the Golden Horn, but his camp was finally broken up and he fled from the city and joined his father-in-law at Mosynopolis. Alexius III treacherously had him blinded; he was caught by the crusaders and finally killed by being hurled from the column of Theodosius in Constantinople. Alexius III fared somewhat better than he deserved: he fell into the hands of Boniface of Montferrat, then took refuge in Epirus with the despot Michael I, who had ransomed him, and finally, after fomenting trouble in Asia Minor, was captured by his son-in-law Theodore Lascaris in 1210; he ended his days in a monastery in Nicaea. It was here that Theodore Lascaris had established his base after the fall of the city, and with courage and astuteness he was now rebuilding the shattered Byzantine state.

[38] See below, chapter V, pp. 184–185.

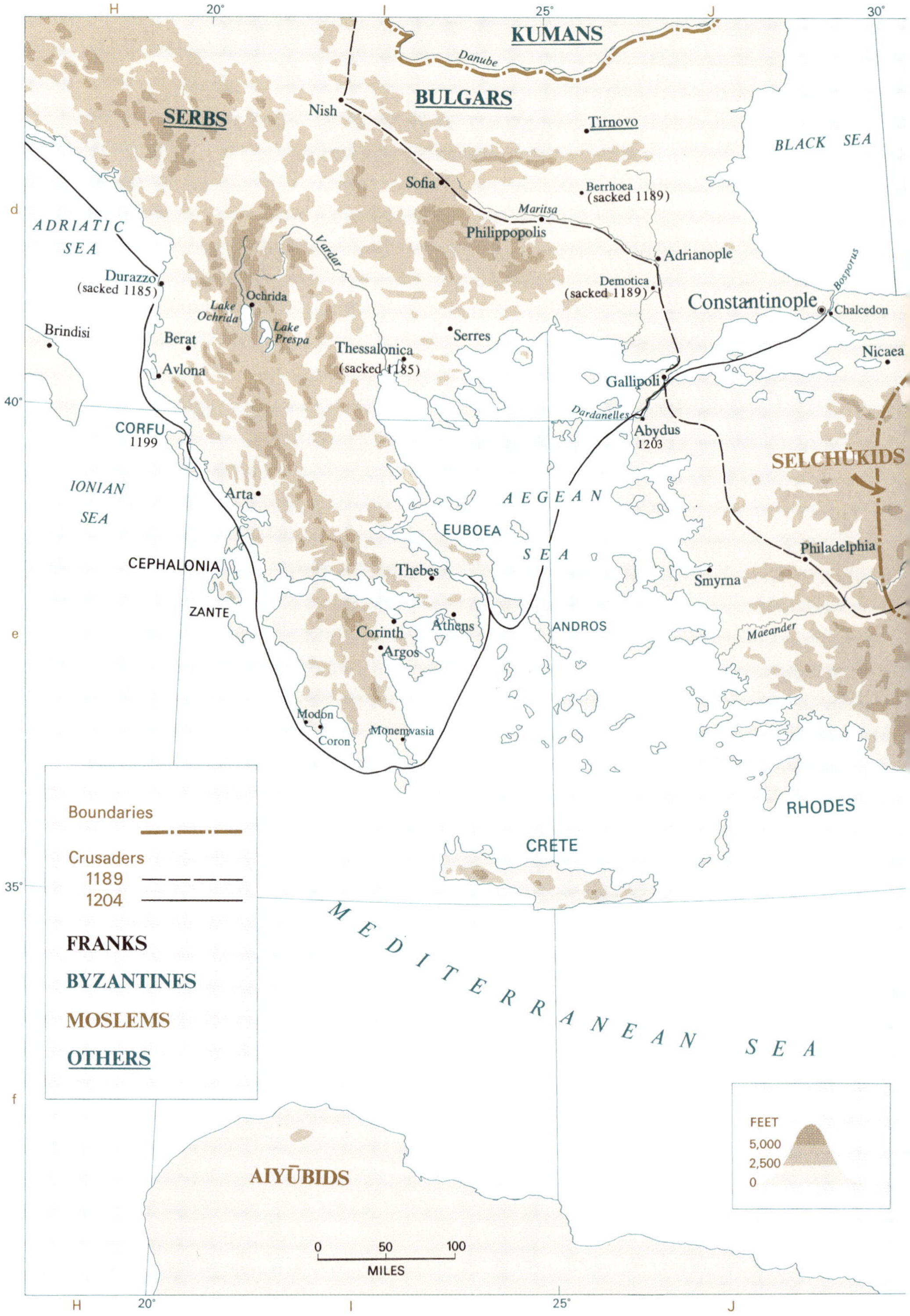

7. The Balkans under the Angeli, 1185–1204 (*Map by the University of Wisconsin Cartographic Laboratory*)

V

THE FOURTH CRUSADE

When Innocent III ascended the papal throne in January 1198, the German crusade planned by Henry VI was still in progress. Within a few months, however, it ended in ignominious

The most important single narrative source for the Fourth Crusade is the famous account by one of its leaders, Geoffrey of Villehardouin, *La Conquête de Constantinople* (ed. and tr. N. de Wailly, Paris, 1874; ed. and tr. E. Faral, Classiques de l'histoire de France au moyen-âge, 2 vols., Paris, 1938–1939). Splendidly complementing this semi-official narrative is the other vernacular work by a French participant, Robert of Clari (Cléry-sur-Somme), *La Conquête de Constantinople* (ed. P. Lauer, Les Classiques français du moyen-âge, Paris, 1924; English translation by E. H. McNeal, Records of Civilization, XXIII, New York, 1936). Shorter accounts in Latin, supplying occasional details, are: the anonymous *Devastatio Constantinopolitana*, ed. C. Hopf, *Chroniques gréco-romanes inédites ou peu connues* (Berlin, 1873), pp. 86–92; and *MGH, SS.*, XVI; Gunther of Pairis, *Historia Constantinopolitana*, ed. P. Riant (Geneva, 1875); also printed in the same editor's *Exuviae sacrae Constantinopolitanae* (Geneva, 1877), pp. 57–126; the Anonymous of Soissons, the Anonymous of Halberstadt (*MGH, SS.*, XXIII), and the Anonymous canon of Langres (all in Riant, *Exuviae*, pp. 3–9, 10–21, and 22–34 respectively), written largely to authenticate relics brought back or sent back to the west by clerics in the crusading armies after the sack of Constantinople. Hopf (*Chroniques*, pp. 93–98) furnishes a Latin translation of the section of the Russian Novgorod chronicle dealing with the capture of Constantinople, the original of which apparently was written by an eyewitness, probably a Russian.

Western chronicles containing accounts of the Fourth Crusade include the *Annales Colonienses maximi* (*MGH, SS.*, XVII); Aubrey of Trois-Fontaines, *Chronica* (*MGH, SS.*, XXIII); Robert of Auxerre, *Chronicon* (*MGH, SS.*, XXVI); Roger of "Hoveden", *Chronica* (ed. W. Stubbs, 4 vols., Rolls Series, LI); Rigord, *Gesta Philippi Secundi* (*MGH, SS.*, XXVI; and ed. H. F. Delaborde, Société de l'histoire de France, I, Paris, 1885). The *Chronique d'Ernoul* (ed. L. de Mas Latrie, Société de l'histoire de France, Paris, 1871), an Old French text written in Syria, reflects the attitudes and interests of the baronage, but it is not accurate for the Fourth Crusade.

The correspondence of Innocent III is, of course, a fundamentally important source (registered in A. Potthast, *Regesta pontificum Romanorum*, 2 vols., Berlin, 1873; texts of letters in *PL*, CCXIV–CCXVII); also valuable is the *Gesta Innocentii III papae* (*PL*, CCXIV), a biography drawn from the letters and containing brief narrative passages. The Venetian documents that survive are printed in G. L. F. Tafel and G. M. Thomas, *Urkunden zur älteren Handels- und Staatsgeschichte der Republik Venedig* (Fontes rerum Austriacarum, 3 vols., Vienna, 1856–1857).

For the Greek point of view, the contemporary eyewitness account of Nicetas Choniates, *Historia* (*CSHB*, Bonn, 1835) is the chief source.

Most modern scholarship on the Fourth Crusade has been preoccupied with the "diversion" problem, which will be discussed below with appropriate references. For accounts of the expedition by secondary authorities one may turn to A. Luchaire, *Innocent III: La Question d'orient* (Paris, 1907), now somewhat out of date, and to the discussions in the standard works of Vasiliev, Kretschmayr, and Norden. See also L. Bréhier, *L'Église et l'orient au moyen-âge: Les Croisades* (Paris, 1928), pp. 152 ff.; *idem, Le Monde byzantin*, I: *Vie et mort de Byzance* (Paris, 1947), pp. 365 ff.; Charles Diehl, "The Fourth Crusade and the Latin Empire," *Cambridge Medieval History*, IV (1927), 415 ff.; R. Grousset, *Histoire des croisades et du*

failure.[1] Thereupon pope Innocent decided to take upon himself the task of arousing Europe to a new effort to recover the Holy Land. In so doing, he was reverting to Urban II's original conception of the crusade as a papal responsibility, and simultaneously revealing his own exalted conception of the role of the papacy in the affairs of Christendom. He announced the project in an encyclical sent out in August 1198 to the archbishops of the west, to be communicated by them to the bishops and other clergy and to the faithful of their provinces.[2] Innocent followed the traditional lines of crusading propaganda, stressing his peculiar grief over the sufferings of Jerusalem, denouncing the princes of the west for their luxury and vice and wars among themselves, and summoning all Christians to win eternal salvation by girding themselves for the holy war. Passing over monarchs and lesser rulers, Innocent sent his summons to all cities, counts, and barons, whom he commanded to raise troops in numbers proportionate to their resources, and to send them overseas at their own expense by the following March, to serve for at least two years. Archbishops, bishops, and abbots were to contribute either armed men or an equivalent amount of money. Two cardinal-legates would proceed to Palestine to act as the pope's representatives there in preparing the way for the coming of the host. The proclamation included the usual inducements: plenary indulgence for crusaders, papal protection for their possessions, and a moratorium on the payment of debts and interest during their absence.

Innocent then wrote to king Philip Augustus of France and king Richard the Lionhearted of England, who had been at war ever since Richard's return from captivity in 1194, admonishing them, under penalty of an interdict to be laid on their lands, to make peace or at least a five years' truce with each other, not only because the war they were waging was causing untold miseries to the common people of their realms, but also because it would interfere with the recruiting of troops for the crusade he was inaugurating.[3] The two cardinals who were eventually to go to Palestine were in the meantime employed on special tasks at home: cardinal Soffredo

royaume franc de Jérusalem, III (Paris, 1936), 173 ff.; F. I. Uspenskii, *Istoriya vizantiiskoi imperii*, III (Moscow-Leningrad, 1948), 367 ff.; M. A. Zaborov, "Krestovye pokhody v russkoi burzhuaznoi istoriografii," *Vizantiiskii vremennik*, n.s., IV (1951), 176 ff.; G. Ostrogorsky, *History of the Byzantine State* (tr. Joan Hussey, London, 1956), pp. 330 ff.; S. Runciman, *A History of the Crusades*, III (Cambridge, 1954), 107 ff.

[1] See above, chapter III, pp. 116–121.
[2] Innocent III, *Epp.*, an. I, no. 336 (*PL*, CCXIV, cols. 308 ff.).
[3] Innocent III, *Epp.*, an. I, no. 355 (*PL*, CCXIV, cols. 329 ff.).

went to Venice to enlist the support of the Venetians, and cardinal Peter Capuano[4] went to France to promulgate the crusade there. Two cardinals were also sent to persuade the Pisans and Genoese to make peace and prepare to take part in the crusade. The pope wrote to the Byzantine emperor, Alexius III Angelus, reproving him for not having long since come to the aid of the Holy Land, and admonishing him as well to acknowledge the primacy of the papacy. Alexius replied in February 1199 with recriminations of his own.[5] Arriving in France late in 1198, Peter Capuano called an assembly of the French clergy at Dijon, where he promulgated the papal bull. He found Philip Augustus, by Christmas 1198, faced with a coalition of French lords whom Richard had won over to his side — including count Baldwin of Flanders and Hainault, count Louis of Blois, and the counts of Boulogne and Toulouse — and therefore eager to listen to Peter's proposals for a truce.[6] Two or three weeks later Peter met with Richard in Normandy. Though Richard maintained that he was only fighting to recover the lands which Philip had perfidiously seized in his absence on the Third Crusade, and accused Philip of responsibility for his captivity in Germany, complaining also that the pope had not given him the protection due him as a returning crusader, he finally yielded to Peter's plea that the war was hindering the recovery of Jerusalem. Late in January 1199 Richard and Philip met and made a truce for five years.[7] But before the end of March Richard was dead, and Philip Augustus soon renewed against John his efforts to seize the Angevin lands on the continent.

The date, March 1199, originally set by the pope for the departure of the armies, passed — as did most of the rest of the year — without even the formation of an expeditionary force.

[4] Sometimes erroneously referred to as Peter of Capua, he came not from Capua but from Amalfi, and belonged to a noble family of that city; see especially M. Camera, *Memorie storico-diplomatiche dell' antica città e ducato di Amalfi*, I (Salerno, 1876), 90, note 1; 383 ff., 665. He was to be Innocent's chief agent in the promotion of the crusade in the west until the spring of 1203, when he was sent on a special mission to the east. At the time of his French mission he held the titular office of cardinal-deacon of St. Mary in Via Lata, and was later advanced by Innocent to the title of cardinal-priest of St. Marcellus. Soffredo was cardinal-priest of St. Praxed.

[5] Innocent III, *Epp.*, an. I, no. 353 (*PL*, CCXIV, cols, 325 ff.); an. II, no. 210 (*ibid.*, cols. 765 ff.).

[6] Both Roger of Wendover, *Flores historiarum*, ad ann. 1198 (ed. H. G. Hewlett, Rolls Series, LXXXIV), I, 280 ff., and the verse biography of William Marshal, *L'Histoire de Guillaume le Maréchal* (ed. P. Meyer, Paris, 1891–1901), lines 11355–11372, ascribe the entire mission of Peter Capuano to a ruse of Philip, who had allegedly begged the pope for a legate to make peace between himself and Richard, and who had paid so well for the favor that Innocent had complied. The verse reflects the English point of view.

[7] Innocent III, *Epp.*, an. II, nos. 23–25 (*PL*, CCXIV, cols. 552 ff.), Innocent's letters of congratulation to Peter, confirming the truce.

Innocent III kept writing letters: to the archbishops and high clergy of the west to spur them to greater efforts; to the patriarch and clergy of the kingdom of Jerusalem, explaining why the crusade had been delayed; and to the princes of "Outremer" to urge them to compose their quarrels and make ready to participate in the coming war on the "infidel". Finally, at the very end of the year, he took a bold and unprecedented step. This was nothing less than an attempt, announced in another circular letter to the archbishops, to finance the crusade by a levy on the incomes of the clergy.[8] The pope announced that he and the cardinals and clergy of Rome had assessed themselves in the amount of a tenth of their revenues for the next year for the expenses of the crusade. Now by his apostolic authority he commanded all the clergy of both orders to contribute a fortieth of their revenues for the following year to the same cause. Exception was made in the case of certain religious orders, like the Carthusians, Cistercians, and Premonstratensians, who were to contribute only a fiftieth.[9] Each archbishop was to call together the bishops of his province in council, and transmit to them the papal command. Each bishop in turn was to summon the clergy of his diocese, and order them to make a true return of one fortieth of their annual revenues, see that the money was collected and deposited in a secure place, and report to the papal court the amount collected. The archbishops were authorized to use some of the money to help pay the expenses of indigent crusaders. In addition the pope commanded that a chest be placed in every parish church to receive the gifts of the faithful, who were to be exhorted in sermons every Sunday to make such contributions, with the promise of papal indulgence in proportion to the amount of their alms.

Innocent recognized the exceptional character of the levy, and assured the clergy that it would not be used as a precedent for establishing a papal tax on their incomes. Nevertheless, the measure seems to have met pretty generally with at least passive resistance. More than a year later, Innocent had to write to the clergy of France reproaching them for their laxity. He reminded them that they had voluntarily promised his legate, at the Council of Dijon, to

[8] See the letter sent to archbishop Ludolph of Magdeburg, dated December 31, 1199 (Innocent III, *Epp.*, an. II, no. 270 [*PL*, CCXIV, col. 828]). Roger of Hoveden, *Chronica* (Rolls Series, LI), IV, 108, quotes the letter sent to England. Potthast, *Regesta pontificum Romanorum*, I, no. 914, lists a copy sent to the archbishop of Ragusa (Dubrovnik).

[9] On the general question of papal taxation for the crusades, see below, chapter X, pp. 347–358. See also M. Villey, *La Croisade, essai sur la formation d'un théorie juridique* (Paris, 1942), pp. 135 ff., and in general A. Gottlob, *Die päpstlichen Kreuzzugssteuern des 13. Jahrhunderts* (Heiligenstadt, 1892).

contribute a thirtieth of their incomes, but had not yet paid even the fortieth he had commanded.[10] Ralph de Diceto reports that the notary sent from Rome to oversee the levy acted high-handedly, and there was a general suspicion that such funds were apt to stick to the fingers of the Roman gentry.[11] In speaking of the levy, Matthew Paris calls it a questionable exaction (*argumentosa extorsio*), which future events were to show was displeasing to God.[12] According to Ralph of Coggeshall the Cistercians protested against the pope's attempt to collect the levy as a persecution of the order.[13]

There is no way of knowing how much money was collected locally under the terms of this levy, or how much was actually transmitted to Rome. With all this opposition, tacit and expressed, on the part of the clergy, the levy was probably not very successful. Nor do we know what pecuniary results, if any, attended the pope's tentative effort to extend the levy to monarchs and nobles. In June 1201 the papal legate, Octavian, cardinal-bishop of Ostia, who had succeeded cardinal Peter in France, made the proposal to the kings of England and France. Philip Augustus and John met together and agreed to contribute a fortieth of a year's income from their lands and the lands of their vassals, on the condition that they should undertake the collection themselves and decide how the money was to be used. The monarchs then issued writs commanding their vassals to assess themselves in this amount.[14] Of any money which may have been raised in this way, probably not much went to defray the expenses of the crusade. Both Philip and John had other and more pressing uses for any revenue they could collect.

As a further recruiting measure in France, on November 5, 1198, Innocent III, presumably acting through Peter Capuano, had commissioned the parish priest, Fulk of Neuilly, to preach the crusade to the people. For some two or three years previously, Fulk

[10] This letter, *Verendum est*, is found only in the *Gesta*, chap. LXXXIV (*PL*, CCXIV, cols. 132 ff.). Potthast (no. 1045) dates it April–May 1200, but it must have been written after April 1201, since it contains an unmistakable reference to the pope's confirmation of the treaty between the Venetians and the French envoys. See below, note 29.

[11] *Opera historica* (Rolls Series, LXVIII), II, 168–169.

[12] *Historia Anglorum* (Rolls Series, XLIV), II, 91.

[13] *Chronicon Anglicanum* (Rolls Series, LXVI), p. 130. Eventually, it seems, the pope accepted a compromise with the Cistercians; Potthast (*Regesta*, no. 1435, July 1201) cites a letter of Innocent thanking abbot Arnold Amalric of Cîteaux and the chapter for the offer of 2,000 marks for the crusade.

[14] Roger of Hoveden (*Chronica*, IV, 187 ff.) tells of the meeting of the kings and gives the writ issued by John. The writ of Philip Augustus is found in Delisle, *Catalogue des actes de Philippe Auguste*, no. 619. See also Delaborde, "À propos d'une rature dans une lettre de Philippe Auguste," *Bibliothèque de l'École des chartes*, LXIV (1903), 306 ff., and A. Cartellieri, *Philipp II. August*, IV, i, 77.

had been conducting a revivalist campaign in the regions around Paris. With the license of his bishop he had been traveling about, preaching to great crowds of people and flaying them for their sins, especially usury and prostitution, and many tales were told of the sudden conversion of moneylenders and harlots, and of the miracles of healing and other wonders that attended his preaching. From November 1198 until his death in May 1202, Fulk devoted himself entirely to the crusade. He undoubtedly succeeded in arousing among the common people an immense, if short-lived, enthusiasm. Contemporaries generally testify to his large influence.[15]

The first nucleus of an expeditionary force came into existence late in November 1199, at a tournament held in Champagne at count Theobald's castle of Écry, attended by counts, barons, and knights from the counties of Champagne and Blois and from the Île de France. There count Theobald himself and count Louis of Blois took the cross, and their example was followed by many other jousters. Geoffrey of Villehardouin, who apparently was present and took the cross with the others, begins his narrative of the actual expedition with this incident; except for the unreliable Ernoul, no other contemporary chronicler mentions it. Nothing in Villehardouin's account implies that Fulk of Neuilly was present at the tournament. Instead, the taking of the cross appears as the spontaneous response of the lords to the prevailing excitement over the crusade. Had Fulk been there, Villehardouin would scarcely have failed to mention it. Yet later historians, especially the nineteenth-century writers of the Romantic school, such as Michaud, have so popularized the legend that Fulk in person won the nobles for the cross at Écry that it still appears in histories of the crusade.[16]

[15] Innocent III, *Epp.*, an. I, no. 398 (*PL*, CCXIV, col. 378), appears to be an abbreviation of Innocent's commission, rather than a later supplement to it, as argued by Gutsch, "Fulk of Neuilly, a Twelfth-Century Preacher," *The Crusades and other Historical Studies Presented to Dana C. Munro* (New York, 1928), pp. 202 ff., and by E. Faral, in his edition of Villehardouin, I, 4, note 1. Villehardouin, Robert of Clari, Gunther of Pairis, Rigord, Otto of St. Blaise, Roger of Hoveden, Robert of Auxerre, and Ralph of Coggeshall all note Fulk's extraordinary success as a preacher. Ralph of Coggeshall, *Chronicon Anglicanum* (Rolls Series, LXVI), p. 130, reports that Fulk himself claimed to have given the cross to 200,000 persons during three years of preaching. He also was a most successful money-raiser. The funds were deposited at Cîteaux for the needs of the Holy Land. Ernoul (p. 338) tells how Cistercians came to the east with some of the money for use in repairing the walls of Acre, Beirut, and Tyre, all damaged by earthquakes. The *Devastatio* (*MGH, SS.*, XVI, 10; ed. Hopf, pp. 86–87) reports that the large sums in Fulk's possession at the moment of his death were turned over by Philip Augustus to Odo of Champlitte and the castellan of Coucy to be spent on the crusade.

[16] E.g., in Jean Longnon, *L'Empire latin de Constantinople* (Paris, 1949), pp. 21 ff. See E. H. McNeal "Fulk of Neuilly and the Tournament of Écry," *Speculum*, XXVIII (1953), 371 ff.

The example set by counts Theobald of Champagne and Louis of Blois inspired neighboring and related princes of northern France to similar action. At Bruges on Ash Wednesday (February 23, 1200), count Baldwin of Flanders and Hainault, who was married to a sister of Theobald, took the cross, together with his brother Henry and many high barons of the region; in Picardy, count Hugh of St. Pol; in Perche, count Geoffrey and his brother Stephen, cousins of Louis of Blois. Thus by the summer of 1200 a considerable crusading army had been formed. An initial meeting at Soissons was adjourned for two months to allow time for further enlistments. At a second meeting, held at Compiègne, each of the three counts, Theobald, Louis, and Baldwin, named two of his barons to act as his agents in contracting for ships to carry the host overseas. Some time around the turn of the year the six envoys set out for Venice.[17]

The forces raised in northern France in this first stage of recruiting were to form the core of the army that went on the Fourth Crusade. The leaders belonged to the very highest rank of the feudal nobility of France. Theobald and Louis were scions of the two branches of the family of Blois-Champagne, one of the great feudal dynasties of France. They were double first cousins, since their fathers were brothers and their mothers were sisters. They were also nephews both of Philip Augustus and of Richard the Lionhearted, their maternal grandmother, the famous Eleanor of Aquitaine, having been married first to Louis VII of France and later to Henry II of England. Thus the mothers of the young counts were half-sisters of Philip Augustus, as well as of Richard and John. Participation in the crusading movement had been a tradition with the family, ever since an ancestor, Stephen of Blois, had taken part in the First Crusade. Theobald's older brother, Henry, had played a prominent role in the Third Crusade, and had been ruler of Jerusalem until his death in 1197.[18] Count Baldwin IX of Flanders, who had married Theobald's and Henry's sister Mary, was also Baldwin VI of Hainault, a fief of the empire, held of the bishop of Liége. All three of the counts were young men, under thirty years of age. Villehardouin's list of the northern French barons who had so far taken the cross includes, notably, Matthew of Montmorency, Reginald of Montmirail, Simon of Montfort, Reginald of Dampierre,

[17] Geoffrey of Villehardouin (*Conquête,* chap. XIV), who was one of the two agents of the count of Champagne, says that the envoys were given only the general instructions to arrange for ships at some seaport, and decided among themselves to apply to Venice. The *Devastatio* asserts that the choice of Venice was dictated by the pope, but this statement is unsupported.

[18] See above, chapter III, pp. 53, 81–85, and below, chapter XV, pp. 522–529.

Guy of Coucy, James of Avesnes, and Peter of Bracieux.[19] The most interesting name is that of the historian himself, Geoffrey of Villehardouin, marshal of Champagne. A man of mature years, he had held high office at the court of Champagne, and from his first responsible task as Theobald's representative in Venice, he was to play an important role in the expedition and in the establishment of the Latin empire.[20] His comrade-in-arms Conon of Béthune, one of Baldwin's barons and his representative on this first mission, was well known as a courtly poet, and had ahead of him a long and distinguished career in the east.[21]

This crusading host resembled the ordinary feudal levy in its composition and organization. The divisions or army corps were the regional contingents, each commanded by the prince of the territory, as the counts of Champagne, Blois, and Flanders. Within each division, the companies were captained by the barons who were the vassals of the count, and the companies were composed of knights and sergeants serving under the banners of their own baron. Thus the bonds which held the host together were essentially feudal in character. Taking the cross was in theory a voluntary act on the part of the individual crusader, but in fact the relationship of vassal to lord had played a decisive part in the enlistment, and it was the determining factor in the exercise of command.

As to numbers, it may be roughly estimated that between eight and ten thousand fighting men had been enrolled by the end of the year 1200. Geoffrey of Villehardouin's list contains the names of some ninety barons, and while he expressly states that he did not name them all, it may be supposed that his list is fairly complete. Robert of Clari later describes the company in which he served under the banner of his lord Peter of Amiens as containing ten knights and sixty sergeants. This first enlistment, therefore, probably consisted of about a hundred barons' companies of some eighty to a hundred men each. The force comprised in the main three categories of troops: armored knights, light-armed squires (sergeants on horseback), and foot-soldiers (sergeants on foot), in the usual proportions of one to two to four.

In seeking transportation overseas at an Italian port, the envoys

[19] See the map showing the fiefs and places of origin of these crusaders in E. Faral's edition at the back of vol. I. This James of Avesnes is the son of the James who died at Arsuf (see above, chapter II, p. 75).

[20] See the introduction to Faral's edition, I, pp. v–xii, and J. Longnon, *Recherches sur la vie de Geoffroi de Villehardouin* (Paris, 1939).

[21] See A. Wallensköld, *Les Chansons de Conon de Béthune* (Helsinki, 1891; new edition, Paris, 1921, with introductory material much abridged). Two of the poems (IV, V) are concerned with the Third Crusade.

were following a well established practice, for the sea route had by now almost entirely superseded the long and difficult land route of the first crusading expeditions. The Italian maritime cities had developed a lucrative passenger traffic in pilgrims and crusaders, along with their carrying trade in the Mediterranean. Individual pilgrims now usually sought passage in the great freighters which set out each year from Pisa, Genoa, and Venice, while bands of crusaders often contracted to hire individual ships at one or another of these ports. In this case, however, the six envoys from the three counts were asking Venice to furnish a fleet large enough to transport a whole army, and the Venetians would certainly consider so serious an undertaking as a matter of state policy, to be determined in the light of their other interests and commitments.

By the end of the twelfth century Venice had already entered upon her greatest age as a commercial, colonial, and maritime power.[22] Her widespread interests in the eastern Mediterranean required the maintenance of a powerful naval establishment and the pursuit of a vigilant and aggressive diplomacy. Like the other Italian maritime cities, Venice had long since acquired valuable trading privileges and exemptions in the ports of "Outremer", such as Acre and Tyre, in return for naval help given to the kingdom of Jerusalem. This had given the Venetians a practical interest in the affairs of the crusader states and had deepened their rivalry with Pisa and Genoa. More recently Venice and her rivals had also developed a profitable trade in Egypt through the port of Alexandria. From the point of view of the crusader states and the papacy, this was traffic with the enemy, especially as Egypt demanded much-needed timber and other naval stores in exchange for the spices of the Far East. Popes and councils had fulminated in vain against this trade in war contraband on the part of Italian cities.

Venice especially had a bad reputation among the Christians of the east as being more concerned with the profits from this trade than with the triumph of the cross.[23] In her trade with Constantinople and other cities of the Byzantine empire, Venice still enjoyed the special advantages granted by emperor Alexius I in 1082 in

[22] On the position of Venice at this time, see H. Kretschmayr, *Geschichte von Venedig*, I (Gotha, 1905), chaps. VII, VIII; W. Heyd, *Histoire du commerce du Levant au moyen-âge*, tr. Furcy Rainaud, I (Leipzig, 1885); and A. Schaube, *Handelsgeschichte der romanischen Völker* (Munich and Berlin, 1906), chaps. X–XIX. A chapter on the Venetians is planned for volume IV of the present work.

[23] It was this feeling presumably that gave rise to the popular story repeated by Ernoul (*Chronique*, p. 345), that the sultan succeeded in bribing the Venetians to turn the projected crusade away from his land.

exchange for Venetian help against Robert Guiscard. John II Comnenus had tried to revoke this grant, and Venice had resorted to war to force him to renew it in 1126. Manuel I had again renewed it in 1148, but Byzantine relations with Venice continued to be strained. Manuel's mass arrest of Venetians in 1171, and his confiscation of their property, coupled with the massacre of all the Latins in 1182, had heightened the tension. Although Isaac II Angelus in 1187 and Alexius III Angelus in 1198 had renewed the privileges, the Byzantines owed Venice much money. Moreover, Alexius III was not only favoring the Pisans and Genoese unduly but also levying tolls on Venetian ships, contrary to the provisions of the treaties. When the six French envoys arrived early in February 1201, Venice was under the governance of one of the greatest personages of her history, the aged, half-blind, but indomitable doge Enrico Dandolo. Elected to this lifetime office in 1192, he had guided the fortunes of the city in troubled times with great craft and vigor. According to Marino Sanudo the younger (d. 1533),[24] he is said to have been 85 years of age at the time of his election as doge. Although this seems scarcely credible, as it would make him 95 at the outset of the Fourth Crusade, in which he was to play so active a part, the sources generally agree on his great age and his badly impaired vision.[25]

The envoys of the French counts presented to the doge and his "small council" of six their request for ships to carry the crusaders oversea. A week later, in reply, the Venetian authorities offered not only to provide transport, for pay, but also to join the crusade as equal partners. They would supply enough transports to carry 4,500 knights and their horses, 9,000 squires, and 20,000 foot soldiers, with their gear and provisions, in return for the sum of 94,000 marks of silver, to be paid in instalments. This estimate of the size of the army for which transportation would be needed must have been made by the envoys themselves. It was at least three times as large as the number of crusaders actually enrolled before the envoys had set out on their mission. They were anticipating many more enlistments of crusaders than in fact they would obtain. This miscalculation was a primary source of the troubles that were to haunt the expedition throughout its whole course. The Venetians

[24] *Vite dei dogi* (*RISS*, XXII, 4), p. 527.

[25] Villehardouin, *Conquête*, chap. LXVII: "si n'en veoit gote, que perdue avoit le veüe par un plaie qu'il ot el chief." The Russian chronicle of Novgorod (ed. C. Hopf, *Chroniques*, p. 98) attributes his partial blinding to a trick with a burning glass perpetrated by the Greeks when he was in Constantinople on a diplomatic mission. On his age and blindness, see H. Kretschmayr, *Venedig*, I, 466, 472.

were to put the transports at the service of the crusaders for a year from the time of departure, which was set for the day of Sts. Peter and Paul of the following year (June 29, 1202), unless that date should be changed by common consent. As their own contribution, the Venetians were to furnish fifty war galleys fully manned and equipped for the same length of service, on condition that Venice should share equally with the crusaders in any conquests or gains made on the campaign.

The envoys accepted the proposal, which the doge then submitted for ratification first to the "large council" of forty, and then to larger bodies of one hundred, two hundred, and a thousand, and finally to the people as a whole, before whom the envoys knelt weeping to loud cries of "We grant it" from more than 10,000 assembled in St. Mark's for mass. After the terms had been accepted by both sides, the covenant was drawn up and signed, on the one hand by the six envoys in the names of the three counts who had accredited them, and on the other by the doge and his council of state and council of forty.[26] The negotiators also agreed secretly that the attack should be directed against Egypt, "because more harm could be inflicted on the Turks there than in any other land." But they would keep up the pretense that the expedition would go direct to Palestine, no doubt to conceal their true intentions from the enemy and to prevent discontent from arising among the rank and file of the crusaders, who naturally expected to be led to Jerusalem.

It was stipulated in the covenant that a copy of it should be transmitted to pope Innocent to secure his confirmation. This joint expedition of a French army and a Venetian fleet, however, arranged for on their own initiative by the French leaders and the government of Venice, was something quite different from the general crusade of western Europe under papal auspices envisaged by the pope. Nevertheless, he felt constrained to accept it as a partial realization of his own project. Not only did he confirm the covenant when it was presented to him at Rome,[27] but he went further and undertook to make the plan his own. In May, a few weeks after receiving a copy of the treaty, he wrote to the clergy in England, instructing them to see to it that those who had taken the cross in that land

[26] Text of the treaty in Tafel and Thomas, *Urkunden*, I, 363 ff.

[27] "Mult volentiers," says Geoffrey of Villehardouin (*Conquête*, chap. XXXI). The *Gesta*, on the other hand (chap. lxxxiii; *PL*, CCXIV, col. 131) asserts that Innocent answered "caute" and made his confirmation conditional on the crusaders' future consultation with the holy see. This author, however, writing after the event, was evidently intent on demonstrating the extraordinary foresight of Innocent (*quod futurorum esset presagiens*). Innocent must surely have welcomed this evidence that some military action was at last preparing.

should be ready to proceed overseas by the next summer, "at the time set by our beloved sons, the counts of Flanders, Champagne, and Blois."[28] He also wrote, about the same time, to the French clergy, endorsing the expedition planned by the envoys and the Venetians.[29] Similar instructions may have been sent to the German clergy, for bishop Conrad of Halberstadt and abbot Martin of Pairis in Alsace were eventually to lead contingents from that country to Venice.

The negotiations at Venice had taken several weeks, and the envoys were not able to set out for home until some time in April 1201. Late in May, after their return, count Theobald of Champagne died. He had been the first to take the cross, and seems to have been regarded as the leader of the crusade. In any event, it was now decided to replace him with a formally elected commander-in-chief. So a council was held at Soissons toward the end of June, which was attended by the counts of Flanders, Blois, St. Pol, and Perche, together with a number of high barons. There Geoffrey of Villehardouin proposed the name of marquis Boniface of Montferrat, "a very worthy man and one of the most highly esteemed of men now living." Villehardouin was able to assure the assembly that Boniface would accept the nomination, so it is clear that somebody had already consulted him about it. After considerable discussion, the barons agreed, and decided to send envoys to Boniface to ask him to come to France and accept the command.[30]

Vassals of the empire for their principality in northern Italy, the members of the house of Montferrat had distinguished themselves as crusaders. Boniface's father, William the Old, had fought in the Second Crusade, and had been captured fighting at Hattin in 1187. His eldest brother, William Longsword, had married Sibyl, daughter of Amalric of Jerusalem (1176), and was posthumously the father of king Baldwin V. A second brother, Renier, had married, in 1180, Maria, a daughter of the emperor Manuel Comnenus, had become caesar, and was poisoned by Andronicus Comnenus in 1183. A third brother, Conrad, had married, in 1185, Theodora, a sister of the emperor Isaac Angelus, had also become caesar, and helped put down a serious revolt against Isaac in 1185.

[28] Roger of Hoveden, *Chronica*, IV, 365. No English contingent actually took part in that expedition.

[29] This is the letter in the *Gesta*, referred to above in note 10. In it the pope mentioned by name three of the six envoys, evidently the delegation sent to Rome with a copy of the covenant for his confirmation, and suggested that their advice should be sought in organizing the crusade in France.

[30] Villehardouin, *Conquête*, chap. XLI.

He had escaped from the fiercely anti-Latin atmosphere of Constantinople, saved Tyre from Saladin in 1187, married Isabel, the heiress to the kingdom of Jerusalem (whose first husband, Humphrey of Toron, was still alive also), and considered himself king from 1190 until his assassination in 1192. The intimate identification of Boniface's whole family with the east, however, could hardly have been the sole reason why the crusaders chose him as their commander. The *Gesta* of pope Innocent III declares that Philip Augustus favored Boniface,[31] but it is not clear why.

We know that, after leaving Venice, four of the six crusader envoys had proceeded to Genoa,[32] and it is possible that the Genoese authorities, intimately linked with the family of Montferrat, had informed them of Boniface's interest. Two historians report, moreover, that Manuel Comnenus had bestowed Thessalonica on Renier of Montferrat, and had crowned him "king".[33] Of course, no Byzantine emperor would have done precisely that, but we know Manuel had made Renier caesar. Nor is there anything inherently improbable about the story that Manuel had given Renier Thessalonica as a *pronoia*: in 1081 Alexius I Comnenus, in the first recorded act of his reign, had made Nicephorus Melissenus caesar, and assigned Thessalonica to him.[34] After the crusade, Boniface of Montferrat was to insist on having Thessalonica,[35] and no other property, for himself, and he did in fact become its first Latin king. We are perhaps justified, therefore, in assuming that, as early as the spring of 1201, his interest in obtaining the command of the crusader armies sprang from a determination to fight on Byzantine soil for what he considered a family fief,[36] and possibly

[31] *Gesta*, chap. LXXXIII (*PL*, CCXIV, col. 132): "cum consilio regis Franciae". Cf. E. Faral, "Geoffroy de Villehardouin: la question de sa sincèreté," *Revue historique*, CLXXVII (1936), 571.

[32] Villehardouin, *Conquête*, chap. XXXII.

[33] Robert of Torigny, *Cronica* (*MGH, SS.*, VI), p. 528; Sicard of Cremona, *Cronica* (*RISS*, VII [1725], col. 612; *MGH, SS.*, XXXI, 173).

[34] Anna Comnena, *Alexiad*, II, viii, 3 (ed. Leib, I, 89).

[35] See below, chapter VI, pp. 190, 192. Boniface made an agreement with the Venetians in August 1204 (printed in Tafel and Thomas, *Urkunden*, I, 512 ff.), the surviving text of which refers to Thessalonica as having been given by Manuel to Boniface's *father*; but the emendation of *patri* to *fratri* clears up this difficulty.

[36] The leading authority on the family of Montferrat, Leopoldo Usseglio, *I Marchesi di Monferrato in Italia ed in Oriente*, II (Turin, 1926), 247, note 2, rejects the story on the ground that no Byzantine emperor ever crowned a subject king. True, but Usseglio fails to see that the ceremonial bestowal of the title of caesar, plus a fief in or near or including Thessalonica (all of which a Byzantine emperor might easily have given), might strike a western historian like Robert or Sicard, unfamiliar with Byzantine protocol, as a royal coronation. Authorities taking this view (and both unknown to Usseglio) are F. Cognasso, "Partiti politici e lotte dinastiche in Bisanzio alla morte di Manuele Comneno," *Memorie della R. Accademia delle Scienze di Torino*, ser. 2, LXII (1912), 220, and J. K. Fotheringham, *Marco Sanudo* (Oxford, 1915), pp. 26 ff.

even for the imperial throne itself. About fifty years old, Boniface apparently had never been overseas or taken part in any crusading movement. He had, however, campaigned in Sicily in Henry VI's war with Tancred, and had also fought a long-drawn-out struggle with the Lombard communes. At his court chivalry flourished and he patronized Provençal troubadours like Peter Vidal. His own court poet was the troubadour Rambald of Vacqueyras.[37]

Boniface now appeared at Soissons, and accepted the command which the crusaders offered him. Villehardouin says that only thereafter did the marquis receive the cross, in a special ceremony; but there is some evidence[38] that he may already have taken it in Italy. From Soissons, Boniface proceeded to Cîteaux at the time of the annual chapter of the Cistercians (Holy Cross day, September 14, 1201). Fulk of Neuilly preached a sermon, and many Burgundians took the cross. The marquis then went on into Germany to attend the Christmas court of his suzerain, the German king, the Hohenstaufen Philip of Swabia, whose loyal friend he was. Philip, brother of the recently deceased emperor Henry VI, had married Irene, daughter of the Byzantine emperor Isaac Angelus, and widow of the Sicilian prince Roger, whom Henry VI had conquered.[39] With his Byzantine bride Philip had acquired the cause of her father Isaac Angelus, who had been deposed, blinded, and relegated to prison with his son Alexius in 1195 by his brother, Alexius III Angelus. Moreover, Philip had inherited from his late brother Henry the traditional enmity toward Byzantium which had expressed itself in Henry's great but abortive plan for an expedition against the Byzantines, a legacy to the Hohenstaufens from their Norman predecessors in Sicily. When Boniface took command of the crusading armies, new interests thus found a voice in the leadership. From Germany he went back to Montferrat to make his final preparations.

The covenant between the Venetians and the crusaders had set the date for the arrival of the host in Venice before the end of April 1202, in order to permit departure at the time of the summer cross-

[37] In addition to the work of Usseglio, see D. Brader, *Bonifaz von Montferrat bis zum Antritt der Kreuzfahrt* (Berlin, 1907); K. Hopf, *Bonifaz von Montferrat und der Troubadour Rambaut von Vaqueiras*, Sammlung gemeinverständlicher wissenschaftlichen Vorträge (ed. R. Virchow and F. von Holtzendorff, Berlin, 1877), 12; O. Schultz [Schultz-Gora] (ed.), *Briefe an Bonifaz I. (II.) Markgrafen von Montferrat* (Halle, 1893); Italian version, ed. G. del Noce (Florence, 1898). See the entry under "Rambaut de Vaqueiras" in A. Pillet and H. Carstens, *Bibliographie der Troubadours*, Schriften der Königsberger gelehrten Gesellschaft Sonderreihe, vol. III (Halle, 1933), pp. 352 ff.

[38] *Gesta*, chap. XLVI (*PL*, CCXIV), cols. xc–xci.

[39] See above, chapter III, p. 119.

ing toward the end of June. In fact, however, the first bands did not leave the various regions of France until April and May, and others straggled along throughout June, July, and August. Boniface himself arrived in Venice with his contingent of Lombards only in the middle of August, and the small bands of crusaders from Germany put in their appearance at about the same time. Worse still, a number of the "high men" from the Île de France, Burgundy, and Provence decided on their own initiative not to sail from Venice at all, but to seek transportation overseas for themselves and their men at other ports, some from Marseilles and some from southern Italy. So when the leaders in Venice were able to make a muster of the forces at their command, they found to their dismay that only about a third of the expected 33,500 men had turned up at Venice. The leaders had counted on raising the large sum of money still owing the Venetians by collecting passage money from the individual crusaders, but they found that, with only ten or twelve thousand troops on hand, they could not meet their obligations. After the individual soldiers had made their contribution, Boniface and the counts and some of the high barons added what money they could spare from their private funds, and pledged their gold and silver plate to the Venetian moneylenders,[40] but in the end they still owed the Venetians some 34,000 marks. Thus the expedition was threatened with failure before it ever got under way, for the Venetians were not likely to go on with it unless they received all the money that was coming to them by the terms of the contract. Villehardouin lays the blame for the threatened fiasco on those who, as he says, were false to their oaths and went to other ports. The primary cause, however, was the excessively high estimate made in the first place by Villehardouin himself and the other envoys as to the size of the army for which transportation would be needed. Even if all the defaulting contingents had come to Venice, they still would not have made up more than half the estimated number of 33,500 men.

At this juncture, doge Enrico Dandolo came forward with a proposal that offered a way out of the impasse. For some time the rulers of Hungary, now in control of the Croatian hinterland, had been encouraging the towns along the Dalmatian coast to rebel against Venetian authority, dominant in Dalmatia for about a

[40] See the document printed in Tafel and Thomas, *Urkunden*, I, no. xcv, in which count Baldwin acknowledges his indebtedness to certain Venetian merchants in the amount of 118 marks, 3 ounces, with interest. Note also R. Morozzo and A. Lombardo, *Documenti del commercio veneziano nei secoli XI–XIII*, I (Turin, 1940), 542, no. 462.

century, and to seek Hungarian protection. In 1186 Zara, one of the most important of these Venetian vassal cities in Dalmatia, had in this way gone over to king Bela III of Hungary. Despite repeated efforts, Venice had failed to recover it. The doge now asked that the crusading army help him regain Zara. In return Venice would allow the crusaders to postpone payment of the debt until such time as they could meet it out of their share of the booty, to be won later during the expedition. Since the alternative was the abandonment of the crusade and the probable forfeiture of the money already paid, the leaders accepted the proposal, although many crusaders objected violently to turning their arms against Christians. With this matter settled, early in September 1202 the doge himself took the cross at a great assembly in St. Mark's, and prepared to go with the expedition as commander of the Venetian forces, leaving the government of Venice to his son Renier in his absence. Then it was that the Venetians began for the first time to take the cross in great numbers, Villehardouin tells us. Apparently they had been waiting for the doge to take the lead.

At this point in his narrative, Villehardouin records what he calls a marvelous and portentous event:[41] the appeal of a Byzantine prince to the crusaders to help him recover his rights in Constantinople. This was the "young Alexius", son of Isaac II Angelus, who had succeeded in escaping to the west to seek the help of his brother-in-law, Philip of Swabia. Landing at Ancona, the party of the young prince traveled north through Italy, and at Verona, according to Villehardouin, encountered some tardy crusaders who were on their way to Venice. Learning from them of the gathering of an army which was preparing to go overseas, Alexius and his advisers decided to send envoys to the leaders of the crusade and ask them for help. Boniface and the counts and high barons were sufficiently interested, Villehardouin tells us, to send envoys of their own to accompany Alexius' party to Philip's court. "If he will aid us to recover the land of Outremer, we will aid him to conquer his land; for we know that it was unjustly taken from him and his father."[42] So Villehardouin reports the response of the crusaders to an appeal which he dates immediately before the departure of the fleet in the fall of 1202. Indeed, if one accepts Villehardouin's version of events, one must assume that the fleet actually sailed on October 1, 1202, without any commitment to the young Alexius,

[41] *Conquête*, chap. LXX: "Or oiez une des plus grant merveilles et des greignor aventures que vos oncques oisiez." The reader will recognize, of course, that this dramatic pronouncement is to some extent a cliché of the literature of the time.

[42] *Conquête*, chap. LXXII.

whose appeal, we are to believe, had only recently been delivered to them.

It was, of course, this appeal and the eventual decision of the crusader chieftains to accede to it that resulted in the "diversion" of the Fourth Crusade from its original purpose of fighting the Moslems in Palestine, or in Egypt, to Constantinople, where the expedition would first restore Isaac and the young Alexius, and then oust them and found a Latin empire on Byzantine soil. This endeavor coincided with the interests of Venice, of Boniface of Montferrat, of Philip of Swabia, and — to the extent that it placed a Roman Catholic dynasty and patriarch on the imperial and ecclesiastical thrones of Constantinople — of Innocent III as well. So modern scholars have often questioned Villehardouin's version of events, which has seemed to them "official" history, concealing behind a plausible narrative a deep-laid secret plot among the interested parties, hatched long before their intentions were revealed to the rank and file of the crusaders, most of whom would have much preferred to carry out a real crusade against the "infidel". Few problems of medieval history have elicited so much scholarly controversy as the "diversion" problem. Though numerous, the sources are often vague or contradictory, naturally enough, since if there was indeed a plot one could hardly expect a contemporary in the secret to reveal it, while one who had no knowledge of it could not reveal any. Both the modern editors of Villehardouin accept his story at face value, and are thus partisans of what has come to be called the *théorie du hasard* or *d'occasion*, according to which the decision to help the young Alexius was really not made until the last moment.[43]

In the early days of the discussion, the Venetians received most of the blame for the diversion. They had, it was alleged, concluded a secret treaty with al-'Ādil, the Aiyūbid sultan, promising not to attack his lands. Indeed, one scholar wrote as if the text of the treaty itself were available. But by 1877, it was clear that the treaty in question actually belonged to a far later date, and that Venice had made no secret promises to the sultan before the Fourth Crusade. Though innocent of this charge, Venice was of course profoundly hostile to Alexius III Angelus; she wished at least to assure herself that the rights owed her by treaty would be respected, and at most to take over the commerce of Constantinople completely. The doge may have lost his eyesight through action by Byzantines,

[43] In addition to the comments by Natalis de Wailly and Edmond Faral in the introductions to their respective editions of Villehardouin, see Faral's article cited in note 31 above.

and in any case hated the Greeks. The Venetians were also deeply concerned with the growing influence of Genoa at Byzantium.[44] Even before the Venetians had been cleared of treason, scholars were shifting the blame for the diversion to Philip of Swabia and Boniface of Montferrat: Philip's kinship with Isaac and the young Alexius, the traditional Norman-Hohenstaufen hostility toward Byzantium, Boniface's family claim to Thessalonica and honors in the Byzantine empire, and Boniface's loyalty to Philip were alleged to be the underlying motives. Innocent III too was declared to be involved in the secret diplomacy.

For so important a project as the diversion of the crusade to be carefully plotted in advance, all agree, one must shake Villehardouin's testimony that the young Alexius landed in Italy as late as August 1202, since, if he really arrived as late as that, there would have been no time to hatch the plot, Villehardouin is correct, and one must accept the *théorie du hasard.* As a matter of fact, however, we have a good deal of evidence tending to show that the young Alexius arrived in the west not in August 1202, but sometime in 1201. If this is accepted, a plot becomes highly plausible but not absolutely certain.[45]

[44] L. de Mas Latrie, *Histoire de l'île de Chypre,* I (Paris, 1861), 162–165, was the first to level the charge against the Venetians, basing it upon the accusation made by the anti-Venetian Syrian source, Ernoul (*Chronique,* pp. 344–346). See also R. Cessi, "Venezia e la quarta crociata," *Archivio veneto,* LXXXI (1952), 1–52. Karl Hopf, "Griechenland im Mittelalter und in der Neuzeit; Geschichte Griechenlands vom Beginn des Mittelalters bis auf unsere Zeit," *Allgemeine Enzyklopädie der Wissenschaften und Künste,* ed. J. S. Ersch and J. G. Gruber, section 1, part 85 (Leipzig, 1867), p. 188, and elsewhere dated the hypothetical treaty so positively in 1202 that it was assumed he had discovered the document; see also L. Streit, *Venedig und die Wendung des vierten Kreuzzugs gegen Konstantinopel* (Anklam, 1877). The decisive refutation of the charge came with the article by G. Hanotaux, "Les Vénitiens ont-ils trahi la chrétienté en 1202?" *Revue historique,* IV (1877), 74–102. But the myth persisted, and is often accepted by later writers, e.g. Alice Gardner, *The Lascarids of Nicaea* (London, 1912), p. 41. It is a surprise, however, to find it in Steven Runciman, *A History of the Crusades,* III (Cambridge, 1954), 113. For Venetian jealousy of Genoa, see J. K. Fotheringham, "Genoa and the Fourth Crusade," *The English Historical Review,* XXV (1910), 20–57.

[45] The first to put the blame on Philip and Boniface were E. Winkelmann, *Philipp von Schwaben,* I (Berlin, 1873), 296, 525 ff.; and P. Riant, "Innocent III, Philippe de Souabe, et Boniface de Montferrat," *Revue des questions historiques,* XVII (1875), 321–374, and XVIII (1875), 5–76. Supporting Villehardouin and the *théorie du hasard* in opposition to these scholars were V. Vasilievskii, "Kriticheski i bibliograficheski zametki," *Zhurnal Ministerstva Narodnago Prosvieshcheniya,* CCIV (1879), 337 ff.; J. Tessier, *La Quatrième croisade* (Paris, 1884); W. Norden, *Der vierte Kreuzzug im Rahmen der Beziehungen des Abendlandes zu Byzanz* (Berlin, 1898) and *Das Papsttum und Byzanz* (Berlin, 1903), pp. 152 ff.; and Kretschmayr, *Geschichte von Venedig,* I, 483. But P. Riant returned to the subject in another article, "Le Changement de direction de la quatrième croisade," *Revue des questions historiques,* XXIII (1878), 71–114, and reaffirmed his earlier arguments. W. Heyd, *Histoire du commerce du Levant,* tr. Furcy Raynaud, I (Leipzig, 1885, reprinted 1936), 265 ff., accepts the date 1201 for Alexius's appearance in the west. So also do P. Mitrofanov, "Izmienenie v napravlenii chetvertago krestovago pokhoda," *Vizantiiskii vremennik,* IV (1897), 461–523, and E. Gerland, "Der vierte Kreuzzug und seine Probleme," *Neue Jahrbücher für das klassische Altertum,*

The contemporary Byzantine historian, Nicetas Choniates, who is reliable, but whose chronology is often difficult to unravel, declares that Alexius III Angelus had freed his nephew, the young Alexius, from prison and taken him along on his campaign against a rebellious official, Manuel Camytzes, in 1201. Early in the campaign (1201), Nicetas says, the young Alexius fled the imperial camp, boarded a Pisan vessel (which had put into the Marmara port of Athyra ostensibly for ballast), escaped his uncle's agents by cutting his hair in western style and dressing in western clothes, and sailed away to the west, where, Nicetas knew, he turned to his sister Irene and her husband Philip of Swabia for help.[46] The *Gesta Innocentii* reports that Boniface of Montferrat visited Innocent in Rome, at a time *after* Boniface "was said to have discussed" with Philip of Swabia a plan to restore the young Alexius; with him he brought a letter from Philip Augustus, to which we have the reply, dated March 26, 1202.[47] This would push the alleged conversations between Boniface, Philip, and the young Alexius back to a date in 1201, certainly long before the summer of 1202, Villehardouin's date for the arrival of the young Alexius in the west.

Then too, Alexius III Angelus, who was of course fully conscious, once his nephew had escaped, of the danger that now threatened him, wrote to the pope, asking for assurances that he would not support Philip of Swabia and the young Alexius against him, and offering to negotiate for a union between the Greek and Latin churches, as the Byzantine emperors usually did when danger threatened. Innocent answered somewhat reassuringly in a letter dated November 16, 1202. He reminded Alexius III that papal policy opposed Philip of Swabia and supported his rival Otto IV for the German imperial throne. Innocent also referred, however, to a visit which the young Alexius had paid him in Rome; and in so doing used the word *olim* to describe the period elapsing since the visit had taken place. It has been cogently argued that the word

XIII (1904), 505–514, an excellent summary of previous scholarship. More emphasis is put on the role allegedly played by Innocent III in the works of F. Cerone, "Il Papa e i Veneziani nella quarta crociata," *Archivio veneto*, XXXVI (1888), 57–70 and 287–297, and J. Güldner, *Über die Versuche Papst Innocenz III. eine Union zwischen der abendländischen und morgenländischen Kirche herbeizuführen* (Tübingen, 1893). See also the two recent articles by the Soviet historian, M. A. Zaborov, "Papstvo i zakhvat Konstantinopolya krestonostsami v nachale XIII v.," *Vizantiiskii vremennik*, n.s., V (1952), 152 ff., and "K voprosu o predistorii chetvertogo krestovogo pokhoda," *ibid.*, n.s., VI (1953), 233 ff.

[46] Nicetas, *Historia*; *De Alexio Angelo*, III (*CSHB*), pp. 711 ff. For the convincing argument against Faral's dating, see H. Grégoire, "The Question of the Diversion of the Fourth Crusade," *Byzantion*, XV (1940–1941), 158–166.

[47] *Gesta*, chap. LXXXIII (*PL*, CCXIV, col. 132).

olim could not refer to anything as recent as August 1202, but must refer to a considerably longer period, as far back as 1201.[48] The *Annals* of Cologne also include a passage which may well date the young Alexius's arrival in the summer of 1201.[49] Finally, Robert of Clari tells us that in mid-December 1202 at Zara, Boniface of Montferrat, in a speech to the crusaders, told them that "last year at Christmas," that is, Christmas 1201, he had seen the young Alexius at the court of Philip of Swabia.[50]

When all these passages are taken together, they strongly suggest that Villehardouin was wrong about the date of the arrival of the young Alexius in the west, and that he had in fact been there since sometime in 1201, or long enough to have launched a plot with Boniface and Philip, and perhaps with the Venetians and the pope. But this is a long way from proving that such a plot was actually launched. Nor need we believe that Villehardouin deliberately lied about the time the young Alexius arrived. He may simply have erred. Moreover, he may be right, and the other evidence misleading. The problem of the diversion is still with us. Though scholars have not heeded a plea made half a century ago to give up trying to solve an insoluble problem,[51] the plea itself makes excellent sense. We are unlikely to be able to go beyond the statement that the diversion which occurred suited the interests of the young

[48] Innocent III, *Epp.*, an. v, no. 122 (*PL*, CCXIV, col. 1124); argument from the word "olim" originated and pressed very hard by Grégoire, *loc. cit.*, 165 f.

[49] *MGH, SS.*, XVII, 810, dealing with the consecration of archbishop Siegfried of Mainz in July 1201, and continuing: "Per idem tempus Alexius . . . venit in Alemanniam ad Phylippum regem sororium suum. . . ." Gerland, "Der vierte Kreuzzug und seine Probleme," p. 510, note 2, points out that there is some ambiguity as to *which* archbishop is meant, Mainz or Magdeburg; and that the date 1201 or 1202 hinges on this question. Faral and Cerone reject the passage; Usseglio (*I Marchesi di Monferrato*, II, 186 f.) refutes their arguments; Grégoire follows Usseglio. It seems likely that the passage really can be used to support the date 1201 for Alexius's journey.

[50] Ed. Lauer, p. 16; tr. McNeal, pp. 45–46.

[51] Luchaire, *Innocent III: La question d'orient* (Paris, 1907), p. 97: ". . . on ne saura jamais, et la science a vraiment mieux à faire qu'à discuter indéfiniment un problème insoluble." The references given above show that scholars did not take his word or his advice. In addition, see H. Vriens, "De Kwestie van den vierden Kruistocht," *Tijdschrift voor Geschiednis*, XXXV (1922), 50–82, and the new and most interesting review of the subject by A. Frolow, "La Déviation de la 4e croisade vers Constantinople," *Revue de l'histoire des religions*, CXLV (1954), 168–187; CXLVI (1954), 67–89, 194–219, who emphasizes the role played by the relics of Constantinople in the motivation of the crusaders. Nor have scholars ceased to take downright positions on the vexed question. See, for example, R. S. Lopez, *Cambridge Economic History*, II (Cambridge, 1952), 311: ". . . the Pope, the Venetians, and a number of feudal lords planned the Fourth Crusade as an expedition against the Byzantine Empire", and note 1: "The legend of a last-minute 'diversion' of the Crusade from the Holy Land to the Byzantine Empire is no longer tenable in the light of decisive Greek and Latin evidence." With such flat statements we must disagree: to us the evidence for a plot seems compelling but not decisive, while we find no evidence that the pope participated in it, though this does not rule out the possibility that he did: no evidence is what one would expect to find if the pope had plotted with the others.

Alexius and Isaac, Philip of Swabia and Boniface of Montferrat, and the Venetians, and that they may therefore have planned it.

Before the fleet sailed on October 1, 1202, Innocent III had learned of the plan to attack Zara. He had sent Peter Capuano to Venice, to accompany the crusaders to the east as papal legate. But the doge and his council, says the author of the *Gesta*, afraid that he would interfere with their wicked plan to attack Zara, told him bluntly that they would not accept him as a legate; he could come along as a preacher if he wished; if not, he could go back to Rome. Insulted, he returned and told Innocent about the proposed attack on a Christian city. The pope wrote instantly, sending the letter by the hand of abbot Peter of Locedio, forbidding the crusaders to attack any Christian city, and mentioning Zara specifically by name as a place in the hands of the king of Hungary, who had himself taken the cross. Peter Capuano also told the pope about the proposals to attack Constantinople on behalf of the young Alexius. Innocent's letter of November 16, 1202, to Alexius III Angelus, already referred to, assures the emperor that Philip of Swabia and the young Alexius had indeed sought to loose the crusading force against Constantinople, that the crusaders had then sent Peter Capuano to the pope to ask his advice, that — despite Alexius III's propensity for fine words and no action — the pope would not permit the attack, although, he said ominously, there were many of his cardinals who thought he ought to allow it because of the disobedience of the Greek church.

But the papal commands, however firmly intended, were disobeyed. During the first week of October 1202, the great fleet (from 200 to 230 ships, including sixty galleys, and the rest transports, some with special hatches for horses)[52] sailed out into the Adriatic. For more than a month it coasted along the Istrian and Dalmatian shores, putting in at various ports in an awesome demonstration of Venetian might. On November 10 it appeared off Zara. Quite probably because of papal warning of excommunication, Boniface had prudently stayed behind, and did not participate in the operations. It was after the landing at Zara that the disaffection that had been brewing in the host came into the open. Some of the barons belonging to the party that had opposed the attack on Zara from the beginning sent word to the defenders not to capitulate,

[52] On this fleet, in addition to the sources already named, see the letter of Hugh, count of St. Pol, written from Constantinople to the "duke of Louvain" (Henry, duke of Brabant and count of Louvain), in Tafel and Thomas, *Urkunden*, I, 304.

for the crusaders, they said, would not take part in the assault. At an assembly of the crusading leaders and the Venetians, abbot Guy of Les Vaux-de-Cernay arose and forbade the attack in the name of the pope. He was supported in his opposition by Simon of Montfort and a number of the high barons. The leaders, however, persuaded the majority of the crusaders that they were bound to help the Venetians capture the city, although Simon of Montfort with his followers withdrew some distance from the walls so as to have no part in the sinful action. After two weeks of siege and assault, Zara surrendered; the garrison and inhabitants were spared, but the crusaders and Venetians occupied the city, dividing the booty between them. By this time (November 24, 1202), it was too late to undertake the passage overseas, and the expedition wintered in Zara. Within three days a major riot broke out between French and Venetians, ending in many casualties.

In mid-December, Boniface of Montferrat arrived. Some two weeks later came envoys bearing proposals from Philip of Swabia and the young Alexius: if the armies would help Isaac Angelus and the young Alexius recover the Byzantine imperial throne, they would bring the empire back into submission to the papacy. Moreover, they would give 200,000 marks of silver, to be divided equally between the crusaders and the Venetians, and would also pay for provisions for the whole expedition for an additional year. The young Alexius would then join the crusade against the Saracens in person, if the leaders wanted him to do so, but in any case he would contribute an army of 10,000 Greeks, and would maintain at his own expense as long as he should live a garrison of 500 knights to serve in Syria in defense of the Holy Land.

At the headquarters of the Venetians, the doge and the leading barons heard this tempting offer. The next day, at a general assembly of the host, the lesser men heard the proposals for the first time. The majority of the rank and file clearly opposed further warfare against Christians, and, supported by some of the clergy, urged that the armies proceed directly to Palestine. Many of the important barons shared this view. But even the clergy was divided, some arguing, like the leaders — whose opinions Villehardouin reflects — that the only way to recover Jerusalem was to begin the war by the Byzantine adventure. Despite the divided opinion, the chiefs of the expedition, including Boniface, Baldwin of Flanders, Louis of Blois, Hugh of St. Pol, and others — fewer than twenty — signed the agreement accepting the offer of the young Alexius and pledging the host to intervention at Constantinople. The move did not end dissension. Many of the lesser people, suffering from hunger and other discomforts while the more important barons monopolized the army's resources, deserted during the winter, fleeing in merchant ships, some of which were lost at sea, or by land through Croatian territory, where the inhabitants massacred them. One group of nobles also departed, swearing that they would return after delivering messages in Syria; but they did not come back. A Flemish contingent, which had been proceeding by sea, arrived safely in Marseilles; although Baldwin commanded its leaders to make rendezvous with the main body off the coast of Greece, they went instead direct to Palestine. Simon of Montfort, Enguerrand of Boves, and other important barons also departed, having made arrangements with king Emeric of Hungary to permit them to pass through his Croatian territories, and thus regain Italy by marching along the shores of the Adriatic. These defections, Villehardouin reports bitterly, hurt the crusader forces seriously.

Those crusaders who had taken part in the attack on Zara, in defiance of the pope's specific commands, had automatically incurred excommunication. The leaders now first secured provisional absolution from the bishops in the host, and then sent a delegation to Rome to explain to Innocent how they had been unwillingly forced into the sin of disobedience, and to ask forgiveness. Eager not to jeopardize the success of the whole crusade, of which he still expected great things, the pope received the delegates kindly. He sent them back with a reproving letter, but not nearly so vigorous in its denunciation of the taking of Zara as one might have expected. After the guilty crusaders should have restored what they had taken illegally, and on condition that they commit no more such offenses, the pope agreed to absolve them.[53] The Venetians, however, could not be let off so easily. They had rebuffed Peter Capuano at Venice, had openly flouted Innocent's warning not to attack Zara, and had shown no signs of repentance. Though the envoys of the crusaders tried to dissuade the pope from excommunicating them, he would not accede. Indeed the papal emissary who brought the letter of absolution for the crusaders bore also a letter of excommunication for the doge and the Venetians. Boniface and his fellow barons, however, took it upon themselves to withhold this letter. They wrote the pope explaining that they had done so to prevent the dissolution of the crusade, and saying that they would deliver it if the pope should still insist.[54]

[53] Innocent III, *Epp.*, an. V, no. 162 (*PL*, CCXIV, cols. 1179 ff.), February 1203.
[54] Innocent III, *Epp.*, an. VI, nos. 99, 100 (*PL*, CCXV, cols. 103 ff.).

The surviving correspondence between pope and crusaders up to this point deals only with Zara. Yet the pope was well aware of the designs upon Constantinople; we have observed his reference to them in his letter of November 1202 to Alexius III. It was not until Innocent received Boniface's letter explaining the withholding of the papal ban from the Venetians that, in June 1203, he finally wrote commanding Boniface to deliver the letter of excommunication on pain of incurring a similar punishment himself, and flatly forbidding the attack on Constantinople.[55] By then it was too late. The fleet had left Zara before the letter was written, much less delivered. How far does the curious papal failure to condemn the diversion in time argue Innocent's complicity in a plot? Some modern historians believe that the pope was protesting "for the record", and had secretly endorsed the attack on Constantinople. The Greeks, from that day to this, have regarded Innocent as the ringleader in a plot. It seems more likely that Innocent rather allowed the diversion to happen. Perhaps he felt he could not prevent it. Moreover, it promised to achieve — though by methods he could not publicly endorse — one of the chief aims of his foreign policy, the union of the churches, and simultaneously to further a second aim, the crusade.

From Zara, most of the army sailed early in April 1203, Dandolo and Boniface remaining behind until the young Alexius could join them. Then they touched at Durazzo (Dyrrachium), where the population received the young Alexius as their emperor. The news that the great expedition had now been launched against him came direct from Durazzo to Alexius III in Constantinople, where bad naval administration had reduced the city's defenses to a pathetically low level. So fond was Alexius III of hunting that the imperial foresters would not permit the cutting of trees for ship-timber, while the admiral of the fleet, Michael Stryphnus, brother-in-law of the empress Euphrosyne, sold nails, anchors, and sails alike for money. Only about twenty rotten and worm-eaten vessels could now be hastily assembled.[56] Meanwhile the advance party of the crusaders had arrived in Corfu, where the inhabitants at first received them cordially. The arrival of the young Alexius, however, spurred the Corfiotes to attack the fleet in the harbor. In revenge, the armies devastated the island. It was already clear that the appearance of a Latin-sponsored claimant to the Byzantine imperial

[55] Innocent III, *Epp.*, an. V, no. 101 (*PL,* CCXV, col. 106).

[56] Nicetas, *Historia*; *De Alexio Angelo,* III (*CSHB*), p. 717.

throne — no matter how legitimate his claim — would arouse only hostility among Greeks.

At Corfu Alexius confirmed his agreements, and, in all probability, undertook to give Crete to Boniface. Here too, the leaders had to face new dissension. A large group of the barons — perhaps half of the total — who had opposed the diversion to Constantinople now withdrew from the host and set up camp by themselves, intending to send over to Brindisi and secure ships to take them direct to Syria. Boniface and the counts and a number of high barons, accompanied by the bishops and abbots and by the young Alexius, went to the camp of these "deserters", and besought them with tears not to break up the host in this way. Finally the recalcitrants yielded; they would stay with the expedition until Michaelmas (September 29), on the solemn assurance that at any time after that date, on two weeks' notice, they would be supplied with ships to transport them to Palestine.

Leaving Corfu on the eve of Pentecost (May 24, 1203), the fleet set sail for Constantinople. It skirted the Morea, entered the Aegean Sea, and made its first landing on the island of Euboea (Negroponte), whence some of the galleys and transports detoured to the island of Andros and forced the inhabitants to recognize young Alexius and pay him tribute. The rest of the ships proceeded to Abydus on the Asiatic shore at the mouth of the Dardanelles, and occupied it without resistance. Taking advantage of the spring harvest, the host took wheat on board. A week later, after the other vessels had come up, the reunited fleet passed through the Dardanelles and the Sea of Marmara, and anchored off the abbey of St. Stephen, seven miles south of Constantinople, now in full view. Having foraged on the Marmara islands, the fleet passed so close to the walls of the capital that some of the defenders opened fire. It then landed and disembarked men and horses at Chalcedon on St. John's day, June 24, just a month after the departure from Corfu. From Chalcedon the crusaders set out by land for Scutari (Chrysopolis), a league to the north, while the ships followed along the shore.

At Scutari, foraging parties raided the land around for provisions, and the crusaders had their first encounter with the armed forces of emperor Alexius III, when a scouting party of some eighty knights attacked and put to flight a much larger body of Greek troops that had been stationed to watch their movements. An envoy from Constantinople now arrived at the camp at Scutari with a message from the emperor. He demanded to know what they were doing in his land, since they were supposed to be on their way to recover the Holy Sepulcher; if they were in need, he would gladly give them provisions for their journey, but if they harbored any hostile intentions toward him or his empire, he would destroy them to a man. The crusader spokesman, Conon of Béthune, answered that Alexius III was a traitor and usurper, and demanded his surrender to his nephew, whom, Conon said, the crusaders would try to persuade to treat him gently.

After sending back this defiance, the leaders decided to appeal to the people of Constantinople to acknowledge their protégé. The galleys set out from the harbor of Scutari, one of them bearing the young Alexius, Boniface, and Dandolo, and sailed as close as they could to the sea walls, while those on board shouted out to the crowds thronging the shore and the walls that they were come to help the people of Constantinople overthrow their tyrant and restore their rightful lord. The demonstration failed, as the only response was a shower of missiles.

So the leaders now made preparations for an attack, mustering their forces (probably something over 10,000) in the plain outside Scutari in seven "battles" or divisions, each containing as far as possible men of the same region and each commanded by one of the counts or high barons. On July 5 the fleet crossed the Bosporus; the French repulsed a Byzantine force and made a landing at Galata, across the Golden Horn from Constantinople. The next day the French stormed and captured Galata's principal defense work, a great tower. The Venetian fleet broke the harbor chain that closed the opening of the Golden Horn, and moved in, sinking or capturing the few Byzantine galleys stationed there as a defending force.[57] They now wanted to concentrate the attack against the sea walls from the waters of the Golden Horn; but the French preferred to fight on land, and agreed to time their assault to coincide with the Venetian action. So the French forces now marched inland from Pera along the shore of the Golden Horn until they came to the little stream at its upper end. Over this they threw a bridge, then crossed and established their camp outside the land walls of the city near the Blachernae palace, at the angle between the land walls

[57] On the topography of Constantinople, see A. M. Schneider, *Byzanz*, Istanbuler Forschungen herausgegeben von der Abtheilung Istanbul des Archäologischen Instituts des deutschen Reiches, vol. VIII (Berlin, 1936); supplemented to some extent by R. Janin, *Constantinople byzantine*, Archives de l'orient chrétien, IV (Paris, 1950). The treatment of A. Van Milligen, *Byzantine Constantinople: The Walls of the City and Adjoining Historical Sites* (London, 1899) is still valuable for its special subject. The large map of the land walls by "Misn" (Nomides), *Χάρτης τῶν χερσαίων τείχων τῆς μεσαιωνικῆς Κωνσταντινουπόλεως* (Constantinople, 1945) is also extremely useful.

and the walls of the Golden Horn. The Venetian fleet moved up to the inner end of the harbor, and maintained contact, preparing scaling ladders and siege artillery, and building platforms high up on the spars of their galleys. Repeated Byzantine sorties kept the land forces engaged, and necessitated the building of palisades around the camp. It was ten days before the preparations for the assault were complete.

It came on July 17. The Varangian guard of English and Danes successfully defended with swords and axes the section of wall chosen by the French crusaders, but the Venetians, with the blind old Dandolo waving the banner of St. Mark in the foremost galley and shouting at his forces, beached their galleys below the sea walls, and with scaling ladders seized first one tower and then another until they held twenty-five along the sea wall, and actually were capturing horses within the walls and sending them to the crusader forces by boat. For defense against the vastly superior Byzantine forces, they set fire to the buildings inside the walls, destroying the whole neighborhood utterly and beginning the tragic ruin of the city. Meanwhile Alexius III with a huge army made a sortie against the crusader battalions attacking the land walls. Wisely refusing to break ranks, the crusaders drew up before their camp, and awaited an onslaught which, in the end, failed to materialize; Alexius III approached close, but then withdrew. At the news of the Byzantine sortie, Dandolo ordered his forces to withdraw from the towers they held, and the Venetians now joined the French. Despite the temporary lodgment of the Venetians on the walls, the action as a whole had failed.

But that night Alexius III fled with his daughter Irene and his jewels to Mosynopolis, a Thracian town. Abandoned, the Byzantine officials released Isaac from prison and restored him to office, sending messengers before dawn to inform the Latins of their action. The wary host sent four representatives, two Frenchmen and two Venetians, to investigate the truth of the report. Through the open gate and between the lines of the axe-bearing Varangians, Villehardouin and his three colleagues came into the Blachernae and the presence of Isaac Angelus. They required him to ratify the obligations which the young Alexius had assumed toward the crusading army, and returned with the proper chrysobull, reluctantly granted. Then the Byzantines opened the city to the entire crusading force, which escorted the young Alexius into the capital. The next day the Latins yielded to the urgent request of Isaac and Alexius to take their forces out of Constantinople proper, in order to avoid a riot, and to lodge them across the Golden Horn in the Jewish suburb of Estanor, now Pera. The object of the expedition attained, the Latins became wide-eyed tourists amid the marvels of Byzantium, wondering at the sacred relics, buying briskly from the Greeks. On August 1, 1203, the young Alexius was crowned co-emperor.[58]

Late in August 1203 the leaders sent to the pope and the monarchs of the west an official circular letter, explaining their decision to go to Constantinople, recounting their experiences since their departure from Zara, announcing the postponement of the attack on Egypt until the spring, and summoning crusading Europe to join the host there in glorious deeds against the "infidel". This letter was apparently the first word Innocent III had had from the expedition since it had left Zara in April. He also received an accompanying letter from Alexius IV, dated August 23, in which the newly elected emperor assured the pope of his filial devotion and of his firm intention to bring the Greek church back into obedience to Rome.[59] Not until February 1204 did the pope reply, reproving the leaders for their disobedience, and commanding them to proceed at once with all their forces to the rescue of the Holy Land. He conjured young Alexius to fulfill his promise in respect to the Greek church, and warned him that, unless he did so, his rule could not endure. To the doge of Venice, who apparently had sent a conciliatory message, he recalled the Venetians' persistent disobedience, and admonished him not to forget his vows as a crusader. He wrote also to the French clergy in the host commanding them to see to it that the leaders did penance for their misdeeds and carried out their professed good intentions.[60] By the time the pope's admonitions and instructions arrived, the dizzy pace of events in Constantinople had presented Christendom with a startling new development.

In the months between August 1203 and March 1204 relations rapidly deteriorated between the crusading armies and the emperors they had restored. Alexius IV began to pay instalments on his debt of 200,000 marks to the crusaders, who in turn paid off their own debt to the Venetians and reimbursed the knights who had paid passage money from Venice. But the leaders once more postponed departure for Palestine, as Alexius IV begged them to

[58] Hereafter we refer to him as Alexius IV.

[59] Innocent III, *Epp.*, an. VI, no. 210 (from Alexius) and 211 (from the crusaders) (*PL*, CCXV, cols. 236–240). Cf. the letter from Hugh of St. Pol in Tafel and Thomas, *Urkunden*, I, 304.

[60] Innocent III, *Epp.*, an. VI, nos. 229–232 (*PL*, CCXV, cols. 259 ff.); an. VII, no. 18 (*ibid.*, cols. 301 ff.); Potthast, *Regesta*, nos. 2122–2125, 2136.

delay until the following March (1204) in order that he might have time to raise the rest of the money he owed them. So greatly did the Greeks hate him, because he had won restoration through a Latin army, that he declared he feared for his life. He hoped, however, to make himself secure within the next seven months. Meanwhile he promised to pay for the Venetian fleet for an additional year, and asked the crusaders to renew their own agreement with the Venetians. The leaders agreed, but when the news became known, those who at Corfu had opposed the entire venture demanded ships for immediate passage to Syria, and were with difficulty persuaded to stay.

While Alexius IV was out of Constantinople with some of the Latins on an imperial progress to receive homage, to assert his sovereignty over disloyal territory, and to try to capture his uncle Alexius III, tension ruled in the city. The Greek clergy were vigorously resisting Alexius' efforts to effect a union with Rome, and smoldered with resentment at his melting down church vessels to get money to pay the Latins. Bitter hatred swept the Greeks at the sight of their new emperor fraternizing with the hated Latins. Greeks pillaged the old quarters of the established Latin merchants. Latins burned down a mosque, and probably started a great conflagration, which lasted a week, endangered Hagia Sophia, did vast damage, and killed many people. To avoid a massacre, the remaining resident Latins took their families and as much as they could of their property, and crossed the harbor to join the crusaders. On his return, Alexius IV changed his attitude towards the Latins, stopped visiting their camp, gave them only token payments, and began to put them off with excuses. In November 1203 a six-man delegation, three French and three Venetian, delivered an ultimatum to Isaac and Alexius. Relations now degenerated into war.

Twice the Greeks sent fire-ships in the harbor down against the Venetian fleet in a determined but unsuccessful effort to burn it. By now a conspiracy had been hatched inside the city against the pro-Latin Alexius IV.[61] At its head was the son-in-law of Alexius III, a Ducas also named Alexius, known as Mourtzouphlus because his bushy eyebrows met.[62] Late in January 1204 a mob in Hagia Sophia told the senate and the high clergy that they would no longer be ruled by the Angeli. An unwilling youth, Nicholas

[61] The only full account of these events is in Nicetas, *Historia*; *De Isaacio Angelo et Alexio filio* (*CSHB*), pp. 741 ff. See also *Devastatio*, ed. Hopf, p. 91; Novgorod chronicle, ed. Hopf, pp. 94–95; and the letter of Baldwin of Flanders to the pope in Tafel and Thomas, *Urkunden*, I, 502–503.

[62] Mourtzouphlus had participated in an abortive palace revolution against Alexius III Angelus as far back as 1201, when he was already leader of an anti-Latin faction. It lasted only a day, and was put down. Mourtzouphlus's "front man" on the earlier occasion was a

Canabus, was put forward and chosen emperor. Alexius IV appealed to the crusaders to occupy the Blachernae and give him protection, but chose as envoy Mourtzouphlus himself, the leading spirit of the conspiracy. Shedding the cloak of deceit, Mourtzouphlus came out into the open, seized the throne late in January, and early in February imprisoned and probably executed Canabus; strangled Alexius IV with a bowstring; possibly murdered Isaac, who in any case soon died; and seized the throne. Alexius V Ducas Mourtzouphlus, a great-great-grandson of Alexius I Comnenus, thus came to power as the avowed leader of the passionately anti-Latin populace. Warfare between the Greeks and the Latins continued. Alexius V restored the sea walls and added new wooden defenses; he took personal command of his troops and in one sharp skirmish against Henry, brother of Baldwin of Flanders, suffered defeat and lost a celebrated icon he was using as a standard.

The leaders of the crusade now decided to take Constantinople for a second time, acting on their own behalf. In March 1204 Dandolo, acting for Venice, and Boniface, Baldwin, Louis of Blois, and Hugh of St. Pol. acting for the non-Venetians, concluded a new treaty regulating their behavior after the city should have fallen.[63] All booty was to be piled up in one place. The Venetians would receive three quarters of it up to the amount needed to pay the remaining debt owed them by the crusaders, while the non-Venetians would receive one quarter. Anything over and above the amount of the debt would be evenly divided between the two parties, but if the total should be insufficient to pay the debt, the non-Venetians would none the less receive one quarter. Food would be divided equally. Venice would retain all titles and property, lay and ecclesiastical, previously held in the Byzantine empire, and all privileges, written and unwritten.

Twelve electors, six Venetians and six non-Venetians, would then proceed to elect a Latin emperor. He would have one quarter of the empire, including the two Byzantine imperial palaces, Blachernae and Boukoleon. The remaining three quarters would be divided evenly between Venetians and non-Venetians. The clergy of the

certain John Comnenus. The most important source is the "Logos Aphegematikos" of Nicholas Mesarites, ed. A. Heisenberg, *Nikolaos Mesarites: Die Palastrevolution des Joannes Komnenos*, Programm des k. alten Gymnasiums zu Würzburg für das Studienjahr 1906–1907 (Würzburg, 1907); see also Nicetas, *Historia*; *De Alexio Angelo*, III (*CSHB*), pp. 697 ff.; his encomium of Alexius III in C. Sathas, *Μεσαιονικὴ Βιβλιοθήκη*, I (Venice, 1872), 84–89; *Nicephori Chrysobergae ad Angelos Orationes* (ed. M. Treu, Breslau, 1892), pp. 1–72. Eudocia, daughter of Alexius III, was successively married to Stephen I of Serbia (who divorced her), Alexius V Mourtzouphlus, and Leo Sgourus of Corinth.

[63] Text in Tafel and Thomas, *Urkunden*, I, 444 ff.

party to which the emperor did not belong, would then have the right to name a cathedral chapter for Hagia Sophia, which in turn would choose a patriarch. Each party would name clergy for its own churches. The conquerors would give to the church only as much of the Greek churches' property as would enable the clergy to live decently. All church property above and beyond this minimum would be divided with all the other booty.

Both parties agreed to remain in the east for one year to assist the new Latin empire and emperor; thereafter, all who might remain would take an oath to the emperor, and would swear to maintain all previous agreements. Each party would select a dozen or more representatives to serve on a mixed commission to distribute fiefs and titles among the host, and to assign the services which the recipients would owe the emperor and empire. Fiefs would be hereditary, and might pass in the female line; their holders might do what they wished with their own, saving the rights of the emperor and the military service owed to him. The emperor would provide all forces needful beyond those owed by his feudatories. No citizen of a state at war with Venice might be received during such a war in the territory of the empire. Both parties pledged themselves to petition the pope to make all violations of the pact punishable by excommunication. The emperor must swear to abide by all agreements between the parties. If any amendment to the present agreement should be thought desirable, it might be made at the discretion of the doge and six councillors, acting together with Boniface and six councillors. The doge would not be bound by any oath to render service to the emperor for any fief or title assigned to him, but all those to whom the doge might assign such fiefs or titles would be bound by oath to render all due service to the emperor as well.

The provisions of this pact of March 1204 foreshadow the future problems of the Latins at Constantinople. Though crusaders and Venetians clearly regarded their operations as a raid for plunder, they nevertheless proposed to found a new state on the very ground they intended to ravage. The future emperor would have only a quarter of the empire; the doge, who would take no oath to him, would have three eighths. Though the doge's own vassals would owe military service, the doge himself would not. The emperor would have to supply all necessary troops and equipment beyond what might be furnished by the feudatories. Yet he himself would not even participate in the distribution of fiefs or the assignment of obligations. Before the first Latin emperor of

Constantinople was even chosen, his fellow-Latins had made it certain that he would be a feudal monarch with insufficient resources and little power. The Venetian establishment in former Byzantine territory, however, was greatly strengthened. No longer dependent upon grants from successive Byzantine emperors, the Venetians had "constitutionally" excluded their enemies from competition. Laymen had disposed, in advance, of the most important ecclesiastical office, and had virtually secularized church property. Taken together with subsequent Venetian behavior, the treaty of March 1204 indicates that Dandolo had little interest in the title of emperor, and was ready to let the crusaders take the post for one of their own candidates, in exchange for the commercial and ecclesiastical supremacy.

This agreement made, the Venetians busied themselves with getting the fleet ready for action. This time a combined force of crusaders and Venetians operating from the ships would launch the assault against the sea walls on April 9. At daybreak the fleet stood out across the harbor on a front a half league long, with the great freighters interspersed between the galleys and the horse transports. The freighters were brought as close to the wall as possible and the flying bridges swung out to reach the tops of the towers, while some of the troops disembarked and tried to scale the walls from the ground. On this day the assault failed and after several hours of desperate fighting the assailants gave up the attempt, reëmbarked on the vessels, and returned to the camp across the harbor. On April 12th they renewed the attack. With a strong wind at its back the fleet crossed the harbor and made for the same section of the wall. The great freighters were able to grapple their flying bridges onto the tops of a few of the towers and the troops swarmed over and drove off the defenders. Others landed, scaled the walls, and broke down the gates from inside. The horses were led ashore from the transports; the knights mounted and rode through the gates. The Greeks retreated farther within the city, and the assailants consolidated their hold on the section in front of the wall they had taken. During the night some of the Germans in the division of the marquis, fearing an attack, set fire to the buildings in front of them, and a new conflagration raged through that part of the city, to add to the terrors of the populace.

That night the crusaders and Venetians slept on their arms, expecting to have to renew the fighting in the morning. In fact, however, Mourtzouphlus had fled the city, and the Latins entered, meeting no further resistance. For three days they indulged in excesses which the Greeks have not forgotten to this day, and which Innocent III himself bitterly condemned when he heard of them. The Latins defiled Greek sanctuaries, murdered and raped, stole and destroyed the celebrated monuments of the capital. The historian Nicetas Choniates wrote a separate treatise on the statues which had perished in the terror.[64] When it was over, Boniface of Montferrat ordered all booty brought in for division. Many risked execution in an effort to keep what they had already seized, and much was doubtless concealed. But what was turned in yielded 400,000 marks and 10,000 suits of armor. The humbler knights resented the greed of the leaders, who took all the gold and silk and fine houses for themselves, leaving the poorer men only the plain silver ornaments, such as the pitchers which the Greek ladies of Constantinople had carried with them to the baths. Sacred relics shared the fate of profane wealth. The Fourth Crusade had come a long way from Écry, and now terminated without having encountered a single armed Moslem.

Indeed, we may regard the momentous events of 1203–1204 as the culmination of an assault of the Latin west upon the Byzantine east that had been intermittently under way for more than a century. Boniface of Montferrat, as ally of Philip of Swabia, had inherited the anti-Byzantine ambitions of Robert Guiscard, Bohemond, the Norman kings of Sicily, and their Hohenstaufen heir, Henry VI, as well as the claims of his own elder brothers, Conrad and Renier. Dandolo was avenging the Byzantine massacre of the Latin residents of Constantinople in 1182, the mass arrest of the Venetians by Manuel Comnenus in 1171 (the bills for this affair had never been settled), and possibly early injuries to himself; these episodes had in turn sprung out of the natural mutual hatred between the Greek population and the pushing, rowdy, shrewd, and successful Italian interlopers in Constantinople, whose privileges and possessions in the capital dated back to the chrysobull of Alexius I of 1082. In the French and German barons of 1204 we may see the successors of all those hosts of crusaders that had poured through Constantinople, with an envious eye to its wealth and a scornful distaste for its inhabitants, since the days of Godfrey of Bouillon, or Louis VII, or Frederick Barbarossa. The sword that had hung precariously over the heads of the Byzantines for so long had fallen at last.

[64] See Innocent's letter, an. VIII, no. 133 (*PL*, CCXV, cols. 710–714); Nicetas's treatise is to be found on pp. 854–868 of the volume of *CSHB* containing his history. See the famous paraphrase of the passages of Nicetas's history in Gibbon's account of the sack.

8. The Balkans in 1216, at the Death of the Latin Emperor Henry (*Map by the University of Wisconsin Cartographic Laboratory*)

VI

THE LATIN EMPIRE OF CONSTANTINOPLE, 1204–1261

On April 13, 1204, the fifth day of the second siege, the crusaders and Venetians took Constantinople. When order had been

Our excellent narrative sources for the Fourth Crusade, both western and Byzantine, break off not long after the foundation of the Latin empire. Villehardouin's account stops with events of the year 1207; Robert of Clari records one event as late as 1216, but after the year 1205 he is writing from hearsay only; Nicetas Choniates closes his history in 1206. None of the narrative sources for the period of the Latin empire is in the same class as these. Villehardouin found his continuator for the years 1207–1209 in the Old French work of Henry of Valenciennes, *Histoire de l'empereur Henri*, ed. and tr. N. de Wailly, in his edition of Villehardouin (Paris, 1874), pp. 304–420; ed. J. Longnon (Paris, 1948), in the Documents relatifs à l'histoire des croisades, publiés par l'Académie des Inscriptions et Belles Lettres. Ernoul continues to furnish information needing confirmation from other sources.

For the period 1220–1242, one must consult the vernacular *Chronique rimée de Philippe Mouskes* (ed. [F.] de Reiffenberg, Brussels, 1838), II, Collection de chroniques belges inédites; also *MGH, SS.*, XXVI (partial text only). The Old French *La Cronique des Vénéciens de Maistre Martin da Canal*, ed. F.-L. Polidori, *Archivio storico italiano*, VIII (1845), 229–798, gives important details, especially naval, from the Venetian point of view. A fourteenth-century Venetian chronicle preserving a good tradition is the Latin *Andreae Danduli chronicon* (*RISS*, XII; new ed., Bologna, 1939 ff.). Aubrey of Trois-Fontaines (*MGH, SS.*, XXIII) continues to be very useful. The work of the Dominican Simon of St. Quentin, which furnishes information on the Latins in Asia Minor unavailable elsewhere, is preserved in Vincent of Beauvais, *Biblioteca mundi* (Douai, 1624). For the complicated but useful Franciscan source material see G. Golubovich, *Biblioteca bio-bibliografica della Terra Santa e dell' Oriente Francescano*, 5 vols. (Quaracchi, 1906–1927); *idem*, "Disputatio Latinorum et Grecorum," *Archivum Franciscanum historicum*, XII (1919), 418–470; L. Wadding, *Annales Minorum*, 27 vols. (Quaracchi, 1931–1934). Three works of the fourteenth-century Venetian, Marino Sanudo (Torsello), are also useful: *Secreta fidelium crucis* (ed. J. Bongars, *Gesta Dei per Francos*, Hanover, 1611, II); *Istoria del regno di Romania* (ed. C. Hopf, *Chroniques gréco-romanes*, Berlin, 1873, pp. 99–170), the Italian version of a lost Latin original, dealing mostly with the Morea; and, short but very valuable, a supplement to Villehardouin (ed. Hopf, *ibid.*, pp. 171 ff.; ed. R. L. Wolff, "Hopf's So-called 'Fragmentum' of Marino Sanudo Torsello," *The Joshua Starr Memorial Volume*, Jewish Social Studies, publication V, New York, 1953, pp. 149–159).

The most important single Greek narrative source for the whole period 1204–1261 is *Georgii Acropolitae opera* (ed. A. Heisenberg, Leipzig, 1903, I), but this deals only occasionally with the Latins, and reveals a detailed knowledge of events only beginning with the 1240's. George Pachymeres, *De Michaele et Andronico Palaeologis, Libri XIII* (2 vols., *CSHB*, Bonn, 1835) is useful for the last years of the Latin occupation; Nicephorus Gregoras, *Byzantina historia* (3 vols., *CSHB*, Bonn, 1829–1855) is occasionally helpful. The Greek verse chronicle of the Morea (ed. J. Schmitt, London, 1904; ed. P. Kalonaros, Athens, 1940) also supplies an occasional detail, as do the French and Aragonese versions (see bibliographical note to chapter VII for full references). A. Heisenberg, "Neue Quellen zur Geschichte des lateinischen Kaisertums und der Kirchenunion," *Sitzungsberichte der Bayerischen Akademie der Wissenschaften*, Philosophisch-philologische und historische Klasse (Munich, 1922–1923), I, II, and III, published very important texts of the Greek archbishop of Ephesus, Nicholas Mesarites. M. A. Andréeva, "À propos de l'éloge de l'empereur Jean III Batatzès par son fils Théodore

restored, and the booty divided, attention turned to the choice of the first Latin emperor. As commander of the host, Boniface of

II Lascaris," *Annales de l'Institut Kondakov (Seminarium Kondakovianum)*, X (1938), 133–144, provides an interesting text.

The principal western documentary sources include the Venetian collections of R. Morozzo della Rocca and A. Lombardo (2 vols., Turin, 1940), as well as Tafel and Thomas, cited in the bibliographical note to chapter V, where the correspondence of Innocent III has also been referred to. For Honorius III, Innocent's successor, we have the incomplete work of P. Pressutti, *Regesta Honorii papae III* (2 vols., Rome, 1888, 1895); some complete texts of letters in *Honorii III Romani pontificis opera omnia* (ed. C. Horoy, Medii aevi biblioteca Patristica seu eiusdem temporis Patrologia, 4 vols., Paris, 1878–1880); and seven previously unpublished or partly published letters dealing with the Latin empire in R. L. Wolff, "Politics in the Latin Patriarchate of Constantinople, 1204–1261," *Dumbarton Oaks Papers*, VIII (1954), 225–303. For the popes who succeeded Honorius we have the splendid editions of the correspondence produced by the École française d'Athènes et de Rome: L. Auvray, *Les Registres de Grégoire IX* (3 vols., Paris, 1899–1910); E. Berger, *Les Registres d'Innocent IV* (4 vols., Paris, 1884–1910); and C. Bourel de la Roncière, *Les Registres d'Alexandre IV* (2 vols., Paris, 1902–1931). For important letters not in the registers, see K. Hampe, "Aus verlorenen Registerbänden der Päpste Innocenz III. und Innocenz IV.," *Mitteilungen des Instituts für Österreichische Geschichtsforschung*, XXIII (1902), 545–567; XXIV (1903), 198–237; F. Schillmann, "Zur byzantinischen Politik Alexanders IV.," *Römische Quartalschrift*, XXII (1908), part 4, 108–131; J. Van den Gheyn, "Lettre de Grégoire IX concernant l'empire latin de Constantinople," *ROL*, IX (1902), 230–234. The letters of the Latin emperors themselves are scattered; see *RHGF*, XVIII, 527 ff.; Tafel and Thomas, *Urkunden*, *passim*; P. Lauer, "Une lettre inédit d'Henri Ier d'Angre, empereur de Constantinople, aux prélats latins," *Mélanges offerts à M. Gustave Schlumberger*, I (Paris, 1924), 190 ff.; A. Teulet, *Layettes du trésor des chartes*, II, III (Paris, 1866), *passim*; [Jean] du Bouchet, *Histoire généalogique de la maison royale de Courtenay* (Paris, 1661), see the "Preuves"; and F. Dölger, *Facsimiles byzantinischer Kaiserurkunden* (Munich, 1931). Other indispensable collections of documentary sources are A. Theiner (ed.) *Vetera monumenta Slavorum meridionalium historiam illustrantia* (2 vols., Rome and Zagreb, 1863–1875), and *Vetera monumenta historica Hungariam sacram illustrantia* (2 vols., Rome, 1859–1860).

Greek documentary materials include V. Vasilievskii, "Epirotica saeculi XIII," *Vizantiiskii vremennik*, III (1896), 233–299, the correspondence of John Apocaucus, metropolitan of Naupactus (Lepanto); J. B. Pitra, *Analecta sacra et classica spicilegio solesmensi parata*, VI (Paris and Rome, 1891), the correspondence of Demetrius Chomatianus, metropolitan of Ochrida; J. B. Cotelerius [Cotelier], *Ecclesiae Graecae monumenta* (Paris, 1686), III. For a bibliography and discussion of the Greek and Latin lists of archbishoprics and bishoprics, see R. L. Wolff, "The Organization of the Latin Patriarchate of Constantinople," *Traditio*, VI (1948), 33–60.

Bulgarian materials bearing on the Latin empire include: M. G. Popruzhenko, "Sinodik Tsarya Borila," *Izvestiya Russkago arkheologicheskago instituta v Konstantinopolie*, V (1900); G. A. Ilinskii, "Gramota Tsarya Ioanna Asienya II," *ibid.*, VII (1902), 25–39; F. I. Uspenskii, "O drevnostyakh goroda Tyrnova," *ibid.*, 1–24; M. Lascaris, *Vatopedskata gramota na Tsar Ivan Asienya II* (Sofia, 1930); V. N. Zlatarski, "Asienoviyat Nadpis pri Stanimaka," *Izvestiya na Bulgarskoto arkheologichesko druzhestvo*, II (1911), 231–247.

Among secondary works, there are only three full-scale treatments of the Latin empire in print, of which two, though still useful, have been superseded. These are C. du F. du Cange, *Histoire de l'empire de Constantinople sous les empereurs français* (1st edition, Paris, 1657; 2nd edition, ed. J. A. Buchon, 2 vols., Paris, 1826); and the pages (67 ff. and 246 ff.) in Hopf's "Griechenland im Mittelalter . . . ," cited above in the notes to chapter V. J. Longnon, *L'Empire latin de Constantinople et la principauté de Morée* (Paris, 1949) provides a consecutive modern treatment. E. Gerland, *Geschichte des lateinischen Kaiserreiches von Konstantinopel* (Homburg v.d. Höhe, 1905) contains only the first part of a study that was never completed, and covers only the years 1204–1216, for which it is excellent. L. Santifaller, *Beiträge zur Geschichte des lateinischen Patriarchats von Konstantinopel* (Weimar, 1938) deals with five surviving documents of the Latin patriarchs, and with the development of the Latin cathedral chapter of Hagia Sophia; see the review by J. Longnon, *Journal des Savants* (1941), pp. 174 ff., printing two new documents.

Montferrat expected to be elected. He occupied the imperial palace of the Boukoleon, reserved by treaty for the successful candidate, and consented to leave it only under pressure of public opinion aroused by the doge. Moreover, Boniface had perhaps already married, and was certainly engaged to marry, Margaret ("Maria"), widow of emperor Isaac II Angelus and sister of king Emeric of Hungary, an alliance surely designed to lend legitimacy to his imperial claims. Even the Greeks of Constantinople, reduced as they now were to those women, children, old men, and members of the lower classes who had not been able to flee the invaders, expected that Boniface would be their new ruler, and when they met a Latin on the street would try to curry favor with him by holding up two fingers in the shape of a cross, saying mournfully "Aiios phasileos marchio", the sacred emperor the marquis.[1]

But Boniface found himself unable to name all six of the crusader electors to the twelve-man commission, and in the end the crusaders picked six churchmen, only three of whom favored Boniface. This sealed his fate, since the six electors chosen by the Venetians, all laymen, unanimously opposed him; the doge did not propose to allow the selection of an old ally of the Genoese. To a man the six Venetians therefore favored count Baldwin of Flanders and Hainault,[2] who also had the support of three of the crusader electors. Boniface's supporters gave up, and joined the others in announcing the unanimous election of Baldwin, at midnight on May 9, 1204. Though bitterly disappointed, Boniface did homage to Baldwin, who was crowned on May 16 at a solemn ceremony in Hagia Sophia by the assembled bishops of the crusading armies acting together, in the absence of a Latin patriarch. The Latins, who had witnessed the coronation of Alexius IV Angelus less than a year earlier, copied Byzantine ceremonial; Baldwin wore the sacred purple boots, and jeweled eagles on his mantle. He and his

[1] Gunther of Pairis, *Historia constantinopolitana* (ed. P. Riant, Geneva, 1875), p. 53. For the sack, which lasted for the three days following the capture, see above, chapter V, pp. 184–185.

[2] Later Venetian tradition as preserved in the still unpublished chronicle of Nicholas Trevisano records a different version of the election: that on the first ballot all six Venetian electors voted for the doge, and all six crusaders for Baldwin; and that then the Venetian Octavian Querini changed his vote, saying that, if the doge should be elected emperor, all the knights from beyond the Alps would desert the empire, and it would be empty and so crushed. Though very interesting, this account of events cannot be accepted unconfirmed, in the face of the general agreement among other sources that the doge never wanted the office of emperor for himself or any other Venetian. But in the reasoning attributed to Octavian Querini by Nicholas Trevisano we may perhaps catch an echo of the doge's own thinking. For the text see F. Thiriet, "Les Chroniques vénétiennes de la Marciana et leur importance pour l'histoire de la Romanie gréco-vénétienne," *Mélanges d'archéologie et d'histoire*, École française de Rome, LXVI (1954), 265.

successors called themselves "Porphyrogenitus, semper Augustus", signed imperial documents in sacred cinnabar ink using Greek letters, and bestowed an occasional Greek title (such as *protovestiarios*, chamberlain) upon their followers. But most of their household retained the familiar western names (seneschal, marshal, butler, constable). Despite the external trappings associated with the divinely ordained power of the Byzantine autocrat, the Latin emperor remained a western feudal ruler, whose power had been sharply limited before he had even been chosen.

The crusader-Venetian treaty of March 1204, which had laid down the procedure for the election of the Latin emperor, had allotted to him, besides the two Byzantine imperial palaces in the capital, only one quarter of the empire. The remaining three quarters were to be divided between the Venetians and the non-Venetian crusaders. The doge himself would take no oath to render service to the emperor, but the doge's vassals would be required to do so. Nor would the emperor participate in the distribution of fiefs; a mixed commission of crusaders and Venetians would have this responsibility, although it would be the emperor who would have to find all necessary troops and equipment beyond what the feudatories might furnish.

The barons had set aside Asia Minor and the Morea (Peloponnesus) as a consolation prize for the unsuccessful candidate for the throne. But Boniface asked instead for the "kingdom of Thessalonica". No doubt he was pursuing the family claim, but he probably also wanted lands bordering on those of his new brother-in-law, the king of Hungary. Boniface's demand precipitated a dangerous quarrel with Baldwin, who disregarded the marquis's request that he not enter Thessalonica, and even issued an imperial edict confirming its traditional Byzantine municipal privileges. In revenge, Boniface asked the Greeks of Adrianople to accept as emperor one of his two young step-sons, children of Isaac Angelus by Margaret of Hungary. Open warfare in Thrace between the two crusader leaders threatened the entire Latin position in the area. Only pressure from the doge and the barons eventually induced Boniface and Baldwin to submit their dispute to arbitration. A joint "parlement" of crusaders and Venetians then awarded Thessalonica to Boniface. Venetian support for the marquis was probably procured by his sale to the doge of the island of Crete, long ago promised to Boniface by Alexius IV. Thus Venice thwarted its chief enemy, Genoa, whose representatives were also negotiating for Crete.

The establishment of the kingdom of Thessalonica and the Venetian purchase of Crete were the initial features of a new territorial settlement. In October 1204 came a wholesale division of Byzantine territory, set forth in a second major treaty, the work of twenty-four commissioners, twelve Venetians and twelve non-Venetians.[3] This pact divided the Byzantine empire into three major shares: one for the Latin emperor (presumably one quarter), and one each for the Venetians and the non-Venetian crusaders, presumably three eighths apiece. The portion of each beneficiary was then further subdivided into a share near Constantinople and a share more remote.

Near the capital, the emperor received a small, roughly triangular piece of territory, the easternmost extension of Thrace, including Constantinople itself, a strip of Black Sea coast running as far north as Agathopolis, and a strip of Marmara coast-line running almost as far west as Heraclea. The Venetians received the remaining coast-line of the Marmara from Heraclea almost to the end of the Gallipoli peninsula, and a strip of territory extending inland to include Adrianople. The non-Venetian crusaders got the tip of the Gallipoli peninsula, and land in Thrace on both sides of the Venetian corridor from the Marmara to Adrianople: south of the corridor their holdings extended west along the Aegean to the boundary of the kingdom of Thessalonica (the Maritsa); north of the corridor the crusaders got a small enclave between the imperial and Venetian territories.

Far from the capital, the emperor received Asia Minor and the Aegean islands of Lemnos, Lesbos, Chios, Scyros, Samos, Samothrace, and Tenos. Venice received the entire east coast of the Adriatic, including places deep in the interior of Albania and Epirus, the Ionian islands, the entire Morea, both shores of the Gulf of Corinth, Salamis, points at both ends of Euboea (the island of Negroponte), Aegina, and the Aegean island of Andros. The crusaders received Macedonia between the Vardar river and

[3] The text is in Tafel and Thomas, *Urkunden*, I, 464–501, also a useful introduction and geographical commentary; see also G. L. F. Tafel, "Symbolarum criticarum geographiam Byzantinam spectantium partes duae: II," *Abhandlungen der historischen Klasse der k. Bayerischen Akademie der Wissenschaften*, V (1848); W. Tomaschek, "Zur Kunde der Hämus-Halbinsel," *Sitzungsberichte der Wiener Akademie der Wissenschaften*, XCIX (1882), 437–507, and CXIII (1886), 285–373; and "Zur historischen Topographie von Kleinasien im Mittelalter," *ibid.*, CXXIV (1891), section 8; K. von Spruner and T. Menke, *Handatlas für die Geschichte des Mittelalters und der neueren Zeit* (Gotha, 1880), pp. 40–41; further commentary in L. de Thalloczy, C. Jireček, and E. de Šufflay, *Acta et diplomata res Albaniae mediae aetatis illustrantia*, I (Vienna, 1913), 41 ff.; and D. A. Zakythinos, "*Μελέται περὶ τῆς διοικητικῆς διαιρέσεως καὶ τῆς ἐπαρχικῆς διοικήσεως ἐν τῷ Βυζαντινῷ κράτει,*" *Ἐπετηρὶς τῆς Ἑταιρείας τῶν Βυζαντινῶν Σπουδῶν*, XXI (1951), 179–217; XXII (1952), 159–182.

Lake Prespa, Thessaly, including the commercially valuable Gulf of Volos, and Attica. Though the text of the treaty awarded them also "Dodecanisos", this does not refer to the islands we now call the Dodecanese, nor to the Cyclades (Naxos, Paros, Delos, etc.) but to the island of Ahil in Little Prespa Lake in Macedonia.[4] The Cyclades not specifically mentioned in the treaty seem to have remained temporarily unassigned. Nor did the treaty mention the region between the Maritsa and the Vardar rivers. This was to be the area of Boniface's new kingdom of Thessalonica. Most of the lands thus lightheartedly allotted remained to be conquered; the Latins were presumptuous indeed, though not as presumptuous as Nicetas Choniates, patriotic Greek observer, accuses them of being; Lydia, Persia, and the Caucasus, which Nicetas in his bitter hyperbole declares they parceled out, do not appear in the text of the partition treaty of October 1204.

After it had been signed, Baldwin awarded many fiefs. We know that his brother Henry obtained Adramyttium in Asia Minor, Peter of Bracieux "another kingdom toward Iconium", Louis of Blois the "duchy" of Nicaea, and Stephen of Perche a "duchy of Philadelphia". In the European sector, a knight of Hainault, Renier of "Trit" (Trith-St. Léger), received Philippopolis (Plovdiv), up the Maritsa in Bulgarian territory. Hugh of St. Pol obtained the Thracian city of Demotica. Each fief was evaluated at so many knights' fees, the basic unit being land worth 300 *livres* of Anjou. Census-takers went out to inquire into the local revenue.

The partition treaty and the award of fiefs marked the official establishment of Latin feudal practices on Byzantine soil. Yet the western system had already been introduced in all its essentials by the Byzantines themselves. Though not hereditary and not subject to subinfeudation, the *pronoia* was in all other respects a fief, and the Byzantine peasants serfs. There is much evidence that in the countryside the Greeks were at first willing to accept their new masters. At Philippopolis they welcomed Renier of Trit and took him as their lord. At Thebes the people hailed Boniface of Montferrat "like one who had just returned from a long absence". In Asia Minor the people of Lopadium, with crosses and bibles, came forth to meet Peter of Bracieux, and at Adramyttium the local

[4] This identification, long ago suggested by Tafel ("Symbolarum . . .", p. 127), has not always been accepted; indeed the suggestion is usually ignored. The author of this chapter feels that explorations of Lake Prespa, made since Tafel wrote, strikingly confirm his identification; see especially I. Ivanov, "Tsar Samuilovata Stolitsa v Prespa," *Izvestiya na Bulgarskoto arkheologichesko druzhestvo*, I (1910), 55–80. The term "Dodecanisos" refers to a church of the twelve apostles, which had become the most important on the island, and by whose name it had become known.

peasants freely brought in their crops to Baldwin's brother Henry, and supplied him and his men with food. It was Latin greed and mistreatment — the Latin sources themselves assure us — that turned the Greek peasants against their new lords, who in many instances proved worse than their old ones. Indeed, the Greeks often found their former Byzantine master confirmed in his lands by the conquerors. Despite the violent mutual antipathy between Latins and Greeks in general, a certain sense of common interest in some instances drew the nobles of both sides together.

The constitution of the curious new hybrid Latin state, developed in the two treaties of March and October 1204, received its finishing touches within the next two years. When the aged Enrico Dandolo died in May 1205, the Venetians in Constantinople, without waiting for word from home, assembled and elected as their chief a certain Marino Zeno, who took the new title of podestà and *dominator* of one quarter and one half of a quarter of "Romania". Zeno surrounded himself with an administration modeled on that at Venice: judges of the commune, councillors, a chamberlain. He issued an edict forbidding any Venetian in the empire to dispose of property except to another Venetian. So independent was Zeno's behavior that the authorities at home grew concerned lest their colonists might intend insubordination. Renier Dandolo, who had been acting as vice-doge in Venice during his father's absence, demanded and received reassurances. Zeno wrote him that he had never intended to challenge the authority of Venice, and added that the Venetians at Constantinople would accept as podestà any appointee whom the authorities at home might send.

After the election of Peter Ziani as doge (August 1205), he required Zeno to cede to Venice the area along the Epirote coast assigned in the partition treaty to the doge. This strategic region, still to be conquered, was thus to be placed directly under the control of the Venetian home authorities. A further edict of Ziani empowered any citizen of Venice or an allied state to conquer any of the Aegean islands or territory formerly Byzantine, and to pass on his conquests to his heirs. The edict does not mention the Venetian colony or podestà at Constantinople. Thus in two sharp actions Ziani limited the power of the outpost and reasserted that of the mother city. The grandiose title of *dominator* over a quarter and half of a quarter of Romania shortly passed from the podestà at Constantinople to the doge himself.

In 1207 Ziani replaced Zeno with a new podestà, and thereafter the doges regularly sent the podestàs out from Venice, requiring each of them first to take an oath[5] to support and uphold the honor of Venice, to obey all commands from the doge and his council, to act as a just civil and criminal judge, to engage in no diplomatic correspondence without the consent of his council, to distribute property of the commune only with the consent of his council, and to pay his own debts while not exacting more than the services due him. His term was to be a short one, as a further precaution against his assuming too much power. Despite the large gaps in our records we know of sixteen different podestà-ships during the years between Zeno's replacement in 1207 and the expulsion of the Latins in 1261. In every important crisis we find the podestà acting as chief of the Venetian colony and as faithful agent of the doge.

While Zeno was still podestà, in October 1205, he signed another important treaty with Baldwin's brother Henry,[6] who was acting as *moderator* or regent of the empire after Baldwin had fallen prisoner to the Bulgarians. The new agreement specified that, whenever the podestà's council and the barons should agree with the emperor that it was time for a campaign, all knights, Venetian and non-Venetian (or Frankish), would have to participate in the campaign from June 1 to September 29 (Michaelmas). If any enemy ruler should have invaded the empire, the knights were further bound to stay in service as much longer as the "aforesaid council" should require. The emperor too was to follow the advice of the "aforesaid council", since it was on this understanding that he had received one quarter of the empire. The emperor might not punish anybody for infraction of these military rules, nor could any individual knight punish him for an infraction. The Franks and Venetians would in each such case appoint judges, and the emperor would have to render satisfaction before them at the bidding of the "aforesaid council".

This new treaty for the first time bound the Venetians to fight for the empire. By regularizing the term of military service it further strengthened the emperor's position. That he was subordinate to the magnates we knew already, but the wording of the new treaty reveals the form of the body to which he was responsible. The "aforesaid council" in the treaty is defined as consisting of the Venetian podestà and his council, acting together with the non-

[5] For text and commentary, see R. L. Wolff, "A New Document from the Period of the Latin Empire of Constantinople: The Oath of the Venetian Podestà," *Annuaire de l'Institut de philologie et d'histoire orientales et slaves*, XII (1952), *Mélanges Henri Grégoire*, IV (Brussels, 1953), 539–573.

[6] Text in Tafel and Thomas, *Urkunden*, I, 571 ff.

Venetian barons. This hybrid group, a curious fusion of Italian municipal and French feudal institutions, formed what may be called the council of the Latin empire. One may compare it to the high court of Jerusalem, where of course the Venetian component was absent. Moreover, the Jerusalemite high court itself heard cases; in Latin Constantinople the Venetians and non-Venetians jointly appointed judges to do so, in accordance with Venetian rather than with feudal practice.

Thenceforth, every time a new Latin emperor was crowned, he was required to swear to uphold all the conditions of the three basic treaties: the pact of March 1204, the partition treaty of October 1204, and this new agreement of October 1205. Henry himself, who had already sworn once, as *moderator*, to observe the Venetians' privileges, had to swear again, before his coronation on August 20, 1206, to abide by all the provisions of these three documents. He swore on the high altar of Hagia Sophia, in the presence of Zeno, the papal legate, and the Latin patriarch. To the Venetians, these three documents formed the constitution of the new state, and they lost no opportunity to remind their partners, the Latin emperors, of the exact nature of their mutual obligations.

At the level of everyday affairs, a further agreement regulated financial claims which might arise between Venetians and Franks in Constantinople.[7] Its most interesting clause provided that a member of either nation might make good his claim against a member of the other by producing a witness *who belonged to the debtor's nationality* who would swear that his fellow-national did in fact owe the money. Thus a Venetian witness against a Venetian, a Frank witness against a Frank: these supplied *prima facie* proof that a claim was justified. Business between Venetians and Franks was brisk, and the national solidarity of each group was vigorous.

The treaty of March 1204, by its provision that the party which should fail to elect the emperor would appoint a cathedral chapter to Hagia Sophia, which would then elect a Latin patriarch, had provided, though most uncanonically, for the ecclesiastical future of the new Latin empire. Indeed, some little time after the choice of Baldwin I the Venetians exercised their right and named a Venetian cathedral chapter, which then chose Thomas Morosini, only a subdeacon but a member of a noble Venetian family, to be Latin patriarch. For some months pope Innocent III remained unaware of the illegal action. When he learned of it, early in 1205,

[7] Text in *ibid.*, II, 49 ff.

he denounced it. But none the less he confirmed Morosini, whom he promoted to be deacon, priest, bishop, and archbishop, and on whom he bestowed certain privileges, including that of anointing kings.

Indeed, Innocent III might have preferred to see the patriarchal throne of Constantinople vacant, and to have had the opportunity to use it as a card in negotiating with the Greeks for a union between the churches. But his hand was forced; he wanted further Venetian assistance in the east. Faced with a *fait accompli*, he made the best of it. He even revised current papal political theory in order to elevate the position of the new Latin patriarch. Most of Innocent's predecessors, especially since the schism of 1054, had held that only Rome, Alexandria, and Antioch, all founded directly or indirectly by Peter, were patriarchates. But the pope now adopted the position that the Byzantine church had held ever since 381: that Constantinople, as new Rome, held second place in the ecclesiastical hierarchy as well as the civil. Innocent III endorsed the theory of five patriarchates. His letters associate Constantinople especially with the apostle John, who preached to the Greeks in Asia; the eagle, which, with the other beasts in Revelation 4, stands close to the throne, represents both John and Constantinople. As the eagle flies higher than other birds, and as John was the last and greatest of the apostles, so the patriarchate of Constantinople is the latest but the greatest of the patriarchates; it owes its elevation, however, to Rome. Innocent adopted the very language of the canon of the Council of Constantinople of 381, and this he later embodied in the fifth canon of the Fourth Lateran Council of 1215. The new political theory was well adapted to the new situation, in which the Latins held actual physical possession of Constantinople, and might use it to favor the twin papal policies of a successful crusade against the Moslems and a union between the Latin and Greek churches.

Innocent continued his efforts to win the Greeks to accept the supremacy of Rome. In December 1204, soon after the Latin conquest, his legate cardinal Peter Capuano summoned the Greek clergy of Constantinople to a colloquy in Hagia Sophia. This interchange was apparently only a long and inconclusive debate, after which Peter commanded the Greeks to conform. In 1205 Benedict, cardinal-priest of St. Susanna, another legate, had stopped in Athens and Thessalonica on his way out to Constantinople, and had held conciliatory discussions with the Greeks on the procession of the Holy Ghost and the use of unleavened wafers for the mass.

Innocent wanted to proceed by persuasion; he quite understood the terrible effect of the sack of Constantinople: "How can the church of the Greeks," he wrote, "be expected to return to devotion to the apostolic see, when it has seen the Latins setting an example of evil, and doing the devil's work, so that already, and with good reason, the Greeks hate them worse than dogs?"[8]

Morosini, who was contentious and hot-tempered, only made matters worse. He quarreled with all his fellow-Latins, even the podestà of the Venetians. On one occasion he stopped Greek services in all churches in Constantinople because the Greek clergy refused to mention his name in their prayers, an act which would have been tantamount to recognizing the Latin patriarch. Nor were repeated debates on the questions at issue, theological and others, of any avail. The Greeks looked across the straits to Nicaea, where a new Greek emperor by 1208 had a new Greek patriarch. Most Greek bishops fled their sees or refused obedience to Morosini. Those few that accepted him balked at accepting a new consecration according to the rites of the Latin church, no doubt feeling that this would constitute a tacit admission that their earlier consecration according to the Greek rite had been uncanonical. The pope commanded Morosini to overlook these refusals of a new consecration. Even in cases where the Greek incumbent refused submission, he was to be summoned thrice before he could be suspended and excommunicated. And only the papal legate might thereafter replace him by a Latin. Everywhere the lower level of the clergy remained Greek, continuing to marry and have families (their sons had to render military service unless they had taken orders), and paying the customary Greek land tax (the *akrostikon*) to the secular authorities.

The Latins did not limit themselves to the substitution of Latin prelates for Greek ones. Largely for financial reasons, they gradually brought about a substantial reorganization of the Byzantine hierarchy of metropolitan sees, with their suffragan bishoprics, and autocephalous archbishoprics without suffragan sees. Sometimes they reduced former Greek metropolitan sees or autocephalous archbishoprics to the level of suffragan bishoprics. Sometimes they elevated to the level of archbishoprics sees which under the Greeks had been suffragan bishoprics only. Sometimes they put suffragan bishoprics under the jurisdiction of former Byzantine autocephalous archbishoprics which had not previously possessed any. Sometimes they founded entirely new bishoprics or even metropolitan

[8] *PL*, CCXV, col. 699 (no. 126); Potthast, *Regesta*, no. 2564, July 12, 1205.

archbishoprics.[9] Western monasticism also took root; the military orders and the Cistercians were followed before long by the Franciscans.

Among the Latins themselves, grave controversies raged on ecclesiastical matters. The pope combatted fiercely the efforts of the Venetians to create a perpetual monopoly of the patriarchate for themselves. Before allowing Morosini to come to Constantinople, the Venetians required him to swear never to accept any non-Venetian as a member of the cathedral chapter of Hagia Sophia. They forced each such newly appointed Venetian canon to swear in turn never to vote for any but a Venetian patriarch. Innocent III secured through his legates the appointment of a few non-Venetians to the cathedral chapter. He further prescribed that the *praepositi* of thirty French churches in Constantinople should participate equally with the predominantly Venetian cathedral chapter in electing future patriarchs. He forced Morosini to abjure his oath publicly. But when Morosini died in 1211, the Venetians forcibly prevented the French clergy from participating in the new election, which thus resulted in a double choice. The pope himself eventually named the new patriarch, after an interval of four years; he chose Gervase, archbishop of Heraclea, a Venetian, but the candidate of the French party. Similarly, in 1219, the papal legate John Colonna sought, by the mass creation of new French *praepositi* entitled to vote in a new election, to swing it away from the Venetians. The new pope, Honorius III, eventually named the third patriarch, Matthew, also a Venetian, and rebellious, money-grubbing, and biased in favor of his fellow-Venetians. Between them, popes Innocent and Honorius and their legates successfully prevented the Venetians from making good their extreme claims. But they thereby weakened the Latin patriarchate as an institution. And by the early 1230's, when pope Gregory IX reversed their policy, permitted the patriarch to appoint to the thirty conventual churches, and even appointed him papal legate, the decline in the fortunes of the Latin empire had gone so far that the act seems only a gesture.

Within the empire itself, Latin clerics and laymen struggled over the question of church property. The treaty of March 1204 had provided that the property of the Byzantine churches be divided among the victors along with the rest of the booty, leaving only enough to permit the clergy to live "honorably". Needless to say, patriarch and pope alike began soon after the conquest to make

[9] R. L. Wolff, "The Organization of the Latin Patriarchate of Constantinople," *Traditio*, VI (1948), 33–60.

vigorous demands for compensation. As early as March 1206, emperor and barons agreed to give the churches, instead of their lost possessions, one fifteenth of all property outside the walls of Constantinople. A commission was to divide all real estate into fifteenths, and award one fifteenth to the churches. Moreover, the Latin laity was to pay tithes as they did in the west, though the Greeks had not yet been compelled to follow this alien custom. Though ostensibly satisfactory, the agreement did not include the Venetians. Moreover, Morosini sequestered all the fifteenths after they had been awarded, because he insisted that he was entitled to one half of the total sum, although the papal legate had fixed his share at only one quarter. A later legate obtained a new settlement (1214–1215) providing that one twelfth should be awarded to the churches. But this too led to quarrels and remained a dead letter. Not until 1219 was a new agreement reached. This provided for the cession of one eleventh of all property to the churches, decreed that cathedral churches were to have their lost property restored, and required cash payments from such villages as paid money rents and could not be divided into elevenths. At the same time, the new agreement provided for two priests in every village of twenty-five hearths, and proportionate numbers for larger settlements. The Greeks were allowed to pay one thirtieth instead of the full tenth for tithes. In 1223 the Venetians adhered to the agreement. The elevenths were distributed, and the property question was settled.[10]

When one considers the fortunes of the crusader state whose secular and ecclesiastical institutions we have been describing, one concludes that its eventual collapse was probably inevitable; founded on alien soil, amid hostile Greeks who soon had leaders around whom they might rally, dependent on a flow of money and men from the west which might be cut off at any time, the Latin empire could have survived, if at all, only through statesmanship so far-sighted and astute that one would be unrealistic in demanding it of flesh-and-blood crusaders and Venetians. Thus, for example, it would probably have been sound policy for the Latin conquerors to exploit the deep social cleavages among the Greeks which had helped bring the Byzantine empire to its ruin. Yet the concept of supporting the peasantry against their former masters, and thus winning favor in the countryside, was so utterly alien to the

[10] R. L. Wolff, "Politics in the Latin Patriarchate of Constantinople," *Dumbarton Oaks Papers*, VIII (1954), 227–303.

westerners that it almost surely never occurred to them as a possibility. But even within the framework of the possible, the Latins, a modern student comes to feel, failed initially to make the most of the diplomatic and military opportunities that lay open to them.

They repulsed advances from the leaders of the recently founded Vlacho-Bulgarian state, blessed by Innocent III himself in 1204 before he knew of the fall of Constantinople; and so they drove these potential allies and dangerous enemies into the arms of the Greeks. The Latins failed to see the benefits which might have accrued to them from an alliance with the Selchükids of Rūm behind the Greeks in Asia Minor. The only allies the crusaders made, the Armenian settlers of the Troad, they betrayed and saw exterminated. Because of their diplomatic ineptitude the Latins found themselves forced to fight on both sides of the straits at once: against Greeks in Europe and in Asia, and against the Vlacho-Bulgarian state with its terrifying Kuman auxiliaries in Europe. The Latins had insufficient manpower for such operations. Again and again they had to interrupt an assault that was going well to rush across the straits to meet a new emergency. Detecting weakness, populations docile in the face of strength went over to the enemy, so that the Latins could never be sure that a conquered town would stay conquered, and often had to conquer it several times. Slow to understand Kuman military tactics, they repeatedly allowed themselves to be drawn into ambushes, and were slaughtered by fast-moving horsemen who peppered them with arrows. They wasted men in expensive and long-drawn-out formal sieges. Their enemies had replacements; they did not. Moreover, from the beginning the Greeks had the services of Latin auxiliaries, usually their best troops. Some of these may have been English or Scandinavian mercenaries formerly in Byzantine service, who continued to fight for the Greeks after the loss of the capital. Others were deserters from the forces of the Latin empire, dissatisfied with their rewards and deaf to all papal admonition.

The Greeks of the Byzantine empire within a short time after the loss of Constantinople had three chief leaders among whom to choose. In April 1204 Trebizond fell to an expedition led by Alexius and David Comnenus, grandsons of emperor Andronicus I (1182–1185), sponsored by their first cousin once removed, queen Tamar of Georgia. David Comnenus continued his conquests westward along the Black Sea coast, taking Oenoë and Sinope — assigned by the partition treaty to Baldwin — and extending the borders of the Trapezuntine state to Pontic Heraclea. This brought him into contact with the Latins. Second among the new Greek leaders to appear was Theodore Lascaris, son-in-law of Alexius III. At the very moment of the crusaders' triumphal entry into Constantinople, after Alexius V Mourtzouphlus had already fled, there was some sort of ceremony in Hagia Sophia, in which Theodore seems to have been chosen emperor in preference to a rival named Theodore Ducas,[11] but refused to accept the insignia. He crossed the straits to Asia Minor, persuaded the inhabitants of Nicaea to shelter his wife Anna and his three daughters, set up headquarters at Brusa (Bursa), reached an understanding with the Selchükids, and defeated three princelings who had set themselves up in the turbulent region of the Maeander valley. By 1208, when he named a new Greek patriarch, who crowned him basileus, Theodore had made Nicaea his capital. The third Greek leader was Michael Ducas Angelus Comnenus, illegitimate son of a high Byzantine official, who suddenly deserted Boniface of Montferrat, in whose service he had been, and at Arta, in southern Epirus, married the daughter of the local governor and soon had extensive holdings there.

In addition to these three local rulers, the former emperors, Alexius III Angelus and Alexius V Ducas Mourtzouphlus, were refugees. Alexius III succeeded in having Alexius V, his son-in-law, blinded; after a series of adventures the former made his way to Iconium, where the Selchükids for some time used him as a threat to Theodore Lascaris, his other son-in-law.

The Vlacho-Bulgarian state, in 1204, had for seven years been in the capable hands of Ioannitsa (1197–1207; "Kaloyan"), younger brother of the two Vlach rebels who had founded it in 1186. Claiming descent from the rulers of the first Bulgarian empire, Ioannitsa had asked Innocent III to crown him emperor, as former popes had done, he said, for his "ancestors", and to consecrate the chief of the Bulgarian church as a patriarch. Innocent had sent a cardinal-legate, Leo, who crowned Ioannitsa king, not emperor, and made the archbishop Basil a primate, not a patriarch (November 1204). The Vlach monarch wrote to the pope, after he learned of the Latin conquest: "Write to the Latins to keep away from my empire, and if they do, my empire will do them no harm. . . . But if they make an attempt against it, and some of them are killed, let not your holiness suspect my empire because it will not

[11] B. Sinogowitz, "Über das byzantinische Kaisertum nach dem vierten Kreuzzuge (1204–1205)," *Byzantinische Zeitschrift*, XLV (1952), 345–351, has tried, but not successfully, to demonstrate that the emperor chosen in Hagia Sophia was Theodore's brother, Constantine Lascaris, who held the throne only until early in 1205.

be my fault."[12] Ioannitsa had already tried to make friends with the Latins, who had contemptuously rejected his advances. He therefore entered into relations with Greek nobles in Thrace, possessing troops of their own, whom the Latins had also rebuffed. The folly of this Latin policy was compounded by their rejection of the offer of an alliance from the Selchükid sultan in exile, Kai-Khusrau I, who was soon afterward restored to power in Iconium.

Yet the consequences of the folly did not manifest themselves at once. The first campaigns of the Latins, in the autumn and winter of 1204–1205, were successful. In Asia Minor, though set back at Brusa, parties of crusaders won notable victories over Lascaris, obtained the alliance of the Armenians of the Troad, seized strong points, and captured the blinded Alexius V Mourtzouphlus. They forced him to climb the great sculptured column in the forum of Theodosius and to jump to his death from the top: "For a high man, high justice", as Dandolo put it in a grim jest.[13] Indeed, one of the scenes carved on the column showed an emperor falling from the summit; so that an old prophecy was now fulfilled. The Latins henceforth called the column "Mourtzouphlus's leap". On the European mainland, Renier of Trit took possession of his dukedom of Philippopolis. Reinforcements from Syria arrived in Constantinople. From Thessalonica, Boniface of Montferrat struck south through Thessaly to Thebes and Athens, building a castle on the bridge across the channel to Euboea, and, at Corinth, driving the local magnate, Leo Sgourus, into the citadel. The impetus of the campaign wore itself out in the sieges of Corinth and Nauplia. A nephew of the historian and marshal, the younger Geoffrey of Villehardouin, landed at Modon (Methone), and the conquest of the Morea was begun. Marco Sanudo, nephew of the doge, seized the island of Naxos, key to the Cyclades, and two years later, in a second expedition, conquered the islands left unassigned by the partition treaty, most of which were thereafter held as fiefs from him. Sanudo himself eventually received from the Latin emperor Henry the title of duke of the Aegean Sea (Αἰγαῖον πέλαγος, "Archipelago"), and held his fief "on a freer tenure than any baron in Romania".[14]

Despite these Latin successes, the year 1205 brought the first of

[12] A. Theiner (ed.), *Vetera monumenta Slavorum*, I, 39. See R. L. Wolff, "The 'Second Bulgarian Empire', Its Origin and History to 1204," *Speculum*, XXIV (1949), 167–206.

[13] Robert of Clari, *Conquête* (ed. Lauer), p. 104.

[14] Text in K. Hopf, "Urkunden zur Geschichte der Insel Andros," *Sitzungsberichte der k. Wiener Akademie der Wissenschaften*, XXI (1856), 243. For the entire early history of the dukedom, see J. K. Fotheringham, *Marco Sanudo* (Oxford, 1915).

a series of setbacks. Ioannitsa and his Greek allies had seized both Demotica and Adrianople, where the new Venetian rulers were allegedly mistreating their Greek subjects. Thrace rose in revolt. Abandoned by most of his men, Renier of Trit and a small force retired into the castle of Stenimaka, deep in Bulgaria. Baldwin did not wait for the return of the Latins summoned from Asia Minor in the emergency, but laid siege to Adrianople. Ioannitsa came with a large force to relieve the siege. The Kuman archers inflicted such heavy punishment upon the Latins that orders were issued that henceforth nobody should be lured away from the main battle line. But at the very next Kuman advance, count Louis of Blois forgot the injunction and pursued the Kuman horsemen. Emperor Baldwin followed him. Louis was killed, and Baldwin captured. Leaving lamps and fires lighted in their tents, at Dandolo's suggestion, the remnants of the Latin armies slipped away at night. Many set sail for the west in panic. Baldwin's brother Henry, arriving from Asia Minor with the needed reinforcements, rushed on ahead of the Armenian foot-soldiers he had brought, and these were massacred with their families by the Greeks. The remaining Latins named Henry regent of the empire. Soon afterwards the aged Dandolo died (May 1205).

Henry appealed for aid to Innocent III, who instructed him to make peace with Ioannitsa (not an easy thing to do), and threatened Ioannitsa with a great phantom army of Latins that would come to aid Constantinople. The pope also asked Ioannitsa to free Baldwin. But the armies from the west did not come. In the summer of 1205 the Kumans, who could not bear the heat, withdrew, and Ioannitsa moved westward against Boniface's kingdom of Thessalonica. Henry strove vainly to reconquer Thrace. At Philippopolis the Paulicians of the city offered to yield it to Ioannitsa; so Renier of Trit emerged from his castle and burned down the Paulician quarter. The Greeks of the city made common cause with Renier's Latins, and thus forced Ioannitsa to besiege a city he had expected to take without effort. Infuriated at what he chose to regard as Greek treachery, Ioannitsa burned Philippopolis and massacred the Greek population. Throughout the winter and spring of 1205–1206 he pursued a campaign of frightfulness in Thrace, destroying most of the towns, exterminating the Greek inhabitants, and taking the sobriquet of *Romaioktonos*, slayer of "Romans", to proclaim himself the counterpart of the Byzantine emperor Basil II *Boulgaroktonos*. To keep Ioannitsa away, the frightened Greeks of Demotica and Adrianople agreed to accept as their lord Theodore Branas, a powerful Greek magnate in the Latin service, married to Agnes, a princess of the French royal house and the widow of Alexius II and of his murderer Andronicus I. Venice formally ceded Branas her rights in Adrianople. For his part, he agreed to protect all Venetians, and to supply 500 armed men for the Latin armies. Ioannitsa's siege of Demotica now failed, and Henry and his forces pursued the Vlachs deep into Bulgaria.

At Stenimaka they rescued Renier of Trit from his castle. From him they heard that Baldwin had died in captivity. According to Nicetas Choniates, Ioannitsa had ordered Baldwin horribly murdered because he was so angry at the Greek-Latin collusion at Philippopolis and the burning of the Paulician quarter. The somewhat later account of Acropolites says that Ioannitsa cut off Baldwin's head, and had the skull hollowed out and adorned with jewels for use as a drinking cup. Perhaps Ioannitsa was deliberately imitating his famous "predecessor" Krum, who in the ninth century had done the same with the skull of the Byzantine emperor Nicephorus I. Or perhaps Acropolites, struck by the parallel between Nicephorus and Baldwin in Bulgarian hands, invented the story for literary effect. In any case, we can hardly doubt that Baldwin died or was killed in captivity. Ioannitsa himself told Innocent III in a letter that he could not set Baldwin free because he had died in prison. The point has some importance, because in 1225 a "false Baldwin" appeared in Flanders and Hainault, and became the protagonist of a local revolution. Some historians have held that he really was the emperor, but our sources for affairs in the east render this virtually impossible. Twenty years after their count had died in Bulgaria, the unhappy Flemings, victims of French aggression and bad government, wanted to believe that Baldwin had returned.[15] Better informed, the sorrowful crusaders in Constantinople in 1206 were convinced that he had died, and chose Henry to succeed him. Morosini crowned Henry in Hagia Sophia on August 20, 1206. This second Latin emperor proved to have the extraordinary personal qualities which alone could have availed in the desperate position of the empire.

Ten days after his coronation, Henry forced Ioannitsa to raise a siege of Adrianople, and pursued the Vlach forces into their own territory. In Asia he entered into relations with David Comnenus, and helped him against Theodore Lascaris. Together Latins and

[15] R. L. Wolff, "Baldwin of Flanders and Hainaut, First Latin Emperor of Constantinople: His Life, Death, and Resurrection, 1172–1225," *Speculum*, XXVII (1952), 281–322.

Trapezuntines attacked Nicomedia, diverting Theodore from an assault on Pontic Heraclea. Theodore did drive the Latins back across the straits, but now David sent supplies to Constantinople, and agreed to become Henry's vassal. During the winter of 1206–1207 the Latins won Pegae, Cyzicus, and Nicomedia. In difficulty, Theodore Lascaris appealed to Ioannitsa to help him by launching an attack on the Latins in Europe. As soon as Ioannitsa did so, and Henry had to weaken his forces in Asia, Theodore attacked. A dash across the straits by Henry in person saved the garrison but not the fortress of Civetot (Cibotus). Another saved Cyzicus from a naval attack led by a Calabrese pirate, Stirione, once admiral of Alexius III and now in Lascaris's service. The Latins chased him out through the Dardanelles into the Aegean. A third expedition saved Nicomedia, and a fourth rescued the survivors of a Latin force which Lascaris had defeated. All this time Ioannitsa was besieging Adrianople, which the Latins could not relieve. When Lascaris proposed a two-year truce, offering to exchange all his Latin prisoners for the right to raze the Latin fortresses at Cyzicus and Nicomedia, Henry accepted the offer. He had nothing left in Asia but Pegae and Charax. The truce almost fulfilled Lascaris's war aims of the moment: to expel the Latins from Asia. Freed for a European campaign, Henry began an advance, but lost many men in a new ambush.

In February 1207 Henry had married Agnes, the daughter of Boniface of Montferrat, at a solemn ceremony in Hagia Sophia, followed by a splendid wedding feast in the imperial palace of the Boukoleon. Now, in the summer of 1207, Henry and Boniface conferred on the banks of the Maritsa; Boniface did homage to Henry, and received Thessalonica from him as a fief, as he had from Baldwin. Soon after the conference, however, Boniface was killed in a skirmish with the Bulgarians. About the same time, Ioannitsa himself died suddenly, of a hemorrhage of the lungs; the death was at once attributed to St. Demetrius, defender and patron of Thessalonica. These two deaths substantially altered the situation.

Ioannitsa's proper heir was his young nephew, John Asen. Too young to make good his claim, however, he fled to Russia, and there ensued a struggle for the throne among three rival chieftains: Slav, a relative of the royal family, with headquarters at Melnik in the Rhodope mountains; Strez, another relative, but the protégé of king Stephen of Serbia, with headquarters in the strong Vardar valley fortress of Prosek; and Boril, Ioannitsa's sister's son, who married his uncle's Kuman widow and seized Tirnovo, the capital.

Henry quickly profited by the disunity. At Philippopolis on August 1, 1208, some 2,000 men, of whom one sixth were Greek, defeated a force of 33,000 under Boril. Henry then had a conference with Slav, who became his vassal and was betrothed to an illegitimate daughter of Henry's. To the pope, Henry wrote that he had added fifteen-days'-journey-worth of territory to his holdings: "Our condition has improved, and gets better every day. We do not attribute this to ourselves but rather to God and to you . . . unless our land of Romania be ruled under your paternal guidance, there is no doubt that it will succumb, but if we have your help, the fortunes of war will be ours."[16] Henry also intervened effectively once more in Asia Minor to support David Comnenus against Theodore Lascaris.

The death of Boniface of Montferrat had raised new problems in the kingdom of Thessalonica. The heir was Demetrius, infant son of Boniface and Margaret. But the most powerful magnates, Oberto of Biandrate, the regent, and Amédée Pofey (Amadeo Buffa), constable of the kingdom, were plotting against Demetrius and against Henry. Henry therefore decided to lead an expedition to Thessalonica to require the Lombard lords to do homage to him for the kingdom on behalf of Demetrius. It was a miserably cold winter journey, made more dangerous by Vlach attacks. Biandrate closed the gates of Thessalonica against the emperor, and demanded all the land between the Vardar and the Adriatic (it "belonged" to Venice, but was in fact ruled by Michael of Epirus), together with all continental Greece and the Morea. He also demanded a corridor to the Black Sea, and asked that Henry accept Philippopolis as the western limit of the Latin empire. The proposals were so outrageous that they were probably intended to be refused. Henry, however, agreed to them, but only as a ruse to win admission to the city, because otherwise he and his men would have died of cold. He did not intend to abide by his promise once he was inside, and the clerics who were with him had absolved him from it. He also stipulated that Margaret must approve the conditions. By this deception he got into Thessalonica, where Biandrate received him with all due honor.

Biandrate and his fellow-plotters intended to turn Thessalonica over to William IV of Montferrat, son of Boniface by an earlier marriage, who was now the marquis at home in Italy. They regarded William as their true lord, and much preferred him to the alien Margaret, regent for a half-alien infant. Indeed, the Lombards hoped to

[16] Text in *PL*, CCXV, col. 1522, no. 207.

make William the emperor of Constantinople, supplanting Henry, and righting what they still felt to be the wrong done to Boniface in 1204. Though they had repeatedly urged William to come out to Greece and assume the imperial power, he cautiously preferred "a pair of oxen and a plow in Montferrat to an emperor's crown abroad".[17] Uncomprehendingly, the few great Lombard nobles who were in on the plot complained that their lord must be a bastard. Hoping that William would reconsider, they had waited, pretending to support Margaret and Demetrius. Now Henry had skillfully turned their embarrassment to his own account. He had accepted Biandrate's humiliating terms, *provided* that Margaret would approve of them. Biandrate had had to accept the proviso for fear of revealing prematurely his disloyalty to Margaret. Once inside Thessalonica, Henry was able to demonstrate publicly that Biandrate's territorial demands had only a limited amount of support among the Lombard nobles, and to persuade Margaret to repudiate them, despite the pressure which Biandrate and his followers had brought to bear on her. Henry thus extracted himself from his dilemma, and without dishonor. Now, on January 6, 1209, he crowned the infant Demetrius as king, and Biandrate took a new oath of homage as regent of the kingdom of Thessalonica.

But Biandrate garrisoned the important fortresses of Serres and Christopolis (Kavalla) with men loyal to William of Montferrat. In the crisis Henry supported Margaret, on whom he conferred great estates in Thessaly, formerly the property of Alexius III's wife Euphrosyne. Biandrate, furious, resigned, and went off to prison. Henry had to fight for Serres, which he took, but Christopolis held out, and the Lombard revolt spread to Thessaly. Henry spent the spring of 1209 campaigning there, taking Larissa but treating the defeated garrison with kindness, and receiving a warm welcome from the Greek population at Halmyros. At Ravennika, the emperor held a "parlement", hoping that the Lombard lords would make peace. Only Amédée Pofey appeared, declared his repentance, did homage, and received his fief once more. Though disappointed, Henry took advantage of the presence of the French lords of southern Greece to receive the younger Villehardouin as his vassal and make him seneschal of the empire, thus attaching Achaea directly to Constantinople instead of to Thessalonica. Villehardouin also recognized that Henry's rights had precedence over those of

[17] V. de Bartholomaeis, "Un Sirventès historique d'Élias Cairel," *Annales du Midi*, XVI (1904), 469 ff.; H. Jaeschke, *Der Troubadour Elias Cairel* (Romanische Studien, ed. E. Ebering, part 20, Berlin, 1921), pp. 149 ff.

the doge; and soon afterwards Venice ceded her rights in the Morea, except for Modon and Coron, to Villehardouin, who gave an annual token tribute to the Venetians and maintained a house in Venice.[18]

Henry then resumed the fight against the remaining Lombard rebels. At Thebes the Greek population welcomed him warmly, but he had to besiege the castle. He forced the surrender of the Lombard defenders, and agreed to give Biandrate a trial before his imperial court. On the way to Thebes, Biandrate escaped to Euboea. Henry then proceeded to Athens, worshiped in the church of the Virgin established in the Parthenon, boldly crossed to Euboea despite the presence of Biandrate, and was preserved from treason by the lord of the island, Ravano dalle Carceri of Verona, until recently one of Biandrate's allies. Biandrate himself now submitted. Henry accepted his new oath of homage, and restored him to office as regent of Thessalonica. It seems probable, however, that Biandrate returned to Montferrat and continued his efforts to induce William to claim Thessalonica. The Lombard revolt in Greece was over.

Henry's successes had alarmed Michael of Epirus, who now sent to request a parley. He agreed to do homage for all his possessions, and married his daughter to Henry's (probably illegitimate) younger brother Eustace. But during the very first year after accepting these arrangements Michael violated his oath. He seized the newly reinstated rebel, Amédée Pofey, now constable of the Latin empire, and one hundred other Latins. He mistreated all of them and crucified Pofey, his chaplain, and three others. This sudden treachery led to warfare between Michael and Henry, in which Michael had the services of some Latin mercenaries, sent across the Adriatic in Venetian ships. By January 1212, Henry commented in a letter, Michael had four separate times broken his oath not to take up arms against him,[19] but we do not know the details of their relationships. In 1210 Venice formally ceded to Michael the Epirote lands obtained by the partition treaty, but it is not clear whether this cession took place during one of the periods of peace between Michael and the Latin empire. In any case, by early 1212 Henry had effectively defeated both Michael and Strez of Prosek.

But his other enemies now threatened once again. Defeated by Henry in 1208, Boril had since occupied himself with a campaign to stamp out Bogomilism among his subjects; the Bogomils were

[18] Text in Tafel and Thomas, *Urkunden*, II, 95 ff.
[19] Text in *RHGF*, XVIII, 531.

perhaps supporters of John Asen. By 1211 Boril had temporarily suppressed them. Theodore Lascaris, for his part, had been engaged against the Selchükids of Rūm. In 1211, with an army almost half of which was made up of Latins, Lascaris defeated the Turks — to whom Henry had also sent Latin auxiliaries — and captured their ally, his contentious father-in-law Alexius III, who was to die in a monastery in Nicaea. After this victory, Theodore issued a general letter to all the Greeks, promising, if they would assist him, to free the land from the Latin "dogs". By 1211, then, both Boril and Theodore were free once again to turn on Henry.

The Latin emperor pursued Boril westward in Bulgaria without coming to grips in a major engagement. Henry's brother Eustace wiped out Strez's forces on the plain of Pelagonia, with the assistance of the mercurial Michael of Epirus, this time assisting his son-in-law. Then Henry turned against Lascaris, who had captured and cruelly killed Peter of Bracieux, one of the leaders of the Fourth Crusade. Lascaris's propaganda was beginning to make the Greeks of Europe restive. On October 15, 1211, on the Asia Minor shore, Henry with 260 knights defeated Lascaris, who had 1,700 men in his own battalion alone, and eighty-nine other battalions also, no doubt much smaller in number, besides 160 Latins. By Henry's own account, his own forces lost not a single man. In the ensuing campaign, Henry took Poemanenum, Lentiana, Adramyttium, and regions still farther south. At Nymphaeum (Kemalpasha), thereafter, he and Lascaris signed a treaty, giving to the Latins the entire Asiatic coast-line of the Sea of Marmara and a considerable stretch along the Aegean. Not only were the towns of Nicomedia, Cyzicus, Pegae, and Adramyttium back in Latin hands, but they also obtained a strip of hinterland stretching as far inland as Achyraūs (Balîkesir). The Nicaeans regained Pergamum and other towns to the south and east. A kind of no-man's-land separated Latin territory from Greek. From Pergamum in January 1212, Henry wrote a triumphant report: "Our four . . . enemies — Boril, Lascaris, Michael, and Strez — are humbled and altogether deprived of strength. Ye must know that there is nothing lacking to the winning of a final victory and complete possession of the empire save an abundance of Latins, to whom we may give the lands we are acquiring, or rather have already acquired, since, as ye know, it does little good to acquire it unless there are those who will protect it."[20] To secure his gains, Henry needed reinforcements that never came. After the siege of Lentiana, he formed his Greek

[20] *Ibid.*, p. 533.

captives into military units, and entrusted to them the defense of his new eastern frontier against Lascaris, which remained stable for the remainder of Henry's reign.

In the west, Eustace and Slav defeated Boril, who also sued for peace. John Asen had returned from Russia with Russian auxiliaries, and civil war had broken out in Bulgaria. As part of the settlement with Boril, Henry, whose Montferrat wife Agnes had died, married Boril's daughter, overcoming his initial reluctance because of her parentage. Sometime thereafter, Henry and Boril went together on an expedition against Stephen I of Serbia, advancing all the way to Nish before the Serbs defeated their forces. King Andrew II of Hungary and Strez of Prosek were also allies of Henry and Boril, but Stephen captured and killed Strez, who had been a vassal of his own. In 1214 the murder of Michael of Epirus by a servant led to the succession of Michael's brother Theodore (1214–1230), an ally of Lascaris. Theodore of Epirus soon secured also the alliance of Slav; Henry's daughter had died, and Slav now married a niece of Theodore. On June 11, 1216, the Latin emperor Henry himself died at Thessalonica, aged only forty. Despite the conjectures of historians that either Henry's Vlacho-Bulgarian wife or his old enemy Oberto of Biandrate was guilty of his murder, there is no evidence that contemporaries ever suspected either of them.

By 1216 Henry had rescued the Latin position from what in 1206 had seemed certain ruin. He had great talents as a soldier: a Greek source calls him "a second Ares".[21] As diplomat, he concluded dynastic alliances with Slav, Michael of Epirus, and Boril, shrewdly reversing the initial haughty attitude of the Latins. Henry gained advantages also from the alliances with David Comnenus and the Selchükids. In his handling of the Lombard revolt he was clever, firm, and generous. But most dramatic of all was his extraordinary reversal of his predecessors' policy toward the Greeks. The coöpting of Theodore Branas, the use of Greek troops against Boril, and the formation of Greek prisoners into a trusted defense corps against a Greek enemy all illustrate a keen sense of political necessity. One might dismiss as mere Latin propaganda the tumultuous receptions which western authorities declare the Greek populations accorded Henry at Halmyros, Thebes, and Negroponte, were it not that the Greek sources also attest to his popularity.

"Henry," says Acropolites, "though a Frank by race, won most cheerful acceptance by the Greeks and the inhabitants of Constan-

[21] Ephraem (*CSHB*), verses 7729 ff.

tinople, for he had installed many of them in high office, and he treated the common people as if they were his own."[22] When the vehement papal legate Pelagius, cardinal-bishop of Albano, exerted pressure on the Greeks of Constantinople in 1214 by closing their churches, Henry received a deputation of leading Greek citizens, who told him frankly that he might rule their bodies but not their souls; they would fight for him in war, but would not give up their faith or alter their way of worship. Henry acceded, defied the papal legate, and reopened the Greek churches. To Innocent III an unknown member of the Greek clergy of Constantinople wrote: "We consider that we have as our lord the emperor, sire Henry, and that we live and labor, till the soil, tend our flocks, and sail the sea beneath his shadow. For without us the granaries will not be filled, or the wine-presses; no bread, no meat, no fish will be eaten, nor can human life and society continue to be maintained."[23] The records of a law-suit tried in Thessalonica in 1213 show that the city had a Greek administration, and that all the Greek bishops of the archdiocese sat in judgment together with the civil administrator. When the case was appealed twenty years later, on the ground that it had been argued during the Latin domination, Greek counsel opposing the appeal argued that during the reign of Henry Greeks had lived without fear, obtaining due and proper justice from fellow-Greeks.[24]

Of course, Henry's work was built on weak foundations. He could not pay his forces. The presence of large numbers of Latin mercenaries in the Nicaean and Epirote armies reflected the basic insecurity of his military position. Both the Nicaeans and the Epirotes, as well as the Vlacho-Bulgarian state, represented indigenous peoples, not rootless interlopers. The Latins might temporarily thwart them by diplomacy, and repeatedly defeat them in the field. Their own domestic concerns might temporarily distract them. Their rivalries among themselves might paralyze them. But they remained to oppose the Latins and eventually to overwhelm them.

On Henry's sudden death Conon of Béthune, distinguished *trouvère* with an accent of Artois which had embarrassed him in his youth, brilliant soldier and diplomat, and trusted leader of the

[22] Acropolites, *Opera* (ed. Heisenberg), I, 28.

[23] J. B. Cotelerius, *Ecclesiae graecae monumenta*, III (Paris, 1686), 516 ff.

[24] *Analecta sacra et profana spicilegio solesmensi parata*, VII (ed. J. B. Pitra, Paris and Rome, 1896), cols. 447–462, in the correspondence of Demetrius Chomatianus, archbishop of Ochrida. See also M. Drinov, "O niekotorykh trudakh Demetriya Khomatiana kak istoricheskom materialie," *Vizantiiskii vremennik*, II (1895), 15 ff.

Latin enterprise against Byzantium since its inception, became bailie of the empire, with the Byzantine title of sebastocrator. The barons chose as the next emperor Peter of Courtenay, count of Nevers and Auxerre, the husband of Yolanda, a sister of Baldwin and Henry. In April 1217 pope Honorius III crowned Peter at Rome in St. Lawrence "outside the walls", deliberately choosing that church lest Peter should later claim that his coronation by the pope as emperor *in* Rome gave him rights over the western empire. Though Honorius wrote of Peter as a "man who hitherto, by the excellence of his magnanimity and the splendor of his actions, has proved himself worthy of an imperial crown",[25] the new Latin emperor, a grandson of king Louis VI, was in fact one of the most notoriously quarrelsome and violent barons in all of France. For many years he had engaged in open warfare against the bishop of Auxerre, and had perpetrated some scandalous atrocities. Another contemporary's judgment seems nearer the mark than that of Honorius: "a man indeed of royal blood and unbounded strength, but with no restraint in his emotions and with a dreadful temper, who would not on any account moderate the force of his anger in the working of harm and the doing of injuries."[26] Though Peter was bringing 6,000 reinforcements, he could hardly have proved a fit successor to Henry.

Before Peter left Rome, the Lombard faction succeeded in obtaining from him the investiture of William of Montferrat with all the rights and duties of the kingdom of Thessalonica, leaving to Demetrius nothing but the empty title. It seems probable that Margaret took refuge in her native Hungary. Thus Peter signed away what Henry had fought to keep. Oberto of Biandrate was surely at the bottom of the affair. We know little about the Lombard seizure of power in Thessalonica itself, but the old feuds there between adherents and opponents of Montferrat probably weakened the kingdom in the face of the onslaught of Theodore of Epirus. Peter also undertook, on behalf of Venice, to besiege Durazzo, which had already fallen to Theodore, whose power extended to much of Thessaly, as well as Ochrida and large parts of Macedonia.

Embarking his pregnant wife Yolanda on a ship bound directly for Constantinople, Peter crossed the Adriatic and laid siege to Durazzo. When it held out, he abandoned the siege and proceeded across Albania. Theodore of Epirus now captured him, together

[25] Pressutti, *Regesta*, no. 497; *Opera* (ed. Horoy), II, col. 360, no. 294.

[26] L-M. Duru, *Bibliothèque historique de l'Yonne* (Auxerre and Paris, 1850), p. 441, who prints the text of the contemporary life of the bishop of Auxerre, Hugh of Noyers.

with his whole army and the new papal legate, cardinal John Colonna. Honorius III immediately began to bring pressure on Theodore for Peter's release. But like Baldwin I, Peter was to die in captivity, probably early in 1219, although as late as 1224 the pope still believed that he was alive and might be set free. Theodore did, however, liberate the papal legate, who had arrived in Constantinople by mid-1218. Although secret negotiations continued for some time, Theodore made no agreement with Rome. Instead, he continued his conquests at the expense of the Latins, taking Neopatras (Hypata), and in 1219 the great Vardar fortress of Prosek, as well as Platamon, which rounded out his holdings in Thessaly. Thessalonica itself was clearly menaced, and Theodore's exultant followers were already predicting its fall.

Meanwhile Yolanda had long since arrived in Constantinople, where she gave birth to a son, the future Baldwin II. She ruled as empress until her death in the summer or fall of 1219. One of her daughters (Agnes) she married to Geoffrey II of Villehardouin, heir to Achaea, and another (Mary) to the Nicaean emperor, Theodore Lascaris. This new dynastic tie reinforced the peaceful relations between Constantinople and Nicaea achieved by Henry after his victory of 1211. And no doubt these were still further strengthened by a five-year treaty concluded in August 1219 between Lascaris and the podestà of the Venetian colony in Constantinople, the future doge Jacob Tiepolo, which opened the territory of each empire to the subjects of the other, freeing the Venetians from tolls and fees in Nicaean lands but requiring the Nicaeans in Constantinople or in other Venetian possessions to pay the legal customs dues. Lascaris also promised not to send warships to Constantinople without the express consent of the podestà, or to enlist Venetian mercenaries without such consent. In March 1220 Tiepolo also concluded a new trade treaty with the Selchükids of Rūm.

Upon Yolanda's death Conon of Béthune was again chosen bailie. The eldest son of Peter and Yolanda, Philip of Namur, refused the imperial throne; so the office fell to his younger brother, Robert of Courtenay. He came east by land to Constantinople, crossing Hungary, where he visited his brother-in-law and sister Yolanda, the king and queen, and then proceeding safely across Bulgaria. This was possible because, after a seven-year siege, John Asen had finally succeeded in capturing Tirnovo. He seized and blinded Boril, and became king of the Vlachs and the Bulgars (1218–1241). Soon thereafter he married Maria, a daughter of king Andrew II of Hungary, and thus became the nephew-in-law of Robert. Taking advantage of Asen's benevolence, Robert entered Constantinople, where he was crowned by the patriarch Matthew on March 25, 1221. In the period of five years since the death of Henry, only the ominous advance of Theodore of Epirus on the west had diminished Latin possessions. So well had Henry done his work that the empire had successfully weathered the dangerous period under bailie, empress, and bailie once more. No doubt Conon of Béthune, the Venetian podestàs, and the papal legate John Colonna among them had provided the necessary strength and wisdom.

But emperor Robert, his contemporaries agreed, had none of the necessary qualities: "*quasi rudis et idiota*" is perhaps their most succinct and damning judgment.[27] In Constantinople, the Venetians extended their possessions. Across the straits fighting broke out, as Theodore Lascaris seized the opportunity provided by the death of Yolanda and broke his treaty with the Latins. Shortly after Robert's coronation, the two sides negotiated for peace. Theodore promised to marry his daughter Eudocia to Robert, and prisoners were exchanged. But the Nicaean patriarch objected to the marriage on grounds of consanguinity: Theodore was married to Robert's sister Mary. The question was still open when Theodore Lascaris died in August 1222. When his daughter Irene's husband, the extraordinarily able John Ducas Vatatzes (1222–1254), succeeded to the throne, two of Theodore's brothers deserted to the Latins. Robert made them commanders in his army.

For a period of two years after his coronation, Vatatzes was unable to attack the Latins. But Theodore of Epirus continued his campaigns against them. By early 1222 he had taken Serres, and Thessalonica was ringed. The pope strove to restrain Theodore and encourage Robert; Oberto of Biandrate and William of Montferrat, Honorius wrote, were on their way east to aid the empire. But in the autumn of 1224, before the western expedition had gotten under way, Theodore's force took Thessalonica. Young king Demetrius and the Latin archbishop fled to Italy. Now master of the second city of the Byzantine empire, Theodore of Epirus assumed the purple. Constantine Mesopotamites, the Greek metropolitan of Thessalonica, refused to crown him, but the learned Demetrius Chomatianus, archbishop of Ochrida, gladly consented to do so. Though the Nicaeans naturally objected, and sneered at Theodore's insufficient acquaintance with protocol, the new "emperor" of Thessalonica secured the support of his own clergy by threatening

[27] Aubrey of Trois-Fontaines (*MGH, SS.*, XXIII), p. 910.

a flirtation with the papacy. A second Greek imperial claimant for the Byzantine heritage had now asserted himself.

Robert not only failed to exploit this division among the Greeks, but reverted to the fatal policy of fighting two-front wars and quickly lost most of what Henry had gained. At Poemanenum in 1225 Vatatzes' forces defeated the Latins so severely that they withdrew another army engaged in besieging Serres. Vatatzes conquered most of the Latin holdings in Asia Minor, built ships, and launched naval attacks on the Gallipoli peninsula. Encouraged, the Greeks of Adrianople asked for troops. Nicaean forces entered the city, an admirable base for the conquest of the remaining Latin possessions in Europe. But this thrust of Vatatzes also threatened Theodore of Epirus, who had by now pushed east from Thessalonica to take most of Thrace. Arrived at the gates of Adrianople, Theodore persuaded the inhabitants to expel Vatatzes' troops, and to open the city to him instead. Thereafter the Latins made peace with Vatatzes, retaining only Nicomedia in Asia, while Theodore of Epirus swept on to Vizya, in Thrace, and to the walls of Constantinople itself. By 1226 the Latin position seemed desperate. The Montferrat crusade to liberate Thessalonica failed, despite the vigorous support of Honorius III. William of Montferrat died in Thessaly in September 1225, and his forces subsequently dispersed.

Probably the only factor that saved the Latins from being driven out of Constantinople in 1225 or 1226 was the benevolence of John Asen. Theodore of Epirus concluded a peace with him, marrying his brother Manuel to Asen's illegitimate daughter Maria. Asen probably demanded that Theodore permit Robert to retain undisturbed the lands the Latins still held. The text of the truce concluded in 1228 between Theodore and the Latins, permitting the free movement of merchants across the frontiers, shows that the Latins still held in Thrace the three towns of Vizya, "Verissa" (Pînarhisar), and "Genua" (Sergen?).[28] The great dated inscription set up in 1230 by John Asen in the church of the Forty Martyrs at Tirnovo speaks of the Latins as possessing their lands only because of his assent.[29]

Asen's benevolence was, of course, far from disinterested. He planned to take over the Latin empire himself. Robert had conceived an infatuation for a French woman of relatively humble birth, whom he had married secretly and taken to live with him in the

[28] R. Predelli, "Il *liber Communis* detto anche *Plegiorum*," *Archivio Veneto*, III–VIII (1872–1874), supplement, pp. 184–185.

[29] F. I. Uspenskii, "O drevnostyakh goroda Tyrnova," *Izvestiya Russkago arkheologicheskago instituta v Konstantinopolie*, VII (1902), 6 ff., and plate 5.

imperial palace. Outraged, his own French knights broke into the imperial bedchamber, mutilated the features of Robert's wife, and seized and later drowned her mother. Unable to avenge himself and full of shame, Robert fled to Rome, and complained to pope Gregory IX, who persuaded him to return to Constantinople. But on the way back in 1228, Robert died in Greece. His sister, Mary of Courtenay, was regent for a time during his absence. After his death the barons chose Narjot of Toucy bailie. The heir, Robert's younger brother Baldwin II, was only eleven years old, and a regency was needed.

This was the moment for which John Asen had been waiting. Like the Bulgarian ruler Symeon some three centuries earlier, Asen hoped that the authorities in Constantinople would arrange a marriage between his daughter Helena and the heir to the imperial throne, and that he would thus become the father-in-law of the future emperor and regent for him. Indeed, the barons approached Asen and made him the offer he wanted. He accepted, and promised to win back all that the Latins had lost to Theodore of Epirus. But those Latins who were guilty of the outrage against Robert's wife began to fear that young Baldwin II, once consolidated in his power by Asen, might punish them for their crime. So they advised that Baldwin reject Asen's daughter, though she was a handsome girl. Like Symeon before him, Asen was thwarted in his ambitions.

To supplant him, as Romanus Lecapenus had once supplanted Symeon, the barons chose John of Brienne, tall and irascible, once king of Jerusalem, claimant to the throne of Armenia, leading participant in the Fifth Crusade, father-in-law of the western emperor Frederick II, and husband of Berengaria, a sister of king Ferdinand III of Castile. John was then commander of the papal troops of Gregory IX, fighting Frederick II in southern Italy. The barons of Constantinople offered the hand of Baldwin II to John's daughter by Berengaria, Mary of Brienne. John would be crowned emperor, and would serve for life; but when Baldwin should reach the age of twenty, he would do homage to John and be invested with the realm of Nicaea and all the land in Asia Minor, except for Nicomedia, which would remain in John's hands. To his heirs John might leave either Asia Minor or the lands of Theodore of Epirus and Slav and Strez. John's heirs would do homage to Baldwin for these lands, none of which were in Latin possession at the time of the new agreement, which drastically revised the partition treaty of 1204.[30] All Venetian possessions were specifically exempted from its provisions. It was ratified by John and pope Gregory IX in April 1229. By the summer of 1231 John had arrived in Constantinople, and he was crowned soon after. Baldwin and Mary were married, and Baldwin did homage to his father-in-law.

John, who was naturally miserly, lost his forces to other employers rather then pay them. He waited until 1233 before crossing the straits to attack Vatatzes, who was engaged in war with the autonomous ruler of Rhodes, Leo Gabalas. The Latins took Lampsacus and campaigned along the shore of the Sea of Marmara. They seized Pegae, and held it briefly, but accomplished nothing lasting.

Meanwhile the balance had markedly shifted. In 1230 Theodore of Epirus broke his treaty with John Asen and invaded Bulgaria, marching up the Maritsa from Adrianople. At a place called Klokotnitsa, John Asen, using as his standard the actual parchment of the violated treaty affixed to a lance, completely defeated and captured Theodore. Asen swept ahead, taking Adrianople, Demotica, and all western Thrace, as well as Serres, Pelagonia, Prilep, Thessaly, and a large part of Albania. This virtually liquidated the holdings of Theodore. Asen garrisoned most of the fortresses in his great new Balkan empire, and treated its inhabitants with rare kindness. He even spared Theodore, until he caught him plotting a rebellion; then he blinded him. Theodore's brother Manuel, Asen's son-in-law, ruled over Thessalonica itself and its immediate neighborhood, using the title despot (1230–1236), and relying on his family relationship with Asen to protect him. Manuel continued to sign official documents with the sacred red letters, however, as if Thessalonica were still the center of an empire.

Like his predecessors of the first Bulgarian empire, and like his own uncle Ioannitsa, John Asen, who had already begun to call himself tsar of the Bulgarians *and the Greeks*, now also wanted an autonomous Bulgarian patriarchate. In 1232 he opened negotiations with the Nicaeans, and transferred from the Latin patriarchate to that of Nicaea some of the bishoprics he had conquered. Between 1232 and 1235 Asen was engaged in trying to build a coalition of Orthodox powers with the object of recovering Constantinople from the Latins. The final conclusion of the agreement between Asen and Vatatzes was delayed until 1235, probably because Vatatzes

[30] R. Predelli, *loc. cit.* (note 28 above), pp. 185–186; Tafel and Thomas, *Urkunden*, I, 265 ff. For John of Brienne in the Fifth Crusade, see below, chapter XI, pp. 389–428; for his reign over the kingdom of Jerusalem, see below, chapter XV, pp. 536–542.

was awaiting the outcome of negotiations he had undertaken with the papacy. The Nicaean patriarch, Germanus, had sent a letter to Gregory IX by the hands of five Franciscan monks who had passed through Nicaea. Soon afterward the pope sent to Nicaea a mission made up of two Franciscans and two Dominicans to confer about ending the schism. Arriving in Nicaea in 1234, they held a series of discussions on the usual questions of the *filioque* and the use of unleavened bread for the sacramental wafer. Vatatzes inquired whether the pope would restore the rights of the patriarch of Nicaea (i.e. of Constantinople) if he should promise obedience to the holy see. The friars answered only that the Greek patriarch would find the pope very well disposed toward him. They refused to attend a general council of the Orthodox churches, since their instructions from the pope had not extended so far, and withdrew to Constantinople.

But Vatatzes put great pressure on them to return to Nicaea. They consented to do so, but, they later reported, this was largely because of the frightening situation they found in Constantinople:

> The land of Constantinople was as if deprived of all protection. The lord emperor John was a pauper. All the paid knights departed. The ships of the Venetians, Pisans, Anconitans, and other nations were ready to leave, and some indeed had already left. When we saw that the land was abandoned, we feared danger because it was surrounded by enemies. Asen, king of the Vlachs, menaced it from the north, Vatatzes from the east and south, and Manuel from the west. Therefore we proposed to negotiate a one-year truce between the emperor of Constantinople and Vatatzes. Indeed, so that we might not seem to be making this effort on our own initiative, we consulted the chapter of Hagia Sophia and the prelates of the land, and the emperor himself on the matter, and all of them unanimously advised us to do so.[31]

With this motive, the friars took part in the council of the Orthodox churches at Nymphaeum, which broke up in mutual violent recriminations, the Greeks reverting to the horrors of 1204, the Latins replying that the crusaders who had perpetrated them had been excommunicated sinners. In the circumstances, the friars paid little heed to Vatatzes' offer to use unleavened bread for the

[31] P. G. Golubovich, "Disputatio . . . ," *Archivum Franciscanum historicum*, XII (1919), 446; M. Roncaglia, *Les Frères Mineurs et l'église grecque orthodoxe au XIIIe siècle, 1231–1274*, Biblioteca bio-bibliografica della terra santa e dell' oriente francescano, ser. 4: *Studi*, II (Cairo, 1954), pp. 23–120; R. L. Wolff, "The Latin Empire of Constantinople and the Franciscans," *Traditio*, II (1944), 213–237.

sacramental wafer if the Latins would drop the *filioque* from the creed. Indeed, the two Franciscans and two Dominicans barely escaped with their lives from the infuriated Greeks, and all negotiations came to nothing.

Almost immediately (1235) Vatatzes concluded the pact with John Asen. The daughter whom Asen had once intended for Baldwin II was now engaged to Vatatzes' son, the young Theodore (II) Lascaris. Driving the Latins from Lampsacus, Vatatzes then crossed the straits and sacked the Venetian town of Gallipoli, massacring the population. Here Asen met him, and Vatatzes took the Bulgarian princess back to Asia, where she married Theodore Lascaris. Simultaneously Vatatzes and the Nicaean clergy raised Joachim, the Bulgarian metropolitan of Tirnovo, to the rank of an autonomous patriarch. Then Vatatzes and Asen joined forces, swept through Thrace, and appeared before the walls of Constantinople. John of Brienne emerged, and with only 160 knights utterly defeated the vastly superior Nicaean-Vlach forces. Even the contemporary Flemish chronicler, Philip Mouskes, often bitterly critical of John's avarice, likens him on this occasion to Hector, Roland, Ogier the Dane, and Judas Maccabaeus.[32] Moreover, the victory on land was accompanied by a decisive Venetian naval triumph over Vatatzes' fleet, and the capture of twenty-five Greek galleys, including the flagship.

But the Greek-Bulgarian assault soon began again. With papal pleas to France and to Hungary ineffectual, the Latin emperor drew his support chiefly from Geoffrey II of Villehardouin and from the Venetians, Pisans, and Genoese, momentarily at peace with one another. Naval contributions probably also came from the duke of the Archipelago, Angelo Sanudo, who intervened with Vatatzes and procured a two-year truce. All parties no doubt welcomed it. John of Brienne's forces, underpaid, tended to "go over into Vlachia". Baldwin II set off for Rome to find some money. On the other side, Asen had begun to fear that only Vatatzes would profit by their joint victory. He asked to have his daughter come home for a visit. Though Vatatzes understood the stratagem, he complied with the request.

In Rome, Gregory IX urged count Peter of Brittany to go to Constantinople instead of Syria on his projected crusading expedition, and commuted the vows of 600 northern French knights on condition that they go to help the Latin empire instead. Hungarian churchmen received similar pleas. But before there had been much

[32] Mouskes (ed. de Reiffenberg), II, 614–615, verses 29068–29079.

response John of Brienne died in Constantinople on March 23, 1237, having taken Franciscan orders shortly before his death.[33]

Now began the last quarter-century of the Latin empire, reduced to the city of Constantinople itself, to which a few wretched Latins clung. Dependent on aid from the west, they had to face the harsh fact that the western states were preoccupied: Louis IX with his own crusading plans, the Hungarians with the Mongol invasions, the popes with their struggle against the Hohenstaufens. Even Venetian commercial interest seems to have slackened. The continued survival of the empire probably reflects the fact that its enemies too were preoccupied: the Bulgarians by John Asen's fear of Vatatzes and, after Asen's death in 1241, by internal weakness, Vatatzes by his distaste for an outright assault on the capital, and by the impact of the Mongol invasions on Asia Minor. Yet Vatatzes' ultimate purpose never wavered; in response to a letter from Gregory IX, summoning him to submit to John of Brienne or suffer blows from new western armies, Vatatzes wrote scornfully that he would never abandon his attacks on the thieves and murderers who occupied a city of which he was legitimate ruler. A real emperor, he told the pope, ruled over people, and not merely over the wood and stone of which fortifications are made.[34]

Vatatzes' ally Asen, however, opened negotiations with the papacy, and allied himself with the Latins. New support came also from bands of Kuman invaders who, in flight before the Mongols, crossed the Danube on inflated skin rafts and poured into the Balkans. Outlandish pagan ceremonies marked the Latin conclusion of an agreement with these savages, and there were even marriages solemnized between noble Latins and daughters of Kuman chieftains. In 1237 a mixed Latin-Kuman-Bulgarian army under the command of Asen besieged Tzurulum (Chorlu), a fortified town in Thrace held by Vatatzes. But Asen broke off the siege on hearing that his wife and son had died. This was a punishment, he decided, for his treachery to Vatatzes. So he returned his daughter Helena to her Greek husband, Theodore Lascaris, and renewed his own alliance with Vatatzes.

Once again the crisis of the Latins in Constantinople became

[33] For details, see article by R. L. Wolff, cited above, note 31; cf. J. M. Buckley, "The Problematical Octogenarianism of John of Brienne," *Speculum*, XXXII (1957), 315–322.

[34] See V. Grumel, "L'Authenticité de la lettre de Jean Vatatzes, empereur de Nicée, au pape Grégoire IX," *Échos d'Orient*, XXIX (1930), 450–458, for discussion and French translation. The Greek text is available in A. Meliarakes, *Ἱστορία τοῦ Βασιλείου τῆς Νικαίας καὶ τοῦ Δεσποτάτου τῆς Ἠπείρου* (Athens and Leipzig, 1898), pp. 276 ff.; also published by I. Sakellion, in the Greek periodical *Ἀθηναῖον*, I (1873), pp. 371–378.

acute. Again the pope spurred on western crusaders, and wrote to the clergy of Greece describing the dreadful food shortages in Constantinople and the weakness of its defenses. He levied a tax of one third of the movable property and income of the clergy of the Morea to help save the capital. Disappointed in Asen, Gregory IX preached the crusade against him too, especially in the lands of Asen's ex-brother-in-law, king Bela IV of Hungary (1235–1270). But Bela refused to fight Asen unless the papacy granted him extensive rights to make ecclesiastical appointments in conquered Bulgarian territory, and also asked to be made papal legate in Hungary. Though Gregory acceded to all Bela's requests except the last, the Mongol invasions effectively prevented Bela from attacking John Asen. And Asen himself, though he had returned to the Nicaean alliance, never again took the field jointly with Vatatzes, and maintained only the semblance of a friendship with him. Gregory IX, not content with striving to raise men and money in the west, issued a series of emergency decrees for Constantinople itself. No litigation might take place for two years, so that all energy would go into defense. The pope agreed to absolve renegade Latins who had fought for the Greeks if they would now repent and fight for the Latin empire again. No item useful for defense might be exported from Constantinople without the special permission of the emperor, the podestà, and the barons.

Baldwin II himself visited Paris, where he appealed to Louis IX and to the queen-mother, Blanche of Castile, great-aunt of his wife, Mary of Brienne. Blanche found Baldwin childish, insufficiently wise and vigorous for his role as emperor; none the less she befriended him. In Flanders, Baldwin had to fight to obtain the marquisate of Namur. In 1238 he visited England, where Henry III at first received him coldly because of an old grudge against John of Brienne, but eventually welcomed him to London and gave him some money. From Constantinople came bad news; Mary and the barons were hungry, the enemy had rolled up movable towers preparatory to a siege, and some of the barons were stealing out through the gates secretly by night to flee to the west. Baldwin decided to dispatch at once part of the army he had been collecting. But Frederick II delayed their passage in northern Italy, where he was besieging Milan. When Gregory IX furiously demanded that Frederick give them safe passage, he consented. But then the commander, John of Béthune, died at Venice while arranging transportation, and the men dispersed. Only a Venetian fleet averted the loss of Constantinople.

In these difficult times, the hard-pressed Latin barons arranged to mortgage the Crown of Thorns to the Venetians. The podestà took over the great relic as surety for a loan of 13,134 hyperpers, a sum originally advanced by four different creditors, including the podestà, but subsequently consolidated by Nicholas Querini, a single Venetian, who thus acquired custody of the crown. Absolute ownership would pass to him if repayment were not forthcoming within a prescribed length of time. Late in 1238 Louis IX redeemed the crown, which proceeded on its famous journey to Paris and its resting-place in the specially built Sainte Chapelle.

Further disappointment awaited Baldwin, who found that most of the great French nobles were unwilling to fight any enemy in the east except the Saracens. Sailing to the Levant in June 1239, they went to Acre instead of Constantinople.[35] Baldwin himself mortgaged Namur to Louis IX for 50,000 *livres parisis*, and then marched out with some 30,000 or more troops, arriving at Constantinople safely in 1239, having received no hindrance but rather help from Asen. In 1240 Latin-Kuman forces took Tzurulum, selling their Greek captives into slavery to their fellow-Greeks. A Venetian fleet once more defeated Vatatzes, whose admiral attributed the loss to the superiority of the Latin vessels.

Meanwhile the widower John Asen had married Irene, the beautiful daughter of his prisoner Theodore of Epirus, and had set Theodore free after ten years in prison. Theodore put himself at the head of a conspiracy of his former favorites and expelled Manuel from Thessalonica. Because he was blind, Theodore could not again become "basileus", but he named his son John (1236–1244) to the office.

The death of Gregory IX in 1241 deprived Baldwin II of his most powerful friend, and the two-year papal interregnum which ensued damaged his prospects. When Baldwin sought to raise money by conferring his western fief of Courtenay on Geoffrey II of Villehardouin, prince of Achaea, Louis IX angrily refused to invest Villehardouin with the estate, which was intimately connected with the French royal family. Baldwin acknowledged the rebuke, but pleaded poverty. The year 1241 brought also the death of John Asen, who was succeeded by his young son Coloman I. This development, together with the reëstablishment of a "basileus" in Thessalonica, naturally aroused Vatatzes' wish to intervene once more in Europe. He made a truce with the Latins to give himself a freer hand. Having secured the person of Theodore of Epirus by

[35] On the 1239 crusade, see below, chapter XIII, pp. 469–481.

trickery, Vatatzes invaded Europe and forced the basileus John to lay down the imperial crown, and to content himself with the title of despot as an award from the Nicaean empire. But a Mongol victory over the Selchükids and the consequent threat to Asia Minor drew Vatatzes back across the straits to Asia.

Our appreciation of Baldwin's poverty is vividly enhanced by the information that there were fighting in the Selchükid armies at this period about 1,000 Latins. They had proved the decisive influence in bringing to the throne sultan Ghiyāth-ad-Dīn Kai-Khusrau II, and enjoyed the special privilege of not kissing his foot. Records of their extraordinary valor against the Mongols reflect the awe in which both their employers and their enemies held them. Indeed, the sultan was so anxious to procure more of these splendid fighters, and so unaware of the weakness of the Latin empire, that about this time he offered Baldwin II an alliance. He asked for a Latin princess as a bride, and promised that she would not have to abandon Christianity, but might have her own chaplain and other clerics and maintain an entire Christian household. Himself the son of a Greek princess,[36] Kai-Khusrau II even offered to build churches in all his cities, and pay Christian priests to officiate in them. He would put the entire hierarchy of Christian bishoprics within his dominions under the jurisdiction of the Latin patriarchate of Constantinople. In fact, he hinted, if his bride should prove truly affectionate, he might himself become a Christian.

Baldwin II was greatly tempted by this offer, and tried to persuade Blanche of Castile of the sultan's great power and high potential usefulness as an ally. He asked that she request one of his sisters to send a daughter out to Constantinople to seal the bargain, since Baldwin and Mary had none of their own. But no more is heard of the proposal. Baldwin's enthusiasm may have abated when he learned more about his prospective ally. Kai-Khusrau was a weak and dissipated man, and was not an enemy of Vatatzes, as he tried to make Baldwin believe, but on excellent terms with him. Moreover, on July 2, 1243, a month before Baldwin wrote to Blanche, the Mongols had defeated the sultan at Köse Dagh in eastern Anatolia, and broken through to Iconium, which they ravaged. It was Vatatzes, anxious to preserve Nicaea from the Mongols, who concluded an alliance with the Selchükids. But the Mongols withdrew from Asia Minor, and thereafter

[36] (Jean) du Bouchet, *Histoire généalogique de la maison de Courtenay* (Paris, 1661), *Preuves*, p. 19, but cf. below, chapter XIX, p. 692, note 12, for a different identification of Kai-Khusrau's mother.

contented themselves with collecting tribute from the Selchükids, who never again regained their former power or prestige.[37] Though the threat to Nicaea was thus averted, it had seemed serious enough to divert Vatatzes' attention for several years from the Latins in Constantinople.

In this period of Baldwin's first sojourn in Constantinople (1239 to 1243 or 1244), he leaned heavily upon Louis IX and Blanche of Castile. He sent relics to Paris, surely in the hope of receiving money in exchange, and also consulted both mother and son about his problems. In a letter of August 1243, he replied to a charge that Blanche had made against him, that he had two Greeks on his council, and governed according to their advice:

> We declare and swear to you that we have never in the past made use in any way of the advice of any Greeks, nor do we now make use of it, nor shall we ever make use of it. On the contrary, whatever we do is done at the counsel of the noble and good men of France who are in our company. . . . Whatever you may find needs correction, we beg you to tell us to correct it, and you will find us ready to follow your advice and your command. . . . All our faith and hope lie in the grace of our lord the king, your most serene son, and in your own.[38]

Baldwin's denial that he had Greek councillors and his insistence that he relied solely on Frenchmen provide a striking commentary on the change in policies since the death of the emperor Henry. In its humility, the letter to Blanche reveals the imperial dependence on Paris, no doubt made even more complete in these years by the vacancy on the papal throne. In 1243 or early 1244, Baldwin returned to the west, to remain until October 1248.

In the spring of 1244, he played a considerable role in the futile negotiations for peace between Frederick II and pope Innocent IV, interceding with Innocent on behalf of Frederick, serving as one of Frederick's envoys and confidants, and obtaining Frederick's intercession with Vatatzes to win a truce for one year, presumably 1244–1245. After the flight of the pope to Lyons in December 1244, Baldwin II remained with Frederick, and may have acted as his representative in the preliminaries to the Council of Lyons. But at the council (June 28, 1245) Baldwin sat at the pope's right hand, holding the place of honor among secular princes. He heard

[37] On the Selchükids, see below, chapter XIX, pp. 682–692; on the Mongols, chapter XXI, pp. 715–718.

[38] A. Teulet, *Layettes*, II, pp. 518–519, no. 3123.

Nicholas, the Latin patriarch of Constantinople, tell the assembled prelates of the aggression of the Greeks, and Innocent preach a sermon on his five great sorrows, one of which was the Greek schism and the Greek threat to Latin Constantinople. Though the main business of the council was the quarrel with Frederick — Innocent had him "deposed", one of the charges being the marriage between his daughter Constance and the recently widowed Vatatzes — it also adopted canons setting aside monies in aid of the Latin empire; these were to include one tenth of the pope's own income and one half of all income from any benefice whose holder had not been in residence for six months or more, unless he had been away on official business.

For the next two years Baldwin's complicated business affairs in the Low Countries detained him in the west, but by October 1248 he was back in Constantinople. Deep in debt, he authorized the empress Mary to mortgage any of his western lands to raise the sum of 24,000 hyperpers which he owed to certain merchants of Constantinople. This large sum may well have been the debt to the Venetian merchant brothers, John and Angelo Ferro, for which, we know, Baldwin at some time mortgaged the person of his only son Philip of Courtenay, who was born about 1240. Early in his childhood Philip was sent off to Venice as surety for his father's debt, and spent many years there in the custody of his father's creditors. His mother, the empress Mary, in 1248, upon Baldwin's return, set off in her turn for the west. She never did mortgage her husband's western lands, probably because of the opposition of Blanche of Castile and Louis IX to such a procedure. Nor did Louis, as has sometimes been asserted, redeem her son, the mortgaged Philip; he did send him in 1258 some money for expenses (1,000 *livres tournois*), but the sum needed to secure Philip's freedom was too large for even Louis's generosity. It was eventually to come from quite another benefactor.[39]

During Baldwin's absence the Mongol danger to Nicaea had subsided, and the despot John of Thessalonica had died and been succeeded by his dissipated younger brother Demetrius. In 1246, therefore, Vatatzes visited Europe. When he heard that Coloman I of Bulgaria had also died, Vatatzes proceeded to take over from the Bulgarians by bloodless conquest Serres, the Rhodope mountains, and most of Macedonia. These great territorial acquisitions led plotters inside Thessalonica to put forward feelers to him.

[39] R. L. Wolff, "Mortgage and Redemption of an Emperor's Son: Castile and the Latin Empire of Constantinople," *Speculum*, XXIX (1954), 45–84.

Vatatzes promised them that he would renew the city's privileges, and the conspirators admitted him. Their leader seems to have been Irene, daughter of Theodore of Epirus and widow of John Asen. Vatatzes, now ruler of Thessalonica, took Demetrius back with him to Asia late in 1246. The Greek "empire" of the west had now virtually disappeared. The aged Theodore clung to his little principality around Ostrovo, but was no real menace to Nicaea. More of a threat was Michael, a bastard son of Michael I, the founder of the Epirote house. Starting in the 1230's in Acarnania, he had reasserted the old Epirote autonomy. The fall of Thessalonica brought despot Michael II (1236–1271) and Vatatzes face to face.

In 1247, the truce procured by Frederick II having expired, Vatatzes attacked the Latins at Tzurulum, capturing it after a major siege. Inside he found his own sister-in-law, Eudocia Lascaris, once intended for the emperor Robert but long since married to a French noble, Anseau of "Cahieu" (Cayeux), who had left her behind in Tzurulum in the hope that her presence there would deter Vatatzes from the siege. But Vatatzes merely sent Eudocia back to Constantinople, and proceeded to take Vizya. Inside the capital, the Latins now feared the worst. But a new emergency on Rhodes, where the Genoese and the prince of Achaea were battling the Greeks, drew Vatatzes away from the attack on Constantinople.

The wretched last years of the Latin empire have left scanty records. Baldwin II was apparently absent from Constantinople much of the time, engaged in a fruitless search for more money and more men than anybody would spare. In 1249 he seems to have visited king Louis's camp at Damietta.[40] In his absence Philip of Toucy acted as bailie in Constantinople. He too borrowed from Loius IX in Palestine in 1251.

As if to symbolize the hopelessness of the Latin position, pope Innocent IV himself reversed the traditional policy of the popes towards Constantinople. As early as 1247 we find him countermanding earlier commands to the clergy to give money for the Latins. He hoped instead to end the schism by direct negotiations with Vatatzes. Queen Maria of Hungary reported that Vatatzes would accept papal supremacy, and in May 1249 Innocent sent the minister-general of the Franciscans, John of Parma, to negotiate directly. He was authorized to call a council in the east, if the Greeks would accept the *filioque*. Vatatzes' return mission was held

[40] For the crusades of Louis IX, see below, chapter XIV.

9. The Balkans in 1237, at the Death of John of Brienne (*Map by the University of Wisconsin Cartographic Laboratory*)

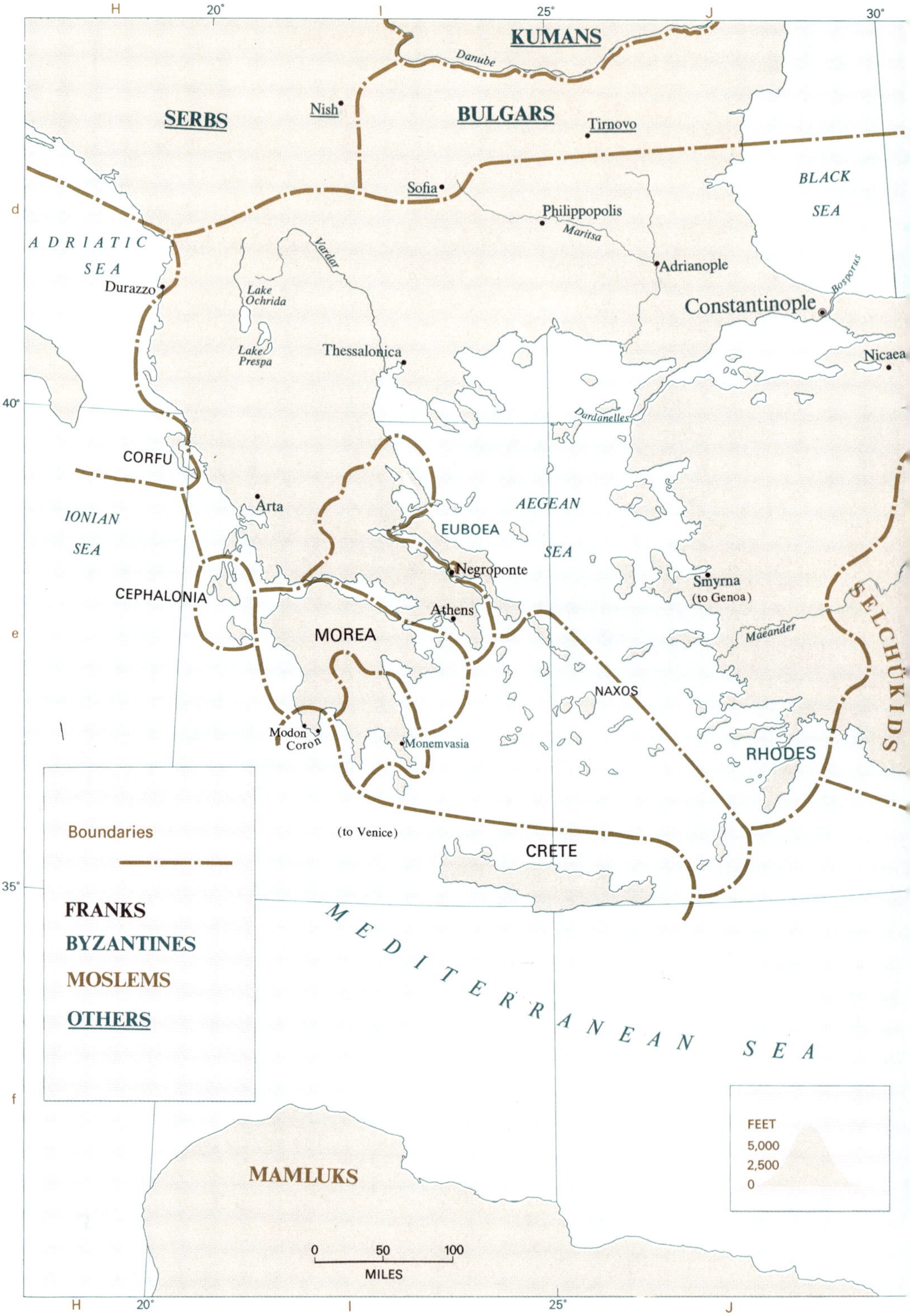

10. The Balkans in 1291, at the Fall of Acre (*Map by the University of Wisconsin Cartographic Laboratory*)

up in southern Italy, first by Frederick II, deeply suspicious of the papal-Nicaean discussions, and, after Frederick's death in 1250, by his successor Manfred. The pope finally received the Greek envoys, and sent them back with new proposals. These long-drawn-out negotiations during the years 1249–1252 gave the Latins a new respite. If Vatatzes could win back Constantinople by diplomacy, he would not launch a full-scale siege.

These years saw an increase in the power of Michael II of Epirus. Though Vatatzes had arranged a dynastic marriage between his own granddaughter, Maria, child of Theodore (II) Lascaris, and Nicephorus, son and heir of Michael II, Michael none the less listened to the siren voice of his aged blind uncle, Theodore of Epirus, who would conspire as long as there was a breath left in his body. In 1252, therefore, Vatatzes' armies ravaged Theodore's appanage at Ostrovo and Michael's territory alike. Michael had to surrender numerous strong points in Epirus and Albania as the price of peace. The presence of so large a Nicaean army in Europe led Innocent IV once again to instruct the clergy to aid the barons and Venetians and the prince of Achaea in any resistance against Vatatzes.

But a new embassy from Nicaea arrived in Rome in 1254. Vatatzes now offered to recognize papal supremacy in matters of faith, and to call a council to consider the *filioque*. In exchange, however, he demanded that Constantinople be restored to him, and its patriarchal throne to his patriarch Arsenius. These demands the papacy had always previously refused to consider. But this time Innocent IV replied only that he could make no promises with regard to Constantinople, because the Latin emperor had not been charged with any offense for which he could be summoned before the papal court and convicted. The pope promised to use his good offices to settle questions at issue between the Latin and the Greek emperors. He also allowed himself to hint that complete Nicaean submission to Rome might be followed by papal support for the resumption of Greek control over the capital. He was prepared to call the Nicaean patriarch "patriarch of Constantinople". Then, "after it had come about by some turn of fortune" that the city of Constantinople had fallen to Vatatzes, Innocent IV would restore the Greek patriarch to his ancient residence, where he would govern the subjects of both Latin and Greek patriarchates.[41]

These guarded words make it clear that Innocent was reconciled

[41] R. L. Wolff, *op. cit.* (in note 39), p. 69, note 54. Text in F. Schillmann, "Zur byzantinischen Politik Alexanders IV.," *Römische Quartalschrift*, XXII (1908), part 4, p. 114.

to the fall of Latin empire and patriarchate if he could obtain union by negotiation. If Nicaea should submit to Rome, Innocent would look the other way while Vatatzes captured Constantinople. But both Vatatzes and Innocent died in 1254, and the negotiations were interrupted. In 1256 pope Alexander IV sent bishop Constantine of Orvieto to Vatatzes' successor, Theodore II Lascaris, with the authorization, if necessary, to repeat the offer of Innocent IV. The discussions apparently came to nothing, but it is clear from the papal correspondence that the Latin empire had failed as an instrument of papal foreign policy. Neither a union of the churches nor a successful crusade had been achieved through its instrumentality, and Innocent IV and Alexander IV therefore wrote it off. Perhaps Baldwin's friendship with Frederick II and his later intimacy with Manfred may have helped the popes reach this decision.

Theodore II Lascaris passed his brief reign (1254–1258) in Balkan warfare against Bulgarians, Epirotes, Albanians, and Serbs, but had no opportunity to move against the Latins. After Lascaris's death Michael Palaeologus, descendant of the Byzantine imperial families, successful and ambitious general, and commander of the Nicaean emperor's Latin mercenaries, succeeded to the throne by an elaborate conspiracy. In 1259, at Pelagonia in Macedonia, he defeated the troops of Michael II of Epirus, Manfred, and William of Villehardouin, prince of Achaea, who had formed a coalition against him. William was taken prisoner.[42] The Greeks who had fought in the armies of the coalition now went over to Michael VIII Palaeologus, whose destiny had become clear.

Soon after the accession of Michael VIII, Baldwin II, who apparently believed that the new Nicaean emperor would be willing to make concessions, sent ambassadors to Michael. First, they asked for the cession of Thessalonica and all the land between it and Constantinople. Michael answered "pleasantly" that he regarded Thessalonica as his own native city, and could not consider abandoning it. The envoys then asked for Serres and the territory from that town east to Constantinople. But Michael declared that this was the site of his first military command, and that he therefore would not give it up. When the Latin envoys reduced their demand to the region from Voleron eastwards, this proved to be Michael's

[42] D. J. Geanakoplos, "Greco-Latin Relations on the Eve of the Byzantine Restoration: The Battle of Pelagonia — 1259," *Dumbarton Oaks Papers*, VII (1953), 101–141. See also the same author's "The Nicene Revolution of 1258 and the Usurpation of Michael VIII Palaeologus," *Traditio*, IX (1953), 420–430. On William of Achaea, see below, chapter VII, pp. 244–259.

favorite hunting preserve. The discouraged Latins then asked what land he would be prepared to concede, and were told none. Indeed, as the price of peace, Michael asked for one half the customs dues and one half the revenue from the mint at Constantinople. The courteous insolence of Michael VIII reflects his certainty of eventual triumph.

At this late stage in the history of the Latin empire, a new source of assistance and protection emerged. In 1258 Mary of Brienne obtained from her cousin, Alfonso X, "the Wise", king of Castile, the money needed to redeem her unfortunate son Philip of Courtenay from Baldwin II's Venetian creditors. By May 1261, at the latest, Philip was free. For the empress Mary, favorite great-niece of Blanche of Castile, it was natural to turn to Alfonso, at whose court her own three brothers were leading nobles. As early as 1246–1247 Baldwin II had tried to obtain military aid from the Spanish order of St. James, but the negotiations had fallen through. Now in the late 1250's, however, Alfonso X was striving to accumulate support enough to obtain general recognition as emperor in the west. Aid to the Latin empire of Constantinople was one of the methods he used to enhance his own prestige. He engaged one of his daughters to Philip of Courtenay. There seemed a lively prospect for a Castilian marriage and perhaps for Castilian military support.[43]

But Baldwin II was not to enjoy the chance to use Castilian aid to redress the balance in the east. Early in 1260 Michael VIII plotted to take Constantinople, not by full-dress siege, but by collusion with a Latin noble who had been taken prisoner at Pelagonia, and who now won his freedom by promising to unlock one of the city gates — his house was in the walls — to admit Michael's forces. But the noble failed to keep his part of the bargain, and Michael had to content himself with seizing the environs of the capital. Galata successfully resisted siege, and a one-year truce was concluded between Greeks and Latins. But Baldwin was so poor that he had to strip lead from the roofs of the palaces of Constantinople to raise money.

In the new crisis, the Venetians took a step which, had it come in time, might have preserved the Latin empire considerably longer. The doge (Renier Zeno) and his council authorized the bailie for the captive prince William of Achaea, the barons of the Morea, the rulers of Athens, Negroponte, Crete, Lemnos, and the duchy of the Archipelago, and others to band together for

[43] R. L. Wolff, *loc. cit.*, note 39 above.

the purpose of stationing a permanent, regularly-paid garrison in Constantinople, to consist of 1,000 men. Venice would pay her share of the stipend, and would secure guarantees from the other partners for their share.[44] But this practical approach to the fundamental problem of defense for the capital came too late. There is no evidence that further action was taken, probably because events supervened.

Before striking at the Latins, Michael VIII Palaeologus rendered himself secure in Europe and Asia by negotiating agreements with the Bulgarians, the Selchükids, and the Mongols. For the actual blow at Constantinople, he believed that he needed naval power not available at Nicaea. He turned to the Genoese, rivals of the Venetians, who had recently expelled the Genoese from Acre (1258). Indeed, the Genoese, quite willing to brave papal displeasure in order to have so useful an ally, seem to have made the initial overtures to Michael. On March 13, 1261, the two powers signed a treaty at Nymphaeum, which was ratified in Genoa on July 10. The Genoese undertook to supply a squadron of up to fifty warships, to be used against the enemies of Genoa, the expense to be borne by Michael. Nicaea would admit Genoese merchants to its territories free of all duties, and would cede to Genoa Smyrna and quarters in all key Byzantine ports, including Constantinople, where they would obtain not only all their own former possessions but all those now belonging to the Venetians. The Black Sea would be closed to all enemies of Genoa, except Pisa. Genoese subjects might serve in the Nicaean armies, and the Nicaean authorities might command the services of Genoese vessels in Nicaean waters to assist in the defense of fortresses.[45]

But before the Genoese fleet could be sent to the east, even before the ratification of the treaty, Michael's troops had taken Constantinople. In the spring of 1261 he sent two armies westward; one, under his brother John, the despot, was to oppose Michael II of Epirus; the other, under the caesar Alexius Strategopoulus, was to oppose the Bulgarians, and on the way to make a demonstration to frighten the Latins at Constantinople. The inhabitants of the immediate environs of the capital, between the Sea of Marmara and the Black Sea, were of course Greek farmers and fishermen, on

[44] Text printed by W. Norden, *Das Papsttum und Byzanz* (Berlin, 1903; reprinted New York, 1958), pp. 759 ff.

[45] Text in C. Manfroni, "Le Relazioni fra Genova, l'impero bizantino e i Turchi," *Atti della Società Ligure di storia patria,* XXVIII (1896), 791 ff.; also see *Liber jurium reipublicae Genovensis* (*Monumenta Historiae Patriae,* VII, Turin, 1854), cols. 1350 ff., no. 945. A discussion of Genoese commercial affairs in the Levant is planned for volume IV of this work.

whom the city relied for food. The historian George Pachymeres calls them *thelematarioi*, or voluntaries, because their allegiance to Greek or Latin was a matter of their own shifting will. The free access to the city enjoyed by the thelematarioi and their natural Greek sympathies made them useful intelligence agents for Michael VIII, who had also established contact with some Greeks living inside the city and nominally loyal to the Latins. On his expedition, Strategopoulus made use of the thelematarioi, who told him of a passageway through or under the city walls, wide enough to admit a single armed man at a time. At the moment of Strategopoulus's arrival, moreover, the Venetian podestà, Marco Gradenigo, a particularly active warrior — no doubt sent out from Venice to act in the spirit of the recent Venetian resolve to defend Constantinople — had loaded most of the Latin defenders aboard ship to attack the island of Daphnusia, in the Black Sea about 70 miles east of the opening of the Bosporus. This virtually stripped Constantinople of its defenders. It is certainly possible that Michael VIII had arranged for Gradenigo to be offered Daphnusia as bait, and had thus lured him into leaving the capital almost undefended.

In these favorable circumstances, Strategopoulus may have infiltrated men through the passageway by night until enough were inside to attack the Latin guards on the walls, open the gates from within, and admit the rest of the Greeks. Or he may have been admitted by some of the thelematarioi who placed ladders inside the walls, killed the guards, and opened the Gate of the Spring to the waiting Nicaean armies. Once the Greeks were inside, a few street fights in the dark completed the operation. Baldwin II fled from the palace of the Blachernae, far up the Golden Horn, to the Boukoleon on the Sea of Marmara. He left behind the imperial purple hat, made according to a Latin design but decorated with a great ruby, as well as the imperial swords wrapped in purple silk and the purple boots. Hastening back from Daphnusia, the fleet found that the conquering Greeks had set fire to the commercial quarter along the Golden Horn, where the families of the Venetian residents lived. This move Strategopoulus took on the advice of John Phylax, a Greek who had been a confidant of Baldwin II, but who now quickly and expediently changed sides. So when the Venetian ships sailed into the harbor, the wives and children of the men aboard were standing on the quays crying for help while their houses and shops burned behind them. The fleet saved the victims, and Strategopoulus's troops completed their occupation of the capital unimpeded.

Some of the Latins rushed to monasteries and tried to disguise themselves in monastic habit, while their women hid in dark corners. One ship belonging to the Venetian firm of Ca' Pesaro rescued Baldwin II, who was wounded in one arm and hungry. The fleet set out for Euboea, but had insufficient provisions, and on the journey many of the refugees died of hunger. At Negroponte Baldwin was welcomed by his vassals, the rulers of the island, by the lord of Athens, and by the duchess of the Archipelago. He created some knights, and sold some relics. Then he sailed away to Italy, where Manfred received him with great friendship and enlisted him among his strong supporters, a relationship which led to the grave suspicions of the papacy and to the weakening of the Castilian alliance sponsored by the empress Mary. Carrying with him "only the shadow of a great name",[46] Baldwin II embarked upon a long series of intrigues to obtain support for the reconquest of Constantinople. Only disappointment and failure lay ahead.

Michael VIII heard of Strategopoulus's victory at Meteorium. On August 15, 1261, preceded by the sacred icon of the "Virgin who points the way", the Hodegetria, he made his ceremonial entry through the Golden Gate into Byzantium, depopulated and in disrepair after the long Latin occupation but always the sacred city of the Greek world. When the procession reached Hagia Sophia, Michael was crowned basileus. The rule of the Latins was over.

Doomed to failure from the first, the Latin empire of Constantinople yet takes its place in history as something more than an outpost of Venetian colonial enterprise and of French and Lombard feudalism on Greek soil. Its freakish constitution claims our interest; the efforts of its wisest emperor and of several popes to heal the breach between Latins and Greeks deserve our attention. Even more arresting: Latin rule deepened and perpetuated the hatred between the two branches of Christendom. Though Michael Palaeologus, in his fear of a renewed assault from the west, would in 1274 actually consent to a union between the churches, he could command very little support for this policy from his people; and in practice the act remained null. One future emperor would in 1369 be personally converted to the Roman faith. No reign would pass without negotiations looking towards unity, and at the Council of Ferrara-Florence a new treaty would in 1439 finally be signed. Yet public opinion could never be won to support reunion with the hated Latins: only extreme danger from the Turks had made it possible, and the rank and file of the Orthodox Greeks on the whole

[46] *Annales S. Iustinae Patavinae* (*MGH, SS.*, XIX), p. 182.

preferred the turban of the sultan to the cardinal's hat. After 1261 the restored Byzantine empire, with its pretensions to world rule undimmed, remained nothing but a Balkan state, shorn of its territories and its resources, plundered and weak. When it eventually fell to the Turks in 1453, its spiritual heirs, the Russians, who had absorbed the Orthodox distaste for the west, attributed its fall to the agreement its emperor had made with the papacy at Ferrara-Florence. Since Constantinople had been punished for its abandonment of orthodoxy, Moscow and Moscow alone, so its churchmen insisted, was the only possessor of the truth. In a very real sense we may trace back to the atrocities of the Fourth Crusade and the persecutions of the period of Latin rule at Byzantium a breach between the Orthodox world and the west that is far from healed in our own day.

11. Frankish Greece (*Map by the University of Wisconsin Cartographic Laboratory*)

VII
THE FRANKISH STATES IN GREECE, 1204–1311

By the partition treaty of October 1204 the western part of the Byzantine empire was to be divided among the conquerors of Constantinople, as we have already seen in the preceding chapter. Venice was assigned Albania, Epirus, Acarnania, and Aetolia, as well as the Ionian islands, the Morea (except for the Argolid and Corinthia), the northern part of Euboea with Oreus and the

The present chapter is based upon a wide range of sources. In addition to the correspondence of pope Innocent III and his successors; the works of Geoffrey of Villehardouin (ed. Edm. Faral, Les Classiques de l'histoire de France au moyen-âge, 2 vols., Paris, 1938–1939), Robert of Clari (ed. P. Lauer, *ibid.*, Paris, 1924), and the later French chroniclers; the German and Italian chroniclers of cities and larger regions; Nicetas Choniates, George Acropolites, George Pachymeres, and Nicephorus Gregoras (all in the *CSHB*, with a later edition of Acropolites by Aug. Heisenberg, 2 vols., Leipzig, 1903), the following are among the more important primary and secondary sources: Henry of Valenciennes, *Histoire de l'empereur Henri de Constantinople* (ed. Jean Longnon in Documents relatifs à l'histoire des croisades, II, Paris, 1948); Aubrey of Trois-Fontaines, *Chronica* (*MGH, SS.*, XXIII), pp. 631–950; Richard of San Germano, *Chronica* [of Sicily] (ed. C. A. Garufi, *RISS*, VII, part 2, 1937); Andrea Dandolo, *Chronicon Venetum* (*RISS*, XII), cols. 13–524; *Chronique rimée de Philippe Mouskes* (ed. Baron Reiffenberg, Commission royale d'histoire [of Belgium], 2 vols., Brussels, 1836–1838); J. A. C. Buchon, *Recherches historiques sur la principauté française de Morée et ses hautes baronnies* (2 vols., Paris, 1845), containing the French and Greek versions of the *Chronicle of the Morea*, now better studied in: *Livre de la conqueste de la princée de l'Amorée: Chronique de Morée (1204–1305)* (ed. Jean Longnon, Société de l'histoire de France, Paris, 1911), and *Τὸ Χρονικὸν τοῦ Μορέως* (*Chronicle of the Morea*, ed. John Schmitt, London, 1904, and also ed. P. P. Kalonaros, Athens, 1940). The Aragonese version of the *Chronicle of the Morea* is called the *Libro de los fechos et conquistas del principado de la Morea* (ed. Alfred Morel-Fatio, Société de l'Orient latin, sér. hist., IV, Geneva, 1885); *Τὸ Χρονικὸν τοῦ Γαλαξειδίου* (*Chronicle of Galaxidi*, dating from the year 1703, ed. K. N. Sathas, Athens, 1865, repr. 1914, and also ed. G. Valetas, Athens, 1944). Important information relating to the years before and after 1200 may be found in Michael Choniates, *Μιχαὴλ Ἀκομινάτου τοῦ Χωνιάτου τὰ Σωζόμενα*, ed. Spyridon P. Lampros (2 vols., Athens, 1879–1880). See also Chas. Hopf, *Chroniques gréco-romanes inédites ou peu connues* (Berlin, 1873), which contains various sources; G. L. Fr. Tafel and G. M. Thomas, *Urkunden zur älteren Handels- und Staatsgeschichte der Republik Venedig* (3 vols., in Fontes Rerum Austriacarum [*Diplomataria et Acta*], vols. XII, XIII, XIV, Vienna, 1856–1857); G. M. Thomas (and R. Predelli), *Diplomatarium Veneto-Levantinum*, Monumenti storici publicati dalla R. Deputazione Veneta di Storia Patria, ser. prima, Documenti, vols. V, IX, (Venice, 1880–1899); Georges Recoura, ed., *Les Assises de Romanie*, Bibliothèque de l'École des hautes études, fasc. 258 (Paris, 1930), and an English translation of the Assizes is provided by Peter W. Topping, *Feudal Institutions as Revealed in the Assizes of Romania*, University of Pennsylvania Translations and Reprints, 3rd series, Philadelphia, 1949; also Paul Riant, *Exuviae sacrae Constantinopolitanae* (2 vols., Geneva, 1877–1878); Franz Miklosich and Joseph Müller, *Acta et*

southern part with Carystus, together with the island of Andros. In 1204, however, Michael Ducas Angelus Comnenus took over the entire area from Albania to the Gulf of Patras. The treaty assigned to the crusaders western Macedonia, Thessaly, Attica, and Megara. The emperor obtained the islands of Tenos and Scyros. Though the treaty made no mention of it, Boniface of Montferrat, already king of Thessalonica and master of the regions of western Thrace and Macedonia, may also tacitly have been allotted the Argolid, Corinthia, Boeotia, and the central portion of Euboea. In October and November 1204, marching by way of the Vale of Tempe, Boniface occupied the plain of Thessaly and, after

diplomata graeca medii aevi sacra et profana (6 vols., Vienna, 1860–1890); J. A. C. Buchon, *Recherches et matériaux pour servir à une histoire de la domination française dans les provinces démembrées de l'empire grec* (2 vols., Paris, 1840); *idem, Chroniques étrangères relatives aux expéditions françaises pendant le XIIIme siècle* (Paris, 1841); *idem, Nouvelles recherches historiques sur la principauté française de Morée et ses hautes baronnies* (2 vols., Paris, 1845). Frequent use should be made of Gustave Schlumberger, *Numismatique de l'Orient latin* (Paris, 1878), and G. Schlumberger, Ferdinand Chalandon, and Adrien Blanchet, *Sigillographie de l'Orient latin* (Paris, 1943).

Karl Hopf, *Geschichte Griechenlands vom Beginn des Mittelalters bis auf unsere Zeit,* in J. S. Ersch and J. G. Gruber, eds., *Allgemeine Encyklopädie der Wissenschaften und Künste* (167 vols., Leipzig, 1818–1889), vols. LXXXV–LXXXVI, 1867–1868, is old but still very valuable. William Miller, *The Latins in the Levant* (London, 1908), excellent in its day but also rather antiquated now; *idem, Essays on the Latin Orient* (Cambridge, 1921); Sir Rennell Rodd, *The Princes of Achaia and the Chronicles of Morea* (2 vols., London, 1907), rather superficial but interesting to read; René Grousset, *L'Empire du Levant* (Paris, 1946); Jean Longnon, *L'Empire latin de Constantinople et la principauté de Morée* (Paris, 1949); Donald M. Nicol, *The Despotate of Epiros* (Oxford, 1957); Ernst Meyer, *Peloponnesische Wanderungen* (Zurich and Leipzig, 1939); Antoine Bon, in *Corinth,* vol. III, part 2: *The Defenses of Acrocorinth and the Lower Town,* American School of Classical Studies at Athens (Cambridge, Mass., 1936); Ferd. Gregorovius, *Geschichte der Stadt Athen im Mittelalter* (2 vols., Stuttgart, 1889), and modern Greek trans. by Sp. P. Lampros (2 vols., Athens, 1904), with a third volume of documents (Athens, 1906, repr. 1917); Kenneth M. Setton, *Catalan Domination of Athens, 1311–1388,* Mediaeval Academy of America (Cambridge, Mass., 1948), which contains also a complete bibliography and critical discussion of the works of the great Catalan historian Antoni Rubió i Lluch, esp. pp. 286–291.

W. Heyd, *Histoire du commerce du Levant au moyen-âge* (trans. Furcy Raynaud, 2 vols. Leipzig, 1885, repr. 1923, 1936), is still the best work on the subject. Note should also be made of: W. Norden, *Das Papsttum und Byzanz* (Berlin, 1903); *idem, Der Vierte Kreuzzug* (Berlin, 1898); John K. Fotheringham, *Marco Sanudo, Conqueror of the Archipelago* (Oxford, 1915); Jean Longnon, *Recherches sur la vie de Geoffroy de Villehardouin* (Paris, 1939); *idem,* "La Reprise de Salonique par les Grecs en 1224," *Actes du VIe Congrès International d'Études Byzantines,* I (Paris, 1950), 141-146; Conrad Chapman, *Michel Paléologue, restaurateur de l'empire byzantin (1261–1282)* (Paris, 1926); Deno J. Geanakoplos, "Greco-Latin Relations on the Eve of the Byzantine Restoration: the Battle of Pelagonia — 1259," *Dumbarton Oaks Papers,* VII (1953), 99–141; Francesco Cerone, "La sovranità napoletana sulla Morea," *Archivio storico per le province napoletane,* new series, II (vol. XLI of the entire collection, Naples, 1916), 5–64, 193–266, and III (1917), 5–67; Jean Longnon, "Le Rattachement de la principauté de Morée au royaume de Sicile en 1267," *Journal des savants* (1942), pp. 134–143; *idem,* "Problèmes de l'histoire de la principauté de Morée," *ibid.* (1946), pp. 77–93, 147–161; Ernst Gerland, *Neue Quellen zur Geschichte des lateinischen Erzbistums Patras* (Leipzig, 1903); Heinrich Kretschmayr, *Geschichte von Venedig* (2 vols., Gotha, 1905–1920); and Georg Caro, *Genua und die Mächte am Mittelmeer, 1257–1311* (2 vols., Halle a.S., 1895–1899).

forcing the pass of Thermopylae, took possession of Thebes and Athens. Then, overcoming the opposition of the Greek tyrant, Leo Sgourus, at the isthmus of Corinth, he pushed on into the Morea and laid siege to Nauplia.

Towards the end of November 1204, however, Geoffrey of Villehardouin, nephew of the historian, having gone first to Syria, was on his way to rejoin the crusaders in Constantinople when he was cast ashore by a storm at the port of Modon in the southern Morea. A Greek noble of the region offered to make an alliance with him for the purpose of conquering the country, a task which they speedily accomplished. When the Greek died soon thereafter, his son betrayed Geoffrey, who then set off for Nauplia to join Boniface. There he encountered an old friend and compatriot in the person of William of Champlitte, grandson of count Hugh of Champagne, with whom he offered to share the conquest of the Morea. With one hundred knights and four hundred mounted sergeants, Geoffrey and William advanced along the northern and western coast of the Morea; they took Patras and Pondikos by assault, and Andravida opened its gates. The people of the countryside came to make their submission and were confirmed in their property and local customs. Only the town of Arcadia (Cyparissia) put up a prolonged resistance (until about February 1205).

Michael of Epirus, established on the other side of the Gulf of Patras, coveted the Morea, for many quite obvious reasons. Wishing to expel William of Champlitte and his companions, he advanced into the peninsula with five thousand men, but the little Latin army defeated him. Then the Latins completed the conquest of Messenia and advanced into the interior of the country, occupying the entire Morea with the exception of Arcadia and Laconia.

William of Champlitte thus became master of the Morea with the title prince of Achaea, which pope Innocent III conferred on him in November 1205. This designation remained the official title, especially in Latin, of his successors; in French they were more often called "princes de la Morée". William divided the unoccupied lands — the imperial demesne and the estates of the great landholders who had fled — among his companions, giving fiefs not only to knights but even to sergeants, as well as to prelates and to the military orders — Templars, Hospitallers, and Teutonic Knights. Even the Greek magnates who had made their submission — the *archontes*, as they were called — received a place in the feudal organization and kept their lands, for which they had the same rights and duties as the French knights. Furthermore, the conquerors left the people of the towns and of the countryside in their former condition, and treated them with such moderation and tolerance as to retain their goodwill.

Meanwhile Boniface of Montferrat, master of all the territory from Thessalonica to the Gulf of Argolis, had distributed the conquered lands to his companions. The Burgundian Othon de la Roche received the lordship of Athens; the Italians Albertino and Rolandino of Canossa, that of Thebes; and the doughty James of Avesnes, that of Negroponte,[1] where he was soon succeeded by the Veronese Ravano dalle Carceri; Guy Pallavicini became marquis of Bodonitsa near Thermopylae, and a knight from the district of Laon, Thomas of Autremencourt (called by his contemporaries "de Stromoncourt"), received Salona, the ancient Amphissa, not far from the ruins of Delphi. In Thessaly and Macedonia, Domokos, Velestinon, Larissa, Platamon, Citrum, and other strongholds became the portions of other crusaders, German, Italian, Burgundian, or Provençal — count Berthold of Katzenellenbogen, Wierich of Daun, Amédée Pofey,[2] Orlando Pescia, Hugh of Coligny, and others — while Boniface reserved for himself, as royal castellanies, a certain number of towns in Macedonia such as Christopolis and Serres. His kingdom of Thessalonica thus extended from the Rhodope mountains to the Morea, where he exercised vague rights of suzerainty over the principality of Achaea.

Venice, traditionally uninterested in the hinterland, proceeded to make good her claims to the important way-stations — already guaranteed her by treaty — along the sea route to Constantinople. In 1206, the Venetians armed a fleet which took Corfu, then seized Modon and Coron in the southwestern part of the Morea, and thence sailed for Crete, purchased from Boniface in 1204, where it embarked upon a long struggle against the Genoese and the Greeks. Elsewhere in the Aegean a rich Venetian, Marco Sanudo, armed a flotilla at his own expense and in 1207, with the aid of several of his compatriots, took possession of Naxos and the principal islands of the Cyclades. His cousin Marino Dandolo became lord of Andros, while Andrew and Jeremiah Ghisi obtained Tenos, Myconos, and the northern Sporades; John Querini received Astypalaea (Stampalia); Jacob Barozzi, Thera (Santorin); and

[1] Euboea: the name "Negroponte" was applied indiscriminately to the island, to the lordship, to the Venetian "bailiwick", and to the capital city (ancient Chalcis).

[2] He is called Buffois, Boffa, Buffedus in texts relating to the Latin empire: see Louis Blondel, "Amédée Pofey, de Cologny, grand connétable de Romanie," *Bulletin de la Société d'Histoire et d'Archéologie de Genève*, IX (1950), 177–200.

Leonard Foscolo, Anaphe. All became vassals of Marco Sanudo, who kept for himself Naxos, Paros, Melos, Siphnos, Cythnos (Thermia), and Syros, to be held by him, with the title duke of the Archipelago, directly from emperor Henry of Constantinople.

By his shrewdness and tolerance, Marco Sanudo was also able to gain the goodwill of his Greek subjects. Finally Marco Venier and Jacob Viaro conquered, respectively, Cerigo and Cerigotto (Cythera and Anticythera) and became vassals of Venice. In Cephalonia, Ithaca, and Zante (Zacynthus), an Italian from Apulia, Maio Orsini, had established himself some time before the capture of Constantinople. He tried to escape the tutelage of Venice by putting himself under the protection of the papacy in 1207, but two years later had to acknowledge himself the vassal of Venice.

By 1209, during the sojourn of the emperor Henry in Greece at the time of his conflict with the Lombard barons of Thessalonica,[3] the prince of Achaea, William of Champlitte, having departed once again for France in 1208, had died, as had his nephew, Hugh of Champlitte, whom he had left as his representative. William's companion, Geoffrey of Villehardouin, either appointed by William or chosen by the barons, had then assumed power. In May 1209 Geoffrey, together with Othon de la Roche, went to Henry's parliament of Ravennika to assure the emperor of his loyalty. Henry confirmed Geoffrey as prince of Achaea and made him his immediate vassal. In June, on the island of Sapientsa off the southwestern coast of the Morea, Geoffrey made a pact with the Venetians; he acknowledged that he had received in fee from the doge of Venice all the lands extending from Corinth to the roadstead of Navarino, being the whole peninsula except the territory of Modon and Coron, which remained in the possession of the Signoria. Geoffrey of Villehardouin thus became the vassal of Venice, saving always the fealty owed to the emperor, his liege lord. But this tie of vassalage was purely theoretical and, in effect, became simply an alliance with Venice, which obtained commercial privileges throughout the whole principality.

A similiar settlement was made at about the same period (March 1209–February 1210) for Euboea, which gave Venice still greater influence there than in the Morea. Ravano dalle Carceri, "lord of Negroponte", had soon extended his authority to the whole island, but, since the north with Oreus and the south with Carystus figured among the territories assigned to Venice in 1204, he acknowledged himself the vassal of the Signoria. Like Villehardouin,

[3] See above, chapter VI, pp. 206–208.

he also was in the position of having two lords: the king of Thessalonica, who had granted him the lordship of Negroponte, and the Signoria of Venice, which was later to exercise powerful influence through its representatives, the bailies of Negroponte.

Finally, in June 1210, taking advantage of the fact that Michael of Epirus had made overtures to the Latin empire, they concluded a treaty by which he acknowledged that he held his lands in fee from the doge of Venice, and granted to the Venetians commercial privileges. But this treaty soon became a dead letter. Michael not only remained completely independent, but shortly thereafter even went so far as to take Corfu and Durazzo from the Venetians.

Thus were constituted, each with its particular status, the various major Frankish states of Greece, which were to maintain themselves for a century and longer: the principality of the Morea and the duchy of the Archipelago, dependent directly on the emperor, but with strong links to Venice; the lordship of Athens, held in vassalage to the king of Thessalonica; Euboea, dependent on both Thessalonica and Venice; and the county of Cephalonia, in theory a satellite of Venice, but always seeking to maintain its autonomy.

Geoffrey I of Villehardouin, recognized by the emperor and by Venice as the master of the Morea, assumed the title prince of Achaea toward the end of the year 1209. He then sent to France for his wife Elizabeth and son Geoffrey. Soon a second son, William, was born to him in the castle of Kalamata in Messenia. He devoted himself to enlarging his possessions. With the aid of Othon de la Roche he seized the fortresses of Acrocorinth (1209), Argos, and Nauplia (1210–1211), where first Leo Sgourus, and then Theodore Angelus Comnenus, brother of Michael of Epirus, had long resisted the attacks of the Latins. He then advanced towards Arcadia and Laconia and made himself master of Sparta (Lacedaemon). The port of Monemvasia and the mountain peoples of Taygetus and Parnon alone succeeded in escaping his domination. He sent to France, mainly to Champagne, for young knights to occupy the newly conquered lands and the fiefs of those who had returned to the west. Women also came out to settle in the Morea, where they founded French families. And gradually there grew up in Greece a chivalric society renowned for its nobility and its refinement.

The lord of Athens, Othon de la Roche, worked hand in hand with Geoffrey of Villehardouin. Since he had helped to reduce

Acrocorinth, Argos, and Nauplia, he received a share of the Argolid with the lordships of Argos and Damala. Furthermore, since Albertino and Rolandino had left Greece, the lordship of Thebes was divided equally between Geoffrey and Othon. As the latter already possessed Lebadea in Boeotia, his holdings were thus almost as extensive as those of the prince of Achaea. Othon made the Acropolis his castle although Thebes was the capital city of his lordship, and it was probably he who erected above the southern wing of the Propylaea the square tower which still stood as late as 1874. The Parthenon became the Latin cathedral, dedicated to Our Lady; and in the monastery of Daphne, on the Sacred Way to Eleusis, Othon established Cistercians from the abbey of Bellevaux. He also sent for relatives and friends from Burgundy, who acquired fiefs and honors in Greece, while his nephew Guy de la Roche became the vassal of Geoffrey for half the lordship of Thebes.

The closing years of the rule of Geoffrey and Othon were marked by two serious developments: a conflict with the church and the downfall of the kingdom of Thessalonica. At the time of the conquest much ecclesiastical property had been secularized and, despite the demands of the clergy, this had not been returned to the churches. Furthermore, the prince of Achaea and the lord of Athens were accused of treating the Greek priests as serfs. Their numbers had considerably increased, since the Greek prelates showed no hesitation in conferring orders on peasants, the *paroikoi*, to permit them to escape the burdens of serfdom and oppressive *corvées*. Finally, the *Chronicle of the Morea* reports that, since the churches had refused to provide their fair share of military aid, Geoffrey had seized their property and devoted the income from it to the construction of the powerful castle of Clermont (Khloumoutsi).

The conflict lasted some five years, from 1218 to 1223. Geoffrey of Villehardouin, whom pope Honorius III had formerly praised for the fervor of his devotion, was now declared by the same pontiff to be an enemy of God "more inhuman than Pharaoh". He was excommunicated and his lands placed under interdict. Finally the prince decided to negotiate and sent one of his knights to Rome. On September 4, 1223, Honorius III confirmed an accord drawn up between the prince and the church of the Morea: Geoffrey restored the church lands and kept the treasures and furnishings of the churches in exchange for an annual indemnity; the number of Greek priests enjoying liberty and immunity was limited in proportion to the size of the community. A similar arrangement was made with Othon de la Roche.[4] In some respects this settlement paralleled that of 1219 in the Latin empire.

Agreements had certainly been expedited by the threat which then hung over the Frankish possessions. Theodore of Epirus, who had succeeded his brother Michael in 1214, had attacked the kingdom of Thessalonica, invaded Thessaly and Macedonia, and taken possession of Serres toward the beginning of 1222. He then laid siege to Thessalonica, which put up a long resistance, but finally surrendered near the end of 1224. All Macedonia and Thessaly fell into his hands. He advanced to the Spercheus river and to central Greece, where marquis Guy Pallavicini was able to hold him, thanks to his strong castle of Bodonitsa. Theodore's southward advance was thus checked, but the danger had been serious, and Honorius III had of necessity been prodigal of encouragement and consolation to Othon and Geoffrey during the years 1224 and 1225.

Soon after, Othon de la Roche returned with his wife Isabel to Burgundy, where he lived a few years longer. He left his extensive holdings to his nephew Guy de la Roche, already lord of half Thebes. Geoffrey I did not long survive the departure of his old friend, with whom he had always acted in perfect accord; he died some time between 1228 and 1230 at the age of about sixty. At approximately the same time another conqueror of Greek lands, Marco I Sanudo, duke of the Archipelago, departed this life after further adventures; he was succeeded by his son Angelo. In Euboea Ravano dalle Carceri had died in 1216 and the island had been partitioned, through the efforts of the Venetian bailie Peter Barbo, among six heirs.

Geoffrey II, elder son of Geoffrey I, succeeded his father at the age of about thirty-five. He had married in 1217 the daughter of emperor Peter of Constantinople, Agnes of Courtenay, and had thus become the brother-in-law of the emperors Robert and Baldwin II. He lived in noble style, keeping always at his court eighty knights with golden spurs, supported on his bounty; many

[4] Othon de la Roche had been present at the second parliament of Ravennika (May 2, 1210), at which most of the important barons of continental Greece had ratified a pact regulating relations between church and state. Prince Geoffrey of Villehardouin had not been, however, a party to the agreement, which thus did not apply to the principality of Achaea. In any event Othon was not himself scrupulous in observing the agreement, and so he and his lands were placed under the same bonds of excommunication and interdict as Honorius levied upon Villehardouin and Achaea. The pertinent documents will be found in the correspondence of Innocent III and Honorius III, a number of them being convenient of access in Sp. P. Lampros, *Ἔγγραφα ἀναφερόμενα εἰς τὴν μεσαιωνικὴν ἱστορίαν τῶν Ἀθηνῶν* (vol. III of Lampros's Greek translation of Ferd. Gregorovius, *Stadt Athen im Mittelalter*), Athens, 1906, reprinted 1917.

came from France to learn the profession of arms or to seek their fortune. He was a humane prince, benevolent and just, solicitous for the condition of the common people. He sent investigators to the courts of the barons to inform him of their way of life and of the manner in which they treated their vassals.

Living on good terms with his Greek neighbors, Geoffrey II assured the peace and prosperity of his principality. His resources permitted him to send financial aid to his liege lord the emperor, John of Brienne. In 1236 he intervened in person to succor Constantinople, besieged by the forces of the Nicaean emperor, John Ducas Vatatzes; with a fleet manned by 100 knights, 300 crossbowmen, and 500 archers, he forced the blockade and then, in conjunction with the Venetians, Pisans, and Genoese, repulsed the Greek fleet and delivered the capital. Two years later, uniting his ships with those of Venice, he again came to the rescue of Constantinople, once more besieged by John Vatatzes. In 1239 he wished to take part in the crusade of his overlord of France, count Theobald of Champagne, but pope Gregory IX ordered him to turn his forces against the Greek emperor in order to ensure the safety of Constantinople. Again in 1243, upon the false rumor of the death of emperor Baldwin II, he returned to the capital of the empire in order to secure the regency during the minority of his wife's nephew, Philip of Courtenay.

Geoffrey II thus emerged as the most powerful vassal of the Latin empire, the person around whom the Frankish states of Greece gradually regrouped themselves. Count Maio Orsini, who had successively acknowledged himself the vassal of the holy see, of Venice, and of Theodore of Epirus, in 1236 placed himself under Geoffrey's suzerainty. Moreover, Baldwin II granted to Geoffrey, as the reward of his services to the empire, suzerainty over the island of Euboea and possibly over the islands of the Archipelago as well, though it was more probably bestowed later on his brother William.

What remained of the old kingdom of Thessalonica, the lordships of Athens and Bodonitsa, had naturally drawn closer to Achaea, yet seemingly with no more formal tie of vassalage than the homage which Guy de la Roche owed to the prince for the lordships of Argos and Thebes. The lordship (commonly called the duchy) of Athens enjoyed the same peace and prosperity as did the Morea. Its chief source of wealth was the flourishing silk industry at Thebes, which turned that city into a commercial center frequented by many foreigners, especially Venetians and Genoese.

In 1240 Guy de la Roche gave the lordship of half Thebes to Bela of St. Omer, a member of the illustrious family of Fauquembergue, castellans of St. Omer in France. Bela had married Guy's sister, Bonne de la Roche. Another of Guy's vassals was the lord of Salona, Thomas II of Autremencourt.

It was reserved for William II of Villehardouin to bring about the unity of Frankish Greece. Geoffrey II died in 1246, leaving no children by his wife Agnes of Courtenay. His brother William was then about thirty-five years old. He had received as appanage the barony of Kalamata, which had been the original fief of his father, and he had been initiated into the government during the lifetime of his brother, who had entrusted the regency to him when he was obliged to go to the rescue of Constantinople. William was more enterprising than Geoffrey II. He resolved first to bring into subjection the peoples of the Morea who were still independent. In the southeast of the peninsula Monemvasia, a nest of corsairs isolated on a rock, still held out against Frankish domination and continued relations with the Nicaean empire. William blockaded it for three years, until famine finally forced the inhabitants to capitulate, yet upon honorable terms, keeping their property, their liberty, and their privileges (1248). Following this surrender, the mountaineers of Parnon made their submission. Then the prince went into winter quarters at Lacedaemon and built nearby, on the edge of the Taygetus chain, the powerful fortress of Mistra (Myzithra). At the other end of this chain, near Cape Matapan, he erected the castle of Maina (Grand Magne). The Slavs of Taygetus, hemmed in by the construction of these two fortresses, came to terms in their turn with the prince, who accorded them privileges. Thenceforth the Frankish domination covered the whole Morea.

During this fortunate winter, prince William of Villehardouin entertained as guests duke Hugh of Burgundy and numerous knights of France who, having taken the cross with king Louis IX, were on their way to meet him in Cyprus. Like his brother Geoffrey II, William wished to join the French crusaders. By marriage he was connected with the royal house of France. His wife, the daughter of Narjot of Toucy, who had served as bailie of the Latin empire of Constantinople, was the granddaughter of Agnes of France and thus the second cousin of Louis IX. William, therefore, armed a squadron of 24 ships, assembled 400 mounted men, and, embarking in the spring with the duke of Burgundy, joined the French royal fleet toward the end of May 1249, just as it was leaving

Cyprus for Damietta. William participated in the whole Egyptian campaign, and stayed with Louis until early May 1250, when the king departed for Acre.[5] At that time William obtained from Louis the right to coin money like that minted in France.

Upon his return to the Morea, William of Villehardouin experienced a few years of tranquillity, during which he and his court led a life of great magnificence. A move of the Greeks against Bodonitsa caused scarcely a ripple, for the prince marched with 800 horsemen to the threatened frontier and easily put the Greeks to rout. The years from 1250 to 1255 mark the zenith of the principality of Achaea: the prince, master of the whole Morea, overlord of the Archipelago, as well as of Euboea and of the county of Cephalonia, and even of Guy de la Roche for Argos and Thebes, dominated all the Frankish states of Greece and was able to make himself respected by the Greeks; because of his gallantry, his *courtoisie*, the brilliance of his court, his alliance with the royal house of France, and his part in the crusade, his renown spread far and wide.

This period of peace ended in 1255 over an incident in the feudal succession which degenerated into a conflict gradually involving all elements of Frankish Greece. Euboea had two overlords, the prince of Achaea and the Signoria of Venice, whose representative, the bailie at Negroponte, had arranged in 1216 the succession to Ravano dalle Carceri by dividing each of the three baronies into two parts and providing that in the event of the death of the possessor of one part the possessor of the other should succeed him. By 1254 William of Verona and Narzotto dalle Carceri each held an entire barony, while the third (Oreus) was divided between Grapella of Verona, nephew of William, and Carintana dalle Carceri. After the death of his first wife, the daughter of Narjot of Toucy, prince William had married Carintana, who died without issue in 1255, making him the heir of her sixth of the island. In accordance with the 1216 agreement, however, William of Verona and Narzotto dalle Carceri gave Carintana's share to Grapella, who thus tried to take over the whole barony of Oreus. Irritated by this decision made for a fief which had belonged to his wife and of which he was the overlord, the prince had William and Narzotto arrested. Their families then asked the aid of the Venetian bailie, Paul Gradenigo, who made himself master of the city of Negroponte. But the prince sent his nephew Geoffrey of Karytaina with a strong force. Geoffrey reoccupied Negroponte, and drove the bailie and the Venetians out.

5 On the crusade to Damietta, see below, chapter XIV, pp. 494–504.

Thus began the conflict between the two overlords of the island, Venice and William of Villehardouin. Each thenceforward tried to find allies in the country. William de la Roche, brother of the lord of Athens and baron of Veligosti and Damala in the Morea, and then Guy de la Roche himself, supported the Venetians, while William of Villehardouin secured the aid of Othon de Cicon, lord of Carystus, and even of the Genoese, four of whose armed galleys he stationed at Monemvasia. From Euboea the war spread into Attica, Corinthia, and Messenia, to the limits of the Venetian possessions, and onto the sea, with varying results in the years 1256 and 1257. In the spring of 1258, prince William resolved to put an end to it. Although his nephew, Geoffrey of Karytaina, went over to Guy de la Roche, whose daughter Isabel he had married, William crossed the isthmus of Corinth with a large force and advanced along the route to Thebes. He met the army of Guy at the foot of Mt. Caryae and, after a severe struggle, William of Villehardouin gained a decisive victory.

Besieged in Thebes and seeing his land devastated, Guy had to make his submission. He went to Nikli in the Morea to do homage to prince William and to submit himself to the judgment of the barons. Since they were not Guy's peers, the barons decided that they could not judge him and referred his case to the court of France. Guy left for the west in the spring of 1259. The court of France decided that, since he had not done liege homage to the prince, he could not be deprived of his fief, and that the fatigue of his journey was punishment enough. After this judgment and a courteous reception by king Louis,[6] Guy set out once more for Greece in the spring of 1260, hastening his return upon receipt of news of a disaster which had just befallen the Latins there.

William of Villehardouin had made a third marriage with Anna Angelina Comnena, daughter of the despot Michael II of Epirus, which union had brought on a disastrous war. Strengthened by his alliance with William and his other son-in-law, king Manfred of Sicily, Michael II wished to profit by the death of the Nicaean emperor Theodore II Lascaris to occupy all Macedonia and to take over Thrace. But Michael Palaeologus had assumed the regency of Nicaea, and had then usurped the imperial crown. After having tried vainly to ward off the danger by negotiations with the three allies — Michael II, William, and Manfred — Michael VIII

[6] The assertion, in *The Chronicle of the Morea,* that Louis made Athens a duchy at this interview (it had always been called a duchy in common parlance) seems to be refuted by the numismatic evidence that this title was not officially used before 1280.

Palaeologus had dispatched a powerful army to Macedonia under the command of his brother, the sebastocrator John. Prince William had, however, assembled his troops early in the spring of 1259 and then, having crossed the Gulf of Corinth, had joined forces with the despot Michael II. In addition to his own troops and those of Thessaly, commanded by his bastard son John, Michael II had 400 knights sent by Manfred from the kingdom of Sicily.

The allied army was concentrated in the western part of Macedonia near Castoria, and soon advanced to meet John Palaeologus, who had pushed into the region of Lakes Prespa and Ochrida. But John avoided battle and confined himself to harassing the allied force with his Turkish and Kuman auxiliaries. At the same time he succeeded in sowing the seeds of disunion among his adversaries by sending emissaries to Michael II. Michael, in the decisive battle which took place some time in the summer of 1259 in the plain of Pelagonia,[7] did abandon his allies; his troops dispersed; and his son John, who had quarreled with the Latins, went over to the enemy. William of Villehardouin, left alone with his vassals and the Sicilian knights, and taken in the rear by the forces of Thessaly, joined battle and tried to pierce the enemy line, but the Franks succumbed to superior force. After escaping from the field of battle and reaching Castoria, William was discovered by the Greeks, taken prisoner, and, with the greater part of the French knights, led before Michael Palaeologus, early in October 1259.

The sebastocrator John was then free to advance across Thessaly to Frankish Greece, where he plundered Thebes, but with the onset of winter the imperial army returned to the headquarters of Michael VIII in Asia Minor. Guy de la Roche, arriving from France the following spring, went to the aid of William's princess, Anna, who was acting as regent, in organizing the resistance of the Frankish states. But Michael, rid of his enemies in the west by the victory of Pelagonia, had by then turned his efforts in the direction of Constantinople. When his troops succeeded in taking it by surprise, on July 25, 1261, he resolved to treat with prince William, who was still a prisoner. For two years the prince had refused to yield to Michael's demands for the surrender of the Morea in exchange for an indemnity, and had offered only a ransom. The fall of Constantinople, which showed him the imminent danger threatening Frankish Greece, reduced him to a somewhat more

[7] For the date of the battle of Pelagonia, see D. M. Nicol, in *Byzantinische Zeitschrift*, XLIX (1956), 68–71, and cf. *idem*, *Despotate of Epiros*, pp. 169 ff.

accommodating frame of mind. He finally agreed to cede the three important strongholds of Monemvasia, Mistra, and Maina; and even consented to hold his principality from Michael, as he had held it formerly from Baldwin II. This accord, concluded towards the end of 1261, was ratified by the parliament of Achaea, composed largely of Frankish ladies acting in the absence of their prisoner husbands. After representatives of the emperor arrived to take possession of the three strongholds and to receive hostages, William of Villehardouin and the knights imprisoned with him were set at liberty.

Thus the first period of the history of Frankish Greece drew to a close: a brilliant period of conquest and of organization, rudely terminated by disaster.[8] Thanks to its restricted and easily defensible frontiers, to its solid military structure, and to the political ability of its leaders, it had for fifty years enjoyed almost complete peace, which had assured the prosperity of the country and had allowed the princes to render aid to Constantinople or to take part in crusades. At its greatest extent — peninsular, continental, and insular — Frankish Greece had comprised as many as a thousand fiefs, whose holders, descendants of the conquerors or newcomers, held more or less directly from the prince of Achaea. Under his overlordship the prince held, in a sort of confederation, the secondary states: the lordship (or "duchy") of Athens, the lordships of Negroponte, the duchy of the Archipelago, and the county of Cephalonia. In his own *seigneurie*, the principality of Achaea, which finally included the whole Morea, he had as immediate or mesne vassals hundreds of feudatories: possibly 500 or 600 knights, as well as esquires and sergeants and Greek *archontes*, these last scattered chiefly in the mountain districts of Arcadia, Triphylia, and Messenia. Many of these feudal lords had erected their own castles like those of the prince, either to speed their conquest or to reinforce weak points: Geoffrey I had built a keep on one of the peaks of Acrocorinth, while Othon de la Roche fortified the Acropolis of Athens. Geoffrey I had also built the powerful castle of Clermont in Elis, and William of Villehardouin that of Mistra on the edge of Mt. Taygetus. These castles of the prince and of the barons often rose upon the foundations of earlier structures — ancient or Byzantine — but at times, as in the case of the two last-named, they

[8] On the social and cultural life of Frankish Greece, note J. Longnon, *L'Empire latin de Constantinople*, pp. 187–216, and cf. K. M. Setton, *The Byzantine Background to the Italian Renaissance* (*Proceedings of the American Philosophical Society*, vol. 100), Philadelphia, 1956, pp. 31–40.

were erected on strategic new sites. They served at once as watch-towers from which to keep the countryside under surveillance, as refuges in case of invasion or revolt, and as points of support to hold important passes.

Thus organized, the principality of Achaea constituted a most unusual sort of feudal state, in which the hierarchy was composed of a series of grades ranging from the prince to the non-noble vassals: high barons, lieges, men of simple homage, *archontes*, and enfeoffed sergeants. The prince himself might disregard his feudal obligations to Venice, as he did in the war of the Euboeote succession, but he always remained the faithful vassal of his liege lord, the Latin emperor of Constantinople, rendering aids in men and money. But the remoteness and weakness of the emperors on the one hand and the strong personalities and initiative of the Villehardouin princes on the other made them in reality quasi-independent.

The power of the prince in respect to his vassals was also limited in theory by the customs of the principality. The prince was the first of the knights of the Morea, presiding over the court of the barons and over the court of the lieges, commanding the army and giving political leadership with the counsel of the lieges. He could not condemn a vassal without the judgment of the lieges or impose the *taille* or *collecte* without their consent. But here again his personal qualities and the prestige of his house assured his moral authority and precluded all conflict with his vassals, except in badly defined cases such as the affair of Euboea. The prince customarily resided at Andravida, an open town, but near his chief fortress, Clermont, and his chief port, Glarentsa (Cyllene). The princely court, which had further increased in magnificence under William of Villehardouin, was famous throughout all Christendom as a school of chivalry. The prince had a constable, who was the most important of the great officials, a marshal, who was second in command of the troops, a chancellor or logothete, a chamberlain or *protovestiarios*, who had charge of the management of the fiefs and of the sale of the products of the demesne, and a treasurer, who looked after receipts and expenditures. His personal domain, which constituted perhaps a quarter of the territory of the principality, comprised several castellanies, the importance of each of which equalled that of a great barony, with its head at one of his principal castles: Corinth, Clermont, Beauvoir (at Pondikos), and Kalamata. These were administered by captains, chosen from among the most distinguished knights, who had powers analogous to those of a baron over his own fief, and who exercised military, judicial, and administrative functions corresponding to those of the *baillis* in northern France. The guard of each castle was entrusted to a castellan, assisted by a constable and sergeants. In addition, Geoffrey II, as we have seen, had instituted *enquêteurs*, whose duty it was to inspect the government of the barons in their fiefs and to make reports to the prince.

The great barons or *bers de terre* were the peers of the prince. They possessed some of his sovereign prerogatives; they shared high justice with him and had the right to construct castles freely. They could be judged only by the court of the barons, consisting of themselves under the presidency of the prince. There were about a dozen high baronies: Patras, Vostitsa (Aegium), Chalandritsa, and Kalavryta in Achaea; Matagrifon (Akova), Karytaina, Veligosti, and Nikli in Arcadia; Gritsena and, in the early years, Kalamata in Messenia; and finally Geraki and Passavant in Laconia. They were of unequal size: Matagrifon, Karytaina, and probably Patras comprised 22 or 24 knights' fees; Kalavryta, twelve; Vostitsa, eight; the others, only four or six. About a third of each of these baronies was subinfeudated to other knights, while the remainder constituted the personal demesne of the baron, who owed service with a number of knights or sergeants in proportion to the importance of his barony.

The lieges formed the most important and possibly the most numerous category of vassals. They had more restricted duties and wider privileges than the men of simple homage. In theory, they owed military service all year round: four months in the field, four months garrison duty, and four months in their own castle or wherever they chose. In addition they owed court and counsel service. Finally, they could be required to serve as hostages or sureties. They were members of the court of the lieges, and each had a court of his own where he judged his own vassals and villeins except for *affaires de sang*. The lieges were not subject to the tax called the *collecte*, and could arrange their daughters' marriages as they chose. The men of simple homage had no court and judged only the civil cases of their villeins; they took no part in counseling their lord and were subject to the *collecte*, which was levied when the prince wished to pay a ransom or marry off his daughter; their women could not marry without the consent of the lord. But they were liable for military service only for the period fixed by their charters of enfeoffment.

The position of the *archontes* and the sergeants is one of the peculiarities of feudalism in the Morea. The *archontes* or *gentils hommes grecs* were the old landed proprietors, incorporated into the feudal organization; they were especially numerous in Arcadia. They had the status of men of simple homage, and, like them, owed the service specified in their charters of enfeoffment; but certain peculiarities, notably in matters of succession, probably carried over from Byzantine law, distinguished them from the men of simple homage. The sergeanties were fiefs worth half a knight's fee and held by esquires or sergeants. Created to reward the mounted sergeants who had taken part in the conquest, they gave to these non-nobles an aristocratic rank in the principality. Their holders did simple homage.

The Latin archbishops and bishops likewise had their place in the feudal organization: they had received fiefs for which they owed *chevauchée* but not garrison duty; they also shared in counsel and in justice. The same was true of the military orders — Templars, Hospitallers, and Teutonic Knights.

Outside the feudal structure Frankish Greece included various categories of privileged persons: the foreign merchants, Venetian, Genoese, and others, gathered together in colonies; the townsmen in the commercial centers, notably Glarentsa, which had been enriched by the growth of trade; the inhabitants of the chief towns, which had preserved their privileges from the Byzantine period; and free peasants or *francs hommes* who could not be taxed without their own consent.

Below them came the great mass of the inhabitants of the countryside, the old *paroikoi*, to whom the Franks gave the name of villein. They had kept their holding, the *stasis*, to which they were attached from father to son and for which they made a fixed payment in proportion to its size; they also owed personal service, cultivating the lord's land, as well as the *corvées* necessary for the construction and upkeep of castles, mills, wine presses, and the like. The villein in the Morea was subject to more or less the same obligations as in France, being unable to quit his land or to contract a marriage or marry off his daughter without authorization; but his *stasis* could not be taken away from him nor could the pair of oxen or the donkey necessary for his work be sold. He could be freed by his lord and even receive land in fee.[9]

Almost all the bishoprics, abandoned by their Greek titularies, had been occupied by the Latins. Yet there remained at Negroponte the Greek bishop, Theodore, who had made his submission to

[9] Cf. in general Peter Topping, "Le Régime agraire dans le Péloponnèse latin au XIVe siècle," *L'Hellénisme contemporain*, ser. 2, X (1956), 255–295.

Rome, while in curious fashion still keeping up close relations with the former Greek metropolitan of Athens, Michael Choniates, who had taken refuge on the island of Ceos. Outside the kingdom of Thessalonica, and Thessaly, there were four ecclesiastical provinces in Frankish Greece: two in the Morea, Patras and Corinth, and two in central Greece, Athens and Thebes. The archbishop of Patras was the primate of the Morea; he had as suffragans, from 1223, the bishop of Olena, whose see was at Andravida, and the bishops of Coron, Modon, and Cephalonia. Dependent upon the archbishopric of Corinth were the bishoprics of Argos and Lacedaemon, as well as that of Monemvasia after its conquest. The archbishopric of Athens included the bishopric of Thermopylae (with the see at Bodonitsa) and the bishoprics of Salona, Daulia, Negroponte, Aegina, and Andros. The archbishop of Thebes had only two suffragans: the bishop of Castoria and the bishop of Zaratovo.

The members of the Greek clergy, regular and secular, who had not fled during the conquest, had been left in their positions. The conquerors, at the time of the submission of the inhabitants, had promised not to force them to change their religion and had manifested much tolerance; nevertheless, as a result of abuses, the concordat of 1223 had limited the number of *papates*, enjoying with their families ecclesiastical exemption. The Greek monks, left undisturbed, were allowed to keep up and even occasionally to expand their monasteries; and the exiled Greek metropolitan of Athens, Michael Choniates, found devious ways to elect new abbots. Only the monasteries abandoned by the Greeks had been occupied by Latin monks. The Cistercians were favored in Greece, as at Constantinople: they took over the abbey of Daphne near Athens and that of Zaraca on the shore of Lake Stymphalus. The Augustinians were established at St. Sauveur in Messenia, the Premonstratensians at Kalavryta, the canons regular of St. Ruf in the cathedral chapter of Patras, the Carmelites at Andravida, and the Temple of the Lord in the chapter of Athens.

Gradually a perceptible rapprochement developed between the various classes of Greeks and the French knights. First the *archontes* achieved a definite status in the feudal order, and Greek officials participated in the administration. Then followed unions between the two races: besides prince William of Achaea, we find duke William of Athens marrying a Greek princess. From illegitimate unions with the women of the land came a race of half-breeds, the *gasmouloi*, who, as the Byzantine historian George Pachymeres remarks, "had the discretion and the cautious spirit of the Greeks, the ardor and pride of the Franks."[10] It is worthy of note that this clever and courageous stock was to play an active part in the struggle of the Byzantines against the Latins in the Morea.

Despite the solemnity of the oaths exchanged by emperor Michael VIII Palaeologus and prince William of Achaea, the peace concluded at the beginning of the year 1262 could scarcely be expected to last. The cession of the three strongholds of Mistra, Monemvasia, and Maina was a direct menace to the whole province of Laconia, where the Franks still held the city of Sparta, dear to the heart of prince William, as well as the great baronies of Passavant and Geraki. It was no longer a question, as it had been at the time of William's succession, of the resistance of a few mountain or maritime people who had succeeded in maintaining their independence; now Michael VIII, who since his recapture of Constantinople was free to intervene in the western part of the old empire, had solid bases from which to attempt the recovery of the rest of Greece, threatening the country simultaneously from the north and from the sea. Here lay the germs of a long struggle which was to embroil the Latins and the Byzantines for many generations.

Prince William was clearly aware of the situation. Freed by pope Urban IV from his promises to Michael VIII, made under duress while in prison, he hastened to make peace with Venice, on May 16, 1262, by a treaty which reëstablished the *status quo ante* in Euboea. While preparing the defenses of the Latin holdings, William visited the region of Lacedaemon, frightened the Greeks, and precipitated events. Michael Cantacuzenus, whom the emperor had chosen as his representative in Monemvasia, alerted his master, who, early in 1263, dispatched an army of Greek soldiers and Turkish mercenaries under the command of his brother, the sebastocrator Constantine. At the same time a fleet, manned largely by *gasmouloi* and Tzacones,[11] proceeded to ravage Euboea and the Archipelago and to take over the coast of Laconia.

Constantine began by occupying and fortifying those of William's lands that lay near his bases. Then he moved up the valley of the Eurotas, gained the valley of the Alpheus, and marched towards Elis. William had gone to Corinth to assemble the forces of Frankish Greece, leaving the defense of the passes of the Alpheus to a knight named John de Catavas, with three hundred knights. John

[10] *De Michaele Palaeologo,* III, 9 (*CSHB*), I, 188.

[11] According to some of the Greek historians (such as Pachymeres, IV, 26, *CSHB,* I, 309), the Tzacones are simply the ancient Lacones or Spartans, a derivation of the name which, despite controversy, a number of modern historians have accepted.

attacked the Byzantine troops at Prinitsa, not far from the ruins of Olympia, and, after a hard struggle, succeeded in forcing them to retreat. Surprised by this attack, the sebastocrator took flight on a swift horse, while his army scattered. In the spring of 1264 Constantine resolved to have his revenge and, following the same invasion route, reached the borders of the plain of Elis at Sergiana, where William took up a position facing him. Michael Cantacuzenus, who commanded the Byzantine vanguard, rode forth to make a demonstration before the front line of the French; his horse stumbled and he was killed before help could reach him. Stunned by this death, Constantine retreated and went to lay siege to Nikli.

There he ran into a new disappointment: the Turkish mercenaries, numbering more than a thousand mounted men, demanded their arrears in pay, and, when Constantine refused, they left him and proceeded to offer their services to the prince of Achaea. Discouraged by all these contretemps, Constantine returned to Constantinople, leaving the command to the grand domestic, Alexius Philes, who marched toward the fertile province of Messenia and occupied the pass of Makryplagi, which controlled its approach. The prince, reinforced by the Turkish mercenaries, had himself reached Messenia, which he was determined to defend. His troops attacked the Greeks in their strong positions and succeeded in dislodging and in putting them to flight. The rout was complete: the grand domestic and numerous other Byzantine dignitaries and officers were taken prisoner. William of Villehardouin advanced to Mistra, and fortified and repopulated Sparta, which had been deserted by its inhabitants; then he withdrew to winter quarters in Elis.

On the sea also, the emperor Michael suffered reverses: the Graeco-Genoese fleet, encountering the Venetian galleys near the island of Hydra, sustained a serious defeat which caused it to lose control of the Aegean. With the failure of all his plans, the emperor came around to the idea of a truce. William of Villehardouin, having seen his knights decimated and a part of his principality devastated by two years of war, was favorably disposed. Pope Urban IV, to whom Michael was now offering a union of the churches, insisted on the ending of hostilities against Frankish Morea as one of the conditions. For its part Venice had already concluded a treaty with the emperor which restored her privileges at Constantinople (1265). As part of this general relaxing of tension between east and west, a reconciliation was brought about between Michael VIII and prince William. To cement the accord, Michael proposed the marriage of his son Andronicus with William's daughter and heir, Isabel. But the barons of Achaea, fearing the seizure of the Morea by the Byzantines, refused to ratify this project.

The truce was, however, bound to be only temporary, and the prince, perforce, had to seek outside aid, which was difficult to find under such circumstances. Since 1262 pope Urban IV had been asking aid for him from France, with little success. The Venetians, who had recovered their privileges in the Byzantine empire, did not wish to compromise their position. King Manfred of Sicily, brother-in-law and former ally of William, was favorably disposed towards the Franks in Greece, but, since the pope had preached a crusade against him, his one thought was to defend himself. The outcome of that crusade eventually solved William's problem.

Charles of Anjou, having become master of the kingdom of Sicily in 1266 by the victory of Benevento, in which Manfred was killed, was naturally inclined to take over Manfred's oriental policy along with the rest of his inheritance, and to cast ambitious glances across the strait of Otranto. Prince William had met Charles of Anjou on the Egyptian crusade, and his first wife, granddaughter of Agnes of France, had been Charles's cousin. Isolated in Greece, William looked with favor on the establishment of a powerful French force on the other side of the Ionian Sea; he resolved, by flattering the ambition of Charles of Anjou, to make certain of his support. Early in 1267, less than a year after the battle of Benevento, he crossed to Italy, got in touch with Charles, and went on to see pope Clement IV at Viterbo.

After long negotiations a treaty was solemnly concluded between Charles of Anjou and William of Villehardouin on May 24, 1267, at Viterbo, at a consistory held in the chamber of the pope in the presence of fourteen cardinals. The clauses of this treaty are rather singular. In exchange for a promise of aid from Charles, William ceded to him Achaea and its dependencies, but he was to retain the usufruct, and his daughter Isabel was to marry one of Charles's sons, who would succeed William in Achaea. If this son should die without children before William, Achaea would revert to Charles himself or to his heir to the kingdom. Three days later, a second treaty between the former Latin emperor of Constantinople, Baldwin II, and Charles of Anjou added the finishing touches to the earlier treaty. In return for a force of two thousand mounted men to help in recovering the empire, Baldwin II ceded to Charles suzerainty over the principality of Achaea, as well as over the islands of the Archipelago and Corfu, and over the Latin possessions in Epirus. All the Greek lands still in the power of the Latins thus passed under the domination of the new king of Sicily.

Frankish Greece had now become a dependency of the kingdom of Sicily. These conditions were hard on William of Villehardouin, who not only lost the quasi-independence which he had enjoyed in relation to his former suzerain Baldwin II, but further sacrificed the rights of the house of Villehardouin to the profit of the house of Anjou. Nevertheless he faithfully fulfilled the conditions, and was himself the first to render aid to his new suzerain the very next year when Conradin came down into Italy. He assumed command of the Angevin forces in Apulia and took part in the battle of Tagliacozzo, where the intervention of a reserve corps, half of it consisting of knights from the Morea, brought victory to Charles (August 23, 1268). Furthermore, in January 1269 William secured by negotiation the surrender of Avlona, thenceforth the advance bridgehead of Charles of Anjou in Albania. William also busied himself with the execution of the clauses of the treaty of Viterbo. In June 1270 a mission arrived in the Morea to receive on behalf of Charles the stipulated oaths and ratifications, and in the spring of the following year William sent to Italy his twelve-year-old daughter Isabel, to wed Philip of Anjou, who was fifteen; the marriage was celebrated with great splendor at Trani on May 28, 1271; thereafter the young Isabel went to live with the royal family at Naples in the Castel dell' Ovo.

Although Charles of Anjou had managed ever since 1269 to send to Achaea some subsidies, provisions, and horses, the expedition of Conradin and the repression of the revolt in Sicily, followed by the Tunisian crusade in 1270,[12] had prevented him in these early years from giving any really extensive aid to the principality. But in 1271 he named as captain-general in the Morea the marshal of Sicily, Dreux of Beaumont, and sent him with troops to Greece. Emperor Michael VIII had given up his attacks in the Morea, and had turned his efforts to Euboea, where he took advantage of a favorable turn of events. A petty knight from Vicenza, Licario by name, fleeing from the resentment of one of the "triarchs" of the island, William II of Verona, and of the latter's brother Gilbert, whose sister Felicia he had secretly married, had offered his services to Michael. With the aid of Byzantine ships, Licario had ravaged the coast of Euboea, taken several castles, and pushed into the interior. Dreux of Beaumont and William of Villehardouin resolved

[12] For the crusade to Tunis, see below, chapter XIV, pp. 508–518.

to take action. Dreux advanced towards Oreus, Licario's naval base, but suffered a severe defeat. William was more fortunate, however, and succeeded in recapturing the castle of La Cuppa near Aulonarion.

In the spring of 1275, the emperor Michael directed his attack against Thessaly, where there ruled the bastard son of Michael II of Epirus, John, duke of Neopatras. Michael VIII sent a fleet into the Gulf of Volos, and a powerful force by land to Thessaly, to blockade John in Neopatras. John managed to escape and went to ask help of the duke of Athens, John de la Roche, who had succeeded at the death of his father Guy in 1263. The latter assembled three hundred experienced knights, joined forces with the troops which John had been able to get together, and, vigorously attacking the Byzantine army, succeeded in putting it to flight. The Byzantines withdrew to Demetrias near their fleet, which the Venetians and Lombards of Negroponte hoped in their turn to destroy. They succeeded in breaking its line and in driving it back on the coast, but John Palaeologus, who commanded the Byzantine army, put his best soldiers on board and, taking the offensive, regained the upper hand, recovering the greater part of the ships. William of Verona was killed, and numerous Latin lords were made prisoner.

The next year Michael VIII, renewing the attack, again sent an army into Thessaly, while a fleet under the command of Licario sailed to Euboea. With the troops which the fleet had transported, Licario ranged over the island up to the very outskirts of the city of Negroponte. Gilbert of Verona, accompanied by John de la Roche, the duke of Athens, marched against him. The engagement took place at Vatonda, about six miles north of Negroponte. In the thick of the fight, John de la Roche was thrown from his horse and made prisoner, together with Gilbert and numerous knights. Meanwhile the Byzantine army had suffered a new disaster in Thessaly, which at first prevented Licario from following up his success, and then allowed the Latins to succor Negroponte. Licario now turned to the southern part of the island, took the castles of La Clisura and Larmena, and occupied Seriphos, Siphnos, and other islands of the Archipelago and spread terror throughout the Aegean.

On the other side of Greece also, in Epirus and Albania, the Latins had found themselves exposed to the attacks of the Byzantines. Already master of Avlona, Charles of Anjou had been busy taking possession of the towns which Manfred had held as the dowry of his wife Helena, daughter of Michael II of Epirus, and of the lands which Baldwin II had ceded to him by the treaty of Viterbo. In 1271 the Albanians had recognized Charles as their king, and Durazzo, Berat, Canina, Butrinto (Buthrotum), and Syvota had fallen into his hands. But three years later Michael VIII had sent an army which had taken Berat and laid siege to Avlona and Durazzo. Thus the Byzantine emperor had succeeded in almost completely encircling the Latin possessions from Albania and Epirus to Thessaly, Euboea, the Archipelago, and Laconia. In the Morea itself, the Byzantines not only held Laconia, but had also infiltrated into Arcadia, where Kalavryta had fallen into their hands by 1277. Nevertheless, William of Villehardouin continued to maintain himself in what constituted the heart of the principality in the Morea: Achaea, Elis, the valley of the Alpheus, and Messenia, to say nothing of the plain of Nikli, the Argolid, and Corinthia. Thanks to aid obtained from Charles of Anjou, William had witnessed no renewal of the terrible invasions of 1263–1264 and the country enjoyed relative quiet.

The last years of the reign of prince William were darkened by bereavements. First he lost two of his chief vassals and faithful companions in arms: Walter of Rosières, baron of Matagrifon, and Geoffrey of Briel, baron of Karytaina, his own nephew, reputed to be the best knight of the Morea. They had no heirs as *bers de terre*, and so the number of great baronies, already diminished by the loss of Passavant and Geraki in Laconia, as well as of Kalavryta, was still further reduced. But worse still, William of Villehardouin lost his son-in-law and heir presumptive, Philip of Anjou, whose death in February 1277 at the age of twenty-one was to have weighty consequences.

A year later, prince William fell ill and, anticipating the approach of death, made his last will; he chose as regent or bailie his nephew the grand constable John Chauderon, provided for legacies to the churches, and selected as his last resting place the church of St. James at Andravida, where his father and brother had already been interred. On May 1, 1278, he died at the castle of Kalamata, where he had been born; he was about sixty-seven years old and had reigned thirty-two years. He had been a brilliant prince, renowned for his magnificence, gallantry, and *courtoisie*. An indefatigable fighter, he had won distinction not only in Greece but also at Damietta and in Italy. On the verge of losing his principality, he had known how to retrieve the situation and to maintain Frankish Morea. But to attain this, he had been forced to sacrifice part of his independence and the interests of his house. According to the provisions of the treaty of Viterbo, the death of Philip of Anjou dispossessed Isabel of Villehardouin, and the principality of Achaea now passed directly to Charles of Anjou, the king of Sicily.

When Charles of Anjou was notified of the death of William of Villehardouin, he added the title prince of Achaea to those he already bore — "king of Jerusalem, of Sicily, of the duchy of Apulia, and of the principality of Capua, count of Anjou, of Provence, of Forcalquier, and of Tonnerre" — and sent the seneschal of Sicily, Galeran of Ivry, to represent him as bailie in the Morea, where he himself was destined never to set foot. Notice of this nomination was sent to the chief barons — the lords of Athens and of Lebadea, the count of Cephalonia, the three lords of Euboea, the lady of Bodonitsa, the constable and marshal of Achaea, the barons of Chalandritsa, Kalavryta, Vostitsa, and Veligosti — as well as to all the cities, lands, castles, towns, and localities of the principality.

The regency of Galeran of Ivry was not a success. Agent of a centralized monarchical regime, he ran afoul of the feudal practices of the Morea; the barons complained to the court of Naples, and Charles ordered Galeran to respect the usages and customs of the principality. However, the Angevin troops in service in the Morea received their pay at irregular intervals and lived off the country. The castles lacked munitions and provisions. In August 1280 Galeran of Ivry was replaced by Philip of Lagonesse, marshal of Sicily, who undertook to remedy the evils of the previous administration by indemnifying the barons, provisioning the castles, and paying the arrears of the castellans and soldiers from the mint of Glarentsa, which Charles of Anjou had had reorganized.

While Philip of Lagonesse was busy improving conditions in the Morea, the Latins of central Greece and Euboea were trying to retrieve their position, undermined by the successes of Michael VIII Palaeologus. William de la Roche, who in 1280 had succeeded his brother John in the duchy of Athens, and who was extending his authority over the whole country from Zeitounion (Lamia) and Gardiki to Argos and Nauplia, lent military support to his father-in-law, the bastard John Angelus Comnenus, duke of Neopatras. And the Venetian bailie of Negroponte, Nicholas Falier, succeeded by secret understandings in recovering some of the castles of Euboea occupied by Licario.

But the struggle between Latins and Byzantines continued,

especially in Albania. Among the problems which engrossed the attention of Charles of Anjou, the Morea ranked well behind the kingdom of Sicily and even Albania, which was nearer home: he not only wished to repair the losses he had suffered in Albania in 1274, but also planned to make it his base of operations for the campaign against the Byzantine empire, envisioned in the treaty he had made at Viterbo with Baldwin II.[13] With a view to recovering the empire of Constantinople, he assured himself of the coöperation of the new despot of Epirus, Nicephorus, the legitimate son of Michael II, he established relations with king Stephen Uroš II of Serbia and tsar George I of Bulgaria, and undertook negotiations with Venice which were to culminate in July 1281 in the treaty of Orvieto.

In 1279 he sent to Durazzo, Avlona, Butrinto, Syvota, and Corfu, as captain and vicar-general in Albania, the energetic Hugh of Sully, with strong reinforcements of troops, materials for war, and provisions. The first objective was Berat, to which Hugh laid siege in 1280. The emperor Michael VIII sent against him an army under the command of the grand domestic, Michael Tarchaniotes, with instructions to wage a campaign of harassment and ambushes, of the sort which had so often proved fatal to the Franks. These tactics succeeded once again: Hugh of Sully, victim of his own impetuosity, fell into a trap and was made prisoner; his disheartened troops fled in disorder and took refuge in their bases of Avlona and Canina (April 1281).

Charles of Anjou did not abandon the struggle. He now regrouped his forces in Albania, assembled new troops, and armed a fleet, while the Venetians mobilized their own. The new expedition against the Byzantine empire had been fixed for April 1, 1283. But Michael VIII lost no time: he got into communication with some malcontents in Sicily, made one of them, John of Procida, his secret agent, and, through him, entered into contact with king Peter III of Aragon, to whom he furnished subsidies. And on Easter Monday 1282, just a year before the date fixed for the expedition against Michael Palaeologus, there took place that spectacular massacre of the French in the island of Sicily known as the Sicilian Vespers.

Thenceforth Charles of Anjou was obliged to abandon any action in the east in order to turn all his efforts against the rebellious Sicilians and the Catalan-Aragonese invaders. Philip of Lagonesse, marshal of the so-called kingdom of Sicily, was recalled from Achaea, and the chief barons of the Morea participated in the war

[13] For the plans of Charles of Anjou, see below, chapter X, pp. 367–370.

in Sicily. The principality was to a certain extent left to itself: king Charles appointed as bailie the baron of Chalandritsa, Guy of Dramelay. Fortunately for the Latins in Greece, Michael VIII died shortly after this last political success. His son, Andronicus II, did not possess his great ability, and was kept busy with his struggle against the Serbs and against the Angeli of Thessaly and Epirus. As a result, the principality of Achaea, as well as Angevin Albania, knew a period of some tranquillity, while the bailie Guy of Dramelay, continuing the tradition of the princes, was conspicuous for his *courtoisie* and munificence.

Charles of Anjou died on January 7, 1285, two years after Michael VIII. His eldest son, Charles II "the Lame", inherited both the kingdom of "Sicily" (Naples) and the principality of Achaea, in conformity with the treaty of Viterbo. But he was hardly prince of Achaea even in name, for, a prisoner of the Catalans since June 1284, he had scarcely been liberated and returned to Italy (in 1289) when one of the first acts of his reign was to restore the principality to its natural heir, Isabel of Villehardouin.

During Charles II's captivity the regent of the kingdom, Robert of Artois, had named as bailie and vicar-general in Achaea the duke of Athens, William de la Roche, now the most powerful personage in Frankish Greece. William profited by the relative quiet which the Morea was enjoying, to protect Messenia against the incursions of the Byzantines of Mistra by constructing the castle of Dimatra. After two years of rule he died, leaving the duchy of Athens to a minor son, Guy II de la Roche; and Nicholas (II) of St. Omer, lord of one half Thebes, was appointed to replace him as bailie of Achaea. Nicholas was, after the duke of Athens, the richest and most powerful of the barons; he had married, successively, Mary, a daughter of Bohemond VI, prince of Antioch and count of Tripoli, and Anna Angelina Comnena, a daughter of Michael II of Epirus and the widow of prince William of Villehardouin. Nicholas continued the program of fortification begun by William of Athens, constructing the castle at Navarino called by the French Port-de-Jonc. "He governed with nobility and wisdom," says the chronicler of the Morea, "and kept the country at peace." In 1289 he was succeeded as bailie by Guy de Charpigny of Lille, baron of Vostitsa, who was to hold office for only a few months.

Charles II of Anjou was not as grasping as his father. He had an amiable disposition and a kind heart. He took a friendly interest in his brother's widow, Isabel of Villehardouin, who had passed twelve sad years at the court of Naples. Immediately upon his return to Italy he gave her, in July 1289, the barony of Karytaina; and two months later, upon the occasion of her second marriage, to Florent of Hainault, he granted her "by pure liberality and special grace" the principality of Achaea, for herself and her direct and legitimate descendants. By this concession Charles II probably wished to compensate for the harshness with which his father had applied the clauses of the treaty of Viterbo upon the death of William of Villehardouin. In fact, Charles II describes his act as one of "restitution and concessions". Its principal conditions were that Florent and Isabel were to hold the principality from Charles II as a fief, and that, if Florent died, Isabel could not remarry without his consent, nor could any daughter who might be heir to the principality marry without his approval under penalty of losing her rights.

Florent of Hainault was the younger brother of the count of Hainault, John of Avesnes; he was also the great-grandson of emperor Baldwin I of Constantinople, the great-nephew of the first lord of Negroponte, James of Avesnes, and a relative of king Charles II. He had abandoned his small inheritance to seek fame and fortune in the Sicilian war. His marriage, it seems, was arranged at the suggestion of the regent, Robert of Artois, who maintained close relations with the house of Hainault, and also with the approval of the barons of the Morea, who wished to have a prince residing in the country who would preserve the rights of the natural heiress. The marriage was blessed by the archbishop of Naples on September 16, 1289; the king invested Isabel with the principality of Achaea and conferred on Florent the office of constable of the kingdom. The new prince was not quite forty years old, the princess hardly thirty.

Florent of Hainault proved to be a wise and prudent prince, as well as a brave and brilliant knight worthy of taking his place in the family of the Villehardouins, into which he had married. Seeing the country ruined by war, pillaged by Angevin as well as Byzantine troops, and ground down by the royal officials, he devoted himself first of all to reëstablishing peace and to securing an accounting from the officials. He made contact with the Byzantine captain of Mistra and, through him, with the emperor Andronicus II, who concluded a firm and lasting accord with Achaea. With peace assured for a long time, prosperity returned to the country, which became "fat and plenteous in all things".

Freed from anxiety as to his own principality, Florent was in a position to aid the despot of Epirus, his wife's uncle Nicephorus, who was exposed to the attacks of the Byzantines and their Genoese allies. With five hundred knights, Florent went to Epirus, raised the siege of Janina, and pursued the Byzantine troops back into imperial territory. But meanwhile Genoese ships ravaged the Gulf of Arta. While the campaign may have been a success for prince Florent, it left the heart of the Epirote despotate in ruins.

Florent also took part in the negotiations for the marriage of Charles II's favorite son, prince Philip of Taranto, with Thamar, daughter of the despot Nicephorus. Thamar received as dowry the chief places of Acarnania. Charles II assigned to Philip all his rights over the eastern dependencies of the kingdom — Albania, Corfu, the principality of Achaea, the duchy of Athens, and the duchy of the Archipelago. Philip of Taranto thus became immediate overlord of all Frankish Greece, as a fief held in chief of the king of Sicily (1294).

Prince Florent's principal difficulty during the course of his government was a long feudal conflict with the duchy of Athens which lasted during his entire reign. Originally independent of the principality of Achaea, and later vassals of the princes only for the lordships of Argos and of Nauplia, the dukes of Athens had always been restive under the pretensions of the Villehardouins to hegemony over all Frankish Greece. When, by the treaty of Viterbo, the principality of the Morea with its dependencies passed under the domination of Charles of Anjou, the duchy of Athens, like Euboea and the county of Cephalonia, was comprised in these dependencies. Likewise, when Charles II returned the principality to Isabel of Villehardouin, he intended to include these same territories. But the old spirit of independence was reincarnated in two persons who then ruled the duchy: the dowager duchess of Athens, Helena Angelina Comnena, resourceful widow of William de la Roche, and her second husband, Hugh of Brienne, a member of the adventurous Brienne family, which had won fame in the east and which, by its pride and intransigence, was destined to bring misfortune on the duchy.

In December 1289, when prince Florent had sent his proxy to receive the homages of the lords of central Greece, Helena, regent for her son Guy II, had refused to do homage. Charles II had intervened to force her submission. In 1291, however, Helena had married Hugh of Brienne, who now became bailie of the Athenian duchy, and forthwith insisted that he had the right to do homage directly to the king. The claim impressed Charles, whose numerous later interventions, marked by uncertainty, if not by actual contradiction, always reflected the latest influence at work on him, whether that of Hugh, or of Florent, or of Philip of Taranto. In the end, Florent of Hainault won; Philip of Taranto renounced his claim to direct homage from the Athenian duchy on condition of receiving that of the prince of Achaea; and Guy II, having reached his majority, received the command to do homage and render service for his duchy to princess Isabel and prince Florent (1296).

Meanwhile peace prevailed in the Morea. In 1292 the privateering of Roger "de Lluria" (of Loria), admiral of James II of Aragon, in the eastern Mediterranean, had spread alarm and provoked an incident where Roger competed first in valor with one of the barons of the Morea, and then in generosity with the princess herself; all ended on the most courteous note in the world. Peace with the Byzantines of Mistra, several times threatened by other incidents, had been maintained through the wisdom and skill of prince Florent. In 1292 or 1293 two rich Slavs of Gianitsa in the Taygetus, aided by about fifty men, had taken the castle of Kalamata by surprise and had there acclaimed emperor Andronicus. It was a grave loss in one of the richest regions of the principality. But Florent of Hainault had sent a mission to the emperor and had succeeded, through the complaisance of an *archon* of Laconia, Sgouromallis by name, in having the castle surrendered to him.

Then, towards 1295, Florent had given up demanding vengeance for the murder of the good baron of Vostitsa and former bailie of Achaea, Guy de Charpigny, by a rich Greek of Kalavryta called Photius, because he had recognized that the murder was the result of an error, and that the primary responsibility for all the trouble rested on the excesses of one of his own relatives, Walter of Liedekerke, captain of the castellany of Corinth: Photius had mistaken Guy de Charpigny for Walter! But in the summer of 1296, Florent could not avoid the grievous consequences of a violent quarrel at the fair of Vervaena between a French knight named Gerard of Remy and a Greek merchant named Corcondylus. The merchant, whom Gerard struck in the course of the quarrel, swore vengeance. With the aid of his son-in-law, cellarer of the castle of St. George, near the valley of the Alpheus, he got possession of the fortress and turned it over to the Byzantine troops of Mistra. Thus war was resumed between the French and the Greeks in the Morea. Prince Florent laid siege to St. George, but despite the siege works which he undertook before the fortress and the assaults made by his troops he could not take it. At the approach of winter he was forced to retire to Andravida. There he fell gravely ill and died, probably on January 23, 1297, leaving, by his union with Isabel, a three-year-old daughter, Mahaut.

Princess Isabel chose as bailie of the principality count Richard of Cephalonia and Zante, son of Maio Orsini. He was a man of experience, who had been ruling his county for forty years, and who was father-in-law of three of the chief barons of the Morea. Isabel retired first to Nisi and then to Kalamata, and busied herself with improving still further the system of defense of Messenia, already reinforced by William de la Roche and Nicholas II of St. Omer. The war with the Byzantines of Mistra, provoked by the taking of St. George, was, moreover, comparatively quiescent. The emperor Andronicus, seeking an accord, entered into conversations for the marriage of his son John to the princess Isabel, but the barons of the Morea gave this project no encouragement. King Charles II also began negotiations for peace with Andronicus, which at the beginning of 1300 were disclosed to the princess Isabel, and which led to a truce that applied to all the Frankish states of Greece and even to Epirus and Thessaly.

Meanwhile, on the advice of Nicholas III of St. Omer, lord of Thebes and marshal of the principality, princess Isabel was planning for her daughter Mahaut a marriage which promised only the happiest results for Frankish Greece. In 1299 the young duke of Athens, Guy II de la Roche, who was a brilliant knight, was solemnly affianced to little Mahaut of Hainault. This union, negotiated without the prior consent of the king of Sicily, aroused Charles II to protest and was for a time endangered, but, upon the intervention of pope Boniface VIII, Charles finally consented. The conflict between the Morea and the Athenian duchy was thus to be allayed, and strong ties were to be formed between the two states.

Isabel also had thoughts of marrying again. Since 1298 Philip of Savoy, count of Piedmont and nephew of count Amadeo V of Savoy, had been engaged in negotiations and had interested the court of Rome in the prospect. In 1300 the princess went to Rome to take part, like many other pilgrims, in the great jubilee, and also to meet Philip of Savoy. The marriage was concluded at the beginning of 1301. The princess was over forty years old, Philip only twenty-two. He was a proud and ambitious young man, tempted by the title of prince and by the Morea's reputation for brilliance. Once again, however, Isabel had neglected to ask the approval of Charles II, and the king, whose interests in Piedmont ran counter to those of Philip, forbade the marriage. Since the princess was already betrothed, however, Charles by a decision of February 6, 1301, declared that she had *ipso facto* forfeited the principality, which he granted to his son Philip of Taranto. But pope Boniface VIII, and probably also Peter Flotte, councillor of king Philip IV of France, intervened; Charles had to yield; and the wedding ceremonies were then celebrated at Rome on February 12. On February 23 in the Lateran king Charles II invested Philip of Savoy with the principality of Achaea.

The new prince had not the qualities of prudence and moderation of Florent of Hainault. He was brave, proud, and obstinate; but his enemies accused him of being fickle, covetous, and double-faced. Moreover, he was of a haughty and autocratic disposition, accustomed to the methods of government of the Italian captains and podestàs. After having gone with Isabel to Piedmont, where he assembled his troops, he crossed over to the Morea, and almost immediately clashed with the feudal traditions of the principality. He demanded the accounts of the chief officials and ordered the arrest of the chancellor, Benjamin of Kalamata, who had been *protovestiarios*. This arbitrary action, contrary to custom, provoked protests from the marshal of the Morea, Nicholas III of St. Omer, who, at the head of his vassals, presented himself in arms before the palace of the prince at Glarentsa. It required the intervention of the princess Isabel and of Philip's wisest councillors to still the conflict.

Soon after, duke Guy II of Athens, who had come to do homage to Philip of Savoy, had to go to Thessaly to defend the lands of his cousin and ward John II Angelus Comnenus against the troops of the *despoina* of Epirus, Anna, widow of the despot Nicephorus. Nicholas of St. Omer, who was a vassal of Guy II for the lordship of Thebes, came to join him with his men. Under his command, the forces of the Athenian duchy and Thessaly pushed the troops of Epirus back into their own country, and then retired after having obtained an indemnity from the *despoina*. They later made an incursion into the territory of the Byzantine empire, as far as the borders of Thessalonica. Then, upon the courteous demand of the empress, Yolanda of Montferrat, who resided in that city, they returned to Thessaly.

During this time, a revolt had broken out among the *archontes* of the mountainous region of Skorta (Gortys), lying on both sides of the Alpheus. Philip of Savoy, greedy for money, had tried to levy an extraordinary tax upon them. Discontented, the *archontes* had waited until the departure of the marshal of the Morea for

Thessaly and had then sent emissaries to the Byzantine captain of Mistra. With the aid of his troops they had gained possession of the castles of St. Helena and Crèvecoeur and had burned them, but had failed before Beaufort, which the captain of Mistra undertook to besiege. Prince Philip assembled the troops of Elis and Achaea and advanced to surprise the Greeks, but, warned by their spies, they decamped, leaving arms and baggage, without waiting for him (1302).

The next year prince Philip campaigned in Epirus. For more than twenty years the despotate of Epirus had been vassal to the Angevins of Naples. The marriage of Philip of Taranto to Thamar, daughter of the despot Nicephorus, and the grant by Charles II to Philip of suzerainty over Epirus had strengthened this tie. In 1302 Charles demanded that the youthful Thomas, son of the late Nicephorus, do homage to the prince of Taranto. But the mother of Thomas, the *despoina* Anna, who was a Palaeologina, in an effort to secure her independence of the Angevins made overtures to the Byzantines, and replied that her son did not need to do homage to Philip of Taranto for lands which he held from the Byzantine emperor. Thereupon Charles II, determined to force her hand, sent troops into Acarnania and asked the aid of the prince of Achaea, who joined these troops with 300 men-at-arms. But the campaign was futile. The Frankish troops besieged Arta, the capital of the despotate, in vain. They lost about a hundred men in a minor action. And with autumn coming on, prince Philip of Savoy returned to the Morea.

This repulse did not discourage Charles II, who planned a new expedition for the following spring. But the *despoina* of Epirus, informed of his intentions, tried to turn aside the threat by the same means she had employed to stop the invasion of Epirus by duke Guy II of Athens: she sent an emissary to Philip of Savoy to offer him a sum of money if he succeeded in avoiding a new campaign. On the advice of the marshal, Nicholas of St. Omer, Philip of Savoy summoned a parliament in the spring of 1304 at Corinth, in order to have an excuse for not going to Epirus. All the chief lords assembled at Corinth: the duke of Athens, the count of Cephalonia, the barons of the Morea. The parliament was the occasion for brilliant festivities, with jousts which lasted for twenty days in which pilgrims passing through participated. It was the last ray of splendor of the court of Isabel, who had maintained the traditions of the Villehardouin princes. It was also the last important act of the reign of Philip of Savoy.

Like Florent of Hainault, Philip had been in no hurry to do homage, as was his duty, to his immediate overlord, prince Philip of Taranto; he meant to lay down his own conditions, especially as in Piedmont Angevin interests ran counter to his own. The reluctance of Philip of Savoy to continue the struggle in Epirus probably decided Charles II to intervene against him. On October 9, 1304, the king revived the act of February 6, 1301, which declared that Isabel had forfeited the principality. Philip of Savoy appointed Nicholas of St. Omer his bailie in Achaea, and went to Italy, possibly to negotiate with Charles II, but also to take action in Piedmont; in December 1304 he arrived in Asti, where the populace named him captain of the commune. The next year, his affairs seemed to take a turn for the better and a temporary accord was made with the Angevins; on November 17, 1305, his proxy was allowed to do homage for him to the prince of Taranto. But in Piedmont, as earlier in the Morea, he continued to combat Angevin policy. A new disagreement arose; and on June 5, 1306, Charles II pronounced the deposition of Philip of Savoy for violation of his feudal oath. In vain Philip sent Isabel and some of his councillors to persuade Charles once more to reverse his decision. Finally he was forced to accept a compromise and to exchange the principality of the Morea for the county of Alba.

Princess Isabel did not resign herself to the loss of the principality, which was her own domain, her patrimony, and her native land. In July 1307 at Poitiers she tried to make a public protest, which the representative of Charles II refused to accept. Her last known act, dated at Valenciennes, April 29, 1311, was to affirm her rights and those of Mahaut, her daughter by Florent, to the principality of Achaea. She died soon after at the age of about fifty-two. Philip of Savoy remarried in 1312, but continued to use the title prince of Achaea, probably because the Angevins did not fulfill their side of the compromise of May 1307. Similarly for the next hundred years his successors, though descended from his second wife, would continue to use the title and some of them would even try to get physical possession of the principality.

After the deposition of Philip of Savoy on June 5, 1306, the principality naturally reverted to its immediate overlord, prince Philip of Taranto, as had in fact been stipulated in the act of February 6, 1301. Philip now ruled directly or indirectly over all Greece from Durazzo and Corfu to the Cyclades. His father, Charles II, gave him the title "despot of Romania". Philip was ambitious and exacting, and the measures taken against Isabel and Philip of Savoy in 1301, 1304, and 1306 must be attributed to his influence. Not content with his somewhat illusory "despotate of Romania", he wished to take effective control of the principality of Achaea. Immediately after the decisions of June 5, 1306, which released the barons of the Morea from the oath of fidelity which they had taken to Philip of Savoy, he went to the Morea to have himself recognized by them as their lord. An army of 10,000 men accompanied him, transported by a considerable fleet. With these troops and those of the principality, he undertook military action in the Morea: the castle of Tripotamos in the valley of the Erymanthus was captured and numerous strongholds surrendered. He left garrisons in the castles and troops to continue the struggle, and went on to Epirus, where he had no success; his army was decimated by disease, and he had to retire to Italy.

The compromise of May 2, 1307, between Charles II and Philip of Savoy made Philip of Taranto definitively prince of Achaea; it is from that year that he began to date his reign. He chose as bailie duke Guy II of Athens, perhaps to satisfy the demands which Guy and his wife Mahaut of Hainault, the natural heirs of Isabel of Villehardouin, are said to have made. The duke, famous for his chivalry and his *courtoisie*, governed the Morea very well, but not for long. He died on October 5, 1308, at the age of only twenty-eight and was interred "in the tomb of his ancestors" in the Cistercian abbey of Daphne near Athens. With him ended the line of the De la Roche dukes, who had for a century raised the duchy of Athens to a high degree of brilliance and prosperity.

Within a year two claimants to the duchy presented themselves before the court of peers of the Morea. Both were cousins of Guy II and, like him, grandchildren of Guy I de la Roche, but in the female line: one was count Walter of Brienne, count also of Lecce in the kingdom of Naples, son of Isabel de la Roche and Hugh of Brienne, who had been bailie of the duchy; the other, Eschiva of Ibelin, lady of Lapithos in Cyprus, was the daughter of Alice de la Roche and John II of Ibelin, lord of Beirut. The court designated Walter of Brienne as heir. Eschiva considered that she had been denied justice; actually, the custom of the Morea required that, between two relatives equal in degree, the male be preferred to the female. As for Guy II's fifteen-year-old widow, Mahaut of Hainault, who might be expected to renew her pretensions to the principality of the Morea, the court of Naples hastened to make certain of her by affiancing her to Charles of Taranto, eldest son of Philip and of Thamar, then twelve years old (1309).[14]

Prince Philip of Taranto was never to return to the Morea. He made plans for a new campaign to continue the reconquest, but, detained in Italy, he sent to the Morea in May 1309, to replace Bertino Visconti as bailie, the marshal of the kingdom of Naples, Thomas of Marzano, with a considerable body of troops. Thomas began the struggle against the Greeks of Mistra. But emperor Andronicus II had sent to the Morea a young captain, active and courageous, of the Cantacuzenus family, possibly the grandson of the member of the family who had been killed at Sergiana in 1264, and the father of the future emperor John VI. Cantacuzenus marched resolutely against Thomas of Marzano and inflicted on him a bloody defeat at the pass of Makryplagi. Continuing his campaign with no respite, he succeeded in retaking the places which Philip of Taranto had captured, and finally forced Thomas to make a truce with him.

At about the same time, Thessaly was invaded by the Catalan Grand Company, which had been spreading terror far and wide in the Byzantine empire. Composed not only of Catalans but also of natives of Aragon, Majorca, and Navarre, the Company was the remnant of the old Catalan bands which had fought for about twenty years against the Angevin troops in Sicily and southern Italy. Finding itself without employ after the peace of Caltabellotta, the Company had hired out its services to the emperor Andronicus to fight against the Ottoman Turks, and its victorious first appearance in the east had taken on the aspect of a crusade. But these adventurers, undisciplined and predatory, were as dangerous to their allies as to their enemies. They had speedily come to blows with the Byzantines: established at Gallipoli, they had pillaged first Thrace and then Macedonia, and had installed themselves at Cassandrea in Chalcidice, whence they threatened Thessalonica. At this point a brother of king Philip IV of France, count Charles of Valois, who, having married Catherine of Courtenay, granddaughter of emperor Baldwin II of Constantinople, wished to establish his claim to the empire, took the Catalan Company into his service and appointed a Picard knight, Theobald of "Cépoy" (Chepoix), to direct it. But Theobald was lost in the midst of that horde of lawless adventurers, and, when they invaded Thessaly in 1309, he left in discouragement and returned to France.

[14] Mahaut's betrothal was dissolved in 1313. She married Louis of Burgundy in November of that year.

The master of Thessaly was then John II Angelus Comnenus, the former ward of Guy II of Athens; he had deserted the Latins in order to enter into relations with the Byzantines. His councillors, seeing the countryside laid waste, tried to get rid of the Company by directing it toward Frankish Greece. The new duke of Athens, Walter of Brienne, wished to avert the danger by making use of the Catalans, in his turn, for his ambitious projects: he planned to reëstablish the protectorate of the Athenian duchy over Thessaly and even, according to the Byzantine historians, to push on toward Thessalonica and Constantinople. He hired the Company and, in the spring of 1310, started on a campaign with them into Thessaly; in six months more than thirty places, including Zeitounion, Domokos, Halmyros, and Demetrias, fell into their hands.

The Catalans hoped to obtain lands in this region of southern Thessaly, which they had helped to conquer. But Walter of Brienne, who was proud and presumptuous, refused not only to give them any land but even to pay the arrears due them, and answered them with threats, thus turning them into mortal enemies. Aware of the danger which they presented, he summoned his vassals and friends from Greece and Italy, assembling a powerful army of seven hundred knights, several thousand other horsemen, and a great number of foot-soldiers.

At the beginning of March 1311 he marched against the Catalan Company, which had succeeded in infiltrating into Boeotia and was entrenched near Skripou (Orchomenus), on the banks of the Cephissus and of Lake Copais, where, as Raymond Muntaner relates, they made use of the swampy land as a "shield". The Company consisted of six to eight thousand men. The army of the duke of Athens was twice as numerous and included in its ranks the most famous barons of the duchy and of the neighboring countries. The encounter took place on March 15, 1311. The duke of Athens dashed forward at the head of his knights into the plain, which looked like a green meadow; but soon the knights slipped, were thrown headlong, and sank in the mud of the swamp, while the Catalans riddled the dismounted knights with arrows and advanced to slaughter them. Almost all the knights were killed, including the lords of Bodonitsa, Salona, Damala, and Tenos. Walter of Brienne had his head cut off. A few just managed to escape from the disaster. Among these were Nicholas Sanudo, eldest son of the duke of Naxos, who was wounded, and Boniface of Verona, lord of Gardiki, Carystus, and Aegina. The Catalans then made themselves masters of Thebes and of the whole duchy.[15] No resistance was offered except at Athens, where the duchess had taken refuge with her children on the Acropolis. But realizing that she could get no help, she soon embarked for the west.

Thus occurred the catastrophe which put an end to the French duchy of Athens, undermined Frankish Greece by its tremendous casualties, and caused a sensation even in the west. And thus ended another period of the history of Frankish Greece. Central Greece, with a territory almost equal to the Frankish possessions in the Morea, was entirely lost to the French forever; the knighthood of the Morea was depleted by perhaps one third of its members, a loss from which it would never recover.

In the Morea, the Byzantines at Mistra had, in the course of these fifty years, gradually gained ground in the southeast of the peninsula: Laconia and the region of Kalavryta had been occupied ever since the reign of William of Villehardouin, and the region of Nikli probably since near the end of the reign of Florent of Hainault. The revolts of the Greeks in 1286 and 1302 had even shaken the chief defense of the Franks in this region of the upper basin and gorges of the Alpheus, called Skorta: the castle of St. George had been taken, those of St. Helena and of Crèvecoeur had been destroyed. But the more important fortresses of Beaufort and Karytaina still held the pass toward Triphylia and Elis; and Messenia, which the Byzantines had not been able to enter, had been reinforced by the construction of new castles.[16]

In the islands, the Latins had reëstablished their position, compromised by the incursions of Licario. In Euboea, some of the castles had been recovered by the Venetian bailie of Negroponte during the principate of Charles I of Anjou; the castles of Carystus and Larmena in the south of the island, by Boniface of Verona in 1296. The duke of the Archipelago, Marco II Sanudo, son of duke Angelo and grandson of the conqueror of Naxos, had seen, toward the beginning of his reign (1262–1303), certain of his islands fall into the power of Licario and the Byzantines, who kept them for twenty years; but just before his death he had been able to recover them, and his son William I inherited the duchy virtually intact. In the Ionian islands, the county of Cephalonia and Zante, situated on the route between southern Italy and the Morea, had

[15] The Catalan duchy of Athens after 1311 will be treated in a chapter of volume III, in preparation.

[16] The Morea after 1311 will be treated in a chapter of volume III.

been drawn increasingly into the life of the principality; and Corfu, which was an Angevin possession, without being directly attached to the Morea, gravitated somewhat into the orbit of Frankish Greece.

In the "despotate of Romania", which Charles II had set up for Philip of Taranto with the idea that it would include all the lands under Angevin influence from Durazzo to Naupactus (Lepanto), there remained under Philip's domination only the territories that formed the Angevin kingdom of Albania, together with the places in Acarnania and Aetolia which had constituted the dowry of his wife Thamar. Between the two, Epirus, which Charles II had succeeded in making a vassal state in 1279, had in 1302 broken away from the overlordship of Philip. Similarly Thessaly, which had been under Angevin influence and under the protection of the dukes of Athens, turned towards the Byzantines at the time of the arrival of the Catalans. Here again the opening of the fourteenth century marked the decline of Frankish power; and the defeat of the eastern policy of Charles of Anjou was consummated under his successor.

Frankish Greece had maintained until the sudden catastrophe of 1311 that state of knightly civilization which had made its reputation in the middle of the thirteenth century. The magnificent appearance of the official charters which had been preserved, as well as the accounts of the chroniclers — Villani, Muntaner, the author of the *Chronicle of the Morea* — all bear witness to its splendor. The court of Isabel of Villehardouin under the reign of Florent of Hainault or that of Philip of Savoy continued the brilliant traditions of the court of prince William, as is shown by Isabel's reception of the Aragonese admiral Roger de Lluria in 1292 and by the parliament of Corinth in 1304; and the splendid festivities during which Guy II de la Roche was knighted at Thebes in 1294 testify to the fact that the court of the dukes of Athens was a close rival to that of the Morea. As soon as peace was reëstablished, prosperity revived; thus the reign of prince Florent was a period of steady recovery. The port of Glarentsa, founded by the Villehardouin princes, had been enriched by commercial traffic between the east and Italy; foreign merchants, Florentine or Sienese bankers, had established themselves there, and the town had become one of the chief commercial centers of the eastern Mediterranean; an admiral was stationed there and the rich bourgeois acted as bankers to the princes.

The Angevin domination had modified the political status of the

Morea. In theory, it remained feudal. Charles of Anjou had charged his bailie Galeran of Ivry to respect the customs of the country, and towards 1320 these were to be codified in the *Assises de Romanie*. But actually at the death of William of Villehardouin the Morea had ceased to be a feudal state grouped around a head who was the peer of his barons, and had become instead a dependency of a highly centralized bureaucratic monarchy. A semblance of autonomy was restored with Florent of Hainault, but the successive interventions of Charles II clearly revealed the Angevin predominance. Increasingly the Morea took on the character of a distant colony, sometimes subject to the excesses of Angevin power, sometimes left to itself when the Neapolitan court had more pressing problems. For the defense of the land against the Byzantines, the feudal army no longer sufficed; the Angevins had been compelled to send mercenaries, and badly paid mercenaries at that; and the Morea had then had a taste of the excesses of the soldiery. By first taking the Catalan Company into his pay and then infuriating them, Walter of Brienne brought on the needless disaster of Lake Copais, which marks the twilight of Frankish chivalry in Greece.

Frederick Barbarossa as a Crusader

12. Languedoc and Central France (*Map by the University of Wisconsin Cartographic Laboratory*)

VIII
THE ALBIGENSIAN CRUSADE

In March 1208 pope Innocent III issued a call for a holy war against the nominally Christian land of southern France. The immediate occasion for the issuance of this summons was the murder at St. Gilles of a papal legate, Peter of Castelnau. But the assassination of the legate was only the match which set fire to tinder which had been accumulating in Languedoc over long years.

Of the narrative sources for the Albigensian Crusade three are most important: (1) The *Hystoria Albigensis* of Peter of Les Vaux-de-Cernay (cited as *Hyst. Alb.*). The latest and best edition of this is by Pascal Guébin and Ernest Lyon (3 vols., Paris, 1926–1939). Volume III contains the introduction, index, and a thirteenth-century French translation of the text. The author was a nephew of Guy, abbot of the Cistercian monastery of Les Vaux-de-Cernay, who became bishop of Carcassonne in 1212. In the spring of that year Peter accompanied his uncle to Languedoc and until his death was an eyewitness of much about which he wrote. He is believed to have died late in 1218 or early in 1219 while still in his early twenties. Factually his account is the best we have for the crusade to the death of Simon of Montfort. It is highly colored in favor of the crusade and its leader, but its author's bias is so genuine and transparent that it is easily discounted. (2) The *Chanson de la croisade contre les Albigeois* (cited as *Chanson*) by William of Tudela, who carried the narrative to the summer of 1213, and an anonymous author who wrote much more fully of events from 1213 to 1219. Two editions of this work may be noted: the one by Paul Meyer (*La Chanson de la croisade contre les Albigeois*, 2 vols,. Paris, 1875–1879), volume I comprising the text in vernacular, volume II, a long introduction and a modern French translation. The second is by Eugène Martin-Chabot (*La Chanson de la croisade albigeoise*, I, II [Paris, 1931, 1957]), the first two volumes of which, bringing the story in text and translation to 1217, have thus far appeared. These two supersede all previous editions; the introduction and notes of both are valuable. The author follows Martin-Chabot (p. xxvii) in believing that the sixteenth-century prose version of the *Chanson* really adds nothing to the poetic version as it has come down to us. Little is known of the authors. William of Tudela was loyal to the south but opposed to heresy; the Anonymous was as partial to the southern cause as Peter of Les Vaux-de-Cernay was to that of Montfort, and he wrote chiefly in hyperbole. Unless indicated to the contrary, references are to the edition by Meyer. (3) The *Cronica* or *Historia albigensium* (cited as *Cronica*) of William of Puylaurens was edited by Beyssier in "Guillaume de Puylaurens et sa chronique," *Troisièmes mélanges d'histoire du moyen âge* (Paris, 1904), pp. 85–175. His edition leaves something to be desired, but supersedes the one in *RHGF*, XIX, 193–225, and XX, 764–776. The author was a native of Languedoc, attached as notary to bishops Fulk and Raymond of Toulouse and later to the court of the Inquisition (see Yves Dossat, "Le Chroniqueur Guillaume de Puylaurens," *Annales du Midi*, LXV [1953], 343–353). Though the *Cronica* continues through 1272, William is thought to have written the portion covering the period of the crusade about 1250. His name appears in documents as a witness as early as 1223, so he may well have had first-hand knowledge of the crusade. He nowhere indicates this, but he does give evidence of an attempt to secure good sources, either verbal or written, and to employ them judiciously. His work is much briefer than that of the other two, but serves as a good corrective to their more partisan approach to the subject.

Of the documentary materials, the most important single body consists in the papal correspondence of Innocent III (1198–1216) and Honorius III (1216–1227). These letters

The real antecedents of the Albigensian crusade lay far back in the economic, political, cultural, and religious history of southern France, but the tracing of these is beyond the scope of the present study.[1] It is perhaps sufficient to point out that, for reasons which

are calendared in August Potthast, *Regesta pontificum Romanorum* (2 vols., Berlin, 1874–1875). The letters of Innocent are published in *PL*, CCXIV–CCXVII; those of Honorius are calendared in P. Pressutti, *Regesta Honorii papae III* . . . (2 vols., Rome, 1888–1895; supplementing at some points Potthast), and published in part by C. A. Horoy, *Honorii III . . . opera omnia* (5 vols., Paris, 1879–1882). Next in importance as a single body of materials are the acts of church councils, general or local, most easily consulted in G. D. Mansi, *Sacrorum conciliorum nova et amplissima collectio*, vols. XXII and XXIII. There are also numerous documents emanating from royal, imperial, feudal, and local ecclesiastical chanceries. Some of these have been calendared: Léopold Delisle, *Catalogue des actes de Philippe-Auguste* . . . (Paris, 1856); Auguste Molinier, "Catalogue des actes de Raimond VI et de Raimond VII," *Histoire générale de Languedoc*, VIII, 1940–2008; *idem*, "Catalogue des actes de Simon et d'Amauri de Montfort," *Bibliothèque de l'École des chartes*, XXXIV (1873), 153–203, 445–501; a large number have been published, notably in: *Histoire générale de Languedoc*, vol. VIII; Alexandre Teulet, *Layettes du trésor des chartes*, vols. I, II, V (cited as Teulet, *Layettes*); and Martin Bouquet, *RHGF*, esp. vols. XVIII, XIX.

The work upon which any careful study of the Albigensian crusade must be based remains the *Histoire générale de Languedoc* by Cl. Devic and J. Vaissete, vols. VI–VIII in the revised edition by Auguste Molinier *et al.* (Toulouse, 1879–1904; cited as *Hist. Lang.*). Achille Luchaire devotes one volume of his six-volume study of Innocent III to the crusade until the death of Innocent (*Innocent III*: *La Croisade des Albigeois*, 3rd ed., Paris, 1911), and more recently there appeared *La Croisade contre les Albigeois et l'union du Languedoc à la France (1209–1249)* (Paris, 1942) by Pierre Belperron. This last is a full and interesting account, but should be used with some caution.

For the background of the crusade the following may be usefully consulted: Hippolyte Pissard, *La Guerre sainte en pays chrétien* (Paris, 1912); Auguste Molinier, "Géographie de la province de Languedoc au moyen âge," *Histoire générale de Languedoc*, XII, 265–319; Paul Dognon, *Les Institutions politiques et administratives du pays de Languedoc du XIIIe siècle aux guerres de religion* (Toulouse, 1895); Charles Higounet, "Un Grand Chapitre de l'histoire du XIIe siècle: La Rivalité des maisons de Toulouse et de Barcelone pour la prépondérance méridionale," *Mélanges . . . Halphen*, pp. 313–322; and several recent essays by Yves Dossat: "Cathares et Vaudois à la veille de la croisade albigeoise," *Revue historique et littéraire de Languedoc*, II (1945), 390–397; III (1946), 70–83; "Le Clergé méridional à la veille de la croisade albigeoise," *Revue historique et littéraire de Languedoc*, I (1944), 263–278; "Le Comté de Toulouse et la féodalité languedocienne à la veille de la croisade albigeoise," *Revue du Tarn*, IX (1943), 75–90; "La Société méridionale à la veille de la croisade albigeoise," *Revue historique et littéraire de Languedoc*, I (1944), 66–87.

For various aspects of the crusade consult: Edgard Boutaric, "La Guerre des Albigeois et Alphonse de Poitiers," *Revue des questions historiques*, II (1867), 155–180; Ferdinand Lot, *L'Art militaire et les armées au moyen-âge* (2 vols., Paris, 1946), I; Charles Petit-Dutaillis, *Étude sur la vie et le règne de Louis VIII* (Paris, 1894); Louis J. Thomas, "Quelques Aspects peu connus de la croisade contre les Albigeois," *Cahiers d'histoire et d'archéologie*, 1931, pp. 257–265; and André Varagnac, "Croisade et marchandise: pourquoi Simon de Montfort s'en alla défaire les Albigeois," *Annales: économies, sociétés, civilisations*, I (1946), 209-218.

For bibliography see: Auguste Molinier, *Les Sources de l'histoire de France* (6 vols., Paris, 1901–1906), III, 63–70; Charles de Smedt, "Les Sources de l'histoire de la croisade contre les Albigeois," *Revue des questions historiques*, XVI (1874), 433–481; and J. Jouhate, "La Croisade contre les Albigeois: Étude bibliographique," *Revue historique, scientifique, et littéraire de département du Tarn*, ser. 2, XXIII (1906), 101–121.

For maps consult: F. Schrader, *Atlas de géographie historique* (Paris, 1896), plate 25; Auguste Molinier, in *Hist. Lang.*, XVI, plates V–VII; Eugène Martin-Chabot, *La Chanson de la croisade albigeoise*, I, facing p. 304; and Pierre Belperron, *La Croisade contre les Albigeois*, at end.

[1] Convenient summaries of the religious, social, and political background of this crusade may be found in the articles by Yves Dossat mentioned in the bibliographical note.

are still not clear, by the latter half of the twelfth century popular heresies had become rooted more widely and deeply in the Midi than in other regions of Europe, and that the institutions of church and state were not so effectively organized as elsewhere to cope with the challenge. The feudal bond, especially in its military aspects, was weaker than in other parts of France; the counts of Toulouse paid only a shadowy allegiance to the king of France; the kings of England and of Aragon possessed substantial holdings in the region and were continually reaching out for more; while the emperor of Germany held suzerainty over the marquisate of Provence east of the Rhone. Thus, the counts of Toulouse, for different parts of their domain, owed allegiance to three rulers in addition to the king of France, while they in turn were constantly embroiled with their own vassals. Though at the turn of the thirteenth century they ruled one of the most considerable vassal states of the crown of France, their lands lacked cohesion. They were cut up into a congeries of lordships, lay and ecclesiastical, many of which recognized only the most nebulous allegiance to the house of St. Gilles. This situation was by no means unique, but was aggravated by the divided allegiance of the counts of Toulouse, the conflicting interests of neighbor states in the territory, the desire of the French king to establish effective hegemony over the Midi, and the determination of the counts of Toulouse to bring their own vassals and the growing towns more firmly under their control. There are indications of efforts on the part of Raymond V and Raymond VI in the twelfth century to improve this condition, but their work was impeded by the rapid growth of heresy in the region and the consequent divisions in the population.

For popular heresy did present a serious challenge. Its manifestations ranged all the way from an effort to return to the simplicity of early Christianity, in a healthy reaction against the temporal power and the presumptions of the ecclesiastical hierarchy, to the setting up what amounted to a rival religion under "Neo-Manichaean" or Catharist leaders. It was this heresy, most firmly entrenched in northern Italy and Languedoc, that clergy and lay rulers by the late twelfth century recognized as the most dangerous to established order. In the earliest extant register of the Inquisition in Languedoc it was referred to as *the* heresy; witnesses before the court were required to tell what they knew of "heresy [i.e., Catharism] and Waldensianism". Although it seems desirable here to outline some of its main features, Catharism is not easily summed up in a few words. Its roots reach back to the eastern Mediterranean world during the early centuries of Christianity, to the religious and philosophical speculations of the so-called Gnostics. Just how the connection between this early gnostic movement and the Catharism in western Europe from the eleventh to the fourteenth century may be traced is still a matter of discussion, which need not be pursued here. Let it be noted merely that observers of the sporadic outbreaks of heresy in France as early as the eleventh century write of it occasionally as "Manichaean".

Basically the Cathars, or the "pure", as they called themselves, were either absolute or modified dualists. These differed in their view of creation. The former believed in two Principles, or Gods, the one creating and ruling an immaterial and suprasensible world which was wholly good, the other creating and ruling this world of sense which was wholly evil. The latter held that all creation was by God, but that Lucifer, who had originally been an angel of light, rebelled, was cast out of heaven, and drew with him a portion of the angels who had been seduced by him. By God he was given dominion over this material universe, which was still in chaos, to shape according to his will. Although there were considerable differences between these two groups, and indeed among members of the same group, they were at one in believing that this world is from the devil, all matter is evil, and the souls of angels who fell from heaven are forcibly implanted in the bodies of men by the devil: the problem of salvation for the individual is to free the soul from the envelope within which it has been imprisoned, which may be accomplished only through the instrumentality of the Catharist church. Both groups denied the Trinity as understood by orthodox Christians, Jesus and the Holy Ghost being created by and inferior to God. Christ had no real existence on this earth, being only a phantom who was not truly born of the Virgin Mary, who did not eat, did not suffer, did not rise from the dead, and did not ascend into heaven. All this occurred in the suprasensible world, wherein was His real existence. The sacraments of the church they held unavailing: the clergy possess no special powers; there is no purgatory and no resurrection of the body. They denied the validity of prayers and offerings for the dead; spurned the veneration of the cross, of images, and of relics; held burial in hallowed ground or belief in the special sanctity of churches and altars to be void of meaning. In addition they were charged with refusal to take oaths; denial of the right of justice to the civil power; condemnation of marriage; and refusal to eat meat, milk, or eggs, which were of sexual origin.

In place of the official church whose foundations they undercut, in both faith and organization, they were in process of setting up a rival church with a hierarchy, consisting of bishops, "elder sons", "younger sons", and deacons; with what may be called sacraments, the most important of which was the *consolamentum*; with a liturgy; and with a membership consisting of a relatively small body of initiates, the "perfected" (*perfecti*), and a much larger group of "believers" (*credentes*). There are occasional references in the sources to a rival "pope", but that is probably due to a misunderstanding of their use of the term "papas". The core of their membership consisted of the perfected. Reinerius Sacconi, who had himself been for many years a member of the sect, but was (when he wrote) a Dominican and an inquisitor, estimated that there were probably about 4,000 perfected in the second quarter of the thirteenth century. They were a picked group of men and women, who had been subjected to a long and rigorous novitiate before they were allowed to receive the consolamentum, a rite somewhat comparable to baptism and ordination in the orthodox church. This rite is carefully detailed in their rituals, two versions of which have come down to us. To them baptism was not material, of water, but spiritual, through the imposition of hands by which they received the Holy Spirit. As a "perfected", one was cleansed from sin and was qualified to preach and to perform the rituals of the church. For one thus consoled a life of great austerity was prescribed. The consolamentum constituted the sole means whereby at death the soul might be freed to return to heaven. But the great majority of believers delayed the rite until they felt death approaching, thus laying themselves open to the charge of licentiousness of life, a charge difficult of proof or denial.

For a clear picture of this heresy much more should be said, but this may suffice to indicate why, having permeated all strata of society in Languedoc, it was considered destructive not alone of orthodox religious faith, but of existing social and political institutions as well.[2] By the middle of the twelfth century, sporadic and

[2] Theoretically, the most useful sources for a knowledge of Catharist heresy are the few pieces of their own writings which have thus far come to light: the *Liber de duobus principiis*, the single MS. of which was discovered and published by A. Dondaine, O.P., under the title *Un Traité néo-manichéen du XIII siècle* (Rome, 1939); a fragment of a Latin ritual, published in the same work (pp. 151–165); and a ritual in Provençal published by L. Clédat in *Le Nouveau Testament, traduit au XIIIe siècle en langue provençale, suivi d'un rituel cathare* (Paris, 1887). But these present only a partial picture, which must be supplemented by reference to the writings of their critics. Two of the best of these are the treatises by Reinerius Sacconi, *Summa . . . de Catharis et Pauperibus de Lugduno* (most recently published by Dondaine in the work cited above, pp. 64–78), and Moneta of Cremona, *Adversus Catharos et Valdenses libri quinque*, published by T. A. Ricchini (Rome, 1743). Of modern works may

uncoördinated efforts on the part of the local clergy and lay officials to contain it had proved clearly inadequate. Preaching missions, such as that of Bernard of Clairvaux in southern France, had yielded negligible results.

The Third Lateran Council in 1179 adopted a decree (canon 27), anathematizing heretics, known variously as Cathari, Patarini, or Publicani, and all who supported them. With these were grouped mercenary soldiers (Latin, *ruterii*; French, *routiers*), who were threatened with the same penalties as were the heretics. An indulgence of two years was offered any who would take up arms against them. At about the same time, the kings of France and England, at the request of Raymond V, united in an agreement to root out heresy from southern France by armed force; but they abandoned the plan in favor of further trial of preaching and disputation. This has been termed the first hint of a crusade in Languedoc.[3] In the years immediately following the Council of Verona (1184), where pope and emperor agreed that the secular power should be employed in the service of the church for the extirpation of heresy, there was developed in addition to ecclesiastical legislation a growing body of secular law in the matter of heresy, which indicates that its suppression was moving from the occasional and the improvised to a conscious policy on the part of church and state looking toward its eradication.

In Languedoc all ranks of society were involved, either as heretics themselves or as harborers or defenders of heretics. Even the ecclesiastical estate was not free from charges either of heresy or of lukewarmness in its pursuit. Raymond VI, who succeeded as count of Toulouse in 1194, lacked his father's interest in rooting out heresy. Indeed, it would be difficult to argue that, given the weakness of his hold upon the lesser nobility in his lands and the autonomous position of the towns, he could have coped effectively with the challenge of heresy, even had he wished to do so.

Immediately upon his accession to the papal throne in 1198, Innocent III took energetic action to stem the spread of heresy in

be mentioned the careful treatment by Hans Söderberg, *La Religion des Cathares* (Uppsala, 1949); Arno Borst, *Die Katharer* (Stuttgart, 1953), which has excellent bibliographical references; A. Dondaine, "L'Origine de l'hérésie médiévale," *Rivista di storia della Chiesa in Italia*, VI (1952), 46–78; and, in English, Steven Runciman, *The Medieval Manichee, A Study in Christian Dualist Heresy* (Cambridge, 1947). The old work by C. Schmidt, *Histoire et doctrine de la secte des Cathares ou Albigeois* (2 vols., Geneva, 1849), is still useful, and has the virtue of presenting a clear picture of their fundamental beliefs in relatively small compass.

[3] *Hist. Lang.*, VI, 78. Three years later there actually was an abortive crusade, led by Henry, cardinal-bishop of Albano, then papal legate (A. Luchaire, *Innocent III*: *La Croisade des Albigeois*, pp. 45–46; cited hereafter as Luchaire, *Croisade*).

southern France. Beginning with the appointment of Renier and Guy, of the Cistercian order, as "commissioners" in southern France, there was a constant succession of papal legates especially appointed to that region primarily for the extirpation of heresy. Renier was raised to the position of legate in 1199; shortly thereafter Peter of Castelnau, archdeacon of Maguelonne and a Cistercian from the monastery of Fontfroide, was associated with him. To the legates already on the ground was added, in 1204, Arnold Amalric, abbot of Cîteaux, who led a mission of twelve Cistercian abbots to the Midi, and who later became one of the most active and prominent of the leaders of the crusade. In 1212 Arnold was chosen archbishop of Narbonne. As these men died or were transferred their places were filled by others, sent from Rome or drawn from the French clergy. They devoted themselves to strengthening the local clergy and introducing reforms, to preaching, and to public disputations with the heretics.

On paper the legates possessed wide authority, but they had a difficult task, not only because of the normal regional resentment of "foreign" reformers, but partially because the very powers conferred upon them by the pope aroused the hostility of many of the local clergy as well as of the nobility. The result was that they had not only to combat heresy, but also to cope with the opposition, covert or declared, of the very element in society from whom they felt they should receive support. Peter of Castelnau in despair asked to be relieved of his mission and be allowed to return to his monastery, a request which Innocent refused.

To the aid of the legates there came in 1206 bishop Diego of Osma and his assistant Dominic. They had been on a mission to Rome, and when that was completed had been urged by the pope to aid in the conversion of heretics in the Midi. They, too, resorted to public disputation with heretics, as a regular part of their procedure. But these debates, like other expedients of the legates, did little to diminish heresy. Feeling toward the legates was in some places so bitter that Peter of Castelnau was advised by his associates in the fall of 1206 to withdraw "for fear of assassination, in that the heretics hated him above all others." This he did and rejoined his fellows only after a period of six months.[4]

Gradually the judgment was forming that heresy could be suppressed only by the use of force. Already in 1204 and 1205 Innocent III had asked Philip Augustus to aid in this task. Finally,

[4] *Hyst. Alb.*, 24 (I, 27, and note 2). References are to numbered sections in the text, followed by volume and page numbers in parentheses.

on November 17, 1207, the pope addressed an open letter to Philip, urging that he and his subjects take up arms to eradicate heresy in Languedoc, offering the same indulgences as those conferred upon crusaders to the Holy Land, and suggesting the confiscation of the lands of heretics.[5] To this letter Philip replied through bishop Odo of Paris. He did not refuse aid, but emphasized his commitments in the north, both military and financial, which would make it impossible, unless the pope could guarantee him a firm truce with John of England, and in addition the clergy and nobility would have to contribute generously to help defray the cost of such an expedition. And, finally, he must be free to recall his troops at any time should the king of England break the truce.[6] The pope was in no position to offer such guarantees, so the matter of the crusade remained in abeyance.

This direct call for a crusade antedates by some months the assassination of Peter of Castelnau, which occurred on January 14, 1208. Peter had attended a conference at St. Gilles which had refused the request of count Raymond VI of Toulouse for absolution from a ban of excommunication which had been pronounced against him the previous year. In confirming this excommunication by letter of May 29, 1207, pope Innocent had written bitterly to Raymond, threatening him with loss of the county of Melgueil, which he held of the holy see, and with the unleashing of other nobles against his lands, to root out heresy and to take what they could conquer.[7] This, together with the pope's appeal to Philip Augustus in November, had stung Raymond to action. Hence his interview with the legates and his request for absolution and the raising of the interdict on his lands. The conference broke up in recriminations and charges of bad faith, and Raymond repeatedly warned the legates that wherever they went they would be under his surveillance. The following morning, while about to cross the Rhone in the neighborhood of Arles, Peter of Castelnau was struck down by the hand of an unknown assassin. Raymond was at once suspected to be the instigator of the crime. The identity of the murderer was never ascertained, nor was the responsibility of Raymond VI ever proved or disproved. Early in March, the pope categorically laid the blame upon him and renewed the anathema of excommunication. But he subsequently modified the charge to one of suspicion of complicity, and Raymond himself steadfastly denied any knowledge of the crime prior to its execution. He was

[5] *PL*, CCXV, 1246–124 [6] *Hist. Lang.*, VIII, 557–558. [7] *PL*, CCXV, 1166–1168.

not an astute politician, but it is improbable that he would have committed such a blunder as to have countenanced so stupid an act on the part of one of his retainers. Indeed, the legate had attracted to himself sufficient ill will to account for the murder as the rash act of an embittered nobleman. But whether Raymond was guilty or not, the only course open to him, under the circumstances, would seem to have been a prompt appeal to the mercy of the church and an assurance of immediate action to discover the murderer and bring him to justice. Instead he temporized.

Raymond's opponents acted without delay. On March 10 pope Innocent wrote to the king, prelates, nobles, and commoners throughout France, denouncing the murder, and declaring Raymond excommunicate as guilty of the crime and of heresy. Innocent invited any and all to take up arms against him and against all supporters of heresy and promised them any lands which they might wrest from the heretics, "saving the right of the *haut suzerain*". To further this cause he urged the conclusion of a truce between the kings of France and England.[8] These letters were followed by a further communication of March 28 addressed to the then legates — Arnold Amalric, Navarre (bishop of Couserans), and Hugh Raymond (bishop of Riez) — calling for a crusade against the heretics of Languedoc and offering, as previously, the same indulgences granted to crusaders to the Holy Land.[9]

The response of the nobility was immediate. William of Tudela writes that he never saw so large a force as gathered in the spring of 1209 to join the attack upon the Midi. The attitude of Philip Augustus was not so favorable. The pope in his letter of March 10 had asked him to lead the expedition for the chastisement of Raymond and the extirpation of heresy. Philip still had his hands full in the north, however, where large issues were at stake in his struggle with John of England and where relations with the empire were not satisfactory. He looked with a critical eye, therefore, upon the drawing off by his vassals of any large number of fighting men for a war in the south. Moreover, his relations with Innocent were strained on more than one point, and the references in the pope's letters of November 17 (1207) and March 10 to the confiscation of the lands of heretics aroused his suspicions at once. He now took occasion to point out firmly that, in the opinion of "learned advisers", the necessary first step was the conviction of Raymond as a heretic: "Only then should you publish the judgment and

[8] *PL*, CCXV, 1354–1362.
[9] Teulet, *Layettes*, I, no. 843.

invite us to confiscate the land, since he holds it of us in fief."[10] At the same time he endeavored, without much success, to limit the numbers of knights who might be drawn off for the southern crusade.

According to William of Tudela, in order to counter these preparations for a crusade Raymond VI sought a meeting with Arnold Amalric, who referred him to Innocent III for a decision in the matter of absolution. Raymond also sought out his nephew Raymond Roger, viscount of Béziers and of Carcassonne, with whom he had been in conflict, and vainly urged upon him a united defense against the threat from the north. Raymond's one remaining recourse lay in a direct appeal to the pope. Already toward the end of 1208 or the beginning of 1209 he had sent representatives to Rome asking for another legate, alleging that it was impossible for him to come to any agreement with Arnold Amalric, and offering to submit in all things to the pope's will. Innocent sent his secretary Milo as legate, with instructions to maintain a conciliatory attitude in his relations with the count, but at the same time to be advised in all things by Arnold Amalric.

Through the instrumentality of the new legate Raymond was dramatically reconciled with the church at St. Gilles (on June 18, 1209). He was made to rehearse the charges preferred against him in the excommunications of 1207 and 1208 and to agree, so far as lay in his power, to correct the abuses therein detailed. These charges run as a refrain through all his subsequent negotiations with the clergy: (1) Raymond had not expelled heretics from his lands, but rather had favored them and had so comported himself as to be suspect of heresy; (2) he had harbored mercenary troops; (3) violated solemn feast days; (4) conferred public office upon Jews; (5) retained the lands of monasteries and churches, especially of St. Gilles; (6) maltreated the clergy, notably the bishops of Carpentras and Vaison, and committed deeds of brigandage against their property; (7) also he had fortified churches; (8) was suspected of involvement in the murder of Peter of Castelnau; (9) and had levied unjust tolls. All these acts he abjured, and as a pledge of good behavior he turned over to the clergy for their administration seven fortresses (mostly in the region of the Rhone), and placed the county of Melgueil, which he held from the holy see, under the virtual control of the clergy.[11] The following day (June 19), at

[10] Léopold Delisle, *Catalogue des actes de Philippe-Auguste* (Paris, 1856), pp. 512–513; *Hist. Lang.*, VIII, 558–559.

[11] *PL*, CCXVI, 89–91. This forms part of a body of materials appearing, under the title *Processus negotii Raymundi comitis Tolosani*, in columns 89 to 98.

the instance of Milo, the count issued a document designed to carry out the terms of his submission, insofar as they concerned his relations with the clergy and their property, and ordered his officials in no way to molest them.

Raymond then asked to be allowed to take the cross against the heretics. The request was granted, and, armed with a papal letter of congratulation for his submission, he shortly went off to join the crusaders, who by this time were moving south through the Rhone valley. He met the approaching army at Valence and appears at once to have established cordial relations with its leaders. His motives in thus throwing in his lot with the invaders from the north are not difficult to guess. He was probably moved less by religious fervor than by a prudent desire to keep watch over the crusaders, to learn their objectives, and to direct their attack against his troublesome nephew and vassal, Raymond Roger, in order to shield his own lands against devastation and conquest.

The crusading army was composed of contingents drawn widely from northern and central France. Despite the determined efforts of the pope over a period of years, it lacked the leadership either of king Philip or of his son Louis, but it did number among its leaders important members of the nobility, chief of whom were duke Odo of Burgundy and the counts of Nevers, St. Pol, and Boulogne (Hervey of Donzi, Walter of Châtillon, and Reginald of Dammartin respectively), together with a considerable number of prelates, including the archbishops of Rheims, Rouen, and Sens, as well as members of the lesser nobility. Acting as overall leaders were the papal legates Arnold Amalric and Milo. No useful estimate of the size of the army can be made; in their report to the pope the legates describe it as the greatest army that had ever been assembled in Christendom.[12]

There is no need to follow in detail the campaigns of the crusade from the capture of Béziers in July of 1209 to the Peace of Paris twenty years later. The more important steps in the conquest of the Midi may be grouped under six general heads: (1) the conquest of the lands of the Trencavel family (1209–1211); (2) the conquest of the Toulousain (1211–1213); (3) the intervention of king Peter of Aragon and the battle of Muret (1213); (4) the triumph of Simon of Montfort: the Lateran Council (1213–1215); (5) the southern

[12] *Chanson*, 279–283 (reference is to lines of the poem); *PL*, CCXVI, 138–139. A second and smaller expedition, under the leadership of the archbishop of Bordeaux and count Guy of Auvergne, entered Languedoc from the west, raided through Quercy and the Agenais, but disappears from the record after laying siege to Casseneuil, on the Lot near its junction with the Garonne (*Chanson*, 300–336).

counter-attack (1215–1225); and (6) the final conquest by the crown (1225–1229).

The first attack of the crusading army was directed against the lands of the Trencavel family, ruled at this time by Raymond Roger, twenty-four years of age, courageous, attractive in personality, but gravely lacking in experience. He ruled as viscount of Béziers and of Carcassonne and lord of the Albigeois and of Razès. His lands formed a solid block, cutting across Languedoc roughly from the Hérault on the east to the Hers on the west, and from the Tarn on the north to the Pyrenees mountains and Roussillon on the south, including within their boundaries the important towns of Albi, Béziers, and Carcassonne, and the strongholds of Cabaret and Minerve to the north, Termes to the south, and Lavaur to the west. Some of these regions were among those most thickly settled with heretics.

For these lands Raymond Roger did homage to count Raymond VI of Toulouse and to king Peter II of Aragon, but he had slight hope of support from either. His refusal to join forces with his uncle, Raymond, against the northerners had apparently been motivated by distrust of the count and undue confidence in his own strength. Although ultimately he did appeal to Peter of Aragon for aid in the defense of Carcassonne, Peter was not yet prepared to cross swords with those who were fighting under the authority of the church, and contented himself with diplomatic protest. Thus left alone, Raymond Roger called upon the citizens of Béziers to defend their city as best they might, while he himself strengthened Carcassonne for a determined stand.[13]

Undaunted by the absence of their prince, the citizens of Béziers prepared for a siege, confident in the strength of their position and believing that they could hold out until the very size of the crusading army would defeat it because of the difficulty of procuring provisions. Their rash over-confidence led them to make a sortie, and in the melee which followed between them and the foot-soldiers of the crusading army the latter forced one of the gates. In the matter of a few hours the city was in the hands of the crusaders; the mounted troops never even saw action (July 22). On the side of the defenders all was confusion; resistance was at an end. The crusaders pillaged

[13] We omit the story, told by the fifteenth-century author of the prose adaptation of the *Chanson* and repeated by most modern historians, to the effect that Raymond Roger sought out the legates at Montpellier and tried unsuccessfully to arrange a peaceful settlement. Though it is reasonable to suppose that he would have made such an effort, no contemporary account mentions it.

and slaughtered at will. Even discounting the lurid exaggerations of our sources — for example, that 7,000 were cremated in burning the church of La Madeleine — the loss of life must have been great, among orthodox as well as heretics.[14] To finish the destruction the foot-soldiers burned one section of the city.

The example of Béziers was sufficient to strike terror into the people of the region, and many places opened their gates to the invaders, whose march from Béziers to Carcassonne was unopposed. The attempt of king Peter of Aragon to aid Raymond Roger by negotiation was fruitless; Carcassonne was invested and for two weeks withstood a siege, August 1–15. Then the summer heat, sickness, and lack of water forced capitulation. Raymond Roger was able to save his people, who were allowed to leave the city, "taking with them nothing but their sins", only by submitting himself as a hostage. His death from dysentery a few months later led to ugly stories of foul play.

The relatively mild treatment accorded Carcassonne, after the destruction wrought at Béziers, is explained by the necessities of the crusaders. Self-interest required that if they were to provision and house themselves, towns and countryside should be preserved rather than destroyed. And it was certainly to the interest of those who hoped to profit by confiscations and to settle in the Midi.

To this point leadership of the crusade had devolved upon the papal legates. By now, however, nearly the whole territory of Raymond Roger was in the hands of the crusaders. Upon whom should these lands be bestowed, and who should assume responsibility for the further prosecution of the war? After some preliminary offers to leading nobles among the crusading forces — the duke of Burgundy and the counts of Nevers and St. Pol — the choice fell upon Simon, earl of Leicester and lord of Montfort,[15] an able and courageous noble from the Île de France, who accepted the honor with some show of reluctance. On the Fourth Crusade Simon had refused to follow the majority in turning aside to conquer Zara,

[14] In their report to the pope, the legates stated that the crusading troops spared no order, sex, or age (*nostrique non parcentes ordini, sexui vel aetati*), putting to the sword nearly 20,000 (*PL*, CCXVI, 139). This is, again, great exaggeration; the total population of Béziers is presumed to have been around eight or nine thousand souls.

[15] His claim to the earldom came through his mother, a daughter of earl Robert III (d. 1204), and was recognized by John of England by the year 1206 (*Pipe Roll, 8 John*, pp. 9, 107). The title "count of Montfort," though in common use by some contemporaries, such as Peter of Les Vaux-de-Cernay, was not used by Simon himself (see Guébin and Lyon edition of *Hyst. Alb.*, I, 82, n. 6).

but had proceeded to Palestine, where for a time he had fought the Moslems. When the call for a crusade against the heretics had been issued, he had gathered a troop from his ancestral lands southwest of Paris, and joined the expedition. He knew well the difficulties of the position offered him, but accepted it on the understanding that those who urged it upon him would stand by him in the hour of need.

Upon the choice of a leader and the completion of their forty-day service, the great majority of the crusaders returned home, leaving Simon with a handful of followers who, after the departure of the duke of Burgundy, numbered only about thirty knights. The winter of 1209–1210 was a difficult period for Simon; his men were ambushed, and one stronghold after another fell away as their holders felt strong enough to break the agreements they had made when menaced by the invading northern host. King Peter of Aragon refused Simon's proffered homage for the viscounty of Carcassonne and the lordship of Razès held of him.

In the spring of 1210 Simon's fortunes took a turn for the better. His wife came south bringing with her much needed reinforcements.[16] With these and other recruits that came later he was able to take the offensive, to reduce the towns and castles which had withdrawn allegiance during the previous winter, and successfully to besiege the two heavily fortified strongholds of Minerve and Termes, the latter capitulating on November 22 after a bitter four-month siege. Simon was now substantially master of the lands of the Trencavel family, Cabaret and Lavaur being the only important strongholds which still held out against him. The decision had to be made whether to rest here or proceed to attack lands held directly by the count of Toulouse.

In the winter of 1210–1211 it appeared for a while as though relations between the southerners and the crusaders might improve. The king of Aragon finally accepted the homage of Simon for Carcassonne and Razès and pursued negotiations looking toward a marriage between his son James and Amicie, a daughter of Simon, who was given custody of the boy, then only three years of age. At the same time the king gave his sister Sancia in marriage to the son of Raymond of Toulouse, the future Raymond VII, who was in his fourteenth year. But friendly negotiation came to nothing when Raymond VI withdrew in bitterness from a council held at Mont-

[16] Simon's wife was Alice of Montmorency, who had remained in the north throughout the first months of the crusade. This was not the only time that she aided her husband by recruiting reinforcements.

pellier early in 1211, at which this momentary rapprochement between Peter of Aragon and Simon had been effected.

The background of that incident was as follows. After the fall of Carcassonne to the crusaders Raymond VI had left their army, but appears to have found difficulty in charting a clear course. According to the prelates, he had not fulfilled the promises made at St. Gilles in 1209. At a series of councils and conferences held at Avignon (September 1209), St. Gilles (June–July 1210), Narbonne (January 1211), and Montpellier (January–February 1211) the accusations were always the same. Raymond sought absolution from the ban of excommunication, under which he had again been placed, and asked to be allowed to purge himself from the charges of heresy, favoring heretics, and complicity in the murder of Peter Castelnau; but for one reason or another his request was consistently disallowed by the prelates. Personally, as Raymond complained and as was surely true of Arnold Amalric and Thedisius (a notary of Genoa who had begun his career in Languedoc as secretary to Milo),[17] some of them may have been haughty and hard men to deal with. As responsible representatives of the church, however, they all seem to have arrived at substantially the same conclusions. The pope had his doubts at times, as when he wrote to Philip Augustus that he felt unsure just who was at fault in the failure of Raymond to purge himself,[18] but he did insist that affirmative action be taken by the clergy on the ground.

Raymond had personally laid his case before his suzerains, Philip Augustus, the emperor Otto IV, and the pope. From them he received advice, but no real support. There is no convincing evidence that he made a genuine effort to fulfill the obligations which he had assumed under the terms of his absolution in June of 1209, or that he made any purposeful move to defend himself in case of direct attack upon his lands by the crusaders. The legates felt confirmed in their judgment of him as a shifty individual whose word was of no value.

With this background the council — or probably more accurately, conference — assembled at Montpellier and held two sessions in late January and early February, 1211. There the clergy laid before Raymond a memorandum of terms upon which he might be reconciled with the church. Peter of Les Vaux-de-Cernay

[17] In *Hyst. Alb.*, 163 (I, 166) Thedisius is depicted as anxious, above all, to devise means by which Raymond might be prevented from securing absolution, and as conferring secretly with Arnold Amalric to this end while they were at Toulouse to reconcile that town to the church in accordance with the pope's instructions.

[18] On August 25, 1211 (*PL*, CCXVI, 524–525).

contents himself with remarking that these were very favorable.[19] William of Tudela, however, paints an entirely different, and probably a far truer, picture.[20] Besides the previous demands upon Raymond, he says that the clergy now required that fortifications be leveled in his territories; imposed limitations on the habitat, food, and clothing of his vassals; required Raymond to allow Simon and his crusaders free passage through his lands so long as they committed no excesses; and bound him to go on a crusade to the Holy Land, after which he should join one of the crusading orders. If Raymond did not accept these demands, he was to be driven from his lands. When this memorandum was read to Peter of Aragon, he is said to have remarked: "By the Lord Almighty, there is here something that needs amendment!" Accounts agree that Raymond left the conference hastily and without further word with the legates; Peter intimates because of an untoward omen; William states to publish the infamous terms of the ultimatum throughout his territories.

These terms have been variously regarded as a product of the poetic imagination of the author of the *Chanson*, as a fabrication of Raymond in an attempt to arouse his vassals to resist an expected attack upon his immediate territories, or as a shrewd plan of the clergy to present conditions which they could be sure he would reject. The real purpose in the action of the legates appears to have been to try to justify a direct attack upon the lands of Raymond, for which Simon now felt himself ready. A fresh sentence of excommunication was directed against the count, already excommunicated, and his lands were laid under interdict. This sentence was later confirmed by the pope.

As a preliminary to the attack, Simon of Montfort turned to the reduction of the two strong points still remaining in the lands of Raymond Roger's son Raymond Trencavel, Cabaret and Lavaur. The former he had attempted to take in 1209, shortly after the capture of Carcassonne, but that attack had failed. Now, with fresh troops from the north under the leadership of bishop Peter of Paris, he was prepared to try again. Peter Roger, lord of Cabaret, shrank from the encounter, yielded without a struggle, and received land elsewhere in compensation. Siege was then laid to Lavaur. The struggle for that stronghold, which lasted from March to May 1211, was bitter. Provisions and troops were sent by one party in Toulouse

[19] *Hyst. Alb.*, 212 (I, 210) and cf. 195.

[20] *Chanson*, 1348–1407, where Arles is indicated as the locale of the conference; but see *Chanson* (ed. Martin-Chabot), I, 144, n. 3.

to support the crusaders. The position of Raymond in this regard is not entirely clear. At first he made no effective move to halt either the provisions or the men. Later, however, he forbade provisioning the crusaders from Toulouse, and he did send some troops to aid in the defense of Lavaur. William of Tudela believed that, had this aid been really substantial, the stronghold would not have fallen.[21]

On behalf of his widowed sister Geralda, countess of Lavaur, the town was defended by Aimery of Montréal, who had twice made his peace with Simon and twice returned to the opposition. His defection, coupled with the ambush and destruction of a column of "pilgrims" at Montgey by count Raymond Roger of Foix, may help to explain Simon's harsh treatment of the defenders when the stronghold was finally rendered. Aimery and some eighty knights were either hanged or put to the sword; a number of heretics, variously estimated at up to 400, were burned. Countess Geralda was cast into a well and covered with stones.[22] This severity represents a change in policy on the part of Simon, who had up to this time made some real attempt to conciliate the southern baronage. Constant defection, however, gradually convinced him of the futility of such a course, and increasingly he turned to harsh treatment of persons and destruction of strongholds which he was unable adequately to garrison.

Reinforced by fresh troops under count Theobald of Bar, Simon of Montfort now essayed a direct attack upon the city of Toulouse. But he quickly recognized that his forces were insufficient adequately to invest the town and to cope with the troops that the counts of Toulouse, Foix, and Comminges were able to bring to its defense. He remained before Toulouse less than two weeks (June 17–29), withdrawing thence to the region of Foix, where he ravaged the territories of count Raymond Roger, and thereafter to Cahors where he accepted the homage of the nobles of Quercy, promised him by bishop William of Cahors while they were before Toulouse.

Already in this campaign of the summer of 1211 may be traced the beginnings of a policy of encirclement of the city of Toulouse, which becomes clearer during the following year. But Simon's position was constantly being undercut by the return north of contingents that had completed their forty-day service; while at the same time Raymond was purposefully gathering reinforcements

[21] *Chanson*, 1527–1529.
[22] *Hyst. Alb.*, 227 (I, 227–228) and n. 2, p. 228.

from the Toulousain, the Agenais, and the territories of Foix, Comminges, and Béarn. He even induced Savary of Mauléon, seneschal of Aquitaine under John of England, to come to his support with a considerable body of mercenaries. The troops thus assembled constituted a respectable force, by the testimony of our sources far superior to any that Simon could put in the field.

Raymond was thus at length in a position to defend his lands and even to assume the offensive. But he was no soldier. Simon elected to stand at Castelnaudary, close to the boundary between the Toulousain and the lands which he had conquered from viscount Raymond Roger. The decisive moment in the engagement came when the count of Foix, who had left the besieging army to attack an escorted convoy of provisions, was defeated and driven from the field while the count of Toulouse remained inactive under the walls of the town. Raymond withdrew, and lost what appears at this distance to have been a good opportunity to defeat and perhaps capture the redoubtable Simon.

This check did not, however, stop the defection of towns and strongholds from Simon; more than fifty are reported to have returned to allegiance to the count of Toulouse during the fall of 1211. Nothing could better illustrate the unstable situation in Languedoc and the inconclusive character of the warfare that was being waged. Despite the astronomical figures mentioned by the sources, the actual troops engaged were few, frequently only a handful. Towns and fortresses would change hands as one or another of the contestants received reinforcements of a few score, or at most a few hundred, real fighting-men. Simon had a small core of faithful associates, drawn largely from among his neighbors in the Île de France, several of whom came with him to the Midi in 1209 and stood by him in fair fortune or foul, frequently until death separated them. These he rewarded with fiefs taken from heretics or rebels.[23] Simon had to depend upon these stalwarts to hold the line as best they might during the long intervals when there were no forty-day "pilgrims" to lend their aid. As time wore on, Simon also had to make increasing use of mercenaries — the employment of whom was one of the bitterest charges brought against Raymond VI and his associates.

[23] Such were his brother Guy, who received Castres and Lombers; the marshal Guy of Lévis, enfeoffed with Mirepoix; Lambert of Thury, who got Limoux; Alan of Roucy, who arrived in 1211 and received Termes, Montréal, and Bram; Bouchard of Marly, given the castle of Saissac and later Cabaret; Robert Mauvoisin, who got Fanjeaux; Guy of Lucy, who became lord of Puylaurens; Hugh de Lacy, enfeoffed with Laurac and Castelnaudary; and perhaps a score of others.

But for offensive purposes a free flow of crusaders seeking the liberal indulgences which could be won by service of only forty days was indispensable. Thus in the winter of 1211–1212 the addition of about one hundred knights led by Robert Mauvoisin turned the balance in favor of Simon;[24] and larger reinforcements in the spring enabled him to reconquer numerous strongholds in the regions of the Tarn and of the Garonne and then to move northwest to the Agenais, whither he had been invited by bishop Arnold of Agen, to receive the submission of that district. In this sweep the most important engagements were the siege and reduction of Penne-d'Agenais on the Lot, northeast of Agen, which capitulated on July 26, 1212, and the capture of Moissac on the Tarn some six weeks later. At Penne a large part of Simon's army, having completed the forty-day service, melted away before the siege ended, and he was constrained to give favorable terms to the garrison, despite the fact that the defenders had been so hard pressed that they had burned a considerable section of the town and had driven out the noncombatants. At Moissac, after a tough fight with much atrocity on both sides, the townsmen, who had employed mercenaries, saved themselves by capitulating and turning their defenders, including some reinforcements from Toulouse, over to Simon, whose forces quickly dispatched them.[25] Other towns in the neighborhood yielded without a fight.

Simon of Montfort now held the territories north and east of Toulouse, except for the fortified town of Montauban, which he avoided. He then proceeded south and southwest, his strategy obviously being to isolate Toulouse and Montauban. He raided south along the Ariège river and then east as far as Tarbes, where he turned north to the Agenais. On this campaign he received the homage of a considerable number of nobles who had supported Raymond. The encirclement of Toulouse was virtually complete.

From conquest Simon now turned to the organization of the lands acquired during the past three years. He called an assembly to meet at Pamiers (November 1212). To this meeting came members of the clergy, the nobility, and some few representatives of the towns, though only the names of the clergy have come down

[24] *Chanson* (ed. Martin-Chabot), I, 245, n. 4.

[25] An accord was drawn up between Simon and abbot Raymond of Moissac on September 14 (*Hist. Lang.*, VIII, 621–626). But Simon seems to have been little more acceptable as a lord than count Raymond. Some time later the abbot wrote to the king (*ibid.*, 635–636) and to the abbot of Cluny (*Recueil des chartes de l'abbaye de Cluny*, ed. A. Bruel, VI, no. 491) complaining bitterly of the treatment accorded the monastery by Simon.

to us.[26] From this group he appointed a commission of twelve to draw up statutes for his conquered territories, composed of four members of the clergy (the bishops of Toulouse and Couserans, a Templar, and a Hospitaller), four from the northern nobility, and four southern laymen, two knights and two burgesses. The document, called the statutes of Pamiers, which resulted from the deliberations of this commission was promulgated on December 1. The essential element in it was the attempt to impose upon the Midi substantially the custom of the region of Paris, with its tighter feudal liens, especially in the matter of military service. What might have been its effect had a longer and more peaceful period of assimilation prevailed can never be known. For the statutes never really took root in the immediate domains of the counts of Toulouse. Simon's conquest of these lands was too fleeting; such elements as were introduced were largely swept away by the return of this part of the ancestral inheritance to Raymond VII by the Peace of Paris in 1229. In the lands directly annexed by the crown, however, they appear to have had a longer life and greater influence.[27]

Simon was given no time for the peaceful organization of his conquered lands. Peter of Aragon, whose effort to this point had been to restrict hostilities, and to effect an accommodation between the conflicting parties, now felt that the activities of Simon had endangered his interests to the point where he must cast his lot more definitely with Raymond of Toulouse and his colleagues. But before committing himself finally to this course he made one last attempt at conciliation at a council held at Lavaur in mid-January of 1213.

Certain events of the months preceding the holding of this council affected the diplomatic moves during and immediately subsequent to its deliberations. After Simon's attack upon Toulouse in June 1211, representatives of that city had written to Peter of Aragon urging his protection from what they considered unjustified persecution by the legates and the crusading forces.[28] Toward the

[26] On this assembly the latest work is Pierre Timbal, *Un Conflit d'annexion au moyen-âge: l'application de la coutume de Paris au pays d'Albigeois* (Toulouse and Paris, 1950), where will be found a convenient edition of the statutes there adopted. Another edition is in *Hist. Lang.*, VIII, 625–635. The best contemporary account is *Hyst. Alb.*, 362–364 (II, 62–64).

[27] Timbal, *Conflit d'annexion*, pp. 26–27.

[28] Letter published in *Hist. Lang.*, VIII, 612–619. It is interesting to note that the Tousans charged Simon with employing against them *routiers*, the harboring of such mercenaries having been cited among the reasons for their own mass excommunication, and with maintaining in his army men who had killed abbot Stephen of Eaunes and mutilated the monks of Boulbonne, just the sort of complaints brought against Raymond VI by his opponents.

end of 1211 Raymond VI had visited king Peter and had solicited his assistance against Simon. In the late spring of 1212 Peter had visited Toulouse, taken the city under his protection, and appointed a vicar to act for him. Shortly thereafter, on July 16, 1212, he had participated in the signal victory of Las Navas de Tolosa over the Spanish Moslems. Peter's position was now much strengthened: he was hailed as a savior of Christendom, and he was free to intervene in the Midi.

Letters of this period indicate the perplexities and uncertainties of papal policy. Innocent III desired to conciliate Philip Augustus, whose assistance he needed in his struggle with Otto of Brunswick and John of England. He also wanted a new crusade against the Aiyūbids, one of his dearest projects. The Albigensian crusade was for him, therefore, a necessary but annoying interruption to larger plans; he must deal with heresy, of course, but at the same time not permit the crusade to proceed to the point of alarming Philip. There was also still in his mind a real question as to the guilt of Raymond and the purity of the motives urging forward Simon and his supporters. In the spring of 1212, he wrote to his legates, Arnold Amalric, now archbishop-elect of Narbonne, and bishop Raymond of Uzès, urgently insisting that they obey his previous orders, to give Raymond of Toulouse an opportunity to clear himself, before confiscating his property or that of his heirs.[29] He thus explicitly denied their previous request for permission to dispose of lands confiscated from Raymond, "since the Apostle enjoins not only avoidance of evil but even the appearance thereof." Innocent concluded with the statement that he had asked bishop Hugh of Riez and master Thedisius to proceed in accordance with his previous instructions. If they found that the delay was Raymond's fault, they should so report, without equivocation, in order that he might act in the matter as the necessities of peace and the faith required.

Sometime in the early winter of 1212–1213, also, king Peter of Aragon sent envoys to represent to the pope how far Simon had overreached himself in attacking Peter's vassals, counts Raymond Roger of Foix and Bernard of Comminges and viscount Gaston of Béarn, and his brother-in-law, the count of Toulouse, none of whom

[29] The letter is undated; Potthast, *Regesta*, I, no. 4517, dates it tentatively between May 25 and June 5; Vaissete, followed by Belperron, thinks it was written in late April (*Hist. Lang.*, VI, 381). Luchaire must surely be wrong in dating it in "late summer" (p. 197). Arnold Amalric left for the campaign against the Spanish Moslems on Tuesday of the octave of Pentecost (May 22). He appears then to have been consecrated; his election took place on March 12 (*Hist. Lang.*, VI, 379, 383).

had ever been convicted of heresy. These emissaries found ready ears for their appeal. In mid-January of 1213, the pope wrote letters to his legates in Languedoc and to Simon of Montfort, the effect of which was to halt the crusade because it had accomplished its objectives; he bade them turn the arms of the crusaders against the "infidel". He scolded Simon for attacking good Christians, and directed him to render to Peter the services which he owed him for the lands of the Trencavel family. He ordered the legates to assemble a council of clerics, nobles, and "other prudent men" to consider proposals which Peter would lay before them, and to report to Innocent their recommendations, that he might thus be enabled to make a proper decision in the matter.

This belated effort to reach an equitable settlement threw the implacable extremists into consternation. In their minds nothing short of the destruction of Raymond and his house would guarantee peace for the clergy in Languedoc and the opportunity for Simon to enjoy the fruits of his hard-fought campaigns.

It was in this climate that the council met at Lavaur in mid-January 1213.[30] Peter II, who had spent several days in Toulouse, requested a hearing before the council and was invited to submit his observations in writing. This he did in a memorandum defending the counts of Comminges and Foix and the viscount of Béarn against the charge of heresy and urging the return of their lands. Count Raymond of Toulouse he pictured as ready to make amends for any injury he might have done the church or the clergy, and as ardently desirous of receiving absolution. If, however, Raymond's lands could not be restored to him personally, Peter asked that he be allowed to go on an extended crusade, either to Spain or to the Holy Land, and that, until convincing proof of his good intentions could be established, his lands be held in trust for his son, who was blameless. The king of Aragon offered to act as trustee.

In a bitter letter the clergy at the council replied to these proposals, refusing to absolve Raymond, on the ground that this matter was no longer within their competence, and maintaining that Comminges, Foix, and Béarn were nests of heresy and their rulers abettors of heretics.[31] They rejected Peter's request for time in which to effect an accord, and warned him that persistence in his present course would invite ecclesiastical censures. Far from being

[30] *Hyst. Alb.*, 368–398 (II, 66–95). The pertinent documents on the council are in *PL*, CCXVI, 833–849.

[31] Charles Higounet (*Le Comté de Comminges de ses origines à son annexion à la couronne* [2 vols., Paris and Toulouse, 1949], I, 90) finds no clear evidence of the truth of this, at least insofar as it refers to Bernard IV of Comminges.

deterred by the firm tone of the prelates Peter appealed his case to the pope and took under his protection the counts of Toulouse, Foix, and Comminges, the viscount of Béarn, and the consuls of Toulouse, all of whom swore fealty to him.

The issue was thus joined. Though probably still unaware of the precise contents of the papal letters favoring the proposals of the king of Aragon, Simon and his supporters were in no doubt as to their general tenor and the necessity of countering the good impression created at Rome by the Aragonese agents. A lengthy memorandum, setting forth their position in the conflict with king Peter, was therefore prepared and placed in the hands of representatives for delivery to the pope. They also took the precaution of securing supporting letters from other members of the clergy of southern France. With greater or less emphasis these all asserted the "necessity" of the destruction of Raymond VI and his house and the conquest and assimilation by Simon of what remained of his lands.

The impact of this delegation, together with the supporting letters, was decisive by the late spring. Letters bearing the papal seals were sent from Rome in late May or early June[32] to king Peter, count Simon, archbishop Arnold Amalric, and bishop Fulk of Toulouse, the tenor of which was quite other than that of the letters dispatched by the pope in mid-January. The crusading party had been completely successful: Luchaire presumes this last series of letters to have been dictated to the papal notaries by the representatives from the Council of Lavaur. Indeed, Innocent harshly upbraided the king of Aragon for having so grossly misinformed him regarding the true state of affairs in Languedoc, bade him withdraw his protection from Toulouse, and declared the rulers of Foix, Comminges, and Béarn under the necessity of securing absolution from the archbishop of Narbonne. He acceded to Peter's request for a special papal emissary to be sent to Languedoc to work for peace. Pending his arrival, the pope enjoined upon Peter the maintenance of a firm truce between himself and Simon (which the king had asked for at Lavaur, but had been refused). Failure to comply with these conditions would lay Peter of Aragon open to ecclesiastical censures.

There is little indication of any real effort toward reconciliation in Languedoc, however. Peter of Les Vaux-de-Cernay reports a suggested conference between Peter of Aragon and Simon of Montfort early in the spring of 1213, but they failed to get together, the upshot being a mutual defiance. Both sides hastened to lay their

[32] The date is variously given. See Potthast, *Regesta*, I, no. 4741; *Hyst. Alb.*, II, 105 note.

cases before Philip Augustus, with no apparent result. The papal letter of January, which the king of Aragon was careful to publish in the north, most certainly reduced the number of new recruits for the army of Simon, and the preaching of Robert of "Courçon" (Curzon), papal legate in France, for a crusade to Palestine served further to turn men's minds from the southland. But Simon was heartened by the news that the son of Philip Augustus, the future Louis VIII, who had for some time contemplated leading an expedition to Languedoc, was now about to take the cross for that purpose. That small hope was dashed, however, when, in view of the threatening situation in the north, his plans were canceled. Simon was therefore compelled to make do as best he might with the slim forces at his command, aided by such few recruits as did arrive. Peter meanwhile returned to Aragon and called upon his nobles to aid him in the defense of Languedoc, justifying his action on the grounds that the count of Toulouse was being unjustly attacked and deprived of his lands, and that family ties required that he go to his assistance.[33]

Both sides looked forward to a decisive engagement. On information that Peter of Aragon had crossed the Pyrenees with a body of troops, Simon of Montfort began pulling in his lines and awaited the movement of Peter and the counts of Toulouse, Foix, and Comminges, who joined forces in Toulouse late in August or early in September, and moved without delay to the investment of Muret, at the junction of the Louge with the Garonne some twelve miles south of Toulouse. Although ill-provisioned and lightly held by crusading troops, Muret constituted a threat to communications between Toulouse and the south, through which Peter had just passed and where his presence had encouraged considerable defection from allegiance to Simon of Montfort.

Simon was at Fanjeaux, some forty miles to the southeast, when he learned of the allied intention to attack Muret. Ordering such aid as could be spared from Carcassonne to follow him, he entered Muret on the afternoon of September 11. The allies had already made a first attack upon the garrison of the town, but had withdrawn, apparently at the suggestion of Peter of Aragon, who decided to allow free entry to the small force under Simon's command, the better to destroy it later.

[33] *Chanson*, 2756–2776. This ends the work of William of Tudela; from this point the poem is continued, in quite different tone and temper, by an anonymous poet who was strongly opposed to the crusade. It will be recalled that one of the king's sisters (Eleanor) was the wife of Raymond VI, and that another sister (Sancia) was married in 1211 to his son, the future Raymond VII.

Much has been written on the battle of Muret.[34] To everyone present except Simon his cause seemed hopeless. He insisted upon his trust in God, and charged that Peter had come to the support of Raymond for frivolous reasons. The clergy advised caution and again strove to deflect Peter of Aragon from the course he had chosen. Though the threat of excommunication did hang over his head, there was no one bold enough to charge him, the warrior of Christendom against Islam at Las Navas de Tolosa, with heresy or even abetting heretics. His championship of the cause of the nobles of Languedoc, therefore, pointed up the hollowness of the oft-reiterated claim that the crusaders were seeking only to root out heresy from the land. The king was not to be turned from his decision by the endeavors of the clergy.

There was dissension among the allies, however, although they knew that provisions were scarce in the town, and that Simon's only hope lay in a quick victory. Raymond's sensible plan for awaiting the inevitable attack in strongly fortified defensive positions was nevertheless scornfully rejected by Peter as unworthy of a soldier. It is probable that the root of this controversy lay deeper than a matter of tactics: the kings of Aragon had long been striving to extend and consolidate their power north of the Pyrenees, and it has been suggested that, though Raymond had welcomed Aragonese aid and had sworn fealty to Peter, he regretted his bargain and distrusted Peter almost as much as he feared Simon.

The battle of Muret was joined on the morning of September 12, 1213, after hope of reaching some accommodation with Peter was abandoned by the prelates who accompanied Simon. Even while the clergy were still attempting to negotiate, some troops from the command of the count of Foix made an exploratory attack upon an open gate of the town. They quickly withdrew and fell out of battle formation. This was the signal for the crusaders to break negotiations and proceed to the attack. With greatly inferior numbers, Simon realized he must catch the allies in the open field and, if possible, off balance, his force being too small to attack

[34] It will suffice to mention a few of the more significant treatments: Henri Delpech, *La Tactique au XIIIe siècle* (2 vols., Paris, 1886), I, 177–265; Auguste Molinier, "La Bataille de Muret d'après les chroniques contemporaines," *Hist. Lang.*, VII, 254–259; Marcel Dieulafoy, "La Bataille de Muret," *Mémoires de l'Institut National de France, Académie des inscriptions et belles lettres*, XXXVI, part 2 (Paris, 1901), 95–134. Ferdinand Lot, in *L'Art militaire et les armées au moyen-âge*, I, 211–216, presents a useful critique, especially on the numbers of troops involved. In English a convenient summary is in Charles Oman, *History of the Art of War in the Middle Ages* (2nd ed., 2 vols., London, 1924), I, 453–467; and see for criticism Hoffman Nickerson, "Oman's Muret," *Speculum*, VI (1931), 550–572. The most important sources are *Hyst. Alb.*, 448–483 (II, 139–176); *Chanson*, 2880–3093; and *Cronica*, xx, xxi.

even a lightly fortified position. In this way Peter's decision to meet him in the field rather than to remain in the protected camp played into his hand.

Surprised, while assembling, by the rapidity of Simon's attack, the troops of the count of Foix received the shock of the first assault, and were hurled back upon the division under the king of Aragon. Here the lack of cohesion on the part of the allies became immediately apparent. Some of the Gascon and Catalan troops under Peter fled the field. Simon's men fought their way to where the king was stationed and, though the Aragonese rallied about him and fought to the last, Peter was struck down; his surviving followers were thrown into confusion by his death. Meanwhile Simon himself led his division on a flanking movement which completed the rout. The engagement lasted only a matter of minutes; there is no record that Raymond and his troops ever got into the fight at all, thus repeating the failure at Castelnaudary two years previously.

The victory was complete. With the mounted troops of the allies in flight from the field, Simon turned to deal with the allies' foot-soldiers who, in the belief that their cavalry were winning the engagement, had proceeded to attack the town. Some were ridden down; others in an attempt to gain their ships, anchored down the Garonne northeast of the town, were drowned in the river. The sources place at 15,000 to 20,000 the numbers of those, mostly foot-soldiers of course, who thus lost their lives. These figures seem very high indeed. There is agreement, however, that losses among the mounted troops were slight for the crusaders, while for the allies, particularly the Aragonese, they were substantial.

However the figures are interpreted, the engagement represented a brilliant victory of a small force (perhaps 800–1,000 mounted men), possessing determination, decision, and discipline, over a larger one (perhaps 2,000–4,000 mounted men), weakened by divided counsels and lacking in leadership and training.[35] The hero of Las Navas de Tolosa presented a sorry spectacle as a commander on the plain of Muret, and the count of Foix, good soldier that he had proved himself in other engagements, failed here to distinguish himself, while, as we have seen, Raymond VI figured not at all in the battle.

The defeat of Muret eliminated Aragon as a threat to the crusaders, and constituted a severe check to the pretensions of

[35] In *L'Art militaire* (I, 214–216) Lot discusses the number of effectives on both sides and indicates the caution necessary in judging the figures.

Aragonese kings north of the Pyrenees; towns and nobles that had faltered in their submission to Montfort were in appreciable numbers again constrained to make terms with him; recruiting in the north for the crusade, which had languished for a time after pope Innocent's letters of the preceding January had, in effect, declared it ended, was again pushed with vigor by Robert of Courçon and other preachers;[36] the leaders of the opposition were for the moment stunned and planless. The counts of Toulouse, Foix, and Comminges met at Toulouse shortly after the defeat at Muret to discuss future action, but nothing seems to have come of this meeting. Raymond VI and his young son withdrew for a few months to the protection of king John of England.

Simon of Montfort, on the other hand, continued the war with renewed vigor, strengthened somewhat by the arrival of a few new crusaders from the north. Completely disillusioned by the recent defections, he now pursued a systematic policy of destroying strongholds which he was unable to garrison. With rapid thrusts he raided through the counties of Foix and Comminges. Thence he turned eastward to the Rhone, where he made alliances designed to bring the marquisate of Provence effectively under his control. From Provence he returned early in 1214 to Narbonne where the viscount, Aimery, influenced by a group of Aragonese who were seeking from Simon the return of their boy king James I, challenged his authority. The quarrel was quieted for the moment by a new papal legate, Peter of Benevento. After this episode Simon proceeded, with considerable reinforcements, on a wide swing through the Agenais, as far as Marmande on the Garonne, a portion of which he destroyed while leaving unmolested the castle, which was held by troops of John of England; to Casseneuil on the Lot, which he reduced after a considerable siege; through Quercy and into southern Périgord, where, on the ground that they harbored heretics, he captured four strongholds on the Dordogne; and thence through Rouergue to Rodez, its capital city, where after considerable dispute he was recognized as overlord by count Henry (November 7, 1214). With the subsequent acquisition of the stronghold of Sévérac, some twenty-five miles to the east of Rodez, Simon could feel himself in effective control of substantially all the lands of Raymond of Toulouse. There remained, however, the problem of securing satisfactory recognition of his conquests.

For such recognition favorable action by pope Innocent III was

[36] *Hyst. Alb.*, 494 (II, 185–186).

essential. This step the pope still hesitated to take. The defeat of the allies at Muret and their appeal for absolution and reconciliation had led him in January 1214 to appoint Peter of Benevento as legate in Languedoc with instructions to follow a conciliatory line. Peter of Les Vaux-de-Cernay exclaims in glee on the astute policy pursued by Peter in dangling before the southerners the hope of reconciliation while Simon employed the time in establishing firmly his hold upon the lands of the count of Toulouse,[37] but there is nothing in the record to indicate that Peter did more than carry out faithfully the pope's instructions. In April he received back into the church the counts of Comminges, Foix, and Toulouse, together with the citizens of Toulouse.[38] Also, in obedience to a letter from the pope, Simon of Montfort met the legate near Narbonne, and finally delivered to him James, the young son of Peter II of Aragon, for return to his homeland.

Peter of Benevento accompanied the young king James I to Aragon and remained south of the Pyrenees for some months. Meanwhile Simon of Montfort had been strengthened by considerable reinforcements from the north, led by Robert of Courçon as papal legate to France, and William, the archdeacon of Paris. Other duties required Robert to leave the crusaders at Le Puy, but there are occasional references to his presence in the south, and in July 1214 at St. Livrade he confirmed Simon of Montfort and his heirs in possession of the lands conquered from the heretics or their supporters in the Albigeois, Agenais, Quercy, and Rouergue, and any others which he might have acquired "within the bounds of our authority".[39] In view of the hesitation of the pope and the reconciliation of count Raymond and other leaders of the resistance some three months previously, such confirmation appears hasty; and it is equally difficult to harmonize it with decisions taken a few months later. There is, however, no record that the legate was disciplined for his action.

At Montpellier, in January of the following year (1215), five archbishops, twenty-eight bishops, and a large number of other clergy and lay magnates met in council under the presidency of Peter of Benevento, by then returned from Aragon, to consider the important question of the disposal of the lands of the count of

[37] *Hyst. Alb.*, 509 (II, 205–206): *O legati fraus pia, O pietas fraudulentia!*

[38] Potthast, *Regesta*, No. 4890; Teulet, *Layettes*, I, nos. 1068, 1069, 1072 (dated April 18 and 25, 1214); *Hyst. Alb.*, 503, 507 (II, 196–198, 201 and n. 5).

[39] *Hist. Lang.*, VIII, 653–655. Robert was papal legate presumably to the whole of France. Therefore, despite the fact that Peter of Benevento was papal legate in the regions concerned, it may be argued that Robert's authority extended over southern France, especially during the absence of Peter in Aragon.

Toulouse. Their recommendation was unanimous; the lands should be given to Simon of Montfort, who should also succeed to all Raymond's honors and titles. In Toulouse and all the lands held by the count, as well as in the other lands occupied by the crusaders, Simon was to be chosen "prince and sole ruler".[40] They requested the legate immediately to invest him with these lands. This Peter was unable to do, however, under the terms of his mission, and the matter had to be referred to the pope. The decision of Innocent III was announced in letters to the legate, the prelates, the nobles, and Simon, all under date of April 2, and all to the same purport:[41] final disposition of the lands which Simon had conquered must await the decision of a general council which the pope had called; pending that decision, Simon was to have custody of these lands, together with the revenues and rights of jurisdiction, and responsibility for defending them, as the legate should determine.

Simon accepted the pope's pronouncement with what grace he could, perhaps constrained to do so by the news, received shortly after the Council of Montpellier, that the long-projected expedition of Louis, heir to Philip Augustus, was actually under way (April 1215). Both Simon and the papal legate probably received the news with some foreboding; the former could not be certain how king Philip might view his conquests, and the latter felt none too sure that his recent decisions, especially regarding Narbonne and Toulouse, would meet with Louis's approval.[42] Both hastened to meet Louis, Simon at Vienne, Peter at Valence, and both were at once reassured by the friendly attitude of the prince royal, who made it clear that he had no wish to upset any of the dispositions already made.

The progress of Louis and his followers across Languedoc, from the Rhone to Toulouse, was in the nature of a triumphal procession. Certain questions involving the disposition of strongholds, which for the time had been kept in the hand of the legate, were settled. Thus it was determined that the walls of Narbonne and Toulouse should be destroyed, greatly to the disgust of their

[40] *Hyst. Alb.*, 545–546 (II, 238–240): the phrase here employed is ". . . ut nobilem comitem Montis Fortis eligerent in tocius terre illius principem et monarcham." This has given rise to considerable speculation whether Simon was actually reaching for a kingdom in Languedoc. Pascal Guébin argues persuasively that *monarcha* then had the meaning of *chef unique* (*Revue historique du droit français et étranger*, ser. 4, X [1931], 417–418; cf. Belperron, *Croisade*, 294, n. 1).

[41] Teulet, *Layettes*, I, nos. 1113–1116.

[42] *Hyst. Alb.*, 552 (II, 244–246): the author discusses at some length the reasons why the legate might feel concern at the approach of Louis, but passes over in silence any similar qualms which Simon of Montfort may have experienced.

citizens, who were, however, for the moment powerless to offer opposition. The castle of Foix was given to Simon, who also obtained, in accordance with instructions in the papal letters of April 2, effective control of all the lands of count Raymond. These dispositions having been effected and Louis and his army having completed the requisite forty-day service, the crusaders turned north again (early June). Within a short time thereafter the legate Peter proceeded to Rome. To consolidate his administration Simon made a tour through the Toulousain, the Agenais, and into southern Périgord.

At the Fourth Lateran Council, which met in November 1215, there was debate as to the final disposition of lands conquered and administered by Simon of Montfort. Of this, two of our chief sources treat only briefly, but the *Chanson* has a lengthy account in which the arguments for and against the claims of Simon are fully stated. How much of this is based on a true report of discussions held during the council, and how much is the product of poetic imagination, it is impossible to say, but the tart admission of Peter of Les Vaux-de-Cernay that there were those, even among the clergy, who opposed attribution of the lands to Simon, and the final decision of the council indicate that there was substantial difference of opinion, and that the pope himself was not entirely happy in the judgment he was called upon to pronounce.[43]

If we are to believe the anonymous author of the *Chanson*, the leading protagonists were bishop Fulk of Toulouse, who spoke hotly for Simon, and count Raymond Roger of Foix, who spoke chiefly for himself; Innocent III is made to assume a mediating position, questioning how Raymond of Toulouse, who had sought and received absolution, and especially his son, who had been guilty of nothing, could justly be deprived of their lands.[44] Simon was not present at the council, but was represented by his brother Guy, and was staunchly supported by the overwhelming majority of the French clergy there present. Raymond VI and his son were both present, but silent, so far as the record indicates. The son's claim was pressed apparently by representatives of his uncle, king John of England; the father's, by several nobles of Languedoc and by a few members of the clergy, chief of whom were archdeacon Hugh

[43] *Hyst. Alb.*, 570–572 (II, 259–263); *Cronica*, xxiv; *Chanson*, 3161–3593.

[44] Already on February 4, in response to the plea of Raymond, who was then in Rome, Innocent had instructed Peter of Benevento to see that proper provision was made for the current needs of the count, "cum autem ignominiosum non solum ei sed nobis etiam videretur, si tanta gravaretur inopia" (Teulet, *Layettes*, I, no. 1099). Raymond, it will be recalled, had been reconciled by Peter in April 1214.

of Lyons and Arnold Amalric, archbishop of Narbonne. Arnold Amalric, from the beginning of the crusade through the Council of Lavaur, had been Raymond's most outspoken enemy among the clergy; but his early insistence that the only possible solution of the problem of heresy in Languedoc lay in the dispossession of the house of St. Gilles and the investment of Simon with its lands seems to have been greatly modified by his recent contest with the latter for prestige and power in Narbonne.

However persuasive may have been the legal argument in favor of the count of Toulouse, and whatever may have been the private preference of the pope, the needs of the church, the diplomatic situation at the moment, and the logic of the crusade demanded that substantial consideration be given to the claims of Simon of Montfort. The final decision of the council on November 30, confirmed by a papal bull of December 14, was therefore to that effect: Raymond VI was declared guilty of harboring heretics and *routiers*, and was deprived of his lands, but so long as he showed himself worthy, he was to receive an annual provision of 400 marks, and his wife was to be protected in her dower rights; all lands conquered from heretics or their supporters were to be assigned to Simon; the remaining lands of Raymond, which had not been conquered by the crusaders, and which consisted chiefly of the marquisate of Provence, were to be held by the church in trust for young Raymond until he should come of age and should show himself worthy to receive them. Lands of Raymond Roger, the count of Foix, were reserved for later consideration.[45] By a letter of December 21, Innocent III appointed bishop Arnold of Nîmes and the archdeacon of Conflans to consider and report upon the claims made by Raymond Roger; pending final decision they were to place the castle of Foix under the jurisdiction of abbot Berengar of St. Thibéry, and Simon of Montfort was to be enjoined from any hostile action against the count. Soon after this, Raymond Roger regained his lands. The disposition made of the county of Comminges is not known, but the presumption is that it was awarded to Simon.[46]

The history of the ten years subsequent to the Fourth Lateran Council is that of the reconquest of their lands by the two Raymonds. The success of Simon of Montfort carried with it certain

[45] Teulet, *Layettes*, I, no. 1152. Under the same date the pope wrote to archbishop Arnold Amalric of Narbonne, directing him to see that countess Eleanor receive 150 marks annual revenue from Beaucaire (*PL*, CCXVI, 992).

[46] Higounet, *Le Comté de Comminges*, I, 99–101.

liabilities. Never a man of easy temper and warm personality, he had experienced difficulty in winning and retaining the support of any large number of those over whom he had extended his rule. As time wore on, the strain under which he lived made him less ready to seek or to accept compromise or accommodation. This heightened the impression, whether justified or no, that he sought power for its own sake and, under the cloak of stamping out heresy, was intent principally upon carving out lands for himself. As noted above, it is not difficult to find in the correspondence of Innocent III indications of hesitancy in supporting this champion of the church, and of fear lest the crusade would proceed — or indeed had proceeded — beyond the objectives which the pope had in mind.

In accordance with the decision of the Lateran Council, Simon took determined steps to strengthen his position in Languedoc, and to secure recognition of his conquests by Philip Augustus. He sought especially to make good his claim to the title duke of Narbonne. He first appealed to the pope against the renewed claims to that title put forth by archbishop Arnold Amalric, and then in February 1216 he marched upon Narbonne, prepared to employ force if necessary. Met at the gates of the city by the archbishop whom he contemptuously thrust aside, despite the excommunication which Arnold pronounced against him, he even went so far as to command the celebration of mass in the ducal chapel, in his disdain for an interdict which the archbishop laid upon the city. Efforts of the clergy to allay the unseemly quarrel were without success. But Simon ultimately established his position; he was granted the title by Philip Augustus some two months later and continued to hold it until his death, as did his son after him.

From Narbonne Simon proceeded to Toulouse, where he received the oath of allegiance of the citizens, ordered them to level their walls, and strengthened the fortifications of the comital residence, the Château Narbonnais. Thence he journeyed to Paris where Philip Augustus invested him with the lands and titles formerly held of him by count Raymond. At no time since the beginning of the crusade had his position appeared so secure as in the spring of 1216. But this was more seeming than real. Crusading recruits were now being deflected elsewhere. Immediately after the close of the Lateran Council, Innocent III had renewed the call for a strong crusading effort to Palestine. Simon was forced more and more to dependence upon mercenary troops.

While Simon was working to establish a firm grip upon his

newly acquired lands, the Raymonds were likewise busy. After conferring with the pope, immediately upon the close of the council, Raymond VI withdrew from Rome to Genoa and was there later joined by his son. Together they journeyed to Marseilles, where they were well received, and thence on invitation to Avignon, where they were acclaimed by nobles and townsmen. From the support there offered them, the immediate assumption of authority in the marquisate of Provence seemed assured of success and the possibility of the reconquest of their lands just west of the Rhone was a hope.

Raymond VI thereupon left for Aragon to seek aid in that quarter, leaving the young Raymond to consolidate his successes in the Venaissin. At this juncture the latter received intimation that the citizens of Beaucaire, the place of his birth nineteen years previously, would open its gates to him. This strongly fortified town on the west bank of the Rhone had been enfeoffed to Simon in 1215 by archbishop Michael of Arles, and he had placed Lambert of Thury over it as seneschal. But there was serious question whether Beaucaire did not properly belong with the Provençal lands which were being held in trust for the young Raymond; so he crossed the Rhone with troops drawn from the nobility and townsmen of the east bank.

The garrison of Beaucaire was quickly driven to the fortress to the north of the town, where it was closely invested by land and water. Repeated sorties failed to break Raymond's lines; the besieged were deprived of access to fresh supplies of food and water. Simon's brother Guy and his son Amalric, who were in the Toulousain, set out with the troops at their command to succor the garrison, and an urgent appeal was sent to Simon to hasten his return from northern France. All efforts, even those of Simon himself when he finally arrived, failed to raise the siege. By the end of August 1216, after an investment lasting some three months, the garrison was reduced by the lack of food and water to such straits that Simon was constrained to yield the stronghold with the understanding that the garrison be allowed to retire unmolested. His decision in this matter was undoubtedly influenced by disquieting reports from Toulouse to the effect that Raymond VI had crossed the Pyrenees from Aragon and had entered that city.

The success of the southern forces at Beaucaire set off a chain reaction. The towns, which from the start of the crusade, and frequently irrespective of their orthodoxy, had shown considerable distrust of Simon of Montfort and his followers, became increasingly opposed to the northern occupation as time wore on and the evidences of lust for power and conquest on the part of the northerners multiplied.[47] The nobility also now began to rally around the house of St. Gilles in the apparent hope that the younger Raymond might prove a leader of sufficient strength to cope with the invaders.

All this called for prompt and decisive action on the part of Simon. By rapid marches he moved on Toulouse, where he found the situation quite out of hand. Raymond VI had withdrawn upon news of his approach, but the inhabitants of the town had forced the crusader garrison to take refuge in the Château Narbonnais. Nor were they cowed by the approach of Simon. They threw barricades across the streets, repaired their dismantled fortifications as best they might, and with determination fought both the attack of Simon's troops and the fires which he had set in several quarters of the town. Resistance was, however, ultimately broken, and through the efforts of the clergy a capitulation was agreed upon. Simon harshly demanded the payment of 30,000 marks' indemnity; the retention of hostages whom he had seized — by some estimated at 400; the further destruction of any edifices that might serve as defensive positions in case of subsequent riots or rebellion; and added strengthening of the Château Narbonnais. The heaviness of the money payment indicates the financial straits to which Simon had been reduced in his attempt to maintain in the field even the semblance of an adequate fighting force. Any thought of conciliation was now at an end. Rebels must submit or accept the consequences.

However, instead of inducing submission this policy merely served to stiffen resistance. As was shown at Beaucaire and at Toulouse, it was in the towns that the increasingly determined resistance of the southern provinces was focussed. The writer of the *Chanson* reports, also, divided counsels among Simon's staunchest lieutenants. The poet tells a long story of debates among the crusading leaders at Beaucaire, and at Toulouse he makes Simon's brother Guy and Alan of Roucy, two of his most devoted followers, heap bitter reproaches upon him for his ruthless methods and severe terms of surrender.[48] Even William of Puylaurens, who felt no undue sympathy for the southern cause, believed that the moral ascendency had now passed from the crusaders, that they had become the slaves of their avarice and their appetites, no longer devoted to the service of Christ and the destruction of the

[47] Cf. *Cronica,* xxvi.

[48] *Chanson,* 4145–4195, 4789–4816, 4930–4937, 5366–5468.

heretics but puffed up in their own pride; "for this reason the Lord will give them to drink to the very dregs of the cup his of wrath."[49]

The fall, winter, and spring of 1216–1217 were employed by both sides in strengthening their positions. The younger Raymond received additional support from town and countryside in the marquisate of Provence and along the right bank of the Rhone. At the same time Simon was actively buttressing his strength, particularly in the southwest and in Provence. The latter territory he was attempting to wrest again from Raymond (VII) when report of a new rising in Toulouse recalled him to the west.

Raymond VI had divided his time since the Lateran Council between Provence and Aragon where, in the late summer of 1217, he was in the process of recruiting troops. Advised of the readiness of the people of Toulouse to place themselves under his command, he hastened to cross the Pyrenees with such Aragonese mercenaries as he had been able to recruit. Arrived in Languedoc, he was joined by Roger Bernard, son of Raymond Roger of Foix, Bernard IV of Comminges, and a very considerable group of lesser nobles from Foix, Comminges, Bigorre, and the southern Toulousain.

On September 13 these allies were able to enter Toulouse under cover of a fog. A majority of the townspeople greeted them with acclaim; others were opposed or attempted to remain neutral, either from prudence or from conviction. These latter were forced to go along with the majority, or fled to the Château Narbonnais (to which the garrison was also driven after an unsuccessful attempt to dispute Raymond's entrance into the town), or were put to the sword. Since all fortifications of the town, except the Château Narbonnais, had been dismantled or destroyed, Raymond's followers hastily dug trenches and erected timbered earthworks. All labored with feverish haste. At the same time for the crusaders countess Alice of Montfort sent an urgent call for help to her brother-in-law Guy and her son of the same name, who were some fifty miles distant in the region of Carcassonne, and dispatched a messenger to her husband on the other side of the Rhone. The forces of the two Guys were insufficient to make headway against the defenders of the town; after two vain attempts to take it by storm, they joined the garrison in the Château Narbonnais and awaited further reinforcements.

Reinforcements appear, however, to have rallied to the southern

[49] *Cronica*, xxv.

cause in more substantial numbers than to the northern. From Quercy, Gascony, the Albigeois, and the region of Carcassonne recruits flocked to the standard of Raymond VI. Many of them were charged with heresy or its support, but there were many others who were orthodox in faith but were determined to break Simon's grip upon the southland, Toulouse now becoming the center of the whole resistance. So widespread was the movement that some historians have seen in it the expression of a new patriotism and solidarity in Languedoc, but it may merely reflect a canny presumption that more might be had from the ineffectual house of St. Gilles than from that of Montfort.

Simon of Montfort, with the forces at his command, made what speed he could in covering the considerable distance from the Rhone to Toulouse. En route he was to suffer the sobering experience of seeing many of the southern recruits in his army desert and return to their homes. When Simon reached Baziège, about twelve miles from Toulouse, he was met by his brother Guy, and together they attacked Toulouse at once, in the hope that the town might be taken before its newly constructed defense system could be consolidated. Their attack failed; it seemed clear that the town would have to be reduced by a siege, and an effective siege required more troops.[50] In an attempt to cut the town's communications with the west and southwest, from which supplies and reinforcements came, Simon attacked St. Cyprien, a suburb of Toulouse on the left bank of the Garonne, joined to the town by two bridges. In this too he was unsuccessful; his need of reinforcements was urgent. To secure these countess Alice, accompanied by the cardinal-legate Bertrand and bishop Fulk of Toulouse, set out for the north to solicit aid from Philip Augustus and again to preach the crusade. Urgent appeals for assistance were also sent to pope Honorius III.

By a series of letters dispatched late in December and early in January (1218) Honorius ordered Toulouse and the towns in the region of the Rhone to desist from rebellion; directed James of Aragon and his counselors to withdraw aid from the rebels; warned young Raymond (VII) of the dire consequences of his present course; and promised Raymond Roger of Foix the prompt return of the castle of Foix if he would withdraw his aid from Toulouse. He requested the clergy of Languedoc to supply all possible help

[50] The story of the siege of Toulouse is told in: *Hyst. Alb.*, 600–612 (II, 293–316); *Chanson*, 5886–8491; *Cronica*, xxviii. The best modern account is by J. de Malafosse, "La Siège de Toulouse," *Revue des Pyrénées*, IV (1892), 497–522, 725–756.

to Simon, and urged Philip Augustus and the clergy of northern France to aid in recruiting forces for the crusade.[51]

There is little indication that the papal letters had much effect. Some southern nobles did join Simon's forces before Toulouse during the winter, either from conviction or from the prudent desire to be on the winning side, for the prestige of his previous successes in the face of great odds was too powerful easily to suffer eclipse. And in the spring there arrived before Toulouse bands of crusaders from the north, the most considerable company being under the command of Ralph of Nesle, count of Soissons. Recruits flowed likewise to the besieged town. Dalmatz of Creixell brought a company of Aragonese mercenaries and Raymond Roger of Foix entered the town with a contingent, but the greatest enthusiasm was created by the appearance in Toulouse of Raymond the younger.

The winter had been spent in thrust and counter-thrust, with neither side gaining any marked advantage. The besieged did, however, seal off the Château Narbonnais from the town by an embankment, strengthened the fortifications hastily thrown up in the autumn, and made good their lack of arms and armor. Contemporary accounts convey the impression that the northern forces had lost the clear supremacy which had been theirs during the first eight years of the conflict, and that the advantage in morale had passed definitely from them to the forces under Raymond. This appears most clearly in the pages of the *Chanson*. But it cannot be ascribed merely to the robust bias of the poet; it is to be found also in the account of William of Puylaurens, who in one place makes the legate chide for his lethargy none less than the redoubtable Simon himself.[52]

After the passing of the Lenten season, the tempo of operations accelerated. Simon's forces succeeded for a time in a second attempt to cut the communications of the town to the west by the occupation of St. Cyprien, but their effort had to be abandoned. A direct attack upon the town gained a momentary foothold within the fortifications, only to be soon lost. Sorties by the besieged kept Simon's troops eternally on the alert. Fighting was rude; losses were severe, the two Guys, brother and son of Simon, being among the wounded. Few prisoners were taken, and there are accounts of

[51] P. Pressutti, *Regesta Honorii papae III*, I, nos. 940, 941, 943, 944, 945, 946, 949, 950. Already, on October 23, the pope had written to his legate ordering him to take measures to halt assistance to the rebels in Provence from Aragon and Catalonia (Pressutti, no. 842). These letters are published in Bouquet, *RHGF*, XIX, 626–647, and in C. A. Horoy, *Honorii III . . . opera* (Paris, 1879–1882), II, 559–576. Cf. also Pressutti, I, nos. 1005, 1006.

[52] *Chanson*, 5886–8491, *passim*, esp. 6482–6504, 6912–6947; *Cronica*, xxviii: "quod ignarus et remissus esset".

the brutal murder of some who did yield themselves.[53] Finally, Simon of Montfort and his counselors determined to construct an enormous cat, under the protection of which ditches might be filled in, and the walls approached and surmounted. This was built and put in operation. The town's defenders centered their efforts upon its destruction. Fighting became hot, and Simon himself hastened to take command. A stone hurled from a mangonel — serviced, it was said, by women — struck him squarely on the head. Thus ended the career of the leader of the crusade, a man whom Raymond VII, albeit his enemy, later praised in the highest terms for his "fidelity, foresight, energy, and all those qualities which befit a prince."[54] He was able to inspire loyalty among a small group of followers whom he rewarded liberally, and who in return served him with singleness of purpose and devotion.

Simon of Montfort was killed on June 25, 1218. The joy of his enemies was unbounded, the grief of his followers unrestrained. There was no one to take up the sword which fell from his hand; leadership devolved upon his eldest son, Amalric, then a young man twenty-six years of age. He had been a faithful lieutenant under his father, and was already a seasoned campaigner, but had never developed the stature necessary to continue his father's work. Almost immediately the edifice which Simon had erected in southern France began rapidly to fall apart. One wonders whether even Simon himself, with inadequate funds, tired followers, and disaffected local nobles, could have maintained it. Forty-day crusaders were of much utility in capturing towns and strongholds, but valueless for policing them when once taken, and Simon had been singularly unsuccessful in winning the lasting support of the southern nobles and knights, whose factious individualism and endemic localism prevented the imposition of strong feudal bonds subordinating them permanently to the ambitious and uncongenial interlopers from northern France.

After one further unsuccessful attack, Amalric raised the siege of Toulouse and retired to Carcassonne. Defection could not be stopped, although Amalric did what he could. Honorius III tried to assist by recognizing his claim to the lands conquered by his father, by soliciting aid for him from the French clergy, and by urging Philip Augustus to prepare, and his son Louis to undertake, a second expedition to Languedoc. For this the pope promised one half of a twentieth then being raised by the clergy of France for

[53] *Chanson*, 6868; *Hyst. Alb.*, 606c (II, 307–309).
[54] *Cronica*, xxviii.

the Holy Land and commanded that the entire yield of the twentieth in Languedoc be delivered to Bertrand, the legate, to be disbursed by him and Amalric for the operations against the Raymonds. But Amalric's financial difficulties seem not to have been greatly ameliorated, and the expedition under Louis was delayed. When he finally did lead it to the south, by the western route, he aided in the capture of Marmande, which had declared again for Raymond, and then moved up the Garonne to Toulouse, which he besieged. But the force at his command was unequal to the task; he soon raised the siege and returned north, having done little harm to the southerners. The Agenais, Quercy, Rouergue, the Albigeois north of the Tarn, Comminges, the Gascon lands which Simon had been able to annex, and the western Toulousain were in large part lost by Amalric, as were the marquisate of Provence and the lands immediately to the west of the Rhone. Such strength as remained to him was centered in lower Languedoc, substantially the lands of the Trencavel family which had been conquered during the first two years of the crusade. And even here there were losses; Castelnaudary, only a few short miles from Carcassonne, fell to young Raymond in 1220 and Montréal in 1221.

It would serve no useful purpose to follow through the petty engagements of the years immediately succeeding the death of Simon. By 1222 Amalric was at the end of his resources. He attempted to turn his lands over to Philip Augustus, but the offer was refused. The death of Raymond VI of Toulouse in August 1222 brought no improvement in Amalric's situation, nor was he aided by the death of Raymond Roger of Foix in the following year. The latter had been a more formidable adversary than had the old count of Toulouse, and he was followed in the county of Foix by a capable and well-tried son, Roger Bernard. Raymond VII, at the age of twenty-five, inspired greater enthusiasm and confidence than had ever been accorded his father. The years 1222 to 1225 constitute a confused period of negotiation among the two principals, the pope, and the king of France, ending with the Council of Bourges, which met on November 30, 1225.

This council was called by Romanus, cardinal-deacon of St. Angelo, the new legate dispatched to "France and Provence,"[55]

[55] For the letters of February 13 and 15 to the clergy, king, nobles, commoners, and Romanus, see Potthast, *Regesta*, I, nos. 7358, 7360, 7361; Pressutti, II, nos. 5305, 5306, 5313, 5314; Horoy, IV, 780, 781–786. The writer finds no evidence that Romanus, mentioned as designated to France in a letter of the pope to Raymond VII, dated January 31, 1224, had actually been functioning in France prior to 1225, but see Zimmermann, *Die päpstliche Legation in der ersten Hälfte des 13. Jahrhunderts* (Paderborn, 1913), p. 81, n. 2.

and was largely attended by prelates or their representatives from all parts of France. First consideration was given to the problem of heresy and the lands of the counts of Toulouse. Raymond urged, as he had at an earlier date, that he be reconciled with the church and enfeoffed with the lands of his father. He repeated his pledge to pursue heretics and to obey in all things the dictates of the church. To this Amalric opposed his claim to the lands which had been adjudged to his father by the church and for which his father had done homage to the king. The judgment of the council was against Raymond. From the negotiations of the preceding months it is clear that, so far as he was concerned, it had been called to give dramatic announcement to a decision already determined in advance. That Raymond had sensed as much may be inferred from his previous negotiation of a secret treaty with Henry III of England[56] and of another with Hugh of Lusignan, count of La Marche, whereby his daughter Joan was betrothed to Hugh's son.[57]

There was no delay in enforcing the decisions against Raymond. At the end of January 1226, Louis VIII proclaimed that he would lead a crusade against the heretics in the southland. The terms of the agreement, negotiated by cardinal Romanus and approved by the pope, were not greatly different from terms which had been rejected by the pope two years previously. A sore point indeed was the stipulation that the clergy of France should contribute a tenth of their revenues for a period of five years in support of the crusade. To clear the ground for the seizure of the lands formerly held by the house of St. Gilles, Raymond was excommunicated by the legate; he was declared a heretic and his lands forfeit. Members of the clergy were sent throughout France to preach the crusade. To stir up enthusiasm, a memorial addressed to the king, and calling upon him to lead such an expedition, was secured from representatives of the nobility.[58]

It was planned that recruits should assemble at Bourges and should proceed thence to Lyons, where the army was to arrive about the first of June. There are no satisfactory estimates of the number of troops which assembled in response to the call. But that it was a respectable force is indicated by the pressures, in the form of heavy financial aids, employed to induce vassals to bring up their

[56] Letter of Henry III in T. Rymer, *Foedera* (Record Commission, London, 1816), I, part 1, p. 179. See also a fragment of an undated letter from Henry, and one issued by his officials on the same subject, published by Charles Petit-Dutaillis, *Étude sur la vie et le règne de Louis VIII* (Paris, 1894), pp. 518–520.

[57] *Chronicon Turonense* (*RHGF*, XVIII), 307. A year later, at the instance of the king and the legate, Hugh returned Joan to her father (*ibid.*, p. 314).

[58] Teulet, *Layettes*, II, no. 1742.

levies; by the wide regional spread shown in the names of participants mentioned by the chroniclers; and probably most significantly by the haste with which towns and individual members of the southern nobility, by letter or by representative or in person, sought to make their peace with the church and their submission to the king. This may probably be explained in large part by the war-weariness of all parties in the south, who had suffered under seventeen years of intermittent warfare, but there is also evident a healthy respect for the power represented by the king's forces.

The crusading army left Lyons early in June and proceeded down the east bank of the Rhone to Avignon, whose representatives had asked the legate for a reconciliation with the church, and had offered the king safe passage across the Rhone. The march to Avignon was without incident, but upon arrival at the town a misunderstanding arose, which resulted in the investment of the city by the king's forces.[59] Avignon was heavily fortified, however, and its citizenry staunch. Siege engines had little effect upon its walls; the stout response of the Avignonese took its toll of the crusading forces; troops of the count of Toulouse, who hovered in the region, made provisioning of the army difficult; and disease of epidemic proportions carried off a considerable number from the invading army. There was lack of unanimity, also, among the king's followers. The clergy were restless under the heavy payments they were called upon to make for the crusade, and some members of the nobility were openly sympathetic toward Raymond VII and his cause.[60] On the other hand provisions in the town failed, and the hope of a successful outcome of the defense gradually faded.

Under the circumstances both sides were ready to negotiate. A capitulation was agreed upon, and the crusaders entered the town on September 9, after a siege lasting three months. By the terms of the surrender the Avignonese were reconciled with the church, and the town was relieved of the interdict which had been laid upon it. In return the townsmen were required to deliver to king and legate a number of hostages, variously estimated from 150 to 300, to destroy the fortifications of the town, to yield without recompense

[59] Charges of bad faith were made on both sides. For the northern point of view, see especially an open letter of the legate Romanus, and another letter of barons and prelates to emperor Frederick II justifying their attack upon a city within the bounds of the empire: Teulet, *Layettes*, II, nos. 1787, 1789; and also *Chronicon Turonense*, pp. 314–315. The southern position is reflected in Roger of Wendover, *Flores historiarum* (ed. H. G. Hewlett, 3 vols., London, 1886–1889; tr. J. A. Giles, London, 1849), II, 309–310. William of Puylaurens reserves judgment, attributing the misunderstanding to divine will (xxxiii).

[60] This picture may be overdrawn, but it is based on *Chronicon Turonense*, p. 316, which is favorable to the crusade and is considered dependable.

Beaucaire and other strong places which had been turned over to them by count Raymond as pledges for debt, and to pay a considerable ransom. A band of mercenaries, who had given excellent service in the defense of the town, were put to the sword, but the oft-repeated statement that entrance into the city was accompanied by a general massacre of the inhabitants rests on no contemporary evidence.

Losses to the crusading army by disease and battle deaths are estimated at about 3,000, which seems a fair price for the capture of Avignon. It is true, however, that the whole of the marquisate of Provence, almost all Languedoc east of Toulouse, the Gévaudan, Rouergue, and much of Quercy now declared for Louis without a further blow being struck. During the siege, count Raymond Berengar of Provence allied with Louis against Raymond of Toulouse. This is not surprising, for the two counts were rivals in Provence and Raymond VII had encouraged the towns in the county of Provence in their sporadic resistance to the authority of their count. But more significant is the fact that two of Raymond's staunchest and most powerful supporters sought peace with the king during this period — Roger Bernard of Foix, who was refused reconciliation with the church,[61] and Bernard V of Comminges, who had succeeded his father in the spring of 1225, and who made his peace at Avignon in September.[62] Thus it may be argued that much bloodshed and destruction were spared by a determined policy at the start.

After its conquest Louis VIII provided for the administration of Avignon and for that of the marquisate of Provence, despite the fact that the emperor was overlord of these territories. He thereafter traversed Languedoc to Pamiers where he made provision for the government of the lands west of the Rhone thus far secured, building upon the plan of Simon of Montfort to establish administrative units under seneschals. Simon's very liberal provision for the church caused him no little embarrassment, but by exchanges of property and money grants he effected amicable adjustments.

The king thereupon left his new conquests to a lieutenant, Humbert of Beaujeu, and proceeded north by easy stages. Toulouse he bypassed, probably because of the approaching winter and the presumption that its capture would require a difficult siege. His

[61] *Cronica*, xxxiii.

[62] Higounet, *Le Comté de Comminges*, II, 111. It should be noted, also, that king James of Aragon and count Nuño Sancho of Roussillon had in April expressed their approval of the crusade (*Hist. Lang.*, VIII, 830–832) and that Henry III of England was won to neutrality by a strongly worded letter from the pope, dated April 27 (*Hist. Lang.*, VI, 602–603).

health was failing and he got no further than Montpensier in Auvergne, where he died on November 8, 1226. He left a son Louis, twelve years of age, and a highly capable widow, the queen-mother, Blanche of Castile.

To Raymond VII of Toulouse the death of Louis VIII offered some respite. In the fall of 1226 he had as allies Roger Bernard of Foix, Raymond Trencavel, a number of other rebels who had been deprived of lands and castles, some towns — notably Toulouse, Agen, and Limoux (which had been reduced by Louis but almost immediately had again revolted), and some portions of the lands of the counts stretching to the west and north. Given the general war-weariness of the whole region, this was not much to build upon. But the French monarchy was so fully engaged with disaffection nearer home, especially the rebellion of the counts of Brittany, Champagne, and La Marche, that it could send little aid to Humbert of Beaujeu and the garrisons in the south. The clergy were also energetically resisting the efforts of the legate to collect the tenth for the crusade.[63] As a result Raymond was able to regain some lost territory. It was impossible, however, to obscure the fact that he was pitting his strength against the much greater potential power of the king of France. Humbert began a program of systematic destruction, laying waste the countryside in the region of Toulouse, and Raymond was powerless to prevent him. There could hardly be any question of the ultimate victor.

Under the circumstances, pope Gregory IX, who succeeded Honorius III in 1227, pressed for final settlement in Languedoc. Cardinal Romanus was retained as legate with instructions to negotiate a peace; to that end he bent his energies, the result being the Peace of Paris of April 12, 1229. On the same date Raymond was absolved from long-standing excommunication and reconciled with the church.[64]

The treaty is a lengthy document, consisting of some twenty-one articles. Raymond swore to be loyal to the king; to obey the dictates of the church; to keep the peace and expel his mercenaries; to pay indemnities amounting to 20,000 marks; to do penance for five years, fighting the "infidel"; and to grant amnesty to those in his lands who had supported church, king, and the house of Montfort against him or his father. Then follow clauses dealing with territorial adjustments. Raymond was to place in custody of the king his

[63] Teulet, *Layettes*, V, nos, 524, 525 (documents dated May 17, 1227).

[64] Texts of the treaty and its preliminaries are published in *Hist. Lang.*, VIII, 878–894. The treaty is also in Teulet, *Layettes*, II, no. 1992. It exists in two forms: the first promulgated by Raymond, the second by the king; but they are identical in content.

daughter Joan, to be married to one of the king's brothers (Alphonse of Poitiers), provided papal sanction for the marriage within prohibited degrees could be secured. In return Raymond would receive the lands of the diocese of Toulouse (with the exception of certain lands granted by the king to Guy of Lévis); would retain the overlordship of the county of Foix; and would receive in addition the Albigeois north of the Tarn, Rouergue, Quercy (except Cahors and some dependent lands), and the Agenais. These are all expressed in terms of ecclesiastical boundaries, and there were a few small exceptions made of lands held of the king, but Raymond received substantially the western and northern portions of the lands controlled by the count of Toulouse prior to the beginning of the crusade. All these lands were to be granted to Raymond as their true lord, and over them he was to have full and free *dominium*, with certain stated exceptions, and the right to make pious bequests. The exceptions were important. Toulouse and its diocese (*Tholosa et episcopatus Tholosanus*) after the death of Raymond could descend only to Alphonse of Poitiers or to his heirs by Joan. Should Alphonse die without heirs by Joan, it was to descend to the king and his heirs; no immediate heirs of Raymond might inherit. That is, in this portion of the county of Toulouse the house of St. Gilles was to die with Raymond. In the other territories named above succession was to go to Joan and her heirs if Raymond died without a legitimate son. In his remaining territories west of the Rhone and south of the Tarn, Raymond ceded all his rights to the king. Similarly, he ceded to the church his rights in lands east of the Rhone, the marquisate of Provence.

Other provisions required restitution to those who, though not heretics, had been deprived of their land by church, king, or Simon of Montfort; obligated Raymond to fight any in his domains who, like the count of Foix, had not made peace with king and church, and to destroy the fortifications of Toulouse and thirty other strongholds within his lands. In addition, pledges, in hostages and castles, were to be held by the king, to assure the faithful fulfillment of the terms of the treaty.

Such were, in outline, the terms of the instrument by which the Albigensian crusade was finally ended. They were severe. Historians from William of Puylaurens[65] to the present have been puzzled to know why Raymond should have agreed to so harsh a settlement. The clauses relative to his loyal submission to king and church were in line with demands that had been made as conditions

[65] *Cronica*, xxxviii.

precedent to reconciliation over the previous twenty years. But the financial provisions, coming at the end of a long period of attrition, owing to costs of war and loss of revenue through the conquests of Simon of Montfort and later of Louis VIII, must have been difficult to meet. They amounted in all to something more than 30,000 marks, most of which sum was payable within a period of four years. This may well have equaled his total income from the lands remaining to him during the period in question. The clauses dealing with the inheritance must have been most difficult of acceptance. The counts of Toulouse had been among the proudest and most independent of the princes owing allegiance to the Capetian kings. Now Raymond VII not only yielded a large portion of the richest of his heritage, but was forced to do homage and swear fealty "according to the customs of Paris" for what was left. He had also to destroy the fortifications of the capital city of his county, Toulouse, and of thirty other towns; to allow the king to garrison, for a period not to exceed ten years, nine of his chief strongholds, including the Château Narbonnais; to renounce forever the hope of handing down to his heirs the heart of his county of Toulouse; and to face the strong likelihood that his heirs would inherit none of his lands. William of Puylaurens felt that he could not have lost more had he risked all and fought to the end. But Raymond appears to have considered it the part of prudence to salvage what he could before the situation deteriorated further.

On the other hand, the question has been raised why Raymond was allowed to retain so much, since utter defeat appeared to be only a matter of time. The answer doubtless lies in the troubled situation of France. Apart from considerations of justice and charity, which seem to have weighed with the queen-mother, and the apparent sympathies and hesitations of some members of the northern nobility, Blanche of Castile, as regent, had the very real problem of establishing her young son firmly upon the throne, in the face of a revolt by some French nobles and the hostile attitude of Henry III of England. She needed a settlement in the south in order to concentrate on other pressing problems.

There are a few further points in connection with the treaty which should not be passed over in silence. By article 7 Raymond agreed to establish a fund, amounting to 4,000 marks, to pay the salaries for ten years of four masters of theology, two decretists, six artists, and two masters-regent of grammar. This clause heralded the establishment of a university at Toulouse, much needed for the training of ecclesiastical personnel in Languedoc. Other clauses of the treaty indicate the drawing together of church and state in the suppression of heresy. Raymond agreed to confiscate the property of anyone who remained excommunicate for a year (art. 3). A bounty of two marks for a period of two years and one mark thereafter was to be paid to anyone apprehending a heretic (art. 2); civil officers (bailiffs) were to be employed to search out heretics and their supporters and bring them to trial (art. 2); and all subjects of the count were required to swear to aid in tracking down heretics and to serve the king in all things, this oath to be renewed every five years (arts. 17, 18). Finally, Raymond acknowledged the king of France as his overlord in the Agenais, a fief which his mother Joan, sister of Richard I, had brought as a dower to Raymond VI, and which was thus held of the king of England, and he yielded all his rights east of the Rhone to the church, despite the fact that he held those lands of the emperor, who had warned him against any form of alienation without imperial consent.[66] That pope Gregory IX found the latter situation anomalous is indicated by his return of the marquisate to Raymond in 1234. This was confirmed, without reference to papal action, by emperor Frederick II in the same year.[67] The Agenais was the subject of discussions between the kings of France and England, finally amicably concluded in the later Peace of Paris (1259) by which Louis IX recognized English claims to the territory.[68]

Thus ended the "Albigensian Crusade". The house of St. Gilles was crushed; a considerable proportion of the lesser nobles of the region were killed or disinherited; a very few of the nobles from the north who had fought under Simon of Montfort, and had been rewarded by the grant of lands, remained and developed new roots in the southland. At least a generation of turmoil succeeded the peace, as is shown by the king's inquests during the second half of the century, before normal feudal relations were reëstablished and injustices at least partially righted. Politically the Capetians were the great gainers. It was now possible to begin actively the assimilation of Languedoc under the crown. From this point of view there is much to be said for the argument that the actual crusade ended with Simon of Montfort's death in 1218, or soon thereafter, and that the subsequent ten years witnessed the fight for effective union of Languedoc with the kingdom of France. But that con-

[66] J. L. A. Huillard-Bréholles, *Historia diplomatica Friderici secundi* (7 vols. in 12, Paris, 1852–1861), II, part 1, 477–478: letter of March 31, 1225.

[67] *Hist. Lang.*, VIII, 979–981.

[68] Rymer, *Foedera* (Record Commission, London, 1816), I, part I, p. 383.

sideration was at least implicit throughout the whole period; it is difficult to disentangle religious and political considerations. Nor can it be said that the Peace of Paris ended the ambitions of other states in the region. The king of Aragon still had claims to lands north of the Pyrenees; the king of England had not lost all interest in the area; and the emperor was still the overlord of Provence.

Nor was Raymond VII disposed to accept without a struggle the terms of the treaty. The twenty years between the signing of that document and his death in 1249 he devoted in large part to three aims: the rehabilitation of his father's memory and the burial of his body in holy ground; the effecting of a marriage that would provide him with a son who might succeed him and thus circumvent, in part at least, the terms of the treaty; and the building of an alliance that could effectively challenge the king's power in Languedoc. In none of these was he successful.

Though the Peace of Paris was a long step in the direction of a political settlement in Languedoc, heresy, which was the avowed reason for the crusade, was by no means eradicated, though its protection by the nobility of the region had been largely broken. There remained the problem of developing machinery to uproot it from town and hamlet, of strengthening local church organization, and of installing more devoted personnel to be maintained by new lands and valuable prerogatives.

At a council, held at Toulouse in November 1229 under the presidency of the cardinal-legate Romanus, there were present numerous clergy, including the archbishops of Narbonne, Bordeaux, and Auch, and a considerable number of laity, including count Raymond, seneschal Odo of Carcassonne, and two consuls of Toulouse. The acts of the council are in forty-five articles, in which the provisions for dealing with heresy are carefully set forth and a program for coöperation of church and state in hunting out the heretic is laid down.[69] In every parish a team consisting of a priest and two or three laymen was to search out heretics; every lord was to be responsible for driving heresy from his lands, failure to do so entailing loss of lands and personal jeopardy; houses in which heretics were found were to be destroyed and the land confiscated; one might seek out heretics in the lands of another, but no one might be punished as a heretic until he had been adjudged such by proper ecclesiastical authority; anyone failing to attend the

[69] Mansi, *Concilia*, XXIII, 191–204. In its provisions for joint action of church and state in the attack on heresy this follows in much the *Ordonnance cupientes*, issued in April 1229 over the name of Louis IX; *Ordonnances des roys de France de la troisième race* (22 vols., Paris, 1723–1847), I, 50–53.

confessional and partake of the eucharist thrice in the year laid himself open to suspicion of heresy; all males after their fourteenth year and females of twelve years and above must take oath to support the church and combat heresy, this oath to be renewed biennially; no heretic might practice medicine or hold public office; a layman might not own a Bible, but exception was made of the breviary and the hours of the Virgin. These latter books in the vernacular were, however, most expressly prohibited.[70]

The Council of Toulouse thus supplemented the Peace of Paris in the program to establish peace, order, and unity of the faith in Languedoc. Military action had not been enough to suppress heresy although it had driven it underground. The problem was still unsolved. A new instrument was now devised to deal with heresy, the Inquisition, but any consideration of its history would carry us beyond the scope of this volume.

[70] It may be of interest to note that this fourteenth canon of the decrees of the council is considered the first instance of the prohibition of the Bible to laymen. It was, however, of only local validity. See Hans Rost, *Die Bibel im Mittelalter* (Augsburg, 1939), pp. 73–78.

IX

THE CHILDREN'S CRUSADE

For more than a hundred years the object of the crusade, the recovery of the Holy Land, had inspired the warriors of western Europe to undertake expeditions of great danger and great cost. From the outset, however, motives were mixed. Many crusaders showed a gross indifference to the purpose of the crusade whenever temptation beckoned, as it did often enough. Even after the fall of Jerusalem to Saladin in 1187, crusading leaders continued to put self-interest ahead of coöperation, and the spectacle of their rivalry was a constant discouragement. The recent diversion of the Fourth Crusade, and the wholesale confiscations of lands in the Midi

The history of the Children's Crusade can be told only from scattered notices in several French, German and Italian chronicles, some more authoritative than others. They have not always been handled with sufficient care, with the result that late and exaggerated accounts, such as that later inserted in the *Chronica majora* of Matthew Paris, have often dominated the story because of their colorful details. A critical assessment of the sources, and of some of the older secondary literature, may be found in Dana C. Munro, "The Children's Crusade," *AHR*, XIX (1913–1914), 516–524, and in Joseph E. Hansbery, "The Children's Crusade," *The Catholic Historical Review*, XXIV (1938), 30–38. Where the present writer ventures to differ with either of these authors is sufficiently indicated below.

In addition to the articles by Munro and Hansbery, the brief account by Reinhold Röhricht, "Der Kinderkreuzzug," *Historische Zeitschrift*, XXXVI (1876), 1–9, is worth mention, though now in the main superseded. There is also the old study by J. F. C. Hecker, still of interest, which attempts to probe the pathological aspect of religious emotionalism, *Child-Pilgrimages*, trans. Robt. H. Cooke, in Hecker, *The Epidemics of the Middle Ages* (3rd ed., London, 1859), pp. 346–360. It includes English translations of some of the longer contemporary, and not so contemporary, accounts. Paul Alphandéry, "Les Croisades d'enfants," *Revue de l'histoire des religions*, LXXIII (1916), 259–282, relies for the events of the crusade (pp. 259–266) on De Janssens, "Étienne de Cloyes et les croisades d'enfants au XIIIe siècle," *Bulletin de la Société dunoise* (Chateaudun, 1891), pp. 32–40, and is of no independent value. However, Alphandéry has essayed an interesting interpretation: ". . . c'est dans un rite de consécration de la jeunesse ou plutôt de l'enfance . . . que nous allons chercher l'origine des croisades d'enfants" (p. 271). This has now been further developed in his *La Chrétienté et l'idée de Croisade*, II (L'Évolution de l'humanité, XXXVIII bis, Paris, 1959), 115–148, where the Children's Crusade is interpreted as an expression of the medieval child cult, related to such movements as that of the child-builders of churches and bridges, and associated in contemporary minds with the now fully developed feast of the Holy Innocents. In effect, it becomes a sacrificial rite, by which the new innocents offer themselves for the salvation of Christendom. A somewhat different contribution to the study of mass movements such as this, however, is that of Norman Cohn, *The Pursuit of the Millenium* (London, 1957), although it has little to say about the Children's Crusade itself (p. 77). Finally there are brief treatments in some of the standard works on the crusades, such as Adolf Waas, *Geschichte der Kreuzzüge*, I (Freiburg, 1956), 253–258, and Steven Runciman, *A History of the Crusades*, III (Cambridge, 1954), 139–144 (a somewhat fanciful version).

during the Albigensian Crusade to reward those who threw in their lot with Simon of Montfort, added much to the general cynicism and disillusion.

It would be a serious mistake, however, to believe that the popular attitude toward the crusade had become worldly or trivial. Some there were who debased its ideals, but the great masses of common people were often bewitched by thoughts of liberating the Holy Land. With each successive proclamation of a crusade, the preachers aroused an excitement shared alike by men and women, the old and the young, all eager to redeem past failures and to drive out the "infidel" from the holy places. Within each crusading army the low-born regarded themselves as the elect of God. This was a cliché of the Middle Ages, but one which never failed to find a response, especially among the poor and the oppressed (to say nothing of the unbalanced) always looking for the millennium. It was a peasant whom St. Andrew chose to receive the news of the Holy Lance at Antioch on the First Crusade, saying to him that God had chosen the poor, who surpassed all others in merit and grace.[1] The "Tafurs", camp-followers from northern France and the Lowlands, who were accused of cannibalism[2] and who frightened their Christian leaders fully as much as they did their Moslem enemies, still felt themselves to be the elect of the army, although they were in fact its very dregs.[3] Now, as time passed, with the obvious failure of knightly arms to free Jerusalem, the idea that the meek might do what the proud and mighty had been unable to do all the more possessed the minds of lesser folk.[4]

During the winter of 1211–1212 William, archdeacon of Paris, and James of Vitry recruited crusaders for Simon of Montfort's army, which was continually being depleted by the withdrawal of those who had completed their forty days' service. Their preaching

[1] Raymond of Aguilers, *Historia Francorum* (*RHC, Occ.*, III), p. 254; see volume I of the present work, pp. 320–322.

[2] Especially by the author of the *Chanson d'Antioche* (ed. Paulin Paris, II [1848], pp. 5–6, and elsewhere), on which cf. Guibert of Nogent, *Gesta Dei per Francos*, VII, 23, ad ann. 1099 (*RHC, Occ.*, IV), pp. 241–243, and Louis Bréhier (ed.), *Histoire anonyme de la première croisade* (Paris, 1924), p. 178: "alii vero c[a]edebant carnes eorum [i.e. Saracenorum] per frusta et coquebant ad manducandum." Bréhier, p. 179, note 4, supplies the other sources for the charge of cannibalism made against the dreaded and despised Tafurs.

[3] See Cohn, *The Pursuit of the Millennium*, pp. 45–48.

[4] Cf. *Annales Reineri Sancti Iacobi Leodiensis*, ad ann. 1212 (*MGH, SS.*, XVI), p. 665: "Erat autem eorum intentio mare se velle transire, et *quod potentes et reges non fecerant*, sepulcrum Christi recuperare"; and also the account in *Chronicae regiae Coloniensis continuatio prima*, ad ann. 1213 (*MGH, SS.*, XXIV), p. 18, in which the failure of so many others, "reges multi, duces plurimi, populi innumerabiles," is contrasted with the children who are weak and unarmed — scornfully, it is true, but revealing an awareness of contrast which must have been general at the time. See also the brief remarks of A. Waas, *Geschichte der Kreuzzüge*, I, 253.

aroused a tremendous response in both France and Germany.[5] The crusade against the Albigensians had already attracted large numbers of common folk, not only *bona fide* crusaders but also the "servientes exercitus", as Peter of Les Vaux-de-Cernay euphemistically calls them, the *ribaldi*, unarmed scavengers and hangers-on who added to the uproar of camp life and the difficulty of keeping any discipline whatsoever. This crusade differed from its predecessors in many ways, not least important being the fact that it ultimately aimed at the destruction of the political authority of a Christian prince, the count of Toulouse. Not that such distinctions made any impress on the masses in the north. For them the crusade was proclaimed to root out heresy and end the scourge of the mercenary troops, variously called *routiers* and *cotereaux*, in southern France — nor were heretics and *routiers* always distinct in their minds.[6] The enemy was near at hand, the goal easy to reach — no long march across the continent, no frightening pull over the treacherous Mediterranean. The first great victory of the Albigensian Crusade, the capture and sack of Béziers in 1209, was made possible by the *ribaldi*, who assaulted the walls on their own, broke into the city, opened its gates to the army, and wreaked terrible havoc on the inhabitants, orthodox and heretic alike.[7]

There had been much preaching of crusade over the past few years, not only against the Albigensians but also against the Muwaḥḥids (Almohads) in Spain, culminating in 1212 in the great Christian victory of Las Navas de Tolosa. It was easy thus to release the religious enthusiasm of the Middle Ages, always close to the surface; it was far more difficult, however, to keep it within bounds when once aroused. Especially was this so in areas of great social ferment such as the Rhine valley and the Lowlands, where old

[5] Peter of Les Vaux-de-Cernay, *Hystoria Albigensis*, 285 (ed. P. Guébin and E. Lyon, I [Paris, 1926], 281–283).

[6] For instance, in the *Annales Marbacenses*, ad ann. 1212 (*MGH, SS.*, XVII), p. 172, occurs this revealing entry: "In this year a crusading expedition was undertaken by the duke of Austria . . . to help the count of Montfort fight the Albigensians, who were *routiers* or *cotereaux*, heretics of the land of St. Gilles." And Walter Map, who should have known better since he attended the Third Lateran Council of 1179 and was an examiner of some Waldensian deputies, could write in his description of what he calls "a certain sect of heretics" that "our king, Henry II, is holding off from all his lands a most damnable sect of a new heresy", and these heretics gather in great bands "which they call *Ruttae*" (*De nugis curialium*, I, xxix [ed. Thomas Wright, Camden Society, London, 1850], p. 60).

[7] Peter of Les Vaux-de-Cernay, *Hyst. Alb.*, 89, 90 (ed. Guébin and Lyon, I, 91); cf. Caesarius of Heisterbach, *Dialogus miraculorum*, V, 21 (ed. Joseph Strange, I [Cologne, Bonn, Brussels, 1851], 302): "Nam quidam satellites zelo fidei accensi, leonibus similes, exemplo illorum de quibus legitur in libro Machabaeorum, scalis appositis, muros intrepide ascenderunt; haereticisque divinitus territis et declinantibus, sequentibus portas aperientes, civitatem obtinuerunt."

social forms were breaking down in the face of increased industrial and urban development, where population was growing rapidly, and where economic insecurity was becoming chronic. The sustained excitement of crusade preaching acted on the people of such areas with explosive force. One could never be certain what form their enthusiasm might take. It was sure to enhance the irritability of those for whom relief from anxiety was often to be obtained only in giving free rein to their passions, and who found in sudden violent action a release from the unbearable insecurity of their dreary lives. But it was a release to be found, then as now, in the crowd, "a device for indulging ourselves in a kind of temporary insanity by all going crazy together."[8] "Around this time," it is reported, "naked women ran through the towns and cities, saying nothing."[9] There was always a touch of madness in the air.

There were many examples of the kind of mass psychosis that might develop when religious enthusiasm ran riot, and wiser heads were constantly reminded of the danger. In Brittany some two generations earlier, for instance, there had been the strange case of that "illiterate idiot", Eon de l'Étoile (Eudo de Stella). Hearing in his church the chant "per Eum qui venturus est judicare vivos et mortuos et seculum per ignem," he thought that the "Eum" referred to himself, since Eudo "sermone Gallico Eun diceretur". Lunacy would be served, even by philology! And so Eon looked upon himself as the son of God, come to judge the quick and the dead. He attracted a following of men as foolish as himself, whom he called his angels and apostles. Soon, however, they degenerated into a band of brigands preying on churches and monasteries. Eon and his company dressed richly, feasted hugely, and led such enviable lives that those who came to arrest him were in turn corrupted by the sight of so much high living and joined him instead. He was finally captured and sent to the Council of Rheims (1148) before pope Eugenius III. He had a forked branch which he explained by saying that should the forked end point heavenward, God would hold two thirds of the world, and he the other third; if earthward, the shares would be reversed — whereupon the entire council burst into laughter. Eon was put in the custody of archbishop Samson of Rheims and died in prison soon after. His followers were more severely dealt with, and the three named "Wisdom",

[8] This definition of a crowd comes from Everett Dean Martin, *The Behavior of Crowds: A Psychological Study* (New York and London, 1920), p. 37, recently quoted in William L. Langer, "The Next Assignment," *AHR*, LXIII (1957–1958), 290.

[9] *Annales Alberti Abbatis Stadensis*, ad ann. 1212 (*MGH, SS.*, XVI), p. 355.

"Knowledge", and "Judgment", and others with "big names", were given to the flames, "since they preferred to burn than to correct their life."[10]

There is another example, from the year 1182, in south central France, where an obscure carpenter, Durand of Le Puy, had a vision in which the Virgin ordered him to exhort the people to peace. She gave him a scrap of parchment upon which was the figure of Mary bearing the infant Jesus in her arms, and the prayer: "Lamb of God, who taketh away the sins of the world, give us peace." There quickly grew up around Durand a large movement, dedicated to the destruction of the brigands of the region, and almost as quickly a "rule" was drawn up. The new confraternity briefly enjoyed the support of all classes of society. Soon, however, it also turned on the established authorities, lost the support of nobility and church, became an outcast and undisciplined mob, and was hunted down and finally destroyed. Later writers would express horror and disgust at this "dangerous presumption", this "rebellion against their betters", in which there was shown "no fear, no reverence, of their superiors".[11]

In the remarkable movement which grew up around the carpenter of Le Puy there is evident the same emotionalism which was to nourish the Children's Crusade. There was also the not untypical *epistola caelestis* so often to be found clutched in the hands of those who seek some visible sign of the continuity of revelation. During the winter and spring of 1211–1212, in the area between the Seine and the Rhine, throughout northeastern France, the

[10] William of Newburgh, *Historia rerum Anglicarum*, I, 19 (ed. Richard Howlett, in *Chronicles of the Reigns of Stephen, Henry II, and Richard I* [Rolls Series, LXXXII], I), pp. 60–64; *The Chronicle of Robert of Torigni* (*ibid.*, IV), pp. 156–157; Otto of Freising, *The Deeds of Frederick Barbarossa*, I, 56, tr. C. C. Mierow and R. Emery (Records of Civilization, New York, 1953), pp. 94–95; *Sigeberti Gemblacensis chronica, continuatio Gemblacensis* (*MGH, SS.*, VI), p. 385; *Sigeberti cont. Praemonstratensis* (*ibid.*), p. 454; cf. Achille Luchaire, *Les Premiers Capétiens* (E. Lavisse, *Histoire de France*, II, Paris, 1901), pp. 360–361. There is no need to follow Cohn (*Pursuit of the Millennium*, p. 38) in attributing to the name Eon "the influence of some Gnostic or Neo-Manichean tradition". Eon is a perfectly good Old French form of the name Odo (Eudo), as the quotation from William of Newburgh itself would clearly indicate.

[11] See in general *Roberti canonici S. Mariani Autissiodorensis chronicon*, ad ann. 1183 (*MGH, SS.*, XXVI), p. 247; Geoffrey of Vigeois (*RHGF*, XVIII), p. 219; *Historia episcoporum Autissiodorensis* (*RHGF*, XVIII), p. 729; *The Chronicle of Robert of Torigni* (*Chronicles of the Reigns of Stephen, Henry II, and Richard I*, IV), p. 309; *The Historical Works of Gervase of Canterbury* (ed. W. Stubbs [Rolls Series, LXXIII], I), pp. 300 ff.; H. F. Delaborde, ed., *Oeuvres de Rigord et de Guillaume le Breton, historiens de Philippe-Auguste* (2 vols., Paris, 1882–1885), I, 38; *Chronicon anonymi Laudunensis canonici* (*RHGF*, XVIII), pp. 705–706. There are many secondary accounts of the movement, e.g. in H. Géraud, "Les Routiers au xiie siècle," *Bibliothèque de l'École des chartes*, III (1841–1842), 138–147; and Achille Luchaire, *Social France at the Time of Philip Augustus*, tr. E. B. Krehbiel (New York, 1929), pp. 12–18.

Lowlands, and western Germany, empty heads throbbed with the feverish exhortations of preachers and burned with zeal for a crusade. Crowds of enthusiasts were soon marching off to Languedoc. Others, from Saxony, Westphalia, and Frisia, were destroying the heretics in their own back yard — the Beguines.[12] Religious sensibilities, however, could stand only so much. The time had come for another of the popular frenzies so characteristic of the period. The time had come, indeed, for another letter from heaven.

The movement which boiled up for a brief moment in 1212 was never, despite the convictions of those who took part in it, a crusade in any legal sense, blessed by the church and encouraged by indulgences. On the contrary, it was deplored by all responsible authority. What has often been looked upon as its "French phase" may not have been considered a crusade even by the participants. In June 1212, it is said, a shepherd boy named Stephen, from Cloyes near Vendôme, beheld a vision of Jesus, who appeared to him in the guise of a poor pilgrim, received some bread from him, and then gave him a letter for the king of France. Soon many of his fellow shepherds gathered about Stephen and accompanied him to St. Denis, and then to Paris to see the king. Meanwhile, a sort of mass hysteria seems to have gripped much of the countryside round about. Many other children were being held in great reverence by the simple crowds, and around these there gathered larger and larger followings of yet more children whose purpose it apparently was to join the "sanctus puer", Stephen.[13] Another source tells of processions of children, and some adults too, carrying banners and candles, crosses and censers, passing through towns and hamlets and chanting in the vulgar tongue (*gallice*), "Lord God, exalt Christianity! Lord God, restore to us the true cross," and other chants also, since there were many such groups, each singing its own variation.[14] That these bands reached the reported number of 30,000 is doubtful;[15] at all events, many of their members were caught up in the recruiting for the Albigensian Crusade,[16] while most of the others returned home. From Jumièges on the lower Seine comes a brief notice that the children claimed to be "seeking

[12] *Annales Colonienses maximi*, ad ann. 1212 (*MGH*, *SS.*, XVII), p. 826.

[13] *Chronicon anonymi Laudunensis canonici* (*RHGF*, XVIII), p. 715.

[14] *Sigeberti Gemblacensis chronica, auctarium Mortui Maris* (*MGH*, *SS.*, VI), p. 467; repeated in *Annalium Rotomagensium continuatio* (*MGH*, *SS.*, XXVI), p. 501.

[15] *Chronica Albrici monachi Trium Fontium*, ad ann. 1212 (*MGH*, *SS.*, XXIII), p. 893; *Chronicon anonymi Laudunensis canonici* (*RHGF*, XVIII), p. 715.

[16] *Sigeberti Gemblacensis chronica, auctarium Mortui Maris* (*MGH*, *SS.*, VI), p. 467.

God".[17] Aside from this vague aspiration, however, there seems to be no contemporary evidence that the children who followed Stephen had any idea of going to the Holy Land.

There is little wonder, however, that in the later accounts of this movement Stephen and his shepherd boys came to be connected with the Children's Crusade. The strange excitement in which they were caught up during that summer of 1212 had already raced swiftly through the region of old Lotharingia between the Rhine and France. There other crowds, young and old, were going far beyond mere processions and chants. To the north and east, in the Benedictine monastery of Andres, near Guines, the monk William was noting the remarkable "peregrinatio", as he called it, of an infinite number of children from various cities and towns, castles and villages, making their way toward the Mediterranean. When asked by their parents and others whither they were going, they too replied as though moved by a single spirit, "to God!"[18] Did they have some notion of going to the Holy Land? It seems almost certain.

Farther east, in the Benedictine house of St. James at Liége, the monk Reiner witnessed a local outbreak of this same movement (*motus mirabilis*). He reports that it embraced not only French but also German children, especially young shepherds and shepherdesses. Those whose parents would not allow them to go wept bitterly. Here at Liége the purpose was clear enough: the children wished to do what princes and kings had failed to do — cross the sea and recover the Sepulcher of Christ. It was another People's Crusade.[19]

South of Liége, at Trier, it was much the same story, though here only German and not French children are mentioned. Their leader was a certain Nicholas, a young boy whose home was Cologne. He bore a cross in the form of a Greek Tau, although the chronicler adds, in words with the sound of an eye-witness report, that it was difficult to make out what material it was made of.[20]

Farther east again, there are additional reports and a few more details. One contemporary, writing in Cologne, provides dates for what he calls "a remarkable, indeed a more-than-remarkable,

[17] *Annales Gemmeticenses*, ad ann. 1212 (*MGH, SS.*, XXVI), p. 510; also *Anonymi continuatio appendicis Roberti de Monte ad Sigebertum* (*RHGF*, XVIII), p. 344.

[18] *Willelmi chronica Andrensis*, 189 (*MGH, SS.*, XXIV), p. 754.

[19] *Annales Reineri* (*MGH, SS.*, XVI), p. 665.

[20] *Gestorum Treverorum continuatio IV*, 3 (*MGH, SS.*, XXIV), p. 399: "nec facile erat discernere, cuius generis et metalli esset."

affair" — around Easter and Pentecost, March 25 and May 13.[21] This is considerably earlier than the date recorded for Stephen's procession in France, and suggests that the movement may have had its origins in the Lowlands and the Rhine valley, and only its outer fringes on the Seine. Many thousands of children ranging from six years to the age of discretion came together, despite the opposition of their parents, relatives, and friends. Some left their plows, others the flocks and herds which had been in their care, and rushed to take the cross. They moved off in groups of twenty, fifty, or a hundred, with Jerusalem their goal. It was unbelievable. How, they were asked, could they expect to do what kings, dukes, and so many others had failed to do. They replied with simplicity that they would obey the divine command and bear with willing spirit whatever God placed upon them.[22] Another Cologne chronicle, quite independently, confirms that French as well as German children were involved, of various ages and conditions. There is the additional note, hardly surprising in view of the circumstances and the times, that some "maligni homines" joined the pilgrimage, pilfered the contributions made to the children by the faithful, and then secretly stole away. One of them was caught and hanged in Cologne.[23]

Here, then, was another eloquent expression of popular piety. It appeared miraculous — but the Devil could work seeming miracles. If it was a sign of the simple faith of the people, it was also a potential threat to established authority. In the somewhat sour account from the monastery of Marbach on the upper Rhine we can sense the conservative distrust for the anti-clerical tendencies of the movement.[24] "As, in the face of such novelties, we become a credulous mob, so indeed many thought that all this arose not from any foolishness but rather through divine inspiration and a kind of piety, and therefore helped them with food and other necessaries. The clergy, however, and certain others, who were more sensible and judged the whole business to be useless, were opposed by the laity, who said that the clergy were unbelievers, and

[21] The chronicler has mistakenly put his account under the year 1213, during which Easter and Pentecost fell on April 14 and June 2.

[22] *Chronicae regiae Coloniensis continuatio prima*, ad ann. 1213 (*MGH, SS.*, XXIV), pp. 17–18.

[23] *Annales Colonienses maximi*, ad ann. 1212 (*MGH, SS.*, XVII), pp. 826–827.

[24] Cf. Cohn, *Pursuit of the Millennium*, p. 66: "Any chiliastic movement was . . . almost compelled by the situation in which it found itself to see the clergy as a demonic factor". It must be added, however, that this one notice from Marbach is the only one which suggests that the Children's Crusade might have turned against ecclesiastical authority. The general silence of the sources, in fact, would indicate that the movement probably never went so far.

that their opposition sprang more from envy and greed than from any love of truth and justice."[25] The "mentes saniores" did not, of course, go completely unheard, and managed to divert many at Cologne into the more official enterprise of the Albigensian Crusade. These went off to join Simon of Montfort's army at Puylaurens.[26] But there were many others set on going to Jerusalem, on joining this "useless expedition" of "children and stupid adults", undertaken more out of foolish curiosity than any real hope for salvation.[27]

The route of the various bands which seem to have gathered and formed in or around Cologne[28] lay up the Rhine and eventually, for most of them, over the Alps into Lombardy. Some of the children were turned back at Mainz;[29] the heat was excessive, and the weak began to fall by the wayside.[30] From Speyer we have a brief notice of their passing — not contemporary, it is true, but of some interest since it preserves the date they went through the town, July 25.[31] At Ebersheim, on a little island in the Ill not far from Schlettstadt, they made a striking impression on the chronicler of the monastery. Nicholas is again named as the leader of this "infinite number" from Germany and France, all convinced that once they reached the sea they could walk across the tops of the waves without wetting their feet.[32]

The expedition passed near Marbach, southwest of Colmar. There the chronicler of the Augustinian house grumbled over the indiscretion and uselessness of such a business, and moralized on the inevitable failure of any such venture undertaken "without the balance of reason or the force of counsel." From Marbach, the

[25] *Annales Marbacenses* (*MGH, SS.*, XVII), p. 172.

[26] Peter of Les Vaux-de-Cernay, *Hyst. Alb.*, 308 (ed. Guébin and Lyon, II, 9, and notes 3 and 4).

[27] So the *Annales Marbacenses* (*MGH, SS.*, XVII), p. 172: ". . . curiositatis causa potius quam salutis".

[28] We cannot accept the account of Joseph E. Hansbery, "The Children's Crusade," *The Catholic Historical Review*, XXIV (1938), 32 ff., that Sens was "one of the points of origin of the real Children's Crusade," and that the children then moved along the route Sens-Troyes-Châlons-Liége-Cologne — certainly a roundabout way of reaching the Holy Land from Sens. All this is based on Richer of Sens, a very late source (see Waitz, in *MGH, SS.*, XXV, 251: "Narrationis telam usque ad a. 1264 deduxit [Richerus]; maiorem libri partem antea, non tamen ante a. 1254 vel 1255 scripsisse videtur"). Richer says nothing of the children being in Sens, but rather gives the impression of a movement abroad (*Richeri gesta Senoniensis ecclesiae*, IV, 3 [*MGH, SS.*, XXV], p. 301).

[29] *Chronicae regiae Coloniensis cont. prima* (*MGH, SS.*, XXIV), p. 18.

[30] *Annales Reineri* (*MGH, SS.*, XVI), p. 665: "Estus Iulii permaximus quindecim primis diebus." Cf. *Annales Colonienses maximi* (*MGH, SS.*, XVII), p. 827: "Multi etiam illorum in silvis et desertis locis estu, fame, et siti perierunt."

[31] *Annales Spirenses* (*MGH, SS.*, XVII), p. 84.

[32] *Chronicon Ebersheimense*, 36 (*MGH, SS.*, XXIII), p. 450; cf. *Sicardi episcopi Cremonensis chronicon* (*RISS*, VII), col. 624 "[dicentes] se per siccum maria transituros."

multitude swarmed through the Alps and into Italy, whether by the St. Gotthard or the Splügen is not known. There they broke up into groups and dispersed among the various towns of Lombardy where they were despoiled by the natives.[33] A notice from Salzburg indicates that some reached Treviso; possibly they hoped to take ship at Venice.[34] But the main body seems to have gone in the other direction, reaching Piacenza on August 20. Nicholas was still the leader of what, despite losses, must even yet have been an impressive pilgrimage, a "great and innumerable multitude of German children, babes at the breast, women and girls," all hastening down to the sea to fulfil the prophecy of an angel of God that they would recover the Holy Sepulcher from the hands of the iniquitous Saracens.[35] Nearby, at Cremona, bishop Sicard also recorded their passage, in drier tones perhaps, but with the authentic note that the company had come from Cologne.[36]

From the valley of the Po, Nicholas and his followers pressed on to the south and the sea. They were in Genoa by Saturday, August 25, bearing crosses, with their pilgrim staves and leathern wallets — more than seven thousand, so it was estimated. They obviously received no encouragement, no offer of sea transportation to the Holy Land, for the very next day most of them were gone again, although many of their number dropped out and remained behind.[37] From Genoa there is no longer any clear trail to follow. The "crusade" had been breaking up all the way from Germany to Italy; many had died, many others had returned home discouraged, or stopped at places such as Genoa and gone no further. A late source reports that two boat-loads sailed from Pisa, of whom nothing more was heard.[38] There are reports that a body of the crusaders went to Rome, where Innocent III relieved of their crusading oaths those who were too young and those weighed down

[33] *Annales Marbacenses* (*MGH, SS.*, XVII), p. 172; cf. *Annales Colonienses maximi* (*MGH, SS.*, XVII), p. 827: "Alii Alpes transgressi, mox ut Ytaliam intraverunt a Longobardis spoliati et repulsi, cum ignominia redierunt."

[34] *Annales Sancti Rudberti Salisburgenses*, ad ann. 1212 (*MGH, SS.*, IX), p. 780: "que [multitudo] et iubente papa Innocentio, missis cardinalibus, apud Tarvisium Ytaliae repellitur."

[35] *Annales Placentini Guelfi*, ad ann. 1212 (*MGH, SS.*, XVIII), p. 426: "Die autem Martis proximo, 13 Kal. Septembris . . .". August 20 was Monday, not Tuesday. The *Chronicae regiae Coloniensis cont. prima* also refers to their reaching Piacenza.

[36] *Sicardi episcopi Cremonensis chronicon* (*RISS*, VII), col. 624. Unfortunately, Sicard says nothing of the outcome, except "demum quasi evanuit universa". Instead, he allows the sad facts of the expedition to remind him of a yet sadder, though less authentic, story of children in Apulia and Sicily, where the famine was so severe that they were eaten by their mothers.

[37] *Annales Ogerii Panis* (*MGH, SS.*, XVIII), p. 131. A tradition of Genoese hostility is preserved in Jacobus de Varagine, *Chronica de civitate Januensi* (*RISS*, IX, i), p. 45.

[38] *Richeri gesta Senoniensis ecclesiae*, IV, 3 (*MGH, SS.*, XXV), p. 301.

by too many years.[39] He is said to have remarked: "These children put us to shame. They rush to recover the Holy Land while we sleep."[40] The chronicler of Trier puts some crusaders ultimately in Brindisi, where the archbishop refused them permission to sail.[41] There are two conflicting accounts of what happened to their leader, Nicholas. One has him going on the Fifth Crusade and fighting at the siege of Damietta, finally returning home safe; the other states that he died in Italy and that his father, who had been guilty of selling some of the children as slaves, committed suicide after returning to Cologne.[42] From these vague and conflicting accounts we may assume that much of the Children's Crusade melted away in Italy. The footsore and deluded crusaders, greatly reduced in number, now began the long trek back over the Alps. They had marched south proudly in great singing crowds. Now, with no dream to sustain them any longer, they made their painful way homeward, barefoot, hungry, objects of scorn and derision to those who had so recently held them in awe and reverence.[43]

One group of these unfortunates remains to be accounted for. It would seem that at some point along the way a party of children headed for Marseilles. Whether this happened before crossing the Alps or after reaching Genoa is impossible to say. The chronicle of Ebersheim refers to their destination as "Vienne, which is a city by the sea."[44] Although the chronicler's geography leaves something to be desired, this seems to indicate a route from Ebersheim by the Doubs and the Rhone. On the other hand, the party which eventually turned up at Marseilles might have been an independent one; the sources do not permit certainty. At all events, the presence of child crusaders in the Rhone valley is certainly indicated, and is supported by two other accounts which put some of them in Marseilles.[45] What happened to this group is best told in the words of Aubrey of Trois-Fontaines.

"In this year [1212] there was a quite miraculous expedition of

[39] *Chronicae regiae Coloniensis cont. prima* (*MGH, SS.*, XXIV), p. 18; *Annales Marbacenses* (*MGH, SS.*, XVII), p. 172.

[40] *Annales Alberti Abbatis Stadensis* (*MGH, SS.*, XVI), p. 355.

[41] *Gestorum Treverorum cont. IV*, 3 (*MGH, SS.*, XXIV), p. 399.

[42] *Annalium Admuntensium continuatio* (*MGH, SS.*, IX), p. 592; *Gestorum Treverorum cont. IV*, 3 (*MGH, SS.*, XXIV), p. 399.

[43] *Annales Marbacenses* (*MGH, SS.*, XVII), p. 172: "Sic ergo decepti et confusi redire ceperunt, et qui prius gregatim et per turmas suas et numquam sine cantu celeumatis transire solebant per terras, modo singillatim et in silentio, nudipedes et famelici redeuntes, facti sunt omnibus in derisum, quia plurime virgines rapte et florem pudicicie sue amiserunt."

[44] *Chronicon Ebersheimense*, 36 (*MGH, SS.*, XXIII), p. 450.

[45] *Chronicae regiae Coloniensis cont. prima* (*MGH, SS.*, XXIV), p. 18; *Chronica Albrici monachi Trium Fontium*, ad ann. 1212 (*MGH, SS.*, XXIII), p. 893.

children, coming together from all around. They first came from the area of the castle of Vendôme to Paris.[46] When they numbered around 30,000 they went to Marseilles, intending to cross the sea against the Saracens. The *ribaldi* and other evil men who joined them sullied the entire army, so that while some perished at sea, and others were sold, only a few of so great a multitude made their way home. Of these, those who had escaped from all this gave the pope their promise that when they became of age they would then cross the sea as crusaders. Now, the betrayers of those children are said to have been Hugh Ferreus and William Porcus, merchants of Marseilles. Since they were the captains of vessels, they were supposed to carry them overseas in the cause of God at no cost, as they had promised to them. They filled seven large ships with them; and when they were two days out, off the island of St. Peter *ad rupem*, which is called Recluse, a storm blew up, two of the ships were lost, and all the children aboard were drowned. It is said that some years later pope Gregory IX built a church of the New Innocents on that island, and installed twelve prebendaries. In the church repose the bodies of the children which the sea threw up there, and up to the present time pilgrims may see them uncorrupted. The betrayers meanwhile sailed the other five ships to Bougie and Alexandria, and there sold all those children to Saracen princes and merchants. From them the caliph [an-Nāṣir] bought four hundred, eighty of them priests and all of them clerics, whom he wished to separate from the others, and he dealt with them more honorably than was his custom. This was the same caliph of whom I spoke earlier as studying at Paris in the guise of a cleric. He learned well those things which are known amongst us, and lately he has given up sacrificing camel's flesh.[47] In the same year in which the children were sold there was a meeting of Saracen princes at Baghdad where they slew eighteen children, who were martyred in various ways, since they were quite unwilling to give up the Christian faith; but they diligently reared the rest of the children in slavery. One of these clerics, who saw all this, and whom the caliph had purchased for himself, has faithfully reported that he heard of absolutely none of these children apostatizing from Christianity. The two betrayers, Hugh Ferreus and William Porcus,

[46] This is a reminiscence of the processions of Stephen and the other shepherds; the explanation of Hansbery, "The Children's Crusade," *The Catholic Historical Review*, XXIV, 33, that Aubrey confused the processions to St. Denis and Paris with the crusade proper, and that here he is reconciling two separate traditions, seems most probable.

[47] At the suggestion of the editor, Paul Scheffer-Boichorst, reading "carnem camelinam" for "panem camelinum" which makes no sense.

afterwards went to the prince of the Saracens of Sicily, Mirabel [the emir Ibn-'Abs], wishing to plan to turn the emperor Frederick over to him; but the emperor, by the grace of God, triumphed over them. He hanged Mirabel, his two sons, and those two betrayers, all from one gallows. Eighteen years after the expedition, adds my informant, Mascemuch of Alexandria still possessed seven hundred — no longer children, but grown men."[48]

Aubrey's account is the classic source for the fate of the Children's Crusade. Together with the various legends which quickly grew up, both in prose and verse, it helped to feed the romantic imaginations of a later day. Dana C. Munro rejected it many years ago, however, on the grounds that it rests solely on the evidence of a single cleric who claimed to have returned, and is full of improbabilities, "such as the facts that eighty of the infants were priests, and that the Moslems tortured the children to make them apostatize." Furthermore, since no chronicle mentions the band of children [here Munro is referring to Stephen of Cloyes' band] at any place between Paris and Marseilles, and no chronicle south of the Loire mentions the movement, there could have been no crusaders at Marseilles and the entire account must obviously be classed with all the other legends obscuring the true facts of the Children's Crusade.[49]

The fact that Aubrey's story seems to describe a French expedition which cannot be confirmed by other sources need cause no difficulty. It has already been suggested that, writing as late as he did, he fused the tradition of Stephen and the shepherd processions around Paris with the story told him by his informant.[50] Furthermore, two independent accounts, one certainly and the other probably written before Aubrey's, put some of the crusaders in the Rhone valley and in Marseilles, as we have seen. There were child crusaders in Marseilles — not from around Paris, to be sure, but from the Lowlands and the Rhine valley, French and German both as so many contemporary observers testify.

Joseph Hansbery has suggested further that, making due allowance for Aubrey's overcredulousness, the main elements of his account may be accepted since it contains statements which can be confirmed by other sources. This is true enough. Unfortunately, as an example, Hansbery chose the founding of the church of the New Innocents, the ruins of which "were discovered by Newton

[48] *Chronica Albrici monachi Trium Fontium* (*MGH, SS.*, XXIII), pp. 893–894.
[49] Dana C. Munro, "The Children's Crusade," *AHR*, XIX (1913–1914), 520.
[50] Above, note 46.

Perkins in 1867."[51] Perkins' letter in which he describes his trip to the island of St. Peter, however, is very slim evidence indeed for any such assertion. Apparently no one on the island ever heard of the church or its ruins, in itself a telling fact against its existence. "Outside the wall . . . we came upon the ruins of something, either a house or a church." The reasons which Perkins adduced for suggesting that this might be the remains of the church of the New Innocents are tenuous indeed, and may be credited to a very obvious desire to tell his correspondent, George Gray, what he wanted to hear.[52]

It is possible, however, to check Aubrey's account at other points. He has referred to Hugh Ferreus (or Ferus) and William Porcus, both well known persons. In the case of the former, at least, it would not be surprising to find him playing the role attributed to him in Aubrey's account. He was *viguier* of Marseilles at the time — not a municipal officer, but rather the representative of the viscount.[53] As such he might have had to deal with the problem posed by the arrival of the child crusaders. William Porcus, however, presents some difficulties. He was not a merchant of Marseilles, as Aubrey says, but a Genoese captain of considerable reputation,[54] and served the emperor Frederick II as admiral[55] before falling into disfavor and having to flee from the kingdom of Sicily in 1221.[56] Aubrey probably knew of this, and knew also that around the same time (in 1222) Frederick captured the Moslem pirate Ibn-'Abs (Mirabellus, Mirabettus, Mirabs in the Latin

[51] Hansbery, "Children's Crusade," p. 33, note 16.

[52] Perkins' letter may be found in App. B of the highly imaginative work of George Zabriskie Gray, *The Children's Crusade* (London, 1871), pp. 234–237. His reasons for thinking the ruins he found were of the church of the New Innocents were, first, that there was no habitation nearby; second, that the building faced due east, "if we may consider the standing wall as the place of the altar" which seemed probable to him since it had no door and had a high window; third, that the stones at the base were large, near the top smaller; and finally, "it had not the appearance of being restored"!

[53] On Hugh, see the notice in August Potthast, *Regesta pontificum Romanorum*, I (Berlin, 1874), 220 (no. 2563): ". . . capella s. Mariae Massiliensis . . . quam Hugo Ferus civis Massiliensis suis sumptibus dicatur construxisse . . ."; also, on the treaty of peace between Pisa and Marseilles dated August 27, 1210, in which Hugh seems to have played a part, Archives municipales de Marseille, AA. 11, cited by Raoul Busquet, "L'Origine des viguiers et des vigueries en Provence," *Provincia*, I (1921), 66, note 7: "Ugo Ferus ejusdem civitatis . . . vicarius". Hugh is, in fact, the prototype of the Provençal *viguier* of the future (*ibid.*); there are several notices of him in H. de Gérin-Richard and Émile Isnard, *Actes concernant les viscomtes de Marseille et leurs déscendants* (Monaco and Paris, 1926), *passim*.

[54] He was active in the Genoese war against Pisa in 1205 (*Annales Januenses*: *Ogerii Panis annales*, ad ann. 1205 [*MGH*, *SS.*, XVIII], p. 123).

[55] See the documents of 1216 and 1218 which he witnessed, in J. L. A. Huillard-Bréholles, *Historia diplomatica Friderici secundi*, I, ii (Paris, 1852), 485, 489, 492, 530.

[56] *Annales Januenses*: *Marchisii scribae annales*, ad ann. 1221 (*MGH*, *SS.*, XVIII), pp. 146–147.

sources), and hanged him and his sons at Palermo.[57] Aubrey apparently tied together three independent incidents to produce a story of two evil merchants selling Christian children into Moslem slavery, plotting against the emperor, and finally meeting a fitting end at the hands of the hangman.

In fact, there is no independent evidence that either was hanged; nor, unfortunately, that Hugh Ferreus, *viguier* of Marseilles, and William Porcus, "amiralio de Misina", even knew one another. If there were, Aubrey's story would be strengthened considerably. If, however, one may accept the suggestion of Reinhold Röhricht, that Aubrey (or, after so many years, his informant) got his names mixed up, and substituted the name of the notorious William Porcus for the obscure William of Posquères, then most of the difficulties disappear. There is evidence that William of Posquères and Hugh Ferreus were associated in 1190, at the siege of Acre during the Third Crusade, when Guy of Lusignan granted commercial privileges in Acre to the citizens of Marseilles.[58]

It was inevitable that Aubrey's account contain some absurdities, depending as it did on the memory of one who was trying to recall events of some eighteen years earlier, and easily tempted into exaggeration. Four hundred clerics, among them eighty priests, is an obvious case in point. But to deny that clerics were present at all would be to misinterpret the temper of the time. Most of the more reliable sources indicate that the expedition included many grown-ups, and one may safely assume that priests and those in lesser orders were no more immune to the contagion of that hot summer than other adults, although the number participating would be small. Aubrey's account also seems to fit with the rest of our meager knowledge: the tradition that the children were sold into slavery; the fact that Bougie and Alexandria were the commercial centers of North Africa most frequented by merchants of Marseilles at this time; that Marseilles was a slave mart of some importance.[59] While we must continue, therefore, to discount what seems

[57] Huillard-Bréholles, *Historia diplomatica Friderici secundi*, II, i, 254; cf. Ernst Kantorowicz, *Frederick the Second (1194–1250)* (New York, 1931), pp. 128–129; Eduard Winkelmann, *Kaiser Friedrich II.*, I (Leipzig, 1889), 188–189; Michele Amari, *Storia dei musulmani di Sicilia*, III, ii (2nd ed., Catania, 1938), 609–612.

[58] J. P. Papon, *Histoire générale de Provence*, II (Paris, 1778), xxiv–xxvi (no. 25); R. Röhricht, *Regesta regni Hierosolymitana* (Innsbruck, 1893), p. 186; cf. *idem*, "Der Kinderkreuzzug," *Historische Zeitschrift*, XXXVI (1876), 5, note 4, citing Louis Méry and F. Guindon, *Histoire analytique et chronologique des actes et des délibérations du corps et du conseil de la municipalité de Marseille*, I (Marseilles, 1841), 190–192, and with incorrect date 1187.

[59] R. Busquet and R. Pernoud, *Histoire du commerce de Marseille*, I (Paris, 1949), 169 ff.

exaggerated and absurd, there is no point in throwing out the baby with the bath. The main lines of the story seem acceptable enough.

The Children's Crusade had a pathetic end, but this did not prevent writers of the thirteenth century, and even later, from drawing the obvious moral. "This work was not of God";[60] the Devil was behind it,[61] or the Old Man of the Mountain,[62] or "a certain evil man";[63] Stephen of Cloyes may have been a boy in years, but he was most vile in his way of life, and his followers perished through the design of Satan.[64] The disapproval, however, though stemming from a well grounded fear of social unrest and popular upheaval, succeeded neither in modifying popular expressions of religious enthusiasm nor in branding the Children's Crusade as devilish work. There would be other examples of mass hysteria of children, not always, to be sure, connected with the crusade. For instance, in 1237 some thousand or so children danced and leaped their way from Erfurt to Arnstadt. Although their parents went out and brought them home the next day, some of the children continued ill for some time, suffering from trembling of the limbs.[65] From the slight notices we have of the matter, it seems to have been an early form of St. Vitus' dance.

This episode has a certain affinity with the legendary case of the children of Hameln, in the diocese of Minden. On the day of Sts. John and Paul, June 26, 1284, there came over the bridge and in through the Weser gate a young man of thirty years, whose beauty and fine dress everyone admired. He had a silver flute, and when he played it all the boys who heard him, to the number of 130, followed him out through the Eastgate to the place where beheadings were held, called "Calvary" by the villagers. There they all disappeared. The mothers of the missing children ran from town to town, but could find no trace of them. And, so the tale goes, as one would

[60] *Annales Reineri* (*MGH, SS.*, XVI), p. 665.

[61] *Annalium Admuntensium cont.* (*MGH, SS.*, IX), p. 592; cf. the late fifteenth-century account of Werner Rolewinck, *Fasciculus temporum*: "Pueri xx milia et amplius de alamania convenientes diabolica machinatione decepti crucesignantur, quasi per eos deus vellet recuperare terram sanctam, secundum illud 'Ex ore infantium' etc. Sed cum ad mare venissent, a piratis dolose in naves rapiuntur quasi eos ad iherusalem ducere promittentibus, verum multos submerserunt alios vendiderunt sarracenis" (University of Pennsylvania MS., Lat. 85, f. 36v).

[62] See Hansbery, "Children's Crusade," p. 31, note 3.

[63] Roger Bacon, *Opus majus ad Clementem IV*, ed. Samuel Jebb (Venice, 1750), p. 189: "post quendam malignum hominem".

[64] Matthew Paris, *Chronica majora* (ed. H. R. Luard [Rolls Series, LVII], II), p. 558: "puer aetate fuit et moribus pervilis". Cf. Rolewinck, *op. cit.*: "Sic patet quomodo diabolus eciam suas cruces predicavit."

[65] J. F. C. Hecker, *Child-Pilgrimages*, pp. 353, 360.

ordinarily reckon the date according to the birth of the Lord, or as such and such a year after a jubilee, in Hameln it is done according to the year of the disappearance of the children.

Here is the earliest surviving version of the well known story of the Pied Piper of Hamelin — without, as yet, any rats. It comes from a fifteenth-century manuscript, but reports an older tradition: "These things I have found in an ancient book. And deacon John of Lügde's mother saw the children go off."[66] What really happened to these children we do not know. The actual event is obscured by the later legend, and there is no contemporary evidence. But it can hardly be doubted that we are in the presence of yet another of the sudden and inexplicable seizures from which juveniles in the mass suffer from time to time — a phenomenon not unknown in our own day.

Even more important than these examples, however, is the rising of the shepherds in France in 1251. They planned to go to the Holy Land to rescue their king, Louis IX. Here again are all the confused elements of restlessness, religious hysteria, and blind violence generally to be feared in movements of this kind. The "Master of Hungary", as the leader was called, had his *epistola caelestis* in a hand which he always kept closed — a command from the Virgin to preach the crusade to the lowly shepherds, since the military pride of the Franks was displeasing to God. The movement is thus akin to the Children's Crusade, all the more so because of the area of its origins (Picardy, Flanders, Brabant, and Hainault) and its heterogeneous composition of men, women, and children. Matthew Paris even accuses the Master of being an old leader of the Children's Crusade "around forty years ago". Though at first favored by the queen, Blanche of Castile, the movement quickly degenerated into a lawless rabble. Everywhere they went there were scenes of terror and bloodshed: at Rouen, where they ejected archbishop Odo and his clergy from the cathedral; at Orléans, where they clashed with the scholars and killed or threw into the Loire some twenty-five of them, wounding many more; at Tours, where they assaulted the Dominican convent, profaned the churches, even mutilated a statue of the Virgin. Later the Master, with the greater number of his followers, occupied Bourges, where one of the

[66] The growth of the legend is traced in Heinrich Spanuth, *Der Rattenfänger von Hameln: vom Werden und Sinn einer alten Sage* (Hameln, 1951), in which there is a photographic reproduction of the page in the MS. in question, giving the earliest form of the legend (at p. 16). See also Waltraud Wöller, "Zur Sage vom Rattenfänger zu Hameln," *Wissenschaftliche Zeitschrift der Humboldt-Universität zu Berlin*, Gesellschafts- und sprachwissenschaftliche Reihe, VI (1956–1957), part 2, 135–146.

citizens, an "executioner with a two-edged sword," says Matthew, "sent him headless to hell"; his body was left to be eaten at the crossroads, while his followers were dispersed "and were everywhere cut down like mad dogs".[67]

The Children's Crusade, while it had chiliastic undertones, never went so far as to invite this kind of destruction. Though opposed by responsible elements of society, it was nevertheless tolerated since it retained the form and appearance of a crusade and did not challenge established authority so far as we know. Seen in its historical setting, however, it remains one of a series of social explosions through which medieval men and women — and children, too, wonderfully sympathetic to the agitations of their elders — found release. But history has not viewed it in this way. Instead, despite the general disapproval of those who lived at the time, it has been the beauty of little children doing God's work, and the pathos of little children sold into slavery, which have stirred the imagination of later ages.

[67] Matthew Paris, *Chronica majora*, V, 246 ff. Cf. Élie Berger, *Histoire de Blanche de Castille, reine de France* (Bibliothèque des Écoles françaises d'Athènes et de Rome, LXX, Paris, 1895), pp. 393–401.

X
THE POLITICAL CRUSADES OF THE THIRTEENTH CENTURY

What is a political crusade? In one sense, of course, every crusade is political, for every crusade aims at conquest, at replacing the rule of unbelievers by that of Christians. But there is an obvious difference between a crusade against the Saracens — or even against the Albigensians — and a crusade against Manfred or Peter of Aragon. In the first case, political means are being used for a

The political crusades are so closely connected with the general history of the thirteenth century that a complete bibliography would be impossibly long. The most important documents are in the papal registers. Those of Innocent III were edited by Bréquigny and reprinted in Migne; the registers of most of the other thirteenth-century popes have been published by the Écoles françaises d'Athènes et de Rome. J. L. A. Huillard-Bréholles published the acts of Frederick II and his sons in the *Historia diplomatica Friderici secundi* (7 vols. in 12, Paris, 1852–1861). J. F. Böhmer, *Regesta imperii*, V: *Die Regesten . . . 1198–1272* (ed. Julius Ficker, 2 parts, Innsbruck, 1881–1882) contains useful material, especially for the period after 1250. The *MGH* for this period give not only important chronicles, but also some collections of documents such as the *Constitutiones et acta publica imperatorum* (Legum Sect., IV), and the *Acta pacis ad S. Germanum anno MCCXXX initae* (Epistolae selectae, IV). Italian chronicles may be found in the *MGH* or in Muratori, *RISS*. The important life of Innocent IV by Nicholas of Carbio (or Curbio) was first published by Muratori (*RISS*, III); there is a better edition by Pagnotti in the *Archivio della Società romana di storia patria*, XXI (1898). English chronicles are in the Rolls Series; of these, Matthew Paris is especially important for the documents given in his *Additamenta* (vol. VI of the Rolls Series edition). French chronicles are printed in the *RHGF*; this series also includes useful documents, especially on the crusade of 1285. The *Layettes du trésor des chartes* and Winkelmann's *Acta imperii inedita* (Innsbruck, 1880–1885) contain less than might be expected. The same may be said of the documents of the Angevin kings edited by G. Del Giudice, C. Minieri Riccio, and G. Silvestri. There is some useful material in I. Carini, *Gli Archivi e le biblioteche di Spagna, in rapporto alla storia d'Italia in generale e di Sicilia in particolare* (Palermo, 1884–1897). Finally, the letters of Albert von Beham, edited by C. Höfler (*Bibliothek des litterarischen Vereins in Stuttgart*, XVI, 1847) throw some light on German affairs in the 1240's.

The only book which gives a general survey of material covered in this chapter is H. Pissard, *La Guerre sainte en pays chrétien* (Paris, 1912), and Pissard is more concerned with the development of canonical doctrine than with the details of the crusades. In spite of its title, O. Volk's *Die abendländisch-hierarchische Kreuzzugsidee* (Halle, 1911) refers to our topic only occasionally. It does discuss the inchoate political crusades of the eleventh century, and for this problem P. Rousset, *Les Origines et les caractères de la première croisade* (Neuchâtel, 1945) and C. Erdmann. *Die Entstehung des Kreuzzugsgedankens* (Stuttgart, 1935) should also be consulted. E. Jordan, *L'Allemagne et l'Italie au XIIe et XIIIe siècles* (Paris, n.d.) and K. Hampe, *Deutsche Kaisergeschichte in der Zeit der Salier und Staufer* (Leipzig, n.d.) are both excellent

religious end — the redemption of the holy places or the destruction of heresy. The political consequences are not part of the primary plan of the church: Urban II is not working for the establishment of a kingdom of Jerusalem, nor does Innocent III particularly desire the creation of a great principality for Simon of Montfort. The second type is doubly political in that neither means nor end has any direct connection with the spiritual objectives of the church. The popes may talk about punishing association with heretics and Saracens, but what they really want to do is to replace a disobedient king with one who will not defy their policies. The crusade against infidel and heretic is waged for the good of

general accounts of the thirteenth-century struggle between the papacy and the Hohenstaufen rulers. The last part of the conflict is discussed in detail in Jordan's very solid work on *Les Origines de la domination angévine en Italie* (Paris, 1909). Information about Innocent III's crusade in Sicily may be found in F. Baethgen, *Die Regentschaft Papst Innocenz III. im Königreich Sizilien* (Heidelberg, 1914) and T. C. Van Cleve, *Markward of Anweiler* (Princeton, 1937). There is no good general account of the crusades against Frederick II; biographers such as Kantorowicz mention them only in passing. W. Koester, *Die Kreuzablass im Kampfe der Kurie mit Friedrich II.* (Münster, 1912) deals with one aspect of the crusades in both Germany and Italy. C. Köhler, *Das Verhältnis Kaiser Friedrichs II. zu den Päpsten seiner Zeit* (Breslau, 1888) is not very helpful. For Italian crusades, see J. Felten, *Papst Gregor IX.* (Freiburg, 1886); H. Frankfurt, *Gregorius de Montelongo* (Marburg, 1898); and, best of all, C. Rodenburg, *Innocenz IV. und das Königreich Sizilien 1245–1254* (Halle, 1892). Material on the crusade in Germany may be found in O. Hintze, *Das Königtum Wilhelms von Holland* (Leipzig, 1885), and F. Reh, *Kardinal Peter Capocci* (Berlin, 1933). The crusade against Ezzelino of Romano is described in O. Canz, *Philipp Fontana, Erzbischof von Ravenna* (Leipzig, 1910). For the crusade against Manfred, see, in addition to Jordan, K. Hampe's fine study on *Urban IV. und Manfred* (Heidelberg, 1905) and R. Sternfeld, *Karl von Anjou als Graf von Provence* (Berlin, 1888). The best account of the brief crusade against Conradin is in Hampe, *Geschichte Konradins von Hohenstaufen* (Leipzig, 1942). The plans of Charles of Anjou to attack the Byzantine empire are discussed in C. Chapman, *Michel Paléologue* (Paris, 1926); F. Carabellese, *Carlo d'Angio nei rapporti politici e commerciali con Venezia e l'Oriente* (*Documenti per la storia di Bari*, X, Bari, 1911); and W. Norden, *Das Papsttum und Byzanz* (Berlin, 1903). There is a good chapter on the crusade against Aragon in Ch.-V. Langlois, *Le Règne de Philippe III le Hardi* (Paris, 1887); see also J. R. Strayer, "The Crusade against Aragon," *Speculum*, XXVIII (1952), and W. Kienast, "Der Kreuzkrieg Philipps des Schönen gegen Aragon," *Historische Vierteljahrschrift*, XXVIII (1933–1934), 673–698. For the historical background to the Sicilian Vespers, with much useful bibliography, see H. Wieruszowski, "Politische Verschwörungen und Bündnisse König Peters von Aragon gegen Karl von Anjou am Vorabend der sizilianischen vesper," *Quellen und Forschungen aus italienischen Archiven und Bibliotheken*, XXXVII (Tübingen, 1957), 136–191. A recent account in English is S. Runciman, *The Sicilian Vespers* (Cambridge, 1958).

Material on the financing of the crusades is collected in W. E. Lunt's fine study of *Financial Relations of the Papacy with England to 1327* (Cambridge, Mass., 1939), and (less satisfactory) in A. Gottlob's *Die päpstlichen Kreuzzugs-Steuern des 13. Jahrhunderts* (Heiligenstadt, 1892). Gottlob's *Kreuzablass und Almosenablass* (Stuttgart, 1906), while dealing more with earlier periods, has some useful data on indulgences for political crusades. The analyses of papal and imperial propaganda, such as F. Graefe, *Die Publizistik in der letzten Epoche Kaiser Friedrichs II.* (Heidelberg, 1909), are not very helpful for our problem. Far more useful is C. Merkel, "L'Opinione dei contemporanei sull' impresa italiana di Carlo I d'Angiò," *Atti della R. Accademia dei Lincei*, ser. 4, Classe di scienze morali, storiche, et filologiche, IV (1888), which gives a good summary of the opinions of chroniclers and poets about the crusades against Manfred and Conradin. Finally, G. Digard's two volumes on *Philippe le Bel et le Saint-Siège* (Paris, 1936), though not definitive, contain much evidence on the deterioration of relations between the papacy and France.

Christendom as the pope understands it. The crusade against Hohenstaufen and Ghibelline is waged to protect the states and the political authority of the papacy.

The difference between the two kinds of crusades is not merely a modern refinement; it was apparent to men of the thirteenth century. The great canonist Henry of Segusio, usually known as Hostiensis, who had seen political crusades at close hand, states the distinction very clearly in his *Summa*.[1] He reports that he found many men in Germany who argued that a crusade against Christians was neither just nor decent. These men admitted that crusades against infidels, or even heretics, were justified, but denied that there was any legal basis for a crusade against rulers who were merely disobedient to the pope. Hostiensis gives the official answer, that disobedience to the commands of Christ's vicar on earth is almost sure to lead to heresy, and that attacks on the unity of the church are far more dangerous than loss of land, however holy, overseas. But he is not very optimistic about the effectiveness of these arguments and concludes that the overseas crusade will always seem more desirable to the "simple", even though the crusade against disobedient Christians is more reasonable.

More reasonable, perhaps, but the church was not so rationalistic before the thirteenth century. There had been some talk of remission of sins for the soldiers who died fighting for Leo IX against the Normans, and Gregory VII had given full absolution to the opponents of Henry IV, but in neither case was there the full equivalent of the crusade indulgence. Moreover, churchmen of the twelfth century were less willing to use force than the eager leaders of the eleventh-century reform movement. Gratian is clearly embarrassed in discussing the problem of the use of force against heretics and excommunicated Christians. He concludes that war against such enemies of God and the church is just, but he does not equate it with the crusade in the Holy Land.[2] Bernard of Clairvaux is even more doubtful. He admits that a defensive war against heretics may at times be necessary, but he prefers the methods of peaceful persuasion.[3] On the whole, except for a half-hearted and unsuccessful attempt of Alexander III (1159–1181) to organize an army to attack the Albigensian heretics, the popes of the twelfth century were not inclined to use the crusade against inhabitants of Christian Europe. Even when Barbarossa drove

[1] Hostiensis, *Summa aurea*, III, 34 (de voto), paragraph 19 (in quo casu).

[2] *Decretum*, secunda pars, causa XXIII. See especially quest. V, c. 47, and quest. VIII.

[3] H. Pissard, *La Guerre sainte en pays chrétien* (Paris, 1912), pp. 22–23.

Alexander from Italy and installed an anti-pope at Rome, there was no talk of a crusade against the emperor.

Here, as in so many other cases, the great innovator was Innocent III (1198–1216). Determined to be obeyed, sure of his rights, he took without hesitation the momentous step of proclaiming a crusade in order to preserve what he regarded as the political rights of the church. In 1199, hardly a year after his election as pope, Innocent first threatened, and then actually ordered, a crusade against Markward of Anweiler and his adherents. The opponents of Markward wore the cross and received the same indulgences as those who fought in Palestine. It is true that Markward had touched Innocent on two of his most sensitive spots. A loyal follower of Henry VI, he had attempted to keep control of the march of Ancona after the emperor's death, even though Innocent was determined to add it to the states of the church. Driven from the mainland by Innocent, Markward took refuge in Sicily and began harassing the regency which Innocent had set up for his ward Frederick II. But why was Innocent so sensitive on these two points? It took almost a decade to convince him that a crusade against the Albigensian heretics was the only solution to a difficult problem. Why did he react so promptly against Markward, who was far less dangerous to the faith? The only possible answer is that Innocent had become convinced, during the pontificate of his predecessor, that it was absolutely essential to the security and independence of the papacy to gain direct control over central Italy and to make the most of its feudal suzerainty over the kingdom of Sicily. These convictions became a settled part of papal policy, and were the cause of most of the political crusades of the thirteenth century.

Innocent's action was more important as a precedent than as a military operation.[4] A few hundred soldiers sent against Markward accomplished nothing. Innocent then turned to Walter of Brienne, who had a claim to Taranto and Lecce, and Walter enlisted a small group of Frenchmen who were given crusading privileges. But Walter was far more interested in conquering his fief of Taranto than in fighting Innocent's enemies, and the affair dragged on until Markward removed the chief reason for a crusade by dying

[4] If Innocent threatened a crusade against John at the height of the crisis over Stephen Langton (1212), then he was ready to follow and expand his own precedent soon after it was made. But it is not certain that he did so; see S. Painter, *The Reign of King John* (Baltimore, 1949), pp. 188–192, and C. R. Cheyney, "The Alleged Deposition of King John," in *Studies . . . presented to F. M. Powicke* (Oxford, 1948). The writer's own belief is that Innocent went no further than to threaten deposition; certainly, no crusade was formally proclaimed.

in 1202. Innocent had not been able to give much support to his Sicilian crusade. The great Fourth Crusade was being organized just at this time, and while Innocent once threatened to divert the whole army to Sicily, it is doubtful that he really meant it. Possibly some of Walter's men had originally taken the vow to go overseas, and were allowed to substitute an expedition to Sicily, but we know nothing of these details. We can say that Innocent, unlike some of his successors, did not sacrifice an overseas crusade to an Italian war, and that he used only the barest minimum of the prestige and money of the church in his attack on Markward.

And yet the precedent was there, and it was to be followed, even down to the excuses which Innocent gave to justify his action — the alliance of Markward with the Saracens of Sicily and the need to have Sicily in friendly hands if the Holy Land was to be saved. During the thirteenth century five popes in succession were to preach political crusades, crusades to preserve the independence of the states of the church and the dependence of Sicily on the papacy. There were good reasons for inaugurating this policy, as for everything Innocent did, and yet one may wonder whether the welfare of the church was really so dependent on political arrangements in Italy. Peter Damian had given a warning at the beginning of papal involvement in Sicilian affairs which should have been remembered: if the martyr may not fight for his faith, how can the church fight for worldly and transitory goods?[5]

Two other precedents set by Innocent were important for the future of the political crusades. In the first place, that same year 1199 which saw the crusade against Markward also saw the first income tax imposed by the pope on the clergy. This tax was for the Holy Land, but it showed later popes how to raise money for the great political crusades against the Hohenstaufens. In the second place, the Albigensian Crusade, while not primarily political, had such important political results that in many ways it set a pattern for the purely political crusades of later years. In order to break the power of feudal rulers who were alleged to be either heretics of abettors of heresy, Innocent elaborated a brief sentence in the *Decretum* into a fully developed theory of what might be called ecclesiastical forfeiture. Gratian said that Catholics might justly take the property of heretics; Innocent claimed the right of "exposition": that is, if a ruler failed to repress heresy, and if his superior would not or could not force him to do his duty, then the pope might offer the territory to any zealous Catholic who

[5] P. Rousset, *Les Origines et les caractères de la première croisade* (Neuchâtel, 1945), p. 48.

would assume the obligation of conquering it.[6] Such a theory allowed the pope to organize armies to carry out his policies in European countries, and by the end of the century it was being used not only against heretics, but also against rulers who were merely disobedient.

Thus Innocent III had worked out all the essential theories and practices of the political crusade. His successors showed, at first, some reluctance to follow his example. Honorius III (1216–1227), in spite of repeated provocation, never found it necessary to preach a holy war against his Italian opponents. The much more sharp-tempered Gregory IX (1227–1241) hesitated to use the full crusade vocabulary in his first struggle with Frederick II from 1228 to 1230. He was thoroughly angry with Frederick for disobeying papal orders, and he was beginning to worry about the strong position which the emperor was acquiring in Italy. Gregory accused Frederick of grave crimes: he was oppressing the Sicilian church and making a mockery of the overseas crusade by iniquitous pacts with the Saracens. He was breaking his most solemn promises by invading the papal states and trying to regain lands ceded to the church. And yet, in his denunciations and appeals for help, Gregory never used the word "crusade". Frederick was denounced unsparingly; he was the enemy of the liberty of the church, he was guilty of lèse-majesté against God. His subjects were released from their oath of fidelity and the pope suggested that he had deprived himself of the imperial dignity through his treaties with the Saracens. These were accusations which in the next decades invariably preceded a political crusade, but Gregory did not take the final step of offering the cross and overseas indulgences to those who fought against Frederick.

Short of this, however, there was nothing which he did not do. He raised, in his own words, "three armies" to clear the papal states of imperialists and to invade the kingdom of Sicily. He asked for military aid from the Lombard League, Genoa, an Infante of Portugal, German magnates, and French bishops. His letters of 1229 to archbishop Robert of Lyons and bishop William of Paris on this subject are especially interesting; they show exactly where Gregory drew the line. They are ordered to bring the pope a suitable number of armed men, in virtue of obedience and for the remission of their sins and those of their soldiers. But while Gregory

[6] Pissard, *La Guerre sainte,* pp. 37–40; *Decretum,* secunda pars, causa XXIII, quest. VII, c. 2.

speaks of remission of sins in general terms, he avoids the precise language of Innocent III, who had promised opponents of Markward the same remission of sins as that granted to those who fought the Saracens in Palestine. Even in writing to the Lombards Gregory shows the same restraint; they are promised remission of sins but not a full crusade indulgence.[7]

This war for defense of the church, to stay within Gregory's terms, did set one important precedent. It was financed, as crusades were coming to be financed, by an income tax imposed on the clergy by the pope. The tax could not be collected in lands which remained under the emperor's power, but we know that the clergy of Sweden, Denmark, England, and northern Italy all paid a tenth of their revenues in 1229 to support the war. The case of the French clergy was a little different since they were already paying a five-year tenth, imposed in 1225 for support of the Albigensian Crusade. That crusade had ended in 1226, and Gregory asked that the final payments be sent to him for the war against Frederick. He was fairly successful in this request and received about 100,000 *livres tournois* from France. At the same time, he asked for financial aid from king Eric Läspe of Sweden, and the king and barons of England. Laymen had no enthusiasm for his war and it is doubtful that he received anything from these sources; the English refused his request with some indignation.

Laymen might protest, but the clergy had to obey. A crusade tax had been used to support a papal war in Italy; a tax for a crusade against heretics in France had been diverted to raise an army to punish a rebellious emperor. The pope had discovered the way to finance his military operations, to pay for the secular support which he had to have in order to achieve his political objectives. For the first time, the papacy could afford a first-class war.

The initial struggle with Frederick II, however, was not entirely successful. The papal armies started with real enthusiasm. Wearing the sign of the Keys of Peter (here again Gregory avoided crusade symbols) they stormed into the mainland territories of the kingdom of Sicily. Frederick's prompt return from Syria frightened them into retreat, and the papal army was getting decidedly the worst of the fighting when peace was arranged in 1230. Frederick was conciliatory and did not, at this time, desire an all-out war with the papacy. Gregory was still suspicious of the emperor, but he was running short of men and money. The bishops of Beauvais and

[7] Lucien Auvray (ed.), *Les Registres de Grégoire IX*, I (Paris, 1896), cols. 211 ff. (nos 350, 351, 352).

Clermont brought a few men from France, but it is doubtful that there was much response to Gregory's appeal in Germany, even though Frederick forgave some Germans for fighting against him. The Lombards were slow in sending help, and in the end gave only a few hundred men. The greater part of the papal army must have been composed of Italians from Tuscany and the papal states, men who were interested primarily in the affairs of their own communes, not in the pope's plans for the future of Italy. Gregory secured a rather favorable peace, considering his military position, and could at least console himself with the thought that prompt defense had saved the states of the church from Frederick's aggression.

Gregory's behavior in 1228 and 1229 suggests that this notable canonist was not quite sure that it was proper to preach a crusade against a Christian ruler, however disobedient. But while Gregory as a canon lawyer may have had scruples, Gregory as a politician must have wondered if a promise of crusade indulgences would have produced a better response to his appeals for aid. At any rate, in his next struggle with Frederick, Gregory no longer tried to make a distinction between a crusade and a war for the defense of the church, and offered the same indulgences as those received by crusaders in Palestine.

The real causes of the great papal-imperial war, which began in 1239, were Gregory's invincible distrust of Frederick, and Frederick's attempts to extend his power to northern Italy. If Frederick had confined himself to Sicily, there would have been friction — since he treated the Sicilian clergy harshly — but perhaps no complete rupture. But when Frederick tried to make good the claims of the empire to rule Lombardy, he created an exceedingly dangerous political situation for the pope. As the emperor himself said, he needed control of Lombardy in order to bring German troops into Italy. With a continuing supply of German soldiers, paid for with the wealth of Sicily, Frederick could dominate the peninsula and wipe out the independence of the papal states. The pope would have had these suspicions in any case; Frederick did his best to confirm them by his singularly tactless behavior. He won a great victory over the Lombard towns in 1237, but instead of accepting a reasonable settlement he insisted on complete submission. He tried to stir up the Romans against the pope; he tried to acquire Sardinia (claimed by the papacy) as a kingdom for one of his illegitimate sons. Gregory could not let the Lombards be crushed; they were the one force in Italy which could fight the emperor on even terms. He could not believe Frederick's promises to respect the rights of the church, for Frederick had already demonstrated an unhealthy ability to wriggle out of the most solemn engagements. So, on March 20, 1239, he excommunicated the emperor, and began a war which was to end only in 1268, with the execution of the last male Hohenstaufen.

From a purely political viewpoint, Gregory was undoubtedly right. Frederick already had nearly absolute power in the south and he was close to gaining full control of the north. If he had been able to dominate Lombardy, it would have been difficult to preserve the independence of the states of the church, and even of the city of Rome. From the viewpoint of the church as a religious organization, the decision was more doubtful. In the first place, Frederick's permanent success was by no means assured. Many able men were to try to unite the turbulent cities of northern and central Italy; none of them ever succeeded in building up more than a temporary and unstable domination. Even if Frederick had been successful and had gained control of all papal territory, he would not have controlled the church. The popes of the twelfth century who had taken refuge in France in times of trouble had gained rather than lost prestige; as Bernard of Clairvaux said, it had not hurt them to exchange the City for the world. The kings of the west would not have tolerated an assertion of imperial authority over the church in the thirteenth century. By making war, Gregory preserved the states of the church and the independence of the Italian towns, but he involved the papacy in political operations which, in the end, weakened its influence.

Gregory, as before, began hostilities with excommunication and the release of Frederick's subjects from the oath of fidelity. He took special pains to make sure that all western Europe learned of his act, and the reasons for it. Frederick, of course, circulated his version of the quarrel, but neither side gained much support by this appeal to public opinion outside Italy. The first mention of a crusade seems to have come early in 1240,[8] almost a year after the excommunication, when the emperor was threatening Rome. Gregory, like every thirteenth-century pope, was not sure of the loyalty of the Romans and tried to stir up their zeal for the church by a great religious procession. At the end he showed them the holiest relics of the Roman church — the heads of the apostles Peter and Paul — and called on them to defend the liberty of the

[8] It is possible that the crusade was first preached in Lombardy late in 1239; see W. Köster *Der Kreuzablass im Kampfe der Kurie mit Friedrich II.* (Munster, 1913), p. 21.

church against this "new Herod". Crosses were distributed among the multitude, and for a brief period the city was almost unanimous in its support of the pope and hostility to the emperor. The papal legate in Milan was permitted to preach a crusade in order to raise an army to support the papal cause in Lombardy, and crusade preaching was also authorized in Germany.

We have no detailed description of the benefits offered in 1240 to crusaders against Frederick, but a papal letter of February 12, 1241, shows that by this time Gregory was making every possible concession to gain support for his crusade. Crusaders against Frederick were to have the same indulgences as those granted to defenders of the Holy Land. When papal agents in Hungary complained that their attempts to gain recruits were hampered by the fact that many Hungarians had taken the vow to go to Palestine, Gregory authorized them to commute such vows to a crusade against Frederick. He also suggested that crusade vows might be redeemed for appropriate sums of money, and authorized such redemptions in order to raise funds for defense. In short, by February 1241 at the latest, he was not only preaching a full-fledged crusade against Frederick, but was giving it priority over a crusade overseas.[9]

Before Gregory had fully developed the idea of a crusade against Frederick, he began to ask the churches of the western kingdoms for financial aid in his war against the emperor. Much of his correspondence on this subject is lost, but while he accused Frederick of heretical behavior and of attacking church lands, he does not seem to have used a crusade as an excuse for his demands. The English clergy were asked for aid late in 1239. A tax of one fifth of their revenues was imposed on foreign clerks beneficed in England, but the native clergy were allowed to discuss the amount they would offer. There was great opposition to the pope's request, and it took most of 1240 to secure grants from the clergy of the different dioceses. Many objected that there was no clear case against the emperor and that the pope was setting a bad example by shedding Christian blood. In the end they all had to agree to make some contribution — in most dioceses a twelfth of their revenues — but collections were slow and Innocent IV was receiving arrears as late as 1244. Grants were also made in Scotland and in Ireland, though the rate is not definitely known. The clergy of France gave the pope one twentieth of their revenues, but some

[9] *Les Registres de Grégoire IX*, no. 5362; the complete letter may be found in A. Theiner, *Vetera monumenta historiam Hungaricam sacram illustrantia*, I (Rome, 1859), 178 (no. 327).

of the money was reserved for other expenses. There was even an attempt to collect a fifteenth in some German dioceses, but Frederick forbade the clergy to pay, and they were probably quite willing to obey. Even in countries which were willing to pay, collection of the grants was slow; at least Gregory was heavily in debt when he died.

The war did not go well for the pope despite his efforts to stir up enthusiasm for the papal cause. The preaching of a crusade had only fleeting results. It roused the people of Rome and of Milan to drive back imperial armies early in 1240, but it did not produce a permanent army which could be used for a long campaign. Outside Italy the crusade had even less effect. The Germans were distressed by the conflict and tried to mediate between pope and emperor. When this effort failed, they gave little support to either side and rejected papal suggestions that they should choose a new king in place of Frederick. In other countries the laity did not even discuss the question of aiding the pope. Meanwhile the war in Italy degenerated into a series of local conflicts in which each side tried to hold its own towns and capture those of the enemy through surprise attacks or alliances with disgruntled minorities. Frederick had somewhat the better of this game, and Gregory realized that a new effort was necessary. On August 9, 1240, he issued a summons for a general council, to be held at Rome in March of the following year.

A general council was a serious threat to Frederick. He had been insisting that his quarrel was with the pope, not the church, that Gregory's personal hostility and vindictiveness were the only cause of the war. Condemnation by a council would make it harder to maintain this position, and might lead to increased support of the pope in the trans-Alpine kingdoms. But while Frederick had reason to fear the meeting of a council, the steps which he took to prevent it hurt him almost as much as the meeting could have done. Many of the clergy called to the council were proceeding to Rome in Genoese ships, since the emperor's control of northern Italy made land travel unsafe. A Pisan fleet, under Frederick's orders, routed the Genoese near Monte Cristo, and captured most of the prelates, including two cardinals. Gregory had to spend the few remaining months of his pontificate in seeking release of the prisoners, and the plans for the council were dropped.

Frederick had killed the council, and in doing so had more or less killed Gregory IX. The old pope, working feverishly to recover from his defeat, wore himself out and died in August 1241. But

Frederick paid a high price for his temporary success. He had attacked the church in the person of its bishops; he had changed his personal quarrel with Gregory into an irreconcilable war with the papacy. He had seriously offended the rulers of the northern kingdoms, notably Louis IX of France, by capturing their subjects. Peace with the church was now almost impossible, and in the long war that was to follow public opinion was less favorable to Frederick than it had been before. The Germans, who had tried to preserve neutrality under extreme papal pressure, began to turn against the emperor after 1241, and opposition in northern Italy became more dangerous.

These were long-run results; the immediate effect of Frederick's blow was to shatter the confidence of the college of cardinals. They were not sure how to deal with their terrible opponent, and their uncertainty made it difficult for them to agree on a new pope. The vacancy lasted almost two years (not counting the fifteen-day pontificate of Celestine IV), but the cardinals finally picked, on June 25, 1243, an able and uncompromising head of the church. Sinibaldo Fieschi, who took the name Innocent IV (1243–1254), was a canonist, like most of the popes of his century, and had worked out a strong theory of papal supremacy. He was also a Genoese and was determined not to sacrifice the people of northern Italy to the emperor. It is difficult to believe that Frederick had any illusions about the pope's pliability, but he at once began negotiations for peace, in line with his contention that Gregory IX alone had been responsible for the quarrel.

As long as the negotiations were confined to generalities some progress was made, but when acts were required, neither side would make real sacrifices. Frederick would not give up the eastern part of the papal states; Innocent would not allow him any real power in Lombardy. The pope finally decided that negotiation was useless, and determined to put himself and the Roman curia in security before renewing hostilities. He slipped away to Genoa and then took refuge in the even safer city of Lyons. There he issued a call for a general council to meet in June 1245.

This time Frederick could not block the meeting. Lyons was not yet French, but it could easily be protected by the French king, and Louis made it clear that he would not permit a repetition of the scandal of 1241. The bishops assembled without difficulty, and accepted the papal decree deposing Frederick from all his thrones — the empire, Sicily, and Jerusalem. The charges were much the same as before — oppression of the clergy, attacks on papal lands, bad faith, undue intimacy with Saracens, and suspicion of heresy — but back of the formal charges lay Innocent's conviction that he could not be really pope while Frederick dominated Italy. The deposition was a declaration of war and was accepted as such by both sides.

There were three main areas where Innocent hoped to weaken Frederick. The first was Germany, where imperial power was already low and where the great princes had virtual autonomy. Here he set up anti-kings — first Henry Raspe of Thuringia, then William of Holland — and used the wealth of the church to buy soldiers and alliances for his puppets. This tactic was never entirely successful, though William of Holland gained control of a large part of northwest Germany, but it did deprive Frederick of badly needed support. He had few ardent adherents in Germany, and these men were so busy defending themselves against papal attacks that they could not send military aid to the emperor.

The next field of action was northern Italy. Here the intensity of local interests and rivalries made it impossible to carry out any general policy. The Lombard League still existed, but it no longer functioned as a unit. Each town had to defend itself; the most it could hope for was to receive reinforcements in time of great danger from a few of its nearest allies. Innocent had a capable legate in Lombardy, Gregory of Montelongo, but Gregory had to spend his energy in organizing the defense of one threatened town after another. Fortunately for the pope, the emperor was in exactly the same situation, and the war in northern Italy resolved itself into a long series of sieges, captures, and defections of individual towns. Frederick had somewhat the worst of the struggle, especially after his defeat at the siege of Parma in 1248, but he always retained the allegiance of parts of Lombardy and Tuscany.

The third area of conflict was the kingdom of Sicily, which included all southern Italy. Legally, Innocent had a better case here than anywhere else. Sicily was a fief of the church, and the pope's right to confiscate the lands of a rebellious vassal was much clearer than his right to depose a hostile emperor. But Frederick had a stronger hold on Sicily than on any other of his domains, and he had protected his frontier by seizing a large part of the papal states. The march of Ancona and the duchy of Spoleto had to be regained by papal forces before anything could be attempted against Sicily, and this task absorbed most of the energy of the papal legates in central Italy. Innocent's only hope of gaining Sicily was through a general rebellion of Frederick's subjects or a full-scale invasion by a papal army. Both methods were tried, and both proved unsuccessful. A rebellion, encouraged by the pope, failed completely in 1246, and an invading army, led by the cardinal-legate Peter Capocci in 1249, never got far beyond the frontier.

During the war with Frederick, Innocent used crusade preaching and crusade propaganda most intensively in Germany. From the middle of 1246 to the death of the emperor in 1250 a steady stream of papal letters urged the preaching of the crusade in Germany and dealt with the financial and administrative problems caused by the taking of crusading vows. In Italy, on the other hand, while the crusade is mentioned occasionally, it seems much less prominent in papal plans. It was not greatly needed in Lombardy, where the towns would fight for independence in any case, and it was of no use in Sicily as long as Frederick kept the clergy of the kingdom under his thumb. It was used mainly as a device for heartening the inhabitants of threatened towns and for enabling papal legates to raise relief expeditions. The crusade was most effective in the papal states, but even there it produced no large, permanent army.

Even in Germany, where the crusade was vigorously preached, and where the energetic legate Peter Capocci used his very full powers to persuade large numbers of men to take the cross, the pope relied on other weapons much of the time. Threats of excommunication or interdict, promises of church offices, and dispensations from impediments to marriage were at least as useful in bringing princes to support the anti-kings as talk of crusade benefits. In the sporadic fighting between the imperialists and William of Holland the crusade was seldom mentioned. The army which took Aachen for William in October 1248 was full of crusaders, and William later received some help from Germans who had taken crusade vows, and who satisfied them by fighting under his banner. But in Germany as in Italy, the crusade produced momentary bursts of enthusiasm rather than a permanent army. The crusaders from the Low Countries went home as soon as Aachen was taken, and William of Holland was often short of soldiers in the following years.

This lack of emphasis on the crusade is curious, given Innocent's conviction that Frederick was the great enemy of the church and that any means could be used against him. It is probable that he was embarrassed by the fact that Louis IX was engaged in an overseas crusade during the very years that the struggle with Frederick reached its climax. The overseas crusade was still the only real crusade in the eyes of the "simple" (as Hostiensis pointed out), and it would have been unwise to push a political crusade at the expense of an expedition against the infidel. As it was, the French were unhappy about the competition between the two movements and Innocent had to act carefully to avoid antagonizing them. Thus, while he ordered his legate in Germany to stop preaching the crusade against the Saracens in order to clear the way for a crusade against Frederick, he also told him to keep the order secret. While, in Germany proper, vows to serve in Palestine could be commuted to vows to fight the emperor, Innocent forbade commutation in the border dioceses. He seems to have been especially bothered by the case of the Frisians, even though they were subjects of William of Holland. He first gave them permission to change their vow, then ordered them to aid William, then reversed himself completely and insisted that they go to Palestine. Such hesitations made it hard to carry on the crusade in Germany with any enthusiasm.[10]

On the other hand, while the crusade against Frederick did not result in any great military operations, it was successful as an excuse for raising money. A contemporary biographer estimates that Innocent spent 200,000 marks in his struggle with Frederick. Some of this may have come from ordinary papal revenues, but the greater part must have been raised by redemptions of crusade vows and by special taxes imposed on the clergy. We know that Italians beneficed in trans-Alpine countries had to contribute a fourth or a half of their income, depending on the value of the benefice. The English clergy promised a subsidy of 11,000 marks, and this did not include payments from exempt monasteries. The clergy of Poland and Hungary also paid a subsidy, and large sums were raised in German dioceses which were not controlled by the Hohenstaufens. But the wealthy church of France could not be asked to contribute, since it was already paying a tenth to Louis for his crusade overseas.

In spending the money he collected, Innocent again concentrated on Germany, where Frederick was weakest. Large sums went to the anti-kings and their supporters: Henry Raspe was given 25,000 marks and William of Holland 30,000. This left the papacy relatively weak in Italy; one reason for the failure of the papal invasion of Sicily in 1249 was lack of money. Innocent needed far more money than he had, but he could not increase his demands on the clergy. There had been violent protests against papal taxation at the Council of Lyons in 1245, and the protests continued during

[10] Élie Berger (ed.), *Les Registres d'Innocent IV*, I (Paris, 1884), cols. 439 ff. (nos. 2935, 3054, 3779, 3967, 3968, 4070).

the next five years. The pope could force the clergy to pay, but he could not force them to be silent, and excessive complaints might have swung public opinion back to the side of the emperor.

When Frederick died at the end of 1250, the pope had not won a clear-cut victory. Sicily was still firmly under Hohenstaufen control, and the imperial position in northern and central Italy, while weakened, was by no means hopeless. Frederick had regained many towns in the march of Ancona in the last year of his life, and he still had allies in Lombardy. The pope had won his greatest advantage in Germany, where William of Holland had gained enough support to absorb most of the energy of the imperialists. After 1250 the popes did not have to worry about Germany, and they chose not to worry about Lombardy. Instead, they concentrated on the strong point in the Hohenstaufen position, the kingdom of Sicily.

This concentration on Sicily forced a change in tactics. As long as the papal-imperial war was fought mainly in northern Italy and Germany, a carefully organized papal army was not absolutely essential. Lombardy and Germany were full of natural enemies of the Hohenstaufens; all they needed was a little papal encouragement. But Innocent had learned that Sicily was so well organized, so bound by its old habits of obedience, that successful rebellion was impossible, and the only way to gain control of the kingdom was to attack it with a large army. The pope could not raise such an army in his own states or in Italy; outside help was needed. And to obtain such an army the full use of crusade techniques was essential. Up to 1250 the political crusade had been a device for stirring up momentary enthusiasm to repel an immediate danger and an excuse for raising money. After 1250 political crusades were planned and organized exactly like overseas crusades; large armies were raised, paid for with clerical tenths, and sent to conquer the enemies of the church.

The need for this new policy was only gradually realized by the popes. To the end of his pontificate, Innocent IV swung back and forth between two plans, now seeking the aid of English or French princes, now attempting to conquer Sicily with his own resources. After his death in 1254 there was less hesitation, and Urban IV (1261–1264) definitely committed the papacy to the policy of calling in a large crusading army to settle the Sicilian affair.

Frederick's death caused a shift in the direction of the papal attack; it did not end the war between the papacy and the Hohenstaufens. Innocent was too deeply committed to the policy of annihilating Hohenstaufen power; as early as 1247 he had promised the Lombards that neither Frederick nor his sons would ever be allowed to rule as king or emperor.[11] Papal prestige was at stake; if Frederick's deposition was valid, his sons could not inherit any of his realms. An atmosphere of suspicion and hate had been created in which it was hard to imagine that any pope could ever trust any Hohenstaufen. Innocent did not hesitate for a moment. In February 1251 he ordered the crusade preached throughout Germany against Frederick's heir, Conrad IV, and authorized the use of all papal letters directed against Frederick for the new war. In March he repeated his solemn promise — this time to the Germans — that the apostolic see would never allow any descendant of Frederick to rule in Germany or Italy. But while he kept up the pressure on Conrad in Germany, Innocent's real interest had shifted to Sicily. Manfred, an illegitimate son of Frederick II, was ruling the kingdom as regent for his half-brother Conrad, and Innocent could hope that an untried ruler with incomplete power might be vulnerable to a papal attack. A rebellion was started in the Terra di Lavoro (Caserta province), and archbishop Marino of Bari was told to encourage the rebels by preaching a crusade against the sons of Frederick. Meanwhile cardinal Peter Capocci was to raise an army in the march of Ancona and invade the kingdom from that base.

Both moves failed. Manfred gradually suppressed the rebellion (except in Naples and Capua), and the cardinal's army was too weak to advance far beyond the border. Innocent then tried negotiating with Manfred, hoping to play on his reluctance to surrender the kingdom to his brother. Manfred might have gone over to the papal side if he had been offered enough, but Innocent promised him only the principality of Taranto, which was his anyway by the terms of Frederick's will. So Manfred continued his resistance, and when Conrad landed at Siponto in January 1252 the regent dutifully surrendered the kingdom. The pope had gained little by his efforts, and when Naples surrendered in 1253, he lost his last foothold south of the papal states.

This experience convinced Innocent, for the moment, that he needed outside help. He continued to talk of the crusade against Conrad—crusade preaching was ordered in Germany in both 1253 and 1254—but he did not take it very seriously. It was little more than a device which made it possible to raise money for William of

[11] *Les Registres d'Innocent IV*, no. 3024.

Holland and his supporters. In 1252 and 1254 he carried on some rather useless negotiations with Conrad, useless because Conrad insisted on being recognized as king of the Romans, and Innocent could not abandon his candidate, William of Holland. But the pope's real policy was to be found in another set of negotiations, which were being conducted, secretly and skillfully, by a papal notary, Albert of Parma. Albert was commissioned to offer the kingdom of Sicily, with proper guarantees of papal rights, to either an English or a French prince and to promise the recipient full crusading privileges and the financial support of the church. This time there was to be a real attack on the center of Hohenstaufen power, not a mere demonstration by a small papal army.

Albert first approached Richard of Cornwall, brother of Henry III of England. Richard showed little interest in the scheme, so Albert turned to the French king's brother, Charles of Anjou. Charles was an ambitious and able politician, always anxious to increase his wealth and power; he was quite ready to listen to Albert's proposition. He carried the negotiations to a point where Innocent was almost sure that he would accept, bargaining shrewdly to decrease the restrictions placed on his power and to increase the financial aid given by the church. But Charles began to lose interest as he realized the difficulties, and a disputed succession in Flanders and Hainault, which gave him an opportunity for easier and quicker gains, made him decide to abandon the project. When he was offered the county of Hainault in return for helping countess Margaret of Flanders, he broke off negotiations with Albert in the fall of 1253.

The pope had to turn back to England. The new candidate was Edmund of Lancaster, the second son of Henry III. He was still too young to lead an army; Henry himself would have to organize the expedition. This was not an ideal solution; Henry had been both incompetent and unlucky as a military leader, and he was not on good terms with his barons. Albert seems to have been a little doubtful, and let the negotiations drag, even though Henry demanded much less than Charles in the way of financial support. Innocent had good reason to be grateful to his envoy for the delays, because Conrad IV died on May 21, 1254, just as the pope was about to confirm the grant of Sicily to Edmund.

This unexpected death — Conrad was only twenty-six — gave Innocent a chance for another quick reversal of policy. Conrad's heir was a baby in Germany, and he left a German, Berthold of Hohenburg, as regent of Sicily because he did not trust his half-brother Manfred. Berthold was not a man of great ability and was handicapped by being a foreigner. Manfred, who was able and popular, had no official position, and was anxious to save his principality of Taranto. Innocent at last had a chance to take over the kingdom peacefully, since there was no strong leader to oppose him. He played skillfully on Sicilian dislike of German rule, and so weakened Berthold's position that he resigned the regency to Manfred. By that time so many nobles had gone over to the pope that Manfred felt he could not risk a war. He made the best bargain he could for himself — he was to keep Taranto and be vicar of most of the mainland — and then surrendered the kingdom to Innocent.

The pope entered the realm on October 11, 1254, and was accepted everywhere as the rightful ruler. Apparently the long struggle had ended with a complete victory; the Hohenstaufens had lost their main source of strength and the pope had added a rich kingdom to the weak and poverty-stricken states of the church. But Manfred had been left in a difficult position; he was not fully trusted by the pope, and his rights were not fully respected by the more ardent supporters of papal rule. A dispute over land led to a fight, and when Manfred's men killed one of his chief adversaries, Manfred was sure that the pope would seize this opportunity to deprive him of all his holdings. After all, he was a Hohenstaufen, even though an illegitimate one, and Hohenstaufen excuses had not been very acceptable to the popes for the last quarter-century. Manfred fled to the hills, raised a rebel army (including his father's old Saracen body-guard), and soon was able to attack the papal forces. A victory early in December almost dissolved the papal army, and Innocent died in Naples a few days later. Manfred gained ground steadily, and it soon became apparent that the church could not keep control of the kingdom. The whole wearisome "Sicilian business" had to be taken up again by the new pope.

As frequently happened, the cardinals chose a mild and easy-going successor to an energetic and uncompromising pope. Alexander IV (1254–1261) had belonged to the party among the cardinals who favored compromise rather than fighting, and as pope he patiently endured aggressions which would have enraged Gregory IX or Innocent IV. That such a man felt that he had to continue the war with Manfred is an indication of the momentum which the Italian policy of the papacy had acquired. At first Alexander kept up the fight with his own resources, but he soon saw that outside help was needed. He turned again to Henry III and Edmund, and on April 9, 1255, formally granted the kingdom of Sicily to the English prince. Henry promised to send an army to Italy by the fall of 1256, and to pay all papal war expenses until his soldiers arrived. These were finally estimated at 135,541 marks. In return, his vow to go to the Holy Land was commuted to a pledge to support the crusade against Manfred. He was to receive a tenth of the revenues of the English clergy for five years, and the usual small change from proceeds of redemption of crusade vows, legacies for the Holy Land, and estates of crusaders who died without fulfilling their vows.

The story of Henry's attempt to fulfill these conditions is more important in English history than in the history of the crusades. He never raised enough money to pay the pope's war expenses, much less enough to send an army to Italy. The collection of the tenths made the English clergy angry with both pope and king, and the request for a grant from the laity led directly to the barons' rebellion in 1258. English money did make possible a brief campaign by a papal army in 1255, but this was completely unsuccessful and ended with the capture of the cardinal-legate Octavian at Foggia. By 1258 both Alexander and Henry were completely discouraged. Henry was ready to give up his son's claims if the pope would restore some of the money he had received. Alexander naturally rejected this request, but in the next year he suspended Edmund's claim to Sicily until Henry paid all he owed.

Meanwhile Manfred had gained complete control of the kingdom. At first he claimed to be acting in the interests of his nephew Conradin, but in 1258 he took the title of king. Even worse, from the papal point of view, he began to form alliances and to claim authority as imperial vicar in Tuscany and Lombardy. There was no legal justification for this claim, since imperial authority was not hereditary, and even if it had been, Manfred was not Frederick's heir. But, in the confused state of politics in northern Italy, no one worried greatly about legality; Manfred was able and successful, and the remnants of Frederick's old party rallied around him.

Alexander had no idea of how to deal with Manfred. When the English alliance, which had been prepared by his predecessor, failed, he could find no substitute. But while he had no success in dealing with Manfred, he was able to gain a little ground in Lombardy, which had been rather neglected by Innocent IV in the last years of his pontificate. There the first tyrants were beginning to appear, and the two most powerful, Ezzelino of Romano and Oberto Pallavicini, were closely connected with Manfred. Ezzelino was a tyrant in every sense of the word, so detested by most of the Lombards that a crusade preached against him late in 1255 stirred up real popular enthusiasm. Venice, Ferrara, and Mantua furnished large contingents; many individuals joined the army, and Alexander picked an able, if worldly, legate, Philip Fontana, to lead the crusade. Padua was taken from Ezzelino in June 1256, but this success exhausted the interest of the Lombards in the crusade. Personal and municipal quarrels broke up the union against Ezzelino, and while the crusade was continued for another three years, it had little effect. In the end Ezzelino was defeated by an alliance between the pro-papal Este family and the pope's other great Lombard enemy, Oberto Pallavicini. This removed the most dangerous tyrant, but Pallavicini remained a power in Lombardy until the advent of Charles of Anjou.

The death of Alexander IV in 1261 enabled the cardinals to make another sharp shift in policy. They chose the patriarch of Jerusalem, James Pantaléon, a prelate who was not a member of their college, but who had gained a reputation as a vigorous administrator. They clearly wanted a more energetic pope; perhaps they also hoped, by electing a Frenchman, to gain the support of the strongest European kingdom for the church's war with the Hohenstaufens. The choice was a momentous one for the future of the papacy and of Europe. James Pantaléon, as pope Urban IV, perfected the technique of the political crusade and prepared the way for the conquest of Sicily by Charles of Anjou. He did this at the price of greatly increasing French influence on church policy and in the college of cardinals.

In the first year of his pontificate, Urban had to adopt a conciliatory policy toward Manfred. The Greeks had just retaken Constantinople, and the Christian foothold in Palestine was threatened by the growing power of the Mamluk sultans. Both the dispossessed Latin emperor Baldwin II of Constantinople and the barons of the kingdom of Jerusalem had powerful friends and relatives in western Europe, especially in France. They could bring great pressure on the pope; they could appeal to the widespread opinion that it was criminal to abandon Latin Christianity in the east in order to gain a political victory in Italy. Urban was forced to negotiate with Manfred, and he did so, though with extreme ill-will. He had no hope and little desire for a peaceful settlement; all he wanted was to demonstrate that it was not his fault if the war continued. Manfred was a little more willing to compromise, but was just as suspicious of the pope as the pope was of him. Real concessions were impossible for either side. Urban was committed to the established papal policy of uprooting the Hohenstaufens and preventing the establishment of a strong secular power in Italy. Manfred felt that he had to keep a foothold in central and northern Italy in order to protect his kingdom from the pope. The negotiations dragged on into 1263, but by this time Urban was already seeking the aid of Charles of Anjou. He had shown that he was a lover of peace, on his own terms; he had proved, to the more pious at least, that Manfred was an incorrigible member of the "viper race". Now he was free to strike.

The negotiations with Charles of Anjou were long and complicated. Charles wanted money for his army and a free hand as king of Sicily; the pope wanted to give as little money as possible and to keep close control over his new vassal. Charles secured some concessions, but the pope gained his main point. Sicily was to be a real vassal kingdom and to give important service to the pope. Neither Charles nor his heirs were ever to acquire the lordship of Tuscany or Lombardy, much less of Germany. Supported by a docile vassal in the south, confronted by only local powers in the north, the states of the church would be entirely safe, and the popes could forget the fear of encirclement which had dogged them since the beginning of the century.

With this important point settled, the pope could be generous in regard to other terms. Charles was to have full crusade privileges for himself and his men, and there was to be crusade preaching in both Italy and France. He was to receive a tenth of the income of the clergy for three years in France and in the ecclesiastical provinces of Lyons, Besançon, Vienne, Embrun, and Tarentaise. Manfred was to be publicly condemned and all those who adhered to him after proclamation of the papal sentence were to forfeit their lands and goods. An argument over Charles's election as a senator of Rome delayed the public announcement of these terms, but essential agreement had been reached by Urban's death on October 2, 1264.

Meanwhile Manfred had begun to harass the pope. He had allies in Tuscany and in the states of the church; his raiders had come very near the city of Rome. Urban had had to preach a crusade against him in central Italy early in 1264. This had produced, as usual, a sudden flash of popular enthusiasm, and Manfred's bands had been driven back from the city. But the war continued, and Urban, in June, had demanded contributions from the Spanish clergy to carry on the fight. Spain had not been asked to contribute to earlier political crusades, but, with England torn by civil war, and French revenues pledged to Charles, it was the only possible source of money.

Urban had been perhaps a little too ready to rely on crusades as a means of achieving his objectives. In 1263 he had had a crusade preached against the Byzantine empire, and another crusade against Manfred's supporters in Sardinia. In the same year he had threatened a crusade against the English barons, if they rejected the efforts of his legates to end their dispute with Henry III. But, while he may have overestimated the efficiency of crusade appeals, he had a clear understanding of the problems of organizing a crusade army. Fervent preaching might recruit soldiers, but only regular pay would keep them beneath the banner of the cross. Papal legates or vicars might beat off a raid on the states of the church, but only an experienced lay general could conquer the kingdom of Sicily. Urban had spent the last months of his pontificate in making sure that Charles of Anjou would have a solid financial base by which to support a large and well trained army. He had not only imposed the tenth on the French clergy (May 3, 1264), but had also used the power of the church to build up a party among Tuscan bankers which would support his plans. By forbidding the faithful to pay their debts to uncoöperative bankers he had almost destroyed the Ghibelline party among Tuscan financiers, and, once these men were committed to the papal side, they were bound to put their resources at the disposal of Charles of Anjou. They made large loans to Charles, guaranteed by the pope, and this money made it possible to carry on through the difficult period before the clerical tenths began to come in. If Charles's expedition was the most successful of all the political crusades, it was largely due to Urban's skill in financing it.

The cardinals hesitated four months before picking Urban's successor. Stronger pressure from Manfred might have prolonged their indecision, but Manfred withdrew most of his troops on hearing of Urban's death. It is difficult, however, to see how basic policy could have been changed; the church was already deeply committed to Charles. In the end the cardinals made as little change as possible: they picked another Frenchman, Guy Foulcois, who became pope Clement IV (1265–1268).

Clement carried on Urban's policy without a break. The formal agreement with Charles was made in April 1265, and Charles himself came to Rome to receive the investiture of Sicily on June 28. He had only a small force with him, and Manfred might have caused him much trouble with a full-scale attack, but the Hohenstaufen ruler merely skirmished in the papal states, and so missed a real opportunity. Meanwhile the main body of Charles's army crossed the Alps in November and marched slowly through Lombardy and Romagna to Rome.

There were still adherents of the Hohenstaufens in these regions, but Clement took the precaution of having a special crusade preached against anyone trying to bar the march of the Angevin army. Papal protection and the strength of the army discouraged opposition; Charles's forces crossed northern and central Italy almost without fighting. In fact, the greatest difficulties during 1265 were financial rather than military; the tenth was paid so slowly that Clement had to pledge the treasures of the churches of Rome for Charles's final loans.

Charles had at least one quality of a great general; he never wasted time. His forces reached Rome only in January 1266; early in February he was already leading them into the kingdom. Manfred met him at Benevento on February 26, with about equal forces, but the French proved superior in fighting ability. Manfred was killed in the battle, and there was no one left to prolong the struggle. The inhabitants of the kingdom accepted Charles as their ruler; the papacy had achieved its great political objective.

Charles's quick success had not completely discouraged the opposition. Two years later the sixteen-year-old Conradin, son of Conrad IV, made a sudden raid into Italy to claim his inheritance. He was received with surprising enthusiasm by many Italians, and was even welcomed in Rome by a friendly senator. Meanwhile a serious rebellion broke out in the island of Sicily and most of the barons of the mainland rose against Charles. Events came so rapidly that there was hardly time to organize a crusade, but Clement did his best for Charles. Crusade preaching was ordered on April 13, 1268, and many Tuscans joined Charles's army as a result. Charles's loans from Sienese bankers were guaranteed by the pope. But Charles was saved by his own generalship and the skill of his French soldiers rather than by the forces recruited through the crusade. He met Conradin near Tagliacozzo on August 23, three days after the young prince had invaded the kingdom. Charles was probably outnumbered, but, by throwing in his reserves at a critical moment, he won a hard-fought battle. Conradin was captured a few days later, and was condemned and executed in Naples in

October. His execution and the fact that the pope made no effort to save him show how badly he had frightened both Charles and Clement.

Charles was an ambitious man, and during the decade and a half which followed the conquest of Sicily the popes at times wondered whether they had really gained by substituting the energetic Frenchman for the rather feckless Hohenstaufen. He was just as eager as Manfred to make his influence felt in northern and central Italy, and his irreproachable orthodoxy, combined with the prestige of his victories, made him much more difficult to oppose. Charles's efforts to extend his power in Italy, however, had no direct influence on the history of the crusades. His other expansionist project, the conquest of the restored Byzantine empire, did have a direct impact on every crusade plan made between 1266 and 1282. It also led, indirectly, to the Sicilian Vespers and thus to the crusade against Aragon in 1285.

In trying to gain control of Greece and the Balkans, Charles was following the example of both his Norman and his Hohenstaufen predecessors. The situation in the east seemed to invite a renewal of Sicilian intervention. Michael VIII Palaeologus held only a fraction of the old Byzantine empire and was especially weak in its western portions. His bitter opponents, the Angeli, ruled Epirus and Thessaly. Western princes, survivors of the Latin empire, held large parts of Greece and many of the islands. The Serbian and Bulgarian states in the northern Balkans were eager to extend their boundaries and were potential allies of any invader. Against this host of enemies the emperor Michael could oppose only his diplomatic skill and his possession of interior lines, which enabled him to use his small army with great effectiveness.

Charles began making plans for an invasion of Byzantine territories within a year of his conquest of Sicily. He realized that his first objective must be to unite all the potential opponents of the Palaeologi. By the treaty of Viterbo (1267) he gained most of the rights of the deposed Latin emperor Baldwin II, including suzerainty over the Frankish principality of Achaea.[12] He also took over Manfred's holdings in Albania, most important of which was Durazzo, and succeeded in having himself elected king of Albania in 1271 or 1272. This title added little to his strength, though he

[12] J. Longnon, "Le rattachement de la principauté de Morée au royaume de Sicile en 1267," *Journal des Savants*, 1942, p. 136; *idem*, *L'Empire latin de Constantinople*, pp. 236–237 On Charles's relations with Achaea, see above, chapter VII, pp. 255–261.

tried to push inland from his Albanian coastal bases on several occasions. Finally, by persistent diplomatic activity, Charles tried to obtain the support of Hungary, Serbia, and Bulgaria, and the assistance of the Venetian fleet.

Charles's plans were perfect in theory, but it was difficult to coördinate all these operations to produce the overwhelming attack which would have annihilated the Byzantine empire. There is an element of high comedy in the diplomatic history of the years between 1267 and 1282; again and again Charles was almost ready to strike when some unforeseen event forced him to postpone his plans. Charles, of course, was not entirely free to concentrate all his attention on the east. He had to safeguard his interests in Italy and he had to have the support, or at least the acquiescence, of the pope. Michael Palaeologus understood this situation perfectly, and many, though not all, of Charles's setbacks were caused by Michael's adroit maneuvers in the west.

The first check was Conradin's invasion in 1268. This was quickly disposed of, but by that time Louis IX was well advanced in his plans for a new crusade. An account of his negotiations with Charles is given elsewhere;[13] it is enough to say here that Charles could not avoid postponing his eastern expedition and joining in the crusade, although he did succeed in modifying its objective. Louis's death at Tunis freed Charles from any obligation to continue the crusade; he made a quick and profitable peace and returned at once to Sicily. He might have persuaded some of his fellow-crusaders to join him in an attack on the Byzantine empire, but the great storm which sank most of the Franco-Sicilian fleet at Trapani made the expedition impossible. By the time that Charles could rebuild his fleet the crusade had long been dispersed. Troubles in northern Italy and a war with Genoa (which was allied to emperor Michael) kept Charles occupied for the next two years.

The next major obstacle to Charles's plans came from an unexpected quarter, the papacy. Both Gregory X (1271–1276) and Nicholas III (1277–1280) were worried by the extent of Charles's power in Italy and saw little advantage to the church in allowing Charles to increase his power by conquests in the east. Gregory X, in addition, was anxious to save what was left of the kingdom of Jerusalem. He had been legate in Syria at the time of his election and he realized that only the united efforts of all western rulers could stem the Mamluk advance; a diversion against Constantinople

[13] See below, chapter XIV, pp. 508–518.

would be fatal to his hopes of restoring the Christian position in Palestine. He devoted his whole pontificate to an attempt to promote a new crusade; he used Charles's ambitions only as a means of furthering his main objective. If the threat of an Angevin invasion could frighten Michael Palaeologus into coöperating with the Roman church so much the better, but Gregory was not going to allow any large expedition to waste western resources in an attack on the Greeks.

Michael made almost the same estimate of the situation as the pope, which made it easy for Gregory to carry out his policy. Faced with the Angevin threat, the emperor agreed to the union of the churches in 1274 and suggested that he might aid the new crusade. The union was bitterly opposed by the Greeks, but Michael was harsh enough with the dissenters to convince the pope of his good faith. Gregory could not prevent minor skirmishes in Greece and the Balkans, but he did restrain Charles from launching a major expedition. Nicholas III followed the same policy, even though by his time it was apparent that the union would be a failure.

Charles must have suffered during these years of frustration, but he never made the mistake of directly and openly opposing the pope. He waited patiently, gained all the support he could in the college of cardinals, and finally reaped his reward. In 1281 the Frenchman Simon of Brie, an old friend of the Capetian family, became pope under the name Martin IV. At last all the pieces of the long-planned combination against the Byzantine empire were going to fit into place.

At first all went well. The Greek emperor was excommunicated for his failure to make the union effective. Venice joined the alliance against the Byzantines and promised important naval support. Charles began to raise money and troops. The pope granted him the crusade tenth in Hungary and Sardinia, and crusade legacies and redemption of vows in Sicily and Provence. There was a certain ambiguity in these grants; Martin IV declared that they were to be used against the "infidel", and thus did not directly sanction a crusade against the schismatic Greeks.[14] The official French historian, William of Nangis, took the same view; he ignored Charles's obvious plans to attack the Byzantine empire and declared that he was going to fight the Saracens and reconquer the kingdom of Jerusalem.[15] But Bartholomew of Neocastro,

[14] *Les Registres de Martin IV*, Bibliothèque des Écoles françaises d'Athènes et de Rome, ser. 2, vol. XVI, part 1 (Paris, 1901), nos. 116, 117.

[15] *RHGF*, XX, 516. For Charles's claim to the kingdom of Jerusalem, see below, chapter XVI, pp. 583–591.

speaking for the Sicilian opponents of the Angevins, was not deceived. He asserted that this would have been a political crusade of the same sort as the one against Manfred. The cross Charles bore was not the cross of Christ, but that of the unrepentant thief, and in its name he was going to attack the friendly Greeks, just as in its name he had shed innocent blood in his earlier wars.[16]

The combination of Charles's careful planning and papal support might have been irresistible; certainly Michael Palaeologus had never been in a more dangerous position. He was saved by the great rebellion known as the Sicilian Vespers, which made it forever impossible for the Angevins to attack the Byzantine empire.

Charles of Anjou had been no easier master to Sicily than his Hohenstaufen predecessors; like them, he had imposed heavy taxes in order to carry on an ambitious foreign policy. His use of French officials added to his unpopularity, especially in the island of Sicily. Many natives hated him; many foreign rulers had cause to fear him. In the period just before 1282 a complicated and still imperfectly known plot was formed against him, involving exiles from the kingdom, old allies of Manfred in northern Italy, the Byzantine emperor, and Peter III of Aragon. Peter was the most dangerous of these enemies; he had a claim to the kingdom through his wife Constance, the daughter of Manfred, and he possessed the best navy in the Mediterranean. The plotters probably hoped that when Charles launched his long-planned attack against Constantinople the kingdom would be left relatively defenseless, but before Charles could sail or they could strike a popular uprising in the island of Sicily upset all plans. The famous Sicilian Vespers of March 30, 1282, wiped out the French garrison of the island, but the king of Aragon did not profit immediately from the rebellion. The rebels at first talked of substituting a league of communes under papal suzerainty for the monarchy; only when Charles launched a dangerous counterattack did they become convinced that they needed a protector. They offered the crown to Peter of Aragon; on August 30 he landed at Trapani and took over the island.

Martin IV, as a Frenchman and supporter of the Angevins, probably reacted more violently to the Sicilian revolution than an Italian would have done. Looked at cold-bloodedly, the establishment of the Aragonese in Sicily was by no means an unmixed evil for the papacy. Charles of Anjou had not been an easy ally; his

[16] *Historia Sicula* (ed. Giuseppe Paladino, *RISS*, XIII, part 3), 10–11.

attempts to gain the hegemony of northern Italy had worried several popes, and his hope of conquering Constantinople had for many years been a disturbing factor in European diplomacy. A reduction in his power could be advantageous to the papacy, especially as it became clear that Peter of Aragon did not have the slightest chance of conquering the mainland and renewing Hohenstaufen aggression against the papal states. But Martin took his stand on higher ground than that of expediency. A papal vassal had been treacherously attacked; the papal sentence denying Sicily to anyone of Hohenstaufen blood had been flouted. The Capetian dynasty, the bulwark of the church, had been injured, and if the injury were not avenged, the French might be less willing to act as champions of the papacy in the future. Martin did not hesitate to take extreme measures. Peter was excommunicated in November 1282, and deprived — in theory — of his kingdom of Aragon on March 21, 1283.

Martin hoped at first that these threats, combined with a new counterattack by Charles of Anjou, would discourage Peter. He soon saw that more force was needed, and sent a legate to France to organize a crusade against Aragon. The negotiations followed closely the pattern set by Urban IV in his dealings with Charles of Anjou. Aragon was to be a papal fief, held by Charles of Valois, the second son of Philip III ("the Bold") of France, on terms very like those under which Charles of Anjou had received Sicily. The French clergy, and those of most dioceses of the old Middle Kingdom, were to pay Philip a tenth of their revenues for four years to finance the expedition. Philip and his followers were to have full crusade privileges. There was some haggling over terms, and some opposition in the royal council, but in February 1284 Philip accepted the throne of Aragon for his son.

Philip faced the same financial problem which had annoyed Charles; he needed large sums of money before the crusade tenths were fully paid. He solved it more easily, thanks to the strength of the French monarchy. An aid was paid by his lay and ecclesiastical vassals, and "gifts" were taken from the towns. His subjects lent him large sums of money, probably on easier terms than the Tuscan bankers had offered Charles. He hired a large number of ships, recruited an army of at least 8,000 men, and was ready to begin his expedition in the spring of 1285.

Peter was in a difficult position. The nobles of Aragon were trying to limit his power and resented his interest in Sicily; they responded badly when he called them to arms. His strongest weapon, the navy, was being used to protect Sicily from the Angevins. In the circumstances, he conducted a remarkably skillful campaign. He delayed Philip as long as he could at the line of the Pyrenees, but refused to risk a pitched battle when his position was turned. Philip advanced rapidly through Catalonia, but was halted again at the strongly fortified position of Gerona. The French army wasted the summer in besieging this town; illness and incessant raids by Peter's troops diminished its strength. By early September Peter was able to recall his fleet to the western Mediterranean, where it almost annihilated the ships in the service of France. Since Philip's army was supplied largely by sea, this blow forced him to retreat. He withdrew most of his army safely, but he himself died at Perpignan on October 5, 1285.

The new king of France, Philip IV ("the Fair"), had probably opposed his father's decision to engage in the crusade. In any case, the events of 1285 must have convinced him that the attack on Aragon was futile. He did enough talking about the crusade to gain a new three-year grant of tenths from the French clergy, but he did not repeat the invasion of Aragon. He was quite ready to make peace, and eventually a settlement was reached in which Charles of Valois was indemnified for his claim to Aragon by receiving the county of Anjou from his cousins of Naples.

The popes were less willing to face facts. For the rest of the century they continued to support the Angevins with men and money, and at one point a quarrel between the heirs of Peter III gave them great hopes of regaining Sicily for their favored dynasty. In the end, however, they had to accept the division of the kingdom. Sicily remained in the hands of a younger branch of the Catalan-Aragonese royal family, while the descendants of Charles of Anjou ruled at Naples. No strong power was left in Italy, either to oppress or to protect the states of the church. This was not an unmixed blessing, as the turmoil of the fourteenth century was to demonstrate, but at least it removed the need for large-scale political crusades.

In spite of the failure of the crusade against Aragon, the papacy had, on the whole, achieved its political objectives. Both the empire and the mainland half of the kingdom of Sicily had been taken away from the unfriendly Hohenstaufens and placed in the hands of rulers who were obedient to the church. Both the empire and the kingdom had been so weakened that they could not threaten the papal states, even if they were to fall again under the control of enemies. But the church had paid a high price for this political victory. It is not fair to blame the disunity of Germany and Italy entirely on the popes of the thirteenth century — tendencies in that direction were already strong before 1200. But, insofar as the thirteenth-century popes encouraged the growth of disunity and opposed efforts toward unification and strong government, they can be blamed for the Italian anarchy which prolonged the Avignonese exile of the papacy and for the German anarchy which made possible the Reformation.

Even more important, the political crusades were one of the factors which weakened the leadership of the church and encouraged the transfer of basic loyalty from the church to the secular state. We know little about the state of public opinion in thirteenth-century Europe, but what little we know suggests a growing antipathy to the political program of the papacy and a weakening loyalty to the ideal of a Christian commonwealth. The complaints of chroniclers and poets about the avarice and ambition of the popes are not conclusive; there are not enough of these to prove general opposition to papal policy. For one Matthew Paris, who criticizes the papacy, there are a dozen chroniclers who give at least tacit approval to the war against the Hohenstaufens. In any case, a chronicler or poet speaks only for himself; we cannot assume that he represents the opinion of a large group. When we turn to protests by churchmen, and official acts of kings, we have better evidence. Bishops and ecclesiastical assemblies did not oppose the pope unless they felt sure of some support; kings did not tax the clergy until they were convinced that their barons would back them in attacking the liberties of the church. During the second half of the thirteenth century we find both protests by large numbers of churchmen and interference with ecclesiastical privileges by kings.

The English clergy made repeated protests against the demands of Innocent IV and Alexander IV for subsidies for their Italian wars. The French clergy paid the tenths for Charles of Anjou grudgingly; Clement IV complained of the ill-will of the bishops and the lack of zeal of the collectors. One cleric of Rheims argued that the claim that the tenth was needed for the defense of the faith was false, since a war against Manfred did not concern the faith. Many pious churchmen agreed with archbishop Giles of Tyre that it was scandalous when men who had taken a vow to go overseas were urged to join the expedition against Sicily or when legacies for the Holy Land were used to make war on Manfred.[17] If the

[17] Pierre Varin, *Archives législatives de la ville de Reims* (Collection de documents inédits sur l'histoire de France, ser. 1, histoire politique, I, Paris, 1840), 452–453; E. Jordan, *Les Origines de la domination angévine en Italie* (Paris, 1909), pp. 538–539.

clergy were discontented, the laity cannot have been enthusiastic about papal policy. Moreover, the more the clergy felt oppressed by the pope, the less they were willing to oppose the growing interference of secular rulers in ecclesiastical affairs. Why should they risk exile and loss of revenue to defend the rights of their churches, when the pope ignored those same rights whenever it suited his interests? The churchmen who had paid tenths to the pope for his wars were not especially shocked when lay rulers demanded similar contributions for their wars.

The behavior of lay rulers supports the conclusion that loyalty to the church had been weakened by the political crusades. The crusades were not the only cause of the decline in papal prestige, but there is a direct connection between them and certain assertions of lay supremacy. From 1245 on, the popes had granted tenths to French and English princes to enable them to fight for the church; by the end of the century the kings of France and England had become accustomed to receiving these subsidies and insisted that they could impose them for their own purposes. The attempt of Boniface VIII (1294–1303), in the bull *Clericis laicos*, to stop this practice was completely unsuccessful. Laymen paid no attention to his orders, and the clergy begged him to revoke a ruling which made them odious to the people. Boniface, in the end, had to admit the right of kings to take tenths for defense of their realms. The use of crusades in secular politics had made it easy for kings to take over the crusade tax on the clergy.

Soon after *Clericis laicos* a political crusade helped revive the quarrel between Philip the Fair and Boniface VIII. Two cardinals who were members of the great Roman family of the Colonna had not been pleased by the election of Boniface VIII. Boniface resented their attitude, and in 1297 used an act of brigandage by a lay member of the family as an excuse to demand the complete submission of the Colonnas. The cardinals, instead of giving in, resisted, and issued public statements claiming that Boniface was not the rightful pope. Boniface preached a crusade against the Colonnas, and succeeded in capturing their castles and driving them into exile. But Philip the Fair did not assist the pope in this political crusade, as his ancestors had done. Instead, he let the Colonnas take refuge in his territory and used them in 1303 in his attack on Boniface at Anagni. And in accusing Boniface of heresy, in trumping up charges and seeking public support against him, Philip used many of the tricks of propaganda which the popes had developed in their political crusades.

Papal taxation and petty crusades in Italy had certainly weakened papal prestige, but it could be argued that the expedition against Aragon in 1285 had done it more harm than had anything else. On the Spanish side, the excommunication of Peter III and the proclamation of a crusade against him had had very little effect. Even though the barons of Aragon had been quarreling violently with their king, they had had no use for an intruder imposed on them by the pope. On the French side, the crusade had led to a strong reaction against papal policy. The expedition had been opposed by Matthew, the influential abbot of St. Denis, and, probably, by the heir to the throne. In any case, the failure of the crusade and the death of his father must have made a strong impression on Philip the Fair. He was only seventeen when he became king; the unhappy memories of the crusade and the diplomatic and financial problems into which he was plunged may well have made him unfriendly to the church. Certainly he began by asserting firmly his authority over his own clergy; during the first five years of his reign the popes made repeated protests against his attacks on the rights of French churches. He showed little interest in crusades or Mediterranean politics. This weakened the alliance between the papacy and France, which had been the dominant feature of European politics for three generations. By depriving the popes of French military support he made it impossible for them to pursue an active policy either in Italy or overseas. Philip was a pious Christian in his private life, but as king he put the interests of the French monarchy far ahead of those of the church. When the two clashed he did not hesitate; he was determined to be master in his own kingdom and to reject any outside interference. Anagni and the exile at Avignon were the logical consequences of the political crusades.

13. The Near East (*Map by the University of Wisconsin Cartographic Laboratory*)

XI
THE FIFTH CRUSADE

A. Preparation and the Efforts of 1217

Although Innocent III had made the best of the results of the Fourth Crusade, he was, of course, disappointed in his hope that the taking of Constantinople would facilitate the conquest of the Holy Land. In the autumn of 1207, however, his former legate to Constantinople, cardinal Benedict, reported on actual conditions in the Latin empire, and thereafter Innocent once more concentrated

The following are the chief primary western sources for the Fifth Crusade: *Chronique d'Ernoul et de Bernard le trésorier* (ed. L. de Mas Latrie, Paris, 1871); *Chronica regia Coloniensis*, in *Scriptores rerum Germanicarum in usum scholarum* (ed. G. Waitz, Hanover, 1880); Emo, *Chronicon* (ed. L. Weiland, *MGH, SS.*, XXIII); *L'Estoire d'Eracles empereur* (*RHC, Occ.*, II) James of Vitry, *Historia Iherosolimitana*, in J. Bongars (ed.), *Gesta Dei per Francos* (Hanover, 1611), I, 1047–1124; Oliver Scholasticus, *Historia Damiatina* (ed. H. Hoogeweg, *Die Schriften des Kölner Domscholasters, späteren Bischofs von Paderborn und Kardinal-Bischofs von S. Sabina Oliverus*, in *Bibliothek des litterarischen Vereins in Stuttgart*, CCII [Tübingen, 1894], 159–282). Of the sources collected in R. Röhricht, *Quinti belli sacri scriptores minores* (Geneva, 1879) and *Testimonia minora de quinto bello sacro* (Geneva, 1882), both published by the Société de l'orient latin, the following are of chief importance: *Gesta crucigerorum*; *Gesta obsidionis Damiate*; John of "Tulbia" (Tolve), *De domino Iohanne rege Ierusalem*; and *Liber duellii Christiani in obsidione Damiate*. The English sources of primary importance are: Matthew Paris, *Chronica majora* (ed. H. R. Luard, 7 vols., 1872–1883, Rolls Series, LVII); Ralph of Coggeshall, *Chronicon Anglicanum* (ed. J. Stevenson, 1875, Rolls Series, LXVI); and Roger of Wendover, *Flores historiarum* (ed. H. G. Hewlett, 3 vols., 1886–1889, Rolls Series, LXXXIV).

The letters of principal value as sources are: *Innocentii III epistolae*, in *PL*, vols. CCXIV–CCXVI, and in *RHGF*, XIX; *Gervasii Praemonstratensis Abbatis epp. ad Innocentium et Honorium*, in *RHGF*, XIX, 604–605, 618–620; and James of Vitry, *Epistolae, 1216–1221* (ed. R. Röhricht, *Zeitschrift für Kirchengeschichte*, XIV [1892–1894], 97–118; XV [1894–1895], 568–587; XVI [1895–1896], 72–114). For Andrew II and the Hungarian Crusade the primary source is *Ex Thomae historia pontificum Salonitanorum et Spalatinorum* (ed. L. von Heinemann, *MGH, SS.*, XXIX, 568–598).

The chief Arabic sources are: Abū-Shāmah, *Kitāb ar-rauḍatain* (Cairo, 1870–1871; extracts tr. in *RHC, Or.*, IV–V); Abū-l-Fidā', *Kitāb al-mukhtaṣar fī akhbār al-bashar* (extracts tr. in *RHC, Or.*, I, 1–165); "Extraits de l'histoire des patriarches d'Alexandrie relatifs au siège de Damiette" (tr. E. Blochet in *ROL*, XI [1908], 240–260); Ibn-al-Athīr, *Al-kāmil fī-t-ta'rīkh* (extracts tr. in *RHC, Or.*, I, II, part 1); al-Maqrīzī, *Akhbār Miṣr* (tr. E. Blochet, "Histoire d'Égypte," *ROL*, VI–XI [1898–1908]).

The principal secondary works for the Fifth Crusade include, first of all, three by R. Röhricht: *Studien zur Geschichte des fünften Kreuzzüges* (Innsbruck, 1891); "Die Belagerung von Damietta (1218–1220): Ein Beitrag zur Kirchengeschichte des Mittelalters," *Historisches Taschenbuch*, ser. 5, V, 6 (1876), 61 ff.; and "Die Kreuzzugbewegung im Jahre 1217," *Forschungen zur deutschen Geschichte*, XVI (1876), 139 ff. Another work of first importance

his efforts on the organization of a new crusade in the west. Yet conditions in western Europe were hardly favorable for the enterprise: Germany was torn by the conflict between Philip of Swabia and Otto of Brunswick, and after the assassination of Philip in 1208, it soon became apparent that Otto's imperial ambitions were irreconcilable with the papal plans. In France the nobility was engaged in the war against the Albigensians, enjoying privileges and immunities similar to those of crusaders in Syria. The bitter territorial conflict between Philip Augustus and John Lackland preoccupied both monarchs, while the attention of Spain was absorbed by the crusade against the Muwaḥḥids (Almohads). The mystical appeal, which had evoked a universal response in earlier crusades, now led only to such fiascos as the Children's Crusade. It was not until 1213 that Innocent III at last sent forth his letters summoning the leaders of Christendom to a great council to be held in November 1215, at the same time announcing that the causes nearest his heart were the reformation of the universal church and the conquest of the Holy Land.[1]

The tone of Innocent's letters leaves no doubt that he was determined to take every precaution to insure that the plans did not miscarry through falling into the hands of others than the chosen agents of the church. What is usually designated as the Fifth Crusade was to be above all else a papal crusade. Innocent

is H. Hoogeweg, "Der Kreuzzug von Damietta," *Mittheilungen des Österreichischen Instituts für Geschichtsforschung* VIII, IX; of lesser importance but useful for details of the expedition and the siege of Damietta is: M. Reinaud, "Histoire de la sixième croisade et de la prise de Damiette d'après les écrivains arabes," *Journal asiatique*, VIII (1826), 18 ff. The financing of the crusade and, particularly, the role of the Templars is treated by L. Delisle, "Mémoire sur les operations financières des templiers," *Mémoires de l'Institut national de France*; *Académie des inscriptions et belles lettres*, XXXIII, part 2 (Paris, 1889), 1–250.

The most thoroughgoing effort to deal with Francis of Assisi and his visit to Damietta is G. Golubovich, "San Francesco e i Francescani in Damiata, 5 Nov. 1219–2 Feb. 1220," *Studi Francescani*, XXIII (n.s., XII; 1926), 307–330; and supplementing this, see P. L. Lemmens, "De Sancto Francisco Christum praedicante coram sultano Aegypti," *Archivum historicum Franciscanum*, XIX (1926), 559–578, and Nazzareno Jacopozzi, "Dove sia evvenuta la visita di San Francesco d'Assisi al Sultano Malek el-Kamel," *Congrès international de géographie, le Caire — Avril, 1925*, V (Cairo, 1926), and more recently M. Roncaglia, "San Francesco d'Assisi in Oriente," *Studi Francescani*, L (1953), 97–106.

Biographical works dealing with leading personages are L. Böhm, *Johann von Brienne* (Heidelberg, 1938); J. Clausen, *Papst Honorius III., 1216–1227* (Bonn, 1895); O. Hassler, *Pelagius Galvani* (Basel, 1902); J. P. Donovan, S.J., *Pelagius and the Fifth Crusade* (diss., University of Pennsylvania; Philadelphia, 1950); D. Mansilla, "El Cardenal hispano Pelayo Gaitán (1206–1230)," *Anthologica Annua*, I (1953), 11–66, a spirited defense, based chiefly on the papal letters; W. Junckmann, "Magister Oliverius Scholasticus, Bischof von Paderborn, Kardinalbischof von S. Sabina, und der Kreuzzug von Damiette," *Katholische Zeitschrift* (Münster, 1851); and L. C. F. Petit-Radel, "Olivier ou Olivarius, écolâtre de Cologne, cardinal-évêque de Sabine," *Histoire littéraire de la France*, XVIII (1895), 14–29.

[1] *PL*, CCXVI, cols. 823 ff.

hoped to inspire all spiritual and temporal leaders with the urgency of the task confronting the church.[2]

He called for energetic action, reminding the faithful of the thousands of Christians languishing in Saracen prisons and of the Moslem fortress recently erected on Mt. Tabor, thought to be the place of Christ's transfiguration — a fortress dominating the city of Acre, through which the Saracens hoped "to invade, unopposed, the remnants of the kingdom of Jerusalem." He summoned bishops, abbots, cathedral chapters, all members of the clergy, the cities and villages in most regions of Europe to furnish armed troops in proportion to their capabilities, together with the necessary arms and supplies for three years' service. He urged maritime cities to provide transportation and naval supplies.

So that the more urgent mission in the orient might not suffer, Innocent suspended the privileges granted to other crusaders, such as those who had elected to fight against the Albigensians and the the Muwaḥḥids, a change in policy which must greatly have disturbed those who in good faith had accepted the pope's own earlier assurances that the heretics were no less dangerous than the "infidels". Kings, princes, counts, barons, and other magnates, unable to take the cross in person, should equip and maintain combatants. Corsairs, pirates, and others guilty of molesting and despoiling pilgrims en route to the Holy Land were to be excommunicated, together with all their associates.

In order that the enterprise might be supported by spiritual as well as by physical weapons, the pope ordered the institution of monthly processionals, men and women marching separately. Public prayers were to be offered beseeching God to restore to the Christians the Holy Sepulcher. During the daily celebration of mass, immediately after communion, men and women were to prostrate themselves humbly while the clergy chanted the 67th (68th) and 78th (79th) Psalms: *Exsurgat Deus, et dissipentur inimici eius*, and *Deus, venerunt gentes in haereditatem tuam*. At the conclusion of the ceremony a special prayer, provided by the pope, was to be offered for the freeing of the land consecrated by the blood of Christ.

To France Innocent sent his former schoolmate Robert of "Courçon" (Curzon) as legate and crusading preacher,[3] and appealed

[2] The following account of the preparations for the crusade is based, in large part, on the letters of Innocent III in *PL*, CCXVI, cols. 817–832, 904–905.

[3] For the following, and many other details, see F. J. G. la Porte du Theil, ". . . Mémoire biographique sur Robert de Courçon, avec l'analyse et l'extrait de dix lettres anecdotes du pape Innocent III," *Notices et extraits des manuscrits de la Bibliothèque Nationale*, VI (Paris, 1800–1801), 130 ff.

to the royal family and to the clergy of France to give him wholehearted support.[4] Soon after Robert's arrival in France, he summoned a council to deal especially with the difficult question of usury, through which many of the nobles and clergy had been pauperized and, as a consequence, could not afford to give the desired support to the crusade. But the clergy of France complained bitterly to the pope of the legate's encroachments upon their authority, of his avarice, and of the slanderous abuse to which they were subjected, both by the legate and by the crusading preachers associated with him. Contemporary sources are in agreement that his imprudent conduct had incurred general hatred. Philip Augustus supported the clergy in their complaints, and the pope, seeing the grave danger to the success of the crusade, acknowledged the excessive zeal of Robert, although pleading extenuating circumstances.[5]

The preaching of Robert of Courçon, like that of his greater contemporary James of Vitry, was most successful among the masses, the unfortunate, and the weak. He permitted all who volunteered to accept the cross: old men, women, children, cripples, the deaf, and the blind. William the Breton, a contemporary historian, alleges that many nobles refused to take the cross because of the difficulties and confusion occasioned by the presence of so many ill-suited to the task of a crusade.[6] But this was largely Innocent's fault: in his anxiety lest aid to the Holy Land be unduly delayed, the pope had expressly admonished his agents not to take the time, at the moment when the cross was assumed, to examine too closely the physical or moral fitness of the crusaders. Exceptions could be made later in all cases of urgent necessity.

In the autumn of 1215, when Robert returned to Rome to participate in the Fourth Lateran Council, the prelates of France, in his presence, placed before the pope their list of grievances, so numerous and, in many instances, so well founded that the pope could only plead with the prelates to forgive the legate's indiscretions.[7] Yet, at the end of 1218, at the request — incredible as it may seem — of the French crusaders, Robert was sent to Palestine by Honorius III as spiritual adviser to the French fleet, but in all things subordinate to the recently chosen papal legate, cardinal Pelagius.[8]

4 *PL*, CCXVI, cols. 827–828; *RHGF*, XIX, 579.

5 Du Theil, "Mémoire," pp. 578–580. See also the letter of Innocent III (May 14, 1214) to Philip Augustus in *RHGF*, XIX, 59.

6 *De gestis Philippi Augusti*, in *RHGF*, XVII, 108.

7 *Ex chronologia Roberti Altissiodorensis*, in *RHGF*, XVIII, 283.

8 P. Pressutti (ed.), *Regesta Honorii papae III* (2 vols., Berlin, 1874–1875), nos. 1498, 1558; O. Rinaldi ("Raynaldus"), *Annales ecclesiastici*, ad ann. 1218, no. 5 (vol. XIII, Rome, 1646).

Meanwhile Simon, the newly appointed archbishop of Tyre, already in France as a crusading preacher and as papal representative at the Council of Melun, had in December 1216 been designated by Honorius as legate in France.[9]

In western Germany, the task of preaching a crusade was entrusted to an impressive array of bishops, abbots, and other high clerics.[10] By far the most successful of these was the scholasticus Oliver of the school of Cologne. The term scholasticus appears to have been employed to designate his role as scholar, teacher, and man of letters, rather than in its narrower significance as a student of scholastic theology.[11] It has been conjectured that Oliver was probably of a noble Westphalian family which had long been in possession of the episcopal see of Paderborn.[12] Innocent again called upon him, this time designating as his province Westphalia, Frisia, Brabant, Flanders, the diocese of Utrecht, and neighboring regions. His success was phenomenal. In the maritime cities and towns fifty thousand are said to have taken the cross; at any rate 300 ships were fitted out in Cologne.[13] As usual, one must accept such figures with reservations.

A third crusading preacher, James of Vitry, had, in the early years of the thirteenth century, come under the influence of the saintly Mary of Oignies, had become a canon regular, and after 1210 had preached the crusade against the Albigensians. His reward was election as bishop of Acre. Honorius III in 1217 summoned him to preach the new crusade in the Latin settlements of Syria, a task all the more difficult because of the widespread corruption prevalent in the cosmopolitan ports of Acre, Tyre, and Sidon, and because of the general use of the Arabic tongue in many communities.[14]

As if determined to prevent the revival of the mercenary interests which had diverted the Fourth Crusade, James unrelentingly attacked the westerners, especially the Venetians, Pisans, and Genoese, who had colonized the port cities. As he traveled through Syria he saw, with rising indignation, the extent to which the colonists had adopted not only the language but the manners and

[9] *Epistolae Honorii papae III*, in *RHGF*, XIX, 616.

[10] Listed by R. Röhricht, *Studien zur Geschichte des fünften Kreuzzuges*, p. 5 and accompanying notes.

[11] Petit-Radel, "Olivier ou Olivarius," *Histoire littéraire de la France*, XVIII, 14 ff.

[12] *Ibid.*, and see also Junckmann, "Magister Oliverius Scholasticus," *Katholische Zeitschrift*, 1851, pp. 101 ff.; H. Hoogeweg, "Die schriften d. Domscholasters Oliverus," *Bibliothek des litterarischen Vereins in Stuttgart*, CCII (Tübingen, 1894), pp. x ff., xx ff.

[13] See the letter of Oliver in *Westdeutsche Zeitschrift für Geschichte und Kunst*, X (1891), 170.

[14] James of Vitry, *Epist.* II, *Zeitschrift für Kirchengeschichte*, XIV, 115.

customs of the Moslems. Perhaps he exaggerated the depravity of the Syrian Christians, especially of the "poulains", the descendants of the first Latin settlers, whose effeminacy and immorality shocked him. But at best he found them a lascivious and treacherous people, always eager to teach the westerners their vicious habits. He charged that they did not scruple at serving as spies for the "infidel" against their own people.[15] In Acre, the key city of the Latin kingdom, where criminals thronged, where women of the street accepted the favors of the clergy, and where the scum of the Mediterranean came to prey upon the newly arrived crusaders, the eloquent James of Vitry restored something of the spiritual ardor of the early crusading era.

In the west troubadours no less than preachers aided the pope in awakening interest in the crusade. Pons of Capdolh (Chapdeuil) expresses the wish that the kings of France and England would make peace, and that the king of Apulia (Frederick II) and the emperor (Otto IV) would become friends until the Holy Sepulcher should be recovered by the Christians. With equal fervor a poem of Aimery of Péguilhan, inspired by the call of Innocent III, urges the young William IV of Montferrat to emulate the deeds of his forebears who had won fame and honor in Syria.[16] An anonymous troubadour appeals to Philip II, Otto IV, and John of England to make peace and go forward together to the conquest of Syria.[17]

Meanwhile the Lateran Council afforded Innocent III an opportunity for arranging the final details.[18] Brindisi and Messina were designated as the places of assembly for departure on June 1, 1217, at which time Innocent himself intended to visit Sicily to bestow his blessings upon the departing pilgrims. The clergy were to urge and, if necessary, compel all crusaders to fulfill their vows, and see to it that the nobles provided and equipped their assigned quotas of armed men. After the expedition was under way the clergy should aid in maintaining discipline through guidance and

[15] James of Vitry, *Historia Iherosolimitana* (ed. Bongars), I, par. 74–79, pp. 1089 ff.

[16] F. Diez, *Die Poesie der Troubadours* (Paris, 1845), pp. 212–213. For the fixing of the dates of these poems see also K. Lewent, *Das altprovenzalische Kreuzlied* (Erlangen, 1905), pp. 28 ff. Cf. A. Pillet and H. Carstens, *Bibliographie des Troubadours* (Halle, 1933).

[17] R. Zenker, "Peire von Auvergne," *Romanische Forschungen: Organ für Romanische Sprachen und Mittellatein*, XII (Erlangen, 1900), 798 ff.:

"Al rei Felip et a'n Oto
et al rei Joan eisamen
laus que fasson acordamen
entr' els. . . ."

[18] J. D. Mansi (ed.), *Sacrorum conciliorum nova et amplissima collectio*, XXII (Venice, 1778; reprinted Paris, 1903), 1058–1067, analyzed in some detail by Röhricht, *Fünft. Kreuz.*, pp. 6 ff. The constitution is also in *PL*, CCXVII, cols. 269 ff. See also W. E. Lunt, *Papal Revenues in the Middle Ages*, II (New York, 1934), 86 ff.

example. All clerics who accompanied the armies were to receive the income from their benefices for three years, even if their properties had previously been encumbered by mortgages.

The apostolic see, which had already appropriated 30,000 pounds to be used in the orient, pledged itself still further to supply equipment and ships for the Roman crusaders and an additional 3,000 marks. The pope mentioned other large sums which were to be paid through the masters of the Temple and the Hospital. In order to obtain other contributions, the pope and the priests of Rome were to pledge a tenth of their incomes. The clergy in general and the religious orders, with the exception of the Premonstratensians, Cistercians, and Cluniacs, who had already been taxed in support of the Albigensian or other crusades, were to pay a twentieth of their incomes for a period of three years. Those refusing to do so would be excommunicated.

As financial officers, the pope used Aimard, treasurer of the Temple in Paris; Martin, the chamberlain of the Temple; John, the marshal of the Hospitallers, and other representatives in the Holy Land; king John of Jerusalem; and the masters of the Templars and Hospitallers.[19] Among the last letters of Innocent III, one addressed to Aimard and another to king John of Jerusalem and the masters advised them that he was sending 9,000 pounds sterling for use in the Holy Land.[20]

The crusaders themselves were to be freed from all other tax obligations, from rents, and from importuning by Jewish moneylenders, and were to receive the special protection of the pope, or of their immediate patrons, until their return home. Maritime trade with the Moslems was to be suspended during four years and severe penalties were to be imposed upon those who engaged in piracy and those who were found selling munitions or essential building materials to the enemy. Finally, special measures applying to the nobility compelled a general peace for four years and forbade the holding of tournaments during a period of three years. All crusaders were to be granted plenary indulgence. Innocent also authorized Ralph of Mérencourt, the patriarch of Jerusalem, to serve as legate in the province of Jerusalem after the arrival of the crusading army. In order to protect Ralph against attacks from Saracen galleys on his return trip to Palestine, the pope called upon John of Brienne, king of Jerusalem, to provide the necessary escort.

[19] Röhricht, *Fünft. Kreuz.*, p. 10 and note 66. Concerning Aimard see Delisle, "Mémoire sur les operations financières des templiers," p. 28, and especially pp. 61 ff. William of Chartres was master of the Temple; Garin of Montaigu, of the Hospital.

[20] A. Potthast, *Regesta pontificum Romanorum*, I (Berlin, 1874), nos. 5180 and 5209.

Since John was himself engaged in a conflict with the kings of Armenia and Cyprus, Innocent peremptorily ordered him to keep the peace.[21]

Despite his efforts, Innocent achieved but partial success. The preaching, the systematic agitation, the efforts to secure temporary peace in the Christian world unquestionably produced a profound impression upon western Europe, but the movement won its chief support among the lowly. Chivalrous society no longer responded with enthusiasm to the call for a holy war, and did not provide the necessary leadership. Mercenary motives persisted among those who took the cross. It was the tragedy of Innocent III that the dominant aim of his pontificate could not be realized within his lifetime. Perhaps, indeed, a crusade undertaken in the spirit in which Innocent conceived it was no longer a possibility. When, in the summer of 1216, he himself set out in an effort to compose, by his own presence, the perennial conflicts of the northern Italian cities, death overtook him at Perugia on July 16, 1216.[22]

His successor, the aged but vigorous Honorius III, devoted himself unsparingly to the realization of Innocent's plans. Despite infirmities, Honorius believed implicitly, according to a contemporary, that it was to be his God-given destiny to free the Holy Land.[23] But the many difficulties of which Innocent III was so keenly aware quickly reappeared and were often accentuated as a result of his death.

Young Frederick II, for example, in a moment of enthusiasm had taken the cross and had appealed to the nobility of Germany to follow his example.[24] But as long as his Welf foe, Otto IV, remained to contest his claim to the throne, Frederick was helpless to embark upon a project which must necessarily remove him so long from Germany. The bitter feuds among the English nobility did not abate with the death of king John on October 16, 1216. Nor were conditions hopeful in France or Spain. Honorius III could not hope for the leadership of the kings and barons of the chief countries of Europe. At best, he could expect immediate assistance only from disparate and ill organized pilgrim groups.

Two significant letters of the Premonstratensian abbot, Gervase, one addressed to Innocent III and the other to Honorius III, reveal the problems facing the promoters of the crusade.[25] Many

[21] Röhricht, *Fünft. Kreuz.*, p. 7.

[22] *Ibid.*

[23] Burchard, *Urspergensium chronicon* (*MGH, SS.*, XXIII), pp. 378–379.

[24] See below, chapter XII, pp. 430–431.

[25] These two letters, analyzed here in some detail, are in *RHGF*, XIX, 604–605, 618–620.

who had taken the vow, Gervase writes, desired to know whether the pope had accorded to the French nobles permission to delay their departure for a year. Archbishop Simon of Tyre, lately arrived as legate in France, had because of his limited authority given no satisfactory reply, merely answering that the pope had changed nothing which had been determined by the council. The inability to obtain sufficient answers to such questions was all the more disturbing because the Parisian doctors had declared that one would be guilty of mortal sin in failing to fulfill his vow within the prescribed year, save with papal dispensation.

The nobles, the powerful men, and even the commoners of the cities had, for the most part, determined not to go at all, having little regard either for spiritual or for temporal penalties. On the other hand, the masses, the "little crusaders", were ardently desirous of fulfilling their vows, but were at a loss as to when to depart. Many had also expressed serious doubts as to their usefulness in the Holy Land in the absence of leaders from their own country who could speak their language. Gervase firmly believed also that the French and the Germans, unable to coöperate in any great enterprise, should not be required to set out together.

The most pressing difficulty, however, was the unequal justice meted out to the upper and lower classes. In France sometimes the clergy had overlooked the failure of the nobles to depart but had threatened the lowly with excommunication, with an eye to filling their own pockets. Gervase advised that the French be permitted to choose their own ports of embarkation. He further recommended the appointment of a special nuncio or legate, acting directly under papal orders, and expressed his disappointment that the new duties of James of Vitry in the Holy Land precluded his returning to France. If the pope felt it inadvisable to send a legate with full powers, Gervase recommended the creation of diocesan commissions empowered to guarantee the privileges of the crusaders, to grant dispensations to the unfit, to collect all accrued sums, and to supervise the distribution of funds. Gervase urged that potential leaders, such as dukes Odo of Burgundy and Theobald of Lorraine, should be compelled to fulfill their vows punctually as a salutary example to all pledged crusaders, whether of high or low degree. He feared that many who had accepted the cross with fervent devotion would now fall "into the abyss of despair", in the belief that the delay in departure, over which they had no control, would deprive them of all privileges and all indulgences. He insisted, however, that the clergy, who were obliged to pay one twentieth without first deducting the ordinary and general taxes, could hardly afford to do so, except for those who had an assured living.

Everywhere indeed the twentieth was regarded as an onerous burden. Its collection often required compulsory measures. In Spain, where a twentieth had already been levied to meet the expenses of the war against the Moors, demands for the collection of another twentieth occasioned bitter protests. In Scandinavia the twentieth had to be levied through payments in kind, and could not be accurately estimated. Generally the twentieth, together with similar taxes, constituted a part of the donation chest maintained in many churches. After collections were made in this manner they were usually sent through Aimard, treasurer of the Temple in Paris, and thence through a duly designated agent to the papal legate in the Holy Land, or directly to the leaders of crusading armies. It was expected that the legate, upon receiving these funds, would distribute them equitably among those crusaders who had taken the cross in the diocese where the taxes had been collected. Exceptions to this practice were authorized in those cases where previous arrangements had been made and sanctioned by the pope, permitting the sending of the money directly to the leaders. The questionable handling of such funds is more than suggested in Gervase's second letter. He complains to Honorius that the people were asking, "What use has been made of the money deposited in the chests of the church, and of the taxes paid by the clergy?" False accounting by some clergymen, even though the culprits were all too frequently absolved, indicates the difficulties in the administration of the finances of the crusades. In at least one instance, there was evidence of actual theft.[26]

Only a few Frenchmen, including archbishop Aubrey of Rheims and bishops John of Limoges and Robert of Bayeux, took part in the expedition of 1217. Most French nobles were pre-occupied in the west, and unwilling to go in the company of Germans and Hungarians.[27] But king Andrew II of Hungary and duke Leopold VI of Austria, in the absence of support from the greater princes of Europe, devoted themselves all the more zealously to assembling and equipping their troops.[28]

Many years before, at the time of his father's death on April 20, 1196, Andrew had assumed the crusading obligation which his

[26] Röhricht, *Fünft. Kreuz.*, p. 10.

[27] *L'Estoire de Eracles* (*RHC, Occ.*, II), p. 322; Aubrey of Trois-Fontaines, *Chronicon* (*MGH, SS.*, XXIII), p. 905 (also in *RHGF*, XVIII, 787).

[28] Röhricht, *Fünft. Kreuz.*, pp. 24–36, is a basic study of the Hungarian crusade.

father had been unable to fulfill. Unstable conditions in Hungary, however, had caused pope Celestine III to consent to the postponement of his departure. Three times thereafter, in 1201, in 1209, and again in 1213, after Andrew had succeeded his brother Emeric on the throne, Innocent had granted further postponements until, at last, he fixed the date of departure for the year 1217.[29] In case he should not return, Andrew's sovereign rights were to descend successively to his three sons, Bela, Coloman, and Andrew, while the actual governance of the kingdom of Hungary was left to John, archbishop of Gran, and that of Croatia and Dalmatia to the master of the Hungarian Templars, Pons of the Cross.

To secure the necessary shipping for his troops Andrew sent to Venice as his agents plenipotentiary the provost Alexander of Siebenbürgen and the prior of the Hospitallers of Hungary, who concluded an agreement with the doge, Peter Ziani. The crafty doge now compelled the king of Hungary to cede the city of Zara in perpetuity to Venice: Hungarians and Venetians, after paying the usual eightieth at the borders, might trade freely in each other's territory; pearls, precious stones and metals, silks, and other luxury products were to be duty-free, clauses which, of course, chiefly benefitted the Venetians, who agreed to supply ten ships of 5,000 hundredweight at a rental of 550 Venetian silver marks each. Other ships were to have carrying capacities of not less than 3,000 hundredweight with rates of hire proportional to their sizes. Rentals were payable in instalments, the first to be made the following Whitsunday, the second not later than May 31, and the last a week before the actual departure. The ships, fully equipped, were to be in the harbor of Spalato (Split) by July 25, and must wait at least thirty days for the arrival of the king.[30]

To raise the necessary funds, Andrew sold and mortgaged property, and resorted to the prevalent custom of debasing the coinage. There is evidence also that he pillaged some of the churches and abbeys of their sacred utensils.[31] At the beginning of July 1217, the crusading army began its march toward Spalato. In company with king Andrew were dukes Leopold of Austria and Otto of Meran, the latter's brother Berthold, archbishop of Kalocsa, and numerous bishops, abbots, and counts from all parts of the empire,

[29] B. Katona, *Historia critica regum Hungariae*, IV (Bratislava and Košice, 1781), pp. 464 ff., gives these preliminaries in detail. See also the letter of Honorius III to Andrew, *3 Idus Febr.* in Fejer, *Codex diplomaticus Hungariae*, III (Budapest, 1829), 189; and I. A. Fessler, *Geschichte von Ungarn*, I (Leipzig, 1867), 276, 313–314.

[30] *Monumenta spectantia historiam Slavorum meridionalium* (ed. Academia scientiarum et artium Slavorum meridionalium), I (1868), 29–31.

[31] Röhricht, *Fünft. Kreuz.*, p. 24.

together with many crusaders from Hungary.[32] The ships sailed from various Adriatic ports to the port of embarkation, Spalato. Supply trains moved overland, followed by large numbers of the German settlers of Transylvania, the so-called Siebenbürgen Saxons.

On August 23, 1217, Andrew, accompanied by a brilliant retinue, arrived at Spalato and was received with pomp and ceremony by the clergy and citizens. As the procession approached, the clergy, clad in silken vestments and bearing censers and crosses, came out to welcome the king. In the church of St. Domnius mass was celebrated. Thomas, archdeacon of Spalato, who describes these events in great detail, relates that the citizens, as a gesture of hospitality, permitted the crusaders to take over their homes in the suburbs of the city. Because of the huge numbers, however, many were compelled to pitch their tents in the surrounding country. The king was deeply moved by the hospitality and generosity of both the clergy and the citizens. In return he offered them as a gift the neighboring castle of Clissa, together with the island in front of it. But they declined, because of the heavy obligations which its maintenance would impose upon them, and therefore Andrew bestowed the castle upon the Templars. So great was the number of crusaders, more than 10,000 mounted men and an unknown number of foot-soldiers, that Andrew and the main body of the crusaders had to wait several weeks for enough ships to transport them. Many knights had to return home or make plans for sailing the following spring.

Duke Leopold of Austria, however, embarked immediately after his arrival in Spalato, and reached Acre after an exceptionally rapid voyage of sixteen days.[33] He had sent an embassy inviting Bohemond IV of Antioch to meet him, and Bohemond, together with his chief vassals, appeared in answer to the invitation. Two German knights were sent to urge Andrew to hasten his embarkation. Meanwhile king Hugh I of Cyprus and his chief vassals and prelates landed at Acre with a large following of Turcopoles, or mounted natives. Shortly afterwards king Andrew arrived. At Acre were assembled the dignitaries of Jerusalem, including the king, John of Brienne, the patriarch, Ralph of Mérencourt, and many others, both laymen and clerics. Military leaders included duke

[32] *Ex Thomae historia pontificum Salonitanorum et Spalatinorum* (*MGH, SS.*, XXIX), pp. 577 ff., is the chief source for the following account. Otto's sister Gertrude had been Andrew's first wife; his sister Agnes had been the third wife of Philip II of France. See also Röhricht, *Fünft. Kreuz.*, p. 24.

[33] Röhricht, *Fünft. Kreuz.*, p. 25.

Leopold of Austria, duke Otto of Meran, Walter of Avesnes, Garin of Montaigu, master of the Hospital, William of Chartres, master of the Temple, and Hermann of Salza, master of the Teutonic Knights. Present also were archbishops Simon of Tyre, Peter of Caesarea, Robert of Nazareth, Berthold of Kalocsa, and Eustorgue of Nicosia, many bishops, including James (of Vitry) of Acre, Egbert of Bamberg, Peter of Raab, Thomas of Erlau, Otto of Münster, Engelhard of Naumburg and Zeitz, Otto of Utrecht, and Robert of Bayeux. A council of war was held in Acre and so great was the number in attendance that the tent, though large, was almost filled.[34] The statement of one contemporary that there were 20,000 knights and 200,000 foot-soldiers is surely an exaggeration,[35] but the number was certainly very great indeed.[36]

The poor harvest of the previous year in Syria had created a famine, a small loaf of bread selling for as much as 12 denarii. So great was the crisis that the patriarch of Jerusalem and other leaders advised many of the pilgrims to return home. During the month of September alone, 66 ships are said to have departed, and 100,000 crusaders to have perished of hunger.[37] Here again is obvious exaggeration, but at the close of 1217, and during much of the following year, the famine helped produce unrest. The scholasticus Oliver mentions especially the lawlessness of the Bavarians who, contrary to the laws of crusaders, committed many acts of violence against the native Christians. Duke Leopold of Austria, however, appears to have conducted himself throughout in an exemplary manner.[38]

Prior to the arrival of the main body of the crusaders, king John of Jerusalem and the masters of the three orders appear to have been contemplating a two-fold plan of attack: an assault by a small force upon al-Mu'aẓẓam Sharaf-ad-Dīn, son of the Aiyūbid sultan al-'Ādil, in his stronghold at Nablus, and a simultaneous landing by the main body at Damietta in Egypt, designed to wrest Egypt from the Moslems and thus to open the door to the conquest of the whole of Syria. The war council in Acre apparently abandoned this project, at least temporarily, probably because of insufficient man-power and ships, but reached no clear and well defined plan of their own. Not improbably the council decided, pending the arrival of

[34] *Eracles* (*RHC, Occ.*, II), pp. 321–323; Oliver, *Historia Damiatina*, pp. 162–163.
[35] *Annales Ceccanenses* (ed. L. C. Bethmann, *MGH, SS.*, XIX), pp. 276 ff.
[36] Röhricht, *Fünft. Kreuz.*, p. 26 and note 30.
[37] *Annales Ceccanenses* (*MGH, SS.*, XIX), p. 302.
[38] Oliver, *Historia Damiatina*, pp. 163, 168.

reinforcements, to carry out a series of petty campaigns designed to keep the enemy occupied and uncertain. Conceivably it regarded Damascus as an ultimate objective.

The Christian camp was located southeast of Acre on the left bank of the Nahr Na'mān at Recordane (Khirbat Kurdānah). On November 3, 1217, the patriarch of Jerusalem appeared bearing the remnants of the True Cross, which had been rescued thirty years before in the battle of Hattin (July 4, 1187) and which were now to become the standard of the army. In intense heat and through revealing clouds of dust the crusaders traversed the plains of Esdraelon and al-Fūlah to 'Ain Jālūt and Tubania ('Ain aṭ-Ṭuba'ūn), their leaders expecting a surprise attack. Indeed, no sooner had the march begun than al-'Ādil had proceeded from Jerusalem towards the region of Nablus, apparently with the intention of intercepting the crusaders in the vicinity of Tubania. When he realized how many and how determined they were, however, he retreated to Baisan (Bethsan), rejecting the proposals of his son al-Mu'aẓẓam, who wanted to attack from the heights of Nain as the pilgrim army crossed the plain of Esdraelon.[39] Ibn-al-Athīr says that the crusaders knew that al-'Ādil's armies were widely dispersed in the provinces.[40]

Observing that the Christians continued their march toward Baisan, al-'Ādil determined to retreat across the Jordan, abandoning Baisan and its terrified inhabitants to the mercy of the invaders. Again his son al-Mu'aẓẓam questioned this decision, but the sultan, with growing impatience, swore at his son in the Persian tongue, evidently desiring to conceal his remarks from his Arab-Turkish followers.[41] As al-'Ādil made good his retreat across the Jordan, the crusaders entered Baisan, where they pillaged unopposed, both within the city and throughout the countryside just south of Lake Tiberias. Al-'Ādil, however, continued his retreat to 'Ajlūn, ordering al-Mu'aẓẓam to cover Jerusalem from a position on the heights of Lubban near Shiloh. From 'Ajlūn the sultan turned northward towards Damascus, proceeding through Ra's al-Mā' to a point some forty miles south of Damascus, Marj aṣ-Ṣuffar.[42]

Meanwhile the crusaders crossed the Jordan, on November 10, 1217, by Jisr al-Majāmi', a bridge some six miles south of Lake

[39] Oliver, *Historia Damiatina*, pp. 163 ff.; *Eracles* (*RHC, Occ.*, II), pp. 323 ff.

[40] Ibn-al-Athīr, *Al-kāmil fī-t-ta'rīkh* (*RHC, Or.*, II, 1), p. 112.

[41] Abū-Shāmah, *Ar-rauḍatain* (*RHC, Or.*, V), p. 162.

[42] Concerning this route see R. Dussaud, *Topographie historique de la Syrie antique et médiévale* (Paris, 1927), p. 385.

Tiberias.[43] The city of Damascus and the surrounding villages were in consternation. The governor of the city was ordered to provision the citadel, to flood the surrounding area, and to take other defensive measures. In response to the call of the sultan, al-Mujāhid Shīrkūh of Homs came to the assistance of the terrified city. But, as the Moslem populace thronged the highway to welcome the reinforcements, the crusaders pursued a leisurely march northward along the Jordan and Lake Tiberias, and then westward across the Jordan at Jacob's Ford, south of Lake Hulah, back to their camp at Acre. From the outset, the expedition appears to have been a mere reconnaissance in force, probably, as the chronicle of Ernoul implies, for want of an acknowledged leader.[44]

For the moment, the zeal of the crusaders was intense, but it was soon to extinguish itself. The author of the *Eracles* relates a conversation reported to have taken place between al-'Ādil and his son al-Mu'aẓẓam, in which the sultan advised against combat while the Christians were filled with crusading ardor; he preferred to wait until they had grown weary when, he said, the land could be freed without peril. As the Christians came to the Jordan and the shores of Lake Tiberias, they found outlets for their religious fervor in bathing in the sacred river and in making numerous pilgrimages to local holy places.[45]

After a brief sojourn there, the crusaders, this time without the king of Hungary, who preferred the comforts of Acre,[46] moved against Mt. Tabor, which al-Mu'aẓẓam, at the direction of the sultan, had fortified some years before as a vantage point overlooking the region traversed by the routes from Acre to Jerusalem. It was this stronghold with its 77 bastions and its garrison of 2,000 men that had caused Innocent III such great concern when in 1213 he had issued his call for a crusade. The fort was regarded by the Moslems as impregnable, and only through information obtained from a native boy were the crusaders encouraged to undertake the assault.[47] On December 3, the first Sunday in Advent, taking as their command the words of Matthew 21:2 ("Ite in castellum, quod contra vos est"),[48] they swarmed up the mountain in an unusually

[43] The *Eracles* (*RHC, Occ.*, II), p. 324, says they crossed "au pont de Judaire". See the note of Röhricht, *Fünft. Kreuz.*, p. 33, note 38.

[44] *Chronique d'Ernoul et de Bernard le trésorier* (ed. L. de Mas Latrie, Paris, 1871), p. 412; see also *Eracles* (*RHC, Occ.*, II), pp. 323–324.

[45] Oliver, *Historia Damiatina*, pp. 164–165.

[46] *Eracles* (*RHC, Occ.*, II), p. 325.

[47] R. Röhricht, *Geschichte des Königreichs Jerusalem, 1100–1291* (Innsbruck, 1898), p. 725.

[48] Oliver, *Historia Damiatina*, p. 165.

heavy fog which hid them from the garrison.[49] The patriarch of Jerusalem, with the fragments of the cross, led the way, while the clergy prayed and sang. The crusaders came so close that they could touch the walls with their lances. Although John of Brienne fought with extraordinary bravery in repelling a sally from the fort, the attack failed.

Upon his descent John took counsel with the master of the Hospitallers and several Syrian barons. Bohemond IV strongly urged the abandonment of the attack, and was supported in this advice by other leaders. Both the scholasticus Oliver and James of Vitry criticized John severely for giving up the attack on Mt. Tabor and for causing others to do so. Yet the courage and wise leadership of John throughout the crusade give the modern historian some confidence in the decision, although one Moslem source implies that the losses of the garrison had been so heavy that it was on the point of surrendering.[50]

Two days later, some of the crusaders, including the Hospitallers and the Templars, dissatisfied with the decision of the leaders, undertook another attack, this time unsuccessfully placing an assault ladder against the walls. But a counterattack from the garrison, using Greek fire, destroyed the ladder and scattered the assailants with heavy losses. Discouraged by this second failure, the crusaders abandoned the siege, and on December 7 they departed for Acre.[51] Shortly after the departure of the attackers, however, al-Mu'aẓẓam decided to destroy the fortifications of Mt. Tabor, yielding evidently to the widespread belief among the Moslems that the mere existence of the fort had subjected them to attack by the Christians.

A third crusader sortie was even more futile, if possible, than the two previous ones. Not more than 500 soldiers, chiefly Hungarian, participated. According to Abū-Shāmah, a son of the sister of the king of Hungary took part in the expedition, presumably as leader, but the author of the *Eracles* identifies the leader only as a certain "rich man called Dionysius".[52] This confusion further suggests that the responsible leaders of the crusade had no hand in the expedition, which appears to have set out to attack the brigands who infested the mountainous region east and southeast of Sidon, contrary to the advice of Balian of Sidon, who knew the difficulties

[49] Abū-Shāmah, *Ar-rauḍatain* (*RHC, Or.*, V), p. 163.

[50] Ibn-al-Athīr, *Al-kāmil* (*RHC, Or.*, II, 1), pp. 113–114.

[51] *Ibid.*, p. 114; Abū-Shāmah, *Ar-rauḍatain* (*RHC, Or.*, V), p. 164.

[52] *Eracles* (*RHC, Occ.*, II), p. 325; *Ar-rauḍatain* (*RHC, Or.*, V), p. 164; Oliver, *Historia Damiatina*, p. 167.

of the country and the cleverness of the brigands.[53] Near Mashgharah, where the crusaders remained for about three days, the mountaineers fell upon them, seizing their horses and slaying or taking captive large numbers of troops. Moslem sources report the nephew of the king of Hungary among the captives. Those who had escaped the massacre endeavored to retrace their steps to Sidon. A Moslem prisoner, known as al-Jāmūs, who had been taken during the battle, agreed to guide them by a shorter route if, in return, they would free him. But he led them into a deep ravine where they were pursued and slaughtered. Al-Jāmūs was slain for his ruse, but very few of the crusaders escaped, although Abū-Shāmah undoubtedly exaggerates when he says that only three of the original 500 returned to Sidon. As the remnants made their way from Sidon to Acre, in the region near Sarepta (Ṣarafand) heavy rains and severe cold on Christmas Eve caused the death of some of the weary stragglers. This expedition marked the close of the crusading efforts of 1217.

King Andrew of Hungary had played no part after the first sortie across the Jordan, but had remained in Acre. Well before the end of the year, he began to make his preparations to return home. His singular inactivity may have resulted, as Thomas of Spalato intimates, from an illness, probably the result of poisoning.[54] In early January 1218, despite the admonitions of the patriarch of Jerusalem threatening excommunication, Andrew took with him many crusaders, beasts of burden, and much military equipment, and "departed stubbornly with his retinue".[55] He proceeded overland along the coast road to Tripoli, accompanied by young king Hugh of Cyprus and Bohemond of Antioch. Andrew remained in Tripoli for the marriage of Bohemond with Melisend, half-sister of the king of Cyprus, and was there when Hugh died suddenly on January 10, 1218. Before leaving Syria, Andrew visited the castles of Krak des Chevaliers and al-Marqab, bestowing gifts upon them to aid in their defense.[56] He then proceeded through Armenia,[57] where he arranged a marriage between his son Andrew and Leon's daughter Isabel, through the territory of the Selchükid sultan of Iconium, into the Nicaean empire of Theodore I Lascaris, whose daughter Maria was betrothed to his eldest son, Bela. After crossing

[53] Abū-Shāmah, *Ar-rauḍatain* (*RHC, Or.*, V), p. 164, describes him as the governor of Sidon. For his identity see C. D. DuCange, *Les Familles d'Outremer* (ed. E. G. Rey, Paris, 1869), p. 434.

[54] *Ex Thomae historia* (*MGH, SS.*, XXIX), p. 578.

[55] Oliver, *Historia Damiatina*, p. 168.

[56] Katona, *Historia critica regum Hungariae*, V (Bratislava and Košice, 1783), 287–288.

[57] *Ex Thomae historia* (*MGH, SS.*, XXIX), p. 579.

into Europe, Andrew continued through Bulgaria, with his army greatly reduced by difficulties and privations, and reached Hungary, bearing numerous relics of the Holy Land. His crusade had achieved nothing and brought him no honor. He returned to an impoverished country whose treasury had been so pillaged, by both lay and spiritual lords, that the debts incurred for the crusade could not be paid.[58] Such was the ineffectual conclusion of the Hungarian phase of the Fifth Crusade. The Latin orient had been deceived in its hopes of the Hungarian king and disillusioned by his conduct, some people believing that his expedition had actually damaged the crusading cause.[59]

Andrew's departure so reduced the numbers of effective troops in Syria that further operations had to be suspended, at least until the arrival of new crusading bands from the west. By now, the crusaders from northwestern Germany and Frisia, many of whom had taken the cross as the result of the preaching of the scholasticus Oliver, were en route by sea to Acre. In the meantime the leaders in Syria, including king John, the duke of Austria, and the members of the military orders, desiring to employ the remnant of the expedition in some useful manner, determined upon the restoration of certain key strongholds. At Caesarea the work of reconstruction was quickly completed with little interference from the Moslems, although their approach was several times reported. On February 2, 1218, the patriarch of Jerusalem, assisted by six bishops, celebrated mass in the church of St. Peter within the newly fortified city.[60]

Meanwhile the Templars, aided especially by Walter of Avesnes, pushed forward the work of restoring the fortifications of Château Pèlerin (Athlith),[61] between Haifa and Caesarea, on a lofty promontory overlooking the sea, which thus protected it on three sides, and sheltered from sudden attack on the fourth by a rugged cliff. The work of restoration required especially the reconstruction of the main tower, known as Destroit, protecting the eastern end of the promontory, and originally constructed by the Templars to guard the narrow road to Jerusalem against the highwaymen who

[58] Fessler, *Geschichte von Ungarn*, I, 319 ff.

[59] Such is the judgment of Oliver, *Historia Damiatina*, p. 168; *Eracles* (*RHC, Occ.*, II), p. 325; James of Vitry, *Epist.* III, *Zeitschrift für Kirchengeschichte*, XV, 569.

[60] Oliver, *Historia Damiatina*, pp. 168–169. The church, formerly a mosque, was dedicated as the church of St. Peter in 1101.

[61] For details of this restoration, see E. G. Rey, *Étude sur les monuments de l'architecture militaire des croisés en Syrie et dans l'île de Chypre* (Paris, 1871), pp. 93 ff., also "Excavations in the Pilgrim's Castle (Athlith)," *Quarterly of the Department of Antiquities in Palestine*, I (Jerusalem–London, 1932), no. 3, pp. 111 ff.

waylaid pilgrims as they passed this point. After weeks of labor, the crusaders had erected a well-nigh impregnable barrier across the promontory, and also built dwellings for the Templars, which were to serve as their quarters until the restoration of Jerusalem. Admirable as was the location of the castle strategically, it also dominated a region rich in fish, salt, wood, oils, vines, grain, and fruits of all kinds. Its harbor, naturally good, admitted of easy improvement.[62] Quite possibly the reconstruction of Château Pèlerin hastened the decision of al-Mu'aẓẓam to destroy the nearby fortifications of Mt. Tabor. In any event it was not until Easter that the crusaders could return to Acre, leaving garrisons in each of the castles.

The work had barely been completed when, on April 26, 1218, the first units of the fleet of the long expected Frisian-German expedition arrived,[63] after an adventurous journey that had lasted nearly a year. Having set sail from Dartmouth early in June 1217, under the command of counts William of Holland and George of Wied, the ships had touched at Brest, at Cape Váres on the Galician coast, and at several Portuguese coastal points before arriving at Lisbon in the third week of July. Here the bishop, Suger, and the masters of the knightly orders and others had urged them to postpone their departure for the east until the following spring, and to join in an attack on the last remaining stronghold of the Moslems in the region of Lisbon, Alcácer (al-Qaṣr) do Sal. The counts of Holland and Wied and many of the German crusaders had accepted the invitation, knowing that the emperor Frederick II would surely not be embarking for the Holy Land before 1218. Some 180 ships had remained in Lisbon. But the Frisians had refused the invitation, mindful of Innocent III's command that nothing be allowed to delay the crusade. With 80 ships, they had continued their voyage immediately.

While the Germans had joined the Portuguese in the siege of Alcácer do Sal, which ended successfully on October 21, 1217, and had then returned to winter in Lisbon, the Frisians had coasted southward along the Portuguese shore, plundering the Moslem ports of Santa Maria[64] and Rota, resting in Cadiz, whose inhabitants had deserted it for fear of them, and sailing through the Strait of

[62] In addition to Oliver, *loc. cit.*, see also *Eracles* (*RHC, Occ.*, II), pp. 325 ff.; James of Vitry, *Epist.* III, pp. 569 ff.; and *Chronique d'Ernoul*, pp. 421 ff.

[63] The following account is based on Emo, *Chronicon* (*MGH*, SS., XXIII), pp. 478 ff., and the *Chronica regia Coloniensis* (*Annales Colonienses maximi*), partim ex *MGH* recusa (*Scriptores rerum Germanicarum in usum scholarum*, Hanover, 1880), pp. 239 ff., the latter text appearing also in the *MGH, SS.*, XVII, 829 ff.

[64] Emo, *Chronicon* (*MGH, SS.*, XXIII), p. 480: "nunc Hairin dicitur"; modern Faro.

Gibraltar, northward along the Mediterranean coast of Spain by Tortosa and Barcelona, and thence, with many delays along the French and Italian shores, to Civitavecchia, in papal territory, where they passed the winter. They set sail once more on March 20, 1218, with a good many Italian crusaders on board, and via Syracuse and Candia reached Acre late in April. On March 31 the German ships set sail from Lisbon, and, though scattered by storms off the Balearic islands and driven to take refuge in various French and Italian ports, also made their way to Acre, arriving during May.[65] Oliver welcomed his countrymen, and assumed a position of leadership among them.

With the gathering of an ever increasing number of crusaders in Acre, the leaders soon decided to employ the expedition against Egypt rather than in Palestine, a plan which king John and the masters of the knightly orders had abandoned a year earlier only for want of sufficient men and ships. Oliver eloquently supported John's proposal to move immediately against Damietta, and appears to have gained unanimous approval for it,[66] and in a letter to the pope dated September 22, 1218, James of Vitry explained that the spring was not a good time for a direct attack on Jerusalem because of the excessive heat and the scarcity of water. Egypt, on the other hand, in contrast to the hot and rugged land of Jerusalem, was a land of great fertility and abundant water. Moreover, it was a level country where the fortifications were chiefly in three cities. The taking of one — Damietta, "the key to Egypt" — would open the way to the others. James recalled also that Egypt was rich in its associations with the life of the infant Jesus and that among its inhabitants were numerous Christians, long under subjugation by the Saracens.[67] No less significant also is the statement of the Arab historian, Ibn-al-Furāt, who quotes the crusading leaders as saying: "It was with the aid of the resources of that rich country [Egypt] that Saladin conquered Syria and subjugated the holy city. If we become masters of it, we can easily retake Jerusalem, with all our former possessions."[68]

[65] *Chronica regia Coloniensis*, pp. 244 ff.; *Annales Colonienses maximi* (*MGH, SS.*, XVII), p. 832.

[66] James of Vitry, *Epist.* III, p. 570, declares the plan to have been "omnibus unanimiter concordatum".

[67] James of Vitry, *Epist.* IV, *Zeitschrift für Kirchengeschichte*, XV, 571–572.

[68] *Ta'rīkh*, excerpts trans. J. F. Michaud, *Bibliothèque des croisades*, IV (Paris, 1829), 388.

B. The Capture and Loss of Damietta

A successful Egyptian campaign might well give the crusaders a foothold of inestimable value in the control of the Near East. The operation called for a forceful and united command, planning of the highest order, assurance of continuous supplies of men and provisions, and enough military discipline to prevent the periodic diminution of the armed forces through the whims of individual leaders or groups of crusaders. The events of the preceding year in Syria must have impressed the experienced leaders with these imperatives.

On May 27, 1218, the vanguard of the crusading fleet arrived in the harbor of Damietta, situated about two miles inland on the right bank of the main branch of the Nile which flows northeastward into the Mediterranean, and is usually described as the Damietta branch. After choosing count Simon (II) of Saarbrücken as temporary leader, pending the arrival of the remainder of the fleet, the forces began preliminary explorations. They met little or no resistance, and chose a site for the camp on the west bank of the river just opposite the city, in a region known as Jīzat Dimyāṭ, a roughly triangular island about three square miles in area, surrounded on the west by an abandoned canal, al-Azraq; on the north by the Mediterranean; and on the south and east by the Damietta branch of the Nile. Defensively, the site was ideal: it had easy access to the source of supplies from the sea, and was protected by the Nile against sudden attack from the south or east. Offensively, however, the location left much to be desired: the armies would have to cross the Nile in the face of enemy resistance. Within a few days, the ships of king John of Jerusalem, duke Leopold of Austria, and the masters of the knightly orders arrived in the harbor.[69] The camp was rapidly fortified by means of a moat and surrounding wall.[70] The Christians thought it a good omen that the water of the Nile, although so near the sea, was fresh. Also an eclipse of the moon, emblem of the Islamic faith, which took place on July 9, was welcomed as a favorable portent.[71]

By now the crusaders had come to recognize the necessity for a superior command: "when the Christians were anchored in the

[69] Oliver, *Historia Damiatina*, pp. 176 ff.; P. Meyer, "La Prise de Damiette en 1219, Relation inédite en Provençal," *Bibliothèque de l'École des Chartes*, XXXVIII (1877), 514–515.

[70] Al-Maqrīzī, "Histoire d'Égypte," *ROL*, IX (1902), 468.

[71] For the date of the eclipse, R. Röhricht, *Beiträge zur Geschichte der Kreuzzüge*, II (Berlin, 1878), 249.

mouth of the river . . . , and were all assembled, they elected a chieftain, and by common accord king John of Jerusalem was chosen. . . ."[72] It was to be the greatest misfortune of the expedition, during its operations in Egypt, that the reinforcements arriving from the west during the next two years were so little experienced in large-scale wars of conquest, or so deeply absorbed in their particular interests, that they failed to appreciate the need for maintaining John in authority.

The arrival of the crusaders at first aroused curiosity rather than apprehension among the Moslems, perhaps because they shared al-'Ādil's view that the Christians would not attack Egypt.[73] Al-'Ādil was still in camp at Marj aṣ-Ṣuffar, south of Damascus, where he had established himself in 1217. His eldest son al-Kāmil, who ruled Egypt in his absence, was near Cairo, and received intelligence of the enemy movements by carrier pigeon. After three days he was prepared to move out of Cairo, at the same time ordering the provincial governors to assemble the nomads. Meanwhile al-'Ādil dispatched all possible reinforcements from Syria, and sent his second son, al-Mu'aẓẓam, to keep watch on the Syrian coast. Al-Kāmil established his camp on the right bank of the Nile, some distance up-river from Damietta at al-'Ādilīyah, where he was able to maintain contact with the city as well as oppose the efforts of the invaders to cross the Nile.[74]

The crusaders admired Damietta for its beauty as well as for the strength of its fortifications.[75] Extending to the water's edge on the east, it was protected by a triple wall and by many towers. Fortified at different times in the past, its three walls were of unequal heights, the first one low to protect the navigable ditch which encircled the city on the land sides, the second one higher and reinforced by twenty-eight towers, each with three *tourelles* or protecting penthouses, and the third, or inner wall, much higher than the other two. In the middle of the Nile, just opposite the city on an island, was the chain tower (Burj as-Silsilah), so called because from the tower to the city walls on the east and probably also to the river bank on the west, there extended huge iron chains which served

[72] *Eracles* (*RHC, Occ.*, II), p. 329.

[73] *Ibid.*, p. 326.

[74] Al-Maqrīzī, "Histoire d'Égypte," *ROL*, IX (1902), 468 ff.

[75] Oliver, *Historia Damiatina*, chaps. 32 and 38, provides a good description of the city and its fortifications. James of Vitry, *Epist. VI*, *Zeitschrift für Kirchengeschichte*, XVI, 79; John of Tulbia, *De domino Iohanne rege Ierusalem* (ed. R. Röhricht, *Quinti belli sacri scriptores minores*, Geneva, 1879), p. 119; the *Liber duellii Christiani* (*ibid.*), p. 143; and the *Gesta obsidionis Damiate* (*ibid.*), p. 73, offer but few additional details. For the chain tower, see Ibn-al-Athīr, *Al-kāmil* (*RHC, Or.*, II, 1), pp. 114–115.

to control traffic in times of peace and to bar the passing of enemy ships in time of war. The tower itself was a formidable stronghold, constructed in 70 tiers and so situated that it could be neither successfully bombarded nor mined from below. It could accommodate a garrison of perhaps three hundred men. Its capture was essential as the preliminary to a siege of the city.

For more than three months the crusaders attacked it intermittently. Though they had eight projectile machines, and poured a barrage of javelins and stones upon the fortifications and into the city, the chain tower held fast. On June 23 the crusaders, in 70 or 80 ships with decks protected by wooden walls and covered with armor, presumably of leather or of hides, approached close to the walls of the city, attacking with extreme violence while simultaneously the ballistae continued to hurl their showers of stones.[76] But this method of assault, although terrifying to the inhabitants, was not effective against the massive fortifications. The duke of Austria and the Hospitallers now erected two scaling ladders, each mounted upon two vessels known as "cogs", well adapted to the supporting of lofty structures by virtue of their broad bows and sterns. At the same time the Germans and Frisians, under the direction of count Adolf of Berg, prepared another ship (called a "maremme", according to the Arabic sources[77]), with shielded bulwarks and a small fortress attached to its mast. With these vessels a new assault was begun on the tower on July 1, 1218.

The maremme was moved into a position between the tower and the city wall, with its ballistae hurling a shower of rocks into the city from the fortified masthead. But an intense counterbombardment from tower and city forced it to withdraw. Meanwhile the scaling ladders of the duke of Austria and the Hospitallers, although secured against the tower walls, broke under the weight of the soldiers, hurling into the water all who had mounted them. The Moslems witnessed this catastrophe with cries of mingled joy and derision, while bugle calls and the roll of kettle drums informed the townsmen of the successful repulse. Far up the river in Cairo, houses were illuminated and banners bedecked the streets. But the artillery continued the incessant barrage against the city.

Now the scholasticus Oliver, the talented mentor of the German and Frisian crusaders, displayed his gift for strategy and military leadership. Perhaps his modest position as scholasticus explains the

[76] "Extraits de l'histoire des patriarches d'Alexandrie relatifs au siège de Damiette sous le règne d'al-Malik al-Kamil," *ROL*, XI (1908), 241–243.

[77] Ibn-al-Athīr, *Al-kāmil* (*RHC, Or.*, II, 1), pp. 114–115.

self-effacing manner in which he, in his *Historia Damiatina*, describes the plan for a new assault. Facts which have come to light, however, through other contemporary sources afford abundant evidence of the significant part which he played in the capture of the chain tower. He was favored also in his efforts by the steadfastness of his Frisian and German followers. Long before, while preaching the crusade, he had inspired his followers with a zeal and loyalty which, in the more active phase of the crusade, made of him a respected and revered leader. Though he himself says only, "with the Lord showing us how and providing an architect", James of Vitry reveals that the architect was Oliver himself. With great labor and expense, he constructed an extraordinary siege machine which brought victory to the Christians. His Frisian and German followers, even the poor, made generous contributions in raising some 2,000 marks to pay the cost of construction.[78] Two cogs were firmly lashed together by means of ropes and wooden beams so that they appeared to be a single structure. Four masts were then erected, with the same number of sail yards. From their tops hung a miniature castle enclosed like a fortified city and shielded with wickerwork. Over its walls and roof, hides were stretched as a protection against Greek fire. Beneath it extended a huge revolving scaling ladder, thrusting forward some 45 feet beyond the prow of the ship and supported by heavy ropes and pulleys.

On August 24, avoiding the dangerous currents flowing west of the tower, the crusaders brought their great machine to anchor to the northeast. While the clergy walked barefoot along the bank praying for the success of the undertaking, the soldiers released the ladder and placed it against the tower. Six Moslem ballistae hurled continuous showers of rocks upon the besiegers; Greek fire streamed down from the chain tower upon the floating castle, and the Christians fought it with salt, acid, and gravel. When at length the Moslem defenders, with fire-brands of burning oil attached to their extended lances, set fire to the ladder, they nearly put an end to the assault.

From his precarious perch the standard-bearer of the duke of Austria was hurled into the river, and the enemy, with cries of victory, fished the banner from the water. The patriarch of Jerusalem, lying in the dust with the fragment of the cross before him and sand covering his head, loudly prayed for divine aid. After an hour of continuous effort crusaders put out the fire, and saved the

[78] *Chronica regia Coloniensis*, p. 445, says: "ex puris elemosinis pauperum edificium construxit." Also in *MGH, SS.*, XVII, 833.

ladder.[79] Now, a young soldier from Liége was first to reach the tower, while a Frisian, one Hayo of Fivelgo, laying sturdily about him with a flail, cut down the Saracen standard-bearer and seized the yellow banner of the sultan. Other crusaders then hurried over the bridge, gaining a foothold in the upper portions of the tower and driving the garrison down to the lower tiers. As night was falling, the cross was planted on the summit, while the Christians on the river bank sang loudly the *Te Deum laudamus*. But from the lower tiers of the tower the Saracens kindled such hot fires that the crusaders were compelled to retreat across the ladder. Once again, however, the ingenious invention of the scholasticus Oliver proved its worth. The crusaders now lowered the ladder and made it fast to the lower walls, which they attacked with iron mallets, while they kept a raging fire burning all night before the entrance. Many of the Moslem garrison, thus trapped, sought safety by leaping from the tower windows, only to drown or to be fished from the river and taken captive. Next morning at ten o'clock the Moslems asked for negotiations and, on the promise that their lives would be spared, surrendered to the duke of Austria. About 100 prisoners were led before king John of Jerusalem.[80] The crusaders cut the chains and demolished the pontoon bridge connecting the chain tower with the city. They closed the door of the tower facing Damietta, and constructed a new pontoon bridge to the west bank of the Nile.[81]

The loss of the chain tower was a staggering blow to the Saracens; the Arabic sources agree that gloom now descended upon the Moslem world. The sultan al-'Ādil, still in Syria, was shocked by the news, and died soon afterwards in his camp (August 31, 1218). Fearful lest the report of his death should lead to revolts throughout his empire, his followers took his body secretly to Damascus, and disposed of his treasure before announcing his death and summoning the citizens of Damascus to "implore the mercy of God for our lord, the sultan *al-malik* al-'Ādil, and pray for your sultan *al-malik* al-Mu'aẓẓam; may God accord to him a long reign!"[82]

[79] *Gesta obsidionis Damiate*, p. 76: "autem per unam horam."

[80] Contemporary sources vary as to numbers: Oliver, *Historia Damiatina*, p. 186, says one hundred men were captured. James of Vitry, *Epist.* IV, p. 575, gives the number as 112. The *Gesta obsidionis Damiate*, p. 76, says "c milites et ccc balistarii." The "Hist. patr. d'Alex.," *ROL*, XI (1908), 243, records that three hundred men were originally in the tower, and that one hundred remained to be captured.

[81] "Hist. patr. d'Alex.", *ROL*, XI (1908), 243.

[82] Al-Maqrīzī, *ROL*, IX (1902), 470. Abū-Shāmah, *Ar-rauḍatain* (*RHC*, *Or.*, V), p. 170, says his death was caused by a "stroke" which came after hearing of the capture of the chain tower.

Al-Kāmil, the eldest son, succeeded in Egypt with the title of sultan; al-Mu'aẓẓam received as his portion Damascus and Palestine; and a third son, al-Ashraf, governed Akhlat in Greater Armenia.

Although the chief barrier to a direct Christian attack upon the camp of al-Kāmil was removed, the crusaders, says Oliver, "fell into idleness and laziness . . ., and they did not imitate Judas Maccabaeus who 'seeing that the time served him' gave no rest to the enemy." James of Vitry, perhaps more plausibly, reports that the leaders thought it inadvisable to undertake to move the army across the constantly rising Nile, but preferred to await more favorable conditions after new crusaders had arrived.[83] Meanwhile the Frisians and many Germans were already making preparations to withdraw during the autumn passage, feeling that they had fulfilled their crusading vows. At the same time the leaders of the crusade had been assured in a letter from the pope dated August 13, 1218, that reinforcements were on the way.[84] Indeed, during the week following the fall of the chain tower a few ships bringing crusaders from Rome appeared in the Nile, and others anchored in the port of Acre. By the end of September many of the new arrivals had crossed over to Damietta,[85] including Pelagius, cardinal-bishop of Albano, sent by Honorius III as papal legate and charged, above all, with maintaining peace and unity among the Christians.[86] With him was his new aide, Robert of Courçon, sent out at the request of the French, as we have already noted, as spiritual adviser to French participants in the crusade. With Pelagius came the Roman crusaders, whom the pope himself had equipped at an expense of some 20,000 silver marks. Shortly afterwards there arrived from England a further group of nobles, including Ranulf, earl of Chester, and Oliver, illegitimate son of king John Lackland. Fewer Englishmen came than were expected because the pope had absolved some, and had allowed others to postpone their departure until the next autumn passage.[87] About the end of October came a large party of French crusaders, who had sailed from Genoa in

[83] Oliver, *Historia Damiatina*, p. 186; James of Vitry, *Epist.* IV, p. 576.

[84] Potthast, *Regesta*, I, 5891; *RHGF*, XIX, 666.

[85] The *Gesta obsidionis Damiate*, p. 77, says merely: "mense Septembris".

[86] Potthast, *Regesta*, I, 4803, and esp. 5810; Richard of San Germano, *Chronicon* (*MGH*, *SS.*, XIX), p. 339.

[87] *Annales de Waverleia* (ed. H. R. Luard, *Annales monastici*, II, London, 1865), pp. 289, 292. The confusion both in English and French chronicles as to the time of the arrival of the English crusaders, i.e., whether at the time of the arrival of Pelagius, shortly after the fall of the chain tower, or in the following year, appears to arise from the assumption that all who were pledged to go actually accompanied the earl of Chester. In some measure, the Annals of Waverley clarifies this, although it leaves some uncertainty as to individual nobles

late August, including archbishop William of Bordeaux, the bishops of Paris, Angers, and Laon, and bishop-elect Milo of Beauvais, together with many prominent nobles.[88]

Far from maintaining peace and unity, the presence of Pelagius appears rather to have fanned partisan differences among the crusaders. Certainly it would be an oversimplification to attribute the quarrels solely to his arrival, or to stress unduly the personal qualities which contemporaries usually ascribed to him. The very tasks imposed upon Pelagius by papal mandate suggest a major inherent weakness not only of the Fifth Crusade, but of all other crusading efforts in the Middle Ages: the absence of a recognized and efficient unified command. Honorius's naive assumption that a common religious motive was a sufficient unifying force inevitably led him and others to ignore more realistic considerations, such as the personal ambitions of individual leaders or the commercial motives of various groups or nationalities. The legate was immediately confronted with these and other distinctly materialistic questions. In order to maintain peace and unity and to further the authentic aims of the crusade, he inevitably had to make military decisions. It was in such matters, requiring cool practical judgment, that his chief failure apparently lay, and in the final analysis, one may argue, this contributed to the disastrous ending of the Fifth Crusade.

Imperious, proud, headstrong, and dogmatic, over-conscious, perhaps, of the lofty position to which he had been elevated by the pope, and literal in his interpretation of his mandate, Pelagius did not hesitate to interfere in the making of military decisions instead of deferring to the judgment of experienced commanders. To him the Fifth Crusade was, above all else, an undertaking of the church — of the whole Christian world. From the outset, therefore, he viewed with suspicion the natural assumption of John of Brienne that the Damietta expedition was a military operation having as its ultimate object the restoration of the kingdom of Jerusalem. It was undoubtedly this that led him, shortly after his arrival, to make clear his position, that the crusaders were subjects not of the kingdom of Jerusalem, but of the church.[89]

who participated in each of the two expeditions, i.e. of 1218 and 1219. For the English crusaders of this time see B. Siedschlag, *The English Participation in the Crusades* (privately printed, Menasha, Wis., 1939), pp. 137 ff.

[88] Concerning the identity of some of the French crusaders, see J. Greven, "Frankreich und der fünfte Kreuzzug," *Historisches Jahrbuch*, XLIII (1923), 45–46 and note 118.

[89] Rinaldi ("Raynaldus"), *Annales ecclesiastici*, ad ann. 1218, no 11. There is perhaps overemphasis on this officiousness of Pelagius by both H. Hoogeweg, "Der Kreuzzug von Damietta," *Mittheilungen des Österreichischen Instituts für Geschichtsforschung*, VIII

The weeks following the fall of the chain tower proved invaluable to the discouraged and demoralized Saracens. Al-Kāmil was so little interrupted that he was able to construct a huge and costly dyke, not far distant from the Christian camp, up the river from the chain tower. After many fierce conflicts on this dyke the crusaders finally cut it. The sultan then ordered a number of ships loaded with stones and had them scuttled about a mile upstream from the city in such manner as to impede navigation.[90] Despite repeated Christian attacks, the Moslems blocked the Nile during the greater part of the winter of 1218–1219, and ships could not reach the upper part of the river.[91] Any ship attempting to pass Damietta itself underwent bombardment by rocks and liquid fire from the city walls.

On October 9, 1218, the Moslems crossed the bridge in the vicinity of Būrah. With some fifty ships, about 4,000 mounted troops, and large detachments of archers and other foot-soldiers, they apparently intended to employ the cavalry for an attack on the southern fortifications of the camp, while the infantry, moving by boats farther down the river, made a thrust at the interior of the camp from the northeast. Only the vigilance of John of Brienne prevented the success of the attack. With a small patrol, he went out to reconnoiter along the west bank of the Nile, and found large numbers of enemy foot-soldiers already ashore. The king and his small detachment hastily attacked the Saracen infantry, while the camp garrison coped as best they could with the mounted attackers. But the Moslem cavalry could make no headway against the fortifications, so the crusaders could concentrate their defense against the infantry. Spurred on by the exhortations of bishop Renier of Bethlehem, John and his companions, although greatly outnumbered, succeeded in slaying most of the invaders. Only a few who plunged into the river were able to escape, and many of these, mostly Syrian archers, unable to swim, perished by drowning. The sultan had to order a retreat.[92]

This action of October 9 discouraged the Saracens, but the crusaders apparently did not win a sufficient advantage to enable

(1887), 205 ff., and L. Böhm, *Johann von Brienne*, pp. 49–50. An interesting interpretation of the position of Pelagius has recently been set forth by J. P. Donovan, S.J., *Pelagius and the Fifth Crusade* (1950), pp. 71 ff.; see also D. Mansilla, "El Cardenal hispano Pelayo Gaitán," *Anthologica Annua*, I (1953), 11–66.

[90] Ibn-al-Athīr, *Al-kāmil* (*RHC, Or.*, II, 1), p. 115; Oliver, *Historia Damiatina*, p. 196.

[91] James of Vitry, *Epist.* V, *Zeitschrift für Kirchengeschichte*, XV, 580.

[92] "Hist. patr. d'Alex.," *ROL*, XI (1908), 244. The same source explains the drowning of so many of the Syrians by the fact that they had been reared in Syria where there were but few rivers suitable for swimming, and had never learned to swim.

them to carry out a general attack. Although the swift current of the Nile made it difficult to move ships upstream to the east bank of the river near the enemy camp at al-'Ādilīyah, some of the more zealous tried to reach it. Pelagius equipped a cog which he sent upstream, apparently to discover whether it was practicable to send ships against the current. The cog made the trip successfully, but the expedition achieved no further result. Shortly afterwards James of Vitry sent another cog manned by 200 men on a similar mission, but they encountered serious resistance and returned with heavy casualties. Next, James tried a "barbote", a smaller and trimmer vessel. Six of its crew were captured, and the remainder perished valiantly while seeking to defend the ship, which was sunk.[93] On October 26 the crusaders successfully repulsed a second Moslem attack.[94] So heavy were the sultan's casualties that he now devoted his efforts to the constructing of barricades and to the setting up of artillery with which to harass Christians seeking to navigate the river or to cross over to the right bank.

Encouraged by the arrival of reinforcements during October and November, the crusaders accelerated their offensive. To avoid al-Kāmil's barricades, they conceived the plan of reconstructing the abandoned canal called al-Azraq ("the Blue") that bounded their camp, by which they could bring ships from the Mediterranean into the Nile at a point well above Damietta. Dredging was completed by early December. Its completion enabled the crusaders to avoid the barriers of the enemy as well as to maintain their camp, but offered few advantages in a direct assault upon the city.[95] Sometime before the end of November,[96] moreover, a large ship, equipped by the Templars, attempted to cross the river, but was driven by contrary winds against the walls of Damietta. There the Saracens attacked it, and eventually the ship was scuttled, either by the enemy or by its Christian crew.[97]

The winter weather brought with it many additional hardships and much suffering. The canal of al-Azraq had barely been opened when on November 29 there began a storm that raged for three

[93] James of Vitry, *Epist.* v, p. 580.

[94] Oliver, *Historia Damiatina*, pp. 190–191; see also "Hist. patr. d'Alex.," *ROL*, XI (1908), 244; *Gesta obsidionis Damiate*, pp. 77–80; James of Vitry, *Epist.* v, p. 581.

[95] Ibn-al-Athīr, *Al-kāmil* (*RHC, Or.*, II, 1), pp. 115–116.

[96] The statement of the *Gesta obsidionis Damiate*, p. 80: "mensi vero Novembris" is supported by the letter of James of Vitry, v, pp. 580 ff., in which he describes this first expedition as taking place shortly after the expedition of his barbote.

[97] James of Vitry, *loc. cit.*, says the Templars scuttled the vessel, while Oliver, *Historia Damiatina*, p. 194, says: "sive ab hostibus sive a nostris incertum habemus." Most of the Christian contemporaries describe the conflict, but are not agreed as to the number participating.

days, with violent winds and torrential rains, causing the Nile to rise rapidly and flood the camps of both the Saracens and the crusaders. Quite unprepared, the Christians suffered intensely. Tents were submerged and food supplies swept away by the raging waters. The sick and wounded, unable to escape the torrent, perished miserably. Transport ships and galleys were torn from their moorings and set adrift, many to be lost. The canal helped to draw off the water, however, and the Moslem camp also suffered.[98]

Shortly before the storm broke, the Christians had built a new floating fortress on a foundation of six cogs to aid in the assault on Damietta. The huge structure was driven by the storm to the east bank of the river, where it was boarded and seized by the Saracens. Its small crew of sixteen men resisted valiantly, but fourteen were slain and two escaped by swimming to the opposite bank. Accused of cowardice, however, and of failing to support their comrades, they were hanged by order of king John.[99] The Moslems, at first overjoyed at the seizure of this prize, soon found they were unable to maneuver the large hulk and decided to burn it lest the crusaders, hoping to recapture it, attack them in overwhelming numbers. In the wake of the storm came disease, and large numbers of Christians perished from cold or from scurvy and pestilence,[100] including Robert of Courçon, so well remembered as the preacher of the crusade in France.[101]

It was during this disastrous storm also that Pelagius took a more active role as the leader of the crusading forces. In the partisan differences which arose between the supporters of king John and the newly arrived crusaders, it was inevitable that the papal legate should find active support among John's opponents. Pelagius' self-confidence was probably heightened by the "discovery" of a book written in Arabic, prophesying the fall of Damietta, whose author was believed to have foretold correctly many events that had already taken place.[102] Such a find must have served to direct the attention of the credulous more and more to the spiritual leader of the expedition, who freely used it as propaganda. Many of the crusaders who had arrived during the autumn of 1218

[98] John of Tulbia, *De domino Iohanne*, p. 123: "Hist. patr. d'Alex.," *ROL*, XI (1908), 245–246.

[99] "Hist. patr. d'Alex.," *ROL*, XI (1908), 245.

[100] The *Gesta obsidionis Damiate*, p. 83, says: "sexta pars exercitus mortua est." John of Tulbia, *De domino Iohanne*, p. 193, says, "quinta pars exercitus mortua fuit." Oliver, *Historia Damiatina*, p. 193: "cum patientia multa migraverunt ad Dominum plurimi."

[101] *Epist.* v, pp. 581–582.

[102] Oliver, *Historia Damiatina*, chap. 35.

were Italians, accustomed from the beginning of their expedition to look upon Pelagius as their leader. Undoubtedly, also, the period of inactivity following the capture of the chain tower and the failure to make appreciable progress against the Saracen camp, followed by the storm, led some to call for new leadership, which gave Pelagius his chance. To the Frisians and Germans, however, who followed the scholasticus Oliver, and had accepted the leadership of John of Brienne, as well as to the close associates of John, who had seen the devastating effects of disunity in 1217, the tension so manifest after the arrival of Pelagius and the new pilgrims must have been more than ominous. As the winter with its winds and rains wore on, discontent reigned among the masses of the troops.[103] At least Pelagius offered a change in leadership, and employed to the limit the authority of his office. When others had failed to find a way of crossing to the opposite bank, he asserted his authority by proclaiming a fast of three days and commanding his followers to stand barefoot before the fragment of the cross while appealing to Heaven for guidance.

A handful of Frisians and Germans aboard the ship "Holy Mother", which had previously been used as an escort in the attack on the chain tower, now went up the Nile and attacked the Moslems' pontoon bridge, returning safely.[104] But now as before the crusaders made no attempt to follow up the victory. It was in fact not until February 2, 1219, that Pelagius ordered a general confession throughout the army, providing at the same time for a new attack upon the enemy camp. On the next day the Christians in cogs, galleys, and barbotes began the ascent of the river in the teeth of a new storm. The cog of the duke of Austria destroyed the palisades which the enemy had erected along the river bank. Blinded by the rain and hail, under heavy fire from the Moslems[105] the crusaders were compelled to withdraw to their camp on the opposite bank of the river. By February 5 conditions were again favorable for the renewal of the attack.[106] The new storm had in any case made the Christian camp untenable.

Now the fortunes of the crusaders improved, largely as the result of developments on the Moslem side. The death of al-'Ādil, who had kept his sons firmly under control although they ruled with royal prerogatives in their respective provinces, had prepared the way for conspiracies and internal conflicts at the very time of

[103] *Gesta obsidionis Damiate*, pp. 80 ff.

[104] Oliver, *Historia Damiatina*, pp. 195–196.

[105] *Gesta obsidionis Damiate*, p. 84.

[106] *Ibid.*, p. 86; Oliver, *Historia Damiatina*, p. 197.

the crusaders' attack.[107] Al-Kāmil, the sultan of Egypt, threatened by the crusaders, had also to face a conspiracy built upon the fears of the people and the discontent of the army (1218–1219). The chief conspirator was 'Imād-ad-Dīn Aḥmad, called Ibn-al-Mashṭūb, emir of Nablus, a Kurd who wielded great influence among the Kurdish troops, which constituted a considerable part of the army. He and other emirs plotted to depose al-Kāmil and to set up in his stead a young brother, al-Fā'iz, whom they believed they could control. By the time al-Kāmil got word of the plot, at his camp at al-'Ādilīyah, preparations for the coup d'état had gone so far that he surprised the conspirators in the very act of taking an oath of fealty to al-Fā'iz, the Koran open before them. At his appearance the conspirators were momentarily awed, but al-Kāmil believed that all was lost. He mounted his horse and fled secretly to Ashmūn, apparently with the intention of taking refuge with his son al-Mas'ūd, the governor of Yemen. At dawn the army along the Nile discovered his flight; their widespread panic led to the complete disruption of the defenses on the right bank of the river and the abandonment of weapons and supplies. At first widely scattered, the Moslem forces gradually reassembled on al-Baḥr aṣ-Ṣaghīr near Ashmūn. But it was only after the arrival of al-Mu'aẓẓam two or three days later that order was restored and al-Kāmil reassured. In a dramatic scene, not without comedy, al-Mu'aẓẓam rushed to the tent of Ibn-al-Mashṭūb at night, forced him to mount his horse while still in night dress, and sent him under heavy escort into exile in Syria.[108]

So it happened that at dawn on February 5, during the heavy wind and rain, a Christian deserter, who had been with the enemy for some time, called across the river to the crusaders to inform them that the Moslem camp had been abandoned.[109] Although king John suspected a ruse, scouts soon confirmed the news.[110] The Christian forces then began crossing the river to the abandoned camp. Their horses had trouble obtaining a foothold in the marshy ground, and a few enemy troops came out of Damietta, but were quickly overcome by the Templars. The crusaders took, from the deserted camp, tents, weapons, gold and silver utensils, livestock, grain and fodder, and even women and children. They also seized

[107] Cf. Ibn-al-Athīr, *Al-kāmil* (*RHC, Or.*, II, 1), pp. 116–117.

[108] *Ibid.*, p. 117; al-Maqrīzī, "Histoire d'Égypte," *ROL*, IX (1902), 475–476; Abū-Shāmah, *Ar-rauḍatain* (*RHC, Or.*, V), pp. 175–176. Arab sources are in essential agreement on the details of this episode.

[109] Oliver, *Historia Damiatina*, p. 198.

[110] *Eracles* (*RHC, Occ.*, II), p. 336.

ships, both large and small, which were moored along the river bank between the camp at al-'Ādilīyah and the city.[111] The crusaders were now encamped on all sides of Damietta: Pelagius with the Roman, Genoese, and other Italian troops on the bank of the river north of the city; the Templars, Hospitallers, and Provençals to the east; and king John of Jerusalem with the French and Pisan troops just south of the city. Across the river, occupying the old camp, were the Frisian and German troops. A bridge was constructed joining the camps on the opposite banks.[112] In February also came reinforcements, especially Cypriote knights commanded by Walter of Caesarea, constable of Cyprus.[113]

It seems likely that al-Kāmil and al-Mu'aẓẓam now decided to follow the advice their father al-'Ādil is supposed to have given them on his deathbed, and to open negotiations with the Christians. Though the *Eracles* alone gives February as the date for the opening of the negotiations, the *History of the Patriarchs of Alexandria*, in referring to the later discussions in August, makes clear reference to these earlier offers.[114] Accordingly, a messenger was dispatched to king John and Pelagius, requesting that ambassadors be sent to discuss terms of peace. When the Christian envoys reached al-Kāmil's camp, the sultan proposed to surrender the kingdom of Jerusalem with the exception of Kerak (Krak des Moabites, al-Karak) and Krak de Montréal (ash-Shaubak), commanding the desert road to Egypt, and offered a thirty-year truce, in exchange for the crusaders' evacuation of Egypt. Representatives of the sultan then returned with the embassy to the Christian camp to receive the reply of the leaders. King John and the French and Syrian leaders favored accepting the offer. They recalled that the Egyptian expedition had been undertaken for the purpose of facilitating the conquest of Jerusalem and argued that the object had now been achieved. But Pelagius, making full use of his powers as legate, and supported by the Italians, as well as by the Templars and Hospitallers, overruled the recommendation of the king. Even when the Moslem emissary returned a second time offering, in addition to the terms already proposed, a tribute of 30,000 bezants as compensation for the two fortresses, he was met

111 "Hist. patr. d'Alex.," *ROL*, XI (1908), 246–247; Ibn-al-Athīr, *Al-kāmil* (*RHC, Or.* II, 1), p. 117. The Arab and Christian sources are in general agreement.

112 Oliver, *Historia Damiatina*, pp. 199 ff.; *Eracles* (*RHC, Occ.*, II), p. 337. Of the bridge James of Vitry, *Epist.* v, p. 583, says: "pontem etiam fortissimum super naves fabricaverunt."

113 *Eracles* (*RHC, Occ.*, II), pp. 339 ff.

114 *Ibid.*, pp. 338 ff.; *ROL*, XI (1908), 253.

with refusal.[115] Had Pelagius now determined to conquer the entire Near East, going far beyond the crusaders' original intentions? Did the Italians support him because of their commercial ambition to establish themselves in the Nile delta? At any rate, the Christian refusal of the Moslem terms sacrificed the attainable to the visionary.

The swift and courageous action of the sultan of Damascus, al-Mu'aẓẓam, had served to stiffen Moslem resistance. Reassembled and reinforced from Syria, the Moslem army took up a new position at Fāriskūr, a short distance up the Nile from al-'Ādilīyah. The Christians had barely consolidated their position under the walls of Damietta when they had to defend their camp against these reorganized enemy forces. The sultans also addressed a joint appeal to the Moslem world, especially to the caliph at Baghdad, an-Nāṣir, who was sometimes called by the Christians the "pope of the Saracens".[116] The crusaders believed Damietta to be strongly fortified and heavily garrisoned, but al-Maqrīzī reports that sickness and death had greatly reduced the garrison, originally some 20,000 strong, and that the survivors were in a weakened condition.[117] An attack on Damietta launched immediately after the crossing of the river might well have been successful, but al-Mu'aẓẓam had ended Moslem panic and enabled the sultan to assume a new position threatening to the Christians. The opportunity had been lost. More than nine months were to pass before the crusaders, after repeated attacks by the Moslems, and after disheartening failures in their assaults on the well-nigh impregnable walls, at last entered Damietta.

While engaged in preparations for attacking the city, the crusaders learned that al-Mu'aẓẓam, who feared that the Christians would obtain possession of several strongholds in Palestine, had ordered the destruction of the fortifications of Mt. Tabor, Toron, Banyas, Safad, and even Jerusalem, whose walls had been strengthened and population greatly increased since the Moslem occupation. On March 19, 1219, the terrified and protesting citizens of Jerusalem witnessed the beginning of the destruction of their city walls.[118] Al-Mu'aẓẓam hoped to make such vantage points in Palestine untenable in the event the Christians should retake them.

[115] *Eracles* (*RHC, Occ.*, II), p. 339. For an interesting interpretation of the historical significance of the policy of Pelagius and his supporters, see R. Grousset, *Histoire des croisades*, III (Paris, 1948), 235.

[116] *Chronique d'Ernoul*, p. 421: "le callife de Baudas qui apostolis est des Sarracens"; and James of Vitry, *Historia orientalis* (ed. J. Bongars, *Gesta Dei per Francos*, I), p. 1125: "sextus filius est nomine Mahomet, qui tenet regnum de Baudas, ubi est Papa Saracenorum."

[117] Al-Maqrīzī, "Histoire d'Égypte," *ROL*, IX (1902), 476–477, 480.

[118] Abū-Shāmah, *Ar-rauḍatain* (*RHC, Or.*, V), p. 173.

He impressed Egyptians into his service, and exacted heavy tribute from Jews and Christians, who made up substantial elements in the populations of Cairo and Fustat, and who now had to mortgage the sacred utensils of gold and silver from their churches and synagogues.[119] As the danger had increased in the delta of the Nile, the beduins on the confines of Egypt had seized the opportunity to block the roads and pillage the countryside, displaying at least as strong hostility toward Moslems as toward the Christian invader.[120] The Moslems suspected that the Christian population — the Copts and the Melkites of the cities — sympathized with the crusaders, and so Christians fell victim to the fanaticism that mounted among the inhabitants as the threat from the invaders increased.[121]

On March 3, 1219, after the arrival of reinforcements from Syria led by al-Muẓaffar, son of al-Manṣūr of Hamah, the Moslems began a series of harassing attacks upon the crusader camp.[122] After repelling two attacks, on March 3 and 17, the crusaders tightened their siege by building a second bridge, almost a mile in length, and mounted on 38 vessels, this time below the city of Damietta. Patrol boats also were constantly active in an effort to prevent the enemy from approaching, and two islands in the Nile were fortified and garrisoned.[123] At dawn on Palm Sunday, March 31, 1219, the Moslems launched a general attack against both the camp and one of the pontoon bridges, part of which they burned before withdrawing with heavy losses.[124] A final attack was repulsed on April 7.

Meanwhile many crusaders had sailed for home. In early May duke Leopold of Austria, who, as Oliver says, "for a year and a half had fought faithfully for Christ, full of devotion, humility, obedience, and generosity", departed. Pelagius employed his full authority to induce the returning crusaders to postpone their departure until the autumn passage, offering plenary indulgence not only for their sins, but for the sins of their immediate families.[125] The departures, however, appear to have been more than offset by

[119] "Hist. patr. d'Alex.," *ROL*, XI (1908), 249 ff.

[120] Ibn-al-Athīr, *Al-kāmil* (*RHC, Or.*, II, 1), p. 118.

[121] "Hist. patr. d'Alex.," *ROL*, XI (1908), 247.

[122] Al-Maqrīzī, *ROL*, IX (1902), 479–480, places al-Muẓaffar's arrival at the beginning of the year 616, which would be early in March of 1219. For details of al-Muẓaffar, see especially Abū-l-Fidā', *Kitāb al-mukhtaṣar* (*RHC, Or.*, I), p. 93.

[123] *Gesta obsidionis Damiate*, p. 88.

[124] Oliver, *Historia Damiatina*, pp. 206–207, says: "ad horam fere decimam," while the author of the *Gesta obsidionis Damiate*, pp. 89–90, says "ante auroram usque ad noctem".

[125] *Gesta obsidionis Damiate*, p. 90.

new arrivals. By May 16 large numbers of reinforcements from the west had arrived, bringing with them supplies and horses. Indeed emergency measures had to be taken to supply the newcomers with provisions. Guy Embriaco of Gibelet (Jubail), a Syrian baron, generously provided sums of money to purchase food supplies from the island of Cyprus.[126]

News of these constant reinforcements may well explain the renewed activity of the sultan who, between May 16 and 18, attacked in force. Moslem "corpses filled the trenches of the Christian camp and covered the field of battle."[127] Evidently in an attempt to prevent the scattering of the enemy during combat, the leaders, employing a well known device of the Lombards, constructed a *carroccio* upon which they placed the standard of the Christians. They instructed the infantry to advance gradually behind it, engaging in combat only when they had attained an advantageous position. During an enemy attack of May 26, the crusaders employed this new device; it bewildered or frightened the Moslems, who abandoned the attack.

Meanwhile the Christians were preparing an assault on the city, constructing battering rams, towers, and other siege machines, and at the same time attempting tunneling operations to undermine the walls. But tunneling was impracticable because of the water in the moat surrounding the outer wall. If the assault was to succeed, it must be made from above, even at the risk of inviting heavy counterattacks from the enemy forces at Fāriskūr. Except for Pelagius the leaders advised against a general attack, saying that they had insufficient troops to assault the enemy camp and the city simultaneously, claiming that the Moslems outnumbered them fifty to one.[128]

Dissatisfied with these objections, Pelagius began a series of direct assaults upon the city from the waterfront. On July 8, 1219, Pisan and Venetian troops, after borrowing anchors, ropes, and other equipment from the various leaders, launched the first attack to the accompaniment of trumpet blasts and the playing of reed pipes and with banners flying. But the garrison sprayed Greek fire upon the scaling ladders and forced the ships to withdraw. At a signal from the besieged garrison, the sultan moved down the river from Fāriskūr, and for two days harassed the Christian camp, so that the defenders could not assist the Italians.

[126] Grousset, *Histoire des croisades*, III, 221.
[127] *Gesta obsidionis Damiate*, p. 91; John of Tulbia, *De domino Iohanne*, p. 127.
[128] *Gesta obsidionis Damiate*, p. 93.

After his first blow had failed, Pelagius, not yet convinced of the futility of his plan, and encouraged by intelligence of the impoverished condition of the garrison, struck again two days later, this time with petraries and mangonels near the city walls. But just before dawn, while the Italian guards were sleeping, eight Saracens succeeded in burning the machine nearest the tower and slaying seven of its defenders. Although delayed in his plans, Pelagius again attacked on July 13 and 31, only to be turned back each time by a deluge of Greek fire. During each of these new efforts signals from the garrison set in motion the troops of the sultan at Fāriskūr. The Moslems concentrated their attacks upon the upper bridge connecting the two camps of the Christians and, on one occasion, were on the point of destroying it when the timely arrival of a detachment of troops drove them back. But even more serious was the counter-offensive of July 31, led by al-Kāmil against the camp of the Templars, which forced a retreat of the defenders on a wide front, and penetrated deep into the camp. Only through the skillful leadership of the new master, Peter of Montaigu, aided by the Teutonic Knights, were the troops reformed and the enemy pursued outside the gates until darkness ended the battle. Pelagius, however, persisted in his assault on the city walls well into the month of August, until the waters of the Nile had so receded that it was no longer possible to reach the walls on the river front with scaling ladders.[129]

Tension between the factions of the crusaders had now almost reached the breaking point. The repeated failures had greatly reduced morale, especially of the masses of infantry. With increasing bitterness they charged the princes and knights with betraying the army, with remaining idly in camp while the Italians besieged the city. They hinted that it was cowardice that had prevented the leaders from attacking the sultan's camp.[130] In their turn, the mounted troops made light of the risks which the foot-soldiers were willing to take in fighting against the Saracens. Mutual recriminations led only to increased bitterness, and mob spirit prevailed, as the disgruntled crusaders muttered their protests at being detained forever from returning home, and clamored for

[129] The most detailed account of these activities during July and August 1219 is that of the *Gesta obsidionis Damiate,* pp. 93–96. The *Eracles* (*RHC, Occ.*, II), p. 340, also reports the signaling between the city and the sultan's camp. The masters of the Hospital and the Temple, Garin and Peter of Montaigu-sur-Champeix, were brothers of archbishop Eustorgue of Nicosia.

[130] *Gesta obsidionis Damiate,* p. 101.

an immediate attack upon the Saracen camp.[131] Goaded on by these complaints, the leaders reluctantly yielded to the very ill-advised plan of attacking the enemy camp at Fāriskūr. They divided the army into three units, one to guard the camp, a second to man the ships, and a third to march overland against al-Kāmil's camp.[132]

On August 29, as the crusaders approached, the Moslems struck their tents and pretended flight, thus leaving the crusaders uncertain whether to continue in pursuit or to withdraw. King John of Jerusalem advised camping overnight, so that in the morning they could better ascertain the intentions of the enemy: there was no fresh water in the region between the Nile and Lake Manzalah, where the Christian forces now stood, and heat and thirst had inflicted heavy suffering on the troops. Many who had clamored loudest to be led to the attack now pleaded insistently to be permitted to withdraw.[133] When the Saracens became aware of this indecision, they halted their pretended retreat, and turned to deliver a smashing attack upon the disorganized and faltering enemy. Oliver says the Cypriotes were the first to flee, and were soon followed in disorderly retreat by the Italians. In vain Pelagius and the patriarch of Jerusalem sought to check the retreat and restore order. Only the intervention of king John, followed by the Templars and Hospitallers, the earl of Chester, and other knights, made it possible to cover the retreat and prevent the destruction of the army. But the losses were heavy, perhaps as high as 4,300, including many of the best of the crusading forces.[134]

The sultan made his victory the occasion for reopening negotiations, evidently believing that the chastening effects of the defeat would make the crusaders more receptive to his proposals. He therefore retained some of the noblest of the captives at his headquarters to serve as emissaries to the crusading leaders while their less fortunate companions were being led in chains through the streets of Cairo.[135] Though the sultan had undoubtedly sustained some losses in the recent battle, and though his own supplies were threatened by the failure of the Nile to rise to its accustomed flood stage during the early autumn, the real reason for his renewal of

[131] *Eracles* (*RHC, Occ.*, II), p. 340.

[132] The *Gesta obsidionis Damiate*, pp. 101 ff., continues to be the most detailed account, although other sources agree in the essentials.

[133] *Eracles* (*RHC, Occ.*, II), p. 340.

[134] *Ibid.*, p. 341, estimates the number killed or dead from thirst and exhaustion at 4,000, in addition to 300 knights who constituted the rear-guard. A number of nobles were captured or missing, and at least one galley, with 200 men aboard, was reported lost (James of Vitry, *Epist.* v, p. 586; Oliver, *Historia Damiatina*, p. 216; *Gesta obsidionis Damiate*, pp. 101 ff.).

[135] "Hist. patr. d'Alex.." *ROL*, XI (1908), 253.

negotiations was the suffering within Damietta. With the river closed, and surrounded by the besieging army, the population was in misery. The streets were filled with the neglected dead and dying, while the scarcity of meat, eggs, bread, and many other foods left no hope to the living save death or surrender.[136] So al-Kāmil sent two of his captive knights, Andrew of Nanteuil and John of Arcis, to renew his former offers of an armistice. In addition to the retrocession of Jerusalem, with the exception of Kerak and Krak de Montréal, the sultan now agreed to pay for the restoration of the walls of Jerusalem, and to permit, or even pay for, the reconstruction of Belvoir (Kaukab al-Hawā'), Safad, and Toron. He also renewed the offer of a thirty-year truce, and agreed to send twenty Moslem hostages of noble birth to remain with the Christians until the fortifications had been restored. In addition, he offered to restore the portion of the True Cross which had been captured many years before at Hattin, together with any prisoners who could be found alive in Egypt and in Syria.[137]

Again king John, the Syrians, the French, and the Teutonic Knights strongly favored accepting the terms. Again Pelagius, most of the clergy, the Italians, the Templars, and the Hospitallers were uncompromising in their refusal. Pelagius' attitude would appear fantastic except for the fact that he was counting on the expected arrival of many crusaders on the imminent autumn passage.[138] Although large numbers had withdrawn from the army, as Oliver states, "before the accustomed passage", many newcomers arrived almost simultaneously with these departures. Above all, Savary of Mauléon, loyal supporter of the late king John of England, arrived with ten or fifteen galleys, giving new encouragement to the crusaders, as did other English arrivals.[139]

It was probably shortly before the battle of August 29 that Francis of Assisi and a brother of his order arrived in the camp of the crusaders, seeking authorization from Pelagius to visit the sultan. After an initial refusal, Pelagius changed his mind and let the pair go on what must have appeared to all observers as a suicidal

136 Al-Maqrīzī, "Histoire d'Égypte," *ROL*, IX (1902), 480.

137 *Eracles* (*RHC, Occ.*, II), pp. 341–343; James of Vitry, *Epist.* VI, pp. 73–74; Oliver, *Historia Damiatina*, p. 218; *Le Menestrel de Reims* (ed. R. Röhricht, *Testimonia minora de quinto bello sacro*, Geneva, 1882), pp. 115 ff.

138 *Gesta obsidionis Damiate*, p. 104.

139 *Ibid.*, p. 104; *Annales de Waverleia* (*Annales monastici*, II), p. 292; *Eracles* (*RHC, Occ.*, II), p. 342 (where some of the English arrivals are confused with those of the previous year). Oliver, *Historia Damiatina*, p. 219, mentions only "Savericus de Mallion cum galeis armatis et bellatoribus plurimis. . . ." John of Tulbia, *De domino Iohanne*, p. 133, says there were fifteen galleys.

mission. Al-Kāmil probably mistook these extraordinary visitors for emissaries from the crusaders and received them courteously, only to find that they had come merely to expose the "errors" of the Moslem faith. Outraged by this impertinence, the companions of the sultan demanded that the friars be summarily executed. Al-Kāmil, however, with a display of affection for his humble visitors, first listened patiently to their message and then had them safely escorted to the outposts of the Christian camp. Francis appears to have remained with the crusaders until after the fall of Damietta before departing for Acre.[140]

Pelagius' opposition did not prevent a protracted discussion of the sultan's offer. Oliver remarks significantly that "during the negotiations we promptly repaired our ramparts and other fortifications." While the negotiations were still in progress, the Moslems, breaking the truce, launched new attacks on the Christian camp and one of the bridges, hoping to get through to Damietta with provisions, but their forces were driven off.[141]

Now the sultan tried bribery. Nine Christians were induced by offers of money to attempt to destroy the bridge, so the Moslems could relieve the city. But one of the Christians revealed the scheme to Pelagius; the others took refuge in the Moslem camp. On the following night a Genoese, acting alone, tried to destroy the bridge and several siege machines. About the same time, a renegade Spaniard was detected in "black market" dealings with the enemy. Both of these traitors, upon detection, were tied to the tails of horses and dragged through the camp as examples. The Christians likewise used Moslem deserters to learn of an impending Moslem attack, and took new precautions to defend both bridge and camp. Pelagius offered two-year indulgences to crusaders who would transport the necessary timbers from the ships to erect emergency fortifications.[142]

[140] The visit is recorded by most of the contemporary sources, perhaps in greatest detail by Ernoul, *op. cit.*, pp. 431 ff. G. Golubovich, *Biblioteca bio-bibliografica della Terra Santa e dell' Oriente Francescano*, I, 94, places the date of the visit between Sept. 1 and 26 (?), 1219. This exhaustive assembling of the pertinent documents has been further supplemented by the same author in *Studi Francescani*, XXIII (n.s., XII; 1926), 307–330. Nazzareno Jacopozzi, "Dove sia evvenuta la visita di San Francesco d'Assisi al Sultano Malek el-Kamel," *Congrès international de géographie*, V, 146, says: "La sua visita a Malek el-Kamel il febbraio del 1220. . . ." For a recent detailed study of the visit see also Roncaglia in *Studi Francescani*, L (1953), 97–106.

[141] Oliver, *Historia Damiatina*, pp. 218–219; *Gesta obsidionis Damiate*, pp. 106–107.

[142] *Gesta obsidionis Damiate*, pp. 108–109. As to the presence of Spaniards see the brief notice of P. Ferdinand M. Delorme, "Les Espagnols à la bataille de Damiette (29 août 1219)," in *Archivum Franciscanum historicum*, XVI (1923), 245. This brief statement of Delorme, based on a bull of Honorius III of March 15, 1219, as well as a remark of Thomas of Celano (p. 149) appears to establish the presence of Spaniards, despite former doubts.

Apparently in desperation al-Kāmil again renewed his offer of peace. In the conference of Christian leaders which followed, king John, who favored acceptance, was strongly supported by the English leaders, particularly by the earls Ranulf of Chester and William of Arundel and Sussex, in addition to his usual following among the French, the Syrians, and the Germans. The partisans of Pelagius argued, not without force, that the sultan's offer was only a crafty maneuver intended to bring about disunity in, and even dissolution of, the Christian army, after which the Moslems would be able, with little difficulty, to regain a Jerusalem whose chief strongholds had already been dismantled. Moreover, they felt, as long as the sultan retained possession of the Transjordanian fortifications of Kerak and Krak de Montréal, he could devastate the surrounding districts at will. The additional offer also to restore the lost fragment of the True Cross must have appeared to others besides Pelagius as essentially fraudulent: Saladin had failed to find the relic many years before when he desperately needed to return it to the Christians in exchange for the lives of his captive subjects.[143]

When these discussions were definitively ended by Pelagius, and the emirs who had come as emissaries had barely departed from the camp, the sultan, in a new effort to supply Damietta, sent a detachment with provisions through the Christian lines November 3, 1219. Passing quietly through the sector held by Hervey of Donzi, count of Nevers, the intruders had actually entered the camp and were moving toward one of the city gates when their presence was detected and the alarm given. Only the swift action of the Templars and Hospitallers, who had risen early for their morning devotions, prevented the complete success of the undertaking. Most of the invaders were slain or put to flight, but a few succeeded in entering Damietta. Charged with inexcusable neglect, the count of Nevers was summarily banished from the camp.[144] For the moment, at least, this incident appears to have created a unanimity of purpose long absent among the crusading leaders. All efforts were devoted to the preparation for a final assault upon Damietta. Severe penalties were ordered for anybody guilty of negligence in the defense of the camp. Guards of the walls and trenches guilty of leaving their posts were to be hanged; recreant knights were to be deprived of horses and arms and banished; while infantrymen, women, and merchant camp-followers assigned to such duty were, if delinquent, to suffer

[143] James of Vitry, *Epist.* VI, pp. 74–75, and Oliver, *Historia Damiatina*, pp. 222 ff.

[144] *Eracles* (*RHC, Occ.*, II), p. 345; Abū-Shāmah, *Ar-rauḍatain* (*RHC, Or.*, V), pp. 176–177.

the amputation of a hand and have their belongings confiscated. Failure to bear arms at all times while guarding the tents would subject every culprit, regardless of rank, to excommunication. Orders were issued also regulating the conduct of the crusaders in case Damietta should be captured.[145]

By now the garrison of Damietta had become so weakened that it was no longer possible to man all the towers. On the night of November 4, 1219, four Christian sentries, while observing a tower which had previously been breached by the machines of the Hospitallers, suspected that it had been deserted. Climbing a long ladder, they found that both wall and tower had in fact been abandoned. They reported their observations, and a sufficient detachment of crusaders occupied the tower while the Christian army entered the city. Much contemporary testimony is written in the spirit of partisanship, for or against Pelagius or John of Brienne. But the ascertainable facts appear to be fairly summarized by the simple statement of Oliver: "On the night of the 5th of November Damietta was captured without treachery, without resistance, without violent pillage and tumult. . . ." According to the author of the *History of the Patriarchs of Alexandria*, however, there were those who said that Damietta was taken only by the treachery of its garrison, who were moved to surrender because of their extreme distress.[146] Seeing the Christian standards flying from the towers on the following morning, the sultan hastily abandoned his camp at Fāriskūr and withdrew to Mansurah. Most of the Arab chroniclers agree that the conquerors either massacred or enslaved the surviving inhabitants. All contemporary sources testify that the few thousands of Saracen survivors, men and women, were all more or less ill. Streets and houses were filled with the dead, whose naked bodies had been partially devoured by ravenous dogs. The dead lay unmoved in the beds of the helpless dying.[147] Oliver says that of the 80,000 people in the city at the beginning of the siege, only 3,000 survived, and of these only 100 were not ill.[148]

Some of the survivors were probably sold into slavery, although many, certainly the prosperous, were retained to be exchanged for

[145] *Gesta obsidionis Damiate*, pp. 110–111.

[146] *Eracles* (*RHC, Occ.*, II), pp. 345 ff.; Oliver, *Historia Damiatina*, pp. 224 ff.; *Chronique d'Ernoul*, p. 426; "Hist. Patr. d'Alex.," *ROL*, XI (1908), 254.

[147] See especially Abū-Shāmah, *Ar-rauḍatain* (*RHC, Or.*, V), p. 177; al-Maqrīzī, "Histoire d'Égypte," *ROL*, IX (1902), 480; and Abū-l-Fidā', *Kitāb al-mukhtaṣar* (*RHC, Or.*, I), p. 91.

[148] Oliver, *Historia Damiatina*, p. 236; cf. *Gesta obsidionis Damiate*, p. 113; James of Vitry, *Epist.* VI, pp. 77–78.

Christians held prisoner by the Moslems. Many of the children were taken by James of Vitry or others and baptized, although most of them were so weakened in health that they succumbed shortly after baptism.[149] There is plausible evidence, however, that many of the surviving adult inhabitants of Damietta were permitted to go into voluntary exile, as the city was repopulated by colonists from the west. In some instances also, the survivors were treated with every consideration, as in the case of the shaikh Abū-l-Ḥasan, who was left unmolested as a man of great charity and virtue.[150] There is little disagreement respecting the rich booty taken in the captured city: precious stones, silks, rich ornaments, quantities of gold and silver utensils. Despite the severe penalties previously decreed, much of this booty fell into the hands of individual looters. The amount which found its way to authorized depositories was estimated by James of Vitry at not more than 400,000 bezants.[151] The fortifications of the city had been but little damaged during the long siege, and the crusaders could turn their attention almost immediately to plundering the surrounding country and to foraging for necessary provisions. By November 23 they had captured the neighboring city of Tinnis without a struggle. The terrified inhabitants, believing the entire crusading army to be moving to the attack, closed the gates and fled. Although the city no longer possessed its ancient splendor, it afforded an additional stronghold of first-rate importance, while its location on Lake Manzalah, with its abundant fish, birds, and salt works, contributed greatly to the food supplies.[152]

But the taking of the city of Damietta inevitably heightened the tension once more between king John of Jerusalem and Pelagius, who assumed that his position as representative of the church gave him full authority to make final disposition of the conquest. Declaring the city to be the possession of the Christians of the west, whose common effort had wrested it from the Moslems, he rejected all proposals which would give John of Brienne control over it, either direct or indirect. John's adherents, on the other hand, envisaged Damietta as a Christian stronghold in Egypt, comparable to Acre in Palestine, and necessarily subject to the king of Jerusalem. It was soon apparent that the question could find no amicable solution except through papal arbitration, or until after the arrival of emperor Frederick II. Meanwhile the partisanship manifested itself on

[149] James of Vitry, *Epist.* VI, p. 79.

[150] Grousset, *Histoire des croisades*, III, 220. Abū-Shāmah, *Ar-rauḍatain* (*RHC, Or.*, V), p. 177, relates this story of Abū-l-Ḥasan.

[151] James of Vitry, *Epist.* VI, p. 78.

[152] Oliver, *Historia Damiatina*, pp. 240 ff.

occasion in actual riots or clashes of arms between the partisans of the king, now including the Templars and Hospitallers as well as the French and Syrians, and the partisans of the legate, chiefly Italians.

In disgust king John equipped three of his ships, and threatened to leave at once. Pelagius at last yielded, and tentatively recognized John's claims to Damietta, pending a final decision by the pope. The Italians, however, insisting that they had been deprived of a fair share in the spoils of Damietta, took arms against the French and all but expelled them from the city. Meanwhile Pelagius, seeking to find a basis for mediation which would prevent the complete demoralization of the expedition, so angered his Italian supporters that they threatened his life. The French, the Templars, and the Hospitallers now, in their turn, routed the Italians. To preserve the peace, however, a redistribution of the spoils, more favorable to the Italians, was made and a semblance of unity restored.[153] It was not until February 2, 1220, that these partisan conflicts were adjusted and the city sufficiently cleansed to permit a formal ceremony signalizing the Christian victory. A solemn procession was led to the splendid mosque, now consecrated as the cathedral of the Blessed Virgin. Individual towers and quarters of the city walls were allotted to the various nationalities participating in the expedition. One tower was reserved for the Roman church and another for the archbishop of Damietta.[154]

Despite the tentative agreement, Pelagius continued to act high-handedly, and John of Brienne to find that his feeble claim to the Armenian kingship demanded his personal attention. Oliver asserts and the Chronicle of Ernoul implies that John employed the Armenian situation merely as an excuse for leaving Damietta.[155] John probably knew that Pelagius' actions merely reflected the will of Honorius III. The capture of Damietta amounted to a personal defeat for John. Pelagius' supporters blamed the subsequent difficulties of the crusade upon John's fit of pique and refusal to subordinate his personal interests. Yet this would have required extraordinary self-abnegation. In any case, John had hardly set sail from Damietta when Honorius, in congratulating the crusaders, gave formal approval to the authority of Pelagius in temporal as in

[153] John of Tulbia, *De domino Iohanne*, p. 139.

[154] Oliver, *Historia Damiatina*, pp. 239–240. G. Golubovich has dealt in some detail with this division of Damietta into quarters according to nationalities, fraternal orders, etc., in his "San Francesco e i Francescani in Damiata, 5 Nov. 1219–2 Feb. 1220," *Studi Francescani*, XXIII (n.s., XII; 1926), 307 ff. No archbishop was elected before the loss of the city.

[155] Oliver, *Historia Damiatina*, p. 248; *Chronique d'Ernoul*, p. 427.

spiritual affairs.[156] Far removed from the scene of action, and dependent upon Pelagius' reports, Honorius doubtless felt the capture of Damietta to be a heroic achievement. Pelagius at Damietta personified the church triumphant; he was Joshua before the walls of Jericho, as the pope had long expected him to be.[157]

The lack of discipline so apparent throughout the ranks of the crusading army may well explain Pelagius' rigorous, if not tyrannical, rule during the months following John's departure. His regulations drastically restricting the movements of ships and the arrivals and departures of pilgrims were emergency measures intended to prevent the disintegration of the army, rather than deliberate acts of tyranny. But his actions probably prevented the adequate safeguarding of the shipping routes between Cyprus and the Syrian ports and the harbor of Damietta, and Saracen ships attacked and destroyed several pilgrim vessels en route to Syria and Egypt. The statement of Ernoul, who is rarely sympathetic toward Pelagius, that more than 13,000 pilgrims were lost in these attacks is probably an exaggeration.[158]

As the crusaders continued inactive in Damietta, dissatisfaction mounted on all sides. The masses of the Christians were convinced that the treasure which had been gathered to pay for the crusade had been misappropriated by various "betrayers, who had kept for themselves the wages of the fighting men." Despite Pelagius' protests and threats, large numbers of crusaders withdrew from the army, and departed for home during the spring passage of 1220, pleading poverty, illness, or other excuses. In their places, however, came many new crusaders, including the archbishops of Milan and Crete, the bishops of Faenza, Reggio, and Brescia, and large numbers of Italian knights.[159]

Ibn-al-Athīr, writing of Moslem tribulation during the year of the Hegira 617 (March 8, 1220–February 24, 1221) declares that while Egypt and Syria were on the point of being conquered by the Franks, the Mongols of Genghis Khan, already in Persia, threatened the whole Islamic world. Yet the threat of the Christians appeared more serious than that of the Mongols, and when al-Ashraf, who ruled in Greater Armenia, received almost simultaneous appeals from the caliph an-Nāṣir for assistance against the

[156] Pressutti, *Regesta Honorii papae III*, I, no. 2338.

[157] See the letter of Honorius in September 1219, *RHGF*, XIX, p. 691: "Quare, sicut alter Josue, populum Domini corrobora et conforta, etc."

[158] *Chronique d'Ernoul*, 429–430. However, Oliver, *Historia Damiatina*, p. 253, mentions 33 galleys of the "king of Babylon . . . which caused us inestimable loss."

[159] Oliver, *Historia Damiatina*, pp. 246–248.

Mongols, and from his brother al-Kāmil for assistance against the crusaders, he was persuaded, albeit with reluctance, by their other brother al-Mu'aẓẓam to employ his army to assist al-Kāmil.[160] Threatening as the Mongol invasion had at first appeared to the Aiyūbids, and above all to the caliph an-Nāṣir, it had actually served to destroy the power of their enemies, the shahs of Khorezm, and left al-Ashraf free to concentrate his forces against the Christian invaders of Egypt. This helped in the end to check the crusaders' threat to Syria.

At Damietta Pelagius was unable to stir the crusaders to action all through the year 1220, save for a pillaging expedition by the Templars against Burlus in July. Christian inactivity lasted until June 1221.[161] As Oliver puts it, "the people were contaminated with gluttony, drunkenness, fornications, adulteries, thefts, and gambling." The departure of king John had left the army without a leader capable of uniting the disparate groups for a common undertaking. Pelagius' efforts to assume such a position met only with rebuffs from the various leaders. At a conference in which Pelagius exhorted them to undertake an attack against the new camp of the sultan at Mansurah, the knights replied that, in the absence of the king, "no other prince was present whom the peoples of different nations were willing to obey."[162]

This long period of inactivity prompted the Moslems to attack the meager garrisons which had been left in the coastal strongholds in Syria. Already, while en route to Syria after the fall of Damietta, al-Mu'aẓẓam had taken the castle of Caesarea, but had failed before Château Pèlerin.[163] In October 1220 al-Mu'aẓẓam further damaged the fortifications of Jerusalem, laid waste the fields and vineyards, and struck at Château Pèlerin. The Templars had prepared for an extended siege, bringing in supplies and men from Acre, and obtaining support from their master, whom Pelagius permitted to withdraw from Damietta for the purpose. Al-Mu'aẓẓam had to abandon the siege.[164]

Moreover, al-Kāmil had ample opportunity, without interruption from the crusaders, to convert his new camp at Mansurah into a veritable city. He employed his soldiers in the construction there

160 Ibn-al-Athīr, *Al-kāmil* (*RHC, Or.*, II, 1), pp. 153 ff.; Abū-l-Fidā', *Kitāb al-mukhtaṣar* (*ibid.*, I), pp. 95–97; see also W. Barthold, *Turkestan down to the Mongol Invasion* (2nd ed., Oxford, 1928), pp. 399 ff.

161 Oliver, *Historia Damiatina*, p. 252.

162 *Ibid.*, pp. 248–249.

163 *Ibid.*, chaps 41, 52–53; Abū-l-Fidā', *Kitāb al-mukhtaṣar* (*RHC, Or.*, I), p. 94.

164 Oliver, *Historia Damiatina*, pp. 254 ff.

of fortifications, palaces, luxurious baths, and many other buildings. Unmolested through the first half of 1221, he found time to make of the new city a stronghold which might well take the place of Damietta in protecting the interior of Egypt, against which, it was clear, Pelagius hoped to move.[165] Arab sources are in agreement that sometime after the fall of Damietta al-Kāmil raised his offer and proposed to surrender to the crusaders Jerusalem, Ascalon, Tiberias, Sidon, Jabala, Latakia, and all other territory which Saladin had conquered in Syria with the exception of Kerak and Krak de Montréal.[166] Pelagius again imposed his view, that by holding Damietta the crusaders could conquer not only the land of Egypt, but Jerusalem also. They were all the more moved to this decision because emperor Frederick II was expected to arrive soon, bringing ample forces for the undertaking.[167] Again the Christians lost the opportunity to regain at one stroke the whole of the territory for whose recovery the expedition had been planned.

The new decision also would soon expose Frederick to the charge that, by delaying to fulfill his vow, taken at the moment of his coronation, he had caused the loss of Damietta and of Egypt.[168] On December 15, 1220, Honorius III had notified Pelagius that Frederick, on receiving the imperial crown, had pledged himself to send a part of his army the following March and to set out for Egypt in person in August.[169] It was not, however, until May 1221 that the promised troops arrived, together with Louis of Bavaria, bishop Ulrich of Passau, and many lords and knights. After their arrival, Pelagius renewed his efforts to carry out his long planned expedition against Cairo. He received the support of the newly-arrived crusaders, especially of Louis of Bavaria, who insisted that he had come for the purpose of attacking the enemy, at the same time urging that the attack should be made before the river had begun its seasonal rise. Yet Louis was a lieutenant of the emperor Frederick, and a few years later Frederick would declare that he had expressly ordered that no important operation be undertaken prior to his own arrival.[170] The attitude of the duke of Bavaria appears

165 Abū-l-Fidā', *Kitāb al-mukhtaṣar* (*RHC, Or.*, I), p. 91.

166 *Ibid.*, p. 97; Ibn-al-Athīr, *Al-kāmil* (*RHC, Or.*, II, 1), p. 122; al-Maqrīzī, "Histoire d'Égypte," *ROL*, IX (1902), 490. Only half of Sidon was then in Moslem hands.

167 *Chronique d'Ernoul*, pp. 435–436.

168 See below, chapter XII, pp. 433–438.

169 Potthast, *Regesta*, I, 6442; J. L. A. Huillard-Bréholles, *Historia diplomatica Friderici secundi* (7 vols. in 12, Paris, 1852–1861), II, 82–83.

170 In addition to the statement of Oliver, *Historia Damiatina*, p. 257, see the letter of Peter of Montaigu (Roger of Wendover, *Flores historiarum*, Rolls Series, LXXXIV, II, 264), and below, chapter XII, pp. 435–436.

to have diminished the doubts in the minds of those who opposed the legate and, in the words of Peter of Montaigu, master of the Templars, "it was agreed by all to make the advance."

Accordingly, on June 29, 1221, the army moved to its old camp in preparation for the advance up the river. On July 6 Pelagius and all the prelates, bringing with them the fragments of the True Cross, appeared. On the following day king John, acting on the sternest commands from the pope, returned from his fruitless voyage to Armenia, bringing with him large numbers of troops.[171] Although still opposing the project, he was too late to change the decision of the other leaders, especially since Pelagius had already threatened with excommunication those who opposed. To every objection John offered, however well founded from the point of view of military strategy, Pelagius turned a deaf ear, allegedly accusing John of treason for his repeated efforts to dissuade him from his plan.

The march of the crusaders, begun on July 17, followed the east bank of the river to Fāriskūr and Sharamsāḥ. Although meeting some slight resistance on the 19th, they occupied Sharamsāḥ on July 21. The sultan was busy at Mansurah, where his own armies, together with those of his brothers al-Mu'aẓẓam and al-Ashraf, were being stationed for resistance. After the capture of Sharamsāḥ, John of Brienne is said to have attempted once more in vain to induce the legate to reconsider his decision. Meanwhile the undisciplined masses, wholly ignorant of the difficulties that lay ahead, and moved solely by the prospect of the rich booty which the city of Cairo would afford them, were not to be denied. A Moslem contemporary remarks that, if king John had not agreed to the continuance of the expedition, the "Franks would have put him to death".[172] Altogether unaware of the hydrography of this area, Pelagius moved his troops on July 24 into the narrow angle where al-Baḥr aṣ-Ṣaghīr separates from the Damietta branch of the Nile, on the opposite bank from Mansurah. Sure of his ability to capture the enemy's stores, Pelagius had neglected to bring adequate food supplies.

No fewer than 600 ships, cogs, galleys, and barbotes had advanced up the river simultaneously with the army, described by Oliver as consisting of 1,200 cavalry, not counting the native Turcopoles and other mounted warriors. The numbers of foot-soldiers were so great that he refrains from an estimate. He speaks, however, of 4,000 archers, including 2,500 mercenaries. From

[171] Oliver, *Historia Damiatina*, p. 257.

[172] "Hist. patr. d'Alex.," *ROL*, XI (1908), 260.

intelligence obtained through interrogation of fugitives, he estimates the enemy mounted troops at 7,000. On the right flank, the ships were drawn up so as to form a protective wall, while the infantry constituted the left flank. The mounted troops occupied the center, stretched out diagonally between the ships and the infantry. In this formation the Christians advanced to a point opposite the camp of the Moslems at Mansurah, where it was clear that the fortifications could be overcome only after a long attack. The crusaders therefore began to erect fortifications around their own camp.

The position occupied by the Christians was, under the most favorable circumstances, a dangerous one. Warnings from Alice, the dowager queen of Cyprus, as well as from the masters of the knightly orders, concerning the huge numbers of Moslem reinforcements were in vain. As Oliver wrote, "sane counsel was far removed from our leaders." Pelagius would of course not accept the advice of John of Brienne, who, as Oliver remarks, "had reflected more deeply on the matter," to seize this opportunity to accept the sultan's offer of peace.[173] Day by day the reinforcements of the enemy multiplied. If we may believe one Egyptian source, the number of horsemen reached no less than 40,000. It is to be assumed that the lesser estimate of Oliver did not take into consideration the forces of al-Mu'aẓẓam and al-Ashraf, recently arrived from Syria.[174] Under these circumstances some of the crusaders showed increasing signs of timidity, and, as the long delay continued, many withdrew from the army to take advantage of the next passage to the west. As the month of August passed, the situation grew more precarious.

As if offering a kind of prelude to the impending disaster, Oliver relates that in their passage along the Nile the crusaders had given little heed to a small canal which enters the Damietta branch of the Nile on the west side of the river opposite Barāmūn. He describes it as "a certain little stream coming from the island of Mahalech" (al-Maḥallah) which, he continues, "is able to bear galleys and other vessels of moderate size."[175] When the Nile was near its crest, as it was in late August, large vessels could navigate this canal. Aided by superior knowledge of the hydrography of the delta area, the emir Badr-ad-Dīn ibn-Ḥassūn brought a number of ships up from al-Maḥallah and moved them in to the Nile by means of this canal opposite Barāmūn. The similarity of this

[173] Oliver, *Historia Damiatina*, pp. 259–261, 268.
[174] Al-Maqrīzī, "Histoire d'Égypte," *ROL*, IX (1902), 482.
[175] *Historia Damiatina*, p. 267.

exploit to that which the Moslems carried out against Louix IX some years later, leads one to assume that on this occasion also the enemy ships were disassembled and transported "on the backs of camels to the canal of al-Maḥallah", where they were launched and then brought secretly into the Nile.[176] In this manner the Moslems were able to block the water route between Damietta and the Christian camp, not only cutting off supplies, but destroying or capturing many vessels.

This was a staggering and unexpected blow to the plans of Pelagius. After numerous consultations with the leaders of the army, he was compelled to order a speedy retreat towards Damietta. Meanwhile the Moslems, employing a pontoon bridge across al-Baḥr aṣ-Ṣaghīr, were able to send considerable numbers of land forces to the rear of the Christian army, blocking their retreat. On August 26 the crusaders endeavored to retreat to Barāmūn by night, but their careless burning of tents and baggage and the great activity in their camp revealed their plan. Many crusaders also, reluctant to sacrifice their supplies of wine, endeavored to consume what they could not carry, drinking themselves into a stupor and falling easy captive to the enemy. Meanwhile the sultan ordered the cutting of the dikes, thus blocking the last hope of escape. In the vicinity of Barāmūn the country had been so flooded that retreat and fighting were alike impossible. Helpless and desperate, Pelagius implored king John of Jerusalem, whose advice thus far he had so stubbornly ignored, to extricate the army from this impossible situation.[177]

But the army was hopelessly trapped. Even when the king endeavored to form a battle line, rather "to die bravely in battle than to perish ignominiously in the flood", the sultan, seeing that the Christian army could be destroyed by flood and famine, refused to do battle. Nothing remained to the crusaders but to sue for peace. William of Gibelet was chosen as emissary, authorized to offer the restoration of Damietta in return for the freedom of the Christian army to withdraw. The sultan al-Kāmil favored the acceptance of the proposal, but his brothers urged the complete annihilation of the invaders. The sultan knew that the city of Damietta was still garrisoned, and that the crusaders had strengthened its fortifications. But a still more important consideration, as the Egyptian historian al-Maqrīzī points out, was the probability that reinforcements,

[176] Al-Maqrīzī, "Histoire d'Égypte," *ROL*, IX (1902), 481, 491; and XI (1908), 223. On the later incident, see below, chapter XIV, p. 502.

[177] *Eracles* (*RHC, Occ.*, II), p. 351.

eager to avenge the humiliation of their fellow Christians, would hasten from the west; al-Kāmil probably knew about the planned expedition of Frederick II. Moreover, the Moslem world was faced with many difficulties arising from unsettled internal conditions and from the Mongol threat. Al-Kāmil's army was weary and desired peace.[178] Accordingly al-Kāmil received the Christian emissary, and later king John himself, with the utmost courtesy, showering upon them many attentions, and sending food and other supplies to the wretched crusaders.[179]

An embassy headed by the masters of the Templars and the Teutonic Knights was sent to Damietta to acquaint the crusaders who had remained in the city with the details of the defeat, and with the terms of the proposed treaty. Meanwhile, in the midst of the disaster, the reinforcements sent by Frederick under the leadership of the chancellor Walter of Palear, the marshal Anselm of Justingen, and the admiral Henry of Malta had arrived in the harbor of Damietta. They were bitter in their denunciation of the leaders who had launched the expedition contrary to the express orders of Frederick that no new undertaking was to be attempted prior to his arrival, and many of the German, Italian, and Sicilian pilgrims shared their views, and opposed the treaty with al-Kāmil. But the French, the Templars, and the Hospitallers, as well as the Syrian, Greek, and Armenian forces, moved by the plight of their countrymen, insisted that the terms of the treaty must be accepted.

At length the difference of opinion manifested itself in acts of violence, particularly on the part of the Venetians, who, together with other disgruntled elements described by the *Chronicle of Tours* as the "emperor's people", attacked the houses of John of Brienne, the Templars, and the Hospitallers, and endeavored to gain control of Damietta. Only when the representatives of the captive leaders of the expedition threatened to surrender Acre to the Saracens if opposition continued, did the Venetians and their supporters agree to the terms of peace.[180] The failure of Walter of Palear and Henry of Malta to prevent the surrender of Damietta subjected them to the extreme wrath of the emperor. The chancellor was deprived of his possessions and condemned to perpetual exile, while the admiral, returning secretly to Sicily, was captured and imprisoned and his fiefs confiscated. Subsequently, however, he was pardoned by Frederick, who not only employed him as commander of the

[178] Al-Maqrīzī, "Histoire d'Égypte," *ROL*, IX (1902), 491–492.

[179] "Hist. patr. d'Alex.," *ROL*, XI (1908), 258; Abū-Shāmah, *Ar-rauḍatain* (*RHC, Or.*, V), p. 183.

[180] *Chronicon Turonense* (*RHGF*, XVIII), p. 302.

fleet but also entrusted him with diplomatic missions of the utmost delicacy.[181]

On August 30, 1221, the fateful terms were drawn up. A peace and armistice of eight years' duration was agreed upon. The Christians agreed to evacuate Damietta, together with all other places in Egypt conquered by them. Mutual surrender of prisoners was to be undertaken without obligation of ransom. The Moslems agreed also to restore that part of the True Cross which had been captured by them at Hattin on July 4, 1187. In earnest of this agreement, hostages were to be exchanged, including king John on the side of the Christians, and al-Kāmil's son aṣ-Ṣāliḥ Aiyūb on the side of the Moslems. These hostages were to be released when Damietta had been evacuated and restored.

The Fifth Crusade had ended in colossal and irremediable failure. Yet, up to the very moment of its catastrophic end, it had held within its easy reach the realization of its goal — the restoration of the Holy Land. The extent to which it failed is perhaps best expressed in the language of the Moslem historian Ibn-al-Athīr, who says: "God gave to the Moslems an unexpected victory, for the acme of their hopes was the recovery of Damietta through restoring to the Franks the cities in Syria which had been taken from them. But God not only gratified them with the restitution of Damietta, but left in their possession also the cities of Syria."[182]

[181] Richard of San Germano (*MGH, SS.*, XIX), pp. 341, 348.
[182] Ibn-al-Athīr, *Al-kāmil* (*RHC, Or.*, II, 1), p. 125.

XII

THE CRUSADE OF FREDERICK II

After the loss of Damietta the Christian world fastened its attention and hopes upon the emperor Frederick II. Less importance might have been attached to his activities had the papal legate

Basic sources include the first three volumes of J. L. A. Huillard-Bréholles, *Historia diplomatica Friderici Secundi* (7 vols. in 12, Paris, 1852–1861); papal correspondence as cited in earlier chapters; several chronicles: *Chronique d'Ernoul et de Bernard le Trésorier* (ed. L. de Mas Latrie, Paris, 1871); *Chronica regia Coloniensis* (*Annales Colonienses maximi*), ed. G. Waitz, *Scriptores rerum Germanicarum in usum scholarum*, Hanover, 1880; *L'Estoire de Eracles empereur et la conquest de la Terre d'Outremer*; *La continuation de l'Estoire de Guillaume arcesvesque de Sur* (*RHC, Occ.*, II); Matthew Paris, *Chronica majora* (ed. H. R. Luard, 7 vols., 1872–1883, Rolls Series, LVII); Philip of Novara, *Mémoires* (ed. C. Kohler, *Les Classiques français du moyen-âge*, Paris, 1913); Roger of Wendover, *Flores historiarum* (ed. H. G. Hewlett, 3 vols., 1886–1889, Rolls Series, LXXXIV); Richard of San Germano, *Chronica* (ed. G. Pertz, 1866, *MGH, SS.*, XIX); and several Arabic sources: Abū-l-Fidā', *Kitāb al-mukhtaṣar fī akhbār al-bashar* (extracts tr. in *RHC, Or.*, I, 1–165); Badr-ad-Dīn al-'Ainī, *'Iqd al-jamān* (extracts tr. in *RHC, Or.*, II, part 1, 181–250); Abū-Shāmah, *Kitāb ar-rauḍatain* (extracts tr. in *RHC, Or.*, IV–V); Ibn-al-Athīr, *Al-kāmil fī-t-ta'rīkh* (extracts tr. in *RHC, Or.*, I, II, part 1); al-Maqrīzī, *Akhbār Miṣr* (tr. E. Blochet, "Histoire d'Égypte," *ROL*, VI–XI, 1898–1908).

The important monographs on the crusades of Frederick II are R. Röhricht, *Die Kreuzfahrt Kaiser Friedrichs des Zweiten* (Berlin, 1872), reprinted with revisions in his *Beiträge zur Geschichte der Kreuzzüge*, I (Berlin, 1874), 1–112; and E. Kestner, *Der Kreuzzug Friedrichs II.* (Göttingen, 1873). General works treating the crusade include: R. Grousset, *Histoire des croisades et du royaume franc de Jérusalem*, III (Paris, 1936); K. Hampe, *Deutsche Kaisergeschichte in der Zeit der Salier und Staufer* (6th ed., Leipzig, 1929, 10th ed., Heidelberg, 1949); E. Kantorowicz, *Kaiser Friedrich der Zweite* (2nd ed., Berlin, 1928; tr. E. O. Lorimer, London and New York, 1931); F. von Raumer, *Geschichte der Hohenstaufen und ihrer Zeit* (3rd ed., 6 vols., Leipzig, 1857–1858, reprinted Berlin, 1943); F. W. Schirrmacher, *Kaiser Friedrich der Zweite* (4 vols., Göttingen, 1859–1865); and E. Winkelmann, *Kaiser Friedrich II.* (2 vols., Leipzig, 1889–1897).

On Frederick and the popes, several of the works listed in the bibliography of the preceding chapter continue to be relevant. In addition, the following are especially useful: C. de Cherrier, *Histoire de la lutte des papes et des empereurs de la maison souabe* (2nd ed., 3 vols., Paris, 1858–1859); A. Hauck, *Kirchengeschichte Deutschlands*, IV (Leipzig, 1903); R. Honig, *Rapporti tra Federico II. e Gregorio IX. rispetto alla spedizione in Palestina* (Bologna, 1896); W. Knebel, *Kaiser Friedrich II. und Papst Honorius III. in ihren gegenseitigen Beziehungen von der Kaiserkrönung Friedrichs bis zum Tode des Papstes 1220–1227* (Münster, 1905); C. Kohler, *Das Verhaltnis Kaiser Friedrichs II. zu den Päpsten seiner Zeit* (Breslau, 1888); J. Marx, *De vita Gregorii IX* (Berlin, 1889); and C. Rodenberg, "Kaiser Friedrich II. und die Kirche" (*Historische Aufsätze, dem Andenken an Georg Waitz gewidmet*, Hanover, 1886).

On Frederick II in relation to Syria and Cyprus see: J. Delaville le Roulx, *Les Hospitaliers en Terre Sainte et à Chypre 1100–1310* (Paris, 1904); G. F. Hill, *A History of Cyprus* (4 vols., Cambridge, 1940–1952); Philip of Novara, *The Wars of Frederick II against the Ibelins in*

Pelagius conquered Cairo and the inland regions of Egypt, or the crusaders accepted the sultan's offer to exchange Damietta for Jerusalem.[1] But now Frederick's chances stood out in bold relief against the background of failure of an expedition which for more than seven years had absorbed the attention of the western world. He alone, the leading sovereign of Europe, emperor of the Holy Roman Empire, was in a position to redeem the losses by employing the resources and the arms of the west in the reconquest of the Holy Land.

Six years before (July 15, 1215), at the height of the efforts of Innocent III to stir the peoples of Europe to take the cross, and while crusading preachers were active throughout Europe, Frederick had received the German crown at Aachen. He had previously been crowned in Mainz on December 9, 1212, but this second coronation was carried out in such a fashion as to emphasize the legitimacy of his election, and to direct the attention of the Christian world to him. The newly crowned king astonished those in attendance at Aachen, as well as the pope, by taking the cross, and called upon the nobles of Germany to follow his example.[2]

At the time, and again some twelve years later, Frederick said that he had taken the cross in order to express his gratitude for the many blessings bestowed upon him. He insisted that in doing so he had placed both his person and the whole of his authority at the service of God by obligating himself to work unremittingly for the recovery of the Holy Land.[3] Later the pope and the curia were inclined to question the sincerity of his motives. In his encyclical of October 10, 1227, pope Gregory IX was to remind Frederick that he had accepted the cross spontaneously, without urging by the apostolic see and without its foreknowledge.[4]

For the moment Innocent chose to ignore the action of his protégé, although he was bending every effort to rally the kings

Syria and Cyprus (tr. with notes and introd. by J. L. La Monte, with verse translation of the poems by M. J. Hubert, New York, 1936); L. de Mas Latrie, *Histoire de l'île de Chypre sous le règne des princes de la maison de Lusignan* (3 vols., Paris, 1852–1861); and R. Röhricht, *Geschichte des Königreichs Jerusalem* (Innsbruck, 1898). For medieval poetry and the crusade of Frederick II see: K. Bartsch and A. Horning, *La Langue et la littérature françaises* (Paris, 1887); J. Bédier, *Les Chansons de croisade* (Paris, 1909); H. E. Bezzenberger (ed.), *Freidankes Bescheidenheit* (Halle, 1872); and F. Diez, *La Poésie des troubadours* (Paris, 1845). Biographical studies include W. Jacobs, *Patriarch Gerold von Jerusalem* (Aachen, 1905); A. Koch, *Hermann von Salza* (Leipzig, 1885); and E. Lavisse, *De Hermanno Salzensi Ordinis Teutonici magistro* (Paris, 1875).

[1] On these events see above, chapter XI, pp. 403–428.

[2] E. Winkelmann, *Geschichte Kaiser Friedrichs des Zweiten und seiner Reiche 1212–1235* (Berlin, 1863), pp. 69–70.

[3] Huillard-Bréholles, III, 39.

[4] *Ibid.*, III, 25.

and princes of Europe to the cross. When setting forth his plans for the crusade during the Fourth Lateran Council, the pope made no mention of Frederick as a crusader. Perhaps Innocent wanted to retain the leadership of the crusade in his own hands, solely as a papal enterprise; perhaps he regarded Frederick's action as the generous but impracticable gesture of a youthful monarch, as yet unaware of the full implications of his obligation. Frederick was useful to Innocent primarily as a foil against his former protégé, Otto IV, now discarded. With conditions in Germany still gravely unsettled, and likely to remain so long after the date designated by the Lateran Council for the departure of the crusade, Frederick could hardly have hoped to go to the east. Indeed, he had no illusions about the difficulties which lay ahead in Germany or about the dangers which might arise in his Sicilian kingdom were he to leave the west. There is abundant evidence that at the time of his coronation Frederick had little enthusiasm for the crusade.[5]

Why did he take the cross? No doubt he was grateful to God for the sudden change of fortune that had restored his heritage, denied him since his father's death in 1197. But it could scarcely have been gratitude alone that moved him. His Hohenstaufen ancestors' ambitions for world empire had necessarily been linked with plans for imperial crusades. Frederick at twenty-one fully realized that the taking of the cross was almost essential to the dignity of his new office, and that Europe expected it of him. The man who aspired to be leader of Europe had also to be leader of the crusade.[6] Moreover, the taking of the cross, insofar as it asserted Frederick's claim to lead the new crusade, as emperor, was a kind of declaration of independence from the papacy, a timely, if not tactful, announcement that he had emerged from papal tutelage. Though a good many German nobles had already taken the cross, Frederick's example now led many others to do so, including archbishop Siegfried of Mainz, four bishops, and the dukes of Lorraine, Meran, Brabant, and Limburg.[7] Little wonder that Innocent was annoyed at the implied menace to his own desire to make the new crusade a purely papal enterprise. Since the pope could hardly express his annoyance, he passed over Frederick's action in silence.

After the death of Innocent (July 16, 1216), his aged successor,

[5] O. Lorenz, "Kaiser Friedrich II.," *Hist. Zeitschr.*, XI (1864), 332.
[6] Kestner, *Der Kreuzzug Friedrichs II.*, pp. 14 ff.
[7] *Chronica regia Coloniensis*, p. 236; *MGH, SS.*, XVII, 828.

Honorius III, at first excluded the emperor from his crusading plans, taking no account of Frederick's action at Aachen. Indeed, it was the emperor himself who took the initiative when he sent an embassy to Rome, at the beginning of the year 1217, to offer his official condolences on the death of Innocent. His envoys reported his desire to discuss with Honorius plans for a new crusade. On April 8, 1217, the pope replied that in the near future he would send a legate to take up with Frederick the question of assistance for the Holy Land.[8] He made no mention of an active role for Frederick as a crusader, and, indeed, there is no evidence that the proposed discussion ever took place.

If Honorius, and Innocent before him, refrained from mentioning Frederick's vow solely out of a considerate realization that, while Otto IV lived, it would be impossible for Frederick to absent himself from his kingdom, then why did neither pope at least praise Frederick's generous gesture, which had influenced so many of the noblest of his German subjects to take the cross? Or are we to assume with von Raumer that almost all the correspondence between Honorius III and Frederick II for the years 1217–1218 is lost?[9] Or did both popes want to preserve the crusade as an exclusively papal enterprise?

In any case between July 15, 1215, and the end of 1218 neither pope made any mention of Frederick's crusading vow. Then, with apparent suddenness, Honorius broke the silence by an urgent appeal to Frederick to fulfill his pledge. Why? Was it because the death of the Welf Otto IV was presumed to have freed Frederick from his preoccupation with Germany? This is unlikely because Henry of Brunswick still actively represented Welf interests and still retained the royal insignia. Was it not rather because the crusading expedition in Egypt was now in dire need of new aid and leadership? Had not the crusading effort, undertaken solely as a papal enterprise, failed, and thus necessitated the appeal to Frederick? Unfortunately, Honorius's appeal itself is lost, but Frederick's reply of January 12, 1219 — the beginning of a regular correspondence on the subject — leaves no doubt that the pope had stressed the urgency of the need of assistance in Egypt.

In December 1218 at Fulda Frederick had already dealt in a preliminary way with the problem of the crusade, and proposed to consider the subject more thoroughly and more fruitfully in a

[8] Huillard-Bréholles, I, part 2, 504: "per quem tam super iis que ex parte tua nobis fuere proposita quam super Terre Sancte succursu. . . ."

[9] Von Raumer, *Geschichte der Hohenstaufen*, III, 117.

diet to be held at Magdeburg the next March. Once more, as at Aachen, he was the independent, self-confident ruler, acting not under pressure from the curia but wholly on his own initiative. He was certain that the nobles would accept his decisions respecting the date and the circumstances of the departure for the Holy Land. He advised the pope to make all princes and prelates who had taken the cross subject to excommunication if they had not fulfilled their vows by the following June 24. No one was to be released from his vow unless, in the judgment of the king and princes, he was considered essential to the protection of the realm. Honorius took immediate steps to put into effect all of Frederick's recommendations.[10]

For reasons which are not apparent in the sources, the meeting at Magdeburg did not take place. Perhaps Frederick was detained in Alsace, or purposely postponed the diet until the papal legate had successfully extracted the royal insignia from Henry of Brunswick. Moreover, shortly afterwards he asked Honorius for a postponement of the crusade to September 29, on the grounds that preparations could not be completed before that time. In a letter of May 18, 1219, the pope agreed. Meanwhile, on May 10, Frederick had acquainted the pope with his desire to have his son Henry crowned before his own departure for the Holy Land. He explained to the pope that his objects were to ensure that the kingdom should be well governed during his absence, and to facilitate Henry's succession to the German heritage in case of his own death while on crusade.[11] The pope appears to have offered no objection to this.

On September 6, Frederick again took up the subject of his son's coronation and requested a further postponement of the crusade to March 21, 1220. Honorius once more yielded to the king's request, indicating that, despite obvious difficulties, the earnestness of Frederick's preparations was indicative of his good intentions. At the same time he warned that further postponement would subject Frederick to the ban which he himself had recommended as the penalty for those who persisted in delaying the fulfillment of their vows.[12]

Through the remainder of 1219, and well into 1220, Frederick, encouraged by Honorius's benevolent comprehension, displayed a

[10] J. F. Böhmer, *Regesta imperii*, vol. V: *Die Regesten des Kaiserreichs unter Philipp, Otto IV., Friedrich II., Heinrich (VII.), Conrad IV., Heinrich Raspe, Wilhelm und Richard, 1198–1272* . . . (eds. J. Ficker and E. Winkelmann, 5 parts, Innsbruck, 1881–1901), part 3 (1892), nos. 6323–6325.

[11] Huillard-Bréholles, I, part 2, 628–629.

[12] *Ibid.*, I, part 2, 691–693.

feverish activity. During a diet at Nuremberg, in October 1219, he gained many recruits from the German nobility for the projected expedition. The port cities of southern Italy were called upon to produce the required ships, and the crusading preachers were urged to greater zeal in their efforts among the people.[13] But on February 19, 1220, Frederick reported to Honorius that he could not launch the crusade at the time agreed upon, because the German nobility had proved so apathetic. Honorius's acceptance of the excuse — though he did warn against further delay — indicated that he was not unaware of the widespread indifference prevalent not only in Germany but throughout Europe. For the fourth time, therefore, he agreed to a postponement, setting the new date for May 1.[14] Even before the arrival of Frederick's letter, Honorius, who by now knew that Damietta had fallen, had sent the scholasticus Conrad of Mainz as crusading preacher to spur on the faltering crusaders of Germany, instructing him to deal gently with dilatory pilgrims, but not to detain them beyond the new deadline even if Frederick should find himself unable to go.[15]

Frederick's own departure clearly depended upon the coronation of his son Henry as king of the Romans, and his own coronation as emperor. It was only after many preliminaries, much negotiation, and the award of special concessions to the spiritual princes that in April 1220 a brilliant diet at Frankfurt elected Henry king, and made arrangements for Frederick's voyage to Rome, which was to culminate in the imperial coronation, and to coincide with the setting out of the crusading expedition. At the same time many thousands took the cross.[16] Although not previously informed and far from pleased with the proceedings at Frankfurt, the curia accepted the *fait accompli*. When Frederick again failed to depart on crusade, however, the pope notified the chancellor, Conrad of Metz, that excommunication impended, but in fact imposed only a penance. All along, Honorius seems to have recognized that he would have to crown Frederick emperor before the latter would go on crusade. Though the pope objected to Frederick's sending a mere abbot to discuss the plans for the coronation, he agreed that the cause of the Holy Land and the general peace required that Frederick be crowned. On August 28 Honorius further consented to crown queen Constance empress. At the end of August Frederick

[13] Röhricht, *Beiträge*, I, 7.
[14] Huillard-Bréholles, I, part 2, 746–747.
[15] *Ibid.*, I, part 2, 783–784.
[16] *Chronicon Leodiense* (*RHGF*, XVIII), p. 635. See also Hampe, *Deutsche Kaisergeschichte*, pp. 222 ff. (10th ed., pp. 262 ff.).

left for Italy, and on November 22, 1220, Honorius crowned him and Constance in St. Peter's.

Honorius had been reminding Frederick that the crusaders at Damietta were in danger so long as their conquests were not extended inland (which was Pelagius' view), and had also notified Pelagius that the emperor's departure was imminent. At his coronation, Frederick took the cross a second time, from the hands of cardinal-bishop Ugolino of Ostia, later his determined adversary pope Gregory IX, and agreed to set sail the following August (1221), meanwhile sending ample reinforcements to Damietta in March.[17]

Having achieved his political aims, Frederick resumed his journey southward. His extraordinary activity must have reassured Honorius that the long delays were over. The emperor ordered the necessary ships made ready in the Sicilian ports; he sent a representative to northern Italy to assemble troops and money; and from Salerno he appealed for support to his faithful subjects of Germany and especially to the cities of Lombardy and Tuscany. Those who would remain in his favor should follow his example: "Therefore, true soldiers of the empire, take up immediately the weapons of Christian knighthood; already the victorious eagles of the Roman empire have gone forth. Twofold rewards await you: the grace of the emperor and eternal bliss. Let yourselves be admonished, let yourselves be moved by entreaty and inspired by the love of Christ, whose bride, the church, your holy mother, is held wretchedly imprisoned in that land: Remember also how the Roman emperor, in ancient days, with the help of his soldiery, loyal unto death, subdued the whole earth."[18]

The princes and nobles who had renewed their crusading vows at the time of the coronation in Rome embarked for Damietta, probably at Taranto, sometime in April 1221, under the leadership of duke Louis of Bavaria, instructed to begin no new undertaking prior to Frederick's arrival.[19] In early June the pope almost apologetically reminded him once more of his obligations, citing the current gossip that he was delaying his preparation and hoped to obtain a new postponement.[20] Shortly afterwards Frederick

[17] Böhmer, *Regesta imperii*, V, part 3, nos. 6366, 6373, 6384, 6394; Winkelmann, *Kaiser Friedrich*, I, 52 ff., 109–111; Huillard-Bréholles, II, part 1, 52 f., and 82 f.

[18] *Ibid.*, II, part 1, 122 ff.

[19] See above, chapter XI, pp. 423–424, and Huillard-Bréholles, III, 40, while for evidence that Frederick had given notice to the army in Damietta to expect his arrival, see *ibid.*, II, part 1, 221: "unde propter expectationem tui subsidii quod etiam per litteras tuas promisisti exercitui sepe dicto."

[20] *Ibid.*, II, part 1, 190.

sent forty more ships, commanded by the chancellor Walter of Palear, the admiral Henry of Malta, and the marshal Anselm of Justingen, who were entrusted with the funds gathered from the crusading tax.[21] On July 20 Honorius thanked Frederick for sending the ships, but reminded him that they should have been sent earlier, all the more so if he had intended to delay his own departure.[22] The readiness with which the pope now forgave the emperor for his failure to accompany the expedition suggests that he was not wholly displeased, and may have hoped that the reinforcements already sent to Damietta could conquer Egypt without Frederick. The extraordinary haste with which Pelagius sought to push forward the conquest of Cairo during July 1221 lends weight to this interpretation.[23]

The virtual anarchy facing Frederick in Sicily after an absence of eight years amply explains his reluctance to depart for the east. He had to redeem the royal lands, which since the death of Henry VI had been recklessly dissipated; reëxamine the systems of taxation and trade regulations, and reassert royal prerogative; break the power of the feudal barons on the mainland and repossess the strategic fortifications which they had taken; subdue the Saracens and drive them from their mountain fastnesses; and rid Sicily of the privileged Genoese and Pisan merchants established in the vital seaports. It was to prove a three-year task. The two fleets which he had dispatched to Egypt during the year 1221 were for the moment his only contribution to the crusade.[24] Yet as these galleys made their way from the Sicilian ports, Pelagius by pressing the attack on Cairo precipitated disaster;[25] so the crusaders were compelled to accept a humiliating truce for eight years (until 1229). However justly Frederick II may be criticized for failing to fulfill his crusading vow punctually, he cannot be held responsible for the loss of Damietta. It was Pelagius and the other crusading leaders who yielded to his insistent demand, or else to his threat of excommunication, who were to blame.

Pelagius' decision to attack Cairo had been taken in Damietta before he could have known that Frederick had remained behind, and at a moment when he had every reason to believe that reinforcements and perhaps the emperor himself were already en

[21] Richard of San Germano (*MGH, SS.*, XIX), p. 341.

[22] Böhmer, *Regesta imperii*, V, part 3, no. 6472; *MGH, Epp. pont.*, I, 124.

[23] See the statement by Winkelmann, *Kaiser Friedrich*, I, 151, in support of this view. See also above, chapter XI, pp. 423–424.

[24] For the details of Frederick's Sicilian problem during these years, see Hampe, *Kaisergeschichte*, pp. 224 ff. (10th ed., pp. 264 ff.).

[25] See above, chapter XI, pp. 424–426.

route. Perhaps Frederick's presence could have given to the Fifth Crusade the unity and coherence and, indeed, the responsible leadership which it had so signally lacked since the capture of the chain tower. No doubt Frederick, like king John of Jerusalem, would have recognized that the Damietta expedition was useful only as a strategic approach to the conquest of Palestine. It is in this negative sense only that Frederick may be held responsible. Honorius and the curia, who certainly must be made to share Pelagius' responsibility, obviously felt compelled to defend him by shifting the blame to Frederick. Although only a short time before Honorius had praised the emperor for his zeal, he now reproached him with the failure. Much contemporary popular criticism was directed at Frederick; it appears in some of the poetry of the troubadours, who reminded him of his repeated failures to fulfill his vow.[26] But Honorius, the curia, and Pelagius bore the brunt of the sharpest attacks. Thus the author of the long poem "The complaint of Jerusalem against the Court of Rome", writes:

> Rome, Jerusalem complains of the greed which dominates you, and Acre and Damietta too, and they say that because of you it continues to be true that God and all his saints are not served in this land — They [the Saracens] are in possession of Damietta because of the legate, our enemy, and Christians are overtaken by death — and know well that this is the way it is: that they have betrayed king John in whom dwells excellence and valiance.[27]

Another sharply attacked the military leadership:

> For, when the clergy take the function of leading knights, certainly that is against the law. But the clerk should recite aloud from his Scripture and Psalms and let the knight go to his great battlefields.[28]

The Christian world was stunned by the reversal in Egypt. Enthusiasm, stirred by the unremitting efforts of propagandists during the previous years, and kept alive by favorable reports from Damietta, now gave way to profound disillusionment. This reaction, perhaps more than anything else in the thirteenth century,

[26] O. Schultz-Gora, *Ein sirventes von Guilhem Figueira gegen Friedrich II.* (Halle, 1902), pp. 3 ff., and F. Diez, *Leben und Werke der Troubadours* (Leipzig, 1882), pp. 259 ff. See also P. A. Throop, *Criticism of the Crusade, a Study of Public Opinion and Crusade Propaganda* (Amsterdam, 1940), pp. 32 ff.

[27] Attributed to Huon of St. Quentin, Bartsch and Horning, *La Langue et la littérature françaises*, col. 373.

[28] Guillaume le Clerc, *Le Besant de Dieu* (ed. E. Martin, Halle, 1869), p. 73, also verses 2547 ff.; tr. Throop, *Criticism of the Crusade*, p. 32.

symbolizes the end of an era. Henceforth, crusades were to receive their impulse, not from papal leadership, but from the realistic policies of ambitious temporal rulers.[29] The bitterness of Honorius III found expression in his letter to the emperor of November 19, 1221, in which he reminded Frederick that for five years the Christian world had hopefully awaited his departure for the Holy Land, and yet he had failed to fulfill his vow, thus subjecting both the pope and himself to criticism. Honorius declared that he himself had been remiss in failing to exert greater pressure, and added that he could no longer remain indulgent. Even before receiving this letter, Frederick had written to the pope in October expressing his desire to take immediate steps to send aid to the Holy Land.[30]

In December Honorius sent cardinal-bishop Nicholas of Tusculum to Frederick, and in the following April (1222) they returned together to Veroli, where Frederick conferred at length with the pope. Honorius informed Pelagius that they had reached agreement on all points, and that Frederick would busy himself speedily with efforts to recover the Holy Land. He mentioned also another meeting to be held in November 1222, at Verona, to which princes, prelates, and vassals had been summoned, to consider the projected expedition.[31] This meeting, however, took place not in Verona but in Ferentino and not until March 1223. It was attended not only by the pope and the emperor, but by king John of Brienne, Ralph of Mérencourt, patriarch of Jerusalem, the masters of the knightly orders, and many others.

Frederick renewed his crusading vows, and the new date for the expedition was set for June 24, 1225. At the same time, as the empress Constance had died in June 1222, arrangements were made for his marriage to Isabel, daughter of John of Brienne and heiress to the kingdom of Jerusalem. This marriage would give Frederick a very substantial interest in the future of Jerusalem, and thus afford a guarantee that he would fulfill his vow. John of Brienne, who was only titular king, might expect to strengthen his own position, while the curia could feel reassured as to the ultimate recovery of the Holy Land.[32] Once more, crusading preachers were sent into all parts of Europe to seek to restore interest in a crusade which, this time, the emperor himself would lead.[33]

[29] See especially the elaboration of this by Kestner, *Kreuz. Fried.*, pp. 15–16.

[30] For the two letters, see Böhmer, *Regesta imperii*, V, part 3, no. 6489, and Huillard-Bréholles, II, part 1, 206–207, 220 ff.

[31] Böhmer, *Regesta imperii*, V, part 3, no. 6510; *MGH, Epp. pont.*, I, 137.

[32] Richard of San Germano (*MGH, SS.*, XIX), p. 343, and Röhricht, *Beiträge*, I, 11.

[33] *Chronica regia Coloniensis*, p. 252: ". . . cum gloriso imperatore Friderico parati sint mare transire." Also in *MGH, SS.*, XVII, 837.

Although still actively employed in disposing of various problems in Sicily, Frederick continued his preparations for the crusade. By the spring of 1224 a hundred galleys and fifty transports, capable of carrying 10,000 foot-soldiers and 2,000 knights, were ready. He offered liberal inducements to crusaders, including free transportation and provisions.[34] King John, recently arrived from Syria, actively furthered the crusading effort by visiting France, England, Spain, and Germany.[35] While received everywhere with acclaim, and enjoying a personal triumph, he had but little success in the main object of his mission. True, Philip Augustus, who died shortly after the arrival of his illustrious guest, made significant bequests to the kingdom of Jerusalem as well as to the Templars and Hospitallers. But the Albigensian war and the hostile relations with England, and a feeling of indifference, if not of positive aversion, toward the crusade, soon convinced John of the futility of his mission in France. In England the regents of young Henry III and the barons were deeply involved in internal quarrels or else engaged in conflicts with the French, while Spain was still occupied with her own fight against the Moslems. The preaching friars were held in contempt, partly because of their lowly origin, partly because of their insufficient ecclesiastical dignity and lack of authority to grant pardon for sins. In many places also the friars had repelled the better classes by their reckless and often obscure statements which encouraged the belief that taking the cross insured immunity from punishment for every sort of criminal action.[36]

Partly of his own choice, and partly as a result of pressure from the curia, Frederick had to push forward by himself his preparations for a crusade. He apparently planned to go into Germany, and by his own presence to influence many of the nobles to take the cross, but was delayed until he could complete the arrangements for the deportation of the Sicilian Saracens into Apulia. Meanwhile he received discouraging reports from king John and the master of the Teutonic Knights, Hermann of Salza. Frederick was too well aware of the determination of Honorius, still mindful of Damietta, to expect that he could be made to understand the seriousness of these difficulties. Accordingly, he moved with the utmost caution in seeking further postponement of the expedition.

[34] Röhricht, *Beiträge*, I, 11 ff.

[35] For his itinerary and his efforts in behalf of the crusade see especially L. Böhm, *Johann von Brienne, König von Jerusalem und Kaiser von Konstantinopel* (Heidelberg, 1938), pp. 69 ff.

[36] See especially the letter of Frederick to the pope (March 5, 1224) in Huillard-Bréholles, II, part I, 409 ff.; also von Raumer, *Geschichte der Hohenstaufen*, III, 158 ff., and Röhricht, *Beiträge* I, 12.

He sent Hermann of Salza to visit the pope and to acquaint him with the true situation. Influenced by Frederick's complaints concerning the shortcomings of the crusading preachers, Honorius sent cardinal-bishop Conrad of Porto as his legate to Germany, at the same time urging the clergy of Germany to put forward their utmost efforts in behalf of the crusade, assuring them that he was sending crusading preachers with full authority. He also wrote an urgent letter to king Louis VIII of France, to order the French crusaders to join the expedition of Frederick, and tried to end the hostile relations between Raymond VII of Toulouse and the church as well as the Anglo-French conflict.[37] But these efforts were vain, and the response in Germany was unsatisfactory.

Not only Frederick but king John, and apparently patriarch Ralph of Jerusalem as well, were convinced that no crusade could be launched at the time agreed upon at Ferentino. Accordingly, Frederick sent an embassy to the pope consisting of Hermann of Salza, king John, and the patriarch to arrange for a postponement. At the same time he summoned the prelates, including many who were likely to influence the pope unfavorably, to a conference in Apulia, where he held them until his embassy to Honorius had successfully accomplished its mission. On July 18, 1225, the pope, at the time in exile at Rieti, at last agreed to postponement, and ordered a conference to be held at San Germano to consider the details.[38] The new agreement respecting the crusade was drawn up at San Germano on July 25, 1225, just ten years after Frederick had received the crown at Aachen and had first taken the crusader's vow.

Frederick promised to depart with an army fitting to his imperial dignity on August 15, 1227, and pledged himself to carry on the war against the Saracens for two years. During this period of two years also he was to maintain in Syria 1,000 knights at his expense or to pay 50 marks in lieu of each combatant wanting to complete this number. He agreed to provide fifty fully equipped galleys and a hundred transport ships sufficient to carry 2,000 armed men with three horses for each, together with their squires and valets. As a special guarantee of his good faith also, he agreed to hand over 100,000 ounces of gold in five installments to the custody of Hermann of Salza, king John of Jerusalem, and the patriarch. This was to be returned to him upon his arrival in Acre to meet the

[37] *Chronica regia Coloniensis*, p. 253; also in *MGH, SS.*, XVII, 835–836. See also Böhmer, *Regesta imperii*, V, part 3, nos. 6569, 6570.
[38] Röhricht, *Beiträge*, I, 12–13.

expenses of the war. If, however, for any reason, including his death, he failed to go on the expedition these funds were to be employed for the needs of the Holy Land.

Upon the completion of the reading of the terms, Frederick advanced to the high altar and, with his right hand upon the Gospels, and in a clear voice, swore to undertake the crusade on August 15, 1227. As double assurance of his sincerity, Reginald of Spoleto swore also "on the soul of the emperor" that the terms of the agreement would be executed, in good faith and without reservations, under penalty of excommunication. Finally, in a letter to the pope, Frederick recapitulated the terms and accepted the ban voluntarily if, in the event of his failure, the crusade did not take place.[39] Since taking the cross at Aachen in 1215, each new postponement had tightened the hold of the curia upon Frederick until, at length, at San Germano he committed himself beyond all retreat.

The terms of the agreement are unique in their harshness, and reveal a want of consideration for the imperial office unparalleled in papal-imperial relations. Frederick pledged the resources of his empire to the limit of its capacity, and assumed as his personal responsibility a burden which the whole of Christendom had been unable to bear. No provision was made to relieve him of the full force of the penalty if, through illness, he should find it impossible to undertake the crusade. In case of his death his successors were bound. Frederick's action at San Germano suggests his acquiescence in a theory of papal-imperial relationships which was to obtain wide currency under Innocent IV and his protégés, the extreme canonists of the later thirteenth century. Although already discernible in the decretals of Innocent III, it is somewhat surprising to find this theory translated into action at San Germano under the milder Honorius III. It is still more surprising that Frederick himself, otherwise the most independent sovereign of the Middle Ages, should, at least where the crusade was concerned, voluntarily have accepted a subservient position as "officialis" and vicar of the holy see, while at the same time recognizing, apparently without protest, the authority of the pope as "judex ordinarius".[40] It seems certain that between the meeting of the emperor's ambassadors with the pope at Rieti, when Honorius was conciliatory, and the conference at San Germano, extraordinary pressure from within the curia had

[39] Richard of San Germano (*MGH, SS.*, XIX), pp. 344–345; Huillard-Bréholles, II, part 1, 501–503; Röhricht, *Beiträge*, I, 13.

[40] See also the interpretation of Kestner, *Kreuz. Fried.*, p. 22, and Röhricht, *Beiträge*, I, 62, n. 77.

been brought to bear upon Honorius to treat Frederick more severely. Probably Pelagius, still smarting under the humiliation of his defeat at Damietta, or else Syrian representatives present at the council were responsible. Only the acceptance of these terms enabled Frederick to obtain the desired postponement. Gregory IX himself several years later referred to the agreement of San Germano as imposing "very great and extraordinary obligations".[41]

In August 1225 Frederick sent fourteen galleys to escort his fiancée, Isabel of Brienne, from Syria. At Acre bishop Jacob of Patti gave Isabel Frederick's ring, and performed the marriage. There were many who marveled, says a contemporary, that two people should thus be married when one was in Apulia and the other in Syria, but "the pope had so ordered it". At Tyre, in accordance with her father's wishes, Isabel received the crown, and sailed for Brindisi, where Frederick and her father met her, and the marriage was celebrated anew on November 9.[42]

If, as has been conjectured,[43] it had been the Syrian nobles who had taken advantage of Frederick's strained relations with the pope to have the harsh terms of San Germano imposed upon him, Frederick was now in a position to adopt a policy no less embarrassing to them. The Syrian magnates and the curia intended Frederick to assume the duties of king of Jerusalem only after his arrival in Syria and his coronation there. But immediately after the marriage Frederick took the title king of Jerusalem, changed his imperial seal to include the new title, and shortly afterwards had himself crowned in a special ceremony at Foggia. John of Brienne had apparently relied upon the assurance, said to have been given him by Hermann of Salza, that the emperor would permit him to hold the kingdom for life.[44] It is probable also that John may have been the more easily persuaded to accept this promise because of the law of the *Assises* that the coronation of the king of Jerusalem should take place in Syria. But Frederick now chose to adopt a purely legalistic attitude. The claims of John of Brienne rested solely upon the inheritance of his late queen Mary and, after her death, upon his rights as guardian of their daughter. Frederick now claimed those rights as his own. Undoubtedly his inconsiderate treatment

[41] Huillard-Bréholles, III, 26.

[42] The details of the marriage are given in the "Relation française du mariage de Frédéric II avec Isabelle de Brienne et ses démêlés avec le roi Jean," in Huillard-Bréholles, II, part 2, 921 ff.

[43] Kestner, *Kreuz. Fried.*, pp. 20–21.

[44] Huillard-Bréholles, II, part 2, 922–923.

of John violated the spirit, if not the letter, of the San Germano agreement, but the legality of his claim appears to have been supported by precedents already established in the cases of Guy of Lusignan, Conrad of Montferrat, and Henry of Champagne.[45]

Such precedents, however, did not serve to reconcile king John, who first remonstrated with Frederick, and then denounced him in unbridled language, calculated to destroy for all time the possibility of a reconciliation. John then fled to Rome to seek the aid of the pope.[46] Honorius sympathized with John, and wrote to Frederick, characterizing his conduct as scandalous — "no less prejudicial to your own reputation than to the interests of the Holy Land."[47] The pope ignored Frederick's assumption of the new title, and that this was an intentional rebuke may be inferred also from the fact that Gregory IX, Honorius's successor, made reference to the title only in August 1231, after Frederick had been reconciled to the church.[48] Meanwhile Frederick sought and obtained the oath of fealty from the Syrian nobles who had accompanied the queen to Brindisi. Although they might well have insisted that, upon a strict interpretation of the *Assises*, the king should be a resident of the kingdom, the barons, with the probable exception of the Ibelins, appear at first to have accepted Frederick as king of Jerusalem without protest.[49]

Both the pope and the Syrian magnates must have recognized that, despite the harsh terms of San Germano, the emperor had made important gains through his marriage. He was now in a position to accomplish the expedition to the Holy Land, not merely as leader of a crusade in the traditional sense, but as a royal conqueror seeking to regain possession of his own. Frederick's first royal decree confirmed the possessions of the Teutonic Knights in Syria, on behalf of Hermann of Salza, the master, and the brothers of that order. At the same time he bestowed new privileges upon them.[50] The Teutonic Knights now won a place in the east comparable to that which the Templars and Hospitallers had so long

45 Von Raumer, *Geschichte der Hohenstaufen*, III, 169.

46 *Ibid.*, and Huillard-Bréholles, II, part 2, 923 and n. 2. See also Salimbene, *Cron.* (*MGH SS.*, XXXII), p. 41.

47 Huillard-Bréholles, II, part 1, 597–598.

48 *Ibid.*, III, 298: "Friderico illustri Romanorum imperatori, semper augusto, Hierusalem et Sicilie regi. . . ."

49 Röhricht, *Beiträge*, I, 15, appears to have little support for his statement that at this time, "Allein der Adel und Klerus des Königreichs Jerusalem war mit Friedrich nicht zufrieden . . . ." It was only later, when there was reason to fear his interference in Cyprus, that there was a definite manifestation of dissatisfaction. Concerning the Ibelins, see G. F. Hill, *History of Cyprus*, II, 90.

50 Huillard-Bréholles, II, part 1, 531 ff.

enjoyed. Although at first he left Odo of Montbéliard unmolested in his duties as bailie, Frederick later replaced him with Thomas of Acerra, whose conduct, as the emperor's representative in Syria, suggests that he had been charged especially with the duty of curbing the power of the Templars.[51]

Frederick's position as king of Jerusalem also influenced the strategy of the new expedition. In 1224 plans for the crusade had still contemplated a return to Egypt, and the ships constructed for the expedition were therefore designed to meet the requirements of a campaign in the delta of the Nile.[52] After Frederick's coronation, however, Jerusalem became his immediate goal, and it was increasingly apparent that, as in most of his imperial projects, "Sicily would supply the money and Germany the men" for the expedition.[53] He looked hopefully also to the Frisians as potential crusaders, recalling their signal successes in the assault on the chain tower, but his call to them evoked only a mild response, since the spiritual impulse from the scholasticus Oliver was no longer effective.[54] In northern Germany only the most earnest appeals of the emperor, combined with offers of fiefs and money, restored some degree of peace among the warring factions. Commissioned by the pope as crusading preacher, bishop Conrad of Hildesheim also won support for Frederick, who later rewarded him richly.[55] Landgrave Louis of Thuringia and duke Walram of Limburg, stimulated by the visit of Hermann of Salza, succeeded in rallying some 700 Thuringian and Austrian knights as well as many prelates and *ministeriales* to the crusade, which also drew forces from Cologne, Worms, and Lübeck. Despite the somewhat disappointing initial outlook, the number and prowess of the crusaders from Germany inspired hope for the success of the expedition.[56]

Crusading preachers, actively engaged in England during 1226–1227, persuaded large numbers to take the cross, although we may well doubt the assertion of Roger of Wendover "that 40,000 tried men marched from England alone". The English were inspired by the apparition in the sky of a shining cross upon which was "the body of Our Lord pierced with nails and with a lance", which

[51] Kestner, *Kreuz. Fried.*, p. 24.

[52] *Chronica regia Coloniensis*, p. 253: "et, si opus fuerit, erectis velis intrare possint flumen Damiate vel aliud aliquod flumen." Cf. also *MGH, SS.*, XVII, 837.

[53] W. K. Nitsch, "Staufische Studien," *Hist. Zeitschr.*, III (1860), 391.

[54] Huillard-Bréholles, II, part 1, 540 ff. See also H. Hoogeweg, "Die Kreuzpredigt des Jahres 1224 in Deutschland . . . ," *Deutsche Zeitschrift für Geschichtswissenschaft*, IV (1890), 74.

[55] Huillard-Bréholles, III, 20, no. 1.

[56] Röhricht, *Beiträge*, I, 18–19.

suggests that the major portion of the crusaders were simple and lowly. Shortly after Easter they left England under the leadership of bishops Peter of Winchester and William of Exeter.[57]

In Lombardy the ancient feud between the cities and the Hohenstaufens could always be easily revived at the slightest evidence of an extension of imperial authority. A summons for Easter 1226 to a diet at Cremona — ostensibly to consider the crusade, and to implement the laws against heresy which had been promulgated at the time of the imperial coronation — occasioned great unrest and suspicion among the Lombard cities, which now re-formed the Lombard League. The cities, led by Milan, were declared guilty of breaking the peace and of hindering preparation for the crusade, and the bishop of Hildesheim, employing his plenary powers as crusading preacher, placed them under the ban. The emperor also declared their privileges forfeited and the terms of the treaty of Constance nullified. With difficulty, Frederick at last succeeded in obtaining the intervention of the pope. The Lombards yielded to papal authority, and peace was temporarily restored. The emperor was assured papal protection of his interests during his absence in the east, and the Lombards were ordered to obey the imperial laws against heresy and to equip 400 men for a period of two years' service on the crusade. The ban was then lifted from the cities, the detailed terms of agreement were prepared, and formal ratification of the document by the various contracting parties was begun.[58]

But the death of Honorius III on March 18, 1227, before the agreement had been ratified, enabled the Lombards to ignore the papal command. The new pope, Gregory IX, forceful, learned, and energetic, included in the letters announcing his election ringing appeals in behalf of the crusade.[59] He admonished Frederick to fulfill faithfully his crusading vow, warning him in unmistakable terms of the penalty of the ban. But circumstantial evidence suggests the possibility of a secret understanding between the curia and the Lombards. Moreover, there is no evidence that the 400 fully equipped crusaders from the towns, required by the papal order, took part in the expedition.[60]

Frederick, however, busied himself with the final preparations

[57] Roger of Wendover, *Flores historiarum*, II, 323 ff.; *Annales monasterii de Waverleia*, in *Annales monastici* (ed. H. R. Luard, 5 vols., 1864–1869, Rolls Series, XXXV), II, 303.

[58] For the compromise, see Huillard-Bréholles, II, part 2, 703 ff. See also Röhricht, *Beiträge*, I, 15–17.

[59] For a brief characterization of Gregory IX see F. Gregorovius, *Geschichte der Stadt Rom im Mittelalter* (4th ed., Stuttgart, 1892), V, 138 ff. For detailed accounts of Gregory see J. Felten, *Gregor IX.* (Freiburg, 1886), and J. Marx, *De vita Gregorii IX* (Berlin, 1889).

[60] Röhricht, *Beiträge*, I, 17, n. 91.

for departure. Crusade taxes were levied, especially against the wealthy cloisters. Monte Cassino is said to have been taxed to the amount of 450 ounces of gold. Frederick took over as mercenaries some 250 mounted troops, formerly in the pay of the pope, from the kingdom of Sicily. Together with the 700 knights from Germany, the 100 in the immediate following of the emperor, and others, the total number may have exceeded the 1,000 required by the agreement of San Germano.[61] By midsummer of 1227, the crusaders had assembled in large numbers in the vicinity of Brindisi, designated by Frederick as the port of embarkation. The Germans arrived in August in far greater numbers than had been anticipated. The crowded conditions, the unbearable heat, the insufficient supplies of food and, above all, the unaccustomed ways of life soon led to widespread disease and to many deaths, including that of bishop Siegfried of Augsburg. Discouraged by the heat, or terrified by the plague, many returned home, leaving numerous ships empty in the harbor. But by the middle of August the main body of the crusaders sailed from Brindisi.[62]

The emperor and his retinue, including many Sicilian knights, were delayed while the fifty ships designed for their use were made ready. On September 8 they also sailed southward along the coast toward Otranto. Both the emperor and the landgrave of Thuringia had been stricken by the plague before sailing from Brindisi. Before reaching Otranto, the landgrave died, while Frederick, whose condition had grown worse, put into port at Otranto, resolved to await his recovery. Fearful that this might delay the sailing beyond the favorable season, he placed twenty galleys at the disposal of Hermann of Salza and Gerald, the new patriarch of Jerusalem, and designated the equally new duke Henry of Limburg as commander of the crusading army pending his own arrival.[63] He immediately sent the archbishops of Reggio and Bari and Reginald of Spoleto to the pope to explain his failure to depart for Syria. Gregory refused to receive them and thenceforth would not listen to Frederick's side of the story. On September 29, 1227, he excommunicated Frederick.

Legally, there can be no question that failure to fulfill his vow subjected the emperor to the ban. Morally, the pope committed an injustice if, as appears to be the case, Frederick was seriously ill and was in fact compelled to stay behind. Gregory apparently did not inquire — or care — whether Frederick was ill or not, and so

[61] Kestner, *Kreuz. Fried.*, pp. 26–27. [62] Huillard-Bréholles, III, 43.
[63] *Ibid.*, III, 44; Richard of San Germano (*MGH, SS.*, XIX), p. 348.

lent weight to the suspicion that he was seizing this opportunity to destroy a political enemy. Perhaps Gregory obtained greater satisfaction from Frederick's failure than he would have from his success. His letter to the emperor, written in late October 1227 and setting forth conditions for the lifting of the ban, referred less to the crusade than to Frederick's alleged violations of papal claims in Sicily.

In his circular letter publishing the excommunication, Gregory branded Frederick as the wanton violator of his sacred oaths taken at Aachen, Veroli, Ferentino, and San Germano, and held him responsible for the sickness and death of innumerable crusaders at Brindisi. Gregory charged him with delay in providing and equipping the necessary ships, and alleged that he had feigned illness, preferring the pleasures of Pozzuoli (where he had moved from Otranto) to the rigors of a crusading expedition. Finally, he accused him of failing to enlist the specified number of troops and to meet the financial requirements imposed upon him at San Germano. Some of these charges, however, are flimsy. The 700 German and Austrian knights, together with the 250 Sicilian mercenaries, the 100 from Frederick's household, and the others recruited probably exceeded the number agreed upon. Moreover, there is no evidence to indicate that the pope, prior to this time, had expressed dissatisfaction with the handling of the pledged sums. The wanton misrepresentation in these instances subjects the entire list of charges to suspicion. In contrast with the pope's unrestrained anger, the defense offered by Frederick in his letter "to all crusaders" of Europe leaves the impression of a straightforward factual statement, the sincerity of which is emphasized by the appeal to the Germans to prepare to join him in May for the expedition which he would lead at that time.[64]

Meanwhile the fleet which had sailed in August 1227 had probably arrived in Syria in early October. The second fleet, that of the Teutonic master and the patriarch, touched first at Limassol in Cyprus, where the constable of Jerusalem, Odo of Montbéliard, Balian of Sidon, and other notables awaited the emperor. Upon learning of his delay, they accompanied the fleet to Syria.[65] The absence of the emperor, "the crowned king from the west", who,

[64] For the pope's circular letter or encyclical of Oct. 10, 1227, see Huillard-Bréholles, III, 23 ff., and for Frederick's letter defending his actions see *ibid.*, pp. 37 ff. The letter of the pope to Frederick concerning his alleged misdeeds in Sicily is in *ibid.*, pp. 32 ff. The contents of this letter clearly indicate the readiness of Gregory to readmit Frederick to the fellowship of the church provided he submit to the papal demands with regard to Sicily. See also Kestner, *Kreuz. Fried.*, pp. 37 ff.

[65] Röhricht, *Beiträge*, I, 20.

by the terms of the agreement of Damietta, alone might break the truce, left to the crusaders a difficult decision. Duke Henry of Limburg, while fully aware of the dangers in breaking the truce, was powerless to resist the demand of the masses of the crusaders: the German knights no less than the ordinary crusaders clamored for either an attack on the Saracens or a speedy return home. Already many crusaders, discouraged by the emperor's delay, had decided to leave, although probably not as many as 40,000, the figure given by the pope in a letter of December 27, 1227. Most likely, large numbers reëmbarked at Acre almost immediately in the ships in which they had arrived.[66] The leaders clearly believed that action was necessary to prevent the disintegration of the army. They decided not to mount a direct attack against Jerusalem. Instead, the duke of Limburg led the main body of the crusader army to Caesarea and Jaffa to carry on the work of restoration of the abandoned fortifications along the coast.

These activities were obviously contrary to the spirit, if not the letter of the treaty, but they did not provoke an attack from the Moslems, because of the sudden death of al-Mu'aẓẓam, the governor of Damascus, in November 1227. This also hastened the decision of a group of French crusaders, who had remained in Acre, to attack and reclaim the whole of Sidon, half of which had been under the jurisdiction of Damascus. They hoped to restore the ancient fortifications, but in the language of Ernoul, "there was too much to do there". They decided instead to fortify the island of Qal'at al-Baḥr, just outside the harbor. About the same time, German crusaders began the reconstruction of the mountain fortress, Montfort (Qal'at al-Qurain), northwest of Acre, later to become "Starkenburg", the headquarters of the Teutonic Knights in Syria.[67]

While the crusaders were thus engaged in Syria, Frederick, now recovered from his illness, was actively preparing to set out the following May (1228). The outlook for the swift reacquisition of the old kingdom of Jerusalem had, however, brightened unexpectedly. For, amazingly enough, at the very moment when the pope was exerting every effort to thwart the plans of the emperor, a representative of the sultan al-Kāmil had arrived in Sicily with an urgent appeal for assistance and with tempting promises in return for immediate aid. After the defeat of the crusaders at Man-

[66] See the pope's letter in Matthew Paris, *Chronica majora* (Rolls Series, LVII), III, 128 ff.
[67] Ernoul, *Chronique*, p. 459; Grousset, *Croisades*, III, 288, and notes 1, 2, 3.

surah in the summer of 1221, the three Aiyūbid brothers, sons of the late sultan al-'Ādil, who had wiped out the threat from the forces of the Fifth Crusade, soon fell out among themselves, al-Kāmil, sultan of Egypt, feuding with al-Mu'aẓẓam, governor of Damascus, while the youngest brother, al-Ashraf, governor of Akhlat, cleverly shifted his allegiance back and forth. By 1225 al-Kāmil was convinced that al-Mu'aẓẓam was plotting to seize the sultanate, while al-Mu'aẓẓam was seeking an alliance with Jalāl-ad-Dīn, the ruthless shah of Khorezm, and so threatening, as al-Kāmil saw, the destruction of the entire Aiyūbid house.

Under these circumstances, almost in desperation, al-Kāmil had in 1226 sent the emir Fakhr-ad-Dīn to the emperor to ask him to come to Acre; he promised to give to him many cities of Palestine which belonged to the Moslems if he would attack al-Mu'aẓẓam.[68] Another Arab historian adds that al-Kāmil specifically promised Frederick Jerusalem.[69] Frederick had sent to al-Kāmil archbishop Berard of Palermo and count Thomas of Acerra, the emperor's bailie in Syria, who had given the sultan rich gifts from Frederick, including a favorite horse with a saddle of gold, inlaid with precious stones. After a ceremonious reception, al-Kāmil had entrusted to them presents of great value from India, Yemen, Iraq, Egypt, and elsewhere in token of his esteem for the emperor.[70] Arabic sources reveal also that archbishop Berard had continued his journey to Damascus in October 1227. Here he had attempted negotiations with al-Mu'aẓẓam, who had dismissed him with the curt message: "Say to your master that I am not as certain others, and that I have nothing for him but my sword."

Al-Mu'aẓẓam had then endeavored, unsuccessfully, to make peace with his younger brother, al-Ashraf; while al-Kāmil, apprehensive over Berard's visit to Damascus, had hastily dispatched Fakhr-ad-Dīn on a second mission to Frederick in the autumn of 1227.[71] It may well have been at this time that Frederick knighted Fakhr-ad-Dīn. For, in describing the emir some years later, Joinville says of him: "his banner was bendy and on one of the bends were the arms of the emperor, who had knighted him."[72] But hardly had Fakhr-ad-Dīn fulfilled his mission when Frederick received word from Thomas of Acerra of the sudden death of al-Mu'aẓẓam. He

[68] Al-Maqrīzī, "Histoire d'Égypte," *ROL*, IX, 509 ff.

[69] Badr-ad-Dīn al-'Ainī, *'Iqd al-jamān* (*RHC*, *Or.*, II, part 1), pp. 185–186. This entire subject is treated by E. Blochet, "Relations diplomatiques des Hohenstaufen avec les sultans d'Égypte," *Rev. historique*, LXXX (1902), 53 ff.

[70] Al-Maqrīzī, "Histoire d'Égypte," *ROL*, IX, 511.

[71] Badr-ad-Dīn al-'Ainī, *'Iqd al-jamān* (*RHC*, *Or.*, II, part 1), pp. 186–187.

[72] John of Joinville, *Histoire de St. Louis* (ed. Natalis Wailly, Paris, 1874), pp. 109–110.

must have perceived at once that the removal of al-Mu'aẓẓam would serve to improve the outlook for al-Kāmil, while weakening his own bargaining power. It was doubtless this realization that led him to send the marshal Richard Filangieri with 500 knights to Syria in the following April and to hasten his own preparations.[73]

In November 1227, an emissary from Frederick, acting "with the consent of the Roman people and the senate,"[74] publicly read in Rome the imperial manifesto explaining and justifying the delay. Perhaps this stimulated the pope to send two cardinals to Frederick in late December, but Frederick refused to receive them. Apparently he had concluded that he could obtain reconciliation with Gregory only on terms that were too humiliating to be acceptable. His diet at Capua in December decreed that each Sicilian fief should provide eight ounces of gold for the crusade, and each group of eight fiefs one armed knight to be ready to sail for Syria in May. In Swabia the emperor's circular letter announcing the departure in May had recruited a good many *ministeriales* for the crusade.[75] But Frederick could not hold the diet at Ravenna, announced in the circular letter, because the Milanese and Veronese blocked the Alpine passes to the Germans, and Gregory IX threatened to place under interdict all villages or towns in which the emperor might stay.[76] We are told, however, that Frederick celebrated Easter 1228 "with all joy and exultation."[77]

In Sicily his measures of retaliation against the papacy, threatening the confiscation of the property of those who obeyed the papal decrees, met with general acceptance.[78] In Rome itself Frederick's powerful supporters, notably the Frangipani, and his many friends among the populace, whom he had fed during the famine of 1227, rioted against Gregory IX and hounded him out of the city, first to Viterbo and then to Rieti.[79] Frederick knew perfectly well that in his absence all his German and Sicilian enemies would join with the pope in an effort to destroy him. Indeed, Gregory had made his plans for the invasion of Sicily, and had been trying to find a Welf protégé in Germany.[80] At Barletta in the late spring of 1228,

[73] Richard of San Germano (*MGH, SS.*, XIX), p. 349.

[74] *Ibid.*, p. 348.

[75] Huillard-Bréholles, III, 57–58. For his circular letter see *ibid.*, pp. 36 ff.

[76] John Codagnellus, *Annales placentini* (Scriptores rerum Germanicarum ad usum scholarum, Hanover, 1901), p. 86.

[77] Richard of San Germano (*MGH, SS.*, XIX), p. 349.

[78] Huillard-Bréholles, III, 50 ff.; Röhricht, *Beiträge*, I, 25.

[79] Richard of San Germano (*MGH, SS.*, XIX), p. 349; Burchard, *Urspergensium chronicon* (*MGH, SS.*, XXIII), p. 383.

[80] Winkelmann, *Kaiser Friedrich*, II, 16 ff.; Kantorowicz, *Friedrich II.*, pp. 163 ff.

Frederick publicly read his will to a huge outdoor assembly. During his absence in Syria, Reginald of Spoleto was to serve as regent. If Frederick should die, his son by Constance, Henry, the king of the Romans, was to be his heir; second in line was the newly born infant Conrad, son of Isabel and so heir to Jerusalem. The nobles present swore to uphold these terms and to secure similar oaths from their vassals.[81]

On June 28, 1228, the emperor with forty ships set sail from Brindisi for Syria. Although Gregory IX, deeply chagrined at Frederick's obstinate determination, said of his departure that he went "without anyone's knowing for certain whither he sailed," actually we are exceptionally well informed by the eye-witness account of a fellow passenger concerning the day-to-day voyage. First pausing at Otranto, the fleet sailed by Corfu, Cephalonia, Crete, and Rhodes, and finally on July 21 entered the harbor of Limassol in Cyprus,[82] where Frederick was met by the marshal Richard Filangieri, who had sailed during the previous April with a considerable part of the army.

On Cyprus he spent five weeks, quarreling with John of Ibelin, lord of Beirut, regent for the young king. John bravely defied Frederick's demand for Beirut and for money, as illegal.[83] Though the episode led to tension, king Henry and John of Ibelin and many Cypriote barons accompanied Frederick when he sailed for Acre on September 2, 1228.

On September 7 they arrived in the port of Acre, where Frederick was received with much ceremony by the Templars and the Hospitallers, as well as the clergy, although he was denied the kiss of peace because of the ban.[84] Thus the shadow of Gregory's hatred darkened the path of the emperor. To show his Syrian subjects his own good-will in the matter, Frederick yielded to the pressure to make overtures to the pope, and sent to Rome the admiral Henry of Malta and archbishop Marino Filangieri of Bari to announce his arrival in Syria and to request absolution, naming duke Reginald of Spoleto, his regent in Sicily, as minister plenipotentiary to negotiate with the pope. The papal decision, however, had already been made. Upon Frederick's departure from Brindisi, Gregory had notified the patriarch of Jerusalem and the masters of

[81] Richard of San Germano (*MGH, SS.*, XIX), pp. 349–350.
[82] *Breve chronicon de rebus Siculis*, in Huillard-Bréholles, I, part 2, 898 ff.
[83] See below, chapter XV, pp. 543–544.
[84] Roger of Wendover, *Flores historiarum*, II, 351: "non ei communicaverunt in osculo neque in mensa . . . ."

the military orders that the ban was to remain despite the emperor's arrival. At the same time he admonished them to have no part in the emperor's Syrian plans.[85]

A sharp division in the crusading army was inevitable. While the German and Sicilian knights stood firmly behind the emperor, the common soldiers, even some Germans, were moved by the religious implications of the expedition and adhered to the papal party, as did the patriarch Gerald, the Templars, and the Syrian bishops. The Pisan and Genoese inhabitants of Syria, doubtless recalling the bungling leadership at Damietta and their resulting commercial losses, supported the emperor, as did the Teutonic Knights, under Hermann of Salza. The English, including the clergy, wavered in their loyalties, at first supporting the emperor but shifting to the papal party. It was this impossible situation which Frederick endeavored to overcome through a clever move. He gave nominal command of various units of the expedition to faithful adherents who were free of the embarrassments of the papal ban: Hermann of Salza, Richard Filangieri, and Odo of Montbéliard.[86] This made it possible for the crusaders to avoid jeopardizing their own position in the eyes of the curia.

Frederick was not in a position to seek a victory through the force of arms. His army was small. Already he was committed to diplomatic rather than military action in his relations with the sultan of Egypt. Since 1226 he had been fully informed of developments in Syria through diplomatic exchanges with al-Kāmil. Indeed his friendly relations with the emir Fakhr-ad-Dīn, begun in 1226, had continued; from the autumn of 1227 until the emperor's arrival in Acre, Thomas of Acerra had carried on the negotiations. We do not know exactly what al-Kāmil had promised, nor whether al-Mu'aẓẓam's death in the previous November had changed his arrangements. At least during the initial stages of the negotiations, Frederick probably hoped to regain the conquests made by Saladin in Syria, and thus to reëstablish the kingdom as it had been before the battle of Hattin. The Arabic sources mention specifically the

[85] Richard of San Germano (*MGH, SS.*, XIX), p. 354; Huillard-Bréholles, III, 83 ff. The choice of Reginald, who even at that time was engaged in combatting the invading forces of the curia in Sicily, indicates how little the emperor was disposed to permit the papal claims in Sicily to be injected into the discussion. Diplomatically, the choice of Reginald would doubtless have destined the negotiations to failure even had the pope been otherwise disposed to a reconciliation. See also Ernoul, *Chronique*, p. 462.

[86] The assumption of Schirrmacher, *Kaiser Friedrich der Zweite*, II, 183, that the pope ordered this arrangement is untenable. For not only would the pope have chosen leaders other than the most faithful of Frederick's followers, but Frederick himself would not have submitted willingly, even meekly, to having the army taken from his command by order of the pope. See Kestner, *Kreuz. Fried.*, p. 43, n. 2.

restoration of Jerusalem, but add the vague mention of "several other places".[87] After al-Mu'aẓẓam's death, an-Nāṣir, al-Mu'aẓẓam's son and his heir as governor of Damascus, endeavored vainly to make peace with his uncle al-Kāmil, who then invaded Syria and took possession of Jerusalem. An-Nāṣir sought aid from his other uncle, al-Ashraf, but the two uncles now joined in plundering their helpless nephew, besieging the city of Damascus, and planning to divide the spoils (early September 1228–May 1229).[88] Al-Kāmil's position was now much stronger than when a year before he had appealed to Frederick for aid. He could now use Jerusalem to bargain with the crusaders for the greater security of Egypt. He could hardly have been fully aware, however, of the weakness of Frederick's forces, nor could he fully have comprehended the seriousness of the singular factional conflict in the ranks of the army arising from Frederick's excommunication, although he had some knowledge of these differences.

Frederick sent Thomas of Acerra and Balian of Sidon to inform al-Kāmil of his arrival and to request the fulfillment of the sultan's promises with respect to Jerusalem. Although receiving the embassy with courtesy, and obviously seeking to impress them by a ceremonial display of his armed forces, al-Kāmil let his visitors depart without committing himself with regard to their mission. His acceptance of Frederick's gifts and his own generous presents in return, including an elephant, ten camels, and ten horses, as well as silks and other rare stuffs, indicate his desire to maintain friendly relations. Shortly afterwards Frederick received the ambassadors of the sultan, including his old friend Fakhr-ad-Dīn, in his camp at Recordane near Acre. Displaying a consummate skill in the usages of Arabic diplomacy, Frederick, through his rare eloquence and extraordinary learning, impressed favorably both al-Kāmil and his clever representative Fakhr-ad-Dīn. Al-Maqrīzī, the Egyptian historian, says the emperor was learned in geometry, arithmetic, and other exact sciences, and reports that Frederick sent several difficult questions on geometry, the theory of numbers, and mathematics to the sultan, who gave them to men of great learning for appropriate answers which he returned to the emperor.[89] His learning as well as his unorthodox views on religion astonished the Moslems as they dismayed the Christians. These, together with the secrecy with which he carried on the negotiations with the

[87] See below, chapter XX, pp. 701–703.
[88] Abū-Shāmah, *Ar-rauḍatain* (*RHC*, *Or.*, V), pp. 190–191.
[89] Al-Maqrīzī, "Histoire d'Égypte," *ROL*, IX, 528–529.

congenial Fakhr-ad-Dīn, aroused the suspicions of the crusaders. Even Freidank, the Swabian poet who "always spoke and never sang", generally well disposed toward the emperor, expressed his sorrow that Frederick veiled his actions in secrecy.[90]

Having committed himself to extensive concessions of territory, al-Kāmil could no longer defend his earlier promises in the face of criticism from his subjects. This consideration for Moslem opinion now became his chief concern. When Thomas of Acerra and Balian of Sidon were again sent to resume the negotiations, the sultan left his headquarters at Nablus and went to his camp at Ḥarbīyah northeast of Gaza in order, as the *Eracles* reports, "to keep at a distance the emperor and his words."[91]

Frederick now prepared to impress the sultan by a show of force. He planned to use, as bases for operations against the city of Jerusalem, the cities of Caesarea and Jaffa, which in October 1227 Henry of Limburg had begun to refortify. In November 1228 Frederick set out on a march from Acre to Jaffa. The masters of the Temple and the Hospital, Peter of Montaigu and Bertrand of Thessy, refused to associate with the excommunicate, but followed at a distance of a day's journey. In the vicinity of Arsuf, however, Frederick, recognizing the dangers to his small following, yielded to pressure from some of the leaders and induced the Templars and Hospitallers to join the main body of the army, agreeing that future orders would be issued not in the name of the emperor but "in the name of God and Christianity".[92] The expedition moved successfully to Jaffa, where the work of fortification was pushed forward. Although at first heavy storms hindered the landing of supplies, by the close of the year 1228 abundant provisions flowed into the city.[93]

As the work on the coastal fortifications was nearing completion in January 1229, disquieting dispatches arrived from Italy, where John of Brienne, who since 1227 had served the curia as Protector of the Patrimony, was reported to have taken San Germano and to be threatening Capua. Ordering a part of the fleet to be held in readiness, the emperor appealed to his loyal subjects in Italy to hold out until his return. At the same time he ordered his admiral, Henry of Malta, to send twenty galleys to Syria by the following Easter.[94] Frederick's situation was now most awkward. If he delayed too long

[90] Bezzenberger, *Freidankes Bescheidenheit*, p. 211. For the attitude of the patriarch toward Frederick's Saracen relations, see Huillard-Bréholles, III, 104.

[91] *Eracles* (*RHC, Occ.*, II), p. 372.

[92] *Ibid.*, pp. 372 ff.

[93] Huillard-Bréholles, III, 90–91.

[94] *Eracles* (*RHC, Occ.*, II), pp. 373–374.

in Syria, he risked losing his Sicilian kingdom, but if he abandoned the Holy Land, he would be dishonored and his position weakened in the eyes of the Christian world. Fortunately for him, al-Kāmil himself was still busy besieging Damascus.

When negotiations were resumed, they led, therefore, to a peace described by an Arabic source as "one of the most disastrous events of Islam".[95] Al-Maqrīzī says that al-Kāmil was universally blamed for the treaty, "and his conduct was severely judged in all countries".[96] Unfortunately, no complete copy of the treaty survives either in Arabic or in Latin. It is possible to reconstruct it only from extracts included in letters to the pope from the patriarch Gerald and the Teutonic master, Hermann of Salza, and in a letter of Frederick to the king of England, as well as from occasional references, with differing emphases, in both Arabic and Christian sources.[97] Al-Kāmil surrendered Jerusalem, giving Frederick the right to make such disposition of it as he desired — obviously including the right to fortify it. In writing to the king of England, Frederick said, "we are allowed to rebuild the city of Jerusalem in as good a state as it has ever been . . . ."[98] Frederick also received Bethlehem and Nazareth, with the villages along the routes to Jerusalem, part of Sidon district, and Toron, dominating the coast. All these places, with the exception of Toron, he could refortify, while al-Kāmil, as Frederick puts it, was not allowed "till the end of the truce, which is agreed on for ten years, to repair or rebuild any fortress or castles".[99]

The settlement with respect to the city of Jerusalem, although drawn up in a spirit of tolerance almost inconceivable of the thirteenth century, evidently proved to be a chief difficulty in the negotiations and the item least acceptable to Christians and Moslems alike. Al-Ḥaram ash-Sharīf, the sacred enclosure, including both the Aqṣâ mosque and the Qubbat aṣ-Ṣakhrah (the Temple of Solomon, or Dome of the Rock) remained in the possession of the Moslems, with full freedom to worship there, provided they were

95 Badr-ad-Dīn al-'Ainī, *'Iqd al-jamān* (*RHC, Or.*, II, part 1), p. 187.

96 "Histoire d'Égypte," *ROL*, IX, 526.

97 For the fragment see Huillard-Bréholles, III, 86 ff.; for the letters of Gerald and Hermann, *ibid.*, pp. 90 ff. and 102 ff. Frederick's letter is in Roger of Wendover, *Flores historiarum*, II, 365 ff. See also the useful analysis of the treaty in J. LaMonte's notes to Philip of Novara, *The Wars of Frederick II against the Ibelins*, pp. 36 ff., n. 4; and below, chapter XX, p. 702.

98 Roger of Wendover, *Flores historiarum*, II, 367. The question of the refortification of Jerusalem is obscure, some of the Arabic sources stating positively that it was not permitted. See Grousset, *Croisades*, III, 318 ff.; and below, chapter XX, p. 702.

99 Roger of Wendover, *Flores historiarum*, II, 367.

unarmed, while the Christians were permitted to enter it to pray.[100] Jerusalem presented a peculiarly difficult problem because of the Moslems who, since 1187, had made their homes there. The sultan endeavored to secure for them a degree of autonomy, safeguarding both their system of justice and their religious customs. A magistrate (*qāḍī*) was to reside in the city to represent their interests, and non-resident Moslems were to receive protection while making pilgrimages to the mosques.

The other Christian states, Tripoli and Antioch, apparently were to receive no aid from Frederick in case of war with the Moslems. Indeed, the emperor seems to have pledged his support to protect the interests of the sultan against all enemies, including Christians, for the duration of the truce. Certain strongholds of the Hospitallers, such as Krak des Chevaliers, al-Marqab, and Chastel Blanc (Burj Ṣāfīthā), as well as Tortosa, held by the Templars, were to be left *in statu quo*, and aid was not to be given them from any source.[101] Finally, prisoners of war, taken either during the Damietta conflict or more recently, were to be released. The provisions relating to the various strongholds of the Templars and Hospitallers suggest that Frederick was revenging himself on them for their long opposition to him. It is less clear why Antioch and Tripoli, the possessions of Bohemond IV, should have been similarly treated, though Bohemond's unwillingness to swear fealty to Frederick may explain it.

The German and Sicilian followers of Frederick were satisfied with the treaty, and Hermann of Salza in his letter to the pope tried eloquently, though in vain, to convince Gregory that much had been gained for the Christian cause. As the crusading poet Freidank put it: "What more could sinners desire than the Holy Sepulcher and the victorious cross?"[102] Frederick himself badly wanted a reconciliation with the patriarch, both because he hoped to be crowned in Jerusalem, in accordance with the honored custom, and because of the urgent necessity of his immediate return to Italy. He was willing to make important concessions if only the patriarch would accompany the army to Jerusalem. Again Hermann of Salza was entrusted with this delicate mission. Gerald declined, however, to give an answer until he had been shown a copy of the treaty. He was then provided, not with the entire treaty, but with an abstract. The contents of this so stirred his anger that he could no longer behave rationally. His condemnation of the treaty was as thorough

[100] Al-Maqrīzī, "Histoire d'Égypte," *ROL*, IX, 525.

[101] See the fragment in Huillard-Bréholles, III, 89, par. 6 and par. 9, and Kestner, *Kreuz. Fried.*, pp. 53 ff.

[102] Bezzenberger, *Freidankes Bescheidenheit*, p. 214, lines 7–32.

as, in many instances, it was unreasonable. Gerald's letter to the pope in particular reveals that he was opposed to the concluding of any sort of peace with the sultan. For him the paramount purpose of a crusade was to shed "infidel" blood, not to engage in conciliatory negotiations that recognized the rights of Moslems within the city sacred to the name of Christ.

The Templars, not wholly for the same reasons, were in sympathy with Gerald's views. It was a tenet of their faith, the *raison d'être* of their order, that they were to fight unremittingly against the "infidel". The acceptance of Frederick's terms would impose upon them peaceful relations with the Moslems for at least ten years. Already they had experienced hardships and suffered disease and privations in winning control of fortified places from which they could pursue the conquest. Now, at a single stroke, a Christian emperor, notoriously friendly with Moslems, had set their achievements at naught, ignored their rights, perhaps, indeed, pledged himself to prevent their further conquests.[103] It is impossible to avoid the conclusion that both the patriarch and the Templars felt keenly that the treaty had ignored their special interests. The patriarch was not secured in his former possessions, and the Templars had profited, at most, to the extent of one or two insignificant villages. Moreover, Frederick had made concessions to the Saracens which, as the Templars believed, would make Christian occupation of the holy city difficult, and expose it to reconquest by the enemy.

It was no difficult matter for the patriarch and his supporters to depict Frederick as a betrayer, an enemy of the church, and to treat his recovery of the Holy Land as an illusion. Even though Gerald may have recognized some positive gains for the emperor, he dismissed them as of no account to the church. When, therefore, Hermann of Salza approached him with a sincere proposal for a reconciliation, Gerald saw only trickery and deceit. From this point on he sought to destroy Frederick and all his works. His first effort was to prevent the emperor's triumphal entry into Jerusalem by forbidding the army, under the threat of excommunication, to follow, and by placing the city itself under interdict. It was with this object that he sent archbishop Peter of Caesarea post-haste to the crusading army. But Frederick had moved more swiftly than the patriarch had anticipated.

When Hermann of Salza had failed to win Gerald over, Frederick set out immediately with the crusading army and a great body of

[103] See Böhmer, *Regesta imperii,* V, part 3, introd., p. xxxvii.

pilgrims for Jerusalem, which he entered on March 17, 1229. Here the agent of the sultan, the qadi Shams-ad-Dīn, awaited his arrival to make the formal surrender. The German pilgrims hailed the event with unbounded rejoicing. In his letter to the pope, Gerald would refer somewhat scornfully to these German pilgrims, "who had fought only to visit the Holy Sepulcher". On the morning of March 18, the army and the pilgrims proceeded to the church of the Holy Sepulcher. Frederick entered and, advancing swiftly to the high altar, took the crown and placed it upon his own head. Hermann of Salza then read to the congregation, first in German and then in French, the emperor's statement reviewing events from the moment of his taking the cross at Aachen. He described the harsh measures of the pope in opposing him, placing the blame not upon the pope, but rather upon those who had falsely informed the pope. By implication then, his bitterest remarks were directed at the patriarch and his followers, described as false Christians who had endeavored to blacken Frederick's character and who had maliciously hindered the peace.[104]

Leaving the church and still wearing the crown, the emperor proceeded to the palace of the Hospitallers, where he began negotiations with the English bishops, the masters of the Teutonic Knights and the Hospitallers, the preceptor of the Templars, and others, respecting the fortifications of the city. No decision was reached, and time was asked for consideration until the following day, March 19. Gerald's plans had gone awry, for it was not until the morning of the 19th that the archbishop of Caesarea arrived to proclaim the interdict. But the time had passed when this could check the plans of the emperor; the interdict could serve only to stir the anger of the people. Frederick was now in a position to place the responsibility for the imbroglio squarely on the patriarch. After his later reconciliation with Frederick, Gregory IX himself had to take steps against the obstinate Gerald as a source of discord in the Holy Land.[105]

It is from the account of Gerald that we learn of Frederick's movements on March 19. Early in the morning he betook himself and his entire following outside Jerusalem. To everyone's astonishment he was preparing for an immediate departure. Perceiving this, the representatives of the orders with whom he had been negotiating concerning the fortifications hastened to him, offering to support

[104] Huillard-Bréholles, III, 100, 109, and Roger of Wendover, *Flores historiarum*, II, 365 ff., 373.

[105] *MGH, Epp. pont.*, I, n. 467. See also Röhricht, *Königreich Jerusalem*, p. 799, n. 7.

his plans. Evidently he suspected an ulterior motive in their sudden change of attitude. He merely replied that he would discuss the plans in detail at another time. Then mounting his horse he rode so rapidly in the direction of Jaffa that those accompanying him had great difficulty in keeping up.

Mysterious as Frederick's conduct appears, his sudden departure is to be attributed not to the interdict, but rather to his urgent desire to return home as swiftly as possible to secure his Sicilian kingdom. He did, however, leave some of the knights of the crusading army behind to defend Jerusalem.[106] Moreover, at least a beginning was made in the restoration of the fortifications, apparently by the Teutonic Knights.[107] The Templars' last-minute offer to coöperate reflected no desire to work with the emperor, but rather their intention of seizing a favorable opportunity to further their own interests. Indeed, both patriarch and Templars had recognized that the gains which Frederick had made could be turned to their own advantage.

Frederick hastened by way of Jaffa to Acre, where he found the patriarch using the funds bequeathed by Philip Augustus to the kingdom of Jerusalem — which had been placed in his hands for safekeeping — in an effort to raise and equip troops, with which he hoped to make himself master of Jerusalem. The Templars were only too eager to lend their aid to such plans. When Frederick demanded an explanation, Gerald offered the excuse that the treaty had been made with the sultan of Egypt, not with the governor of Damascus, who was still in a position to attack Jerusalem. When the emperor ordered him to desist, the patriarch replied that he owed no obedience to an excommunicate. Through heralds Frederick now summoned the crusaders and the inhabitants of the city and, in a large assembly before the city gates, attacked the patriarch and Templars for their recalcitrance. He ordered all knights who were armed against him to leave the country, and authorized Thomas of Acerra to inflict severe punishments upon those who resisted the order.[108]

Despite these measures, the opposition continued and Frederick now resorted to force. He had the gates of the city guarded by his followers and forbade anyone of the opposing party to enter. In the city itself his men occupied positions from which to attack the palace of the patriarch and the houses of the Templars. Gerald

[106] This is revealed in a letter of the pope to the Templars, February 26, 1231: Huillard-Bréholles, III, 267.

[107] Huillard-Bréholles, III, 98.

[108] *Ibid.*, III, 137 ff.

complained that even the churches were taken over as vantage points. Monks who had been authorized by the patriarch to preach in opposition to the emperor were seized and whipped. Messages sent by Gerald to the pope were intercepted by Frederick; Gerald had to send multiple letters, employing several messengers.[109] But Frederick was unable to check the opposition, and Gerald was now so angry that he would accept nothing short of abject surrender.

From Italy came word that John of Brienne, leading the papal forces, had entered Apulia, and now was in the process of seizing the ports with the object of taking the emperor prisoner upon his arrival.[110] Forced to sail for the west, Frederick ordered all surplus weapons, siege machines, and other instruments of war taken to the ships or destroyed to keep them out of Gerald's hands. He named Balian of Sidon and Warner the German as bailies of Jerusalem, and sold the bailliage of Cyprus for a term of three years to longstanding foes of the Ibelins. He left a strong garrison to protect the imperial interests in Acre and, as a counterbalance to the Templars, helped the Teutonic Knights to redeem the territory around their stronghold, Montfort, which dominated the city of Acre.[111]

On the first day of May the emperor embarked from Acre, not without some hostile demonstrations from the inhabitants. Cypriote sources relate that, although Frederick had arranged to depart secretly at an early hour, he was followed to the harbor, through the street of the butchers, and pelted "with tripe and bits of meat most scurrilously." John of Ibelin, who accompanied the emperor to his galley, had to intervene with force to restore order.[112] These accounts, however, appear to have been written deliberately to emphasize the degradation of the emperor and the strength and gallantry of John of Ibelin. The seven galleys proceeded first to Cyprus, where Frederick was present at the marriage — apparently by proxy — of the king to Alice, the sister of the marquis of Montferrat. Then, after a rapid voyage, the emperor landed secretly, on June 10, at Brindisi. Frederick had been in Apulia a month before Gregory IX had even heard of his departure from Acre.[113]

Although the emperor's coming had taken the pope unawares, his subjects in Sicily responded so fast and so favorably to his

[109] Huillard-Bréholles, III, 110 and 138 ff.

[110] *Ibid.*, III, 112. One must conclude with Kestner, *Kreuz. Fried.*, Beilage 1, p. 70, that this information came directly from Reginald of Spoleto.

[111] *Eracles* (*RHC, Occ.*, II), p. 375; Huillard-Bréholles, III, 117 ff.

[112] Philip of Novara, *Mémoires*, p. 24, par. XLIII. See also F. Amadi, *Chron.* (ed. R. de Mas Latrie, *Documents inédits sur l'histoire de France*, 1st ser., Paris, 1891), I, 135–136.

[113] *Breve chronicon de rebus Siculis*, in Huillard-Bréholles, I, part 2, 902–903; Burchard, *Urspergensium chronicon* (*MGH, SS.*, XXIII), p. 383; Huillard-Bréholles, III, 146.

appeals that, with German troops driven into Brindisi by storms on their way home from the east, they scored success after success against the papal forces. By the autumn of 1229 Frederick stood in full possession of his kingdom. It was now only necessary for him to make his peace with the defeated pope. Although rebuffed in his first efforts, the faithful master of the Teutonic Knights, Hermann of Salza, eventually obtained an armistice, Frederick displaying conciliatory behavior and refraining from encroachments upon the papal domains. The German princes guaranteed the emperor's good faith. In May 1230 peace terms were drawn up, and on August 28 the ban was lifted; on September 1 at Anagni the "disciple of Mohammed" was once more received as the "beloved son of the church".[114]

The crusade of Frederick II is unique in the history of the Middle Ages, reflecting not so much the spirit of the age as the complex and cosmopolitan character of the emperor. The primary aim of any crusade was the restoration of Jerusalem to the Christians, and this had been achieved with a skill and brilliance all the more remarkable because the methods of accomplishing it were so little characteristic of the thirteenth century. Opposed at every step by the church, whose interests the crusade was intended to serve, Frederick achieved, without bloodshed, the object which the whole of Christendom most ardently desired. But in doing so, he earned for himself only opprobrium in the eyes of the leaders of the church. He was charged with sacrilege, with preferring the worship of Islam to the Christian faith, with betrayal of the crusading cause, with plundering, and with blasphemy. His outlook on life, the result of his contact since infancy with the rich and varied culture of the orient, elevated him far above the bigotry and the narrow prejudices so characteristic of Gregory IX, of the patriarch Gerald — indeed, of most of the clergy of the age. Again and again Frederick's letters, no less than his deeds, reveal his sympathies with the recovery of the Holy Land as a symbol of the Christian faith. But loyalty to this ideal did not deprive him of his capacity to understand that many of the places within Jerusalem were no less sacred to the mind and heart of the Moslem.

It is perhaps paradoxical that Frederick II, subjected to the bitterest reproaches for his anticlericalism, was able to attain

[114] For details of the reconquest, see Richard of San Germano (*MGH, SS.*, XIX), 355 ff. See Röhricht, *Beiträge*, I, 48 ff. For the reconciliation with the pope, see *Chronica regia Coloniensis*, pp. 262–263; also in *MGH, SS.*, XVII, 842; *Brev. Chron. Sic.* (Huillard-Bréholles), pp. 903–904.

through tolerance and conciliation what the leaders of the church believed to be possible and desirable only through the shedding of blood. For, in all the denunciations of Frederick by the patriarch, none was more bitter than the charge that he came not to slay the Moslem but to treat with him as a friend. It is a flaw in Frederick's achievement that his failure to arrive earlier, before the death of al-Mu'aẓẓam, when his presence in Syria would have aided al-Kāmil, deprived him of the opportunity to regain the unconditional possession of all the former Christian lands in Syria. It is also to his discredit that he displayed no capacity for conciliation with the Franco-Syrian knights who might well have become his staunch allies in the maintenance of his conquest. Failure to achieve this friendly alliance, indeed his almost contemptuous and brutal treatment, particularly of the Cypriotes, contributed immeasurably to subsequent conflicts and to the ultimate loss of Syria.

The greatness of Frederick's achievement was marred, above all, by the impossible situation in which he found himself as an excommunicate. Inability to unite the forces of Christendom, to enter upon the expedition with the full authority of the church behind him, compelled him to accept not the settlement which he most desired, but rather that which the sultan felt compelled to grant. One may well inquire with Freidank:

> "O what in the world can a kaiser do,
> Since Christians and heathen, clergy too,
> Are striving against him with might and main?"[115]

For the imperfections of the treaty the pope and the curia, far more than Frederick II, were responsible. At the most crucial moment in the crusading efforts of the thirteenth century, so vigorously launched by Innocent III, so zealously supported by Honorius III, the opportunity for a lasting success was sacrificed by Gregory IX to what, in his view, was a more desirable end, the chastisement of the Hohenstaufen emperor. Twice during the first three decades of the century the recovery of the Holy Land lay within easy grasp of the Christians through conciliation. Both times the curia failed to accept it. Pelagius had nullified the successes in Egypt, and Gregory IX, in his unyielding hatred of Frederick II, had deprived the Christian west of the full benefits of his achievement.

[115] From the translation by T. L. Kington, *History of Frederick II, Emperor of the Romans* (2 vols., Cambridge and London, 1862), I, 334, from Freidank's *Bescheidenheit*:

> "Waz mac ein kaiser schaffen
> Sit kristen, heiden unt pfaffen
> Streitent gnuoc wider in?"

XIII
THE CRUSADE OF THEOBALD OF CHAMPAGNE AND RICHARD OF CORNWALL, 1239–1241

The crusade of 1239–1241 was indeed a strange expedition. Prepared and launched in a maze of confusion and cross-purposes, it was viewed without enthusiasm, if not actually with distaste, by the two chief potentates of Christendom, the pope and the emperor of the Holy Roman Empire. Its two leaders, Theobald, king of Navarre and count of Champagne, and Richard Plantagenet, earl of Cornwall, never met during the course of the expedition. The crusaders spent most of their time peacefully in camp at Acre, Jaffa, and Ascalon, confining their military activities to two skirmishes — one a minor victory, the other a disastrous defeat. The crusading barons were divided by mutual jealousy and paid little or no attention to the orders of their chosen leader. The prelates and barons of the kingdom of Jerusalem and the masters of the three military orders disagreed with the crusaders on most questions of diplomacy, strategy, and tactics, and quarreled furiously among themselves. Many of them were at open war with the official representative of

The chief sources for the crusade of 1239–1241 are two continuations of William of Tyre, *Le Livre d'Eracles* and *Le Livre d'Eracles*, Rothelin manuscript. The former will be referred to as *Eracles*, the latter as *Rothelin Eracles*. Both are printed in *RHC, Occ.*, II. Additional useful information may be found in al-Maqrīzī, *Akhbar Miṣr* (tr. E. Blochet, "Histoire d'Égypte," *ROL*, VI–XI, 1898–1908); the anonymous *Histoire des patriarches d'Alexandrie*, quoted in footnotes to al-Maqrīzī's work; *Les Gestes des Chiprois* (*RHC, Arm.*, II); *Annales de Terre Sainte* (ed. R. Röhricht, *Archives de l'orient latin*, II); the chronicle of Aubrey of Trois-Fontaines (*MGH, SS.*, XXIII); the *Annales prioratus de Dunstaplia* in *Annales monastici*, III (ed. H. R. Luard, Rolls Series, XXXVII); and Matthew Paris, *Chronica majora* (ed. H. R. Luard, Rolls Series, LVII).

The fullest secondary account of the crusade is found in R. Röhricht, "Die Kreuzzüge des Grafen Theobald von Navarra und Richard von Cornwallis nach dem heiligen Lande," *Forschungen zur deutschen Geschichte*, XXVI (1886), 67–81. A section is devoted to it in R. Grousset, *Histoire des croisades et du royaume franc de Jérusalem*, III (Paris, 1936), 372–396. This crusade is discussed in its relation to the career of Peter of Dreux in S. Painter, *The Scourge of the Clergy, Peter of Dreux, Duke of Brittany* (Baltimore, 1937), pp. 110–117. There is also a useful account in H. d'Arbois de Jubainville, *Histoire des ducs et des comtes de Champagne* (Paris, 1861–1865), V, 277–326.

their young king's father and guardian, the Hohenstaufen Frederick II. In short, if one wished to write a burlesque of the crusades, one could do no better than to give an accurate account of this expedition. Yet this crusade accomplished more for the Christian cause in terms of lands and fortresses recovered from the Moslems than any other except the First Crusade. One can easily understand why Armand of Périgord, master of the Knights Templar, called the outcome a pure miracle wrought by God.

The background of every crusade consisted of three chief elements — the situation in the Holy Land, the policy and actions of the pope and the secular princes of Europe, and the motives, resources, ability, character, and political position of the crusaders. The third of these elements was always complicated, but the first two were often fairly simple. In the case of the expedition of 1239–1241 all three were truly magnificent mixtures of confusion, uncertainty, and cross-purposes.[1]

In November 1225 emperor Frederick II had married Isabel of Brienne, queen of Jerusalem, daughter of Mary of Montferrat and John of Brienne. Isabel had died in 1228 leaving her son Conrad as heir to the throne under the guardianship of his father. In 1229 Frederick had concluded a truce for ten years with al-Kāmil, sultan of Egypt, by which he had obtained possession of Jerusalem, Bethlehem, and Nazareth with corridors connecting these places with the sea-coast. But Frederick had no intention of contenting himself with the carefully limited suzerainty enjoyed by the kings of Jerusalem. As a result he had soon fallen out, before leaving Syria for the west in 1229, with most of the prelates and barons of the kingdom. The quarrel had grown more bitter when Frederick seized control of Cyprus by replacing John of Ibelin, lord of Beirut and regent for the young king Henry of Lusignan, with Cypriote lords who supported the imperial cause. John — the ablest, most influential, and most powerful of the barons of Jerusalem — reconquered Cyprus in 1233 after a long and savage war.[2] Until his death in 1236 he led the opposition to Frederick, who was far too occupied at home to give adequate support to his agents in the Levant. In the Holy Land itself, the Christians were thus divided not only by the chronic quarrels between the Templars and Hospitallers but also by those between the barons of the kingdom and the agents of Frederick II.

[1] The major part of the material for the discussion of the background of the crusade has been drawn from the *Registres de Grégoire IX* (ed. Lucien Auvray, Bibliothèque des Écoles françaises d'Athènes et de Rome, 2nd series).

[2] On the kingdom of Cyprus during this period, see below, chapter XVII, pp. 610–613.

The death of al-Kāmil (1238) led to an equally grave division among the Moslems.[3] His two sons, al-'Ādil Abū-Bakr and aṣ-Ṣāliḥ Aiyūb, became respectively masters of Egypt and Damascus, but their uncles and cousins immediately prepared to contest this division of the Aiyūbid domains.

The treaty of San Germano in July 1230 had temporarily reconciled Frederick II and pope Gregory IX, who now sincerely tried to bring peace to the kingdom of Jerusalem. But the pope was never really reconciled either to the truce with the Moslems or to Frederick's attempts to rule in Jerusalem. On September 4, 1234, Gregory dispatched a letter to the people of England to urge them to prepare for a new crusade. He pointed out that when the truce between the emperor and the sultan should expire in July 1239, the Holy Land would have need of Christian troops. All who went on the crusade would receive indulgence for all venial sins duly confessed. Those who could not go but contributed money would receive the same benefits. The persons and property of crusaders would come under papal protection. No usury was to be collected from crusaders. In November similar letters were sent to the people of France. All the clergy were directed to preach the crusade, but apparently the pope's chief reliance was on the Dominican friars. The preaching was so successful that in September 1235 the pope was obliged to order the prelates of France to prevent crusaders from starting before the appointed time.

Pope Gregory well knew that one could always persuade a fair number of barons to embark on a crusade. But few barons could afford it. Hence the chief problem was to raise money, as became particularly apparent in the summer of 1235. The most important lord who had assumed the cross was Amalric, count of Montfort and constable of France, who not only had no money but was overwhelmingly in debt. The pope had already authorized the men preaching the crusade to permit those who could not go in person to buy absolution from their oaths, but he doubted that these "redemptions" would yield enough. In June 1235 he wrote to all prelates to say that he hoped to maintain an army in Palestine for ten years after the end of the truce (1239). Every Christian who was not a crusader was to pay a denarius a week for this purpose. For each year in which this tax was paid the payer would be relieved from two years in purgatory. As time went on and more and more impecunious barons took the cross, Gregory was obliged to think of other financial expedients. The clergy were asked to pay a series

[3] For a detailed account of Aiyūbid affairs, see below, chapter XX, pp. 705–706.

of subsidies varying from one twentieth to one thirtieth of their annual incomes. In 1237 king Louis IX of France wrote to the pope to say that his conscience was troubled. When he received money from his Jews, how could he be sure some of it was not the product of usury? Gregory suggested that he could solve this by giving a generous sum for the crusade. In the autumn of the same year the episcopal sees of southern France were asked to pay off the debts of Amalric of Montfort.

It was usual to assign to a crusading baron the money collected in one or more dioceses except for sums that came from lands of other crusaders. As a rule part was to be given to the baron to prepare for the crusade and the rest sent to him after he reached the Holy Land. It is not surprising that this practice should have led to considerable confusion. The papal records were not kept very carefully. In February 1238 Gregory was obliged to admit that he had assigned the revenues from the diocese of Poitiers to both Geoffrey of Argentan, an English knight, and Peter of Dreux, count of Brittany (termed duke by the Bretons). Peter had the prior claim. The count of Mâcon was assigned the money raised in the province of Lyons, but later three of its dioceses were ordered to give their funds to the duke of Burgundy.

By the 1230's, the Albigensian Crusade was over as far as the need for armed force was concerned — it was in the hands of the Inquisition. Although the continuous wars against the Moslems in Spain and the attacks on the Prussians continued to call for men and funds, the chief rival for the resources and men destined to relieve the Holy Land was the Latin empire of Constantinople, where the emperor John of Brienne was facing a Bulgarian-Nicaean coalition. He had sent his son-in-law and co-emperor, Baldwin II, to the west to get help.[4] In the late summer of 1236 pope Gregory decided to assist the Latin empire. On October 23 he wrote to Peter of Dreux, who had apparently already agreed to lead an expedition to Constantinople, to assure him that he would not be obliged to obey the orders of the emperor, the patriarch, or the doge of Venice. On December 9 the pope wrote a rather vague letter to the most important French baron who had taken the cross, Theobald, king of Navarre and count of Champagne. He did not actually ask Theobald to go to Constantinople instead of to Palestine, but he begged him in general terms to aid Baldwin in any way he could. On May 9, 1237, Henry of Dreux, archbishop of Rheims and brother of Peter, was directed to finance the count of Bar if he

[4] See above, chapter VI, pp. 218–220.

decided to go to the aid of Constantinople. The next day a letter to bishop Hugh of Sées directly ordered him to change his vow and go to Constantinople. The expedition was to start in March 1238.

Thus by the spring of 1237 pope Gregory had two crusades on his hands. If he had hoped to persuade all the crusading barons to go to Constantinople, he had not succeeded. This situation led to some confusion. On May 27, 1237, Gregory wrote Louis IX, asking him to see that crusaders going to *either* the Holy Land or Constantinople were given a respite in payments on their debts. In February 1238 the pope wrote the archbishop of Rheims that count Henry of Bar was going to lead one hundred knights on one of the two crusades. In March bishop Aimo of Mâcon was authorized to permit Humbert, lord of Beaujeu, to change his destination from the Holy Land to Constantinople. In short there were a number of crusading barons in France, but no one was quite sure who was going to Palestine and who to Constantinople.

The next problem was to decide when the armies should start. The first change in plan seems to have been made suddenly. On October 30, 1237, Gregory directed the prior of the Dominicans in Paris to urge all crusaders to Constantinople to be ready in March. The next day he directed Baldwin to defer his journey until August. On December 17 he wrote to the bishop of Sées informing him of the new date and indicating that the change had been made at duke Peter's suggestion. Meanwhile in November 1237 the expedition to Palestine had encountered a serious obstacle. The French barons who were to lead the crusade had pointed out to the pope that they would need the coöperation of the German emperor — passage through his lands, shipping facilities, and supplies. But Frederick II had no desire to see a crusading army in Palestine a full year before his truce with the sultan expired. He refused all aid. Hence on November 4 the pope informed the archbishops of Sens and Rheims that the Syrian crusade was postponed for a year, until August 1239. On December 7 the emperor wrote to the pope stating that he had promised the crusaders not to ask for another delay beyond the year. When the time came, he would give them every assistance. In fact he would either lead them in person or send his son Conrad as his representative. Thus by the end of 1237 the departure for Constantinople was set for August 1238 and that for the Holy Land for August 1239.

The expedition to Constantinople did not start in August 1238 nor was it led by Peter of Dreux. Just what did happen is obscure.

On January 12, 1238, the pope wrote to Peter asking him to reduce the contingent he expected to lead to Constantinople in August. The bishop of Sées was informed that the emperor Baldwin II needed money more than troops. On May 14 the bishop was directed to give Peter at once one third of the funds collected by him for the relief of Constantinople and to pay him the rest when he reached his destination. Nothing more is heard of this expedition until July 5, 1239, when Louis IX sent agents to count the crusaders who had gathered around the banner of Baldwin.[5] Sometime later Baldwin set out for Constantinople. The only barons known to have been with him were Humbert of Beaujeu and Thomas of Marly. Peter of Dreux was in the host bound for Palestine.

During the years 1234 through 1238 pope Gregory had been devoting a large part of his attention to his plans for the two crusades. But early in 1239 came a serious diversion in the form of a renewal of his quarrels with Frederick II: the basic issue between them remained unsolved, as Frederick was resolved to make himself absolute master of Italy, and the pope felt obliged to support Frederick's enemies in northern Italy. On March 20, 1239, he excommunicated Frederick.

This situation was, to say the least, confusing to the crusaders who were bound for the Holy Land. The pope was the initiator and patron of the expedition. Many of the usual ports of departure for Palestine were in Frederick's domains, and he was the guardian of his son Conrad, the young king of Jerusalem. While the barons had probably never expected that Frederick would actually lead their host, his coöperation was extremely important. Hence the crusaders must have been sadly perplexed when they gathered at Lyons in July 1239. Matthew Paris, who was no friend to Gregory, states that both the pope and the emperor asked the barons to postpone the crusade.[6] But in a letter of April 1240 addressed to king Henry III of England, Frederick himself stated specifically that he had asked the crusaders to wait until he or Conrad could lead them, and that they had been about to accede to his request, but that the firm insistence of Gregory had persuaded them to start.[7] When Frederick wrote this letter, the expedition had met a serious reverse, and he may well have wanted to throw the blame on the pope, whose own letters to the crusaders have not survived.

[5] *RHGF*, XXII, 596.
[6] Matthew Paris, *Chronica majora*, III, 614–616.
[7] *Ibid.*, IV, 26–29.

If Frederick did indeed ask the crusaders to delay their departure, he took it in good part when they refused to follow his advice. He wrote to them that the pope's support of the Lombard rebels had thrown his realm into such confusion that he could give them little aid. He offered them passage through his lands and ports. Moreover, he would write to his bailie of Jerusalem directing him to aid them. The emperor closed with some sharp remarks about the citizens of Acre, who had steadfastly refused to acknowledge his sovereignty. Some months later he congratulated the crusaders on their safe arrival at the city he had warned them against. He was much too short of funds to finance the fortification of Jerusalem, but they could buy what supplies they needed from his domains. In January 1241 he directed his agent in Sicily to allow the purchase of supplies for the crusading army in Palestine.[8] In view of the difficulties besetting Frederick, he seems to have done what he could for his not entirely welcome allies.

The crusading barons who gathered at Lyons formed an imposing group. At their head stood two peers of France, one of whom wore a crown — count Theobald IV of Champagne, since 1234 king of Navarre, and Hugh IV, duke of Burgundy. With them were two great officers of the realm, Amalric, count of Montfort and constable of France, and Robert of Courtenay, butler of France. Below these lords in feudal and official dignity but fully their equal in prestige came Peter of Dreux, once count (duke) of Brittany and earl of Richmond. Although by 1239 Peter was simply lord of La Garnache and Montaigu, he was generally called count of Brittany. Then there were a group of counts of secondary rank — Guigues of Forez and Nevers, Henry of Bar, Louis of Sancerre, John of Mâcon, William of Joigny, and Henry of Grandpré. Among the important men below comital rank were Richard, viscount of Beaumont; Dreux of Mello, lord of Loches and Dinan; Philip of Montfort, lord of La Ferté-Alais; Andrew, lord of Vitré; Ralph, lord of Fougères; Simon, lord of Clermont; Robert Malet, lord of Graville; and William, lord of Chantilly. With some overlapping these lords fall into three classes — officials and servants of the French crown, relatives and former vassals of Peter of Dreux, and vassals of Theobald.

Theobald IV was an excellent poet, an ineffective warrior, and an irresolute and shifty politician. By 1234 he had lost through a

[8] J. L. A. Huillard-Bréholles, *Historia diplomatica Friderici II* (Paris, 1852–1861), V, 360–362, 645, 646–647.

combination of ineptness and bad luck an important part of his vast patrimony, and had earned the distrust of every group in the feudal politics of France. Only his status as a crusader had saved him from severe punishment for rebellion against Louis IX. One can only guess at Theobald's motives in taking the cross. He came of a crusading family. His uncle count Henry had been ruler of Jerusalem, and his father Theobald III had died while preparing to go to the Holy Land. Theobald quarreled with the church less than most feudal princes and was an enthusiastic burner of heretics. Perhaps he felt grateful to Divine Providence for the kingdom of Navarre. Perhaps he was chiefly interested in papal protection in case his rebellion against king Louis failed. Certainly nothing in his record gave any hope that he would furnish wise, determined, or consistent leadership to the crusading host.

Peter of Dreux was a noted soldier and a skillful and unscrupulous politician. He loved power, wealth, prestige, and strife of all kinds. Born a younger son of the house of Dreux, and hence a relative of the Capetian kings, he had spent his life struggling to obtain and keep a position that would satisfy his ambitions. Husband to Alice, the heiress of Brittany, he had forced its almost independent counties into a centralized feudal state. Her death reduced his rights in the duchy to those of guardian of his young son John. Having failed at rebellion against Blanche of Castile and Louis IX, Peter retired to his second wife's domains in Poitou. His reasons for taking the cross are not hard to guess. He needed the pope's friendship to aid him in settling his numerous quarrels with the church, and he wanted more action than his petty fiefs in Poitou would be likely to supply. Few barons can have had greater need of the crusader's indulgences. As an experienced and competent soldier with no affection for useless risk Peter was a valuable addition to the crusading host.

Amalric of Montfort was a bankrupt hero. Son of Simon, who had led the Albigensian Crusade and won the title count of Toulouse, Amalric had been obliged to surrender his rights in Toulouse to the French crown.[9] Although he enjoyed the dignity of constable of France, his lands were small and he was deeply in debt. His crusade was financed by the pope and king Louis. Perhaps his reputation as a soldier was more a reflection of his father's glory than the result of his own prowess, but he was undoubtedly considered the first soldier of France. Duke Hugh of Burgundy had little fame as either a soldier or a statesman. But he came of a family

[9] See above, chapter VIII, pp. 314–324.

noted for its enthusiasm, courage, and perseverance as crusaders, and he was to prove himself a worthy member of it. Count Henry of Bar had probably done more fighting with less success than any other baron of France.

In a letter which we should probably date October 6, 1237, the chief barons and prelates of Jerusalem who were opposed to Frederick II gave Theobald advice, in answer to questions he had asked them.[10] They saw no point in delaying the expedition until the end of the truce, as Saracens never kept truces anyway. Marseilles or Genoa seemed the best ports of departure for a French army. They then suggested that the crusaders land at Cyprus and there take counsel with the leaders of the Christians in Palestine. At Cyprus supplies were plentiful and the army could rest after its voyage. Moreover from Cyprus it was equally easy to strike for Syria or Egypt, whichever seemed more promising.[11] Apparently Theobald had not asked about political conditions in either the kingdom of Jerusalem or the Aiyūbid state, but if the advice to stop at Cyprus had been followed, the crusaders would have been able to inform themselves on these matters before they reached Palestine.

In another letter Armand of Périgord, master of the Knights Templar,[12] informed Walter of Avesnes that the sultan of Egypt was a man of no valor and was held in general contempt. The lord of Transjordania was at war with the sultan of Damascus. Several of the Aiyūbid lords whom Armand would not yet name were anxiously awaiting the coming of the crusaders and had promised to submit to them and receive baptism. The references to a feeble sultan of Egypt and to an independent sultan at Damascus show that this letter was written after the death of the sultan al-Kāmil in March 1238. It is not clear that Walter of Avesnes was connected with the barons who were planning the crusade, but the letter appears in the chronicle of Aubrey of Trois-Fontaines, whose chief interest lay in Champagne and its vicinity. It may well have been the knowledge that different sultans ruled at Damascus and in Egypt that led the crusaders to abandon any idea of attacking Alexandria or Damietta and moved them to sail directly to Acre.

[10] E. Martène and U. Durand, *Thesaurus novus anecdotorum*, I (Paris, 1717), 1012–1013.

[11] R. Röhricht, *Regesta regni Hierosolymitani*, p. 282, dates this letter 1238. The letter tells the crusaders not to delay because of the truce. But the crusaders had postponed their departure to August 1239 as early as November 4, 1237. To accept the date of 1238 it is necessary to believe that this news took eleven months to reach Acre. Moreover, to justify his date Röhricht makes an emendation in the list of men who sent the letter. October 1237 seems an acceptable date that removes all difficulties.

[12] Aubrey of Trois-Fontaines (*MGH, SS.*, XXIII), p. 945.

There was little point in attacking Egypt if its sultan did not control the Holy Land.

The crusaders left France in August 1239. While a few took advantage of emperor Frederick II's offer to use the ports of southern Italy, the majority sailed from Marseilles. As the fleet neared its destination, a storm scattered it over the shores of the Mediterranean. If one is to believe the Rothelin manuscript, some ships were driven as far as Sicily and Sardinia. Theobald reached Acre on September 1, and soon the army was concentrated there. At Acre the crusaders were met by the potentates of the Holy Land — the prelates and barons of the kingdom of Jerusalem and the masters of the three great military orders, the Templars, the Hospitallers, and the Teutonic Knights. The most prominent of the local barons as far as relations with the crusaders were concerned was a recent arrival in Palestine to whom Frederick had given the county of Jaffa, Walter, count of Brienne, nephew of John of Brienne, former king of Jerusalem. Walter was a vassal of Theobald for his county of Brienne and must have been well known to most of the crusading lords. With him were Odo of Montbéliard, constable of Jerusalem, and two of the chief members of the great house of Ibelin, Balian, lord of Beirut, and John, lord of Arsuf, as well as their cousin, Balian of Sidon. Balian of Sidon also had connections in the crusading host. His mother Helvis of Ibelin's second husband had been Guy of Montfort, younger brother of Simon, count of Toulouse, and he was thus a half-brother of Philip of Montfort, lord of La Ferté-Alais.

The most immediate necessity facing the crusaders was to attempt to secure the safety of Jerusalem. Frederick had obtained possession of the holy city by his truce with al-Kāmil, but either because of penury or from a desire not to annoy the Moslems he had neglected to fortify it. When the truce expired, the only defensible post in the city was the Tower of David, which was held by a small garrison under the command of an English knight, Richard of Argentan. Although the alarmed citizens had done what they could to improve the defenses, they had succeeded only in erecting some flimsy works at St. Stephen's Gate. As soon as Theobald landed at Acre, he wrote to Frederick II to notify him of his safe arrival and to ask for money to rebuild the walls of Jerusalem. Meanwhile the Moslems had decided to anticipate any possible action by the crusading host. Attacking the city in force, they easily overthrew the light works that had recently been erected, but the Tower of David held out against them. Soon imperial agents arrived to ask for an extension of the truce. Although these officers persuaded the Moslems to abandon their attack on the Tower of David, it is not clear whether or not they retired from the city.[13]

The news of the attack on Jerusalem reminded the crusaders who were resting quietly at Acre that they had come to the Holy Land to conduct a campaign against the Moslems. Theobald summoned a council of the crusading lords and the prelates and barons of the kingdom of Jerusalem to decide on a course of action. The chroniclers tell us that a whole day was passed in fruitless debate, and that many divergent views were presented, but they do not say what these views were. Presumably the possibility of fortifying Jerusalem was discussed. Perhaps the local barons, who were all members of the anti-imperial party, had no enthusiasm for saving the city for Frederick, with whom they were at war. Perhaps Theobald felt that he lacked the resources required for so great a task. Then it seems likely that there were some who wanted to attack the sultan of Damascus, while others preferred a campaign against Egypt. As the two sultans were on very bad terms, a good argument could be advanced for a vigorous attack on one of them in the hope that the other would stay neutral. The final decision looks like a compromise. The army would first march down the coast to Ascalon and build a castle there, a scheme that was of particular interest to the chief local lord in the council, Walter of Brienne, as Ascalon covered his county of Jaffa from Egyptian attacks. Then the host would proceed against Damascus itself. The chief objection to this plan was that it was likely to antagonize both sultans. The sultan of Egypt would naturally be alarmed at having the host camp on his frontier, and he probably had no desire to see a castle built at Ascalon. Under the circumstances annoying the sultan of Egypt seems a poor way to prepare for an attack on Damascus.

It was November 2 before the army commenced its march toward Ascalon. Except for the two days spent debating their plan of campaign there is no information about the barons' activities during the two preceding months. Acre was a pleasant city, noted

[13] It is impossible to reconcile fully the different accounts of the events in Jerusalem during this crusade. *Rothelin Eracles*, pp. 529–530, states clearly that both the city and the Tower of David were taken shortly after the crusaders arrived at Acre. All the other chroniclers both Christian and Moslem place the fall of Jerusalem after the battle of Gaza. The only possible solution seems to lie in a passage of the *Annales de Dunstaplia*, p. 150. It tells how Richard of Argentan and his men were saved by the imperial envoys. Obviously the *Rothelin Eracles* may have confused this Moslem attack with the later one that captured and destroyed the Tower of David. As Richard's lands lay near Dunstable, the priory's chronicler may well have based its account on a letter from him or a report by one of his men.

for its easy moral standards. Theobald was a poet and had in his train two fellow rhymers, Ralph of Nesle, younger brother of count John of Soissons, and Philip of Nanteuil. Peter was probably not a poet himself, but he was a patron and friend of poets. The town was full of noble ladies such as Alice of Champagne, daughter of count Henry by Isabel, queen of Jerusalem. The widow of king Hugh I of Cyprus, she had been briefly married to Bohemond V, prince of Antioch and count of Tripoli. Before the crusade was over she was to marry Ralph of Nesle. Although Theobald composed a poem bemoaning his absence from his lady, it seems likely that local consolation was available.[14] Certainly the ordinary knights whose funds were rapidly being spent were impatient at the leisureliness of their noble leaders.[15]

On November 2, 1239, the host left Acre on its march towards Ascalon. There were some 4,000 knights, of whom more than half were supplied by the local barons and the military orders. Like most crusading armies it was short of horses and provisions. Apparently the sultan of Damascus had learned that the crusaders planned to lay siege to his capital, and ordered his vassal chieftains to bring supplies to the city. On the second day after leaving Acre, Peter of Dreux learned that a large convoy of edible animals bound for Damascus was passing within striking distance. The army's need for supplies and probably his own desire for action and glory moved Peter to decide to intercept the convoy. As he was unwilling to share either the glory or the booty, he did not mention his plan to his fellow barons. Late that evening he left camp with a force of two hundred knights and mounted sergeants. At dawn they reached the castle where the convoy had spent the night. Apparently there were two possible routes from the castle toward Damascus. Hence Peter divided his forces. A party under the poet Ralph of Nesle lay in ambush on one road while Peter himself watched the other. At sunrise the Moslems left their stronghold and took the road held by Peter's party. When their leader found that he was intercepted by a force smaller than his own, he decided to give battle rather than risk the loss of his convoy by retreating to the castle. Peter had taken up a position where the road emerged from a narrow defile. This gave him a great tactical advantage. By catching his lightly armed foes in a narrow place, he had robbed them of their chief asset, speed of maneuver. The Moslem leader sent forward his archers in the hope of holding off the French knights until his

[14] Joseph Bédier, *Les Chansons de croisade* (Paris, 1909), pp. 197–206.
[15] *Ibid.*, pp. 229-234.

cavalry could clear the defile, but Peter's charge cut them to pieces and caught the main body in the pass. The fight became a hand-to-hand combat with sword and mace—the type of struggle most favorable to the heavily armed crusaders. But the Moslems fought well, and Peter felt obliged to sound his horn to call up his other contingent. The arrival of Ralph and his party decided the battle. The enemy was routed and fled toward the castle. Peter and his men entered the castle with the fugitives, killing many and taking the rest. Then he returned to camp with his booty. The fresh supplies, to say nothing of the victory, were very welcome to the crusading host.

By November 12 the crusading army had reached Jaffa. There they learned that the sultan of Egypt had sent a strong force to the vicinity of Gaza to hold the frontier of his lands. A number of barons, jealous of the glory that Peter of Dreux had acquired by his raid, decided to go out ahead of the army, attack the enemy, and rejoin the host at Ascalon. Apparently the two most ambitious leaders were the counts of Bar and Montfort, but they were joined by Hugh, duke of Burgundy; Walter of Brienne, count of Jaffa; Balian, lord of Sidon; John of Ibelin, lord of Arsuf; Odo of Montbéliard; the viscount of Beaumont; and many lesser lords. Estimates of their force range from 400 to 600 knights. When Theobald, Peter of Dreux, and the masters of the three military orders learned of the plan, they protested strenuously. They wanted the whole army to move as a unit to Ascalon and then attack the enemy if it seemed feasible. But the adventurous barons would not listen. Not even Theobald's plea that they remember the oath they had taken to obey him as leader of the crusade had any effect. Not only did they defy Theobald as leader of the army, but even some of his own vassals were among the rebels.

The party left Jaffa in the evening and rode all night. They passed Ascalon and came to a brook that formed the frontier of the kingdom of Jerusalem. The count of Jaffa's desire for adventure had cooled by this time. He pointed out that the horses were tired and suggested that they retire to Ascalon. But the crusaders insisted on going on. Count Walter led his men over the stream, deployed them, and covered the crossing. Once across the brook the army halted. The barons spread cloths on the ground and dined. They had chosen a most unfortunate spot for their rest, a sandy basin surrounded by high dunes. Apparently not even the count of Jaffa, who had conducted the crossing in so military a manner, thought to send out patrols or even to post sentries on the dunes.

The Egyptian commander had not been so negligent, and his scouts soon informed him of the crusaders' position. He promptly covered the dunes with crossbowmen and slingers. Their presence was first discovered by Walter of Jaffa; perhaps he had belatedly sent out a scout. The call to arms was given, and the leaders assembled in council. Walter and the duke of Burgundy wanted to retreat, but the counts of Bar and Montfort refused to do so. They said that the enemy was so near that only the cavalry could hope to escape. Retreat would mean sacrificing the infantry. Thereupon Walter of Jaffa and Hugh of Burgundy departed for Ascalon, leaving their colleagues to fight the battle. It seems likely that Balian of Sidon, John of Ibelin, and Odo of Montbéliard went with them. Walter's objections to crossing the Egyptian frontier lead one to wonder whether he and his fellow Syrian barons had not joined the expedition in the hope of curbing the recklessness of the crusaders, and saved themselves when they found it impossible.

Amalric of Montfort ordered his crossbowmen to clear the foe from the dunes. The men opened fire and were making good progress until they ran out of crossbow bolts. Amalric then noticed a deep, narrow passage between two dunes where his troops would be sheltered from the enemy's fire. The knights charged toward this place and easily scattered the infantry holding it. By this time the Egyptian cavalry had arrived on the scene, but its leader knew better than to charge the heavily armed knights in their narrow pass. Instead he tried the time-worn trick of a feigned retreat. Completely duped, the crusaders rode out of their position in full pursuit while the Moslem infantry seized the pass behind them. The battle was over. The Moslem cavalry turned around, surrounded the crusaders, and cut them to pieces. Count Henry of Bar was killed. The count of Montfort, the viscount of Beaumont, some eighty knights, and many serjeants were captured.

When the main body of the army reached Ascalon, it met the count of Jaffa and the duke of Burgundy, who told them of the desperate situation of the counts of Bar and Montfort. With the Teutonic Knights in the vanguard, the army at once moved toward Gaza. Soon they met scattered fugitives and then the pursuing Moslems. But the Egyptian commander did not feel strong enough to fight the whole crusading army, and he retired while the crusaders occupied the corpse-strewn battlefield. Theobald was inclined to pursue the retreating enemy, but the Templars and Hospitallers pointed out that in that case the prisoners would probably be killed by their captors. Reluctantly Theobald accepted their advice and returned to Ascalon. Soon the army retired up the coast to Jaffa and then went all the way back to Acre.

This retirement to Acre is extremely puzzling. The army had marched to Ascalon in order to build a castle there. Certainly the loss of a few hundred men did not weaken it so seriously that it could not carry out its plan. One reason for the retreat may well have been lack of supplies. The army had started from Acre without enough provisions, and Peter's booty cannot have lasted long. But it seems likely that the perpetual conflict between crusaders and local lords was an even more important factor. The barons of Jerusalem and the military orders were in general inclined to let the Moslems alone when they could. Their interest lay in defending their own lands rather than in aggression, and long experience had given them a deep respect for the military capacity of their foes. No doubt the Templars and Hospitallers considered the idea of pursuing the victors of Gaza into Egypt utterly foolhardy. The prisoners captured at Gaza blamed the two orders for their plight.[16] While this was obviously unfair, it seems clear that the orders saw no reason for risking a large army in the vague hope of rescuing a small number of prisoners. But not even the non-aggressive tendencies of the orders and the local barons explain the retirement to Acre. The fortification of Ascalon was to their interest. It seems more likely that the determining factor was the civil war between the local barons and Richard Filangieri, the imperial bailie. Filangieri was holding Tyre, and the local barons were anxious to recover it. The Ibelins and Odo of Montbéliard may well have felt that they had spared enough time from their private war. It is interesting to notice that Philip of Novara in his chronicle mentions the crusade of Theobald only in connection with the arrival in the Holy Land of Philip of Montfort, who was to become an important baron of Jerusalem.[17]

At Acre the crusaders settled down once more to enjoy the pleasures of the city. Either they had forgotten the plight of Jerusalem or they were too discouraged to attempt to do anything to save it. A month or so after the battle of Gaza, an-Nāṣir Dā'ūd of Kerak, lord of Transjordania, advanced into the city and laid siege to the Tower of David. The garrison was small and poorly furnished

[16] Joseph Bédier, *Les Chansons de croisade* (Paris, 1909), pp. 217–225.

[17] This rests on a distinction drawn between Philip of Novara's own work and later additions to it. See Charles Kohler's edition of *Les Mémoires de Philippe de Novare, 1218–1243* (Les Classiques français du moyen-âge, no. 10, Paris, 1913), p. xii, and cf. in general John L. LaMonte and Merton J. Hubert, translators, *The Wars of Frederick II against the Ibelins in Syria and Cyprus by Philip of Novare* (Records of Civilization, no. XXV, New York, 1936).

with provisions. When an-Nāṣir offered them safe passage to the coast in return for the surrender of the fortress, they felt obliged to accept. The Moslems then razed the Tower to the ground. The holy city was once more in the hands of the Saracen.

While Theobald and his followers were sitting in Acre for two months, marching down the coast to Ascalon, and retiring ingloriously to their starting point, fortune was at work paving the way for them to achieve an entirely undeserved success. During these months the confusion in the Aiyūbid states had been steadily increasing. About the time the crusaders arrived at Acre, aṣ-Ṣāliḥ Ismā'īl, brother of the late sultan al-Kāmil, had driven his nephew, aṣ-Ṣāliḥ Aiyūb, from Damascus. Late in October the unfortunate Aiyūb had been captured and imprisoned by his cousin, an-Nāṣir Dā'ūd of Transjordania. Ismā'īl had promptly set to work to consolidate his position as sultan of Damascus. This led to a fierce civil war between his supporters and those of Aiyūb. From this quarrel came the crusaders' first promising opportunity.[18]

Al-Muẓaffar Taqī-ad-Dīn, lord of Hamah, who had been a loyal supporter of Aiyūb, found himself attacked by the lord of Homs, al-Mujāhid Shīrkūh, who had joined the new sultan of Damascus. Al-Muẓaffar looked around for aid and decided to deal with the crusaders. He sent a Tripolitan clerk named William to Acre to ask Theobald to march towards his lands. When the crusaders arrived, he would turn his fortresses over to them and turn Christian. If Theobald was still seriously thinking of attacking Damascus, this offer deserved investigation. Otherwise the lord of Hamah was not important enough to waste time on. In any event, Theobald led his forces northwards and camped before Pilgrim Mountain just below Tripoli. From there he sent messengers to al-Muẓaffar. As the crusaders' advance into Tripoli had diverted the attention of al-Mujāhid of Homs, al-Muẓaffar of Hamah felt no further need for aid and refused to carry out his promises. Annoyed and discouraged, the crusaders stayed a while at Tripoli as guests of its count, Bohemond V, prince of Antioch, and then returned to Acre. The sources supply no dates for this period. All one can say is that Theobald was back in Acre by early May 1240.

About this time, an-Nāṣir Dā'ūd of Transjordania and his prisoner Aiyūb came to an agreement. An-Nāṣir was to back Aiyūb in an attempt to conquer Egypt. Their project met with immediate success. The sultan of Egypt, al-'Ādil Abū-Bakr, was deposed by

[18] See below, chapter XX, pp. 706–707.

his men, who promptly welcomed aṣ-Ṣāliḥ Aiyūb as their new sultan. This sudden reversal of fortune was most disturbing to sultan aṣ-Ṣāliḥ Ismā'īl of Damascus. The man he had driven from Damascus had become master of Egypt. Ismā'īl immediately decided to seek the aid of the crusading host.

The sultan's offer was very tempting. He would surrender at once the hinterland of Sidon, the castle of Belfort (Shaqīf Arnūn), Tiberias, and Safad. Eventually he would turn over to the Christians more lands and fortresses. The master of the Templars writing to the preceptor of the Templars in England stated that all the territory between the coast and the river Jordan was to be recovered.[19] Certainly the sultan promised to return all Galilee, Jerusalem and Bethlehem with a wide corridor to the coast, Ascalon, and the district of Gaza without the city itself. Although the lists of places mentioned in the chronicles include several fortresses in Samaria, there is no evidence that this district as a whole was to be ceded to the Christians.[20] As all these regions except Galilee were actually in the hands of the lord of Transjordania and the sultan of Egypt, their return to Christian rule would have to await the victory of the new allies. The crusaders were to be allowed to buy supplies and arms in Damascus. They were to promise not to make any peace or truce with the sultan of Egypt without the consent of the sultan of Damascus. The crusading army was to go to Jaffa or Ascalon to coöperate with the sultan in defending his lands from the Egyptians. Theobald accepted the terms and marched his army south once more.

This truce between the crusading leaders and the sultan of Damascus met with opposition in both camps. The Moslem religious leaders in Damascus protested against it as treason to their faith. The garrison of Belfort refused to surrender the castle, and the sultan was obliged to reduce it by siege in order to turn it over to its Christian owner, Balian of Sidon. On the Christian side there were two centers of opposition, the Knights Hospitaller and the friends of the men captured at Gaza. The reasons for the Hospitallers' attitude are not clear. Safad was a great Templar castle, and the Hospitallers may have felt that they had been neglected. Perhaps the mere fact that the Templars favored the truce may have turned the rival order against it. The protests of the other group

[19] Matthew Paris, *Chronica majora*, IV, 64.

[20] This account of the lands promised by the sultan of Damascus is based on the assumption that the chroniclers were correct in stating that the later agreement with the sultan of Egypt conveyed the same territories as the truce with Damascus. The longest list of places recovered is found in Matthew Paris, *Chronica majora*, IV, 141–143.

are easily understood: the truce condemned the count of Montfort and his fellow prisoners to indefinite captivity.

In accordance with his agreement Theobald led his host down the coast to the vicinity of Jaffa, where he was joined by the army of the sultan of Damascus. An Egyptian force advanced to meet them there. Just what happened is far from clear. Apparently the followers of the sultan resented the alliance with the crusaders, and deserted in large numbers to the other side. The Christians, left without allies, took refuge in Ascalon. Moslem writers speak of crusaders killed and captured, but the Christian historians fail to mention any serious fighting.

Meanwhile the Hospitallers and the friends of the count of Montfort had been at work on the irresolute Theobald. Without too much difficulty they persuaded him to make advances to the sultan of Egypt. The sultan was anxious for peace. He had not yet had time to consolidate his control over the vast lands ruled by his deposed brother, and he had many problems more pressing than the situation on the Palestinian coast. If he could obtain peace by freeing his prisoners and confirming the lands the crusaders had already been promised by his rival at Damascus, it was well worth his while. An agreement was soon reached, and a truce concluded on these terms.

This treaty also met fierce opposition in the Christian army. The Templars and some of the local lords refused to accept it, and insisted on keeping the previous agreement with Damascus. Both parties could advance excellent arguments. From the point of view of the crusading barons who had come to the Holy Land to extend the territory held by the Christians, Theobald's action was wise. The sultan of Damascus had already surrendered Galilee, which was in Christian hands. But he had also shown that he could not persuade his army to coöperate with the crusaders against the sultan of Egypt and the lord of Transjordania, who controlled Jerusalem, Bethlehem, and the Gaza region. The truce with these two princes secured the rest of the lands that had been promised, and freed the prisoners. The question of good faith is more difficult to assess. Theobald could argue that the desertion of the crusaders by the sultan's troops released him from his agreement. Moreover, there is a suggestion in the chronicles that Ismā'īl of Damascus had been negotiating privately with an-Nāṣir of Transjordania. In any event, Theobald's truce with the sultan of Egypt secured for Christendom the lands and fortresses obtained by Frederick II in 1229 and about as much more in addition. Nevertheless it is not hard to understand the position of the Templars and the local lords. The Templars had received Safad, and the lord of Sidon had possession of Belfort. They might well feel obliged to hold to the agreement that gave them these places. The sultan of Damascus was nearer at hand than the sultan of Egypt and hence a more direct threat to the orders and the barons of Jerusalem. Certainly a war with him would hamper the barons in their contest with Frederick's officials.

The agreement between Theobald and the sultan of Egypt provided that the lands, castles, and prisoners should be surrendered within forty days. But Theobald and many of his fellow barons were thoroughly tired of the expedition. The endless quarrels of the orders and the local lords would have been enough to discourage a far more determined man than the king of Navarre. Perhaps too there was some truth in Matthew Paris' suggestion that Theobald had no desire to face the debates over the chief command that were bound to arise when earl Richard of Cornwall arrived with his English crusaders. Whatever their reasons may have been, Theobald and Peter of Dreux did not wait to see the agreement carried out. They made a pilgrimage to Jerusalem, and embarked at Acre about the middle of September 1240. It is not clear how many of the crusaders went with them. The duke of Burgundy and count Guigues of Nevers stayed at Ascalon to build the castle there. There is conclusive evidence that Theobald left some of his own followers there under the command of a deputy.[21]

Theobald and his fellow crusaders had won no glory. Their own very moderate efforts had accomplished nothing whatever. But the presence of their host, while there was bitter rivalry between the Aiyūbid princes, had brought great gains to the Christian cause. Without either fighting or active diplomacy Theobald had achieved far more than had Frederick II in 1229. One must not dismiss the possibility that this was according to Theobald's plan. He was no ardent lover of battle. He had arrived at Acre to find the barons of Jerusalem and the imperial bailie in the midst of a bitter civil war. The master of the Templars had been saying for some time that the quarrels of the Aiyūbid princes would give great opportunities to the crusaders. Very possibly Theobald decided that his best course was to do little or nothing and wait for his chance.

The master of the Templars wrote an exultant letter to his preceptor in England announcing the truce with the sultan of

[21] Arbois de Jubainville, *Histoire des ducs et des comtes de Champagne*, IV, 315–316.

Damascus. As the messenger who bore it sailed over the Mediterranean, he passed the crusading fleet of Richard, earl of Cornwall, brother of king Henry III of England. Richard's preparations had been fully as confused as those of his French colleagues.[22] He had taken the cross as early as 1236 with his brother-in-law, Gilbert Marshal, earl of Pembroke, John le Scot, earl of Chester and Huntingdon, and William Longsword, usually called earl of Salisbury. In January 1237 king Henry III expressed his pleasure that the Jews of England had offered an aid of 3,000 marks for Richard's crusade.[23] But the king and the English barons were doubtful of the wisdom of letting the earl go. The official reason was that he was the heir apparent to the throne. This may have had some weight, but it seems far more likely that he was the only effective balance between the king and the baronial opposition headed by Gilbert Marshal. At any rate on February 25, 1238, earl Richard, William Longsword, and Simon of Montfort, earl of Leicester, younger brother of count Amalric, were informed by the pope that their vows were suspended, as the king needed them in England. Apparently this did not please the earl, for on April 20 the pope ordered Henry III to give every assistance to his crusading brother.

Meanwhile Frederick II had informed Richard of the postponement of the crusade to August 1239. The emperor hoped that Richard would join in this postponement, and, when he started, would pass through Frederick's lands. By November there was more to confuse the poor earl. Pope Gregory suggested that he give up his crusade, and contribute to the aid of Constantinople the money he would have spent. But Richard's determination was immovable. Matthew Paris suggests a possible reason. When some of the English barons tried to persuade him to stay home, the earl replied that England was in such a mess that he would have gone even if he had not taken the crusader's vow. He was tired of trying to arbitrate between the king and his advisers and the baronial opposition. On November 17, 1238, the pope granted him protection as a crusader and protection for his heir until he reached the age of 25. In a rather mournful letter to his legate in England the pope directed that, as Richard refused to commute, he would have to be given the money raised in England for Constantinople.

As his quarrel with Frederick II grew more acute, Gregory

[22] The background of earl Richard's crusade is drawn chiefly from the *Registres de Grégoire IX* and Matthew Paris, *Chronica majora*.

[23] *Calendar of Patent Rolls, 1232–1247* (Rolls Series), p. 173.

was less anxious to have the English crusaders pass through his Italian domains. The empress, Isabel Plantagenet, was the sister of Richard and the sister-in-law of the other English leader, Simon of Montfort. Early in February 1240 Gregory ordered archbishop Walter of York to see that the crusaders did not start until the pope gave the word. Apparently this had no effect on the crusaders, and they continued their preparations. Simon sold his wood of Leicester for £1,000 to raise money for the expedition. After a series of conferences in which he made at least temporary peace between the king and Gilbert Marshal, who had apparently given up his crusading plans, Richard of Cornwall left England on June 10. With him were William Longsword and some dozen English barons. Simon of Montfort seems to have gone by himself with his own party. Together they are said to have led 800 knights. Richard was well received by king Louis and proceeded to southern France. According to Matthew Paris, he was met there by archbishop John of Arles, who in the pope's name forbade him to cross, but there is no other evidence to support this, and Matthew must be used with caution because of his violent anti-papal bias. In any event Richard kept carefully out of the quarrel between Frederick and the pope. Despite his brother-in-law's invitation, he did not enter the imperial lands, but sailed from Marseilles about the middle of September and landed at Acre on October 8. Simon of Montfort, on the other hand, went to Brindisi. While there is no positive evidence that he ever reached Palestine, one document suggests his presence there. In May 1241 a group of Palestinian barons wrote to the emperor requesting that earl Simon be made bailie of the kingdom.

When Richard of Cornwall reached Acre he found the situation extremely discouraging.[24] Theobald of Champagne and Peter of Dreux had sailed for home some two weeks before his arrival, taking with them a fair part of their troops. The two great military orders were engaged in a bitter feud. The Hospitallers, who favored the truce with Egypt, had withdrawn their forces to Acre, while the Templars, who supported the agreement with Damascus, were at Jaffa. Richard seems to have asked the lord of Transjordania whether or not he considered the truce in force and to have received a negative answer. At any rate he marched down the coast to Jaffa. There he was met by the envoys of the sultan of Egypt, who conveyed their master's offer to confirm the truce made with Theobald.

[24] The fullest account of earl Richard's crusade is found in the earl's own letter to Baldwin de Redvers, earl of Devon. Matthew Paris, *Chronica majora*, IV, 138–144.

Richard took counsel with the duke of Burgundy, the leader of the French crusaders, Walter of Brienne, and the masters of the two great orders. All except the Templars agreed that it was wise to accept the sultan's offer. Late in November earl Richard dispatched messengers to Cairo to notify the sultan of his decision. Then he marched to Ascalon and set about completing the castle.

The sultan of Egypt was apparently in no great hurry to complete the negotiations for the truce. It was not until February 8, 1241, that Richard's messengers returned to Ascalon to report that the agreement was finally concluded. Meanwhile the earl had been pressing the work on Ascalon castle. The chroniclers note that he restored it just as it had been built by his uncle, king Richard I. By the middle of March the task was done. Then Richard faced a perplexing problem — to whom should he entrust this important frontier fortress? According to the custom of the kingdom of Jerusalem the liege men, that is the barons, of the realm should have custody of the royal fortresses during the minority of king Conrad.[25] But this theory had never been accepted by Frederick II, and Richard was the emperor's brother-in-law. Hence the earl sent a messenger to Jerusalem to summon Walter Pennenpié, the emperor's agent in the city, to come to Ascalon and take custody of the castle. Just how Walter had become installed in Jerusalem is unknown. Presumably Theobald and Peter of Dreux had decided to stay neutral in the contest between the barons of the kingdom and the emperor, and had returned the holy city to its most recent Christian guardians, the imperial agents.

On April 13, 1241, the Christian prisoners captured at Gaza were finally exchanged for the Moslem captives in the hands of the crusaders. Earl Richard had already done what he could for those who had been slain in the battle. He had sent men with carts to collect their bones and bury them solemnly in the cemetery of Ascalon. Then he made provision for daily masses for their souls. Matthew Paris assures us that this act of considerate piety gained the earl great popularity in France. Once the prisoners had been returned, Richard felt that his work in the Holy Land was finished. On May 3 he took ship at Acre for the journey home.

Richard had accomplished nothing that Theobald could not have easily done had he been less impatient to get home. He had simply completed with efficiency and resolution the tasks that Theobald had left unfinished. But he could have thrown the whole situation into

[25] John L. La Monte, *Feudal Monarchy in the Latin Kingdom of Jerusalem* (Cambridge, Mass., 1932), p. 73.

confusion by listening to the Templars and renewing the alliance with Damascus against Egypt. While Richard's vanity moved him to attempt to minimize Theobald's accomplishment, he did not try to undo his work in the hope of achieving glory for himself. Theobald's truce with Egypt was a great victory for the Christian cause, and Richard had the good sense to satisfy himself with consolidating the gains made by it. In short, Richard of Cornwall deserves some credit for what he did but far more for the mistakes he did not make.

The kingdom of Jerusalem had been strengthened by the addition of lands and castles. The truce would give the Christians time to fortify the places that had been recovered. This had been done at a considerable cost in money and men. The crusade also supplied the kingdom of Jerusalem with a future very feeble bailie, Ralph of Nesle, husband of Alice of Cyprus, and one of its most effective barons, Philip of Montfort. But all the results both major and minor were produced by fate — or in the words of Armand of Périgord, by God's will. The crusaders themselves had had little to do with their own accomplishments.

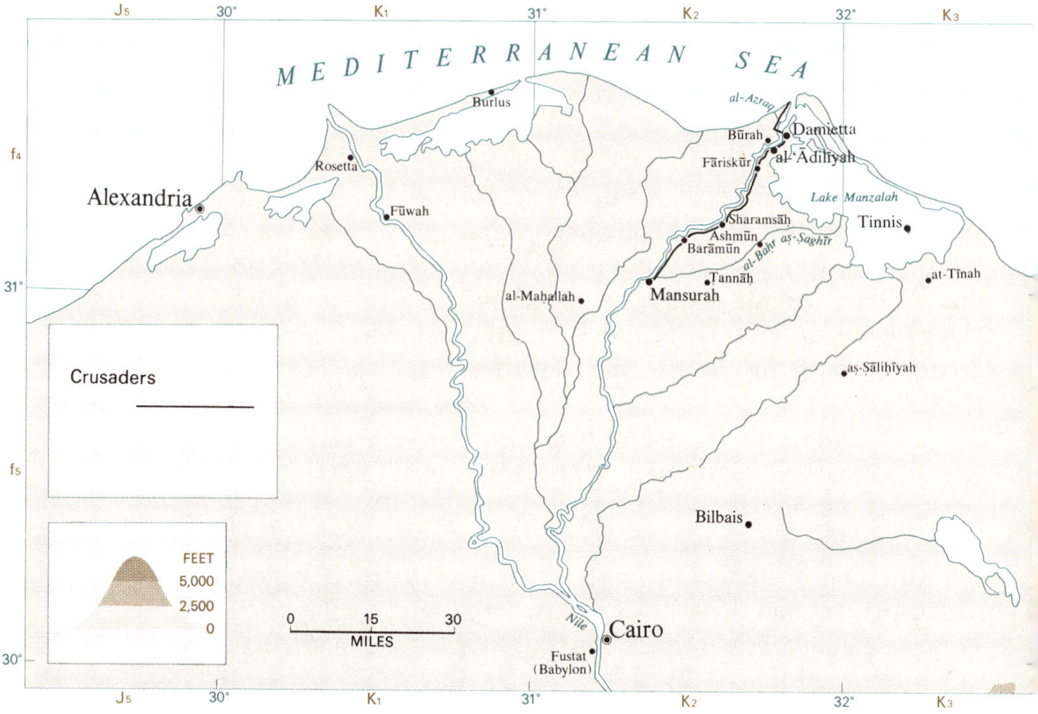

14. The Fifth Crusade, 1218–1221 (*Map by the University of Wisconsin Cartographic Laboratory*)

15. The Crusade of Louis IX, 1249–1250 (*Map by the University of Wisconsin Cartographic Laboratory*)

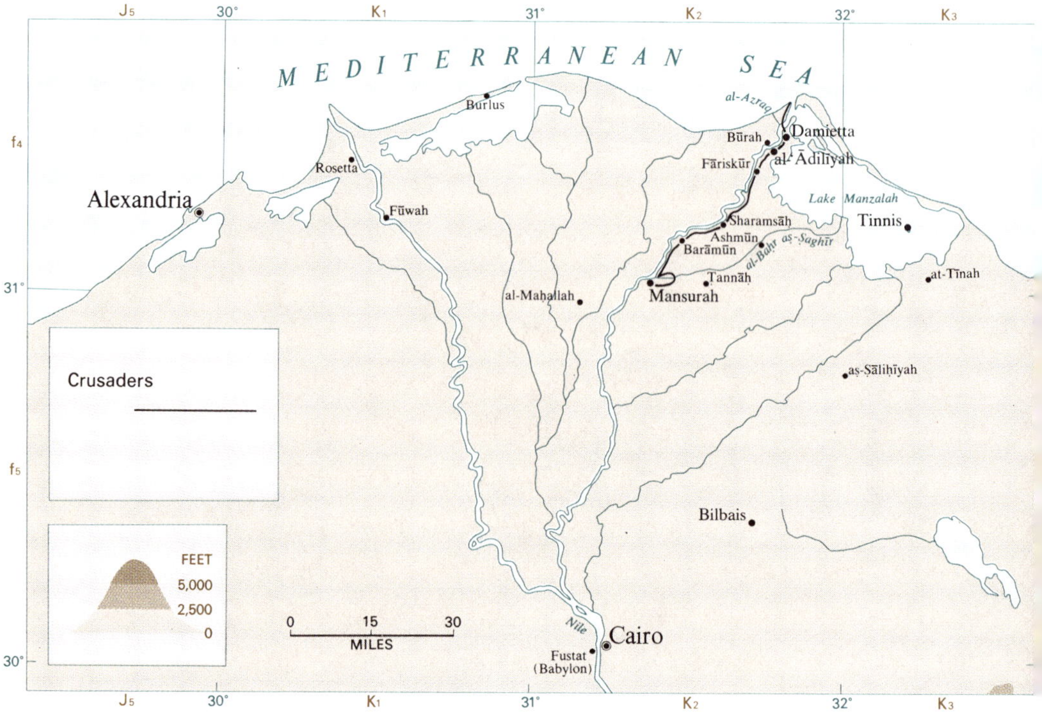

XIV
THE CRUSADES OF LOUIS IX

The crusades of Louis IX mark both the culmination and the beginning of the end of the crusading movement. None of the earlier expeditions was as well organized or financed, none had a more inspiring leader, none had a better chance of success. The crusade of 1249 was the last whole-hearted effort of Christendom against the infidel — it was watched with friendly interest even

The two chief narrative sources for the first crusade of Louis IX are John of Joinville's *Vie de St. Louis* (many editions, the most valuable being that of Natalis de Wailly, Paris, 1874) and the continuation of William of Tyre known as the Rothelin manuscript (published in *RHC, Occ.*, II, 483–639). Louis himself gave a good brief account of his adventures in Egypt in a letter printed in Duchesne, *Historiae Francorum scriptores* (Paris, 1649), V, 428–432. The French chroniclers and writers of pious lives (William of Nangis, Geoffrey of Beaulieu, et al.) appear in *RHGF*, XX, XXII, and XXIII; they contribute little additional information. Matthew Paris gives a tendentious account of the crusade but includes valuable documents in the *Additamenta* (vol. VI of the Rolls Series edition). Most of the fragmentary financial records of the crusade are collected in *RHGF*, XXI, 264–280, 283, 404, 513–515, 530–537. The *Layettes du trésor des chartes*, II and III, contain scattered material on financial aspects of the crusade, but there is less than might have been expected from these royal archives. L. T. Belgrano's *Documenti inediti riguardanti le due crociate di S. Ludovico* (Genoa, 1859) is difficult both to find and to use; fortunately his valuable material on Louis's financial arrangements with the Genoese was summarized by A. Schaube, "Die Wechselbriefe König Ludwigs des Heiligen," *Jahrbücher für Nationalökonomie und Statistik*, LXX ([3rd series, XV], 1898), 603–621, 730–748. Contracts for ships were published by Belgrano (*op. cit.*, and in *Archives de l'orient latin*, II [1884], 230–236) and by Jal (*Pacta naulorum*, *Collection de documents inédits: Documents historiques*, I, Paris, 1841). R. Röhricht's *Kleine Studien zur Geschichte der Kreuzzüge* (*Wissenschaftliche Beilage zum Programm des Humboldts-Gymnasiums zu Berlin*, Easter, 1890) include accounts of Louis's two crusades "in Regestenform" which include valuable bibliographical references. No secondary work has treated adequately all aspects of the crusade; the most readable accounts are in H. Wallon, *Saint-Louis et son temps*, I (Paris, 1875), and R. Grousset, *Histoire des croisades*, III (Paris, 1936), 426–531.

For the Tunisian expedition, the primary narrative source is the chronicle of Primat, published in *RHGF*, XXIII. The other chronicles give briefer accounts; all are published in *RHGF*, XX, XXII, or XXIII. Information about finance and shipping may be found in books listed above. Most modern writers have passed over this crusade very rapidly; the one full account is by Richard Sternfeld, *Ludwigs des heiligen Kreuzzug nach Tunis, 1270, und die Politik Karls I. von Sizilien* (Berlin, 1896). Sternfeld's attempt to minimize the responsibility of Charles of Anjou is not wholly convincing, but he gives valuable material on papal and Angevin diplomacy, and his summary of the events of the crusade is good. The old *Vie de Saint Louis* by Le Nain de Tillemont (vol. V, ed. J. de Gaulle, Paris, 1849) gives an account of the crusade which is still useful. R. Röhricht sums up all available information about the crusade of Edward I in his "Études sur les derniers temps du royaume de Jérusalem," *Archives de l'orient latin*, I (1881), 617–632.

in regions which were jealous of the leadership of the French king and suspicious of the policy of the pope. But the very magnitude of the undertaking brought disillusion when it failed. If Louis, the richest and most powerful ruler in western Europe, could not conquer the Moslems and recover the holy places, who could? Thus the failure of Louis contributed to the loss of confidence, the hesitations, and even the cynicism which weakened all later crusades.

The high hopes with which this crusade began were due in large part to the character and abilities of the leader. Louis's devotion to the crusading ideal was evident even to the skeptical Frederick II. Neither the pressure of public opinion nor the emotional exhortations of the clergy was responsible for his taking the cross. Love of glory and hope of profit were equally foreign to his nature. He made his decision unaided by his family and advisers, but once he decided that the welfare of his soul and of Christendom required a crusade, he never looked back. He was not a reluctant crusader like Philip Augustus, nor an impatient one like Richard the Lionhearted. He was willing to devote all the time, money, and energy to the crusade which the business required. The loss of opportunities for expanding his kingdom, the boredom of a long period of purely defensive operations, did not cause him to lose interest. From 1245 to 1270 the crusade was the basis of his foreign policy; he made every effort to keep peace in Europe, so that Christendom could unite in an attack on the Saracens. His singleness of purpose and his freedom from selfish motives gained him the devotion of many of his followers and the respect of all.

To these qualities of character were added real abilities as a war minister. Louis had both the experience and the patience needed for organizing an army, and he had surrounded himself with men who knew how to carry out his plans. He overcame almost completely the material difficulties which had plagued earlier crusaders — finance, transportation, supply. He not only raised and equipped a large army; he succeeded in bringing most of it to the point of attack without the tremendous losses of men and supplies which had characterized earlier overseas expeditions. His courage was an inspiration to his army, but he never fell into the foolhardy rashness which destroyed other brave leaders. His one great weakness was in generalship — he was better at organizing an army than in commanding it in the field — but even in this respect he was no worse than most crusading leaders.

It is also true that the situation in the Near East in the 1240's was not unfavorable to the Christians. Saladin's empire had been divided among heirs who hated one another as only relatives can hate. They were incapable of uniting against an invader; some of them were even ready to make an alliance with the crusaders against their rivals. The sultan of Egypt, whose outlying possessions included the holy places, was a sullen, suspicious tyrant; his heir had been sent out of the country and was almost unknown to his future subjects; his slave army of mamluks was becoming conscious of its power and resentful of a regime of many punishments and few rewards. Farther east the thunder-cloud of Mongol invasion was about to break over Baghdad. The Syrian Moslem princes could not face their Christian enemies squarely with this menace rumbling behind their backs. All in all, the Moslem world was weakened and divided as it had not been for a century, so weak and divided that even when Louis went down to unexpected defeat it could not fully exploit the victory.

Louis took the cross in December 1244. A serious illness was the immediate occasion for his decision, but the events which had taken place during the year must have impressed any sincere Christian with the need for a new crusade. The persistent quarrels of the descendants of Saladin had twice enabled the Christians to recover Jerusalem and a large part of Galilee, but the equally persistent quarrels between imperialists and Ibelins, Temple and Hospital, Acre and Tyre, had prevented any solid reorganization of the recovered territories. As a result, when the Aiyūbid sultan of Egypt formed an alliance with the Khorezmian bands of northern Syria against a coalition of Syrian princes and Christians, the inland parts of the kingdom were almost defenseless. The Khorezmians took Jerusalem, massacred a large part of the garrison, and destroyed the few remaining fortifications during the summer of 1244. Then they joined an Egyptian army coming up from the south and inflicted a complete defeat on the Christian-Syrian Moslem army at Ḥarbīyah, northeast of Gaza, on October 17, 1244. The work of the last two decades was undone. All that had been gained by the diplomacy of Frederick II in 1229, the crusade of Theobald of Champagne and Navarre in 1239–1240, and the negotiations of Richard of Cornwall in 1240–1241 was swept away. The holy city was lost, and the Christians, still bickering among themselves, were thrown back to their fortified coastal cities.[1]

The need was great, but the situation in western Europe was not

[1] See below, chapters XVI and XX. On the Khorezmians, see below, chapter XIX, pp. 668–674.

entirely favorable to a new crusade. Italy and Germany were torn by the conflict between pope and emperor, and neither Innocent IV nor Frederick II was anxious to send supporters away on an expedition to the east. In England Henry III and his barons were on such bad terms that a concentrated effort for a crusade was almost impossible. Spain, as usual, had her own problems, and the king of Norway contributed only empty promises. France alone had both the will and the resources for a crusade, and Louis's army was almost entirely French. Yet in spite of troubles outside France, the church was able to secure some financial contributions from other countries, and small groups of Englishmen and Lorrainers took part in the expedition.

Preparations began early in 1245. Odo of Châteauroux, cardinal-bishop of Tusculum, was given charge of preaching and organizing the crusade in France, and preachers were also sent to England, western Germany, and the Scandinavian countries. Innocent IV tried to ensure sufficient funds for the army, even though he had great need of money for his war on Frederick II. The Council of Lyons ordered a grant of one twentieth of ecclesiastical revenues for the support of the crusade, and the French clergy voluntarily[2] increased the rate to one tenth of their revenues. In addition many minor revenues, such as redemptions of crusade vows and legacies for the Holy Land or unspecified pious uses, were assigned to the king, his brothers, and other leaders. These grants produced important sums, even though the twentieth was not a success outside the French-speaking provinces bordering on Louis's realm. Lunt and Powicke agree that the subsidy was never collected in England.[3] Haakon V of Norway managed to convert the levy in his kingdom to his own purposes, and in Germany proper the little that was received was used for the war against Frederick II. But the dioceses of the old kingdoms of Lorraine and Burgundy paid sizeable sums which were given to Louis and his brothers. This was an important precedent; throughout the rest of the century the clergy of these districts were taxed for the benefit of the French king, and French influence grew in the lands beyond the Meuse and the Rhone. In

[2] "Voluntarily" may be a little too strong. Certainly both pope and king put pressure on the clergy. The archbishop of Narbonne and his suffragans protested that since they had not attended the assembly which raised the rate from a twentieth to a tenth they were not bound to pay. Innocent IV hesitated a little but finally ruled in July 1247 that, since they were "in prefato regno constituti" they must pay at the same rate as the other clergy of the realm (E. Berger, *St.-Louis et Innocent IV*, Paris, 1893, p. 195).

[3] W. E. Lunt, *Financial Relations of the Papacy with England* (Cambridge, 1939), p. 254; F. M. Powicke, *King Henry III and the Lord Edward* (Oxford, 1947), I, 366.

France itself the tenth was eventually extended to five years, and it became the chief source of revenue for the crusade.

Unfortunately we do not have a complete record of the income produced by the tenth, but it is possible to compare the payments made by some dioceses with those made in 1289 when a total is available. The average payment for the first tenth is about 74% of that for the second, and since the tenth in 1289 produced 256,613 *livres tournois* net, the earlier levy should have yielded about 189,894 *livres* a year or roughly 950,000 *livres* for the five years. Since the total cost of the crusade to the king was estimated in the fourteenth century as 1,537,570 *livres*, it is evident that the French clergy paid by far the largest share of the expenses.[4] This view is supported by Joinville, who told the king at Acre in 1250 that people believed that so far he had spent none of his own money on the crusade but had relied on the contributions of the clergy. This assertion was not literally true, and there is room for a considerable number of errors in our earlier calculations; but, no matter how the figures are cast, the church made a notable contribution to the financing of the crusade. No earlier crusade was as well supported; the system of taxing the incomes of the clergy reached its full development only in the middle years of the thirteenth century, and the 1249 crusade was the first overseas expedition to profit from the new techniques.

The king also tried to increase his income from other sources. Most of the revenues from the royal domain were fixed, either by custom or through long-term leases, but the towns could be pressed to give money to the king. A very incomplete account shows that the towns of the old domain paid at least 66,000 *livres tournois*.[5] This excludes the towns of Normandy and Languedoc, which must have paid something to the king. Even with these omissions it is a respectable sum; the king's annual income at this time was probably not more than 240,000 to 250,000 *livres tournois*.[6] Moreover, the towns continued to send money to the king once he had gone overseas. When their accounts were being

[4] The evidence on which these calculations are based may be found in *RHGF*, XXI, 404, 513–515, 533–536, 542, 556. The figures for total expense may well be inflated; the French government had reason to overestimate its expenditures on behalf of the church in order to justify new requests for assistance.

[5] *RHGF*, XXI, 264–280.

[6] Schaube, "Die Wechselbriefe König Ludwigs des Heiligen," *Jahrbücher für Nationalökonomie und Statistik*, LXX, 614, estimates the expenditure of the French government, 1256–1259, at an average of 113,785 *livres tournois* a year. *RHGF*, XXI, p. LXXVI, gives a higher estimate of royal income for 1238 and a lower one for 1248 than the average stated above. 5 *livres tournois* were equivalent to 4 *livres parisis*.

examined in 1260, many of them complained that they were heavily in debt, because they had contributed two or three times to the expenses of the crusade.[7]

Lesser sums were raised by the great counts and the barons who accompanied the king. As we have seen, the church gave generous grants to the king's brothers, and most lords could expect some contribution from their domains. Few could imitate Alphonse of Poitiers, who received 7,500 *livres tournois* from Auvergne alone, but anything which they could collect was a gain for the crusade. In the end king Louis had to assist most of the barons through gifts, wages, or loans, but the fact that they could support themselves for the first weeks or months of the expedition eased the drain on his resources.

While money was being raised, the king arranged for transportation and supply. In 1246 his agents hired sixteen ships from Genoa and twenty from Marseilles. The contracts were drawn up with great care, with exact descriptions of equipment, provisions for defense, and number of seamen. The continued support of Genoa was assured by giving the inhabitants of the city many opportunities for profit. For example, two Genoese, Hugo Lercari and Jacob di Levanto, were made admirals of the royal fleet. This position was more that of business manager than naval officer. The two admirals received important contracts, for example one for supplying cross-bow bolts, and acted as bankers for the king on many occasions. Most other Genoese businessmen, great and small, had some share in the profitable work of exchanging or lending money to the king. The good relations between Louis and Genoa meant that the king was always well supplied with transportation and always able to secure money for his immediate needs. Even after his capture and ransom, his credit was good, and his drafts on the Paris treasury were promptly honored by Italian bankers in the Holy Land.

While the work of securing ships was going on, the king sent agents to Cyprus to lay in a store of provisions. They did their work well; Joinville speaks with admiration of the mountains of grain and wine-barrels which the crusaders found when they reached the island. Except when they were cut off from the sea by the Saracens' naval victory on the Nile, Louis's troops seem to have been well supplied with food.

Raising money, securing ships, and buying supplies took about a year longer than the king had first expected. The first contract

[7] *Layettes*, III, nos. 4598, 4609, 4611, etc. Roye, for example, gave 1,200 *livres parisis* to the king before he sailed and 1,100 *livres parisis* on three occasions while he was overseas.

for ships called for them to be ready by midsummer of 1247; Louis actually embarked at Aigues-Mortes on August 25, 1248. It is difficult to know how much of the army sailed with him; certainly many crusaders either took ship later or embarked at other ports. Cyprus was the rendezvous, and the king, who reached Cyprus on September 17, had a long wait before his forces were fully assembled.

The delay in Cyprus was costly to the crusade in many ways. Many crusaders died, including important men such as counts John of Montfort and Peter of Vendôme and the lord of Bourbon. Others ran out of money and had to borrow from Italian bankers or enter the king's service and so add to his expenses. Worst of all was missing a favorable opportunity to attack Egypt. The sultan aṣ-Ṣāliḥ Aiyūb had taken most of his army to Syria to attack an-Nāṣir, the ruler of Aleppo, and his troops were occupied with the siege of Homs during the winter of 1248–1249. It was precisely during those months that there was some chance for a rapid march up the Nile. To wait for spring meant that the crusaders could hardly hope to establish a beachhead before the regular summer rise of the Nile made progress through the Delta impossible.

To counterbalance these disadvantages the king and his advisers had one great argument. The longer Louis remained in Cyprus, the larger his army became. Belated barons from France, seasoned warriors from Syria and the Morea, the troops of the Temple and Hospital more than made up for the losses caused by sickness. Even at its maximum size, which was probably attained in the spring of 1249, the crusading army was barely large enough to carry out its mission. As usual, the totals given by chroniclers (50,000 and the like) are mere guesses without authority. Most of the Christian writers obtained their information at second hand, and the Arabs had an obvious incentive to exaggerate the size of the defeated forces. Statements about the number of knights, mounted sergeants, and crossbowmen are worthy of a little more consideration — these specially trained men were set apart from the bulk of the army in many ways and might have been roughly counted by men like Sarrasin and Joinville. If we accept Sarrasin's estimate of 2,500 knights (Joinville says 2,800) and 5,000 crossbowmen, and assume that there were about two mounted sergeants and four foot-soldiers for each knight, we would come out close to Wallon's figure of a total force of 25,000 men.

Even this seems high in view of what we know of the cost of the crusade. Knights were paid at least 160 *livres tournois* a year (many received more), and crossbowmen and men-at-arms about 90 *livres* a year. If Louis had supported 1,500 of the 2,500 knights and 3,000 of the 5,000 bowmen and men-at-arms, he would have spent over half a million *livres* a year or about a million *livres* for the two years devoted to the Egyptian campaign. This would leave only half a million *livres* for shipping, the ransom, the long stay in Syria, and the cost of fortifying coastal cities, since we know that the treasury estimated his total expenses at 1,537,540 *livres*. This is clearly impossible; we have accounts for the Syrian period of the crusade showing that the king spent well over a million *livres* after he left Egypt. The discrepancy is too great to be explained away. It is possible that Louis supported less than three fifths of the army, though even the greatest lords called on him for financial assistance. It is possible that French officials, working years after the crusade, inadvertently omitted part of the expenses, though they had every reason to exaggerate, since they were trying to impress the papacy with the sacrifices which French kings had made for the faith. Making all possible allowances for error, it still seems that Louis must have supported at least half the army and that he could not have spent much more than 350,000 *livres* a year during the Egyptian campaign, in view of what we know about his potential sources of income. This would indicate an army of some 15,000 men — a large force for the time, but one which could not stand many losses without falling below the level needed for the conquest of Egypt.[8]

By spring of 1249 the last troops, coming from Acre, had joined, and the fleet was ready. According to one source[9] the mariners had spent the winter in repairing and building small boats for landing operations — a very natural occupation, even if unrecorded by men like Joinville who had little understanding of naval matters. Either at this time or earlier, Damietta was selected as the point of attack. Some chroniclers give an elaborate story of sealed letters containing the destination, which were to be opened only when the captains had put to sea, but it is unlikely that any such complicated device was used. It was obvious that the crusade was going to Egypt, for

[8] The best discussions of the size of the army are L. de Mas Latrie, *Histoire de Chypre*, I, 350, and Wallon, *St.-Louis et son temps*, I, 284. Schaube, *op. cit.*, p. 615, has some interesting calculations about Louis's expenditures in Syria. The essential figures are in *RHGF*, XXI, 404, 513, 530. Material on pay for military service may be found in E. Boutaric, *St. Louis et Alfonse de Poitiers* (Paris, 1870), pp. 115, 116, and in J. Strayer, *Administration of Normandy under St. Louis* (Cambridge, 1932), p. 65.

[9] *RHGF*, XXIII, 119, chronicle of John de Columna, an Italian Dominican who wrote before 1275.

there was no other reason for wintering in Cyprus, and the only alternative in Egypt to Damietta was Alexandria. Damietta had been taken once before by a crusade, and most of the chroniclers seem to think its choice for Louis's expedition inevitable. Whatever precautions were taken were useless. The sultan was convinced the attack was to be made on Damietta, put a garrison into the city, and lay with the rest of his army a little farther up the Nile.

The army sailed from Cyprus at the end of May, after a false start, broken up by a storm, a week or two earlier. They reached the Damietta mouth of the Nile on June 4 (according to most of the sources), and a council of war decided on an immediate attack. This boldness had its reward; the landing on June 5 was the one completely successful operation of the crusade. The beach picked for landing was on the west bank of the Nile, across the river from the town. It was guarded by a strong detachment of the enemy, but some troops had to be left in the city and even more remained with the sultan in his camp up the Nile. The crusaders probably had a large numerical superiority, and they planned their landing skillfully enough to make the most of this advantage. They had a sufficient number of shallow-draft craft to embark a large part of the army simultaneously, and efforts were made to hold the force together instead of letting it waste its strength in piecemeal attacks. The Saracen defenders either failed to use their bowmen efficiently, or else were checked by the counter-blast of crossbow bolts from the boats. In any case, they did little damage to the men afloat. Then, as the Christians began to jump out of the boats, often waist-deep in water, the defenders tried a cavalry charge. The horsemen were no more effective than the bowmen. The crusaders braced the butts of their lances against the sand and the light-armed Saracens, whose horses were probably hampered by bad footing, were unable to ride them down. The king, with the courage he showed throughout the crusade, came ashore as soon as his men had planted his standard on the beach, and had to be restrained from rushing at once on the enemy. The beachhead was soon well established, and the Saracens withdrew. The Christians had had only minor losses, but two of the Saracen emirs were killed.

Good planning and brave fighting now brought an extra dividend. The Moslem coastal defense units, which retreated across the Nile on a bridge of boats, did not join the garrison of threatened Damietta, but sought safety further up the river. This was not very encouraging to the garrison, the Arab tribe of the Kinānah, who must have felt that they were being sacrificed to gain time for the rest of the army. They joined the retreat, apparently in a state of panic, since no one thought of destroying the bridge of boats.[10] The Christians soon discovered that the town was abandoned and entered it the next day.

This was a great achievement. Damietta was a good and easily defensible base, full of food and plunder. It had resisted the Fifth Crusade under John of Brienne for over a year before yielding. It was important enough to Egypt to be used as a hostage to secure the surrender of Jerusalem — this offer had been made to John of Brienne after the first capture of the city.[11] And Louis had gained all this at the cost of a single skirmish — his army was intact, better supplied than he could ever have hoped, and absolutely secure while it planned its next move.

If the decisive boldness which had led to a landing on a hostile shore the day after arrival had continued, the crusade might have achieved its objective at once. The Egyptians were terribly discouraged — they had counted on a long siege of Damietta which would waste the Christian army while they gathered strength. The unpopular sultan was seriously ill, and the heir to the throne, living in semi-exile in Syria, was an unknown quantity. Christian morale was at its peak; an immediate attack might have broken all opposition. Instead the crusading army remained in Damietta for five and a half months.

There were good reasons for delay, as there always are in war. Alphonse of Poitiers, the king's brother, was expected daily, with a large body of troops. He had benefitted more from papal generosity than any other crusader, save Louis himself; he had raised large sums of money from the laymen of his provinces; his forces would be a welcome addition to the army. The Nile was about to overflow, and only a rapid march would bring the crusaders out of the Delta before the floods began. Perhaps the risk was too great, yet nothing went well after the decision to spend the summer in Damietta. The sultan in a last burst of energy restored discipline in his army by hanging the leaders of the runaway garrison of Damietta. He concentrated troops and supplies at the strategic point of Mansurah and sent raiding parties down to the crusading lines. Meanwhile morale among the crusaders declined. The usual vices of garrison life appeared in Damietta and, when part of the army was moved

[10] This may have been unimportant; a Genoese chronicler (*MGH, SS.*, XVIII, 227) states that the Christian fleet was forcing an entrance to the Nile while the army landed. In any case, Louis had complete control of local waters, and could have ferried his army to the other shore; the bridge was merely a convenience.

[11] See above, chapter XI, pp. 419, 423.

out of town to get food and exercise for the horses, Saracen raids became annoying. It was hard to restrain young knights, bored by the long delay, angered by loss of friends, from making wild sorties among the enemy, and this resentment against discipline asserted itself later in more dangerous circumstances. No great physical damage was done the army during the summer, but when it moved again it had lost some of its edge.

Alphonse arrived on October 24, just as the best season for fighting in Egypt began. Discussions during the summer had made it clear that one group among the barons preferred an attack on Alexandria to a march through the Delta, and a council of war was held to decide between the two plans. There were strong arguments in favor of seizing Alexandria. The crusaders had full control of the sea, they could probably reach Alexandria before the sultan could move his army there from Mansurah, and possession of the chief Egyptian port would put tremendous pressure on the enemy. If an earlier sultan had been willing to surrender Jerusalem to regain Damietta, even greater concessions could be expected in exchange for Alexandria. Safe behind their fortifications, sure of ample supplies by sea, the crusaders could hold the key positions of Alexandria and Damietta until the Egyptians surrendered all their conquests in the kingdom of Jerusalem. This seemed both safer and surer than a repetition of the dangerous march through the Delta which had led the Fifth Crusade to disaster.

The arguments on the other side are not as well known; the chroniclers who reported the discussion favored the attack on Alexandria and gave little space to the ideas of the opposing group. It seems clear that the party which wished to strike through the Delta at Cairo invoked the sound military principle of seeking the main force of the enemy. Why had they come to Egypt instead of Palestine? Was it not because any gains in the Holy Land were precarious if the main Egyptian army remained undefeated? And would the situation be any better if the crusaders forced the surrender of Jerusalem by occupying Egyptian seaports without destroying the forces of the enemy? The Christians in the Holy Land were bound to be inferior in numbers to the Saracens who surrounded them; the only way to give them any security was to destroy the military and political organization of the chief Saracen state. As the king's brother, count Robert of Artois, said, the best way to kill a snake is to smash its head. Joinville, who reports this phrase, also claims that Artois was the only prominent supporter of the Delta route, and that it was only because he was the king's brother that he succeeded in convincing Louis despite the opposition of most of the other barons. This may be a little unfair; there is a tendency in Joinville and some of his contemporaries to blame all the misfortunes of the crusade on Robert of Artois because of his fatal disobedience of orders later in the campaign. But though the advice to push on against the main Egyptian army conforms perfectly to Artois's impetuous character, the same advice might have been given by more sober councillors. It might have proved the best advice, had the terrain been favorable and supply assured. Even with tenuous lines of communication and the watery Delta to hamper their heavy-armed host, the crusaders brought Cairo to the edge of panic before they were turned back.

The advance began on November 20; a few days later the crusade had its last piece of luck when the sultan died. This caused a political and military crisis among the Egyptians. The heir to the throne, Tūrān-Shāh, was far away, and it was many weeks before he could reach Egypt to take over the government. To avoid a panic the sultan's widow, Shajar-ad-Durr, with the aid of a few high officials, concealed the ruler's death and succeeded in forging an order which placed the emir Fakhr-ad-Dīn in command of the army. By the time the news leaked out, the regency was in full control of the situation, and the army had become accustomed to obeying its new commander. This adjustment was aided by the slow advance of the crusaders. It was difficult to move an army across the streams of the Delta; one canal had to be dammed in order to let them proceed. It proved equally difficult to bring a fleet of galleys and small craft up the Nile, and yet the fleet was absolutely essential to insure supply, since no garrisons were left along the way to keep open communications by land. As a result, it took the crusaders a full month to reach the main Egyptian defensive position at Mansurah, protected by the Ashmūn-Ṭannāḥ branch of the Nile.

Here the Christians met a serious obstacle. They could not cross a river with a powerful enemy holding the opposite shore, and they were pinned down in the triangle between the Nile and the Ashmūn-Ṭannāḥ branch where raiders could nibble away at their forces. They held their own in the skirmishes which followed during the next few weeks, but fighting in detail was dangerous to the crusaders. Some troops had had to be left behind to garrison Damietta; others had been lost during the advance; and the remaining forces were too small to stand the attrition caused by frequent skirmishing. Louis realized the danger and issued strict orders to remain on the defensive; but he was not always obeyed, and even when he was, there were bound to be some losses. Another ominous sign was the beginning of attacks on the fleet bringing supplies up the Nile. The crusaders made a prolonged attempt to build a causeway across the Ashmūn-Ṭannāḥ branch, but the works protecting the causeway were swept by missiles and Greek fire, and what little progress had been made was negated when the enemy dug away the bank on the opposite side.

The situation was serious when Louis discovered a way to turn the Saracen position. A native revealed, for a substantial reward, the existence of a ford further down the Ashmūn-Ṭannāḥ branch. Here, after weeks of waiting, was a wonderful opportunity to take the enemy by surprise, attack him in the rear, and win a complete victory. The operation was planned for February 7, 1250. An advance-guard composed of the best cavalry, including the force under count Robert of Artois, the Templars, and an English contingent led by William of Salisbury, was to cross the ford at dawn, secure the further bank, and wait for the rest of the army. The king would then bring over the rest of the cavalry, with some of the infantry crossing last. Duke Hugh of Burgundy was left to guard the camp, with a few horsemen and a strong contingent of crossbowmen. This detachment of a camp-guard, though necessary, still further reduced the size of the crusading army and made it absolutely essential for it to act as a unit. Louis realized the danger, and issued strict orders for all groups to remain in contact and to advance only under his orders.

The attack was made the next day, and this rapid execution of the plan gained the advantages of complete surprise. The ford proved difficult, but was crossed successfully by the advance-guard. Once on the other side, Robert of Artois became completely intoxicated with the excitement of combat. He refused to wait for the rest of the army and led a wild charge against the Saracen camp. The movement was completely successful; the enemy had had no warning, and the Egyptian commander, Fakhr-ad-Dīn, was killed before he could arm himself. This victory deprived Artois of what little discretion he still possessed. The camp on the river was merely an outpost; the bulk of the Saracen army was quartered in the fortified town of Mansurah. Artois insisted on attacking this position at once, though he should have known, as many of his followers did, that cavalry was of little use in the narrow streets of a medieval town. He led his forces into a trap where the enemy was protected by house-walls, where the Christians were exposed to missiles from the roofs, and where it was almost impossible to keep formation. The Saracens saw their opportunity, rallied, and destroyed most of the advance-guard. This success gave them encouragement and time to reform under subordinate leaders, most notable of whom was Baybars, the future sultan.

Meanwhile the king had crossed with the rest of the cavalry. He did not yet know of the disaster which had overtaken the advance-guard, though he must have been disturbed to see no sign of it near the ford. He had barely time to form his troops in order of battle when the Saracens came down on him from Mansurah. Following their usual tactics, they fired repeated volleys of arrows to break the crusaders' ranks. This was an especially effective maneuver on this occasion, since few, if any, of the Christian bowmen had yet been able to cross the river, and the Saracen archers were not disturbed by counter-fire. Retreat was impossible; the crusaders had to advance, but as they came into contact with the enemy their lack of numbers exposed them to new dangers. The Egyptians pressed them so closely that they could hardly move, and fresh enemy troops waited to take the place of weary units.

Louis kept his courage, and through his own calm bravery held his army together. He soon saw that his best plan was to fight his way through the enemy till he reached a point opposite his old camp. There he might get some cover from his bowmen and reinforcements might be ferried across. But this sensible maneuver was halted repeatedly. The king, in typical feudal fashion, had to consult his chief subordinates before making any decision, and this meant that group commanders had to be sought out in the heat of battle and brought to him for hasty conferences. Then he heard, belatedly, that his brother Robert of Artois was trapped in Mansurah, and halted while a small detachment went out in the forlorn hope of rescuing him and his troops. Joinville, who took part in this sortie, gives the impression that it was overwhelmed, almost before it started, by superior numbers. Meanwhile, however and wherever the king moved, his rear-guard was under heavy pressure and was more than once in danger of being cut off. Here again Joinville gives a vivid picture of how he and a few companions, returning from their sortie, held a small bridge over a little stream which protected the king's rear. Thus the Christian host fought its way doggedly along, now decimated with arrows, now swaying back and forth under the shock of hand-to-hand fighting. Toward evening reinforcements of crossbowmen arrived under the constable Humbert of Beaujeu. According to one source, they were brought across the river on a wooden bridge hastily constructed by the men who had remained behind to guard the Christian camp.[12] This would indicate that the king had already fought his way through the enemy to a point opposite his old quarters. Wherever they came from, the reinforcements turned the tide. The Saracens withdrew to Mansurah, and Louis had the satisfaction of camping amid the wreckage of the Egyptian outposts.

Crusading heroism had won the battle, but chivalrous folly had already lost the campaign. The only chance for success had been to destroy the Egyptian army, and that army, relatively stronger than ever, still lay at Mansurah, between the Christians and Cairo. If Artois had not lost the advance-guard, a more complete victory might have been gained, though it is doubtful whether the crusaders had ever had a large enough force effectively to cut the enemy's line of retreat. As it was, the Saracens had preserved their morale and most of their forces, while Louis's army had fallen below the level necessary for offensive operations.

The events of the next weeks showed that the Egyptians understood how to profit from the situation. They kept up steady pressure on the crusaders without ever committing themselves so far that they risked a serious defeat. On February 11 they mounted a strong attack, in the hope of capturing the camp, or at least of cutting off some sections of the Christian army. The crusaders had to fight desperately to beat off the attack, and Louis again proved his high courage in rescuing the unit commanded by his brother, Charles of Anjou. In the end the Saracens withdrew in good order to Mansurah, leaving the Christians once more victorious, but reduced in numbers. Lesser raids also took their toll, while dysentery, scurvy, and all the other diseases of the camp began to weaken the forces which had survived the battles.

Prudence dictated a retreat, but at this point the piety of Louis overcame his generalship. He could not believe that the army had been brought so far, through so many dangers, only to fail at the last. He might still have gained large concessions by walling himself up in Damietta, but instead he remained obstinately in his positions on the Nile. His only hope was an outbreak of civil war among the

[12] Other sources put the building of the bridge later, and it does seem difficult to believe that it could have been constructed so promptly, especially as the workmen would have been under enemy fire for part of the time.

leaders of the Egyptian army. Instead, there was a momentary solidifying of forces around the new sultan. Tūrān-Shāh appeared at Mansurah on February 28, and a few days later the enemy discovered a new means of harassing the crusaders. The Moslems took boats to pieces, carried them on camel-back around the Christian position, and relaunched them further down the Nile. This flotilla soon gained complete control of the river, and cut off the provisions which had been coming up from Damietta. Dozens of Christian ships were captured, and so few escaped the blockade that the crusading camp was soon on desperately short rations. It is hard to understand why more attention had not been given to securing the line of supply, or why the excellent sailors in the king's service found it impossible to arm galleys which could break the blockade. It may be that the commanders of a feudal army showed their usual lack of understanding of naval power, and that the shipmen were never given the materials or the money needed to create an effective river fleet. Many of the Christian chroniclers do not even mention the blockade, which would indicate that their sources of information in the army failed to understand its importance. The Moslem writers, on the other hand, stress the closing of the river and consider it one of the chief causes of the Christian collapse.

Despite death, sickness, and starvation, Louis held out until the end of March. Then, far too late, he began a withdrawal. Skillful planning and heroic fighting by the rear-guard brought the army safely across the bridge over the Ashmūn-Ṭannāḥ branch, but the crusaders were not much better off in their old camp than they had been before. About this time there were some half-hearted negotiations with the Saracens on a proposal to exchange Damietta for Jerusalem, but it is difficult to believe that the sultan and his advisers took the proposals very seriously. The crusaders' position was hopeless, and a council of war soon decided to fall back on Damietta. The weaker members of the host were placed in the few galleys which remained, while the rest of the army withdrew by land. They left their fortifications on April 5, and the full weakness of the crusaders was soon revealed. Outnumbered, faint from illness and lack of food, they struggled halfway to Damietta, with the Saracens swarming around them like flies, to use Joinville's expression. At that point they could do no more. Louis, who had refused to try to escape by boat, surrendered with the land forces. Most of the galleys were captured at the same time, though one, carrying the legate, escaped.

Except for the garrison in Damietta, the crusading army had

ceased to exist as a fighting force. And even Damietta was not entirely secure; when news of the surrender came, some of the sailors talked of abandoning the town. Fortunately for Louis, he had left queen Margaret in Damietta, and she succeeded in stopping the proposed flight. Though she had just given birth to a son, she called in the Pisan and Genoese leaders, begged them not to leave her, and clinched the argument by raising a large sum of money for their wages and supplies.

The Saracens were somewhat embarrassed by the completeness of their victory. They had to provide for thousands of prisoners, though they simplified the problem by massacring the sickly and the poor. The greatest possible profit had to be made from the capture of the king and the great barons, and there was difficulty in deciding how this could be done. The fact that Louis had no authority in the kingdom of Jerusalem made it useless to ask for cessions of territory there. The fact that his troops still held Damietta made it necessary to moderate extreme demands; a prolonged siege of the town might well cost more than could be gained from the prisoners. It was clearly to the interests of the Egyptians to get Louis and his army out of the country as soon as possible, before expeditions for rescue or revenge could be organized in France. Difficulty in deciding on terms was perhaps increased by the hostility to Tūrān-Shāh which was beginning to appear in the Egyptian army. Finally, an agreement was reached toward the end of April. After asking for a million bezants as ransom, the sultan reduced his demand to 800,000 bezants. Damietta was to be surrendered, and half the ransom paid before the king left Egypt. In return all surviving captured crusaders were to be freed, and the supplies stored in Damietta were to be preserved until ships could be sent for them.

No sooner had this agreement been reached than it was threatened by a revolt of the Egyptian army. The mamluks had been restive under the old sultan, whom they feared; for Tūrān-Shāh they had only contempt, and they were quick to strike for power. On May 2 the young sultan was assassinated in the presence of the whole army. Baybars was conspicuous in the plot (according to some sources he dealt the final blow as Tūrān-Shāh pleaded for his life), but it was another mamluk, Aybeg, who became commander of the army, and soon husband of Shajar-ad-Durr, and co-sultan with the youthful Aiyūbid al-Ashraf Mūsâ. The blood-lust and the indiscipline caused by the revolt led to threats against the prisoners, but the army commanders soon realized that it would be foolish to sacrifice valuable captives. They decided to maintain the treaty; on May 6 Damietta was surrendered and the king was set free.

Half the ransom (400,000 bezants) was paid during the next two days. There is some dispute as to its exact value in French money, but it is fairly clear that Joinville, who helped collect the money, thought it amounted to 200,000 *livres tournois*. Royal accounts, prepared much later, value it at only 167,000 *livres tournois*, but this could easily have resulted from writing the sum in terms of the more valuable *livres parisis* (which would amount to 160,000), and then failing to make the necessary adjustment when adding it to other expenses stated in *livres tournois*.[13] (The odd 7,000 *livres* could be interest on loans or cost of exchange.) Whether 167,000 or 200,000 *livres tournois*, it was a large, but not impossible, sum to pay. As we have seen, the king's annual revenue was probably somewhat larger, and the tenth being paid by the French church brought in about as much each year. The fact that the money could be collected so quickly shows that the king's resources and credit were still intact. It is true that, to complete the payment, the king had to seize 30,000 *livres* from deposits entrusted to the Temple, but Joinville, who accomplished this mission, makes it clear that his use of force was merely symbolic, and that the Templars had no great objection to providing the money as long as they were freed from blame. The best proof that the ransom did not bankrupt Louis is found in the hundreds of drafts on the French treasury which were issued in the following years while the king stayed in Palestine. These drafts were honored by Italian bankers without question, and the charges for exchange and interest were kept at the very low figure (for the Middle Ages) of ten to fifteen per cent. Whether royal credit would have remained so good had the full ransom been paid is another question, but, as we shall see later, Louis was eventually freed from his obligation to pay the remaining 400,000 bezants.

As soon as the ransom was paid, Louis sailed for Acre. He had few troops with him, since only the greater men had been released from prison, and some of these had headed directly for France. Nevertheless, he was received with joy by the inhabitants of Acre; a few hundred men were always a welcome reinforcement to the hard-pressed kingdom of Jerusalem. Louis was to remain in Palestine for almost four years (about May 13, 1250, to April 24,

[13] The value of the ransom is discussed by Schaube, *op. cit.*, p. 615; Wallon, *St.-Louis et son temps*, I, 370, 389; N. de Wailly in his edition of Joinville, pp. 461–462.

1254). It seems doubtful that he had at first planned so long a stay, but he had certainly determined to salvage what he could from the wreckage of the crusade. The release of the remaining captives had to be secured, and something might be done to ensure the safety of the remnants of the kingdom of Jerusalem. Both operations took longer than had been expected, and before they were completed political events in the Arab world gave the king some hope of regaining the holy city. So his stay was prolonged, month after month, much to the benefit of the crusading kingdom, and, despite the fears of his advisers, not greatly to the detriment of France.

The moral greatness of Louis never appeared more clearly than in this decision to remain overseas. Most of his predecessors, when defeated in battle, had run for home as soon as possible; most of his followers were desperately anxious to return to France. Joinville gives a graphic description of the councils in which the king's decision was discussed. He may have exaggerated the importance of his own arguments, but it is clear that many great barons wanted the king to leave, and that Louis was grateful to Joinville for supporting the opposite point of view. But while Louis could not be persuaded to depart, he could not prevent the departure of most of his followers. His own brothers, Charles of Anjou and Alphonse of Poitiers, sailed on August 10, and the king had great difficulty in retaining even a small body of troops. No one had any money left; Louis had to meet all expenses and pay excessively high wages to the men who entered his service. According to Joinville, the king never had more than 1,400 troops at any one time in Palestine, and even this figure may be exaggerated.

Fortunately for the Christians, the assassination of Tūrān-Shāh had started a bitter quarrel between the Syrian and the Egyptian Moslems. Loyalty to the house of Saladin still existed, and the most prominent representative of the Aiyūbid family, an-Nāṣir, the prince of Aleppo, knew how to profit from it. He seized Damascus in July 1250 and began planning an attack on the upstart Mamluk rulers of Egypt. This quarrel put Louis in a much stronger position than he could have expected when he went to Acre. He occupied a strategic block of territory between Cairo and Damascus and his small army of seasoned warriors might hold the balance of power in a war between two equally matched adversaries. As a result, both Syrians and Egyptians began to seek his support. The Syrians offered him Jerusalem while the Egyptians began to concern themselves with the fate of the Christian captives. The Mamluks had been rather careless at first about obeying the terms of the treaty;

the king's war machines and food stored in Damietta had been destroyed and many of the prisoners slain. Now they began to restore the captives, in larger and larger groups, as they saw the need to conciliate the king. More than this, soon after the invading Syrian army had been driven back (February 2 or 3, 1251), the Egyptians began negotiating with Louis for an alliance, holding out the hope that he could recover all Palestine up to the Jordan as a price for his aid.

Some of the royal advisers, notably the Templars, favored an agreement with the Syrians, but Louis seems to have had little hesitation in choosing the Egyptian side. This was probably a wise decision, though it did not produce all the results which had been expected. Egypt was unified as Syria was not, and the Egyptian army had just inflicted a decisive defeat on the Syrians. It looked as if Cairo would, in the long run, dominate Damascus, and it was well for the Christians to be on the winning side. More important, perhaps, to the king, was the fact that the Egyptians could offer him concrete advantages while the Syrians merely gave promises. An eventual cession of Jerusalem was an uncertain basis for policy. The wheel of fortune turned with extraordinary rapidity in Moslem countries; the rise of a new military leader, the advent of a new sultan, the creation of a new alliance might upset any arrangement. But the Egyptians had both Christian captives and the king's promise to pay the second half of the ransom, and once these were surrendered no political upheaval could bring them back. Louis secured all he could ask for on both these points. All the surviving captives, even those who had been converted to Islam, were returned. The payment of the remaining half of the ransom was canceled. With these tangible gains, Louis had no hesitation in making an alliance with the Egyptians early in 1252. He agreed to support their invasion of Syria in return for the cession of Jerusalem, Bethlehem, and most of the lands west of the Jordan.

The new allies were to meet in May between Jaffa and Gaza, to combine operations against the Syrians. The king, with as large a force as he could raise, was in Jaffa in good time, but the Syrians blocked the union of the two forces by occupying Gaza. Louis did not give up hope. but remained in Jaffa for over a year. Meanwhile al-Musta'ṣim, the caliph in Baghdad, did his best to end a war which might have had disastrous results for Islam. Since neither adversary had been able successfully to invade the other's homeland, they were not unwilling to listen to proposals of peace. A treaty was finally made about April 1, 1253, which ended the war between

Syria and Egypt, and, at the same time, destroyed Louis's last hope of regaining Jerusalem.

While negotiating with the Moslems, Louis had worked steadily to improve the defenses of the coastal strip still remaining in Christian hands. His mere presence in Palestine had done much to suspend the bickering among Christians which had made coöperative efforts almost impossible. Under his leadership the fortifications of Acre, Caesarea, Jaffa, Sidon, and some smaller places were rebuilt or strengthened. The value of this work was shown when the Syrian army, free to harass the Christians after the peace of 1253, made demonstrations along the coast. They did not dare attack Jaffa and Acre, which were well fortified, but did a good deal of damage to the people of Sidon, where the work of fortifying the town had just begun. Louis also tried to protect the northern flank of the crusading kingdom by strengthening the principality of Antioch. He reconciled the young prince of Antioch, Bohemond VI, with his mother Lucienne, and encouraged close relations between Antioch and the Christian kingdom of Armenia. Finally, Louis made earnest, if rather uncomprehending, efforts to come to some sort of understanding with the Mongols. He had begun the exchange of messages with the Great Khan Göyük while still in Cyprus in 1248 and knew by this time that the Mongols had some leanings toward Nestorian Christianity and fairly definite plans to attack the Moslems of the Near East. Here were the raw materials for an alliance, but neither people could understand the other. Louis thought primarily of conversion, the Mongols of conquest. Louis was annoyed by Mongol attempts to treat him as a vassal prince, and the Mongols were irritated by French independence. A working agreement between Mongols and Christians was not entirely impossible, as was shown by king Heṭoum I of Armenia a few years later, but it required a knowledge of the orient and a flexibility which Louis did not possess.

Most of the work of fortification was finished by the time that peace was made between Damascus and Cairo. It soon became apparent that there was little more for the king to do. He sent part of the army on an unsuccessful raid on Banyas and learned that the enemy was now too strong to be shaken even by a surprise attack. There was no possibility of maneuver; the Christians could do little more than defend what they had. The king of France was not needed for garrison work. He was needed at home. The regent Blanche of Castile had died at the end of 1252, and the king's brothers, able though they were, could not quite fill her place. Some time toward the end of 1253 or early in 1254 Louis decided to return to France as soon as good weather had set in. He left Geoffrey of Sargines with 100 knights to reinforce the garrison of Acre and sailed from that port on April 24, 1254. After a long and dangerous voyage he landed at Hyères in Provence early in July.

King Louis often thought of the Holy Land during the prosperous years which followed his return to France. He maintained the French garrison in Acre under Geoffrey of Sargines, and helped the hard-pressed Christians raise money to defend their last fragments of territory. The French treasury later estimated that this assistance in men and money cost the king an average of 4,000 *livres tournois* a year between 1254 and 1270. The consciences of most rulers were satisfied with considerably less, but Louis was not content with such routine expressions of piety. He felt responsible for the failure of the 1249 crusade and longed to redeem himself by a successful expedition. He was encouraged in this hope by his brother Alphonse, who began planning a new crusade almost as soon as he returned from Syria. But, as usual, the internal politics of the commonwealth of Christendom interfered with its foreign policy. The popes were spending most of their time and all the money they could raise on the old quarrel with the Hohenstaufens. Louis's younger brother, Charles of Anjou, was drawn into the struggle; and, when he set off to conquer the kingdom of Sicily from Manfred, he took with him some of the best fighting men of France. Only when he had won his decisive victory at Benevento in 1266 was it possible to consider the needs of the Holy Land.

It was time, and past time, to think of the Christian outposts in the Levant. Baybars, sultan at Cairo since 1260, had revealed his great qualities as a military leader. Just before assassination had cleared his way to the throne, he had been largely responsible for defeating a Mongol army which had occupied Syria. There were few men, from the Mediterranean to the Yellow Sea, who could claim such a victory, and Baybars had greater prestige and authority than any Moslem ruler since Saladin. With Egypt and Syria united under him, Baybars began a steady attack on the Christian fortresses. One by one they fell, Caesarea and Arsuf in 1265, Safad in 1266, Jaffa and Antioch in 1268. Undermanned, divided by political and economic rivalries, the remaining towns were in no condition to defend themselves. A new effort was needed if any Christian states were to survive in the eastern Mediterranean.

With Charles of Anjou as king of Sicily, the pope no longer had to concentrate all his resources on Italy, but it seems doubtful that Clement IV planned a full-scale crusade as a result of the victory at Benevento. He continued the policy of the last few years, raising a little money for Palestine through a one per cent tax on ecclesiastical income, and encouraging individuals to redeem their crusading vows by spending a few months fighting around Acre. It was not lack of energy which made him hold back, but rather the complicated political situation in Italy and the Levant. There was still a Hohenstaufen heir, young Conradin, around whom all the opponents of the papacy and the Angevins might unite. War or rebellion in Italy was not merely possible; it was probable. There was a difficult decision to be made about Constantinople. Charles of Anjou, hardly secure on his new throne, was planning a reconquest of Byzantine lands, and a revival of the Latin empire of Constantinople. Michael VIII Palaeologus, who had only recently regained the great city on the Bosporus, was countering with an offer to reunite the Greek and Latin churches. The old plan of persuading the Mongols of Persia to form an alliance with the Christians against Baybars, had been revived and had to be investigated. The pope wanted to be very sure where the most effective blow could be struck before he called out the forces of western Europe. But Louis, always disdainful of power politics, saw only the captivity of the holy places and the oppressions of Baybars. Late in 1266 he secretly told the pope his intentions, and on March 24, 1267, at a great meeting of his barons, he and his three sons took the cross.

There was little enthusiasm for the new crusade among the nobility of France. Joinville flatly refused to follow the king to whom he was bound by so many ties of memory and affection, and said bluntly that the new expedition was a mistake. Jongleurs and troubadours, who wrote for the upper classes, criticized the whole crusading idea. For generations the only successful crusades had been those directed against Europeans, and Frenchmen were becoming cynical about the reasons for, and pessimistic about the results of, overseas expeditions. One chronicler reports that the royal council was unanimously opposed to the crusade, and several say that the king had to make repeated efforts to persuade a respectable number of barons and knights to take the cross. Even the royal family was not united on the plan. A special embassy was sent to Charles of Anjou, and the terms of the king's letter indicate that he knew that his brother had no great liking for the expedition.

The one favorable element in the situation was that there was some hope of securing aid from other countries. King James I of Aragon was dreaming of ending his long reign with a victorious expedition to the east, and Henry III of England, as he grew old, began to think that it was time to redeem the crusading vow he had taken so many years before.

In view of the general lack of enthusiasm it seems likely that Louis had to bear even more of the expenses than he had on his previous crusade. We know that the duke of Burgundy received a generous stipend from the king, and if so great a man could not or would not rely on his own resources, the poorer crusaders must have leaned heavily on the king. Even prince Edward, who was to lead the English forces in place of his father, borrowed 70,000 *livres tournois* from Louis for crusading expenses in 1268, though the English clergy and laity were about to make large payments for his expedition. It may be that this money was to be used primarily to secure the aid of Edward's Gascon vassals, since the prince agreed to give 25,000 *livres tournois* to Gaston of Béarn and to repay the loan from Gascon revenues. When Louis did not make direct grants, he paid indirectly by allowing the pope to divert revenues to great lords. Thus Alphonse of Poitiers, Theobald V of Champagne, count John of Brittany, count Guy of Flanders, and other lords of the Low Countries all received large sums from grants which had been made to the king by the pope.[14]

To meet these expenses the king had the same revenues as before. Grants by the church were once again the largest single source of income. A tenth of the revenues of the ecclesiastics of France and a twentieth of the revenues of churchmen in the border dioceses (Liége, Metz, Toul, Verdun, and the non-French parts of the province of Rheims) were conceded soon after Louis took the cross. Since money for the Sicilian war was still being collected, the crusade tenth could not begin until 1268 — it then ran for three years. The king also received the small change of papal income in France — the remnants of the one hundredth of 1262, redemptions of crusading vows, indeterminate legacies, and the like. The towns were asked to pay an aid for knighting the king's eldest son and for the crusade, and this levy was extended as widely as possible, despite claims to exemption. At the same time it was far from covering all laymen, in contrast to the twentieth granted to Henry III by the English parliament. The royal ambassadors reminded

[14] The king, however, would not assent to Alphonse's request that he be given the proceeds of the tenth in all his lands: see Boutaric, *St.-Louis et Alfonse de Poitiers*, p. 315.

Charles of Anjou that he owed his brother 49,000 *livres*, but Charles made no effort to pay the debt until 1270. Alphonse of Poitiers relieved the king of a considerable expense by making energetic efforts to raise money in his own domains. He took aids from the nobles and received 30,000 *livres tournois* from the pope, as well as indeterminate legacies and redemption of vows in his lands. The non-nobles paid heavily; there was a double *cens* in the northern counties, and a *fouage* for three years in his southern holdings. The Jews were seized and forced to ransom themselves. Altogether, Alphonse must have raised well over 100,000 *livres tournois*, which left him in a much better financial position than most of the crusaders.[15]

King Louis began to spend his money as soon as the first sums from the tenth became available. Contracts were made with the leaders of feudal contingents, and agents were sent to the Mediterranean to secure ships. Venice and other maritime cities were approached, but in the end the contracts went to Genoa (19 ships) and Marseilles (20), just as they had before. The admiral, this time, was to be a French subject, Florent of Varennes, but the Genoese chose two consuls who were in virtual command of their ships. Chartering old vessels and commissioning the building of new ones were an immediate drain on the king's resources, since the Genoese demanded down payments of one third to one half of the total sum. Prices were somewhat lower than in the 1240's, but new ships still cost 7,000 *livres tournois* apiece, while old ones were chartered at prices running from 850 to 3,750 *livres tournois*. It is not surprising that the French envoys were occasionally short of money. Louis, however, still had good credit in Genoa, and by the summer of 1269 most of the arrangements for the fleet had been made. The ships were to be at Aigues-Mortes by early summer in 1270.

These contracts are much more specific than those of the 1240's, and in some of the details we may see the first signs that the king was thinking of Tunisia as a possible objective of the crusade. The king is given a very free hand in controlling the movements of the fleet. He may ask it to stop briefly at some port or island so that he may hold a council. He may land his army once, reëmbark it after a month, and land it a second time, at no extra cost. If his operations are so prolonged that he needs the fleet during and after the winter months, he may keep the ships by making an additional payment of two fifths of the base price. No destinations are mentioned, but these provisions would permit a quick blow against a nearby

[15] See Boutaric, *op. cit.*, pp. 280 ff. for a description of Alphonse's financial expedients.

enemy, such as Tunisia, to be followed, if possible, by a longer expedition to the east. They might also be interpreted as envisaging a stopover at some eastern base such as Cyprus or Crete in order to reassemble and reprovision the army before a landing in Egypt or Syria. The precedents of 1248 favor this second interpretation, but there are strong reasons for believing that no landing at an eastern base was contemplated in 1270. In the first place, no supplies were shipped ahead of the army to Cyprus, though Louis had found this very helpful for his earlier attack on Egypt. In the second place, these contracts, so specific in all other respects, are remarkably vague about the destination of the fleet. This could hardly have been accidental, since in the negotiations with Venice which immediately preceded those with Genoa, a voyage to the Holy Land and a halt in Cyprus or Crete were specifically mentioned. It looks as though Louis changed his plans some time in 1268 to include an attack on Tunis. If he did, there was every reason to keep his destination secret, not only to deceive the enemy but to avoid alienating his friends. The Genoese had no desire to ruin their trade with Tunisia, and the crusade was unpopular enough without trying to explain an unprecedented diversion to the western Mediterranean. So the contracts were drawn in such a way that the king was free to move against Tunisia, while those who were not in on the secret could still think that an ordinary expedition against Egypt or Syria was planned.[16]

It may seem unfair to accuse an honest man of such tortuous behavior on very slender evidence, but it is difficult to come to any other conclusion. Certainly the attack on Tunisia must have been decided on before the army sailed in the summer of 1270. The fact that the rendezvous for the fleet was fixed at Cagliari proves this; Sardinia was impossibly remote from any eastern objective. Louis never made important decisions on the spur of the moment; it is difficult to believe that he made no plans about Tunisia until the spring of 1270. We know that he was in constant contact with Charles of Anjou, and Charles had had trouble with Tunisia from the beginning of his reign in the kingdom of Sicily. He must have told his brother of his difficulties, and the fact that a Tunisian embassy visited Paris in 1269 after negotiating with Charles shows that Louis was taking some interest in the problem. No one of these arguments is decisive, but the cumulative effect is strong. Louis

[16] The contracts with Genoa and Marseilles are published in the books by Jal and Belgrano cited in the bibliographical note. The contract proposed by the Venetians is in Duchesne, *Historiae Francorum scriptores*, V, 435–436.

must have decided on the Tunisian diversion late in 1268, or early in 1269.

It is easier to accept the fact of an early decision to attack Tunisia than to understand the reasons which led to it. Contemporaries of Louis and modern historians have been equally puzzled by the act.[17] Scholars of great ability have even denied that Charles of Anjou influenced the decision, and have claimed that he merely followed his brother reluctantly into the adventure. But can anyone believe that Louis would have concerned himself with Tunisia if Charles had not been king of Sicily? France had no political or economic relations with Tunisia, and Louis was interested in the Holy Land, not in the conquest of North African ports. Sicily, on the other hand, had an important trade with Tunisia and was immediately affected by unfriendly acts of the Ḥafṣid ruler, Muḥammad I. Charles had every reason to be dissatisfied with the behavior of the emir. He had been a friend of the Hohenstaufens; he had allowed supporters of Conradin to sail from his ports in 1268 to stir up rebellion in Sicily. Even after the shattering defeat of Tagliacozzo the emir had sheltered these enemies of Charles in his domains. Moreover, he had refused Charles the annual payments which he had regularly made to the Hohenstaufen emperors for free access to Sicilian waters and markets. Charles had been demanding these payments since he became king, and an attack, or at least a demonstration against Tunisia, was an obvious way of backing up his diplomacy.

It is true that Tunisia was not a major objective and that Charles's policies at this time were aimed primarily at the reconquest of the Latin empire of Constantinople. But the crusade planned by Louis imposed a serious obstacle to this plan. Charles knew that his brother would keep his vow, and that many of the French warriors who might have joined an expedition to Romania would follow their king instead. He knew that Louis was anxious to have his support, and family pride, gratitude for recent assistance, and political expediency forbade him to reject the request. Charles could hardly escape a crusade, but he could hope to make it brief and profitable to himself. Louis was always willing to listen to advice from his brothers, and in this case he greatly needed the assistance which Charles could give. By himself he could hardly raise a respectable army; with Sicilian assistance he might be able to strike a real blow against the Moslems. Under these conditions Charles could argue

[17] The fullest discussion of the problem is in Sternfeld's *Ludwigs des heiligen Kreuzzug nach Tunis*. H. F. Delaborde gives a useful criticism of Sternfeld's thesis in *ROL*, IV (1896), 423–428. The Moslem interpretation is treated in the chapter on North Africa in volume III of the present work (in preparation).

that Louis should consider the interests of Sicily and strike a blow against the infidels across the strait.

The chroniclers report some of the reasons which may have persuaded Louis to attack Tunisia. He had no very clear picture of the geography of North Africa, and he probably thought that Tunisia was closer and more accessible to Egypt than was actually the case. He was told that the Mamluk army drew military supplies from Tunisia, and he may have believed that Tunisia would furnish a base from which pressure could be exerted on Egypt. The rather remote danger of the Tunisian navy blocking the straits of Sicily was also mentioned. The payment owed by Tunisia for access to Sicilian ports may have been represented as a service owed by a vassal to his lord. Louis had strong feelings about disloyal vassals — witness his attitude to the English barons during their rebellion — and he would certainly have felt that a vassal who denied service to a Capetian prince deserved punishment. There was a rumor that the emir of Tunisia was ready to become a Christian if he could be assured protection, and it is quite possible that Muḥammad I himself started the story in order to gain time in his negotiations with Charles. Louis may not have fully believed the report, but it would have quieted his religious scruples and made it easier for him to convince others. It was generally believed that Tunisia could be easily and quickly conquered, so that Louis could still hope to take his army to the east after an inspiring and profitable victory.

All this is speculation, but behind the speculation lie the hard facts of Capetian family loyalty and the dependence of the two brothers on each other. Tunisia was the only objective which satisfied both the religious policy of Louis and the political needs of Charles. Each king could hope that after the Tunisian raid his interests would prevail. Louis could dream of a united French-Sicilian army sailing on to attack the Egyptians, while Charles, wise with his years of military experience, could feel sure that the crusade would break up after one campaign and that he might then recruit knights and bowmen for a war on the Greeks.

Louis had planned his troop movements so well that he and the larger part of the army arrived in Languedoc several weeks ahead of the ships. The Genoese were late, and the king was not able to sail until July 2, 1270. This was at least a month behind schedule, and it was a month which Louis could ill afford to lose. Not only would he land in Tunisia during the worst of the summer heat; he would also have very little good weather left for the second stage of the voyage to the east.

Most of the army seems to have embarked at Aigues-Mortes or Marseilles at about the same time; there were very few laggards compared to 1248. This would indicate a relatively small force, since it was very difficult, under thirteenth-century conditions, to embark a large number of men within a limited period. Other evidence supports the conclusion that Louis had a smaller army in 1270 than in 1248. The king's own household included only about 327 knights, and yet this should have been one of the largest divisions of the army. The lower cost of shipping also indicates a small force; with no great demand for vessels, Genoa and Marseilles had to deflate their prices. Troops from the Latin states of the east, which had played a prominent role in the Egyptian campaign, were not present in Tunisia. Louis's great reluctance to undertake any important operations before the arrival of Charles of Anjou also suggests a small army. It is true that he had waited for Alphonse at Damietta, but he had been willing to risk a pitched battle and a siege upon landing, and the sultan of Egypt was a far more dangerous foe than the ruler of Tunisia. The Arabic historian al-Maqrīzī regularly exaggerates the size of crusading forces, but his figures, for what they are worth, indicate a smaller army in Tunisia than at Damietta. Altogether, a very rough guess might place the number of men who sailed with the king at no more than 10,000.[18]

The rendezvous for the fleet was at Cagliari, in southern Sardinia. Here the final council was held, and the decision to attack Tunis was announced. The secret had been well kept, and both the sailors and the rank and file of the army were surprised. Many of the Genoese seamen were so sure that they were going to the Holy Land that they had contracted loans payable in Syria. No chronicler gives a very full account of the arguments used to persuade the men, but it is clear that the wealth and weakness of Tunis were stressed. There was also talk of the conversion of the emir and the value of Tunis as a Christian base against the Moslems. Pious crusaders were assured that they would receive the same indulgences for fighting western Moslems as for service in the Holy Land. There seems to have been no real opposition to the plan; Louis's reputation stood so high that few men could question his decisions.

It took about a week to assemble the fleet at Cagliari. The run across to Tunisia was made quickly, and a landing was made on

[18] See the estimates of F. Lot, *L'Art militaire et les armées au moyen-âge* (Paris, 1946), I, 196.

July 18 without serious opposition. Tunisian outposts harassed the crusaders, and tried to cut them off from water, but after the Genoese had taken the fort built on the site of ancient Carthage the Christian camp was reasonably secure. Then both sides settled down to a waiting game. Louis, conscious of the smallness of his army, remembering his experiences in Egypt, issued strict orders against any sorties. He was determined not to risk a pitched battle until Charles of Anjou arrived, and he did not wish to dribble away his forces in indecisive fighting. He was better obeyed than he had been in Egypt, and the army on the whole resisted the temptation to attack Moslem skirmishers. As for Muḥammad I, he realized that he was reasonably safe behind the walls of his city, and that his greatest danger was to risk his army in the open. So he limited his operations to aggressive patrolling of the Christian lines and small-scale attacks on foragers.

Meanwhile heat, lack of sanitation, and scarcity of fresh food brought the usual diseases to the Christian camp. The royal family itself was stricken. The king's eldest son, Philip, was too weak to lead his division, and young John of Nevers soon became mortally ill. Born in Damietta during the dark days of the retreat from Mansurah, John died just as the king himself fell ill. Louis, no longer strong enough to fight off disease, weakened gradually, and on August 25 he died, as he had lived, in the service of the faith.

Just as the king's death was being announced, the vanguard of the Sicilian fleet appeared. Charles of Anjou was saddened by his brother's death, but had no intention of becoming a martyr himself. The new king of France, Philip III, was in nominal command, but his illness and lack of experience forced him to leave everything to his determined uncle. Charles soon decided, after a few more skirmishes, that the crusaders' position was untenable. The army must either risk a full-scale attack on Tunis, or withdraw. The Ḥafṣid emir was also anxious to end hostilities. Sickness had appeared in his army, and he had no desire to face a prolonged siege. With both leaders in this state of mind, it was not difficult to arrange a peace. There was a good deal of indignation among the lesser men in the camp, but Charles had no great difficulty in persuading the leaders to follow his plans. The treaty was ratified on November 1, and seventeen days later the crusaders embarked for Sicily.

A large part of the indignation against the treaty was caused by the fact that Charles was the only one to derive much benefit from its terms. True, Tunisia paid a war indemnity of 210,000 gold-ounces, but even if these were worth 50 *sous tournois* apiece,[19] they amounted to only 525,000 *livres*. This was far less than the crusaders' expenses, especially since the king of Sicily received one third of the sum. Charles, on the other hand, regained all the old privileges of the kings of Sicily in Tunisia. His subjects and friends could trade freely in Tunisian ports, and could exercise their faith freely in Tunis. The supporters of the Hohenstaufens were to be expelled from the lands of the emir. The annual payment for the right to trade with Sicily was doubled and arrears were to be made up. On the whole, Charles had gained most of his objectives. He had engaged in a crusade at a minimum cost in time and money, and in return he had restored his position in Tunisia and broken up a possible center of opposition there. Of all the crusaders, he was the only one who had reason to be pleased.

The unsatisfactory results of the crusade were emphasized by the events of the return. Edward of England arrived just as the final negotiations with Tunisia were being concluded. He was not pleased with a peace which prevented him from fighting, but he could do nothing but accompany Charles and Philip to Sicily. When the fleet reached Trapani, it was struck by a storm which did great damage to the French and Italian vessels, but left Edward's ships unscathed. Pious crusaders were quick to see in this disaster a divine judgment on the faint-hearted. In spite of the warning, all the leaders except Edward agreed to put off further expeditions for three years. More misfortunes were not slow in coming. Theobald of Champagne and Navarre died of an illness contracted in Africa. With many of his ships out of commission and the winter storms beginning, Philip had to take the difficult land route back to France. The hardships of the journey were too much for his pregnant queen, Isabel of Aragon, and she died after giving birth to a dead child. It was not an army but a great funeral procession which returned to France. The young king carried with him the remains of his father, his wife, his stillborn son, his brother, and his brother-in-law. It is not surprising that the next appeal for an overseas expedition drew little response from the French.

The final episode of the crusade was Edward's journey to the Holy Land. Deprived of all outside support, he was accompanied by only a few hundred of his own countrymen. This was too small an army for any effective fighting, as he soon discovered. A few raids in 1271 accomplished nothing, and a truce in 1272 between

[19] This may have been their nominal value, but actual exchange rates at this time give a value closer to 40 *sous tournois*. See Belgrano, *Documenti inediti*, pp. 136, 142, 324–325.

Acre and Baybars ended hostilities. True to his principles, Edward refused to accept the truce, but he could hardly continue fighting when the town which was his chief base of supplies was at peace. He finally followed Louis's example, and left a garrison in Acre at his expense when he sailed at the end of the summer. As a military expedition, his crusade had been useless, but as a political gesture it was a great success. Edward's steadfastness and devotion to the Holy Land were contrasted with the weakness and political maneuverings of Philip and Charles. He gained a reputation for pious zeal which was to be of assistance to him in his later quarrels with Scotland, France, and the papacy. But while his record was better than that of the other kings he had drawn much the same conclusion from his experiences. Like Philip and Charles, he would talk of regaining the Holy Land, but he would always find some reason why it was impossible to make the effort. The age of the great crusades, led by the kings of the west, had ended.

16. Palestine (*Map by the University of Wisconsin Cartographic Laboratory*)

17. Northern Syria (*Map by the University of Wisconsin Cartographic Laboratory*)

John II Comnenus and His Wife Irene

XV
THE CRUSADER STATES
1192–1243

After the Third Crusade, the kingdom of Jerusalem faced conditions less favorable than those prevailing before the battle of Hattin. It was surrounded by strong Aiyūbid states while its own territory was confined to the coast of the Levant. Its armed forces and diplomatic influence were small. Within the kingdom, the transfer of the capital to Acre symbolized the shift in emphasis from religious to economic and commercial interests that would characterize the thirteenth century.

When Philip Augustus left Acre in 1191, Richard the Lion-hearted remained in nominal command, although a remnant of the French forces under duke Hugh of Burgundy allied itself with

Among the sources for this period, especial importance attaches to the *Chronique d'Ernoul et de Bernard le trésorier* (ed. L. de Mas Latrie, Paris, 1871), and to the *Estoire de Eracles* (*RHC, Occ.*, II). For the relations of Jerusalem with the Hohenstaufens and, indeed, for most of the happenings of the early thirteenth century, see Philip of Novara, *The Wars of Frederick II against the Ibelins in Syria and Cyprus* (tr. J. L. La Monte and M. J. Hubert, Records of Civilization, New York, 1936) which, though invaluable, is biased in favor of the Syrians. Concerning the text history of Philip's work, see *ibid.*, pp. 3 ff., and C. Kohler, *Les Mémoires de Philippe de Novare, 1218–1243* (Les Classiques français du moyen-âge, X, Paris, 1913).

Inevitably the papal correspondence must be studied in connection with this as with all crusading activities: P. Jaffé, *Regesta pontificum Romanorum ad annum MCXCVIII* (ed. S. Loewenfeld, F. Kaltenbrunner, *et al.*, II, Leipzig, 1888), and A. Potthast, *Regesta pontificum Romanorum inde ab anno post Christum natum MCXCVIII ad annum MCCCIV* (2 vols., Berlin, 1874–1875). The full texts of Innocent III's correspondence may be found, although in a faulty edition, in *PL*, CCXIV–CCXVII; better versions of certain letters are specified in the footnotes to this volume. For Honorius III and Gregory IX, see *I regesti del pontefice Onorio III* (ed. P. Pressutti, I, Rome, 1884); *Regesta Honorii papae III* (*ed.* P. Pressutti, 2 vols., Rome, 1888–1895); and *Les Registres de Grégoire IX* (ed. L. Auvray, 4 vols., 1896–1955).

Among the Arabic chroniclers the most useful are Abū-l-Fidā', *Kitāb al-mukhtaṣar fī akhbār al-bashar* (extracts tr. in *RHC, Or.*, I); Ibn-al-Athīr, *Al-kāmil fī-t-ta'rīkh* (extracts tr. in *RHC, Or.*, II, part I); and Usāmah Ibn-Munqidh, *An Arab Gentleman and Warrior in the Period of the Crusades* (tr. and ed. P. K. Hitti, Records of Civilization, New York, 1929).

The *Assises de Jérusalem* (*RHC, Lois*, I, II) are extremely useful for the legal aspects of Jerusalem in relation to the other principalities and for the position of the king and the barons in the thirteenth century. In connection with this work, M. Grandclaude, *Étude critique sur les livres des Assises de Jérusalem* (Paris, 1923), is very helpful.

Principal secondary works are R. Röhricht's monumental *Geschichte des Königreichs Jerusalem* (Innsbruck, 1898), and R. Grousset, *Histoire des croisades*, III (Paris, 1936). The best secondary account of the principality of Antioch and its tangled relations with Jerusalem, Tripoli, and the Moslem states is to be found in C. Cahen, *La Syrie du nord à l'époque des croisades* (Paris, 1940).

Conrad of Montferrat in opposition to Richard and to Guy of Lusignan. Increasingly anxious to leave the unhealthy Syrian shores and return to the west to deal with John and Philip Augustus, Richard gradually inclined to the politic settlement of Christian differences in Syria. Guy resigned his pretensions to Jerusalem and purchased from Richard the more attractive Cyprus, for which he departed in May 1192. Richard was then free to agree to Conrad's election as king of Jerusalem. Husband of Isabel, heiress to the throne, Conrad was not only an able soldier and statesman, but leader of the majority Syrian party in opposition to the incompetent and luckless Guy. Richard sent Henry of Champagne to Tyre to escort Conrad to Acre for his coronation, but Conrad was killed by an Assassin on April 28. Although both Richard and Saladin were accused by some of instigating the murder,[1] it was apparently the result of a quarrel with the Assassins over Conrad's seizure of a merchant ship belonging to the order. His death removed the one competent candidate for the throne who was primarily interested in the power of Jerusalem. Others looked upon the kingship as a duty or as an addition to their holdings.

The exigencies of Jerusalem's situation made inadvisable the possible conflicts and uncertainties of a regency. The newly reconciled factions would scarcely have agreed upon a council or regent without further bitterness. Therefore Henry of Champagne, the wealthy nephew of the kings of France and England, was hastily selected to be the queen's new husband and to share the throne. Henry would have preferred to return to the west, but appeals from Richard, the Syrian barons, and the remaining crusaders prevailed, and when Richard promised to return with reinforcements, Henry accepted. He and Isabel were married in Tyre, according to *Eracles*, two days after Conrad's death, and then proceeded to Acre to take over the government. Henry's accession was hailed for ending the internal conflict which had persisted since the reign of Baldwin IV and had divided Christian efforts in the crusade. He was never crowned, and we know of his using the title lord of Jerusalem only once (in March 1196). He usually called himself count of Troyes.

By the treaty of September 2–3, 1192, drawn for a term of three years and three months, the Franks had received the littoral from north of Tyre to south of Jaffa. Lydda-Ramla was to be divided and Ascalon, Darum, and Gaza were to be dismantled for the duration. Jerusalem was to be accessible to Christians, and the

[1] See above, volume I, pp. 125–126.

pilgrim route to Mecca open to Moslems. Separate treaties were reserved for Antioch and Tripoli. After Richard's departure on October 9, 1192, Saladin revised the peace even more generously for certain Frankish barons, giving Sarepta and half the district of Sidon to Reginald Grenier, and the castle and surrounding lands of Caymont to Balian of Ibelin. Henry took possession of Jaffa, and restored Haifa, Caesarea, and Arsuf to their respective lords. Peace with Antioch and Tripoli followed on October 30, when Saladin met with Bohemond III in Beirut.

The generally effective peace brought relief to the people, and crowded the roads with pilgrims. Within a short time old commercial routes were reopened for a flourishing trade. The Italian cities — Pisa and Genoa in particular — gained greater privileges and lands in Syria than ever before, inasmuch as the reorganized kingdom depended greatly on their navies for protection from the Moslems by sea. Jerusalem now became embroiled in their feuds and rivalries for commercial supremacy. Although their navies helped to reëstablish the kingdom, their abuse of power within the kingdom and their preoccupation with their own economic interests weakened the state and helped produce its final fall.

The general situation immediately after the Third Crusade, however, did not appear hopeless. The reduced Latin territory and its compactness meant fewer surprises in the hinterland for the Franks, who were eager to reconquer the remainder of the coast between Jerusalem and Tripoli, and looked to an early renewal of crusading enthusiasm in Europe. Saladin's death in 1193, threatening Aiyūbid unity, seemed to promise them ultimate success. The Franks were unable, however, to take advantage of Moslem disunity then and later because of Jerusalem's own political troubles; a series of female successions, minorities, and regencies made long-range policies difficult to plan or execute.

Henry of Champagne faced the immediate problem of consolidating his position and strengthening the crown before he could take any action outside Jerusalem. He learned in May 1193 that the Pisans, old allies of the Lusignan faction, were plotting to seize Tyre for Guy. Henry immediately forbade that more than thirty Pisans reside in the city at any one time. When the Pisans retaliated by ravaging the coast up to Acre, Henry expelled them from Acre and all the kingdom, threatening to hang any who should return. He thus canceled the previous grants to the Pisans by former rulers, which he and Richard had confirmed in 1192. Throughout his reign, Henry was often forced to renounce policies and friendships favored by Richard, to turn from the Lusignans and Pisans to the Monferrine-Genoese-Syrian Frank faction.

The affair of Tyre spread to include Guy's brother Aimery, constable of Jerusalem and lord of Jaffa. When he intervened with Henry for the Pisans, Henry charged him with complicity in the plot and imprisoned him. Aimery appealed to the laws of the kingdom, protesting such treatment, especially as Henry was acting without the consent of the high court. In this Aimery was upheld by the barons and the masters of the Temple and Hospital. Henry was persuaded to free Aimery, who gave up the constableship and all he held from Henry to retire to Cyprus, where he succeeded to the throne and to the leadership of the Lusignan-Pisan party at Guy's death in 1194.

When Aimery ascended the Cypriote throne, Henry still claimed Cyprus as part of the kingdom of Jerusalem. Many nobles and merchants held fiefs and privileges in both states because of Guy's success in drawing colonists from the devastated mainland. Aimery and Henry, recognizing that the rivalry was injurious to both Cyprus and the kingdom of Jerusalem, reached an accord when Henry visited Cyprus in 1194, after his return from Armenia. The three daughters of Henry were to marry Aimery's three sons and establish one ruling family, concentrating Frankish power in the east. Henry was to give his own city, Jaffa, for dowry. In addition, at the first marriage he would cancel the 60,000 dinars which Guy had owed Richard for Cyprus, a debt which Richard had passed on to Henry.[2] The accord also paved the way for Henry's reconciliation with the Pisans, who were now pardoned and restored to their old lands and privileges.

During this early period, Henry quarreled also with the canons of the Holy Sepulcher over the election of a new patriarch. Basically, the trouble stemmed from the ruler's attempt to maintain royal rights over the clergy, and is noteworthy as one of the last instances of violent disagreement between throne and church in Jerusalem. On the whole, relations between the two were harmonious and cordial in the reorganized kingdom. However, when the patriarch Ralph died in 1194, the canons of the Holy Sepulcher elected Aymar the Monk, archbishop of Caesarea and partisan of the Pisans, without consulting Henry. When Henry objected that they had encroached upon crown rights, they replied that the customs of the kingdom gave them the right to elect a patriarch at once.

[2] See below, chapter XVII, pp. 599–604.

They added that they had not asked his approval of the candidate because he had not been regularly crowned king; this was an obvious evasion, since the holy city, where the king ought by law to have been crowned, was held by Moslems. Henry again acted swiftly and impulsively, arresting the canons and threatening them for usurping the royal prerogative. They were immediately released on the advice of the chancellor Joscius, archbishop of Tyre, and Aymar was further pacified by a grant and a prebend to his nephew. The canons sent a delegation to pope Celestine III, who concluded the affair by confirming Aymar and censuring Henry for brutality.

Henry also reasserted in some measure hegemony over the northern principality of Antioch, which had drifted far from Jerusalem's sphere of influence following Saladin's destruction of the centralized power of the early kingdom. Bohemond III (1163–1201) had initiated policies which Antioch would follow for the next half century: he annexed Tripoli, gained Moslem friendship, particularly in Aleppo, quarreled with his prelates, and began intermittent warfare with Armenia. The union with Tripoli was a personal one, resulting from the bequest of the county by Raymond III to his godson Raymond, eldest son of Bohemond. As Raymond was also heir to Antioch, where frontier conditions were unstable, Bohemond III deemed it wiser for his second son, Bohemond, to take Tripoli.[3] Bohemond III signed a two-year truce with Saladin in 1187, followed by a ten-year treaty in 1192. A treaty with Aleppo was more than a mere pact of non-aggression; aẓ-Ẓāhir of Aleppo feared the Armenians, his uncle Saif-ad-Dīn, and Turkish interference, so he concluded an alliance with Antioch which reached its zenith during the early years of Bohemond IV's rule. To Antioch the defensive alliance with Aleppo meant an ally against Armenia when the principality could not depend upon Jerusalem, from which it was separated by Latakia (Laodicea) and other Moslem holdings. Internally the small group of Latins controlling the political life of the principality were inextricably involved in the bitter rivalries between the much larger Greek and Armenian populations. The racial and religious hatreds between the Greeks and the Armenians split the ruling Franks, who were to be found in both parties. Antiochene-Armenian relations were further complicated by claims of the Templars to the fortress of Baghrās, which

[3] On the union of Antioch and Tripoli, cf. in general Jean Richard, *Le Comté de Tripoli sous la dynastie toulousaine (1102–1187)* (Bibliothèque archéologique et historique, XXXIX, Paris, 1945).

they had possessed until 1188, when it was captured, dismantled, and then restored by Saladin. Armenia refused to return it to the Templars because it guarded the entrance to Syria. The Antiochenes felt uneasy with the strategic stronghold in Armenian hands; this had been one of the reasons why Bohemond III had not included his vassal Leon II in the treaty of 1192 with Saladin. Saladin himself had objected to Leon's holding Baghrās, which lay on the route from Cilicia to Antioch.

Open conflict with Cilician Armenia came in 1194. Leon of Armenia, after long service in the court of Bohemond III, returned to Armenia as regent for his niece Alice. In 1194 he lured Bohemond and his family to Baghrās, perhaps by a false promise to surrender the fortress. He hoped to gain release from homage to Bohemond, and to seize Antioch. Leon took Bohemond's family and court off to Sis as prisoners. Bohemond agreed to surrender Antioch in exchange for his freedom, sending the marshal Bartholomew Tirel and Richard of L'Erminet to turn the city over to Armenian troops under Heṭoum of Sasoun. After their initial entry, Antiochene resistance was whipped up by the clergy and the Greeks. The citizenry ousted the invaders and, under the venerable patriarch Aimery, formed a commune which recognized Raymond as lord until his father should be released. Heṭoum stationed his troops outside the city walls.

Antioch then asked aid of Henry of Jerusalem and Bohemond of Tripoli. Despite the weakness of his forces, Henry went as arbitrator, following the old tradition that the ruler of Jerusalem should answer Antioch's appeals. He was undoubtedly also influenced by the broader view that war between Christian states would help the Moslems. He sailed to Tripoli, where young Bohemond joined him, and then went on to Antioch and Sis. There Leon was persuaded to negotiate peace with Antioch. All the prisoners captured at Baghrās were released; Leon was quit of homage to Bohemond; Bohemond gave up the frontier territory he held in the plain of Armenia up to the Syrian Gates; and arrangements were made for the marriage of Raymond of Antioch to Alice of Armenia (1195). Bohemond was certain that a son of the union would inherit Armenia, and that his Latin upbringing would render him an ally of Antioch. But Raymond soon died, and Bohemond III sent Alice back to Leon with her infant son Raymond Roupen. Leon determined that this great-nephew of his should inherit Antioch on the death of Bohemond III.

In 1198 Bohemond of Tripoli, trying to insure his succession to Antioch, attempted to take the city in his father's lifetime. While az-Ẓāhir of Aleppo detained Leon of Armenia, the young Bohemond entered Antioch, summoned the commune, and persuaded it to renounce in his favor its oath to his father. The basis of his claim to the title prince of Antioch thus became popular election instead of inheritance. Within three months, however, Leon settled his Moslem troubles, made peace with the military orders, and marched on Antioch. There was no resistance to his army or to its restoration of Bohemond III. Bohemond of Tripoli was more interested in securing his own eventual accession than in deposing his father, now old, easily led, and tiring of Leon's brief protection. The son could also count on support against Leon from the Templars, whose claims to Baghrās were still unsatisfied.

While Antioch remained troubled, the kingdom enjoyed the results of Henry's foreign policy. As a wise diplomat, he gained peace to rebuild the shattered strength of his land, accepting the friendship of Moslem and Christian alike. On his journey back from Antioch in 1194 he passed through Assassin territory and was welcomed by the master of that order, which owed its independence to a balance of power in Syria between the Franks and the Aiyūbids. At this time it was turning to Jerusalem to counter the power of Damascus.[4] Similarly, after Saladin's death in March 1193, Henry took advantage of internecine Moslem struggles to play one Aiyūbid against the others. The Franks seldom attempted attacks on Moslems, however, being more concerned with the restoration of prosperity in their own cities and fiefs. Thus for a half century there was no concentrated war between Frank and Aiyūbid in Syria. Breaches of the peace were usually precipitated by the arrival of fresh crusaders from Europe.

In 1197, when the treaty signed by Henry and Saladin was about to expire, the Hohenstaufen emperor Henry VI had mustered huge forces for an eastern expedition.[5] Already lord of Sicily through his marriage to the Norman heiress Constance, Henry VI had arranged to assume suzerainty over Cyprus and Armenia by conferring crowns upon the rulers of each state.[6] Aimery of Cyprus, wishing to clarify the status of his island domain, had sent an embassy to the pope and Henry VI in 1195; both had agreed that he should have the crown, and he assumed the royal title in the spring of 1196 while his coronation awaited the arrival of Henry

[4] See volume I, chapter IV, for a general treatment of the Assassins, where, however, this episode is not discussed.

[5] See above, chapter III, pp. 117–121.

[6] For the crown of Cyprus, see below, chapter XVII, p. 604.

VI or imperial envoys. Leon of Armenia, after uniting the Armenian church with Rome, likewise requested a crown from the emperor, promising to hold Armenia from him. Henry received Leon's homage and promised a coronation. Not content with this, Leon also received a crown from the Byzantine emperor Alexius III Angelus. Aimery was crowned in September 1197 by the imperial chancellor, Conrad of Querfurt, when the first contingent of the projected imperial crusade stopped at Cyprus for that purpose. Leon was crowned January 6, 1198, at Tarsus, in the presence of the Armenian clergy, the Franco-Armenian nobility of the land, the Greek archbishop of Tarsus, the Jacobite patriarch, and the caliph's ambassadors. While he was crowned by the catholicus, Gregory Abirad, Leon received the other royal insignia from archbishop Conrad of Mainz in Henry's name.

The German crusaders who landed at Acre in the summer of 1197 were soon so seriously at odds with the Syrian Franks that their leaders moved their camp to the outskirts of the city to avoid a clash. Relations between Moslems and Christians were uneasy, and the new arrivals seemed bound to precipitate some change in the Syrian situation. The first change, however, was independent of the crusade: Stephanie of Milly, widow of Hugh (III) Embriaco, the last lord of Jubail, bribed the Kurdish emir of that town to leave his stronghold. The Moslems left and Stephanie's forces took possession of Jubail in the autumn of 1197. The Christians were beginning to dislodge the Moslems from their few ports along the Syrian coast, holdings which had separated Antioch and Tripoli from the kingdom since the days of Saladin.

In September the German crusaders, without notifying Henry of Champagne, attacked in Moslem territory. They were encircled by Moslems, but eventually saved by Henry, who proceeded to reorganize them on the advice of Hugh of Tiberias. Fearing a surprise move by al-'Ādil Saif-ad-Din, Henry's forces returned to Acre, where they learned that the Moslem leader was attacking Jaffa. While Henry was preparing to go to the defense of his city, he fell from a tower window in Acre and died (September 10, 1197). His death removed the unifying force holding the barons and crusaders together. Jaffa had already fallen to the Moslems, but the news was delayed; the host dispersed, and affairs came to a virtual standstill pending the selection of a new consort for queen Isabel.

Two candidates were considered: Ralph of Tiberias and Aimery of Lusignan. Ralph, a distinguished legist, had been born in the east, knew the country well, and would devote his entire life to its interests. His brother Hugh was the leader of the barons. But the family was poor, had lost its great fief, and had no means to support the army and the court. Considering this, the Hospitallers and the Templars opposed Ralph. They favored Aimery, who had money and support from Cyprus, and was known as a good administrator. As liegeman of Henry VI, Aimery was also backed by the imperial chancellor. He was finally approved, married to Isabel, and crowned by the patriarch Aymar (October 1197). This was also Isabel's official coronation, although she had ruled jointly with her two previous husbands for several years.

Even before formally taking over the kingdom, Aimery held a council of war to consider the best use of the forces then in the country. Jaffa was lost and further warfare there seemed pointless. The most important place still in Aiyūbid hands was Beirut, lying between Tyre and Tripoli, and so dividing the Christian holdings. The host reassembled and marched up the coast, including the German crusaders under duke Henry of Brabant and Cypriote reinforcements. The fleet sailed parallel to the army. By mid-October of 1197 they had passed through Tyre and had reached Sidon, deserted after being destroyed by the Moslems. On October 22–23 they met the enemy between Sidon and Beirut. A short delaying action ended when Saif-ad-Dīn withdrew. He had sent forces on to destroy Beirut on October 21, but these were halted in their work by Usāmah, emir of the city, whose wealth depended on pirate ships based at Beirut which attacked shipping along the coast. When the Christians appeared before his gates October 23, Usāmah and his men went forth to fight, leaving a virtually undefended citadel to be taken over by a Christian carpenter and slaves. Usāmah fled and the Christians entered a deserted but intact city. The slaves hastened to surrender the tower to Aimery. The Franks now ruled the coast from Acre to Tripoli, and could extend their control to the coastal waters. Aimery profited greatly from the large store of arms left by Usāmah, and by having at his disposal a large fief.

Leaving a garrison at Beirut, the army pushed on to Toron and besieged it (November 28–February 2), but halted operations when the news of Henry VI's death on September 28 reached them. The Germans retired hastily to Tyre, whence they sailed almost immediately to Italy and Germany; Aimery could not continue the siege alone. He quickly came to terms with Saif-ad-Dīn, concluding a treaty much like the old one, but keeping Beirut and Jubail. The crusade had thus increased Jerusalem's holdings. It had also introduced Hohenstaufen ambitions as a new and important factor in the subsequent history of Jerusalem and Cyprus.

Aimery was now ready to turn his attention to the administration of his new kingdom. He early refused to unite Jerusalem and Cyprus; each continued to maintain its own court, finances, and army, and his successors would abide by the principle of separation. Rivalry between the two states almost ceased, and Cyprus often gave of its resources to Jerusalem. In return, Cyprus drew from Syria many Franks who were pleased by the economic and commercial advantages of the island.

Much was hoped of a new crusade which the pope was preaching in Europe. Some of its members who refused to be "diverted" to Byzantium arrived at Acre as early as 1202.[7] As usual, they understood little of politics, diplomacy, or military affairs in the Near East. Reginald of Dampierre, leader of 300 knights, announced to king Aimery that existing treaties with the Moslems should be broken so that he and his men could begin fighting immediately. Aimery replied that more than 300 men were necessary to fight the Aiyūbids, and that he would wait for further evidence of a large crusade. Meanwhile he counseled the impatient westerners to wait. Instead, most started northward to join the war raging between Bohemond IV and Leon of Armenia in Antioch, but many were massacred crossing into Latakian territory; a few stayed peaceably in Jerusalem.

Aimery did undertake one reprisal against Moslems during this time. An Egyptian emir, holding a castle near Sidon, sent out corsairs much as Usāmah had from Beirut. When Aimery's protests to Saif-ad-Dīn failed to stop the piracy, he launched a naval raid which netted twenty Egyptian ships, with supplies valued at 60,000 bezants, and 200 captives. Then he led the barons, Templars, and Hospitallers on land raids into Galilee, while Moslems under Saif-ad-Dīn's son al-Mu'aẓẓam raided near Acre. Each military force carefully avoided the other; Aimery was still waiting for larger forces, and Saif-ad-Dīn did not want to provoke the arrival of more Europeans. In May 1204 Aimery showed further naval strength by raiding Fūwah in the Nile delta.

These actions, however, almost ceased with the diversion of the Fourth Crusade and the realization that the Holy Land was not to profit from it. Indeed, for Jerusalem the Fourth Crusade was a tragedy. The Latin empire of Constantinople was never strong

[7] See above, chapter V, pp. 173–175.

enough to aid Syria; it dispersed western Christian efforts in men and wealth, and even attracted some nobles already established in Syria.[8] Since most of the armies had gone to Constantinople, Jerusalem again sought peace with a willing Saif-ad-Dīn. The peace of September 1204, for six years, gained for the Franks the halves of Sidon, Lydda, and Ramla previously held by the Moslems, as well as the return of Jaffa and the extension of religious privileges and pilgrim facilities in Nazareth.

Aimery died on April 1, 1205, shortly after peace had been established. He had been self-assured, politically astute, sometimes hard, seldom sentimentally indulgent. He had found his greatest test in upholding crown rights against baronial privilege without provoking revolt. It was not his fault that he failed to strengthen the crown; a series of female and minority successions to the throne would gravely weaken the kingdom; and conditions on the frontier were very unsettled. With his death, Cyprus and Jerusalem were again separated, the former going to Hugh I, his son by his first marriage, while Isabel ruled Jerusalem until her own death soon after. An infant son died about the same time.

John of Ibelin, lord of Beirut and Isabel's half-brother, was elected by the high court of Acre to be bailie of the kingdom for Isabel and then for her heiress Mary, Isabel's daughter by Conrad of Montferrat. Ibelin's regency lasted from 1205 to 1210, when Mary married John of Brienne. It was a period of prosperity and peace for Jerusalem, although there was some trouble with Saif-ad-Dīn when pirates from Cyprus captured several Egyptian vessels. Saif-ad-Dīn led an army up to Acre before Ibelin convinced him that Jerusalem had not been responsible for the Cypriote actions. After exchanging prisoners, Saif-ad-Dīn went north to Tripoli, where Homs was under attack from Krak des Chevaliers. He campaigned in the area, captured 'Anaz, and finally agreed to a peace with Bohemond IV which relieved pressure on Homs.

Although the kingdoms of Cyprus and Jerusalem had found some stability under Aimery and after him, the principality of Antioch had been torn by wars of succession. The death of Bohemond III in April 1201 precipitated action by both Bohemond of Tripoli and Leon of Armenia. Informed of his father's illness, young Bohemond rushed to Antioch, arriving on the day of the funeral. He immediately sounded the bell of the commune and demanded recognition as the rightful heir. The right of succession followed

[8] See above, chapters VI and VII.

as yet no absolutely fixed principle in feudal law. John of England and Arthur of Britanny were at this time contending for the throne of England in a situation analogous to that of Bohemond and Raymond Roupen. It would have been normal for Raymond Roupen to become prince, as the son of Raymond, the eldest son of Bohemond III. Many nobles had taken oaths of homage to him and were loyal to the elder line. His uncle, the younger Bohemond, on the other hand, was the closest living relative of the last holder of the title and could, besides, fall back on his former popular election by the commune. While Raymond Roupen was not personally objectionable to the population of Antioch, many feared Armenian influence in his court. So Bohemond IV was accepted as prince, although not consecrated by the church, and those who favored Raymond fled to exile in Armenia.

Bohemond's position in Antioch was further strengthened by his allies. The Templars backed him, as did the Hospitallers for the moment, won over by the settlement of an old debt of Raymond III of Tripoli. Aẓ-Ẓāhir of Aleppo again promised aid, and the Greek and Frankish elements remaining in the seignory supported him. Leon of Armenia heard of the death of Bohemond III late, but then hurried to Antioch with Alice and Raymond Roupen to claim it for his great-nephew. When he found Bohemond IV already installed, he sent back for reinforcements, while Bohemond called on Aleppo. Despite his war with Damascus, aẓ-Ẓāhir invaded Armenia in July 1201, and Leon had to lift his siege of Antioch.

The war was renewed by Leon in 1202. During the following summer Aimery intervened, in the hope of settling the affair before the expected Fourth Crusade arrived. Accompanied by the papal legate, cardinal Soffredo, the masters of the Hospital and the Temple, and the high barons of the kingdom, he induced Leon to grant a short truce. After Leon had agreed to accept the decision of barons and legate, the barons, possibly under Bohemond's influence, announced that the question at issue was purely one of feudal law in which the legate should have no say. Angered, Leon ended the truce and on November 11, 1203, entered the city, and asked the patriarch to arrange peace between him and the commune. Bohemond IV was busy in Tripoli at the time, but the commune and Templars held the citadel stoutly, and were able to expel the Armenians. Their appeals to Aleppo were answered when aẓ-Ẓāhir started again into Armenia. Leon left Antioch in December, when aẓ-Ẓāhir's army reached the Orontes.

In his struggle with Antioch, Leon had striven to gain papal support. In 1194–1195, when he was planning to get the title of king, he had instituted a union of the Armenian church with Rome; pope Celestine III had concurred in 1196 when Leon requested and received the royal title and crown from Henry VI. Throughout his pontificate, Innocent III tried to handle the problem of northern Syria so as to keep Armenia's adherence while not alienating Antioch. Leon clearly expected to receive tangible political benefits for his loyalty to Rome, and when Bohemond IV took Antioch, Leon had demanded "justice" of Innocent. Bohemond's actions had upset the papal plan for peaceful negotiations under the church, but, however much Innocent favored Leon in this affair, he could not condone his retention of Baghrās nor could he condemn Bohemond out of hand. The papal legates, cardinals Soffredo of St. Praxed and Peter Capuano of St. Marcellus, only succeeded in antagonizing Leon and giving Bohemond an opportunity to show his judicial agility.

While the legates were negotiating, Christians, Moslems, and the military orders fought among themselves with indiscriminate enthusiasm. Bohemond was forced to leave Antioch to defend Tripoli during the feudal rebellion of Renart of Nephin, who in 1203 without his suzerain's approval married Isabel, the heiress of 'Akkār (Gibelcar). Bohemond had the right to seize Renart's fiefs after he had been cited before the baronial court of Tripoli and condemned by default. Leon of Armenia supported Renart, while Bohemond relied on the Templars, the Hospitallers, the Genoese, and Aleppo. King Aimery, however, and certain barons, like Ralph and Hugh of Tiberias, supported Renart, because they disliked Bohemond's pretensions to autonomy in Antioch and Tripoli.

Toward the end of 1204, Renart raided up to the gates of Tripoli. Bohemond lost an eye in the battle which followed. After Aimery's death in April 1205, the regent, John of Ibelin, hostile to Renart, withdrew royal favor. Bohemond went over to the offensive, and by the end of the year captured both Nephin and 'Akkār. The baronial revolt collapsed, and in 1206 Bohemond was able to return to Antioch, which in the interim had been more or less protected from Leon by the watchfulness of az̧-Z̧āhir.

Between 1203 and 1205 the Hospitallers made several vain efforts to recapture some of their former territories in the north. The garrisons of Krak des Chevaliers and al-Marqab failed twice in 1203 to retake Ba'rīn (Montferrand), then held from Aleppo by al-Manṣūr of Hamah. They were so badly defeated that they requested the Templars to mediate for them. The Templars, making much of the arrival of Aimery and other lords in Antioch that summer, persuaded al-Manṣūr to sign a peace not unfavorable to the Hospitallers in September 1203. In 1204 and 1205 the Hospitallers renewed their raids against Ba'rīn, and attacked Jabala and Latakia. They finally subsided in 1205 when the Moslems attacked al-Marqab.

Although the Fourth Crusade had given little comfort to Jerusalem, Bohemond IV was able to draw from the capture of Constantinople a certain political profit. To offset the vassalship of his rival, Leon of Armenia, to the western emperor Henry VI, Bohemond in 1204 did homage for Antioch to Mary, wife of the first Latin emperor Baldwin, who had come to Acre unaware that her husband had been "diverted" to Constantinople and had there become emperor. Bohemond thus made the new Latin dynasty the "legitimate" heirs of its Byzantine predecessors as suzerains of Antioch.

When Bohemond returned to Antioch in 1206, he found a clerical quarrel raging in the city. Peter Capuano had returned as papal legate to mediate between Bohemond and Leon but had fallen out with Peter of Angoulême, patriarch of Antioch, over clerical appointments in the principality. The legate excommunicated the cathedral chapter and took from Peter his patriarchal rights. The patriarch could expect no assistance from Bohemond, with whom he was already at odds. Indeed the patriarch had come to favor the Armenians against the Greeks, and had extended this preference so far as to support Raymond Roupen and friendship with Leon, who was again in communion with Rome. Early in 1207 Bohemond completely alienated the Latin church and most of the Franks in Antioch by enthroning the Greek patriarch, Symeon II, who was violently opposed to the Latin patriarch Peter. But in 1208 Peter of Angoulême submitted to the legate and received a favorable judgment from Rome, whereupon he excommunicated Symeon, Bohemond, and their followers, and placed Antioch under an interdict. Most of the population merely changed over to another communion, but Bohemond went further by allying himself with the Greek emperor Theodore Lascaris of Nicaea.

The unpopularity of Bohemond's behavior made it possible for Leon to plan a revolt within the city. Led by Peter of Angoulême and dissatisfied Latin nobles, the city rose, and Bohemond took refuge in the citadel. Leon entered with some of his army, just as Bohemond felt strong enough to emerge, expel the invaders, and crush the revolt. Leon had held Antioch only a few days. Bohemond blamed the rebellion on the unfortunate Latin patriarch, who was imprisoned and tortured by thirst until he finally was driven to drinking lamp oil, and died in July 1208. Later that year Bohemond was excommunicated by patriarch Albert of Jerusalem under orders from Innocent III. This apparently meant little to him, for he kept the Greek patriarch Symeon in Antioch until 1213, and meanwhile refused to accept Peter, abbot of Locedio, who was appointed patriarch of Antioch by the pope.

Bohemond's danger in Antioch in 1208 induced aẓ-Ẓāhir once more to invade Cilicia in 1209. Leon had to agree to return Baghrās to the Templars and to renounce his claims to Antioch. To offset this defeat, Leon sought to tie the Hospitallers closer to him by giving them fortresses to enable them to hold the march on the west of Cilicia against the Selchükids and to free himself for action on the southeast.

In the kingdom of Jerusalem, John of Ibelin concluded his regency in 1210 by negotiating a marriage for Mary. The barons sought a man able to protect the land in peace and in war. They sent Aymar of Lairon, lord of Caesarea, and Walter of Florence, bishop of Acre, as ambassadors to the court of Philip Augustus to request him to nominate such a man. They were a trifle disconcerted by the nominee: John of Brienne, younger son of a noble family of Champagne, perhaps elderly,[9] without substantial means. Despite these drawbacks, however, he was a courageous, able, and determined knight. As king he resembled Aimery in balance and wisdom; financially he was endowed with 40,000 *livres tournois* from Philip and an equal sum from Innocent III, who also gave him 300 knights. John landed at Haifa September 13, 1210, and proceeded to Acre, where a grand welcome awaited him. On September 14 he married Mary, and on October 3 was crowned with her at Tyre and received the homage of his new subjects.

The situation facing the new king was grave, and complicated by headstrong elements within the kingdom itself. The treaty with the Moslems signed by Aimery was to expire in September 1210, if Saif-ad-Dīn's offer to renew it with ten additional villages near Acre were not accepted. John of Ibelin, the barons, the Hospitallers, and the newly formed Teutonic Knights urged its acceptance, while the Templars, the patriarch, and many of the clergy strenuously opposed it. Saif-ad-Dīn continued to restrain his men. But the

[9] On his alleged age, however, see the interesting article of J. M. Buckley, "The Problematical Octogenarianism of John of Brienne," *Speculum*, XXXII (1957), 315–322.

Franks raided up to the Jordan, and forced many Moslems to leave the area west of the river. With this the war started. The situation, despite promises, was not good; Jerusalem had but a toehold in Syria. John of Brienne asked aid, especially men, from the west, and Innocent III had the crusade preached once more throughout Europe, but the response was slow. Before the Franks could prepare, al-Mu'aẓẓam, viceroy of Damascus, had reached Acre itself, although he contented himself with raids and prisoners. The Franks struck a blow in June 1211 by sending another raiding expedition under Walter of Montbéliard to the Nile delta. When the French knights at Acre prepared to leave, however, the kingdom sought peace. Saif-ad-Dīn received a delegation at his new fortress on Mt. Tabor in Galilee, and signed a treaty to last until 1217. This ushered in a new peaceful period during which the commerce and prosperity of Jerusalem expanded under John, who, after the death of queen Mary in 1212, continued to rule as regent and bailie for the heiress, his infant daughter Isabel.

No such peace existed, however, between Antioch and Armenia, and John of Brienne was shortly involved in their quarrel. Leon's attempts to keep the fortress of Baghrās, despite his promise in the treaty with aẓ-Ẓāhir to return it to the Templars, led to a war in Cilicia and in the Antiochene plain until in 1211 the master of the Temple was wounded in an ambush, and Innocent III published the old excommunication against Leon. Leon sent Raymond Roupen against the Templars while he gave former Latin posts and possessions to the Greeks. He even received Symeon, Greek patriarch of Antioch. In 1211 John of Brienne and Bohemond both gave the Templars such effective aid that Leon finally returned Baghrās. But the new treaty was abruptly broken the next year with further actions against the Templars. This time the interdict was strictly enforced until Leon was reconciled with Rome in March 1213.

Several factors combined to make Leon's position much stronger than Bohemond's in northern Syria in the years immediately following the new rapprochement with Innocent. Bohemond was estranged from aẓ-Ẓāhir, his strongest Moslem ally, just as the announcement of a new crusade drew aẓ-Ẓāhir closer to Saif-ad-Dīn who favored Leon. Leon also won the favor of John of Brienne, who in 1214 married Leon's daughter Rita ("Stephanie") and expected to inherit Armenia. In Antioch morale was low; the population, exhausted by strife and alarmed at prospects of a new religious war, felt deserted by Bohemond IV, who preferred to reside in the richer and more centrally located Tripoli. Leon's intrigues rebuilt a strong party in favor of Raymond Roupen, who was already backed by the clergy and some of the barons and who now promised richer fiefs to Hospitallers, justice to the Latin patriarch Peter and to the Antiochene exiles in Armenia, and fiefs to some nobles in Antioch. The most important of the latter group was the seneschal, Acharie of Sermin (Sarmīn), who was also mayor of the commune. Bohemond IV was in Tripoli when the plot reached fruition. On the night of February 14, 1216, Leon entered Antioch with his army and within a few days held the city, persuading the Templars in the citadel that aid was not coming. Raymond Roupen paid homage to patriarch Peter and was consecrated prince of Antioch, a confirmation of his office which had been denied Bohemond. For a time Leon's dreams seemed realized: Raymond Roupen, his own designated heir, was at last installed as prince of Antioch.

The new order began auspiciously. Raymond Roupen rewarded the church and the orders; the regular clergy regained possessions confiscated by Bohemond, while the Teutonic Knights and Hospitallers were well treated. The latter were made guardians of the citadel and confirmed in all the fiefs promised them earlier. Exiled Antiochenes returned to their possessions; Pisan privileges, which had been curtailed by Bohemond, were restored. But the mixed character of Raymond's support, combined with an empty treasury and lack of good counsel, alienated the good will the new reign had enjoyed in its first days. Raymond Roupen even quarreled with Leon, thus losing military strength as well as the hope of inheriting Armenia. In Antioch both nobles and commune objected to heavy taxation, and the commune became increasingly restive as the early prosperity of the reign faded. Another loss was the good council of the patriarch Peter, who died in 1217, and whose office was not filled until 1220. The young prince seems to have surrounded himself with men who aroused his suspicions of the people to such an extent that he demanded extraordinary oaths of loyalty from laymen and clergy alike.

John of Brienne was to be, in theory at least, commander-in-chief of the Fifth Crusade, which Innocent III launched in 1215 at the Fourth Lateran Council.[10] In Syria the crusade was vigorously preached by James of Vitry, appointed bishop of Acre by the new pope, Honorius III, in order to prepare the land for the crusade. The first European arrivals were the Hungarians under Andrew II

[10] On the preparations for the Fifth Crusade, see above, chapter XI, pp. 377–388.

and the Austrians under Leopold VI. Others followed slowly. At a general council at Acre held in October 1217 the Syrian and Cypriote barons and the crusaders jointly agreed to attack the strong new Moslem castle on Mt. Tabor, but the affair degenerated into a large raid. The armies took Baisan, looted across the Jordan, returned, and then unsuccessfully besieged Mt. Tabor (November 29–December 7).[11]

Thereafter the Christians decided on the strategy which was to be followed in most of the later crusades. They would concentrate on capturing an important commercial city in Egypt, in this case Damietta on the Nile, and then exchange it for Jerusalem and Palestine. The Syrian Franks now built fortresses at Caesarea and Château Pèlerin between Caesarea and Acre. The latter was to be garrisoned by Templars, and was the most important gain to Jerusalem from the Fifth Crusade. Then the main body of the crusade, accompanied by most of the Syrian and Cypriote forces, left Acre on May 27, 1218. They left a moderately strong garrison, headed by 500 knights, to defend Acre. In August the Franks near Acre escaped an ambush by al-Mu'aẓẓam. The Moslem leader then took his troops to Caesarea, which called on Acre for aid. Acre sent some ships, but advised that the castle be abandoned. The garrison left secretly, and Moslem forces destroyed the castle. A further siege of Château Pèlerin was abandoned when al-Mu'aẓẓam was called to aid his brother al-Kāmil in Egypt. Before leaving he followed his father's advice and dismantled most of his best fortresses in Syria: Mt. Tabor, Toron, Safad, and Jerusalem. Kerak alone escaped. The Moslem leaders hoped that when news of such action reached the crusaders they would return, make a pilgrimage to Jerusalem, and then go back to Europe. The walls of Jerusalem began to fall on March 19, 1219.

In Egypt, instead of taking advantage of the death of al-'Ādil Saif-ad-Dīn on August 31, 1218, the Christians allowed a stalemate to develop before Damietta. John of Brienne, previously elected to lead the crusade, found his authority questioned and nullified by Pelagius, the papal legate. Disgusted, John left the forces in Egypt on the pretext of claiming Armenia in the name of his wife Rita, daughter of Leon of Armenia, who had died on May 2, 1219.[12] John was rejected by the Armenians; upon his return to Acre, Rita died. When he returned to Damietta, which the crusaders had meanwhile taken, and opposed Pelagius's plan of marching on Cairo, he

[11] For details see above, chapter XI, pp. 388–394.
[12] Röhricht, *Geschichte des Königreichs Jerusalem*, p. 741.

was ignored. Defeat followed, but al-Kāmil agreed to return all prisoners. The treaty was to last until 1229 and to be on the same terms as the treaty which had expired in 1210.

This crusade had brought Bohemond IV of Antioch into closer relationship with the kingdom. While Raymond Roupen was proving incompetent in Antioch, Bohemond was free to act in the south. He was on excellent terms with the crusaders in 1217, and allied himself with Cyprus in 1218 by marrying Melisend, sister of Hugh. His suspect alliance with Aleppo definitely ended in 1216 at aẓ-Ẓāhir's death, and he fought the Moslems in 1218 when they raided Tripoli. This helped him gain Frankish support when Antioch rose against Raymond Roupen. The plot to reinstate Bohemond IV was led by William Farabel (1219). Antioch sent for its old prince while Raymond first sought refuge in the citadel, only to leave it to the Hospitallers and flee to Cilicia. There he found Leon still unwilling to forgive him, although on his deathbed. Raymond Roupen then went to Damietta, where he was protected by Pelagius in the name of Honorius III. There was no resistance to Bohemond IV when he appeared in his old city, and he remained prince of Antioch until his death. This long struggle over the succession of Antioch had divided the Christians, and had weakened Christianity in Syria, while the Armenians could not prevent the Selchükids of Rūm from taking the whole of western Cilicia.

Armenia was further disrupted by its own war of succession, which followed Leon's death in 1219. Leon had designated as his heiress Isabel, his five-year-old daughter by his marriage to Sibyl of Lusignan. Her claim was contested by Raymond Roupen and by John of Brienne. Raymond had the better claim: Leon had begun his reign nominally as regent for Alice, Raymond's mother, and he had long been considered Leon's heir. John's claim was based on his marriage to Leon's older daughter Rita, as we have just noted. John was forced to abandon his claim, however, with her death and that of their young son. Raymond Roupen approached the crusaders at Damietta in 1219 for support in claiming Armenia, and was able to return in 1221 with some of them and promises from Pelagius. Meanwhile in Armenia the first regent, Adam of Gaston (Baghrās), had been assassinated and Constantine of Lampron, founder of the powerful Heṭoumid house, ruled in his stead. Raymond Roupen found some Armenian support in and around Tarsus, notably from Ṿahram, castellan of Corycus, who insisted upon marrying princess Alice. Together they conquered from Tarsus to Adana, then met reverses. Forced to retire to Tarsus, they called on Pelagius and the Hospitallers at Damietta, but reinforcements arrived too late. The people of Tarsus opened the gates to Constantine of Lampron; Raymond Roupen was captured and ended his days in prison in 1222.[13]

Armenia, weakened by wars and in need of a strong ally, found a temporary solution in a tie with Antioch. Philip, the young son of Bohemond IV, agreed to adopt the Armenian faith, communion, and customs and to respect the privileges of all nations in Armenia. In June 1222 Philip married Leon's small heiress, Isabel, at Sis, and was accepted as prince-consort. His first action was to halt, with Bohemond's aid, a Selchükid attack in the west.

But Philip surrounded himself with Franks, introduced Latin customs, and showed disdain for the Armenians. When it was rumored that he wanted to give the crown and throne to Antioch, Constantine of Lampron led a revolt (at the end of 1224). Philip and Isabel were seized at Tall Ḥamdūn on their way to Antioch, and taken back to Sis, where Philip was imprisoned. His father moved cautiously in an attempt to save the young man's life, even trying humble negotiations, but Constantine knew Antioch's military strength was not enough for an immediate attack, so refused to return the prince. Philip was poisoned in prison, probably at the beginning of 1225. Bohemond, in anger, determined on war, although such a conflict had been expressly forbidden by the pope as harmful to all Christendom. He called in as ally the sultan at Iconium, 'Alā'-ad-Dīn Kai-Qobād I, and ravaged upper Cilicia in 1225. Constantine of Lampron reversed the former alliance by bringing in Aleppo as well as the Hospitallers and Teutonic Knights. When Aleppo attacked Baghrās, Bohemond had to return to his own lands. There was uneasy peace during the rest of his reign.

John of Brienne hoped to find his daughter, the heiress Isabel, a husband who would contribute men and supplies to Jerusalem, but would leave control of affairs in John's hands. In October 1222, leaving Odo of Montbéliard as bailie, and accompanied by the patriarch Ralph and the master of the Hospital, Garin of Montaigu, John traveled to Italy. In Apulia he met emperor Frederick II, and arranged for the latter's marriage to Isabel. Frederick had professed himself a crusader since his coronation in 1215[14] and, as the husband of the heiress to Jerusalem, would have an additional

[13] Röhricht, *Geschichte des Königreichs Jerusalem*, pp. 741–742.

[14] See above, chapter XII, pp. 430–438. John of Brienne's daughter Isabel is sometimes called Yolanda.

personal interest in helping to rehabilitate the kingdom. But Frederick was not the man to leave the actual power to John. In Rome, John asked pope Honorius III's consent to the contemplated union, and seems to have agreed to conclude his regency in 1226 when Isabel would be fifteen years of age. In 1223, when John left Italy for France and Spain, where he married Berengaria of Castile (1224), he asked Hermann of Salza, master of the Teutonic Knights, to conclude arrangements for Isabel's marriage, expecting to remain as king of Jerusalem while he lived, with Frederick and Isabel to succeed him on the throne.

Hermann of Salza was a loyal servitor of the German empire, however, and drew up the contract to the effect that Frederick and Isabel were to rule in their own names as soon as they were married. In 1225, at thirteen, Isabel was married by proxy in Acre, crowned at Tyre, and escorted overseas to Brindisi where, on November 9, she was married to Frederick in person and crowned Roman empress and queen of Sicily.

Once the ceremony was concluded, Frederick demanded that he be put in possession of the kingdom of Jerusalem and receive the homage of the Syrian barons. Helpless because his interests had not been safeguarded in the contract, John had to surrender the bailliage and regency of Jerusalem to the queen's husband, who, however, had to comply with the law of the land and appear within a year and a day to claim his rights. Balian of Sidon and other Jerusalemite barons in Italy gave their oaths of homage to Frederick, who then sent Richer, bishop of Melfi, to Syria to receive the homage of the rest. With him went 300 knights as escort and as a garrison in Syria in Frederick's name. For the moment Odo of Montbéliard continued as bailie, but in 1226 Frederick appointed Thomas of Acerra, a devoted servant of the Hohenstaufen ruler. With Frederick absorbed in imperial affairs, Jerusalem was to be ruled by his lieutenants, and the kingdom was therefore unable to act in its own interests even when the Moslems were divided.

Early contingents of crusaders left the west in 1226; and during 1227 Germans under the command of Thomas of Acerra and Henry of Limburg, and Frenchmen and Englishmen under bishops William of Exeter and Peter of Winchester arrived at Acre. They joined the forces of the kingdom in fortifying Caesarea, Jaffa, and other coastal towns. In Sidon, they forced the Moslems of Damascus from the part of the town they held, and fortified the small island of Qal'at al-Baḥr, which controlled the harbor. The Germans rebuilt Montfort, northeast of Acre, for the Teutonic Knights, who called it Starkenburg. Meanwhile Frederick himself had been drawn into his celebrated correspondence with al-Kāmil, and had received at least a general promise of Jerusalem in exchange for an undertaking to direct the onslaught against al-Mu'aẓẓam, al-Kāmil's brother and rival in Syria.[15] The final delays caused by Frederick's illness, however, prevented him from taking full advantage of the divisions among the Aiyūbids, as al-Mu'aẓẓam died before Frederick's forces could reach the east.

The diplomatic approach to the conquest of Jerusalem distressed the crusaders and the Syrian Latins even before the emperor himself arrived. Richard Filangieri, Frederick's marshal, who reached the east in the spring of 1228 with an advance party of 500, punished a group of knights for raiding Moslem territory, and returned the booty they had taken. He also repeatedly rode out of Acre and — so the crusaders said — consulted secretly with envoys from al-Kāmil. Knowing nothing of the previous negotiations, the crusaders complained to the pope, and charged Frederick's agents with being evil bailies. Frederick's own departure (June 28, 1228), undertaken after Gregory IX had excommunicated him, only added to the tensions and the frictions among the Christians in the east. At the first port of call — Cyprus — came Frederick's violent quarrel with John of Ibelin, essentially a head-on conflict between the imperial interpretation of Frederick's powers and the traditional feudal role of the Jerusalemite king.[16]

John of Ibelin was willing to do homage to Frederick as the king of Jerusalem and to serve him for the fief of Beirut, which he held from the king. But Frederick demanded the immediate surrender of Beirut, claiming it to be part of the royal domain. In fact the imperial view was that Jerusalem was now part of the empire and subject to Roman imperial law. By the law of Jerusalem, however, a liegeman was protected in his possession of a fief against the arbitrary exactions of the king. It was stipulated, without question, that a liegeman could be disseised of his fief only by action of the high court of Jerusalem. Frederick tried to ride roughshod over the feudal limitations upon his powers as king of Jerusalem. Ibelin claimed to hold Beirut as a fief from his half-sister Isabel and her husband Aimery. He had fortified it and defended it himself. If the emperor thought he held it wrongly, he would give reason and right before the court of the kingdom of Jerusalem in Acre. Frederick replied with a show of force, and an uneasy peace was

[15] For a full account, see above, chapter XII, pp. 448–449.
[16] See below, chapter XVII, pp. 610–612.

established only by the call of the crusade. Disturbed by reports of papal armies under John of Brienne in his Italian territories, Frederick agreed to accept the decision of the high court of Acre.

Other barons in the east soon took sides. Bohemond IV had received an embassy from Frederick in 1227, and readily sympathized with a fellow-excommunicate. Tripoli, Bohemond's favorite possession, was already pro-imperial and anti-Ibelin, especially since the marriage of his son, Bohemond, with Alice of Cyprus. Alice was thwarted by her Ibelin bailies in Cyprus, who would not allow her new husband to replace them. Tripoli thus became a center of refuge for the anti-Ibelin faction. With Guy Embriaco of Gibelet (Jubail) and Balian of Sidon, Bohemond IV went to Cyprus to greet Frederick, not as a liegeman, because Antioch was held of Constantinople and not of Jerusalem, but as a tentative ally. In the midst of his quarrel with the Ibelins, Frederick abruptly demanded of Bohemond an oath of homage for both Tripoli and Antioch. The frightened prince feigned mental and physical illness and fled to Nephin, where he immediately recovered. Frederick could not insist, at a time when he needed a show of unity among the Franks during his negotiations with al-Kāmil. He persuaded Bohemond to appear with him at Acre in 1229, although misunderstanding probably continued between them, and Bohemond's territories were pointedly excluded from the later peace with Egypt.

Most of the Syrian and Cypriote barons landed with Frederick and the imperial forces at Acre on September 7, 1228. There they found the annual pilgrims ready to embark for Europe, but the emperor persuaded many to remain in the interest of the crusade. Most of the barons accepted his position as regent for his infant son Conrad (Isabel had died in early May 1228),[17] and Balian of Sidon and Odo of Montbéliard surrendered the bailliage. Because of his excommunication, however, the clergy and the military orders, except the Teutonic Knights, refused to obey Frederick. Although the Templars and the Hospitallers rode parallel to his forces, they would not place themselves under his authority; the population as a whole, lately enthusiastic, turned against him when Franciscan friars spread the news of his status.

With such divided forces the crusade had no hope of attaining any measure of success through military action alone. But negotiations with al-Kāmil culminated in the treaty of Jaffa (February 18,

[17] Frederick's son Conrad was born on April 25, 1228, and his wife Isabel died on May 4; for further details, see Röhricht, *Königreich Jerusalem*, p. 769.

1229) to last for ten and a half years, really a personal pact between the emperor and the sultan, enforceable by their good will. Frederick gained the city and surroundings of Jerusalem, although the Moslems retained important rights within the city and it was not to be refortified.[18] Besides the states of Antioch and Tripoli, several of the most important strongholds of the Templars and Hospitallers were specifically omitted from the agreement, with the provision that the emperor would prevent his subjects from aiding the lords of these lands against the sultan. The treaty contrasted greatly with all earlier ones, which had been made in the interests of the kingdom as a whole. The kingdom, with the exception of areas held by certain rebellious emirs, was now almost as large as it had been before Saladin. But the treaty proved especially unacceptable to the Christian clergy and the military orders, except for the Teutonic Knights. The war would be continued around the great fortresses of the Templars and Hospitallers.

On March 17 Frederick entered a Jerusalem free of Moslems save in the Temple. With the ban of excommunication still upon him, the emperor crowned himself the next day in the church of the Holy Sepulcher. Most of the Syrian barons had been ordered back to Acre by the patriarch Gerald, and on March 19 the prelate sent an emissary, archbishop Peter of Caesarea, to place the Temple and holy places of Jerusalem under an interdict while Moslem or emperor remained there. To Frederick such action meant little; his interest in Jerusalem waned rapidly with success, and he was in haste to return to the pressing problems that confronted him in Europe. He made rapid and sketchy plans to reinforce the city's defenses, giving the king's house before the Tower of David to the Teutonic Knights, and then left abruptly. Odo of Montbéliard, constable of the kingdom, remained in Jerusalem for a short time with a token garrison, but was soon replaced by an imperial bailie.

The emperor remained a turbulent month in Acre, seemingly intent on forcing the Syrian Franks into the mold of his empire. The previous difficulties on Cyprus and the open antagonism of the clergy and friars made an understanding between imperial and baronial forces impossible. Instead, there developed an extension of the Guelf-Ghibelline struggle in the Levant. Frederick placed most of the blame for his trouble in Acre on the patriarch, the Templars, who had refused to surrender Château Pèlerin to imperial forces, and the Ibelins. He closed the gates of Acre early in April, and put guards around the houses of the Templars and the patriarch.

[18] But see above, chapter XII, pp. 455–456.

When friars preached against him on Palm Sunday, April 8, 1229, they were pursued. But attempts to capture the houses of the Templars, their master, and John of Ibelin ended in failure, and the episode served only to alienate most of the remnants of Syrian sympathy for Frederick.

On May 1, 1229, Frederick left for his troubled Italian territories, which papal armies under John of Brienne had successfully invaded. In the high court of Acre, before departing, he conferred the bailliage of Jerusalem on Balian of Sidon and Warner the German, later replaced by Odo of Montbéliard. Then he arranged to sell the bailliage of Cyprus to enemies of the Ibelins, left a strong imperial garrison in Acre, and sailed, to the jeers and catcalls of the population. He never returned, nor did his heirs Conrad and Conradin ever appear among their people.

If Frederick's crusade represented a diplomatic victory, it was also a moral disaster for an excommunicate to have won back the holy city, which symbolized so much for the kingdom. By importing into the Levant the imperial absolutistic onslaught on local custom and autonomy, he made Syrian unity impossible. The bitter division was seen at once in the varying attitudes of the Syrians toward the treaty of Jaffa and toward the imperialists. The Templars were openly hostile toward both; barons and imperialists had already joined battle over the Ibelin case, which had never — as Frederick had promised — been presented before the high court. No general policy for the welfare of the kingdom could be established; nobody was capable of enforcing one. The barons found it impossible even to take advantage of the new treaty. Aiyūbid Islam recovered from its civil wars, but Jerusalem's leadership continued divided, and the territory regained by Frederick was not protected.

The first serious raid on the city of Jerusalem was made in 1229 by a mass of unorganized beduins, plunderers of pilgrims from Jaffa to Jerusalem. The few Christian guards retreated to the Tower of David while the governor, Reginald of Haifa, called on Acre for aid. An advance guard reached Bethlehem in two days, thus encouraging the Christians to emerge and expel the Moslems. The Christians, however, even after this scare, left Jerusalem almost undefended for another ten years, when it was easily taken by an-Nāṣir Dā'ūd of Transjordania. Frederick used the raid as an excuse to send to the east reinforcements, which were diverted to the imperialist war in Jerusalem and Cyprus.

Frederick's supporters and his enemies carried on the contest by legal and diplomatic as well as military means. The anti-imperialists sought, for instance, to deprive Frederick of the title king of Jerusalem, which he used as regent for Conrad. In 1229 they persuaded Alice of Cyprus to advance her claim to the throne as the daughter of Isabel and Henry of Champagne, and therefore the closest living heir of king Amalric. Her lawyers challenged Conrad's claim, since he had not appeared in the realm within the required year and a day. The high court, not yet ready to renounce the Hohenstaufens, temporized, but the issue remained alive. An embassy reached Frederick at Foggia in May 1230, asking that Conrad appear in Acre as soon as possible, but was answered with vague promises. However, the imperial bailies ruled efficiently and maintained imperial prestige.

The year 1230 also saw small, bitter campaigns in the areas not covered by the treaty. The Hospitallers of Krak des Chevaliers allied themselves with the Moslems of Damascus against al-Kāmil, and with their tributaries, the Assassins, against Bohemond IV. They raided Ba'rīn, the only stronghold left to Dā'ūd. They joined with the Templars of Tortosa only to be defeated in attacking Hamah, but continued to raid Jabala, Aleppo, and the area around al-Marqab until they finally made peace in the late spring of 1231. In its efforts to regain lost lands in Tripoli and Antioch, the order persuaded Gregory IX to publish the excommunication of its ancient enemy, Bohemond IV, in March 1230. The pope gave the patriarch Gerald the right to lift the ban if Bohemond proved repentant, a state of mind which Gerald tried to induce, as did the Ibelins, with whom Bohemond was then friendly. Gregory IX wished, moreover, to settle these disputes among the Christians in the east, having now reached an understanding with Frederick. Bohemond himself, who was aging and wanted to die in the fold, signed a treaty with the Hospitallers (October 26, 1231) in which the latter renounced all the privileges granted to their order by Raymond Roupen, and recognized Bohemond's feudal rights. In return they retained Jabala and Château de la Vieille and were granted two large money fiefs in Tripoli and Antioch. Bohemond was finally recognized by the church as prince of Antioch, and was granted absolution.

During the next decade central authority virtually collapsed, in the absence of a king and with the "imperialist" or "Lombard" war continuing. Supporting Frederick's cause were western troops under the imperial agents the Filangieri brothers, the Teutonic Knights, several Jerusalemite barons, and the Pisans. The imperialist forces held Tyre and Sidon. Their opponents included the Ibelins, supported by the majority of the baronage of Jerusalem and Cyprus, forty-three major lords in all, king Henry of Cyprus, the commune of Acre, and the Genoese. They held Cyprus, Acre, and Beirut. A third group, composed of the Templars, the Hospitallers, the Venetians, and certain barons such as Odo of Montbéliard and Balian of Sidon, together with many of the clergy, originally took a position between the two extremes and strove to keep the peace, but eventually were driven to join the Ibelins.

In June 1230 the first stage of the war ended in a year's truce when Frederick's bailies in Cyprus were defeated. The emperor was unable to supply assistance until a Ghibelline victory in Italy, marked by the treaty of San Germano (July 9, 1230), put an end to his excommunication, terminated the interdict on Jerusalem, and forced all in Syria to submit to the treaty of Jaffa. Preparing to establish his rule firmly in Syria and suppress opposition, Frederick ordered the confiscation of the lands of the Ibelin leaders, including John of Beirut and his nephews, John (later count of Jaffa) and John of Caesarea. To effect this a sizable expedition sailed for the Levant under Richard Filangieri, imperial bailie for the kingdom of Jerusalem and imperial legate in the Levant. He found Ibelin forces massed on Cyprus, and therefore went on to besiege Beirut, where the lower city was surrendered by the bishop.[19] The fortress now underwent a long siege under the direction of Filangieri's brother Lothair, while Filangieri went on to accept the surrender of Tyre, which he placed under another brother, Henry.

In 1231 Filangieri presented his credentials before the high court of Acre and was accepted. But his siege of Beirut had violated the law that a vassal's fief could be declared forfeit only by action of the high court of Jerusalem, and not by the mere will of the king. Although anxious for peace, many barons were alienated by the siege, and protested vehemently. Balian of Sidon stated the barons' position — the kings of Jerusalem, including Frederick, had always sworn to observe the assizes and usages of the kingdom, which included of course the law in question. Ibelin had offered to prove his case before the high court, but had been disseised with no semblance of a trial. As loyal lieges of the realm, the barons would assist in punishing Ibelin if the court should decide against him, but until such a decision they could not permit the bailie's action. Balian asked that Beirut be returned to Ibelin, and that Filangieri

[19] Probably Galeran, known to be bishop by 1233; J. LaMonte, notes to Philip of Novara, *The Wars of Frederick II against the Ibelins*, p. 121, note 1, citing Eubel, *Hierarchia Catholica*.

then bring the case for Frederick before the high court. Such a strong protest showed a growing belief among the baronial class that it represented the real strength of the kingdom when the king was a non-resident foreigner. Filangieri promised to consider the plea, but continued the siege and clearly intended to obey only Frederick's orders. He told baronial representatives who appeared at Beirut that the emperor's wishes would be observed; if the barons wished to appeal the case they should send an embassy to Italy. It was the failure of that embassy in the winter of 1231 that now threw the moderate party to the Ibelins.

The new commune of Acre, growing from the old brotherhood of St. Andrew, now became a base of anti-Ghibelline activity. Knights, bourgeois, and citizens, loyal to the Ibelins, formed an association against the imperialists, and asked instructions from John of Ibelin in Cyprus. Their professed purpose was to guard the rights and liberties of the kingdom, acting legally as an autonomous commune similar to those of Lombardy and Tuscany. The commune finally offered the mayoralty to Ibelin, who arrived in Acre in April 1232 and received the communal oath. The next act of the sworn association or commune was to seize the imperial fleet in the harbor. Before the establishment of the commune, the Ibelin cause had been waning. Leaders of the church and military orders had favored Frederick, but their efforts at mediation failed, as did those of Venice, Genoa, and Pisa. The Ibelins withstood Filangieri, reinforced the citadel of Beirut, and created a diversion by attacking Tyre. Followed by Ibelin's forces and the Genoese fleet, the imperialists hastened to protect their base. At Casal Imbert the imperialists turned, surprised the Ibelins, and defeated them. Only reinforcements from Acre saved them from complete disaster. The main campaign then shifted to Cyprus, where by April 1233 the Ibelins had won, while the imperialists still held only Tyre on the mainland. Filangieri tried desperately but without success to get aid from Armenia, Antioch, and Tripoli. Even his appeals to Frederick failed.

The Ibelins also tried to gain Antioch's help, offering a marriage alliance and great fiefs in Cyprus. But the defeat at Casal Imbert rendered these proposals unattractive to Bohemond, who nonetheless did not ally himself with Filangieri. Bohemond's death early in 1233 removed him from any further part in the Lombard war. By his long and active rule he had proved himself a capable prince of Antioch — the last in fact — subtle, without scruple, often violent, but withal one of the great Syrian jurists.

Bohemond V inherited an Antioch impoverished by wars, open to Moslem incursion, deserted by commerce, and isolated from Tripoli and the kingdom by Moslem Latakia. By contrast, his county of Tripoli was, as a neighbor of the kingdom, flourishing, with a prosperous port and excellent defenses. He also found the north virtually controlled by the military orders, in whose wars and raids he had to participate. With the Hospitallers and Templars he was defeated in 1233 by al-Muẓaffar Taqī-ad-Dīn II of Hamah, who owed revenues to Krak des Chevaliers. Christian support came from Jerusalem and Cyprus in October. A great coalition of Moslem forces had assembled to attack the Selchükids in Iconium (Konya),[20] and, to be free of Christian annoyance, al-Kāmil told Taqī-ad-Dīn to pay his debt and make peace. Bohemond V also joined the Templars against the Armenians, who raided Baghrās and killed some members of the order. Heṭoum avoided war by yielding, and Bohemond agreed reluctantly; he would have liked to avenge his brother Philip. The Templars fought the Moslems of Aleppo over Darbsāk, and Baghrās was saved only by the intervention of Bohemond. In 1237 the order made its last great effort against Aleppo, but was so badly defeated that thereafter it remained at peace with that Moslem state for many years.

Bohemond V followed the general policies of his father; he modified only slightly the anticlericalism, usually having minor troubles with the church and orders, and he tried to maintain the old neutrality with the south. In 1243 he gave refuge but no aid to Lothair Filangieri. However, Antioch was prevented from regaining importance in Syrian politics when Bohemond and his men took part in the Frankish-Syrian coalition which was destroyed at Gaza in 1244. This was catastrophic for the chivalry of Antioch and Tripoli at the moment when the two states needed all their defenders.

With Tyre alone of the great cities loyal to Frederick, while an imperial governor still ruled the city of Jerusalem, Frederick tried vainly to win back the barons (in 1232–1233). He offered to appoint as bailie a Syrian baron, Philip of Maugastel, and to pardon the Ibelins, and asked only the dissolution of the commune of Acre. All proposals were rejected amid scenes of riot in Acre. The high court then decided that Balian of Sidon and Odo of Montbéliard were the true bailies, having been appointed by Frederick in person before the court. No appointment by letter was deemed valid; thus only Conrad, before the high court, could make a new appointment.

[20] See below, chapter XIX, p. 684.

This continued suspicion of Frederick was eventually to prove costly to Syria, which lost the protection of his prestige when the barons were not strong enough to furnish adequate protection.

In 1234, at the request of the high court, Hermann of Salza, ignoring the military defeats suffered by the imperialists, proposed a settlement restating the imperial position, and adding only a vague commitment that Frederick and Conrad should observe the ancient laws of the kingdom. The draft was directed principally toward the moderates and was approved by pope Gregory IX, now reconciled with Frederick. Necessity forced pope Gregory IX to cite John of Ibelin as treasonous and rebellious (1235). Gregory sent a legate, archbishop Theodoric of Ravenna, who placed an interdict on the traditionally Guelf city of Acre for refusing to dissolve its commune. Although Gregory instantly countermanded the order, he failed to placate the Syrians. By 1237, when Gregory had once more broken with Frederick, he abandoned his vain effort to force a compromise between imperial absolutism and Jerusalemite feudal principles, and he promised his support to the baronial cause. In advising the Ibelins to continue their course, he stressed the usefulness of a close union between Jerusalem and Cyprus against the emperor and the Moslems.

John of Ibelin had died in 1236. Besides defending baronial rights against imperial aggression, he had stressed baronial responsibilities, and had for a while checked anarchy. With him died much of his party's spirit, although leadership devolved upon his son Balian and Philip of Montfort. Frederick was too occupied in the west to attempt to recapture authority in Syria just then. The Latin orient was left without definite central or political authority, and the uneasy truce between the barons and Filangieri revealed the impotence of both groups. Jerusalem had now two bailies within the kingdom: Filangieri considered himself the only imperial representative and ruled in Tyre, while Odo of Montbéliard governed in Acre as bailie for Conrad with the support of the high court.

When the treaty of Jaffa expired in 1239, several European expeditions, notably those of Theobald of Champagne and Richard of Cornwall, arrived to engage in another crusade,[21] hopeful of the opportunity offered by the death of al-Kāmil in March 1238. His son al-'Ādil II severed Frankish-Aiyūbid relations before he was deposed in June 1240 in favor of his brother, aṣ-Ṣāliḥ Aiyūb.

[21] See above, chapter XIII.

Theobald of Champagne arrived in 1239 to find the Templars leading a faction that supported the Moslems at Damascus against those of Egypt, and the Hospitallers supporting the Egyptians. The Moslems overran the city of Jerusalem, whose small garrison was permitted to evacuate under a safe-conduct. One party of crusaders fell into an Egyptian trap at Gaza, where many were killed or captured. Theobald and his remaining troops retreated to Acre, where he finally accepted an offer from Damascus of all the old kingdom west of the Jordan in return for Frankish protection of the southern frontier of Palestine. The treaty met with opposition from some Damascenes as well as from the Hospitallers, who preferred an agreement with Egypt to release the captives taken at Gaza. Before leaving the Holy Land in September 1240, Theobald concluded just such a peace with Egypt, but made no arrangements for its enforcement. The unpopular Theobald's departure took place just fifteen days before the arrival of Richard of Cornwall on October 8.

Before deciding on a Moslem alliance, Richard of Cornwall helped refortify Ascalon and Jaffa, giving the former to Walter Pennenpié, imperial governor of Jerusalem. Then, advised by duke Hugh of Burgundy, count Walter of Jaffa, and the Hospitallers, he signed the treaty with Egypt, after aṣ-Ṣāliḥ had agreed to make good the territorial promises of Damascus. Thereupon prisoners were finally exchanged. On paper, at least, the old kingdom was reconstituted except for parts of Nablus and of Hebron and all of Transjordania. But appearances were deceptive; intensified divisions were at work within the country, although Richard temporarily strengthened the imperial position and prestige in Syria because of his wisdom and justice. At all times he acted as a friend of Frederick. Inasmuch as aṣ-Ṣāliḥ had also shown his wish to continue his father's friendship with the emperor, by acting so generously toward Jerusalem, there was now a chance for peace between the barons and the emperor. Richard secured the submission of the Ibelin leaders, who agreed to accept Frederick's rule if he would appoint Simon of Montfort, earl of Leicester, as bailie of Jerusalem until Conrad was of age and came to receive his kingdom. When Richard left on May 3, 1241, it seemed that the old kingdom was virtually restored and peace assured. Instead the Franks ignored the great territorial gains and drifted into a new phase of the struggle with the empire, which was to end with a definite rejection of Frederick's regency and the loss of any real central authority.

While waiting for Frederick's answer to Richard's proposals, the barons kept in reserve Alice of Champagne's claim to the throne. Filangieri stayed in Tyre; the baronial leaders dispersed to attend to neglected fiefs on the mainland and in Cyprus; and Acre was left to the leadership of Philip of Montfort, a nephew of John of Ibelin, the "old lord" of Beirut. Philip had arrived with Theobald, and had married Mary, daughter of Raymond Roupen and heiress of the rich seignory of Toron, close to Tyre. The calm was broken when the Templars, dissatisfied with the Hospitaller-inspired Egyptian treaty, besieged the Hospitallers in Acre in 1241, and then raided in Hebron. Dā'ūd of Transjordania answered by attacking Christian pilgrims and merchants. Then on October 30, 1242, the Templars sacked Nablus, burned the mosque, and let not even native Christians escape. This brought 2,000 troops from Egypt to join Dā'ūd at Gaza for a brief action against the Templars. Many Moslems were not unreasonably convinced that peace with the Franks was impossible.

Among the Latins internal strife continued. At Acre the commune permitted the Templars to besiege the house of the Hospitallers, some of whom now joined with Richard Filangieri and several bourgeois of Acre in a conspiracy to surrender the city to the imperialists. But Filangieri was surprised incognito in Acre; the plot was revealed, and swift action by Philip of Montfort, the citizens, the Genoese, and the Venetians kept Acre out of imperial hands. Filangieri escaped, while baronial forces besieged the few Hospitallers in the place. Most of the Hospitallers were at al-Marqab for a local war with Aleppo, and when the master disavowed the plot and all in it, the barons lifted the siege. The episode reinforced Ibelin control over Acre, a strong Guelf commune. Filangieri was recalled to Italy.

Tyre was left under Lothair Filangieri. When the *pullani* (half-castes) of the city asked the barons to help them drive out the imperialists, the barons decided to act. They had the support of Marsiglio Giorgio, the new Venetian bailie, who resented Filangieri's acquisition of some Venetian possessions in Tyre. Instead of attacking Tyre, the barons adopted the more subtle plan of Philip of Novara, outstanding legist, who suggested how they could gain the city legally. On April 25, 1243, he pointed out, Conrad would come of age, Frederick's regency would end, and Filangieri would have no legal position in Jerusalem. In accepting Philip's plan, the barons also revived the claims of Alice, lately married to Ralph of Nesle, a rather poor knight who had come to the east on Theobald's crusade. Philip of Novara successfully presented her petition, arguing that, as the nearest heir present in the country, she and her husband should be bailies. Her first act was to demand the surrender of the city and castle of Tyre, a demand naturally refused by the imperialists. The barons then completed negotiations with the citizens and were able to take the city, while Lothair and his men held the citadel. This they lost when Richard Filangieri, forced back by storms, sailed unsuspectingly into the harbor and was captured by the barons. Lothair surrendered the citadel to save his brother. With the fall of Tyre, on July 10, 1243, the barons were at last completely victorious. Imperial rule in Jerusalem was ended, and the central Jerusalemite monarchy received a blow from which it never recovered.

Alice and her husband Ralph were in an ambiguous position. They had the title of bailies, but no power. Power belonged to the barons, who refused to release to the new bailies any cities, especially Tyre, on the ground that, during a regency, authority should reside in the lieges, who were subject only to the high court. In reality, it seems that Philip of Montfort wanted possession of Tyre to round out his wife's territory of Toron. When he installed himself in Tyre, Ralph of Nesle left Syria and Alice to return to France, protesting baronial usurpation of his power as bailie. Balian of Ibelin established himself in Acre to complete the superiority of baronial power. As a result, Jerusalem became a sort of feudal republic, lacking real unity or leadership. The baronial victory saved the liberties of the kingdom at the expense of its unity and strength; imperial prestige had gone, rivalries among the diverse factions intensified, and no central authority could act to prevent encirclement by a revived Moslem empire.

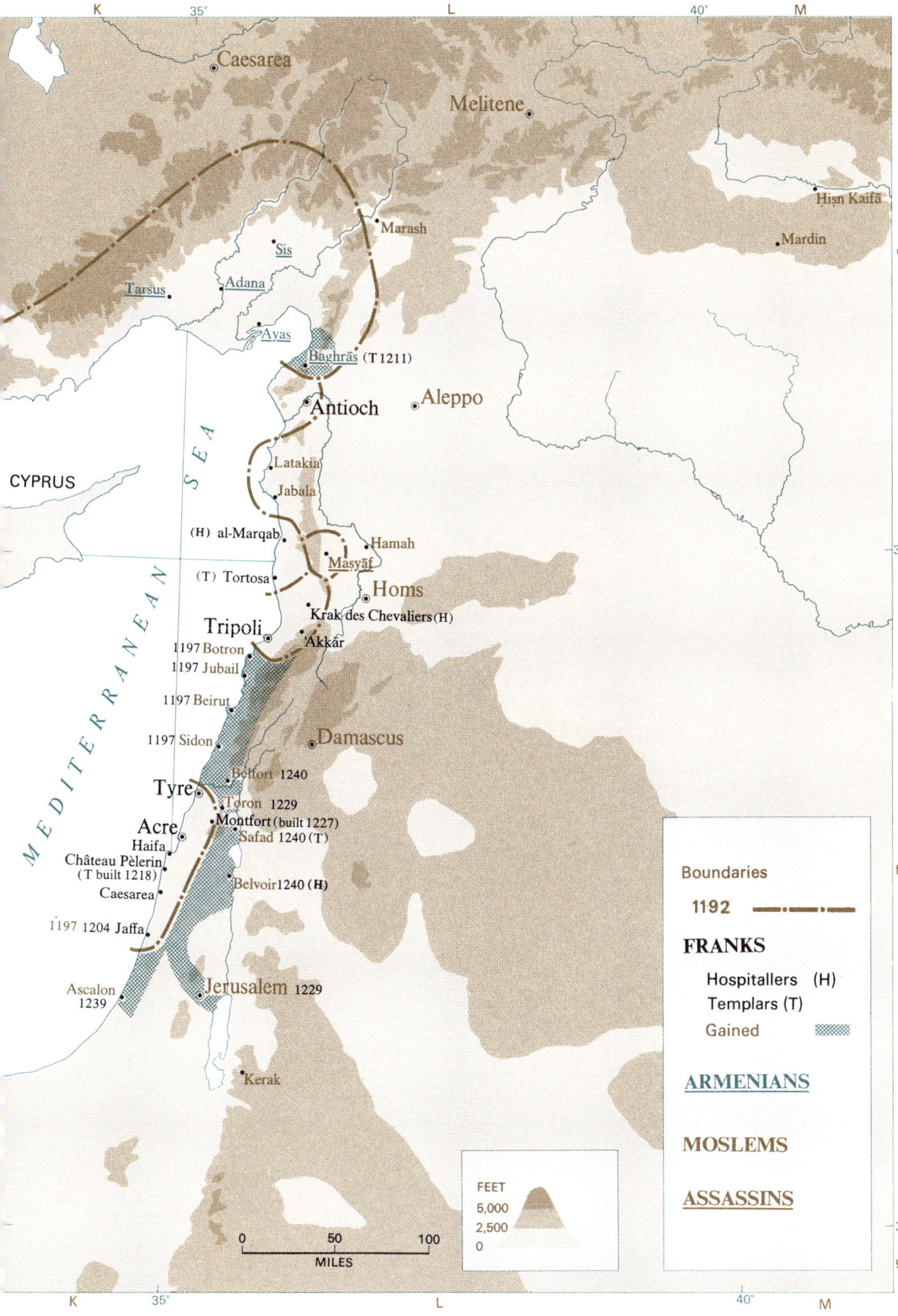

18. The Latin States, 1192–1243 (*Map by the University of Wisconsin Cartographic Laboratory*)

19. The Latin States, 1243–1291 (*Map by the University of Wisconsin Cartographic Laboratory*)

XVI
THE CRUSADER STATES
1243–1291

The attempt of the emperor Frederick II to rule the kingdom of Jerusalem ended with the surrender of Tyre by the brothers Filangieri and their departure from the country. Thenceforward the kingdom was to be governed according to the lawyers' strict interpretation of the constitution, which meant that the land continuously hovered on the edge of anarchy.

The chief collections of relevant sources are: Vincenzo de Bartholomaeis, *Poesie provenzale storiche relativa all' Italia* (*FSI*, LXXI–LXXII, Rome, 1931); J. Bongars, *Gesta Dei per Francos* (2 vols., Hanover, 1611); E. Martène and U. Durand, *Thesaurus novus anecdotorum* (5 vols., Paris, 1717); Martène and Durand, *Veterum scriptorum et monumentorum amplissima collectio* (9 vols., Paris, 1727–1733); Louis de Mas Latrie, *Histoire de l'île de Chypre sous le règne des princes de la maison de Lusignan*, II, III: *Documents et mémoires* (Paris, 1852–1855); Louis de Mas Latrie, "Nouvelles preuves de l'histoire de Chypre," *Bibliothèque de l'École des chartes*, XXXII (1871), 341–378; XXXIV (1873), 47–87; and XXXV (1874), 99–158; J. F. Michaud, *Bibliothèque des croisades*, IV: *Extraits des historiens arabes*, ed. M. Reinaud (Paris, 1829); and G. L. F. Tafel and G. M. Thomas, *Urkunden zur älteren Handels- und Staatsgeschichte der Republik Venedig mit besonderer Beziehung auf Byzanz und die Levante* (Fontes rerum Austriacarum: Österreichische Geschichtsquellen, 2 abt., Diplomataria et acta, XII, XIII, XIV, Vienna, 1856–1857).

Reference should also be made to the papal correspondence published in the second series of the Bibliothèque des Écoles françaises d'Athènes et de Rome, specifically: *Les Registres d'Innocent IV* (ed. Élie Berger, 4 vols., Paris, 1884–1921); *Les Registres d'Alexandre IV* (ed. C. Bourel de la Roncière, J. de Loye, P. de Cenival, and A. Coulon, 3 vols., Paris, 1902–1953); *Les Registres d'Urbain IV* (ed. Jean Guiraud, 4 vols., Paris, 1899–1929); *Les Registres de Clément IV* (ed. Édouard Jordan, 6 fasc., Paris, 1893–1945); *Les Registres de Grégoire X et de Jean XXI* (ed. Jean Guiraud and L. Cadier, 4 fasc., Paris, 1892–1906); *Les Registres de Nicolas III* (ed. Jules Gay [and Suzanne Vitte], 5 fasc., Paris, 1898–1938); *Les Registres de Martin IV* (ed. F. Olivier-Martin *et al.*, 3 fasc., Paris, 1901–1935); *Les Registres d'Honorius IV* (ed. Maurice Prou, Paris, 1886–1888); *Les Registres de Nicolas IV* (ed. Ernest Langlois, 9 fasc., Paris, 1886–1893). See also René de Mas Latrie (ed.), *Chroniques d'Amadi et de Strambaldi* (Collection de documents inédits sur l'histoire de France, 2 vols., Paris, 1891–1893); *Annales Januenses* (*MGH, SS.*, XVIII); *Annales de Terre Sainte* (ed. R. Röhricht [and G. Raynaud], *Archives de l'orient latin*, II [1884], 427–461); *Assises de Jérusalem* (*RHC, Lois*, I, II); Jacobus Auria, *Annales* (*MGH, SS.*, XVIII); Bartholomew of Neocastro, *Historia Sicula* (ed. Giuseppe Paladino, *RISS*, XIII, iii, Milan, 1920); Florio Bustron, *Chronique de l'île de Chypre* (ed. René de Mas Latrie, Paris, 1884); *Chronica de Mailros* (ed. Joseph Stevenson, Bannatyne Club, Edinburgh, 1835); Bartholomew Cotton, *Historia Anglicana* (ed. H. R. Luard, Rolls Series, XVI); Andreas Dandolo, *Chronicon Venetum* (ed. E. Pastorello, *RISS*, XII, 1938 ff.); *De excidio urbis Acchonis* (Martène and Durand, *Veteres scriptores*, V); *Estoire d'Eracles* (*RHC, Occ.*, I, II); *Les Gestes des Chiprois* (*RHC, Arm.*, II, to which all references in this chapter are made; also ed. G. Raynaud, Geneva, 1887); Hetoum ("Hayton"), *La Flor des estoires de la terre d'orient* (*RHC, Arm.*, II); John of Ypres, *Chronicon Sythiense Sancti*

The kingdom of Jerusalem was by 1243 reduced to a narrow strip stretching up the coast from Ascalon to Beirut. Besides the coastal strip it included Jerusalem and Bethlehem, won back by Frederick's treaty of 1229, with a precarious corridor leading up to the holy city from Jaffa. Jerusalem itself, which had already been sacked by the Moslems in 1239, was without defenses, apart from the Tower of David. Farther north, the whole of Galilee had recently been recovered by the diplomacy of Richard of Cornwall. On the north, between Beirut and Jubail the kingdom marched with the county of Tripoli, now ruled by Bohemond V of Antioch. The county comprised the coast-lands as far as Valania and extended inland to the castles of 'Akkār and Krak des Chevaliers, on either side of the plain of the Biqā'. Still farther to the north, and separated from the county by the Moslem ports of Jabala and Latakia and

Bertini (Martène and Durand, *Thesaurus novus anecdotorum*, III); John of Joinville, *Histoire de Saint Louis* (ed. N. de Wailly, Paris, 1874); Joseph de Cancy, letter to Edward I of England, and Edward's reply, tr. Wm. B. Sanders, in Palestine Pilgrims' Text Society, V (London, 1896), 1–16 (at the end of the volume); Bertrandon de la Broquière, *Voyage d'outremer* (ed. C. H. A. Schéfer, Paris, 1892); H. F. Delaborde (ed.), "Lettre des chrétiens de Terre-Sainte à Charles d'Anjou, 22 avril, 1260," *ROL*, II (1894), 206–215; *Lignages d'outremer* (*RHC, Lois*, II); Ludolph of "Suchem" (Sudheim), *Description of the Holy Land and of the Way Thither* (tr. Aubrey Stewart, Palestine Pilgrims' Text Society, XII, London, 1895); Manuscript of Rothelin in *RHC, Occ.*, II; Matthew Paris, *Chronica majora* (ed. H. R. Luard, Rolls Series, LVII); Ramón Muntaner, *Cronica* (ed. Coroleu, Barcelona, 1886); Marino Sanudo (Torsello), *Istoria del regno di Romania* (ed. Charles Hopf, *Chroniques gréco-romanes inédites ou peu connues*, Berlin, 1873, pp. 99–170); Sanudo, *Liber secretorum fidelium crucis* (in Bongars, *Gesta Dei*, II); and Thaddeus of Naples, *Hystoria de desolacione et conculcacione civitatis Acconensis* (ed. Paul Riant, Geneva, 1873).

Among the oriental sources, special note should be made of: Abū-l-Fidā', *Kitāb al-mukhtaṣar* (extracts in *RHC, Or.*, I); Abū-l-Maḥāsin Yūsuf, *An-nujūm az-zāhirah fī mulūk Miṣr wa-l-Qāhirah* (extracts tr. in Michaud, *Bibliothèque*, IV); Abū-Shāmah, *Kitāb ar-rauḍatain* (extracts in *RHC, Or.*, IV, V); Badr-ad-Dīn al-'Ainī, *'Iqd al-jamān* (extracts in *RHC, Or.*, II, 1); *The Chronography of Gregory Abû'l Faraj the Son of Aaron, the Hebrew Physician commonly known as Bar Hebraeus* (ed. and tr. E. A. W. Budge, 2 vols., London, 1932); Ibn-al-Furāt, *Ta'rīkh ad-duwal wa-l-mulūk* (extracts tr. in Michaud, *Bibliothèque*, IV); Ibn-Khallikān, *Wafayāt al-a'yān* . . . (tr. MacG. de Slane, *Biographical Dictionary*, 4 vols., London, 1842–1871); Kamāl-ad-Dīn, *Zubdat al-ḥalab fī ta'rīkh Ḥalab* (tr. E. Blochet [later chapters only], "Chronique de l'Alep," *ROL*, III [1895], 509–565, and VI [1898], 1–49; al-Jazarī, *Ḥawādith az-zamān* (tr. J. Sauvaget, *Chronique de Damas*, Paris, 1949); al-Maqrīzī, *Akhbār Miṣr* (tr. E. Blochet, "Histoire d'Egypte," *ROL*, VIII [1900–1901], 165–212, 501–553; IX [1902], 6–163, 466–530; X [1903–1904], 248–371); al-Maqrīzī, *Al-mawā'iẓ wa-l-i'tibar fī dhikr al-khiṭaṭ wa-l-āthār* (tr. E. M. Quatremère, *Histoire des sultans mamlouks*, 2 vols., Paris, 1837–1845); Muḥī-ad-Dīn, *Sīrat al-malik aẓ-Ẓāhir* (extracts tr. in Michaud, *Bibliothèque*, IV; English translation by S. F. Sadeque, *Baybars I of Egypt* [Karachi et alibi, 1956], pp. 75–239).

In addition to Claude Cahen's *La Syrie du nord à l'époque des croisades et la principauté franque d'Antioche* (Paris, 1940), and Sir George Hill's *A History of Cyprus*, II: *The Frankish Period, 1192–1432* (Cambridge, 1948), mention need be made only of the following: C. L. Kingsford, "Sir Otho de Grandison, 1238?–1328," *Transactions of the Royal Historical Society*, 3rd ser., III (1909), 125–195; R. Röhricht, "Études sur les derniers temps du royaume de Jérusalem," *Archives de l'orient latin*, II (1884); G. Schlumberger, "Prise de Saint-Jean d'Acre en l'an 1291," in *Byzance et croisades: Pages médiévales* (Paris, 1927); and, of course, F. M. Powicke, *King Henry III and the Lord Edward* (2 vols., Oxford, 1947).

the Ismā'īlite strongholds in the Nuṣairī mountains, was the principality of Antioch, which consisted of little more than the plain of Antioch, with an outlet to the sea at St. Simeon.

The lawful king of Jerusalem was the Hohenstaufen Conrad, son of Frederick II and Isabel of Brienne (Yolanda), who had died giving birth to him. Conrad had arrived at his legal majority, at the age of fifteen, on April 25, 1243. This had removed the juridical right of his father, the emperor, to govern in his name and had provided the lawyers of "Outremer" with the occasion for ridding themselves of his nominees. The young king at once sent Thomas of Aquino, count of Acerra, to be his representative; but at a meeting of the high court, held in the patriarch's palace at Acre on June 5, 1243, and attended by all the barons and bishops of the kingdom as well as the officials of the commune of Acre and the presidents of the Venetian and Genoese colonies, the lawyer Philip of Novara argued that homage could not properly be paid to Conrad until he came in person to receive it, and that in the meantime the regency ought to be entrusted to the next available heir to the crown. Odo of Montbéliard, who led the moderate faction amongst the barons, suggested that Conrad should be sent an official invitation to visit his kingdom and that no further action be taken until he replied. But Philip, with the Ibelin family backing him, won his point.[1]

The next heir was Alice, dowager queen of Cyprus, the eldest surviving daughter of queen Isabel I and Henry of Champagne. She and her third husband, Ralph of Nesle, were accepted as regents, and the members of the high court swore allegiance to them, saving king Conrad's rights. As we have seen in the preceding chapter, this action legally entitled them to strip Filangieri of his authority. But when Tyre was recaptured from him, it was not handed over to the regents, as they expected, but was allotted by the high court to Philip of Montfort, lord, in his wife's right, of Toron and son of an Ibelin lady. Ralph of Nesle saw that his regency was intended to be purely nominal, and soon retired to France. Alice remained titular regent until her death in 1246, with her cousin Balian of Ibelin, lord of Beirut, acting as her bailie. When she died, the high court gave the regency to the next heir, her son king Henry I of Cyprus, in spite of a protest from her half-sister Melisend, dowager princess of Antioch, the daughter of queen Isabel I and Aimery of Cyprus, who claimed that, as she was a generation

[1] *Gestes des Chiprois*, 225–226 (*RHC, Arm.*, II), pp. 730–732; *Estoire d'Eracles* (*RHC, Occ.*, II), p. 240; Amadi, *Chronique*, pp. 190–191; *Assises de Jérusalem*, II, 399; Tafel-Thomas, *Urkunden*, II, 351–389, giving an account written by a Venetian eye-witness, Marsiglio Giorgio.

nearer to the absentee king, she ought to have precedence. King Henry retained Balian of Ibelin as his bailie, and confirmed Philip of Montfort in the possession of Tyre.[2] When Balian died in 1247 he was succeeded as bailie by his brother John, lord of Arsuf. King Henry, who was indolent and immensely fat, seldom stirred from his kingdom of Cyprus, leaving the mainland kingdom to govern itself.[3]

The high court was dominated by the great family of Ibelin, whose connections covered the whole lay nobility of Outremer. The head of the house was Balian of Beirut, eldest son of John, the "old lord" of Beirut. His brother John, who succeeded him as bailie, was lord of Arsuf. A cousin, another John, was the leading lawyer in the kingdom, and was soon to acquire the fief of Jaffa. Two younger sons of the "old lord" of Beirut, Baldwin and Guy, were the most prominent nobles in Cyprus. Balian, the late lord of Sidon and Belfort, his half-brother Philip of Montfort, lord of Tyre and Toron, and John, the late lord of Caesarea, were sons of sisters of the "old lord". Odo of Montbéliard was a close relative of Balian of Ibelin's wife Eschiva. Every lay tenant-in-chief was a member of this one clan, which for the moment worked in unison.[4]

There was less unity between the military orders, which now controlled as much of the country as the lay baronage. The Hospital and Temple had come together to oppose Frederick II, but latterly the Hospital had supported Filangieri and advocated Frederick's policy of friendship with Egypt rather than with Damascus, while the Templars, who favored alliance with Damascus, worked in with the Ibelins. The Teutonic Knights tended to back the Hospital against the Temple, but played a smaller part in the politics of the kingdom.

The quarrels between the orders were parallelled by the quarrels between the Italian commercial colonies, whose power had been enhanced by the years of comparative peace that had followed the Third Crusade. The Genoese tended to ally themselves with the Hospital, and the Venetians with the Temple. The Provençal merchants regularly opposed the Genoese, and the Catalans opposed the Provençals. The Pisans stayed between the two parties.

[2] *Gestes des Chiprois*, 257 (p. 741); Röhricht, *Regesta*, pp. 315–316; *Les Registres d'Innocent IV*, II, 60 (no. 4427). Innocent told Odo of Châteauroux to investigate Melisend's claim, but did not pursue the matter.

[3] *Annales de Terre Sainte*, p. 442; Amadi, *Chronique*, p. 198.

[4] For the Ibelin family connections, see Ducange, *Les Familles d'Outremer*, under "Garnier", "Ibelin", "Montfort"; also Runciman, *History of the Crusades*, III, appendix III (genealogical trees). Balian's son Julian was now lord of Sidon; and John's son-in-law John l'Aleman of Caesarea.

The final defeat of the imperialists meant the triumph of Templar foreign policy. The Aiyūbid world was divided between aṣ-Ṣāliḥ Aiyūb of Egypt and his uncle, aṣ-Ṣāliḥ Ismā'īl of Damascus, with his cousin an-Nāṣir Dā'ūd of Kerak as an unstable third party in their disputes. The Templars at once offered their friendship to Ismā'īl, and obtained from him and an-Nāṣir the withdrawal of the Moslems from the Temple area at Jerusalem and its restoration to the order. Aiyūb, in his anxiety at losing the friendship of the Franks, announced that he would confirm the arrangement. The reëntry of the Templars to their original home was triumphantly reported by the master to pope Innocent IV.[5]

Next spring (1244) war broke out between Aiyūb of Egypt and Ismā'īl of Damascus, who was supported by an-Nāṣir of Kerak and by the young prince of Homs, al-Manṣūr Ibrāhīm. The Templars persuaded the barons to offer their alliance to Ismā'īl, and the prince of Homs came in person to Acre to complete the negotiations and to offer the Franks a share of Egypt when Aiyūb should be defeated. He was received with honor and entertained sumptuously by the Temple. But Aiyūb too found allies. Since the death of the Khorezm-Shāh Jalāl-ad-Dīn in 1231, his army, some ten thousand strong, had been wandering leaderless through the Jazira, ready to hire itself to the highest bidder. The Khorezmians gladly accepted Aiyūb's offer to enter his service against Ismā'īl and the allies of Damascus.[6]

It had been arranged that the Franco-Damascene forces should assemble outside Acre in the summer of 1244. While they were gathering, the Khorezmians flooded into Syria from the north. They swept down past Homs and Damascus, ravaging the countryside but not venturing to attack the cities till they came into Galilee. There they captured and sacked Tiberias and passed on to sack Nablus. Early in July they appeared before Jerusalem. The Franks realized the danger too late. The patriarch, Robert, hastened to the city with Armand of Périgord and William of Châteauneuf, masters of the Temple and the Hospital, and reinforced the garrison in the Tower of David, but slipped away just before the enemy arrived.

[5] Matthew Paris, *Chronica majora* (Rolls Series, LVII), IV, 289–298; Abū-l-Fidā', *Kitāb al-mukhtaṣar* (*RHC, Or.*, I), p. 122; Badr-ad-Dīn al-'Ainī, *'Iqd al-jamān* (*RHC, Or.*, II, 1), p. 197; al-Maqrīzī, *Akhbār Miṣr* (tr. Blochet, *ROL*, X), pp. 355–357. The master of the Temple was Armand of Périgord.

[6] Joinville, *Histoire de St. Louis*, ed. Wailly, p. 290; Matthew Paris, *Chronica majora*, IV, 301 (Frederick II blames the barons for provoking the Egyptian-Khorezmian alliance); Abū-l-Fidā', *Kitāb al-mukhtaṣar* (*RHC, Or.*, I), p. 119; al-Maqrīzī, *Akhbār Miṣr* (*ROL*, X), p. 358; Kamāl-ad-Dīn, *Ta'rīkh Ḥalab* (tr. Blochet, *ROL*, VI), pp. 3–6, 13. On the Khorezmians, see below, chapter XIX, pp. 668–674.

On July 11 the Khorezmians burst into the city. There was some fighting in the streets and a massacre of all the inmates of the Armenian convent of St. James. But the citadel held out. When no help seemed to be coming from Acre, the garrison sent a desperate appeal for help to an-Nāṣir of Kerak, the nearest ally of the Franks. An-Nāṣir disliked the alliance, but he sent some troops towards the city. The Khorezmians, anxious to avoid a battle, then offered the garrison a safe-conduct to the coast in return for the surrender of the citadel. On August 23 the Tower of David was handed over to the Khorezmians, and the Frankish population of the city, some six thousand men, women, and children, marched out on the road to Jaffa. When they paused to take a last look at Jerusalem, they saw Frankish flags waving from the towers. Thinking that somehow rescue had arrived, most of the armed men turned back, only to fall in an ambush beneath the walls. Two thousand of them perished. The remainder journeyed painfully towards Jaffa, continually harassed by brigands. Only three hundred survivors reached the coast.

Meanwhile the Khorezmians sacked Jerusalem. The churches were burnt, including the shrine of the Holy Sepulcher, where the tombs of the kings of Jerusalem were desecrated, and the few Latin priests who had stayed behind were murdered. Houses and shops were pillaged. Then, when the city was desolate, the Khorezmians rode on to join the Egyptian army before Gaza.[7]

So Jerusalem passed finally from the Franks. But it was thought at Acre that the city would soon be re-occupied after the coming victory. Meanwhile al-Manṣūr Ibrāhīm arrived before Acre at the head of the armies of Damascus and Homs, and an-Nāṣir brought up his troops, who were mostly beduins. On October 4, 1244, the allies began to march southward. The Christian army was the largest that Outremer had put into the field since the Third Crusade. The cavalry numbered about a thousand, six hundred provided by the lay barons and the remainder by the military orders. The Hospital and the Teutonic Knights, though they disapproved of the war, sent all the men that they could spare. The infantry was probably about five thousand strong. The army was under the command of Philip of Montfort, lord of Tyre, Walter of Brienne, count of Jaffa, and the three masters. The patriarch Robert, archbishop

[7] *Chronica de Mailros*, pp. 159–160; Matthew Paris, *Chronica majora*, IV, 308, 338–340; Ms. of Rothelin, pp. 563–565; al-Maqrīzī, *Akhbār Miṣr* (*ROL*, X), pp. 358–359; Badr-ad-Dīn al-'Ainī, *'Iqd al-jamān* (*RHC*, *Or.*, II, 1), p. 198.

Peter of Tyre, and bishop Ralph of Lydda and Ramla accompanied the troops; and Bohemond of Antioch sent his cousins, John and William of Botron (al-Batrūn), and Thomas, constable of Tripoli. The Moslem troops were rather more numerous but lightly armed. There was perfect fellowship between the Franks and the men of Homs; but an-Nāṣir and his beduins kept themselves apart.

The Egyptian army was commanded by a young mamluk emir, Rukn-ad-Dīn Baybars. It consisted of about five thousand picked troops, mostly infantry, the cavalry arm being provided by the Khorezmians.

The armies made contact at the village of Ḥarbīyah (La Forbie), a few miles northeast of Gaza, on October 17. The allied commanders held a council of war, at which the prince of Homs recommended that they should fortify their camp and remain on the defensive. He knew that the Khorezmians disliked attacking a strong position, and inaction soon made them restless. As the Egyptians were too few to attack without them, it was probable that the Khorezmians would soon melt away and the Egyptians be forced to retire. But Walter of Brienne urged an immediate attack. The allied army was the stronger, and it would be wrong to miss an opportunity of destroying the Khorezmian menace. After some discussion he had his way, and orders were given to advance. The Franks were on the right flank, the armies of Damascus and Homs in the center, and an-Nāṣir and his beduins on the left.

While the Egyptian troops held the Frankish attack, the Khorezmians counterattacked the Damascene army. The Damascenes could not stand the shock and turned and fled, followed by an-Nāṣir and his beduins, who had never liked the war. The army of Homs, which had held its ground, found itself between the fleeing armies of Damascus and Kerak and had to cut its way out. The Franks were isolated, and the Khorezmians then wheeled round to attack their flank and drive them on to the Egyptians. Though they fought bravely, they were hopelessly trapped. Within a few hours the army was destroyed. Philip of Montfort and the patriarch escaped to Ascalon, where they were joined by the survivors of the military orders: thirty-three Templars, twenty-seven Hospitallers, and three Teutonic Knights. The dead were said to number well over five thousand, and included the master of the Temple, the archbishop of Tyre, the bishop of Lydda and Ramla, and the two young lords of Botron. Eight hundred prisoners were taken by the Egyptians, including the master of the Hospital and the constable of Tripoli. The count of Jaffa was captured by the

Khorezmians, who hurried with him to Jaffa, threatening to kill him unless the garrison surrendered. But he shouted to his men to hold firm, and the Khorezmians were awed by the strength of the fortifications. They retired, sparing the count's life because of the ransom that he would bring. He was taken with the other captives to Egypt. The Egyptian army meanwhile marched on Ascalon, which was now garrisoned by the Hospital. The first attempts to take it by storm failed. The Egyptians therefore encamped before it, hoping soon to bring up a fleet and to blockade it into surrender.[8]

The losses suffered by Outremer at Ḥarbīyah were surpassed only by those at Hattin. But, fortunately for the Franks, Aiyūb was in a less formidable position than Saladin had been. He still had to conquer Damascus and establish himself over his cousins, and he had to deal with his embarrassing mercenaries, the Khorezmians. They had hoped to be rewarded by the grant of lands in Egypt, but he refused to allow them across the isthmus of Suez. They contented themselves meanwhile in raiding the Frankish countryside, and then joined the army that Aiyūb sent against Damascus in the spring of 1245. Damascus surrendered to Aiyūb in October, Ismā'īl being compensated with the principality of Baalbek. An-Nāṣir's lands west of the Jordan, including Jerusalem, had already passed to the Egyptians, and by 1247 the Aiyūbid princes of the north recognized Aiyūb's suzerainty. The Khorezmians joined Ismā'īl in an attempt to recover Damascus in 1246, but al-Manṣūr Ibrāhīm of Homs and an-Nāṣir Yūsuf of Aleppo, subsidized by Aiyūb, sent an army to its relief, and this army routed the Khorezmians near Baalbek. They were almost annihilated, and their few survivors disappeared back into the east.[9]

In the summer of 1247 Aiyūb was able to resume operations against the Franks. An Egyptian army moved into Galilee and attacked Tiberias, which Odo of Montbéliard had recently refortified. The town and castle were soon captured, and Mt. Tabor and the castle of Belvoir were occupied a few days later. The Franks were too short of manpower to defend their outlying fortresses. From Galilee the Egyptians moved to the siege of Ascalon, while their fleet sailed up from Egypt to blockade it from the sea. The Hos-

[8] *Estoire d'Eracles*, II, 427-431; Ms. of Rothelin, pp. 562–566; *Gestes des Chiprois*, 252 (p. 740); *Chronica de Mailros*, pp. 159–160; Joinville, *St. Louis*, pp. 293–295; Matthew Paris, *Chronica majora*, IV, 301, 307–311; al-Maqrīzī, *Akhbār Miṣr* (*ROL*, X), p. 360; Abū-Shāmah, *Ar-rauḍatain* (*RHC, Or.*, V), p. 193. Walter of Brienne was killed in prison.

[9] Ibn-Khallikān, *Wafayāt*, tr. de Slane, III, 246; al-Maqrīzī, *Akhbār Miṣr* (*ROL*, X), pp. 361–365; Abū-Shāmah, *Ar-rauḍatain* (*RHC, Or.*, V), p. 432; *Estoire d'Eracles*, II, 432.

pitallers of the garrison appealed to Acre and to Cyprus for help. King Henry sent eight galleys and a hundred knights under his seneschal, Baldwin of Ibelin, and Acre sent seven galleys and fifty light vessels. The Egyptian fleet of twenty-one galleys set out to meet them, but was scattered by a sudden storm, and many of the ships were wrecked. The relieving force was able to reach Ascalon and land the knights and supplies, but the weather was too bad for the ships to remain in the open roadstead. They returned to Acre. Meanwhile the Egyptians, who had lacked wood for siege engines, were able to use the timber from their own wrecks. They constructed a great battering-ram, which at last, on October 15, broke a way through the walls, and the Egyptians passed within. The defenders were taken by surprise, and were all slaughtered or made prisoner. At Aiyūb's orders the fortress was dismantled and the town deserted.[10]

The occupation of Ascalon and eastern Galilee satisfied Aiyūb for the moment. He was too unsure of his Moslem vassals to go farther. The Franks had a breathing-space, which they badly needed. The disaster at Ḥarbīyah had seriously reduced their manpower. Few fresh colonists arrived to fill the depleted ranks of the baronage. Only the military orders could obtain recruits in the west, and as a result more and more of the defenses of the kingdom were given over to them. The mutual jealousies of the orders were in no way diminished, while the absence of a royal or baronial militia removed the only effective curb on the Italian colonies, whose rivalries were even more intense.[11]

Farther north Bohemond V, prince of Antioch and count of Tripoli, tried to keep out of his neighbors' troubles. Through his wife, Lucienne of Segni, great-niece of Innocent III and cousin of Gregory IX, he kept on good terms with Rome, but he sought to please Frederick II also by giving asylum to Thomas of Acerra and Lothair Filangieri. He was friendly with Henry of Cyprus, but had been openly hostile to the Armenians ever since the death of his brother Philip there. But the pope forbade him to go to war, and there was a gradual reconciliation after the marriage of Henry to the Armenian princess Stephanie in 1237. His only military enterprise during these years was to send a contingent, probably

[10] *Estoire d'Eracles*, II, 432–435; *Gestes des Chiprois*, 258 (p. 741); *Annales de Terre Sainte*, p. 442; Badr-ad-Dīn al-'Ainī, *'Iqd al-jamān* (*RHC, Or.*, II, 1), p. 200; al-Maqrīzī, *Akhbār Miṣr* (*ROL*, X), p. 315.

[11] The situation as regards manpower and discipline in Syria must be viewed in connection with the whole history of the military orders, the Italian colonies, and the Frankish enterprises in Greece and elsewhere, for all of which see above, chapters VI and VII, and chapters in forthcoming volume IV.

at the request of the pope, to join in the disastrous campaign of 1244. His relations with his vassals were good, though his wife was beginning to fill the county of Tripoli with her Roman relatives, which was to cause trouble later. He seldom visited Antioch, preferring to live at Tripoli.[12] The city of Antioch was almost entirely administered by its commune, in which the Greeks were powerful, and Bohemond seems to have been friendly with the Greek church. During these years Rome decided to try to solve the religious problems of Antioch by encouraging uniate churches, which could be self-governing and use their own language and ritual so long as they recognized the supreme authority of Rome. The Greek patriarch of Antioch, Symeon II, whom Bohemond seems to have allowed to reside at Antioch, would have nothing to do with the scheme. But his successor, David, submitted to the pope in 1245 and for two years was the only patriarch in Antioch, the Latin, Albert, having retired to Europe to complain of the arrangement at the Council of Lyons, where he died. The next Latin patriarch, the pope's nephew Opizon, reached Antioch in 1248. Soon afterwards he quarreled with David's successor, Euthymius, who rejected papal supremacy and was banished from the city.[13] A similar attempt to make the Jacobite church uniate was only partly successful, as half the Jacobites refused to follow the Jacobite patriarch Ignatius when he submitted to Rome. The work of conciliation was conducted by Franciscan and Dominican friars, whose orders the patriarch Albert had greatly favored.[14] On the other hand the Latin patriarchate had considerable trouble with monasteries recently established in the principality by the Cistercian order.[15] Bohemond V died in 1252, when the government of Outremer was in the hands of king Louis of France.[16]

Louis IX came to the east in 1248. During the six years that he remained there he was entrusted with the administration of the kingdom of Jerusalem. Though his unhappy Egyptian campaign cost Outremer more men than it could now afford, his administration, particularly during the four years of his residence at Acre, gave the kingdom peace and security. He also intervened usefully in Antiochene affairs on Bohemond V's death, to end the unpopular

[12] For Bohemond V's reign, see the general summary in Cahen, *La Syrie du nord*, pp. 650–652.

[13] *Ibid.*, pp. 684–685. See also Pressutti, *Regesta Honorii papae III*, II (Rome, 1895), 352, and Bar Hebraeus, *Chronography* (tr. Budge), p. 445.

[14] Cahen, *La Syrie du nord*, pp. 681–684, a fully referenced account.

[15] *Ibid.*, pp. 668–671, 680–681.

[16] *Ibid.*, p. 702.

regency of the dowager princess Lucienne, and to arrange the marriage of the young prince Bohemond VI with Sibyl, a daughter of king Heṭoum of Armenia, which resulted in a close political alliance between Bohemond and his father-in-law.[17] Louis could not, of course, remain permanently in the east, and his departure left Outremer in a precarious position. King Henry of Cyprus, regent of Jerusalem, died in January 1253, leaving a child of a few months to succeed him, under the regency of the dowager queen, Plaisance of Antioch. The infant king, Hugh II, could not act as regent of Jerusalem, and queen Plaisance was accepted as regent, though she did not come to Acre to have oaths of allegiance sworn to her. The bailie in the kingdom of Jerusalem was John of Ibelin, lord of Arsuf, till 1254 and again from 1256 to 1258. John of Ibelin, count of Jaffa, was bailie from 1254 to 1256, when John of Arsuf was probably in Cyprus. To help in the government Louis left behind one of his most trusted captains, Geoffrey of Sargines, with a regiment of soldiers paid for by the French crown. Geoffrey was appointed constable of the kingdom.[18]

The death of Conrad of Germany in May 1254, when Louis was on his way home, gave the crown of Jerusalem to his two-year-old son Conradin, whose nominal rights were scrupulously regarded by the lawyers of Outremer, though there was no change in the government of the kingdom.[19]

While Louis was still in Egypt, the situation in the Moslem world had been altered by the Mamluk revolution in Cairo, which gave Egypt to a series of rulers far more bellicose and intolerant than the Aiyūbids. Meanwhile Damascus had passed to the Aiyūbid ruler of Aleppo, Saladin's great-grandson an-Nāṣir Yūsuf. He was desperately nervous of the Mamluk sultan Aybeg and was therefore eager to keep on good terms with the Franks. Since Aybeg had no wish to drive them into a close alliance with Damascus, they found themselves in an advantageous position. Shortly before he left Acre, Louis arranged a truce with Damascus, to last from February 21, 1254, for two years, six months, and forty days.[20] The next year Aybeg made a ten years' truce with Acre, from which he excluded the town of Jaffa, whose reduction he considered necessary if he were to hold Palestine against an-Nāṣir Yūsuf. The Franks therefore used Jaffa as a base for raiding Mamluk caravans, and an

[17] For Louis's policy with regard to Antioch, see above, chapter XIV, p. 507.

[18] See La Monte, *Feudal Monarchy*, pp. 74–75.

[19] Matthew Paris, *Chronica majora*, V, 459–460. See below, note 24.

[20] Matthew Paris, *Chronica majora*, V, 522; Ms. of Rothelin, p. 630; *Annales de Terre Sainte*, p. 446.

attempt by the governor of Jerusalem, in May 1256, to punish the raiders ended in disaster. When on its expiry the truce was renewed for ten years, Jaffa was included.[21]

The forebearance of the Moslems was also largely due to the imminence of Mongol invasions. The caliph at Baghdad, al-Musta'ṣim, who saw himself in the front line, made every effort to maintain peace in Islam. His anxiety was well founded, for in January 1256 a vast Mongol army, under Hulagu, brother of the Great Khan Möngke, crossed the Oxus on its westward march.[22]

The respite did not bring peace to Outremer, where the rivalry of the Venetian and Genoese colonies flared up in a civil war that involved the whole kingdom. The Venetian and Genoese districts in Acre were divided by the hill of Montjoie, which belonged to the latter, except for its summit, occupied by the old monastery of St. Sabas, to which both colonies laid claim. One morning early in 1256, while the case was before the courts, the Genoese, with the prearranged support of the Pisans, suddenly occupied the monastery, and when the Venetians protested, they rushed down into the Venetian quarter, sacking the houses there and burning the ships tied up at the quay. It was only after heavy fighting that the Venetians drove them out. When the news reached Tyre, Philip of Montfort, who had been contesting the right of the Venetians to certain neighboring villages, forcibly ejected them from the third of the town that was theirs by the treaty of 1124.

The government at Genoa, unwilling to start a war with Venice, offered to mediate all around, but by then it was too late. The Venetian consul at Acre, Marco Giustiniani, was a man of resource. He managed to persuade the Pisans that the Genoese were untrustworthy allies. He then made friends with the Ibelins. John of Arsuf, the bailie, and John of Jaffa both opposed Philip of Montfort's anti-Venetian action, the former because he feared that Philip intended to declare Tyre independent of Acre, the latter because of its shocking illegality. Moreover, a Genoese had recently tried to assassinate John of Jaffa, which naturally strengthened his preference for Venice. The fraternities of Acre, nervous lest Philip should make Tyre a successful commercial rival to their own city, joined the Venetian camp, as did the Templars and the Teutonic Knights, whereat the Hospitallers supported the Genoese. The Provençal colonists inevitably opposed Genoa, and the Catalan

21 Ms. of Rothelin, pp. 631–633; *Annales de Terre Sainte*, p. 446; Abū-l-Fidā', *Kitāb al-mukhtaṣar* (*RHC, Or.*, I), pp. 133–134.

22 See below, chapter XXI, pp. 717, 726.

colonists the Provençals. Farther north, Bohemond VI tried to remain neutral and forbade his vassals to take part. But his Embriaco cousins of Jubail remembered their Genoese origin and defied his ban, thus earning his hatred and turning his own sympathies towards the Venetians. The only other neutrals were the queen-regent in Cyprus and Geoffrey of Sargines, who had neither the position nor the material means to restore order. There was no patriarch at hand. James Pantaléon (later pope Urban IV), who was appointed in December 1255, did not reach Acre till 1260.

Most of the fighting in the so-called war of St. Sabas was done by the Italians. When the Pisans deserted them, the Genoese overran their quarter of Acre, which gave them command of the harbor. But a large Venetian squadron arrived and landed men who cleared the Genoese from the Venetian and Pisan quarters and captured the hill of St. Sabas, but could not dislodge them from their own quarter, which was protected on the rear by the Hospital. During the next two years the Genoese and Venetians preyed on each other's shipping and brought the foreign trade of Outremer almost to a standstill. In June 1258 there was a great sea battle off Acre, in which the Genoese were severely defeated. A simultaneous attempt by Philip of Montfort to march on Acre was halted by the militia of the fraternities. As a result the Genoese decided to abandon their quarter in Acre and to concentrate on Tyre. But the acts of reciprocal piracy continued.[23]

There had been several attempts to restore peace. Queen Plaisance of Cyprus had crossed to Tripoli, and come with her brother Bohemond VI to Acre in February 1258 to receive oaths of allegiance as regent. But when Bohemond put forward her claims as her son's guardian, and the Ibelins and Templars and Teutonic Knights concurred, the Hospitallers and Philip of Montfort suddenly became conscientious about Conradin's rights. Nothing, they said, should be done in his absence. Plaisance was eventually accepted by a majority vote, but she had unwillingly been forced to take sides in the conflict, and was powerless to stop it.[24] Next, the absentee patriarch appealed to Rome on Plaisance's behalf; and pope Alexander IV ordered two Venetian and two Pisan delegates to sail to Syria in a Genoese ship and two Genoese in a Venetian ship, to make peace. Both parties sailed in July 1258, but on their

[23] *Estoire d'Eracles*, II, 443–447; *Gestes des Chiprois*, 267–270, 275–290 (pp. 742–748); *Annales Januenses* (*MGH, SS.*, XVIII), pp. 239–240; Dandolo, *Chronicon Venetum*, pp. 365–367. See Heyd, *Histoire du commerce du Levant*, I, 344–354.

[24] *Assises de Jérusalem*, II, 401; *Estoire d'Eracles*, II, 443; Ms. of Rothelin, p. 643; *Gestes des Chiprois*, 268, 271 (pp. 742–744).

way they learnt of the sea battle off Acre, and returned to Italy.[25] In April 1259 the pope sent a special legate, Thomas Agni of Lentini, to Acre to settle the quarrel. The bailie, John of Arsuf, having died, Plaisance came again to Acre to appoint as bailie the less controversial Geoffrey of Sargines (May 1, 1259). Neither he nor the legate could achieve anything at first. It was only after the arrival of the patriarch James the next year that negotiations could seriously proceed. Eventually, in January 1261, plenipotentiaries from the Venetians, the Pisans, and the Genoese attended a meeting of the high court at Acre and were officially reconciled, together with the quarreling nobles and the military orders. It was agreed that the Genoese should have their establishment at Tyre and the Venetians and Pisans theirs at Acre.[26] Neither Venice nor Genoa regarded the arrangement as final. Occasional acts of piracy continued. But the main interest of both cities was now centered farther north, where the Greeks of Nicaea, who were negotiating an alliance with Genoa, were planning the stroke that would recover Constantinople and end the Latin empire, in which Venice had so large a stake.[27]

Bohemond of Antioch had been able to do little to help his sister Plaisance as he was by now involved in a feud with the Embriaco family. Its head, Henry of Jubail, rejected Bohemond's suzerainty and ruled as an independent lord, with the help of the Genoese. Meanwhile the other native barons of the county of Tripoli were offended by the favor shown to the Roman friends of Bohemond's mother Lucienne. In 1258, led by Bertrand Embriaco, head of the younger branch of the family, and his son-in-law John, lord of Botron, they marched on Tripoli in open revolt. Bohemond was defeated just outside the gates and wounded by Bertrand himself, and Tripoli was saved only by a contingent of Templars. A few weeks later Bertrand was murdered in one of his villages by some armed peasants, whom everyone believed to have been instigated by Bohemond. His death cowed the rebels, who retreated, but the whole Embriaco clan burned for revenge.[28]

Queen Plaisance died in 1261. Her son, Hugh II of Cyprus, was now eight years old, and a new regent was needed for Cyprus

[25] For references, see above, note 23.

[26] Tafel-Thomas, *Urkunden*, III, 39–44; *Gestes des Chiprois*, 290 (p. 748); *Annales de Terre Sainte*, pp. 448–449.

[27] See above, chapter VI, pp. 229–233.

[28] *Gestes des Chiprois*, 291–297 (pp. 748–750). See E. G. Rey, "Les Seigneurs de Giblet," *ROL*, III (1895), 399–404.

and Jerusalem. Hugh's father, Henry I, had had two sisters. The elder, Mary, had married Walter of Brienne, and was now dead, leaving a son, Hugh. The younger, Isabel, was married to Henry of Antioch, Bohemond V's brother, and was still living with a son, also called Hugh, who was slightly older than his cousin of Brienne. Isabel had brought the two boys up together after her sister's death. If the children of a deceased elder sister ranked above a living younger sister and her children, Hugh of Brienne was heir to the Cypriote throne and second heir, after Hugh II, to the throne of Jerusalem, and was therefore entitled to the double regency. But he was unwilling to compete against his aunt. The high court of Cyprus accepted the claim of Isabel's line but, preferring a male to a female regent, gave the regency to her son Hugh. The high court of Jerusalem took longer over its deliberations. It was not till 1263 that Isabel and her husband came to Acre, and were formally recognized as regents, though the barons showed scruples that had hitherto been ignored, and refused her an oath of allegiance because of the absence of king Conradin. Isabel appointed her husband bailie, while Geoffrey of Sargines returned to his old post of seneschal.

Isabel died the next year in Cyprus. Hugh of Antioch, regent of Cyprus, then claimed the regency of Jerusalem as her heir. But now Hugh of Brienne put in a counter-claim. After some discussion, in which he maintained that by the custom of France, which was followed in Outremer, the children of an elder sister took precedence over those of a younger, the high court decided that the decisive factor was kinship to the last holder of the office. Isabel had been regent, and her son took precedence over her nephew. Hugh of Antioch was unanimously accepted, and the barons paid him the homage that they had refused to his mother. The Italian colonists offered him fealty, and the military orders gave him recognition. There was a superficial atmosphere of reconciliation all round. Hugh removed his father from the post of bailie, preferring to spend half his time himself at Acre. During his absences in Cyprus the seneschal Geoffrey acted for him.[29]

During these years the neighbors of Outremer had been undergoing a long and serious crisis. In February 1258 the Mongols under Hulagu sacked Baghdad, ending forever the long history of the 'Abbāsid caliphate. From Iraq they moved on into Syria. In January 1260 they captured Aleppo and came into direct contact

[29] See La Monte, *Feudal Monarchy*, pp. 75–77, and Hill, *History of Cyprus*, II, 151–154, for discussions of the legal points and for references.

with the Franks.[30] Heṭoum I, king of Armenia, had long been an advocate of alliance with the Mongols. In 1254 he had himself visited the Great Khan Möngke at Karakorum. In return for calling himself the Khan's vassal he was promised increase of territory and protection against the Anatolian Turks.[31] He persuaded his son-in-law Bohemond VI, who seems in some way to have regarded him as overlord, to follow his policy. When Hulagu appeared in northern Syria, Heṭoum and Bohemond hastened to pay a deferential visit to his camp. They were both rewarded with some of the spoils taken by the Mongols at Aleppo. Heṭoum was further given back territory that he had lost to the Turks in Cilicia, and Bohemond received towns and forts that Antioch had lost to the Moslems in Saladin's time, including the port of Latakia. In return, Bohemond was requested to admit the Greek patriarch Euthymius back into Antioch. When the Mongol army moved on southwards towards Damascus, under the Nestorian Christian general Kitbogha, the king of Armenia and the prince of Antioch accompanied it; and when Damascus was captured in March 1260, the three Christian potentates rode side by side in triumph through the streets.[32]

To the Franks at Acre Bohemond's friendship with the Mongols seemed disgraceful. The recovery of Latakia was unimportant in their minds in comparison with the insult done to the Latin church by the reintroduction of the Greek patriarch. The pope hastened to excommunicate Bohemond, while the barons at Acre wrote a letter to king Louis's brother, Charles of Anjou, to describe the dangers, political and moral, of the Mongol advance and to ask for his help. It is probable that the barons were influenced by the Venetians, who saw with growing concern how the Genoese were strengthening their hold on the Far Eastern trade through their friendship with the Mongols, and through their new monopolies in the Black Sea since the Greek recapture of Constantinople in July 1261. But a general fear of the Mongols was not unreasonable. They seemed to be determined to achieve world-conquest, and experience showed that they could not tolerate the existence of independent states: their allies had to be their vassals. Moreover, though there were Christians amongst them, such as Hulagu's wife, Toqūz Khātūn, and the general Kitbogha, these Christians were

[30] See below, chapter XXI, pp. 717–719, 726.

[31] See below, chapter XVIII, pp. 652–653.

[32] *Gestes des Chiprois*, 302–303 (p. 751); letter to Charles of Anjou in *ROL*, II, 213; Bar Hebraeus, *Chronography*, p. 436. The cession of Latakia is never specifically recorded, but it must have been part of the unspecified territory returned to Bohemond. When next mentioned, it is in Frankish hands.

"heretic" Nestorians and showed an unwelcome sympathy with the Greek church. Nor were accounts of the sack of Baghdad calculated to give a high impression of Mongol civilization. When therefore it seemed likely that there was to be a clash between the Mongols and the Mamluks, sympathy at Acre was given to the latter.[33]

The Mongols had no intention of attacking the Franks, and the government at Acre sought to avoid provocation. But one of the more irresponsible lords, Julian of Sidon, could not resist the temptation to conduct a raid into the Biqā'. The Mongols, who had just taken over the district, sent a small company to drive him back, but its leader, who was Kitbogha's nephew, was ambushed and killed by Julian. Kitbogha angrily sent troops which penetrated to Sidon and sacked the town. A raid into Galilee led by John II of Beirut and the Templars was severely punished by the Mongols. John was captured and had to be ransomed.[34]

The Mongol capture of Damascus impelled Kutuz, the Mamluk sultan of Egypt, to take action to stem the Mongol conquest. He put to death an ambassador sent by Hulagu to demand his submission, and in July 1260 his army crossed the Egyptian frontier into Palestine. The moment was well chosen, for news had reached Hulagu that his brother Möngke had died and civil war had broken out in Mongolia, four thousand miles to the east, and he felt obliged to move with the greater part of his forces to the eastern confines of his government. Kitbogha was left to hold Syria with an army far smaller than that which the Mamluks could muster.

From his camp at Gaza Kutuz sent envoys to Acre to ask permission to march through Frankish territory and to obtain provisions there and even military aid. When the high court met, the barons were inclined to offer the sultan all that he requested. But the master of the Teutonic Knights, Anno of Sangerhausen, opposed the decision, warning them that it would be foolish to trust the Moslems far, especially if they were elated by victory. His order had strong Armenian connections, and he probably sympathized with Hetoum's pro-Mongol policy. His words so far moved the assembly that the military alliance was rejected, but the sultan was given authority to pass through Frankish lands and to buy food there. In August the Egyptian army marched up the coast and encamped

[33] For a defense of the Frankish attitude, see Cahen, *La Syrie du nord*, pp. 708–709.

[34] *Gestes des Chiprois*, 303–307 (pp. 752–753); *Annales de Terre Sainte*, p. 449 (dating the raids, wrongly, after the battle of 'Ain Jālūt); Hetoum, *Flor des estoires*, p. 174.

for some days in the orchards outside Acre. Many of the emirs were hospitably entertained within the city, and one of them, Baybars, pointed out to Kutuz how easily it could be taken by surprise. But the sultan considered such treachery inopportune. The Franks had been slightly alarmed by the size of the Egyptian forces, but were cheered by a promise that they should buy at reduced rates the horses that would be captured from the Mongols.

The decisive battle of 'Ain Jālūt, on September 3, 1260, when the Christian Kitbogha was defeated and slain by the Mamluks, produced exactly the results that Anno had feared. The whole Syrian hinterland passed into Egyptian hands, and the treacherous murder and replacement of Kutuz by the energetic and fanatical Baybars led to a determined policy of aggression against the Franks. None of the spoil of 'Ain Jālūt found its way to Frankish hands.[35] When in 1261 John of Beirut and John of Jaffa visited the new sultan's camp to arrange for the release of Frankish prisoners in Egypt and for the cession of the little fort of Zir'īn in Galilee, which sultan Aybeg had promised a few years before, Baybars refused to listen to them, and merely sent the prisoners to labor camps.[36] In February 1263 John of Jaffa, whom Baybars seems to have liked, interviewed him at Mt. Tabor and secured the promise of an exchange of prisoners. But the Moslems owned by the Temple and the Hospital were useful trained craftsmen; and the orders refused to give them up. Baybars, expressing disgust at such mercenary greed, canceled the arrangement. Instead, he invaded Frankish territory, sacking Nazareth in April and then marching on Acre. It was suspected that he had been promised help by Philip of Tyre and the Genoese, but if so, at the last moment their consciences were too strong for them. After wounding Geoffrey of Sargines in a skirmish outside the walls, he retired.[37]

The Franks were now thoroughly alarmed. In 1261 Balian of Arsuf leased his fief to the Hospital, fearing that he could not defend it himself. Julian of Sidon had already in 1260 mortgaged his castles of Sidon and Belfort to the Templars, who had since foreclosed. But the orders were almost as impotent as the lay lords. In 1264 the Hospital and the Temple united to capture the little

[35] For the battle of 'Ain Jālūt, see below, chapter XXI, pp. 718–719. For the Frankish attitude to the campaign, *Gestes des Chiprois*, 308–310 (pp. 753–754); Ms. of Rothelin, p. 637.

[36] *Annales de Terre Sainte*, p. 450; Badr-ad-Dīn al-'Ainī, *'Iqd al-jamān* (*RHC, Or.*, II, 1), pp. 216–217, saying that a truce was made all the same.

[37] *Gestes des Chiprois*, 318–320 (p. 756); *Annales de Terre Sainte*, p. 450; al-Maqrīzī, *Al-khiṭaṭ* (tr. Quatremère), I, i, 194–197; Badr-ad-Dīn al-'Ainī, *'Iqd al-jamān* (*RHC, Or.*, II, 1), pp. 218–219.

fort of al-Lajjūn, the ancient Megiddo, and a little later raided Moslem territory as far south as Ascalon, while Geoffrey of Sargines' French regiment penetrated to Baisan. But such fruitless excursions only served to irritate the sultan.[38]

Early in 1265 Baybars set out from Egypt at the head of a great army. He had been alarmed by news of a Mongol invasion of northern Syria, but his troops at Aleppo had held it. He could therefore attack the Franks in the south. After feigning to go on a hunting expedition, he swooped on Caesarea. The town fell to him on February 27 and the citadel a week later. From Caesarea he crossed Mt. Carmel to Haifa, which was hastily abandoned by its inhabitants. Next, after an unsuccessful attack on the Templar stronghold of Château Pèlerin (Athlith), he marched on Arsuf. The garrison of 270 Hospitaller Knights fought well, but lost too many men to continue the defense for long. Their commander surrendered on April 29, on the promise that the survivors should go free. Baybars broke his word and took them all into captivity. The sultan then moved towards Acre. The regent Hugh, who had been in Cyprus, hastened across the sea with all the troops that he could muster; and Baybars found the defenses too well manned for an attack to be worth while. After garrisoning the newly conquered territory he returned to Egypt. His frontier now ran within sight of the Frankish capital.[39]

The sultan's main animosity was directed against the Mongols' allies, Heṭoum of Armenia and Bohemond of Antioch. His opportunity to punish them came in 1266. Already in 1261, soon after 'Ain Jālūt, his troops had ravaged their territories, sacking the port of St. Simeon. In February 1265 their protector Hulagu died in Azerbaijan. Both Heṭoum and Bohemond had remained his faithful vassals, though the latter offended him in 1264 by banishing the Greek patriarch Euthymius and reintroducing the Latin Opizon. Hulagu was succeeded as Il-khan, or governor of the Mongol provinces of southwest Asia, by his son Abagha. But Abagha's authority was not established for some months, and then he was involved in a war with his cousins, the khans of the Golden Horde, the Kipchaks, with whom Baybars, himself a Kipchak Turk

[38] *Estoire d'Eracles*, II, 444, 449; *Annales de Terre Sainte*, p. 451.

[39] *Gestes des Chiprois*, 328 (pp. 758–759); *Annales de Terre Sainte*, pp. 451–452; *Estoire d'Eracles*, II, 450; Badr-ad-Dīn al-'Ainī, *'Iqd al-jamān* (*RHC*, *Or.*, II, 1), pp. 219–221; Abū-l-Fidā', *Kitāb al-mukhtaṣar* (*RHC*, *Or.*, I), p. 150; al-Maqrīzī, *Al-khiṭaṭ*, I, ii, 7–8. The loss of the fortresses inspired a bitter poem by the Templar Ricaut Bonomel, printed in Vincenzo de Bartholomaeis (ed.), *Poesie provenzale storiche relative all' Italia*, II (*FSI*, LXXII), 222–224: "Ir' e dolors s'es e mon cor asseza . . . ."

by birth, was in diplomatic relations. The Īl-khan could not afford to give his vassals much assistance.[40]

In the early summer of 1266 two great Mamluk armies set out from Egypt. The first, under the sultan, marched on Acre. Geoffrey of Sargines had recently received reinforcements from France, and the city was well garrisoned. So Baybars turned into Galilee. After demonstrating in front of the Teutonic castle of Starkenburg, he suddenly appeared before the huge Templar castle of Safad, which dominated the whole district. The garrison was numerous, but consisted largely of Syrian and half-breed troops. After his first assaults, on July 7, 13, and 19, failed, the sultan offered an amnesty to any native soldiers who would surrender. The Templar knights were at once suspicious. There were recriminations between them and the native troops, and the latter began to desert. The Templars soon found that they could no longer man the defenses. They sent a native sergeant called Leo to arrange terms of surrender, and trusting his word that their lives would be spared, they yielded up the castle. Baybars had them all decapitated, while Leo promptly became a convert to Islam. The capture of Safad gave Baybars control of all Galilee. Philip of Montfort's castle of Toron surrendered to him without a struggle. He then proceeded to massacre the inhabitants of various Christian villages. When envoys came from Acre to ask leave to bury the Christian dead in Galilee, he retorted that they would find enough to bury nearer home, and marched down to the coast, slaughtering every Christian that he met. But once again he found Acre strongly garrisoned, and retired towards Egypt.[41]

While the sultan thus diverted the main attention of the Franks, his second army, under the emir Kalavun, assembled at Homs and entered the county of Tripoli, where it captured the forts of al-Qulai'ah and Ḥalbah and the town of 'Arqah, thus isolating the coast from the valley of the Buqai'ah and the Hospitaller castles of 'Akkār and Krak des Chevaliers. Kalavun then turned north to join the army of the prince of Hamah, al-Manṣūr II, and to march with him to Aleppo. From there he turned west to cross the Amanus mountains into Cilician Armenia. King Heṭoum was away begging for help from the Īl-khan. When he returned, he found that his sons had been routed in a battle near Sarvantikar; Ṭoros was dead, Leon a prisoner. His capital, Sis, and all his chief cities

[40] See below, chapter XXI, p. 722.

[41] *Gestes des Chiprois*, 346–353 (pp. 764–768); *Estoire d'Eracles*, II, 484–485; al-Maqrīzī, *Al-khiṭaṭ*, I, ii, 28–30; Abū-l-Fidā', *Kitāb al-mukhtaṣar* (*RHC, Or.*, I), p. 151; Badr-ad-Dīn al-'Ainī, *'Iqd al-jamān* (*RHC, Or.*, II, 1), pp. 222–223.

had been thoroughly sacked and the whole country devastated. It was a blow from which the Cilician kingdom never recovered.[42]

The victorious army was ordered by Baybars to move next against Antioch. But the soldiers were tired and sated with loot. A little judicious bribery from Bohemond and the commune of Antioch induced the commanders to retire towards Damascus.[43]

Early in 1268 Baybars set out once more. The only Christian possessions south of Mt. Carmel now were Château Pèlerin, which the sultan considered too strong to attack, and Jaffa, which belonged to the lawyer John of Ibelin's son Guy. Guy's hope that his father's prestige and the personal truce that he had made with Egypt would spare the town were disappointed. It fell to the sultan after twelve hours' fighting on March 7. Most of the citizens were slain, but the garrison was allowed to go unharmed. The castle was destroyed, and its wood and marble were sent to Cairo for the great mosque that Baybars was building there. From Jaffa Baybars moved into Galilee, to attack Belfort. After a bombardment of ten days, the Templars there surrendered on April 15. The women and children were sent to Tyre, but the men kept as slaves. On May 1 the Mamluk army was before Tripoli, but the city was well garrisoned, and Baybars turned northward. The Templars of Chastel Blanc and Tortosa sent to beg him to spare their territory. He agreed, and moved inland, down the Orontes valley.[44] On May 14 he was within sight of Antioch. There he divided his forces. While one detachment was sent to capture St. Simeon and cut the city off from the sea, and a second to guard the passes over the Amanus and prevent help coming from Cilicia, the sultan and the main force launched an attack on the walls of Antioch.

The siege began on May 14. Prince Bohemond was at Tripoli, and the city was commanded by its constable, Simon Mansel. On the first day's fighting he led an unsuccessful sortie and was captured outside the walls. At his captors' request, he tried to arrange for the surrender of the city, but the officers within the walls would not listen to him. The defense was gallant, but there were not enough troops to man the whole circuit of the fortifications. There was a general assault on May 18, and after a fierce struggle a breach was made in the walls on the slope of Mt. Silpius, through which the Moslems poured into the city.

42 See below, chapter XVIII, pp. 653–654.

43 See Cahen, *La Syrie du nord*, p. 716, citing a ms. of Muḥī-ad-Dīn ibn-'Abd-ar-Raḥīm.

44 *Gestes des Chiprois*, 364–365 (p. 771); *Estoire d'Eracles*, II, 456; Abū-l-Fidā', *Kitāb al-mukhtaṣar* (*RHC, Or.*, I), p. 152; al-Maqrīzī, *Al-khiṭaṭ*, I, ii, 50–51; Badr-ad-Dīn al-'Ainī, *'Iqd al-jamān* (*RHC, Or.*, II, 1), pp. 226–228.

The horrors of the sack of Antioch shocked even the Moslem chroniclers. The sultan remembered the crusaders' sack of Jerusalem nearly two centuries before and the recent sack of Baghdad by the Mongol allies of Antioch. He showed no mercy. He closed the city gates, that no citizen might escape. Anyone found in the streets was slaughtered. Those who cowered in their houses were either slain or made slaves. Some thousands, with their families, had fled for refuge to the huge citadel on the mountain-top. They were parceled out among the leading emirs. The riches found in the city were astounding. The commercial prosperity of Antioch had been declining recently, but its stores of treasures were untapped. The sultan's officers carefully collected the loot, and it was distributed next morning to the soldiers. Coin was so plentiful that it was handed out in bowlfuls. Every soldier acquired at least one slave, and so many remained over that the price of a boy fell to twelve dirhems and of a girl to five. A few notables were allowed to ransom themselves, but many of the leading citizens and ecclesiastics perished without a trace.[45]

The principality of Antioch, the oldest of the Frankish states in the east, had lasted for 171 years. Its sudden destruction in 1268 was a bitter blow to the prestige of the Christians, and it was followed by a rapid decline of Christianity in northern Syria. The Franks were ejected, and the native Christians, suspect to the Moslems because of their support of the Mongols, fared little better. The sultan made no attempt to repopulate Antioch. Its commercial value was no longer great enough, and it was useful to him only as a fortress. The city quickly dwindled till it was little more than a village. The eastern patriarchs, Greek, Armenian, and Jacobite, soon moved their headquarters to Damascus.[46]

On the fall of Antioch, the Templars abandoned their castles in the Amanus mountains, Baghrās and La Roche de Russole. All that was left of the principality was the enclave of Latakia, which Hulagu had won back for Bohemond, and the castle of Quṣair, whose lord was a friend of the local Moslems; it was allowed to remain undisturbed for seven more years.[47]

[45] *Gestes des Chiprois*, 365 (pp. 771–772); *Estoire d'Eracles*, II, 456–457; Bar Hebraeus, *Chronography*, p. 448; Abū-l-Fidā', *Kitāb al-mukhtaṣar* (*RHC, Or.*, I), p. 152; al-Maqrīzī, *Al-khiṭaṭ*, I, ii, 52–53; Badr-ad-Dīn al-'Ainī, *'Iqd al-jamān* (*RHC, Or.*, II, 1), pp. 229–234. See other references in Cahen, *La Syrie du nord*, p. 717 and notes.

[46] Bertrandon de la Broquière, who visited Antioch in 1432, reported that the walls were intact but there were only about three hundred houses standing within, almost entirely inhabited by Turcomans (*Voyage d'Outremer*, ed. Schéfer, pp. 84–85).

[47] *Gestes des Chiprois*, 365 (pp. 771–772); *Estoire d'Eracles*, II, 457; Cahen, *La Syrie du nord*, p. 717, note 17.

After his triumph Baybars was ready to make a truce. The Mongols showed signs of stirring, and there were rumors that Louis IX was returning to the east. At the regent Hugh's request an Egyptian embassy arrived at Acre to discuss a truce. When Hugh tried to impress the ambassador by displaying his troops in battle array, the Egyptian retorted that the whole army was not as numerous as the Christian captives at Cairo. A year's truce was arranged between Acre and Cairo, and Bohemond, though offended at being addressed by Baybars merely as count, not prince, was by his wish included in it.[48]

Hugh was grateful for the peace. He had not been able to end the fighting between the Venetians and Genoese, which had flared up again in 1267.[49] His one reliable lieutenant, Geoffrey of Sargines, was mortally ill and died in the spring of 1269,[50] and his own position, though nominally greater, was insecure. Young king Hugh II of Cyprus died in December 1267, aged fourteen, and he succeeded to his throne. This gave his authority a more permanent basis, but he found the Cypriote barons less willing to coöperate with a king than with a regent. They reminded him that they were not obliged to follow him overseas. If he wanted an army to fight on the mainland, it had to be composed of volunteers.[51] In October 1268 Conradin, titular king of Jerusalem, was put to death after an attempt to wrest back the kingdom of Sicily from Charles of Anjou, who had, with papal approval, conquered it from Frederick II's bastard, Manfred, less than three years before.[52]

On the news of Conradin's death Hugh assumed the title king of Jerusalem. His cousin, Hugh of Brienne, who had gone to Greece and married the heiress of Athens, Isabel de la Roche, did not contest his claim. But now a new claimant appeared, whom Hugh did not at first take seriously, but who was to cause him far more trouble. Of queen Isabel I's four marriages Conradin was descended from the second and Hugh from the third. But a daughter of the fourth, Melisend, had been the second wife of Bohemond IV of Antioch, and had left a daughter Mary of Antioch. She now declared that, as she was a generation nearer than Hugh

48 Muḥī-ad-Dīn, *Sīrat al-malik aẓ-Ẓāhir* (Michaud, *Bibliothèque des croisades*, IV), pp. 513–515.

49 *Gestes des Chiprois*, 354 (pp. 768–769); *Estoire d'Eracles*, II, 455–456.

50 *Gestes des Chiprois*, 368 (p. 772).

51 *Gestes des Chiprois*, 359 (p. 769). See Hill, *History of Cyprus*, II, 178.

52 *Gestes des Chiprois*, 363 (p. 771), reports festivities at Acre when the news of Conradin's death arrived. They were held in order to please the church.

to their common ancestress Isabel I, she took precedence over him. The case was brought before the high court. Hugh's argument was that his grandmother Alice had been accepted as next heir and regent, and after her her son Henry of Cyprus, then Henry's widow Plaisance, acting for his infant son, then Hugh's own mother Isabel, Henry's sister, then Hugh himself. Mary answered that there had been a mistake; her mother Melisend should have succeeded Alice as regent. Mary's only supporters were the Templars. Hugh had just reconciled himself with Philip of Montfort and the Hospital, and they were annoyed. No one else was prepared to admit that a mistake had been made in 1246 or in 1264. Moreover, a vigorous young man was obviously better suited to be monarch than a middle-aged spinster. Hugh was crowned in the cathedral at Tyre, the traditional coronation-place of the kings, on September 24, 1269, by bishop John of Lydda, acting for the patriarch William. Mary issued a formal protest, and hurried off to plead her cause at Rome.[53]

Hugh had been able to go to Tyre because of his reconciliation with Philip of Montfort, whose pride had been humbled by the loss of Toron. The older Ibelins had died, John of Arsuf in 1258, John of Beirut in 1264, and John of Jaffa in 1266. As a result of Baybars's conquests, the only lay fiefs left on the mainland were Beirut, which had passed to John of Beirut's elder daughter Isabel, and Tyre. To cement the general pacification king Hugh married his sister Margaret, the loveliest girl of her time, to Philip's elder son John, while Philip's younger son, Humphrey, married Isabel of Beirut's sister Eschiva. The king himself married one of the Ibelins of Cyprus.[54]

For the moment all seemed well. Baybars was quiescent. The Il-khan was said to be sympathetic to the Christian cause. Louis IX was known to be planning another crusade. In September 1269 king James I of Aragon sailed from Barcelona at the head of a great squadron to go crusading, but ran into so fearful a storm that he turned back home. Only two of his bastard sons continued the journey. They arrived at Acre in December, to find that Baybars had just broken his truce with the Franks. He made a demonstration in front of Acre, while others of his troops lay hidden in the hills, where they ambushed the French regiment, which had been raiding in Galilee. The princes of Aragon, who had arrived eager

[53] *Gestes des Chiprois*, 369 (pp. 772–773); *Assises de Jérusalem*, I, 415–419. See La Monte, *Feudal Monarchy*, pp. 77–79, and Hill, *History of Cyprus*, II, 161–165.
[54] *Gestes des Chiprois*, 370–371 (pp. 773–774); *Lignages*, p. 462.

to fight the enemy, now counseled caution, and soon went home having achieved nothing. But Baybars withdrew his army, for fear of Louis's crusade.[55]

The year 1270 was full of tragedy. Louis's crusade set out, not for Palestine but for Tunis, where the king and most of his army died of disease.[56] Baybars, too prudent to go campaigning till he knew of the movements of the French, arranged for his friends of the Ismā'īlite sect to assassinate Philip of Montfort at Tyre.[57] Next spring Baybars knew that he could safely attack the Franks again. In February he marched into the county of Tripoli and appeared before the Templar castle of Chastel Blanc. After a short but spirited defense, the garrison was advised by the Templar commander at Tortosa to surrender. The survivors were allowed to retire unharmed. The sultan then turned against the huge Hospitaller fortress of Krak des Chevaliers, where al-Manṣūr II of Hamah joined him. The siege began on March 3. Heavy rains at first prevented the Moslems from bringing up siege engines, but on March 15, after a short but heavy bombardment, they broke into the outer enceinte. The inner enceinte held out for another fortnight and the great south tower till April 8. On its surrender the few survivors were given a safe-conduct to go to Tripoli. Krak, which had defied Saladin, had been considered the strongest fortress in the east. Its loss was a severe blow to Frankish prestige. 'Akkār, the Hospitaller castle on the south side of the Buqai'ah, was attacked next and fell on May 1, after a fortnight's siege.[58]

Prince Bohemond, who was at Tripoli, sent to beg the sultan for a truce. Baybars mocked him for his cowardice, and insultingly ordered him to pay the expenses of the Mamluk campaign. Bohemond refused. But, after a failure to capture the little island fortress of Maraclea, whose lord had gone to seek help from the Mongols, Baybars suddenly offered a ten years' truce, which Bohemond accepted. The Mamluk army moved southward, pausing only to besiege the Teutonic fortress of Starkenburg, which surrendered on June 12. There were now no inland castles left to the Franks. But a naval expedition sent from Egypt against Cyprus failed, owing to bad seamanship. Eleven ships ran

[55] *Gestes des Chiprois*, 350–351 (pp. 766–768) (wrongly dating the episode 1267); *Estoire d'Eracles*, II, 457–458; *Annales de Terre Sainte*, p. 454.

[56] See above, chapter XIV, pp. 514–516.

[57] *Gestes des Chiprois*, 374 (pp. 775–777).

[58] *Gestes des Chiprois*, 376 (p. 777); *Estoire d'Eracles*, II, 460; al-Maqrīzī, *Al-khiṭaṭ*, I, ii, 84–85; Abū-l-Fidā', *Kitāb al-mukhtaṣar* (*RHC, Or.*, I), p. 154; Badr-ad-Dīn al-'Ainī, *'Iqd al-jamān* (*RHC, Or.*, II, 1), pp. 237–239.

aground near Limassol, and the crews fell into the hands of the Cypriotes.[59]

Baybars's willingness to make a truce was due to the arrival in the east of a small but efficient crusading army led by Edward of England, eldest son of king Henry III. Edward had left home in the summer of 1270, intending to join Louis IX, but had arrived too late at Tunis, and had spent the winter in Sicily. He had about a thousand men from England with him, and a small number of Flemings and Bretons. His brother, Edmund of Lancaster, followed close behind with a few reinforcements.

Edward arrived at Acre on May 9, 1271. He was horrified by the state of affairs. The hopes raised at the time of Hugh's coronation had been disappointed. Hugh was unpopular with the commune at Acre, which he seems to have offended by his arrogance and tactlessness. The Templars and the Teutonic Knights resented his reconciliation with the Montforts and the Hospitallers. His friend Philip of Montfort was dead, leaving two untried sons, and the Hospital, crippled by the loss of Krak, could give him little support. The Cypriote nobles still refused to serve on the mainland, and were angered by his high-handed attitude towards them. It was only in 1273 that they agreed to follow him abroad for four months in the year, provided that the king or his heir led the army in person. The Venetians and Genoese were still quarreling, and both were trading freely with the enemy, with licenses from the high court to do so. The Venetians provided the Mamluks with arms and the Genoese furnished slaves. Edward with his tiny army found that he could do nothing. Even his attempt to capture the little Moslem fortress of Qāqūn on Mt. Carmel came to nothing. His only success was diplomatic. His envoys persuaded the Mongol Īl-khan to send an expedition into Syria in the autumn of 1271. An army of Mongol horsemen swept across the Euphrates, past Aleppo, from which the garrison fled, and penetrated as far south as Apamea. But Baybars, who was at Damascus, gathered a large army and marched to meet them. The Mongols knew that they would be outnumbered and retired swiftly back over the river-frontier, laden with booty. Abagha apologized to Edward that he had not been able to spare a larger force.

Edward soon saw that he was wasting his time. He advised the Franks to make peace with Baybars, and his agents arranged a

[59] *Gestes des Chiprois*, 377–378 (pp. 777–778); *Estoire d'Eracles*, II, 460; *Annales de Terre Sainte*, p. 455; al-Maqrīzī, *Al-khiṭaṭ*, I, ii, 84–86, 88, 100; Abū-l-Fidā', *Kitāb al-mukhtaṣar* (*RHC, Or.*, I), p. 154; Badr-ad-Dīn al-'Ainī, *'Iqd al-jamān* (*RHC, Or.*, II, 1), pp. 239–240.

treaty guaranteeing the integrity of the remaining lands of the kingdom of Jerusalem for ten years and ten months. It was signed at Caesarea on May 22, 1272. As a special concession, pilgrims were to be allowed free passage to Nazareth. Edward then prepared his departure. On June 16 an Assassin, disguised as a native Christian, attempted to murder him in his tent. It seems that Baybars feared him sufficiently to wish to see him eliminated. But he recovered from the wound, and sailed from Acre in September. He arrived back in England to find his father dead and himself king.[60]

Edward was the last crusader prince to come to Palestine. It was not for lack of crusading propaganda that no others followed. Among Edward's companions had been the archdeacon of Liége, Theobald Visconti, who returned home soon after his arrival, on the news that he had been elected pope. As Gregory X he took a deep personal interest in the east, and did all that he could to encourage the crusading movement, collecting advice and reports from every appropriate authority, and placing the question of the crusade at the head of the agenda to be discussed at the great council that he summoned to Lyons in May 1274. But though expressions of good-will came from every side, no one offered to set out himself. Gregory was sadly disappointed but could do nothing.[61]

While the council was meeting, Mary of Antioch, claimant to the throne of Jerusalem, came to lay her case before it. She seems to have enjoyed the sympathy of the pope, who had probably formed a poor impression of king Hugh when he met him in Palestine in 1271. The high court of Jerusalem sent representatives to say that it alone could decide on the succession to the throne. The council therefore did not intervene. But Mary continued to enjoy the pope's favor, and he suggested that, as she was unlikely to establish herself at Acre, she should sell her rights to Charles of Anjou. It was questionable whether such rights could be sold, but the pope doubtless thought that, as he was protector of the kingdom, such a transaction done with his approval would be legal. The sale was

[60] *Gestes des Chiprois*, 376, 379–382 (pp. 777–779); *Estoire d'Eracles*, II, 460–464; *Annales de Terre Sainte*, p. 455; *Assises de Jérusalem*, I, 347, 626; II, 427–434; Dandolo, *Chronicon Venetum*, p. 380; al-Maqrīzī, *Al-khiṭaṭ*, I, ii, 102; Badr-ad-Dīn al-'Ainī, *'Iqd al-jamān* (*RHC, Or.*, II, 1), p. 207. See Powicke, *King Henry III and the Lord Edward*, II, 597–603, also Hill, *History of Cyprus*, II, 168–170. Powicke (II, 603) discusses the legend of Edward's wife Eleanor sucking the poison from his wound. It was first told by Ptolemy of Lucca a century later.

[61] For Gregory X's crusading activities and the reports which he received, see Throop, *Criticism of the Crusades*, *passim*.

not completed till 1277, after Gregory X's death. Mary received a thousand gold pounds and the promise of an annuity of four thousand *livres tournois*, and Charles assumed the title king of Jerusalem.[62]

The papacy had reason to encourage the transaction. Charles of Anjou, king of Sicily and Naples, was proving as formidable as the Hohenstaufens whom the papacy had called him in to replace. He sought to dominate Rome and all Italy, and his particular ambition was to conquer Constantinople. The Byzantine emperor Michael VIII Palaeologus had offered the submission of his church to Rome at the Council of Lyons; and the pope knew that the slender hope of the Byzantine people accepting the union depended on the protection that he provided against Charles. It was desirable to distract Charles's attention elsewhere. Moreover, the actual government at Acre left much to be desired. Hugh was proving very unsuccessful as a king. In 1273, for example, he had lost control of the fief of Beirut. Its heiress, Isabel of Ibelin, had been married as a child to the child-king of Cyprus, Hugh II. On his death she remained unmarried for some time, enjoying a liaison with Julian of Sidon. Then she married Hamo the Stranger, who seems to have been one of Edward of England's knights. He mistrusted king Hugh, and on his deathbed, in 1273, put his wife and her fief under the protection of Baybars. When Hugh tried to take the widow to Cyprus to marry her to a man of his choice, Baybars protested. The high court gave Hugh no support, and Isabel returned to Beirut with a mamluk guard to protect her.[63] Baybars's protectorate ended with his death, and Isabel married two more husbands, of her own choice, before she died in 1282, when the fief passed to her sister Eschiva, wife of Hugh's friend Humphrey of Montfort.[64]

Hugh's next rebuff was over Tripoli. Bohemond VI died in 1275, leaving a son Bohemond VII, aged fourteen, and a daughter Lucy, a few years younger. Hugh at once claimed the regency as the next adult heir to the house of Antioch. But custom gave the regency to the ruler's mother, and the dowager princess Sibyl at once assumed the office, naming Bartholomew, bishop of Tortosa, as her bailie. When Hugh arrived at Tripoli, he found the bishop administering the government, and the young prince in Armenia, under the protection of king Leon III, his uncle. No one supported Hugh, as Bartholomew was extremely popular at the moment, being the

[62] *Gestes des Chiprois*, 375 (p. 777), and references in note 53 above.
[63] *Estoire d'Eracles*, II, 462; Ibn-al-Furāt, *Ta'rīkh* (Michaud, *Bibliothèque*, IV), p. 532.
[64] *Lignages*, p. 462; Ducange-Rey, *Familles d'outremer*, pp. 235–236.

known enemy of the hated Roman faction introduced by Lucienne of Segni, Bohemond V's widow, and headed by her brother Paul, bishop of Tripoli.[65] Hugh's only success was to preserve Latakia from an attack by the Mamluks. He arranged a treaty which spared the town in return for a tribute of twenty thousand dinars annually and the release of twenty prisoners.[66]

In 1276 Hugh quarreled openly with the Temple. Its master since 1273 had been William of Beaujeu, a cousin and friend of Charles of Anjou. He was staying with Charles at the time of his election and only came to the east in 1275. In October 1276 the order purchased a farm called La Fauconnerie from its lay lord, and deliberately omitted to secure Hugh's consent to the transaction. Hugh's complaints were ignored, and he obtained no sympathy from the high court or the fraternities of Acre. In his rage he packed up his belongings and moved to Tyre, intending to sail to Cyprus and never to return. The Templars and the Venetians were delighted, but the patriarch, the commune, the Hospitallers, the Teutonic Knights, and the Genoese sent to Tyre to beg him at least to appoint a bailie. After some hesitation he consented, and named Balian of Ibelin, son of John of Arsuf. He also nominated judges for the courts of the kingdom. Then he sailed secretly for Cyprus, and wrote from there to the pope to justify his actions.

Balian had a difficult task. Hostilities broke out again between the Venetians and the Genoese. There were riots in the streets of Acre between merchants from Bethlehem supported by the Temple and merchants from Mosul supported by the Hospital. He could count on the good-will only of the patriarch, the former legate Thomas Agni of Lentini, and the Hospital. But before he had been in office for a year the government was taken out of his hands.[67]

As soon as his purchase of Mary's rights was completed, Charles of Anjou sent a small armed force to Acre under Roger of San Severino, whom he named as his bailie. With the help of the Venetians and the Temple, Roger was able to land at Acre, where he produced credentials signed by Charles of Anjou, by Mary of Antioch, and by the pope, John XXI. The bailie Balian, finding that the Temple and the Venetians were ready to use force to support Roger, and that neither the patriarch nor the Hospital would promise to intervene, admitted the Angevins into the citadel

[65] *Estoire d'Eracles*, II, 466–467; *Gestes des Chiprois*, 385 (p. 780).

[66] Al-Maqrīzī, *Al-khiṭaṭ*, I, ii, 125; Muḥī-ad-Dīn, *Sīrat al-malik aẓ-Ẓāhir* (Michaud, *Bibliothèque*, IV), p. 685.

[67] *Estoire d'Eracles*, II, 474–475; *Gestes des Chiprois*, 396 (p. 783) (post-dating the episode).

under protest. There Roger raised Charles's standard, and ordered all the barons to give him oaths of allegiance as the king's bailie. The barons hesitated, unwilling to admit that the crown could be transferred without a decision by the high court. They sent to Cyprus to ask Hugh to release them from their oath, so that they could consider the throne vacant. Hugh refused to receive their envoy. Roger then threatened to confiscate the fiefs of anyone who did not pay him homage. As the fiefs all now lay in the suburbs of Acre or were money-fiefs attached to the city's revenues, Roger could have carried out his threat. He allowed the barons to make one more fruitless appeal for guidance to Hugh. They then acknowledged him. It is doubtful whether he received homage from the Montforts of Tyre or the lady of Beirut; but even Bohemond of Tripoli recognized him as *de facto* ruler of Acre.[68]

Roger's government lasted for five years. It was a period of comparative peace. Baybars died in 1277, and it was not till the summer of 1280 that the emir Kalavun was securely established as sultan of the Mamluk empire.[69] In September 1281 there was another great Mongol invasion of Syria. Kalavun was seriously alarmed, but in October he managed to defeat the invaders in a fierce battle near Homs. The more responsible statesmen of western Europe, such as Edward of England, advocated alliance with the Mongols, but the only allies that the Il-khan found in Syria were the Armenians of Cilicia and the order of the Hospital, which sent a contingent of knights from its headquarters at al-Marqab to join in the battle at Homs.[70] Charles of Anjou had always been on good terms with Egypt; and Roger carried out his instructions. When Kalavun sent in May 1281 to suggest the prolongation of the truce with Acre for another ten years, Roger's government gladly agreed, and Bohemond of Tripoli made a similar truce two months later. Kalavun was delighted, as a Frankish attack on his left flank would have seriously embarrassed him. After his victory at Homs he received a visit from Roger, who came in person to his camp to congratulate him.[71]

Roger's policy was short-sighted. But that Bohemond should

[68] *Estoire d'Eracles*, II, 478–479; *Gestes des Chiprois*, 398 (pp. 783–784); Sanudo, *Liber secretorum fidelium crucis* (Bongars, *Gesta Dei*, II), pp. 227–228; Amadi, *Chronique*, p. 214; John of Ypres, *Chronicon*, in Martène and Durand, *Thesaurus anecdotorum*, III, col. 755.

[69] See below, chapter XXII, p. 751.

[70] *Gestes des Chiprois*, 407–408 (pp. 786–787); letter of Joseph de Cancy to king Edward I and the king's reply, in Palestine Pilgrim's Text Society, V (London, 1896): Joseph apologizes because king Hugh and prince Bohemond were unable to arrive in time to help the Mongols. See also the references in chapter XXI below, pp. 715, 722.

[71] Al-Maqrīzī, *Al-khiṭaṭ*, II, i, 28–34; Röhricht, *Regesta*, p. 374.

wish for a truce was understandable, for he was in trouble with his vassals in Tripoli. He had returned from Armenia to take over the government in 1277, when he was sixteen. His bailie, bishop Bartholomew of Tortosa, had been popular as the enemy of the Roman faction. But the leader of the Roman party, Paul of Segni, bishop of Tripoli, had attended the Council of Lyons and there made friends with the new master of the Temple, William of Beaujeu. The Templars therefore turned against the prince's government. Guy (II) Embriaco, lord of Jubail, had been ready to be friendly with Bohemond as the opponent of the Romans, but Bohemond infuriated him by refusing to let his brother John marry a local heiress, giving her instead to a nephew of bishop Bartholomew. Guy and John then kidnaped the girl and retired with her to the protection of the Templars. There they were joined by members of the younger branch of the Embriaco family, who had not forgiven the murder of their father Bertrand by Bohemond's father. Bohemond retorted by burning the Templars' buildings at Tripoli, and cutting down a forest that they owned nearby. The Templars made a demonstration outside Tripoli and burned the castle of Botron but failed to take the fort of Nephin, where twelve of their knights were captured by Bohemond's men. Bohemond then marched to attack Jubail, but was defeated near Botron. The combatants numbered only about two hundred on each side, but the carnage was tremendous. Bohemond accepted a truce, and the Templars recovered their quarters in Tripoli.[72]

In 1278 Guy of Jubail and the Templars attacked Tripoli again. Bohemond was defeated outside the walls, but twelve Templar galleys that tried to force the harbor were scattered by a storm, while fifteen of Bohemond's galleys succeeded in doing some damage to the Templar port of Sidon. A truce was arranged by the master of the Hospital, Nicholas Lorgne. But three years later, in January 1282, the Embriaco brothers and their distant cousin William smuggled themselves into Tripoli, hoping to take the town with the help of the Templars. The plot had been mismanaged, however, and the Templar commander, Reddecoeur, was away. The conspirators panicked and fled to the buildings of the Hospital. Bohemond was warned and sent troops against the Hospital, which surrendered the refugees on condition that their lives be spared. Thereupon, Bohemond took Guy of Jubail, his brothers John and Baldwin, and his kinsman William to Nephin, where they were buried in the sand up to their necks and left to starve. He claimed

[72] *Estoire d'Eracles*, II, 481; *Gestes des Chiprois*, 390–393 (pp. 781–783).

that he had not himself put them to death. The less important conspirators were blinded. The Genoese, who regarded Guy as a compatriot, became openly hostile to Bohemond, and John of Montfort, the devoted ally of the Genoese, planned to march on Jubail, but Bohemond arrived there first.[73]

Roger of San Severino's government at Acre was more tranquil, though it was resented by the local nobility. It was the Templar master, William of Beaujeu, who kept the country loyal to Roger. William managed to reconcile John of Montfort with the Venetians, who were allowed to return to their old premises at Tyre. But when in 1279 king Hugh suddenly arrived at Tyre, hoping to recover his mainland kingdom, only John offered him support. The king remained for four months at Tyre; then as he could not force his Cypriote vassals to stay longer away from their island he returned to Cyprus, rightly blaming the Templars for his failure.[74]

The massacre of the Sicilian Vespers, on March 30, 1282, forced Charles of Anjou out of Sicily and put him on the defensive. He could no longer afford to keep many troops in the east. At the end of the year Roger was summoned back to Italy with most of his forces. He left as his deputy the seneschal Odo Poilechien, a Frenchman in the Angevin service who had come with him to the east.[75] No one at first challenged Odo's power, but he was insecure. When, in June 1283, envoys came from the sultan to confirm the renewal of the truce, he gladly accepted the proposal, but had the treaty signed by the commune of Acre and the Templars of Château Pèlerin and Sidon. It guaranteed the integrity of the Frankish coast from Mt. Carmel to the Ladder of Tyre, and of Château Pèlerin and Sidon. Tyre and Beirut were excluded. The right of pilgrimage to Nazareth was confirmed.[76]

In 1283 king Hugh took advantage of Roger's departure to come once again to the mainland. His friend John of Montfort's brother Humphrey had just succeeded in his wife's right to Beirut, and the moment seemed opportune. He was obliged by the weather to land at Beirut, where he was received as king. But when he sent his troops by land to Tyre, they were mauled by Moslem raiders, instigated, he suspected, by the Templars of Sidon. When he

[73] *Gestes des Chiprois*, 409–413 (pp. 787–789).

[74] *Ibid.*, 401 (p. 784).

[75] *Ibid.*, 418 (p. 789); Sanudo, *Istoria del regno di Romania*, in C. Hopf, *Chroniques gréco-romanes inédites ou peu connues* (Berlin, 1873), pp. 138–139, 165: ". . . miser Otto de Pillicino, il qual si dicea ch' era nipote di papa Martino [IV] . . . ." Cf. Mas Latrie, "Nouvelles preuves," *Bibliothèque de l'École des chartes*, XXXIV (1873), 47–48.

[76] Al-Maqrīzī, *Al-khiṭaṭ*, II, i, 60, 179–185, 224–230.

himself landed at Tyre, the omens were unfavorable. His standard fell into the sea, and the great cross carried by the clergy who met him broke off and killed his Jewish court physician. No one moved in his favor at Acre. After four months his Cypriotes returned home, but he stayed on at Tyre. His favorite son Bohemond died there, then his friend and brother-in-law, John of Montfort. Tyre officially passed to John's brother Humphrey of Beirut, who was made to promise to sell it if required to the crown. But Humphrey died in February 1284. His widow, Eschiva, was left to govern Beirut; she later married Hugh's youngest son, Guy. Tyre was left to John's widow, the princess Margaret.[77]

Hugh himself died at Tyre on March 4, 1284.[78] He was succeeded by his eldest son John, a delicate boy of seventeen, who was crowned king of Cyprus at Nicosia on May 11 but was recognized on the mainland only at Tyre and Beirut. He died in Cyprus on May 20, 1285, and was succeeded by his brother Henry, who was crowned king of Cyprus next month but for the moment did not venture to cross to the mainland.[79]

Meanwhile Kalavun prepared to attack the Frankish possessions not covered by the recent truce. The ladies of Tyre and Beirut hastened to make their own truce with him, and the sultan concentrated his efforts against the Hospital, which he wished to punish for its constant support of the Mongols. Its one great remaining castle was al-Marqab, on a high hill overlooking Valania, on the coast north of Tortosa. On April 25, 1285, the Mamluk army arrived below the castle, and toiled up the mountainside with the greatest number of siege engines that had ever been seen in the east. But the castle was superbly sited and well equipped. It held out for a month before a mine under the north salient made further defense impossible. On their surrender the knights of the Hospital were allowed to leave fully armed on horseback with all their portable possessions, and the lives of the rest of the garrison were spared, as a tribute to their gallantry.[80]

The fall of al-Marqab alarmed the citizens of Acre. They had recently learned of the death of Charles of Anjou, and the whole west was distracted by the war of the Sicilian Vespers. The time had come to compose differences, and accept a monarch nearer at

[77] *Gestes des Chiprois,* 419–423 (pp. 789–791); Amadi, *Chronique,* pp. 214–215.

[78] *Gestes des Chiprois,* 424 (p. 791); Amadi, *Chronique,* p. 216.

[79] *Gestes des Chiprois,* 425, 431 (pp. 791–792); Amadi, *loc. cit.*

[80] *Gestes des Chiprois,* 429 (pp. 791–792); Amadi, *loc. cit.*, al-Maqrīzī, *Al-khiṭaṭ,* II, i, 80; Abū-l-Fidā', *Kitāb al-mukhtaṣar* (*RHC, Or.*, I), p. 161; Muḥī-ad-Dīn, *Sīrat al-malik aẓ-Ẓāhir* (Michaud, *Bibliothèque,* IV), pp. 548–552.

hand. On the advice of the Hospital young king Henry sent an envoy from Cyprus to Acre to negotiate for his recognition there. The commune, the Hospitallers, and the Teutonic Knights at once offered their support, and the Templars followed suit after a little hesitation. But Odo Poilechien, with the sole support of the French regiment (still paid for by the king of France) refused to resign his office. King Henry landed at Acre on June 4, 1286. The representatives of the three orders cautiously did not come to welcome him, but when they saw with what impatient enthusiasm he was received by the citizens, who threatened to take up arms to drive Odo out of the citadel, they persuaded Odo to hand it over to them, and they handed it on to the king. Odo and his Frenchmen were allowed to leave unharmed with all their possessions.[81]

On August 15 Henry was crowned at Tyre by the archbishop, Bonnacorso, acting for the patriarch Elias. The court then moved to Acre, where there was a fortnight of frivolous festivity, with tournaments and pageants and banquets. The fifteen-year-old king, who had not yet begun to suffer from the epilepsy that crippled his life, was immensely popular. His advisers were his uncles Philip and Baldwin of Ibelin. On their advice he soon returned to Cyprus, leaving Philip as bailie. It seemed to them clear that Acre preferred an absentee monarch.[82]

The hopes raised by the new reign were not fulfilled. Next spring (1287) war broke out between the Genoese and Pisan colonies all along the coast, and the Genoese, who had obtained the friendly neutrality of the sultan, blockaded the seaports and, after a victory over the Pisans and the Venetians who had joined them, planned to force their way into Acre. Only the intervention of the masters of the Temple and the Hospital persuaded them to raise the blockade and withdraw to Tyre.[83]

While this war was raging, the sultan annexed the last remnant of the principality of Antioch. The Moslem merchants of Aleppo had long complained of the inconvenience of having to send their goods through the Christian port of Latakia. In March 1287 its defenses were seriously damaged by an earthquake. Kalavun took advantage of this and, claiming that Latakia, as part of the principality of Antioch, was not covered by his truce with Tripoli, sent an army to take over the town. It fell at once, and the garrison,

[81] *Gestes des Chiprois*, 435–438 (pp. 792–793); Amadi, *Chronique*, pp. 216–217; Sanudo, *Liber secretorum*, p. 229; Mas Latrie, *Documents*, III, 671–673.

[82] *Gestes des Chiprois*, 439 (p. 793); *Annales de Terre Sainte*, p. 548; Amadi, *Chronique*, p. 217.

[83] *Gestes des Chiprois*, 440–460 (pp. 793–799); *Annales Januenses*, p. 317.

which had retired to a fort at the end of the mole, surrendered a few days later, on April 20.[84]

Bohemond VII did not long survive its loss. He died childless on October 19, 1287. His heir was his sister Lucy, who was married to a former grand admiral of Naples, Narjot of Toucy, and lived in Apulia. She was unknown to the citizens of Tripoli, who therefore decided to invite the princess-mother, Sibyl of Armenia, to take over the government. But her one idea was to restore to power the discredited bishop of Tortosa, Bartholomew. Her letter inviting him to be bailie was intercepted. After an angry scene, when the nobles told her that he was unacceptable, they and the merchants of Tripoli declared the dynasty dethroned, and set up a sovereign commune, whose mayor was Bartholomew Embriaco, son of the Bertrand whom Bohemond VI had had murdered and brother of the William whom Bohemond VII had starved to death.

Princess Sibyl retired to Armenia, but early in 1288 Lucy arrived at Acre, intending to take up her inheritance. The Hospitallers received her with honor and escorted her to Nephin, the frontier town of the county. There she issued a proclamation of her rights. The commune countered by a proclamation citing its grievances against the dynasty, and put itself under the protection of Genoa. While messengers went to Genoa to inform the council, who ordered their admiral in the east, Zaccaria, to proceed to Tripoli to make arrangements with the commune, the masters of the three orders visited Tripoli to plead Lucy's cause. The Templars and the Teutonic Knights joined chiefly because of their alliance with Venice, the enemy of Genoa. Their mission was in vain. When Zaccaria arrived at Tripoli, he would recognize the commune only on condition that Genoa was granted a larger quarter there and the right to have a podestà. Meanwhile Bartholomew Embriaco, who planned to secure the county for himself, sent secretly to Cairo to ask the sultan for support if he should proclaim himself count. Public opinion in Tripoli grew suspicious of both Bartholomew and the Genoese, and Lucy was invited to the city. She tactfully informed Zaccaria, who was in Cilicia, of her invitation and secured his approval. A general compromise was reached. The Genoese were allowed their additional streets and their podestà. The privileges of the commune and its right to administer the city were admitted, and Lucy became countess of Tripoli.[85]

[84] *Gestes des Chiprois*, 462 (pp. 799–800); Abū-l-Fidā', *Kitāb al-mukhtaṣar* (*RHC, Or.*, I), p. 162.

[85] *Gestes des Chiprois*, 464–472 (pp. 800–802); Amadi, *Chronique*, pp. 217–218; Sanudo, *Liber secretorum*, p. 229; *Annales Januenses*, pp. 332–336.

Her reign was brief. In the winter of 1288 two Frankish envoys came to Cairo and warned the sultan that, if the Genoese were allowed to control Tripoli, they would dominate the whole Levant, and the export trade of Egypt would be at their mercy. It was thought that the envoys came from the Venetians, but they may have been Bartholomew Embriaco's men.[86] The sultan, whose policy was to play Venice off against Genoa, was delighted with the excuse for intervention. In February 1289 he moved a great army into Syria. One of his emirs who was in the pay of the Templars went to the master, William, to tell him that the objective was Tripoli. But when William tried to warn the governments of Acre and Tripoli, no one believed him. They had faith in the treaties that Kalavun had made with them. When in March the Mamluk army marched down the Buqa'iah towards Tripoli, nothing had been done for its defense. The Temple and the Hospital hastily sent detachments under their marshals, and the French regiment came up from Acre under its commander, John of Grailly. From Cyprus king Henry sent his young brother Amalric, whom he appointed constable of Jerusalem, with some knights and five galleys. The Genoese admiral Zaccaria had four galleys in the port, and the Venetians two, and there were various smaller boats, some local and some Italian. There had been others, but they sailed, with many civilians on board, to Cyprus.

Medieval Tripoli stood on the peninsula where the modern al-Mina now stands. It was detached from the castle of Pilgrim Mountain, which rises above the modern town. The castle was undefended, and in the last days of March 1289 Kalavun moved his whole army up to the city walls. The Christians commanded the sea, and could pour provisions into the harbor. But the land fortifications could not stand up against the sultan's pitiless bombardment. When two of the towers on the southeastern wall crumbled, the Venetians decided that further defense was useless and retired with their portable possessions to their ships. The Genoese then followed suit, fearing that the Venetians might steal some of their ships. The Italians' defection threw the defense into disorder. When the sultan ordered a general assault that morning, April 26, 1289, there was no organized opposition. His troops poured into the city, and a panic-stricken horde of soldiers and civilians fled before them to the harbor. The countess escaped in a Cypriote

[86] *Gestes des Chiprois,* 473 (p. 802) (the author says that he knows the envoys' names but prefers not to tell); abū-l-Maḥāsin, *An-nujūm az-zāhirah* (Michaud, *Bibliothèque,* IV), p. 561, says that they were sent by Bartholomew.

galley with prince Amalric and the two marshals, but there were few other survivors of the general massacre that followed. A few refugees rowed across to the tiny island of St. Thomas, off the point, but the Mamluk cavalry crossed the shallow water after them and slew them all. Their corpses were left to rot in the sun.[87]

A few days later the sultan's troops occupied Botron and Nephin. All that was left of the county of Tripoli was Jubail, whose lord, Peter Embriaco, was allowed to remain there under strict Moslem supervision for another eight or nine years.[88]

The fall of Tripoli presaged an attack on Acre. Yet its citizens could not believe that the sultan would really eliminate a center which was of commercial convenience to everyone. King Henry had gone to Acre, and there he received envoys from Kalavun, who reproached him for having broken his truce by going to the rescue of Tripoli. He replied that, if Tripoli had been included in the truce, the sultan had no right to attack it. His excuse was accepted, and a new truce, in which the lady of Tyre joined, was signed for ten years, ten months, and ten days. But Henry had lost confidence in the sultan's word. Before he returned to Cyprus in September, leaving his brother Amalric as bailie, he sent John of Grailly to the west to beg for urgent help.[89]

John of Grailly obtained sympathy but no material response in the west. The Genoese, who had suffered serious losses at Tripoli, had countered by attacking Egyptian merchant shipping and raiding the Delta village of at-Tīnah. But when Kalavun closed Alexandria to them, they hastened to make peace. When their envoys came to Cairo, they found embassies from both the German and the Byzantine emperors waiting upon the sultan.[90] The Venetians had not much regretted the fall of Tripoli but were nervous for Acre, where they held the commercial hegemony. They agreed to send twenty galleys, under Nicholas Tiepolo. The pope entrusted him and John of Grailly and Hugh of Sully, who sailed with him, with a thousand pieces of gold each. His fleet was joined by five galleys sent by king James of Aragon. The only other answer to the

[87] *Gestes des Chiprois*, 474–477 (pp. 802–804); *Annales Januenses*, pp. 322–326; Amadi, *Chronique*, p. 218; Auria, *Annales* (*MGH*, *SS.*, XVIII), p. 324; al-Maqrīzī, *Al-khiṭaṭ*, II, i, 101–103; Abū-l-Fidā', *Kitāb al-mukhtaṣar* (*RHC*, *Or.*, I), pp. 163–164.

[88] Sanudo, *Liber secretorum*, p. 230; al-Maqrīzī, *Al-khiṭaṭ*, II, i, 103–104. For Jubail, see Grousset, *Histoire des croisades*, III, 745, note 3.

[89] *Gestes des Chiprois*, 479 (p. 804); Amadi, *loc. cit.*; Odorico Rinaldi ("Raynaldus"), *Annales ecclesiastici post Baronium ab anno 1198 usque ad annum 1565*, XIV (Cologne, 1692), 421 (ad. ann. 1289, cap. 68).

[90] Heyd, *Histoire du commerce du Levant*, I, 416–418.

appeal that the pope sent out after hearing John of Grailly's tale came from a rabble of peasants and unemployed townsfolk from Lombardy and Tuscany, men eager to find adventure and loot and the reward of spiritual merit. The pope had little confidence in them, but he put them under the command of Bernard, the refugee bishop of Tripoli, who, he hoped, would keep them under restraint. These reinforcements arrived at Acre in August 1290.[91]

The truce between the sultan and king Henry had restored confidence at Acre. There was a good harvest that year in Syria. Trade was booming, and Acre was full of merchants from the interior. But the arrival of the Italian crusaders at once caused trouble. They were drunken, disorderly, and irrepressible. One day at the end of August a riot started between them and some Moslem merchants. Soon the Italians were rushing wildly through the streets of Acre slaughtering everyone that they saw who wore a beard or eastern dress. Many local Christians perished along with the Moslems. The barons and the knights of the military orders were horrified. They managed to give refuge to a few Moslems within the castle, and eventually stilled the riot and arrested the ringleaders.

When Kalavun heard of the massacre, he decided that the time had come to eradicate the Franks. The government at Acre hastened to send him apologies. He replied with an embassy demanding that the ringleaders should be handed over to him. The bailie Amalric called a council, at which William of the Temple suggested that all the criminals in the jails of Acre should be sent to Cairo as being the guilty men. But no one else supported a proposal to send Christians to certain death. Instead, there was an attempt to persuade the ambassadors that Moslem merchants had started the riot. Receiving no satisfaction from Acre, Kalavun consulted his qadis, who told him that he would be justified in breaking the truce. He gathered together his army.

Once again Templar agents at the Mamluk court warned William of Beaujeu, who sent a personal envoy to Cairo. Kalavun offered to spare Acre in return for as many Venetian sequins as the city had inhabitants. But when William put this proposal before the high court, it was scornfully rejected, and he himself was insulted as a traitor.[92]

[91] *Gestes des Chiprois*, 480 (pp. 804-805); Dandolo, *Chronicon venetum*, p. 402; Sanudo, *Liber secretorum*, p. 229; Amadi, *Chronique*, pp. 218–219.

[92] *Gestes des Chiprois*, 480–481 (pp. 805–806); Amadi, *Chronique*, p. 219; Bustron, *Chronique de l'île de Chypre*, ed. Mas Latrie, p. 118; al-Maqrīzī, *Al-khiṭaṭ*, II, i, 109; Muḥī-ad-Dīn, *Sīrat al-malik aẓ-Ẓāhir* (Michaud, *Bibliothèque*, IV), pp. 567–568; Ludolf of Suchem, *Description of the Holy Land* (tr. Stewart, Palestine Pilgrims' Text Society, XII), pp. 54–56.

Kalavun no longer hid his intentions. On November 4 he left Cairo at the head of his troops. But he suddenly fell ill, and six days later he died. The people at Acre considered that their troubles were over.[93]

But there was not the usual disputed succession in Egypt. Kalavun's son al-Ashraf Khalīl dealt at once with the inevitable palace conspiracy, and within a few days was firmly established on his father's throne. But it was now too late in the year to start the campaign against Acre. The government there hoped to find the new sultan more pacific and sent an embassy to congratulate him and ask for peace terms. The ambassadors were thrown at once into prison, where they died.[94]

After careful preparations the Moslem army moved from Egypt in March 1291. On March 6 the sultan left Cairo for Damascus, where he deposited his harem. Meanwhile men and siege machines were gathered from all over his empire. The army from Hamah was so heavily laden that it took a month to travel over the muddy roads from Krak down to Acre. The sultan collected almost a hundred machines, including two vast catapults called the Victorious and the Furious, and a new efficient type of light mangonel called the Black Oxen. His forces were said to number 60,000 horsemen and 160,000 infantrymen. However exaggerated these numbers may be, the Moslems must have outnumbered the Christian forces by about ten to one. On April 5 this huge army encamped before the walls of Acre.

By now the Franks had realized their plight. The military orders summoned all their available members from Europe, to serve under their respective masters, the Templar William of Beaujeu, the Hospitaller John of Villiers, and the Teutonic Conrad of Feuchtwangen, whose predecessor Burkhard had made a bad impression by choosing to resign his office a few months before. There were a few English knights sent by Edward I under the command of the Swiss Otto of Grandison. King Henry, who was ill, sent troops from Cyprus and promised to follow with reinforcements as soon as he could. Meanwhile his brother Amalric was in command. Every able-bodied man in Acre was enlisted for the defense. In all, the garrison numbered about a thousand horsemen and twelve to fourteen thousand foot-soldiers. The defenses were in good condition. The government had never neglected them, and visiting

[93] *Gestes des Chiprois*, 482 (p. 806); Amadi, *Chronique*, p. 219; al-Maqrīzī, *Al-khiṭaṭ*, II, i, 110–112; Abū-l-Fidā', *Kitāb al-mukhtaṣar* (*RHC, Or.*, I), p. 163. Other Arabic sources give Kalavun's death date as December 6.

[94] *Gestes des Chiprois*, 483–487 (pp. 806–807); al-Maqrīzī, *Al-khiṭaṭ*, II, i, 120.

pilgrims had helped to pay for their upkeep and repair. On the west and south the city was protected by the sea. On the north and east a double line of walls ran encasing both the city and its northern suburb Montmusart. The two quarters were separated by a single wall and the castle. The north and east walls met at a salient, at the end of which jutted out a great tower recently built by king Henry II, opposite the so-called "accursed tower" on the inner wall. Projecting from king Henry's tower was a barbican built by king Hugh. This salient was considered the most vulnerable section of the defense. It was therefore entrusted to the bailie Amalric and the royal troops. On his right were the French and English knights, under John of Grailly and Otto of Grandison, then the Venetian and Pisan troops, and, next to the sea, those of the commune of Acre. The Teutonic Knights supplemented the royal troops, and on their left, along the walls of Montmusart, were the Hospitallers, then the Templars. The army of Hamah was opposite the Templars, that of Damascus opposite the Hospitallers, and the Egyptian army stretched from the salient to the bay of Acre, with the sultan's tent pitched near the shore.

The Christians had command of the sea. Many women and children had already been transferred to Cyprus, and the ships had returned laden with provisions. A considerable flotilla lay off the harbor and at the quays. It was later believed that many able-bodied men had slipped away with the refugees. But the taunts of cowardice that were freely exchanged afterwards seem to have had small foundation.

The siege began on April 6 with a bombardment from the sultan's catapults and mangonels that was maintained day and night, while his archers poured their arrows at the galleries on the walls and over them into the town. On April 15 the Templars made a moonlight sortie into the camp of the Hamah army, which began well, till the knights and their horses became entangled in the tent ropes and were forced back in confusion. A sortie by the Hospitallers in pitch darkness a few days later failed completely. It was then decided that sorties were too expensive, for the defense realized that men and armaments were both running short. Meanwhile the sultan's sappers were at work. There were said to be a thousand employed against each tower of the enceinte.

King Henry arrived on May 4, with a hundred horsemen and two thousand infantrymen, and with John Turco, archbishop of Nicosia. In a last effort to make peace he sent envoys to the sultan, who merely asked them if they had brought the keys of the city.

He added that as a tribute to the king, who was so young and so ill, he would spare the lives of the defenders. All that he wanted was the place. As he spoke, a stray catapult-stone fell among the bystanders. Al-Ashraf in his rage wanted to kill the envoys, but was persuaded to send them back to Acre.

By May 8 the barbican of king Hugh was so badly damaged that it had to be abandoned. On May 15 the outer wall of the tower of king Henry collapsed, and the Mamluks passed in over its ruins. The towers on either side, that of St. Nicholas to the south and those of the English and the countess of Blois on the west, were already undermined. The defense was forced back to the inner enceinte. A fierce attack on St. Anthony's gate, where the wall of Montmusart met the city wall, was beaten back by the Templars.

The sultan ordered a general assault for the morning of Friday the 18th. It was launched against the whole length of the walls from St. Anthony's gate to the bay of Acre on the south, but concentrated on the "accursed tower" at the salient. Wave after wave of turbaned assailants were hurled against the walls to the din of trumpets and drums and battlecries. It was not long before the tower fell and the royal troops were pushed back on to the Templars. There they made a stand. The Hospitallers came up to their support, but neither Templars nor Hospitallers could recover any lost ground. The enemy poured into the city, cutting off John of Grailly and Otto of Grandison on the eastern wall. There was furious fighting in the streets, but Acre was lost. King Henry and his brother Amalric managed to reach a ship at the quay. The master of the Hospital was carried wounded and protesting by his followers to another ship. The master of the Temple was taken mortally wounded to the buildings of the Temple. John of Grailly was severely wounded, and led by Otto of Grandison to a Venetian ship. There was a ghastly panic on the quays. The aged patriarch, Nicholas of Hannapes, was rowed out towards a ship in the roadstead, but he allowed so many refugees to crowd into his boat that it sank and he was drowned. The Templar Roger de Flor managed to seize a ship and made a fortune out of the money that he extracted from the noble ladies to whom he gave refuge. No one knew how many people perished, drowned or slaughtered by the Moslems. Very few lives were spared. The number of prisoners taken was comparatively small.

By evening all Acre was in the sultan's hands, except for the Templar building which jutted out into the sea at the southwest corner of the city. There several knights and a number of civilians had taken refuge, and ships that had landed refugees in Cyprus came back to its aid. After a week of fruitless attack the sultan offered to let the inmates go free if the building were surrendered to him. His offer was accepted, but the Moslem soldiers who entered the building began to molest the Christian women and boys. The Templars in their fury turned them out and prepared to renew the fight. The Mamluks laid mines, and on May 28 the landward walls began to crumble. The Moslems were rushing in through the widening breach when the whole edifice collapsed killing defenders and assailants alike.[95]

Tyre had already fallen. When Mamluk troops appeared there on May 19, the garrison abandoned the town without a struggle, for all that it was the strongest fortress on the coast and had successfully defied Saladin. Sidon was occupied at the end of June, though its Castle of the Sea was held by the Templars till July 14. Beirut surrendered on July 31, after the commanders of the garrison had been tricked into placing themselves in the Mamluks' power. The Templars did not attempt to hold either of their great castles, Château Pèlerin and Tortosa. The latter was evacuated on August 3 and the former on August 14.[96] All that was left to them now was the waterless island of Ruad, two miles off the coast opposite Tortosa. They held it for twelve more years.

When the whole country was in his power, the sultan al-Ashraf ordered the systematic destruction of every castle on the coast, so that the Franks might never again establish a foothold in Outremer. Nor did they.

[95] The story of the siege and fall of Acre is told on the Frankish side by the *Gestes des Chiprois*, 489–508 (pp. 808–817) (the author, the so-called "Templar of Tyre", who was not a Templar but the secretary of the master of the Temple, was present and gives a fairly impartial account); Marino Sanudo, *Liber secretorum*, pp. 229–331 (he was a contemporary but not himself present, and bases his account chiefly on the *Gestes*); *De excidio urbis Acchonis*, *passim*, in Martène and Durand, *Veteres scriptores*, V, whose anonymous author, also a contemporary but not himself present, is very free with accusations of treachery and cowardice, in order to arouse the conscience of the west; and Thaddeus of Naples, *Hystoria de desolacione Acconensis*, ed. Riant, *passim*, which was written a little later and is equally abusive, also for propaganda purposes. Chroniclers such as Amadi and Bustron give short second-hand accounts. A short account in Greek, written by the monk Arsenius, is quoted by Bartholomew of Neocastro (ed. Paladino, *RISS*, XIII, iii), p. 132; it accuses the Franks of laziness and evil living but not of cowardice. Ludolf of Suchem's account (pp. 54–61) gives traditions learnt in the east a few years later. Roger de Flor's adventures were recorded by Muntaner, *Cronica*, ed. Coroleu, p. 378. Of the Arabic writers, the account of Abū-l-Fidā', *Kitāb al-mukhtaṣar* (*RHC, Or., I*), pp. 163–164; is brief, but he was an eye-witness. The fullest account is that given by al-Maqrīzī, *Al-khiṭaṭ*, II, i, 120–126, which correlates all the Arab chroniclers. A letter from the sultan to the Armenian king Heṭoum II, full of boastful details, is quoted in Bartholomew Cotton, *Historia Anglicana* (Rolls Series, XVI), p. 221.

[96] *Gestes des Chiprois*, 504, 509–513 (pp. 815, 817–818); *Annales de Terre Sainte*, p. 460; al-Maqrīzī, *Al-khiṭaṭ*, II, i, 126–131; Abū-l-Fidā', *Kitāb al-mukhtaṣar* (*RHC, Or.*, I), p. 164; al-Jazarī, *Ḥawādith az-zamān*, tr. Sauvaget, pp. 6–8.

XVII
THE KINGDOM OF CYPRUS
1191–1291

From the moment when Richard the Lionhearted arrived with his fleet off Limassol on May 6, 1191, the island of Cyprus was destined to take an increasingly large place in crusading history.

For an almost exhaustive bibliography, see Sir George Hill, *A History of Cyprus* (4 vols., Cambridge, 1940–1952; vol. IV edited by Sir Harry Luke), II, xiii–xl, with a commentary on the sources, III, 1143–1155. Cf. reviews of Hill's work by J. L. LaMonte in *Speculum*, XXIII (1948), 704–706, and by V. Laurent in *Revue des études byzantines*, VI (1948), 269–272. Besides Hill, see: J. L. LaMonte, "Chronology of the Latin Orient," *Bulletin of the International Committee of Historical Sciences*, XII (Paris, 1942–1943), 141–202; V. Laurent, "Les Fastes épiscopaux de l'église de Chypre," *Revue des études byzantines*, VI (1948), 153–166; *idem*, "La Succession épiscopale des derniers archevêques grecs de Chypre, de Jean le Crétois (1152) à Germain Pésimandros (1260)," *ibid.*, VII (1949), 33–41; J. Darrouzès, "Évêques inconnus ou peu connus de Chypre," *Byzantinische Zeitschrift*, XLIV (1951), 97–104 (mostly from fourteenth century and later); J. Richard, "Pairie d'orient latin: Les Quatre baronies des royaumes de Jérusalem et de Chypre," *Revue historique de droit français et étranger*, XXVIII (1950), 67–88; *idem*, "Nouveaux documents des archives italiennes concernants l'orient latin," *Procès-verbaux de l'Académie des Inscriptions et Belles-lettres* (Paris, 1948), pp. 258–265; and J. P. Donovan, *Pelagius and the Fifth Crusade* (Philadelphia, 1950).

Among earlier authorities cited by Hill, the following are of special value for this period in addition to the general sources for the history of the crusades: *Les Gestes des Chiprois; Recueil de chroniques françaises écrites en orient aux xiiie et xive siècles (Philippe de Novare et Gérard de Monréal)* (ed. G. Raynaud, Société de l'orient latin, Geneva, 1887; and another edition, *RHC, Arm.*, II, 651–872); Philip of Novara, *Mémoires, 1218–1243* (ed. Ch. Kohler, Les Classiques français du moyen-âge, X, Paris, 1913) (the central portion of the *Gestes des Chiprois*); Philip of Novara, *The Wars of Frederick II against the Ibelins in Syria and Cyprus* (tr. and ed. J. L. LaMonte, with verse translation of the poems by M. J. Hubert, Records of Civilization, XXV, New York, 1936); Louis de Mas Latrie, *Histoire de l'île de Chypre sous le règne des princes de la maison de Lusignan* (3 vols., Paris, 1852–1861); Leontios Makhairas, *Recital concerning the Sweet Land of Cyprus, entitled "Chronicle"* (ed. and tr. R. M. Dawkins, 2 vols., Oxford, 1932); Francesco Amadi, *Chroniques d'Amadi et de Strambaldi* (ed. R. de Mas Latrie, Collection de documents inédits sur l'histoire de France, Paris, 1891); Estienne de Lusignan, *Description de toute l'isle de Cypre et des roys, princes, et seigneurs . . . iusques en l'an . . . mil cinq cens soizante et douze* (Paris, 1580); *Excerpta Cypria, Materials for a History of Cyprus* (tr. C. D. Cobham, Cambridge, 1908); J. L. LaMonte, "A Register of the Cartulary of the Cathedral of Santa Sophia of Nicosia," *Byzantion*, V (1929–1930), 439–522; and J. Delaville le Roulx, *Cartulaire général de l'ordre des hospitaliers de S. Jean de Jérusalem (1100–1310)* (4 vols., Paris, 1894–1906).

For modern works, in addition to Mas Latrie's and Hill's histories cited above, see: N. Iorga, *France de Chypre* (Paris, 1931) (interesting viewpoints, though many inaccuracies); J. Hackett, *A History of the Orthodox Church in Cyprus* (London, 1901; Greek translation by C. I. Papaïoannou, 3 vols., Athens and Peiraeus, 1923–1927); Sir Ronald Storrs, *A Chronology of Cyprus* (Nicosia, 1930) (useful, though a few inaccuracies); M. Grandclaude, *Étude critique sur les livres des Assises de Jérusalem* (Paris, 1923); C. Enlart, *L'Art gothique et de la renaissance en Chypre* (2 vols., Paris, 1899); and G. Jeffery, *A Description of the Historic Monuments of Cyprus* (Nicosia, 1918).

Whether one holds with Iorga that the conquest of Cyprus was an integral part of Richard's grand strategy for the crusade, or with Hill that the conquest was only a "side-issue", which later developed into a major operation, still the position and resources of the island were obviously bound to involve it eventually in the fortunes of the crusader states on the mainland.[1] Cape Andreas, the easternmost tip of the island, lies only a day's sail, with favoring winds, from the coast of Syria less than seventy miles distant; and the northern coast of the island approaches to within forty miles of the coast of Anatolia. In clear weather from the height of Stavrovouni one can see Mt. Lebanon, and from the peaks of the northern range of mountains, the summits of the Taurus range eighty miles away. For centuries a way-station for pilgrim traffic to the Holy Land, Cyprus, since the First Crusade, had intermittently provided ships and supplies to the crusaders. In 1155 or 1156, it suffered from a devastating raid, condemned alike by Greeks and Latins, at the hands of the freebooting Reginald of Châtillon.

In 1191 Cyprus had been subject for almost seven years to the tyranny of a great-nephew of emperor Manuel I, Isaac Ducas Comnenus, who had assumed the title *basileus* and had thwarted all efforts of the emperors Andronicus I Comnenus and Isaac II Angelus to dislodge him. An enemy of the Latins and an ally of Saladin, Isaac Comnenus of Cyprus prevented the Franks in Syria from procuring provisions, and gave orders that no ship of the crusaders was to be allowed to enter any port of the island.[2] Toward the end of April 1191, two of the ships accompanying that in which Richard's sister, Joan of Sicily, and his betrothed, Berengaria, had sailed from Messina, were wrecked on the southern coast near Limassol. Isaac robbed and mistreated the survivors, endeavored to entice the ladies ashore in order to hold them for ransom, and, upon

[1] Iorga, *France de Chypre*, pp. 16–17; Hill, *History of Cyprus*, I, 315–316.

[2] Hill, *History of Cyprus*, I, 317, cites only English sources for the league with Saladin; cf. Hackett, *Orthodox Church in Cyprus*, p. 60; R. Grousset, *Histoire des croisades*, III, 47; and Mas Latrie, *Histoire de l'île de Chypre*, I, 21 (the last cites also the Continuator of William of Tyre and William the Breton). But see Abū-Shāmah, *Ar-rauḍatain* (*RHC*, *Or.*, IV), pp. 508–510, quoting a letter of the qadi al-Fāḍil, secretary of state under Saladin, who refers to the "liberated king from Cyprus", his opposition toward the king of England, and his offer of friendship to the sultan. The editors of *ar-Rauḍatain*, p. 510, note 1, say that the phrase "roi affranchi" (Arabic, *al-malik al-'atīq*, involving a play on words with another meaning of "good" or "precious") refers to Guy of Lusignan, liberated after Hattin, but this makes little sense since Guy aided Richard in taking Cyprus. It seems probable that it refers to Isaac who, before going to Cyprus, had been taken prisoner and liberated by the Armenians. A reference to a *roi affranchi* at the siege of Acre undoubtedly does refer to Guy: see p. 413 and note 2, with reference to another possible translation: "ancien roi". The index, s.v. "Chypre" and "Guy de Lusignan", continues the confusion. Cf. A. Cartellieri, *Philipp II. August* (4 vols., Leipzig, 1899–1921), II, 189, note 1, who identifies the "liberated king from Cyprus" as Isaac. On the Byzantine situation, see above, chapter IV, pp. 145–148.

their refusal, denied them supplies of fresh water. At this juncture, Richard with the rest of his fleet arrived from Rhodes (May 6).

Within a month the whole island had fallen to Richard.[3] On May 12 he married Berengaria at Limassol and had her crowned queen of England. At Famagusta envoys arrived from Philip Augustus to press Richard to hurry on to Acre, but the latter sent word:

> 'Twas vain to urge him on to haste;
> The words they spake were but a waste.
> Himself had made swift action,
> And, having with the Greeks begun,
> The half of Russia's wealth he'd spurn
> Before to Syria he would turn
> Till he had crushed the Cypriot
> From whose isle rich supplies are got.[4]

During the conquest Guy of Lusignan, anxious to gain Richard's support against Philip Augustus and the party of Conrad of Montferrat, arrived with a contingent from the mainland. Familiar with the "passable roads and difficult places" of the island,[5] he helped in the reduction of the great northern castles of Kyrenia, Kantara, Buffavento, and St. Hilarion (Dieudamour to the Franks).

When Isaac was captured, he asked Richard, according to the popular legend, not to place him in irons. Richard, accordingly, turned him over in silver chains to the custody of the Hospitallers, who imprisoned him in their castle of al-Marqab until shortly before his death, probably in 1195. With all Cyprus in his hands, including enormous booty, Richard sailed for Acre on June 5, after appointing Richard de Camville and Robert of Turnham to administer the island, with orders to send supplies to Syria. Thereafter "the Franks received reinforcements by sea, as well food as soldiers and arms, to such an extent that fresh vegetables and early fruits were sent to them from the island of Cyprus and arrived within forty-eight hours."[6]

The Cypriotes, embittered by the despotic rule of Isaac, had put up little opposition to Richard, but they were speedily disillusioned. Neophytus, the saintly hermit of the Enkleistra, in a

[3] See Hill, *History of Cyprus*, I, 317 ff. and notes for variant versions of the conquest, which is discussed in the context of the Third Crusade in chapter II, above, pp. 62–64.

[4] Ambroise, *The Crusade of Richard Lion-Heart* (tr. and ed. M. J. Hubert and J. L. LaMonte, Records of Civilization, XXXIV, New York, 1941), lines 1895–1902.

[5] *Itinerarium perigrinorum et gesta regis Ricardi*, in *Chronicles and Memorials of the Reign of Richard I* (ed. W. Stubbs, 2 vols., Rolls Series, XXXVIII), I, 202.

[6] Kamāl-ad-Dīn, *Zubdat al-ḥalab fī ta'rīkh Ḥalab*, tr. and ed. E. Blochet, "L'Histoire d'Alep," *ROL*, IV (1896), 195.

letter to a friend, after describing the misrule of Isaac, writes: ". . . lo, the Englishman lands in Cyprus, and forthwith all ran unto him! Then the king [Isaac], abandoned by his people, gave himself also unto the hands of the English. Him the English king bound in irons and having seized his vast treasures, and grievously wasted the land, sailed away to Jerusalem, leaving behind him ships to strip the country . . . . The wicked wretch achieved nought against his fellow wretch Saladin, but achieved this only, that he sold our country to the Latins for two hundred thousand pounds of gold. Whereon great was the wailing . . . ." The hermit took bitter satisfaction in the inconclusive outcome of the Third Crusade, for "Providence was not well pleased to thrust out dogs, and to bring wolves in their room."[7]

An unsuccessful revolt by the disaffected Greeks led Richard, anxious to avoid further difficulties with his new conquest, to sell Cyprus to the Templars for a down payment of 40,000 dinars, with 60,000 more to follow from the revenues of the island. Having attempted to exploit the island to the limit, the Templars were faced in April 1192 with a new revolt, which they suppressed mercilessly, with much indiscriminate bloodshed. Disgusted with their purchase, they then, possibly at the suggestion of the dispossessed king of Jerusalem, Guy of Lusignan, turned the island over to him. He paid them 40,000 dinars, borrowed either from the burgesses of Tripoli or from the Genoese, and assumed responsibility for the remaining 60,000 still owing to Richard.[8]

Thus by a strange series of chances, Cyprus, permanently separated from the Greek empire, fell under the dynasty of the Lusignans, who ruled it for close on three hundred years. In the thirteenth century it became a "staging area" for crusading operations, and in the fourteenth and fifteenth centuries, the easternmost outpost of Christendom.

In May 1192, at about the time when Henry of Champagne became ruler of Jerusalem, Guy, having taken possession of the island from Richard I, crossed over to Cyprus. He found vacant lands to be distributed: the ancient public domain, and the lands of those who had fled before or after Richard's conquest.[9] He found

[7] *Excerpta Cypria* (tr. Cobham), pp. 12, 10. For dating of this letter about 1196, see Hill, *History of Cyprus*, I, 309, note 2.

[8] See note on the sale in Hill, *History of Cyprus*, II, 67–69.

[9] The chroniclers of the conquest speak of Greek magnates who, at Nicosia, gave Richard half their lands in return for confirmation of their privileges. Since no further mention of them is found, it is probable that those who submitted kept their lands and the rest lost all. See Mas Latrie, *Histoire de l'île de Chypre*, I, 46–47.

a terrified population to be reassured, for the ferocity of the Templars had caused inhabitants of both town and country to seek refuge in the mountains. When Guy "had the land, he sent out word to restore confidence to the villeins and he repeopled the cities and the castles; and he sent word to all the countries round about that all knights and Turcopoles and burgesses who wished fiefs and lands should come to him and he would give them to them. So they came from the kingdom of Jerusalem, from Tripoli, from Antioch, and from Armenia. And there were established fiefs worth four hundred white bezants for a knight and worth three hundred for a turcopole with two horses and a coat of mail; and they were assigned lands and he gave burgages in the cities."[10] Guy enfeoffed knights dispossessed by Saladin; widows, whom he dowered and married off; orphans; and even "Greeks, cobblers, masons, and writers of the Saracen tongue." In all he parceled out about three hundred fiefs to knights and two hundred to men-at arms, besides further grants to burgesses and to the common people, so that he had left scarcely the wherewithal to support twenty knights.[11] The *Eracles* compares this policy favorably with that of the first Latin emperor at Constantinople a decade later: "And I tell you truly that if count Baldwin had thus peopled the land of Constantinople, when he was emperor, he would never have lost it. But, by bad advice, he coveted all and so lost all, both his body and his land."[12]

Having laid the foundations of a new feudal monarchy in Cyprus, Guy died some time after August 18, 1194.[13] He had never assumed the title king of Cyprus, but only that of *dominus*. His contemporaries judged him weak and lacking in discernment, even simpleminded, yet unquestionably he possessed considerable courage. Though possibly he was too open-handed in his distribution of lands, he showed wisdom and common sense in his arrangements for Cyprus. Richard had granted the island to Guy for life only and, upon quitting the Holy Land, had transferred his rights to Henry of Champagne, but neither Richard nor Henry claimed

[10] *Eracles* (*RHC, Occ.*, II), pp. 191–192.

[11] *Ibid.*, pp. 188–189 (MS. G).

[12] *Ibid.*, p. 189 (MS. D); Mas Latrie, *Histoire de l'île de Chypre*, II, 9. Baldwin I of Constantinople did of course distribute fiefs, but chiefly to Latins, thus alienating many Greeks (see above, chapter VI, pp. 192–193, 199).

[13] Until recently the accepted date of Guy's death has been April 1194, but Jean Richard has discovered in the State Archives of Genoa the only known charter of Guy as Lord of Cyprus, dated August 18, 1194: his "Nouveaux documents," *Procès-verbaux*, p. 261. For varying estimates of Guy, see M. W. Baldwin, *Raymond III of Tripolis and the Fall of Jerusalem (1140–1187)* (Princeton, 1936), pp. 62 ff., and volume I of the present work, chapter XIX, pp. 603, 611.

the reversion. Guy was succeeded by his younger brother Aimery (1194–1205).

After being duly chosen by the barons of Cyprus, Aimery's first task was to replenish his treasury, badly depleted by Guy's generosity. Since his brother had given away almost all the land (and at fixed values, while the lands had appreciated to almost double), Aimery called together the knights and said: "You are my men. You know well that I have so little land that each one of you has more than I. How should it be that I, who am your lord, should be so poor and you so rich? That is not seemly. Therefore, I ask that you take counsel among yourselves and that each man of you surrender to me some of your rents and of your land." After each had done "what he could", Aimery took measures "either by force, or by friendship, or by agreement", so that at his death his revenues in Cyprus had risen to at least 200,000 bezants.[14]

Since Aimery "feared the emperor of Constantinople, who was a Grifon",[15] he determined to strengthen his position by asking for the crown of Cyprus from emperor Henry VI. The emperor, prevented by illness from leading his projected crusade, appointed the imperial chancellor, bishop Conrad of Hildesheim, to head the expedition, and entrusted the coronation to him. In the autumn of 1197, Aimery did homage to the chancellor in Nicosia and was crowned. This coronation was to bear bitter fruits in the Lombard war of Frederick II.

Meanwhile Henry of Champagne died in September 1197, and the high court of Jerusalem, prompted by the imperial chancellor, offered the crown to Aimery. Aimery accepted, but disappointed Innocent III, who saw the potential advantage to the Holy Land of a king with the resources of Cyprus at his command, by stipulating that the revenues of the kingdom of Cyprus should not be used to bolster up the kingdom of Jerusalem. He married the widowed queen Isabel (his first wife Eschiva of Ibelin had died), and was crowned with her in October 1197. Thenceforth he resided more frequently at Acre than at Nicosia. He proved himself a notable ruler until, in the Lenten season of 1205, he died of overindulgence in the choice *daurades* which the fisherfolk brought him. "King of the two kingdoms, first of Cyprus and then of Syria,"

[14] *Eracles* (*RHC, Occ.*, II), pp. 190–191 (MS. C gives 300,000 bezants; MS. G, 200,000). Before Henry of Champagne died, he and Aimery, who had been at odds, patched up their differences in an agreement which remitted the 60,000 dinars which Aimery still owed; it also provided that Aimery's three sons marry Henry's three daughters, but when the time arrived for this, Hugh (see below, p. 605) was the only surviving son.

[15] I.e., a Greek, Alexius III Angelus (1195–1203): *Eracles* (*RHC, Occ.*, II), p. 209. For the plans of Henry VI, see above, chapter III, pp. 116–120.

wrote John of Ibelin in the *Livre des Assises*, "he governed both well and wisely until his death."[16]

Aimery's heir for the crown of Cyprus was his ten-year-old son by Eschiva, Hugh I (1205–1218). In violation of the rule that the regent to administer the kingdom should be the nearest relative on the side through which the throne escheated, and that the guardian of the minor king should be the nearest relative on the other side, the high court of Nicosia appointed Walter of Montbéliard, constable of Jerusalem and husband of Hugh's elder sister Burgundia, to both positions.[17] In 1208, when Hugh attained the marriageable age of fourteen, Walter negotiated the marriage of the young king with Alice, daughter of Henry of Champagne and Isabel of Jerusalem. Hugh's first act upon reaching his majority in 1210 was to demand from Walter an accounting of his administration. Breaking his promise to the high court to render an account, Walter decamped with his family and valuables to Acre, where he was welcomed by his cousin, John of Brienne, king of Jerusalem. Until his death, probably in 1212, Walter stirred up trouble for Hugh in his relations with the church. Hugh's short reign was brought to a close by his death in Tripoli on January 10, 1218, while on the Fifth Crusade. He "was very ready to undertake anything which concerned him and might turn to his honour. He was very fond of the company of knights and all kinds of men of arms. He was irascible and violent, but his anger soon passed."[18] He left an heir, Henry I, about eight months old.

The barons of Cyprus entrusted the guardianship of the infant king to his mother Alice, and also recognized her as regent "but as the mother and not as any possible heir to the throne."[19] Fearing her inexperience, they associated with her as administrative bailie first her uncle, Philip of Ibelin (1218–1227), and then his brother John, the "old lord" of Beirut (1227–1228). Alice kept the guardianship and the whole of the royal revenues, but when difficulties arose between her and the Ibelins she finally left for Syria, probably in 1223.[20] Though John was forced to turn the king over to the emperor Frederick and his bailies in 1228, the Ibelins worked

[16] *Livre de Jean d'Ibelin*, 273 (*RHC, Lois*, I), p. 430.

[17] See J. L. LaMonte, *Feudal Monarchy in the Latin Kingdom of Jerusalem* (Cambridge, Mass., 1932), p. 52 and note 1.

[18] *Eracles* (*RHC, Occ.*, II), p. 360, quoted in Hill, *History of Cyprus*, II, 83, where he corrects the translation of Mas Latrie, *Histoire de l'île de Chypre*, I, 182.

[19] LaMonte, *Feudal Monarchy*, p. 52, note 2. The documents call Alice simply "queen of Cyprus" and call the Ibelins "bailie".

[20] See Hill, *History of Cyprus*, II, 88, note 3, for the disputed date of Alice's break with her uncles.

together to govern the island during the critical years of the Lombard war, and John continued, until his death in 1236, to exercise practical control over king Henry I.

Politically the middle third of Henry I's long reign (1218–1253) was dominated by the Lombard war (1229–1243), so fateful for the Latin kingdoms in the east. Anticipating the claims which Frederick II might raise when he embarked on his crusade, the Ibelins had had Henry crowned in 1225, though he did not officially come of age until 1232. The war ended, as far as operations in Cyprus were concerned, in 1233, when effective imperial suzerainty over the island ceased.

In the earlier years of his reign Henry was too young to play an active role; even later on he never seems to have assumed a commanding position. The barons of Jerusalem in 1243 chose his mother Alice to be regent of their kingdom until Frederick II's son Conrad should come to claim it. Henry succeeded his mother as regent when she died in 1246, and added to his title king of Cyprus that of lord of Jerusalem. Yet he was a singularly colorless figure. Hill, noting that Joinville does not even mention Henry, has suggested that "the corpulence, which won for him the nickname of 'the Fat', may have been connected with mental lethargy".[21]

In January 1253 Henry I died in Nicosia, leaving the kingdom to his infant son Hugh II (1253–1267), under the regency of his queen, Plaisance, sister of Bohemond VI of Antioch. Seemingly it was to this young Hugh, who did not live to attain his majority, that Thomas Aquinas dedicated the *De regimine principum*.[22] In 1257 Bohemond took Hugh and Plaisance to Acre, and succeeded in having Hugh recognized as heir to the kingdom of Jerusalem, and Plaisance as regent for her son. But her death in 1261 brought up again the question of the regencies of both Cyprus and Jerusalem. There were at least three possible claimants: Isabel, sister of Henry I of Cyprus, who had married Henry of Antioch, younger son of Bohemond IV; her son, Hugh of Antioch-Lusignan; and Hugh of Brienne, the son of her deceased elder sister Mary and Walter of Brienne, count of Jaffa. Isabel's claim to the regency of Cyprus was passed over by the high court in favor of a male, her son Hugh of Antioch-Lusignan, while Hugh of Brienne, possibly in deference to his aunt who had brought him up, did not press his claim. In Jerusalem, however, Isabel and her husband were

[21] Hill, *History of Cyprus*, II, 83; cf. 148.

[22] See Thomas Aquinas, *On the Governance of Rulers* (*De regimine principum*) (tr. G. B. Phelan, St. Michael's College Philosophical Texts, published for the Institute of Mediaeval Studies, London and New York, 1938), introd., pp. 4, 8–11.

The Battle of Hattin

Frankish Prisoners Freed from the Saracens

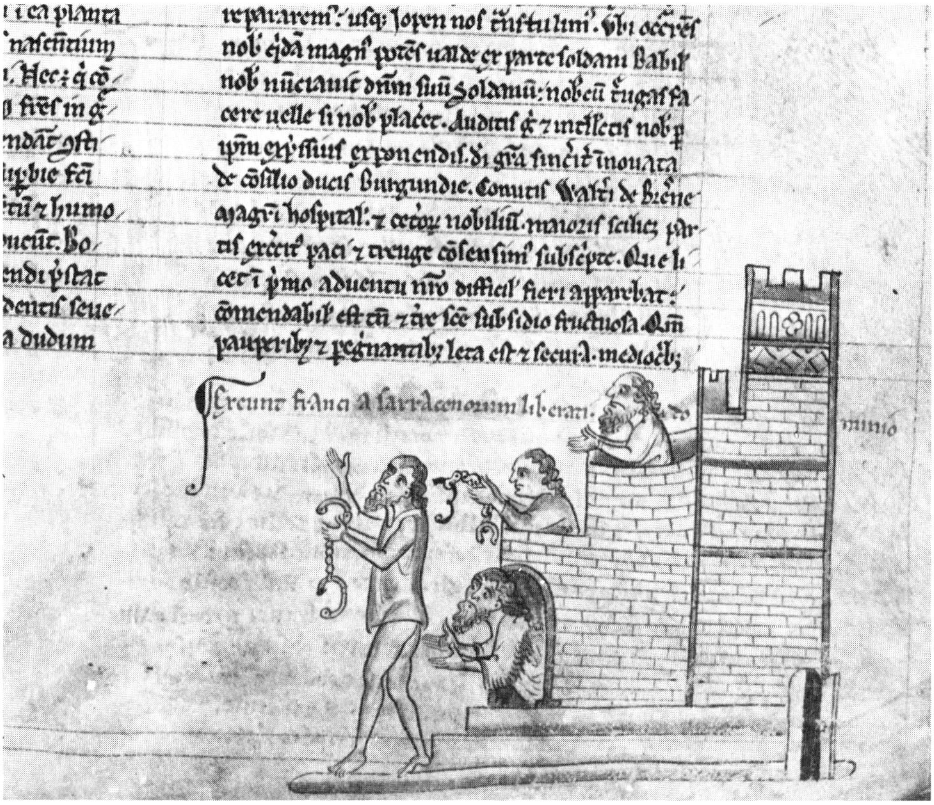

20. Cyprus (*Map by the University of Wisconsin Cartographic Laboratory*)

recognized as regent and bailie in 1263, but, upon her death in 1264, a contest arose over the claims of the two Hughs. The high court of Jerusalem decided in favor of Hugh of Antioch-Lusignan on the grounds that "he was the eldest living male relative in the first degree of relationship to the minor, and was most closely related to the person last seised of the office."[23] This significant decision became a precedent in later cases in Cyprus, notably at the succession of Hugh IV in 1324.

The death of Hugh II in 1267 brought to an end the series of Lusignans directly descended in the male line from Hugh (VIII), ancestor of the counts of La Marche. The high court chose as king Hugh of Antioch-Lusignan, who adopted his mother's name and thenceforth called himself Hugh of Lusignan. In 1268 Charles of Anjou executed Conradin, last of the Hohenstaufens, and Hugh became also king of Jerusalem. The reigns of Hugh III (1267–1284) and his sons, John I (1284–1285) and the epileptic Henry II (1285–1324), kings of Cyprus and Jerusalem, were to witness the death throes of Frankish Syria.[24]

The establishment of a Latin kingdom in Cyprus presented certain advantages to the crusaders of the thirteenth century. It constituted an ideal advance base of operations, where successive expeditions might rendezvous, recuperate from the rigors of the long sea voyage, and concert plans for attack on Egypt or Syria. As a source of supplies, the island, "mout riche et bone et bien plaintive de tous biens," was no less important.[25] Furthermore, protected by the surrounding seas, it furnished for harried fighters from the mainland an ideal retreat, where they might rest and recover their spirits before returning to the struggle. Of much assistance, then, to the crusaders, "the possession of Cyprus allowed them to prolong for another century their occupation of the Syrian seaports."[26]

On the other hand its occupation led to certain distinct disadvantages. Secure and prosperous, it proved to be an irresistible attraction not only to the barons of Syria, but even to the common people on their Syrian estates, to whom the liberal policies of Guy

[23] LaMonte, *Feudal Monarchy*, p. 76; see above, chapter XVI, pp. 570–571.

[24] Hill, *History of Cyprus*, II, 179, seems to have erred in stating that John was crowned king of Jerusalem. Of all the authorities he cites, only the late writer Lusignan speaks of his being proclaimed king in Tyre (*Description de toute l'isle de Cypre*, f. 137^{v}). The testimony is discounted by other modern authorities; cf. LaMonte, "Chronology," *Bulletin of the International Committee of Historical Sciences*, XII (1942–1943), 148.

[25] *Gestes des Chiprois*, 514 (*RHC*, *Arm.*, II), p. 818.

[26] Grousset, *Histoire des croisades*, III, 137.

and his successors made available lands in Cyprus, free from the menace of incessant Moslem raids. Merchants also were attracted, and the various towns of the island became thriving centers of trade, though Famagusta had to await the fall of Acre to enter upon its great commercial role. The mainland thus lost badly needed colonists and defenders. As the century advanced, the Cypriote knights became increasingly loath to leave the comfort and safety of the island in order to defend the few ports remaining to the Christians in Syria. After the final catastrophe of 1291, planners of future crusades still looked to Cyprus as their advance base, but the emphasis among Europeans in general shifted from crusading zeal to lust for commercial profit.

Aimery of Lusignan, in accepting the crown of Jerusalem, had made clear that he did not intend to mortgage the revenues of Cyprus to support the kingdom of Jerusalem, now threatened by the successors of Saladin, but he promised as much help as possible. He at once crossed to the mainland with a Cypriote contingent to reinforce the Germans and the military orders, but when the news of the death (September 28, 1197) of emperor Henry VI reached Palestine early in 1198, it effectively took the heart out of the German crusade. In the following summer Aimery concluded a truce with al-ʻĀdil, and, when that expired, a further favorable one in 1204.

Meanwhile preparations for the Fourth Crusade were well advanced. In the spring of 1201, Alexius III appealed to Innocent III. If the pope would help him to recover Cyprus by excommunicating Aimery, Alexius would give aid to the crusaders. The pope refused, stating that Byzantium had already lost Cyprus when Richard I conquered it, that "the western princes have asked us, since in the island of Cyprus no modest aid is supplied to the eastern province, to warn your imperial magnificence, given the present state of the Holy Land, not to molest the king of that island . . .," and that it would be most unwise to divert Aimery from the defense of the Holy Land to the protection of his Cypriote realm.[27] When the main body of crusaders was detoured to Constantinople in 1203, Cyprus was militarily little affected, though the excesses committed by the Latins against the Greek church, after the fall of the city, had repercussions on Orthodox believers in the island.

Faced with delays in the army's assembling in the ports of Italy for the Fifth Crusade, Honorius III, in July 1217, decided to

[27] *Gesta Inn. III* (*PL*, CCXIV), cols. cxxiii–cxxv. See Hill, *History of Cyprus*, II, 62, note 3 for further references.

dispatch to the east the inadequate forces already collected. It was the intention of duke Leopold of Austria and king Andrew of Hungary to meet at Cyprus on September 8, and the pope wrote to archbishop Otto of Genoa instructing him to direct the crusaders gathered at Genoa to sail for Cyprus if they would avoid pirates and Saracens. He also wrote the king and patriarch of Jerusalem, and the masters of the Hospital and Temple, to meet Leopold and Andrew at Cyprus. These plans do not seem to have materialized. Leopold, after a swift passage from the Adriatic of only sixteen days, went straight to Syria, which he reached in mid-September, and Andrew followed in October.[28] Hugh I had already crossed with a Cypriote force, including Eustorgue of Montaigu, Latin archbishop of Nicosia, Walter of Caesarea, constable of Cyprus, and the Ibelins, who formed part of the Cypriote rather than of the Jerusalemite contingent.[29] Without effective leadership, the crusade degenerated into a series of fruitless attacks. In early January 1218 Hugh accompanied Andrew from Acre to Tripoli to witness the marriage of Bohemond IV of Tripoli and Melisend of Lusignan. On January 10 Hugh died suddenly. Andrew departed for Hungary, and most of the Cypriotes seem to have returned home.

When the remaining crusaders in Syria decided to transfer their activities to the Nile, archbishop Eustorgue sailed with the king of Jerusalem, John of Brienne, to the siege of Damietta. Shortly before the capture of that city, the constable Walter arrived with a band of one hundred Cypriote knights and their men-at-arms. During the siege, Cyprus proved a welcome source of supply to the besiegers, often hard pressed for provisions. When John left Egypt in the spring of 1220 to uphold his claim to the throne of Armenia, the Cypriotes also departed. In John's absence, the legate Pelagius left the sea routes between Acre and Damietta unguarded, with the result that a Saracen squadron of ten armed galleys surprised

[28] Potthast, *Regesta*, nos. 5585–5587; Delaville le Roulx, *Cartulaire*, nos. 1580–1582; Pressutti, *Regesta Honorii papae III*, nos. 672–673; cf. Mas Latrie, *Histoire de l'île de Chypre*, II, 36; Hill, *History of Cyprus*, II, 82. Although Hill (*loc. cit.*) puts Leopold, and Delaville le Roulx, on the basis of the intentions announced by pope Honorius, puts Andrew on Cyprus (Delaville le Roulx, *Cartulaire*, no. 1582: ". . . qui vient de débarquer en Chypre"; *idem*, *Les Hospitaliers en Terre Sainte et à Chypre* (*1110–1310*) [Paris, 1904], p. 142), there really is no clear evidence that either stopped at the island; cf. Mas Latrie, *Histoire de l'île de Chypre*, I, 193. Hill's authority is A. W. A. Leeper, *A History of Medieval Austria* (Oxford, 1941), p. 300, which in turn leans on the *Annales Claustro-neoburgenses* (*MGH, SS.*, IX), p. 622, which refers to the swift passage of Leopold without once mentioning Cyprus. On Andrew's crusade, see above, chapter XI, pp. 386–394.

[29] See J. L. LaMonte, "John d'Ibelin, the Old Lord of Beirut, 1177–1236," *Byzantion*, XII (1937), 425; seemingly, after the accession of John of Brienne, John of Ibelin, ". . . crowded out of his important position, . . . began . . . to be more interested in Cyprus than in Jerusalem."

a crusading fleet in the harbor of Limassol, burnt a large number of vessels, and took prisoner or killed a reported thirteen thousand Christians.[30] In July 1221 John returned to Egypt by way of Cyprus, and probably brought some Cypriotes with him to take part in the fatal advance towards Cairo. Upon the evacuation of Damietta in September 1221, even "the earth, by a divine miracle, was saddened", for in the following year an earthquake shook Cyprus, and a tidal wave submerged Limassol and Paphos.[31]

Among the participants in the Damietta campaign was the young Philip of Novara, in the service of the Cypriote knight Peter Chappe. Born apparently in Novara around 1195, Philip went to the east and eventually settled in Cyprus. While in Egypt, he received instruction from Ralph of Tiberias, the great jurisconsult of Jerusalem. In his later years, Philip wrote not only one of the legal treatises making up the *Assises de Jérusalem*, but also a highly colored narrative of the war between Frederick II and the Ibelins.

When, in June 1228, Frederick II finally set out on his long-delayed crusade, he set in motion the train of events leading to the Lombard war — a war in which the "Ibelins, like the Guelphs in Germany, maintained the constitutional rights of the feudal baronage against the imperialists, and, more successful than their western counterparts, established in Jerusalem and Cyprus that rule of law so well illustrated by the *Assises* which were written by the most famous member of their family."[32]

As early as 1225 the bailie of Cyprus, Philip of Ibelin, fearing that Frederick would claim the wardship of king Henry, still a minor, had him crowned. Frederick considered Cyprus an imperial fief, since king Aimery in 1197 had recognized the suzerainty of his father, the emperor Henry VI. After Henry's coronation, Frederick had written protesting that he alone had the right to bestow the crown and demanding the regency; but he could take no action until he reached Limassol in July 1228. Encouraged by Amalric Barlais, a Cypriote baron who had gone to meet him with a group of other anti-Ibelin barons, Frederick determined to exercise his rights over the island.

[30] The figure is probably exaggerated by the chroniclers; it may well include not only the casualties at Limassol, but others captured on the sea lanes between Acre, Cyprus, and Egypt. For Pelagius and the Fifth Crusade at Damietta, see above, chapter XI, pp. 397–428.

[31] R. Röhricht, *Testimonia minora de quinto bello sacro* (Geneva, 1882), p. 240; see Hill, *History of Cyprus*, II, 87 and note 5 for other accounts.

[32] LaMonte, *Feudal Monarchy*, p. 60. These "Lombards" or "Longobards" are not to be confused with the natives of northern Italy; they were the inhabitants of the old Byzantine theme of Longobardia in southern Italy. Cf. LaMonte's introduction to Philip of Novara, *The Wars*, pp. viii–ix.

Immediately he wrote his "dear uncle", John of Ibelin, bailie since the death of Philip in 1227, asking him to join him and bring the young king. Though many of the Cypriote barons distrusted the emperor, Ibelin determined to obey the summons, for he did not wish "that people could say throughout the world: 'The emperor of Rome came across the sea in great force and would have conquered all, but that the lord of Beirut and other disloyal men of Outremer loved the Saracens better than the Christians, and because of this they revolted against the emperor and did not wish that the Holy Land should be recovered.' "[33]

Frederick received Ibelin cordially, invited him to a banquet, and persuaded him and his retinue to put off their mourning garments for more cheerful robes of scarlet. But at the banquet, after filling the hall with armed men, Frederick made three demands: that John surrender the person of king Henry to him as suzerain of Cyprus; that John render an accounting of the bailliage since the death of Hugh; and that he surrender Beirut, which, as a fortress of Conrad's kingdom, should be in Frederick's hands as regent for his young son, since Isabel had died before Frederick sailed for the east. John reluctantly conceded the emperor's right to the custody of king Henry. As for the second demand, he declared that he was not responsible for accounting for the revenues of Cyprus, which had been given to queen Alice, and offered to prove his case before the high court of Nicosia, by whose authority he held the bailliage. As for Beirut, he held it as a fief, granted by queen Isabel and king Aimery, and appealed to the high court of Acre, which alone should judge matters of feudal tenure in Jerusalem: "Et sire, vous soiès certains que pour doute de mort ou de prizon je ne feray plus, se jugement de boune court et de loyale ne la me faisoit faire."[34] Thus the issue was joined.

After giving hostages for his appearance in the high courts of Cyprus and Jerusalem, the "old lord" withdrew to Nicosia, whither Frederick followed him. Refusing to take up arms against his lord (for Frederick, as overlord of the king of Cyprus, could claim John's allegiance as a Cypriote vassal), the lord of Beirut withdrew to the fortress of Dieudamour. At this point, Frederick received word of the rebellion fomented against him by Gregory IX in Italy. He was anxious to finish his crusade and return to the west, and made a treaty with John by which the hostages were returned, and

[33] Philip of Novara, *The Wars* (tr. LaMonte), pp. 75–76. For this situation and the ensuing conflict as it affected the kingdom of Jerusalem, see above, chapter XV, pp. 543–554.

[34] *Gestes des Chiprois*, 127 (*RHC, Arm.*, II), p. 679; Philip of Novara, *The Wars* (tr. LaMonte), p. 79.

the castles of Cyprus surrendered to liegemen selected by Frederick. John promised to accompany him on his crusade. On September 3, 1228, Frederick, taking king Henry with him, sailed for Syria.

After he had concluded the treaty of Jaffa with the sultan al-Kāmil on February 18, 1229, and had crowned himself king of Jerusalem in the church of the Holy Sepulcher, Frederick was eager to start home. He sold the bailliage of Cyprus to the anti-Ibelin Amalric Barlais and four colleagues. The revenues of Cyprus were farmed to them for three years for 10,000 marks. The Ibelin case was still undecided when, on May 1, the emperor sailed from Acre.

From 1229 to 1233 Cyprus was torn by Frederick's war with the Ibelins. While the imperial bailies in Syria were gaining adherents by their wise rule, the reverse was true in Cyprus. To raise funds to pay the emperor, the five bailies imposed heavy taxes, and despoiled the estates of the Ibelins and their supporters. In June 1229 John of Ibelin crossed from Syria, raised the countryside and, after a battle near Nicosia on July 14, drove the bailies to take refuge in the northern castles. Kantara and Kyrenia were quickly taken. Besieged in Dieudamour, the surviving bailies finally surrendered after Easter in 1230, gave up the person of king Henry, and relinquished all claims to the bailliage.

By then Frederick, successful against the papal armies in Italy, and, after the treaty of San Germano in July 1230, once again restored to the bosom of the church, was ready to turn his attention eastward. He sent out an army under Richard Filangieri, the imperial marshal. The first contingent under the bishop of Melfi arrived off Cape Gata near Limassol in September 1231. Envoys dispatched to king Henry at Kiti demanded in the name of the emperor that Henry banish John of Ibelin and all his relatives from Cyprus. Henry replied that he could not banish Ibelin since he was his liegeman and so deserving of his protection, and that, since he himself was Ibelin's nephew, he could not banish all the relatives of the house of Ibelin from the island. The "old lord" had disposed a force at Limassol to prevent a landing; so the imperial fleet sailed on to capture the town of Beirut, and lay siege to its castle. When Filangieri arrived in Syria, he summoned the high court, which accepted his credentials as bailie of the kingdom of Jerusalem. Yet, as we have seen,[35] when the barons realized that he was not going to submit to them the case of the seizure of Beirut, the majority turned against him.

John of Ibelin, having assembled the Cypriote host at Famagusta

[35] See above, chapter XV, pp. 548–549.

to go to the relief of Beirut, crossed to the mainland in the spring of 1232, whereupon Barlais and his confederates promptly deserted to the imperialists. John reinforced his castle and then went to Acre, where, in April 1232, he received the oath of the recently established commune and seized the imperial fleet in the harbor. Since Ibelin had stripped Cyprus of most of its defenders, Filangieri sent over a force under Barlais, which overran the island and took all the castles except Dieudamour and Buffavento. In retaliation, Ibelin planned an attack on the imperialist base at Tyre, but at Casal Imbert, north of Acre, the Cypriotes, while Ibelin was absent in Acre, were surprised on the night of May 3–4, and were badly routed. Filangieri then dispatched the main body of his troops to finish the reduction of Cyprus. Ibelin at once collected his scattered forces and, toward the end of May, crossed over in Genoese ships and captured Famagusta by surprise. Most of the Cypriote population welcomed the Ibelins as deliverers. On June 15, at Agridi, the Cypriotes completely defeated the imperialists, who retreated to the castle of Kyrenia. Its capitulation in the spring of 1233 brought to a close the imperialist threat to the island.

The struggle on the mainland continued for another ten years, though after the death of John of Ibelin in 1236 an uneasy truce was maintained. Finally, in 1243, Philip of Novara suggested that, since Conrad would come of age on April 25, 1243, Frederick's regency would thereby end and with it Filangieri's appointment as bailie; so the barons would be acting legally if they should drive Filangieri out. In June 1243 a full meeting of the vassals of Jerusalem and Cyprus at Acre accepted the claim of Alice of Champagne, as nearest heir of Conrad present in the country, to the regency of Jerusalem.[36]

With the capitulation of Tyre the baronial party in the east triumphed and the imperial rule almost ceased. In 1247 Innocent IV absolved Henry of Cyprus from any oath he might have taken to the emperor, and took him and his kingdom under the protection of the holy see. Alice and then Henry I were regents for Conrad, still legally king; it was not until after the death of Conradin in 1268 that Hugh III of Cyprus, proclaimed by the high court in 1269, could style himself "twelfth Latin king of Jerusalem and king of Cyprus."

The struggle with Frederick had exacerbated the factions in the kingdom of Jerusalem and weakened its fabric. We are reminded,

[36] See above, chapter XV, pp. 553–554, and chapter XVI, p. 559.

however, that if that kingdom, "for which the Ibelins and their allies fought so stubbornly in the thirties and forties was lost before the end of the century, the institutions which they fought to preserve continued in Cyprus for two centuries more, and the rights of the individual and the limitation of the crown were the cornerstones of the Cypriot constitution as long as the Lusignan dynasty lasted."[37]

In 1239, during the Lombard war, the truce which Frederick II had made with al-Kāmil, the sultan of Egypt, had expired, and, as we have seen, the crusade of Theobald of Champagne and Richard of Cornwall had followed.[38] The most tangible result of their efforts was the fortification of Ascalon. Cyprus remained largely apart from all this, however, and in 1244 king Henry ignored an appeal for aid when Jerusalem was threatened by the Khorezmians, and finally fell on August 23, though he later sent over a force of three hundred men, who all perished at the disaster of Ḥarbīyah (La Forbie) on October 17.[39] In 1247 Henry furnished eight ships under Baldwin of Ibelin, seneschal of Cyprus, to aid in the attempt to relieve Ascalon, which fell on October 15.

A year or two before he sailed on his crusade, Louis IX sent a sergeant, Nicholas of Choisy, to Cyprus to collect provisions. Tuns of wine were stacked in great piles along the seashore. "Wheat and barley they had put in heaps amid the fields; and when one saw them, it seemed as if they were mountains; for the rain which had beaten on the grain for a long time had made it sprout on top, so that there appeared there only green grass. So it happened that when they wished to take the grain to Egypt, they cut down the top layers with the green grass and found the wheat and barley as fresh as though it had just been threshed."[40] Louis landed on September 18, 1248, at Limassol, where he was welcomed by king Henry and the Ibelin lords. John of Ronay, vice-master of the Hospital, and William of Sonnac, master of the Temple, came from Acre to plan the campaign. Louis "was eager to press on to Egypt without stopping,"[41] but his barons persuaded him otherwise, and not until May 13, 1249, did he depart. The long delay was costly in money and bad for morale. An epidemic broke out in the French camp and, though the troops were dispersed around the island, many died. Diplomatic activity, however, did not slacken. In

[37] LaMonte's introduction to Philip of Novara, *The Wars*, p. 56.

[38] See above, chapter XIII.

[39] See above, chapter XVI, pp. 561–564.

[40] Joinville, *Histoire de Saint Louis*, 130–131 (ed. N. de Wailly, Paris, 1874), pp. 72–74. For this crusade, see above, chapter XIV, pp. 493–495.

[41] *Ibid.*, 132 (ed. Wailly), p. 74.

December, envoys arrived with a letter alleged to be from the Great Khan Göyük to initiate the first of the abortive pourparlers for an alliance with the Mongols. Later, the emperor Baldwin II of Constantinople sent his wife, Mary of Brienne, to ask for aid to ward off the threatened attack of the Greeks on Constantinople.[42]

When Louis finally sailed from Cyprus, the island chivalry sailed with him — king Henry, the seneschal Baldwin of Ibelin, the constable Guy of Ibelin, and the archbishop Eustorgue, who died at Damietta. King Henry rode with king Louis on the solemn entry into Damietta, on June 6, but soon departed for Cyprus, leaving one hundred and twenty knights to serve for a year under Baldwin and Guy, who were also in command of one thousand knights from Syria. After the surrender at Mansurah (April 6, 1250), the Ibelins narrowly escaped with their lives from the massacre planned by the mamluks subsequent to the murder of the sultan Tūrān-Shāh. "There came at least thirty [mamluks] to our galley, with naked swords in their hands and Danish axes round their necks. I asked my lord Baldwin of Ibelin, who knew Saracen well, what these people were saying; and he replied that they were saying that they were coming to cut off our heads."[43] The Ibelin brothers were among the negotiators for the renewal of the agreement which Louis had made with Tūrān-Shāh, and returned to Cyprus with the other Cypriote captives who were released on May 6.

Hugh III, first as regent and later as king of both Cyprus and Jerusalem, had to deal with the fanatical and determined Mamluk sultan Baybars (1260–1277). His task was formidable. Hugh tried to reconcile warring Christians — Venetians, Genoese, Templars, Hospitallers, and others — for a concerted effort against Baybars, but even his Cypriote vassals, preferring the relative security of their island estates to the ceaseless struggle on the mainland, would not always support him.

In the spring of 1271, when prince Edward of England (afterwards king Edward I) arrived from Tunis with one thousand men, Hugh crossed from Cyprus to plan a campaign with Edward and Bohemond VI of Tripoli. Baybars took the opportunity of Hugh's absence from Cyprus to fit out seventeen galleys camouflaged as

[42] Hill, *History of Cyprus*, II, 144, errs in his interpretation of Joinville when he says that Mary's ship was torn from its mooring at Paphos and driven to Acre "whence she was fetched back to Lemesos by Joinville." Actually, Joinville met Mary at Paphos, where she was left with nothing to wear but the clothes she had on, since her ship with all her "harnois" had been driven off. Joinville brought her to Limassol, and later sent her fine cloth for new clothes (Joinville, 137 [ed. Wailly], p. 76). On the situation of Baldwin and the Latin empire, see above, chapter VI, pp. 225–226.

[43] Joinville, *Histoire de Saint Louis*, 354 (ed. Wailly), p. 192.

Christian ships to carry the war into the island, but most of them were wrecked off Limassol. Meanwhile, Edward and Hugh with their inadequate forces could do little more than raid.[44]

At this inauspicious moment occurred the celebrated dispute in which the Cypriote knights, whose one desire was to return home, claimed that their liability for their fiefs was limited to service in the island. The case was referred to Edward. Hugh maintained that the knights owed service at the desire and need of the king outside the realm as well as within, that the barons of Jerusalem had served at Edessa and elsewhere outside the kingdom of Jerusalem, and that Cyprus was ruled by the same laws as Jerusalem. He then cited instances, going back to the reign of Aimery, when the Cypriote knights had served outside Cyprus. James of Ibelin, author of one of the legal treatises of the *Assises*, presented the knights' case, arguing that they were not bound by their oaths to unlimited service at the king's discretion, nor were they bound to serve outside the realm. In citing instances of former service Hugh was taking advantage of their former good deeds, for in the past they had voluntarily served for love of God and of their lord, and never because of the summons of the king. "And further we show certainly by men who are still full of life, that the men of the realm of Cyprus have served more often outside the realm the house of Ibelin than [they have served] my lord the king or his ancestors; and if the usage of their service subjects them to service, by such reasoning the Ibelins could demand of them what my lord the king demands."[45] James chided Hugh for his tactlessness when he concluded that the king could have their service "par biau parler, qui poi coste." Edward seems to have made no decision, but in 1273 a compromise was reached, by which the barons agreed that they owed the king service outside Cyprus for four months a year and that they must serve in person wherever the king or his son went.

Such a debate was hardly likely to encourage Edward or Hugh to aggressive action against Baybars, and in April 1272 they signed a truce for ten years, ten months, ten days, and ten hours (renewed in 1283 with Baybars' successor Kalavun) to cover the plain of Acre and the road to Nazareth. In September Edward sailed for home, leaving Hugh to continue the struggle to maintain his authority against the factions, complicated by the arrival in Acre in 1277 of Roger of San Severino with letters from pope John XXI,

[44] On Edward's crusade, see above, chapter XIV, pp. 517–518, and chapter XVI, pp. 582–583; on the Mamluks, see below, chapter XXII, p. 749.

[45] *Document relatif au service militaire*, II, 25 (*RHC, Lois*, II), p. 434; quoted in LaMonte, *Feudal Monarchy*, p. 157, note 1.

Charles of Anjou, and Mary of Antioch, to take possession as bailie for Charles. Appeals to Hugh in Cyprus went unanswered and the lieges of Jerusalem finally did homage to Charles's representative. In 1279 Hugh crossed over to try to restore his authority, but, when the four months' service of his Cypriote vassals ended, he was forced to return home. Again in August 1283 he crossed for a final effort, but died in Tyre in March 1284. If Hugh III had proved unequal to the task of reconciling the quarreling factions, he had been withal a competent king.

With the death on January 7, 1285, of Charles of Anjou, whose son Charles II showed no interest in the crown of Jerusalem, the factions were gradually brought round to acceptance of Hugh's son, Henry II, as king of Jerusalem. He was crowned in the cathedral of Tyre on August 15, 1286. The chivalry of Cyprus and Syria celebrated the event with festivities for fifteen days at Acre, where, in the *Auberge* of the Hospital, they enacted scenes from the romances of the Round Table, "et contrefirent Lanselot et Tristan et Pilamedes, et mout d'autres jeus biaus et delitables et plaissans."[46] And this less than five years before the final catastrophe. The epileptic Henry, probably on the advice of his counselors, who feared that his popularity might evaporate as had Hugh's before him, soon returned to Cyprus.

The expulsion of the Angevins, who had had an understanding with Egypt, freed Kalavun's hands. Latakia fell on April 20, 1287. When Kalavun threatened Tripoli, Henry sent a Cypriote force in four galleys, but the city fell on April 26, 1289. Refugees were pouring into Cyprus. Three days after the fall of Tripoli, Henry arrived in Acre to patch up a truce with Kalavun, and then returned to Cyprus. In answer to appeals to the west, the pope had managed to collect and send a fleet manned by a nondescript rabble of Italians, whose undisciplined conduct in Syria provided Kalavun, as we have seen,[47] with grounds for asserting that the truce had been violated. Kalavun's sudden death at the end of 1290 left his son al-Ashraf to finish the destruction of the kingdom. The investment of Acre on April 5, 1291, finally achieved the union of all the Latin factions in one last heroic stand. On May 4, when Henry arrived with reinforcements, he was welcomed with *feux de joie*, but found the besieged in a bad way, with no agreement on a single command. Though accused of deserting the siege with three thousand men on May 15, the king of Cyprus seems to have

[46] *Gestes des Chiprois*, 439 (*RHC*, *Arm.*, II), p. 793.
[47] See above, chapter XVI, pp. 593–594.

remained until the grand assault of May 18, when it was clear that the city was lost.[48] One by one during the summer the remaining cities fell, while their inhabitants escaped to live for years in Cyprus in poverty and distress. Cyprus went into mourning, and, as late as 1394, the traveler Martoni noted that when the Cypriote ladies went out, they wore long black cloaks showing only their eyes "on account of the sorrow and dire grief for the loss of that city of Acre and other cities of Syria."[49]

The kingdom of Jerusalem had fallen, but its institutions, with some modifications, were to live on for two more centuries in the kingdom of Cyprus. In its earlier years Cyprus seems to have had its own customs, similar to, but distinct from, those of Jerusalem. The chronicler Makhairas, after speaking of the settlement made by Guy, says that the lords "made assizes for their advantage, and made the king, when he would put on the crown in the church, swear upon the (holy) Gospel to accept and to maintain the assizes and all the good customs of the said kingdom, and to maintain the privileges of the holy church of Christ . . . . Then the kings and the lords one after another built churches and many monasteries . . . . And they made the assizes, and arranged that they should have their revenue to live upon."[50]

It is difficult to trace the evolution of Cypriote law and the transmission of the customs of Jerusalem to Cyprus during the thirteenth and fourteenth centuries, since court records are lacking and it is necessary to rely largely on theoretical legal treatises.[51] Philip of Novara states that Henry I of Cyprus and his lieges swore an oath to keep "the assizes and good customs of the kingdom of Jerusalem"; this took place between 1230 and 1233, when a general meeting in Syria of the barons of Cyprus decided to prepare an expedition to oust Frederick II's partisans from Cyprus.[52]

[48] For a discussion of this point, with references, see Hill, *History of Cyprus*, p. 186.

[49] *Excerpta Cypria*, p. 24; see also p. 17.

[50] Makhairas, *Chronicle*, 27, 29 (ed. and tr. Dawkins, I), pp. 25, 27; quoted in Grandclaude, *Étude critique*, p. 114, note, following edition of Miller and Sathas.

[51] See the significant article of Jean Richard, "Pairie d'orient latin," *Revue historique de droit français et étranger*, XXVIII (1950), p. 80, and especially note 3, where he states that he is preparing an edition of Cypriote documents found in the Vatican Archives, which show the existence of certain institutions in Cyprus somewhat different from those set forth in the *Assises*. Although M. Richard, in reply to my inquiry, was kind enough to inform me that his edition was scheduled to appear in the *Bibliothèque de l'Institut français d'archéologie à Beyrouth*, it had not done so by 1957. These documents, as well as various other articles of M. Richard, largely concern the fourteenth century.

[52] *Documents relatifs à la successibilité au trône*, 5 (*RHC, Lois*, II), p. 406; *Livre de Philippe de Navarre* [sic], 47 (*RHC, Lois*, I), p. 521, cited in Grandclaude, *Étude critique*, p. 115.

Frederick had obtained from king Henry fealty and homage and from the men of Cyprus fealty without homage, and had then taken seisin, without judgment, of several fiefs, and even of the kingdom of Cyprus contrary to the Jerusalemite *Assise sur la Ligèce* established by king Amalric. According to this assise, all holders of fiefs in the kingdom owed liege homage to the chief lord, i.e. to the king or regent, but if the king failed to aid a vassal, threatened in person or in his goods, or if he imprisoned him without judgment, all the lieges of the kingdom, who were peers, should unite and arm to restore the liberty or possessions of their fellow and might even deprive the king of his lordship. This assise was obviously an excellent weapon to use against Frederick and seems to explain the formal adoption of the law of Jerusalem by the Cypriotes.

At their coronation, the kings of Cyprus swore: "les previleges des beneurés reis mes devanciers et les assises dou royaume et dou rei Amauri et dou rei Baudoyn son filz et les ancienes costumes et assises dou roiaume de Jerusalem garderai; et tot le peuple crestien dou dit roiaume, selonc les costumes ancienes et approvéez de ce meisme roiaume, et selonc les assises des devant dis rois en lors dreis et en lor justices garderai, si come roi crestien et feil de Dieu le doit faire en son roiaume, et totes les autres choses dessus dites garderai feaument. Ensi m'ait Dieu et ces saintes Evangiles de Dieu."[53] Though many of the men responsible for the legal treatises which make up the *Assises de Jérusalem* held fiefs on the mainland and were active in the affairs of that kingdom, they also had strong ties with Cyprus. King Aimery ordered the compilation of the *Livre au roi* to preserve the memory of the old laws, lost when Jerusalem fell in 1187. Philip of Novara in the middle of the thirteenth century wrote the *Livre de forme de plait*. John of Ibelin, count of Jaffa, was probably brought up in Cyprus while his father Philip was bailie (1218–1227); he wrote, shortly before his death in 1266, the *Livre des assises de la haute cour* (which, together with some later assises, was given official sanction by the high court of Cyprus in 1369).[54] James of Ibelin, author of one of the less important treatises, was spokesman for the barons of Cyprus when they refused the demands of Hugh III for military service in Syria.

[53] *Livre de Jean d'Ibelin*, 7 (*RHC, Lois*, I), p. 30, quoted in Grandclaude, *Étude critique*, p. 155. This is the Jerusalemite oath.

[54] Hill, *History of Cyprus*, II, 165, adheres to the old view that John was still alive in 1268, ignoring the evidence for 1266 cited in Grandclaude, *Étude critique*, p. 141. Richard, *loc. cit.* (note 51, above), remarks that John's book was not in regular use in the early fourteenth century for it took months, in 1369, to find a good text of the manuscript.

The law, as expounded in these and other treatises of the thirteenth century, was the law laid down by the high courts of Jerusalem and Nicosia; it was the feudal law of the west modified by conditions in the east; not French, as Hugh of Brienne found out when he appealed to that law in 1264; not imperial, as Frederick II learned when he tried to claim the regency of Cyprus without reference to the high court of Nicosia. Only in the *Assises de la cour des bourgeois*, where the Franks took over from the law in use in the east rules applicable to the lower classes, is much Roman law to be found.[55]

The chief governing body in Cyprus was the high court of Nicosia, composed of the Cypriote barons and presided over by the king or his representative. It chose the king, and, when necessary, a regent for the kingdom. It had jurisdiction over the nobles in all questions, except religion, marriage, and testament, which were reserved to the ecclesiastical courts, and except for cases involving the nobles with their inferiors, which were dealt with by the cour des bourgeois or low court. The latter, consisting of twelve "jurats", chosen by the king, and presided over by the viscount of Nicosia, a knight also chosen by the king, exercised jurisdiction likewise in all cases concerning non-noble Franks. The viscount, head of the police and collector of dues from the bourgeois, was assisted by an official with the title of *mathesep*.[56] The grand officers of the crown were the seneschal, constable, marshal, chamberlain, and chancellor.[57] The thirteenth-century registers of the *secrète royale*, the central office of the treasury, have unfortunately been lost, and other accounts are lacking; so information on the revenues of the kings of Cyprus is scarce, except for casual mention of customs duties, special taxes, and the like. Besides the regular feudal levies, the army included the *arrière ban* of all men capable of bearing arms, and the mercenaries. Important among the latter were the light-armed native horsemen, the Turcopoles. For a fleet, the thirteenth-century rulers of Cyprus depended largely on procuring ships from the Genoese.

The general lines of Cypriote institutional development had been marked out by the first two Lusignans. Whatever the chroniclers may say about Guy's generous concessions even to artisans, the territorial fiefs were probably granted largely to French barons, many of whom had lost their lands on the mainland though they

[55] LaMonte, *Feudal Monarchy*, pp. 100–101; Grandclaude, *Étude critique*, pp. 123 ff.

[56] For special privileges of the Syrians, see Hill, *History of Cyprus*, II, 52. *Mathesep* derives from Arabic *muḥtasib*: inspector of weights and measures.

[57] For lists of the holders of these offices, see LaMonte, *Feudal Monarchy*, pp. 256–257.

often kept their Palestinian titles. These fiefs were hereditary, but, unlike the system in the kingdom of Jerusalem, where the fief descended to all heirs of the first holder, in Cyprus, from the time of either Guy or Aimery, in the event of the failure of a direct heir, born in wedlock, the fief reverted to the crown. This custom proved a distinct advantage to the crown. Contributing also to its strength was the fact that, while such a noble house as the Ibelins might acquire much wealth and exercise great influence, there never developed in Cyprus great territorial fiefs such as weakened the position of the kings of Jerusalem. Furthermore, unlike the latter, the rulers of Cyprus kept the prerogative of coinage in their own hands. Yet the island was small; practically all the nobles were immediate vassals of the king; all were equally concerned in maintaining their interests against their lord. So a compact and united group developed, which could on occasion be extremely dangerous to the crown.[58]

To non-noble Europeans and easterners, Guy and his successors granted burgage tenements in the towns or rents in money or in kind (grain, sugar, olives, etc., for sale or for immediate consumption). As in Jerusalem, rents came to be habitually granted also to knights and were regarded as true fiefs.

Between the French ruling class and the native Graeco-Cypriotes no fusion, such as occurred in England between Normans and English after 1066, and to a lesser extent in Syria and in Frankish Greece between French and natives, ever took place. Religious differences, exacerbated by the Latin policy of forcing the Greek church into obedience to Rome, were too great.[59] Many Greek landholders had fled the island during Isaac's rule or at the time of Richard's conquest; others lost their lands because of opposition to the new rulers. Numbers of the remaining free Greeks seem to have fled to the towns, where, subject to arbitrary tallages and other exactions, they suffered a loss in status.[60] Wilbrand of Oldenburg, who visited Cyprus in 1211, recorded his rather prejudiced impressions of the island and its native population: "There is one archbishop, who has three suffragans. These are Latins. But the

[58] See Grandclaude, *Étude critique*, pp. 151 ff. for this point and a technical discussion of the effect of the *Assise sur la Ligèce* on Cyprus and Jerusalem respectively. See also Richard, *op. cit.*, pp. 81 ff.

[59] For other elements — Syrians, Maronites, Armenians, Jews, etc — fused in varying degrees with the native Greek population, see Hill, *History of Cyprus*, II, 1 ff.

[60] For the view that the leading Greek families maintained their former rank and prerogatives in the bosom of the native population, hostile to the conquerors, and bided their time until their position was restored, partially under the Venetians and more fully under the Turks, see Laurent's review in *Revue des études byzantines*, VI (1948), 270.

Greeks, over whom throughout this land the Latins have dominion, have thirteen [sic] bishops, of whom one is an archbishop. They all obey the Franks, and pay tribute like slaves. Whence you can see that the lords of this land are the Franks, whom the Greeks and Armenians obey as serfs. They are rude in all their habits and shabby in their dress, sacrificing chiefly to their lusts. We shall ascribe this to the wine of that country which provokes to luxury, or rather to those who drink it. . . . For the wines of this island are so thick and rich that they are sometimes specially prepared to be eaten like honey with bread."[61]

According to the writers of the Frankish period, the classes of the Cypriote population on the land remained the same as under Byzantium. They fell into three categories. At the lowest level were the *paroikoi*, similar to the *adscriptitii glebae* in the west, who paid a yearly head-tax, rendered a corvée (*angarion*) of two days' labor a week to their lord, and surrendered to him one third of the produce, except seed. Under the Lusignans, they were made subject to the jurisdiction of their lord, who treated them as mere chattels and could inflict any punishment short of mutilation or death. Next higher in the social scale were the *perpyriarii*, so called from an annual tax of fifteen hyperpers (the gold nomisma or bezant) paid to their lord. They had risen from the class of *paroikoi* by compounding with the Byzantine dukes or *katapans* for their personal freedom and that of their descendants, but their crops were still subject to the one-third tribute. Above the *perpyriarii* were the *eleutheroi* or *francomati*, who had bought emancipation, or obtained it by free grant, from their lord. He still took from a fifth to a tenth of the produce of their lands, which were free, and, if he asked them to work, paid them wages, usually nominal. They came under the jurisdiction of the ordinary magistrates, and paid tribute to the king for salt and various privileges.

The population and prosperity of the towns increased after Richard's conquest, with the establishment of colonies from the great mercantile communities of the west. The Latin penetration of Cyprus had begun even prior to the Lusignan period, for in 1148 Manuel Comnenus had granted to the Venetians the same commercial privileges in Cyprus as they enjoyed elsewhere in the empire.[62] And Latin merchants had welcomed Richard at Limassol. In 1196 Aimery conferred privileges on the merchants of Trani, whose archbishop had brought the scepter for his coronation.

[61] *Excerpta Cypria*, p. 13.

[62] See Hill, *History of Cyprus*, I, 306, note 2, for the possibility of Amalfitans by 1168.

Two years later Aimery granted to the men of Marseilles freedom of trade and a village or manor (casale) in Cyprus in exchange or as a reward for 2,800 bezants contributed to the defense of Jaffa.

With the turn of the century, grants to foreign merchants become more numerous. The first recorded act of the queen-mother Alice of Champagne (July 1218) was the concession, made to the Genoese upon the advice of the bailie Philip of Ibelin and her lieges, of extensive privileges: freedom of trade, free jurisdiction in all cases concerning their nationals, except treason, rape, and homicide; two plots of land, one in Limassol and one in Famagusta, with rights to build thereon; and protection of life and property in wrecks.[63] Since Cyprus had no fleet at the time, the grant was doubtless motivated by the desire to obtain the assistance of Genoese ships, but it marked the first of a long series of concessions, which were to end disastrously in 1377 with the Genoese seizure of Famagusta. In October 1291 Henry II granted consular courts and commercial privileges to the Pisans and Catalans. These privileges included large reductions in import and export duties, which, by then, were assuming important proportions in the revenues of the kings of Cyprus.

The inevitable counterpart of the establishment of a Latin kingdom in Cyprus was the establishment of the Latin church and the attempt to convert the Greek Orthodox to Roman Catholicism, and to bring into obedience to the Latins not only the Greek clergy, but also the clergy of the Syrian, Nestorian, and Armenian rites. The tactlessness of many emissaries of the holy see was countered by the obstinate opposition of the Cypriotes. The extreme zeal of such popes as Honorius III and Gregory IX increased the bitterness of the struggle, which the more moderate policy of Innocent IV and the *Constitution* of Alexander IV did little to allay. The Lusignan rulers made generous grants, as loyal sons of Rome, to the Latin churches and religious orders, but did not wish to see the native population driven in desperation to emigration or revolt. They

[63] LaMonte, *Feudal Monarchy*, in Appendix D, summarizing grants to Italian and Provençal communes in the Latin states, on page 268 gives Nicosia instead of Limassol, seemingly following Ricotti's edition of the *Liber jurium reipublicae Ianuensis* (*Historiae patriae monumenta*, 2 vols., Turin, 1845), I, cols. 625–626, doc. 544, which reads: "apud niccosiam", though LaMonte refers also to Mas Latrie and Röhricht. But Mas Latrie's edition of this document in his *Histoire de l'île de Chypre*, II, 39, reads: "apud Nimociam [Limassol]", and his reading is followed by most modern authorities. Cf. Röhricht, *Regesta*, no. 912; Hill, *History of Cyprus*, II, 85; W. Heyd, *Histoire du commerce du Levant au moyen-âge* (tr. F. Reynaud, 2 vols., Leipzig, 1885–1886; reprinted, Leipzig, 1923), I, 362.

tried with only partial success to hold the balance between the unevenly matched contestants.

In February 1196, at about the time when Neophytus was writing his bitter denunciation of the Latin conquest, pope Celestine III addressed to the clergy, magnates, and people of Cyprus a bull stating that, at the request of Aimery, who, "recognizing the Roman church as head and mistress of all churches", desired to recall the schismatic Greeks to the true church, the pope had given full powers to the archdeacon of Latakia and to Alan, archdeacon of Lydda and Aimery's chancellor, to establish the Latin church in Cyprus.[64] The two commissioners set up the archbishopric of Nicosia with the three suffragan dioceses of Paphos, Limassol, and Famagusta, and began gradually to despoil the Greek church. Alan became the first Latin archbishop of Nicosia, while his fellow-commissioner was elected bishop of Paphos. The four sees were endowed in part from the property of the Greek church and in part from lands abandoned by their Cypriote holders and from the public domain.

The Latin clergy who were introduced into the island ministered largely to the conquerors and their descendants. As in the Latin patriarchate of Constantinople, "traces of Latin secular clergy below the level of cathedral chapters are few."[65] When members of the Latin aristocracy found it difficult to attend cathedral services, they often endowed private priests.[66] Regular clergy swelled the ranks of the Latins. Even before the arrival of the Lusignans, the Templars had begun a church in Nicosia, which Guy continued and in which he was buried. Hugh I made important donations to the Hospitallers. During the thirteenth century numerous monastic orders received endowments in the island and, with the fall of Acre, a flood of regular clergy arrived from the mainland.

The establishment of the Latin church in Cyprus led to difficulties on two fronts. On the one hand the Latin clergy were soon involved in disputes with the secular authorities. The clergy complained that the lay lords and the crown were not enforcing the collection of tithes on domainial and baronial lands as was the custom in the kingdom of Jerusalem; the clergy further objected to having serfs on church lands liable to royal tallages and *angaria*

[64] *PL*, CCVI, cols. 1147-1148; LaMonte, "Register of the Cartulary of Santa Sophia," *Byzantion*, V (1929–1930), no. 2; Jaffé, *Regesta*, no. 17329. B., archdeacon of Latakia, has not been identified.

[65] R. L. Wolff, "The Organization of the Latin Patriarchate of Constantinople, 1204–1261 Social and Administrative Consequences of the Latin Conquest," *Traditio*, VI (1948), 41.

[66] See LaMonte, "Register of the Cartulary of Santa Sophia," *Byzantion*, V, nos. 14, 16.

(corvées). On the other hand, overshadowing the differences with the secular authorities, was the struggle with the Greek church. As in Constantinople and other Latin states in the east, the Latins were at first prepared to allow some differences in rite, though they tried unceasingly to convert the Greeks, from whom they also insisted on absolute obedience. The Latin archbishop was to be metropolitan of all Christians in Cyprus, and the Greek bishops were to do homage and fealty to the Latin bishops.

An attempt to settle some of these questions was made by an agreement at Limassol in October 1220 between Alice and the Cypriote barons on one side and Eustorgue, archbishop of Nicosia, and his three suffragans on the other. The crown confirmed to the Latin church the tithes on all domainial and baronial lands according to the custom of Jerusalem and remitted services and dues owed the crown by ecclesiastical serfs. The agreement stated that the Greek clergy owed obedience to the Latin archbishop, and made rules to check the practice of Greeks' taking minor orders to avoid taxation and service. The agreement did not work. The papal registers abound in repeated admonitions to the secular authorities urging them to enforce collection of tithes and other payments due the church. The Greeks proved recalcitrant.

In 1222 the legate Pelagius, on his way back to Italy, stopped in Cyprus, and, in association with Eustorgue's brothers Peter and Garin of Montaigu, the masters of the Temple and of the Hospital, tried to arbitrate. An accord concluded at Famagusta renewed the Limassol convention and enacted numerous provisions to tighten the hold of the Latins on the Greek church. Most important was the provision made "at the wish of both parties" (i.e. the lay authorities and the Latin ecclesiastics, for the Greeks were not represented) that the fourteen Greek bishoprics be reduced to four; that the bishops obey their Latin ordinaries according to the usage of Jerusalem; that their sees be transferred to secondary towns — Soli in the diocese of Nicosia, Arsinoë (modern Polis) in that of Paphos, Lefkara in that of Limassol, and Karpassia (Rizokarpasso) in that of Famagusta; and that existing incumbents retain their estates for life, while their successors would receive for their support the payments from their priests and deacons which were customary for the Greeks in other places. The provision for the reduction of the Greek dioceses, which seems not to have been immediately put into effect, was probably an attempt to mitigate the demand of Honorius III that all the Greek bishops be expelled. It was obvious to the queen and her counselors that the Greeks could not be converted *en masse* and could not be left wholly without pastors.[67]

The Greek archbishop Neophytus (not to be confused with the hermit of the Enkleistra) refused to submit and was banished.[68] The Cypriotes then sent a deputation to Germanus, the Greek patriarch of Nicaea, to ask for guidance. In a letter of 1222–1223 Germanus directed the Greek bishops to refuse to do homage to the Latins, but to yield in such matters as obtaining leave from the Latin ordinary to take possession of their offices and admitting appeals to the ordinaries from decisions of Greek bishops. Some of the Greek clergy seem to have submitted, for in 1229 Germanus wrote a second letter, addressed this time to Syrians as well as Greeks, denouncing the unbridled ambition of the Roman church, which was trying to set up the pope in place of Christ, and forbidding the clergy and laity to have any dealings with those who had given in to the demands of the Latins.

In the ensuing years the martyrdom of thirteen Greeks further inflamed the struggle. Two monks from Mt. Athos, wishing to share the sufferings of their cobelievers, had settled in the monastery of Kantara with a small group of disciples. A Dominican friar named Andrew entered into a disputation with them on the long-vexed question of the "azymes" (whether it was proper to use unleavened bread for the sacramental wafer as was done in the Roman church). Summoned before archbishop Eustorgue for opposing the Roman practice, they were thrown into prison, where they suffered manifold hardships and one died. Gregory IX sent orders to treat them as heretics if they persisted in their "error". When Eustorgue had to retire for a time to Acre because of a quarrel with Balian of Ibelin, whom he had excommunicated for marrying within the prohibited degrees of consanguinity, he left friar Andrew to deal with them. When they were brought before the high court, king Henry allowed Andrew to impose sentence. They were to be dragged through the market-place or river-bed at the tails of horses

[67] See Hill, *History of Cyprus*, III, 1047 and 1044–1045, referring to Honorius' letters of December 30, 1221 (Potthast, no. 6747), and of January 3, 1222 (Potthast, no. 6755). Pressutti, no. 3663, summarizing the letter of December 30 to queen Alice, notes that Potthast, in nos. 6747 and 6748, makes two letters to the queen out of "one and the same letter", a point not noticed by LaMonte ("Register of the Cartulary of Santa Sophia," *Byzantion*, V, p. 451, note 2).

[68] Laurent, in his review of Hill in *Revue des études byzantines*, VI (1948), 271, and in his article, "La Succession épiscopale," *ibid.*, VII (1949), 37, does not credit the story given in Hackett, *Orthodox Church in Cyprus*, pp. 84 and 309, and in Hill, *History of Cyprus*, III, 1044, based on the evidence of the 17th-century Orthodox patriarch of Jerusalem, Dositheus, that an earlier archbishop, Esaias, submitted in 1220, then repented and sought pardon at Nicaea for his apostasy.

and mules, and then burnt. Sentence was carried out, but since some of their bones remained unconsumed, they were mixed with the bones of unclean animals, so that they might not be venerated as relics, and burned again (1231).[69] The Orthodox world was stirred to its depths. Germanus wrote Gregory IX a letter singularly mild, considering the provocation, and the pope in 1233 dispatched two Dominicans and two Franciscans to confer with the patriarch, but their mission accomplished little.[70]

In 1240 Gregory sent new instructions to Eustorgue not to allow Greeks to celebrate mass unless they had taken an oath of obedience to the Roman church, and had renounced their heretical opinions, especially in regard to unleavened bread (azymes). In answer, the Greek bishops stripped the churches and monasteries of their remaining treasures and, together with the principal monks and priests, secretly left the island. Gregory then directed Eustorgue to fill the vacancies with Latins.

Innocent IV decided to try a more conciliatory policy. In 1247 he appointed his penitentiary, the Franciscan Lawrence, as legate to the east with instructions to protect the Greeks from molestation by the Latins. In 1248 a new legate, Odo of Châteauroux, cardinal-bishop of Tusculum, arrived in Cyprus with Louis IX to continue the work of conciliation. Many Cypriote ecclesiastics returned. Odo's task was complicated by the death of archbishop Eustorgue in April 1250 at Damietta and by the election in his place of Hugh of Fagiano, who, with fanatical zeal, chose to ignore the pope's injunctions to leave the Greeks in peace, and issued various harassing orders. Odo allowed the Greek bishops to elect and consecrate a new metropolitan, Germanus Pesimandrus, with the understanding that the Greek suffragan bishops might ignore the Latin archbishop and promise obedience directly to Germanus, while the latter was to promise obedience directly to the holy see. Archbishop Hugh was so angry that he placed the kingdom under an interdict and retired temporarily to his native Tuscany.

Odo continued his attempt to carry out the papal policy of tolerating the rites and usages of those Greeks who had returned to the Roman obedience, but he soon had to leave Cyprus, and Innocent IV died in December 1254. Nothing now stood in the way

[69] The legate Pelagius has been charged with responsibility for the death of these Greeks, but he himself died in 1230, a year before their execution: see Donovan, *Pelagius and the Fifth Crusade*, p. 104, and Hill, *History of Cyprus*, III, 1049, note 1, correcting H. T. F. Duckworth, *The Church of Cyprus* (London, 1900).

[70] For fuller details of this mission than are given by Hackett or Hill, see R. L. Wolff, "The Latin Empire of Constantinople and the Franciscans," *Traditio*, II (1944), 225–227.

of Hugh's burning desire to root out what he regarded as heretical opinions. Latin and Greek archbishops hurled excommunications at each other, while the secular authorities tried vainly to keep the peace. Finally Germanus appealed to Rome, and Alexander IV referred the matter to Odo, whose decision was embodied in the *Constitutio Cypria* or *Bulla Cypria* of Anagni (July 3, 1260). Thereupon Hugh retired again to Tuscany, though he kept his title of archbishop of Nicosia until his death in 1267.

The *Constitutio Cypria* attempted to settle the relationship of the two churches for the future, but it could not eliminate all seeds of controversy. It confirmed the reduction of the Greek sees to four and provided that after the death of Germanus, who was made independent of the Latin hierarchy in the island, the Latin archbishop should be sole metropolitan. A series of lengthy articles dealt with the oath of obedience to be taken by newly elected Greek bishops, their rights and jurisdiction.[71]

Alexander IV's constitution brought no peace. "Heresy" still flourished; the schism endured. Greeks who conformed were excommunicated by Greeks who resisted. The civil arm refused to intervene to punish recusant Greeks. The fear that, with the fall of Latin Constantinople, the new Byzantine emperor might take advantage of Cypriote disaffection to make a landing in the island proved unfounded, but discontent smouldered on, though no acute outbreak occurred until early in the next century. In about 1280 or shortly thereafter the Latin archbishop, Raphael, issued a constitution giving instructions to the Greek clergy for their discipline, ritual, and administration, which was to be read four times a year by the Greek bishops to clergy and laity. The tone of the document, which speaks of the Greek prelates as merely "tolerated", while the Latin were "ordained", was not such as to assuage the bitter feelings of the Greeks. It charged the Greek clergy with being ignorant and slack, but perhaps such a charge could have been brought with equal justice against the Latin clergy. The struggle continued and was ended only with the expulsion of the Latins by the Turks in the sixteenth century. Today such monuments as the noble thirteenth-century cathedral of Hagia Sophia (now a mosque) in Nicosia and the magnificent fourteenth-century ruins of the Premonstratensian abbey of Bellapais in the north alone bear witness to the once dominant position of the Latin church in the island.

[71] For a summary of the *Constitutio Cypria*, see Hill, *History of Cyprus*, III, 1059 ff., and Hackett, *Orthodox Church in Cyprus*, pp. 114–123.

Secure behind its sea walls, Cyprus played a significant role in thirteenth-century crusading history. When the Latin states on the mainland fell, it offered asylum to the hordes of refugees. The kingdom of Cyprus became the heir, in its institutions, of the kingdom of Jerusalem. Succeeding centuries were to witness bitter struggles — the Greek church against the Latin, and Cypriote barons against their rulers. In a wider sphere, however, Cyprus was to become the great emporium for commerce between east and west, and was to loom large in the projects of those who planned future crusades.

XVIII
THE KINGDOM OF CILICIAN ARMENIA

In the course of the eleventh century large numbers of the Armenian population left their homeland and migrated west and southwest of the Euphrates, to regions already settled by Armenians at an earlier period. The first important wave of emigrants accompanied the kings of Vaspurkan, Ani, and Kars, and other

Extracts and translations of the principal Armenian sources are collected in *RHC, Arm.*, I. To these should be added: V. A. Hakopian, *Short Chronicles* (in Armenian; 2 vols., Erevan, 1951–1956; the first volume of this publication has a critical edition of the *Chronology* of Heṭoum [pp. 65–101], attributed by the editor to king Heṭoum II instead of to Heṭoum ["Hayton"] the historian); and R. P. Blake and R. N. Frye (eds.), *History of the Nation of the Archers (the Mongols) by Grigor of Akanc'* (Cambridge, Mass., 1954).

The anonymous Cilician Chronicle, preserved in a manuscript of the Mekhitharist Library in Venice and referred to by Alishan as the Royal Chronicle, is a most important source. The complete photographs, made for the late Robert P. Blake and lent by him to Professor Joseph Skinner, were put at the author's disposal by the latter, together with his translation; she wishes to express her sincere thanks to him. Since the present chapter was written, the Venice manuscript has been published by S. Akelian, under the title *Chronicle of the General Sempad* (in Armenian; Venice-San Lazzaro, 1956). Miss Der Nersessian, the author of this chapter, has retained in both the text and the footnotes the former designation of "Cilician Chronicle" but has given the page references to Akelian's edition. For an identification of this published text with Alishan's "Royal Chronicle" and its attribution to Sempad, cf. S. Der Nersessian, "The Armenian Chronicle of the Constable Smpad or of the 'Royal Historian'," *Dumbarton Oaks Papers*, XIII (1959), 143–168.

Among the sources one should include the colophons of manuscripts, which often give valuable historical information: Garegin I Hovsepian, *Colophons of Manuscripts* (in Armenian; Antilias, 1951), with colophons down to the year 1250; and L. S. Khachikian, *Colophons of Armenian Manuscripts of the XIVth century* (in Armenian; Erevan, 1950). For various charters and other acts, see: V. Langlois, *Le Trésor des chartes d'Arménie* (Paris, 1863); Cornelio Desimoni, "Actes passés en 1271, 1274 et 1279 à l'Aïas (Petite Arménie) et à Beyrouth par devant des notaires génois," *Archives de l'orient latin*, I, 434–534; and L. Alishan, *L'Armeno-Veneto* (2 vols., Venice - San Lazzaro, 1893).

The principal Syriac sources are the anonymous chronicle translated by A. S. Tritton and H. A. R. Gibb, "The First and Second Crusades from an Anonymous Syriac Chronicle," *Journal of the Royal Asiatic Society*, 1933, pp. 69–101, 273–305; Michael the Syrian (tr. J. B. Chabot, *Chronique de Michel le Syrien, Patriarche Jacobite d'Antioche*, 3 vols., Paris, 1899–1905; Armenian version, tr. V. Langlois, *Chronique de Michel le Grand*, Venice, 1868); and Bar Hebraeus (tr. E. A. Wallis Budge, *The Chronography of Gregory Abû 'l Faraj . . . commonly known as Bar Hebraeus*, Oxford, 1932).

The principal Arabic sources are: Abū'l-Fidā', *Kitāb al-mukhtaṣar* (extracts in *RHC, Or.*, I, 1–115); Ibn-al-Athīr, *Al-kāmil fī-t-ta'rīkh* (extracts in *RHC, Or.*, I, 187–744, and II, part 1); Ibn-al-Qalānisī, *Dhail ta'rīkh Dimashq* (extracts translated by H. A. R. Gibb, *The Damascus Chronicle of the Crusades*, London, 1932, and by R. Le Tourneau, *Damas de 1075 à 1154*, Paris, 1952); al-Jazarī, *Ḥawādith az-zamān* (extracts and summaries by J. Sauvaget, *La*

minor rulers whose lands had been seized by the Byzantine emperors and who had been granted, in return, domains in Cappadocia and Asia Minor. A second wave followed the conquest of Armenia by the Selchükid Turks and the disaster of Manzikert in 1071.[1] It is probable that by far the greater number of those who fled the Turkish domination sought refuge in the cities and regions of the Taurus, the Anti-Taurus, and northern Syria held by Armenian chieftains, where they were joined towards the end of the century by some Armenians of Cappadocia who moved southward after the death of the last Armenian kings. A considerable number still remained, however, north of the Taurus; according to the *Gesta* when the crusaders approached Caesarea of Cappadocia (Kayseri) they entered "the country of the Armenians", and when they reached Comana and Coxon they were welcomed by the Armenian population of these cities.

In order to secure the defense of their eastern borders, the Byzantine emperors had appointed some Armenians as governors of important cities, entrusted them with the command of their armies, or ceded large tracts of land to them. But gradually, taking advantage of the unsettled conditions of these outer regions and the weakening of the central authority, some of these chieftains had broken the ties that bound them to the empire. At the time of the

Chronique de Damas, Paris, 1949); Abū-Shāmah, *Kitāb ar-rauḍatain* (*RHC, Or.*, IV–V); Kamāl-ad-Dīn, *Zubdat al-ḥalab fī ta'rīkh Ḥalab* (tr. E. Blochet, "Histoire d'Alep," *ROL*, III–VI, 1895–1898); al-Maqrīzī, *Al-mawā'iẓ wa-l-i'tibar fī dhikr al-khiṭaṭ wa-l-āthār* (tr. E. M. Quatremère, *Histoire des sultans mamlouks de l'Égypte*, 2 vols., Paris, 1837–1845); and al-Maqrīzī, *Akhbār Miṣr* (tr. E. Blochet, *Histoire d'Égypte*, Paris, 1908). In Persian, there is Ibn-Bībī, *Saljūq-nāmeh* (ed. Th. Houtsma, Leyden, 1902; extracts tr. C. Schéfer, Paris, 1889). There is a German translation of Ibn-Bībī by H. W. Duda, *Die Seltschukengeschichte des Ibn Bibi*, Copenhagen, 1959.

The Byzantine and western writers include: Anna Comnena, *Alexiad* (ed. B. Leib, 3 vols., Paris, 1937–1945); Cedrenus-Skylitzes, *Historiarum compendium*, vol. II (*CSHB*, Bonn, 1839); Nicetas Choniates, *Historia* (*CSHB*, Bonn, 1835); and William of Tyre, *Historia rerum in partibus transmarinis gestarum*, and French translation, *L'Estoire de Eracles empereur* (*RHC, Occ.*, *I*).

Among the principal secondary sources which should be consulted in addition to the general histories of the crusades are the following: Leonce M. Alishan, *Léon le Magnifique, premier roi de Sissouan ou de l'Arméno-Cilicie* (Venice, 1888); Leonce Alishan, *Sissouan ou l'Arméno-Cilicie* (Venice, 1899); Claude Cahen, *La Syrie du nord à l'époque des croisades et la principauté franque d'Antioche* (Paris, 1940); F. Chalandon, *Les Comnène: Jean II Comnène et Manuel Comnène* (Paris, 1913); N. Iorga, *Brève histoire de la Petite Arménie* (Paris, 1930); J. Laurent, "Les Croisés et l'Arménie," *Handes Amsorya*, XLI (1927), 885–906; G. G. Mikaelian, *Istoriya kilikiiskogo armyanskogo gosudarstvo* (Erevan, 1952); J. de Morgan, *Histoire du peuple arménien* (Nancy-Paris, 1919); Malachia Ormanian, *Azkabadoum* (in Armenian), vols. I and II (Constantinople, 1912–1914); M. Tchamtchian, *History of the Armenians* (in Armenian; 3 vols., Venice, 1784–1786); and Fr. Tournebize, *Histoire politique et religieuse de l'Arménie* (Paris, n.d.).

[1] For the Selchükid victory at Manzikert, see volume I of the present work, chapter V, pp. 148–150; for the Armenian princelings in 1097, see *ibid.*, chapter IX, pp. 299–301.

First Crusade there were many such chieftains, some in key positions, who gave important assistance to the Latin armies. The governor of Melitene, Gabriel, was an Armenian of the Greek Orthodox faith whose daughter Morfia married Baldwin of Le Bourg. The Armenian Constantine was lord of Gargar. Ṭaṭoul had been appointed governor of Marash by Alexius Comnenus and was confirmed in this position by the crusaders. Ablgharib (Abū-l-Gharīb) was master of Bira (Birejik). At Edessa, where the Armenian element was particularly numerous, the governor was Ṭoros, son-in-law of Gabriel of Melitene, who had received the title *curopalates* from Alexius Comnenus.

However, the most important chieftain in these parts had been Philaretus, whose authority, at the time of his greatest power, between 1078 and 1085, had extended over a vast area which comprised the cities of Melitene, Marash, Edessa, and Antioch. After the death of Philaretus, the remnants of his armies gathered around Kogh Ṿasil, ruler of Kesoun and Raban, who for a time also held Hromgla. Among those who fought at his side was Dgha Ṿasil, whom he adopted and who succeeded him.

The Armenian possessions in Cilicia, which were to endure much longer than these ephemeral principalities, were at first far less important. Here also the Armenian immigration had begun at a fairly early date. The historian Mkhiṭar of Ayrivanḳ records that in the first years of the tenth century fifty noblemen of Sasoun, fleeing from the Turks, had crossed the Taurus; doubtless they were accompanied by their followers as well as by their families. By the latter part of the century the Armenians of Cilicia and northern Syria were sufficiently numerous to warrant the appointment of a bishop at Tarsus and of another at Antioch.[2] This increase in the population coincided with the Byzantine reconquest and, according to Bar Hebraeus, the Byzantines stationed the Armenians "in the fortresses which were in Cilicia, and which they took from the Arabs." No names of Armenian officials are recalled, however, before the second half of the eleventh century, when the population had been further increased by the arrival of new immigrants from Cappadocia and Armenia. When in 1067 the Turks, having pillaged Iconium, were returning home by way of Cilicia, Romanus Diogenes, in order to stop them, sent the commander of Antioch, the Armenian Khaçhadour, to Mamistra, but there is no mention of any local Armenian chieftain. There may have been an Armenian governor at Tarsus before 1072, for according to the Cilician

[2] Étienne Asotik de Tarôn, *Histoire universelle* (tr. F. Macler, Paris, 1917), p. 141.

Chronicle, whose account differs from that of Matthew of Edessa, the anti-catholicus George came there, seeking the protection of Kakig, son of Kourkēn. Nothing further is known about this Kakig, and a few years later, in 1079, the governor of Tarsus was Ablgharib.

Ablgharib belonged to a family which had long been in the service of Byzantium. His grandfather, Khoul Khachig, prince of the region of Ṭornavan in the province of Vaspurkan, was a vassal of the Byzantine emperors; his father, Hasan, had served under Michael V; and Ablgharib himself had received the governorship of Tarsus from Michael VII. Ablgharib also held the two important forts of western Cilicia, Babaṛon and Lampron, which he ceded later to one of his generals, Ōshin, founder of the powerful feudal family of the Heṭoumids.

Some modern historians have identified Ōshin I with the general Aspietes, whose exploits are told by Anna Comnena, and with Ursinus, mentioned by Radulf of Caen and Albert of Aix (Aachen), and have credited him with all their deeds. But as Laurent has convincingly proved, there are no valid grounds for this identification and very little is known about him.[3] According to Samuel of Ani, Ōshin had left his hereditary possessions in the region of Ganja in 1073, had come to Cilicia accompanied by his family and his followers, and had wrested Lampron from the Saracens. But the Armenian sources that are closer to the Heṭoumids speak of him merely as one of the faithful chieftains of Ablgharib to whom the latter ceded Lampron,[4] while Matthew of Edessa and the Cilician Chronicle mention him only in passing, together with two other princelings who came to the assistance of the crusaders when they crossed the Taurus.

The early history of the rival family of the Ṛoupenids is equally obscure. Samuel of Ani considers Ṛoupen I a relative of the last Bagratid ruler, but he was, in all probability, a chieftain of minor importance who, some time after the death of king Gagik (1071), had settled in the region of Gobidaṛa, where we find his son Constantine in the last years of the eleventh century.[5] It was this Constantine who, by seizing, in 1091, the castle of Vahka on the Gök river, laid the foundations of Ṛoupenid rule in Cilicia. We

[3] J. Laurent, "Arméniens de Cilicie: Aspiétès, Oschin, Ursinus," *Mélanges Schlumberger*, I (1924), 159–168. Ōshin and "Ursinus" may be the same man; Aspietes is clearly distinct.

[4] Garegin I Hovsepian, *Colophons*, col. 542, 552; L. Alishan, *Hayabadoum* (in Armenian; Venice, 1901), II, 414.

[5] N. Adontz, "Notes arméno-byzantines: VI. L'aïeul des Roubéniens," *Byzantion*, X (1935), 185–203.

do not know the actual extent of his possessions. The historians speak in vague terms of his capture of many castles from the Turks; he probably had control over part of the mountainous region southwest of Vahka, perhaps as far as the Cilician Gates, for the Cilician Chronicle in referring to a letter sent by Constantine and Ṭoros of Edessa to the crusaders seems to imply that the peaceful passage through Podandus was due to the influence of these two men.[6]

Constantine, Ōshin of Lampron, and Pazouni, as well as the monks living in the Black Mountains, in the Taurus, provisioned the crusaders during the siege of Antioch, and they all welcomed as liberators the Christian armies who had come to fight against the Moslems. These feelings are reflected in the colophons of contemporary Armenian manuscripts; the scribes hail the "valiant nation from the west" whose arrival shows that "God has visited his people according to his promise", they speak again of "the valiant nation of the Franks who . . . through divine inspiration and the solicitude of the omnipotent God took Antioch and Jerusalem."[7] The crusaders, too, were happy to find a friendly population and at first rewarded the services rendered to them, but the cordial relations lasted only as long as the interests of both parties did not clash.

In order to obtain a clear idea of future development in the Armenian principality, one should consider the outstanding geographical features of Cilicia. The Armenian possessions, though limited, were of strategic importance. A son-in-law of Ōshin who had succeeded Ablgharib at Tarsus was not able to hold it against the Turks, but the fortresses of Babaṛon and Lampron, erected on crags at the foot of Bulgar Dagh, could not be taken. Thus the Heṭoumids commanded the southern exit of the Cilician Gates, the route which led directly to Tarsus. Vassals of Byzantium, to which they remained faithful, they do not seem to have had marked ambition for territorial expansion. In the long struggle with the Ṛoupenids, which came to an end only through the marriage of Heṭoum I to the daughter and heiress of Leon II, the Ṛoupenids were almost always the aggressors, and when the Heṭoumids attacked it was usually within the framework of Byzantine invasions and not as an independent act. The aim of the Ṛoupenids, on the other hand, was to become masters of Cilicia.

The Cilician plain is divided into two main parts: the lower or western plain stretches from the foothills of the Taurus to the sea,

[6] Cilician Chronicle, p. 102; cf. also the *Anonymous Syriac Chronicle*, pp. 70–71.
[7] Garegin I Hovsepian, *Colophons*, cols. 261, 265.

and is watered by the Cydnus, Sarus, and Pyramus; its principal cities in the medieval period were Adana and especially Tarsus; Seleucia was its chief port. The upper or eastern plain is separated from the western and the sea by the ridge called Jabal Nūr. The city of Mamistra commands the passage of the Pyramus on its way from the upper to the lower plain; Anazarba and Sis are farther north on tributaries of the Pyramus. To the east the plain is limited by the range of the Amanus, and it is here that Cilicia was more vulnerable, for the passes which lead into Syria are broader and shorter than the famous Cilician Gates.

The policy followed, with varying fortunes, by the Ṛoupenid princes was determined to a great extent by the configuration of the land. It was an absolute economic necessity to descend from the mountain strongholds into the arable lands of the plain; to have control of the large cities which were situated on the trade routes; to reach the coast and have an outlet on the sea. To protect themselves from attacks from the northwest and west complete control of the Cilician Gates was essential, and this brought them into conflict with the Heṭoumids; to safeguard their eastern borders control of the passes of the Amanus was essential, and this brought them into conflict with Antioch. But their principal adversary during the entire twelfth century was Byzantium, to which Cilicia belonged.

Ṭoros I (1100–1129), the son and successor of Constantine, proceeded carefully. He refrained from taking part in the struggle between the Greeks and Latins over the possession of the principal cities of the plain, and captured only Anazarba. He strengthened that city and made it the seat of his barony; he erected a church dedicated to St. George and St. Theodore on the ruined remains of which part of his dedicatory inscription is still visible. He remained on good terms with the Byzantines in spite of the seizure of Anazarba and the plunder and destruction of Heraclea, where he killed the sons of Mandalē to avenge the murder of king Gagik. His chief concern, however, was to maintain friendly relations with the Latin princes who had been enlarging their possessions at the expense of the Armenians.

In 1098 Baldwin of Boulogne became master of Edessa, following the murder of Ṭoros by the populace. In 1104 Ṭaṭoul of Marash, after successfully resisting the attacks of Bohemond I and his kinsman Richard of the Principate, was forced to cede the city to Joscelin I of Courtenay. Between the years 1115 and 1118 Baldwin of Le Bourg seized the domains of Dgha Ṿasil and those of

Ablgharib, lord of Bira; he imprisoned Constantine of Gargar in the fortress of Samosata, where he died; he captured Ravendan near Cyrrhus, and the territories ruled by Pakrad.[8] Thus, with minor exceptions, all the Armenian possessions outside Cilicia passed into Latin hands, and it must have become evident to Ṭoros I that if he wished to remain free and master of his lands, he would have to be careful not to antagonize his powerful and ambitious neighbors.

Therefore, realizing the weakness of his position, he pursued a cautious policy. His land had been plundered by the Moslems in 1107 and again in 1110/1111 when a larger army descended on Anazarba without meeting any resistance. Ṭoros kept aloof also from the battles fought against the Turks in 1112/1113 within his own territories, but in 1118 he took part in the siege and capture of 'Azāz by Roger of Antioch, sending a contingent of troops under the leadership of his brother Leon. Ṭoros gave assistance also to Arab, one of the sons of Kilij Arslan I, when Arab revolted against his brother Mas'ūd. Mas'ūd was the son-in-law and ally of Gümüshtigin Ghāzī, the Dānishmendid, which was probably the principal reason for the Dānishmendid invasion of Cilicia early in the reign of Leon I (1129–1137). While Gümüshtigin Ghāzī was invading from the north, Bohemond II of Antioch entered Cilicia from the east. The reasons for the break with Antioch are not known; the anonymous Syrian Chronicle reports that Armenian brigands had been plundering the lands of Gümüshtigin Ghāzī and that Bohemond had suffered similarly. The two invading armies, unaware of one another's advance, met in the plain north of Mamistra, and Bohemond was killed in the encounter. While the Franks, deprived of their leader, hastily retreated, Leon occupied the passes and killed many of the fugitives. Gümüshtigin Ghāzī withdrew without pursuing Leon, but returned the following year (1131), seized several forts, and imposed a tribute on the Armenians.

Leon did not long remain inactive. In 1132, taking advantage of the fact that both Gümüshtigin Ghāzī and the Franks were occupied elsewhere, he seized Mamistra, Adana, and Tarsus, and he followed these conquests in 1135 with the capture of Sarvantikar, a fortress built near the point of convergence of the northern routes that crossed the Amanus. His growing power, and especially the foothold he had gained on the Syrian border, alarmed the Franks; the combined forces of Raymond of Poitiers, the new prince of Antioch, and Baldwin of Marash, with contingents sent by king Fulk of Jerusalem, entered Cilicia. Leon, assisted by his nephew

[8] See volume I of the present work, chapter XII, pp. 387–391, 405.

Joscelin II of Edessa, was at first able to withstand their attack, but finally was surprised in an ambush and was taken to Antioch. His captivity lasted only two months. The menace of a Byzantine expedition, directed against Antioch as well as Cilicia, probably hastened his release and, according to Cinnamus, the Latins and Armenians even established some kind of alliance against the Greeks.

As soon as he was set free, Leon rushed to the western borders of Cilicia and laid siege to Seleucia in the vain hope of stopping the Greek advance, but was soon forced to raise the siege. In a rapid march across the plain John Comnenus recovered Tarsus, Adana, Mamistra, and finally Anazarba, Leon's only point of stiff resistance. John also took Tall Ḥamdūn and, without pausing to pursue Leon and his sons, who had fled to the mountains, marched on Antioch. The conquest of Cilicia was completed in the winter of 1137–1138; Vahka fell in spite of its strong position and the prowess of a nobleman called Constantine; the fort of Raban and the surrounding areas were also seized.[9] Leon, his wife, and two of his sons, Ṛoupen and Ṭoros, were carried in chains to Constantinople, and Armenian rule in Cilicia seemed destroyed for ever.

Very little is known about internal conditions during the Byzantine occupation. The Greek garrisons do not seem to have been very strong, for even before John's return to Constantinople, while he was besieging Shaizar, the Selchükid Mas'ūd had seized and held Adana for a short time, carrying some of its inhabitants as captives to Melitene; and in 1138–1139 the Dānishmendid emir Muḥammad took Vahka and Gaban and various localities in the region of Garmirleṛ (Red Mountains). But, with the captivity of Leon I, the center of Armenian resistance was destroyed; the only strong princes who remained in Cilicia, the Heṭoumids and their allies, were vassals of Byzantium and always faithful to their suzerain. John crossed Cilicia peacefully at the time of his second expedition to the east (1142). When, after his death and the departure of his son Manuel, Raymond of Antioch captured some of the castles along the Syrian border, the Armenians of that area took no part in the battle, nor did they when the Byzantine forces sent by Manuel defeated Raymond.

However, the situation was soon to change. Leon's younger son, Ṭoros, had been allowed to live at the imperial court after the

[9] Nicetas Choniates, *Historia: De Johanne Comneno* (*CSHB*, Bonn, 1835), pp. 29-33. The Cilician Chronicle (p. 160) and Sempad (*RHC, Arm.*, I, 616) also mention three other localities: Khalij, Amayḳ, Ṭsakhoud. The first two have not been identified, the last is probably the province which lies roughly to the east of Sis.

deaths of his father and his brother Ṛoupen. He was then able to make useful contacts and to escape, probably in 1145. Neither the circumstances of his escape nor those of his arrival in Cilicia are clearly known; legendary and romantic stories distorted the facts and several traditions were already current in the following century. Ṭoros probably came by sea to the principality of Antioch and entered Cilicia secretly. A Jacobite priest, Mar Athanasius, is reported to have led him by night to Amoudain, a castle on the river Pyramus, southeast of Anazarba, and from there he proceeded to the mountainous region which had been the stronghold of his family but which was still held by the Turks. He lived there in disguise, and little by little rallied around him the Armenians of this eastern section of Cilicia. His brother Stephen (Sdefanē), who had been living at the court of his cousin Joscelin II of Edessa, also joined him, and in the course of a few years Ṭoros recovered Vahka, the castles in the vicinity of Anazarba such as Amoudain, Simanagla, and Arioudzpert, and finally Anazarba, the seat of the Ṛoupenid barony. These conquests were probably completed by 1148, the date given by Michael the Syrian and Bar Hebraeus for the beginning of Ṭoros II's reign.

Ṭoros and his small band had fought with great courage and energy, and the general situation in the Levant had favored him. His Latin neighbors had not fully recovered from the destruction of Edessa and the losses suffered during the siege of Antioch; above all, the growing power of Nūr-ad-Dīn forced them to concentrate their efforts on the defense of their own principalities. Joscelin II of Edessa, the most powerful Latin prince of this area, was Ṭoros's friend, and the ties between the two cousins were further strengthened when Ṭoros married the daughter of Simon of Raban, one of Joscelin's vassals.

Ṭoros had also been free from Moslem attacks. The armies of 'Ain-ad-Daulah, Kara Arslan, Mas'ūd, and Nūr-ad-Dīn had seized the territories once held by Kogh Ṿasil, but they did not enter Cilicia. Ṭoros was thus able to strengthen his position. About the year 1151 he took Tall Ḥamdūn and Mamistra, imprisoning the governor, Thomas.

If the immediate neighbors of Cilicia were too busy to interfere with Ṭoros's progress, Byzantium could not allow him to keep the cities still claimed by the empire.[10] In 1152 a Byzantine army under

[10] On Byzantine policies in Cilicia and Antioch, see volume I of the present work, chapter XIII, pp. 439-440, 445, and chapter XVI, pp. 530, 540-546, 560; see also above, chapter IV, pp. 130-137.

the command of Manuel's cousin Andronicus Comnenus, supported by contingents from the Armenian chieftains of western Cilicia, besieged Mamistra. Ṭoros sallied forth under cover of darkness, routed the Byzantine army, and took many prisoners. Andronicus fled to Antioch and from there returned to Constantinople. Among the prisoners were three of Byzantium's principal Armenian allies: Ōshin II of Lampron, Vasil of Partzapert, and Dikran of Bṛagana; Ōshin's brother, Sempad of Babaṛon, was killed in battle. Ōshin was released after he had paid half of a ransom of 40,000 tahegans and left his young son Heṭoum as hostage. A marriage was negotiated between Heṭoum and one of the daughters of Ṭoros, who agreed to forego the remainder of Ōshin's ransom, counting it as his daughter's dowry.

Ṭoros II was now master of a large section of the plain. No new expedition was sent to Cilicia; Manuel tried instead an indirect method of defeating Ṭoros. At Manuel's instigation Mas'ūd of Iconium invaded Cilicia; he demanded that Ṭoros recognize him as his suzerain and that Ṭoros return to the Greeks the cities he had captured. Ṭoros agreed to do the first, and since this was the only condition which directly interested Mas'ūd, he withdrew without further resort to arms. However, after Ṭoros raided Cappadocia in the winter or early spring of 1154, Mas'ūd was quite ready to listen to Manuel's renewed request, which was accompanied by costly gifts. The Moslem armies met with severe reverses. Ṭoros's brother Stephen, assisted by the Templars of Baghrās (Gaston), surprised the general Ya'qūb in the Syrian Gates, killed him, and routed his men. A terrible plague of gnats and flies decimated the Selchükid forces before Tall Ḥamdūn, and the remnants of the army were destroyed by Ṭoros on his return from a raid into enemy territory that had reached as far as Gabadonia.[11]

The Byzantine plans had failed once again. Ṭoros established cordial relations with Ma'sūd's successor Kilij Arslan II. When Stephen seized Coxon and Pertous, and supported the Christian population of Behesni, who had been aroused by the cruel treatment of their new governor, Ṭoros recovered Pertous by a ruse and returned the city to Kilij Arslan. On his part Kilij Arslan, anxious to rally forces against Nūr-ad-Dīn, made every effort to maintain

[11] Michael the Syrian, *Chronique* (tr. Chabot), III, 311; Bar Hebraeus, *Chronography* (tr. Budge), p. 281. The Armenian sources do not mention an attack by Ṭoros (*RHC, Arm.*, I, 175). The Cilician Chronicle states that the enemy fled in disorder "as if they were pursuing their own selves. For Ṭoros was not in his country, but had gone to Dzedz. And when he returned and saw how things were, they all gave thanks to God that they [the enemy] had been routed without arms or human combat" (p. 173). On the Selchükids and Dānishmendids, see below chapter XIX, pp. 675–692.

peace with his Christian neighbors, and even sent ambassadors to Ṭoros, as well as to Antioch and Jerusalem, with the idea of forming an alliance.

Seeing that he could no longer count on the Selchükids, Manuel turned to the Latins; he promised Reginald of Antioch to defray his campaign expenses if he would march against Ṭoros, but once again, Byzantium did not obtain the desired results. For, having seized the castles of the Amanus taken by Ṭoros from the Greeks, Reginald ceded them to the Templars, their previous owners, and when Manuel failed to send the promised sums, Reginald reversed his stand, allied himself with Ṭoros, and the two princes raided Cyprus (1155). Ṭoros remained on good terms with the Latins, and in 1157 took part in the allied attack on Shaizar and Ḥārim.

Byzantium did not immediately react to the plunder of Cyprus; the expedition prepared in great secret a few years later (1158) took Ṭoros and Reginald completely by surprise. Warned by a Latin pilgrim, Ṭoros had barely time to flee to a small castle built on an almost inaccessible crag called Dajig. The Byzantine armies swept through the Cilician plain without meeting any resistance. Reginald, fearing the emperor's revenge, proceeded to Mamistra dressed in a penitent's garb, and humbled himself before Manuel, promising to remain his vassal and to cede the citadel of Antioch. Shortly thereafter Ṭoros also arrived dressed as a penitent; the Templars and Baldwin III, who in the meantime had come from Jerusalem, interceded for him. Ṭoros promised submission; he presented to the emperor abundant supplies and horses for the army, and received his pardon; Manuel is said even to have bestowed upon him the title *sebastos*.

Cilicia was once again under Byzantine domination. As in the days of Leon I, no sooner had Ṛoupenid control extended into the plain than Byzantium had intervened. But the disaster this time was not complete. Ṭoros II was free, his cavalry was still intact, and he retained his mountain strongholds, for Manuel realized that it was more important to have him in Cilicia, as a vassal who could take part in the fight against the Moslems, than in Constantinople as a captive. We thus see Armenian contingents in the Graeco-Latin expedition against Nūr-ad-Dīn in 1159, and, the following year, among the allied troops led by John Contostephanus against Kilij Arslan.

A break between the Greeks and Armenians, which might have

had serious consequences, occurred in 1162. The governor of Tarsus, Andronicus Euphorbenus, invited Stephen to a feast, and when the latter's body was found the next day outside the city gates, Andronicus was accused of the murder. Ṭoros and Mleh immediately took up arms to avenge their brother; they massacred the garrisons of Mamistra, Anazarba, and Vahka. But in the face of the constant Moslem menace it was most important to maintain the alliance between the Christian forces. King Amalric of Jerusalem assumed the role of mediator, as his predecessor had done; Andronicus was recalled and replaced by Constantine Coloman. Nor did Manuel raise any objections the following year when Ṭoros helped the barons of Antioch to install Bohemond III, and to expel Constance, who had appealed for help to Coloman. Ṭoros continued to fight side by side with the Greeks and the Latins. He joined the allied forces against Nūr-ad-Dīn (1164) and he and his brother Mleh were among the few leaders who escaped the disaster of Ḥārim.

We have little information about the internal affairs of Cilicia during this period. The Byzantine occupation had no doubt strengthened the position of their Armenian allies of western Cilicia, but after his return from Ḥārim and perhaps after his successful raid on Marash, when he captured four hundred Turks, Ṭoros felt sufficiently strong to attack Ōshin of Lampron. The struggle between the two princes alarmed the catholicus, Gregory III, whose family was allied to the house of Lampron, and he sent his brother, Nersēs the Gracious, to bring about a reconciliation.[12] It was during this journey to western Cilicia that Nersēs met Manuel's kinsman Alexius Axouch at Mamistra; this encounter proved to be the starting point of the negotiations between the Greek and Armenian churches, which were to last several years without success.[13]

The see of the catholicus had been transferred in 1151 to Hromgla (Qal'at ar-Rūm), a fortified position on the Euphrates north of Bira. Ever since 1125 the head of the Armenian church had been residing at Dzoyḳ, but his position had become almost untenable after the conquests of Mas'ūd and particularly after the capture of Duluk. The catholicus Gregory, seeking refuge elsewhere, had gladly accepted the offer of Hromgla made to him by Beatrice, the wife of Joscelin II of Courtenay, at that time a prisoner of the Turks. Hromgla seems to have been given at first "in trust", but later the

[12] Garegin I Hovsepian, *Colophons*, col. 385.

[13] S. Der Nersessian, *Armenia and the Byzantine Empire* (Cambridge, 1945), pp. 42–52.

catholicus purchased it from Joscelin III for 15,000 tahegans; the official deed of transfer was kept in the archives of Hromgla, so that — adds the Cilician Chronicle — no member of the Courtenay family should ever claim the castle.

Ṭoros II had accomplished a remarkable piece of work. He had reëstablished the Armenian barony of Cilicia, and, although the territories over which he had control were limited and he was a vassal of the Byzantine emperor, he had laid foundations on which his successors could build. His work was almost undone, however, in the years immediately following his death (1168), by the actions of his brother Mleh, whom, a few years earlier, Ṭoros had expelled from Cilicia. Mleh had gone to the court of Nūr-ad-Dīn and had been appointed governor of Cyrrhus. As soon as news of the death of Ṭoros reached him, he invaded Cilicia with the help of Turkish contingents provided by Nūr-ad-Dīn. A first attempt to seize power there proved unsuccessful, though he took numerous prisoners; he was preparing to return with larger forces when the Armenian nobles ceded the barony to him in order to avoid further bloodshed.[14] The regent Thomas fled to Antioch, and Ṭoros's young son Ṛoupen II was carried for safety to Hromgla, where, however, Mleh's agents succeeded in killing him.

From the outset Mleh antagonized the notables and the population by his rapaciousness and his wanton cruelty. His ambition and his confidence in the support of his powerful friend Nūr-ad-Dīn encouraged him to undertake at once the extension of his possessions. Using as a pretext the repudiation by Heṭoum of his wife, who was Mleh's niece, he beleaguered Lampron, but in spite of a long siege he was unable to capture this strong position; so he turned to the east and wrested from the Templars the castles of the Amanus. With the help of Turkish forces he seized Adana, Mamistra, and Tarsus (December 1172–January 1173), routed the hastily assembled army of Constantine Coloman, made him a prisoner, and sent him to Nūr-ad-Dīn, together with other prominent captives and much booty. Mleh's growing power disturbed the Latins, already aroused by such acts as the seizure and robbing of count Stephen of Sancerre in 1171, while he was proceeding from Antioch to Constantinople. Mleh's hold over the castles of

[14] The "Brief History of the Ṛoupenians", attributed to Heṭoum ("Hayton"), is the only Armenian source which mentions Mleh's first, unsuccessful attempt to seize the throne. According to it when the Armenians heard that Mleh was making ready to return, they asked him "to come peacefully to be master of the country, so that the Christians should not suffer from the soldiers of the infidels. And he [Mleh], hearing this, sent back the soldiers to the sultan with many thanks." Cf. V. A. Hakopian, *Short Chronicles*, II, 102–103. On Mleh and Nūr-ad-Dīn, see volume I of the present work, chapter XVI, p. 527.

the Amanus constituted a direct threat to the principality of Antioch. Bohemond III and some of the neighboring barons marched, therefore, against Mleh in the spring of 1173, but apparently were not successful at first.[15] When news of the conflict reached Jerusalem, Amalric decided to intervene in person, though he invaded Cilicia only after Mleh had eluded his repeated attempts to meet with him personally. Avoiding the difficult mountainous regions, Amalric advanced through the plain, destroying the villages and setting fire to the crops as he progressed. But Mleh was saved once again by Nūr-ad-Dīn, who created a diversion by marching against Kerak. Amalric hastened back to Jerusalem; the other Latin forces probably withdrew at the same time, and Mleh remained master of Cilicia.

The death of Nūr-ad-Dīn in May 1174 spelled the end of Mleh's fortunes. When they no longer had reason to fear Nūr-ad-Dīn's intervention, the Armenian nobles rebelled, and killed Mleh in the city of Sis, which had become his residence. They chose as his successor Ṛoupen III (1175–1187), the eldest son of Stephen, who, since his father's death, had been living with his maternal uncle Pagouran, lord of Babaṛon.

True to the ideas which had guided most of his predecessors, Ṛoupen reverted to the policy of collaboration with the Latins, and he strengthened these ties in 1181 by marrying Isabel, the daughter of Humphrey III of Toron. He had already taken part in the expedition against Ḥārim, and the withdrawal of the Frankish troops before they had attained their goal must have been a bitter disappointment to the Armenians, for whom the Moslems were then the chief enemy. The Turkoman tribes of Anatolia had been crossing the northern borders for some time. Ṛoupen tried to rid his land of these marauding groups; he killed a large number of them, and took many prisoners and considerable booty. Kilij Arslan II complained to Saladin, who, in the fall of 1180, entered Cilicia. He established his camp near Mamistra, made rapid raids in different directions, and withdrew only after Ṛoupen had promised to release the Turkoman prisoners and to return the booty he had taken. Ṛoupen made his peace with Kilij Arslan, and we find the two fighting side by side at the time of the revolt of Isaac Comnenus, who, late in 1182, after the seizure of the imperial

[15] Michael the Syrian dates the Latin expedition in 1170 and says that Mleh, abandoned by his Turkish allies, was besieged in a fortress, and was forced to surrender and promise submission to the king of Jerusalem (*Chronique*, III, 337), but the other sources and the sequence of events show that the correct date is 1173. Cf. C. Cahen, *La Syrie du nord*, p. 414, note 7.

throne by Andronicus, had returned to Cilicia. It was probably during this period that Ṛoupen recovered Adana and Mamistra, which had once again been taken by the Byzantines. As for Tarsus, still in Greek hands in 1181, it had passed later to Bohemond, who sold it to Ṛoupen in 1183.

The Byzantine forces in Cilicia were now depleted and the moment seemed opportune to Ṛoupen to overthrow their Armenian allies, the rival house of Lampron, to whom Ṛoupen was related through his mother. Hard pressed by Ṛoupen's siege and no longer able to count on Byzantine help, Heṭoum of Lampron appealed to Bohemond III. Officially Ṛoupen and the prince of Antioch were allies, but Bohemond resented the cordial welcome extended by Ṛoupen to the Antiochene barons who had disapproved of his marriage to Sibyl and had fled to Cilicia. Moreover, any increase of Ṛoupenid power was always viewed with suspicion by the princes of Antioch. Under cover of friendship Bohemond invited Ṛoupen to a banquet and, after imprisoning him, invaded Cilicia. However, Bohemond was able neither to relieve Lampron, nor to capture a single town or castle, for Leon, to whom Ṛoupen, his brother, had succeeded in sending a message, and other Armenian barons, valiantly continued to fight.[16] Seeing that his efforts were fruitless, Bohemond, having kept Ṛoupen prisoner for a year, decided to release him. Pagouran of Babaṛon, related both to the Heṭoumids and to Ṛoupen, acted as intermediary; he sent several hostages including his own sister Rita, Ṛoupen's mother. Ṛoupen promised to pay a ransom of 1,000 tahegans and to cede the castles of Sarvantikar and Tall Ḥamdūn, as well as Mamistra and Adana. But soon after the ransom had been paid and the hostages had been returned, he reconquered all that he had ceded, and Bohemond was not in a position to retaliate beyond making a few ineffectual raids.

The barony was thus in a strong position when Ṛoupen III transferred the power to his brother Leon II (1187) and retired to the monastery of Trazarg. The menace of the recent alliance between Isaac Angelus and Saladin, and the more immediate threat of the Turkomans, led to a rapprochement between Leon and Bohemond. Large bands of these nomads had again been crossing the northern borders, advancing almost as far as Sis and laying waste on all sides. Leon could muster only a small force, but he attacked them with such energy that he routed the bands, killed their leader Rustam, and pursued the fugitives as far as Sarvantikar,

[16] L. Alishan, *Hayabadoum*, p. 347.

inflicting heavy losses on them. The following year (1188), taking advantage of the troubled condition in the sultanate of Rūm that preceded the death of Kilij Arslan II, Leon turned against the Selchükids. A surprise attack on Bragana was unsuccessful, and the constable Baldwin was killed, but Leon returned two months later with a larger army, killed the head of the garrison, seized the fortress, and marched into Isauria. Though we find no specific mention of it, Seleucia must have been captured about this time, for the city was in Armenian hands when Frederick Barbarossa came in 1190. Proceeding northward, Leon seized Heraclea, gave it up after payment to him of a large sum, and advanced as far as Caesarea. It is probably about this time that Shahnshah, brother of Heṭoum of Lampron, took, on behalf of Leon, the fortress of Loulon, covering the northern approach to the Cilician Gates, and fortified it.[17]

On the eve of the Third Crusade the Armenian barony of Cilicia could be considered one of the vital Christian states of the Levant, and its strong position was particularly noticeable at a time when the Latin principalities, reduced almost exclusively to the three large cities of Antioch, Tyre, and Tripoli, were hard pressed by Saladin. The letters sent in 1189 by pope Clement III to Leon II and to the catholicus Gregory IV Dgha are a clear indication of this, for, while previously the Armenians had been asking for help, now it was the pope who urged them to give military and financial assistance to the crusaders.[18]

When Frederick Barbarossa approached the Armenian territories, Leon sent an embassy composed of several barons, with presents, ample supplies, and armed troops. A second embassy, headed by the bishop Nersēs of Lampron, arrived too late and returned to Tarsus with the emperor's son Frederick, the bishops, and the German army. Barbarossa's death made a profound impression on the Armenians; we find it recorded in the colophons of many manuscripts written during these years in Cilicia. It was a particularly cruel blow for Leon, in whom Barbarossa's presence and influence had bred high hopes of obtaining the royal crown which he so greatly desired. Nersēs of Lampron claims that Frederick had promised this "in a writing sealed with a gold seal," but when Leon asked for the fulfillment of the promise, the German leaders

[17] *Ibid.*, p. 432; colophon of a manuscript written by Nersēs of Lampron at Loulon in 1196.

[18] The letter of Clement III is preserved only in an Armenian translation. See the French translation in L. Alishan, *Léon le Magnifique*, pp. 163–165.

demurred, stating that, since the emperor was dead, they could not act.[19]

Leon participated in the wars of the crusaders; his troops were present at the siege of Acre, and he joined Richard the Lionhearted in the conquest of Cyprus. He was intent, at the same time, upon insuring the security of his own realm, and some of his actions undertaken for this purpose ran counter to the interests or aspirations of his neighbors. In 1191 he captured the fortress of Baghrās, taken from the Templars by Saladin and dismantled after the arrival of the Third Crusade, and he refused to cede it to the Templars. This brought to a head the growing antagonism between Leon and Bohemond III, and the possession of Baghrās was to be one of the principal points of contention in the long struggle between Cilicia and Antioch. For the moment Leon was the stronger of the two. Annoyed by the fact that Bohemond had signed a separate peace with Saladin and had complained to him of the seizure of Baghrās, annoyed also by Bohemond's continued delays in repaying the sums lent to him in 1188, Leon hatched a plot to seize Bohemond and to free himself of the suzerainty of Antioch. Soon after the death of Saladin he invited Bohemond to Baghrās and seized him, just as several years earlier Bohemond himself had made prisoner Leon's brother Ṛoupen III.[20] His attempt to annex Antioch was unsuccessful; though many of the nobles were favorable to Leon, the citizens set up a commune which took an oath of allegiance to Raymond, Bohemond's eldest son, and messengers were sent to the other son, Bohemond of Tripoli, and to Henry of Champagne, ruler of Jerusalem. Leon took his prisoners to Sis, where Henry came to negotiate Bohemond's release in the spring of 1194. Bohemond renounced his rights as a suzerain, and in return for this was allowed to go back to Antioch without paying a ransom; Leon retained Baghrās and the surrounding territory. To seal the new friendship, a marriage was arranged between Leon's niece Alice, the heiress-presumptive, and Bohemond's eldest son and heir, Raymond.

Although Leon had not attained his ultimate purpose, that is, mastery or at least suzerainty over Antioch, his position was stronger than it had been before, and he pressed with renewed energy his claims for a royal crown, seeking the assistance of the two most powerful rulers of the time, the pope and the German

[19] Colophon written by Nersēs of Lampron at the end of his translation of the letters of Lucius III and Clement III. Cf. Garegin I Hovsepian, *Colophons*, col. 538. For Frederick Barbarossa, and the situation after his death, see above, chapter III, pp. 113–116.

[20] For the relations between Leon and Antioch see C. Cahen, *La Syrie du nord*, and above, chapter XV, pp. 526–528, 532–541.

emperor. The embassies sent to Celestine III and to Henry VI met with success; in 1197 the imperial chancellor, Conrad of Hildesheim, left for the east, taking with him two crowns — one for Aimery of Cyprus, another for Leon. Aimery was crowned in September, but Leon's coronation was slightly delayed, partly through political circumstances — Conrad had gone directly from Cyprus to Acre — partly for religious reasons. The emperor demanded merely to be recognized as Leon's suzerain, but the pope required submission of the Armenian church to Rome, and this created considerable difficulty; there was marked opposition not only from the clergy of Greater Armenia, but from the majority of the clergy and the people of Cilicia. John, archbishop of Sis, was sent to Acre, and shortly thereafter a delegation headed by Conrad, archbishop of Mainz, arrived at Sis.

The bishops called together by Leon at first refused the papal demands, and are said to have agreed to them only after Leon told them that he would submit merely in word and not in deed. But the conditions listed by the historian Kirakos deal with disciplinary regulations rather than with matters of dogma.[21] One may wonder whether the first demands, against which the Armenian bishops rebelled, did not directly concern their creed, and whether these demands were not later abandoned, leaving only the clauses to which the bishops, carefully selected by Leon among those more favorable to Rome, could truthfully subscribe. This hypothesis gains strength from the fact that in the subsequent correspondence exchanged between pope Innocent III and his successors on the one hand, and the Armenians on the other, there is no direct reference to any of the points of dogma which separated the two churches, and which had proved such serious stumbling blocks in all the attempts at union between the Greeks and Armenians. Both king and catholicus are lavish in their expressions of respect and submission to the papacy, but this submission must have been considered by them as the homage due to a suzerain lord, and the respect due to the successor of the apostle Peter. Some minor new usages were introduced into the liturgical practices, but there were no basic changes. In a letter written to the pope in 1201 the catholicus Gregory VI tactfully and discreetly explains that the Armenian faith remains what it had always been "without any additions or deletions". The union with the church of Rome is not a conversion, but a union

[21] *RHC, Arm.*, I, 422–423. According to Vincent of Beauvais (*Speculum historiale*, XXI, 29) a condition set by the papal legate was that all school children aged twelve should be taught Latin. Another source adds that the catholicus was required to send a legate to the pope at set dates to render his homage (L. Alishan, *Léon le Magnifique*, p. 167).

within the universal church to which they all belong, since the regeneration through baptism has caused all men to become the sheep of the same fold, namely the church of the living God.[22]

Leon II was crowned with great solemnity in the cathedral church of Tarsus, on January 6, 1198, in the presence of the Syrian Jacobite patriarch, the Greek metropolitan of Tarsus, and numerous church dignitaries and military leaders.[23] The catholicus Gregory VI Abirad anointed him and the royal insignia were presented by Conrad of Mainz. There was great rejoicing among the Armenians, who saw their ancient kingdom restored and renewed in the person of Leon.

The Armenian historians and the scribes of contemporary manuscripts also refer to a crown sent by the Byzantine emperor, Alexius III Angelus. But there does not seem to have been a separate coronation ceremony, for the crowns sent by Byzantium, for instance, to the kings of Hungary or to petty rulers, had a symbolic and honorific character, and were not intended to show the promotion of a prince to the dignity of a king. The evidence concerning the date is contradictory, some placing it as early as 1196, some as late as 1198.[24] In 1197 Leon sent an embassy to

[22] *PL*, CCXIV, col. 1008.

[23] Sempad and the Cilician Chronicle date the coronation of Leon on January 6, 647, of the Armenian era, which would correspond to the year 1199 (the year 647 goes from January 31, 1198, to January 30, 1199); all the other Armenian sources — histories, chronicles, as well as a number of colophons of manuscripts — give January 6, 646, of the Armenian era which corresponds to 1198. Many modern historians have given preference to the date mentioned by Sempad; one of the principal reasons for this being that the name of Nersēs of Lampron, who died in July 1198, does not appear among those of the dignitaries present at the coronation, listed by the constable Sempad, and other bishops are mentioned in his place for the sees of Tarsus and Lampron (L. Alishan, *Léon le Magnifique*, pp. 168–180). But it is not proved that this is actually the list of the persons present at the coronation. Sempad, after mentioning the coronation and the death of Nersēs of Lampron, gives a general picture of Leon's personality, then comes the sentence: "and at the coronation of Leon there were many bishops and chieftains, whom I shall mention briefly here, for the information of the readers" (*RHC, Arm.*, I, 634). This sentence does not occur in the Cilician Chronicle, and the list there, which in several instances is more accurate than Sempad's, is preceded by the words: "And the land of Cilicia was adorned and embellished by all the orders of clerics and noble chieftains, and I shall give their names one by one" (p. 208). The list is, therefore, not connected with the coronation festivities and the omission of the name of Nersēs of Lampron cannot be used as an argument for dating the coronation after his death, especially as Nersēs himself refers to Leon as king in several colophons, one of which, written in 1198, is particularly explicit. "In this year," he writes, "the king of the Armenians was greatly honored . . .; the fame of his bravery moved the great rulers of Ancient Rome, Henry, and of New Rome, Alexius, who crowned him with precious jewels in the church of Tarsus, of which I am the unworthy pastor " (Garegin I Hovsepian, *op. cit.*, col. 624). For the German imperial ambitions which motivated the granting of this crown, see above, chapter III, pp. 116–120.

[24] Sempad (*RHC, Arm.*, I, p. 633) and the Cilician Chronicle (p. 207) report that the king of the Greeks sent a magnificent crown to Leon, and Leon is given the title of king in a colophon of the same year (Garegin I Hovsepian, *Colophons*, col. 599). According to Kirakos Alexius sent a crown to Leon only when he heard that the German emperor had already sent one (*RHC, Arm.*, I, 424).

Constantinople composed of Nersēs of Lampron and other dignitaries, and it has been said that the purpose of this embassy was to thank the emperor for the crown that Leon had received. But neither Nersēs nor the other contemporaries who speak of this embassy refer to a crown; all of the discussions centered on religious questions, and the sending of the embassy was the last of several fruitless efforts to achieve a union between the two churches.[25] Whatever the actual facts concerning the Byzantine crown may have been, it is evident that Leon was much more anxious to be crowned by the western emperor, for this put him on an equal footing with the Latin princes of the Levant.

The succession to Antioch was the main problem of Leon's reign. Raymond had died early in 1197, and in accordance with the feudal laws his son Raymond Roupen, Leon's great-nephew, became Bohemond's heir. The barons had sworn allegiance to Raymond Roupen, but his succession to Antioch was opposed by Bohemond's second son, Bohemond of Tripoli; by the Templars, who could not forgive Leon for keeping Baghrās; and by the commune, which was hostile to any Armenian interference. The war of succession, which began after the death of Bohemond III in 1201 and was to continue for almost a quarter of a century, concerned Antioch even more than it did Cilicia and has been discussed elsewhere in this volume.[26] Suffice it to say here that, in spite of momentary successes, Leon's plans were defeated in the end; Raymond Roupen, crowned prince of Antioch in 1216, was ousted three years later by his uncle, Bohemond of Tripoli, and all hope of Armenian supremacy over Antioch was lost.

Syrian affairs also involved Leon in warfare with aẓ-Ẓāhir of Aleppo and the Selchükid Rukn-ad-Dīn Sulaimān II, whom Bohemond of Tripoli had summoned to his aid. In 1201 he repulsed a Selchükid invasion of Armenia, but he was less successful two years later when he had to confront the Aleppine forces on the banks of the Orontes. Hostilities broke out again late in 1205. Leon made a surprise attack on Darbsāk, and although he could not take the fort, he laid waste the surrounding territory and inflicted heavy losses. Aẓ-Ẓāhir sent fresh contingents and assumed their command in person in the spring of 1206. Victorious at first, Leon had to retreat before the superior forces when the Antiochene armies joined the Moslems. An eight-year truce was signed, but in 1208–1209 aẓ-Ẓāhir and the Selchükid Kai-Khusrau I, whom

[25] L. Alishan, *Hayabadoum*, pp. 424–425.

[26] See above, chapter XV, pp. 532–541; also C. Cahen, *La Syrie du nord*, pp. 596–635.

Leon had befriended earlier and received at his court, made a sudden attack and seized the fort of Pertous.

However, these were minor reverses and Cilician power was at its apogee during the reign of Leon II. His kingdom extended from Isauria to the Amanus. He had become master of Lampron by seizing and imprisoning Heṭoum, whom later he freed and sent as his ambassador to the pope and to the emperor.[27] A skilled diplomat and wise politician, Leon established useful alliances with many of the contemporary rulers. Through his second marriage he became the son-in-law of Aimery of Lusignan, king of Cyprus and Jerusalem; his daughter by his first marriage, Rita ("Stephanie"), was wedded to John of Brienne, king of Jerusalem; his niece Philippa married Theodore I Lascaris, emperor of Nicaea. In spite of the difficulties caused by the wars of the succession to Antioch and by the religious problems, Leon maintained, on the whole, his good relations with the papacy. He gained the friendship and support of the Hospitallers and the Teutonic Knights by granting considerable territories to them. To the Hospitallers, already established in Cilicia in 1149, he gave Seleucia, Norpert (Castellum Novum), and Camardias, thus constituting a march on the western borders of Cilicia and thereby protecting the country from the Selchükids.[28] He also ceded castles in the Giguer and along the Antiochene frontier. The Teutonic Knights received Amoudain and neighboring castles.[29] The master of the order may even have resided in Cilicia for a while; Wilbrand of Oldenburg, who describes in great detail the ceremonies of the feast of the Epiphany held at Sis in 1211, saw him riding next to the king.[30]

Commerce was greatly developed during the reign of Leon II, who granted special privileges to the Genoese and Venetian merchants.[31] The important land routes that crossed Cilicia brought there many products from Central Asia, and these, in addition to local products, were exported or exchanged for the wares of the European traders. Corycus and especially Ayas (Lajazzo) had good harbors; moreover, many of the inland cities were connected with the sea through navigable rivers.

The transformation of the Armenian court, following the pattern

[27] N. Akinian, "Heṭoum Heghi, Lord of Lampron 1151–1218(?)" (in Armenian), *Handes Amsorya*, LXIX (1955), 397–405.

[28] V. Langlois, *Le Trésor des chartes d'Arménie*, pp. 74–77 and special charters. G. Delaville Le Roulx, *Les Hospitaliers en Terre Sainte et à Chypre* (Paris, 1904).

[29] V. Langlois, *Le Trésor des chartes d'Arménie*, pp. 81–82 and special charters.

[30] J. C. M. Laurent, *Peregrinatores medii aevi quatuor* (Leipzig, 1864), pp. 177–179. The master was Hermann of Salza, who may merely have been visiting Sis at this time.

[31] V. Langlois, *Le Trésor des chartes d'Arménie*, pp. 105–112, 126.

of the Frankish courts, proceeded at a more rapid pace after Leon came to power. Many of the old names of specific functions or the titles of dignitaries were replaced by Latin ones and the changes in nomenclature were often accompanied by changes in the character of these offices. The ancient feudal system of Armenia was also gradually modified in imitation of western feudalism; the barons lost some of the independence which the *nakharars* had enjoyed and were bound by closer ties to the king. Finally, in matters of law, the authority of the Latin Assizes constantly increased until the Armenians fully adopted the Assizes of Antioch, translated by the constable Sempad during the reign of Leon's successor.[32]

Leon died in 1219. He had named his young daughter Isabel as his rightful heiress and had released the barons from their oath of allegiance to Raymond Roupen. But the latter had several strong supporters and he tried to seize the power with their assistance. He was defeated, however, after a few initial successes, and died in captivity.[33] To avoid further complications, the regent, Constantine of Lampron, decided to find a husband for the young princess; his choice fell on Philip, the fourth son of Bohemond IV of Antioch.[34] The joint rule of Isabel and Philip lasted only a short while; Philip's disdain for the Armenian ritual, which he had promised to respect, and his marked favoritism to the Latin barons angered the Armenian nobility; he was deposed, imprisoned, and died in captivity through poisoning.[35]

Despite her determined resistance[36] Isabel was next married to

[32] The Assizes of Antioch, which have survived only in the Armenian version, were translated by the constable Sempad, king Heṭoum's brother, before the year 1265: (L. Alishan), *Assises d'Antioche reproduites en français et publiées au sixième centenaire de la mort de Sempad le Connétable* (Venice, 1876); Joseph Karst, *Armenisches Rechtsbuch: Sempadischer Kodex aus dem 13. Jahrhundert in Verbindung mit dem grossarmenischen Rechtsbuch des Mechithar Gosch* (Strassburg, 1905).

[33] John of Brienne, who had married Rita ("Stephanie"), Leon II's daughter by his first marriage, also made a claim for the throne, but he was rejected by the barons, and Rita's death, followed soon after by the death of their son, deprived him of his title to the succession. Raymond Roupen's chief supporter was Vahram, lord of Corycus, who married Raymond Roupen's mother, the princess Alice. They seized Tarsus and Adana, which were recaptured by the regent, Constantine of Lampron, in 1221; Raymond Roupen died the following year. See above, chapter XV, pp. 539–541.

[34] Negotiations for a marriage with Andrew the son of king Andrew II of Hungary, begun in the lifetime of Leon II, were not pursued.

[35] Bohemond IV tried in vain to obtain the liberation of his son. His appeal to the pope, Honorius III, after Philip's death, did not have any positive results. He turned to the Selchükids and, urged by him, Kai-Qobād I ravaged northern Cilicia, Constantine retaliating in kind; the latter appealed to al-'Azīz of Aleppo and Bohemond was forced to desist from further action.

[36] Isabel fled to Seleucia and sought refuge with the Hospitallers; the latter were unwilling to give her up to Constantine but feared the powerful regent; they eased their conscience by selling him the fortress, with Isabel in it. She is said to have refused to consummate the marriage for several years.

the regent's own son Heṭoum, and the long antagonism between the two powerful feudal families of the Ṛoupenids and the Heṭoumids of Lampron was thus brought to an end (1226). The early years of Heṭoum I's reign were relatively peaceful. Relations with Antioch, though strained, did not lead to hostile acts, for Bohemond IV was beset by too many difficulties to resort to arms.[37] There was greater unrest along the Selchükid border. In 1233 Kai-Qobād I invaded Cilicia and imposed a tribute upon the Armenians.[38] Selchükid troops entered the country again (1245–1246), after Heṭoum had acceded to the Mongol general Baiju's demand and delivered to him the wife and daughter of Kai-Khusrau II, who had sought refuge at the Armenian court at the time of the Mongol attack on Iconium. Though helped by the Armenian baron, Constantine (II) of Lampron, the regent's namesake, in revolt against king Heṭoum, Kai-Khusrau could only seize a few forts which the Mongols, some years later, forced him to return.

The Mongols were the most serious menace, and it was Heṭoum's realization of this that had forced him to betray the laws of hospitality and to send a deferential message to their general Baiju. The Mongol hordes had swept through Armenia and Georgia, far into Anatolia, and Heṭoum early recognized that only an alliance with them could save his kingdom. Consequently he sent his brother, the constable Sempad, on an official embassy to Karakorum.[39] Sempad left Cilicia in 1247 and returned in 1250 with a diploma guaranteeing the integrity of the Cilician kingdom, and the promise of Mongol aid to recapture the forts seized by the Selchükids.

In 1253 Heṭoum himself set out to visit the new Great Khan Möngke at Karakorum. He was the first ruler to come to the Mongol court of his own accord, and was received with great honors. The assurances given by Möngke's predecessor Göyük were renewed and expanded; Möngke further promised to free

[37] Heṭoum I established alliances with many of the Frankish princes. His sister Stephanie married Henry I of Cyprus; another sister, Maria, married John of Ibelin, count of Jaffa. His daughters were also given in marriage to Latin princes: Sibyl to Bohemond VI of Antioch; Euphemia to Julian, count of Sidon; and Maria to Guy of Ibelin, son of Baldwin, seneschal of Cyprus. Heṭoum's daughter Rita, however, married an Armenian, the lord of Sarvantikar (either Sempad or his brother Constantine).

[38] The coins struck by Heṭoum I at Sis during this period bear the names of Kai-Qobād I and Kai-Khusrau II in Arabic script on the reverse; two of the latter are dated 637 and 641 AH (=1239/1240, 1243/1244). On the Selchükids at this period, see below, chapter XIX, pp. 683–684.

[39] Letter written by Sempad to his brother-in-law, Henry I of Cyprus: see William of Nangis, *Vie de saint Louis* (*RHGF*, XX), 361–363; Kirakos, *History* (Tiflis, 1909), pp. 301–302. On the Mongols, see below, chapter XXI.

from taxation the Armenian churches and monasteries in Mongol territory.[40] Heṭoum's dominating idea was not merely to preserve his own kingdom and to obtain protection for the Christians under Mongol rule, but to enlist the Khan's help in freeing the Holy Land from the Moslem.

Heṭoum returned in 1256 encouraged by these promises and laden with gifts. On his way out he had passed through Greater Armenia; on his return voyage he remained much longer there, receiving visits from many of the local princes as well as from the bishops and abbots. Leon II had considered himself king of all the Armenians, and had stamped this title on some of his coins, but this was the first time that a ruler of Cilicia had come into direct contact with the population of the mother country.

Heṭoum tried to win the Latin princes over to the idea of a Christian-Mongol alliance, but could convince only Bohemond VI of Antioch. For his part, he remained faithful to the clauses of the understanding with the Mongols. He visited several times the court of the Il-khans and gave his military assistance whenever it was needed. Armenian troops fought side by side with the Mongols in Anatolia and in Syria, and the successes of the Mongols enabled Heṭoum to recover, in addition to the Cilician forts taken by the Selchükids, some of the territories which had once belonged to Kogh Ṿasil.

Thus the Armenians at first benefitted from their alliance with the Mongols. Heṭoum was also successful in his encounters with Kilij Arslan IV, whom he defeated in 1259, and with the Turkomans established on the western borders of Cilicia. He routed their bands, mortally wounded their leader Karaman, and freed the region of Seleucia from their attacks (1263).[41] But the Armenians were soon to experience the counter-effects of their alliance, especially when, after the defeat of Kitbogha at 'Ain Jālūt and the loss of Damascus and Aleppo, Mongol power weakened in Syria; they were to be among the principal victims of the formidable enemy of both Mongols and Christians, the Egyptian sultan Baybars.[42]

Heṭoum tried to negotiate with Baybars, and embassies were exchanged, but the sultan made excessive demands and Heṭoum, seeing that war was imminent, went to Tabriz to seek Mongol help. However, Baybars precipitated his action; the Mamluk armies

[40] Kirakos, *History*, pp. 350–357; Heṭoum, *La Flor des estoires de la terre d'orient* (*RHC, Arm.*, II), 163–168; *Cilician Chronicle*, pp. 229–231.

[41] *Cilician Chronicle*, pp. 238–240; C. Cahen, "Quelques textes négligés concernant les Turcomans de Rūm," *Byzantion*, XIV (1939), 133–134.

[42] For Baybars, see below, chapter XXII, pp. 745–750.

and their ally al-Manṣūr II of Hamah invaded Cilicia, passing through the Amanus Gates instead of trying to force a passage through the Syrian Gates (1266). The Armenians, commanded by the constable Sempad and the two young princes, Ṭoros and Leon, resisted valiantly, but they were hopelessly outnumbered. Ṭoros was slain, Leon and Sempad's son Ṿasil, surnamed the Tatar, were taken prisoner, and the enemy armies devastated the entire country for twenty days without meeting further resistance. They sacked Mamistra, Adana, Ayas, Tarsus, and smaller localities; at Sis they set fire to the cathedral and forced the treasury, taking all the gold that had been assembled there. They slaughtered thousands of the inhabitants and carried many more as captives to Egypt. When Heṭoum returned he found his country in ruins, and distraught by this fatal blow and by his personal sorrow, he waited only for the return of Leon from captivity to abdicate and seek solace in a monastery.

Baybars imposed very heavy conditions; the Armenians were forced to cede all the forts of the Amanus and their conquests along the Syrian border, with the exception of Behesni. Leon was set free only when Heṭoum had been able to obtain from Abagha, after repeated requests, the release of Baybars' favorite, Shams-ad-Dīn Sungur al-Ashkar, captured by the Mongols at Aleppo.

Cilicia was now surrounded by the Moslems; Antioch had fallen, the Templars had abandoned Baghrās and the neighboring forts, the road thus lay open before Baybars. The Mongols were the only allies who could give effective assistance against the Egyptians, even though their position was much less strong than it had been at the time of Hulagu. When Leon was freed, Heṭoum, therefore, took him to Abagha in order to have him recognized as his heir, and after Heṭoum's abdication (1269) Leon returned to the court of the Īl-khans to have his title confirmed. Leon III believed, as his father had, in a Mongol-Christian alliance which would save the Holy Land; he made repeated pleas to the western powers; Abagha also sent envoys to the popes and to Edward I of England, without any success. It is not certain that common action was possible or would have been successful, but in the absence of any concerted opposition the Mamluks were free to continue their conquests, to seize, as they did a few years later, all the Latin possessions in Syria and Palestine, and in the latter part of the fourteenth century to destroy the Armenian kingdom of Cilicia.

The wars waged by Baybars elsewhere gave Leon III a few years' respite at the beginning of his reign, and he tried to heal the ravages caused by the Mamluk invasion. New privileges were granted to the Venetian merchants in 1271; Ayas was rebuilt and became again an active commercial center. Marco Polo, who visited it in 1271, speaks of it as "a city good and great and of great trade", adding that "all the spicery and the cloths of silk and of gold and of wool from inland are carried to this town".[43] As the Egyptians captured the Syrian and Palestinian sea ports the importance of Ayas grew; it was one of the chief outlets to the Mediterranean for the goods brought from Central Asia, but its importance and wealth made it at the same time one of the principal targets of the Egyptians.

Mamluk attacks began again in 1275; in a rapid but devastating raid they advanced as far as Corycus. At the same time the Turkomans entered Cilicia from the west and, though repulsed, continued to raid the border lands year after year. Internal dissension and revolts of some of the barons created further difficulties for Leon during these years when there was almost no direct Mongol assistance. The invasion of Syria in 1281 was the most serious undertaking by the Īl-khans in these parts since the death of Hulagu; the Armenians fought at the side of the Mongols, but the Egyptian sultan Kalavun, having won the neutrality of the Franks, was able to defeat the Mongol and Armenian forces.

Lawless bands of Mongols, Egyptians, Turkomans, and Kurds pillaged Cilicia; they set fire to Ayas and looted the warehouses abandoned by the population, who had fled to a new fortress built out in the sea. The emissaries sent to Egypt by Leon to ask for peace were detained as prisoners until the master of the Templars intervened. Another factor may have been instrumental in modifying the Egyptian attitude: the new Mongol Īl-khan, Arghun, was favorable to the Christians; Leon had gone to his court to pay his respects, and Kalavun may have feared Mongol intervention. A ten-year truce was signed on June 6, 1285; the conditions were extremely onerous — an annual tribute of one million dirhems — moreover, numerous privileges were granted to the Egyptians.[44] The peace won at such high cost was to be broken before the ten years had elapsed.

After the fall of Acre and Tripoli, when Egyptian armies had reached Homs, Heṭoum II, who had succeeded his father Leon III in 1289, tried to appease them by offering a large sum of money;

[43] Marco Polo, *The Description of the World*, ed. A. C. Moule and Paul Pelliot (London, 1938), p. 94. For the importance of Ayas see W. Heyd, *Histoire du commerce du Levant* (reprinted Leipzig, 1936), II, 73–92.

[44] Al-Maqrīzī (tr. Quatremère), *Histoire des sultans mamlouks*, II, i, 201–212.

the sultan al-Ashraf accepted this, merely postponing his invasion until he had completed the conquest of the Frankish territories. In the spring of 1292, he marched on the patriarchal see of Hromgla. The citadel resisted for thirty-three days and was finally taken by assault on May 11. Terrible slaughter followed; many of the monks were killed, others were carried into captivity together with the catholicus Stephen IV himself. The Egyptians looted the churches and the residence of the catholicus; they destroyed or stole the precious relics and church treasures.[45] The capture of Hromgla was celebrated as a great victory; the sultan wrote to the qadi Ibn-al-Khuwaiyī to announce the event; he was received with special honors at Damascus, and for seven days the trumpets continued to sound in the cathedral and candles burned all through the night.[46]

The Egyptians did not immediately enter Cilicia, but in May 1293 the army stationed at Damascus received orders to march on Sis. Ambassadors were sent in great haste by the Armenians; they were forced to cede the remaining fortresses on the eastern front — Behesni, Marash, and Tall Ḥamdūn, and to double the tribute they had been paying theretofore.

The murder of the sultan al-Ashraf late in 1293, the troubled reign of the usurper Kitbogha, and the famine and plague which spread in Egypt and Syria gave a breathing-spell to the Armenians. Heṭoum, who had abdicated in favor of his brother Ṭoros III in 1292, was urged to return two years later.[47] He strengthened the ties with Cyprus — the only other Christian kingdom surviving in the Levant — by giving his sister Isabel in marriage to Amalric, the brother of king Henry II. He also tried to revive the Mongol alliance and set out to visit the Il-khan Baidu. While he was waiting at Maragha, where he was able to save from destruction the Syrian church erected by Rabban Ṣaumā and to protect the Nestorian patriarch Mar Yabhalāhā III, Ghazan wrested the power from Baidu. Heṭoum went to pay him homage. From Ghazan he received the assurance that the Christian churches would not be destroyed, and it is probable that he also received the promise of military assistance.[48] On his return to Sis in 1295 he arranged a marriage

[45] L. Alishan, *Hayabadoum*, pp. 500–502.

[46] Al-Jazarī (tr. Sauvaget), *La Chronique de Damas*, pp. 15–16 and appendices I and II.

[47] Heṭoum II, converted to the Roman church, had entered the Franciscan order. A brave soldier and a devout Christian, his frequent vacillations between the throne and the monastery weakened the royal authority at a time when a strong hand and an uninterrupted policy were sorely needed.

[48] J. B. Chabot, "Histoire du patriarche Mar Jabalaha III," *ROL*, II (1894), 137–139; Bar Hebraeus, *Chronography*, p. 506.

between his sister Rita and Michael IX, the son and associate of Andronicus II Palaeologus; in order to establish an alliance with the Byzantine empire, he went in person to Constantinople, accompanied by his brother Ṭoros. But during his absence another brother, Sempad, who had won the support of the catholicus Gregory VII and of pope Boniface VIII, seized power (1296).

Cilicia was torn by this internal strife. Heṭoum, returning from his fruitless journey to obtain the support of the Mongols, was intercepted near Caesarea by Sempad, and imprisoned together with his brother Ṭoros; Ṭoros was strangled and Heṭoum partially blinded. Sempad was overthrown by his younger brother Constantine, who freed Heṭoum but retained the power (1298). A year later Heṭoum, having recovered his sight, resumed the kingship for the third time and exiled his brothers Sempad and Constantine to Constantinople, where they died.

These fratricidal wars and the discords which reigned also among the Mongols encouraged the Egyptians to invade Cilicia once again. In 1298 their armies sacked Adana and Mamistra and took eleven fortresses. Among these were Marash and Tall Ḥamdūn, which the Armenians had ceded some years earlier, but which they had apparently recovered in the meantime.

Heṭoum still counted on the Mongols to defeat the Egyptians, and it seemed, for a short time, that his hopes were to be fulfilled. The Syrian expedition led by the Il-khan Ghazan, whom Heṭoum joined at the head of 5,000 men, routed the Mamluk army near Homs in December 1299. But Ghazan departed shortly after and the Egyptians recovered Syria. A second campaign in 1301 was seriously hampered by bad weather, and the third expedition, in 1303, ended in disaster. The Mongol forces were decimated, many of the soldiers were drowned in the flooded waters of the Euphrates; Heṭoum retreated with the remnants of the Mongol army and went to the court of Ghazan before returning to Cilicia.

The road to Cilicia again lay open before the Moslems. Already in 1302 the emir of Aleppo had made a rapid raid, burning the harvest and gathering vast booty. In July 1304 the Egyptians took Tall Ḥamdūn, which Heṭoum had recovered after the Mongol victory of 1299. They returned to Cilicia the following year and, although the Armenians, helped by a company of Mongols who had come to collect the annual tribute, inflicted heavy losses on them, they were defeated after the arrival of fresh Egyptian troops. Marino Sanudo summarizes in graphic terms the unhappy state of the country. "The king of Armenia," he writes, "is under the fangs of four ferocious beasts—the lion, or the Tartars, to whom he pays a heavy tribute; the leopard, or the Sultan, who daily ravages his frontiers; the wolf, or the Turks, who destroy his power; and the serpent, or the pirates of our seas, who worry the very bones of the Christians of Armenia."[49] The difficulties increased when the Mongols were converted to Islam, for then the Armenians not only lost all hope of assistance but were subjected to religious persecution.

In 1305 Heṭoum abdicated in favor of his nephew Leon IV and once again retired to a monastery, but Leon's reign, already troubled by internal strife, in particular the opposition which the pro-papal policy of Heṭoum and the catholicus had stirred up, came to an abrupt end on November 17, 1307. The Mongol emir Bilarghu treacherously killed Heṭoum, king Leon, and about forty of the dignitaries and nobles who accompanied them.[50]

The Armenian barony, later the kingdom of Cilicia, fighting against tremendous odds, had not only maintained its existence for over two centuries, but had attained an important position during the reign of Leon II and part of that of Heṭoum I. It had valorously played its part in the crusades, continuing the struggle, together with the kingdom of Cyprus, after the destruction of the other Christian realms of the Levant.

The history of constant warfare, invasions, destructions, and plunder, briefly sketched above, may tend to obscure the very real cultural achievements of the period, which can only be recalled here in a few words. Along with original histories, literary works, and theological writings, we find numerous translations from Greek, Syriac, and even Arabic, but the most significant are the translations from Latin which appear for the first time in Armenian

[49] Quoted by Henry H. Howorth, *History of the Mongols*, III (1888), 579.

[50] Tchamitch, without giving his source, says that the Armenians, who were angered by the changes that Heṭoum, king Leon IV, and the catholicus wished to introduce into the Armenian ritual, in order to conform to Roman usage, aroused Bilarghu against Heṭoum and Leon and thus caused their death (*History of the Armenians*, III, 311). He has been followed by most modern historians, but this interpretation of Bilarghu's action does not rest on any text known so far. The Armenian sources recall the murder very briefly without giving a specific reason (*RHC, Arm.*, I, 490, 664; Khachikian, *Colophons*, pp. 55–56; Hakopian, *Short Chronicles*, I, 88, 89, 99; II, 188, 512–513), or say that Bilarghu wished to become master of Cilicia (*RHC, Arm.*, I, 466). Jean Dardel (*RHC, Arm.*, II, 16–17), the Moslem sources (al-Maqrīzī, *Histoire des sultans mamlouks*, II, ii, 279; the continuation of Rashīd-ad-Dīn, cited in *RHC, Arm.*, I, 549, note 1; the *Tarikhi Oldjaïtou*, cited in *RHC, Arm.*, II, 16, note 3), and the Latin sources ("Les Gestes des Chiprois," *RHC, Arm.*, II, 867–868; the "Chronicle of Cyprus," cited in Howorth, *History of the Mongols*, III, 771) give different reasons, but nowhere is there the slightest hint that the Armenians who were opposed to Heṭoum and Leon for religious reasons were in any way responsible for their murder.

literature. Various members of the house of Lampron figure prominently among the authors of this period, both as original writers and as translators, and it is worthy of note that some of them, like the constable Sempad, were laymen.

The Armenian rulers founded and endowed numerous monasteries. It can be seen from the ruined remains, as well as from literary evidence, that these monasteries and churches, and even the military constructions, did not compare favorably with the splendid monuments erected in the past in Armenia proper, but some of the foundations of this period are interesting from a different point of view, for instance, the hospital founded by queen Isabel, where she herself often tended the sick and the poor. If architecture did not develop greatly in the Cilician kingdom, the minor arts on the other hand attained a degree of excellence. The illuminated manuscripts of this period, which rival in quality the best products of medieval art, are also outstanding witnesses of the remarkable resilience of the people, for many of the finest examples were produced in the most adverse circumstances, and at times when the very existence of the country was threatened.

21. Persia and Adjacent Regions (*Map by the University of Wisconsin Cartographic Laboratory*)

XIX
THE TURKS IN IRAN AND ANATOLIA BEFORE THE MONGOL INVASIONS

A. *The Iranian Principalities, Georgia, and the Caliphate*

At the conclusion of the chapter on the Selchükids, we remarked that the history of the eastern Moslem countries in the twelfth century had little direct connection with that of the Mediterranean region.[1] A few pages must be devoted to it, however, for the thirteenth century would see the brusque reëntry of Central Asia into

For a summary chapter of this kind, a bibliography can only be indicated in an even more summary way. The sources are for the most part those already noted in the chapter on the Selchükids in volume I, together with, for the western continuation of Irano-Mesopotamian history dealt with here, those indicated in the various chapters relative to Syria in the twelfth and thirteenth centuries; for the Selchükids of Anatolia see below, p. 675. For Iran especially, see the history of the Khorezmians contained in al-Juvainī, *Ta'rīkh-i-Jahān-Gushâ* (ed. Mirzā Muḥammad Qazvīnī, vol. II, Gibb Memorial Series, XVI, 2, Leyden and London, 1916, now translated by J. A. Boyle, *The History of the World Conqueror* [Manchester, 2 vols., 1958]) and an-Nasawī, *Sīrat as-sulṭān Jalāl ad-Dīn Mankubirtī* (ed. and tr. O. Houdas, Publications de l'École des langues orientales vivantes, series 3, vols. 9–10, Paris, 1891–1895); and, for Mesopotamia, Sibṭ Ibn-al-Jauzī, *Al-muntaẓam*, vols. IX and X (Hyderabad, India, 1940), and Ibn-as-Sā'ī, *Al-jāmi' al-mukhtaṣar* (ed. Père Anastase-Marie and Mustafâ Jawād, Baghdad, 1934). On the other hand we have the good fortune to possess three collections of *inshā'* (administrative correspondence) emanating from the government of Sanjar and the first Khorezmians. The appreciable results of the latest archaeological researches on Khorezm are collected in S. P. Tolstov, *Po sledan drevne Khorezmiiskoi tsivilizatsii* [*On the Traces of the Old Khorezmian Civilization*] (Moscow, 1948); in German translation by O. Mehlitz, *Auf den Spuren der Altchorezmischer Kultur* (Berlin, 1953).

As for secondary works, there exist only a few studies other than partial or superficial ones which need not be cited here. Besides W. Barthold's *Turkestan down to the Mongol Invasion*, cited in volume I, we need note only the article by Fuad Köprülü, "Hârizmšâhlar," in *İslâm ansiklopedisi* (Istanbul, 1941 ff.; in Turkish); M. Altay Köymen, *Buyuk Selçuklu imparatorluğu tarihi* (Ankara, 1955; in Turkish); and, for an-Nāṣir, F. Täschner, "Futuwwa, eine gemeinschaftbildende Idee im mittelalterlichen Orient und ihre verschiedenen Erscheinungsformen," *Schweizerisches Archiv für Volkskunde*, LII (1956), 122–158; and Claude Cahen, "Note sur les débuts de la futuwwa d'an-Nâcir," *Oriens*, VI (1953), 18–22. On Georgia, see W. E. D. Allen, *A History of the Georgian People* (London, 1932); Alexandre Manvelichvili, *Histoire de Géorgie* (Paris, 1951); J. Djavakhichvili, *History of the Georgian Nation* (2nd ed., Tiflis, 1948; in Georgian); and V. Minorsky, *Studies in Caucasian History* (London, 1953).

[1] See volume I of the present work, p. 175.

Mediterranean history, briefly with the Khorezmians, and then more lastingly with the Mongols, and the reader should be provided with sufficient data to preserve continuity between the Selchükid invasions in the eleventh century and those of the thirteenth, described in a later chapter.[2]

What gradually replaced the disintegrating state in the western half of the Selchükid territories was a cluster of principalities, some originating with officials of the sultanate appointed as atabegs (regents) for minors, others founded by chiefs of the freed Turkomans — a Turkoman resurgence connected with the successes achieved at the same time by the Oghuz in Khurasan, though not materially dependent on them. The progress of these Turkomans did not take the same form everywhere. On the Azerbaijan-Armenia frontier, the powerful Īva groups agreed to serve the princes of Azerbaijan and of Mosul, and even the 'Abbāsid caliph in Mesopotamia, before becoming the irreconcilable adversaries of the Khorezmians, who eventually decimated them. In Khuzistan, the Avshars of Shumlah resisted both the last Selchükid sultans and the caliphs, but their lands lay too near the latter, and so they were finally subjected at the close of the twelfth century. In Fars a true principality was established, first through the growing autonomy of its Selchükid governors, then through the emergence of a Turkoman tribe, the Salgurs, who preserved it up to the beginning of the fourteenth century, at first independently but later as vassals of the Mongols. Elsewhere the new principalities were founded by atabegs. The atabeg of Damascus, Tughtigin, has already been dealt with, as has Zengi of Mosul and Aleppo, who divided his activities between Syria and Mesopotamia;[3] his successors at Mosul, as distinct from those at Aleppo, pursued a lack-luster existence into the thirteenth century, by chance finding a historian, however, in the great Ibn-al-Athīr. The regime was to continue into the time of the first Mongols under a former slave of the last Zengids, Lu'lu'.

In the first half of the twelfth century Azerbaijan gradually became autonomous, ruled at first by Selchükid princes holding appanages or in rebellion, and later by enfeoffed military chiefs. In the middle of the century the atabeg of one of these Selchükids, Īldegiz (or Eldigüz), founded a dynasty there which, together with the last sultans, controlled all of central Iran; weakened, however, at the beginning of the thirteenth century by the same causes which weakened the sultans themselves, it collapsed before the

[2] See below, chapter XXI.

[3] Volume I, chapters V and XIV.

Khorezmian assaults. To the west of Azerbaijan the "Shāh-i-Armīn" of Akhlat maintained an autonomous principality on Lake Van up to the beginning of the thirteenth century.

These changes on the political scene were relatively superficial; they did not entail any changes of fundamental importance beneath the surface. The atabegs, possibly even the Salgurids, essentially continued the trends of the Selchükid administration, in their military organization, their orthodox religious orientation, and the like. In some respects the Turkish conquest, though now roughly stationary in extent, continued in depth. Where the Turks were few in number, Selchükid decadence did, it is true, allow strong native groups to acquire a certain independence. Typical were the Shabānkārah Kurds and the Lurs, the former in Fars, the latter in the Zagros mountain ranges to the east of Baghdad. But elsewhere the Turkish chiefs worked tenaciously toward the gradual elimination of local Arab or Kurdish lords and the substitution of their own men. Even in Iraq, after the death of Dubais following the downfall of the caliph al-Mustarshid, neither the Mazyadids nor any other Arabs played a role comparable to that of the 'Uqailids when Malik-Shāh had been obliged to leave Mosul in their hands. Nor would the revival of the caliphate in any way herald an Arab renascence.

From another point of view, it is noteworthy that the political fragmentation of the Iranian domain did not result in a cultural decline: this was the time when the poet (an-)Niẓāmī of Ganja was living on the northwest frontier, and when Sa'dī was born. It was also the period when there flourished several of the great mystics, such as 'Abd-al-Qādir (al-)Gīlānī, well-springs of popular Iranian religion down to our own day.

The chiefs of Azerbaijan and their Moslem neighbors to the west faced a task somewhat comparable to that which challenged their fellows in Syria. A Christian state existed at their very door, the kingdom of Georgia — an indigenous state, but just as enterprising as the Frankish principalities. The history of the Franks and that of Georgia are linked not only by their parallel struggle against the Moslem princes, but by the modest assistance they rendered each other, to the point at least of forestalling a complete coalition of enemy forces on either of their two fronts. One of them might even draw off an enemy dangerous to the other: thus in 1121 Īl-Ghāzī, having beaten the Franks, was called on to participate in an anti-Georgian coalition and was there defeated in turn. In spite of the near impossibility of direct contact, such a sense of solidarity developed on each side that early in the thirteenth century they could envisage concerted operations. Moreover, the Georgians had already engaged Frankish mercenaries, for example in 1121, undoubtedly in the Constantinopolitan market.

In a sense the Turks themselves had contributed to the power of the Georgian kingdom. They had destroyed the feudal principalities on its periphery without touching the very heart of the country, protected by its forests, its mountains, and its access to the sea. Thus by the time of the First Crusade David the Restorer (1089–1125) had been able to establish a relatively strong monarchy, cementing his power by leading his diverse subjects to the reconquest of lost lands and the expulsion of Turkoman raiders. David's victories had reached their climax in 1122 when, after crushing the combined Azerbaijan and Artukid armies, he had been able to make Tiflis, after four centuries of Moslem domination, a Christian city once again, and thereafter his capital. He had concluded alliances with the Byzantines as well as with the Moslem Shirvān-Shāh Minūchihr, whose lands lay between Georgia and the Caspian. David had repeopled the newly won provinces while assuring them military protection by maintaining a large establishment of Kïpchaks — those same Kïpchaks of the north Caucasian steppes among whom the Moslem states regularly recruited a large proportion of the slaves destined for their armies. His successes had made him master also of the Armenian peoples. Unable to regain their own lost national independence, they willingly rallied to him, though he was a Christian of another church. And he knew quite well how to treat the Moslems of old stock living in his territories, with a tolerance which won for him the astonished approval of their co-religionists elsewhere.

For the next hundred years the Georgians warred intermittently with the Moslems of Erzerum, Kars, and Ani, and especially of Akhlat and Azerbaijan; during this century Islam appears to have been, on the whole, rather on the defensive. In the twelfth century the stake was often possession of Ani, where the old Kurdish dynasty of the Shaddādids, though on good terms with its Armenian subjects, had difficulty in maintaining itself. At one time briefly held by David, the town was again taken by the Georgians in 1161 after a victory over the combined forces of Azerbaijan and eastern Anatolia, but was lost once more in a return engagement four years later with the same coalition. It was finally annexed by the Georgians at the beginning of the thirteenth century, when, under the illustrious queen Tamar, Georgian policy was particularly expansionist, owing to the decadence of the Azerbaijan principality and regional quarrels over the possession of Akhlat, which the distant Aiyūbids eventually acquired. Tamar carried on vigorous operations, sometimes in the direction of Erzerum, but generally against the more accessible Akhlat and the towns of Azerbaijan — less campaigns of conquest than raids intended to intimidate and to obtain booty. Sometimes Georgian territory suffered Moslem raids too; in general, however, Georgian attacks and counter-attacks were the more violent, to say nothing of an almost lunatic escapade which once took a Georgian force up to the very borders of Khurasan.

It is impossible to say how much headway Georgian power might have made had it survived the disastrous Khorezmian and Mongol invasions. It was a golden age in the history of this small Caucasian people, a period which saw, aside from its military exploits, a remarkable development in art and literature in which native traditions blended with Byzantine and Iranian influences, and which saw also the birth of the national epic, *The Knight in the Panther's Skin* by Shoṭa Rusṭveli, reflecting, like those of so many other countries, the character of a fighting aristocracy.

In Mesopotamia, Selchükid decay benefited the caliphate, the full restoration of which culminated in the long reign (1180–1225) of the only caliph after the ninth century to emerge as a really strong personality, an-Nāṣir. He carried on the work of his predecessors by liquidating the last of the unsubdued Turkomans, making Iraq a state truly subject to the caliphate. In Iran itself he conducted, first against the last Selchükid, Tughrul III, and then against the Khorezmians, diplomatic and military policies more effective than any which had been associated with the Commanders of the Faithful for some decades. Moreover, and most important, he took full advantage of the implications of this title and, while resigning himself to the inevitable political fragmentation of Islam, at least attempted to repair the religious divisions of the Moslems under his personal moral leadership.

The destruction of the Fāṭimid caliphate, which had come about just before his succession, favored his efforts, but he was prompted especially by the Mesopotamian and Iranian situations. The Shī'ites, although politically shackled by the Selchükids, remained numerous. In sympathy with their views, an-Nāṣir at one time entertained the idea of having himself recognized as their head as well as that of the Sunnites. Orthodox opposition was so violent, however, that he was forced to give up this scheme. Still, he reached an accord with the Ismā'īlites of Alamut, among whom there was a growing inclination towards compromise, and obtained from the grand master, Jalāl-ad-Dīn al-Ḥasan, a recognition which made him something like the head of this autonomous sect. But the achievement best known today and possibly the most fruitful, though in a way he undoubtedly could not foresee, was his reorganization of the *futūwah*.

This was the word long used for the moral principle of chivalric fraternity on which the organizations of "youths" were based and from which they often derived their name (a concept also implicit in the etymological root of *futūwah*). These groups primarily embraced important segments of the small artisan class in the towns, for whom such organizations represented a mixture of initiatory and interconfessional brotherhoods, societies for mutual aid, and semiprivate militias. They were in general frowned upon by men of social standing, who gave them names signifying bandit or footpad. At Baghdad, however, among other places, they acquired such strength that when constituted authority failed they actually took over certain quarters of the city and eventually drew to themselves some important people. Moreover, among the many *futūwah* organizations in Baghdad and throughout Islam there was considerable diversity, ranging from the strictly orthodox to the extremely heretical.

It was an-Nāṣir's ambition to unite this entire conglomeration, to reorganize it into cadres dependent upon himself, and to use these organizations of the "masses", hitherto disruptive of order, to establish order. Under his influence various accounts were written, developing the principles of the *futūwah*. Moreover, he tried to associate in his undertaking the princes whose coöperation would be necessary to extend the reform beyond the boundaries of Iraq. To conform with their customs he made of the *futūwah* something of a chivalric order, whose members were distinguished by a special costume and were accorded the exclusive right to participate in certain of their favorite sports. This aspect, because of its superficial similarity to certain elements of western chivalry, has often caused a misunderstanding of the nature of an-Nāṣir's work; it was, however, its most ephemeral characteristic. On the other hand, the "democratic" organizations of the *futūwah*, in certain areas such as Anatolia, followed a development certainly attributable to greater and more profound influences than the personality of a single caliph, but the place always reserved for an-Nāṣir in their traditions shows that in some respects he was indeed the renovator of the institution.

One can discern the efforts of an-Nāṣir throughout the whole range of Islamic religious life. He strove to control education by granting licenses to teach. He encouraged his spiritual collaborator Shihāb-ad-Dīn 'Umar (as-)Suhrawardī to found a religious order. But in completing the practical development of a society in Iran and Mesopotamia distinct from that of Syria, he was remarkably indifferent to the idea of a Holy War against the Franks. The Moslem princes of Syria respected him and notified him of their victories; he sent them some assistance, but the *jihād* never played a part in his religious propaganda.

It was inevitable that an-Nāṣir's activity, in some respects such a novel departure, won him many enemies. When the Mongols suddenly burst on the scene, he would be accused of having deliberately brought on the disaster in order to crush the Khorezmians.

B. *The Khorezmian Empire*

Once again it was in Central Asia that violent upheavals occurred, the repercussions of which would ultimately spread to the shores of the Mediterranean. One such repercussion resulted in the replacement of the Ghaznavids by the Ghūrids. It was among the recently subdued and converted wild men of the upper valleys of the Hindu Kush that the Ghaznavids recruited a part of their forces, as the caliphal generals had done among the tribes of Dailam at an earlier time, and as the Turkish chiefs of the Zagros mountains often did among the Kurds. The chiefs of the valleys of Ghūr thus came to sense their own strength, established autonomous principalities, and finally, after the total destruction of Ghaznah, supplanted the Ghaznavids throughout all their Hindu possessions. Their military flair even led them to extend their conquests into the upper valley of the Ganges, representing a new political extension of Islam in India. No more than the other rulers of their time, however, could they avoid using Turkish slaves for a large part of their army. At the beginning of the thirteenth century, profiting from the crushing of the Ghūrids outside of India by the Khorezmians, these "mamluks" carried their chiefs to power in India proper, and set up a military regime somewhat analogous to that which the more famous Mamluks of Egypt would establish a half century later. The slave dynasty at Delhi endured until the beginning of the sixteenth century, when it was destroyed by the Mughuls ("Grand Moguls", from "Mongols").

Much more serious consequences for Iran, however, resulted from changes in Central Asia by which Islam, no longer victorious, found itself on the defensive and forced to retreat. A Mongol people, whom Moslem authors call the Kara-Kitai (Persian, Qarā-Khitāy, or Black Cathayans), driven from China, where at one time they had carved out a vast kingdom, now turned back to the west, destroying the Kara-Khanid kingdoms, which had been weakened by internal rivalry and tribal disorder. In vain did the Kara-Khanids of Transoxiana call the Selchükid Sanjar to their aid; in 1141 he was crushed. Although for the most part pagan, the Kara-Kitai numbered in their ranks many of those Nestorians who were for many centuries so influential, from the point of view of religion, in Central Asia, and who periodically renewed their ties with their brethren of Iran and Mesopotamia. The defeat inflicted by this partially Christian army on Sanjar, until then the most powerful prince of Islam, made a considerable impression everywhere. The chief of the Kara-Kitai bore the title Gur-Khan, and the accounts of his victory, spreading throughout the west, gave rise to the legend of the famous "Prester John", who would later be sought wherever there was believed to be, far to the rear of the Moslems, a powerful Christian kingdom, still thought in Marco Polo's time to be just beyond the Mongols, but later transferred to Abyssinia.

The subjection of Transoxiana as far as Khorezm by the Kara-Kitai had little effect on the life of these areas, where the conquerors allowed the princes to reign as vassals whom they controlled firmly. By the very nature of things, however, it marked a certain decrease in the amount of assistance which Islam could count on from these lords against other faiths, or orthodox Islam against heretical sects. On the other hand, it brought about a new southward movement by a certain number of Oghuz Turkomans, some of them perhaps still pagan. They took refuge in the territories of Sanjar. But his strength had just been shattered, and these Turkomans, like their ancestors under the Ghaznavids, could only be a still further cause for concern, finally breaking out in open revolt. Sanjar, forced to fight, became their captive in 1153. Although they apparently always recognized him as sultan, he could not prevent their subjecting the country to their exactions. He escaped in 1156 but died soon afterwards, and his nephew and successor Maḥmūd Khan, a Kara-Khanid whom he had adopted, could not repair the damage.

Unlike their eleventh-century predecessors, the Oghuz masters of Khurasan proved to be incapable of producing founders of states. Their victory was one of destruction and anarchy only. It extended to Kerman, where the local Selchükid line was destroyed; and it may have had repercussions, though how great we cannot tell, on the Turkoman movements in areas further west. This victory, however, had an opposite and profitable effect on a dynasty located to their rear. Once again Khorezm, protected by its girdle of desert, became a secure and prosperous oasis.

In spite of all its progressive Turkification and manorialization, Khorezm apparently still preserved the essence of its traditional agricultural, commercial, and cultural prosperity. It was governed by a family which was descended from Anushtigin, a Turkish slave installed there by Malik-Shāh, and which, though it had revived the old native title Khorezm-Shāh, had remained more or less vassal to Sanjar despite periodic friction. The Khorezmian dynasty had to become vassal to the Kara-Kitai also, which made it possible for it to complete its emancipation from Sanjar when his power declined. Amid the disasters of Oghuz victories, the Khorezm-Shāhs maintained a solid and undivided principality, indeed strengthened by the fact that to all those who desired the restoration of order it seemed the only hope. And at this very moment the disintegration of the power of the Kara-Kitai themselves, brought on at the end of the twelfth century and the beginning of the thirteenth by new movements of peoples in the Asian steppes, resulted in the complete independence of the Khorezm-Shāhs.

This situation apparently forced the Khorezm-Shāhs to develop a powerful army. Its maintenance meant exactions difficult for the population to endure, but bearable thanks to growing prosperity and victories abroad. This army was composed primarily of a huge recruitment of Turks from their neighbors to the northwest, the Kïpchaks. There was not always time to buy them young and bring them up as proper Moslems, a practice generally followed by those princes who employed such Turkish warriors. Those who came to be called Khorezmians on battlefields far distant from Khorezm were not such ethnically or culturally. They were to acquire a reputation for ferocity; but circumstances would allow them no means of subsistence other than this very ferocity.

In these circumstances the Khorezm-Shāh Tökiish (or Takash) managed, around 1190, to occupy Khurasan, where he brought the Oghuz under control. With Iran in an extreme state of fragmentation at the time, this conquest immediately made him the great power of the day, to whom one could turn in case of need. The last Iranian Selchükid, Tughrul III, tried to rebuild his authority at the expense of the atabeg Abū-Bakr of Azerbaijan and the caliph an-Nāṣir. The latter appealed to Tökiish, who conquered Raiy and Hamadan, and it was thus that in 1194 the namesake and last descendant of Tughrul-Beg was killed. But Tökiish then felt himself called upon to take up the Selchükid heritage, and demanded of the caliph an-Nāṣir his own recognition as sultan at Baghdad. This was certainly distasteful to an-Nāṣir, who was not incapable of resistance. A rupture ensued which, at the outset, differentiated the political position of Tökiish, enemy of the caliph, from that which Tughrul-Beg had enjoyed as the caliph's protector — a situation rife with consequences for the Khorezm-Shāh, who thus alienated the orthodox Moslem groups.

It was during the reign of Muḥammad, who succeeded his father Tökiish as Khorezm-Shāh in 1200, that all the effects of this policy made themselves strikingly evident, a policy the success of which derived more from the existence of a political vacuum abroad than from any compelling drive from within. In fact Khorezmian rule was now the reign of an army encamped on hostile soil. The Khorezmians occupied Transoxiana and almost all the non-Hindu regions of the Ghūrid states; they extorted recognition from the independent Kïpchaks; they contributed to the ruin of the Kara-Kitai, with the exception of some who entered Khorezmian service and ended by founding an autonomous dynasty at Kerman, destined to last as a vassal of the Mongols down to the fourteenth century; they became masters of all central Persia; they fought the Kurds in al-Jibāl. In brief, they established a wide-flung empire which, though it included neither Azerbaijan nor any Arab country, extended in the opposite direction to the very confines of India, thus joining to much of the former Selchükid dominions a part of the territories of the Ghaznavids and the Kara-Khanids.

But this military state was supported by none, opposed by all. A new struggle with the caliph, from which he managed to emerge undefeated, completed the Khorezmian break with orthodoxy. On the grounds of alleged contacts of the caliph with Kara-Kitai pagans directed against himself, a Moslem, Muḥammad declared an-Nāṣir dethroned, and proclaimed an anti-caliph chosen from the descendants of ʿAlī, son-in-law of the prophet Mohammed, whom the Shīʿites had always considered the prophet's legitimate heirs, as opposed to the ʿAbbāsids. But since the initiative had been taken on no doctrinal basis and without any previous agreement with the Shīʿites, there was no real rapprochement with this sect, which had in any event been somewhat weakened by a century and a half of orthodox repression.

Meanwhile the Kïpchak soldiery was making itself more and more unbearable to the population. The Khorezm-Shāhs had preserved the Selchükid administrative system, which could not fail to conflict with the growing exactions of the military horde. For a long time Muḥammad's mother Turkān Khātūn, who enjoyed great prestige, defended the vizir Niẓām-al-Mulk and his principles of administration. But the break with orthodoxy served also as the pretext for a break with this princess and the vizir and for the dislocation of the existing bureaucracy, for which there was no substitute available. Among the people — as much the civil aristocracy, of Bukhara for example, as the general mass — there was a longing for liberation. When it became known that the governor of a frontier post, whose action the Khorezm-Shāh did not repudiate, had ordered the massacre, ostensibly for spying, of a whole caravan of Moslem merchants returning from Mongol territory, this caused a rupture with the commercial classes, and the feeling spread that the Islamic cause might be revenged upon Muḥammad, the pseudo-Moslem, through the pagan Mongol Genghis Khan (Chinggis Khan or Qan). Possibly Mongol strength would have broken Khorezmian power anyway; it is difficult to say, since Khorezmian power was only in its infancy. In any case things would not have happened as they did, that immediately after the first defeat by the Mongols it became obvious that there was no resistance to them anywhere, and that the Khorezmian edifice no longer rested on any foundation whatsoever. Muḥammad, a hunted man abandoned by all, died in 1220 on an island in the Caspian Sea.

This still did not mark the end of "Khorezmian" history, or at least of the princes and bands to whom posterity has given this name. There followed an era of savagery comparable to that of the Italian or German condottieri, or the Grand Companies of the Hundred Years War. And chance has decreed that it would be better known than earlier Khorezmian history, thanks to the talented narrator it found in the person of an-Nasawī, secretary of the last Khorezm-Shāh. The Mongols gave no quarter when resisted, and the Kîpchak warriors had no alternative but to flee, try to regroup elsewhere, plunder everywhere in order to exist, and try to conquer other territories to put under tribute. Muḥammad had given his son Jalāl-ad-Dīn Mangubertī (or Mangbartī, Mengübirdi) the rule of the lands taken from the Ghūrids. It was around him that the "Khorezmians" gathered. Now came a succession of barbarous raids, and of desperate flights before the Mongols alternating with hasty and destructive conquests, always further westward, of new kingdoms which there was never time to organize.

Jalāl-ad-Dīn escaped Mongol pursuit by fleeing across the Indus. He tried to deprive the slave kings of their kingdom, but then abruptly wheeled about and made for Kerman, then on to Fars and al-Jibāl where his brother Rukn-ad-Dīn Ghūrshānchī had blazed the trail for him. In his turn he naturally clashed with the caliph, and then with the caliph's ally Uzbeg, the atabeg of Azerbaijan. He did not invade Iraq, but defeated the atabeg himself and annexed Azerbaijan (1225), which promptly became the base for a destructive but ephemeral conquest of Georgia. No sooner was this achieved than suddenly the Mongols appeared just behind him on the Iranian plateau, though at this time merely a vanguard which could be checked in battle.

Still the Khorezmians sought safety farther west, and so began a new struggle, now with the Aiyūbids of Mesopotamia, from whom they wrested Akhlat on Lake Van, not without still more devastation. It must be said that among the Aiyūbids, as among the Syrian and Mesopotamian princes in general, there was no concord, and that some had appealed to Jalāl-ad-Dīn. Al-Mu'aẓẓam of Damascus, in league with the lord of Irbil, Gökböri, and with the Artukids of Mardin and Ḥiṣn Kaifā, systematically used the Khorezmians against his brother al-Ashraf of the Jazira and Lu'lu' of Mosul. Al-Ashraf once had to get help against them from the Selchükid sultan of Rūm (Anatolia), Kai-Qobād I. The Khorezmians, masters of one of the principal routes into Asia Minor by virtue of their possession of Akhlat, planned to conquer Rūm, and Jahān-Shāh of Erzerum, the enemy of his cousin Kai-Qobād, made an advance agreement with the would-be conquerors. Kai-Qobād was the most powerful Selchükid Anatolia had known, but this did not stop him from appealing to al-Ashraf; together they crushed the Khorezmians west of Erzinjan in 1230. Now the Mongols appeared again, and fell on Azerbaijan itself; the Khorezm-Shāh had no time to regroup his forces, and fled to Diyār-Bakr. There, in 1231, the man who had struck fear into half the Moslem world met an obscure death at the hands of a Kurdish peasant.

But the Khorezmians were still not destroyed. Their chiefs, thenceforth without fixed bases, saw no hope but to offer their services to any prince who might agree to give them semi-autonomous refuge in his territories; and princes were to be found who thought it better in this way to avoid their depredations and especially their employment as a military force by rivals. For a time they served al-Ashraf, but soon accepted a more advantageous offer sent them by Kai-Qobād, who hoped to use them to defend his Armenian frontier against the Mongols. It would soon be obvious, however, that they had no stomach for the job, and he had to establish them, mingled with the rest of his forces, in the interior of his states. They at least played a prominent role in the struggle he now had to sustain against the Aiyūbids in Anatolia and in upper Mesopotamia. But the successor of Kai-Qobād, Kai-Khusrau II, fell out with them, whereupon they withdrew, and went off to write yet another chapter of adventure in the Jazira.

Here they fell anew into a hot-bed of intrigue. For a while at first they fought for anyone; finally they joined the Aiyūbid aṣ-Ṣāliḥ, against whom almost all the other princes of Syria and upper Mesopotamia were leagued. It was a lasting alliance which earned the Khorezmians possession of Diyār-Muḍar, lying within the great bend of the Euphrates, and allowed aṣ-Ṣāliḥ Aiyūb to extricate himself from some difficult situations first in the Jazira, then in

Syria, whence he finally took Egypt (in 1240, without Khorezmian aid) from his brother al-'Ādil II. The Khorezmians were then used to round out this victory by bloody operations against the principality of Aleppo, with some early success which soon turned into defeat, however, forcing them to retreat to the Euphrates boundary of Iraq in the territory of the caliph. From there they were recalled by another Aiyūbid, Ghāzī of Maiyafariqin, in his turn at war with Aleppo, Mosul, and the Selchükids of Rūm. Again, disaster. But their old ally, aṣ-Ṣāliḥ, now hoped to take Syria from his relatives and enemies of Kerak and Damascus, and called upon them. They were guilty of frightful excesses when they fell on Syria, took Jerusalem from the Franks, who had been called to the rescue by the princes threatened by aṣ-Ṣāliḥ, and finally inflicted on this coalition the terrible rout near Gaza in 1244. Naturally it was aṣ-Ṣāliḥ's turn to fear their exactions, all the more terrible for their sense of revived strength. He came to an understanding with the Aleppans, who were used to fighting the Khorezmians; the latter now suffered a new and final disaster under the walls of Homs in 1246. Decimated, with their chiefs slain and their ranks thinned by the toll of warfare and age, some of the Khorezmians hired themselves out to the Mongols, others to an-Nāṣir Dā'ūd, prince of Kerak, who, two years earlier, had resisted aṣ-Ṣāliḥ, while still others served in the regular army of aṣ-Ṣāliḥ in Egypt. Their last survivors would be found at the victory of 'Ain Jālūt over the Mongols in 1260. Forty years earlier Khorezm, their starting point, had become a Mongol province.

Not only did their trek result in the spread of ruin and the destruction of old kingdoms, facilitating the more lasting Mongol conquest which ensued, but in their passing they had also jostled Turkomans such as the Ivas of eastern Armenia. Either drawn forward or pushed back, these Turkomans, when the Khorezmians had passed, remained to constitute, together with the new migrations forced by the Mongol conquests, a reinforced Turkoman element in the western areas, with all the difficulties of adjustment which would follow. The effects of this were felt in Selchükid Anatolia, for instance, which they would weaken on the very eve of the Mongol assault, and also in Syria at the time of the crusade of Louis IX.

Thus the eruptions of Central Asia, moving westward step by step, brought chaos even to the Mediterranean countries; but it would not be for the Khorezmians to give a new and stable form to this world in upheaval. That would be the role of the Mongols, pressing on their heels.

C. *The Selchükid State of Rūm*[4]

Those interested in the history of the crusades may know the princes of Arab Syria and Egypt, but they are often unaware that in Anatolia at this time a Turkey was being born quite unlike the rest of the Moslem world. Obviously the Turks of this region did not have the same day-to-day contacts with the Franks of Syria and Palestine as did the Moslems of Aleppo and Damascus. As we have seen, however, they at least fought with them and made peace with them, and moreover their contacts with the Byzantines would naturally interfere with the course of Franco-Byzantine relations.

Even in histories of the Moslem world Selchükid Rūm appears only as a country cousin, except of course in those works specifically dealing with Turkey. Nor is this by chance. On the contrary, it reflects the basic fact of a Turkey growing up as something of a stranger to the traditional Moslem world, which has consequently left us almost no reliable information about it. Since for the twelfth century we do not yet have any historical literature written in the Selchükid milieu, we are forced to rely on Byzantine or native Christian sources of information, as prejudiced as they are precious. Indigenous Moslem materials on Anatolia do exist for the thirteenth century, but the historians of the rest of the Moslem world ignore them. The fact that they are not even written in Arabic, but in Persian, reinforces the impression of belonging to another world, one of minor interest only. It goes without saying that this very

[4] For the twelfth century, the sources are primarily Christian: Byzantine (Anna Comnena, John Cinnamus, Nicetas Choniates), Armenian (Matthew of Edessa), and above all Syriac (Michael the Syrian), to which may be added some data of a numismatic, epigraphic, and archaeological nature.

For the pre-Mongol thirteenth century we finally have a Moslem chronicle from Anatolia, that of Ibn-Bībī, composed, however, under the Mongol regime: *Saljūq-nāmeh* (ed. Th. Houtsma, Leyden, 1902; tr. by H. W. Duda, *Die Seltschukengeschichte des Ibn Bibi* [Copenhagen, 1959]); to this might be added the evidence of Arab historians such as Ibn-al-Athīr, *Ta'rīkh ad-daulah al-atābakīyah mulūk al-Mauṣil* [*History of the Atabeg State of the Lords of Mosul*] (*RHC, Or.*, II, part 2), of Kamāl-ad-Dīn ibn-al-'Adīm, *Zubdat al-ḥalab fī ta'rīkh Ḥalab* [. . . *History of Aleppo*] (*RHC, Or.*, III), and of the Syriac historian Bar-Hebraeus, *Chronography* (tr. E. A. W. Budge, London, 1932), as well as the account of the missionary Simon of St. Quentin as preserved by Vincent of Beauvais, and a few archival pieces.

There exists no thorough history of medieval Turkey. *Gosudarstvo Seldzhukidov Maloi Azii* [*Selchükid Rule in Asia Minor*] by V. Gordlevskii (Moscow, 1951) unfortunately was written before documentary publications of more recent date, and like its predecessors incorrectly confounds, it would seem, the pre-Mongol and post-Mongol periods. Important discussions can be found in *İslâm ansiklopedisi*; in Paul Wittek, *The Rise of the Ottoman Empire* (London, 1938); in Fuad Köprülü, *Les Origines de l'empire ottoman* (Paris, 1937); and in a review of some problems in two articles published by the present writer in the *Journal d'histoire mondiale* (UNESCO), II (1954), nos. 2–3, and in *Mélanges L. Halphen* (Paris, 1951). See also O. Turan, "Les Seljukides et leurs sujets non-musulmans," *Studia Islamica*, I (1953), 65–100; and C. Huart, "Épigraphie arabe d'Asie Mineure," *Revue sémitique*, II (1894) and III (1895).

fact ought, paradoxically, to attract us to the history of Turkish origins, and that a treatment of the medieval Near East would be incomplete which does not give their due to the founders of one of the more vital states of the modern world. Furthermore, it is obvious that a knowledge of these origins is indispensable to a larger understanding of the history of the crusades and the Latin east itself.

The basic facts of Turkish settlement in Anatolia have been given in the preceding volume:[5] established, yet shut in, in the area of the plateaus; cut off from the coasts; almost cut off from the Arab world; and maintaining only a precarious though real tie with the Iranian lands behind. Furthermore, they were divided into the more numerous true Turkomans, devoted to raiding the "infidel" and hostile to all ideas of an administrative state, and the Selchükids, seeking to form in Anatolia for their own benefit a state like that of their Iranian cousins, at least insofar as persistent Byzantine tradition and the absence of non-Turkish Moslems experienced in territorial administration might allow.

The Selchükids pursued a policy of neutrality — even temporary alliance — with the Greeks, in the interests of establishing their domination over the greatest number of Moslems possible. The usual Turkoman tendency was to favor the Dānishmendid family, which controlled the routes throughout the north; that of the Selchükids, to follow the descendants of Sulaimān, established for the most part around Iconium (Konya). Admittedly, the distinction between the two was not always clear; and it certainly came to be blurred, first because Selchükid strength itself was to a large extent based upon the Turkomans, who were consequently given a free hand, especially in the frontier marches called *uj*; also, because the leading Turkoman chiefs themselves, such as the Dānishmendids, could not avoid gradually becoming Moslem territorial princes; and finally, because the rivalries of cliques and individuals within each camp led to permanent alliance between the main adversaries. Still it may be said that the struggle between Selchükids and Dānishmendids dominated the first three quarters of the twelfth century, roughly divisible into two periods.

For the major portion of the reign of the Selchükid Mas'ūd (1116–1155), who, following a few chance-comers, eventually succeeded his father Kilij Arslan I, the Dānishmendids formed a united front under a single head, Gümüshtigin Ghāzī (1105?–1134 or 1135), and then Muḥammad (d. 1140). They constituted the

[5] See volume I, chapter V.

dominant power in central Anatolia. Mas'ūd actually accepted the protection of Gümüshtigin Ghāzī, which he paid for by allowing the latter to retake Melitene (Malatya) at the expense of a Selchükid cadet (Tughrul Arslan) in 1124; and, in spite of a temporary rupture, he maintained the alliance with Muḥammad. From the outset hostilities continued without cease against the Franks and Armenians to the south and the Byzantines to the west, and periodically against Trebizond to the northeast. Mas'ūd's predecessor Shāhan-Shāh paid with his throne and his life for attempting a reconciliation with Alexius Comnenus. There followed a revolt against Mas'ūd and Gümüshtigin Ghāzī by one of Mas'ūd's brothers, Arab, and then momentary discord between Mas'ūd and Muḥammad. This allowed John Comnenus, less trammeled on his European side than his father had been, and with no thought of undertaking any Syrian enterprise before clearing the routes of Anatolia, to convert into an effective and fortified reoccupation the ill-defined reconquest of the western areas effected on the morrow of the First Crusade, and to push his inland frontier northeastward as far as the province of Kastamonu. Given the nature of Dānishmendid power, this was not much of a set-back. In 1135 the caliph consecrated their position with the title *malik*, reconciled, it is not known how, with Selchükid authority, which the caliph surely did not contest, although it is not certain that he recognized their title of sultan.

After 1140, however, the Dānishmendids were divided, Yaghi̊-Basan,[6] a brother of the dead Muḥammad, against Dhū-n-Nūn, the son, and other princes of his family. True, at the death of Mas'ūd in 1155 his son Ki̊li̊j Arslan II was in his turn opposed by a brother, who possessed Ankara as an appanage and enjoyed the support of Yaghi̊-Basan. The latter's death in 1164 clearly swung the balance in favor of Ki̊li̊j Arslan. During these struggles Mas'ūd and Ki̊li̊j Arslan tried to conclude peace with the new Byzantine emperor, Manuel Comnenus, who at first continued to press hard — the expedition of 1146 reached the very gates of Iconium. The news of the approach of the Second Crusade made agreement more attractive to both parties, and not only did peace reign between Greeks and Selchükids in subsequent years, but the Selchükids occasionally assisted the Greeks against their enemies, such as the Armenians of Cilicia. Still, aside from the hostilities which continued

[6] Yaghi̊-Basan's father Gümüshtigin Ghāzī was the son of Malik-Ghāzī.

sporadically to pit Byzantines against Dānishmendids on the Black Sea coast, there were other local but constantly spreading struggles between Byzantines and the frontier Turkomans who threatened either the Byzantine borders or the routes of communication between Constantinople and Syria, and it was difficult for Kîlîj Arslan to keep these Turkomans under control. Finally, around 1160, Manuel Comnenus prepared an expedition of considerable size to reconquer part of the Anatolian plateau. Kîlîj Arslan then gambled everything on one throw: he made formal promises to Manuel to guarantee his frontiers; he promised to send contingents against the imperial enemies in Europe; he offered, by a visit to Constantinople itself, to proclaim to the world his deference to the empire.[7] Like all Byzantines, Manuel was fond of prestige, and in addition he was nagged by the persistence of other imperial problems; he accepted, and there followed a sensational reception in 1162 which changed nothing basically, but prolonged the official peace between the two sovereigns for fourteen years.

The relative sacrifices this policy cost Kîlîj Arslan were compensated for, as under Mas'ūd before him, by the new opportunity it afforded for meddling in the Dānishmendid conflicts — which had led, under Mas'ūd, to recognition of his suzerainty by the Dānishmendid Dhū-l-Qarnain of Melitene and to the annexation of Ankara, the appanaged holder of which, Shāhan-Shāh, would, however, ally himself with Yaghî-Basan — and for interfering on the Syrian and Euphrates borders of his kingdom. Like Mas'ūd, Kîlîj Arslan profited from the successes of Nūr-ad-Dīn against the Franks, in which he had assisted by taking the Franks in the rear, by claiming, along with the northern places of the ex-county of Edessa to the west of the Euphrates, a fringe of territories on the north Syrian plain neighboring the mountains of Anatolia.

It is evident that Nūr-ad-Dīn could not allow this new power to compete for influence in territory he considered his own. Hence relations between them quickly cooled, and making a show of a furious desire for the Holy War, the Syrian prince soon caused the condemnation of Kîlîj Arslan, in the eyes of pietists, as a friend of the Greeks. In 1164, thanks to the growing division among the Dānishmendids, Kîlîj Arslan took Ankara from his brother, and from Dhū-n-Nūn his territories in Cappadocia. Naturally the latter appealed to his only possible ally, Nūr-ad-Dīn, who, having conquered Egypt, no longer had to exercise great caution on his northern frontier, and who apparently obtained very large territorial

[7] On this visit, see volume I of the present work, chapter XVII, p. 545.

concessions in this direction by official act of the caliph. Reinforced by contingents of his vassals or allies of the Jazira and Cilicia, his armies three times from 1171 to 1173, and finally he himself, invaded Selchükid territory.[8] Kîlîj Arslan had to agree to allow Dhū-n-Nūn to be installed at Sebastia (Sivas) with a garrison and an agent representing his protector Nūr-ad-Dīn. Always the diplomat, Kîlîj Arslan paid this price for a reconciliation with his Moslem neighbors, possibly exchanging mutual promises with them, in order to maintain the balance requisite for a common renewal of the Holy War against the Christians of both Syria and Byzantium. Then fate smiled on Kîlîj Arslan. In 1174 Nūr-ad-Dīn died, and the unity of Moslem Anatolia, except Armenia, could be molded to the benefit of the Selchükids without fear of resistance.

But as might be expected, relations with Manuel Comnenus worsened. All the old differences persisted. The treaty of 1173 between the Moslems had of course aroused the suspicion of the emperor and had brought a menacing demonstration. Now the death of Nūr-ad-Dīn seemed to provide a favorable opportunity, since it deprived Kîlîj Arslan of a possible ally, while the Selchükid unification of Anatolia seemed likely to result if the Byzantines continued their policy of toleration toward Kîlîj Arslan. The threat demanded quick action. For once, Europe was tranquil. The invasion bases of western Anatolia had been strengthened. Any uprising of Dānishmendid subjects could be discounted in advance. All these reasons incited Manuel Comnenus to undertake a powerful expedition, the major army of which, in 1176 under his personal command, moved on Iconium. Partly through his own fault the army met with irreparable disaster in the defile of Myriokephalon. It was a replica of the defeat at Manzikert a century earlier. Myriokephalon marked the complete collapse of Byzantine pretensions, never renounced in theory, to dominion in Anatolia, and foreshadowed the ascendancy of the Selchükid state of "Rūm". Kîlîj Arslan did not want to annex the devastated west, but in 1177 he did annex Melitene to the east and resumed his policy of extending his influence in the countries of the Euphrates. Moreover, in 1180 Manuel Comnenus died, and the troubles which followed upon his death weakened Byzantium seriously in the face of pressure from frontier Turkish elements.

As scanty as our documentation may be, it is at least sufficient to show not only that Myriokephalon was an obvious manifestation of Selchükid military strength, but that beneath the surface the

[8] On Nūr-ad-Dīn and Kîlîj Arslan, see volume I, chapter XVI, p. 527.

Selchükid state was also beginning to establish administrative institutions, develop Moslem forms of culture, and stimulate economic activity, the full development of which is clearly visible in the following century, thanks to the greater adequacy of our sources. And yet this time of expansion was also a time of crisis — a duality which runs through the whole of the history of Selchükid Rūm. The submission of the Dānishmendids had added to the Turkoman element within the Selchükid dominions. In addition, the Turkomans of eastern Anatolia may have been influenced by the agitations of their Iranian cousins; at all events, there began in 1185, to continue for several years, a vast Turkoman movement. Starting from upper Mesopotamia, it spread through Armenia as far as the Georgian border, and down into Selchükid Cappadocia, with extensions into Cilicia and northern Syria. The chief was one Rustam, of whom we know nothing else.

At this critical moment Kîlîj Arslan, getting on in years and possibly obliged to satisfy the demands of impatient sons, thought it wise to divide his entire realm, under his continuing suzerainty, into eleven appanages for the benefit of his nine surviving sons, one brother, and a nephew (1190). But immediately jealousy sprang up among the brothers, and with it a strong temptation to employ Rustam's Turkomans. This is what Quṭb-ad-Dīn Malik-Shāh of Sebastia, the eldest son, did. Anxious to obtain the future succession, he forced Kîlîj Arslan to take him as his associate in the capital of Iconium, which the old prince had kept for himself.

It was in this situation that the crusade of Frederick Barbarossa supervened. For twelve years the German emperor had maintained good relations with Kîlîj Arslan against the common enemy, the Byzantine empire; in 1189–1190 the old sultan still asked nothing more than to arrange a passage for the crusaders under his friend. But this attitude was naturally not shared by the Turkomans, eager to pillage the Christian army, nor by Saladin's emissaries, influential among the pietists and seeking to break up the expedition before its arrival in Syria. The German army thus clashed with the *uj* Turkomans, and then, more seriously, with Quṭb-ad-Dīn himself, supported by the troops of Rustam. The German attack on Iconium forced him to let his father arrange matters after a fashion; Barbarossa reached Cilicia. Considerably weakened, Quṭb-ad-Dīn now engaged in rather pointless hostilities with certain of his brothers, in the course of which his father escaped the semi-captivity in which his son had held him. The old sultan led a wandering life, from son to son, seeking to reconcile them. He was finally taken in by

Ghiyāth-ad-Dīn Kai-Khusrau (I), to whom, perhaps because of his Greek mother, he had given the government of the new acquisitions on the western border. After promising him the succession, Kilij Arslan died in 1192 at the age of seventy-seven.

Naturally, the inevitable war matched Kai-Khusrau with Quṭb-ad-Dīn, and then, when he died in 1192, with their brother Rukn-ad-Dīn Sulaimān II, who finally expelled Kai-Khusrau from Iconium (1196) and forced him to seek refuge in Byzantine territory. Sulaimān then refashioned the unity of Selchükid territory to his own advantage at the expense of his other brothers. Hardly had he done so when he died, however (1204), and Kai-Khusrau, recalled from his asylum among the Greeks, with the support of the *uj* Turkomans and the descendants of the Dānishmendids, fell heir to the entire realm, which thereafter was to remain undivided in his hands and in those of his descendants. If this crisis proves clearly the weakness of the monarchical institution, it is typical, however, that far from interrupting the Selchükid and Turkoman expansion it actually encouraged it.

During the lifetime of Kilij Arslan the Selchükid administration had established itself behind the Turkomans in Greek strongholds which, surrounded by flat country impossible to hold, had finally had to surrender. Sozopolis, at first held of Kai-Khusrau as a fief, under the new name of Burghlu (modern Uluborlu), provided a base upon which a new province was organized. Meanwhile, to the southwest, the Turkomans reached the coast stretching east from the shore facing Rhodes up to the environs of Adalia (Antalya). In the disorders of the Byzantine empire under the Angeli, Greek frontier lords rebelled and paid homage to the Turks in order to obtain reinforcements; it was through a suppliant of this kind that Kai-Khusrau obtained Laodicea, soon to be supplanted by the new town of Denizli which would menace all the area of the Maeander. Farther north, Dorylaeum ceased to be Greek; the Byzantines held only the shore line of the Black Sea without any part of the hinterland at all; and even here, in the center, the Turks had reached the sea, possibly occupied Samsun briefly, and cut distant Trebizond off from its dependence on Constantinople. All this was expansion of the Turkoman type, yet always to the profit of the Selchükids.

Rukn-ad-Dīn, more faithful to the paternal tradition, appears to have sought to turn his energies toward acquisitions in Moslem areas to the east; as a result, he took the principality of the local Saltukid dynasty of Erzerum, whence, it is true, he next made a demonstration in force against the Christians of Trebizond and

Georgia. He did not think it judicious, however, to annex Erzerum outright for the moment, but installed his brother Mughīth-ad-Dīn Tughrul-Shāh there, in exchange for his appanage. At Erzinjan the Mengüchekid dynasty continued but, thenceforth surrounded, was reduced to the role of vassal.

Thereafter, the frontier to the west for more than half a century not only found a new stability in fact, but, it seems, was officially recognized by both sides. It would appear that, for Byzantium, or rather for the Nicaean empire (the Asian successor of Byzantium as opposed to the Latin empire of Constantinople created by the Fourth Crusade in 1204),[9] this policy involved the recognition of a free hand for the Selchükids in the east, perhaps including the lands of other Greeks there who were hostile or indifferent to the Lascarids. Although Kai-Khusrau was led once again to break with his old supporters the Greeks, and in 1211 fell in battle against them on the western front, no hostility would mar the relations between his descendants and Nicaea thereafter. No major crusade after that of Frederick Barbarossa crossed Anatolia.

The Selchükids now were concerned first with acquiring a firm hold on the coasts, south and north; next, with renewing the policy of conquest of, or influence over, Moslem countries to the southeast. Already in 1207 Kai-Khusrau had been able to annex Adalia without arousing any Nicaean reaction, providing a Selchükid base for trade with Egypt. His son 'Izz-ad-Dīn Kai-Kā'ūs I (1211–1220) added Sinope on the Black Sea, a stronghold on which a Selchükid military, and to some extent commercial, domination could be based. His brother 'Alā'-ad-Dīn Kai-Qobād I (1220–1237), whose reign was the most glorious of his dynasty, extended his possessions on the southern coast of Anatolia up to the shore opposite Cyprus and to the Cilician Gates, and in a place which he renamed 'Alāyā (originally 'Alā'īyah, from his honorific; modern Alanya) established one of his principal residences. On the Black Sea he took those Greek towns of the Crimean coast which had swung to Trebizond after the fall of Constantinople and had hampered merchants from Selchükid territory; this was the object of a memorable maritime expedition. In another direction, Kai-Khusrau I, Kai-Kā'ūs I, and Kai-Qobād I pacified and consolidated the Taurus frontier facing the Armenian kingdom of Cilicia, also at the height of its development. They aligned themselves with the Franks of Antioch against Cilicia, with the Latins and Venetians of Constantinople against the Greeks of Nicaea, and with the Cypriotes; they hired Frankish

[9] See above, chapters V and VI.

mercenaries; and they corresponded with the papacy and welcomed Latin missionaries, in an effort to detach their Greek subjects from their Byzantine connections. These three Selchükids, and their successors under Mongol domination, may thus be said to have been generally favorable to Franks, neutral toward Greeks, and hostile primarily to their fellow-Moslems. In particular, they again undertook, on a large scale, the policy of expansion southeastward, begun in the middle of the twelfth century but abandoned during the dynastic troubles; they were helped now by the discord of the princes of Syria and the Jazira.

With aẓ-Ẓāhir Ghāzī of Aleppo both Kai-Khusrau and Kai-Kā'ūs pursued a policy of alliance against Leon II of Armenia. From this alliance the Aiyūbid hoped also to derive some protection eventually against his uncle al-'Ādil I. On the death of aẓ-Ẓāhir in 1216, Kai-Kā'ūs wished to support the candidature of another son of Saladin, al-Afḍal, vassal of the Selchükids at Samosata since 1203, but lost out because of the intervention of al-Ashraf, son of al-'Ādil. Kai-Qobād returned to the old policy and in alliance with al-Ashraf took from the Artukid Maudūd of Amida and Ḥiṣn Kaifā his strongholds beyond the Euphrates as far as Chemishkezek to the south of Erzinjan. He annexed Erzinjan at the same time (1228), three years after the death of its elderly lord Bahrām-Shāh. In the midst of all this there appeared a new factor in west Asian politics, the Khorezmians led by Jalāl-ad-Dīn Mangubertī.

So long as the Khorezmians threatened only Erzerum, with whose prince Kai-Qobād was embroiled, or even the northeastern possessions of al-Ashraf, such as Akhlat on Lake Van, the Selchükid sovereign had no reason to be ill disposed to Jalāl-ad-Dīn. Things changed when it appeared that Jalāl-ad-Dīn, become master of Akhlat and seconded by Jahān-Shāh of Erzerum, now his client, prepared to invade Anatolia. Kai-Qobād succeeded in persuading not only al-Ashraf, who came in person, but the government of Aleppo, and the head of the Aiyūbid family, al-Kāmil of Egypt, to send reinforcements, and the combined armies routed the Khorezmians to the west of Erzinjan in 1230. Dragged down in the defeat, Jahān-Shāh lost Erzerum, which this time was annexed outright; the territory of Kai-Qobād now stretched to the borders of Azerbaijan. The Georgians perforce had also sided with the Khorezmians; an energetic demonstration forced them, as well no doubt as their allies of Trebizond, to adopt thenceforth a more favorable attitude toward Kai-Qobād.

But the victors soon fell out. Al-Ashraf, wrapped up in Syrian affairs, lost interest in his distant states, now devastated by the approaching Mongols. Kai-Qobād thought he could employ the Khorezmians, who had no leader and no lands, to occupy Akhlat, a key to the invasion routes. On the other hand, al-Kāmil took Amida and Ḥiṣn Kaifā from their Artukid ruler Maudūd (1232) because of his alleged pro-Khorezmian leanings. Thereafter, with no motive for coöperation, Selchükid and Aiyūbid ambitions were diametrically opposed.[10] In 1233 al-Kāmil hoped to invade Selchükid territory, which some Syrians who had been there in 1231 said was poorly defended; stopped in the mountains north of Syria, he swung toward the northeast, where the Artukid al-Khiḍr of Kharput had called upon him for assistance. The two allies were crushed and Kai-Qobād annexed Kharput, thus moving across the Euphrates. He even briefly put a garrison in the heart of Aiyūbid country, at Harran (which al-Kāmil was able to recover, however, without trouble), and then besieged Amida.

After the death of Kai-Qobād I in 1237, his son Ghiyāth-ad-Dīn Kai-Khusrau II broke with the Khorezmians, who fled to the Jazira; but thanks to the deaths, one after the other, of al-Ashraf and al-Kāmil, he was able, by taking part in an almost general coalition of Syrian and Jaziran princes against al-Kāmil's son aṣ-Ṣāliḥ Aiyūb and the Khorezmians, to enter Amida itself, the strongest place in Diyār-Bakr, and to lay siege to Maiyafariqin beyond the Tigris. Selchükid territory thus reached in Armenia almost those boundaries which the Byzantine empire had had, and, toward Mesopotamia, even surpassed them (attaining almost those of modern Turkey), corresponding closely to the area of relatively strong Turkoman settlement.

Under Kai-Qobād I and, in spite of the growing Mongol danger, at the beginning of the reign of Kai-Khusrau II, the Selchükid state thus stood at the height of its military power and territorial expansion, ringed by vassals or allies, Moslem Aleppo and the Jazira, Christian Cilicia, even briefly Trebizond, Nicaea, and Cyprus, which sent contingents of military reinforcements when called on. This was also the period when the organization of institutions was perfected, and when economic life and civilization came of age. We know much of this now from the chronicles, some archival documents (exceptional for the Moslem world), and accounts of such travelers as Simon of St. Quentin. It is to this aspect that we now turn.

[10] On the Aiyūbids, see below, chapter XX, pp. 703–704.

D. *Selchükid Society in Anatolia*

First of all, we are in "Turkey" — contemporary observers are all in accord here. Undoubtedly there remained important groups of earlier peoples, often in the majority: Greeks to the west, Armenians to the east, Monophysite Syrians in the upper Euphrates districts. There were, however, many reasons why the name Turkey was commonly applied to the Selchükid state of Rūm, but not to any of the neighboring states no less ruled by Turkish dynasties. Turkish settlement, particularly in the frontier zones dominated by Turkomans and in the few large towns on which the administrative institutions of the regime were based, very quickly became relatively important, following the thinning out of the older population. The other peoples formed only local agglomerations cut off from contact with any greater whole, with no political role, those Armenians with a desire for independence having emigrated to Cilicia, and the Greeks having collaborated willingly, it would seem, with the new masters. And as a result of mixed marriages, of the taking of prisoners in frontier warfare, and of religious conversions, a part of the native population had been more or less made over and absorbed into the new regime.

It is noteworthy, however, that in the upper ranks of society this Turkish character made less impression within the Selchükid state than outside it. As we shall see, the administrative personnel and the culture of the urbanized Turks were Iranian, to the extent that within leading circles there was a tendency to restrict the appellation "Turk" to the rough uncivilized Turkomans, and to look down on them with contempt. This proved to be a source of difficulty, and we shall note the fragility it imparted to the Selchükid structure despite its many elements of strength.

As for the native populations, though they had obviously suffered much in the anarchy of the conquests, they later had no more cause for complaint than those of neighboring Moslem states. So long as they were not connected with foreign political powers, their religious leaders, who were at the same time directors of their communities in all matters of civil law, could carry on. The Monophysites, for whom there was no foreign support, kept intact their clergy, and the churches and monasteries which they had held before the Turkish conquest. The Armenian and Greek groups were much more disorganized, but not systematically eliminated, and worship was in no wise impossible for any religious group. Nevertheless, the Selchükid state was a resolutely Moslem one. In the beginning, in the Turkoman principalities, the ineptitude of the conquerors had left in Christian hands what remained of local administration; eventually, the systematic call for Iranians or their spontaneous influx allowed the Selchükids to build a state based essentially on Moslems. Moreover, the heresies which tore the old Moslem countries had little effect among the aristocracy, which was morally united behind the principles of Ḥanafite jurisprudence.

It does not follow, however, that the Selchükid state of Rūm was a carbon copy of the state of the Great Selchükids. The present condition of scholarship hardly lets us frame questions, let alone suggest answers, but it is evident that the settlement of the Turks in a territory with a background other than Moslem brought them face to face with problems with which the traditions of old Moslem countries were not prepared to cope; on the other hand, the new conditions could suggest to them original solutions. One might then ask what part was played in these solutions by Byzantine, Iranian, and Turkish influences, and what was new; and national or religious prejudices have not always been absent in such discussion. To be sure, the central and provincial adminstration corresponded in the main with the model of the Great Selchükids of Iran; the only thing original was the office of the *pervāneh*, who distributed the sultan's concessions. But the economic and social realities upon which the regime was based are almost completely obscured. It is likely that the desertion of fields at the time of the conquests, and the collectivist traditions of the tribes, subsequently put a considerable proportion of the land into the hands of the state (to the extent that the state was organized) without, however, destroying either the large individual holdings of Moslem magnates or, around the towns, the small holdings available without religious distinction to townsmen. The state thus had the means of making large land-grants (Arabic singular, *iqṭā'*) to its soldiers and officials without unduly weakening itself; but no doubt wages in specie also played an important role. Indeed, it seems to have been original with the Selchükid state of Rūm as compared with the neighboring Moslem states, to have maintained numerous foreign mercenaries alongside a servile military establishment, in this perhaps following the Byzantine example. It could afford to do this because it did not lack other resources.

We know almost nothing about the incidence of taxes, except that the large number of "infidels" made the head tax, which fell on such people in all Islamic countries, an important source of revenue. But what was the land tax? Were the taxes levied on

Turkoman herds and flocks regularly collected? We do not know. What we do know, however, is that, thanks to the maintenance of public order, the mineral resources and the commercial possibilities of Anatolia were intensively exploited, and brought considerable revenue to the state. Iron, copper, alum, salt, and wood were products all the more valuable for the fact that the Moslem areas to the south were almost entirely without them. In addition, products of Russia, in particular slaves destined for Egypt, often crossed Selchükid territory, while caravans passed through carrying the luxuries of the Far East from Iran to Sinope or Constantinople for reëxport, or to the court of Iconium and major centers like Caesarea (Kayseri). Sebastia was one of the great commercial crossroads of the Near East. On the main routes the Selchükid sultans and the magnates had mighty caravanserais built, serving as inns, entrepôts, and fortresses combined. Even allowing for exaggeration in the enthusiastic descriptions of, say, Simon of St. Quentin, it is sure that in the first half of the thirteenth century the Selchükid state of Rūm was one of the richest in the east.

An exact appreciation of the character of this state is made difficult because most of the documents date from the period of the Mongol protectorate, that is, at the beginning of a process of disintegration and the substitution of new forms. On the other hand, there has been too great a tendency to apply to the Selchükids of Rūm what is known about the Selchükids of Iran, of which, we believe, the features have not themselves always been clearly visualized. The result is that some have professed to see in the Selchükid state of Rūm a feudal state, for example, or, to be more precise in terms of eastern institutions, a state conceding to high officers, mostly military officers, large quasi-autonomous holdings which were more or less inheritable. The author hopes to suggest, in connection with the research he has done on this problem in the rest of the Moslem world, that the facts, *before* the Mongol period, are quite different.

For the Turkoman chiefs who were gradually subdued in the twelfth century, the Selchükids substituted appanaged members of their own family; then these, who became too independent, gave way to military commanders primarily of servile origin. They were able to constitute hereditary seignories in certain marches (for example, at Marash), and to endow with extensive powers the commanders of the *uj* territories or of the coastal provinces. Nevertheless it appears very likely that in most cases these commands were effectively bestowed and exercised in conditions permitting central control and revocation at any moment, and excluding all inheritance. Even in the special cases of districts formally granted as *iqṭāʿ*, it is apparent that these grants were never so absolute as to confer on their holders independent power, and were only exceptionally passed on to their children. In sum, we are dealing with a strong state comparable in this respect to the state of the Great Selchükids before its disintegration, or that of the Comneni as it still was in the twelfth century, and, within its narrow limits, that of the Lascarids of Nicaea in the thirteenth — without, however, our being able to decide to what extent their examples may have affected the policy of the Selchükids of Rūm. It is evident, however, that this policy would have been impossible without the resources they had at their disposal.

The towns were the pivot of the system. Several of them, not to mention the capital Iconium, acquired or regained, under their old names now Turkified, or under entirely new names (there were also some cases of a really new town replacing an old ruined town near by), an importance for which there is still evidence in the impressive succession of mosques, schools, caravanserais, walls, and the like, remains of which cover Anatolia.

It was in the towns that the *akhi* ("brotherhood") was organized, an institution which took full form and is well known to us only during the Mongol period, although its first development came earlier. The akhis were connected with the general mass movement of the *futūwah* groups discussed above in connection with the caliph an-Nāṣir. The name appears to have designated the superior initiates in a kind of mystical order which had probably developed in northwest Iran in the eleventh century. But why did the akhis (the brothers) here form around themselves groups on which they even bestowed their name, groups like those which evolved elsewhere without akhis as a nucleus? It is impossible to say. We can only note the unparalleled development of the institution to the point where, after the disintegration of the realm, the akhis would become the dominant force in certain towns. We may note also their apparent unity, explained by the homogeneity of members' backgrounds, unlike corresponding organizations in the rest of the Moslem world. Finally, though they represented a popular element which the aristocracy and sometimes the government distrusted, and tended to accept religious traditions of every origin, heretical as well as orthodox (and sometimes not even Moslem), they were organized by leaders who for the most part did belong to the Sunnite aristocracy, and they certainly did not systematically oppose the government. In the thirteenth century they were one element the government could apparently play off against others, and they defended Selchükid urban civilization on occasion as well against the Mongols as against the Turkomans. This last feature would evidently change when, in the fourteenth century, the Turkomans became masters almost everywhere. In brief, we have here an institution which in principle is related to the rest of the Moslem world but which in Anatolia in the course of the thirteenth century took an entirely original bent.

In the domain of culture, there is no doubt of the predominant, almost exclusive, influence of Iran, or more precisely of Khurasan, at least among the aristocracy. But here lay one of the weaknesses of this aristocracy and of this culture: the gulf between the upper classes and their Persian culture on the one hand, and the masses, Turk and Turkoman, on the other. For although the latter spoke only Turkish, in upper circles everything written was in Persian (except works of theology and law, and some public acts, for which Arabic, the language of the Koran, was used). The national Persian literature so thoroughly permeated the culture that the Selchükid sultans of the thirteenth century bore names of historic or legendary Iranian heroes. This Persian influence continued to grow as a result of the influx of refugees from Transoxiana and Khurasan fleeing the Khorezmians and the Mongols. In particular they brought with them the latest developments of the great mystic movement in which Iran was caught up at the time. They found a rich soil in which to resow its seeds in this new Moslem society which had in its traditions none of the "rationalist" movement of the Islam of earlier centuries. It was during the reign of Kai-Qobād I that one of the greatest "Persian" mystics, Jalāl-ad-Dīn (ar-)Rūmī, began his activity, which would culminate after the Mongol conquest in the creation of that order of "whirling dervishes" which has colored a part of Turkish life down to modern times.

In the realm of art the orientation was the same, although more subtly so. Here also we lack data which might justify firm conclusions. The relations of Selchükid art with the art which flourished simultaneously in Iran are obvious. But our conclusions tend to vary, depending on whether, in this larger artistic realm, we accord a more or less prominent place to earlier Iranian traditions, or to Turkish methods, or to the methods of Central Asia, Moslem or not, introduced by the Turkish conquest into the whole Moslem world, such as the use of bare brick. We can be sure that the general conception of the mosques and madrasahs is that of the whole Irano-Turkish world of the time. Though many of the architects who built them and artists who decorated them came from Iran, many were either natives or local Moslems. It is *a priori* very likely, therefore, that the modes of construction or decoration of Byzantine times were conserved in Selchükid buildings. As for figured ornamentation, however, this was common, as we know, to all works of art influenced by the Turks and Iran (each in their own way) as opposed to Semitic Moslem art. Be this as it may, the remains of mosques and other monuments in Iconium, Caesarea, Sebastia, Divrighi, and elsewhere bear witness to the degree of technical perfection and artistic delicacy which the builders of the Selchükid monuments of Rūm had attained; and the same can be said respecting their ceramics, metal wares, carpets, and other products.

But as we have noted, there was in all this civilization a serious weakness: it had not assimilated the Turkomans. These, the conquerors of the country, could no longer participate in the regime which they had established there. They clung to their own form of popular Islam, mixed with pre-Islamic customs and beliefs transported from Turkestan, and they listened to their *babas*, the preachers-sorcerers-judges who lived among them in their tribes. Certainly, in the rest of the Moslem world, the cultural cleavage between townsmen and beduins was hardly less; but at least the former wrote the same language the latter spoke, and prided themselves on being part of a common tradition. In Anatolia, on the contrary, there was no such contact. Even before the Mongol period the Turkomans did not have the beginnings of a Moslem Turkish literature which their Transoxian brothers could understand, and what literature did exist was written in a language they themselves did not comprehend. We need not dwell on the evident contrasts in social structure and manner of life; they are characteristic of that whole Moslem world where sedentary people and nomads live in proximity, the nomads hostile to the administrative procedures, conceptions of property, and taxes, to the blessings of which the settled population tries to introduce them. We shall see this gulf more clearly under the Mongol protectorate because, with the Selchükid aristocracy crushed, the Turkomans then developed quite differently. But the gulf existed before this, and had already manifested itself at the time of a grave crisis under Kai-Khusrau II.

It was at this very moment, in fact, that the links binding the Turkomans to the Selchükid state weakened and snapped. The Khorezmians and Mongols had driven into flight a great number of Turkomans who had been living in Central Asia or Iran, and who now flocked into Anatolia. Unable to adjust to Selchükid institutions, these newcomers reinforced the anti-Selchükid attitude of the Turkomans of Rūm. In addition, the settlement of these "displaced persons" posed difficult economic and social problems which were aggravated, in the eastern provinces, by the ravages of Khorezmians and Mongols. Partly perhaps to dam this movement from the east, the last Selchükids annexed the Armenian principalities. By doing so, however, they incorporated into their state more Turkomans than other Moslems. They spread them around as best they might, in part apparently to the newly conquered frontier provinces, but often this seems only to have extended the difficulties over a wider area. All we know for certain is that around 1239 all central Anatolia was caught up in a vast Turkoman revolt, led by one Baba Isḥāq, about whom we know very little. They resisted the entire army for two years, and Frankish mercenaries among others were needed to put an end to the revolt. But this was not merely an isolated episode. Obscure as the origins of the religious and political movements of the Turkomans during the Mongol period may be, there is no doubt that many of their founders had been connected in one way or other with the circles in which Baba Isḥāq had been nurtured, or with those which he had himself created. And this confers on him an importance certainly greater than one might think on first reading the few bald comments of the aristocratic chroniclers.

Unfortunately for the Selchükid state, at the very moment when, behind its imposing façade, it was thus weakened internally, the Mongol danger loomed in the east.[11] Their raiders had already penetrated Selchükid territory in the last days of the reign of Kai-Qobād I; internal difficulties of the Mongols gave Kai-Khusrau II a few years of respite. But in 1242 Erzerum succumbed, and in 1243 the great invasion was on. Taken up with his wars in Diyār-Bakr, Kai-Khusrau had made no provision for it. He hastily collected the largest force possible, comprising contingents of every origin including the Franks again, and met the Mongols at Köse Dagh on the traditional invasion route between Sebastia and Erzinjan. The morale of these troops was perhaps better than that of many others, who were beaten in advance by the reputation of the Mongols for an almost supernatural invincibility and the fact that they had never been defeated even by the greatest princes. On the morrow of the battle, however, nothing remained of the

[11] For the Mongols in Anatolia, see below, chapter XXI, pp. 725–732.

Selchükid army, and the Mongols gave themselves up to the pillage of Sebastia and Caesarea, while the panic-stricken Kai-Khusrau abandoned all his treasures and fled to Adalia and from there toward the Greek frontier. His vizir Muhadhdhib-ad-Dīn was made of sterner stuff, however, and went to the victorious Mongol general Baiju, and with him to the Mongol prince Batu Khan, whom Baiju served. From the prince he got a treaty of peace which allowed the Selchükid state to continue in exchange for a tribute and undoubtedly a promise of reinforcements whenever called for. And so Kai-Khusrau reëntered Iconium, and soon was even able to revenge himself on the Armenians, who had handed over to the conquerors his mother,[12] a refugee among them. In appearance things went on as usual, and one might speak of the date 1243 only as that of a lost battle. In reality, it sounded the knell of the Selchükid state. It marked the beginning of a long process of Mongol encroachment which gradually grew into direct administrative control. But even that remnant of the state which the Mongols were quite willing to let endure was internally so feeble that it disintegrated rapidly under the impact of forces which the Selchükids were too weak to contain, the Mongols too indifferent.

[12] Cf. above, chapter XVIII, pp. 652–653, where other sources indicate that Kai-Khusrau's wife and daughter, rather than his mother, were handed over to Baiju. On Māh-Perī Khātūn, mother of Kai-Khusrau, see *Encyclopaedia of Islām*, II, 639, citing her tomb at Caesarea, and Vincent of Beauvais's remark that she was a concubine.

XX
THE AIYŪBIDS

During his lifetime Saladin had already distributed the provinces incorporated in his empire to members of his own family, with virtually sovereign powers. Three of his sons held the chief governments in Egypt and Syria: al-Afḍal ʿAlī, the eldest, at Damascus, aẓ-Ẓāhir Ghāzī at Aleppo, and al-ʿAzīz ʿUthmān in Egypt.[1] The fourth major government, that of the Jazira with upper Mesopotamia and Diyār-Bakr (with its capital at Maiyafariqin) was held by his brother al-ʿĀdil Saif-ad-Dīn, whose son al-Muʿaẓẓam ʿĪsâ governed his second province of Kerak and Transjordan as al-ʿĀdil's deputy. Three lesser provinces in Syria were held by other relatives: Hamah by al-Manṣūr Muḥammad (son of Saladin's nephew Taqī-ad-Dīn), Homs by his cousin's son al-Mujāhid Shīrkūh II, and Baalbek by al-Amjad Bahrām-Shah (son of his nephew Farrūkh-Shāh).[2]

On Saladin's death (March 4, 1193) the unity imposed by his personality and authority was disrupted, and all the provinces (except that of Kerak) became in effect separate and independent principalities. The consequence was to endow Syria with a new kind of political structure. Outwardly it resembled in its fragmentation

No detailed study of the Aiyūbid period has yet been made, and many of the principal contemporary sources are still in manuscript, particularly the history of Ibn-Wāṣil of Hamah (partially reproduced in the chronicle of Abū-l-Fidā'), the chronicle of Sibṭ Ibn-al-Jauzī (facsimile ed., Chicago, 1907), and that of Kamāl-ad-Dīn ibn-al-ʿAdīm of Aleppo (tr. E. Blochet, Paris, 1900). Of less importance are the *Kāmil* of Ibn-al-Athīr (vol. XII, Leyden, 1853; portions ed. and tr. in *RHC, Or.*, II, 1; ends in 1231), the continuation of the *Rauḍatain* of Abū-Shāmah (Cairo, 1947; portions ed. and tr. in *RHC, Or.*, V), and other surviving minor chronicles. Some materials from sources no longer extant are found in later general chronicles, especially those of adh-Dhahabī and al-Maqrīzī. For general European works covering the period see the bibliography to chapter XV.

[1] All the Aiyūbid princes were designated by an attribute following the title *al-malik*, and by an honorific substantive compounded with "ad-Dīn", followed by the proper name. For brevity and consistency their names will be given as above (where al-Afḍal ʿAlī, for example, stands for *al-malik* al-Afḍal Nūr-ad-Dīn ʿAlī ibn-Yūsuf), except in the few cases where the compounded title is the more commonly used, as in the case of Saladin himself (an-Nāṣir Ṣalāḥ-ad-Dīn Yūsuf ibn-Aiyūb) and his brother al-ʿĀdil Saif-ad-Dīn (Abū-Bakr ibn-Aiyūb).

[2] The ninth Aiyūbid province in southern Arabia (Yemen) lasted only until 1229, generally under Egyptian suzerainty, but in 1232 another was set up at Ḥiṣn Kaifā in Mesopotamia, which lasted until the Ottoman conquest of Iraq under Sulaimān the Magnificent.

the pre-Selchükid period; and the superficial disturbances caused by rivalries within the Aiyūbid family, by the ambitions of some of its members, and by the struggles of the princes of Damascus and Aleppo to maintain their independence against their more powerful kinsmen in Egypt and Mesopotamia, give the history of the Aiyūbid period an appearance of anarchical disorder. But in reality it was closely knit together by a basic family solidarity, reinforced by intermarriages and by the moderating influence of a powerful religious bureaucracy, which carried on the traditions of Nūr-ad-Dīn and Saladin. The lesser princes, especially those of Hamah and Homs, played an important part in maintaining the balance between rival forces (primarily in order to preserve their own principalities from absorption); and even when the Aiyūbids themselves were crushed out of existence between the Mamluks and the Mongols, the structure which they created survived in the institutions of the Mamluk empire.

The stability of the Aiyūbid regime is shown further by the rapid growth of material prosperity in Syria and Egypt, and the remarkable expansion of literary, artistic, and intellectual culture. The former was due largely to the enlightened policy of the princes in promoting agricultural and economic development and their fostering of commercial relations with the Italian states. The corollary of this policy was the maintenance of peaceful relations, as far as possible, with the Frankish states in Syria, and there are few, if any, occasions during the whole period on which Aiyūbid princes took the offensive against the Franks.

A further stabilizing factor, at least in the long run, was the emergence in each generation of one leading member of the family, who succeeded in time in imposing his authority over all or most of the others, though at the cost of increasingly violent effort and opposition in successive generations. In the first generation the keystone of the whole Aiyūbid structure was Saladin's brother al-'Ādil Saif-ad-Dīn, who had been during Saladin's reign his chief counselor and, next to him, the strongest and most able personality in the family. Not only did he enjoy great prestige, as against the youth and inexperience of Saladin's sons, but, having at different times governed Egypt, Aleppo, and Kerak, he was familiar with the internal conditions of all the principalities. As prince of the Jazira, his immediate task after Saladin's death was to defeat the attempt of the Zengids 'Izz-ad-Dīn of Mosul and 'Imād-ad-Dīn of Sinjar to exploit the opportunity to recover their former possessions in Mesopotamia. With the aid of his nephews at Aleppo and

Damascus, he stabilized the situation in the eastern provinces, although the Zengids regained for a time their independence in their own territories.

During the next six years al-'Ādil extended and consolidated his power in Syria and Egypt. Averse to warfare, he used as his chief weapons diplomacy and intrigue, for the exercise of which the rivalries of Saladin's sons gave him ample scope. Al-Afḍal 'Alī at Damascus, as the eldest, was regarded as head of the Aiyūbid house, but his misgovernment and weakness turned Saladin's troops against him and led to an expedition against Damascus by al-'Azīz of Egypt in May 1194. Al-'Ādil joined the coalition of Syrian princes against al-'Azīz, and on his withdrawal remained with al-Afḍal in Damascus. A second attempt was made by al-'Azīz in 1195, this time in concert with aẓ-Ẓāhir of Aleppo; after breaking up the coalition by intrigue, al-'Ādil followed al-'Azīz to Egypt and stayed with him until the next year, when they combined to drive al-Afḍal out of Damascus (June 1196); al-'Ādil remained in Damascus as viceroy of al-'Azīz. When the war with the crusaders was renewed in 1197, therefore, he was able to take the field at once, to capture Jaffa (September 5), and to send troops to reinforce Egypt against an invasion. After the surrender of Beirut by its commander to the German crusaders and their investment of Toron at the end of November, he obtained reinforcements from Egypt and all the Syrian princes, forced the raising of the siege (February 2, 1198), and negotiated a fresh truce in June for five and a half years.[3] Then, leaving his son al-Mu'aẓẓam 'Īsâ as his deputy in Damascus, he returned to the Jazira to complete the restoration of Aiyūbid control in the east.

On the death of al-'Azīz (November 29, 1198), leaving only a minor son, al-Manṣūr Muḥammad, there was a split in the Aiyūbid forces. The Asadī regiment called in al-Afḍal as regent; the Ṣalāḥī emirs in the meantime summoned his uncle al-'Ādil from Mesopotamia, while al-Afḍal, at the instigation and with the support of his brother aẓ-Ẓāhir, marched on Damascus. Al-'Ādil had barely time to throw himself into the city before it was invested by al-Afḍal, and was besieged for six months until the arrival of his son al-Kāmil Muḥammad with the Mesopotamian troops; he then pursued al-Afḍal to Egypt, defeated him at Bilbais, and entered Cairo (February 6, 1200).

[3] A report of al-Maqrīzī states that in the same year the fortifications of Ascalon were razed by agreement between al-'Ādil and al-'Azīz. On this truce see above, chapter XV, pp. 530–531.

On August 4 al-'Ādil was formally proclaimed sultan of Egypt and Syria. All the territorial princes recognized him except aẓ-Ẓāhir of Aleppo, who now joined with al-Afḍal in a last attempt to assert the claims of the house of Saladin. In the spring of 1201, after seizing Manbij and Qal'at Najm, they made the mistake of attacking Hamah, but, failing to capture it, marched on Damascus in August, supported by the Ṣalāḥī troops in Palestine, who joined themselves to al-Afḍal in resentment at the deposition of young al-Manṣūr Muḥammad by al-'Ādil. Once more al-'Ādil succeeded by intrigue in breaking up the coalition, at the end of September, and, having regained the adherence of a section of the Ṣalāḥīyah, determined to pursue his advantage. At the invitation of al-Manṣur of Hamah he followed aẓ-Ẓāhir and threatened to besiege Aleppo until he agreed to recognize al-'Ādil as sultan (end of January 1202). In return aẓ-Ẓāhir was left in undisturbed possession of Aleppo, and al-Afḍal was given the minor fief of Samosata, where he died in 1225. Hamah and Homs were left to their own princes, and the other provinces were distributed to sons of al-'Ādil: Damascus to al-Mu'aẓẓam 'Īsâ, Egypt to al-Kāmil Muḥammad, the Jazira to al-Ashraf Mūsâ, Diyār-Bakr to al-Auḥad Aiyūb, and the fortress of Qal'at Ja'bar to al-Ḥāfiẓ Arslan.

Although a final rupture between Saladin's sons and al-'Ādil was thus averted, the continued distrust of aẓ-Ẓāhir was shown by his activity in fortification, notably the reconstruction of the walls and the powerful citadel of Aleppo, and of the frontier fortresses of Qal'at Najm on the Euphrates and Apamea on the Orontes. The principal theater of al-'Ādil's activities, on the other hand, was Mesopotamia, where his sons were in conflict not only with the Zengids but also (after al-Auḥad's occupation of Akhlat in 1207) with the Georgians. In 1209 he led the combined armies of the Aiyūbids in an attack on Sinjar; but the arrival of a coalition of the eastern princes and a direct order from the caliph to withdraw led him to make peace, the more readily as aẓ-Ẓāhir was being tempted to combine with the Zengids and to join them in substituting the suzerainty of the Selchükid sultan of Rūm for that of al-'Ādil. Before the latter's return to Syria, however, the Georgians were crushingly defeated (1210) by al-Auḥad, and compelled to sign an undertaking to maintain peace for thirty years. With this success the Aiyūbid supremacy in Mesopotamia was definitely assured, and on al-Auḥad's death shortly afterwards the whole province was placed under al-Ashraf.

All these preoccupations played a large part in determining the policy of the Aiyūbids towards the Franks. The reduction of the outlying Frankish possessions, especially in the south, had removed any real menace from their local forces; the only danger to be apprehended (and it remained vividly present to al-'Ādil, with his memories of the Third Crusade) was the possibility of fresh crusades from overseas. Like Saladin before him, al-'Ādil's chief concern was for Egypt (no doubt reinforced by the naval raids on Rosetta in 1204 and Damietta in 1211), and his Egyptian troops were for the most part retained on garrison duty in Egypt. His fear of stirring up new invasions, together with his habitual aversion to becoming involved in serious warfare, even led him to make concessions for the sake of peace, as in the retrocession of Jaffa and Nazareth in 1204. Like Saladin again, he favored the commercial interests of the Italian states, with the double object of increasing his own revenues and war potential, and discouraging them from supporting fresh crusades. Commercial treaties with Venice and Pisa are attested in 1207–1208, and when in 1212 the Frankish merchants at Alexandria were arrested as a precautionary measure their number is put at 3,000. The greater part of his reign was covered by a series of truces with the kingdom (1198–1204, 1204–1210, 1212–1217), during which the defenses of Jerusalem and Damascus were reorganized, notably by the construction of a new fortress at Mt. Tabor (aṭ-Ṭūr), begun in 1211. Most of the active fighting during this period was between the Hospitallers of Krak des Chevaliers or Bohemond IV of Antioch and Tripoli and the princes of Hamah and Homs, who could rely if necessary on the support of aẓ-Ẓāhir. Only once, in 1207, was al-'Ādil himself drawn into active intervention, when he captured al-Qulai'ah, besieged Krak des Chevaliers, and advanced up to the walls of Tripoli before making peace with Bohemond on payment of an indemnity.

Meanwhile aẓ-Ẓāhir at Aleppo also had his own reasons for maintaining peace with Antioch. Alarmed by the growing power of the Armenians of Cilicia, and always on the look-out for potential allies against his uncle, he had readily answered Bohemond of Tripoli's call for reinforcement against the Armenians in 1201; and again in 1203 and in 1205–1206 he was instrumental in defending Antioch against Leon II.[4] A combined invasion of Cilicia by Selchükid and Aleppine forces in 1209 compelled Leon to sue for terms, but the struggle in and for Antioch continued, and

[4] On this alliance, see above, chapter XV, pp. 533–537.

in 1211 pope Innocent III himself appealed to aẓ-Ẓāhir to support the Templars. Aẓ-Ẓāhir also was in treaty relations with the Venetians at Latakia, who were permitted to maintain a *fondaco* in Aleppo.

Al-'Ādil, however, had long disapproved of his nephew's alliance with Bohemond and had discouraged it by diplomatic means. In 1214 Bohemond, after the murder of his eldest son Raymond by Assassins in Tortosa, led a combined attack on the Ismā'īlite castle of al-Khawābī. The Assassins appealed to aẓ-Ẓāhir, who sent reinforcements and enlisted al-'Ādil's support for a diversionary raid in the south. This ended the alliance, and when Leon entered Antioch in February 1216 aẓ-Ẓāhir, anxious to secure the succession for his infant son by al-'Ādil's daughter Ḍaifah, was obliged to refuse the invitation of sultan Kai-Kā'ūs I to coöperate in an invasion of Cilicia. A few months later, on November 11, 1216, aẓ-Ẓāhir died, leaving the reputation of an energetic and capable, but harsh, sovereign.

A mass exodus of the merchants of Alexandria to Acre in 1216 gave the Moslem princes sufficient warning of the approaching crusade. Al-'Ādil remained on guard in Egypt until the crusaders mustered at Acre (1217) and began operations towards the east; even then he left the great bulk of his forces with al-Kāmil and moved up with a small contingent to support al-Mu'aẓẓam.[5] The troops at his disposal were too few to oppose the crusaders, and while they besieged Banyas and raided over the Jordan he guarded the approaches to Damascus, detached al-Mu'aẓẓam to Nablus to screen Jerusalem, and called for reinforcements from the northern princes.

After a brief respite during the winter (1217–1218), and as al-Ashraf was moving down to support the defense, the situation was suddenly transformed; the Aiyūbids found themselves engaged on three fronts simultaneously. On learning of the descent on Damietta al-'Ādil sent back the Egyptian troops under his command and instructed al-Mu'aẓẓam to destroy the fortress of Mt. Tabor, as it locked up too many men and military stores. Al-Ashraf was diverted to attack the northern territories of the Franks, and raided Chastel Blanc and Krak des Chevaliers. But in the meantime a party at Aleppo, opposed to the child prince al-'Azīz Muḥammad and his atabeg Shihāb-ad-Dīn Tughrul, seized the opportunity of al-'Ādil's difficulties to negotiate with al-Afḍal and the Selchükid sultan. Early in June Kai-Kā'ūs seized Raban and Tell Bashir and

[5] On the operations in Palestine in 1218 and 1219, see above, chapter XI, pp. 389–396.

marched on Aleppo; al-Ashraf hastened up to its defense and with the aid of Arab contingents defeated the sultan and his allies at Buzā'ah (early July) and regained the captured territories. From this time he was regarded as suzerain of Aleppo, but left its government in the loyal and capable hands of Tughrul and sent the rebellious emirs to join al-Kāmil's army in Egypt.

Al-Mu'aẓẓam at first remained on guard in Palestine, and gained a minor success towards the end of August at Caymont (Qaimūn) near Ramla. Immediately afterwards he was recalled to Damascus by the news of al-'Ādil's death there (August 31, 1218) and resumed its government, but loyally recognized his brother al-Kāmil as successor to the sultanate. As the situation in Syria was again stabilized, al-Kāmil, faced with a worsening position at Damietta, sent out fresh appeals for assistance and received reinforcements from Hamah and Homs. Before al-Mu'aẓẓam could arrive, however, al-Kāmil himself withdrew from Damietta in consequence of a plot to dethrone him, led by the son of Saladin's Kurdish emir al-Mashṭūb.[6] Al-Mu'aẓẓam's arrival in February 1219 was followed by the banishment of Ibn-al-Mashṭūb and the renewal of operations before Damietta, but al-Ashraf was engaged in Mesopotamia by conflicts at Mosul, followed by disturbances in northern Syria due to Ibn-al-Mashṭūb's intrigues with al-Afḍal. So few troops were now left in Syria that it was decided to dismantle Jerusalem and remove all military stores (March 1219), in case it should be attacked by the Franks.

The capture of Damietta in November 1219 seems to have led, curiously, to a relaxation of tension on the Moslem side. Al-Kāmil, it is true, disappointed by the rejection of his peace offers, called for a general levy of combatants "from Cairo to Aswan"; but a similar call by al-Mu'aẓẓam at Damascus met with no response, and al-Mu'aẓẓam himself returned to Syria, where during the next year (1220) he harassed the crusaders, capturing and destroying Caesarea and twice attacking Château Pèlerin (Athlith). Al-Ashraf was still detained in Mesopotamia by operations against the Artukids of Mardin and Amida and Ibn-al-Mashṭūb, who had rewarded the sultan's clemency in the previous year by allying himself with the princes of Mardin and Sinjar. After capturing Sinjar (July 1220), al-Ashraf marched to Mosul with the army of Aleppo and remained in its vicinity for several months, engaged in negotiations with the

[6] On the early stages of the crusade at Damietta, the death of al-'Ādil, and the plot against al-Kāmil, see above, chapter XI, pp. 397–408. That Ibn-al-Mashṭūb's punishment was banishment rather than death is typical of mild Aiyūbid justice.

Zengid princes and with Gökböri at Irbil. By the beginning of 1221 he felt so secure in his province that he yielded, though unwillingly, to the arguments of al-Mu'aẓẓam; leaving Akhlat and Diyār-Bakr under the government of his brother al-Muẓaffar Shihāb-ad-Dīn Ghāzī, he accompanied al-Mu'aẓẓam and the other Syrian princes to Egypt and rejoined al-Kāmil at Mansurah at the end of July.

In the interval, al-Kāmil, lacking effective support from his brothers and with an increasingly disaffected and war-weary army,[7] had continued to negotiate with the crusaders for the sake of peace. Even after the arrival of al-Mu'aẓẓam and al-Ashraf he was in no mood to become involved in heavy fighting, and in spite of their remonstrances and the hopeless position of the invading army willingly accepted the crusaders' offer of surrender rather than face the prospect of a prolonged siege to recover Damietta. At the end of August the terms of peace were duly signed for a period of eight years, with provision for a general release of prisoners, and Damietta was reoccupied on September 8, 1221.[8]

With the removal of the crusading threat the minor causes of friction between the Aiyūbids reasserted themselves. Al-Ashraf had remained in Egypt with al-Kāmil, and al-Mu'aẓẓam felt himself in danger of being squeezed between his more powerful brothers in Egypt and Mesopotamia. After a successful expedition in June 1222 to force Guy of Jubail to adhere to the peace, he made the false step of attempting to seize Hamah (January 1223) and of occupying Ma'arrat-an-Nu'mān and Salamyah. Forced to desist from the siege of Hamah and to surrender his conquests by order of al-Kāmil, he revenged himself by forming an alliance with Gökböri of Irbil (possibly with the connivance of the caliph an-Nāṣir) against al-Ashraf, and by encouraging Ghāzī to revolt at Akhlat. The rebellion was quickly put down by al-Ashraf with the assistance of Aleppine troops, and al-Mu'aẓẓam, after a demonstration at Homs, was again restrained from further operations by the threats of al-Kāmil (1224). In order to escape from this unwelcome control, he entered into communication with disaffected elements in the Egyptian army and paralyzed al-Kāmil by openly boasting of the success of his intrigues and challenging him to march into Syria if he dared. Against al-Ashraf he adopted the dangerous

[7] Al-Maqrīzī notes that at Mansurah more fighting with the crusaders was done by the "commons", i.e. the auxiliaries and volunteers, than by the regular troops (*Sulūk*, I, 206). On this phase of the crusade, see above, chapter XI, pp. 408–423.

[8] See above, chapter XI, pp. 423–428.

policy of inviting the Khorezm-Shāh Jalāl-ad-Dīn (whose ruffianly adventures with his Khorezmian bravoes are related in another chapter)[9] to seize Diyār-Bakr. In 1226 he again attacked Homs, while Gökböri moved on Mosul and the Artukids on the Jazira. Al-Ashraf parried the attack on Homs with the troops of Aleppo and appealed to the Selchükid sultan Kai-Qobād I for aid against the Artukids, but himself subsequently came into conflict with him. In desperation he made his submission to al-Mu'aẓẓam, but too late to prevent Jalāl-ad-Dīn from investing Akhlat, the garrison of which, however, not only held the city but retaliated by occupying Khoi and other places in Azerbaijan after the Khorezm-Shāh's withdrawal.

It was now al-Kāmil's turn to feel alarmed at the coalition between the Syrian princes (from which, however, Aleppo held aloof), especially when al-Mu'aẓẓam recognized the suzerainty of Jalāl-ad-Dīn. At the same time he was aware of the preparations of emperor Frederick II for a crusade. In the early months of 1227 the only avenue that seemed open to him was to renew to Frederick the offer, which he had already made to the crusaders at Damietta, to cede Jerusalem with part of Palestine. But in a few months the whole situation changed. In May al-Ashraf succeeded in escaping from his gilded captivity at Damascus, at the price of breaking his solemn engagements. As the princes of Homs and Hamah also turned against al-Mu'aẓẓam, he, finding himself isolated in opposition to the crusading armies now beginning to assemble at Acre, destroyed the fortifications of Jerusalem and other castles. But before Frederick's arrival, and to the deep distress of the troops and citizens of Damascus, he died on November 12, 1227, and was succeeded, with al-Kāmil's approval, by his son an-Nāṣir Dā'ūd.[10]

The restored concord between the princes did not last long. Dā'ūd began badly by refusing al-Kāmil's request for the cession of Krak de Montréal (ash-Shaubak), but the *casus belli* was supplied by a conflict over Baalbek, where al-Amjad was attacked by al-'Azīz 'Uthmān of Banyas. When Dā'ūd ordered al-'Azīz to desist, he appealed to al-Kāmil, who marched into Palestine in July 1228 and occupied Nablus and Jerusalem. Al-Ashraf, summoned by Dā'ūd, came down to Damascus from Mesopotamia; al-Kāmil fell back to Tall al-'Ajūl and was there joined by al-Ashraf. The conclusion of their conference was that al-Ashraf should take over the

[9] See above, chapter XIX, pp. 672–674.

[10] On the varying circumstances of al-Kāmil's negotiations with Frederick, see above, chapter XII, pp. 448–450.

government of Damascus, while al-Kāmil should occupy Palestine, and their nephew Dā'ūd be given the Jazira in compensation. When Dā'ūd refused these terms, al-Ashraf laid siege to Damascus towards the end of the year, with the support of the troops of Aleppo.

During all this time the Syrian princes seem to have paid little attention to the crusaders; except for a skirmish at Acre in February by the troops of al-'Azīz of Banyas, they did not interfere with the works of fortification on the coast, nor even when the Moslem population of Sidon was driven out. After Frederick's arrival al-Kāmil remained in Palestine to conduct negotiations over the fulfilment of his offer in the altered circumstances. Five months of hard bargaining resulted in the compromise treaty of February 18, 1229, which was received in most Moslem circles with violent indignation and certainly helped to stiffen the resistance to al-Ashraf at Damascus.[11] Nevertheless, the qadi of Hamah, in what may be a transcript of al-Kāmil's circular letter, applauds the statesmanship of the sultan in securing at such small cost the supreme boon of peace for the Moslems of Syria; he adds, as a summary of the terms, that the cession was limited to Jerusalem alone, "including neither much nor little of its territories and dependencies", and on the stipulations that Franks should not rebuild in it anything whatsoever, "neither wall nor dwellings", nor pass beyond its moat, that Friday prayer should be observed in it for the Moslem population, that no Moslem should be hindered from visiting it at any time, and that no money should be exacted from any visitor.[12] Certainly, after Frederick's visit to Jerusalem[13] and return to Acre in March, al-Kāmil was able, at al-Ashraf's request, to join in the siege of Damascus (April), and prosecuted it with such severity and destructiveness that Dā'ūd was forced to surrender the city on June 25 in return for the grant of Transjordan and eastern Palestine, including Nablus and the district of Jerusalem.

Al-Ashraf's occupation of Damascus was followed by a major redistribution of territory. He remained in possession of Akhlat and Diyār-Bakr and retained his suzerainty over Aleppo, but surrendered the Jazira to al-Kāmil, who also annexed western Palestine along with Tiberias. It is not quite clear what was the purpose of

[11] On this treaty, see above, chapter XII, pp. 452–458.

[12] Shihāb-ad-Dīn Ibn-abī-d-Damm, Bodl. MS. Marsh 60, ad annum 625. The clauses quoted by Gerald do not seem to be mentioned in any Arabic source.

[13] The original text of Sibṭ Ibn-al-Jauzī, in which the incidents of Frederick's visit are described, differs to some extent from the free adaptations derived from later sources in Michaud (*Bibliothèque*, IV, 431–432) and Grousset (*Histoire des croisades*, III, 316–317). Ibn-Wāṣil also gives a first-hand account of the visit.

this interweaving of the possessions of the two most powerful Aiyūbid princes. Most probably it was a device to reinsure each against the other, but in effect it gave al-Kāmil an indisputable supremacy—a supremacy further enhanced by his siege of Hamah in August 1229 and reinstatement of the lawful heir al-Muẓaffar Taqī-ad-Dīn II, whose place had been usurped by his younger brother an-Nāṣir Kilij Arslan during the Damietta campaign, under the protection of al-Ashraf. Then, while al-Ashraf was expending his forces on a lengthy siege of Baalbek, al-Kāmil occupied his new possessions in the Jazira. Simultaneously Jalāl-ad-Dīn attacked Akhlat again; the garrison, receiving no support from their own prince al-Ashraf and only belated and insufficient help from al-Kāmil, surrendered after a seven-months' siege (April 1230), and the entire population was massacred or carried off. At this juncture the Selchükid sultan Kai-Qobād offered an alliance to al-Kāmil against Jalāl-ad-Dīn; al-Ashraf, hurrying to the north, took command of the Aiyūbid armies and joined the sultan near Erzinjan. In a furious battle the Khorezmians were totally defeated (August 10); Jalāl-ad-Dīn fled to Tabriz and al-Ashraf reoccupied the ruins of Akhlat.[14]

The opportunity of al-Kāmil's absence in the north was seized by the military orders (who were not covered by the treaty) to make attacks on Ba'rīn (December 1229) and Hamah (July 5, 1230), which were repulsed by al-Muẓaffar. In the following year they raided Jabala, and there were counter-raids on al-Marqab and Valania from Aleppo (February 1231), until a truce was signed in June. On the other side, Arab tribesmen, stirred up by demagogic preachers, attacked pilgrims in Jerusalem and on the roads until they were brought under control. But on the whole public security was completely reëstablished, and in 1232 al-Kāmil and al-Ashraf were able to resume their campaign to strengthen Aiyūbid control in Mesopotamia and Diyār-Bakr, which were threatened by the Mongol armies in Persia and Transcaucasia. The Artukids were finally deprived of their strongholds of Amida and Ḥiṣn Kaifā, and the latter was bestowed on al-Kāmil's eldest son, aṣ-Ṣāliḥ Aiyūb.

Al-Kāmil was now at the height of his power, courted by the princes of Persia, and visited by ambassadors even from India and Spain. It would not be surprising if, as is sometimes suggested, his head was turned and his ambitions excited by this success. A crisis was not long in coming. The Selchükid sultanate also had reached an apogee of power under sultan Kai-Qobād, and now

[14] For the Khorezmians and Selchükids in 1230, see above, chapter XIX, pp. 673, 683.

shared a common frontier with the Aiyūbids. To find employment for the Khorezmian bands who had been driven by the Mongols, after the death of Jalāl-ad-Dīn, into Anatolia, Kai-Qobād seized Akhlat (1233). All the Aiyūbid princes rallied to al-Kāmil's summons in the summer of 1234, but against the Selchükid defenses their armies could not force a way through the Taurus passes. As he withdrew al-Kāmil sent a detachment to defend Kharput; it was routed and Kharput itself captured in August by the Selchükid forces. These reverses added fuel to the private resentments of the princes of Syria against al-Kāmil, and al-Muẓaffar of Hamah (who had been the chief sufferer from the failure at Kharput) took the lead in opening negotiations with Kai-Qobād. The intrigue was discovered by al-Kāmil, who returned to Egypt in anger, and the armies broke up. Without resistance Kai-Qobād overran the whole of al-Kāmil's province of the Jazira and carried off its population. In the next year, however, al-Kāmil made his peace with the Syrians; in concert with al-Ashraf he reoccupied the Jazira in January and February 1236, sent 3,000 Selchükid prisoners to Egypt, and invested aṣ-Ṣāliḥ Aiyūb with the government of all his eastern possessions. After his withdrawal the Selchükids again attacked Amida and destroyed Dara (August), probably in retaliation for the destruction of several fortresses belonging to Mardin, the only remaining Artukid principality in Diyār-Bakr.

On November 26 al-'Azīz Muḥammad of Aleppo died, leaving a seven-year-old son, with the name and honorific epithets of his great-grandfather Saladin, an-Nāṣir Ṣalāḥ-ad-Dīn Yūsuf, under the regency of his grandmother Ḍaifah, the sister of al-Kāmil. Suspecting, rightly or wrongly, that al-Kāmil had designs upon Aleppo, she formed an alliance with al-Ashraf, who for his part was dissatisfied with the division of the Artukid territories. Al-Kāmil riposted by inviting an-Nāṣir Dā'ūd from Kerak to Egypt and investing him with the government of Damascus. As on the previous occasion, the Syrian confederates sought the support of the Selchükid sultan Kai-Qobād, and on his death (May 31, 1237) that of his successor Kai-Khusrau II, against the intervention of al-Kāmil, to whom they addressed a warning not to move into Syria. Only three months later (August 28), however, al-Ashraf died, leaving the government of Damascus to his brother aṣ-Ṣāliḥ Ismā'īl. The Syrian confederacy was weakened by the defection of al-Muẓaffar of Hamah to the side of al-Kāmil, who laid siege to Damascus in November and pressed the attack until Ismā'īl surrendered on December 29 and was transferred to Baalbek. The troops of his Syrian allies were allowed to withdraw unmolested, but al-Muẓaffar was dispatched to exact retribution from Homs, while al-Kāmil prepared to march on Aleppo. Its governors made all preparations for the expected siege and had enrolled Turkoman and Selchükid troops for the defense of the city, when al-Kāmil himself died at Damascus on March 9, 1238.

The character of al-Kāmil is one of the most complex problems of Aiyūbid history. Even Sibṭ Ibn-al-Jauzī, who preached the sermon against him at Damascus when news arrived of his treaty with Frederick, speaks of him in admiring terms as brave and sagacious, a lover of learning, and just and generous in the highest measure. He imposed such respect and awe as no Aiyūbid before him, and such discipline that on his expeditions none of his soldiers, it was said, dared take a blade of straw from a peasant. Loyal to his own word, he exacted from his kinsmen the loyalty due him as sultan; in warfare he was always victorious in the end, but he detested war and intrigue, and preferred to gain his objects by negotiation. He was remarkably matched with Frederick in some respects, especially, perhaps, in his aloofness from the passions of his age and his cold superiority to his contemporaries. It was not only for his outrage to public opinion by the cession of Jerusalem, but rather by contrast with the open and warmly human character of his brother al-Mu'aẓẓam, that he was regarded without affection by his subjects and never sure of the loyalty of his troops. Four years before his death he had even had to remove his eldest son and heir, aṣ-Ṣāliḥ Aiyūb, from Egypt on suspicion of enrolling mamluks to revolt against him, but characteristically reconciled him by giving him a new and open field for his talents in Mesopotamia.

The removal of al-Kāmil's controlling personality at once threw the Aiyūbid princes into violent and confused rivalries. His son al-'Ādil Abū-Bakr II, whom he had appointed as his successor in place of aṣ-Ṣāliḥ Aiyūb, was recognized as sultan by the Egyptian officers, who also nominated al-Jauwād Yūnus (a grandson of al-'Ādil I and the husband of al-Ashraf's only daughter) as prince of Damascus, and drove an-Nāṣir Dā'ūd back to Kerak. The army of Aleppo turned from the defensive to the offensive, seized Ma'arrat-an-Nu'mān, and besieged Hamah, while its governors renewed the alliance with sultan Kai-Khusrau II and rejected the overtures successively of aṣ-Ṣāliḥ Aiyūb, al-'Ādil II, and al-Jauwād. Aṣ-Ṣāliḥ Aiyūb was in difficulties with the Khorezmians, who had left the service of Kai-Khusrau and joined Artuk Arslan of Mardin; he fled to Sinjar, but when Badr-ad-Dīn Lu'lu' of Mosul besieged him there he dispatched the qadi of Sinjar in disguise to appeal to the Khorezmians to take his part. They marched on Sinjar, defeated the forces of Mosul, then drove out a Selchükid army which had laid siege to Amida, and captured the fortress of Nisibin and the Khabur province for aṣ-Ṣāliḥ Aiyūb; in return he made over to them the province of Diyār-Muḍar (the western Jazira).

Towards the end of the year 1238 al-Jauwād, fearing an Egyptian invasion in concert with an-Nāṣir Dā'ūd, invited Aiyūb to take possession of Damascus in return for certain districts in Mesopotamia. But already Aiyūb had acquired a reputation which gave alarm to the neighbors of Damascus. Consequently, when, after establishing himself in Damascus, he advanced into Palestine to organize an invasion of Egypt, his uncle aṣ-Ṣāliḥ Ismā'īl reappeared from Baalbek, accompanied by al-Mujāhid of Homs, and seized Damascus from Aiyūb's son al-Mughīth 'Umar (September 30, 1239). Aiyūb, deserted by all his troops except eighty mamluks, was captured at Nablus by an-Nāṣir Dā'ūd and imprisoned in Kerak.

At this juncture the treaty negotiated with Frederick for a period of ten years, five months, and forty days from February 18, 1229, expired, and crusading activities were resumed under Theobald of Champagne.[15] In October al-'Ādil II sent a force into Palestine which inflicted such severe losses near Ascalon on the crusaders (November 13) that they abandoned their project of refortifying it. In the same month, after the Franks had begun to rebuild the defenses of Jerusalem, an-Nāṣir Dā'ūd laid siege to it, and in the middle of December succeeded in storming the Tower of David and reoccupying the city. In spite of these local successes, however, the Aiyūbid princes and principalities were in no trim to engage in any serious operations. In Egypt especially, under the young sultan al-'Ādil II, things were going from bad to worse. By reckless extravagance he dissipated the considerable reserves (estimated at six million dinars and twenty million dirhems) left by al-Kāmil, and between the Kurds and the Turks in the Egyptian army there was open hostility. The mamluks were aggrieved and mutinous, and the contempt of the troops for al-'Ādil went so far that when his black ewer-bearer on one occasion gleefully showed the patent which he had just received for a military fief to the emir Rukn-ad-Dīn al-Hījāwī (the general who had defeated the crusaders at Ascalon), the emir slapped his face and took the patent out of his hands.

[15] See above, chapter XIII.

The initiative in injecting some new vigor and purpose into the Aiyūbid system was taken by al-Muẓaffar Taqī-ad-Dīn II of Hamah. Faithful to the policy of alliance with Egypt against the now traditional confederacy of Damascus, Homs, and Aleppo, it was for him a matter of the first importance to have a strong sultan installed in Egypt, and all his hopes were centered on aṣ-Ṣāliḥ Aiyūb. His appeals to an-Nāṣir Dā'ūd were successful; on April 11, 1240, Dā'ūd released Aiyūb on a sworn agreement that in return for Dā'ūd's assistance in establishing him in Egypt he would make over Damascus and Mesopotamia to Dā'ūd. At the same time messages were sent to the Khorezmians, urging them to attack Aleppo and Homs. Fortune, hitherto so perverse towards Aiyūb, now suddenly smiled; as al-'Ādil prepared to march into Palestine to meet Dā'ūd and Aiyūb, he was arrested at Bilbais by his Turkish troops on May 4, and an urgent call was sent to Aiyūb. On May 18 he entered Cairo and was saluted as sultan.

Aṣ-Ṣāliḥ Aiyūb's success in Egypt was profoundly alarming to his uncle aṣ-Ṣāliḥ Ismā'īl at Damascus, who feared, not without reason (although Aiyūb had already quarreled with Dā'ūd), that he was determined to oust him also. As the Khorezmians were already operating on the frontiers of Aleppo, he could hope for little support in that quarter. He turned accordingly to the crusaders, and in return for the surrender of Safad, Belfort, the rest of Sidon, and Tiberias, Theobald and the Templars agreed to a defensive alliance against Egypt; the joint armies assembled at Jaffa. Ismā'īl even allowed the crusaders to enter Damascus to purchase arms, an action which gave great offense to its Moslem population.

Aṣ-Ṣāliḥ Aiyūb, however, was fully occupied in reorganizing his kingdom and his army. His experience with the Kurds, who had deserted him in Palestine in the previous year, and the indiscipline and disloyalty of the Aiyūbid regiments in Egypt towards his father and his brother, had convinced him that no reliance could be placed upon them. After dealing vigorously with the disorders of the Arabs in upper Egypt and restoring financial stability, he set himself systematically to create a new regiment of picked Turkish mamluks, to appoint them to fiefs and offices in place of the emirs of the Kāmilī and Ashrafī regiments, and to construct a new citadel and barracks for them on the island of Roda, close to Cairo. So far from concerning himself over events in Syria,[16] such of his attention

[16] On the supposed battle between the Egyptians and the crusaders and forces of Damascus in the summer of 1240 see Stevenson's note in *The Crusaders in the East*, p. 321, n. 1.

as aṣ-Ṣāliḥ Aiyūb gave to foreign affairs was directed to sending a mamluk force to drive the Yemenites out of Mecca and to preparing a fleet at Suez for an expedition to Yemen. The negotiations opened by Richard of Cornwall in December 1240 doubtless removed any fears he may have entertained, and his delay in agreeing to recognize the crusaders' occupation of Ascalon and to release the prisoners held in Egypt was perhaps due to the employment of the prisoners on his military works.

During these negotiations aṣ-Ṣāliḥ Aiyūb's northern allies, the Khorezmians, attacked the territories of Aleppo, severely defeated the army of Aleppo (commanded by Saladin's son al-Mu'aẓẓam Tūrān-Shāh) at Buzā'ah on November 11, 1240, plundered the countryside of Aleppo, and captured Manbij. The new prince of Homs, al-Manṣūr Ibrāhīm, whose father al-Mujāhid had just died, moved up to support his kinsmen, and additional troops were sent from Damascus.[17] When the Khorezmians made a second plundering raid in January, in the course of which they devastated the regions of Sarmīn and Shaizar, the allied forces pursued them across the Euphrates and defeated them near Edessa on March 6, 1241. The cities of the Jazira were divided between the victors and Badr-ad-Dīn Lu'lu' of Mosul; the army of Aleppo then combined with a Selchükid force against aṣ-Ṣāliḥ Aiyūb's son and deputy Tūrān-Shāh, who was compelled to surrender Amida to the Selchükid sultan Kai-Khusrau II. A few months later the Khorezmians, after refitting at Ana, allied themselves with al-Muẓaffar Ghāzī of Maiyafariqin and attacked Amida (August 1241); after an indecisive campaign of Aleppine and Selchükid troops in the autumn, al-Manṣūr of Homs again came to the rescue in the following spring, and defeated them even more signally near al-Majdal on the Khabur on August 22, 1242. But their depredations in the Jazira continued until in the spring of 1243 the Selchükid sultan, threatened by a Mongol invasion of Anatolia, hastily concluded an agreement by which the Khorezmians were given Kharput, and Akhlat was assigned to al-Muẓaffar Ghāzī. With the crushing defeat of Kai-Khusrau by the Mongols on July 2,[18] however, the situation in the north was entirely transformed; the Mongols occupied both Amida and Akhlat and seriously threatened the whole of Mesopotamia.

[17] The historian of Aleppo, Kamāl-ad-Dīn, links up the agreement with Damascus with the release of the Templars imprisoned at Aleppo, though not directly: *Zubdat al-ḥalab* (tr. Blochet), p. 213.

[18] *Ibid.*, p. 226; Ibn-Bībī gives June 26. On the battle of Köse Dagh and its consequences, see above, chapter XIX, pp 691–692, and below, chapter XXI, pp. 725–732.

The struggle in the north had its repercussions also in the south. Ismā'īl of Damascus, deprived of the support of Homs, remained inactive, and operations were reduced to mere skirmishing. An Egyptian expedition from Gaza was met and defeated near Jerusalem by Dā'ūd of Kerak and the Templars in May 1242; a few months later, however, after a raid by the crusaders on Nablus (October 31), Dā'ūd joined with the troops of Gaza in retaliatory raids on their territories. The victory of the Mongols momentarily shocked the Aiyūbids into an attempt to compose their rivalries, but negotiations fell through owing to aṣ-Ṣāliḥ Ismā'īl's suspicions of Aiyūb. He renewed instead the alliance with the Franks and in the spring of 1244 gave them full possession of Jerusalem, in agreement with Dā'ūd of Kerak and al-Manṣūr of Homs. What had been outrageous perfidy in al-Kāmil fifteen years before was now taken for granted, even to the extent of surrendering the Dome of the Rock.

Aṣ-Ṣāliḥ Ismā'īl's suspicions were well-founded. In June 1243 al-Muẓaffar of Hamah, almost certainly acting in concert with aṣ-Ṣāliḥ Aiyūb, had dispatched an embassy to the eastern princes and Baghdad, with instructions to its leader to contact the Khorezmians on his way, and to invite their chief Berke Khan to support Aiyūb against his Syrian enemies. In the summer of 1244 over 10,000 of them swept down through the Biqā', captured Jerusalem after a short siege (August 23), occupied Palestine, and joined the Egyptian troops at Gaza. Al-Manṣūr of Homs again took the lead in organizing a coalition of Syrian Moslems and Franks against them, and the combined armies of Homs, Damascus, Kerak, and Acre advanced to Gaza. The Khorezmians and the Egyptians under the emir Rukn-ad-Dīn Baybars[19] broke through the Moslem troops on the left and center; the Khorezmians then surrounded the Franks, and only some fifty of the Templars and Hospitallers escaped (October 17).[20]

Baybars at once led his contingent to besiege Ascalon, while Palestine was taken over by aṣ-Ṣāliḥ Aiyūb's governors. Shortly afterwards Aiyūb's son al-Mughīth, who had been held in Damascus ever since 1239, died in prison; Aiyūb, in violent anger, reinforced his troops and directed them, along with the Khorezmians,

[19] This Baybars is not to be confused with the Mamluk sultan of the same name and honorific; after his treacherous alliance with the Khorezmians a few months later he was seized and died in prison. The future sultan entered the service of aṣ-Ṣāliḥ Aiyūb only in 1247, when his master al-Bunduqdār was exiled and al-Bunduqdār's mamluks were enrolled in Aiyūb's guard (adh-Dhahabī, ad annum 645) — hence his epithet Bunduqdārī.

[20] On the battle of Ḥarbīyah, see above, chapter XVI, pp. 562–564.

to march on Damascus. After a bitter siege, which lasted the whole of the following summer, Ismā'īl and al-Manṣūr surrendered on terms (October 2, 1245), Ismā'īl being assigned Baalbek and Bosra, to Aiyūb's intense displeasure. Damascus was occupied by the Egyptian commander Mu'īn-ad-Dīn ibn-ash-Shaikh, whose first action was to bar the Khorezmians from entering the city, in order to save it from their violence, and to assign western Palestine to them. The Khorezmians, balked of their anticipated booty, mutinied and, after sacking part of the Ghūṭah, won over the Egyptian commander at Gaza, Rukn-ad-Dīn Baybars, allied themselves with Dā'ūd of Kerak (who in consequence regained Jerusalem, Nablus, and Hebron), took service under aṣ-Ṣāliḥ Ismā'īl, and besieged their former associates in Damascus on his behalf.

But the prospect of a Khorezmian sack of Damascus was too much for al-Manṣūr of Homs. Breaking with Ismā'īl, he allied himself with Aleppo and prepared to coöperate with the Egyptians in raising the siege. Before they could unite, the Khorezmians, who had besieged the city for three months, withdrew to deal with al-Manṣūr, plundering and destroying as they went. Outside Homs they were met by the troops of Homs and Aleppo, reinforced by squadrons of Arabs and Turkomans, and totally defeated (May 19 or 26, 1246). This was the end of them as a fighting force; the remnants dispersed to find what service they could. Aṣ-Ṣāliḥ Ismā'īl fled to Aleppo, leaving Baalbek to be occupied by the governor of Damascus, and his sons to captivity in Egypt, but an-Nāṣir Yūsuf refused Aiyūb's demand that he should surrender Ismā'īl to him. Dā'ūd of Kerak was met and defeated by an Egyptian force at as-Salṭ on September 11 and besieged in Kerak, which he was at length allowed to keep at the price of surrendering all his other territories and the Khorezmians who had joined him. In March 1247 aṣ-Ṣāliḥ Aiyūb began a progress round his Syrian dominions, making benefactions to schools, religious establishments, and notables, while his troops under Fakhr-ad-Dīn ibn-ash-Shaikh captured Tiberias in June after a spirited defense, and went on to besiege, capture, and dismantle the newly-rebuilt castle of Ascalon (October 24).

A month after his victory over the Khorezmians al-Manṣūr of Homs had died of consumption, and his young son al-Ashraf Mūsâ II was completely dominated by Aiyūb. The reduction of Homs to vassal status and the virtual elimination of Kerak gravely altered the balance of forces in Syria to the disadvantage of the young and ambitious an-Nāṣir Yūsuf of Aleppo. In 1247 the fourteen-year-old prince of Hamah, al-Manṣūr Muḥammad (who had succeeded on al-Muẓaffar's death in October 1243), was drawn into the orbit of Aleppo by a marriage with his cousin, Yūsuf's sister 'Ā'ishah. In the next year, when aṣ-Ṣāliḥ Aiyūb, already suffering from his fatal disease, had returned to Egypt, an-Nāṣir Yūsuf formed an alliance with Badr-ad-Dīn Lu'lu' of Mosul and laid siege to Homs. Since the promised Egyptian reinforcements were delayed, al-Ashraf Mūsâ was compelled to surrender Homs and to accept instead Tell Bashir as Yūsuf's vassal. In spite of his severe illness, Aiyūb marched to Damascus and laid siege to Homs in midwinter, but the state of his health and the reports of the massing of the crusaders in Cyprus induced him to accept the intercession of an envoy from the caliph al-Musta'ṣim and come to terms with Yūsuf. On April 19, 1249, he was carried back to Egypt, and at once gave orders to furnish Damietta with stores of weapons and provisions and to fit out a river fleet at Cairo.[21]

The unexpected and unexplained retreat from Damietta of the Egyptian commander Fakhr-ad-Dīn ibn-ash-Shaikh on the day after the arrival of the crusading fleet, and the consequent evacuation of the city, left aṣ-Ṣāliḥ Aiyūb with no option but to concentrate his forces at the fortified camp of Mansurah. During the long pause that followed, his Damascus troops besieged and captured Sidon (July–August), and Dā'ūd went to join an-Nāṣir Yūsuf at Aleppo, leaving Kerak to be fought over by his sons and eventually occupied by an Egyptian governor. Aiyūb's death on November 22 did not affect the immediate situation, thanks to the efficient fighting machine that he had created and the strong personality of his concubine Shajar-ad-Durr, who concealed his death and controlled the administration in his name. In concert with the Baḥrī mamluks, she summoned his son Tūrān-Shāh from Ḥiṣn Kaifā, but he did not arrive until the end of February.

In the meantime the strenuous campaign at Mansurah, in which the regular troops were supported by bands of Egyptian volunteers, stirred up to enthusiasm by the preaching of the Moroccan shaikh Aḥmad al-Badawī, had produced a significant realignment of forces in the Egyptian army. During the battle on February 8, 1250, when the crusaders crossed by a ford and attacked the Egyptian camp, the death of Fakhr-ad-Dīn was followed by a panic among his troops, but the position was restored by a vigorous counterattack of the Baḥrī mamluks, led by Rukn-ad-Dīn Baybars Bunduqdārī. From this moment the Baḥrīyah were in the saddle, and it was they who

[21] On the crusade of Louis IX, see above, chapter XIV, pp. 494–504.

reaped the greatest credit from the destruction of the crusading army at Fāriskūr on April 6. They were in no mood, consequently, to submit to Tūrān-Shāh's attempts to replace them in the offices of state by his own Mesopotamians. Tempers rose on both sides, and when Tūrān-Shāh sent a threatening message to Shajar-ad-Durr it was the last straw. Believing themselves marked down for removal, the mamluk officers, led by Baybars, attacked and killed Tūrān-Shāh on Monday, May 2, and proclaimed Shajar-ad-Durr sultanah of Egypt and queen of the Moslems. The negotiations with Louis IX were brought to a conclusion by Aiyūb's former deputy, al-Hudhbānī, and Damietta was reoccupied on May 6.[22]

The theatrical manner in which the Aiyūbid dynasty of Egypt was terminated tends to conceal the evolution which reached its climax with the murder of Tūrān-Shāh. In effect, aṣ-Ṣāliḥ Aiyūb had already broken with the principles of the Aiyūbid regime. Lacking the personal qualities upon which the authority of his predecessors had rested, and which had maintained the solidarity of the Aiyūbid house, he attempted to supply the deficiency by building up a military machine (which he controlled with merciless severity) to impose his will. The other Aiyūbid princes he treated not as kinsmen but as enemies (with the exception, perhaps, of al-Muẓaffar of Hamah), and thus inaugurated a personal regime not unlike that of the Mamluk sultans who followed him. The officers and troops of his new mamluk corps had no sense of loyalty to the Aiyūbid house, but only to their own leaders; and as soon as their position was challenged they asserted themselves and disposed of the royal power in their own interests.

It was not to be expected that the Aiyūbids of Syria or their Kurdish supporters would tamely accept the extinction of their Egyptian branch at the dictation of the Turkish mamluks. The governor of Kerak set up al-Mughīth 'Umar, a son of al-'Ādil II, as sultan in Transjordan, while the Kurdish troops at Damascus invited an-Nāṣir Yūsuf of Aleppo to take over the city, admitting him into it on July 11. On July 30 Shajar-ad-Durr married the Turkoman generalissimo Aybeg and abdicated in his favor. He was at once recognized as sultan by the troops, with the honorific of al-Mu'izz, but in view of the reactions in Syria the emirs decided to associate an Aiyūbid prince with him and selected for the purpose a grandson of al-Kāmil, al-Ashraf Mūsâ III, then six

[22] On this settlement, see above, chapter XIV, pp. 503–504; on the Mamluk sultans, see below, chapter XXII.

years of age. A short time later he was quietly dropped again and disappeared.

The first movement of an-Nāṣir Yūsuf's forces from Damascus to Gaza was countered by the Baḥrīyah in October. He then formed a coalition of all the Syrian Aiyūbids and again set out for Egypt in December. It is admitted that the sympathies both of the population and of most of the army were on his side; but on February 2, 1251, after a confused fight on the Egyptian border, he was put to flight by the mamluks. In the rout of the Syrian army many of the Aiyūbid princes were captured, among them aṣ-Ṣāliḥ Ismā'īl, who was executed by order of Aybeg, and the veteran Tūrān-Shāh, son of Saladin, who was honorably set free, together with the other Aiyūbids. The Egyptian forces then moved up into Palestine, but withdrew again as an-Nāṣir Yūsuf marched on Gaza for the third time and occupied Darum, apparently before the end of the same year. From the western sources it appears that this third expedition was aimed not at an invasion of Egypt, but at preventing the junction of the Egyptian army with Louis IX, who, having received satisfaction from Aybeg of his demand for the release of all Christian prisoners, had rejected an-Nāṣir's offer to cede Jerusalem in return for an alliance. The Arabic sources scarcely mention the activities of Louis in Palestine during these years.[23] For more than a year the Egyptian and Syrian armies lay opposite one another while negotiations were proceeding; finally, about the end of March 1253, an-Nāṣir conceded Jerusalem to Aybeg,[24] and made peace. Except for the harassing actions of the Syrian forces on their way back to Damascus, Louis was left to pursue his work of fortification undisturbed, and before returning to France signed a peace with Damascus for ten years, six months, and forty days.

In 1255 the violence and indiscipline of the Baḥrī mamluks in Egypt led to an open breach with Aybeg. After his execution of their commander the majority of the Baḥrīyah fled to Damascus, where an-Nāṣir Yūsuf welcomed them as allies against Egypt. During the renewed tension John of Ibelin engaged the Egyptians at Gaza in skirmishes and border raids, but when Aybeg restored peace with an-Nāṣir in 1256 by surrendering Palestine to him, the ten-year treaty with the Franks was renewed and extended to include Egypt also.

For nearly four years more the house of Saladin, in the person

[23] See above, chapter XIV, pp. 504–508.

[24] Adh-Dhahabī (ad annum 650) states definitely that Nablus and its regions were to remain under an-Nāṣir, but cf. below, chapter XXII, pp. 742–743.

of his great-grandson an-Nāṣir Yūsuf, was supreme in Syria, although involved from time to time with al-Mughīth of Kerak, chiefly owing to the capricious transfer of their services from one prince to another by the Baḥrī mamluks. Summoned to present his homage to the Mongol Hulagu after the capture of Baghdad in 1258, an-Nāṣir sent his son al-'Azīz Muḥammad in his place, but when Hulagu opened his western campaign in 1259 an-Nāṣir left Aleppo to be defended by Tūrān-Shāh and took up a position outside Damascus, with al-Manṣūr II of Hamah, at the same time sending an envoy to the new Mamluk sultan Kutuz to beg for help. After the Mongol sack of Aleppo in January 1260 al-Manṣūr withdrew with the Syrian troops and the Baḥrīyah to join the army of Kutuz. Damascus was occupied on March 1, and Banyas, 'Ajlūn, Nablus, and other fortresses fell in their turn; an-Nāṣir, who had fled to Transjordan, was seized and surrendered to the Mongol general Kitbogha by his own Kurdish attendants.[25] In August Kutuz marched into Syria, accompanied by al-Manṣūr, who distinguished himself in the decisive battle at 'Ain Jālūt (September 3) and was restored to his principality of Hamah. Al-Ashraf Mūsâ II of Homs, though he had at first joined Hulagu, was also restored to Homs, but Aleppo was placed under non-Aiyūbid government.

A year later a second Mongol army was dispatched from Mesopotamia into Syria and recaptured Aleppo (November 1261). Al-Manṣūr fell back to Homs and there joined forces with al-Ashraf. In a battle outside Homs the two Aiyūbid princes defeated the Mongol forces (December 10) and drove them back beyond the Euphrates. With this not inglorious exploit the active history of the Aiyūbids in Syria comes to an end. In 1263 the Mamluk sultan Baybars perfidiously killed al-Mughīth and seized Kerak, and on the death of al-Ashraf Mūsâ in the same year the principality of Homs was suppressed. Al-Manṣūr alone, in consideration of his loyalty and his services, was allowed to retain his principality at Hamah, where, with one short interruption, the house of Taqī-ad-Dīn survived until 1341.

[25] He was executed by Hulagu on receiving the news of the defeat of the Mongol army at 'Ain Jālūt.

XXI
THE MONGOLS AND THE NEAR EAST

The Mongol empire, the most extensive known to history, stretched from Korea to Poland, and from Tonkin to the Mediterranean. Its birth, like that of so many empires of nomadic origin, had all the earmarks of the miraculous, but while others vanished as quickly as they appeared, leaving few traces worth noting, the Mongol empire lasted no little while and placed its stamp on many generations to come. Needless to say, its formation marked a critical moment in the history of the crusades and of the relations between east and west. Although we cannot trace the history of the Mongol empire here, even in general, we can sketch those of its features of greatest importance for the subjects dealt with in these volumes.

Before the thirteenth century, the Mongols were hardly known except to their immediate neighbors in China and Central Asia, and to a few merchants and missionaries, Moslem or Nestorian.

For Anatolia, see the bibliography given above for the Selchükids of Rūm, chapter XIX, p. 675. Up-to-date references are furnished in the Turkish *İslâm ansiklopedisi* and, to the extent that it has appeared, the new edition of the *Encyclopaedia of Islam*. There exist only special studies, often in Turkish; one may find, however, some important general observations, not always in agreement, in F. Köprülü, *Les Origines de l'empire ottoman* (Paris, 1937), and P. Wittek, *The Rise of the Ottoman Empire* (London, 1938). As for the sources, one may read the English translation of Bar Hebraeus by Sir Ernest A. Wallis Budge, *The Chronography of Gregory Abû'l Faraj, the Son of Aaron, the Hebrew Physician, commonly known as Bar Hebraeus* (2 vols., London, 1932); the French translation by C. Defrémery and B. R. Sanguinetti (4 vols., Paris, 1853–1858, reprinted 1879–1914, 1954) of the *Voyages* of Ibn-Baṭṭūṭah, now being translated into English by H. A. R. Gibb, *The Travels of Ibn Baṭṭūṭa, A.D. 1325–1354*, I, Works Issued by the Hakluyt Society, 2nd series, CX (Cambridge, 1958); and for a translation of Ibn-Bībī's chronicle, see H. W. Duda, *Die Seltschukengeschichte des Ibn Bibi* (Copenhagen, 1959). The works of W. Barthold, *Histoire des Turcs de l'Asie centrale* (Paris, 1946), and *Turkestan down to the Mongol Invasion* (London, 1928), remain indispensable, as do his numerous articles in Russian.

For the Īl-khanid state, one need only refer to Bertold Spuler, *Die Mongolen in Iran* (2nd ed., Berlin, 1955), where there may be found all the bibliographical references necessary; to which add, for the Mongol thrust toward western Asia, R. Grousset's and S. Runciman's histories of the crusades, and C. Cahen's *La Syrie du nord*. One of the principal sources, part I of the *Ta'rīkh-i-Jahān-Gushâ* of Juvainī, has been translated into English by J. A. Boyle (Cambridge, 1957). See also D. Sinor, "Les Relations entre les Mongols et l'Europe jusqu'à la mort d'Arghun," in *Cahiers d'histoire mondiale*, III (1956), 39–62.

Their social ideas and way of life differed little from those of the Turkish nomads to the west of them. Their religion consisted merely of a few vague notions and animistic practices directed by magic-working wise men or shamans, and left them highly susceptible to foreign beliefs. There was nothing readily apparent to mark out one of their tribal chieftains, Temüjin, for a noteworthy role in history, but he succeeded, after about twenty years of petty warfare and intrigue, in uniting a certain number of tribes which were attracted by his success and the lure of booty and new pasturages. To this nucleus, he rapidly added neighboring peoples who had been a part of former Turkish or Turco-Mongol (Kitai) kingdoms. The influence of the traditions of these peoples, as well as his own victories, bred in him an ambition for conquest which, as always with nomads, scorned political frontiers. In 1206 he took the title of Genghis Khan (Chinggis Khan or Qan), the Universal Emperor. Then his followers set out to conquer the world.

The swift mobility and apparent invincibility of these men from an unknown land, who overthrew one "eternal" empire after another, filled their victims with a terror which was in itself one of the principal factors in their victories. Genghis Khan, like other leaders of anarchic nomads in the first flush of victorious conquest, succeeded in imposing discipline on his men, and a respect for the law formulated in the *yasak*. The army had a simple organization in groups of tens, hundreds, and thousands. Its extreme mobility usually allowed it to launch an attack before the enemy could have adequate warning. Furthermore, the Mongol chief was adept in obtaining information from merchants, and in using agents, spies, and accomplices. Thanks to his conquered subjects, he was able to transport swiftly unheard-of quantities of siege material. Finally, the alternatives of protection or massacre and frightful ravage, depending on whether one submitted completely or resisted, speeded the surrenders. The Mongols, or Tatars as they were sometimes called after one of their component groups, also joined a certain prudence to their daring. They did not try to establish their dominion in any area where they could still only make advance raids. They backed off when destruction seemed to threaten. But their courage was boundless; there were no captive Mongols, only victors or dead.

It was in 1211–1212 that northern China, including Peking, fell to some tens of thousands of these men. The occupation of the territories in Central Asia recently subject to the Kara-Kitai soon put the Mongols in contact with the Khorezmian empire. In 1219–1220 they conquered Transoxiana and Khurasan, and launched raids across Iran as far as Azerbaijan. In 1221 Ghaznah fell, and Jalāl-ad-Dīn Mangubertī escaped the invader only by putting the Indus between them.[1] Meanwhile another force set out from Azerbaijan, this time without Genghis Khan, and undertook a remarkable expedition from 1220 to 1223, crossing the Caucasus and spreading terror across southern Russia, in the Crimea, and then among the Bulgars along the middle Volga, before returning to Central Asia around the northern end of the Caspian Sea without having made a geographic mis-step. The death of Genghis Khan in 1227 hardly interrupted the conquests. His four sons, with the third, Ögödai, as suzerain, continued them. From 1231 to 1234 came the liquidation of the Kin dynasty of northern China and the annexation of Korea, and about the same time, from 1230 to 1233, the occupation of all Iran. From 1237 to 1239 the Mongols conquered central Russia, and in 1240 the Ukraine. The invasion of Poland and Hungary and the defeat of the German armies at Liegnitz in Silesia came the next year. The death of Ögödai in 1242 resulted in the evacuation of central Europe, but not of Russia, which would remain under the Mongol sway. And in 1243, the Mongols of Iran destroyed the Selchükid army of Rūm at Köse Dagh, transforming Anatolia into a Mongol protectorate.

Dissensions between Ögödai's successors stopped the advance briefly, but under Möngke it started again. One of his brothers, Kubilai, carried on long and difficult operations in China which were to lead, around 1280, to the Mongol conquest of all southern China and even the establishment of a protectorate over Tonkin and Cambodia. Meanwhile another brother, Hulagu, achieved in western Asia victories of major import for Moslems and Christians alike. The Assassins of Alamut, before whom all rulers had trembled for a century and a half, fell in 1256.[2] In 1258 the caliphate of Baghdad, five centuries old, perished in a blood-bath inflicted by an army to which Moslem vassals had had to supply reinforcements. Between 1258 and 1260 upper Mesopotamia succumbed, and in 1260 the Mongols invaded Syria, sacked Aleppo, frightened Damascus into subjection, and destroyed the Aiyūbid principalities of Syria and Palestine.[3] After 1243 the Armenians of Cilicia did

[1] On his further exploits, and those of his "Khorezmian" Kîpchaks, see above, chapter XIX, pp. 672–674.

[2] On the Assassins, their overthrow at Alamut, and their later activities in Syria, see volume I of the present work, chapter IV.

[3] For the Aiyūbid principalities, see above, chapter XX, pp. 712–714.

homage to the Mongols, and brought in their wake the Franks of Antioch, who participated in Mongol operations in Syria.[4]

It was in Palestine, however, that the Mongol advance was finally stopped. The death of Möngke in 1259 had obliged Hulagu to leave too few forces for his general Kitbogha to hold the country effectively. Egypt remained a powerful point of defense, strengthened by the very collapse of the Syrian principalities. In September of 1260, at 'Ain Jālūt, the Mamluks crushed Kitbogha, and occupied almost all of Syria. The moral effect of the victory was considerable, but the material effect was not overly great, since Mesopotamia remained Mongol, and Syria itself was often threatened and invaded. Nevertheless, trial and error gradually taught the best defense against the Mongols. Possibly, too, the invaders lost certain elements of their initial superiority, since they now began a struggle among themselves over the division of their conquests. They were never able to surpass the western frontier established in 1260, nor the eastern frontier of about 1280. Of course, it was physically impossible to expand indefinitely an empire in which a commander on the western frontier already needed almost two years to travel to and from the capital of the Great Khan, Karakorum in Mongolia.

The Mongol conquest represented far more than a simple change in overlordship. For a time the political unity of the Mongol state allowed travel through Asia from east to west without the crossing of a single political boundary; and this endured even after the empire was divided into four realms following Möngke's death. This gave trans-Asian commerce a new lease on life, and made possible cultural exchanges throughout the entire area from Peking to Tabriz. The conquest had brought widespread destruction, of course, but the return to stability often allowed the rebuilding of ruined cities, although not always completely. With regard to Moslems in particular, while a great number of Turkomans had been pushed back (with serious consequences on the Byzantine frontier), many others, more numerous than the Mongol tribesmen themselves, were caught up and swept along with the conquerors. As a result the nomadic element increased in places, preventing the return to agriculture of lands emptied by the first devastations. Furthermore, just as the indifferent regime of the Kara-Kitai had tolerated all faiths and, as far as Islam was concerned, all its rival branches, so now this was repeated throughout a much vaster area and under a much more effective government.

[4] For Armenian-Mongol relations, see above, chapter XVIII, pp. 652–659.

The Mongols also finished what the Selchükids had started, the separation of Iran from the Arab world. Arab Baghdad became nothing more than a peripheral dependency of Iran, no longer the heart of Islam. In opposition to this Iranian Mongol world, the bastion of orthodox Islam and of Arabic culture now became Mamluk Egypt, which itself was altered by the reaction against the Mongols, the Mongol destruction of Moslem Syrian states, and to some extent the Mongol example.[5] The Mongols now cast their shadow over "international" relations, particularly those between the Mamluks and the crusaders. One's attitude toward the Mongols became the decisive criterion. In contrast to the forbearance of the Aiyūbids, the Mamluks were grimly determined to finish once for all with the Franks, who had helped bring in the Mongol hordes, considered by the Mamluks the destroyers of all civilization. There is hardly an area where the arrival of the Mongols did not mark the opening of a new period.

Neither Mongol unity, however, nor certain of the features of the primitive Mongol regime were to last forever. Of the four realms into which the empire was divided under the theoretical suzerainty of the Great Khan at Peking, we are interested here only in the state of the Īl-khans of Persia, occupying Iran, Mesopotamia, and Moslem Anatolia.

The Īl-Khanid state, so called from the title of its rulers, was established by the descendants of Hulagu, who died in 1265. At first its capital was at Tabriz; later, after the reign of Öljaitu (1304–1316), it was transferred to the new city of Kangurlan (Persian, Sulṭānīyeh), still flourishing in northwestern Iran. Its foreign policy encompassed endless hostilities with the Mongols of Russia, better known as the Golden Horde;[6] sporadic enmity with the state of Chaghatai in Turkestan; attacks and counter-attacks against the Mamluks for possession of the borderlands between Syria and Mesopotamia; and finally, rather good diplomatic relations with the Byzantine state in common opposition to the Golden Horde and the Mamluks, and also with the western Christians specifically against the Mamluks. Of especial interest, however, are the religious and economic policies of the Mongols, because these had the greatest international repercussions.

As already noted, the Mongols originally had no religion, at

[5] On the Mamluks, see below, chapter XXII.

[6] For the Golden Horde, see B. Spuler, *Die goldene Horde* (Leipzig, 1943), and G. Vernadsky, *The Mongols and Russia* (New Haven, 1953).

least in the sense of the great universal religions. As a result, they had tolerated these great religions indifferently. From the very beginning, however, they tended for political reasons to lean on the Christians or the non-orthodox Moslems, since these groups had suffered under the old regime and therefore were more likely to support the new. There is no doubt whatsoever that the Nestorians in Iran and Central Asia, as well as the Armenians in Cilicia, supported the Mongols and were favored in turn. Though Hulagu personally leaned toward Buddhism, his wife Toqūz Khātūn was a Nestorian, and the Īl-khanid household included many Christians. On the other hand, Sa'd-ad-Dīn, vizir under Arghun (1284–1291), was a Jew who remained unconverted.

As had happened elsewhere, however, it was Islam which finally won the Mongols over, although not without difficulty. Hulagu's son Tegüder (1282–1284), probably with some hope of bringing the war with the Mamluks to an end, embraced Islam, and paid with his life for his premature step. But Ghazan (1295–1304) could become a Moslem without danger, and all his successors would follow him. There were many reasons for Islam's victory among the Mongols. That it was the dominant religion among their subjects was a factor, but the importance of this must not be exaggerated, since conquering minorities, beginning with the Arabs, did not always adopt the religion of the conquered majorities, even though it might be on a spiritual level equal to or surpassing their own. The Mongols of the Golden Horde had been converted to Islam even more quickly than the Īl-khanids, thus creating a barrier between themselves and the indigenous Russian populations, who were, it is true, primarily subjects of vassal principalities which the Mongols did not administer directly. Insofar as the influence of native peoples is concerned, in fact, we must concentrate chiefly on the Turkomans if we are to explain the Islamization of the Mongols. In southeastern Russia, as well as in Iran, the Turkomans were much more numerous than the Mongols themselves. They were almost all resolute Moslems, and because of the similarity in way of life they largely absorbed their conquerors very early. Modern Iran conserves scarcely any trace of the Mongols, and in southern Russia those today called Tatars are all Turkish-speaking people. Essentially, the Islamization of the Mongols thus appears as one aspect of their Turkification.

Even though they became Moslems in faith, however, the Mongols did not act like the Moslem rulers whom they had replaced. While reëstablishing the legal inferiority of non-Moslems in a Moslem state, they strove to favor them as much as possible in order to get the diplomatic support of Christendom. The Mamluks were therefore justified in looking with suspicion on these Mongol converts to Islam; the convert Ghazan carried out in Syria the most formidable of the Mongol invasions, and took as vizir Rashīd-ad-Dīn, also a convert, but thought to be covertly loyal to his original Jewish faith. In addition, some of the Mongols became Sunnites and others Shī'ites. Since Hulagu, as a patron of the astrologers, had protected the great Khurasanian Shī'ite scholar, Nāṣir-ad-Dīn (aṭ-)Ṭūsī, for whom he had founded the observatory of Maragha, the Shī'ites had regained some of the ground lost in the two preceding centuries. This was a prelude to that evolution which, from the sixteenth century to the present, was to make of Persia officially a Shī'ite Moslem state, cut off in consequence from the rest of the Moslem world, and especially from its neighbor the Ottoman empire, where Shī'ism was persecuted.

The diplomatic effects of this religious toleration were widespread, and were of special significance for relations with the west. At the first appearance of the Mongols, westerners had been of varying opinions. They were not unaware of the frightful ravages perpetrated by the invaders, and knew that in Europe these fell on Christian peoples and churches. On the other hand, they quickly saw that a Mongol defeat of nearby Moslems was almost as good as a Frankish victory, and Franks who derived their information from the Nestorian Christians of Central Asia were aware of the advantages which a Mongol occupation brought to Christians. Those who had allied themselves with the Armenians of Cilicia were inclined to share the pro-Mongol attitude held by the Heṭoumid dynasty since its inception. Further, the legend of Prester John helped to fashion prevailing attitudes. We have noted its Kara-Kitai origin in the twelfth century,[7] but in the west the legend had become — and all the more so since the Kara-Kitai had departed from the scene — a manifestation of an ardent but confused belief and hope, fed periodically by distant echoes of the Nestorian church, in the existence of a Christian power lying beyond Islam. That there were Nestorians among the Mongols who publicly practised their religion helped to confer upon them this role. Added to which, there was the incredible simplicity of missionaries who, convinced of the obviousness of their Truth in the eyes of all men of good will, took for an imminent, inward conversion to the faith of Christ even the tritest expression of friendliness.

[7] See above, chapter XIX, pp. 668–669.

The approach of the Mongols happened to coincide with the moment when, under the combined effect of the failure of the crusades and the spirit of the growing mendicant orders, the papacy undertook a missionary policy which, if not at first aimed at the Mongols, could not avoid establishing contacts with them and the Christians under their domination. Innocent IV later sent to Mongolia, through Russia, the Franciscan John of Pian del Carpine, and through Anatolia the Dominican William of Rubrouck, whose accounts remain priceless sources of information. The Mongol response was somewhat disconcerting. The Great Khan, drunk with victory, demanded the submission of all — kings,[8] emperors, and pope — as though they were ordinary lords, without obliging himself to offer them, as he might to lesser lords, even a distant protection. As can be imagined, this demand met with a rather chilly reception, but relations were reëstablished on a more realistic basis after 'Ain Jālūt (1260).

The Mongols now sought an alliance which would produce a concerted effort by the Christians of Europe and themselves against the Mamluks. Abagha (1265–1282) sent ambassadors to the pope (Clement IV) in 1267, to king James I of Aragon in 1269, and to the Council of Lyons in 1274, proposing campaigns against the common enemy — campaigns which, however, it was impossible to organize in sufficient strength or to synchronize, owing to the great distances involved and the many internal difficulties of the parties concerned. Pope Nicholas IV took up the idea once more, however, and Arghun's response went west in the hands of the Nestorian Mar Yabhalāhā III, who visited the Genoese, the kings of France and England, and the pope in the course of an embassy the valuable account of which we still possess.[9] Negotiations still went on under Ghazan and even, somewhat perfunctorily, between pope John XXII and Abū-Sa'īd (1316–1335), who had, however, made his peace with the Mamluks. The presence of western negotiators facilitated contacts with the Mongols, as did the sending of missionaries such as Ricold of Monte Croce, and even the constitution, officially accepted by the Īl-khan, of a hierarchy of bishops *in partibus infidelium*, under an archbishop of Sultaniyeh.

[8] On the efforts of Louis IX of France, and later of Edward I of England, to concert operations with the Mongols against the common Moslem foe, see above, chapter XIV, p. 507, and chapter XVIII, p. 654.

[9] P. Pelliot, "Les Mongols et la papauté," *Revue de l'orient chrétien*, XXIII (1922/1923), XXIV (1924), and XXVIII (1931/1932); the Syriac *Histoire de Mar Jabalaha III* (tr. J. B. Chabot, Paris, 1895); and E. A. W. Budge, *The Monks of Kublai Khan* (London, 1928). The kings were Philip IV and Edward I; the pope was Honorius IV, who had just died when Mar Yabhalāhā reached Rome (1287).

In the territory of the Golden Horde missionaries compiled the Codex Cumanicus (a Latin-Turco-Tatar dictionary). It was, in fact, a prince of Chaghatai's house who communicated to Philip IV the Fair of France an unrealistic plan for Asian peace, inviting him to prepare a European equivalent. And it was under the Mongols that Christian missions and a Latin episcopate were established in China.

In the commercial sphere, there was a parallel growth. The Mongol concern for traders from the very outset is illustrated by the episode of the caravan massacred under the Khorezm-Shāh,[10] or, in the early years of the state of Chaghatai, by the long administration of a vizir of merchant origin, Mas'ūd-Beg. This interest in trade was to some extent common to all nomads, and was naturally emphasized by the immensity of the Mongolian conquests. It is difficult to know whether or not trans-Asian commerce in the Mongol period was substantially greater than that of preceding periods. There was no Iranian or Mesopotamian maritime rebirth; in fact, it was to the Genoese that the Mongols looked on one occasion to challenge the Mamluk fleet in the Indian Ocean.[11] The land caravans were perhaps more direct now; instead of turning their goods over to others in the passes between Chinese Turkestan (Sinkiang) and Moslem Central Asia, as they had formerly had to do, merchants could go from the Mediterranean as far as Peking if they chose. The rise of the Italians, Mongol toleration, and this characteristic of caravan unity explain how Italian merchants could penetrate deep into Asia — even, like Marco Polo, as far as China — and thus bring back new and valuable information. It does not necessarily follow that there was any significant economic change in this trade; Asians had hitherto carried it on exclusively and continued for the most part to dominate it.

It is not our concern here to deal with Italian mercantile activity, either along the northern routes controlled by the Golden Horde, or along the southern, controlled by the Il-khanids.[12] We need only point out that because these routes ran from west to east, the state of quasi-permanent war between the Golden Horde to the north and the Il-khanids to the south had little effect on this commerce. The routes which originated along the north shore of the Black Sea crossed the lower Volga at Serai, the capital of the Golden Horde. Those which passed through Iran began either at Trebizond on

[10] See above, chapter XIX, pp. 671–672.
[11] Bar Hebraeus, *Chronography* (tr. Budge), p. 575 (ad annum 1290).
[12] This trade will be treated in a chapter of volume IV, in preparation.

the south shore of the Black Sea, or else at Ayas (Lajazzo) in Cilicia. The real meeting-places for the traders were Sebastia (Sivas) in Anatolia, and especially Tabriz, even after it had ceased to be the political capital. For political as well as economic reasons the Mongols improved the organization of transportation and communications. The establishment of relays, caravanserais, and highway police benefited merchants as well as the state. More debatable, however, was their fiscal policy, the merits of which did not outweigh its defects. This led to a brief experiment which, from our point of view, is particularly interesting — the use of paper money, or to be more exact, silk money, already common in China. In the unprepared climate of Iran, however, and because of an undeveloped technique, the scheme collapsed before the unanimous opposition of the merchant class.[13]

Even in the realm of culture the horizons broadened. We need note only that the Mongol period saw the culmination of Sa'dī's life and the early career of Ḥāfiẓ, two universally recognized poets. It has left to us some of the most notable masterpieces of Iranian architecture. Persian miniature painting now took its rise from the fusion of the Iranian heritage with Chinese contributions, while Bar Hebraeus combined elements of Syriac, Arabic, and Persian culture in his writings. The Mongol period also witnessed the composition, under the direction of Rashīd-ad-Dīn, of the only history of completely universal scope (and not strictly limited to the Moslem world) that Islamic culture has produced, in which, side by side with some rather perfunctory notices of the "Franks",[14] there is much more complete and valuable information on the Chinese and the peoples of Central Asia, especially the Turks and the Mongols.

If the influence of the Mongol conquest was lasting, the political structure of the Mongols was not. Though stable, the regime could not avoid the economic and military difficulties which had paralyzed its predecessors, aggravated by the growth of a nomadic element which was always ready for new adventures. In the second quarter of the fourteenth century the Il-khanid state passed away. The state, if we can call it that, of Chaghatai collapsed at about the same time. A half century later, however, there would emerge from its ruins the last of the great leaders of Central Asia, Tamerlane (Timur-Lenk). The atmosphere, however, would be quite different, marked especially by Moslem fanaticism. The Timurids could play

[13] K. Jahn, "Das iranische Papiergeld," *Archiv Orientalny*, X (1938), 308–340.
[14] Tr. K. Jahn, *Histoire des Francs* (Leyden, 1951).

the part of restorers of the Mongol empire, and witness the spread of a healthy Iranian culture; but nothing could revive the exceptional climate of religious interpenetration and the free movement of men and goods which had characterized the Mongol period.

Consequently, there is little point in dealing here with the history of Iran and more distant Asia after the fall of the Īl-khanids. One of their dependencies, however, although remote from the focus of their empire proper, deserves a special and more detailed treatment. Not only was Anatolia, because of its location, in constant touch with the Christian west, but it was under the conditions created there by Mongol rule that there arose the Ottoman empire, whose impact on European history was to be so great.

To summarize the chaotic events which followed the catastrophe of Köse Dagh in 1243 and the death, two years later, of Kai-Khusrau II, is very difficult. Anatolia was so removed from the center of their empire that it never occurred to the Mongols to suppress the Selchükid government. Mongol exactions made its effective continuance impossible, however, even though no Mongol administration was set up to replace it at the outset. In addition, and unfortunately for Rūm, Kai-Khusrau II left only minor heirs, giving free rein to the rival ambitions of the magnates. Some of these advocated submission to the Mongols; others looked to the Turkoman instinct to resist, or hoped for Greek aid. The anarchy allowed Turkoman emancipation on the borderlands and the organization of akhis in some towns. Only gradually did order return, under a condominium of one of the Selchükid magnates and a group of Mongol generals, but the situation remained precarious and soon dissolved again. Only then did the Mongols turn their attention to the establishment of a direct administration, during which the puppet Selchükid dynasty died out. Since, however, Anatolia continued to be of secondary importance to the Mongols, and since they themselves were divided and weakened, there could be no regaining of lost ground, and the beginning of the fourteenth century saw a new situation out of which the Ottoman state would gradually take shape.

The principal stages of this evolution were as follows. From 1246 to 1256 the vizir Shams-ad-Dīn al-Iṣfahānī, and after his death (1249) the old emir Kara-Tai, beneficiaries of the Selchükid regime and the real heads of government, succeeded after a fashion in maintaining the old order of things, except where the Turkomans were concerned on the Cilician, Syrian, and Euphrates borders. This they did in spite of opponents who obtained the intervention of the Mongols in support of Kai-Khusrau's second son, Rukn-ad-Dīn Kilij Arslan IV, at the expense of the first-born, 'Izz-ad-Dīn Kai-Kā'ūs II, who alone had been proclaimed sultan at first.

In 1256, the arrival of new Mongol armies in Iran, under the command of Hulagu, and the preparations for the conquest of Mesopotamia and Syria, led Baiju, the Mongol chief of Azerbaijan, to demand permanent quarters in Anatolia for his troops. On the whole, the proponents of submission were dominant in the more immediately threatened eastern part of Anatolia, while the resistance party's strength lay in central Anatolia. Within this latter group were orthodox Moslems, disturbed by the "paganism" of the Mongols and the favor they showed Christians, who were still very numerous in Anatolia; Christian Greeks, who counted on assistance from Nicaea; and finally the Turkomans, whose pasturages were threatened and who were always ready for a brawl anyway. Moreover, many Turkomans had only recently fought the Mongols in other areas whence they had been driven west. Naturally there was no question of a real alliance among these diverse groups, with their generally conflicting interests. It was this irreconcilability which gave to the resistance organized around Kai-Kā'ūs its complexity and its weakness. He was defeated and fled to Byzantine territory while the Mongols enthroned his younger brother Kilij Arslan.

The Mongols, however, soon accepted the idea of a division between the two sultans, the more submissive Kilij Arslan receiving the eastern part of the Selchükid state, the more important part as far as the Mongols were concerned. They needed security on their flank while, from 1258 to 1260, they invaded Mesopotamia and Syria. In 1261, however, they took steps to get rid of Kai-Kā'ūs permanently. The unhappy sultan fled first to Constantinople and then, his hopes dashed by Michael VIII Palaeologus, who had become reconciled with the Mongols of Persia, ended his life as an exile in the Crimea under the protection of the Golden Horde, who were on bad terms with their cousins of Iran. From this crisis, enemies and refractory subjects derived most of the profit. Trebizond retook Sinope. The anarchy of the Turkomans, buttressed by Kurdish anarchy to the east, reigned from the Euphrates to the Byzantine frontier. An autonomous group organized itself between the upper Maeander and the Mediterranean shore across from Rhodes. Another mastered the Taurus, from its Isaurian end to the approaches of the Cilician Gates; its chief was Karaman, whom a tradition, acceptable in its wider implications, at least, associated with the heretical circles stirred up by Baba Isḥāq.[15] Others, on the Syrian borders, plundered indiscriminately the subjects of the Selchükids, the Aiyūbids of Aleppo, the Armenians of Cilicia, and the Franks of Antioch, not to mention the Mongols themselves when their power declined. It seemed as if everything were falling apart.

From 1261 to 1275, however, there was a certain steadying, associated with the person of Mu'īn-ad-Dīn Sulaimān, called the Pervāneh from the name of the first high office of state which he had held. The Pervāneh seized and wielded power as a dictator with Mongol backing, first under the nominal rule of the sultan Rukn-ad-Dīn Kilij Arslan IV, then under his son Ghiyāth-ad-Dīn Kai-Khusrau III. He maintained his position with the aid of Mongol armies, in place of the old Selchükid army, which could no longer be relied on. He was a firm Moslem, raised in the Selchükid state, who exercised authority to the apparent satisfaction of Mongol financial and military demands, but strove at the same time to preserve Selchükid traditions and institutions, at least as far as possible. He was unable to suppress the Turkomans, but at least he kept them within tolerable limits. He retook Sinope and reëstablished order. Favored by the general growth of trade among the Mongols of Persia, commerce in Anatolia developed equally. Cultural and religious life returned to the norms of the preceding period. It was difficult, however, to maintain unity. The magnates had profited from the financial disorganization to get provinces which they now held as quasi-fiefs in lieu of salaries. The Pervāneh himself held the old Dānishmendid province and Sinope, and the vizir Fakhr-ad-Dīn 'Alī had had his children invested with the whole Byzantine border area to the west. And there were others, not least of all the representative of the Mongol fisc who administered the province of Kastamonu directly as security for the repayment of loans. If these personages had their petty disputes, they at least managed to avoid outright civil war. There followed fourteen years of relative stability.

In 1276, however, came a new and more serious crisis, stemming from the growing rivalry between the Pervāneh and certain other magnates. Moreover, the terrible Mamluk sultan Baybars, who had already expelled the Mongols, harried the Franks and Armenians, and established his authority throughout Egypt and Syria

[15] See above, chapter XIX, p. 691.

with effective brutality, now sought to deal permanently with the Mongol menace by cultivating all their adversaries.[16] Both the Pervāneh and his rivals followed the two-faced policy of negotiating with Baybars in case they should fall out with the Mongols, while denouncing to the Mongols such negotiations by the other side. Finally Baybars was provoked into launching a campaign against Caesarea (Kayseri) in 1277, which opened with a bloody victory over the Mongols. Besides this, the Turkomans were still very much in evidence, and the Karamanids in particular constituted an available force which certain of the Pervāneh's enemies, as well as Baybars himself, tried to stir up. It goes without saying that they asked for nothing better than to fish in troubled waters, obviously with their own interests in mind. All told, this was the most serious aspect of the crisis. Baybars, getting less support than he had hoped for from the Selchükid provinces, where fear of the Mongols persisted, was unable to hold his own; but the Karamanids held the field for two years. They put forward a Selchükid pretender known as Jemri, the "poor fellow", a sobriquet given by his enemies. They succeeded in occupying Iconium (Konya) briefly (1276). Almost all the Turkomans of southwestern Anatolia participated in the movement, and while after a long, hard struggle the Selchükid-Mongol government did wrest back the great towns of the plateau, nothing could dislodge the Turkomans in the frontier zones, especially in the Karamanid Taurus.

Though order was finally reëstablished, Anatolia was left in a situation quite different from that which had prevailed under the Pervāneh. Since he was considered responsible for the initial Mongol set-back, he was executed. He had no successor. Rather than restore those of high rank such as Fakhr-ad-Dīn 'Alī, who had given no cause for suspicion, the Mongols gradually themselves took over the high offices of state, controlled them, introduced their own fiscal institutions, and, in short, slowly took over the direct administration of the country. For some time Selchükid sultans continued to reign, chosen and replaced by the Mongols at will, and exercising less and less authority. The last sultan disappeared at the beginning of the fourteenth century so obscurely that most of the chroniclers know neither the date nor the circumstances of the end of this once-glorious dynasty, now more than two centuries old. Nevertheless, the Mongol seizure of power did not have the characteristics it might have had fifty years earlier; the Mongols,

[16] For Baybars, see below, chapter XXII, pp. 745–750, and above, chapter XVI, pp. 574–586 (for the Franks), and chapter XVIII, pp. 653–655 (for the Armenians).

in fact, were becoming more and more converts to Islam, and their government therefore no longer aroused in rigorist circles the same resentment that it had.

Yet the authority of the Mongols, the heirs of the Selchükids, did not extend over the same area nor penetrate as deeply. Though they held eastern Anatolia firmly, they were concerned with the more remote west only to the extent that they thought they could derive from it profits greater than the costs of occupation. In other words, they were concerned with holding the large towns of the plateau, but had little interest in the peripheral Turkomans. At the same time, Byzantine defenses in Asia Minor were weakening. When, therefore, the eastern Turkomans fled westward before the next wave of invading Mongols, under Timur, there soon appeared outlines of Turkoman principalities as far west as the Aegean coast. Furthermore, the Karamanids were far from being destroyed, and at the beginning of the fourteenth century they finally occupied Iconium. Other principalities emerged, especially in the mountains of southern Anatolia, not to mention that of the Germiyan Turkomans, who had been brought in from the border region between Armenia and the Jazira in 1276 to combat a Turkoman revolt in western Anatolia, and naturally became in their turn quite independent.[17] These principalities, much less affected by Iranian or Mongol influences than the large towns of the old Selchükids, constituted a refuge and a base for the rise of a sort of "Turkism", thus accentuating the ever-present contrast between the Selchükid cities and the *uj* territories of the Turkomans.[18]

Even over these towns and cities of the plateau, however, the Mongol hold remained relatively lax. The akhis were less circumscribed and held in check than under the Selchükid regime. Without in any way constituting actual "communes", as some scholars once thought, they became, in the absence of any real authority, an element of great influence in the life of the cities. Although their influence was exercised, in general, against the Turkomans, it also tended toward the limitation of Mongol power, though without going so far as revolt. Later, when there emerged Turkoman principalities, in which the towns enjoyed a good deal of internal independence because of the non-urban character of the Turkomans, the movement would be able to accommodate itself to their domination without difficulty.

[17] For details, see C. Cahen, "Notes pour l'histoire des Turcomans d'Asie mineure . . .; III," *Journal asiatique*, CCXXXIX (1951), 349–354.

[18] A chapter on these principalities and their Ottoman successors is planned for volume III of this work.

Thus, there was no real substitution of a Mongol state for the old state of the Selchükids. Of course, certain Mongol institutions left a strong impress on the country, but politically Mongol unity fell far short of what had prevailed under their predecessors. New poles of attraction appeared: Armenia gravitated toward Iran or Mesopotamia, while Anatolia was drawn to the Turkoman principalities on its periphery. Nor did the disintegration stop there, for in the fourteenth century the Mongols became weak and divided in turn. In Anatolia their generals struggled against one another, as elsewhere in the Il-khanid empire, to such an extent that there was a tendency toward disintegration even in the area which remained Mongol. In some cases Mongol chiefs seized power, as did Eretna at Sebastia, or local notables succeeded in elevating themselves as petty princes, as did the vizir of Eretna's grandson, the qadi Burhān-ad-Dīn, at Sebastia in the last decades of the fourteenth century.

Except for a few lasting institutions of a fiscal nature, then, the Mongol regime in Anatolia represents on balance a destruction of the territorial and human collectivity which the Selchükid sultanate of Rūm had gradually built up. The interior was now divided into three parts, themselves in political disintegration: the eastern portion, no longer looking to the west, but rather to the east and south; the great central cities, which maintained Selchükid-Mongol traditions, though reduced now to regional importance only; and the domain of the Turkomans in the west, with the plateau no longer the focal point, but rather a dependency, of the frontier areas.

Economic developments reflect this political evolution. Not that commercial activity declined prior to the fall of the Il-khanid empire. On the contrary, the favorable conditions created by Mongol unification and toleration, and the development of western undertakings, created a current of exchange from Central Asia to the Mediterranean probably greater than before. But the direction of the carrying trade through Anatolia was thrown into confusion. The north–south trans-peninsular route across Anatolia toward Egypt via Adalia declined considerably, as did the drawing-power of the court of Iconium. The caravans now made for Trebizond, only touching a corner of the old Selchükid territory at Erzerum, or for Ayas in Cilicia. Despite political discord, however, trade continued between the north and south shores of the Black Sea, above all in Armenian and Italian hands. Sebastia therefore remained an important crossroads for international commerce. The more western areas, however, were forsaken, and meanwhile the dislocation of the Mongol empire likewise endangered the commerce of the eastern areas.

We are too poorly informed on social changes to do more than suggest one or two hypotheses. In part, the Mongol state replaced the Selchükid state, and Mongol magnates replaced Selchükid magnates, as the proprietors of the soil. This altered the pattern of development from one adapted to the promotion of general prosperity within the country to one of exploitation for the benefit of foreigners, who were for the most part in temporary residence only. The final disintegration of the Īl-khanid empire, however, made this feature transitory. It would be more important to know in what measure the anarchy, especially the disbursements and speculations, of the Mongol chiefs converted into private property the properties of the old state and in particular the old *iqṭā‘* grants. Probably we shall be able to answer this question only after a complete study of conditions in the Ottoman period. Joined with this is the question, to what extent Moslem institutions were deprived of their endowments (Arabic singular, *waqf*) by the neutral, even anti-Moslem, religious policy of the first Īl-khanids. And also, during the same period, what changes were made by the westward extension of Turkoman domains. The impression of the present writer is that there was no radical upset, but much remains to be learned. The condition of agricultural workers, in any case, must have been little modified by changes which for them meant simply an exchange of masters. As for the towns, the development of the akhis, which reached its apogee in the fourteenth and fifteenth centuries, is naturally of great importance.

Finally, the cultural continuity with the preceding period was quite marked, but here too there was evolution and a fusion of the inheritances of the past. Even though, in the eastern provinces, the policy of the first Īl-khanids encouraged a fleeting restoration of the Armenian communities, the Moslem character of the upper classes and of the institutions was in no way compromised. The illustrious Moslem vizir of Mongol sovereigns, Shams-ad-Dīn (al-)Juvainī, himself helped to multiply and consolidate Islamic foundations in Anatolia. It is not certain that common Mongol rule facilitated the continuation of contacts with Iran, for the Iranian scholars remained at home. What contacts there were, however, at least served to accentuate the division from the Arab world.

Literature, too, remained Persian, and indeed now bore the full fruit of the growth begun in the Selchükid period. It was now that

Jalāl-ad-Dīn (ar-)Rūmī composed the greater part of his mystical poems, to which may be added those of his son, Sulṭān Veled, and the literature of mysticism was enriched, with the growth of the akhis, by the invaluable *futūwah* books. It was now, too, that the chroniclers Ibn-Bībī and (al-)Aqsarāyī produced those works without which we would know so little about the society in which they lived. Moreover, contact was now established between the mystical currents of the Iranized elements and the Turkish masses. More popular than Jalāl-ad-Dīn was Hajjī Bektash, of whom we know nothing except that his name would later serve to designate one of the most important dervish orders in the organization of Ottoman society. What is even more important, there began to appear works in Turkish which adapted for a Turkish public the offerings of Persian mysticism. If we are still far from the time when Turkish would become a literary language, authors such as Yūnus Emre and Shaiyād Ḥamzah nevertheless bear witness to a cultural elevation of the Turkish masses connected with their political rise in the Turkoman principalities.[19] And it was also around 1300 that the semi-legendary Naṣr-ad-Dīn Khoja lived. He has remained from that time forward the symbol of the bantering common-sense of the people.

The successive collapses of the Selchükid and Mongol regimes should not, therefore, be looked upon as the collapse of a civilization, but rather as its progressive rearrangement along new territorial lines and in new cultural patterns. The picture we get from Ibn-Baṭṭūṭah and the Egyptian official al-ʻUmarī, in the years 1330–1340, shows how completely the Anatolian world was cut off from Arab Islam. To a lesser extent, the fall of the Mongol empire would cut it off from Iran also. Though held fast by certain old traditions, the independent Ottoman state would take its rise on the frontiers of a sealed-off world.

[19] A. Bombaci, *Storia della letteratura turca* (Milan, 1956).

22. The Mongols in the Near East, to 1291 (*Map by the University of Wisconsin Cartographic Laboratory*)

23. The Mamluks in the Near East, to 1291 (*Map by the University of Wisconsin Cartographic Laboratory*)

XXII
THE MAMLUK SULTANS TO 1293

The immediate aftermath of victory over the crusade of Louis IX in 1250 was the establishment in Egypt of a Mamluk sultanate, which blossomed out into an empire on the lines of its Aiyūbid predecessor in the Near East. It included Egypt, Palestine, and Syria, with a sovereignty less permanent and less well defined over certain regions and fortress towns in the upper Euphrates valley, southeastern Anatolia, Hejaz, the northern Sudan, and Cyrenaica. Mamluk Egypt, the first power to break the spell of Mongol invincibility in a pitched battle, then took the lead in the expulsion of the crusaders from the Holy Land. Moreover, this Mamluk sultanate proved to be of considerable importance in Arabic learning and culture in the later Middle Ages, in part because of the transfer of the political center of gravity and the seat of the 'Abbāsid caliphate from Baghdad to Cairo. It also had an active share in international trade from the thirteenth century down to the days when the Cape of Good Hope was rounded two hundred years later.

The word *mamlūk* is the passive participle of the verb "to own" in Arabic, meaning a person (or chattel) owned through deed of sale, barter, capture in war, or presentation as a gift or tribute from a provincial governor or subject community. All mamluks

First among contemporary sources for Mamluk history is Ibn-Wāṣil's chronicle entitled *Mufarrij al-kurūb fī akhbār Banī Aiyūb*, here cited from MS, though volume I was edited by Jamāl-ad-Dīn ash-Shaiyāl and published at Alexandria in 1953, and further volumes are expected. Equally important is *Zubdat al-fikrah fī ta'rīkh al-hijrah*, by Baybars ad-Dawādār, still in MS. Besides Abū-Shāmah's well known *Kitāb ar-rauḍatain* (*RHC*, *Or.*, IV–V), a sequel entitled *Dhail ar-rauḍatain* was recently published in Cairo, without date. A study of Mamluk history must also rely on al-Maqrīzī's *Kitāb as-sulūk li-ma'rifat duwal al-mulūk* (edited by the author of this chapter, Cairo, 1956–date), and on *An-nujūm az-zāhirah* by Abū-l-Maḥāsin Ibn-Taghrī-Birdī, edited in 11 volumes by the staff of the National Library in Cairo (1929–1950), portions edited (1909–1936) and translated (1954–1957) by W. Popper at Berkeley.

Modern works in European languages include G. Wiet, *L'Égypte musulmane . . .*, in *Précis de l'histoire d'Égypte*, vol. II (1932), ch. VII: "Les Sultans mamlouks" (pp. 237–285); A. N. Poliak, *Feudalism in the Middle East* (London, 1939); and P. K. Hitti, *History of Syria* (2nd ed., London, 1957). As all three of these have full bibliographies, this footnote is intended merely as an introduction guiding the reader to them.

thus were slaves, but not all slaves were called mamluks. The term was applied only to white slaves, not to negroes: at first especially to Turks from Central Asia, but later embracing slaves from western Asia, as well as from many parts of Europe, including the lands of the Baltic Sea.[1] These mamluks had been numerous and powerful since the great days of the 'Abbāsid caliphate in Baghdad, when they formed a large part of the army. Their variety increased with every opening up of a new geographical area through raid, conquest, or trade; but whatever their origin, they all proudly called themselves "Turks".[2] The Turkish mamluk exercised great influence on Moslem polity in the Middle Ages, and his manner of life was the subject of discussion among contemporary Arabic writers from the ninth century onward.[3] Ibn-Ḥassūl, who died in 1058, described the Turkish mamluk as a haughty creature "who would not allow himself to be treated as less than equal to his master in food, drink, dress, or riding equipment. He would never deign to perform menial service, such as sweeping and cleaning a dwelling, or attending to horses and cattle, as others in bonded slavery would be expected to do. As soon as he was made free, he would not be satisfied with anything less than leadership of an army, appointment to a court office, [or] command of a regiment . . . ."[4]

We have abundant evidence of the remarkable degree of care with which these mamluks were brought up and trained to become the main soldiery of independent provincial dynasties throughout the Moslem world, some of which were themselves of mamluk origin. The Selchükid empire, whose rulers were not mamluks, relied extensively on this type of soldiery; in his "Treatise on Government" (*Siyāsat-Nāmeh*) the illustrious vizir Niẓām-al-Mulk (d. 1092) gives a detailed account of the probation of a mamluk, from the moment he came into his master's possession until the time he was considered free and horseworthy, after which he could rise to any eminence in the military or political scale.[5]

The Aiyūbid dynasty relied on mamluk officers and troopers for at least half of its army. Saladin himself was surrounded by select companies of these mamluks, splendidly equipped and thoroughly trained in the art of war. The system was continued, and intensified,

[1] Wiet, *Les Sultans mamlouks*, p. 241.

[2] On these Turkish elements in Islam, see volume I of the present work, chapter V, pp. 136–139.

[3] Al-Jāḥiz, *Majmū'at rasā'il* . . . (Cairo, 1934), pp. 2–53.

[4] Ibn-Ḥassūl, *Risālah fī tafḍīl al-Atrāk* . . . (ed. 'Abbās al-Azzawī, *Türkiye Belleten*, no. 14–15 [1940]), p. 42.

[5] Niẓām-al-Mulk, *Siyāsat-Nāmeh* (tr. C. Schéfer, Paris, 1893), pp. 130–141.

under his successors. Each mamluk company was designated by the honorific of its owner, as for example the Asadīyah, belonging to Asad-ad-Dīn Shīrkūh, Saladin's uncle and predecessor in the government of Egypt, and the Ṣalāḥīyah, belonging to Ṣalāḥ-ad-Dīn (Saladin) himself. These mamluk companies had a considerable share in Saladin's wars before and after the battle of Hattin, and the roll of their dead and their casualties in his many campaigns bears impressive witness to Saladin's dependence on mamluk soldiery, besides other troops of free status, mostly Kurds.[6] More concrete evidence of the influence and weight of these mamluks in Saladin's empire is to be found in the lists of monuments and pious endowments that bore their names, in Cairo, Damascus, and elsewhere.[7]

Fragmentization of the Aiyūbid empire after Saladin's death (1193), and the ensuing wars among Aiyūbid princes in Egypt, Syria, and the Jazira, served to augment the numbers and powers of mamluks everywhere, until often they became kingmakers in those countries.[8] For instance, it was due to the 'Ādilīyah, mamluks of sultan al-'Ādil Saif-ad-Dīn, who for a time had almost reintegrated his brother's empire, that his own son and successor al-Kāmil nearly lost his throne.[9] A little later, it was the Kāmilī mamluks who, together with some black slaves, enabled al-Kāmil's son aṣ-Ṣāliḥ Aiyūb (1240–1249) to depose and succeed his younger brother al-'Ādil II, in spite of the opposition of the free Kurdish soldiers in the army.[10]

Aṣ-Ṣāliḥ Aiyūb, the last effective sultan of the Aiyūbid dynasty in Egypt, developed the system of employing mamluks for his army and bodyguard to the highest pitch of efficiency. As an aspirant to the sultanate he had had early bitter experience of the jealousies of his kinsmen, and feared them still, now that he had become master in Egypt and in much of Syria, including Damascus. He had no love for the free Kurds of the army, nor had he much trust in the Kāmilīyah and other mamluk groups, to whom he partly owed his good fortune. He was therefore determined to surround himself with mamluk troops of his own creation; he imported them from various markets, but wherever they were

[6] Ibn-Wāṣil, *Mufarrij al-kurūb* (Bibl. Nat. MS., used in a photographic copy), I, folios 70, 78, 89, 90–91, 96, 101–102, 126, 130–131.

[7] Al-Maqrīzī, *Al-mawā'iẓ wa-l-i'tibār fī dhikr al-khiṭaṭ wa-l-āthār* (Būlāq, A.H. 1324–1326), II, 38, 41, 80, 83, 87–88, 367.

[8] On these wars, see above, chapter XX.

[9] Al-Maqrīzī, *As-sulūk* (ed. Ziada), I, 222–223.

[10] Ibn-Waṣil, *op. cit.*, folio 37; al-Maqrīzī, *As-sulūk*, I, 294–296. See also above, chapter XX, p. 707.

bought the great majority were Turks, and a Turkish dialect was their common language. He then built himself a castle on the island of Roda, overlooking the Nile (Baḥr an-Nīl), and had those who proved to be the most hardened and reliable of these new mamluks stationed there as his bodyguard. They were known as al-Baḥrīyah aṣ-Ṣāliḥīyah, signifying, however, not their relation to the barracks overlooking the river, as is reiterated by almost all secondary authorities, but apparently their importation from across the sea (*baḥr*).[11] This meaning of *baḥrīyah*, reminiscent of the crusaders' "outremer", is confirmed by its application to the crusaders themselves by Arabic authors,[12] as well as to mamluks in other places and at other periods,[13] and its survival in modern Arabic usage.

From the number of madrasahs (schools), public baths, water fountains, mosques, caravanserais, and other buildings bearing the names of leading Ṣāliḥī mamluks (Baḥrīyah and others) we can be sure that these men wielded considerable wealth and power in Cairo in the middle of the thirteenth century.[14] But the Baḥrīyah especially became the terror and scourge of older mamluk groups as well as of the people of Cairo, giving a foretaste of one of the bad features of mamluk rule in Egypt and Syria in years to come. Apparently aṣ-Ṣāliḥ Aiyūb built the castle on the island of Roda in a deliberate effort to get them away from the streets of Cairo.[15]

These Baḥrī mamluks acquitted themselves well in the victory over the crusaders at Mansurah (February 1250), a victory all the more remarkable in that Egypt had lost its sultan in November of the previous year.[16] Pending the arrival of the son and heir to the throne, Tūrān-Shāh, from his governorship near Mosul, the conduct of operations and civil affairs of the realm were in the hands of a singularly capable woman, Shajar-ad-Durr (Spray of Pearls). She had been a *mamlūkah* (fem. of *mamlūk*) in the harem first of the caliph and then of sultan aṣ-Ṣāliḥ Aiyūb, bearing him a son, Khalīl, who had died in infancy; but she had become the sultan's favorite wife in his aging years. When he died, she had concealed his death, giving out that he was seriously ill. Regular meals were brought

[11] Their sole duty was to guard the person of the sultan; see M. Ziada, "New Notes on Mamluk History [in Arabic]," *Bulletin of the Faculty of Arts of the University of Egypt*, IV, 1 (1936), 72.

[12] Abū-Shāmah, *Dhail ar-rauḍatain*, pp. 10–11, 52, 151; Ibn-Wāṣil, *op. cit.*, I, folio 150.

[13] See al-Khazrajī, *History of the Rasūlids of Yemen* (Arabic text, ed. G. Shaikh M. 'Asal, London, 1906–1913), part 2, pp. 5, 11, 13.

[14] Al-Maqrīzī, *Al-khiṭaṭ*, II, 43–44, 46, 82, 83, 116, 290, 420; Ibn-Duqmāq, *Kitāb al-intiṣār* . . . (Būlāq, A.H. 1309), IV, 44.

[15] Abū-l-Maḥāsin, *An-nujūm*, VI, 319; Ibn-Iyās, *Badā'i'* . . . (Būlāq, A.H. 1311), I, 83.

[16] For this crusade, see above, chapter XIV, pp. 494–504.

in to where he was supposed to lie, and the necessary orders of state duly appeared, bearing his forged signature. It was under these adverse conditions that, during the crusaders' attack on Mansurah, the commander-in-chief of the forces of Egypt, Fakhr-ad-Dīn, was taken by surprise and slain beside his bath. His loss, however, was something of a blessing to the Baḥrī mamluks, if not for the morale of the forces as a whole, for he had been plotting to acquire the sultanate for himself.[17]

Significantly enough the new commander-in-chief was the leader of the Baḥrī mamluks, Ak-Tai, who had been secretly dispatched post-haste after the sultan's death to bring Tūrān-Shāh back with all speed, but who was nevertheless appointed to the high command *in absentia*.[18] Ak-Tai also had designs on the sultanate, but was biding his time, as was the Kurdish vizir Ibn-Abī-'Alī al-Hudhbānī, the sultan's deputy in Cairo.[19] There were other men of ability and potential ambition, such as the young mamluk leader Baybars, to whom most of the credit for the victory over the crusaders was due, although Ak-Tai, now returned from northern Iraq, had skillfully arranged the order of the day.[20]

A few days later Tūrān-Shāh arrived, and Shajar-ad-Durr relinquished to him the reins of power, which she had manipulated so well, with the aid of her mamluk associates. News of the old sultan's death was then made public. In the decisive victory of Fāriskūr, in which Louis was captured and his army destroyed, it was Baybars who so distinguished himself that the eye-witness historian Ibn-Wāṣil called him and the other Baḥrīyah the Templars of Islam.[21]

With the crusading peril overcome, the victors turned to settle what seem to have been old accounts among them. Sultan Tūrān-Shāh, who had been disliked and distrusted by his own father, could not have had much love either for his stepmother Shajar-ad-Durr or for her friends the Baḥrīyah. In his two-months' reign, he made himself generally hated, first by accusing Shajar-ad-Durr of concealing his father's treasure, and then by breaking his word to Ak-Tai, to whom he had promised a certain governorship. He made matters worse by appointing many of his own recently arrived mamluks to posts that by custom belonged to older and more

[17] Abū-l-Maḥāsin, *An-nujūm*, VI, 332–333, 358, 363; al-Maqrīzī, *As-sulūk*, I, 345.

[18] *Ibid.*, I, 345, 358.

[19] *Ibid.*, I, 343; Ibn-Wāṣil, *op. cit.*, II, folios 343, 361–362.

[20] *Ibid.*, II, folio 367.

[21] *Ibid.*, II, folio 370. On this victory, see above, chapter XIV, pp. 501–504, and chapter XX, pp. 711–712.

deserving men. Plots and counterplots culminated in the murder of Tūrān-Shāh at Fāriskūr in the opening days of May 1250, at the hands of the mamluk generals and with the collusion of his stepmother, whom he had so badly rewarded for her loyalty to him at a very critical moment in the history of Egypt.[22] He died unmourned, except by those who felt that events were marching a little too quickly for their own private purposes, and by a party of Kurdish officers and soldiery, the Qaimarīyah, who thought that the Turkish mamluks had overstepped the mark.[23]

The murder of Tūrān-Shāh, which ended Aiyūbid rule in Egypt, left a void that had to be filled quickly by the men who had created it. The Aiyūbid princes in Syria had been casting covetous eyes on Egypt for many years; moreover, the mamluks feared a possible crusade to avenge the failure and secure the release of king Louis. It was obviously in the interest of the Baḥrīyah to choose a successor to Tūrān-Shāh while they controlled the situation. Their choice fell on Shajar-ad-Durr herself, mainly as a stop-gap and a counter against the inevitable claims of Aiyūbid princes to the throne of Egypt, and also perhaps as a means to put an end to the dreams of such men as al-Hudhbānī and Ak-Tai, who seemed to entertain the hope of ruling Egypt singlehanded on autocratic lines. It was therefore not quite in her own right that she became *sulṭānah* of Egypt, but rather as the widow of aṣ-Ṣāliḥ Aiyūb, and the mother (*umm*) of his son who had died in infancy. She was styled not merely "sulṭānah Shajar-ad-Durr", but also "Umm-Khalīl aṣ-Ṣāliḥīyah", in order to assert the legitimacy of her succession, and to thwart in advance any Aiyūbid claims of illegality. The mamluks offered the post of commander-in-chief, the most important appointment in the realm, to al-Hudhbānī, who declined it out of pique.[24] Ak-Tai, who had actually held the post under Tūrān-Shāh, was passed over, perhaps in fear of his ambitions and ability. It was next offered to a hitherto unknown mamluk emir, Aybeg the Turkoman, who readily accepted.

Such was the birth of the Mamluk dynasty (May 1250). Though the sultanah was of Armenian or Turkish origin, the new dynasty could not be but a continuation of the Aiyūbids in political background and outlook: the mamluks themselves were the creation of

[22] Many contemporary accounts of the killing of Tūrān-Shāh have been collected in Abū-l-Maḥāsin, *An-nujūm*, VI, 328, 370–372; see also Ibn-Wāṣil, *op. cit.*, II, folios 370–371; al-Maqrīzī, *As-sulūk*, I, 358–359; Abū-Shāmah, *Dhail ar-rauḍatain*, p. 185.

[23] *Ibid.*, p. 185; al-Maqrīzī, *As-sulūk*, p. 366.

[24] Ibn-Wāṣil, *op. cit.*, II, folio 373.

their late masters, and their experience in government and administration was limited to the established order in Egypt and Syria.

Shajar-ad-Durr's first act of government was the peaceful liquidation of the crusade, by confirming the terms of ransom which had been settled between Tūrān-Shāh and Louis. Half of the stipulated sum was scraped together in Damietta by Louis's queen, and the French king was allowed to sail away to Acre with the remnant of his army, only a few days after the setting up of the new dynasty.[25] Shajar-ad-Durr then went out of her way to shower favors and appointments with suitable fiefs on the Baḥrī mamluks, to whom she owed her exalted position.

Disgruntled murmurs began to be heard in many quarters in Cairo regarding the installation of a woman on the throne, but the first serious note of disapproval came from Damascus, where the Kurdish Qaimarīyah refused to take the oath of allegiance. They called upon an-Nāṣir Yūsuf of Aleppo to chastise the daring upstarts of Cairo, and to recover Egypt for its rightful heirs. An-Nāṣir marched on Damascus, which opened its gates to him, and all the Baḥrī mamluks stationed there were arrested. Thus an-Nāṣir became lord of the two principal cities of Syria, but reprisals against the Qaimarīyah took place in Cairo.

Meanwhile the 'Abbāsid caliph at Baghdad, al-Musta'ṣim, still the titular head of the Moslem world, did not relish the idea that the new ruler of Egypt should be a woman who had once been in his own harem;[26] there was also some learned opinion against the setting up of any woman on the throne of a Moslem country.[27] It was finally agreed that Shajar-ad-Durr should marry the commander-in-chief, Aybeg, and abdicate the throne in his favor; both ceremonies took place in July 1250, and the eighty days of sole rule of Shajar-ad-Durr came to a peaceful end. This arrangement, however, was not to the satisfaction of the Baḥrīyah and their leader Ak-Tai, who acknowledged Aybeg as sultan only for reasons of expediency, having sized him up as a mediocrity who could easily be removed at a more convenient time. Al-Hudhbānī was first among the emirs to hold the state parasol in the coronation procession, in token of his support and assent. He served Aybeg well

[25] See above, chapter XIV, pp. 504–505.

[26] She had been a gift from al-Musta'ṣim to aṣ-Ṣāliḥ Aiyūb, who had on at least one occasion sent her to brighten the exile of a relative, an-Nāṣir Dā'ūd; now the caliph inquired whether among the emirs of Egypt there was not at least one man fit to rule them, offering to send one if they could not agree on one; Hitti, *History of Syria*, p. 629, and *Encyclopaedia of Islām*, IV, 249.

[27] Ibn-Wāṣil, *op. cit.*, II, folios 373, 376; al-Maqrīzī, *As-sulūk*, I, 368–369; as-Suyūṭī, *Husn al-muḥāḍarah* . . . (Cairo, A.H. 1327), II, 34.

until he fell out of favor and died a disappointed man later in the reign.[28] But whether it was due to a sudden awakening of the Baḥrīyah to their mistake, or to an ominous increase in Aiyūbid opposition, it was decided within a few days of Aybeg's elevation that some Aiyūbid prince should be set up as joint ruler. An Aiyūbid child of less than ten years, named al-Ashraf Mūsâ, was duly chosen, and official proclamations were issued under the two names, though power remained ostensibly in the hands of Aybeg, with the masterful Shajar-ad-Durr unwilling to relinquish any part of her real control.[29]

This arrangement, however, could hardly be expected to placate Aiyūbid legitimists, who were already on the march towards Egypt, headed by an-Nāṣir of Aleppo and Damascus. Besides, a handful of mamluks in Cairo itself now proclaimed as sultan another young Aiyūbid prince of Kerak, al-Mughīth 'Umar (September 1250). Aybeg, who had been taken for an easy-going person, at once proved his true mettle by declaring Egypt to be an appanage of the 'Abbāsid caliphate in Baghdad, from which he held the reins of power as viceroy. He then forestalled the possibility of any Aiyūbid approaches to Louis IX in Acre by the friendly gesture of releasing a number of French prisoners still in Egypt. Still taking no chances, Aybeg ordered the razing of old Damietta and its fortifications (October 1250), in case of a breach of faith on the part of Louis, or any other crusaders.[30] Meanwhile preparations were being completed for the dispatch of an expedition to repel the Aiyūbid invaders, whose vanguard was put to flight by Ak-Tai in the vicinity of the frontier town of Gaza. A battle was fought shortly afterwards (February 1251) near aṣ-Ṣāliḥīyah, within Egyptian territory, where the invading forces were routed; many Aiyūbid princes were captured, but an-Nāṣir managed to escape. None too content with this result, Aybeg sent Ak-Tai to ferret out the nests of Aiyūbid resistance in Palestine, so that no future invasion should reach the Egyptian frontiers so easily.

By this time, the Mongol danger had begun to loom large in western Asia, threatening the very existence of the caliphate in Baghdad.[31] The caliph deemed it vital that Moslem dynasts should sink their differences before the advancing peril, and unite in an effort to repel it when it came. Much to the advantage of the

[28] Al-Maqrīzī, *As-sulūk,* I, 373, 376–377, 381, 386.

[29] Ibn-Wāṣil, *op. cit.,* II, folio 376; al-Maqrīzī, *As-sulūk,* I, 368–369; Abū-l-Maḥāsin, *An-nujūm,* VII, 5–6. Mūsâ was either the son or the grandson of al-Kāmil's son al-Mas'ūd, who had briefly governed Yemen.

[30] Al-Maqrīzī, *As-sulūk,* I, 372.

[31] See above, chapter XXI, p. 717.

nascent Mamluk state in Egypt, a treaty was concluded (April 1253) between Aybeg and an-Nāṣir, by which the former would hold Egypt and a slice of Palestine at the banks of the Jordan, including Jerusalem as well as the coastline, while the latter, together with other Aiyūbid princes in Syria and Palestine, would be left undisturbed in their several principalities.

Aybeg's reliance on the Baḥrīyah for the whole campaign against the Aiyūbids had increased their power unduly, making them unmanageable and disdainful of everybody except Ak-Tai. So long as the Aiyūbid threat remained, Aybeg had had to behave warily towards them; but no sooner was the treaty concluded than he began to move fast. He removed the child Mūsâ, and appointed his own mamluk Kutuz to the post of deputy sultan, much to the indignation of the Baḥrīyah. Extraordinary taxes which Baḥrī emirs had levied on certain districts precipitated a revolt headed by an Arab chief named Ṭālib, whose slogan was that mamluks (slaves) should not rule over free men. Aybeg had to call upon Ak-Tai for the suppression of this dangerous movement, which had mustered great numbers of beduins; Ak-Tai crushed it near Bilbais with a force smaller but better armed and disciplined (June 1253).

From this new success Ak-Tai emerged as a personal rival to the sultan. He began to arrogate to himself powers belonging only to the head of the state, and to ride in pomp and circumstance from his dwelling in Cairo to the sultan's palace in the citadel. With his connivance the Baḥrīyah, who called him *al-malik al-jawād* (the generous king), indulged in atrocious acts of violence. Next, Ak-Tai was betrothed to a princess of the Aiyūbid house of Hamah; he demanded that Aybeg allow him and his bride to reside in the citadel, on the ground of her royal descent.[32] Aybeg now felt he had no choice but to get rid of Ak-Tai before it was too late; he summoned him on official business to the citadel, where he had him trapped and murdered, and his head thrown to his escort standing below the walls (September 1254).

Many of the Baḥrīyah, appalled at the news of this sudden blow, fled the country; some of those who stayed behind were arrested and their property was confiscated. For the moment Aybeg saved his throne, but only by scattering the Baḥrīyah among the courts of his Aiyūbid enemies in Syria. There they lived as political refugees, trying to incite an-Nāṣir of Aleppo (and others) to make another bid for Egypt, and raiding Palestine like robber barons, hovering all the time on the Egyptian border. Aybeg spent the best part of

[32] Al-Maqrīzī, *As-sulūk*, I, 388–390; Abū-l-Maḥāsin, *An-nujūm*, VII, 10–12, 30.

three years (1254–1257) in frontier camps to guard against their movements, but also sought external support; he resorted to the old device of declaring himself viceroy of the caliph, sending an embassy to Baghdad for the traditional robes of honor and other insignia of investiture. He also renewed an old truce with the crusaders,[33] and proposed an alliance with Lu'lu', the powerful atabeg of Mosul, whose daughter he proposed to marry, if only to break away from the domination of Shajar-ad-Durr and her open sympathies with the exiled Baḥrīyah. The news of this last move on the part of Aybeg produced an irretrievable rupture; Shajar-ad-Durr felt herself a woman wronged, and Aybeg stayed away from her. Yet he allowed himself to be lured to a meeting of reconciliation, where he was savagely murdered in his bath (April 1257). She announced that he had died a natural death, but the truth soon leaked out, and she met an equally brutal end three days later.

Young 'Alī, Aybeg's son, of course had no "right" to the succession in a military oligarchy of mamluks, despite the fond wishes of his father, but he suited the devious strategems of the leading emirs. They accepted the youngster as successor, not in real earnest, but as a substitute to be quietly removed as soon as they decided which of them should mount the throne. This feature of mock primogeniture was meticulously repeated time and again after the demise of almost every sultan, with the same purpose in view. After his deposition each of these shadow successors would live in retirement somewhere in Egypt, or in exile abroad. That some sons of sultans were able to remain on the throne for a time was due more to the inability of the emirs to agree among themselves than to any staying qualities inherent in these sons. Yet all outward ceremonials of a new reign were observed on each such occasion. 'Alī ibn-Aybeg, a lad of fifteen years, was raised to his father's throne; the senior member of his father's own mamluks, Kutuz, was retained in the post of deputy sultan. But the destruction of Baghdad by the Mongols played into the hands of Kutuz, who convinced the council of state in Cairo that the Mongol threat made it urgently necessary to have a strong man at the helm, not a helpless playboy of no worth or experience. 'Alī was deposed, and Kutuz was proclaimed sultan (November 12, 1259).

After Hulagu destroyed Aleppo (January 1260), he had to return to Karakorum to take part in the choice of a successor to the supreme khanate. The command of the Mongol army in Syria

[33] See al-Maqrīzī, *As-sulūk*, I, 393; and above, chapter XVI, pp. 567–568.

was left to Kitbogha, a Nestorian Christian Mongol. Meanwhile such Aiyūbid forces as an-Nāṣir was reputed to have gathered near Damascus, to oppose the Mongol advance, dwindled rather quickly. Men like Baybars and other Baḥrī mamluk exiles left an-Nāṣir's court in disgust, offering their services to Kutuz, who welcomed them back to Cairo. Damascus soon surrendered to Kitbogha without resistance (March 1260), and was spared some of the usual Mongol indignities. Kutuz realized his danger to the full, and anticipated further Mongol progress southward by marching from Egypt to Palestine at the head of a considerable army, but not before he had ordered the public execution of the Mongol envoys in Cairo. His vanguard under Baybars, now fully restored to his old position in the Mamluk army, drove advance Mongol troops out of Gaza, where Kutuz himself then arrived to prepare the main advance northward along the Palestinian coast. Kitbogha offered alliance and protection to the crusader barons at Acre if they would refuse passage to the Mamluks, but Kutuz secured the Christians' neutrality, and was thereby able to surprise the Mongols in Galilee.

Aided by this initial advantage, the Mamluks defeated the Mongols in a pitched battle (September 1260), at 'Ain Jālūt, not far from Nazareth.[34] The bravery of Kutuz, and of his general Baybars, won the day; Kitbogha was slain. For the first time in history the Mongols had been indisputably beaten in a decisive encounter; their spell was broken at last, and Damascus rose and cast off their heavy yoke. But Kutuz did not rest satisfied until the Mongols, completely crushed and crestfallen, were driven out of Syria beyond the Euphrates. He then restored, where possible, all the Aiyūbid princes and other officials to their former places as governors under his command. In this way he extended the suzerainty of the Mamluk sultanate over Syria and Palestine, except for the small principality of Kerak. Far more important was the universal prestige which Kutuz gained for the Mamluks by this victory, for 'Ain Jālūt had warded off the Mongol danger not only from Egypt but from European Christendom as well, though there were some Christian princes who clung to the idea of an alliance with the Mongols. Yet the reward meted out to Kutuz was murder; on his triumphant return to Egypt he was treacherously stabbed to death (October 1260) by Baybars, who immediately afterwards rode into Cairo and usurped the Mamluk throne.[35]

[34] See above, chapter XXI, p. 718.

[35] Baybars ad-Dawādār, *Zubdat al-fikrah*, X, folios 32–33.

Within a single decade, and in spite of three regicides, the Mamluks had proved themselves a power capable of withstanding both internal and external threats of disruption. Granting that they had inherited a ready-made and well developed governmental machine, based on military principles which suited the purposes of an oligarchy, the variety of problems which they had so successfully tackled had none the less been a real test of their strength and ability to govern. Sultan Baybars, whose ascent to the throne meant the return of the Baḥrīyah,[36] was to give further proof of these qualities in his crowded reign of seventeen years (1260–1277).[37] His achievements merit his recognition as founder of the Mamluk state, and he indeed was the organizer of its military and administrative machinery on imperial lines.

Kutuz had no son to be used as a foil against the coup d'état which Baybars had so swiftly accomplished; but the governor of Damascus, 'Alam-ad-Dīn, whom Kutuz had reinstated in the Syrian capital, refused to recognize what had taken place in Cairo, proclaiming himself sultan and calling upon Aiyūbid princes and Mamluk governors of Syrian provinces to acknowledge him. His summons met with little or no response, and Baybars forthwith sent against him an expedition which brought him to Cairo in chains (January 1261), installing in Damascus as governor al-Bunduqdār, the one-time master of Baybars.[38] Meanwhile in Cairo a nascent beduin insurrection was quickly stifled; the rebels were surrounded; and their Shī'ite leader al-Kūrānī was hanged with many of his associates.

Baybars repeatedly demonstrated quickness of action, resolution, courage, shrewdness, prescience, and determination. He seemed to be able to accomplish many things almost at the same time, and to be always on the move directing affairs of state in his travels in Egypt and Syria. In these opening months of his reign he badly needed to put his house in order, so that he might deal with a problem created by the extinction of the 'Abbāsid caliphate in Baghdad; various dynasts were now contemplating its revival in their own countries, and for their own advantage. An-Nāṣir of Aleppo and Damascus may have toyed with the idea of attracting a refugee 'Abbāsid to his court to bolster up his own waning fortunes by acknowledging him as caliph, but the march of events overwhelmed

[36] Al-Maqrīzī, *As-sulūk*, I, 437.

[37] On Baybars see Muḥyī-ad-Dīn, *Sīrat al-malik aẓ-Ẓāhir* (ed. and tr. S. F. Sadeque, Dacca, 1956).

[38] 'Alam-ad-Dīn was later restored to favor and appointed governor of Aleppo by Baybars.

the Aiyūbid prince. Baybars promptly put the same idea into effect; he proclaimed an 'Abbāsid refugee caliph with the honorific al-Mustanṣir (1261), and supplied him with armed forces in a vain effort to regain Baghdad.[39] Al-Mustanṣir's death did not discourage Baybars, who in 1262 set up another 'Abbāsid, less closely related to the murdered al-Musta'ṣim, as the caliph al-Ḥākim in Cairo in 1262.[40] He thus made Egypt the seat of the caliphate and the cynosure of Moslem eyes. Cairo, the new focus of Islam, was nearer Europe and more accessible to many Moslem countries than was Baghdad. Moslem savants flocked to Cairo, where they found plenty of patronage and encouragement, and the learning they spread elsewhere in the process of migrating to Egypt gave impetus to a sort of renaissance in Islam. But the 'Abbāsid "caliphs" in Cairo were to be mere court functionaries of the Mamluk sultans.

Baybars had another pressing problem to solve before he felt wholly secure. The Aiyūbid prince of Kerak, al-Mughīth 'Umar, continued to assert his own legitimist claims, persisting in serious schemes of acquiring Egypt, unlike the other Syrian Aiyūbids, who now lived in peace with the Mamluk sultanate. Baybars knew him well, having taken refuge at his court as an exile in previous years, and collaborated with him in several raids on the Egyptian border. At the first move of Baybars against the fortress principality of Kerak, al-Mughīth caused the caliph to intercede for him, without any lessening of his pretensions. Eventually Baybars had him entrapped, and sent him a prisoner to the citadel of Cairo, where he was executed on a charge of treasonable correspondence with the Mongols (April 1263).

During these three years of general consolidation of his empire, Baybars had also been busy with the organization of a regular Mamluk army, the levying of Arab contingents, the rebuilding of a navy, the redistribution of fiefs among the army commanders and the soldiery, the building of roads and bridges, and the digging of irrigation canals in various parts of Egypt. He also strengthened the fortresses of Syria, garrisoned them with mamluks, and connected Damascus and Cairo by a twice-weekly postal service. Moreover, the fortifications of Alexandria were carefully repaired and inspected, and the estuaries of the Nile at Damietta and Rosetta were protected by watchtowers. To those years also belong the building of the mosque and college (*madrasah*) of Baybars, besides

39 Muḥyī-ad-Dīn, *Sīrat al-malik* (tr. Sadeque), pp. 123–134.
40 *Ibid.*, pp. 158–160; adh-Dhahabī, *Ta'rīkh al-Islām*, folio 257.

a free cemetery with an endowment for the burial of poor Moslems.[41]

Having disposed of the last recalcitrant Aiyūbid in Syria, Baybars now felt able to embark upon a vigorous foreign policy that had the double purpose of keeping the Mongols away from Mamluk border territories in northern Iraq, and of punishing those crusader states which had made common cause with them, while suitably preparing against any crusading expedition from Europe. He naturally had little knowledge of what had been taking place in the west to make the formation of a European crusade on the old grand scale almost an impossibility; but it was in consonance with his policy of thoroughness to have the Egyptian coasts well manned and fortified. He then initiated amicable relations with the Byzantine emperor Michael VIII Palaeologus, and with Manfred of Sicily, who could be relied upon to inform Baybars of any European activity intended to help the crusader states in Syria.[42] Manfred's enemy Charles of Anjou accordingly sent a friendly embassy to Cairo, which Baybars received in 1264.[43] Even earlier Baybars had allied himself with the chief of the Golden Horde of Kîpchak Mongols in the valley of the Volga, Berke Khan, a grandson of Genghis Khan who had embraced Islam in his youth and was now the inveterate enemy of the Īl-khanids of Persia. Equally important for Baybars was the alliance with the Selchükids of Rūm, whose strategic position threatened both the northern Mongol flank and the Christian kingdom of Cilician Armenia. In order to forestall any surprise Mongol attack on his eastern frontiers through northern Iraq Baybars had the earth scorched along the invasion route between Amida and Akhlat, and repaired the Syrian fortifications that the Mongols had once destroyed.

Small wonder that by 1265 Baybars was able to launch a vigorous military offensive in more than one direction. He began by capturing the ports of Caesarea, Haifa, and Arsuf, razing their fortifications to the ground, and returning to Egypt to resume an unfinished inspection of fortifications and waterways in Alexandria, and to replenish his forces with a new Mamluk army.[44] In 1266 he gave orders for intensive raids against the crusader towns along the Syrian coast, while he himself took Safad, returning to Damas-

[41] K. A. C. Creswell, *The Works of Sultan Baibars* (Cairo, 1926).

[42] The embassy to Manfred included the historian Ibn-Wāṣil.

[43] Al-Maqrīzī, *As-sulūk*, I, 513. On Charles of Anjou, see above, chapter X, pp. 363–371, and chapter XVI, pp. 583–590.

[44] On this and subsequent campaigns of Baybars against the crusaders, see above, chapter XVI, pp. 575–582.

cus to prepare for an expedition against Armenia, whose capital, Sis, he next sacked in a swift campaign.[45] After a brief sojourn in Cairo, where he generally passed the winter months to rest his troops, he repaired to Syria in 1267 to inspect the new fortifications of Safad, going back to Cairo highly elated with the results of his campaign. Early in 1268 he again went to Syria, where he took Jaffa, Belfort, and, after a strenuous siege, Antioch, chief city of the strongest crusading principality in those years. He could well afford to spend 1269 in leisurely travels in Egypt, Syria, and Arabia, performing the pilgrimage to Mecca with great pomp, and incidentally realizing his dream of extending Mamluk sovereignty over the holy cities of Islam. He left the emir Shams-ad-Dīn Marwān in Mecca as governor, to present the Ka'bah with a covering embroidered with the sultan's name in letters of gold.

In 1270 Baybars conducted negotiations with the Syrian branch of the Assassins, forcing the Old Man of the Mountain to pay tribute as the price of peace. In that same year Louis IX led his fateful crusade into Tunisia; Baybars stayed in Cairo closely watching events, and even considered giving help to his fellow Moslems against the invaders.[46] But the death of the French king on the Tunisian coast dispelled all his anxiety, and in 1271 the sultan marched to Syria, where he took Chastel Blanc, Krak des Chevaliers, and 'Akkār, followed by the swift conquest of several fortresses of the Assassins. In that year a flotilla of eleven ships attacked the shores of Cyprus, but was repulsed and wrecked in a storm.[47] Baybars went back to Cairo late in the year, but returned to Syria in 1272 to make a general inspection of Syrian garrison towns. He left Damascus in 1273 for Bira on the Euphrates, where he inflicted a severe defeat on the Mongols, after swimming the river to meet them at the head of his troops. On his way back to Damascus he seized the remaining fortresses of the Assassins, while other Mamluk troops were operating in Cyrenaica, Cilicia, and Nubia.[48]

The crusader principalities now felt that their only safety lay in a general truce, which Baybars concluded with them in 1274, and a year of calm ensued. In 1275, however, Baybars was again in Cilician Armenia, where he seized and sacked Sis and Ayas; other

[45] For Baybars' attacks on Cilician Armenia, see above, chapter XVIII, pp. 653–655.

[46] On the crusade against Tunisia, see above, chapter XIV, pp. 508–518, and chapter on North Africa in the forthcoming vol. III.

[47] Al-Maqrīzī, *As-sulūk*, I, 593–594; on Cyprus during this period, see above, chapter XVII, pp. 615–616.

[48] For Baybars' Nubian operations, see al-Maqrīzī, *As-sulūk*, I, 608, 621–623; and J. S. Trimingham, *Islam in the Sudan* (London, 1949), pp. 69, 79. For a spirited treatment of Baybars' campaigns, see also Wiet, *Les Sultans mamlouks*, pp. 252–254.

Mamluk troops were once more in Nubia in that year. In 1277 Baybars was again in the north, to meet combined Mongol and Selchükid forces in Anatolia, where he won a signal victory in a battle near Albistan. He then entered Caesarea, in Cappadocia, where he received the homage of the people and caused coins to be struck in his name as suzerain of the Selchükids of Rūm.[49] By June of 1277 Baybars was back in Damascus, where he died at the height of his eventful career, after a short illness following a bout of drinking fermented mare's milk, in which a poisoned cup was rumored to have figured.[50]

Berke Khan, the eldest son of Baybars, reigned for only a little more than two years, during which the usual Mamluk plotting and wirepulling came into full play. The young sultan was acquainted with the art of government, since his father had appointed him co-sultan early in his reign, and had left him as virtual ruler of Egypt during his frequent campaigns in Syria. Yet neither his experience, nor his too literal interpretation of his father's instructions to execute potential rivals,[51] availed him in keeping the throne for long. Berke Khan was deposed in August 1279 by his own father-in-law Kalavun, and was given the province of Kerak in Transjordan as an independent principality. Salamîsh, another son of Baybars, only seven years old, was solemnly proclaimed sultan at the suggestion of Kalavun, now appointed guardian and commander-in-chief, with all the trappings of a co-sultan. Kalavun placed his own supporters in most of the key offices of the administration in Egypt and Syria, thus preparing the way for the inevitable next step. Salamîsh was quietly deposed (December 1279), and was sent later to join his brother in Transjordan. Baybars had a third son, Khiḍr, but there was no need any longer to resort to the pitiful farce of setting up child sultans on the throne. Kalavun had made all his dispositions to become sultan himself; Khiḍr was given Krak de Montréal (ash-Shaubak) near Kerak, to rule after the fashion of his eldest brother.[52]

Sultan Kalavun was a Baḥrī mamluk like Baybars, and followed closely in his steps. He had witnessed the coming of the Mamluk sultanate into power, and had played an active though unspectacular part in its fortunes.[53] Having acceded to the throne, Kalavun had to

[49] See above, chapter XXI, pp. 727–728.

[50] On Baybars' death, and the rumors of poison, see the account by Sadeque in his edition of Muḥyī-ad-Dīn, *Sīrat al-malik*, p. 11.

[51] See the letter in Ibn-Wāṣil, *op. cit.*, II, folio 440A.

[52] Abū-l-Maḥāsin, *An-nujūm*, VIII, 27.

[53] On this phase of his career, see al-Maqrīzī, *As-sulūk*, I, 436, 445, 528.

face a double measure of the usual opposition, which chose for its own ends to feign loyalty to the house of Baybars. Several Mamluk emirs who had participated in the military triumphs of Baybars felt that they had as good a claim to the sultanate as did Kalavun; notably Sungur al-Ashkar, governor of Damascus, who proclaimed himself sultan immediately after the mysterious death of Berke Khan in his principality of Kerak. Sungur found support among the beduins of Syria as well as the remaining sons of Baybars, Khiḍr and Salamîsh, whose adherents were by no means negligible. Sungur was routed by Kalavun's forces in a battle south of Damascus, but he escaped and appealed for help to the Îl-khan Abagha, son and successor of Hulagu. Abagha had been one of the most persistent protagonists of the scheme of crusader-Mongol alliance against the Mamluk empire; he had seen with his own eyes the havoc wrought on Mongol armies at Albistan, and was only too eager to aid Sungur or any other rebel from Egypt or Syria in any plan to disrupt the Mamluk empire.

Mongol troops thereupon invaded northern Syria (September 1280), causing much destruction around Aleppo. Kalavun marched to Syria to meet a second Mongol invasion on a larger scale, but before the clash took place Sungur had made peace with the sultan, in exchange for the promise of certain north Syrian fortress towns to rule independently, and of an unprecedented rank in the Mamluk hierarchy that would make him second only to the sultan. Kalavun was thus able to concentrate his whole attention upon the Mongols, who had mustered a formidable army under Mengü-Timur, brother of Abagha, with contingents of Armenians, Georgians, and others. The contending forces met at Homs (October 1281), where the Mongols were defeated and compelled to withdraw from Syria. In 1282 Abagha died, and was succeeded in the Mongol Îl-khanate of Persia by Tegüder ("Aḥmad"), who had recently embraced Islam, and showed his devotion to the religion he had adopted in friendly letters to Kalavun, expressing his ardent desire to live on terms of peace and amity with all Moslem countries. The Mongols as a people were far from sharing these sentiments, and when the pagan Arghun came to the throne in 1284, Tegüder's policy was reversed, for Arghun revived Abagha's old scheme of a crusader-Mongol alliance to crush the Mamluk empire. To block it Kalavun, like Baybars, entered into diplomatic relations with the Mongols of the Golden Horde, the Byzantine emperor, the kings of France, Castile, and Aragon-Sicily, the republic of Genoa, and the German emperor, Rudolph of Hapsburg.

On the way to meet the invading Mongols, Kalavun had prudently renewed the general truce concluded by Baybars towards the end of his reign with crusader cities anxious for peace. That truce was nominally for ten years, and some of the new terms added to it by Kalavun were none too favorable or reassuring to the crusaders.[54] But Kalavun had no intention of respecting his word the moment his lands were free of the Mongols. He had made known his intentions against the crusaders in the first year of his reign in a letter to Sungur al-Ashkar;[55] so when the fear of the Mongols was finally abated, his first target was the Hospitallers' fortress of al-Marqab, covering the northern frontiers of the county of Tripoli. Kalavun fell upon it suddenly, and undermined its walls so rapidly that the garrison had to surrender and depart (May 1285). He then marched against Maraclea, a strong castle built in the sea, belonging to a vassal[56] of Bohemond VII of Tripoli. The sultan warned the latter that unless the castle was dismantled and abandoned, he would make war upon the county itself, and Bohemond had to give the necessary instructions (1286), if only to save his own shrunken territory. About that time Margaret of Tyre had to purchase a treaty of peace with Kalavun on humiliating terms, and a similar treaty was made with king Leon III of Cilician Armenia, in return for a heavy yearly tribute.

Having achieved so much against the crusaders at little cost to himself, Kalavun was able to think of ousting his old rival, Sungur al-Ashkar, from his vast principality in Syria, ultimately compelling him to give it up and retire to obscurity in Cairo (1287). Kalavun also harassed Khiḍr, prince of Kerak, until he too yielded and came to Cairo. Khiḍr and his brother Salamîsh were sent much later to honorable exile in Constantinople. In 1288, Kalavun sent two disciplinary expeditions southward to regulate Nubian relations with the Mamluk sultanate, though no serious attempt was made to turn the country into a dependency.[57] About the same time, succession disputes in Tripoli, following the death of Bohemond VII without male issue, decided Kalavun to capture the city for himself. But he had to lay siege to it, storm it, and level it to the ground, before he could claim it as his own (1289). Shortly afterwards the fortress of Botron south of Tripoli was taken, and also

[54] For Kalavun's attacks on the crusading states, see above, chapter XVI, pp. 589–595.

[55] Al-Maqrīzī, *As-sulūk*, I, 641.

[56] Identified by Röhricht, *Königreich Jerusalem*, pp. 988–989, as Bartholomew Embriaco (see above, chapter, XVI, p. 591), but by Rey (p. 387) as Meillor III of Ravendel.

[57] Al-Maqrīzī, *As-sulūk*, I, 736–737, 743, 749–755; Trimingham, *Islam in the Sudan*, p. 70.

demolished; but this was Kalavun's last feat of arms. He went back to Egypt to prepare for the siege of Acre, on the convenient pretext that Moslem traders in the city had been mistreated; but when about to depart with his army he fell ill and died in camp (November or December 1290) at the age of seventy.

Kalavun had followed Baybars' example in embellishing Egyptian and Syrian towns with buildings and renovations, including a mosque, a mausoleum, and a general hospital in Cairo which brought special credit to its founder.[58] He had given much attention to discipline and efficiency in the Mamluk army, a third of which he organized for duty in the citadel of Cairo; the name Burjīyah (men of the tower) was thenceforward attached to the new corps.

It was perhaps likewise in imitation of Baybars, but in hope of better family luck, that Kalavun appointed his eldest son, 'Alī, as his successor in the Mamluk sultanate. When 'Alī died mysteriously, a second son, al-Ashraf Khalīl, was made heir, though Kalavun, whether from dislike of Khalīl's violence and alleged immorality, or because he suspected him of poisoning the elder brother, could not be induced to sign the formal deed of appointment. Yet Kalavun consented to have Khalīl solemnly declared his successor, and had him made deputy-sultan before leaving for his last campaign in Syria. Even after Khalīl had been cleared of the charge of causing the death of his brother, Kalavun left the diploma of appointment unsigned, partly because of the mixed advice of his ministers, such as the emir Turun-Tai, who detested Khalīl and used every possible occasion to slight him.[59] It also seems likely that Kalavun was withholding his signature for the benefit of a younger son, Muḥammad, who was born to him by a young wife in his later years; but the sultan's unexpected death left no time for hesitation, and Khalīl duly succeeded to the throne, which was to be held thereafter by Kalavun's descendants for nearly a hundred years.

When sultan Khalīl saw his father's unsigned diploma at the first meeting of the council of state in Cairo (November 1290) he quietly remarked: "My father refused to bestow on me what God had ordained to give me", and threw the scrap of paper away.[60] It was an appropriately regal remark for a young sultan of twenty-seven, notoriously accused of ungodliness, violence, and unnatural vice. Khalīl pursued a vindictive course of action against those of

[58] For a graphic description of this hospital and other buildings of Kalavun, see al-Maqrīzī, *As-sulūk*, I, appendix IX, 997–1001.

[59] *Ibid.*, I, 757.

[60] *Ibid.*, I, 756; Abū-l-Maḥāsin, *An-nujūm*, VIII, 4.

his father's men whom he had known to be the source of his own unpopularity and who had accused him of fratricide. The consequent executions, imprisonments, and confiscations of property turned Khalīl's short reign of three years into a long nightmare, in which the sultan's favorite minister and lifelong companion, Ibn-as-Sal'ūs, grotesquely lorded it over the court.[61] Khalīl's old enemy, the emir Turun-Tai, was the first to suffer death after terrible torture; yet the sultan provided amply for the dead man's blind son.[62] Khalīl even remitted some arrears of taxes in Egypt and Syria to alleviate hardship, and was remarkably respectful to the memory of his father Kalavun, observing the anniversaries of his death with much solemnity and ceremonial.[63]

In external affairs, Khalīl had courage, ability, and vigor. He took up his father's plan of besieging Acre, after careful additional preparations in men and material. The siege engines which he finally assembled before the city, in the spring of 1291, numbered more than were known to have been employed at any previous operation in the crusades. On the other hand, Acre was splendidly fortified, and it withstood fierce bombardment for ten consecutive days, after which Khalīl decided to storm it. The final assault took place in the early morning of Friday, May 18, 1291, while the doomed city was shrouded in mist; effective resistance soon became hopeless, and for ten days longer Acre was subjected to fire and sword as well as plunder, followed by the dismantling of its fortifications. Within a few months after the fall of Acre, all the other coastal towns still in the possession of the crusaders were taken in turn by a small army force, and all were demolished except Beirut, which capitulated as soon as it was summoned to surrender.[64]

The sultan returned to Damascus with a multitude of captives in his train; the news that preceded his triumphal progress caused feasts and festivities to be held everywhere in Egypt and Syria. Poets sang the praises of the sultan who had made an end of the last crusaders in Syria, and the sultan's cruelties towards his father's men were for the time forgotten. Khalīl then busied himself with renovating and developing fortifications and public buildings in Aleppo, Baalbek, Damascus, and Tripoli; but he returned to Cairo early in 1292, apparently full of dreams of further conquest.

He caused the 'Abbāsid caliph al-Ḥākim to preach a holy war against the Mongols, but his subsequent march to the upper

[61] Al-Maqrīzī, *As-sulūk*, I, 760–763, 771. [62] *Ibid.*, I, 757–759.

[63] *Ibid.*, I, 759, 764, 774–775.

[64] On the fall of Acre and other cities of Frankish Syria, see above, chapter XVI, pp. 595–598.

Euphrates to challenge them to fight was limited to the siege and capture of Hromgla (July 1292), a fortress town opposite Bira. He signaled this victory in Cairo by arresting a number of leading emirs of his government, whom he suspected of making trouble for him in his absence, and imprisoning them.[65] The following spring he prepared for an invasion of Cilician Armenia, but he moved no farther than Damascus, where envoys sent by the Armenian king, Ṭoros III, ceded to him the towns of Marash and Behesni as the price of peace.[66] He returned to Cairo to review his troops in preparation for a campaign apparently against the Mongols, for no sooner had he settled in his capital than some Mongol envoys arrived with daring demands for the surrender of Aleppo, on behalf of the Il-khan Gaikhatu. The sultan dismissed the envoys with the threat that he would march upon Baghdad. This idle exchange of bluster led to no hostilities. Some of Khalīl's own men who could no longer tolerate his abnormality, capriciousness, and suspicion lured him into a hunting party northwest of Cairo, where he was taken unawares and brutally cut to pieces (December 1293).

Mamluk polity was that of a military oligarchy, in which the sultan, a mamluk by origin (unlike his successor sons) was surrounded by a caste of emirs, who had been mamluks themselves. Like the sultan, these emirs were foreigners of various origins, but in the thirteenth century mostly Kipchaks like both Baybars and Kalavun. The emirs, who were organized as cavalry of well defined grades and services, held all military commands and court offices, as well as high administrative appointments in the provinces of Egypt and the rest of the Mamluk empire. They were all Moslems, nominally at least, and were collectively called Men of the Sword, to distinguish them from Men of the Pen, who were the native holders of civil appointments, many of whom were non-Moslems. For their services, and in proportion to their grades, the emirs were rewarded with fiefs (Arabic singular *iqṭā'*), which might be landed estates (compact or scattered), towns, villages, or even annual allowances from the revenue of a tax, customs duty, or excise levied by the central government.[67] Each emir was obliged to divide two thirds of his fief among his own private mamluks, by granting them either portions of the fief, or pecuniary allowances from its revenue. Allocation and supervision of fiefs and sub-fiefs

[65] Al-Maqrīzī, *As-sulūk*, I, 781. [66] See above, chapter XVIII, pp. 655–656.

[67] Poliak, *Feudalism in the Middle East*, p. 18. This work is an exhaustive study of the whole subject, based on all the available material, and the writer is indebted to it for several ideas expressed here.

were the charge of the state department for the army, the *dīwān al-jaish*, called also the *dīwān al-iqṭā'*; but there were other grants, in money and in kind, which were made at certain times by the sultan to the emirs through other departments of the state.[68]

The rudiments of the system go back to the days of Saladin in the twelfth century. But it should be made clear that though the Mamluk system of the late thirteenth century bore striking resemblance to that of feudalism in western Europe, the two systems differed fundamentally and essentially in regard to the theory of land tenure. Thus the fief, which formed the backbone of the feudal order in the west, was in the Mamluk system no more than a land or other endowment, significantly called in French "une dotation foncière", which gave the holding emir, in the words of an eminent French scholar, "ni la propriété, ni la possession, ni la jouissance du fonds; elle fait seulement participer le titulaire aux revenus du sol, dont elle lui confère l'impôt".[69]

Springing from a stratum common to the rest of the military oligarchy, the sultan came to the throne by no hereditary right of succession. He was simply chosen by the common consent of the emirs in council, and on his elevation to the dignity he was duly recognized by the 'Abbāsid "caliph" in Cairo, from the time of Baybars onwards. Thus in fact the sultan was rather a head Mamluk or a chief emir than king in the absolute sense of the word, though men like Baybars and Kalavun had no great difficulty in towering high above their entourage, and Kalavun's progeny, to the fifth generation, would hold the Mamluk sultanate in their hands in almost unbroken succession.

The Mamluk army consisted of three principal units: the knights who were in the sultan's service without being his freedmen, the royal mamluks who were the freedmen of the reigning sultan, and the private mamluks of the emirs. There were sub-units within these categories, with special assignments of service in peace and war, such as the Baḥrī corps, which had produced Baybars and Kalavun. There were also auxiliary troops of Arab beduins, Turkomans, Kurds, Syrians, and Palestinians as well as small native Egyptian levies.[70] Otherwise the rest of the population of the Mamluk empire had little in common with their stern foreign masters, to whom they were useful as city artisans supplying the ruling Mamluk fraternity with all their needs in peace and war, or

[68] Poliak, *Feudalism in the Middle East*, pp. 4–5, 20–22.

[69] M. Gaudefroy-Demombynes, *La Syrie à l'époque des mamelouks* (Paris, 1923), p. cxiv; see also Poliak, *op. cit.*, p. 18, for a clear definition of the Mamluk fief.

[70] *Ibid.*, pp. 9–15.

as servile tenants and serfs in the countryside, cultivating the land and paying the various taxes. Beyond these functions, and that of filling judicial, religious and minor offices in administrative departments of the Mamluk empire, the native population in general had no part in the business of the state.

Such was the impression which the socio-economic historian Ibn-Khaldūn formed for himself, on his visit to Cairo and Alexandria at the beginning of the fifteenth century: "The sultan of Egypt," he noted, "lives in perfect tranquillity; so rare is the spirit of faction or rebellion among the people of that country, where one sees nothing but a ruling sultan and submissive subjects. The government of the country is in the hands of Turkish Mamluk sultans and their appertaining bands of similar Turkish stock, succeeding each other, family after family, with a caliph who is denoted ʻAbbāsid, and is a descendant of the caliphs of Baghdad."[71] Ibn-Khaldūn has another acid remark, in which he describes the good people bearing themselves in life as if they had finished with the Day of Judgment.[72] But if this description of placidity held true of the people of Cairo, who would nevertheless join in public rejoicings when the sultan came back from a victorious campaign or had his son circumcised, it certainly applied neither to the turbulent mamluk companies in the city, nor to the peasantry, rife with economic unrest caused by bad agrarian conditions in the provinces, where Mamluk tyranny bore down more heavily.[73]

For all their tyranny and stiff social isolation from their subjects, however, the Mamluk sultans and their emirs were active patrons of art, architecture, and solid learning. The latter field would claim a splendid array of biographers, theologians, historians, geographers, and encyclopaedic scholars in the fourteenth century; but the preceding fifty years, though not devoid of learned men of distinction in Egypt and Syria, saw especially the building of magnificent mosques, graceful colleges, stately tomb chapels, and other foundations attesting to the splendor of Mamluk rule. The enthusiasm which produced these monuments, in increasing number and variety throughout the Mamluk period, has been somehow attributed partly to an instinct for architecture, partly to a passion for display. But having been the creation of the Aiyūbids, who were themselves great builders of pious works, the Mamluks evidently aped their masters in this respect, before and after the establishment of the Mamluk sultanate, in much the same way as they generally

[71] Ibn-Khaldūn, *Al-muqaddimah*, quoted by Wiet, *Les sultans mamlouks*, p. 249.
[72] Al-Maqrīzī, *Al-khiṭaṭ*, I, 50.
[73] Poliak, *op. cit.*, p. 66.

imitated them in methods of government and administration. The Mamluk sultans and their emirs, however, surpassed their Aiyūbid predecessors in pious works, apparently because as a group they were recently converted Moslems, with additional zeal for their adopted religion. Because of their imperfect understanding of the tenets of Islam owing to the paucity of their Arabic, and because of their over-literal interpretation of the precepts of the Moslem religion as regards reward and punishment for deeds and actions in this world, they apparently indulged in these material manifestations of piety as a guarantee for their own salvation in the hereafter. This theory is supported by the low standard of their private morals. Their abundant wealth and prosperity, acquired especially through the international transit trade, enabled them to atone for such shortcomings by lavish expenditures for public works.

IMPORTANT DATES AND EVENTS

1187 July 4	Saladin defeats the army of Jerusalem decisively at Hattin
1187 July 14	Conrad of Montferrat lands at Tyre, takes command of defense
1187 October 2	Jerusalem surrenders to Saladin
1187 October 20	Urban III dies; Gregory VIII becomes pope (October 21)
1187–1190	Saladin conquers almost all the territory of the Latin states
1187 Nov.–Dec.	Saladin unsuccessfully besieges Tyre
1187 December 17	Gregory VIII dies; Clement III becomes pope (December 19)
1188 March 27	Emperor Frederick I Barbarossa takes the cross at Mainz
1189 January 22	Henry II of England and Philip II of France take the cross
1189 May 11	Frederick I leads German crusaders overland from Regensburg
1189 July 6	Henry II dies; son Richard I becomes king of England
1189 August 27	Guy of Lusignan begins siege of Acre; Pisan fleet blockades it
1189 September 6	English crusaders aid Portuguese to recapture Silves from Moors
1189 November 18	William II of Sicily dies; Tancred of Lecce seizes throne
1190 March 22–28	German crusaders cross Dardanelles, start march across Anatolia
1190 May 18	German crusaders defeat Selchükid Turks, take Iconium
1190 June 10	Frederick I drowns in Cilicia; army proceeds to Antioch, disbands
1190 July 4	Richard I and Philip II start on crusade from Vézelay
1190 July 27	Crusaders led by Henry of Champagne arrive at Acre
1190 September	Richard I and Philip II arrive at Messina by different routes
1190 November 24	Conrad of Montferrat marries Isabel of Jerusalem, claims throne
1191 March 28 (or 20)	Clement III dies; Celestine III becomes pope (March 30, or 24)
1191 March 30	Philip II sails from Messina to Acre, arriving April 20
1191 April 10	Richard I sails from Messina to Crete, Rhodes, Cyprus
1191 May 6–June 5	Richard I conquers Cyprus from Isaac Comnenus, sails to Syria
1191 July 12	Acre surrenders after assaults by combined crusading armies
1191 July 31	Philip II sails from Acre, leaving Richard I in sole command
1191 September 6	Richard I defeats Saladin's forces at Arsuf, on way to Jaffa
1192 April 28	Conrad of Montferrat is killed at Tyre by Assassins
1192 May 5	Henry of Champagne marries Isabel, rules kingdom of Jerusalem
1192 May	Guy of Lusignan buys Cyprus from Templars, founds dynasty
1192 August	Death of Selchükid (of Rūm) Kîlîj-Arslan II disrupts Anatolia
1192 October 9	Richard I sails from Acre; Third Crusade ends
1193 March 4	Saladin dies; Aiyūbid and Zengid princes struggle for provinces
1194 February 20	Tancred dies; Sicily comes under Hohenstaufen emperors
1194 March 25	Tökish (Khorezm-Shāh) kills Tughrul III (last Iranian Selchükid)
1194 autumn	Guy of Lusignan dies; brother Aimery inherits Cyprus
1195 April 8	Isaac II Angelus is deposed and blinded by brother Alexius III
1197 September 10	Henry of Champagne dies from fall, leaving no heir to Jerusalem
1197 September	Aimery is crowned king of Cyprus by German crusaders
1197 September 28	Emperor Henry VI dies, causing collapse of German crusade
1197 October	Aimery weds Isabel; they are crowned king and queen of Jerusalem
1198 January 6	Leon II is crowned king of Armenia by German crusaders
1198 January 8	Innocent III becomes pope, soon after death of Celestine III
1199	First political "crusade" is proclaimed, against Markward
1199 late November	French counts at Écry take cross for Fourth Crusade
1200 August 4	Saladin's brother al-'Ādil is proclaimed sultan of Egypt and Syria
1201 April	Bohemond III of Antioch dies; succession is disputed until 1219

1201 (probably)	Alexius [IV] escapes to Italy, asks crusaders to oust Alexius III
1202 early Sept.	Venetians under doge Enrico Dandolo take cross
1202 October 1	Crusaders sail on Venetian ships to attack Zara
1202 November 24	Zara falls, is looted and given to Venice; crusaders winter there
1203 April–June	Crusaders sail from Zara to Corfu to Euboea to Chalcedon
1203 July 6	French and Venetians begin siege of Constantinople
1203 July 17	Major assault fails, but Alexius III Angelus flees
1203 August 1	Alexius IV Angelus is crowned co-emperor with blinded Isaac II
1204 February 1	Alexius V Ducas deposes Isaac II, strangles Alexius IV
1204 March	Crusaders plan attack, sign treaty dividing potential spoils
1204 April 13	Constantinople is taken by Latins, sacked; Fourth Crusade ends
1204 April	Trebizond is captured by Comneni with Georgian support
1204 May 9	Baldwin of Flanders is elected Latin emperor by crusaders
1204 October	Byzantine empire is partitioned among crusaders
1204 November	Ioannitsa is crowned king of Bulgaria by Catholic primate Basil
1204–1205	Geoffrey of Villehardouin and William of Champlitte conquer Morea
1205 April 1	Aimery dies, leaving Cyprus and Jerusalem under separate regencies
1205 April 14	Baldwin is captured by Ioannitsa, slain; brother Henry is regent
1205 November	William of Champlitte becomes prince of "Achaea" (Morea)
1206 August 20	Henry is crowned Latin emperor of "Romania"
1207	Deaths of Ioannitsa and Boniface disrupt Bulgaria and Thessalonica
1208 January 14	Murder of Peter of Castelnau touches off Albigensian Crusade
1208 spring	Theodore I Lascaris is crowned Greek emperor at Nicaea
1209 May	Geoffrey I rules Achaea as vassal of Latin empire, founds dynasty
1209 July 22	Béziers is taken and sacked by northern French crusaders
1209 August 15	Carcassonne surrenders to crusaders, who overrun Trencavel lands
1210 October 3	John of Brienne and wife Mary are crowned rulers of Jerusalem
1212 spring	German phase of Children's Crusade starts in Rhine valley
1212 June	Stephen of Cloyes starts French phase of Children's Crusade
1212 July 16	Peter II of Aragon defeats Moors at Las Navas de Tolosa
1212 August 25	Nicholas of Cologne and German pilgrims reach Genoa, disperse
1213 September 12	Peter II is slain as Simon of Montfort wins battle of Muret
1215 November	Fourth Lateran Council considers Languedoc, Fifth Crusade, etc.
1216 February 14	Leon II of Armenia installs Raymond Roupen at Antioch (to 1219)
1216 June 11	Latin emperor Henry dies; Peter of Courtenay is named emperor
1216 July 16	Innocent III dies; Honorius III becomes pope (July 18)
1217 early July	Hungarian crusaders under Andrew II start on Fifth Crusade
1218 early January	Andrew II leaves Acre for Hungary, having accomplished nothing
1218 January 10	Hugh I of Cyprus dies, leaving infant son Henry I under regency
1218 May 27	Fifth Crusade arrives off Damietta to attack Aiyūbid Egypt
1218 June 25	Simon of Montfort is killed while besieging Toulouse
1218 August 31	Al-'Ādil dies; sons divide realm, al-Kāmil ruling Egypt as sultan
1218	John Asen takes Tirnovo, becomes king of Bulgaria
1219 early	Peter of Courtenay dies in captivity; son Robert is named emperor
1219 May 2	Death of Leon II of Armenia occasions struggle for succession
1219 November 5	Damietta is abandoned to crusaders by Egyptian garrison
1220 November 22	Frederick II is crowned Holy Roman emperor by Honorius III
1221 August 30	Crusaders surrender to al-Kāmil, evacuate Damietta (September 8)
1222 August	Theodore I Lascaris dies; son-in-law John Ducas Vatatzes succeeds
1222 August	Raymond VI of Toulouse dies; son Raymond VII succeeds as count
1224 autumn	Thessalonica falls to Theodore of Epirus, who assumes purple
1225 October 6	An-Nāṣir, last strong 'Abbāsid caliph (from 1180), dies
1225 November 9	Frederick II marries Isabel of Brienne, claims throne of Jerusalem
1226 early June	Louis VIII of France leads crusade against Languedoc
1226 June	Heṭoum I marries Ṛoupenid heiress Isabel, becomes king of Armenia
1226 November 8	Louis VIII dies, leaving young son Louis IX under regency
1227 March 18	Honorius III dies; Gregory IX becomes pope next day
1227 September 29	Frederick II is excommunicated by Gregory IX (to August 28, 1230)
1228 January (?)	Robert of Courtenay dies; brother Baldwin II is under regency
1228 June 28	Frederick II sails on crusade in belated fulfillment of 1215 vow
1229 February 18	Frederick II gains Jerusalem under terms of treaty with al-Kāmil

1229 April 12	Peace of Paris ends Albigensian Crusade
1229 May 1	Frederick II sails from Acre to save Apulia from John of Brienne
1229 (about)	Geoffrey I of Achaea dies; son Geoffrey II succeeds
1230 April	John Asen of Bulgaria defeats Theodore of Epirus at Klokotnitsa
1231 August 15	Jalāl-ad-Dīn, last Khorezm-Shāh, is slain fleeing from Mongols
1231 September	Baldwin II marries Mary of Brienne; her father John is co-emperor
1232 April	Commune of Acre supports John of Ibelin against imperialists
1232 May 3	Imperialist forces defeat Cypriotes at Casal Imbert in Palestine
1232 June 15	Cypriotes defeat imperialists at Agridi in Cyprus
1233 winter	Bohemond IV of Antioch and Tripoli dies; son Bohemond V succeeds
1233 early April	Surrender of Kyrenia ends imperialist threat to Cyprus
1236	John of Ibelin, bailie of Cyprus and mayor of Acre, dies
1237 March 23	John of Brienne dies, leaving Baldwin II as sole Latin emperor
1238 March 9	Death of al-Kāmil touches off struggle among Aiyūbid princes
1239 March 20	Frederick II is again excommunicated by Gregory IX
1239 September 1	Crusaders under Theobald IV of Champagne arrive at Acre
1239 November 13	Crusading barons are defeated near Gaza by Aiyūbid army
1239 December 7	Jerusalem surrenders to Aiyūbids, who dismantle fortifications
1240 early	Gregory IX preaches a "crusade" against Frederick II
1240 summer	Theobald IV concludes favorable treaty with Aiyūb of Egypt
1241 April 13	Richard of Cornwall confirms treaty; Aiyūb returns Gaza prisoners
1241 June	John Asen of Bulgaria dies; son Coloman I succeeds
1241 August 22	Gregory IX dies; Celestine IV becomes pope (October 25)
1241 November 10	Celestine IV dies; 19-month papal interregnum ensues
1243 April 25	Conrad comes of age, ending Frederick II's claim on Jerusalem
1243 June 25	Innocent IV becomes pope, ending interregnum
1243 July 2	Mongols defeat Selchükids at Köse Dagh, make them vassals
1243 July 10	Fall of Tyre ends imperialist power in Syria
1244 August 23	Jerusalem is sacked by Khorezmians (never regained by Franks)
1244 October 17	Egyptians and Khorezmians shatter Frankish-Syrian forces near Gaza
1245 June 28	Council of Lyons considers Latin empire, "deposes" Frederick II
1246	Coloman I dies; most of Balkans fall to Nicaean empire
1246 summer	Geoffrey II of Achaea dies; brother William II succeeds
1248 August 25	Louis IX sails to Cyprus, winters there preparing crusade
1249 June 5	French crusaders land in Egypt, capture Damietta next day
1250 April 6	Louis IX and crusaders surrender to Egyptians
1250 May 2	Mamluks kill Aiyūbid Tūrān-Shāh; widow Shajar-ad-Durr rules
1250 May 6	Crusaders surrender Damietta, ransom Louis IX and other leaders
1250 July 30	Shajar-ad-Durr marries Aybeg, first Mamluk sultan of Egypt
1250 December 13	Frederick II dies; son Conrad IV (king of Jerusalem) succeeds
1252 January	Bohemond V of Antioch and Tripoli dies; son Bohemond VI succeeds
1253 January 18	Henry I of Cyprus dies, leaving infant son Hugh II under regency
1254 April 24	Louis IX sails for France after strengthening Palestine
1254 May 21	Conrad IV dies, leaving infant son Conradin as heir
1254 November 3	John Ducas Vatatzes dies; son Theodore II Lascaris succeeds
1254 December 7	Innocent IV dies; Alexander IV becomes pope (December 12)
1255	Civil war splits Frankish Greece
1256 December 20	Mongols under Hulagu take Alamut, end Assassins' sway in Persia
1257 April 11	Aybeg is murdered; son 'Alī becomes nominal Mamluk sultan
1258 February	Mongols under Hulagu sack Baghdad, kill last 'Abbāsid caliph
1258 August	Theodore II dies; Michael VIII Palaeologus seizes Nicaean throne
1259 summer	Michael VIII defeats Franks at Pelagonia, captures leaders
1259 November 12	Kutuz deposes 'Alī and becomes Mamluk sultan
1260 January 24	Mongols devastate Aleppo; Hulagu withdraws to Iran
1260 March 1	Mongols under Kitbogha take Damascus
1260 September 3	Mamluk army under Baybars routs Mongols at 'Ain Jālūt
1260 October 23	Baybars kills sultan Kutuz, seizes Mamluk throne
1261 May 25	Alexander IV dies; Urban IV becomes pope (August 29)
1261 July 25	Greeks reconquer Constantinople; Latin empire ends
1261 August 15	Michael VIII Palaeologus is crowned emperor in Constantinople
1264 October 2	Urban IV dies; Clement IV becomes pope (February 5, 1265)

1265 February 8	Hulagu dies; son Abagha establishes Il-Khanid dynasty in Iran
1266 February 26	Charles of Anjou defeats Manfred at Benevento, wins Sicily
1266 Aug.–Sept.	Mamluks under Kalavun devastate Armenia
1267 May 24	William II of Achaea becomes vassal of Charles of Anjou
1267 December 5	Hugh II of Cyprus dies; cousin Hugh III is chosen king
1268 May 18	Antioch is overwhelmed by Mamluks, completely sacked
1268 August 23	Charles of Anjou and William II defeat Conradin at Tagliacozzo
1268 October 29	Conradin is executed; Hugh III of Cyprus becomes king of Jerusalem
1268 November 29	Clement IV dies; 3-year papal interregnum ensues
1270 July 18	Louis IX and French crusaders land in Tunisia
1270 August 25	Louis IX dies; Charles of Anjou negotiates peace with Ḥafṣid emir
1270–1272	Edward [I] of England leads crusade to Tunisia and Palestine
1270 November 18	Crusaders leave Tunisia after ratifying treaty (November 1)
1271 April 8	Baybars takes Krak des Chevaliers after month's siege
1271 September 1	Gregory X becomes pope, ending interregnum
1273 July 9	Last Assassin stronghold in Syria surrenders to Mamluks
1274 July 6	Union of Latin and Greek churches takes place at Lyons
1275 May 11	Bohemond VI of Tripoli dies; son Bohemond VII is under regency
1276 January 10	Gregory X dies; three short pontificates follow
1277 March 18	Charles of Anjou purchases claim to throne of Jerusalem
1277 April 18	Mamluks under Baybars defeat Mongols at Albistan
1277 May 20	John XXI dies; Nicholas III becomes pope (November 25)
1277 July 1	Baybars dies; sons become nominal Mamluk sultans in turn
1278 May 1	William II dies; Achaea reverts to Charles of Anjou
1279 December	Kalavun seizes Mamluk throne, subdues revolt (1280)
1280 August 22	Nicholas III dies; Martin IV becomes pope (February 22, 1281)
1281 late Oct.	Mamluks under Kalavun rout invading Mongols near Homs
1282 March 30	Angevin garrison in Sicily is massacred (Sicilian Vespers)
1282 December 11	Michael VIII dies; son Andronicus II becomes emperor
1284 March 4	Hugh III of Cyprus and Jerusalem dies; son John I succeeds
1284 June 26	Pied Piper incident at Hameln recalls Children's Crusade
1285 January 7	Charles of Anjou dies, leaving realm to son Charles II
1285 March 28	Martin IV dies; Honorius IV becomes pope (April 2)
1285 May 20	John I of Cyprus dies; brother Henry II succeeds (to 1324)
1285 summer	Philip III of France leads fruitless crusade against Aragon
1286 August 15	Henry II of Cyprus is crowned king of Jerusalem at Tyre
1287 April 3	Honorius IV dies; Nicholas IV becomes pope (February 15, 1288)
1287 October 19	Bohemond VII of Tripoli dies childless, leaving disputed succession
1289 April 26	Mamluks under Kalavun take Tripoli, sack it, massacre Franks
1289 September 16	Florent of Hainault marries Isabel of Villehardouin, rules Achaea
1290 Nov. or Dec.	Kalavun dies while marching on Acre; son al-Ashraf Khalīl succeeds
1291 May 18	Mamluks under Khalīl take Acre, ending kingdom of Jerusalem
1291 May–August	Remaining Frankish towns in Syria surrender to Mamluks
1292 April 4	Nicholas IV dies; 2-year papal interregnum ensues
1293 December 13	Murder of Khalīl touches off struggle among Mamluks for throne
1294 July 5	Celestine V becomes pope, ending interregnum
1294 December 13	Celestine V abdicates; Boniface VIII becomes pope (December 24)
1297 January 23	Florent dies, leaving Achaea under regency
1298	Mamluks sack Adana, Mamistra, and other Cilician cities
1301 February 12	Philip of Savoy marries Isabel, rules Achaea under Charles II
1303 October 11	Boniface VIII dies; Benedict XI becomes pope (October 22)
1304 July 7	Benedict XI dies; Clement V becomes pope (1305–1314)
1306 June 5	Charles II deposes Philip of Savoy from Achaean rule
1307–1314	Templars suppressed by Philip IV of France and pope
1307 November 17	Mongol Bilarghu kills Armenian rulers, crippling Cilician state
1309 August 15	Rhodes surrenders to Hospitallers, who establish their order there
1311 March 15	Catalans overwhelm Franks (under Walter of Brienne), win Attica

GAZETTEER
AND NOTE ON MAPS

This gazetteer has been prepared to fill a variety of functions. Every place name found in the text or on the maps is here alphabetized and identified, variant spellings and equivalent names in other languages are supplied, and the map location is indicated by key letters. Thus it not only serves as an index to the maps, and a supplement to them, but is in itself a source for reference on matters of historical geography and changing nomenclature. Names originating in Arabic, Turkish, Persian, or Armenian have been carefully transliterated according to the systems described in the prefatory note on transliteration and nomenclature.

In the gazetteer, alphabetization is by the first capital letter of the form used in maps and text, disregarding such lower-case prefixes as *al-* and such geographical words as Cape, Gulf, Lake, Mount, and the like. The designation classical may mean Greek, Latin, biblical, or other ancient usage, and the designation medieval generally means that the name in question was in common use among speakers of various languages during the crusades, or appears in contemporary sources.

The maps themselves fall into two groups: ten locational and thirteen historical. On the locational maps may be found nearly every place name occurring in the text, except a few whose exact locations are unknown, a few outside the regions mapped, several in areas overcrowded with names, some of minimal importance or common knowledge, and many which occur only in names of crusaders or other persons. The six locational maps appearing in volume I have been revised, and maps of the Straits and Aegean, Frankish Greece, Languedoc, and Cyprus have been added.

The historical series comprises maps showing the changing fortunes of the crusaders and their Christian rivals and Moslem enemies between 1189 and 1311. All place names on this series (except in the Nile delta) also occur on the locational maps.

All maps for the second edition have been newly designed and prepared in the University of Wisconsin Cartographic Laboratory under the direction of Randall D. Sale, assisted by Michael P. Conzen. Base information was compiled from U.S.A.F. Jet Navigation Charts at a scale of 1:2,000,000. Historical data have been supplied by Dr. Harry W. Hazard from such standard works as Sprüner-Menke, Stieler, Andree, and Baedeker for Europe, Miller, Rubió y Lluch, and Bon for Frankish Greece, and Ramsey, Honigmann, Dussaud, Deschamps, Cahen, and LeStrange for the Near East. Additional information was found in *The Encyclopaedia of Islam* and *İslâm Ansiklopedisi*, in Yāqūt and other Arabic sources, in *The Columbia Lippincott Gazetteer of the World*, and on Michelin road maps of France and adjacent countries.

Aachen (German), Aix-la-Chapelle (French): city — F2b5, 1, 2.
Abenberg (German): town 15 miles SSW of Nuremberg.
Ablasṭa: town — see Albistan.
Abydus or Abydos (classical): town, now abandoned — J2d5, 6.
Abyssinia: region south of the Sudan — not in area mapped.
Acarnania (classical), Akarnanía (modern Greek): district of western Greece — I1e2, 11.
Acerra (Italian): town 8 miles NNE of Naples.
Achaea or Achaia (classical), Akhaïa (modern Greek): district of northern Morea — Ie, 11.
Achrida: town — see Ochrida.
Achyraūs (classical), Balikesir (Turkish): town — J3e1, 6.
Acre; Ptolemaïs (classical), Saint John or Saint Jean (medieval), ʿAkkā (Arabic): city, port — L1f3, 3, 4, 5, 13, 16, 18, 19, 22, 23.
Acrocorinth; Akrokorinthos (Greek): rock — I3e3, 11.
Adalia (medieval), Attalia (classical), Antalya (Turkish): port — K1e4, 1, 13.
Adana (classical, West Armenian, Turkish): city — L1e3, 3, 5, 13, 18, 23.
Ādharbādhagān: region of NW Persia — see Azerbaijan.
al-ʿĀdilīyah (Arabic): town — K2f4, 14, 15.
Admont (German): town — G5c3, 1.
Adramyttium (classical), Edremit (Turkish): town — J3e1, 1, 6, 8, 13.
Adrianople; Hadrianopolis (classical), Edirne (Turkish): city — J2d4, 1, 4, 6, 7, 8, 9, 10, 13, 22, 23.
Adriatic Sea — 1.
Aegean Sea — 6, 7, 8, 10, 11, 13.
Aegilia: island — see Cerigotto.
Aegina (classical), Aíyina (modern Greek): island — I4e3, 11.
Aegium: town — see Vostitsa.
Aenus: town — see Enos.
Aetolia (Latin), Aitōlia (ancient Greek): district of central Greece — I2e2, 11.
Afāmiyah: town — see Apamea.
Afula: village — see al-Fūlah.

Agathopolis (classical), Akhtopol (Bulgarian): town — J3d3, 6.
Agen (French): town — E1d1, 12.
Agenais (French): district around Agen — E1d1, 12.
Agridi (Greek): village — K4e5, 20.
Aguilers (medieval), Aighuile or Aiguilhe (French): village just north of Le Puy.
Ahasi; al-Aḥāsī (Arabic): small island just off Mahdia.
Ahil; Hagios Akhillēos (medieval Greek): island in Little Prespa Lake.
Ahlat: town — see Akhlat.
Aiello or Ajello Calabro (Italian): village — H2e1, 1.
Aighuile or Aiguilhe: village — see Aguilers.
Aigues-Mortes (French): town — E5d2, 12.
'Ain aṭ-Ṭuba'ūn — see Tubania.
'Ain Jālūt (Arabic: well of Goliath), Well of Harod (medieval): village — L1f3, 16, 22, 23.
'Ain Zarbâ or 'Ain Zarbah: town — see Anazarba.
Aintab; 'Aintāb (Arabic: spring of good taste), Anṭap (Armenian), Gaziantep (modern Turkish: warrior Aintab): city — L3e3, 17.
Aitōlia: district of central Greece — see Aetolia.
Aix-la-Chapelle: city — see Aachen.
Aíyina: island — see Aegina.
Aíyion: town — see Vostitsa.
Ajello Calabro: village — see Aiello.
'Ajlūn (Arabic): town — L1f3, 16.
Akarnanía: district of western Greece — see Acarnania.
Akhaïa: district of northern Morea — see Achaea.
Akhlat or Ahlat (Turkish), Akhlāṭ or Khilāṭ (Arabic), Khlaṭ (Armenian): town — M3e2, 13.
Akhtopol: town — see Agathopolis.
'Akkā: city, port — see Acre.
'Akkār (Arabic), Gibelcar (medieval): fortress — L2f1, 5, 17, 18, 19.
Akova or Ákovos: castle — see Matagrifon.
Ákra Maléas — see Malea, Cape.
Ákra Taínaron — see Matapan, Cape.
Akrokorinthos: rock — see Acrocorinth.
Akshehir: town — see Philomelium.
Alamannia or Allemania: medieval name for Germany.
Alamut; Alamūt (Persian, Arabic): fortress — O1e4, 4, 13, 21, 22.
Alashehir: town — see Philadelphia.
'Alāyā (Arabic), Alanya (Turkish): port — K2e4, 1, 13.
Alba (Italian): town — F4d1, 2.
Albania; Shqipni or Shqipri (Albanian): region NW of Epirus — Hd, 1, 11.
Albano Laziale (Italian): town 14 miles SE of Rome.
Albi (French): town — E3d2, 12.
Albigeois (French): district around Albi — Ed, 12.
Albistan; Arabissus (classical), Ablasṭa (West Armenian), Elbistan (Turkish): town — L3e2, 13, 22, 23.
Alcácer do Sal (Portuguese), al-Qaṣr or Qaṣr Abī-Dānis (Arabic): town — C2e2, 2.
Alençon (French): town — E1c2, 12.
Aleppo; Beroea or Chalybon (classical), Ḥalab (Arabic), Haleb (Turkish): city — L3e4, 3, 5, 13, 17, 18, 19.
Alexandretta; İskenderun (Turkish): port — L2e4, 17.
Alexandretta, Gulf of; Sinus Issicus (classical), İskenderun Körfezi (Turkish) — L1e4, 17.

Alexandria (classical), al-Iskandarīyah (Arabic): city, port — J5f4, 1, 4, 13, 14, 15, 22, 23.
Algeria; al-Jazā'ir (Arabic), Algérie (French): modern name for region east of Morocco.
Allemania — see Alamannia.
Almirós: town — see Halmyros.
Alpheus or Alpheios (classical), Alfiós (modern Greek): river — K2e3, 11.
Alps: mountain range — FGc, 1, 2.
Alsace (French), Elsass (German): region west of the upper Rhine — Fc, 1, 2.
Altenburg (German): town — G3b5, 2.
Altwied: town — see Wied.
Amalfi (Italian): port — G5d5, 1.
Amanus (classical), Gavur Daghi or Elma Daghi (Turkish): mountain range — L2e4, 17.
Amanus Gates; Maṛi (Armenian): pass south of Marash — L2e3, 17.
Amayḳ or Amoyḳ (Armenian): unidentified town in Cilicia.
Ambracia: town — see Arta.
Amida (classical), Āmid or Diyār-Bakr (Arabic), Diyarbekir or Diyarbakir (Turkish): town — M1e3, 3.
Amiens (French): city — E3c1, 2.
Ammōkhostos: port — see Famagusta.
Amoudain (Armenian): fortress 2 miles south of Anazarba.
Amoyḳ: town — see Amayḳ.
Amphissa: town — see Salona.
Amu Darya: river — see Oxus.
Amvrakikós Kólpos — see Arta, Gulf of.
Ana; 'Ānah (Arabic): town — M2f1, 13.
Anadolu: region — see Anatolia.
Anafah: town — see Nephin.
Anagni (Italian): town — G4d4, 1.
Anaphe; Anaphē (ancient Greek), Anáfi (modern Greek): island — J1e4, 6.
Anatolia; Romania (medieval), Anadolu (Turkish): region south of the Black Sea, now Asiatic Turkey.
'Anaz (Arabic): village 4 miles ESE of Krak des Chevaliers.
Anazarba; Anazarbus (classical), Anavarza (Armenian), 'Ain Zarbâ or 'Ain Zarbah (Arabic): town, now abandoned— L1e3, 17.
Ancona (Italian): port — G4d2, 1, 2.
Ancyra: town — see Ankara.
Andikíthira: island — see Cerigotto.
Andravida (medieval), Andravídha (modern Greek): town — I2e3, 11.
Andreas, Cape: NE tip of Cyprus — K5e5, 20.
Andres (French): monastery 15 miles NE of Boulogne.
Andros; Ándros (modern Greek): island — I5e3, 6, 7.
Angers (French): town — D5c3, 2, 12.
Angoulême (French): town — E1c5, 12.
Ani (Armenian), Ānī (Arabic): town, now unimportant — M4d5, 13.
Anjou (French): region of NW France — D4c3, 2, 12.
Ankara (Turkish), Ancyra (classical), Angora (medieval): town — K3e1, 1, 13.
Annweiler: town — see Anweiler.
Anṭākiyah or Antakya: city — see Antioch.
Antalya: port — see Adalia.
Anṭap: city — see Aintab.
Antaradus or Anṭarṭūs: port — see Tortosa.

Anti-Lebanon; al-Jabal ash-Sharqī (Arabic: the eastern mountain) — L2f1, 16, 17.
Anti-Taurus: mountains — L1e3, 17.
Anticythera: island — see Cerigotto.
Antioch; Antiochia (classical), Anṭākiyah (Arabic), Antakya (Turkish): city — L2e4, 3, 4, 5, 13, 17, 18, 19, 22.
Antioch, Principality of — Le, 19.
Anweiler or Annweiler (German): town 22 miles WSW of Speyer.
Apamea (classical), Afāmiyah or Qal'at al-Muḍīq (Arabic): town, now unimportant — L2e5, 17.
Apollonia-Sozusa: town — see Arsuf.
Apulia (classical), Puglie (Italian): region of SE Italy — Hd, 1.
Aquino (Italian): village 39 miles NW of Capua.
Aquitaine (French): region of western France — DEc, 12.
Arabia: peninsula — LMNgh, 13, 21.
Arabissus: town — see Albistan.
Aradus: island — see Ruad.
Aragon; Aragón (Spanish): region of NE Spain — Dd, 2, 12.
Aral Sea — PQcd, 21.
Arbela: town — see Irbil.
Arca: town — see 'Arqah.
Arcadia (classical), Messarea (medieval), Arkadhía (modern Greek): district of northern Morea — Ie, 11.
Arcadia (medieval), Cyparissia (classical), Kiparissía (modern Greek): town — I2e3, 11.
Arcadiopolis (medieval), Bergulae (Latin), Bergoulē (ancient Greek), Lüleburgaz (Turkish): town — J3d4, 6.
Arcis-sur-Aube (French): town — E5c2, 12.
Ardeal: region — see Transylvania.
Arevintan: fortress — see Ravendan.
Argentan (French): town — D5c2, 12.
Argolid or Argolis (classical), Argolís (modern Greek): district of eastern Morea — Ie, 11.
Argolis, Gulf of; Argolikós Kolpós (modern Greek) — Ie, 11.
Argos; Árgos (modern Greek): town — I3e3, 7, 11.
Ariège (French): river — E2d2, 12.
Arīḥā: town — see Jericho.
Arioudzpert (Armenian): fortress near Amoudain.
Arkadhía: district of northern Morea — see Arcadia.
Arles (French): town — E5d2, 2, 12.
Arm of Saint George (medieval): the Sea of Marmara and Bosporus.
Armena: castle — see Larmena.
Armenia; Hayastan (Armenian), Ermenistan (Turkish): region north of Lake Van — Mde, 13.
Arminaz: village — see L'Erminet.
Arnissa: town — see Ostrovo.
Arnstadt (German): city — G1b5, 1.
'Arqah or 'Irqah (Arabic), Arca or Irqata (classical): town — L2f1, 17.
Arsinga: town — see Erzinjan.
Arsinoë (classical), Polis (medieval): town — K3e5, 20.
Arsuf; Apollonia-Sozusa (classical), Arsur (medieval), Arsūf (Arabic): town, now unimportant — K5f3, 4, 16.
Arta; Ambracia (classical), Árta (modern Greek): town — I1e1, 1, 7, 8, 9, 10, 11.
Arta, Gulf of; Amvrakikós Kólpos (modern Greek) — Ie, 11.

Artois (French): district of northern France — E3b5, 2.
Arundel: town in sw Sussex.
Arwād: island — see Ruad.
Ascalon; Ashkelon (classical), ʿAsqalān (Arabic): port, now abandoned — K5f4, 3, 4, 5, 13, 16, 18, 19.
Ashmūn ar-Rummān (Arabic): town — K2f4, 14, 15.
al-ʿĀṣī: river — see Orontes.
Asia Minor (classical): region equivalent to western Anatolia — JKde, 1.
Assisi (Italian): town — G3d2, 2.
Asti (Italian): town — F4d1, 2.
Astypalaea (classical), Stampalia (medieval), Astipalaia (modern Greek): island — J2e4, 6.
Aswan; Uswān (Arabic): town in southern Egypt.
Athens; Athēnai (ancient Greek), Athínai (modern Greek): city — I4e3, 1, 7, 8, 9, 10, 11.
Athlith or ʿAtlīt: castle — see Château Pèlerin.
Athos, Mount; Áyion Óros (modern Greek): monastery — I5d5, 6, 11.
Athyra (classical), Büyük Chekmeje (Turkish): port — J4d4, 6.
Atlantic Ocean — 2, 12.
al-Aṭrūn: village — see Latrun.
Attalia: port — see Adalia.
Attica (Latin), Attikē (ancient Greek), Attikí (modern Greek): district of eastern Greece — Ie, 6, 11.
Auch (French): town — E1d2, 12.
Augsburg (German): city — G1c2, 1, 2.
Aulon (classical), Avlón (modern Greek): town — I4e2, 11.
Aulon: port — see Avlona.
Aulonarion (classical and medieval), Avlonárion (modern Greek): town — I5e2, 6, 11.
Aumale (French): village 25 miles wsw of Amiens.
Austria; Ostmark (German): region east of Bavaria, smaller than modern nation — GHc, 1.
Autremencourt (French): village 13 miles NNE of Laon.
Auvergne (French): region of southern France — Ecd, 2, 12.
Auxerre (French): town — E4c3, 12.
Avarinos: port — see Navarino.
Avesnes-sur-Helpe (French): town 45 miles NNE of Laon.
Avignon (French): town — E5d2, 2, 12.
Avlón: town — see Aulon.
Avlona (medieval), Aulon (classical), Valona (Italian), Vlonë (Albanian): port — H5d5, 1, 7, 8, 9, 11.
Avlonárion: town — see Aulonarion.
Axius: river — see Vardar.
Ayas (medieval), Lajazzo (Italian), Yumurtalik (Turkish): port — L1e4, 3, 5, 17, 18, 22.
Áyion Óros: monastery — see Athos, Mount.
Ayrivanḳ: town — see Erivan.
ʿAzāz (Arabic), Hazart (medieval): town — L3e4, 17.
Azerbaijan; Ādharbādhagān or Āẕerbaijān (Persian): region of NW Persia — Ne, 13, 21.
al-Azraq (Arabic: the blue): canal — K2f4, 14, 15.

Baalbek; Heliopolis (classical), Baʿlabakk (Arabic): town — L2f1, 3, 16, 17.
Babaṛon (Armenian): fortress NE of Lampron.

Babenberg (German): castle at Bamberg.
Babylon: town — see Fustat.
Bacon: town — see Batkun.
Bactra: city — see Balkh.
Baden or Baden-Baden (German): city — F4c2, 1, 2.
Baghdad; Baghdād (Arabic): city — M5f2, 4, 13, 22, 23.
Baghrās (Arabic), Pagrae (classical), Gaston (medieval), Baghra (Turkish): town — L2e4, 3, 4, 5, 17, 18, 19.
Bagnara Calabra (Italian): port 17 miles NE of Reggio di Calabria.
Baḥr an-Nīl: river — see Nile.
al-Baḥr aṣ-Ṣaghīr (Arabic: the small sea): canal — K2f4, 14, 15.
Baḥr Lūṭ — see Dead Sea.
Bairūt: port — see Beirut.
Baisan; Scythopolis or Bethshan (classical), Bethsan or Bessan (medieval), Baisān (Arabic): town — L1f3, 16.
Bait Laḥm: town — see Bethlehem.
Bait Nūbā (Arabic), Betenoble (medieval): village — L1f4, 16.
Baʿlabakk: town — see Baalbek.
Balansiyah: city, port — see Valencia.
Balarm: city, port — see Palermo.
Baleares (Spanish): island group — Ee, 2.
Balıkesir: town — see Achyraūs.
Balkans: mountain range and peninsula — Id, 1, 6, 13.
Balkh (Persian, Arabic), Bactra (classical): city, now unimportant — R2e4, 21.
Baltic Sea — 1, 2.
Bamberg (German): city — G1c1, 2.
Banduci: town — see Voden.
Bāniyās: port — see Valania.
Banyas; Paneas or Caesarea-Philippi (classical), Belinas (medieval), Bāniyās (Arabic): town — L1f2, 16.
Bar-le-Duc (French): town — F1c2, 2, 12.
Barāmūn (Arabic): village — K2f4, 14, 15.
Barbary: the coast of North Africa.
Barcelona (Spanish), Barshilūnah (Arabic): city, port — E3d4, 2.
Bari (Italian): port — H2d4, 1.
Baʿrīn or Bārīn (Arabic), Montferrand (medieval): fortress — L2f1, 17.
Barletta (Italian): port — H2d4, 1.
Barqah: region — see Cyrenaica.
Barshilūnah: city, port — see Barcelona.
Basel (German), Basle (French): city — F3c3, 1, 2.
Basra; al-Baṣrah (Arabic): city, port — N3f5, 13.
Bath: city — D3b4, 2.
Batkun (Bulgarian), Batkounion (Greek), Bacon (medieval): town, now abandoned — I5d3, 6.
al-Batrūn: town — see Botron.
Bavaria; Bayern (German): region of southern Germany — Gc, 1, 2.
Bayeux (French): town — D5c1, 2.
Bayonne (French): town — D4d2, 2.
Baziège (French): town — E2d2, 12.
Béarn (French): district of SW France — Dd, 12.
Beaucaire (French): town — E5d2, 12.
Beaufort (French): castle near St. George, SW of Karytaina.
Beaufort: castle at Leuctrum — I3e4, 11.
Beaufort: crusader castle — see Belfort.

Beaujeu (French): town — E5c4, 12.
Beaumont-sur-Oise (French): town 20 miles north of Paris.
Beaumont-sur-Sarthe (French): town — E1c2, 12.
Beauvais (French): town — E3c1, 2.
Beauvoir (French): castle at Pondikos.
Beauvoir: crusader castle — see Belvoir.
Behesni; Behesnou (West Armenian), Besni (modern Turkish): fortress, now town — L3e3, 17.
Beirut; Berytus (classical), Bairūt (Arabic): port — L1f2, 3, 4, 5, 13, 16, 17, 18, 19, 23.
Belen Boghazi: pass — see Syrian Gates.
Belfort or Beaufort (medieval), Shaqīf Arnūn or Qal'at ash-Shaqīf (Arabic: fort of the rock): crusader castle — L1f2, 3, 4, 16, 18, 19.
Belgrade; Beograd (Serbian): town — I1d1, 1.
Belinas: town — see Banyas.
Bellagrada: town — see Berat.
Bellapais (medieval): monastery — K4e5, 20.
Bellevaux or Vellefaux (French): abbey 32 miles NW of Toul.
Belvoir or Beauvoir (medieval), Kaukab al-Hawā' (Arabic: star of the sky): crusader castle — L1f3, 3, 16, 18, 19.
Benevento (Italian): city — G5d4, 1.
Beograd: town — see Belgrade.
Berat; Pulcheriopolis (classical), Bellagrada (medieval): town — H5d5, 1, 7, 11.
Berg (German): medieval county — F2b4, 1.
Berg (German): town — G5c2, 1.
Bergama: town — see Pergamum.
Bergoulē or Bergulae: town — see Arcadiopolis.
Beroea: city — see Aleppo.
Berrhoea or Beroea (classical), Stara Zagora (Bulgarian): town — J1d3, 6, 7.
Berytus: port — see Beirut.
Besançon (French): town — F2c3, 2.
Besni: fortress, now town — see Behesni.
Betenoble: village — see Bait Nūbā.
Bethlehem; Bait Laḥm (Arabic: house of flesh): town — L1f4, 16.
Bethsan, Bethshan, or Bessan: town — see Baisan.
Béthune (French): town 20 miles WSW of Lille.
Beyoghlu: port — see Pera.
Béziers (French): town — E4d2, 12.
Biandrate (Italian): village 24 miles north of Montferrat.
Bigha: town — see Pegae.
Bigorre (French): district of SW France — E1d3, 12.
Bijāyah: port — see Bougie.
Bikīsrā'īl: castle — see Château de la Vieille.
Bilbais or Bilbīs (Arabic): town — K2f5, 14, 15.
Binkath: city — see Tashkent.
al-Biqā' (Arabic: the hollow), Coele-Syria (classical): district of central Lebanon — L1f2, 16, 17.
Bira; al-Bīrah (Arabic), Birtha (classical), Bir (West Armenian), Birejik (Turkish): town — L3e3, 13, 17.
Bizyē: town — see Vizya.
Black Sea — KLd, 1, 4, 6, 7, 8, 10, 13, 22, 23.
Blois (French): town — E2c3, 12.
Bodonitsa (medieval), Pharygae (classical), Mendhenítsa (modern Greek): village — I3e2, 9, 11.

Boeotia (Latin), Boiōtia (ancient Greek), Voiotía (modern Greek): district of eastern Greece — I4e2, 11.
Bohemia; Čechy (Czech): region north of Austria — Gb5, 1, 2.
Bokhārā: city — see Bukhara.
Bolkar Dagh: portion of Taurus range — see Bulgar Dagh.
Bon, Cape; Ra's Addār (medieval Arabic), Ra's aṭ-Ṭīb (modern Arabic): NE tip of Tunisia — G2e3, 1.
Bona (medieval), Hippo Regius (classical), Būnah (Arabic), Bône (French): port — F3e4, 1, 2.
Bordeaux (French): city, port — D5d1, 2, 12.
Bosnia; Bosna (Serbian): region south of Croatia — Hd, 1.
Bosporus (classical), Karadeniz Boghazi̊ (Turkish: Black Sea strait) — J5d4, 6, 13.
Bosra; Buṣrâ (Arabic): town — L2f3, 13, 16.
Botron (medieval), Botrys (classical), al-Batrūn (Arabic): town — L1f1, 3, 5, 16, 18, 19.
Boudantē: town — see Podandus.
Bougie (French), Saldae (classical), Bijāyah (Arabic): port — F1e4, 2.
Bouillon (French): town — F1c1, 1.
Boulbonne (French): abbey — E2d2, 12.
Boulogne-sur-Mer (French): port — E2b5, 2.
Bourbon (French): town — E4c4, 12.
Bourges (French): town — E3c3, 2, 12.
Bourgogne: region — see Burgundy.
Bouthrōton: town — see Butrinto.
Boves (French): village 5 miles SE of Amiens.
Brabant (French, Flemish): district east of Flanders — E5b4, 1, 2.
Bracieux (French): village — E2c3, 12.
Bṛagana (Armenian): unidentified fortress between Lampron and Seleucia.
Bram (French): village — E3d2, 12.
Brandoveus: town — see Voden.
Branits; Viminacium (classical), Brandiz or Branichevo (medieval), Brnjica (Serbian): town — I3d1, 1.
Bratislava: city — see Pressburg.
Braunschweig: city — see Brunswick.
Breiz: region of NW France — see Brittany.
Bremen (German): city, port — F4b2, 1, 2.
Brenthē: town — see Karytaina.
Brescia (Italian): city — G1c5, 1.
Brest (French): port — D1c2, 2.
Bretagne: region — see Brittany.
Brie (French): district ENE of Paris.
Briel (French): village — E5c2, 12.
Brienne-la-Vieille (French): town — E5c2, 12.
Brindisi (Italian): port — H3d5, 1, 7.
Brittany; Bretagne (French), Breiz (Breton): region of NW France — Dc, 2, 12.
Brnjica: town — see Branits.
Bruges (French), Brugge (Flemish): port, now city — E4b4, 2.
Brunswick; Braunschweig (German): city — G1b3, 2.
Brusa; Prusa (classical), Bursa (Turkish): town — J5d5, 1, 6, 13.
Brygēis Limnē or Brygias Lacus — see Prespa, Lake.
Buda (Hungarian): city — H5c3, 1.
Buffavento (Italian): castle — K4e5, 20.

Buḥairat al-Ḥūlah — see Hulah, Lake.
Buḥairat al-Manzalah — see Manzalah, Lake.
Buḥairat Ṭabarīyah — see Tiberias, Lake.
Bukhara; Bokhārā (Persian), Bukhārā (Arabic): city — Q5e1, 21.
Bulgar Dagh or Bolkar Dagh (Turkish): portion of Taurus range west of Lampron — K4e3, 20.
Bulgaria: region south of the lower Danube, larger than modern nation — Id, 1, 6, 13.
Bullis: town — see Canina.
Bulunyās: port — see Valania.
Būnah: port — see Bona.
al-Buqai'ah (Arabic: the little hollow): valley — L1f1, 17.
Būrah (Arabic): town — K2f4, 14, 15.
Burgos (Spanish), Burghush (Arabic): city — D2d3, 2.
Burgundy; Bourgogne (French): region of eastern France, extending farther south than now — Ec, 2, 12.
Burj Ṣāfīthā: crusader castle — see Chastel Blanc.
Burlus (Arabic): town — K1f4, 14, 15.
Bursa: town — see Brusa.
Buṣrâ: town — see Bosra.
Butrinto (Italian), Buthrotum (Latin), Bouthrōton (ancient Greek), Butrint (Albanian): town — I1e1, 11.
Büyük Chekmeje: port — see Athyra.
Büyük Menderes: river — see Maeander.
Buzā'ah (Arabic): town — L3e4, 17.
Byblos: town — see Jubail.
Byllis: town — see Canina.
Byzantium: city — see Constantinople.

Cabaret (French): castle — E3d2, 12.
Caco: fortress — see Qāqūn.
Cadiz; Cádiz (Spanish): port — C4e4, 2.
Caen (French): city — D5c1, 2.
Caesarea (classical), Qaisārīyah (Arabic): port, now unimportant — K5f3, 3, 5, 16, 18, 19, 23.
Caesarea ad Argaeum or Caesarea-Mazaca (classical), Kayseri (Turkish): city — L1e2, 3, 4, 5, 13, 18, 22, 23.
Caesarea-Philippi: town — see Banyas.
Cagliari (Italian): port — F5e1, 1, 2.
Cahieu: town — see Cayeux-sur-Mer.
Cahors (French): town — E2d1, 12.
Caiffa or Caiphas: port — see Haifa.
Cairo; al-Qāhirah (Arabic): city — K2f5, 1, 4, 13, 14, 15, 22, 23.
Calabria (Italian): region of SW Italy — He, 1.
Callipolis: peninsula — see Gallipoli.
Caltabellotta (Italian): town — G4e3, 1.
Calycadnus (classical), Saleph (medieval), Selef or Gök(-Su) (Turkish): river — K5e4, 20.
Camardias (Armenian): unidentified castle in western Cilicia.
Cambodia; region of SE Asia — not in area mapped.
Cambrai (French): town — E4b5, 2.
Candia: medieval name for Crete.
Canina (medieval), Bullis or Byllis (classical): town — H5d5, 11.
Canossa (Italian): town, now unimportant — G1d1, 2.

Canterbury: town — E2b4, 2.
Capdolh: village — see Chapdeuil.
Cappadocia (classical): region of central Anatolia — KLe, 13, 20.
Capua (Italian): town — G5d4, 1.
Carcassonne (French): city — E3d2, 2, 12.
Carinthia; Kärnten (German): region south of medieval Austria — Gc, 1, 2.
Carmel, Mount; Jabal Mār Ilyās (Arabic: Mount St. Elias) — K5f3, 16.
Carpathians : mountain range — Ic, 1, 13.
Carpentras (French): town — F1d1, 12.
Carrhae: town — see Harran.
Carthage; Carthago (Latin): town — G1e4, 1.
Caryae, Mount; Kariaí (modern Greek) — I5d5, 6, 11.
Carystus (classical), Káristos (modern Greek): town — I5e2, 6, 11.
Casal Imbert (medieval), az-Zīb (Arabic): castle — L1f2, 16.
Caspian Sea — NOde, 4, 13, 21, 23.
Cassandrea, Pallene, or Potidaea (classical), Kassándra or Potídhaia (modern Greek): peninsula — I4e1, 11.
Casseneuil (French): village — E1d1, 2, 12.
Castellum Novum: castle — see Norpert.
Castelnau-le-Lez (French): village on outskirts of Montpellier.
Castelnaudary (French): town — E2d2, 12.
Castile; Castilla (Spanish): region of north central Spain — D2d4, 2.
Castoria (medieval), Celetrum (classical), Kastoría (modern Greek): town — I2d5, 11.
Castra Comnenon: town — see Kastamonu.
Castres (French): town — E3d2, 12.
Castri: town — see Delphi.
Castrum Cepha: town — see Ḥiṣn Kaifā.
Catalonia; Cataluña (Spanish), Catalunya (Catalan): region of NE Spain — Ed, 2, 12.
Caucasus; Kavkaz (Russian): mountain range — MNd, 13, 21.
Cayeux-sur-Mer (French), Cahieu (medieval): town 40 miles south of Boulogne.
Caymont (medieval), Tall Qaimūn (Arabic): castle — L1f3, 16.
Čechy: region — see Bohemia.
Celetrum: town — see Castoria.
Central Asia: region extending from Mongolia to the Oxus.
Ceos; Keōs (ancient Greek), Kéa (modern Greek), Tzia (medieval): island — I5e3, 6, 11.
Cephalonia; Kephallēnia (ancient Greek), Kephallōnia (medieval Greek), Kefallinía (modern Greek): island — I1e2, 7, 8, 9, 10, 11.
Cephissus (medieval), Kēphisos (ancient Greek), Kifissós (modern Greek): stream — I4e2, 11.
Cépoy: town — see Chepoix.
Cerigo (Italian), Cythera (Latin), Kythēra (ancient Greek), Kíthira (modern Greek): island — I3e4, 1, 11.
Cerigotto (Italian), Aegilia (classical), Anticythera (medieval), Andikíthira (modern Greek): island — I4e5, 1.
Chahan: river — see Pyramus.
Chalandritsa (medieval), Khalandrítsa (modern Greek): town — I2e2, 11.
Chalcedon; Kalkhēdōn (ancient Greek), Khalkēdōn (medieval Greek), Kadıköy (Turkish): town — J5d5, 1, 6, 7.
Chalcidice; Khalkidikē (ancient Greek), Khalkidhikí (modern Greek): peninsula — I4d5, 11.

Chalcis: town — see Negroponte.
Chalon-sur-Saône (French): town — E5c4, 12.
Châlons-sur-Marne (French): town — E5c2, 2.
Chalybon: city — see Aleppo.
Champagne (French): region of NE France — Ec, 2, 12.
Champlitte-et-le-Prélot (French): town — F1c3, 12.
Chanakkale Boghazî: strait — see Dardanelles.
Chantilly (French): town 24 miles NNE of Paris.
Chapdeuil (French), Capdolh (medieval): village — E1c5, 12.
Charax (medieval), Hereke (Turkish): village — J5d5, 6.
Chardak Boghazı: pass — see Myriokephalon.
Chartres (French): town — E2c2, 2, 12.
Chastel Blanc (medieval), Burj Ṣāfīthā (Arabic): crusader castle — L2f1, 17.
Château de la Vieille (French), Bikīsrā'īl (Arabic): castle — L2e5, 17.
Château Pèlerin (French), Athlith (medieval), 'Atlīt (Arabic): castle — K5f3, 16, 18, 19.
Châteauneuf (French): unidentified castle, possibly Norpert in Cilicia.
Châteauroux (French): town — E2c4, 12.
Châtellerault (French): town — E1c4, 12.
Châtillon-sur-Loing (French): town — E3c3, 12.
Châtillon-sur-Sevre: town — see Mauléon.
Chauvigny (French): town — E1c4, 12.
Chelebiköy (Turkish), Colla or Culos (medieval): village — J2d5, 6.
Chemishkezek (Turkish): town — L4e1, 13.
Chepoix (French), Cépoy (medieval): town 17 miles NE of Beauvais.
Cher (French): river — E1c3, 12.
Chester: city — D3b2, 2.
China: region of eastern Asia — not in area mapped.
Chinese Turkestan; Sinkiang (Chinese): region east of Turkestan — not in area mapped.
Chinon (French): town — E1c3, 12.
Chios; Khíos (modern Greek), Scio (Italian), Sakîz (Turkish): island — J1e2, 6.
Choisy-le-Roi (French): town — E3c2, 12.
Chorasmia: region — see Khorezm.
Chorlu: town — see Tzurulum.
Chorsa: town — see Kars.
Choson: region of east Asia — see Korea.
Christopolis (medieval), Neapolis Datenon (classical), Kaválla (modern Greek): port — I5d5, 6, 11.
Chrysoceras: bay — see Golden Horn.
Chrysopolis: port — see Scutari.
Cibotus: port — see Civetot.
Cilicia (classical): region of southern Anatolia — KLe, 17, 20.
Cilician Gates; Pylae Ciliciae (classical), Külek Boghazî (Turkish): pass — K5e3, 20.
Circuiz (medieval): plain of the upper Maritsa in Bulgaria.
Cîteaux (French): abbey — F1c3, 12.
Citrum (Latin), Kítros (modern Greek): town — I3d5, 11.
Civetot (medieval), Cibotus (classical): port, now abandoned — J5d5, 6.
Civitavecchia (Italian: old city): port — G2d3, 1.
Clairvaux (French): abbey — E5c2, 12.
Clarence: town — see Glarentsa.
Clermont (French): town — E4c5, 2, 12.

Clermont (French), Khelōnatas (ancient Greek), Khloumoutsi (medieval Greek): castle — I2e3, 11.
Clermont de l'Oise (French): town 15 miles ESE of Beauvais.
Cléry-sur-Somme (French): town 27 miles east of Amiens.
Cloyes (French): village — E2c3, 12.
Cluny (French): abbey — E5c4, 12.
Cocussus: town — see Coxon.
Coele-Syria: district of central Lebanon — see al-Biqā'.
Coggeshall: town 40 miles NE of London.
Coible: fortress — see al-Khawābī.
Coliat: fortress — see al-Qulai'ah.
Coligny (French): town — F1c4, 12.
Colla: village — see Chelebiköy.
Colmar (French), Kolmar (German): city — F3c2, 1.
Cologne (French), Köln (German): city — F2b5, 1, 2.
Comana or Placentia (medieval): town, now abandoned — L2e2, 13.
Comminges (French): medieval county — E1d3, 12.
Compiègne (French): town 33 miles east of Beauvais.
Conflans-Sainte Honorine (French): town 15 miles NW of Paris.
Conserans: bishopric — see Couserans.
Constance (French), Konstanz (German): town — F5c3, 1, 2.
Constantinople; Byzantium or Constantinopolis (classical), İstanbul (Turkish): city, port — J4d4, 1, 4, 6, 7, 8, 9, 10, 13, 22, 23.
Copais, Lake; Kōpais Limnē (ancient Greek): lake, now filled in — I4e2, 11.
Cordova; Córdoba (Spanish), Qurṭubah (Arabic): city — D1e3, 2.
Corfu (Italian), Corcyra (Latin), Kerkyra (ancient Greek), Kérkira (modern Greek): island — H5e1, 1, 7, 8, 9, 10, 11.
Corice: town — see Cyrrhus.
Corinth; Korinthos (ancient Greek; now Palaiá Kórinthos: Old Corinth): town — I3e3, 1, 7, 11.
Corinth, Gulf of; Korinthiakós Kólpos (modern Greek) — I3e2.
Corinth, Isthmus of; land connection between Morea and central Greece.
Corinthia (classical), Korinthía (modern Greek): district around Corinth — I3e3, 11.
Cornwall: region of SW England — CDb, 2.
Coron; Korōnē (medieval Greek), Koróni (modern Greek): town — I2e4, 8, 9, 10.
Corsica; Corse (French): island — Fd, 1, 2.
Corycus (classical), Goṛigos (West Armenian), Korgos (Turkish): port — K5e4, 13, 20.
Coucy-le-Château (French): village 15 miles west of Laon.
Courçon: manor — see Curzon.
Courtenay (French): village — E4c2, 12.
Couserans or Conserans (French): bishopric — E2d2, 12.
Coutances (French): town 37 miles WSW of Bayeux.
Coxon (medieval), Cocussus (classical), Gogison (West Armenian), Göksun (Turkish): town — L2e2, 13.
Crac — see Krak.
Creixell (Spanish): town 35 miles WSW of Barcelona.
Cremona (Italian): town — G1c5, 2.
Crete; Candia (medieval), Krētē (medieval Greek), Kríti (modern Greek): island — IJe, 1, 4, 7, 8, 9, 10, 13.
Crèvecoeur (French): castle — I3e3, 11.
Crimea; Krym (Russian): peninsula — K4c5, 1, 13.

Croatia: Meran (medieval), Hrvatska (Croatian): region north of Dalmatia — Hcd, 1.
Culos: village — see Chelebiköy.
Cursat: town — see Quṣair.
Curzon; Courçon (medieval): manor at Kedleston, 4 miles NW of Derby.
Cuyk or Kuik (Dutch): town — F1b4, 1.
Cyclades (classical), Kikládhes (modern Greek): island group — I5e3, 1, 6.
Cydnus (classical), Tarsus-Chayi (Turkish): river — K5e4, 20.
Cyllene: town — see Glarentsa.
Cynaetha: town — see Kalavryta.
Cyparissia: town — see Arcadia.
Cyprus; Kypros or Kipros (Greek), Kibris (Turkish): island — Kef, 3, 4, 5, 13, 18, 19, 20, 22, 23.
Cyrenaica (classical), Barqah (Arabic): region — If, 1.
Cyrrhus (classical), Corice (medieval), Qūris (Arabic): town 11 miles west of Ravendan.
Cythera: island — see Cerigo.
Cythnos (classical), Thermia (medieval), Kíthnos (modern Greek): island — I5e3, 6, 11.
Cyzicus (classical): town, now abandoned — J3d5, 6.

Dailam (Persian): district of northern Persia — N4e3, 13, 21.
Dajig (Armenian): crag in Cilician Taurus east of Lampron.
Dalmatia; Dalmacija (Croatian): region east of the Adriatic Sea — Hd, 1.
Damala (medieval), Troezen (Latin), Troizēn (ancient Greek): town — I4e3, 11.
Damascus (classical), Dimashq or ash-Sha'm (Arabic: the left): city — L2f2, 3, 4, 5, 13, 16, 18, 19, 22, 23.
Damietta; Dimyāṭ (Arabic): port — K2f4, 13, 14, 15, 23.
Dammartin-en-Goële (French): village 20 miles NE of Paris.
Dampierre; Le-Vieil-Dampierre (French): village 23 miles east of Châlons.
Dampierre-le-Château (French): village 20 miles ENE of Châlons.
Danmark: region — see Denmark.
Danube: river — J5c5, 1, 2, 13.
Daphne; Daphnē (ancient Greek), Dhafní (modern Greek): village — I3e3, 11.
Daphnusia (medieval), Thynias (classical), Kefken (Turkish): island — K1d4, 6.
Dara (classical), Dārā (Arabic): town — M1e3, 13.
Darbsāk (Arabic), Trapesac (medieval): town, now unimportant — L2e4, 17.
Dardanelles; Hellespontus (classical), Chanakkale Boghazi (Turkish): strait — J2d5, 6.
Darsous: city — see Tarsus.
Dartmouth: port — D2b5, 2.
Darum or Daron (classical), ad-Dārum (Arabic): town, now unimportant — K5f4, 16.
Daulia (medieval), Dhávlia (modern Greek): town — I3e2, 11.
Daun (German): town — F2b5, 2.
Deabolis: town — see Devol.
Dead Sea; Baḥr Lūṭ (Arabic: sea of Lot) — L1f4, 13, 16.
Delhi: city in NW India — not in area mapped.
Delos; Dēlos (ancient Greek), Dhílos (modern Greek): island — J1e3, 6.
Delphi (classical), Castri (medieval), Dhelfoí (modern Greek): town — I3e2, 11.
Delta (classical): region at mouth of the Nile.
Dēmatra: castle — see Dimatra.
Demetrias; Goritsa or Dēmētrias (medieval Greek): town, now abandoned — I3e1, 11.

Demotica; Dēmotika (medieval Greek), Dhidhimótikhon (modern Greek): town — J2d4, 1, 6, 7, 13.
Denizli (Turkish): modern town near medieval Laodicea.
Denmark; Danmark (Danish): region, then including the southern part of Sweden — Ga, 1, 2.
Derby: town — D4b3, 2.
Deutschland: region — see Germany.
Develi: village — see Gabadonia.
Devol; Deabolis or Diabolis (medieval): town, now abandoned — I1d5, 11.
Devon: region of SW England — D2b4, 2.
Dhafní: village — see Daphne.
Dhávlia: town — see Daulia.
Dhelfoí: town — see Delphi.
Dhidhimótikhon: town — see Demotica.
Dhílos: island — see Delos.
Dhodhekánisoi: the southern Sporades — see Dodecanese.
Diabolis: town — see Devol.
Dicetum (Latin): unidentified locality, probably in France.
Dietz; Diez (German): town 29 miles NNW of Mainz.
Dieudamour: castle — see Saint Hilarion.
Dijlah or Dijle: river — see Tigris.
Dijon (French): city — F1c3, 1, 2, 12.
Dillingen (German): town 65 miles SSW of Nuremberg.
Dimas; ad-Dīmās (Arabic): headland 8 miles north of Mahdia.
Dimashq: city — see Damascus.
Dimatra (medieval), Dēmatra (Greek): castle — I3e3, 11.
Dimyāṭ: port — see Damietta.
Dinan (French): town — D3c2, 2.
Divrighi (Turkish): town — L4e1, 13.
Diyār-Bakr, Diyarbakır, Diyarbekir: town — see Amida.
Diyār-Bakr (Arabic): region of the upper Tigris — L5e2, 13.
Diyār-Muḍar (Arabic): the western Jazira, east of the Euphrates — L4e4, 13, 17.
Djerba: island — see Jerba.
Dodecanese; Dōdekanēsos (medieval Greek), Dhodhekánisoi (modern Greek): the southern Sporades.
Doliche: town — see Duluk.
Dollnstein (German): castle — G1c2, 2.
Domokos; Thaumacia (classical): town — I3e1, 11.
Donzi or Donzy (French): town — E4c3, 12.
Dordogne (French): river — D5d1, 12.
Dornberg (German): castle 28 miles WSW of Nuremberg.
Dorset: region of southern England — D3b4, 2.
Dorylaeum (classical): town, now abandoned in favor of Eskishehir — K1e1, 1, 13.
Doubs (French): river — F1c4, 12.
Douro (Portuguese), Duero (Spanish): river — C2d4, 2.
Dramelay or Tremelay (French): village — F1c4, 12.
Dreibrunnen: village — see Trois-Fontaines.
Dreux (French): town — E2c2, 12.
Dubrovnik: port — see Ragusa.
Duero: river — see Douro.
Duluk; Doliche (classical), Dulūk (Arabic), Dülük (Turkish): town — L3e3, 17.
Dunstable: town 32 miles NW of London.
Durazzo (Italian), Epidamnus or Dyrrachium (classical), Durrës (Albanian): port — H5d4, 1, 7, 8, 9, 10, 11.

Durham: city — D4b1, 2.
Dzedz (Armenian): unidentified district, probably NW of Vahka.
Dzoyḳ (Armenian): monastery on islet in lake (Göljük) 18 miles SE of Kharput.

Eaunes (French): abbey — E2d2, 12.
Ebersheim (German): town 20 miles NNE of Colmar.
Eboli (Italian): town 17 miles ESE of Salerno.
Ebro (Spanish): river — E1d5, 2.
Ecbatana: city — see Hamadan.
Écry (French): castle at Asfeld — E5c1, 2.
Edessa (medieval), ar-Ruhā' (Arabic), Urfa (Turkish): city — L4e3, 3, 13, 17.
Edirne: city — see Adrianople.
Edremit: town — see Adramyttium.
Eger: city — see Erlau.
Egypt; Miṣr (Arabic): region of NE Africa — Kfg, 1, 13.
Eire: island — see Ireland.
Elbe (German), Labe (Czech): river — F5b2, 1, 2.
Elbistan: town — see Albistan.
Eleusis (classical), Elevsís (modern Greek): town — I4e2, 11.
Elis; Ēlis (ancient Greek), Ilía (modern Greek): district of NW Morea — I2e2, 11.
Elma Daghi: mountain range — see Amanus.
Elsass: region west of the upper Rhine — see Alsace.
Ely: city — E1b3, 2.
Embrun (French): town — F2d1, 2.
Emesa: city — see Homs.
England: region — Db, 2.
Enkleistra (Greek): monastery — K3f1, 20.
Enos; Aenus (classical), Menas (medieval), Enez (Turkish): town — J2d5, 6.
Epaktos: port — see Naupactus.
Ēpeiros: region — see Epirus.
Ephesus (classical): town, now abandoned — J3e3, 6.
Ephraim: hills NE of Caesarea in Palestine.
Epidamnus: port — see Durazzo.
Epiphania: city — see Hamah.
Epirus; Ēpeiros (ancient Greek), Ípiros (modern Greek): region west of Thessaly — I1e1, 1, 8, 9, 11.
Erdély: region — see Transylvania.
Ereghli: port — see Heraclea.
Ereghli: port — see Heraclea, Pontic.
Ereghli: town — see Heraclea-Cybistra.
Erfurt (German): city — G2b4, 1, 2.
Erivan; Ayrivanḳ (East Armenian), Yerevan (modern Armenian): city — M5d5, 13.
Erlau (German), Eger (Hungarian): city — I1c3, 1.
Ermenistan: region — see Armenia.
Erymanthus (classical), Ōlonos (medieval Greek), Erímanthos (modern Greek): mountain and adjacent stream — I2e2, 11.
Erzerum; Theodosiopolis (classical), Garin (West Armenian), Erzurum (Turkish): city — M2e1, 4, 13, 22.
Erzinjan (Turkish), Arsinga (classical): town — L5e1, 4, 13, 22.
Esdraelon or Jezreel (biblical): plain SE of Haifa.
Eski Manyas: village — see Lentiana.
Eskihisar: town — see Laodicea.

España: region — see Spain.
Essex: region of SE England — Eb, 2.
Estanor: port — see Pera.
Esztergom: town — see Gran.
Étampes (French): town — E3c2, 12.
Euboea (classical), Evripos (medieval Greek), Negroponte (Italian), Évvoia (modern Greek): island — I5e2, 1, 6, 7, 10, 11.
Euphrates (classical), al-Furāt (Arabic), Fırat Nehri (Turkish): river — N4f5, 13, 17, 21.
Eurotas (classical), Evrótas (modern Greek): river — I3e4, 11.
Évreux (French): town — E2c1, 2.
Evros: river — see Maritsa.
Évvoia or Evripos: island — see Euboea.
Exeter: city — D2b5, 2.

Faenza (Italian): town 18 miles SW of Ravenna.
Fagiano (Italian): village near Pisa.
Falkenstein (German): village 19 miles ENE of Regensburg.
Famagusta; Ammōkhostos (ancient Greek), Famagosta (medieval Italian): port — K4e5, 13, 20.
Fanjeaux (French): village — E3d2, 12.
Fāriskūr (Arabic): town — K2f4, 14, 15.
Faro: port — see Santa Maria do Algarve.
Fars; Fārs (Persian), Fāris (Arabic): region of SW Persia — Og, 21.
Fās: city — see Fez.
Faustinopolis: town — see Loulon.
Feke: fortress — see Vahka.
Ferentino (Italian): town 6 miles ESE of Anagni.
Ferrara (Italian): city — G2d1, 2.
Feuchtwangen (German): town 40 miles WSW of Nuremberg.
Fez; Fās (Arabic): city — D1f1, 2.
Fília: district — see Triphylia.
Filistīn: region — see Palestine.
Fırat Nehri: river — see Euphrates.
Fivelgo or Fivelingo (Dutch), Violgama (Latin): district of Frisia — EFb, 2.
Flanders; Vlaanderen (Flemish) : region of northern France and Belgium — Eb, 2.
Florence; Firenze (Italian): city — G2d2, 1, 2.
Foggia (Italian): city 33 miles north of Melfi.
Foix (French): town — E2d3, 12.
Fokís: district — see Phocis.
Fontfroide (French): abbey — E3d2, 12.
Forcalquier or Forcalquiers (French): town — F1d2, 12.
Forez (French): district east of Clermont — E4c5, 12.
Fors (French): village — D5c4, 12.
Fougères (French): town — D4c2, 12.
France: region, smaller than modern nation.
Franconia; Franken (German): region of western Germany — FGbc, 2.
Frankfurt am Main (German): city — F4b5, 1, 2.
Freising (German): town 45 miles SSW of Regensburg.
Frisia; Friesland (Dutch, German): region of northern Netherlands and NW Germany — Fb, 1, 2.
al-Fūlah (Arabic: the bean), La Fève (medieval), Afula (modern): village — L1f3, 16.

Fulda (German): town — F5b5, 2.
al-Furāt: river — see Euphrates.
Fustat; al-Fusṭāṭ (Arabic), Babylon (medieval): town — K2f5, 13, 14, 15.
Fūwah (Arabic): town — K1f4, 14, 15.

Gabadonia (Armenian), Develi (Turkish): village in Anatolia, 22 miles south of Caesarea.
Gabala: port — see Jabala.
Gaban (Armenian), Geben (Turkish): fortress — L2e3, 17.
Gabes; Qābis (Arabic): port — G1f2, 1, 2.
Gabes, Gulf of — Gf, 1, 2.
Gadres: town — see Gaza.
Galata (medieval), Sycae (classical): part of Constantinople south of Pera.
Galicia (Spanish): region of NW Spain — Cd, 2.
Galilee: region of northern Palestine — L1f3.
Galilee, Sea of — see Tiberias, Lake.
Gallipoli; Callipolis (classical), Gelibolu (Turkish): peninsula — J2d5, 4, 6, 7.
Ganges: river in India — not in area mapped.
Ganja; Gandzak (East Armenian), Yelisavetpol or Kirovabad (Russian): town — N2d5, 13, 21.
Gardiki (medieval), Larisa Kremastē (ancient Greek): town — I3e2, 11.
Gargar; Gargaṛ (West Armenian), Karkar or Qarqar (Arabic), Gerger (Turkish): town — L4e3, 13.
Garin: city — see Erzerum.
Garmirleṛ (Armenian: red mountains): foothills between Vahka and Gaban.
Garonne (French): river — D5c5, 2, 12.
Gascony; Gascogne (French): region of SW France — Dd, 2, 12.
Gaston: town — see Baghrās.
Gata, Cape: southern tip of Cyprus — K4f1, 20.
Gavur Daghi: mountain range — see Amanus.
Gaza; Gadres (medieval), Ghazzah (Arabic): town — K5f4, 16.
Gaziantep: city — see Aintab.
Geben: fortress — see Gaban.
Gelderland: district east of Utrecht — see Guelders.
Gelibolu: peninsula — see Gallipoli.
Gelnhausen (German): town 12 miles east of Frankfurt.
Genoa; Genova (Italian): city, port — F4d1, 1, 2.
Genua (Latin): town in Thrace, possibly Sergen 12 miles NNW of Vizya.
Georgia; Sakartvelo (Georgian): region east of the Black Sea and south of the Caucasus range — Md, 13.
Geraki (medieval), Geronthrae (classical), Yeráki (modern Greek): town — I2e3, 11.
Geranea: pass — see Makryplagi.
Gerger: town — see Gargar.
Germanicia: town — see Marash.
Germany; Alamannia or Allemania (medieval), Deutschland (German): region of north central Europe.
Gerona (Spanish): town — E3d3, 2, 12.
Geronthrae: town — see Geraki.
Gévaudan (French): district of south central France — E4d1, 12.
Gharnāṭah: city — see Granada.
Ghaudesh: island — see Gozo.
Ghaznah (Arabic), Ghaznī (Persian): town — R4f2, 21.
Ghazzah: town — see Gaza.

Ghūr or Ghōr (Persian): city, now a village — Q5f2, 21.
al-Ghūṭah (Arabic): district SE of Damascus — L2f2, 16.
Gianitsa (Greek): town, now abandoned, 3 miles east of Kalamata.
Gibelcar: fortress — see ʿAkkār.
Gibelet: town — see Jubail.
Gibraltar, Strait of — C5e5, 2.
Giguer (medieval), Jger (Armenian): fief on Gulf of Alexandretta north of Syrian Gates.
Gisors (French): town 17 miles SW of Beauvais.
Glarentsa or Clarence (medieval), Cyllene (Latin), Kyllēnē (ancient Greek), Killíni (modern Greek): town — I2e3, 11.
Gloucester: city — D3b4, 2.
Gobidaṛa (Armenian): fortress east of Mamistra.
Gogison or Göksun: town — see Coxon.
Gök[-Su] (Turkish: sky-blue): river flowing past Vahka into the Sarus.
Gök[-Su]: river — see Calycadnus.
Golden Horn; Chrysoceras (classical), Halich (Turkish): bay between Constantinople and Pera.
Gönen: town — see Poemanenum.
Gonesse or Lagonesse (French): town 10 miles NNE of Paris.
Good Hope, Cape of: southern tip of Africa — not in area mapped.
Goṛigos: port — see Corycus.
Goritsa: town — see Demetrias.
Gortys: district — see Skorta.
Gournay-en-Bray (French): town 17 miles WNW of Beauvais.
Gozo; Ghaudesh (Maltese): island — G5e4, 1.
Gradets (Bulgarian), Graditz (medieval): town — J2d3, 6.
Grailly or Grilly (French): manor 55 miles east of Mâcon.
Gran (German), Esztergom (Hungarian): town — H4c3, 1.
Granada (Spanish), Ighranāṭah or Gharnāṭah (Arabic): city — D2e3, 2.
Grand Magne: castle — see Maina.
Grandison or Grandson (French): town — F2c4, 1.
Grandpré (French): village 40 miles east of Rheims.
Graville-Sainte Honorine (French): village 32 miles west of Rouen.
Greece; Hellas (Greek): region west of the Aegean Sea, smaller than modern nation — Ie, 1.
Grilly: manor — see Grailly.
Gritsena: district of Messenia, 20 miles NW of Kalamata.
Guelders; Gelderland (Dutch): district east of Utrecht — F2b3, 2.
Guines or Guînes (French): town 16 miles NE of Boulogne.
Györ: town — see Raab.

Habor: river — see Khabur.
Ḥabrūn: town — see Hebron.
Hadrianopolis: city — see Adrianople.
Hadrumetum: port — see Susa.
Hafsa (Turkish), Nicaea Minor (classical), Nikiz (medieval): town — J2d4, 6.
Hagios Akhillēos: island — see Ahil.
Haifa; Caiphas or Caiffa (medieval), Ḥaifā (Arabic): port — L1f3, 3, 5, 13, 16, 18, 19.
Hainault; Hainaut (French), Henegouwen (Flemish): district east of Artois — EFb, 1.
Ḥalab or Haleb: city — see Aleppo.
Ḥalbah (Arabic): town — L2f1, 17.

Halberstadt (German): city — G2b4, 1.
Halich: bay — see Golden Horn.
Hallermund (German): castle 14 miles WNW of Hildesheim.
Halmyros (ancient Greek), Almirós (modern Greek): town — I3e1, 11.
Hamadan; Ecbatana (classical), Hamadān (Persian): city — N4f1, 4, 13, 21.
Hamah; Epiphania or Hamath (classical), Ḥamāh (Arabic): city — L2e5, 3, 4, 5, 13, 17, 18, 19, 22.
Hameln (German), Hamelin (English): town — F5b3, 2.
Hannapes (French): village 35 miles ENE of Laon.
Ḥarbīyah (Arabic), La Forbie (medieval): village — K5f4, 16.
Ḥārim (Arabic), Harenc (medieval): town — L2e4, 17.
Harput: fortress — see Kharput.
Harran or Haran (Turkish), Carrhae (classical), Ḥarrān (Arabic): town — L5e4, 3, 13.
Hasankeyf: town — see Ḥiṣn Kaifā.
Hattin; Madon (classical), Ḥaṭṭīn or Ḥiṭṭīn (Arabic): village — L1f3, 16.
Hauran; Ḥaurān (Arabic): district of southern Syria — L2f3, 16.
Hausen (German): village 15 miles SW of Worms.
Hauteville (French): village 30 miles WSW of Bayeux.
Hayastan: region — see Armenia.
Hazart: town — see 'Azāz.
Hebron; Ḥabrūn or Khalīl (Arabic), Saint Abraham (medieval): town — L1f4, 16.
Hebrus: river — see Maritsa.
Hejaz; al-Ḥijāz (Arabic): region of western Arabia — Lgh, 13.
Heliopolis: town — see Baalbek.
Hellas: region — see Greece.
Hellespont or Hellespontus: strait — see Dardanelles.
Henegouwen: district — see Hainault.
Henneberg (German): village 31 miles ESE of Fulda.
Heraclea; Perinthus (classical), Ereghli (Turkish): port — J3d5, 6.
Heraclea, Pontic; Hērakleia (Greek), Ereghli (Turkish): port — K2d4, 1.
Heraclea-Cybistra (classical), Ereghli (Turkish): town 50 miles NE of Laranda.
Heraclea Pelagoniae: town — see Prilep.
Hérault (French): river — E4d2, 12.
Hereford: town — D3b3, 2.
Hereke: village — see Charax.
Hermon, Mount; al-Jabal ash-Shaikh or Jabal ath-Thalj (Arabic: the hoary, or snow-covered, mountain) — L1f2, 16.
Hers (French): river — E2d2, 12.
Hierapolis (classical): ancient city near medieval Laodicea.
Hierapolis: town — see Manbij.
Hierosolyma: city — see Jerusalem.
al-Ḥijāz: region — see Hejaz.
Hildesheim (German): town — F5b3, 2.
Ḥimṣ: city — see Homs.
Hindu Kush: mountain range — Re, 21.
Hippo Regius: port — see Bona.
Ḥiṣn al-Akrād: fortress — see Krak des Chevaliers.
Ḥiṣn Kaifā (Arabic), Castrum Cepha (classical), Hasankeyf (Turkish): town — M2e3, 3, 13, 18.
Ḥiṭṭīn: village — see Hattin.
Hohenburg (German): castle — G2c3, 2.
Holin: city — see Karakorum.
Holland (Dutch): region north of Brabant — Eb, 1, 2.

Holstein (German): region south of Denmark — FGb, 1, 2.
Homs; Emesa (classical), Ḥimṣ (Arabic): city — L2f1, 3, 4, 5, 13, 17, 18, 19, 22, 23.
Howden; Hoveden (medieval): town 39 miles SE of Thirsk.
Hromgla; Qal'at ar-Rūm (Arabic: fort of Rome), Ranculat (medieval), Hṛomgla (West Armenian), Rum Kalesi (Turkish): fortress — L3e3, 13, 17.
Hrvatska: region north of Dalmatia — see Croatia.
Hulah, Lake; Buḥairat al-Ḥūlah (Arabic) — L1f2, 16.
Hungary; Magyarország (Hungarian): region of central Europe — HIc, 1.
Huntingdon: town 20 miles WSW of Ely.
Hwang Hai — see Yellow Sea.
Hydra (ancient Greek), Hydrea (Latin), Ídhra (modern Greek): island — I4e3, 11.
Hyères (French): town — F2d2, 2.
Hypatē: town — see Neopatras.

Ibelin (medieval), Jabneel or Jamnia (classical), Yabnâ (Arabic): town — K5f4, 16.
Iconium (medieval), Konya (Turkish): city — K3e3, 1, 4, 13, 20, 22, 23.
Ídhra: island — see Hydra.
Ieper: town — see Ypres.
Iesi or Jesi (Italian): town — G4d2, 1.
Ifrīqiyah: region of North Africa — see Tunisia.
Ighranāṭah: city — see Granada.
Île de France (French): region around Paris.
Ilía: district of NW Morea — see Elis.
Ill (French): river flowing past Strassburg.
India: region of southern Asia — not in area mapped.
Indian Ocean — 21.
Indus: river — Rgh, 21.
Ioánnina: town — see Janina.
Ionian Islands — island group from Corfu to Zante.
Ionian Sea — HIe, 7, 8, 9, 10, 11.
Ipáti: town — see Neopatras.
Ípiros: region west of Thessaly — see Epirus.
Iqlībiyah: village — see Kelibia.
Iran: modern nation holding most of medieval Persia.
Īrān: region of SW Asia — see Persia.
Iraq: modern nation, approximately equivalent to Mesopotamia.
al-'Irāq — see Mesopotamia.
Irbil (Arabic), Arbela (classical): town — M5e4, 13.
Ireland; Eire (Irish): island — Cb, 2.
'Irqah or Irqata: town — see 'Arqah.
Isauria (classical): region of southern Anatolia — K3e3, 13, 20.
Isfahan; Iṣfahān or Ispahān (Persian), Iṣbahān (Arabic): city — O2f3, 21.
Ishbīliyah: city — see Seville.
al-Iskandarīyah: city, port — see Alexandria.
İskenderun: port — see Alexandretta.
İstanbul: city, port — see Constantinople.
Istria (classical): peninsula — G5c5, 1, 2.
Italy; Italia (Italian): peninsula, now a nation.
Ithaca; Ithakē (ancient Greek), Itháki (modern Greek): island — I1e2, 11.
Itil: river — see Volga.
Ivry-sur-Seine (French): town 5 miles SSE of Paris.
İzmir: city, port — see Smyrna.

İzmit: town — see Nicomedia.
İznik: town — see Nicaea.

Jabal Anṣārīyah (Arabic: mountain of the Nuṣairis) or Jabal Bahrā' (Arabic): mountain — L2e5, 17.
al-Jabal ash-Shaikh or Jabal ath-Thalj — see Hermon, Mount.
al-Jabal ash-Sharqī: mountain — see Anti-Lebanon.
Jabal Lubnān — see Lebanon, Mount.
Jabal Mār Ilyās — see Carmel, Mount.
Jabal Nūr (Arabic): offshoot of the Taurus range NE of Adana.
Jabal Tābūr or Jabal aṭ-Ṭūr — see Tabor, Mount.
Jabala; Gabala (classical), Jabalah (Arabic): port — L1e5, 3, 5, 17, 18, 19.
Jabneel: town — see Ibelin.
Jacob's Ford; now Jisr Banāt Ya'qūb (Arabic: bridge of the daughters of Jacob): ford across the upper Jordan — L1f2, 16.
Jadera: port — see Zara.
Jaffa or Joppa; Yāfā (Arabic): port — K5f3, 3, 4, 5, 13, 16, 18, 19.
Jaiḥūn: river — see Oxus.
Jamnia: town — see Ibelin.
Janina (medieval), Ioánnina (modern Greek): town — I1e1, 11.
Jarbah: island — see Jerba.
Jaxartes (classical), Saiḥūn (Persian, Arabic), Syr Darya (modern): river — Q2c4, 21.
al-Jazā'ir: region — see Algeria.
Jazira; al-Jazīrah (Arabic: the island, or peninsula): the upper Mesopotamian region.
Jerba; Meninx (classical), Jarbah (Arabic), Djerba (French): island — G1f2, 1, 2.
Jericho; Arīḥā or ar-Rīḥā (Arabic): town — L1f4, 16.
Jerusalem; Hierosolyma (classical), al-Quds (Arabic: the holy): city — L1f4, 3, 4, 5, 13, 16, 18, 19, 22, 23.
Jerusalem, Kingdom of — KLf, 19.
Jesi: town — see Iesi.
Jeyhan: river — see Pyramus.
Jezreel: plain — see Esdraelon.
Jezreel: village — see Zir'īn.
Jger: fief — see Giguer.
al-Jibāl (Arabic: the mountains): district of western Persia — N2e5, 13, 21.
Jisr al-Majāmi' (Arabic): bridge — L1f3, 16.
Jisr Banāt Ya'qūb: bridge — see Jacob's Ford.
Jīzat Dimyāṭ (Arabic): island across Nile from Damietta.
Joigny (French): town — E4c3, 12.
Joinville (French): town — F1c2, 12.
Joppa: port — see Jaffa.
Jordan; al-Urdunn (Arabic): river — L1f4, 13, 16.
Jubail (Arabic: small mountain), Byblos (classical), Gibelet (medieval): town — L1f1, 3, 5, 13, 16, 17, 18, 19.
Jumièges (French): village 12 miles west of Rouen.
Justingen (German): town 54 miles WNW of Augsburg.

Kadiköy: town — see Chalcedon.
Kairawan; al-Qairawān (Arabic): city — G1e5, 1, 2.
Kaisūn: fortress — see Kesoun.
Kalamata (medieval), Pharae (classical), Kalámai (modern Greek): town — I3e3, 11.

Kalavryta (medieval), Cynaetha (classical): town — I3e2, 11.
Kalden (German): castle at Pappenheim, 40 miles north of Augsburg.
Kalkhēdōn: town — see Chalcedon.
Kalocsa (Hungarian): town — H4c4, 1.
Kangurlan (Mongol), Sulṭānīyeh (Persian): town — N4e4, 13, 21, 22.
Kantara; al-Qanṭarah (Arabic: the bridge): town — K4e5, 20.
Karadeniz Boghazi: strait — see Bosporus.
al-Karak: fortress — see Kerak.
Karakorum (Turkish), Holin (Chinese): city in Mongolia — not in area mapped.
Karaman: town — see Laranda.
Kariaí — see Caryae, Mount.
Káristos: town — see Carystus.
Karítaina: town — see Karytaina.
Karkar: town — see Gargar.
Kärnten: region — see Carinthia.
Karpassia (medieval), Rizokárpasso (modern Greek): town — K5e5, 20.
Kars (East Armenian, Turkish), Chorsa (classical): town — M4d5, 13.
Karytaina (medieval), Brenthē (ancient Greek), Karítaina (modern Greek): town — I3e3, 11.
Kassándra: peninsula — see Cassandrea.
Kastamonu (Turkish), Castra Comnenon or Kastamuni (medieval): town — K4d4, 13.
Kastoría: town — see Castoria.
Katzenellenbogen or Katzenelnbogen (German): town 25 miles NW of Mainz.
Kaukab al-Hawā': castle — see Belvoir.
Kaválla: port — see Christopolis.
Kavkaz: mountain range — see Caucasus.
Kayseri: city — see Caesarea.
Kéa: island — see Ceos.
Kefallinía: island — see Cephalonia.
Kefken: island — see Daphnusia.
Kelibia; Iqlībiyah (Arabic): village — G2e4, 1, 2.
Kemalpasha: town — see Nymphaeum.
Keōs: island — see Ceos.
Kephallēnia or Kephallōnia: island — see Cephalonia.
Kēphisos: stream — see Cephissus.
Kerak; Kir-hareseth (classical), Krak des Moabites or Krak of Moab (medieval), al-Karak (Arabic): fortress, now town — L1f4, 3, 5, 13, 16, 18, 19, 23.
Kerkyra or Kérkira: island — see Corfu.
Kerman; Kirmān (Persian): region of southern Persia — Pg, 21.
Kesoun; Ḳesoun (West Armenian), Kaisūn (Arabic), Keysun (Turkish): fortress, now town — L3e3, 17.
Khabur; Habor (classical), Khābūr (Arabic): river — M1e5, 13.
Khalandrítsa: town — see Chalandritsa.
Khalij or Khaliōn (Armenian): unidentified town in Cilicia.
Khalīl: town — see Hebron.
Khalkēdōn: town — see Chalcedon.
Khalkidikē or Khalkidhikí: peninsula — see Chalcidice.
Khalkís: town — see Negroponte.
Khwārizm: region at mouth of Oxus River — see Khorezm.
Kharput or Harput (Turkish), Kharpert (West Armenian): fortress, now town — L5e2, 3, 13.
al-Kharrūbah (Arabic): hill 11 miles SE of Acre.
al-Khawābī (Arabic), Coible (medieval): fortress — L2f1, 17.

Khelōnatas or Khloumoutsi: castle — see Clermont.
Khilāṭ or Khlaṭ: town — see Akhlat.
Khíos: island — see Chios.
Khirbat Kardānah: mills — see Recordane.
Khoi; Khūy (Persian): town — M5e2, 13, 21.
Khorezm; Chorasmia (classical), Kh^{w}ārizm (Persian): region at mouth of the Oxus river — Q1d3, 21.
Khurasan; Khorāsān (Persian): region of NE Persia — PQe, 21; misapplied to Pontus in the medieval period.
Khuzistan; Susiana (classical), Khūzistān (Persian, Arabic): region of SW Persia — Nf, 21.
Kı̊brı̊s: island — see Cyprus.
Kiev (Russian): city — K1b5, 1.
Kifissós: stream — see Cephissus.
Kikládhes: island group — see Cyclades.
Killíni: town — see Glarentsa.
Kiparissía: town — see Arcadia.
Kipros: island — see Cyprus.
Kir-hareseth: fortress, now town — see Kerak.
Kirmān: region of southern Persia — see Kerman.
Kirovabad: town — see Ganja.
Kíthira: island — see Cerigo.
Kíthnos: island — see Cythnos.
Kiti (Greek): village — K4f1, 20.
Kítros: town — see Citrum.
Klisoura: castle — see La Clisura.
Klokotnitsa (Bulgarian): village — J1d4, 6.
Kolmar: city — see Colmar.
Köln: city — see Cologne.
Konstanz: town — see Constance.
Konya: city — see Iconium.
Kōpais Limnē — see Copais, Lake.
Köprülü: town — see Prosek.
Korea; Choson (Korean): region of east Asia — not in area mapped.
Korgos: port — see Corycus.
Korinthía: district — see Corinthia.
Korinthiakós Kólpos — see Corinth, Gulf of.
Korinthos: town — see Corinth.
Korōnē or Koróni: town — see Coron.
Köse Dagh (Turkish): peak NE of Sebastia — L3e1, 22.
Koulourē: island — see Salamis.
Kozan: town — see Sis.
Krak de Montréal (medieval), ash-Shaubak (Arabic): fortress — L1f5, 3, 13.
Krak des Chevaliers (medieval), Ḥiṣn al-Akrād (Arabic: stronghold of the Kurds): fortress — L2f1, 3, 5, 17, 18, 19, 23.
Krak des Moabites: fortress — see Kerak.
Krētē or Kríti: island — see Crete.
Krym: peninsula — see Crimea.
Kufa; al-Kūfah (Arabic): town — M5f3, 13.
Kuik: town — see Cuyk.
Külek Boghazı̊: pass — see Cilician Gates.
Kurdistan; Kurdistān (Persian, Arabic): region between Armenia and Persia — MNe, 13.
Kyburg (German): village 25 miles ESE of Colmar.

Kyllēnē: town — see Glarentsa.
Kypros: island — see Cyprus.
Kyrenia (medieval): town — K4e5, 20.
Kythēra: island — see Cerigo.

L'Erminet (medieval), Arminăz (Arabic): village — L2e4, 17.
La Clisura (medieval), Klisoura (medieval Greek): castle — I4e2, 11.
La Cuppa (medieval): castle near Aulonarion.
La Fauconnerie (French): farm 6 miles north of Caymont.
La Ferté-Alais (French): village 27 miles south of Paris.
La Fève: village — see al-Fūlah.
La Forbie: village — see Ḥarbīyah.
La Garnache (French): village 75 miles SW of Angers.
La Marche: district — see Marche.
La Portelle: pass — see Syrian Gates.
La Roche: castle in Burgundy, on the upper Ognon river.
La Roche de Russole or de Roissel (French): fortress — L1e4, 17.
Labe: river — see Elbe.
Lacedaemon: town — see Sparta.
Laconia; Lakōnia or Lakōnikē (medieval Greek): district of SE Morea — I3e4, 11.
Laconia, Gulf of; Lakōnikos Kolpos (medieval Greek) — I3e4, 11.
Ladder of Tyre: ascent south of Tyre.
al-Lādhiqīyah: port — see Latakia.
Lagonesse: town — see Gonesse.
Lairon or Laron (French): village — E2c5, 12.
Lajazzo: port — see Ayas.
al-Lajjūn (Arabic), Megiddo (medieval): village — L1f3, 16.
Lakedaimōn: town — see Sparta.
Lakōnia or Lakōnikē: district of SE Morea — see Laconia.
Lakōnikos Kolpos — see Laconia, Gulf of.
Lamia or Lamía: town — see Zeitounion.
Lampron (West Armenian), Namrun (Turkish): fortress — K5e3, 13, 20.
Lampsacus (classical), Lapseki (Turkish): village — J2d5, 6.
Lancaster: city — D3b1, 2.
Landsberg (German): town — G3b4, 1.
Langres (French): town — F1c3, 12.
Languedoc (French): region of southern France — Ed, 2.
Laodicea: port — see Latakia.
Laodicea ad Lycum (classical), Eskihisar (Turkish): town, now abandoned in favor of Denizli — J5e3, 1, 6, 13.
Laon (French): town — E4c1, 2.
Lapithos; Lapēthos (medieval Greek): town — K4e5, 20.
Lapseki: village — see Lampsacus.
Laranda (classical), Karaman (Turkish): town — K4e3, 13, 20.
Larisa Kremastē: town — see Gardiki.
Larissa (medieval), Lárisa (modern Greek): town — I3e1, 11.
Larissa: fortress — see Shaizar.
Larmena (medieval), Armena (medieval Greek): castle on Mt. St. Nicholas — I5e2, 6, 11.
Laron: village — see Lairon.
Las: castle — see Passavant.
Las Navas de Tolosa (Spanish): battlefield — D2e2, 2.
Latakia; Laodicea (classical), al-Lādhiqīyah (Arabic): port — L1e5, 3, 5, 13, 17, 18, 19, 23.

Latrun; al-Aṭrūn (Arabic), Le Toron des Chevaliers (medieval): village — L1f4, 16.
Laurac (French): village 4 miles NW of Fanjeaux.
Lauria: town — see Loria.
Lavaur (French): town — E2d2, 12.
Le Bourg (French): castle 25 miles NE of Rheims.
Le Mans (French): city — E1c3, 2, 12.
Le Petit Gerin: village — see Zirʿīn.
Le Puiset (French): castle — E2c2, 12.
Le Puy (French): town — E4c5, 12.
Le Toron des Chevaliers: village — see Latrun.
Le-Vieil-Dampierre: village — see Dampierre.
Lebadea (classical), Levádhia (modern Greek): town — I3e2, 11.
Lebanon, Mount; Jabal Lubnān (Arabic) — L2f1, 16, 17.
Lecce (Italian): town — H4d5, 1.
Lefkara (medieval Greek): town — K4f1, 20.
Legnica: city — see Liegnitz.
Leicester: town — D4b3, 2.
Lemesós: port — see Limassol.
Lemnos; Lēmnos (medieval Greek), Límnos (modern Greek): island — J1e1, 6.
Lentiana (medieval), Eski Manyas (Turkish): village — J4e1, 6, 8.
Lentini (Italian): town — H1e3, 1.
Leon; León (Spanish): region of northern Spain — Cd, 2.
Lepanto: port — see Naupactus.
Les Barres (French): village — E1c4, 12.
Les Vaux-de-Cernay (French): abbey — E2c2, 12.
Lesbos (classical), Mytilēnē (medieval Greek), Lésvos (modern Greek): island — J2e1, 6.
Leuven: city — see Louvain.
Levádhia: town — see Lebadea.
Lévis-Saint Nom (French): village — E2c2, 12.
Levkōsia: town — see Nicosia.
Liebenau (German): castle 38 miles ENE of Regensburg.
Liedekerke (Flemish): town 44 miles SE of Bruges.
Liége or Liège (French), Luik (Flemish): city — F1b5, 1, 2.
Liegnitz (German), Legnica (Polish, Czech): city — H2b4, 1.
Lille (French), Ryssel (Flemish): city — E4b5, 2.
Limassol; Nemesos (medieval Greek), Lemesós (modern Greek): port — K4f1, 13, 20.
Limburg (Flemish): district east of Liége — Fb, 1.
Límnos: island — see Lemnos.
Limoges (French): city — E2c5, 2, 12.
Limoux (French): town — E3d2, 12.
Lisbon; Lisboa (Portuguese): city, port — C1e2, 2.
Lisieux (French): town 45 miles WSW of Rouen.
Little Prespa Lake; Mikrē Prespa Limnē (medieval Greek) — I2d5, 11.
Lloria: town — see Loria.
Locedio (Italian): abbey 12 miles WNW of Montferrat.
Loches (French): town — E1c3, 12.
Loire (French): river — D3c3, 2, 12.
Lombardy; Lombardia (Italian): region of NW Italy — Fc, 1, 2.
Lombers or Lombez (French): village — E1d2, 12.
London: city, port — D5b4, 2.
Lopadium (classical), Ulubad (Turkish): town — J4d5, 6.

Loria (medieval), Lauria (Italian), Lloria (Catalan): town — H1d5, 1.
Lorraine (French), Lothringen (German): region of eastern France — EFc, 1, 2, 12.
Lot (French): river — E1d1, 12.
Louge (French): river flowing into the Garonne at Muret.
Loulon (Armenian), Faustinopolis (classical), Lu'lu'ah (Arabic): town —K5e3, 13, 20.
Louvain (French), Leuven (Flemish): city 41 miles WNW of Liége.
Lower Lorraine: district of southern Belgium.
Lubban; al-Lubbān (Arabic): village — L1f3, 16.
Lübeck (German): city, port — G1b2, 1, 2.
Lucca (Italian): town — G1d2, 2.
Lucy-le-Bocage (French): town 18 miles NW of Montmirail.
al-Ludd: town — see Lydda.
Lügde (German): town 13 miles SW of Hameln.
Luik: city — see Liége.
Lüleburgaz: town — see Arcadiopolis.
Lu'lu'ah: town — see Loulon.
Lusignan (French): town — E1c4, 12.
Lycaonia (classical): region of central Anatolia — Ke, 13, 20.
Lychnidus: town — see Ochrida.
Lychnitis Lacus — see Ochrida, Lake.
Lydda; Saint George (medieval), al-Ludd (Arabic): town — K5f4, 16.
Lydia (classical): region of western Anatolia — Je, 13.
Lyons; Lyon (French): city — E5c5, 2, 12.

Ma'arrat-an-Nu'mān (Arabic): town — L2e5, 17.
Maas: river — see Meuse.
Macedonia (classical): region around Vardar river — Id, 11.
Mâcon (French): town — E5c4, 12.
al-Madīnah: city — see Medina.
Madon: village — see Hattin.
Maeander (classical), Büyük Menderes (Turkish): river — J3e3, 1, 6, 13.
Magdeburg (German): town — G2b3, 1, 2.
al-Maghrib al-Aqṣâ: region of NW Africa — see Morocco.
Maguelonne (French): port, now unimportant — E4d2, 12.
Magyarország: region of central Europe — see Hungary.
al-Maḥallah (Arabic, now al-Maḥallah al-Kubrâ): city — K2f5, 14, 15.
Mahdia; al-Mahdīyah (Arabic): city, port — G2e5, 1, 2.
Maina; Mainē (medieval Greek), Máni (modern Greek), Grand Magne (French): castle — I3e4, 11.
Maine (French): region of NW France — Dc, 2, 12.
Mainz (German), Mayence (French): city — F4b5, 1, 2.
Maiyafariqin; Martyropolis (classical), Maiyāfāriqīn (Arabic), Miyafarkin or Silvan (Turkish): town — M2e2, 3, 13.
al-Majdal (Arabic: the place of contention): unidentified battlefield on the Khabur river.
Majorca; Mallorca (Spanish): island — Ee, 2.
Makkah: city — see Mecca.
Makryplagi (medieval), Geranea (classical), Makripláyi (modern Greek): pass — I4e2, 11.
Malatya: city — see Melitene.
Malazgirt: town — see Manzikert.
Malea, Cape; Ákra Maléas (modern Greek) — I4e4, 11.

Mallorca: island — see Majorca.
Malta; Māliṭah (Arabic): island — G5e5, 1.
Malvasia: village — see Monemvasia.
Mamistra (medieval), Mopsuestia (classical), Msis (Armenian), Misis (Turkish): town — L1e4, 3, 13, 17.
Manbij (Arabic), Hierapolis (classical): town — L3e4, 17.
Mandzgerd or Mantskert: town — see Manzikert.
Máni: castle — see Maina.
Mansurah; al-Manṣūrah (Arabic): town — K2f4, 14, 15.
Mantua; Mantova (Italian): city — G1c5, 1.
Manzalah, Lake; Buḥairat al-Manzalah (Arabic) — K3f4, 14.
Manzikert; Mandzgerd (West) or Mantskert (East Armenian), Malazgirt (Turkish): town — M3e1, 13.
Maraclea (medieval), Maraqīyah (Arabic): port — L1e5, 17.
Maragha; Marāgheh (Persian): town — N2e3, 13, 21, 22.
Marash (Armenian, Turkish), Germanicia (classical), Mar'ash (Arabic): town — L2e3, 3, 5, 13, 17, 18.
Marbach (German): monastery 5 miles sw of Colmar.
Marche; La Marche (French): district of NW France — E2c4, 2, 12.
Mardin (Turkish), Māridīn (Arabic): town — M1e3, 3, 4, 13, 18, 22.
Margat: fortress — see al-Marqab.
Margiana: city — see Merv.
Maṛi: pass south of Marash — see Amanus Gates.
Maritsa (modern), Hebrus (classical), Evros (medieval Greek), Merich (Turkish): river — J2d5, 1, 6.
Marj aṣ-Ṣuffar (Arabic): plain — L2f2, 16.
Marly-le-Roi (French): town 12 miles west of Paris.
Marmande (French): town — E1d1, 12.
Marmara, Sea of; Propontis (classical), Marmara Denizi (Turkish) — J4d5, 6.
al-Marqab (Arabic: the watch-tower), Margat (medieval): fortress — L1e5, 3, 5, 17, 18, 19, 23.
Marrakesh; Marrākush (Arabic): city — C2f4, 2.
Marseilles; Marseille (French): city, port — F1d2, 2, 12.
Martyropolis: town — see Maiyafariqin.
Marv: city — see Merv.
Marzano di Nola (Italian): town 18 miles east of Naples.
Mashgharah (Arabic): village — L1f2, 16.
Maṣyāf or Maṣyāth or Maṣyād or Miṣyāf (Arabic): fortress — L2e5, 3, 4, 5, 17, 18, 19, 23.
Matagrifon (medieval), Akova (medieval Greek), Ákovos (modern Greek): castle — I2e3, 11.
Matapan, Cape; Taenarum (classical), Metōpon (medieval Greek), Ákra Taínaron (modern Greek) — I3e4, 11.
Maugastel (French): unidentified castle near Tyre.
Mauléon (French, until 1736), Châtillon-sur-Sevre (modern French): town — D5c4, 12.
al-Mauṣil: city — see Mosul.
Mauthausen (German): town — G5c2, 1.
Mayence: city — see Mainz.
Mecca; Makkah (Arabic): city — L5h4, 4, 13, 22, 23.
Medina; al-Madīnah (Arabic: the city): city — L5h1, 4, 13, 22, 23.
Mediterranean Sea — 1, 2, 3, 5, 7, 8, 9, 10, 11, 13, 14, 15, 16, 17, 19, 20, 22, 23.
Megara; Mégara (modern Greek): town — I4e3, 11.
Megiddo: village — see al-Lajjūn.

Meissen (German): town — G4b4, 2.
Melenicum: town — see Melnik.
Melfi (Italian): town — H1d4, 1.
Melgueil (French): medieval county around Mauguio, 7 miles east of Montpellier.
Melitene (classical), Melden (West Armenian), Malatya (Turkish): city — L4e2, 3, 4, 5, 13, 18, 22.
Melk (German): town — H1c2, 1.
Mello (French): town 28 miles north of Paris.
Melnik (Bulgarian), Melenicum (medieval): town — I4d4, 1, 8.
Melos; Mēlos (ancient Greek), Mílos (modern Greek): island — I5e4, 6, 11.
Melun (French): town — E3c2, 12.
Menas: town — see Enos.
Mendhenítsa: village — see Bodonitsa.
Meng-ku: region — see Mongolia.
Meninx: island — see Jerba.
Meran: medieval name for Croatia.
Mérencourt (French): unidentified locality in France.
Merich: river — see Maritsa.
Merseburg (German): city — G2b4, 2.
Merv or Marv (Persian), Margiana (classical): city — Q2e3, 21.
Mesopotamia (classical), al-'Irāq (Arabic): region between the Euphrates and the Tigris — Mf, 13.
Messarea: district of northern Morea — see Arcadia.
Messenia; Messēnia (medieval Greek): district of sw Morea — I2e3, 11.
Messina (Italian): port — H1e2, 1.
Messíni: town — see Nisi.
Meteorium (Latin), Meteōrion (medieval Greek): unidentified castle, probably about 40 miles east of Pergamum.
Methōnē or Methóni: port — see Modon.
Metōpon — see Matapan, Cape.
Metz (French): city — F2c1, 1, 2.
Meuse (French), Maas (Flemish, Dutch): river — E5b4, 1, 2, 12.
Midi (French): southern France.
Mignano (Italian): village 10 miles SE of Monte Cassino.
Míkonos: island — see Myconos.
Mikrē Prespa Limnē — see Little Prespa Lake.
Milan; Milano (Italian): city — F5c5, 1, 2.
Milly (French): village 50 miles NE of Châlons.
Mílos: island — see Melos.
al-Minā' (Arabic): modern port in Lebanon, on site of medieval Tripoli.
Minden (German): town — F4b3, 1.
Minerve (French): castle — E3d2, 12.
Minho (Portuguese), Miño (Spanish): river — C2d3, 2.
Minōa: village — see Monemvasia.
Mirepoix (French): town — E2d2, 12.
Misis: town — see Mamistra.
Miṣr: region of NE Africa — see Egypt.
Mistra; Myzithra (ancient Greek), Mistrás (modern Greek): town — I3e3, 11.
Miṣyāf: fortress — see Maṣyāf.
Miyafarkin: town — see Maiyafariqin.
Modon (medieval), Methōnē (medieval Greek), Methóni (modern Greek): port — I2e4, 7, 8, 9, 10, 11.
Moissac (French): town — E2d1, 12.

Monemvasia; Monemvásia (modern Greek), Minōa (ancient Greek), Malvasia (medieval): village — I4e4, 7, 8, 9, 10, 11.
Monferrato: district of NW Italy — see Montferrat.
Mongolia; Meng-ku (Chinese): region north of China — not in area mapped.
Mons Pelegrinus — see Pilgrim Mountain.
Montaigu (French): town 50 miles SW of Angers.
Montaigu-sur-Champeix or Montaigut-le-Blanc (French): castle — E4c5, 12.
Montauban (French): town — E2d1, 12.
Montbéliard (French): town 36 miles west of Basel.
Monte Cassino (Italian): abbey — G4d4, 1.
Monte Cristo (Italian): island — G1d3, 2.
Monte Croce (Italian): village near Florence.
Montelongo or Montelungo (Italian): castle 7 miles SW of Anagni.
Montferrand: fortress — see Ba'rīn.
Montferrat (French), Monferrato (Italian): district of NW Italy — F4c5, 1.
Montfort (French), Starkenburg (German), Qal'at al-Qurain (Arabic): castle — L1f2, 16, 18, 19.
Montfort-l'Amaury (French): town — E2c2, 12.
Montgey (French): village — E2d2, 12.
Montmirail (French): town — E4c2, 12.
Montmorency (French): village 10 miles north of Paris.
Montmusart (French): northern suburb of Acre.
Montpellier (French): town — E4d2, 2, 12.
Montpensier (French): town — E4c4, 12.
Montréal (French): village — E3d2, 12.
Mopsuestia: town — see Mamistra.
Moravia; Morava (Czech): region SE of Bohemia — Hc, 1.
Morea (medieval), Peloponnesus (Latin), Peloponnēsos or Moreas (medieval Greek): peninsular region of southern Greece — Ie, 1, 8, 9, 10.
Morocco; al-Maghrib al-Aqṣâ (Arabic: the farthest west): region of NW Africa — Cf, 2.
Moscow; Moskva (Russian): city — not in area mapped.
Mosul; al-Mauṣil (Arabic), Musul (Turkish): city — M4e4, 4, 13, 22, 23.
Mosynopolis (Greek): town, now abandoned — J1d4, 6.
Msis: town — see Mamistra.
Münster (German): city — F3b4, 1, 2.
Muret (French): town — E2d2, 12.
Musul: city — see Mosul.
Myconos (classical), Míkonos (modern Greek): island — J1e3, 6.
Myriokephalon (classical), Chardak Boghazi̇ (Turkish): pass — K4e1, 13.
Mytilēnē: island — see Lesbos.
Myzithra: town — see Mistra.

Nablus; Neapolis (classical), Nābulus (Arabic): town — L1f3, 16.
Nahr Na'mān (Arabic): stream debouching 1 mile SE of Acre.
Nain (Arabic): village 4 miles ENE of al-Fūlah.
Naissus: town — see Nish.
Namrun: fortress — see Lampron.
Namur (French): town — E5b5, 2.
Nangis (French): town — E4c2, 12.
Nanteuil-le-Haudoin (French): town 29 miles NE of Paris.
Naples; Napoli (Italian): city, port — G5d5, 1.
Narbonne (French): town — E4d2, 12.
Naṣībīn: town — see Nisibin.

an-Nāṣirah: town — see Nazareth.
Nassau (German): medieval duchy — Fb, 1, 2.
Naumburg an der Saale (German): city — G2b4, 2.
Naupactus (classical), Lepanto (Italian), Epaktos (medieval Greek), Návpaktos (modern Greek): port — I2e2, 11.
Nauplia (classical), Návplion (modern Greek): port — I3e3, 11.
Navarino (Italian), Avarinos (medieval Greek), Pílos (modern Greek): port — I2e4, 11.
Navarre; Navarra (Spanish): region of northern Spain — Dd, 2.
Naxos; Náxos (modern Greek): island — J1e3, 6, 8, 9, 10.
Nazareth; an-Nāṣirah (Arabic): town — L1f3, 16.
Néa Artáki: village — see Vatonda.
Neapolis: town — see Nablus.
Neapolis Datenon: town — see Christopolis.
Near East: region from Egypt to Persia and Turkey to Aden.
Nederland: nation — see Netherlands.
Negroponte (medieval), Chalcis (classical), Khalkís (modern Greek): town — I4e2, 8, 9, 10, 11.
Negroponte: island — see Euboea.
Nemesos: port — see Limassol.
Neocastro or Nicastro (Italian): town 15 miles SSE of Aiello.
Neopatras (medieval), Hypatē (ancient Greek), Ipáti (modern Greek): town — I3e2, 1, 11.
Nephin (medieval), Anafah (Arabic): town — L1f1, 16.
Nēsi: town — see Nisi.
Nesle (French): village 28 miles ESE of Amiens.
Netherlands; Nederland (Dutch): modern nation, larger than medieval Holland.
Neuenburg (German): town 19 miles north of Basel.
Neuilly-sur-Marne (French): town 10 miles east of Paris.
Nevers (French): town — E4c4, 12.
Nicaea (classical), İznik (Turkish): town — J5d5, 1, 4, 6, 7, 8, 9, 10, 13.
Nicaea Minor: town — see Hafsa.
Nicastro: town — see Neocastro.
Nicomedia (classical), İzmit (Turkish): town — J5d5, 1, 6, 8, 13.
Nicosia; Levkōsia (medieval Greek): town — K4e5, 13, 20.
Nicotera (Italian): town 35 miles NNE of Reggio di Calabria.
Nif: town — see Nymphaeum.
Nikiz: town — see Hafsa.
Nikli (medieval), Palaio-Episkopi (medieval Greek): town, now abandoned — I3e3, 11.
Nile; Baḥr an-Nīl (Arabic): river — K3f4, 1, 13, 14, 15.
Nimburg (German): town 33 miles south of Strassburg.
Nîmes (French): city — E5d2, 12.
Nish (Turkish, Serbian), Naissus or Nissa (classical): town — I2d2, 1, 7, 8, 9, 10.
Nisi (medieval), Nēsi (medieval Greek), Messíni (modern Greek): town — I3e3, 11.
Nisibin or Nusaybin (Turkish), Nisibis (classical), Naṣībīn or Nuṣaibīn (Arabic): town — M2e3, 13.
Nonancourt (French): town — E2c2, 12.
Norge: region of western Scandinavia — see Norway.
Normandy; Normandie (French): region of northern France — DEc, 2, 12.
Norpert (Armenian), Castellum Novum (Latin): castle NE of Vahka.
North Africa: region from Morocco to Cyrenaica, north of the Sahara.
North Sea — 1, 2.

Norway; Norge (Norwegian): region of western Scandinavia — not in area mapped.
Novara (Italian): town — F4c5, 1.
Novgorod (Russian): city in northern Russia — not in area mapped.
Novi Pazar: town — see Rascia.
Noyers (French): town — E4c3, 12.
Nubia (classical): region south of Egypt, equivalent to northern Sudan.
Numidia (classical): region west and south of Tunisia.
Nuremberg; Nürnberg (German): city — G2c1, 1, 2.
Nuṣaibīn or Nusaybin: town — see Nisibin.
Nymphaeum (classical), Nif or Kemalpasha (Turkish): town 14 miles east of Smyrna.

Ochrida (medieval), Lychnidus or Achrida (classical), Ohrid (Serbian): town — I1d4, 1, 7, 11.
Ochrida, Lake; Lychnitis Lacus (classical), Ohridsko Jezero (Serbian) — I1d4, 11.
Oea: city, port — see Tripoli.
Oenoë (Latin), Oinoē (medieval Greek), Ünye (Turkish): port — L3d4, 13.
Oignies (French): village 13 miles SSW of Lille.
Oldenburg (German): city — F4b2, 2.
Olena; Ōlena (medieval Greek): town, now abandoned — I2e3, 11.
Ōlonos: mountain — see Erymanthus.
Olympia (classical): ruined city near Prinitsa.
Oporto; Pôrto (Portuguese): port — C2d4, 2.
Orchomenus: town — see Skripou.
Oreus (Latin), Ōreos (medieval Greek), Oreoí (modern Greek): town — I4e2, 11.
Orléans (French): city — E2c3, 2, 12.
Orontes (classical), al-ʿĀṣī (Arabic: the rebellious): river — L1e4, 13, 16, 17.
Orvieto (Italian): town — G3d3, 1, 2.
Osma (Spanish): town — D2d4, 2.
Osnabrück (German): town — F4b3, 2.
Ostia (Italian): village — G3d4, 1.
Ostmark: region east of Bavaria — see Austria.
Ostrovo (medieval), Arnissa (classical): town — I2d5, 11.
Otranto (Italian): town 22 miles SE of Lecce.
Otranto, Strait of: southern entrance to Adriatic Sea.
Öttingen (German): village 40 miles SSW of Nuremberg.
Oultrejourdain: region — see Transjordania.
Outremer (French: over seas): the Latin states in Syria and Palestine.
Oxus (classical), Jaiḥūn (Persian, Arabic), Amu Darya (modern): river — P5d2, 21.

Paderborn (German): town — F4b4, 1.
Padua; Padova (Italian): city — G2c5, 1, 2.
Pagasētikos Kolpos — see Volos, Gulf of.
Pagliara: village — see Palear.
Pagrae: town — see Baghrās.
Pairis: village 45 miles NNW of Basel.
Palaeokastro Hagios Geōrgios or Palaiókastron Áyios Yeóryios: castle — see Saint George.
Palaestina: region west of the Jordan — see Palestine.
Palaiá Kórinthos: town — see Corinth.
Palaio-Episkopi: town — see Nikli.
Palear (German), Pagliara (Italian): village 38 miles WSW of Montferrat.
Palermo (Italian), Balarm (Arabic): city, port — G4e2, 1.

Palestine; Palaestina (classical), Filistīn (Arabic): region west of the Jordan — KLf, 13.
Pallene: peninsula — see Cassandrea.
Pamiers (French): town — E2d2, 12.
Paneas: town — see Banyas.
Pantelleria (Italian): island — G3e4, 1, 2.
Paphlagonia (classical): region of northern Anatolia — Kd, 13.
Paphos (medieval Greek): town — K3f1, 13, 20.
Paris (French): city — E3c2, 2, 12.
Parma (Italian): town — G1d1, 1.
Parnon; Parnōn (medieval Greek), Párnon Óros (modern Greek): mountain range — I3e3, 11.
Paros (ancient Greek), Páros (modern Greek): island — J1e3, 6.
Partzapert (medieval), Partsrpert (West Armenian): fortress 20 miles SW of Vahka.
Passau (German): town — G4c2, 1, 2.
Passavant (medieval), Las or Passava (medieval Greek): castle near Gythium — I3e4, 11.
Patmos (classical), Pátmos (modern Greek): island — J2e3, 6.
Patras (medieval), Pátrai (modern Greek): port — I2e2, 11.
Patras, Gulf of; Sinus Calydonius (classical), Patraïkós Kólpos (modern Greek) — I2e2, 11.
Patti (Italian): town 32 miles west of Messina.
Pegae (Latin), Pēgai (medieval Greek), Bigha (Turkish): town — J3d5, 6, 8.
Péguilhan (French): village — E1d2, 12.
Peking or Peiping: city in China — not in area mapped.
Pelagonia (classical): district NW of Macedonia.
Peloponnesus or Peloponnēsos: peninsula — see Morea.
Pembroke: town — D1b4, 2.
Penne-d'Agenais (French): town — E1d1, 12.
Pentedaktylon: mountains — see Taygetus.
Pera or Estanor (medieval), Beyoghlu (Turkish): port east of the Golden Horn — J4d4, 6.
Perche (French): district west of Chartres — E1c2, 12.
Pergamum (classical), Bergama (Turkish): town — J3e1, 1, 6, 13.
Perigord; Périgord (French): district south of Limoges — Ec, 2, 12.
Perinthus: port — see Heraclea.
Pernis: castle — see Petrich.
Perpignan (French): town — E3d3, 12.
Persia; Īrān (Persian): region of SW Asia — NOf, 13, 21.
Persian Gulf — NOg, 21.
Pertous (Armenian): fortress 15 miles NW of Marash.
Perugia (Italian): town — G3d2, 2.
Peterborough: town 25 miles NW of Ely.
Petrich (Bulgarian), Petritzos (medieval Greek), Pernis (medieval): ruined castle 2 miles south of Stenimaka.
Pharae: town — see Kalamata.
Pharygae: village — see Bodonitsa.
Phea: castle — see Pondikos.
Pherae: town — see Velestinon.
Philadelphia (classical), Alashehir (Turkish): town — J4e2, 1, 4, 6, 7, 13.
Philippopolis (classical), Plovdiv (Bulgarian): town — I5d3, 1, 6, 7, 8, 9, 10, 13.
Philomelium (Latin), Philomēlion (medieval Greek), Akshehir (Turkish: white city): town — K2e2, 4, 13.
Phocis; Fokís (modern Greek): district west of Lake Copais — I3e2, 11.

Piacenza (Italian): town — F5c5, 2.
Pian del Carpine or Piano della Magione (Italian): village 9 miles WNW of Perugia.
Picardy; Picardie (French): region of northern France — Eb, 2.
Piedmont; Piemonte (Italian): district of NW Italy — Fcd, 1, 2.
Pilgrim Mountain; Mons Pelegrinus (medieval): hill overlooking Tripoli.
Pílos: port — see Navarino.
Pinarhisar; Verissa (medieval), Pınarhisar (Turkish): town — J3d4, 6.
Pisa (Italian): port, now city — G1d2, 1, 2.
Placentia: town — see Comana.
Platamon; Platamōn (ancient Greek), Platamón (modern Greek): town — I3e1, 11.
Plovdiv: town — see Philippopolis.
Po (Italian): river — G3d1, 1, 2.
Podandus (classical), Boudantē (West Armenian), Pozantı (Turkish): town — K5e3, 20.
Poemanenum (Latin), Poimanēnon (medieval Greek), Gönen (Turkish): town — J3d5, 6.
Poitiers (French): town — E1c4, 2, 12.
Poitou (French): region of western France — Dc, 2, 12.
Pola (Italian), Pula (Croatian): port — G4d1, 1, 2.
Poland; Polska (Polish): region east of Germany — HIb, 1.
Polis: town — see Arsinoë.
Pondikos (medieval), Phea (classical), Pontikókastron (modern Greek): castle — I2e3, 11.
Ponthieu (French): district of western Picardy.
Pontus (classical): region of northern Anatolia — Ld, 13.
Port-de-Jonc (French): castle at Navarino.
Porto (Italian): village 13 miles SW of Rome.
Pôrto: port — see Oporto.
Portugal: region south of Galicia — Cde, 2.
Posquères (French): village near Vauvert, 12 miles SSW of Nîmes.
Potenza (Italian): town 26 miles SSE of Melfi.
Potidaea or Potídhaia: peninsula — see Cassandrea.
Pozantı: town — see Podandus.
Pozsony: city — see Pressburg.
Pozzuoli (Italian), Puteoli (classical): town 7 miles WSW of Naples.
Prague; Praha (Czech): city — G5b5, 1, 2.
Prespa, Lake; Brygias Lacus (Latin), Brygēis Limnē (medieval Greek), Prespansko Jezero (Serbian) — I1d5, 11.
Pressburg (German), Pozsony (Hungarian), Bratislava (Czech): city — H3c2, 1.
Prilep (Bulgarian), Heraclea Pelagoniae (classical), Prilapum (medieval): town — I2d4, 1, 11.
Prinitsa (medieval Greek): village — I2e3, 11.
Probaton (medieval), Provadiya (Bulgarian): town — J3d2, 6.
Procida (Italian): island 14 miles WSW of Naples.
Propontis — see Marmara, Sea of.
Prosek (Serbian), Prosacum (medieval), Köprülü (Turkish), [Titov] Veles (modern): town — I2d4, 1, 8.
Provence (French): region of SE France — EFd, 1, 2, 12.
Prusa: town — see Brusa.
Ptolemaïs: city, port — see Acre.
Puglie: region of SE Italy — see Apulia.
Pula: port — see Pola.
Pulcheriopolis: town — see Berat.
Puteoli: town — see Pozzuoli.

Puylaurens (French): village — E3d2, 12.
Pylae: pass — see Thermopylae.
Pylae Ciliciae: pass — see Cilician Gates.
Pyramus (classical), Chahan (West Armenian), Jeyhan (Turkish): river — L1e4, 13, 17.
Pyrenees: mountain range — DEd, 2, 12.

Qābis: port — see Gabes.
al-Qāhirah: city — see Cairo.
al-Qairawān: city — see Kairawan.
Qaisārīyah: port — see Caesarea.
Qal'at al-Baḥr (Arabic: castle of the sea): islet off Sidon.
Qal'at al-Muḍīq: town — see Apamea.
Qal'at al-Qurain: castle — see Montfort.
Qal'at ar-Rūm: fortress — see Hromgla.
Qal'at ash-Shaqīf: crusader castle — see Belfort.
Qal'at Ja'bar (Arabic): fortress — L4e5, 17.
Qal'at Najm (Arabic: fort of a star): fortress — L4e4, 17.
al-Qanṭarah: town — see Kantara.
Qāqūn (Arabic), Caco (medieval): fortress — L1f3, 16.
Qarqar: town — see Gargar.
al-Qaṣr or Qaṣr Abī-Dānis: town — see Alcácer do Sal.
al-Quds: city — see Jerusalem.
Quercy (French): district around Cahors — E2d1, 12.
Querfurt (German): town 36 miles NE of Erfurt.
al-Qulai'ah (Arabic: the small fort), Coliat (medieval): fortress — L2f1, 17.
Qūriṣ: town — see Cyrrhus.
Qurṭubah: city — see Cordova.
Quṣair (Arabic: little castle), Cursat (medieval): town, now unimportant — L2e4, 17.

Raab (German), Györ (Hungarian): town — H3c3, 1.
Raban (Turkish), Ṛaban (West Armenian), Ra'bān (Arabic): fortress — L3e3, 17.
Ragusa (medieval), Rhausium (classical), Dubrovnik (Serbian): port — H4d3, 1.
Raiy (Persian), Rhages or Rhagae (classical): town, now abandoned in favor of Teheran — O2e5, 21.
Ramerupt (French): village — E5c2, 12.
Ramla; Rama or Rames (medieval), ar-Ramlah (Arabic: the sandy): town — K5f4, 16.
Ranculat: fortress — see Hromgla.
Ra's Addār or Ra's aṭ-Ṭīb — see Bon, Cape.
Ra's al-Mā' (Arabic: headland of the water): village — L2f3, 16.
Rascia (Latin), Rashka (Serbian): medieval state and town (now Novi Pazar) — Id, 1.
Rashīd: port — see Rosetta.
Ratisbon: town — see Regensburg.
Rauḍah: island — see Roda.
Ravendan; Rāwandān (Arabic), Arevintan (West Armenian), Ravendel (medieval), Ravanda (Turkish): fortress — L3e4, 17.
Ravenna (Italian): port, now town — G3d1, 1, 2.
Ravennika (medieval): town, now abandoned — I3e2, 8, 11.
Razès (French): medieval county — E3d2, 12.
Recordane (medieval), Khirbat Kardānah (Arabic): mills — L1f3, 16.
Red Sea — Lgh, 4, 13, 22, 23.

Redvers: village — see Reviers.
Regensburg (German), Ratisbon (medieval): town — G3c1, 1, 2.
Reggio di Calabria (Italian): port — H1e2, 1.
Reggio nell' Emilia (Italian): town — G1d1, 1.
Reichersberg (German): village 16 miles south of Passau.
Reims: city — see Rheims.
Remy (French): town 27 miles east of Beauvais.
Reviers (French), Redvers (medieval): village 11 miles east of Bayeux.
Rhages or Rhagae: town, now abandoned in favor of Teheran — see Raiy.
Rhausium: port — see Ragusa.
Rheims; Reims (French): city — E5c1, 2.
Rhine; Rhin (French), Rhein (German), Rijn (Dutch): river — E5b4, 1, 2.
Rhinelands: district along both sides of the Rhine.
Rhodes; Rhodus (classical), Ródhos (modern Greek): island — Je, 1, 4, 6, 7, 8, 9, 10, 13.
Rhodope; Rhodopē (ancient Greek), Rodhópi (modern Greek), Rodopi (Bulgarian): mountains — I5d4, 6.
Rhone; Rhône (French): river — E5d2, 2, 12.
Richmond: town 25 miles south of Durham.
Rieti (Italian): town 40 miles NNE of Rome.
Riez (French): village — F2d2, 2.
ar-Rīḥā: town — see Jericho.
Rijn: river — see Rhine.
Rizokárpasso: town — see Karpassia.
Roda; Rauḍah (Arabic): island in the Nile opposite Fustat.
Rodez (French): town — E3d1, 12.
Ródhos: island — see Rhodes.
Rodopi or Rodhópi: mountains — see Rhodope.
Romagna (Italian): region south of the lower Po — Gc, 1.
Romania: medieval name for Anatolia.
Romano d'Ezzelino (Italian): village 36 miles NW of Venice.
Rome; Roma (Italian): city — G3d4, 1, 2.
Ronay or Rônai (French): town 27 miles SSE of Caen.
Rosetta; Rashīd (Arabic): port — K1f4, 13, 14, 15.
Rosières-sur-Mance (French): village 39 miles NE of Châlons.
Rota (Spanish), Rūṭah (Arabic): village — C4e4, 2.
Roucy (French): village 14 miles NW of Rheims.
Rouen (French): city — E2c1, 2.
Rouergue (French): district around Rodez — Ed, 12.
Roussillon (French): district north of the eastern Pyrenees — E3d3, 12.
Roye (French): village 26 miles SE of Amiens.
Ruad; Aradus (classical), Arwād or Ruwād (Arabic): island — L1f1, 17.
Rubrouck (Flemish): village 33 miles WNW of Lille.
ar-Ruhā': city — see Edessa.
Rum Kalesi: fortress — see Hromgla.
Russia: region of eastern Europe — JKb, 1.
Rūṭah: village — see Rota.
Ruwād: island — see Ruad.
Ryssel: city — see Lille.

Saarbrücken (German), Sarrebruck (French): town 38 miles SSE of Trier.
Sabina (Italian): district 35 miles north of Rome.
Sablé-sur-Sarthe (French): town — D5c3, 12.
Sachsen: region — see Saxony.

Safad; Saphet (medieval), Ṣafad (Arabic): town — L1f3, 3, 16, 18, 19, 23.
Safāqus: town — see Sfax.
Sagitta or Ṣaidā': port — see Sidon.
Sahan: river — see Sarus.
Sahara; aṣ-Ṣahrā' (Arabic): desert — EFGf, 1, 2.
Ṣahyūn: crusader castle — see Saone.
Saiḥūn: river — see Jaxartes.
Saijar: fortress — see Shaizar.
Sailūn: plain — see Shiloh.
Saint Abraham: town — see Hebron.
Saint Cyprien (French): suburb of Toulouse, across the Garonne — E2d2, 12.
Saint Denis (French): town 7 miles north of Paris.
Saint George: town — see Lydda.
Saint George; Palaeokastro Hagios Gēorgios (medieval Greek), Palaiókastron Áyios Yeóryios (modern Greek): castle — I2e3, 11.
Saint Gilles (French): village — E5d2, 12.
Saint Gotthard; Sankt Gotthard (German), San Gottardo (Italian): pass — F4c4, 2.
Saint Helena: castle — I2e3, 11.
Saint Hilarion or Dieudamour (French): castle — K4e5,
Saint John or Saint Jean: city, port — see Acre.
Saint Livrade; Sainte Livrade-sur-Lot (French): village — E1d1, 12.
Saint Omer (French): town 30 miles east of Boulogne.
Saint Omer: castle 16 miles ENE of Andravida.
Saint Peter; San Pietro (Italian): island — F4e1, 2.
Saint Pol-sur-Ternoise (French): town 34 miles north of Amiens.
Saint Quentin (French): town 26 miles NW of Laon.
Saint Sabas: monastery on Montjoie, overlooking Acre.
Saint-Sauveur (French: Holy Saviour): abbey at Modon.
Saint Simeon (medieval), as-Suwaidīyah (Arabic), Süveydiye (Turkish): port — L1e4, 17.
Saint Thibéry (French): abbey — E4d2, 12.
Saint Thomas: islet off Tripoli in Lebanon.
Saissac (French): village — E3d2, 12.
Sakartvelo: region east of the Black Sea — see Georgia.
Sakiz: island — see Chios.
Salamis (classical), Salamís (modern Greek), Koulourē (medieval Greek): island — I4e3, 11.
Salamyah or (colloquial) Salamīyah (Arabic): town — L3e5, 17.
Saldae: port — see Bougie.
Saleph: river — see Calycadnus.
Salerno (Italian): port — G5d5, 1.
aṣ-Ṣāliḥīyah (Arabic): town — K3f5, 14, 15.
Salisbury: city — D4b4, 2.
Salm (German): castle 30 miles WSW of Strassburg.
Salona (medieval), Amphissa (classical): town — I3e2, 9, 11.
Salonika: port — see Thessalonica.
as-Salṭ (Arabic): town — L1f3, 16.
Salza (German): town — G1b4, 1.
Salzburg (German): city — G4c3, 1, 2.
Samaria: district of northern Palestine — L1f3, 16.
Samarkand; Samarqand (Persian, Arabic): city — R2e1, 21.
Samos; Sámos (modern Greek): island — J2e3, 6.

Samosata (medieval), Samousad (West Armenian), Samsat (Turkish): town — L4e3, 3, 17.
Samothrace or Samothrakē (classical), Samothráki (modern Greek): island — J1d5, 6.
Samsun (Turkish): port — L2d4, 13.
San Germano Vercellese (Italian): village 22 miles NW of Montferrat.
San Gottardo: pass — see Saint Gotthard.
San Pietro: island — see Saint Peter.
San Severino Marche (Italian): town 32 miles SW of Ancona.
Sancerre (French): town — E3c3, 12.
Sangerhausen (German): town 31 miles SSE of Halberstadt.
Sankt Gotthard: pass — see Saint Gotthard.
Santa Maria do Algarve (medieval Portuguese; from Arabic *al-Gharb*: the west), Faro (modern): port — C3e3, 2.
Santorin: island — see Thera.
Saone (medieval), Ṣahyūn or Ṣihyaun (Arabic): crusader castle — L2e5, 17.
Saône (French): river — F1c5, 12.
Saphet: town — see Safad.
Sapientsa; Sapiéntza (modern Greek), Sapienza (Italian): island — I2e4, 11.
Saragossa; Zaragoza (Spanish), Saraqusṭah (Arabic): city — D5d4, 2.
Sardica: city — see Sofia.
Sardinia; Sardegna (Italian): island — Fde, 1, 2.
Sarepta (medieval), Zarephath (classical), Ṣarafand (Arabic): town — K5f3, 16.
Sargines or Sergines (French): village — E4c2, 12.
Sarmīn (Arabic), Sermin (medieval): town — L2e5, 17.
Sarrebruck: town — see Saarbrücken.
Sarus (classical), Sahan (Armenian), Seyhan (Turkish): river — K5e4, 13, 17, 20.
Sarvantikar; Sarouantiḳar (Armenian): fortress — L2e3, 17.
Sasoun (Armenian), Sasun (Turkish): town — M2e2, 13.
Ṣatīf: town — see Setif.
Savona (Italian): port — F4d1, 1, 2.
Savoy; Savoie (French): region of SE France — F2c5, 1, 2, 12.
Saxony; Sachsen (German): region then of NW Germany — F5b3, 1, 2.
Sayn (German): town — F3b5, 2.
Schaumburg (German): medieval county NW of Hameln.
Schlesien: region north of Moravia — see Silesia.
Schlettstadt (German), Sélestat (French): town 14 miles north of Colmar.
Schwaben: region of SW Germany — see Swabia.
Scio: island — see Chios.
Scotland: region north of England — Da, 2.
Scribention: town — see Sopot.
Scutari (Italian), Chrysopolis (classical), Üsküdar (Turkish): port — J5d4, 6.
Scyros (classical), Skíros (modern Greek): island — I5e2, 6.
Scythopolis: town — see Baisan.
Sebastia (classical), Sivas (Turkish): city — L3e1, 4, 13, 22.
Sées (French): town — E1c2, 12.
Segni (Italian): town 30 miles ESE of Rome.
Segusio (classical), Susa (Italian): town — F3c5, 2.
Seine (French): river — E1c1, 2, 12.
Selef: river — see Calycadnus.
Sélestat: town — see Schlettstadt.
Seleucia (medieval), Selevgia (West Armenian), Silifke (Turkish): port, now town — K4e4, 13, 20.

Sens (French): town — E4c2, 12.
Serai or Serai-Berke: stronghold 45 miles east of modern Stalingrad — not in area mapped.
Serbia; Srbija (Serbian): region east of Croatia and Dalmatia — HId, 1.
Sergiana or Serviana (medieval): village — I2e3, 11.
Sergines: village — see Sargines.
Seriphos (ancient Greek), Sérifos (modern Greek): island — I5e3, 6.
Sermin: town — see Sarmīn.
Serres (medieval), Sérrai (modern Greek): town — I4d5, 1, 6, 7, 8, 9, 11.
Serviana: village — see Sergiana.
Sestus (Latin), Sēstos (medieval Greek): town, now abandoned — J2d5, 6.
Setif; Ṣatīf (Arabic): town — F1e4, 2.
Sévérac-le-Château (French): village — E4d1, 12.
Seville; Sevilla (Spanish), Ishbīliyah (Arabic): city — C5e3, 2.
Seyhan: river — see Sarus.
Sfax; Safāqus (Arabic): town — G1f1, 1, 2.
Shaizar (medieval Arabic), Larissa (classical), Saijar (modern Arabic): fortress — L2e5, 17.
ash-Sha'm: city — see Damascus.
ash-Sha'm: region — see Syria.
Shaqīf Arnūn: crusader castle — see Belfort.
Sharamsāḥ (Arabic): town — K2f4, 14, 15.
ash-Shaubak: fortress — see Krak de Montréal.
Shilb: town — see Silves.
Shiloh; Sailūn (Arabic): plain — L1f3, 16.
Shiraz; Shīrāz (Persian, Arabic): city — O3g1, 21.
Shqipni or Shqipri: region NW of Epirus — see Albania.
Shumlah (Arabic): district of Khuzistan.
Sibilla: town — see Zawila.
Sicily; Sicilia (Italian), Ṣiqillīyah (Arabic): island — Ge, 1, 2.
Sidon; Ṣaidā' (Arabic), Sagitta (medieval): port — L1f2, 3, 5, 13, 16, 18, 19.
Siebenbürgen: region SE of Hungary — see Transylvania.
Siena (Italian): town — G2d2, 1.
Sifanto or Sífnos: island — see Siphnos.
Ṣihyaun: crusader castle — see Saone.
Silesia; Schlesien (German), Śląsk (Polish), Slezsko (Czech): region north of Moravia — Hb, 1.
Silifke: port, now town — see Seleucia.
Silpius, Mount (classical), Ziyaret Daghî (Turkish) — L2e4, 17.
Silvan: town — see Maiyafariqin.
Silves (Portuguese), Shilb (Arabic): town — C2e3, 2.
Simanagla (Armenian): fortress near Amoudain.
Sind: region west of the Indus — Rg, 21.
Sinjar; Sinjār (Arabic): town — M2e4, 13.
Sinkiang: region east of Turkestan — see Chinese Turkestan.
Sinope; Sinōpē (medieval Greek), Sinop (Turkish): port — L1d3, 13.
Sinus Calydonius — see Patras, Gulf of.
Sinus Issicus — see Alexandretta, Gulf of.
Siphnos (classical), Sifanto (Italian), Sífnos (modern Greek): island — I5e4, 6.
Siponto (Italian): town, now abandoned for Manfredonia — H1d4, 1.
Ṣiqillīyah: island — see Sicily.
Siracusa: town — see Syracuse.
Sirmium (classical), Sremska Mitrovitsa (Serbian): town — H5d1, 1.
Síros: island — see Syros.

Sis (Armenian, medieval), Kozan (Turkish): town — L1e3, 3, 4, 5, 17, 18, 19, 22, 23.
Sivas: city — see Sebastia.
Skíros: island — see Scyros.
Skorta (medieval), Gortys (Greek): district around Karytaina.
Skripou (medieval Greek), Skripoú (modern Greek), Orchomenus (classical): town — I3e2, 11.
Ślaşk or Slezsko: region north of Moravia — see Silesia.
Smyrna; İzmir (Turkish): city, port — J3e2, 1, 4, 6, 7, 8, 9, 10, 13.
Sofia; Sardica (classical), Sofiya (Bulgarian): city — I4d3, 1, 7, 8, 9, 10.
Soissons (French): town 20 miles sw of Laon.
Soli (Greek): town, now abandoned — K3e5, 20.
Somerset: region of southern England — D2b4, 2.
Sonnac (French): village — E3d3, 12.
Sopot (Bulgarian), Scribention (medieval): town — I5d3, 6.
Sozopolis (medieval), Uluborlu (Turkish): town — K1e2, 13.
Spain; España (Spanish): region south of the Pyrenees.
Spalato (medieval), Split (Serbian): port — H2d2, 1.
Sparta or Lacedaemon (Latin), Spartē or Lakedaimōn (ancient Greek), Spárti (modern Greek): town — I3e3, 11.
Spercheus (classical), Sperkhiós (modern Greek): river — I3e2, 11.
Speyer (German), Spires (French): town — F4c1, 1, 2.
Split: port — see Spalato.
Splügen (German): pass — F5c4, 2.
Spoleto (Italian): town 32 miles east of Orvieto.
Sponheim (German): town 27 miles wsw of Mainz.
Sporades; Sporádhes (modern Greek): island group — Je, 1.
Srbija: region east of Croatia and Dalmatia — see Serbia.
Sremska Mitrovitsa: town — see Sirmium.
Stampalia: island — see Astypalaea.
Stara Zagora: town — see Berrhoea.
Starkenburg: castle — see Montfort.
Stavrovouni (medieval Greek): mountain — K4f1, 20.
Stenimaka or Stanimaka (Bulgarian): town — I5d4, 6.
Stimfalías Límní — see Stymphalus, Lake.
Straits — see Bosporus, Dardanelles.
Strassburg (German), Strasbourg (French): city — F3c2, 1, 2.
Strymon; Strymōn (ancient Greek), Strimón (modern Greek), Struma (Bulgarian): river — I4d5, 11.
Stymphalus, Lake; Stimfalías Límni (modern Greek) — I3e3, 11.
Sudan; as-Sūdān (Arabic: the Negro-lands): region south of Egypt — Kh, 13.
Suez; as-Suwais (Arabic): isthmus and port — K3g1, 13.
Sully (French): town — E3c3, 12.
Sulṭānīyeh: town — see Kangurlan.
Sulzbach (German): town — G2c1, 1.
Ṣūr: port — see Tyre.
Sūriyah: region — see Syria.
Susa; Hadrumetum (classical), Sūsah (Arabic): port — G1e5, 1, 2.
Susa: town — see Segusio.
Susiana: region of sw Persia — see Khuzistan.
Sussex: coastal region of SE England, south of London.
Sutri (Italian): town 28 miles NNW of Rome.
as-Suwaidīyah or Süveydiye: port — see Saint Simeon.
as-Suwais: isthmus and port — see Suez.

Swabia; Schwaben (German): region of sw Germany — Fc, 1, 2.
Sweden; Sverige (Swedish): region of eastern Scandinavia, smaller than modern nation — not in area mapped.
Sybota: island, and mainland port — see Syvota.
Sycae: part of Constantinople south of Pera — see Galata.
Syr Darya: river — see Jaxartes.
Syracuse; Siracusa (Italian): town — H1e3, 1.
Syria (classical), ash-Sha'm or Sūriyah (Arabic): region — Lf, 13.
Syrian Gates; La Portelle (medieval), Toun̦ (Armenian), Belen Boghazi̊ (Turkish): pass over Amanus range — L2e4, 17.
Syros (classical), Syra (medieval), Síros (modern Greek): island — I5e3, 6.
Syvota (medieval), Sybota (classical): island, and mainland port (now abandoned) — I1e1, 11.

Ṭabarīyah: town — see Tiberias.
Tabor, Mount; Jabal Tābūr or Jabal aṭ-Ṭūr (Arabic) : mountain — L1f3, 16.
Tabriz; Tabrīz (Persian): city — N2e2, 13, 21, 22.
Taenarum — see Matapan, Cape.
Tagliacozzo (Italian): town — G4d3, 1.
Tagus (classical), Tajo (Spanish), Tejo (Portuguese): river — C1e2, 2.
Taïyetos: mountains — see Taygetus.
Tall al-'Ajūl (Arabic): hill — K5f4, 16.
Tall Bāshir: fortress — see Tell Bashir.
Tall Ḥamdūn (Arabic), Tilhamdoun (Armenian), Toprakkale (Turkish): castle 18 miles east of Adana.
Tall Qaimūn: castle — see Caymont.
Ṭannāḥ (Arabic): village — K2f4, 14, 15.
Ṭarābulus: city, port — see Tripoli.
Ṭarābulus al-Gharb: city, port — see Tripoli.
Taranto (Italian): port — H3d5, 1.
Tarbes (French): town — E1d2, 12.
Tarentaise (French): district SE of Savoy.
Tarn (French): river — E1d2, 2, 12.
Tarsus (classical, Turkish), Darsous (West Armenian): city — K5e4, 3, 4, 5, 13, 18, 20, 23.
Tarsus-Chayi̊: river — see Cydnus.
Ṭarṭūs: port — see Tortosa.
Tashkent; Binkath or Tāshkand (Arabic): city — R5d4, 21.
Taurus (classical), Toros Daghlari̊ (Turkish): mountain range — KLe, 13, 20.
Taygetus (classical), Pentedaktylon (medieval Greek), Taïyetos (modern Greek): mountains — I3e3, 11.
Tbilisi: city — see Tiflis.
Tejo: river — see Tagus.
Tell Bashir; Tall Bāshir (Arabic), Turbessel (medieval), Tilbeshar (Turkish): fortress — L3e4, 17.
Tempe, Vale of; Tempē (ancient Greek), Témbi (modern Greek): defile — I3e1, 11.
Tenos; Tēnos (ancient Greek), Tínos (modern Greek): island — J1e3, 6.
Termes (French): village — E3d3, 12.
Ternovum: town — see Tirnovo.
Terra di Lavoro (Italian): district east of Capua.
Tevere: river — see Tiber.
Thabaria: town — see Tiberias.
Thaumacia: town — see Domokos.

Thebes; Thēvai (ancient Greek), Thívai (modern Greek): city — I4e2, 7, 11.
Theodosiopolis: city — see Erzerum.
Thera; Thēra (ancient Greek), Santorin (medieval), Thíra (modern Greek): island — J1e4, 6.
Thermia: island — see Cythnos.
Thermopylae (classical), Pylae (medieval): pass — I3e2, 11.
Thessalonica (medieval), Salonika (Italian), Thessaloníki (modern Greek): port — I3d5, 1, 7, 8, 9, 10, 11.
Thessalonica: kingdom — Id, 8.
Thessaly; Thessalia (classical): region of northern Greece — I3e1, 1, 11.
Thessy: probably Theix, 65 miles NW of Le Puy.
Thēvai or Thívai: city — see Thebes.
Thíra: island — see Thera.
Thirsk: town — D4b1, 2.
Thornham: town — see Turnham.
Thrace; Thracia (Latin), Thrakē (ancient Greek), Thráki (modern Greek), Trakya (Turkish): region south of Bulgaria — Jd, 1, 6, 13.
Thuringia; Thüringen (German): region of central Germany — Gb, 1, 2.
Thury-en-Valois (French): town 36 miles NE of Paris.
Thynias: island — see Daphnusia.
Tiber; Tevere (Italian): river — G3d4, 1.
Tiberias; Ṭabarīyah (Arabic), Thabaria (medieval): town — L1f3, 13, 16.
Tiberias, Lake, or Sea of Galilee; Buḥairat Ṭabarīyah (Arabic) — L1f3, 16.
Tickhill: town 39 miles NNE of Derby.
Tiflis; Tiflīs (Persian, Arabic), Tbilisi (Georgian): city — M5d4, 4, 13, 21, 22, 23.
Tigris (classical), Dijlah (Arabic), Dijle (Turkish): river — N4f5, 13, 21.
Tilbeshar: fortress — see Tell Bashir.
Tilhamdoun: castle — see Tall Ḥamdūn.
at-Tīnah (Arabic): village — K3f4, 14, 15.
Tinnis; Tinnīs (Arabic): town, now unimportant — K3f4, 14, 15.
Tínos: island — see Tenos.
Tirnovo; Ternovum (Latin), Trnovo (Bulgarian): town — J1d2, 1, 6, 7, 8, 9, 10, 13.
Tonkin: region of SE Asia — not in area mapped.
Tonnerre (French): town — E4c3, 12.
Torigny-sur-Vire (French): village 24 miles SW of Bayeux.
Ṭornavan (East Armenian): district of Vaspurkan.
Toron (medieval): fortress — L1f2, 3, 5, 16, 18, 19.
Toros Daghlari: mountain range — see Taurus.
Tortosa; Antaradus (classical: opposite Aradus), Anṭarṭūs or Ṭarṭūs (Arabic): port — L1f1, 3, 4, 5, 13, 17, 18, 19.
Toscana: region of central Italy — see Tuscany.
Toucy (French): village — E4c3, 12.
Toul (French): town — F1c2, 1, 2, 12.
Toulousain (French): district around Toulouse.
Toulouse (French): city — E2d2, 2, 12.
Touraine (French): region of central France — E1c3, 12.
Touṛn: pass over Amanus range — see Syrian Gates.
Tours (French): town — E1c3, 2, 12.
Trabzon: city, port — see Trebizond.
Trakya: region south of Bulgaria — see Thrace.
Trani (Italian): port — H2d4, 1.
Transcaucasia: region including Georgia and parts of Armenia and Azerbaijan.

Transjordania or Transjordan; Oultrejourdain (medieval): region east of the Jordan.
Transoxiana: region NE of the Oxus — QRde, 21.
Transylvania; Siebenbürgen (German), Erdély (Hungarian), Ardeal (Rumanian): region SE of Hungary — IJc, 1, 13.
Trapani (Italian): port — G3e2, 1, 2.
Trapesac: town — see Darbsāk.
Trazarg (Armenian): monastery west of Sis.
Trebizond; Trapezus (classical), Trapezunt (medieval), Trabzon (Turkish): city, port — L5d5, 4, 13, 22, 23.
Tremelay: village — see Dramelay.
Treviso (Italian): town 16 miles NNW of Venice.
Trier (German), Trèves (French): city — F2c1, 1, 2.
Triphylia (classical), Trifília or Fília (modern Greek): district of western Morea — I2e3, 11.
Tripoli; Tripolis (classical), Ṭarābulus (Arabic): city, port — L1f1, 3, 4, 5, 13, 16, 17, 18, 19, 22, 23.
Tripoli; Oea (classical), Ṭarābulus al-Gharb (Arabic): city, port — G4f3, 1.
Tripotamos (medieval Greek): castle and village — I2e3, 11.
Trith-St. Léger (French): village 31 miles SE of Lille.
Trnovo: town — see Tirnovo.
Troad; Trōas (ancient Greek): district south of the Dardanelles — Jde, 1, 6, 13.
Troezen or Troizēn: town — see Damala.
Troina (Italian): town — G5e3, 1.
Trois-Fontaines (French), Dreibrunnen (German): village 30 miles WNW of Strassburg.
Troyes (French): town — E5c2, 2, 12.
Ṯsakhoud (Armenian): district south of Partzapert.
Tubania (medieval), 'Ain aṭ-Ṭuba'ūn (Arabic): well 1 mile NE of 'Ain Jālūt.
Tudela (Spanish), Tuṭīlah (Arabic): town — D4d3, 2.
Tunis; Tūnis (Arabic): city — G1e4, 1, 2.
Tunisia; Ifrīqiyah (Arabic): region of North Africa — Fe, 2.
Turbessel: fortress — see Tell Bashir.
Turenne (French): village — E2c5, 12.
Turkestan: region NE of Transoxiana — QRc, 21.
Turkey: modern nation, holding Anatolia and parts of Thrace and Armenia.
Turnham or Thornham: town 21 miles west of Canterbury.
Tuscany; Toscana (Italian): region of central Italy — Gd, 1, 2.
Tusculum (Latin): town, now abandoned, 12 miles SE of Rome.
Tuṭīlah: town — see Tudela.
Tyre; Tyrus (classical), Ṣūr (Arabic): port — L1f2, 3, 4, 5, 13, 16, 18, 19, 22, 23.
Tzia: island — see Ceos.
Tzurulum (classical), Chorlu (Turkish): town — J3d4, 6.

Ukraine; Ukraina (Russian): region of SW Russia — Kc, 1, 13.
Ulubad: town — see Lopadium.
Uluborlu: town — see Sozopolis.
Ünye: port — see Oenoë.
al-Urdunn: river — see Jordan.
Urfa: city — see Edessa.
Üsküdar: port — see Scutari.
Uswān: town in southern Egypt — see Aswan.

Utrecht (Dutch): city — F1b3, 1, 2.
Uzès (French): town — E5d1, 12.

Vacqueyras (French): town — F1d1, 12.
Vahka; Vahga (West Armenian), Feke (Turkish): fortress — L1e3, 13.
Vaison-la-Romaine (French): town — F1d1, 12.
Valania (medieval), Bulunyās (medieval Arabic), Bāniyās (modern Arabic): port — L1e5, 17.
Valence (French): town — E5d1, 12.
Valencia (Spanish), Balansiyah (Arabic): city, port — D5e1, 2.
Valenciennes (French): town 28 miles SE of Lille.
Valois (French): district NE of Paris.
Valona: port — see Avlona.
Van, Lake; Van Gölü (Turkish) — M3e2, 13.
Vardar (medieval, modern), Axius (classical): river — I3d5, 1, 11.
Varennes-sur-Allier (French): town — E4c4, 12.
Váres, Cape: northernmost point of Galicia — C3d2, 2.
Vaspurkan; Vaspourakan (East Armenian): region east of Lake Van — Me, 13.
Vatonda (medieval), Néa Artáki (modern Greek): village — I4e2, 11.
[Titov] Veles: town — see Prosek.
Velestinon (medieval), Pherae (classical): town — I3e1, 11.
Veligosti (medieval), Veligostē (medieval Greek): castle — I3e3, 11.
Vellefaux: abbey — see Bellevaux.
Venaissin (French): district around Avignon and Carpentras.
Vendôme (French): town — E2c3, 12.
Venice; Venezia (Italian): city, port — G3c5, 1, 2.
Verden (German): town — F5b3, 1.
Verdun (French): town 35 miles west of Metz.
Verissa: town — see Pinarhisar.
Veroli (Italian): town 26 miles NW of Monte Cassino.
Verona (Italian): city — G2c5, 2.
Vervaena (classical): village — I3e3, 11.
Vexin; Véxin (French): district NW of Paris — Ec, 2.
Vézelay (French): town — E4c3, 12.
Vicenza (Italian): town — G2c5, 1, 2.
Vienna; Wien (German): city — H2c2, 1.
Vienne (French): town — E5c5, 12.
Vieste (Italian): town — H2d4, 1.
Vigeois (French): village — E2c5, 12.
Villehardouin (French): castle near Troyes.
Villiers-le-Bel (French): town 10 miles NNE of Paris.
Viminacium: town — see Branits.
Violgama: district of Frisia — see Fivelgo.
Viterbo (Italian): town — G3d3, 2.
Vitré (French): town — D4c2, 12.
Vitry-en-Artois (French): village 25 miles south of Lille.
Vizya (Latin), Bizyē or Vizyē (Greek), Vize (Turkish): town — J3d4, 6.
Vlaanderen: region of northern France and Belgium — see Flanders.
Vlachia: region north of Bulgaria — see Wallachia.
Vlonë: port — see Avlona.
Voden (Bulgarian), Banduci (classical), Brandoveus (medieval): town — J2d3, 6.
Vohburg (German): village 28 miles SW of Regensburg.
Vöhringen (German): town 38 miles west of Augsburg.
Voiotía: district of eastern Greece — see Boeotia.

Voleron or Volerum (medieval): district in Thrace — J1d4, 6.
Volga (Russian), Itil (Tartar): river — N3c4, 13, 21.
Volos, Gulf of; Pagasētikos Kolpos (ancient and medieval Greek) — I3e1, 11.
Vostitsa (medieval), Aegium (classical), Aíyion (modern Greek): town — I3e2, 11.

Wales: region west of England — Db, 2.
Wallachia; Vlachia (medieval): region north of Bulgaria — Jd, 1, 13.
Waverley: abbey 35 miles SW of London.
Wendover: town 34 miles NW of London.
Weser (German): river — F5b2, 1, 2.
Westphalia; Westfalen (German): region of NW Germany — Fb, 1, 2.
Wied or Altwied (German): town 39 miles SE of Cologne.
Wien: city — see Vienna.
Wiesenbach (German): village in Baden, probably Wiesenbach über Neckargemünd, 18 miles ENE of Speyer.
Winchester: city — D4b4, 2.
Wittelsbach (German): castle 16 miles ENE of Augsburg.
Wöltingerode (German): castle 22 miles west of Halberstadt.
Worms (German): town — F4c1, 1, 2.
Würzburg (German): city — F5c1, 1, 2.

Yabnâ: town — see Ibelin.
Yāfā: port — see Jaffa.
Yāzūr (Arabic): castle — K5f3, 16.
Yelisavetpol: town — see Ganja.
Yellow Sea; Hwang Hai (Chinese) — not in area mapped.
Yemen; al-Yaman (Arabic: the right hand): region of SW Arabia — not in area mapped.
Yeráki: town — see Geraki.
Yerevan: city — see Erivan.
York: city in central Yorkshire.
Yorkshire: region of NE England — D5b2, 2.
Ypres (French), Ieper (Flemish): town 17 miles NNW of Lille.
Yumurtalik: port — see Ayas.

Zagros (Persian): mountain range — NOef, 21.
Zante (Italian), Zacynthus (classical), Zákinthos (modern Greek): island — I1e3, 7, 11.
Zara (Italian), Jadera (classical), Zadar (Croatian): port — H1d1, 1.
Zaraca (classical): village — I3e3, 11.
Zaragoza: city — see Saragossa.
Zaratovo (Greek): suffragan see under bishop of Thebes.
Zarephath: town — see Sarepta.
Zawila; Sibilla (medieval), Zawīlah (Arabic): town — G2e5, 1.
Zeitounion; Lamia (classical), Zitouni (medieval Greek), Lamía (modern Greek): town — I3e2, 11.
Zeitz (German): town — G3b4, 2.
Zeta (Serbian): district south of Rascia — HId, 1.
az-Zīb: castle — see Casal Imbert.
Zir'īn (Arabic), Jezreel (classical), Le Petit Gerin (medieval): village — L1f3, 16.
Zitouni: town — see Zeitounion.
Ziyaret Daghi — see Silpius, Mount.

Important Towns and Fortresses

In this position in volume I, there appeared a list of 100 of the most important towns and fortresses in or near the crusaders' states, showing changes in control of each place for the period 1097–1189. Since the crusading area expanded in the thirteenth century, while the Frankish holdings in Syria and Palestine contracted, we have eliminated 50 of the less significant places there, and have added a similar list of 50 from the Aegean area.

In the first list below, as in volume I, the initials of Armenians, Byzantines, Franks, and Moslems, and X for the Assassins, indicate their possession of a place in 1189 or its subsequent acquisition or construction by them in the year given. Within the Frankish period Hospitallers and Templars are similarly designated by initials, and Teutonic Knights by K. After 1291, when this list closes, the only places in this area remaining in Frankish hands were Cyprus, Jubail (for a few years under Mamluk suzerainty), and the tiny island of Ruad (unlisted, under the Templars until 1303).

In the second list, the same meanings apply to B (for Byzantines; subdivided after 1204 into E for Epirus, N for Nicaea, and G for other Greek states) and F (for Franks, with R for Romania, V for Venice, M and A used here for Morea and Athens, as the Moslems and Armenians did not affect this area, and O for others), while S (for Slavs) covers Bulgars, Vlachs, and Serbs in the Balkan peninsula.

The Near East 1189–1291

Acre	M → F 1191 → M 1291
Adana	A (sacked 1266 by Mamluks)
'Akkār	M → F 1192? → M 1271
Alamut	X → Mongols 1256
Aleppo	M (sacked 1260, 1261, 1280 by Mongols)
Antioch	F (occupied 1194, 1208, 1216 by A) → M 1268
Arsuf	M → F 1191 (H 1261) → M 1265
Ascalon	M (occupied 1192 by F) → F 1239 → M 1247
Ayas	A (sacked 1266, 1275 by Mamluks)
Baalbek	M (occupied 1260 by Mongols)
Baghdad	M → Mongols 1258
Baghrās	M → A 1191 → F(T) 1211 → M 1268 (occupied 1280 by Mongols)
Beirut	M → F 1197 → M 1291
Belfort	F → M 1190 → F 1240 (T 1260) → M 1268

Belvoir M → F(H) 1240 → M 1247
Bethlehem M → F 1229 → M 1239 → F 1240 → M 1244
Botron M → F 1197 → M 1289

Caesarea M → F 1191 (occupied 1220 by M) → M 1265
Chastel Blanc F(T) → M 1271
Château Pèlerin F(T) built 1218 → M 1291
Cyprus B (Isaac Comnenus) → F 1191

Damascus M (occupied 1260 by Mongols)
Damietta M → F 1219 → M 1221 → F 1249 → M 1250

Gaza M (occupied 1192 by F, 1260 by Mongols)

Haifa M → F 1191 → M 1265
Hamah M (occupied 1260 by Mongols)
Homs M (occupied 1260 by Mongols)

Iconium M (sacked 1243 by Mongols)

Jabala M (occupied 1231 by F)
Jaffa M → F 1191 → M 1197 → F 1204 → M 1268
Jerusalem M → F 1229 → M 1239 → F 1240 → M 1244
Jubail M → F 1197 → M 1291 (Embriacos stay a few years as vassals)

Krak des Chevaliers F(H) → M 1271

Latakia M → F 1260 → M 1287

Mamistra A (sacked 1266 by Mamluks)
al-Marqab F(H) → M 1285
Maṣyāf X → M 1270
Montfort F(K) built 1227 → M 1271

Nablus M (sacked 1242 by F, occupied 1260 by Mongols)
Nazareth M → F 1229 → M 1263

Safad M → F(T) 1240 → M 1266
Sidon M → F 1197 (half), 1204 (rest; abandoned, retaken 1227) (occupied 1249, 1253 by M, sacked 1260 by Mongols, T 1260) → M 1291
Sis A (sacked 1266, 1275 by Mamluks)

Tarsus A (sacked 1266 by Mamluks)
Tiberias M → F 1240 (sacked 1244 by M) → M 1247
Toron M → F 1229 → M 1266
Tortosa F(T) → M 1291
Trebizond B (Comneni 1204)
Tripoli F → M 1289
Tyre F → M 1291

The Aegean and Balkans 1189–1311

Adrianople B (occupied 1189–1190 by F) → F(R) 1204 (occupied 1205 by S) → N 1225 → E 1225 → S 1230 → N 1247? (B 1261)
Andravida B → F(M) 1204

Andros B → F(O) 1207
Arcadia B → F(M) 1205
Argos B → F(A) 1210 (M 1311)
Arta B → E 1204 → N 1259 (B 1261)
Athens B → F(A) 1204 (→ Catalans 1311)
Avlona B → E 1204 → F(O) 1258 (Angevins 1269) → B 1281?

Berat B → E 1204 → F(O) 1258 (Angevins 1271) → B 1274
Bodonitsa B → F(O) 1204 (→ Catalans 1311)

Cephalonia F(O) from 1185
Cerigo B → F(O) 1207 → B 1275?
Cerigotto B → F(O) 1207 → B 1275?
Chios B → F(R) 1204 → N 1247 (B 1261)
Constantinople B → F(R) 1204 → B(N) 1261
Corfu B → F(O) 1199 (V 1206) → E 1214 → F(O) 1259 (Angevins 1267)
Corinth B → F(M) 1205 (Acrocorinth 1209)
Coron B → F(V) 1206
Crete B → F(V) 1207

Durazzo B → F(V) 1204 → E 1210 → S 1230 → E 1237 → N 1256 → F(O) 1258 (Angevins 1271)

Euboea B → F(O) 1205 → B 1276?

Geraki B → F(M) 1204 → B 1263

Kalavryta B → F(M) 1204 → B 1277

Lemnos B → F(O) 1205 → B 1269?
Lesbos B → F(R) 1204 → N 1224 → F 1230? → N 1247 (B 1261)

Maina F(M) built 1249 → B 1262
Mistra F(M) built 1249 → B 1262
Modon B → F(V) 1206
Monemvasia B → N 1205 → F(M) 1248 → B 1262

Nauplia B → F(A) 1211 (M 1311)
Naxos B → F(O) 1207
Negroponte (town) B → F(O) 1205 (V 1216)
Neopatras B → F(O) 1205 → E 1218 → G 1271
Nicaea B → F(R) 1204 → N 1205 (B 1261)
Nicomedia B → F(R) 1204 → N 1205 → F(R) 1207 → N 1208 → F(R) 1211 → N 1235 (B 1261)
Nikli B → F(M) 1207
Nish B → F(O) 1189 → S 1189

Patras B → F(M) 1204
Philippopolis B → F(O) 1189 → S 1189 → F(R) 1204 → S 1205 → N 1246? (B 1261)

Rhodes B → G 1204 → F (Genoese) 1246 → N 1247 (B 1261) → F (Hospitallers) 1309

Salona B → F(O) 1204 (→ Catalans 1311)
Samos B → F(O) 1204 → N 1247 (B 1261)
Serres B → F(R) 1204 → E 1222 → S 1230 → N 1246 (B 1261)
Smyrna B → N 1205 → F (Genoese, under B) 1261
Sofia B → F(O) 1189 → S 1189
Sparta B → F(M) 1211 (occupied 1263 by B)

Thebes B → F(A) 1204
Thessalonica B → F(O) 1204 → E 1224 → N 1246 (B 1261)

Veligosti B → F(M) 1207

Zante F(O) from 1185

INDEX

Aachen, 356, 430, 432, 433, 440, 441, 447, 458; *and see* Albert of Aix

Abagha, son of Hulagu; Il-khan of Persia 1265–1282: 575, 576, 580, 582, 586, 654, 722, 751, 762

'Abbāsids, Arab caliphal dynasty at Baghdad 749–1258: 17, 27 note, 34, 571, 662, 665, 671, 717, 735, 736, 742, 746, *and see* al-Qā'im 1031–1075, al-Mustarshid 1118–1135, al-Mustaḍī 1170–1180, an-Nāṣir 1180–1225, al-Musta'ṣim 1242–1258; at Cairo 1261–1519: 747, 756, 757, *and see* al-Mustanṣir 1261–1261, al-Ḥākim 1262–1302

'Abd-al-Mu'min, Muwaḥḥid caliph 1130–1163: 28, 30–32

'Abd-al-Qādir Gīlānī, Persian mystic (d. 1166), 663

Abenberg, count of, *see* Frederick

Ablgharib (Abū-l-Gharīb), son of Hasan; Armenian lord of Bira (to 1117), 632–634, 636

Abū-Bakr, Naṣrat-ad-Dīn, grandson of Ildegiz; atabeg of Azerbaijan 1191–1210: 670

Abū-l-Ḥasan, shaikh at Damietta, 419

Abū-Sa'īd, son of Öljaitu; Il-khan of Persia 1316–1335: 722

Abū-Shāmah, Arabic chronicler (d. 1268), 392, 393

Abydus, 103, 108, 177

Abyssinia, 669

Acarnania, 13, 226, 235, 263, 267, 273

Acerra, count of, *see* Thomas of Aquino

Achaea, bailies of, *see* Hugh of Champlitte, John Chauderon, Galeran of Ivry, Philip of Lagonesse, Guy of Dramelay, William de la Roche, Nicholas II of St. Omer, Guy de Charpigny, Richard Orsini, Nicholas III of St. Omer, Guy II de la Roche, Bertino Visconti, Thomas of Marzano; barons of, 255, 264, 265, 267, 269; parliament of, 248; princes of, *see* William I of Champlitte 1205–1209, Geoffrey I of Villehardouin 1209–*c.* 1229, Geoffrey II of Villehardouin *c.* 1229–1246, William II of Villehardouin 1246–1278, Charles I of Anjou 1278–1285, Charles II 1285–1289, Florent of Hainault 1289–1297, Philip of Savoy 1301–1306, Philip of Taranto 1306–1313, Louis of Burgundy 1313–1316; princesses of, *see* Isabel of Villehardouin 1289–1306, Mahaut 1313–1318; principality of, 207, 213, 238–240, 242 note, 243, 245, 248, 249, 255, 256, 258–269, 272–274, 367, 760, 762; regent of, *see* Anna Angelina Comnena 1259–1261; *see also* Morea

Acharie of Sermin (Sarmīn), seneschal of Antioch, 538

Achyraūs, 209

Acre: under Saladin 1187–1191: 39 note, 40, 41, 46, 51–54, 61, 63–69, 75, 115, 116, 339, 600 note, 601, 646, 759; under Franks 1191–1210: 69–73, 77, 78, 80–85, 120, 121, 158 note, 161, 522–524, 529–532, 604, 647, 759; 1210–1225: 379, 381, 382, 388–396, 402, 416, 419, 422, 427, 437, 440, 536–538, 605, 609, 610 note, 698, 760; 1225–1243: 222, 442, 448, 449, 451, 454, 459, 460, 463, 469, 471–474, 477, 478, 481, 483, 484, 489, 542–554, 612, 613, 626, 701, 702, 761; 1243–1268: 230, 245, 491, 494, 504, 505, 507–509, 554, 559, 561, 562, 565–576, 606, 613, 614, 615 note, 709, 741, 742, 745; 1268–1291: 518, 579, 580, 582–586, 588–590, 592–598, 608, 616–618, 624, 655, 753, 754, 762; bay of, 596, 597; bishops of, 381, 389, 536, 538; high court of, *see under* Jerusalem, kingdom

Acrocorinth, 14, 240, 241, 248

Acropolis, at Athens, 241, 248, 272

Acropolites, George, Byzantine historian (d. 1282), 204, 210

Adalbert III, count of Dillingen 1185–1198: 92, 93

Adalia, 133, 681, 682, 692, 730

Adam of Gaston (Baghrās), regent of Armenia 1219–1221: 540

Adana, 540, 635–637, 642, 644, 651 note, 654, 657

Adela, sister of Henry I of Champagne; 3rd wife of Louis VII of France 1160–1180; regent 1190–1191 (d. 1206), 54, 70

Adelaide of Montferrat, wife of Roger I of Sicily 1090–1101, regent 1101–1112, 3rd wife of Baldwin I of Jerusalem 1113–1116 (d. 1118), 5, 7, 18, 19 note

al-'Ādil Abū-Bakr I, Saif-ad-Dīn ("Saphadin"), brother of Saladin; Aiyūbid governor of the Jazira 1186–1193: 77, 78, 693; ruler 1193–1198: 117, 526, 529, 694, 695; ruler of Damascus 1198–1200: 121, 530, 608, 695; sultan of Egypt and Syria 1200–1218: 161 note, 169, 531–533, 536, 537,

683, 696–699, 737, 759, 760; and fifth crusade, 389–391, 398, 401, 407, 409, 449, 539, 698, 699; daughter of, 113 note
al-ʿĀdil Abū-Bakr II, Saif-ad-Dīn, son of al-Kāmil Muḥammad; Aiyūbid sultan of Egypt 1238–1240 (d. 1247), 465, 471, 473, 475, 478, 480, 551, 674, 705–707, 737; son of, 712
ʿĀdilī mamluks, 737
al-ʿĀdilīyah, town, 398, 405, 408–410
Admont, abbot of, 92
Adolf (of Altena), archbishop of Cologne 1193–1205 (d. 1220), 117
Adolf III, son of Engelbert I; count of Berg 1189–1218: 399
Adolf III, count of Schaumburg and Holstein 1164–1203 (d. 1205), 92, 115, 121
Adramyttium, 192, 209
Adrianople, 190, 191, 203–205, 215, 217; third crusade at, 104–111, 113, 148
Adriatic Sea, 173, 206, 208, 212, 609; coasts of, 13, 29, 175, 191; ports on, 3, 10, 388; region of, 14, 127
Aegean Sea, 177, 191, 205, 209, 238, 254, 257, 729; dukes of, *see* Archipelago; islands in, 191, 193; map of, 152
Aegina, 191; bishopric of, 252; lord of, 271
Aetolia, 235, 273
Afāriqah, Christians of Tunisia, 27 note
al-Afḍal ʿAlī, Nūr-ad-Dīn, son of Saladin; Aiyūbid governor of Damascus 1186–1193, ruler 1193–1196, regent of Egypt 1198–1200, lord of Samosata 1203–1225: 683, 693, 695, 696, 698, 699
Africa, *see* North Africa, Tunisia
Agathopolis, 191
Agen, 319; bishop of, 295
Agenais, 287 note, 294, 295, 303, 304, 306, 315, 320, 322
Aghlabids, Arab dynasty in Tunisia 800–909: 17
Agnes (of Andechs), daughter of Berthold IV of Meran; 3rd wife of Philip II of France 1196–1200 (d. 1201), 388 note
Agnes ("Anna") of Châtillon, daughter of Reginald and Constance; 1st wife of Bela III of Hungary 1172–1184: 139
Agnes of Courtenay, daughter of Latin emperor Peter and Yolanda; wife of Geoffrey II of Achaea 1217–1246 (d. 1247), 213, 242–244
Agnes ("Anna") of France, daughter of Louis VII and Adela; wife of Alexius II Comnenus 1180–1183, wife of Andronicus I Comnenus 1183–1185, wife of Theodore Branas after 1205 (d. 1220), 134, 141, 145, 204, 244
Agnes of Montferrat, daughter of Boniface (II) of Thessalonica; 1st wife of Latin emperor Henry 1207–*c.* 1210: 205, 210
Agridi, 760; battle (1232), 631, 761
Ahasi, 21
Ahil, 192
Aḥmad al-Badawī, Moroccan shaikh, 711
Aiello (Calabro), count of, 41 note
Aigues-Mortes, 493, 511, 515
Aimard, Templar, 383, 386
Aimery, lord of Montréal (d. 1211), 293
Aimery III, viscount of Narbonne 1194–1236: 303
Aimery of Limoges, Latin patriarch of Antioch 1139–1196?: 527
Aimery of Lusignan, son of Hugh VIII; constable of Jerusalem 1181–1194: 45, 48, 50, 65; count of Jaffa 1193–1194: 525; ruler of Cyprus 1194–1197: 42, 82, 118–120, 149, 525, 528, 604, 622, 624, 647, 759; king 1197–1205: 121, 529–532, 559, 604, 605, 610, 616, 619–623, 759; king of Jerusalem 1197–1205: 82, 121, 530–536, 543, 604, 608, 611, 650, 759, 760; son of (by Isabel), *see* Amalric; wives of, *see* Eschiva of Ibelin, Isabel (of Jerusalem)
Aimery of Péguilhan, troubadour (d. *c.* 1255), 382
Aimo, bishop of Mâcon 1228–1242: 467
ʿAin Jālūt, 390; battle (1260), 574, 575, 653, 674, 714, 718, 722, 745, 761
ʿAin-ad-Daulah, son of Malik-Ghāzī; Dānishmendid emir at Melitene 1140–1152: 638
ʿĀʾishah Khātūn, daughter of al-ʿAzīz Muḥammad of Aleppo; wife of al-Manṣūr Muḥammad II (after 1247), 711
Aix, *see* Aachen; *see also* Albert
Aiyūbids, Kurdish dynasty, xviii, 422, 449, 465, 471, 481, 489, 505, 522, 528, 530, 531, 543, 546, 561, 564, 608, 673, 693–714, 717, 719, 735–737, 740, 742, 743, 745–748, 759, 761; sultans of Egypt 1174–1252: 297, 560, 567, 694, 712, 757, 758, *and see* Saladin 1174–1193, al-ʿAzīz ʿUthmān 1193–1198, al-Manṣūr Muḥammad 1198–1200, al-ʿĀdil (Abū-Bakr I) Saif-ad-Dīn 1200–1218, al-Kāmil Muḥammad 1218–1238, al-ʿĀdil Abū-Bakr II 1238–1240, aṣ-Ṣāliḥ Aiyūb 1240–1249, (al-Muʿaẓẓam) Tūrān-Shāh 1249–1250, al-Ashrāf Mūsâ 1250–1252; rulers of Damascus 1174–1260: 448, 560, 674, 694, *and see* Saladin 1174–1193, al-Afḍal ʿAlī 1193–1196, al-ʿAzīz ʿUthmān 1196–1198, al-ʿĀdil (Abū-Bakr I) Saif-ad-Dīn 1198–1218, al-Muʿaẓẓam ʿĪsâ 1218–1227, an-Nāṣir Dāʾūd 1227–1229, al-Ashrāf Mūsâ 1229–1237, aṣ-Ṣāliḥ Ismāʿīl 1237–1237, 1239–1245, al-Kāmil Muḥammad 1237–1238, al-Jauwād Yūnus 1238–1238, aṣ-Ṣāliḥ Aiyūb 1238–1239, 1245–1249, (al-Muʿaẓẓam) Tūrān-Shāh 1249–1250, an-Nāṣir Yūsuf 1250–1260; rulers of Aleppo 1183–1260: 526, 540, 674, 694, 714, 727, *and see* Saladin 1183–1193, aẓ-Ẓāhir Ghāzī 1193–1216, al-ʿAzīz Muḥammad 1216–1236, an-Nāṣir Yūsuf 1236–1260; rulers of the Jazira (at Maiyafariqin) 1185–1260: 665, 672, 673, 683, 694, *and see* Saladin 1185–1193, al-ʿĀdil (Abū-

Bakr I) Saif-ad-Dīn 1193–1198, al-Auḥad Aiyūb 1198–1202, al-Ashraf Mūsâ 1202–1229, al-Muẓaffar Ghāzī 1229–1244; rulers of Homs 1174–1263: 694, 714, *and see* Saladin 1174–1193, al-Mujāhid Shīrkūh 1193–1240, al-Manṣūr Ibrāhīm 1240–1246, al-Ashraf Mūsâ 1246–1263; rulers of Hamah 1174–1341: 694, 714, 743, *and see* Saladin 1174–1193, al-Manṣūr Muḥammad I 1193–1221, an-Nāṣir Ḳilij Arslan 1221–1229, al-Muẓaffar Maḥmūd 1229–1243, al-Manṣūr Muḥammad II 1243–1284; rulers of Baalbek 1174–1260: *see* Saladin 1174–1193, al-Amjad Bahrām-Shāh 1193–1230, al-Ashraf Mūsâ 1230–1237, as-Ṣāliḥ Ismā'īl 1237–1246, aṣ-Ṣāliḥ Aiyūb 1246–1249, (al-Mu'aẓẓam) Tūrān-Shāh 1249–1250, an-Nāṣir Yūsuf 1250–1260; rulers of Transjordania (at Kerak) 1188–1263: 714, *and see* Saladin 1188–1193, al-Mu'aẓẓam 'Īsâ 1193–1227, an-Nāṣir Dā'ūd 1227–1249, al-Mughīth 'Umar 1250–1263; rulers of Ḥiṣn Kaifā 1232–1534: 693 note, *and see* aṣ-Ṣāliḥ Aiyūb 1232–1239; rulers of Yemen 1174–1229: 693 note, *and see* Saladin 1174–1193, al-Mas'ūd Yūsuf 1215–1229; *see also* al-'Azīz Muḥammad, al-'Azīz 'Uthmān, al-Fā'iz Ibrāhīm, Farrūkh-Shāh Dā'ūd, al-Ḥāfiẓ Arslan, Khalīl, al-Mughīth 'Umar, al-Muẓaffar 'Umar, (al-Manṣūr) Shīrkūh, (al-Mu'aẓẓam) Tūrān-Shāh, *and* 'Ā'ishah Khātūn, Ḍaifah Khātūn

'Ajlūn, 390, 714

Ak-Tai, Mamluk general (d. 1254), 713, 739–743

Akhi (Turkish, brotherhood), 688, 725, 729, 731, 732

Akhlat, 665, 672, 673, 683, 684, 696, 700–704, 708, 748; rulers of, 402, 663, 664, *and see* Aiyūbids (of the Jazira)

'Akkār, 534, 558, 576, 581, 749, *and see* Isabel of Gibelcar

Akrostikon (Greek, land tax), 197

'Alā'-al-Mulk, 'Alid anti-caliph (*c.* 1218), 671

'Alam-ad-Dīn al-Ḥalabī, governor of Damascus (to 1261), 746

Alamannia: "emperor of", 104; "king of", 103; *see also* Germany

Alamut, 665, 717, 761

Alan, archdeacon of Lydda (to 1196), Latin archbishop of Nicosia 1196–*c.* 1205: 624

Alan of Roucy, lord of Termes, 294 note, 310

'Alāyā, 682

Alba, county of, 268

Albania, 191, 212, 217, 227, 235, 236; Angevins in, 256–258, 260, 261, 263, 273, 367, 368; people of, 228

Albano (Laziale), 761; cardinal-bishops of, *see* Henry, Pelagius

Albert (Rezzato), bishop of Brescia 1213–1226, Latin patriarch of Antioch 1226–1245: 421, 566

Albert (Avogadro), patriarch of Jerusalem 1205–1213: 536

Albert of Aix (Aachen), German chronicler (d. after 1120), 633

Albert of Parma, papal notary, 360

Albert Pallavicini, marquis of Bodonitsa (d. 1311), 271

Albertino of Canossa, co-lord of Thebes, 238, 241

Albi, 288

Albigensian crusade (1209–1229), 277–324, 326, 327, 330, 333, 347, 349, 378, 381, 383, 439, 466, 470, 760, 761

Albigensian heresy, heretics, xvii, 279–291, 293, 294, 297, 298, 301, 303, 304, 307, 308, 311, 312, 316, 322–324, 327, 343–346, 379

Albigeois, 304, 312, 315, 320; lord of, 288

Albistan, battle (1277), 728, 750, 751, 762

Alcácer do Sal, 395

Alençon, *see* John

Aleppo, 576, 675, 684, 696–699, 704, 705, 707, 710, 711, 754; atabegs of, 662, 698; attacks on, 547, 550, 708; emirs of, 657, 746 note; merchants of, 590; Mongols at, 571, 572, 575, 582, 653, 654, 714, 717, 744, 751, 755, 761; rulers of, *see* Aiyūbids (1183–1260); troops from, 533, 550, 674, 697, 699–703, 705, 708, 710; Venetians at, 698

Alexander III (Orlando de' Bandinelli), pope 1159–1181: 137, 141, 345, 346

Alexander IV (Reginald de' Conti de Segni), nephew of Gregory IX; pope 1254-1261: 228, 361–363, 373, 569, 570, 572, 623, 628, 761

Alexander of Siebenbürgen, provost of Hungary, 387

Alexandria, 747, 748, 757, 761; attacks on, 30, 34 note, 35, 471, 495, 497; emir at, 337; merchants at, 697, 698; patriarchate of, 196; trade with, 161, 336, 339, 593

Alexiad, 127, 128; *see also* Anna Comnena

Alexius III Angelus, brother of Isaac II; Byzantine emperor 1195–1203: 118, 148–150, 155, 162, 205, 529, 604, 648, 649, 759; and Henry VI, 42, 119, 149; and fourth crusade, 150, 166, 169, 171, 173, 176–179, 608, 760; after 1203: 151, 181, 201, 209; wife of, *see* Euphrosyne Ducaena

Alexius IV Angelus, son of Isaac II; Byzantine co-emperor 1203–1204: 150, 151, 166, 168–174, 176–182, 189, 190, 760

Alexius Axouch, Byzantine duke at Mamistra, 641

Alexius Branas, Byzantine general (d. 1186), 147

Alexius I Comnenus, Byzantine emperor 1081–1118: 5, 123–132, 135, 138, 142, 161, 165, 185, 632, 677; and first crusade, 126, 134; wife of, *see* Irene Ducaena

Alexius II Comnenus, son of Manuel I and Maria; Byzantine emperor 1180–1183, co-emperor 1183–1183: 134, 137, 139, 141, 144, 145, 204; wife of, *see* Agnes of France
Alexius Comnenus, nephew of Manuel I; Byzantine pretender 1184–1186: 36
Alexius Comnenus, grandson of Andronicus I; emperor of Trebizond 1204–1222: 200, 760
Alexius V Ducas ("Mourtzouphlus"), Byzantine emperor 1204–1204: 150, 151, 181, 182, 184, 201, 202; wife of, *see* Eudocia Angelina
Alexius Philes, Byzantine official, 254
Alexius Sebastus, Byzantine prince, 99, 101
Alexius Strategopoulus, Byzantine caesar, 230–232
Alfonso X ("the Wise" or "the Learned"), son of Ferdinand III; king of Castile 1252–1284, co-emperor (Holy Roman) 1257–1273: 229, 751
Algeria, 17, 19, 28, 30, 31
'Alī, al-Manṣūr Nūr-ad-Dīn, son of Aybeg; Mamluk sultan of Egypt 1257–1259: 744, 761
'Alī, aṣ-Ṣāliḥ, son of Kalavun (d. before 1290), 753
'Alī, son-in-law of Mohammed; caliph at Kufa 656–661: 671
'Alī, son of Yaḥyâ; Zīrid emir at Mahdia 1116–1121: 20
'Alī ibn Yūsuf, Murābiṭ ruler in Morocco and Spain 1106–1143: 20
Alice, daughter of Henry II of Champagne and Isabel of Jerusalem; wife of Hugh I of Cyprus 1208–1218: 605; 1st wife of Bohemond V of Antioch 1225–1228: 544; wife of Ralph of Nesle 1241–1246: 474, 485, 553; regent of Cyprus 1218–1232: 425, 544, 547, 605, 611, 623, 625; regent of Jerusalem 1243–1246: 559, 580, 606, 613
Alice, daughter of Louis VII of France, 48, 49, 61
Alice, daughter of Ṛoupen III; wife of Heṭoum of Sasoun 1189–1194, wife of Raymond of Antioch 1195–1197, wife of Ṿahram after 1221 (d. 1236), 527, 533, 540, 646, 651 note
Alice (Plantagenet), niece of Arthur of Brittany; 1st wife of Peter of Dreux 1213–1221: 470
Alice de la Roche, daughter of Guy I of Athens; wife of John II of Ibelin (to 1264), 269
Alice of Montferrat, daughter of William IV; 1st wife of Henry I of Cyprus 1229–1233: 460
Alice of Montmorency, sister of Matthew II; wife of Simon IV of Montfort 1191–1218 (d. 1221), 290, 311, 312
Almohads, *see* Muwaḥḥids
Almoravids, *see* Murābiṭs
Alpheus river, 253, 258, 264, 266, 272
Alphonse, son of Louis VIII of France; count of Poitiers 1241–1271: 320, 492, 496, 497, 505, 508, 510, 511, 515; wife of, *see* Joan (of Toulouse)
Alps, 118, 189 note, 333–335, 366, 450
Alsace, 164, 433, *and see* Margaret, Philip
Altenburg, count of, 50, 115
Amadeo V, count of Savoy 1285–1323: 265
Amalfi, 6, 155 note; merchants from, 27 note, 622 note
Amalric, son of Fulk; king of Jerusalem 1163–1174: 34, 35, 65, 140, 164, 547, 619, 641, 643; wife of, *see* Maria Comnena
Amalric Barlais, Cypriote baron, imperial bailie (with 4 associates) 1229–1230: 610, 612, 613
Amalric of Lusignan, son of Aimery and Isabel (d. *c.* 1206), 532
Amalric "of Lusignan", son of Hugh III; bailie of Jerusalem 1289–1291, regent of Cyprus 1306–1310: 592–597, 656; wife of, *see* Isabel (Heṭoumid)
Amalric VI of Montfort, son of Simon IV; count of Montfort and duke of Narbonne 1218–1241, earl of Leicester 1218–1239, constable of France 1230–1241: in Languedoc, 308, 309, 314, 315, 470; and crusade of 1239: 465, 466, 469, 470, 475, 476, 480, 482
Amanian (of Grisinhac), archbishop of Auch 1226–1242: 323
Amanus Gates, pass, 654
Amanus mountains, 576–578, 635, 636, 650; castles of, 640, 642, 643, *and see* Baghrās, Darbsāk
Amayḳ, 637 note
Amédée Pofey (Amadeo Buffa), constable of Thessalonica (d. 1210), 206–208, 238
Amicie of Montfort, daughter of Simon IV (d. 1253), 290
Amida, 684, 703, 704, 706, 708, 748; lords of, 683, 699
Amiens, *see* Peter
'Āmil (Arabic, official), 22, 26, 30, 31
al-Amjad Bahrām-Shāh, Majd-ad-Dīn, son of Farrūkh-Shāh Dā'ūd; Aiyūbid governor of Baalbek 1183–1193, ruler 1193–1230 (d. 1231), 693, 701
Amoudain, 638, 650
Ana, 708
Anacletus II (Peter of Leon, "Pierleone"), anti-pope 1130–1138: 7, 8 note
Anagni, 374, 375, 461, 628
Anamur, fortress, plate 1B
Anaphe, 239
Anatolia, 144, 664, 666, 673, 688, 704, 722, 735, 759; Byzantines and, 125, 127, 132, 133, 140, 141, 676–679; coast of, 600; Mongols in, 652, 653, 690–692, 708, 717, 719, 724–732, 750; third crusade in, 114, 680, 682, 759; Turkomans in, 643, 653, 676, 680, 685–691; Turks of, *see* Sel-

chükids of Rūm, Dānishmendids; *see also* Asia Minor
'Anaz, 532
Anazarba, 635–638, 641
Ancona, 96, 168, 218; march of, 346, 355, 358, 359
Andravida, 237, 249, 252, 258, 265
Andreas, Cape, 600
Andres, monastery, 331
Andrew, Dominican friar, 626
Andrew II, son of Bela III and Agnes; king of Hungary 1205–1235: 210, 213, 386–388, 391–394, 538, 609, 651 note, 760; wives of, *see* Gertrude (of Andechs), Yolanda of Courtenay
Andrew, son of Andrew II of Hungary and Gertrude (d. 1234), 387, 393, 651 note
Andrew, lord of Vitré, 469
Andrew Ghisi, co-lord of Tenos 1207–1259: 238
Andrew of Brienne, brother of count Erard; lord of Ramerupt (d. 1189), 50, 52
Andrew of Chauvigny, Poitevin baron, 58
Andrew of Nanteuil, brother of bishop Milo of Beauvais; French crusader, 415
Andronicus I Comnenus, grandson of Alexius I; before 1182: 145, 639; Byzantine regent 1182–1183, co-emperor 1183–1183, emperor 1183–1185: 36, 62, 139, 145, 146, 164, 204, 600, 644; and Saladin, 37, 146, 148; grandsons of, 200; wife of, *see* Agnes of France
Andronicus Euphorbenus, governor of Tarsus (to 1162), 641
Andronicus II Palaeologus, son of Michael VIII, 255; Byzantine emperor 1282–1328 (d. 1332), 261, 262, 264, 265, 267, 270, 593, 657, 751, 762; wife of, *see* Yolanda of Montferrat
Andros, 177, 191, 236, 238; bishopric of, 252
Angarion (Greek, corvée), 622, 624
Angelo Ferro, brother of John; Venetian merchant, 225
Angelo Sanudo, son of Marco I; duke of the Archipelago *c.* 1227–1262: 219, 242, 272; wife of, 232
Angelus, Byzantine imperial dynasty at Constantinople 1185–1204: 146–151, 681, *and see* Isaac II 1185–1195, Alexius III 1195–1203, Isaac II and Alexius IV 1203–1204; *see also* Anna, Eudocia, Irene (2), Theodora Angelina
Angelus "Comnenus", Byzantine dynasty in Epirus 1204–1461: *see* Michael I "Ducas" 1204–1214, Theodore 1214–1230, Michael II 1236–1271, Nicephorus 1271–1296, Thomas 1296–1318; at Thessalonica 1224–1246: *see* Theodore 1224–1230, Manuel 1230–1236, John 1236–1244, Demetrius 1244–1246; at Neopatras 1271–1318: *see* John I 1271–1295, John II 1303–1318; *see also* Anna, Helena (2), Irene Angelina "Comnena"
Angers, bishop of, *see* William
Angevins, French dynasty in Sicily 1268–1282 and Naples 1265–1442: 256, 267, 268, 270, 273, 274, 370, 372, 509, 617, 762, *and see* Charles I 1268–1285, Charles II 1285–1309, Philip of Anjou, Philip I of Taranto, Charles of Taranto; *see also* Plantagenets
Angoulême, *see* Peter
Ani, 664, *and see* Samuel; king of, 630
Anjou, 372, *and see* Charles, Philip; crusaders from, 56, 74; house of, 49, *and see* Plantagenets, Angevins; livres of, 192; lord of, 48; pennies of, 60
Ankara, lord of, 677, 678
Anna Angelina, daughter of Alexius III; wife of Isaac Comnenus (to 1195), 1st wife of Theodore I Lascaris (after 1199), 201
Anna Angelina Comnena, daughter of Michael II of Epirus; 3rd wife of William II of Achaea 1259–1278, 2nd wife of Nicholas II of St. Omer 1280–1284; regent of Achaea 1259–1261: 246, 247, 261
Anna Cantacuzena (Palaeologina), niece of Michael VIII Palaeologus; 2nd wife of Nicephorus of Epirus 1272–1296, despoina (after 1296), 266, 267
Anna Comnena, daughter of Alexius I; Byzantine historian (d. after 1148), 125, 633
Anna Dalassena, mother of Alexius I Comnenus (d. after 1095), 125, 128
Anno of Sangerhausen, master of the Teutonic Knights 1257–1274: 573, 574
Ansbert, Austrian priest and chronicler (d. after 1196), 92, 109, 114
Anseau of Cahieu (Cayeux), French baron, 226; wife of, *see* Eudocia Lascaris
Anselm (of Mauny), bishop of Laon 1215–1238: 403
Anselm of Justingen, German marshal, 427, 436
Anti-caliph, *see* 'Alā-al-Mulk
Anti-catholicus, *see* George
Anti-popes, *see* Anacletus II 1130–1138, Victor IV 1159–1164
Anti-Taurus mountains, 133, 631
Antioch, city, 196, 632, 634, *and see* George; under Franks 1098–1189: 10, 38, 39, 46, 47, 50, 52, 126, 127, 133, 134, 326, 637–639, 642, 645; under Franks 1189–1268: 49, 113, 115, 508, 527, 528, 532–538, 540, 541, 559, 566, 577, 698, 749, 759, 762; under Moslems after 1268: 578, 654; Greek patriarchs of, *see* Athanasius, Symeon II, David, Euthymius; Latin patriarchs of, *see* Bernard of Valence 1100–1135, Ralph (of Domfront) 1135–1139, Aimery of Limoges 1139–1196 ?, Peter of Angoulême 1201–1208, Peter (of Locedio) 1209–1217, Albert (Rezzato) 1226–1245, Opizon (Fieschi) 1247–1268
Antioch, principality, before 1189: 5, 9–12,

127, 132–134, 572, 635–638, 640–643; 1189–1243: 456, 522 note, 524, 526–529, 531–538, 540, 541, 544, 545, 547, 549, 550, 603, 646, 648, 652, 682, 697, 760; 1243–1268: 507, 559, 566, 578, 718, 727, 749; after 1268: 590; princes of, *see* Bohemond I 1099–1111, Bohemond II 1126–1130, Raymond of Poitiers 1136–1149, Bohemond III 1163–1201, Bohemond IV 1201–1216, 1219–1233, Raymond Roupen 1216–1219, Bohemond V 1233–1252, Bohemond VI 1252–1268, *and also* Henry, Philip, Raymond (2), William; princesses of, *see* Constance 1136–1163, *and also* Alice, Lucienne of Segni, Lucy, Margaret, Maria, Mary (3), Melisend of Lusignan, Plaisance, Sibyl (2); regents of, *see* Tancred 1101–1103, 1104–1112, Roger of Salerno 1112–1119, Constance 1149–1153, 1160–1163, Reginald of Châtillon 1153–1160, Lucienne of Segni 1252–1252
Anushtigin (of Gharcha), slave of Malik-Shāh; founder of Khorezm-Shāhs (*c.* 1078, d. 1098), 669
Anweiler, *see* Markward
Apamea, 582, 696
Apulia, 239, 334 note; under Normans, 5–9, 13, 15, 25, 29–31, 41, 132, 136, 137; under Hohenstaufens, 109, 439, 440, 442, 460, 541, 761; under Angevins, 256, 259, 591; barons of, 7, 9, 21, 29; dukes of, *see* Robert Guiscard, Roger Borsa, William, Roger; "king of", 382
Aqṣâ mosque, at Jerusalem, 455; *see also* Temple
Aqsarāyī, chronicler (d. after 1323), 732
Aquino, *see* Thomas
Aquitaine, 56, *and see* Eleanor; duke of, 48, 54; seneschal of, 294
Arab, son of Kïlïj Arslan I; Selchükid rebel (in 1126), 636, 677
Arabia, 749
Arabic language, transliteration and nomenclature, xix–xxi
Arabs, Semitic people, xx, xxi, 671, 676, 720, 731, 732; in North Africa, 17–23, 25, 28, 29; in Egypt, 495, 675, 707, 743; in Syria, 390, 675, 699, 703, 710, 747; in Cilicia, 632; in Mesopotamia, 663, 719; *see also* Beduins, Melkites
Aragon, 300, 304, 309, 311, 367, 371, 372, 375, 762; kings of, 33, 279, 301, 303, 323, *and see* Peter II 1196–1213, James I 1213–1276, Peter III 1276–1285, James II 1291–1327; princesses of, *see* Constance, Eleanor, Isabel, Sancia; soldiers from, 260, 270, 302, 311, 313
Arcadia, district, 237, 240, 248, 251, 258
Arcadia, town, 237
Arcadiopolis, 105
Archibald X, lord of Bourbon 1242–1249: 493
Archipelago, 253, 257, 258; duchy of, 202, 229, 240, 243, 245, 248, 256, 263, 272; dukes of, *see* Sanudos
Archontes (Greek, magnates), 237, 248–252, 264, 266
Arcis (-sur-Aube), *see* John
Argentan, *see* Geoffrey, Richard
Arghun, son of Abagha; Il-khan of Persia 1284–1291: 655, 720, 722, 751
Argolid, 235, 236, 241, 258
Argolis, Gulf of, 238
Argos, 240, 241, 243, 245, 259, 263; bishopric of, 252
Ariège river, 295
Arioudzpert, 638
Arles, 284, 292 note; archbishops of, 309, 483
Arm of St. George, 96, 104
Armand of Périgord, master of the Temple 1232–1244: 463, 464, 471, 472, 475, 479, 481, 484, 485, 561–563
Armenia (Greater), 653, 659; Aiyūbids in, 402, 421, *and see* Akhlat; Armenians of, 630–632, 647, 653; Mongols in, 652, 730; Turks in, 631, 662, 673, 674, 680, 684, 691, 729
Armenia, Cilician (or Lesser), 393, 424, 525, 533, 538, 584, 587, 591; barony of (to 1198), 526–529, 603, 634–647, 658; kingdom of, xvii, 507, 529, 537–541, 549, 577, 609, 647–659, 679, 682, 748, 749, 755, 762; kings of, *see* Ṛoupenids, Heṭoumids; princes of, *see* Ṛoupenids, Philip of Antioch 1222–1224; regents of, *see* Thomas 1168–1170, Adam of Gaston 1219–1221, Constantine I 1221–1226; *see also* Cilicia
Armenian church, 529, 534, 541, 578, 623, 641, 647, 649, 653, 658 note; *see also* Catholicus
Armenian language, transliteration and nomenclature, xxii
Armenians, Indo-European people, 630, 631, 636, 640, 653, 730, 740, 751; in Armenia, 664, 685, 731; in Cilicia, xviii, 112, 133, 526, 533, 535, 539–541, 550, 565, 573, 586, 600 note, 632–659, 677, 692, 697, 717, 720, 721, 727; in Cyprus, 621 note, 622, 623; in Palestine, 562, 646; in Latin empire, 108, 200, 202, 203; on fifth crusade, 424, 427
Arnold (of Rovinjan), bishop of Agen 1209–1228: 295
Arnold, bishop of Nîmes 1212–1242: 307
Arnold (of Altena), bishop of Osnabrück 1173–1191: 92, 93
Arnold Amalric, abbot of Cîteaux 1200–1212: 157 note; papal legate in Languedoc, archbishop of Narbonne 1212–1225: 283, 285–287, 291, 297, 299, 307, 308
Arnold of Lübeck, German abbot and chronicler (d. 1212), 120
Arnstadt, 340
ʿArqah, 576
Arsenius (of Apollonia), Orthodox patriarch

at Nicaea 1255–1259, at Constantinople 1261–1265 (d. 1273), 227
Arsinoë, 625
Arsuf, 74, 454, 508, 524, 575, 748; battle (1191), 74, 75, 759; forest of, 75; lords of, *see* Thierry d'Orques *c.* 1192–*c.* 1205, John of Ibelin 1236–1258, Balian of Ibelin 1258–1265
Arta, 201, 267
Arta, Gulf of, 263
Arthur, nephew of Richard I; Plantagenet duke of Brittany 1196–1203: 53, 54, 59, 533
Artois, 70, 211; counts of, 261, 262, 497–501
Artuk Arslan, Nāṣir-ad-Dīn, Artukid ruler of Mardin *c.* 1200–*c.* 1240: 705
Artukids, Turkoman dynasty in Mesopotamia 1101–1408: 664, 673, 699, 701, 703, 704, *and see* Īl-Ghāzī, Artuk Arslan, Maudūd, al-Khiḍr
Arundel, earl of, 417
Asadī mamluks, 737
Ascalon: under Franks 1153–1187: 50; under Moslems 1187–1239: 71, 76–79, 82, 83, 85, 423, 473, 474, 523, 695 note, 706; under Franks 1239–1247: 463, 475–481, 484, 552, 558, 563–565, 614, 708–710; under Moslems after 1247: 575
Asen, Vlach tsar of Bulgaria 1186–1196: 100, 102, 147, 148, 201
Ashmūn (ar-Rummān), 408, 498, 499, 502
al-Ashraf Khalīl, Ṣalāḥ-ad-Dīn, son of Kalavun; Mamluk sultan of Egypt and Syria 1290–1293: 595–598, 617, 656, 753–755, 762
al-Ashraf Mūsâ, Muẓaffar-ad-Dīn, son of al-ʿĀdil I Saif-ad-Dīn; Aiyūbid ruler of the Jazira 1202–1229: 673, 696, 698–701; lord of Akhlat 1210–1233: 402, 421–426, 449, 453, 683, 684; ruler of Damascus 1229–1237, of Baalbek 1230–1237: 547, 702–704; daughter of, 705
al-Ashraf Mūsâ, Muẓaffar-ad-Dīn, son of al-Manṣūr Ibrāhīm; Aiyūbid ruler of Homs 1246–1263: 710, 711, 714
al-Ashraf Mūsâ, Muẓaffar-ad-Dīn, son (or grandson) of al-Masʿūd Yūsuf; Aiyūbid co-sultan of Egypt 1250–1252: 503, 712, 742, 743
Ashrafī mamluks, 707
Asia Minor, 12, 125, 151, 200, 201, 247, 631, 673, 729; first crusade in, 126; third crusade in, 49, 91, 92, 110, 148; Latins in, 190–192, 202–206, 209, 215, 216; Mongols in, 220, 223; *see also* Anatolia
Aslun Khātūn, 3rd wife of Kalavun, 753
Aspietes, Armenian governor of Tarsus, 633
Assassins (Arabic, Ḥashshāshīn), Ismāʿīlite quasi-Moslem sect, 788; in Persia, 665, 666, 717, 761; in Syria, 34, 80, 81, 523, 528, 547, 581, 583, 698, 749, 759, 762; masters in Syria, *see* Rāshid-ad-Dīn, Naṣr, Najm-ad-Dīn
Assisi, *see* Francis
Asti, 268
Astypalaea, 238
Aswan, 699
Atabeg (Turkish, regent), 133, 662, 670, 672, 698, 744
Athanasius, Orthodox patriarch of Antioch 1165–1170: 140
Athens, 13, 14 note, 196, 202, 208, 237, 248, 272; archbishopric of, 252; bailie of, 263; duchy of, 229, 246 note, 261, 263–265, 269, 271, 272; dukes of, 273, *and see* lords of; lords of, *see* De la Roches (1205–1308), Walter of Brienne 1309–1311; lordship of, 238, 240, 243, 248; metropolitan of, 252; regent of, *see* Helena Angelina Comnena 1287–1296
Athos, Mount, monastery, 128, 626
Athyra, 171
Attica, 192, 236, 246, 762
Aubrey (of Humbert), archbishop of Rheims 1207–1218: 287, 386
Aubrey Clement of Metz, marshal of France (d. 1191), 68
Aubrey of Trois-Fontaines, French chronicler (*c.* 1240), 335, 337–339, 471
Auch, archbishop of, *see* Gerard, Amanian
Augsburg, bishop of, 446
Augustinians, order, 252, 333
al-Auḥad Aiyūb, Najm-ad-Dīn, son of al-ʿĀdil I Saif-ad-Dīn; Aiyūbid ruler of the Jazira 1198–1202, of Diyār-Bakr 1202–1210, lord of Akhlat 1207–1210: 696
Aulonarion, 257
Aumale, count of, 49
Austria, crusaders from, 444, 447, 539; dukes of, *see* Babenberg
Autremencourt, *see* Thomas I, Thomas II, Thomas III
Auvergne, 319, 492; count of, 287
Auxerre, bishop of, 212; count of, 212
Avesnes (-sur-Helpe), *see* James I, James II, John II, Walter
Avignon, 291, 309, 317, 318, 373, 375
Avlona, 3, 127, 256–258, 260
Avshars, Turkoman people, 662
Ayas, 650, 654, 655, 724, 730, 749
Aybeg, al-Muʿizz ʿIzz-ad-Dīn, Mamluk co-sultan of Egypt 1250–1252, sultan 1252–1257: 503, 567, 574, 712, 713, 740–744, 761; wife of, *see* Shajar-ad-Durr
Aymar ("the Monk"; dei Corbizzi), patriarch of Jerusalem 1194–1202: 156, 525, 526, 530
Aymar of Lairon, lord of Caesarea 1192–1213, marshal of the Hospital *c.* 1216–1219: 524, 536
Ayrivank, *see* Erivan; *see also* Mkhiṭar
ʿAzāz, 636
Azerbaijan, xxii, 575, 662–665, 671–673, 683 701, 717; rulers of, 662, 670, 672, 726; troops from, 664

al-ʿAzīz, Ḥammādid emir at Bougie 1105–1121: 20
al-ʿAzīz Muḥammad, son of aẓ-Ẓāhir Ghāzī; Aiyūbid ruler of Aleppo 1216–1236: 541, 651 note, 683, 698, 704
al-ʿAzīz Muḥammad, son of an-Nāṣir Yūsuf; Aiyūbid prince (d. after 1258), 714
al-ʿAzīz ʿUthmān, ʿImād-ad-Dīn, son of Saladin; Aiyūbid governor of Egypt 1186–1193, sultan of Egypt 1193–1198, ruler of Damascus 1196–1198: 693, 695
al-ʿAzīz ʿUthmān, ʿImād-ad-Dīn, son of al-ʿĀdil I Saif-ad-Dīn; Aiyūbid lord of Banyas *c.* 1211–*c.* 1233: 701, 702
al-Azraq canal, 397, 405

B—, archdeacon of Latakia, Latin bishop of Paphos (after 1196, d. before 1220), 624
Baalbek, 564, 693, 701, 703, 704, 706, 710, 754; rulers of, *see* Aiyūbids (1174–1260)
Baba (Turkish, old man), 690
Baba Isḥāq, Turkoman rebel (d. 1241), 691, 727
Babaṛon, 633, 634; lord of, 639, 643, 644
Babenberg, *see* Leopold V, Frederick I, Leopold VI
Babylon, 27, *and see* Cairo, Fustat
Bacon, 106, *and see* Batkun
Baden, margrave of, 92, 93, 115
Badr-ad-Dīn ibn-Ḥassūn, Egyptian emir, 425
Baghdad, 336, 663, 666, 709, 735, 736, 744, 747; caliphs at, *see* ʿAbbāsids; Mongols at, 489, 571, 573, 578, 714, 717, 719, 744, 755; sultans at, 670
Baghrās: under Franks to 1188: 639; under Saladin 1188–1191: 527, 646; under Armenians 1191–1211: 526–528, 534, 537, 646, 649, *and see* Adam of Gaston; under Franks 1211–1268: 537, 541, 550, 578, 654; *see also* Amanus mountains, castles of
Bagnara (Calabra), 59
Bagratids, Armenian dynasty at Ani 885–1064: *see* Gagik
Bahā'-ad-Dīn, Arabic biographer (d. 1234), 77, 82
al-Baḥr aṣ-Ṣaghīr, canal, 408, 424, 426
Bahrām-Shāh, Fakhr-ad-Dīn, Mengüchekid lord of Erzinjan *c.* 1160–1225: 683
Baḥrī mamluks, 711–714, 738–746, 750, 756
Baidu, grandson of Hulagu; Īl-khan of Persia 1295–1295: 656
Baiju, Mongol general, 652, 692
Baisan, 390, 539, 575
Bait Nūbā, 82, 83
Baldwin, archbishop of Canterbury 1184–1190: 47, 58, 64–66; chaplain of, 65
Baldwin, constable of Armenia (d. 1188), 645
Baldwin, count (V) of Hainault 1171–1195, count (VIII) of Flanders 1191–1194: 70; wife of *see* Margaret of Alsace
Baldwin I, son of Baldwin V of Hainault; count (IX) of Flanders 1194–1205 and (VI) of Hainault 1195–1205: 155, 159, 160, 164, 167 note, 174, 175, 181 note, 182; Latin emperor of Romania 1204–1205: 189–195, 200, 203–205, 212, 213, 236, 262, 603, 760; wife of, *see* Mary (of Champagne)
Baldwin II, son of Peter of Courtenay and Yolanda; Latin emperor of Romania 1228–1231: 213, 216, 219, 242, 760; co-emperor 1231–1237: 217, 466, 467, 761; emperor 1237–1261: 221–229, 231, 243, 248, 256, 468, 615, 761; titular emperor 1261–1273: 232, 255, 258, 260, 270, 363, 367; wife of, *see* Mary of Brienne
Baldwin I (of Boulogne), count of Edessa 1098–1100, king of Jerusalem 1100–1118: 7, 635; wife of, *see* Adelaide of Montferrat
Baldwin II (of Le Bourg), count of Edessa 1100–1118, king of Jerusalem 1118–1131: 632, 635; wife of, *see* Morfia
Baldwin III, son of Fulk; king of Jerusalem 1143–1163: 134, 140, 640
Baldwin IV ("the Leper"), son of Amalric; king of Jerusalem 1174–1185: 523, 619
Baldwin V, son of William "Longsword" and Sibyl; king of Jerusalem 1185–1186: 46, 164
Baldwin, lord of Marash (d. after 1146), 636
Baldwin de Redvers (of Reviers), earl of Devon 1245–1262: 483 note
Baldwin Embriaco, son of Henry (d. 1282), 587
Baldwin of Ibelin, son of Guy; constable of Cyprus, 590
Baldwin of Ibelin, son of John I; seneschal of Cyprus 1246–1267: 560, 565, 614, 615, 652 note
Baleares, 32, 36, 396; governor of, 20
Balian (I) Grenier, son of Reginald and Helvis; lord of Sidon *c.* 1204–1240: 392, 447, 453, 454, 479, 481, 542, 560; co-bailie of Jerusalem 1228–1228, 1229–1231: 460, 544, 546, 548; baronial co-bailie 1233–1240: 472, 475, 476, 550
Balian II of Ibelin, lord of Ibelin and Ramla *c.* 1187–1193: 46, 66, 524; wife of, *see* Maria Comnena
Balian III of Ibelin, son of John I; lord of Beirut 1236–1247, bailie of Jerusalem 1243–1247: 472, 551, 554, 559, 560, 626; wife of, *see* Eschiva of Montbéliard
Balian of Ibelin, son of John, of Arsuf; lord of Arsuf 1258–1265 (titular 1265–1277), bailie of Jerusalem 1276–1277: 574, 585; wife of, *see* Plaisance (of Antioch)
Balkans, 367, 369, 761; and Byzantine empire to 1204: 110, 118, 125–128, 131, 139, 140, 142, 144, 146–149, 220; third crusade in, 97, 110, *and see* Bulgaria; maps of, 186
Baltic Sea, region of, 122, 736
Bamberg, bishop of, 389

Banū-Hilāl, Arab tribe in North Africa, 18, 20
Banū-Khurasān, Arab family at Tunis, 25
Banū-Maṭrūḥ, Arab family at Tripoli (in Africa), 23
Banū-Sulaim, Arab tribe in North Africa, 18
Banyas, 410, 507, 698, 714; lord of, 701, 702
Bar (-le-Duc), counts of, *see* Henry I, Theobald I, Henry II
Bar Hebraeus, Gregory Abū-l-Farāj, Jacobite patriarch at Aleppo 1252–1286: 632, 638, 724
Barāmūn, 425, 426
Barbary, *see* North Africa
Barcelona, 396, 580
Bari, *see* Maio; archbishop of, 359, 446, 451; diet at (1195), 118
Ba'rīn, 534, 535, 547, 703
Barletta, 450
Bartholomew (of Vendôme), archbishop of Tours 1174–1206: 56
Bartholomew (Mansel ?), bishop of Tortosa 1263–after 1287, bailie of Tripoli 1275–1277: 584, 587, 591; nephew of, 587
Bartholomew, lord of Maraclea (to 1286), 581, 752
Bartholomew Embriaco, son of Bertrand; mayor of Tripoli 1287–1288: 591, 592, 752 note
Bartholomew of Neocastro, Sicilian chronicler (*c.* 1285), 369
Bartholomew Tirel, marshal of Antioch, 527
Basel, bishop of, *see* Henry
Basil, archbishop of Tirnovo 1186–1203 (Orthodox), 1203–1204 (Latin), primate of Bulgaria 1204–1217 ?: 147, 149, 201, 760
Basil II ("Boulgaroktonos"), Byzantine co-emperor 963–976, emperor 976–1025: 123, 124, 130, 203
Basil Xeros, Byzantine envoy (d. *c.* 1145), 11
Bath, bishop of, *see* Reginald fitz Jocelyn
Batkun, 106
al-Batrūn, *see* Botron
Battles, *see* Manzikert (1071), Myriokephalon (1176), Hattin (1187), Arsuf (1191), Las Navas de Tolosa (1212), Muret (1213), Klokotnitsa (1230), Casal Imbert (1232), Agridi (1232), Gaza (1239), Liegnitz (1241), Köse Dagh (1243), Ḥarbīyah (1244), Pelagonia (1259), 'Ain Jālūt (1260), Benevento (1266), Tagliacozzo (1268), Albistan (1277), Cephissus (1311)
Batu Khan, grandson of Genghis Khan; ruler of the Golden Horde 1243–1256: 692
Bavaria, *see* Welf VI; crusaders from, 92, 93, 109, 389; duke of, 423, 435
Baybars ("al-Bunduqdārī"), an-Nāṣir Rukn-ad-Dīn, slave of al-Bunduqdār, xviii; Mamluk general (to 1260), 500, 503, 508, 574, 709 note, 711, 712, 739, 745, 761; Mamluk sultan of Egypt and Syria 1260–1277: 574, 586, 714, 745–753, 755, 756, 761, 762; and Franks, 508, 509, 518, 574–584, 615, 616, 727, 748–750, 762; and Armenians, 575–577, 653, 654, 727, 749; and Selchükids, 728, 748, 750; and Golden Horde, 575, 748; and Mongols, 508, 575, 582, 727, 728, 749, 750, 762
Bayeux, bishop of, 386, 389
Bayonne, bishop of, 56
Baziège, 312
Béarn, 294, 298; viscounts of, 297–299, 510
Beatrice, wife of Joscelin II; regent of Edessa 1150–1150 (d. after 1152), 641
Beaucaire, 309, 310, 318
Beaufort (near St. George), 267, 272
Beaujeu, lord of, *see* Humbert
Beaumont (-sur-Oise), *see* Dreux
Beaumont (-sur-Sarthe), viscount of, 469, 475, 476
Beauvais, bishops of, 50, 66, 80, 349, 403
Beauvoir, 249
Beduins, desert Arabs, 18, 411, 546, 562, 563, 690, 743, 746, 751, 756; *see also* Arabs
Beguines, order, 330
Behesni, 639, 654, 656, 755
Beirut, 71; under Moslems 1187–1197: 120, 121, 524, 530, 531, 695; under Franks 1197–1291: 121, 158 note, 451, 543, 548, 549, 558, 580, 584, 588, 589, 598, 611–613, 754; bishop of, 548; ladies of, *see* Isabel of Ibelin 1264–1282, Eschiva of Ibelin 1282–1291; lords of, *see* John I of Ibelin *c.* 1205–1236, Balian III of Ibelin 1236–1247, John II of Ibelin 1247–1264, Humphrey of Montfort 1282–1284
Bela II ("the Blind"), king of Hungary 1131–1141: 131; wife of, *see* Helena (of Rascia)
Bela III, brother of Stephen III; king of Hungary 1173–1196: 47, 91, 94, 137–141, 168, 386, 387; wives of, *see* Agnes of Châtillon, Margaret (of France)
Bela IV, son of Andrew II and Gertrude; king of Hungary 1235–1270: 221, 387, 393; wife of, *see* Maria Lascaris
Bela of St. Omer, lord of half of Thebes 1240–1258 ?: 244; wife of, *see* Bonne de la Roche
Belfort, 51, 479, 481, 560, 574, 577 707, 749
Bellapais, monastery, 628
Bellevaux, abbey, 241
Belvoir, 415, 564
Benedict, abbot of Peterborough (d. 1193), 45 note
Benedict, cardinal-deacon 1200–1201, cardinal-priest 1201–1212, cardinal-bishop (of Porto) 1212–1216, papal legate at Constantinople, 196, 199, 377

Benedict XI (Nicholas Boccasini), pope 1303–1304: 762
Benedictines, order, 331
Benevento, 8 note, 29, *and see* Peter; battle (1266), 255, 366, 508, 509, 762
Benjamin of Kalamata, chancellor of Achaea (to 1302), 266
Benjamin of Tudela, Jewish traveler and author (*c.* 1160), 142
Berard (Costa, of Castacca), archbishop of Bari 1207–1213, of Palermo 1213–1252: 449
Berat, 258, 260
Berbers, Hamitic people, 17, 18, 20, 21, 26, 28, 32
Berengar, abbot of St. Thibéry, 307
Berengaria, daughter of Sancho VI of Navarre; wife of Richard I of England 1191–1199 (d. 1230), 61–64, 77, 600, 601
Berengaria, sister of Ferdinand III of Castile; 3rd wife of John of Brienne 1224–1237: 216, 542
Berg, county: counts of, *see* Engelbert, Adolf
Berg, town, *see* Frederick
Berke Khan, as-Saʿīd Nāṣir-ad-Dīn, son of Baybars; Mamluk sultan of Egypt and Syria 1277–1279, lord of Kerak 1279: 750, 751
Berke Khan, chieftain of Khorezmians, 709
Berke Khan, brother of Batu Khan; ruler of the Golden Horde 1256–1266: 748
Bernard, abbot of Clairvaux (d. 1153), 7, 9, 11 note, 12 note, 282, 345, 351
Bernard, agent of Frederick I at Venice, 96
Bernard, archbishop of Ragusa 1189–1203 (d. *c.* 1216), 156 note
Bernard (of La Carra), bishop of Bayonne *c.* 1185–after 1204: 56
Bernard, bishop of Tripoli 1286–1288 (d. after 1295), 594
Bernard IV, count of Comminges 1181?–1225: 293, 297–300, 303, 304, 311, 318
Bernard V, son of Bernard IV; count of Comminges 1225–1241: 318
Bernard of Valence, Latin patriarch of Antioch 1100–1135: 127
Berrhoea, 96, 102, 103
Bertha of Sulzbach ("Irene"), 1st wife of Manuel I Comnenus 1146–1160: 10, 11, 15, 133, 134, 136
Berthold V (of Andechs), son of Berthold IV; archbishop of Kalocsa (and Bacs) 1206–1218, patriarch of Aquileia 1218–1251: 387, 389
Berthold, bishop of Naumburg and Zeitz 1186–1206: 120
Berthold I, count of Katzenellenbogen 1173?–1217?, lord of Velestinon 1205–1217?, regent of Thessalonica 1207–1217?: 238
Berthold V, nephew of bishop Rudolph of Liége; count of Nimburg (and Zähringen) 1186–1218: 92, 93
Berthold, count of (Künsberg and) Tuscany (in 1189), 108
Berthold IV (of Andechs), duke of Dalmatia and Meran (Croatia) and margrave of Istria 1188–1204: 92, 93, 100, 102, 104, 106, 107, 111, 120
Berthold, margrave of Vohburg (d. 1204), 92, 93
Berthold of Hohenburg, regent of Sicily 1254–1254 (d. 1256), 360, 361
Bertino Visconti, bailie of Achaea 1308–1309: 270
Bertrand (Savelli), cardinal-priest 1217–1221, papal legate in Languedoc, 312–314
Bertrand Embriaco, second cousin of Guy I (d. *c.* 1258), 570, 587, 591
Bertrand of Thessy, master of the Hospital 1228–1230: 452, 454, 458
Besançon, 364
Bethlehem, 455, 464, 479, 480, 506, 546, 558; bishop of, 404; merchants from, 585
Béthune, *see* Conon, John
Béziers, 287–289, 327, 760; viscount of, 286, 288
Biandrate, *see* Oberto
Bigorre, 311
Bilarghu, Mongol emir, 658, 762
Bilbais, 695, 707, 743
al-Biqāʿ, 558, 573, 709
Bira, 641, 749, 755; lord of, 632, 636
Blachernae, palace at Constantinople, 14, 150, 178, 179, 182, 190, 231
Black Sea, 206, 230, 231, 572; coasts of, 191, 200, 678, 681, 682, 723, 724, 730
Blanche of Castile, aunt of Ferdinand III; wife of Louis VIII of France 1200–1226, regent of France 1226–1236, 1248–1252: 221, 223–225, 229, 319, 321, 341, 470, 507
Blois, countess of, 597; counts of, *see* Stephen, Theobald V, Louis I; county of, 158
Bodonitsa, 242, 243, 245, 252; lady of, *see* Isabel Pallavicini; marquis of, *see* Guy Pallavicini, Albert Pallavicini
Boeotia, 13, 236, 241, 271
Bogomil heresy, heretics, 128, 144, 208
Bohemia, crusaders from, 93, 105; duke of, 93
Bohemond I, son of Robert Guiscard; prince of Antioch 1099–1111: 5, 6, 10, 125–127, 132, 185, 635
Bohemond II, son of Bohemond I; prince of Antioch 1126–1130: 10, 133, 636
Bohemond III, son of Raymond of Poitiers and Constance; prince of Antioch 1163–1201: 63, 85, 524, 526–528, 532, 533, 641, 643, 644, 646, 649, 759; wife of, *see* Sibyl
Bohemond IV ("the One-Eyed"), son of Bohemond III; count of Tripoli 1187–1233: 85, 388, 392, 393, 456, 526–528, 532, 540, 609, 646, 649; prince of Antioch 1201–1216: 531–538, 697, 698; 1219–

1233: 456, 541, 544, 547, 549, 652, 761; sons of, 606, 651; wife of, *see* Melisend (of Lusignan-Jerusalem)
Bohemond V, son of Bohemond IV: 544; prince of Antioch and count of Tripoli 1233–1252: 474, 478, 550, 558, 563, 565, 566, 571, 585, 761; wives of, *see* Alice (of Champagne-Jerusalem), Lucienne of Segni
Bohemond VI, son of Bohemond V and Lucienne; prince of Antioch 1252–1268 (titular to 1275), 507, 567, 569, 570, 572, 575, 577, 587, 591, 653, 761; count of Tripoli 1252–1275: 578, 579, 581, 584, 615, 762; daughter of, 261; sister of, 606; wife of, *see* Sibyl (Heṭoumid)
Bohemond VII, son of Bohemond VI; count of Tripoli (and titular prince of Antioch) 1275–1287: 584, 586–588, 591, 752, 762
Bohemond "of Lusignan", son of Hugh III of Cyprus (d. 1283), 589
Bon, Cape, 18, 25, 31
Bona, 25 note, 27 note, 28, 29
Boniface II, son of William III; marquis of Montferrat 1192–1207: 143, 164–178, 182–185, 188–190, 207; king of Thessalonica 1204–1207: 151, 165, 190, 192, 201–203, 205, 206, 236–238, 240, 760; wife of, *see* Margaret (of Hungary)
Boniface III, son of William IV; marquis of Montferrat 1225–1253, (titular king of Thessalonica 1230–1253), 460
Boniface VIII (Benedict Gaetani), pope 1294–1303: 265, 266, 374, 657, 762
Boniface (dalle Carceri) of Verona, grandson of William I; lord of Gardiki and Aegina 1294–1317: 271, 272
Bonnacorso (of Gloria), archbishop of Tyre 1272–after 1286: 590
Bonne de la Roche, sister of Guy I of Athens; wife of Demetrius of Montferrat (to 1227), wife of Bela of St. Omer (after 1240), 244
Bordeaux, archbishops of, *see* William, Gerald
Boril, nephew of Ioannitsa; Vlach tsar of Bulgaria 1207–1218: 205, 206, 208–210, 213; wife of, 205
Bosnia, 131, 139; ban of, 149
Bosporus, 197, 214; city on, 37, 509, *and see* Constantinople; crossing of, 178, 200, 201, 205, 217, 223; mouth of, 231
Bosra, 710
Botron, 587, 593, 752, *and see* John; lords of, 563, 570
Bouchard of Marly, lord of Cabaret, 294 note
Bougie, 23, 27 note, 336, 339; rulers of, *see* Ḥammādids
Bouillon, *see* Godfrey
Boukoleon, palace at Constantinople, 182, 189, 190, 205, 231
Boulbonne, abbey: monks of, 296 note
Boulogne (-sur-Mer), 48, *and see* Baldwin (I, of Jerusalem); count of, 155, 287
Bourbon, lord of, *see* Archibald
Bourges, 316, 341; council of (1225), 315, 316
Boves, *see* Enguerrand
Brabant, 341, 381; duke of, *see* Henry
Bracieux, *see* Peter
Bragana, 645; lord of, 639
Bram, 294 note
Branas, *see* Alexius, Theodore
Brandoveus, 102, *and see* Voden
Branits, 94, 98, 100; "duke" of, 98, 99
Bremen: archbishop of, 120; burghers from, 115
Brescia, bishop of, *see* Albert
Brest, 395
Brie, *see* Martin IV (Simon of)
Briel, *see* Geoffrey
Brienne (-la-Vieille), counts of, *see* Erard II, Walter III, Walter IV, Hugh, Walter V, *and also* Andrew, Isabel, John, Mary; county of, 472
Brindisi, 29, 137, 446, 447, 483, *and see* Margarit; as seaport, 115, 177, 382, 442, 443, 446, 451, 460, 461, 542; archbishops of, *see* Peter, Dominic
Brittany, 328; counts of, *see* Peter of Dreux, John; crusaders from, 50, 74, 582; duke of, 59, 533, *and see* count of; heiress of, 470
Bruges, 159
Brunswick, duke of, 432, 433, *and see* Otto
Brusa, 201, 202
Buddhism, religion, 720
Buffa, Amadeo, *see* Amédée Pofey
Buffavento, 601, 613
Bukhara, 671
Bulgar Dagh, 634
Bulgaria: before 1189: 128, 144, 146, 147; third crusade in, 91, 94–98, 100, 101, 105, 106, 109, 147; 1189–1204: 119, 148, 149; 1204–1261: 192, 194, 200, 201, 203–205, 209–211, 213, 217, 219–221, 225, 228, 230, 394, 466, 760; after 1261: 367, 368; king of, *see* Ioannitsa 1204–1207, John Asen 1218–1241; patriarch of, *see* Joachim; primate of, *see* Basil; princesses of, *see* Helena, Maria (2); tsars of, *see* Symeon 893–927, Asen 1186–1196, Peter 1196–1197, Ioannitsa 1197–1204, Boril 1207–1218, Coloman I 1241–1246, George I 1280–1292
Bulgars, Turkic people, 97, 98, 100, 116, 147, 213, 717
al-Bunduqdār, 'Alā'-ad-Dīn Aytigin, governor of Damascus (in 1261), 709 note, 746
al-Buqai'ah, valley, 576, 581, 592
Būrah, 404
Burgundia of Lusignan, daughter of Aimery and Eschiva; wife of Walter of Montbéliard, 605
Burgundy, 242, 490; crusaders from, 166,

167, 238, 241; dukes of, *see* Hugh III, Odo III, Hugh IV, *and also* Louis
Burhān-ad-Dīn, qadi at Sebastia (d. 1398), 730
Burjī mamluks, 753
Burkhard IV (of Querfurt), burggrave of Magdeburg 1179–1190: 93, 115
Burkhard, count of Wöltingerode (in 1189), 92
Burkhard of Schwanden, master of the Teutonic Knights 1283–1290 (d. after 1304), 591, 595
Burlus, 422
Butrinto, 258, 260
Buzā'ah, 699, 708
Byzantine emperors, before 1204: 5, 8–11, 171, *and see* Nicephorus I 802–811, Romanus I (919–944), Basil II (963) 976–1025, Michael V (1041–1042), Romanus IV 1068–1071, Michael VII 1071–1078, Alexius I 1081–1118, John II 1118–1143, Manuel I 1143–1180, Alexius II 1180–1183, Andronicus I 1183–1185, Isaac II 1185–1195, (1203–1204), Alexius III 1195–1203, Alexius IV (1203–1204), Alexius V 1204–1204; at Nicaea 1208–1261: *see* Theodore I 1208–1222, John III 1222–1254, Theodore II 1254–1258, Michael VIII (1258–1261); after 1261: *see* Michael VIII 1261–1282, Andronicus II 1282–1328, Michael IX (1295–1320), John V 1341–1347, 1354–1376, 1379–1390, 1390–1391, John VI 1347–1354, John VIII 1425–1448
Byzantine empire, 214; to 1204: xvii, 5, 9, 11, 13, 14, 24, 29–31, 36–38, 88, 90–92, 94, 96–110, 116–119, 122–151, 161, 162, 166, 170, 172 note, 182, 185, 191–193, 200, 235, 602, 608, 622, 631–635, 637, 638, 640, 664, 675–681, 760; 1204–1261, *see* Nicaea, empire; after 1261: 233, 255, 260, 270, 365, 367–370, 657, 718, 719, 727, 729
Byzantines, *see* Byzantine emperors, Greeks, Orthodox Christians
Byzantium, *see* Byzantine empire, Constantinople

Ca' Pesaro, Venetian firm, 232
Cabaret, 288, 290, 292, 294 note
Cadiz, 395
Caen, *see* Radulf
Caesarea (in Anatolia), 631, 645, 657, 687, 690, 692, 728, 750
Caesarea (in Palestine): under Saladin 1187–1191: 84; under Franks 1191–1265: 394, 422, 448, 454, 507, 524, 539, 542, 699; under Moslems after 1265: 508, 575, 583, 748; archbishops of, 389, 457, 458, 525, 545; lords of, *see* Aymar of Lairon 1192–1213, Walter 1213–1229, John 1229–1241, John l'Aleman 1241–1265
Cagliari, 512, 515
Cahieu, *see* Cayeux; *see also* Anseau
Cahors, 293, 320; bishop of, 293
Cairo, 398, 399, 414, 567, 577, 695, 699, 707, 711, 737–739, 741, 743–749, 752–755, 757; attacks on, 423, 424, 430, 436, 497, 498, 501, 539, 610; caliphs at, *see* Fāṭimids; government at, 17, 484, 505–507, 579, 591–595, 735; people of, 35, 411, 738, 757; sultans at, *see* Aiyūbids, Mamluks; trade with, 22
Calabria, 7, 13, 15, 20, 59, 61, 136; pirate from, 205
Caliphate, caliphs (Arabic singular, *khalīfah*), early, *see* 'Alī 656–661; of Baghdad, *see* 'Abbāsids; of Cairo, *see* Fāṭimids, 'Abbāsids; of Morocco, *see* Muwaḥḥids; *see also* Anti-caliph
Calixtus II (Guy of Vienne), pope 1119–1124: 132
Caltabellotta, peace of (1302), 270
Calycadnus river, 49, 114
Camardias, 650
Cambodia, 717
Cambrai, bishop of, *see* Roger
Candia, 396; *see also* Crete
Canina, 258, 260
Canossa, *see* Albertino, Rolandino
Cantacuzenus, 270, *and see* John VI 1347–1354, Michael; *see also* Anna Cantacuzena
Canterbury, archbishop of, 47, 58, 64, 66; chapter of, 65
Capdolh, *see* Chapdeuil; *see also* Pons
Capetians, dynasty in France 987–1848: 11, 54, 57, 59, 244, 245, 279, 321, 322, 369, 371, 470, 490, 514, *and see* Louis VI 1108–1137, Louis VII 1137–1180, Philip II 1180–1223, Louis VIII 1223–1226, Louis IX 1226–1270, Philip III 1270–1285, Philip IV 1285–1314; *see also* Agnes, Alice, Alphonse of Poitiers, Charles of Anjou, Charles of Valois, Margaret, Mary, Robert of Artois
Cappadocia, 144, 631, 639, 678, 680, 750
Capua, 155 note, 359, 450, 454; principate of, 8, 259
Carcassonne, 288, 289, 291, 292, 300, 311, 312, 314, 315, 760; bishop of, 277 note; seneschal of, 323; viscounts of, 286, 288, 292; viscounty of, 290; walls of, plate 1A
Cardinals, 156, 173, 353, 354, 363, 365, 369, *and see* Peter Damian 1058–*c.* 1066, Conrad of Wittelsbach 1163–1200, Henry 1179–1188, Octavian (Conti) 1182–1206, Soffredo (of Pisa) 1182–1208, Peter Capuano 1192–1214, Ugolino (de' Conti) 1198–1227, Benedict 1200–1216, Leo (Brancaleone) 1200–*c.* 1230, Pelagius (Galvani) 1205–1230, Stephen Langton 1205–1228, John Colonna 1212–1245, Robert of Courçon 1216–1219, Romanus (Bonaventura) 1216–1243, Bertrand (Savelli) 1217–1221, Conrad (of Urach) 1219–1227, Nicholas (of Claromonte) 1219–1227, Oliver (Saxo) 1225–1227, James of

Vitry 1228–1240, Octavian (Ubaldini) 1244–1273, Odo of Châteauroux 1244–1273, Peter Capocci 1244–1259
Carintana dalle Carceri, cousin of Narzotto; hexarch of northern Euboea 1220–1255, 2nd wife of William II of Achaea, 245
Carinthia, duke of, 120
Carmel, Mount, 575, 577, 582, 588
Carmelites, order, 252
Carpentras, bishop of, *see* Geoffrey
Carthage, 27 note, 516
Carthusians, order, 156
Caryae, Mount, 246
Carystus, 236, 239, 272; lords of, 246, 271
Casal Imbert; battle (1232), 549, 613, 761
Caspian Sea, 664, 672, 717
Cassandrea, 270
Casseneuil, 287 note, 303
Castelnau (-le-Lez), *see* Peter
Castelnaudary, 294, 302, 315
Castile, 232; kings of, *see* Ferdinand III 1217–1252, Alfonso X 1252–1284; princesses of, *see* Berengaria, Blanche, Eleanor
Castoria, 274; bishop of, 252
Castres, 294 note
Catalonia, 372; merchants from, 560, 568, 623; soldiers from, 260, 261, 270–274, 302, 313 note, 762
Cathars, *see* Albigensian heretics
Catherine of Courtenay, daughter of titular Latin emperor Philip; 2nd wife of Charles of Valois 1301–1308, titular empress of Constantinople 1285–1308: 270
Catholicus, *see* Gregory III 1133–1166, Nersēs 1166–1173, Gregory IV 1173–1193, Gregory VI 1194–1203, John 1203–1206, 1208–1229, Stephen IV 1290–1292, Gregory VII 1292–1307; *see also* Anticatholicus, Armenian church
Caucasus mountains, 192, 665, 717
Cayeux (-sur-Mer), *see* Anseau of Caheiu
Caymont, 524, 699
Celestine III (Hyacinthus Bobo Orsini), pope 1191–1198: 118, 149, 387, 526, 528, 534, 624, 646, 647, 759
Celestine IV (Godfrey Castiglione), pope 1241–1241: 354, 761
Celestine V (Peter of Morrone), pope 1294–1294 (d. 1296), 762
Central Asia, 661, 668, 674, 689, 691, 715–717, 724, 736; Nestorians in, 668, 720, 721; steppes of, 670; trade with, 650, 655, 723, 730
Ceos, 252
Cephalonia, 13, 239, 451; bishop of, 252; counts of, *see* Orsinis; county of, 240, 245, 248, 263, 272
Cephissus, stream; battle (1311), 271, 762
Cépoy, *see* Chepoix; *see also* Theobald
Cerigo, 239
Cerigotto, 239
Chaghatai, son of Genghis Khan (d. 1242), house of, 723; state of, 719, 723, 724
Chalandritsa: baron of, 259, 261; barony of, 250
Chalcedon, 177, 760
Chalcidice, 270
Chalon (-sur-Saône), count of, 53
Châlons (-sur-Marne), 333 note
Champagne, 68, 158, 240, 471, 536; counts of, *see* Hugh I, Henry I, Henry II, Theobald III, Theobald IV, Theobald V, *and also* Adela, Alice, Mary; marshal of, 160
Champlitte (et-le-Prélot), *see* Hugh, Odo, William
Chantilly, lord of, 469
Chapdeuil, 766, *and see* Pons of Capdolh
Charax, 205
Charistikion (Greek), 129, 145
Charles, son of Philip III of France; count of Valois (d. 1325), 270, 371, 372; wife of, *see* Catherine of Courtenay
Charles I of Anjou, son of Louis VIII of France: 360, 363–366, 501, 505, 572, 748; king of Sicily (crowned 1266) 1268–1282: 42, 255–258, 366–370, 373, 508–518, 579, 607, 762; pretender to Jerusalem 1277–1285: 259, 583–586, 588, 589, 617, 762; prince of Achaea 1278–1285: 259–263, 272–274, 762; king of Naples ("Sicily") 1282–1285: 371, 372, 588
Charles II ("the Lame", of Anjou), son of Charles I; Angevin king of Naples 1285–1309, prince of Achaea 1285–1289: 261–269, 273, 274, 617, 762
Charles of Taranto, son of Philip I (d. 1315), 270
Chartres, *see* William
Chastel Blanc, 456, 577, 581, 698, 749
Château de la Vieille, 547
Château Pèlerin, 545, 575, 577, 588; construction (1218), 394, 395, 539; siege (1220), 422, 539, 699; fall (1291), 598
Châteauneuf, *see* William
Châteauroux, *see* Odo
Châtellerault, viscount of, *see* William
Châtillon (-sur-Loing), *see* Agnes, Joan, Reginald, Walter
Chauvigny, 766, *and see* Andrew
Chelebiköy, 105
Chemishkezek, 683
Chepoix, *see* Theobald of Cépoy
Cher river, valley of, 56
Chester, earls of, 402, 414, 417, 482
Children's crusade (1212), xviii, 325 note, 329–342, 378, 760, 762
China, 668, 715–717, 723, 724
Chinese Turkestan, 723
Chinon, 49, 56
Chios, 191
Choisy (-le-Roi), *see* Nicholas
Christian III, count of Oldenburg 1167–1192: 92
Christodoulus, Sicilian admiral 1119–*c.* 1139: 21
Christopolis, 207, 238
Church, *see* Armenian, Greek, Latin

Cilicia, xviii, 527, 536, 537, 540, 541, 577, 586, 632–659, 679, 684, 685, 717, 720, 724, 730; Byzantines in, 134, 140, 637–644; third crusade in, 113, 115, 680, 792; Turks in, 132, 572, 632, 634, 636, 637, 639, 642, 649, 651 note, 652, 653, 655, 680, 682, 697, 698, 725, 727; Mamluks in, 576, 577, 654–657, 749, 762; *see also* Armenia, Cilician
Cilician Gates, pass, 634, 635, 645, 682, 727
Cinnamus, John, Byzantine historian (d. *c.* 1190), 11, 133, 134, 136, 637
Circuiz, 95
Cistercians, order, 156, 157, 158 note, 166, 198, 277 note, 283, 383; in Sicily, 11 note, 12 note; in Frankish Greece, 241, 252; in Spain, 566
Cîteaux, abbey, 158 note, 166; abbots of, 157 note, 283
Citrum, 238
Civetot, 205
Civitavecchia, 396
Clairvaux, abbot of, *see* Bernard
Clari, *see* Cléry; *see also* Robert
Clement III (Paolino Scolaro), pope 1187–1191: 58, 96, 645, 646 note, 759
Clement IV (Guy Foulcois), pope 1265–1268: 255, 365–367, 373, 509–511, 722, 761, 762
Clement V (Bertrand de Gouth), pope 1305–1314: 762
Clermont (de l'Oise), count of, *see* Ralph, *and also* Simon
Clermont (in Auvergne), bishop of, *see* Hugh
Clermont (in Greece), 241, 248, 249
Cléry (-sur-Somme), *see* Robert of Clari
Clissa, castle at Spalato, 388
Cloyes, 330, *and see* Stephen
Cluny: abbots of, *see* Peter, William; monks of, 383
Coggeshall, *see* Ralph
Coligny, *see* Hugh
Colmar, 333
Cologne, 115, 331–335, 444, *and see* Nicholas; annals of, 172; archbishops of, 90, 117; scholasticus of, 381
Coloman, son of Andrew II of Hungary and Gertrude; duke of Croatia (d. 1241), 387
Coloman I, son of John Asen II and Maria; Vlach tsar of Bulgaria 1241–1246: 222, 225, 761
Colonna, family, 374, *and see* John
Comana, 631
Comminges, 294, 298, 303, 307, 311, 315; counts of, *see* Bernard IV, Bernard V
Comnenus, Byzantine imperial dynasty at Constantinople 1057–1185: 123–146, 688, *and see* Alexius I 1081–1118, John II 1118–1143, Manuel I 1143–1180, Alexius II 1180–1183, Andronicus I 1183–1185; *see also* Alexius, Isaac, *and* Anna, Maria (2) Comnena; at Trebizond 1204–1461: *see* Alexius 1204–1222, David; at Epirus, Thessalonica, and Neopatras, *see* Angelus "Comnenus"
Compiègne, 159
Conflans (-Sainte Honorine), archdeacon of, *see* William Jordan
Conon of Béthune, French baron and poet, regent of Romania 1216–1217, 1219–1221: 160, 178, 211, 213, 214
Conrad (of Krosigk), bishop of Halberstadt 1201–1209 (d. 1225), 164
Conrad, bishop of Hildesheim 1221–1246: 444, 445
Conrad (of Laichling), bishop of Regensburg 1187–1204: 92, 93, 105, 120
Conrad (of Urach), cardinal-bishop of Porto 1219–1227: 440
Conrad, count of Dornberg (in 1189), 92, 93
Conrad, count of Öttingen (in 1189), 92, 93
Conrad III, Hohenstaufen king of Germany 1138–1152: 10–12, 15, 16, 131, 133, 135, 136; and the second crusade, 12, 15, 90, 117, 121, 135, 136
Conrad IV, son of Frederick II and Isabel of Brienne; Hohenstaufen king of Jerusalem 1228–1254: 451, 464, 467, 468, 484, 544, 546, 547, 550–553, 559, 560, 567, 606, 611, 613, 761; emperor (uncrowned) of Germany and Sicily 1250–1254: 359, 360, 761; son of, 366
Conrad, margrave of Landsberg 1190–1210: 120
Conrad, scholasticus of Mainz, 434
Conrad of Feuchtwangen, master of the Teutonic Knights 1290–1296: 595
Conrad of Metz, chancellor of Germany, 434
Conrad of Montferrat, son of William III: 38, 46, 47, 164, 165, 185; marquis of Montferrat 1188–1192: 51, 52, 62, 63, 65, 66, 601, 759; claimant to throne of Jerusalem 1190–1192: 66–68, 70, 71, 78–81, 116, 165, 443, 523, 530, 759; daughter of, 532; wives of, *see* Theodora Angelina, Isabel (of Jerusalem)
Conrad of Querfurt, bishop of Hildesheim 1194–1198, of Würzburg 1198–1202, chancellor of Germany, 120, 121, 529, 530, 604, 647
Conrad (landgrave) of Thuringia, master of the Teutonic Knights 1239–1240: 463, 472, 475
Conrad of Wittelsbach, archbishop of Mainz 1183–1200, cardinal-bishop (of Sabina) 1163–1200: 91, 120, 121, 529, 647, 648
Conrad Otto, duke of Moravia 1182–1191, of Bohemia 1189–1191: 93
Conradin, son of emperor Conrad IV; Hohenstaufen duke of Swabia: 256, 351, 360, 362, 366–368, 509, 513; king of Jerusalem 1254–1268: 546, 567, 569, 571, 579, 607, 613, 761, 762
Constance, treaty of (1183), 445
Constance (Hohenstaufen), daughter of

Manfred of Sicily; wife of Peter III of Aragon 1262–1285 (d. 1302), 370
Constance, daughter of Roger II of Sicily; wife of emperor Henry VI 1186–1197 (d. 1198), 41, 59, 117, 130, 147, 528
Constance ("Anna"), legitimized daughter of emperor Frederick II; 2nd wife of John III Ducas Vatatzes (after 1244), 225
Constance of Antioch, daughter of Bohemond II; wife of Raymond of Poitiers 1136–1149, regent of Antioch 1149–1153, 1st wife of Reginald of Châtillon 1153–1164?, regent of Antioch 1160–1163: 10, 133, 134, 140, 641
Constance of Aragon, sister of Peter II; wife of Emeric I of Hungary 1178–1204, 1st wife of emperor Frederick II 1209–1222: 434, 435, 438, 451
Constantine, Armenian leader at Vahka, 637
Constantine, Armenian lord of Gargar (to 1117), 632, 636
Constantine, bishop of Orvieto *c.* 1250–1257: 228
Constantine, son of Leon III; Heṭoumid king of Cilician Armenia 1298–1299: 657
Constantine I, grandson of Sempad of Barbaṛon; Heṭoumid lord of Lampron, regent of Armenia 1221–1226 (d. 1261), 540, 541, 651, 652
Constantine II, son of Heṭoum of Lampron; Heṭoumid lord of Lampron, 652
Constantine, grandson of Sempad of Babaṛon; Heṭoumid lord of Sarvantikar, 652 note; wife of, *see* Rita?
Constantine, son of Ṛoupen I; Ṛoupenid lord of Partzapert 1092–1100: 633–635
Constantine Coloman, Byzantine governor of Tarsus 1162–1173: 641, 642
Constantine Lascaris, brother of Theodore I; Byzantine leader, 201 note
Constantine Mesopotamites, Orthodox metropolitan of Thessalonica (to 1224), 214
Constantine Palaeologus, brother of Michael VIII; sebastocrator (d. 1306), 253, 254
Constantinople: under Comneni 1081–1185: 3–5, 11–14, 29, 37, 38, 62, 126–128, 130–133, 138–142, 144–146, 637, 639, 640, 642, 664, 678; under Angeli 1185–1204: 37, 42, 46, 92, 97, 98, 101, 103–109, 147–151, 161, 165, 169, 173, 174, 176–185, 197, 239, 531, 532, 608, 649, 681, 760; under Latins 1204–1261: 187, 189, 191, 193, 195–205, 210–233, 235, 238, 243, 244, 247, 248, 252, 377, 466–468, 482, 535, 544, 570, 682, 687; under Greeks after 1261: 232, 233, 253, 254, 271, 363, 368, 370, 371, 509, 513, 572, 584, 628, 657, 726, 752, 761; council of (381), 196; Greek patriarchs of, *see* Nicetas II 1186–1189, Arsenius 1261–1265, *and* patriarchs of Nicaea; Latin patriarchs of, *see* Thomas Morosini 1205–1211, Gervase 1215–1219, Matthew 1221–1226, Simon (of Maugastel) 1227–1232, Nicholas *c.* 1234–1251
Constantinople, empire, *see* Byzantine empire, Latin empire
Copais, Lake, 271, 274
Copts, Christian sect, 411
Corcondylus, Greek merchant, 264
Corfu: before 1199: 13, 14, 24, 25, 135, 138, 146; under Franks 1199–1214: 176, 177, 181, 238, 760; under Epirus 1214–1259: 240, 451; under Franks after 1259: 256, 260, 263, 268, 273
Corinth: under Greeks to 1205: 13, 14, 202; under Franks after 1205: 239, 253, 264, 267; archbishopric of, 252; castle at, 249; parliament at (1340), 267, 273
Corinth, Gulf of, 13, 191, 247
Corinth, Isthmus of, 237, 246
Corinthia, 235, 236, 246, 258
Cornwall, 54; earl of, *see* Richard
Coron, 208, 238, 239; bishop of, 252
Corycus, 650, 655; castellan of, 540, 651 note
Cosmas, bishop of Mahdia 1148–1159 (d. 1160), 27, 31 note
Coucy (-le-Château), castellan of, 158 note, 160
Councils, ecumenical, *see* Constantinople (381), Third Lateran (1179), Fourth Lateran (1215), Lyons (1245, 1274), Ferrara-Florence (1438–1442); other, *see* Rheims (1148), Verona (1184), Dijon (1198), Lavaur (1213), Melun (1216), Bourges (1225), Toulouse (1229)
Courçon, *see* Curzon; *see also* Robert
Courtenay, 222; house of, 642, *and see* Agnes, Baldwin II, Catherine, Joscelin I, Joscelin II, Joscelin III, Mary, Peter, Philip (2), Robert (2), Yolanda
Couserans, bishops of, *see* Navarre, Sancho
Coutances, *see* Walter
Coxon, 631, 639
Creixell, 767, *and see* Dalmatz
Cremona, 334; bishop of, 334; diet at (1226), 445
Crete, 62, 177, 190, 191, 229, 238, 451, 512, 759; archbishop of, 421 (identity unknown); *see also* Candia
Crèvecoeur, 267, 272
Crimea, 682, 717, 726
Croatia, 139, 146, 167, 175, 387; *see also* Meran
Crown of Thorns, 222
Crusade of 1197: 6 note, 42, 117–122, 149, 153, 528–531, 604, 608, 695, 759; map, 86
Crusade of Frederick II (1228–1229), xvii, 429–451, 460–462, 541–543, 701; in Cyprus, 451, 543, 544, 610–612; in Syria, 349, 451–460, 544–546, 612, 702
Crusade of 1239–1241: xviii, 463–469, 551, 614; French phase, 222, 243, 469–481, 706, 707, 761; English phase, 482–485, 708
Crusade of 1249–1250: 356, 487, 488, 674; preparations, 488–493, 614; in Cyprus, 244, 493–495, 614, 761; in Egypt, 226,

245, 255, 495–504, 515, 566, 615, 711, 712, 735, 738, 739, 741, 761; in Syria, 504–508, 566, 567; map, 486
Crusade of 1270, *see* Tunisian crusade
Crusade of prince Edward (1270–1272), 510, 517, 518, 582–584, 615, 616, 762
Crusades, *see* First crusade, Second crusade, Third crusade, Crusade of 1197, Fourth crusade, Albigensian crusade, Children's crusade, Political crusades, Fifth crusade, Crusade of Frederick II, Crusade of 1239–1241, Crusade of 1249–1250, Tunisian crusade, Crusade of prince Edward
Culos, 105, *and see* Chelebiköy
Curia Christi (Latin, court of Christ), 89
Curzon, *see* Robert of Courçon
Cuyk, count of, *see* Henry
Cyclades, 192, 202, 238, 268
Cydnus river, 635
Cyprus: under Greeks to 1191: 37, 62–64, 133, 146, 599–602, 621, 622, 640, 646, 759; under Franks 1191–1218: xviii, 64, 67, 68, 81, 82, 118, 120, 148, 523, 525, 528–532, 540, 601–605, 607–609, 620–624, 647, 759, 760; 1218–1233: 412, 421, 443 note, 447, 451, 460, 462, 464, 543–546, 548, 549, 605, 606, 609–613, 618, 619, 623, 625–627, 682, 761; 1233–1253: 244, 245, 471, 492, 493, 495, 507, 512, 550, 551, 553, 560, 565, 606, 614, 615, 627, 684, 711; 1253–1291: 567, 571, 575, 581, 584–586, 588–590, 592, 593, 595, 596, 598, 606, 607, 615–617, 619, 620, 628, 749; after 1291: 269, 608, 618, 619, 623, 629, 656, 658; bailies of, *see* Philip of Ibelin, John I of Ibelin, Amalric Barlais (with 4 associates); barons of, 462, 464, 544, 548, 582, 588, 589, 604, 608, 610, 611, 616, 617, 619, 620, 624, 625, 629; crusaders from, 409, 414, 530, 539, 608–610, 614, 615, 617; high court of, 571, 605–607, 611, 619, 620, 626; kings of, *see* Aimery 1197–1205, Hugh I 1205–1218, Henry I 1218–1253, Hugh II 1253–1267, Hugh III 1267–1284, John 1284–1285, Henry II 1285–1324, Hugh IV 1324–1359; other rulers of, *see* Isaac Comnenus 1184–1191, Richard I (of England), Guy of Lusignan 1192–1194, Aimery of Lusignan 1194–1197; people of, 62–64, 582, 601, 603, 613, 621–624; regents of, *see* Walter of Montbéliard 1205–1210, Alice 1218–1232, Plaisance of Antioch 1253–1261, Hugh III 1261–1267, Amalric "of Lusignan" 1306–1310; map of, 556
Cyrenaica, 735, 749
Cyrrhus, 636; governor of, 642
Cythnos, 239
Cyzicus, 205, 209

Ḍaifah Khātūn, daughter of al-ʿĀdil I Saif-ad-Dīn; wife of aẓ-Ẓāhir Ghāzī (to 1216), regent of Aleppo (after 1236), 698, 704
Dailam, tribes of, 668
Dajig, 640
Dalle Carceri, *see* Carintana, Narzotto, Ravano; *see also* Boniface, Felicia, Gilbert, Grapella, William I, William II of Verona
Dalmatia, 131, 138, 139, 146, 167, 168, 173, 387; duke of, *see* Berthold IV
Dalmatz of Creixell, Aragonese captain, 313
Damala, 241; barons of, *see* William de la Roche, James de la Roche, Reginald de la Roche
Damascus: under Aiyūbids 1174–1260: 38, 71, 390, 391, 398, 401, 402, 449, 453, 455, 473, 474, 479, 505, 506, 561, 564, 567, 675, 695–699, 701, 702, 704–713, 737, 741; under Mamluks after 1260: 577, 578, 582, 595, 656, 745–751, 754, 755; atabeg of, 662; Mongols at, 572, 573, 653, 714, 717, 745, 761; rulers of, *see* Aiyūbids; troops from, 67, 542, 561–563, 596, 708, 709, 711
Damietta, 30, 34, 37, 389, 448, 471, 697, 742, 747; fifth crusade at, 335, 396–430, 434–439, 442, 452, 456, 539–541, 609, 610, 698–701, 703, 760; crusade of 1249 at, 226, 245, 258, 494–498, 501–504, 506, 515, 516, 615, 627, 711, 712, 741, 761; archbishops of, 420, *and see* Giles
Dammartin (-en-Goële), *see* Reginald
Dampierre, (Le-Vieil-), *see* Guy
Dampierre (-le-Château), *see* Guy, Reginald
Dandolo, *see* Enrico, Marino, Renier
Dānishmendids, Turkoman dynasty at Sebastia 1063–1174: 132, 133, 140, 636, 676–681, 727, *and see* Malik-Ghazi 1097–1105?, Gümüshtigin Ghāzī 1105?–*c.* 1134, Muḥammad *c.* 1134–1140, Yaghi-Basan 1140–1164; *see also* ʿAin-ad-Daulah, Dhū-l-Qarnain, Dhū-n-Nūn
Danube river, 92, 131, 220; island in, 94; region north of, 125
Daphne, 241, 252, 269
Daphnusia, 231
Dara, 704
Darbsāk, 550, 649; *see also* Amanus mountains, castles of
Dardanelles, 101–103, 110, 116, 177, 205, 219, 759
Dartmouth, 50, 395
Darum, 79, 82, 83, 523, 713
Daulia, bishopric of, 252
Daun, *see* Wierich
David II ("the Restorer"), king of Georgia 1089–1125: 664
David, Orthodox patriarch of Antioch *c.* 1242–after 1247: 566
David Comnenus, grandson of Andronicus I; leader at Trebizond (d. 1214), 200, 204–206, 210
De la Roches, Burgundian dynasty at Athens 1205–1308: 269, *and see* Othon 1205–1225, Guy I 1225–1263, John 1263–1280, William 1280–1287, Guy II 1287–

1308; *see also* Alice, Bonne, Isabel, James, Reginald, William
Deabolis, *see* Devol
Dead Sea, 82
Delhi, slave kings of, 668, 672
Delos, 192
Delphi, 238
Delta, *see* Nile, delta of; maps of, 486
Demetrias, 257, 271
Demetrius Angelus Comnenus, son of Theodore of Epirus; despot of Thessalonica 1244–1246: 225
Demetrius Chomatianus, Orthodox archbishop of Ochrida (in 1224), 214
Demetrius of Montferrat, son of Boniface II and Margaret; king of Thessalonica 1209–1224 (d. 1227), 206, 207, 212, 214; wife of, *see* Bonne de la Roche
Demosiakoi (Greek, state *paroikoi*), 143
Demotica, 105, 106, 192, 203, 204, 217
Denizli, 681
Denmark: axes from, 615; clergy of, 349; crusaders from, 50, 51, 65; mercenaries from, 179
Derby, earl of, 50
Devol, treaty of (1108), 127, 132
Devon, 54; earl of, 483 note
Dgha Ṿasil (Basil "the Younger"), adopted son of Kogh Ṿasil; Armenian lord of Kesoun 1112–1116: 632, 635
Dhū-l-Qarnain, son of 'Ain-ad-Daulah; Dānishmendid emir at Melitene 1152–1162: 678
Dhū-n-Nūn, 'Imād-ad-Dīn, son of Muḥammad; Dānishmendid emir in Cappadocia 1140–1164 (d. 1174), 677–679
Dicetum, *see* Ralph de Diceto
Diego (of Acebes), bishop of Osma 1201–1207: 283
Dietpold (of Bergen), bishop of Passau 1172–1190: 92, 93, 102, 104, 106, 115
Dietrich, count of Wied 1158–1189: 92, 105
Dietrich I, margrave of Meissen 1195–1221: 120
Dietz, *see* Henry
Dieudamour, 611–613; *see also* Saint Hilarion
Dijon, council of (1198), 155, 156
Dikran, Armenian lord of Bṛagana (d. after 1198), 639
Dillingen, count of, *see* Adalbert
Dimas, 21
Dimatra, 261
Dinan, lord of, 469
Dionysius, treasurer of Hungary, 392
Divrighi, 690
Diyār-Bakr, 673, 684, 691, 693, 700–704
Diyār-Muḍar, 673, 706
Dodecanese, 192
Dollnstein, count of, *see* Gebhard
Dome of the Rock (Qubbat aṣ-Ṣakhrah), at Jerusalem, 455, 709
Dominic (?), archbishop of Brindisi 1203?–*c.* 1216: 335
Dominic, assistant to bishop Diego of Osma, 283
Dominicans, order, 341, 465, 467; individual friars, 218, 219, 281, 494 note, 566, 626, 627, 722
Domokos, 238, 271
Donzi, *see* Hervey
Dordogne river, 303
Dornberg, count of, *see* Conrad
Dorset, 54
Dorylaeum, 681
Dositheus, Orthodox patriarch of Jerusalem 1669–1707: 626 note
Doubs river, 335
Dramelay, *see* Guy
Dreux: count of, *see* Robert II; house of, 470, *and see* Henry, Peter, Philip
Dreux of Beaumont (-sur-Oise), marshal of Sicily (in 1271), 256, 257
Dreux of Mello, French commander, 69
Dreux of Mello, lord of Loches and Dinan, 469
Dubais, Mazyadid ruler of Hilla 1107–1134 (d. 1135), 663
Ducas, *see* Alexius V, John, John III, Michael I, Theodore; *see also* Euphrosyne, Irene Ducaena
Duluk, 641
Dunstable, 473 note
Durand (Chapuis) of Le Puy, carpenter and visionary, 329
Durazzo, 3, 36, 118, 146, 176, 212, 240; Angevins at, 258, 260, 268, 273, 367
Durham, bishop of, 54
Dzedz, 639 note
Dzoṿḳ, monastery, 641

Eaunes, abbey, abbot of, 296 note
Ebersheim, 333, 335
Écry, 158, 185, 759
Edessa, city, 11, 134, 616, 632, 635, 638, 708, *and see* Matthew; lord of, 632, 634
Edessa, county, 126, 678; counts of, *see* Baldwin I 1098–1100, Baldwin II 1100–1118, Joscelin I 1119–1131, Joscelin II 1131–1150; regents of, *see* Richard of the Principate 1104–1108, Beatrice 1150–1150
Edmund Plantagenet, son of Henry III of England; count of Lancaster, titular king of Sicily 1255–1259 (d. 1296), 360, 362, 582
Edward I ("Longshanks"), son of Henry III; as crusader 1270–1272: 510, 517, 518, 582–584, 615, 616, 762; Plantagenet king of England 1272–1307: 374, 518, 586, 595, 654, 722; wife of, *see* Eleanor of Castile
Egbert (of Andechs), son of Berthold IV of Meran; bishop of Bamberg 1203–1237: 389
Egypt, 19, 76, 78, 79, 82, 83, 106, 449, 453, 505–508, 514, 564, 567, 574, 575, 595, 610, 654, 656, 674, 678, 695, 697, 700,

704, 707, 708, 711, 718, 719, 735, 737, 738, 740–751, 753–755, 757; attacks on, xvii, 30, 34, 140, 163, 169, 180, 245, 389, 396–428, 430, 432, 444, 462, 471–473, 477, 493–504, 512, 516, 539, 566, 607, 609, 698, 706, 713, 760, 761; ships from, 53, 531, 532, 564, 565, 581, 593; sultans of, *see* Aiyūbids (1174–1252), Mamluks (1250–1390); trade with, 22, 23, 27, 161, 592, 593, 682, 730; troops from, 67, 476, 479, 480, 489, 553, 562–565, 573, 574, 576, 596, 655, 657, 674, 687, 697, 698, 700, 705, 706, 709–711, 713, 739, 756, 761, *and see* Mamluks

Elbe river, 121

Eleanor, sister of Peter II of Aragon; 5th wife of Raymond VI of Toulouse, 300 note, 307

Eleanor of Aquitaine, 1st wife of Louis VII of France 1137–1152, wife of Henry II of England 1152-1189 (d. 1204), 12, 15, 61, 159

Eleanor of Castile, granddaughter of Alfonso IX; 1st wife of Edward I of England 1254–1290: 583 note

Eleusis, 241

Eleutheroi or *francomati* (Greek, freemen), 622

Elias (Peleti), patriarch of Jerusalem 1279–*c.* 1287: 590

Elis, 248, 253, 254, 258, 267, 272

Elizabeth (of Chappes), wife of Geoffrey I of Achaea 1210–1218: 240

Ely, bishop of, 54, 79

Embriacos, Genoese family at Jubail 1109–1298?: 569, 570, 587, *and see* Hugh III 1184–1186, Guy I 1186–1241, Henry 1241–*c.* 1271, Guy II *c.* 1271–1282, Peter 1282–*c.* 1298; *see also* Baldwin, Bartholomew, Bertrand, John, William

Embrun, 364

Emeric I, son of Bela III and Agnes; king of Hungary 1196–1204: 173, 175, 189, 190, 387; wife of, *see* Constance of Aragon

Engelbert I, count of Berg 1166–1189: 92

Engelhard, bishop of Naumburg and Zeitz 1207–1242: 389

England, 10, 49, 53–55, 61, 79, 82, 89, 91, 120, 156, 221, 362, 365, 384, 431, 479, 482, 533, 583, 621; clergy in, 163, 349, 352, 357, 362, 373, 465, 510; crusaders from, on third crusade, 47, 50, 56, 58–60, 63, 65, 67, 69, 74, 85, 114–116, 602, 792; on fourth crusade, 164 note; on fifth crusade, 402, 415, 417; on crusade of Frederick II, 444, 445, 452, 458, 542; on crusade of 1239–1241: 466, 472, 481, 483; on crusade of 1249–1250: 490, 499; on crusade of prince Edward, 510, 517, 582, 584; at defense of Acre, 595–597; great seal of, 62; kings of, *see* Plantagenets; mercenaries from, 179, 200

Enguerrand of Boves, French baron, 175

Enkleistra, monastery, 601, 626

Enos, 105

Enrico Dandolo, doge of Venice *c.* 1193–1205: 162, 163, 167–169, 173; on fourth crusade, 151, 174–176, 178–180, 182–185, 760; at Constantinople 1204–1205: 183, 184, 189, 190, 193, 202, 203

Eon de l'Étoile, fanatic in Brittany (d. 1148), 328

Ephraim, hills, 73

Epirus, 191, 193, 235; Angevins in, 256–258, 263, 265–269, 273; despoina of, *see* Anna Cantacuzena; despots of, *see* Michael I 1204–1214, Theodore 1214–1230, Michael II 1236–1271, Nicephorus 1271–1296, Thomas 1296–1318; despotate of, 151, 201, 208, 226–228, 266–269, 273, 367; troops from, 211, 228, 266

Epistola caelestis (Latin, letter from heaven), 329, 341

Erard II, count of Brienne 1161?–1189: 50, 51

Eretna, ʿAlā'-ad-Dīn, Mongol emir at Sebastia 1335–1352: 730

Erfurt, 340

Eric Läspe, king of Sweden 1223–1250: 349

Erivan, *see* Mkhiṭar of Ayrivanḳ

Erlau, bishop of, 389

Ernoul, French chronicler (d. after 1229), 158, 391, 420, 421, 448

Erymanthus, stream, 269

Erzerum, 664, 665, 682, 683, 691, 730; lord of, 673, 681

Erzinjan, 673, 682, 683, 691, 703

Esaias, Orthodox archbishop of Cyprus *c.* 1205–*c.* 1220: 626 note

Eschiva of Ibelin, niece of Balian II; 1st wife of Aimery of Lusignan (d. *c.* 1196), 604, 605

Eschiva of Ibelin, daughter of John II and Alice; wife of Humphrey of Montfort 1269–1284, wife of Guy "of Lusignan" *c.* 1285–1303, lady of Beirut 1282–1291, lady of Lapithos (d. 1309), 269, 580, 584, 588, 589

Eschiva of Montbéliard, daughter of Walter and Burgundia; wife of Balian III of Ibelin (after 1230), 560

Esdraelon, plain, 390

Essex, earl of, 49

Este, family, 363

Estonians, Finnic people, 122

Étampes, 12, 40

Euboea: under Greeks to 1205: 13, 29, 177, 191, 202, 235, 236, 760; under Franks 1205–1276?: 208, 229, 232, 238–240, 242, 243, 245, 246, 248, 249, 253, 256, 257, 263; under Greeks after 1276?: 257–259, 263, 272

Eudocia Angelina, daughter of Alexius III; wife of Stephen I of Serbia (to 1202), wife of Alexius V Ducas 1202–1204, wife of Leo Sgourus 1204–1207: 148, 149, 182 note

Eudocia Lascaris, daughter of Theodore I;

wife of Anseau of Cahieu (after 1227), 214, 226
Eugenius III (Peter Bernardo), pope 1145–1153: 11, 12, 15, 16, 27, 136, 328
Eugenius, Sicilian admiral, possibly "Hugo Falcandus" (d. *c.* 1203), 3 note
Euphemia (Femyē), daughter of Heṭoum I; wife of Julian of Sidon (after *c.* 1252), 652 note
Euphrates river, 641, 685, 696, 725, 755; crossings of, 582, 657, 708, 714, 745, 749; region east of, 673, 674, 679, 683, 684, 735; region west of, 630, 678, 679, 726
Euphrosyne Ducaena, wife of Alexius III Angelus (d. 1215), 176, 207
Europe, map of central, 2; map of western, 44
Eurotas river, 253
Eustace, (illegitimate?) son of Baldwin V of Hainault; commander of Latin forces, 208–210; wife of, 208
Eustorgue of Montaigu (-sur-Champeix), brother of Garin; Latin archbishop of Nicosia *c.* 1215–1250: 389, 413 note, 609, 615, 625–627
Euthymius, Orthodox patriarch of Antioch (before 1260–after 1264), 566, 572, 575
Évreux, bishop of, 58, 63
Exeter, bishop of, 445, 542
Ezzelino III of Romano, tyrant of Padua 1237–1256, of Verona 1237–1259: 363

al-Fāḍil, qadi at Cairo, 600 note
Faenza, bishop of, *see* Roland
Fagiano, *see* Hugh
al-Fā'iz Ibrāhīm, son of al-'Ādil I Saif-ad-Dīn (d. 1220), 408
Fakhr-ad-Dīn 'Alī, vizir of Selchükids, 727, 728
Fakhr-ad-Dīn ibn-ash-Shaikh; Egyptian emir (d. 1250), 449, 452–454, 498, 499, 710, 711, 739
Falkenstein, count of, *see* Kuno
Famagusta, 64, 601, 608, 612, 613, 623–625
Fanjeaux, 294 note, 300
Fāriskūr, 410, 412–414, 418, 424, 712, 739, 740
Farrūkh-Shāh Dā'ūd, 'Izz-ad-Dīn, nephew of Saladin; Aiyūbid governor of Damascus 1178–1183: 693
Fars, 662, 663, 672
Fāṭimids, Arab caliphal dynasty in Tunisia 909–972 and Egypt 969–1171: 17, 18, 19 note, 27 note, 30, 35, 665, *and see* al-Mu'izz 953–975, al-Mustanṣir 1036–1094, al-Ḥāfiẓ 1130–1149
Fauquembergue, family, 244
Felicia (dalle Carceri), daughter of William I of Verona; wife of Narzotto dalle Carceri (to 1264), wife of Licario: 256
Ferdinand III, king of Castile 1217–1252, of Leon 1230–1252: 216
Ferentino, 438, 440, 447
Ferrara, 363; council of (1438–1442), 232, 233
Ferro, *see* Angelo, John
Feuchtwangen, *see* Conrad
Fifth crusade (1217–1221), 216, 297, 760; preparations, 300, 308, 378–388, 432, 434, 537, 538, 608, 609; Syrian phase, 388–396, 538, 539, 605, 609, 698; Egyptian phase, 335, 397–428, 434–437, 449, 452, 496, 497, 539–541, 609, 610, 698–700; map, 486
Filangieri, *see* Henry, Lothair, Marino, Richard
First crusade (1096–1099), 5, 6, 125, 134, 159, 326, 464, 600, 631–634, 664, 677
Fivelgo, *see* Hayo
Flanders, 68, 70, 204, 221, 341, 360, 381; countesses of, *see* Margaret (I) of Alsace, Margaret II; counts of, *see* Philip (I) of Alsace, Baldwin (VIII), Baldwin (IX), Guy; crusaders from, 47, 50, 65, 115, 175, 582, *and see under* Low Countries; seneschal of, *see* Hellin
Flemings, Flemish, *see* Flanders
Florence, *see* Walter; bankers from, 273; council of Ferrara– (1438–1442), 232, 233
Florent (or Floris) III, count of Holland 1157–1190: 92, 93, 106, 115
Florent of Hainault, brother of count John II; prince of Achaea 1289–1297: 262–266, 268, 272–274, 762; wife of, *see* Isabel of Villehardouin
Florent of Varennes, French admiral, 511
Foggia, 362, 442, 547
Foix, 293; castle of, 306, 307, 312; counts of, *see* Raymond Roger, Roger Bernard; county of, 294, 298, 303, 311, 315, 320
Fontfroide, abbey, 283
Forcalquier, count of, 259
Forez, count of, 469
Fors, *see* William
Fougères, lord of, 469
Fourth crusade (1202–1204), xv, 37, 119, 138, 144, 209, 289, 533; preparations, 154–167, 347, 608, 759; diversion, 150, 167–173, 325, 381, 531, 608; at Zara, 173–176, 760; at Constantinople, 150, 151, 177–185, 760; results, xvii, 38, 88, 151, 185, 233, 377, 531, 535, 608, 682; map of, 186
France, 5, 11, 12, 16, 48, 49, 55, 57, 89, 137, 155, 157, 195, 204, 212, 219, 222, 239, 240, 245–247, 250, 251, 255, 270, 321, 322, 327, 329, 341, 351, 363, 364, 371, 378, 381, 384, 385, 439, 465, 467, 470, 483, 484, 490, 503–505, 508–510, 513, 517, 518, 542, 554, 559, 571, 713, 761; clergy of, 155, 156, 164, 283, 299, 306, 313, 314, 316, 319, 348, 349, 352, 357, 365, 371–375, 380, 490, 491, 504, 510; crusaders from, 121, 224, 252, 326, 508, 537, 575, 576, 580, 590, 592, 596; on third crusade, 47, 50, 60, 65, 70, 74, 75, 78–83,

85, 114, 116, 522; on fourth crusade, 88, 150, 157 note, 159, 162, 163, 167, 174, 178, 179, 181, 185, 198, 207, 232, 238, 759, 760; on children's crusade, 331–333, 337, 760; on political crusades, 287, 346, 350, 372; on fifth crusade, 380, 385, 386, 402, 409, 415, 417, 420, 427; on crusade of Frederick II, 440, 448, 542; on crusade of 1239–1241: 219, 243, 471, 482, 484; on crusades of Louis IX: 244, 490, 493, 581, 614, 742, 761, 762; kings of, *see* Capetians; peers of, 54, 469; regents of, *see* Adela and William, archbishop of Rheims (1190–1191), Blanche of Castile (1226–1236, 1248–1252); map of central, 276
Francis of Assisi, founder of Franciscan order (1209, d. 1226), 378 note, 415, 416
Franciscans, order, 198, 226, 415, 544, 566, 656 note; individual friars, 218–220, 627, 722
Frangipani, family, 450
Frankfurt (am Main), 434, 770
Franks, 11, 144, 724; in Africa, 22, 23; in Cyprus, 599–629; in Greece, 235–274, 621, 761, 762; in Syria, 34, 35, 46, 522–598, 663, 667, 674–678, 682, 683, 694, 697, 709, 713, 718, 719, 721, 727, 761, 762, plate 2B; *see also* Latins
Frederick I, count of Abenberg (in 1189), 92, 105
Frederick I ("Barbarossa"), nephew of Conrad III; Hohenstaufen emperor of Germany 1152 (crowned 1155)–1190: 32, 33, 47, 282, 345, 346, 759; and Byzantines (to 1188), 15 note, 88, 90, 130, 136–138, 140, 141; on third crusade, frontispiece, xvii, 49, 55, 57, 88–104, 107–121, 146–148, 185, 645, 646, 680, 682, 759
Frederick, son of Frederick I; Hohenstaufen duke of Swabia and Alsace 1169–1191: 49, 53, 65, 91–93, 96, 100, 102, 105, 109–116, 645
Frederick II, son of Henry VI and Constance: 117; Hohenstaufen emperor of Germany and Sicily 1211 (crowned 1220)–1250: xviii, 337, 338, 463, 488, 541, 565, 760, 761; and papacy, 216, 221, 224, 225, 227, 346, 348–359, 429–442, 445–447, 450, 461, 462, 465, 490; and fifth crusade, 382, 384, 395, 419, 423, 427, 434–437; and Albigensian crusade, 317 note, 318, 322, 323; and Latin empire, 221, 224, 226, 228; king of Jerusalem 1225–1228: xvii, 42, 442–451, 464, 542, 543, 606, 610, 701, 760; regent 1228–1243: 451–462, 464, 467–469, 471–473, 480–484, 489, 543–553, 557–560, 561 note, 604–606, 610–614, 618–620, 702, 705, 706, 760, 761; wives of, *see* Constance of Aragon, Isabel of Brienne, Isabel (Plantagenet)
Frederick I of Babenberg, son of Leopold V; duke of Austria 1194–1198: 120
Frederick of Berg, advocate of Passau and Melk (d. 1190), 93, 100, 105, 106, 115
Frederick of Hausen, minnesinger (d. 1190), 111
Freidank, Swabian poet and crusader, 454, 456, 462
Freising, bishop of, 11
Frisia, 330, 381; crusaders from, 50, 51, 65, 115, 357, 394, 395, 399–402, 407, 409, 444; *see also* Low Countries
al-Fūlah, 390
Fulda, 432
Fulk (of Marseilles), bishop of Toulouse 1205–1231: 277 note, 296, 299, 306, 312
Fulk, son-in-law of Baldwin II of Jerusalem; count (V) of Anjou 1109–1129, king of Jerusalem 1131–1143: 10, 134, 636
Fulk of Neuilly, priest (d. 1202), 157, 158, 166
Fustat, 35, 411
Futūwah (Arabic, magnanimity), 666, 688
Fūwah, 531

Gabadonia, 639
Gaban, 637
Gabes, 20, 24, 25, 27 note
Gabes, Gulf of, 22
Gabriel (Khōril), Armenian lord of Melitene (to 1103), 632
Gagik (East Armenian), Bagratid king of Greater Armenia (d. 1071), 633, 635
Gaikhatu, son of Abagha; Īl-khan of Persia 1291–1295: 755
Galata, 178, 229
Galeran, bishop of Beirut (before 1233–after 1245), 548 note
Galeran of Ivry, seneschal of Sicily, bailie of Achaea 1278–1280: 259, 274
Galicia, coast of, 395
Galilee, 479, 480, 489, 531, 537, 558, 561, 564, 565, 573, 574, 576, 580, 745
Gallipoli, 108, 109, 191, 215, 219, 270
Ganges river, valley of, 668
Ganja, 633, *and see* Niẓāmī
Gardiki, 259; lord of, 271
Gardolph (of Harpke), bishop of Halberstadt 1193–1201: 120
Gargar, lord of, 632, 636
Garin, Latin archbishop of Verissa 1207–1210, of Thessalonica 1210–1224: 214
Garin fitz Gerald, Norman baron, 58
Garin of Montaigu (-sur-Champeix), master of the Hospital 1207–1227: 383, 389, 392, 397, 413 note, 425, 438, 541, 609, 625
Garmirleṛ hills, 637
Garnier, *see* Grenier
Garonne river, 287 note, 300, 302, 303, 312, 315; region of, 295
Gascony, 315; soldiers from, 302, 312, 510
Gasmouloi (Greek, half-breeds), 252, 253
Gaston, *see* Baghrās; *see also* Adam
Gaston VI, viscount of Béarn 1173–1215, count of Bigorre 1196–1215: 297–299

Gaston VII, great-nephew of Gaston VI; viscount of Béarn 1229–1290: 510
Gata, Cape, 612
Gaza, 479, 480, 506, 523, 553, 562, 573, 709, 710, 713, 742, 745; battle (1239), 473 note, 475–477, 479, 484, 552, 761; battle (1244), 489, 550, 563, 674, 709, 761, *and see* Ḥarbīyah
Gebhard II, count of Dollnstein (in 1189), 92, 93
Gelasius II (John Coniulo), pope 1118–1119: 132
Gelnhausen, 770; diet at (1195), 118, 119
Genghis Khan (Temüjin), Great Khan of the Mongols 1206–1227: 421, 672, 716, 717, 748
Genoa, 57, 58, 165, 230, 309, 334, 335, 402, 471, 591, 609, 760; archbishop of, 609; client city of, 21; crusaders from, 65, 68, 409, 503, 516; government of, 8, 9, 104, 125, 132, 138, 155, 161, 165, 170, 189, 190, 238, 348, 368, 492, 512, 549, 568, 570, 591, 592, 722, 751; individuals from, 291, 338, 354, 416, 492, 569; merchants from, 572; in Africa: 27 note; in Byzantine empire: 132, 138, 162, 230, 572; in Cilicia: 650; in Cyprus: 623; in Frankish Greece: 243, 251; in Sicily: 436; in Syria: 230, 381, 452, 534, 548, 553, 559, 560, 568–570, 574, 579, 582, 585, 588, 590–593, 602, 615; ships from, 53, 56, 57, 96, 161, 219, 226, 230, 243, 246, 254, 263, 353, 492, 511, 514, 515, 549, 569, 592, 613, 620, 623, 723; trade with, 524
Genua, 215
Geoffrey, bishop of Carpentras (to 1211 ?), 286
Geoffrey III, son of Rotrou III; count of Perche 1191–1202: 159, 164
Geoffrey of Argentan, English crusader, 466
Geoffrey of Briel, nephew of William II of Achaea; baron of Karytaina 1255–1275: 245, 246, 258; wife of, *see* Isabel de la Roche
Geoffrey of Donjon, master of the Hospital 1193–1202: 525, 533
Geoffrey of Lusignan, son of Hugh VIII; count of Jaffa 1191–1193 (d. after 1197), 48, 52, 63, 65, 68, 71
Geoffrey of Sargines, seneschal of Jerusalem 1254 ?–1269, bailie 1259–1263: 508, 567, 569–571, 574–576, 579
Geoffrey of Tournai, baron of Kalavryta 1260–1263 (titular to 1283), 259
Geoffrey of Villehardouin, marshal of Champagne, chronicler (d. *c.* 1213), 150, 158–160, 164, 166–172, 174, 175, 202, 237
Geoffrey I of Villehardouin, nephew of Geoffrey the chronicler; prince of Achaea 1209–*c.* 1229: 202, 207, 208, 237, 239–242, 244, 248, 760, 761; wife of, *see* Elizabeth (of Chappes)
Geoffrey II of Villehardouin, son of Geoffrey I; prince of Achaea *c.* 1229–1246: 213, 219, 222, 240, 242–244, 761; wife of, *see* Agnes of Courtenay
Geoffrey Plantagenet, illegitimate son of Henry II of England; archbishop of York 1191–1212: 79
George (Gēorg: East Armenian), Armenian anti-catholicus, 633
George, son of Dietrich; count of Wied 1189–1218 ?: 395
George I, tsar of Bulgaria 1280–1292 (d. 1295), 260
George Ghisi, grandson of Andrew; lord of Tenos 1303–1311: 271
George of Antioch, Sicilian admiral 1126–*c.* 1150: xviii, 14, 19, 21–24, 26, 29
Georgia, 652, 663–665, 672, 680, 682, 683, 696; king of, *see* David II 1089–1125; queen of, *see* Tamar 1184–1212; troops from, 751, 760
Geraki, barony of, 250, 253, 258
Gerald (of Malemort), archbishop of Bordeaux 1227–1261: 323
Gerald (of Lausanne), bishop of Valence 1220–1225, patriarch of Jerusalem 1225–1239: 446, 447, 451, 452, 455–462, 545, 547, 702 note
Geralda, sister of Aimery of Montréal; countess of Lavaur (d. 1211), 293
Gerard (of La Barthe), archbishop of Auch 1173–1192: 56
Gerard of Malberg, master of the Teutonic Knights 1241–1244: 562
Gerard of Remy, French knight, 264
Gerard of Ridefort, master of the Temple 1185–1189: 45, 50
Germanus, Orthodox patriarch at Nicaea 1222–1240: 218, 626, 627
Germanus Pesimandrus, Orthodox archbishop of Cyprus *c.* 1254–after 1260: 627, 628
Germany, 10, 16 note, 89–91, 115–119, 132, 133, 139, 155, 166, 327, 330, 345, 352, 355–360, 364, 372, 373, 378, 381, 431, 433, 435, 439, 450, 490, 610, 717; clergy of, 164, 353, 440; crusaders from, on second crusade, 90; on third crusade, 50, 65, 88, 90–94, 97–116, 148, 645, 680, 759; on crusade of 1197: 118–122, 529, 530, 608, 695, 759; on fourth crusade, 167, 184, 185, 238; on children's crusade, 331–334, 337, 760; on fifth crusade, 385, 386, 388, 394, 395, 399, 400, 407, 409, 417, 427, 432, 434; on political crusades, 350; with Frederick II, 444, 446–448, 450, 452, 456, 458, 461, 542; emperors of, 8, 29, 279, *and see* Henry IV 1056–1106, Henry V 1106–1125, Lothair II 1125–1137, Frederick I 1152–1190, Henry VI 1190–1197, Otto IV 1201–1211, Frederick II 1211–1250, Conrad IV 1250–1254, *and* Holy Roman empire; kings in, *see* Conrad III 1138–1152, Philip (of Swabia) 1197–1208, Henry VII 1220–1232, Henry Raspe

1246–1247, William (of Holland) 1247–1256; magnates of, 348, 354, 430, 461; *see also* Alamannia
Germiyan, Turkoman state, 729
Gerona, 372
Gertrude (of Andechs), daughter of Berthold IV of Meran; 1st wife of Andrew II of Hungary *c.* 1205–1213: 388 note
Gervase (of Chichester), abbot (of St. Just of Thenailles), general of Premonstratensians 1210–1220, bishop of Séez 1220–1228: 384–386
Gervase, archbishop of Heraclea, Latin patriarch of Constantinople 1215–1219: 198
Gévaudan, 318
Ghazan ("Maḥmūd"), son of Arghun; Il-khan of Persia 1295–1304: 656, 657, 720–722
Ghaznah, 668, 717
Ghaznavids, Turkish dynasty in Afghanistan and India 962–1186: 668, 669, 671
Ghibellines, pro-Hohenstaufen faction, 345, 365, 545, 548
Ghisi, *see* Andrew, George, Jeremiah
Ghūr, 668
Ghūrids, Afghan dynasty in Persia and Afghanistan 1149–1215: 668, 671, 672
al-Ghūṭah, 710
Gianitsa, 264
Gibelcar, *see* ʿAkkār; *see also* Isabel
Gibelet, *see* Jubail; *see also* William
Gibraltar, Strait of, 396
Giguer, 650
Gilbert Horal (or Roral), master of the Temple 1193–*c.* 1198: 525
Gilbert Marshal, earl of Pembroke 1234–1241: 482, 483
Gilbert (dalle Carceri) of Verona, son of William I; triarch of central Euboea 1275–1279: 256, 257, 259
Giles, bishop of Damietta 1249–1254, archbishop of Tyre 1254–*c.* 1265: 373
Gisors, 48
Glarentsa, 249, 251, 266, 273; mint of, 259
Gloucester, countess of, 66; earldom of, 54
Gnostics, early Christian sect, 280, 329 note
Gobidaṛa, 633
Godfrey, bishop of Langres *c.* 1140–1164: 12
Godfrey (of Spitzenberg, count of Helfenstein), bishop of Würzburg 1184–1190: 90–93, 105, 115
Godfrey III, duke of Lower Lorraine and count of Louvain 1142–1190: 93
Godfrey of Bouillon, brother of Baldwin I of Jerusalem; advocate of the Holy Sepulcher 1099–1100: 185
Godfrey of Wiesenbach, knight from Franconian Rhineland, 91, 111, 112
Gök river, 633
Gökböri, Muẓaffar-ad-Dīn, emir of Irbil *c.* 1191–*c.* 1233 (d. 1242), 673, 700, 701
Golden Horde, Mongol-Turkish force, 575, 719, 720, 723, 726, 748, 751; rulers of, *see* Batu Khan 1243–1256, Berke Khan 1256–1266; *see also* Kïpchaks
Golden Horn, 151, 178–180, 231
Gonesse, *see* Philip of Lagonesse
Good Hope, Cape of, 735
Gournay (-en-Bray), *see* Hugh
Göyük, son of Ögödai; Great Khan of the Mongols 1246–1248: 507, 615, 652, 722
Gozo, 21
Gradenigo, *see* Marco, Paul
Graditz (Gradets), 106
Grailly, *see* John
Gran, 94; archbishop of, 387
Grandison, *see* Otto
Grandpré, count of, 469
Grapella (dalle Carceri) of Verona, nephew of William I; triarch of northern Euboea 1255–1264: 245
Gratian, Francis, compiler of canon law (*c.* 1140), 345, 347
Graville (-Sainte Honorine), lord of, 469
Greece, before 1203: 5, 9, 13, 14, 24, 127; 1203–1311: 175, 206–208, 216, 221, 235–274, 367, 369, 565 note, 579, 621; map of, 234; *see also* Byzantine empire
Greek church, union with Armenian church, 641, 647, 649; union with Latin church, 171, 180, 181, 196, 228, 232, 369, 509, 584, 762; in Byzantine empire, 128, 130, 143, 144, 147, 173, 218; in Latin empire, 183, 196, 197, 211, 608; in Frankish Greece, 251, 252; in Cyprus, 621–629; in Syria, 127, 566, 578; and Mongols, 573; *see also* Orthodox Christians, Patriarchs
Greek language, transliteration and nomenclature, xix
Greeks (or "Byzantines"), 125, 136, 138, 139, 142, 149, 150, 170, 177, 196, 199–204, 209–211, 215, 217–232, 363, 369, 514, 570, 584, 615, 635, 637, 641, 761; of Cyprus, 601–603, 621, 622, 625–628; of Anatolia, 676–678, 681–683, 685, 725; and third crusade, 92, 98, 100, 101, 103, 106–110; and fourth crusade, 174, 176, 180–182, 184, 185; and fifth crusade, 427; in Latin empire, 189, 192, 193, 199, 203, 204, 206–211, 224, 230–232; in Frankish Greece, 237–239, 242, 245, 247, 252–267, 270–274; in Sicily, 5, 19; in Syria, 133, 526, 527, 533, 535, 537, 566; *see also* Orthodox Christians, Byzantine empire, Nicaea
Gregory III (Bahlavouni), Armenian catholicus 1133–1166: 641, 642
Gregory IV Dgha, nephew of Gregory III; Armenian catholicus 1173–1193: 645
Gregory VI Abirad, nephew of Gregory III; Armenian catholicus 1194–1203: 529, 647, 648
Gregory VII, Armenian catholicus 1292–1307: 657, 658
Gregory VII (Hildebrand), pope 1073–1085: 345

Gregory VIII (Albert di Morra), pope 1187–1187: 89
Gregory IX (Ugolino de' Conti de Segni), cousin of Innocent III; pope 1227–1241: 319, 322, 336, 361, 547, 623, 626, 627, 760, and Latin empire, 198, 216, 217, 219–222, 243, 466–468, 482; and Frederick II, 216, 221, 348–354, 430, 435, 442, 443, 445–448, 450–452, 455–458, 460–462, 465, 467–469, 482, 543, 551, 611, 760, 761; and crusade of 1239: 219, 243, 463, 465–468, 470, 482, 483; cousin of, 565
Gregory X (Theobald Visconti, archdeacon of Liége), pope 1271–1276: 368, 369, 583, 584, 762
Gregory of Montelongo, papal legate in Lombardy (d. 1269), 355
Grenier, *see* Reginald, Balian, Julian
Gritsena, barony of, 250
Guelders, count of, 50, 51, 65, 115
Guelfs, anti-Hohenstaufen faction, 545, 551, 553, 610, *and see* Welfs
Guigues, count of Forez 1203–1241, of Nevers 1226–1241: 469, 481
Guines, 331
Guiscard, *see* Robert Guiscard
Gümüshtigin Ghāzī, son of Malik-Ghāzī; Dānishmendid ruler 1105 ?–*c.* 1134: 133, 636, 676, 677
Guy, abbot of Les Vaux-de-Cernay, bishop of Carcassonne 1211–1223: 174, 277 note
Guy, nephew of Matthew of Montmorency; castellan of Coucy, 158 note, 160
Guy, Cistercian monk, papal commissioner, 283
Guy II, count of Auvergne 1195–1224, of Rodez 1208–1209: 287 note
Guy (of Dampierre-le-Château), son of Margaret II; co-count of Flanders 1251–1279, count 1279–1304, count of Namur 1263–1304: 510
Guy de Charpigny of Lille, baron of Vostitsa 1278–1295, bailie of Achaea 1289–1289: 259, 261, 264
Guy I de la Roche, nephew of Othon; lord of half of Thebes, lord of Athens 1225–1263: 232, 241–247, 269
Guy II de la Roche, son of William; duke of Athens 1287–1308, bailie of Achaea 1307–1308: 261, 263–267, 269, 271, 273; wife of, *see* Mahaut of Hainault
Guy I Embriaco, son of Hugh III; lord of Jubail 1186–1187, 1197–1241: 412, 544, 700
Guy II Embriaco, son of Henry; lord of Jubail *c.* 1271–1282: 587, 588
Guy of (Le-Vieil-)Dampierre, knight from Champagne, 50, 51
Guy of Dramelay, baron of Chalandritsa 1278–1288, bailie of Achaea 1282–1285: 259, 261
Guy of Ibelin, son of John I; constable of Cyprus (in 1249), 560, 615
Guy of Ibelin, son of John, of Jaffa; count of Jaffa 1266–1268 (titular 1268–1304), 577
Guy of Ibelin, son of seneschal Baldwin, 652 note; wife of, *see* Maria (Heṭoumid)
Guy of Lévis, lord of Mirepoix, 294 note, 320
Guy of Lucy, lord of Puylaurens, 294 note
Guy of Lusignan, son of Hugh VIII; king of Jerusalem 1186–1190: 45, 46, 48, 50–53, 65, 66, 81, 85, 443, 523; and third crusade, 63–68, 71, 74, 77, 339, 600 note, 601, 759; ruler of Cyprus 1192–1194: 81, 82, 148, 523–525, 602–604, 607, 618, 620, 621, 624, 759; daughters of, 65; wife of, *see* Sibyl (of Jerusalem)
Guy "of Lusignan", son of Hugh III; constable of Cyprus (d. 1303), 589; wife of, *see* Eschiva of Ibelin
Guy of Montfort, son of Simon IV; count of Bigorre 1216–1220: 311, 313
Guy of Montfort, brother of Simon IV; lord of Castres (d. 1229), 294 note, 306, 309–313, 472; wife of, *see* Helvis of Ibelin
Guy Pallavicini, marquis of Bodonitsa 1204–after 1237: 238, 242

Haakon V, king of Norway 1217–1263: 490
Hadrian IV (Nicholas Breakspear), pope 1154–1159: 29, 137
al-Ḥāfiẓ, grandson of al-Mustanṣir; Fāṭimid caliph at Cairo 1130–1149: 22, 27
Ḥāfiẓ, Persian poet (d. 1388), 724
al-Ḥāfiẓ Arslan, son of al-'Ādil I Saif-ad-Dīn; Aiyūbid lord of Qal'at Ja'bar 1202–*c.* 1242: 696
Hafsa, 106
Ḥafṣids, Berber dynasty in Tunisia 1230–1574: *see* Muḥammad I 1249–1277
Hagia Sophia (Greek, holy wisdom), cathedral in Constantinople, under Greeks to 1204: 96, 109, 128, 144, 181, 201; under Latins 1204–1268: 183, 189, 195, 196, 198, 204, 205, 218; under Greeks after 1268: 232
Haifa, 394, 524, 536, 575, 748, *and see* Reginald; lord of, *see* Pagan
Haimo (of Briançon), archbishop of Tarentaise 1179–*c.* 1210: 92, 93, 104
Hainault, 204, 341, 360, *and see* Florent, Isabel, Yolanda; counts of, 155, 159, 189, 262; crusaders from, 192
Hajjī Bektash, Turkish mystic (d. after 1330), 732
al-Ḥākim, descendant of al-Mustarshid; 'Abbāsid "caliph" at Cairo 1262–1302: 747, 754
Ḥalbah, 576
Halberstadt, bishops of, *see* Gardolph, Conrad
Hallermund, count of, 92, 115
Halmyros, 207, 210, 271
Hamadan, 670
Hamah, 67, 547, 693, 696, 700, 703, 705; qadi of, 702; rulers of, *see* Aiyūbids (1174–1284); troops from, 595, 596, 699

Hameln, 340, 341, 771
Ḥammādids, Berber dynasty in Algeria 1014–1152: 17, 19, 25, 28, *and see* al-'Azīz 1105–1121
Hamo "the Stranger", English crusader (d. 1273), 584; wife of, *see* Isabel of Ibelin
Ḥanafites, Moslem legal school, 686
Hannapes, *see* Nicholas
Harbīyah, 454; battle (1244), 489, 563–565, 614, 709 note, *and see* Gaza
Ḥārim, 640, 641, 643
Harran, 684
Hartwig (of Utlede), archbishop of Bremen 1184–1207: 120
Hasan, son of Khoul Khachig; Armenian in Byzantine service, 633
al-Ḥasan, son of 'Alī; Zīrid emir at Mahdia 1121–1148: 20, 21 note, 22, 24
Hattin, 771; battle (1187), 45, 46, 52, 85, 164, 390, 415, 428, 452, 522, 564, 600 note, 737, 759, plate 2A
Hausen, *see* Frederick
Hauteville, house of, 5, 6, 8 note, 11, 34, 36, 41, *and see* Tancred
Hayo of Fivelgo, Frisian crusader, 401
Hebron, 552, 553, 710
Hejaz, 735
Helena, daughter of John Asen of Bulgaria and Maria; wife of Theodore II Lascaris (after 1235), 216, 219, 220
Helena, daughter of Uroš II of Rascia; wife of Bela II of Hungary 1130–1141: 131
Helena Angelina Comnena, daughter of John I of Neopatras; wife of William de la Roche of Athens 1275–1287, regent of Athens 1287–1296, 2nd wife of Hugh of Brienne 1291–1296 (d. after 1299), 252, 263
Helena Angelina Comnena, daughter of Michael II of Epirus; 2nd wife of Manfred of Sicily 1259–1266 (d. 1271), 257
Hellespont, *see* Dardanelles
Hellin (of Wavrin), seneschal of Flanders, 65
Helvis of Ibelin, daughter of Balian II; wife of Reginald of Sidon, wife of Guy of Montfort (after 1202), 472, 559, 560
Henneberg, count of, 92, 115
Henry (of Septala), archbishop of Milan 1213–1230: 421
Henry (of Horburg), bishop of Basel 1181–1191: 92, 93
Henry, bishop of Prague 1182–1197, duke of Bohemia 1193–1197: 120
Henry (of Hasenburg), bishop of Strassburg 1181–1190: 90
Henry, cardinal-bishop of Albano 1179–1188, papal legate to France and Rhinelands, 89, 90, 282 note
Henry, count of Altenburg (in 1189), 50, 115
Henry I, count of Bar 1170–1191: 50
Henry II, son of Theobald I; count of Bar 1214–1239: 466, 467, 469, 471, 475, 476
Henry I, grandson of Stephen of Chartres and Blois; count of Champagne 1152–1181: 159; wife of, *see* Mary (of France)
Henry II, son of Henry I; count of Champagne and count-palatine of Troyes 1181–1197: 53–55, 65, 68, 74, 78–81, 85, 759; ruler of kingdom of Jerusalem 1192–1197: 81, 82, 84, 159, 443, 470, 523–530, 602–604, 646, 759; daughter of, 474, 547, 559, 605; wife of, *see* Isabel (of Jerusalem)
Henry II, count of Cuyk 1166–1204: 92
Henry VI, count of Grandpré 1231–after 1287: 469
Henry (Pescatore), count of Malta, imperial admiral, 427, 436, 451, 454
Henry I, count of Rodez 1214–1227: 303
Henry, count of (Upper) Salm 1163–1204: 105
Henry II, count of Sayn 1172–1203: 92
Henry I, count of Sponheim 1191–1197: 92, 105
Henry, count of Vöhringen (in 1189), 92, 93
Henry I, son of Godfrey III of Lower Lorraine; duke of Brabant and count of Louvain 1190–1235: 120, 121, 173 note, 431, 530
Henry III, duke of Limburg 1167–1221: 93, 431
Henry IV, son of Walram IV; duke of Limburg 1226–1247: 446, 448, 454, 542
Henry IV, emperor of Germany 1056 (crowned 1084)–1106: 345
Henry V, son of Henry IV; emperor of Germany 1106 (crowned 1111)–1125: 132
Henry VI, son of Frederick I; 55, 94, 96, 103, 104, 109, 147, 148; Hohenstaufen emperor of Germany 1190 (crowned 1191)–1197: 41, 59, 116, 130, 166, 346, 759; king of Sicily 1194–1197: 41, 88, 117, 149, 166, 185, 436; and crown of Cyprus, 82, 118, 119, 149, 528, 604, 610, 647; and crown of Cilicia, 119, 149, 528, 534, 535, 647, 648 note, 649; and crusade of 1197: xvii, 6 note, 42, 117–121, 149, 153, 528–530, 604, 608; wife of, *see* Constance (of Sicily)
Henry VII, son of Frederick II and Constance; Hohenstaufen duke of Swabia 1216–1235, king of Germany 1220–1232 (d. 1242), 433, 434, 451
Henry, son of Baldwin V of Hainault: 159, 182, 192–195, 203; Latin emperor of Romania 1205–1216: xviii, 195, 202, 204–212, 214, 215, 224, 232, 239, 240, 760; wives of, *see* Agnes of Montferrat, Maria (of Bulgaria)
Henry II, Plantagenet king of England 1154–1189: 47–49, 55, 64, 88, 89, 93, 159, 759; legacy to, 40, 41, 59; and heretics, 282, 327 note; wife of, *see* Eleanor of Aquitaine
Henry III, son of John; Plantagenet king of England 1216–1272: 221, 321, 349, 365, 439, 482, 483, 490, 510, 583; and Lan-

guedoc, 316, 318 note, 322, 323; and Sicily, 360, 362; letters to, 455, 468; sons of, 360, 582
Henry XII ("the Lion"), nephew of Welf VI; Welf duke of Saxony 1142–1180, of Bavaria 1156–1180, of Brunswick 1180–1195: 89, 90, 115, 121
Henry IV, son of Henry "the Lion"; Welf duke of Brunswick and count-palatine of the Rhine 1195–1227: 120, 432, 433
Henry Dandolo, *see* Enrico Dandolo
Henry Embriaco, son of Guy I; lord of Jubail 1241–*c.* 1271: 570
Henry Filangieri, brother of Richard (d. after 1231), 547, 548
Henry of Antioch, son of Bohemond IV; bailie of Jerusalem 1263–1264 (d. 1276), 571, 606, 607; wife of, *see* Isabel of Lusignan
Henry of Dietz, count of Birstein 1189–1234: 91, 92
Henry of Dreux, son of count Robert II; archbishop of Rheims 1227–1240: 466, 467
Henry of Kalden, marshal of Frederick I and Henry VI, 94, 102, 120
Henry I of Lusignan, son of Hugh I; king of Cyprus 1218–1253: 451, 460, 464, 548, 565, 567, 605, 606, 610–615, 618, 619, 626, 652 note, 760, 761; regent of Jerusalem 1246–1253: 559, 560, 580, 606, 613; sisters of, 571; wives of, *see* Alice of Montferrat, Stephanie (of Lampron), Plaisance (of Antioch)
Henry II "of Lusignan", son of Hugh III; king of Cyprus 1285–1324, of Jerusalem 1286–1291 (titular 1291–1324), 589, 590, 592–597, 607, 617, 623, 656, 762
Henry of Saarbrücken, uncle of Simon II; count of Zweibrücken 1180–1225: 92
Henry of Segusio ("Hostiensis"), Italian canonist (d. 1271), 345, 356
Henry Raspe IV, son of Hermann I; landgrave of Thuringia 1242–1247, king in Germany 1246–1247: 355, 357
Heraclea (in Thrace), 191; archbishop of, 198
Heraclea (-Cybistra), 635, 645
Heraclea, Pontic, 200, 205
Hérault river, 288
Hereford, prior of, 79
Heresy, heretics, 445, 470, *and see* Albigensian (Catharist), Bogomil, Massalian, Neo-Manichean, Paulician, Waldensian
Hermann (of Katzenellenbogen), bishop of Münster 1174–1203: 92, 93, 95, 96, 104, 109, 120
Hermann I, brother of Louis III; landgrave of Thuringia 1190–1218: 120
Hermann IV, margrave of Baden 1160–1190: 92, 93, 115
Hermann of Salza, master of the Teutonic Knights *c.* 1210–1239: 542, 551, 650; and fifth crusade, 389, 427; and crusade of Frederick II, 438–440, 442–444, 446, 447, 452, 455–458, 461
Hers river, 288
Hervey of Donzi, son-in-law of Peter of Courtenay; count of Nevers 1199–1223: 287, 289, 417
Hetoum ("Hayton"), son of Adām of Gaston; Armenian historian (d. after 1307), 630 note
Hetoum (Heghi), son of Ōshin II; Hetoumid lord of Lampron 1168–1218?: 639, 642, 644, 645, 650; wife of, 639, 642
Hetoum I, son-in-law of Leon II; king of Cilician Armenia 1226–1269: 550, 567, 634, 651–654, 658, 760; and Mongols, 507, 572, 573, 575, 576, 652–654; wife of, *see* Isabel (Roupenid)
Hetoum II, son of Leon III; king of Cilician Armenia 1289–1292, 1294–1296, 1299–1305 (d. 1307), 598 note, 630 note, 655–658
Hetoum of Sasoun, Armenian commander (d. 1194), 527; wife of, *see* Alice (Roupenid)
Hetoumids, Armenian dynasty in Cilicia 1226–1342: 540, 633–635, 637, 641, 644, 652, 659, 721, *and see* Hetoum I 1226–1269, Leon III 1269–1289, Hetoum II 1289–1292, 1294–1296, 1299–1305, Toros III 1292–1294, Sempad 1296–1298, Constantine 1298–1299, Leon IV 1305–1307; *see also* Constantine (3), Euphemia, Hetoum, Isabel, Maria (2), Nersēs, Ōshin (2), Pagouran, Pazouni, Rita (3), Sempad (3), Shahnshah, Stephanie, Toros, Vasil
Hierapolis, 110
Hildesheim, bishops of, 120, 444, 445, 604, 647
Hindu Kush range, 668
Hindus, religious community, 668, 671
Ḥiṣn Kaifā, 684, 693 note, 703, 711; lords of, *see* Artukids, Aiyūbids
Hodegetria, icon, 232
Hohenburg, *see* Berthold
Hohenstaufens, imperial dynasty in Germany and Italy 1138–1268: 59, 88, 117, 166, 170, 220, 431, 445, 508, 513, 517, 531, 547, 584, 759, *and see* Conrad III, Conrad IV, Conradin, Constance (2), Frederick I, Frederick II, Frederick, Manfred, Philip; "crusades" against, 345, 347, 357–367, 370–373
Holland, counts of, *see* Florent III, William I, William II, John II of Avesnes
Holstein, count of, 92, 115, 121
Holy Land, *see* Palestine
Holy Roman empire, 88, 121, 212, 285, 317 note, 354, 372, 387, 430, 435, 543, 545; emperors of, before 1257: *see* emperors of Germany; after 1257: *see* Richard Plantagenet (of Cornwall) 1257–1272 and Alfonso X of Castile 1257–1273, Rudolph I 1273–1291; vassals of, 159, 164
Holy Sepulcher, church at Jerusalem, under Latins: 33, 456, 458, 545, 612; under

Moslems: 47, 99, 178, 326 note, 331, 334, 379, 382, 562; canons of, 525
Homs, 493, 532, 561, 576, 586, 655, 657, 674, 693, 696, 700, 701, 705, 707, 710, 711, 751, 762; rulers of, *see* Aiyūbids (1174–1263); troops from, 562, 563, 699, 709, 710
Honorius II (Lambert of Fagnano), pope 1124–1130: 7, 132
Honorius III (Cencio Savelli), pope 1216–1227: 462, 540, 541, 651 note, 760; and Frederick II, 348, 432–445, 542, 760; and Latin empire, 198, 212–215; and Frankish Greece, 241, 242; and Albigensian crusade, 277 note, 312–316, 318 note, 319; and fifth crusade, 380, 381, 384, 386, 396, 402, 403, 416 note, 420–424, 538, 608, 609; and Cyprus, 623, 625, 626 note
Honorius IV (Jacob Savelli), pope 1285–1287: 722, 762
Hospital of St. John, at Jerusalem, knights of, *see* Knights Hospitaller; masters of, *see* Roger of Les Moulins 1177–1187, Geoffrey of Donjon 1193–1202, Garin of Montaigu 1207–1227, Bertrand of Thessy 1228–1230, Peter of Vieille Bride 1239–1242, William of Châteauneuf 1243–1258, Nicholas Lorgne 1277–1284, John of Villiers 1285–1293; other masters were Armengaud of Aspe 1188–1190, Warner of Nablus 1190–1192, Alfonso of Portugal 1203–1206, Geoffrey le Rat 1206–1207, Guerin 1230–1236, Bertrand of Comps 1236–1239, Hugh Revel 1258–1277
Hoveden, *see* Howden; *see also* Roger
Howden, *see* Roger of Hoveden
Hromgla, 632, 641, 642, 656, 755
Hubert, *see* Oberto
Hubert Walter, nephew of Ranulf de Glanville; bishop of Salisbury 1189–1193, archbishop of Canterbury 1193–1205: 58, 64, 65, 71, 85
al-Hudhbānī, Ḥusām-ad-Dīn, ibn-abī-ʿAlī; Kurdish vizir (d. before 1257), 712, 739–742
Hugh, archdeacon of Lyons, 307
Hugh (de la Tour), bishop of Clermont (in Auvergne) 1227–1249: 350
Hugh (Pierrepont), bishop of Liége 1200–1229: 159
Hugh, bishop of Sées 1229–1240: 467, 468
Hugh I, count of Champagne 1089–after 1125: 237
Hugh IV, count of St. Pol 1174–1205, ruler of Demotica 1204–1205: 159, 164, 173 note, 174, 180 note, 182, 192
Hugh III, duke of Burgundy 1162–1192: 54, 56, 60, 70–72, 74, 75, 78, 79, 81-83, 85, 522
Hugh IV, son of Odo III; duke of Burgundy 1218–1273, titular king of Thessalonica 1266–1273, and crusade of 1239: 466, 469–471, 475, 476, 481, 484, 552; and crusade of 1249: 244, 499; and Tunisian crusade, 510
Hugh, stepson of Raymond III of Tripoli; titular lord of Tiberias 1187–1197 (d. 1205), 529, 530, 534; wife of, *see* Margaret of Ibelin
Hugh de Lacy, English knight, lord of Laurac, 294 note
Hugh de Puiset, bishop of Durham 1153–1195, justiciar to Richard I, 54
Hugh III Embriaco, lord of Jubail 1184–1186: 529; wife of, *see* Stephanie of Milly
Hugh Ferreus (or Ferus), viguier of Marseilles, 336–339
Hugh of Brienne, son of Walter IV; count of Brienne and Lecce 1250–1296, bailie of Athens 1291–1296: 263, 264, 269, 571, 579, 606, 607, 620; wives of, *see* Isabel de la Roche, Helena Angelina Comnena
Hugh of Champlitte, nephew of William I; bailie of Achaea 1208–1209: 239
Hugh of Coligny, French knight, 238
Hugh of Fagiano, Latin archbishop of Nicosia 1251–1267: 627, 628
Hugh of Gournay, English commander, 69
Hugh VIII of Lusignan, lord of Lusignan 1152?–1165?: 607
Hugh X of Lusignan, nephew of Guy and Aimery; count (II) of Marche and (I) of Angoulême 1219–1248: 316, 319
Hugh XI of Lusignan, son of Hugh X; count (III) of Marche and (II) of Angoulême 1248–1260: 316
Hugh I of Lusignan, son of Aimery and Eschiva; king of Cyprus 1205–1218: 384, 388, 393, 532, 604 note, 605, 609, 611, 624, 760; half-sister of, 393, 540; wife of, *see* Alice (of Champagne-Jerusalem)
Hugh II of Lusignan, son of Henry I and Plaisance; king of Cyprus 1253–1267: 567, 570, 571, 579, 580, 584, 606, 607, 761, 762; wife of, *see* Isabel of Ibelin
Hugh III "of Lusignan", son of Henry of Antioch and Isabel of Lusignan; regent of Cyprus 1261–1267: 571, 606; king 1267–1284: 579, 607, 613, 615–617, 762; regent of Jerusalem 1264–1269: 571, 575, 579, 607, 615; king 1269–1284: 579, 580, 582–586, 588, 589, 596, 597, 613, 616, 762; physician of (d. 1283), 589; wife of, *see* Isabel of Ibelin
Hugh IV "of Lusignan", son of Guy; king of Cyprus 1324–1359: 607
Hugh of Noyers, bishop of Auxerre 1183–1206: 212
Hugh ("le Roux") of Sully, Angevin commander, 260, 593
Hugh Raymond, bishop of Riez 1202–1223, papal legate in Languedoc, 285, 297
Hugo Falcandus (possibly admiral Eugenius), Sicilian historian, 3 note, 25, 31 note
Hugo Lercari, Genoese admiral, 492
Hulagu (Hülegü), brother of Möngke; Il-khan of Persia 1258–1265: 568, 571–573,

575, 578, 654, 655, 714, 717–721, 726, 744, 751, 761, 762; wife of, *see* Toquz Khātūn
Hulah, Lake, 391
Humbert V, lord of Beaujeu 1216–1250: 318, 319, 467, 468, 501
Humphrey of Montfort, son of Philip; lord of Beirut 1282–1284, of Tyre 1283–1284: 580, 582, 584, 586, 588, 589; wife of, *see* Eschiva of Ibelin
Humphrey III of Toron, lord of Montréal 1168–1173: 643; wife of, *see* Stephanie of Milly
Humphrey IV, son of Humphrey III; lord of Toron 1179–1198: 63, 66, 81, 165; wife of, *see* Isabel (of Jerusalem)
Hundred Years War, 672
Hungary, 47, 91, 98, 127, 131, 136, 139, 141, 146–149, 167, 168, 212, 213, 219–221, 352, 357, 368, 369, 387, 394, 609, 717, 760; crusaders from, 93, 352, 386, 388, 392, 538, 760; third crusade in, 49, 94, 95, 147; kings of, 648, *and see* Bela II 1131–1141, Stephen III 1162–1173, Bela III 1173–1196, Emeric I 1196–1204, Andrew II 1205–1235, Bela IV 1235–1270; "Master of", 341, 342; princesses of, *see* Margaret, Maria, Piriska
Huntingdon, earl of, 482
Hydra, 254
Hyères, 508

Ibelin, house of, 443, 460, 477, 489, 544–553, 559, 560, 568, 569, 580, 605, 606, 609–614, 616, 621, *and see* Baldwin (2), Balian (3), Eschiva (2), Guy (3), Helvis, Isabel (2), James, John (4), Margaret, Philip (2)
Ibn-abī-Dīnār, Arabic historian (d. *c.* 1700), 26
Ibn-ʿAbs, Sicilian emir and pirate (d. 1222), 337–339
Ibn-al-Athīr, Arabic historian (d. 1234), 25, 390, 421, 428, 662
Ibn-al-Furāt, Arabic historian (d. 1405), 396
Ibn-al-Khuwaiyī, qadi, 656
Ibn-as-Salʿūs, Shams-ad-Dīn, vizir of Mamluks (to 1293), 754
Ibn-Baṭṭūṭah, Arab traveler (d. 1378), 732
Ibn-Bībī, Persian chronicler (d. after 1282), 732
Ibn-Ḥassūl, Arabic historian (d. 1058), 736
Ibn-ʿIdhārī, Arabic historian (d. *c.* 1300), 23
Ibn-Khaldūn, Arabic historian (d. 1406), 30, 757
Ibn-Maimūn, *see* Muḥammad ibn-Maimūn
Ibn-Wāṣil, Arabic historian (in 1250), 739, 748 note
Iconium, 192, 201, 223, 550, 632, 652, 676, 677, 679–681, 687, 688, 690, 692, 728–730; third crusade at, 111–115, 759; sultans at, 91, 132, 140, 141, 147, *and see* Selchükids of Rūm
Iesi, 117
Ifrīqiyah, 17, *and see* Tunisia
Ignatius, Jacobite patriarch 1222–1252: 566
Īl-Ghāzī, Artukid ruler of Mardin 1107–1122: 663
Īl-khans, Mongol dynasty in Persia 1258–1349: 653, 655, 719, 720, 723–727, 730, 731, 748, 762, *and see* Hulagu 1258–1265, Abagha 1265–1282, Tegüder 1282–1284, Arghun 1284–1291, Gaikhatu 1291–1295, Baidu 1295–1295, Ghazan 1295–1304, Öljaitu 1304–1316, Abū-Saʿīd 1316–1335; *see also* Mengü-Timur
Īldegiz (Eldigüz), Shams-ad-Dīn, atabeg of Azerbaijan *c.* 1137–1172: 662
Île de France, 158, 167, 289, 294
Ill river, 333
ʿImad-ad-Dīn Aḥmad, son of al-Mashṭūb; emir of Nablus, 408, 699
ʿImād-ad-Dīn Zengi II, brother of ʿIzz-ad-Dīn; Zengid lord of Sinjar *c.* 1170–1197: 694
Imām (Arabic, leader), 30
India, 449, 668, 671, 703
Indian Ocean, 723
Indus river, 672, 717
Innocent II (Gregory Papareschi), pope 1130–1143: 7, 9, 132 note
Innocent III (Lothair de' Conti de Segni), pope 1198–1216: xviii, 149, 153, 237, 334, 336, 462, 534, 536, 537, 604, 647, 650, 698, 759; and fourth crusade, xv, 154–159, 163–165, 169–176, 180, 185, 531, 608; and Latin empire, 195–198, 200, 201, 203, 204, 206, 211; and Albigensian crusade, 277, 282–287, 289 note, 291, 292, 297–299, 303–309, 344; and Hohenstaufens, 346–349, 430–432, 441; and fifth crusade, 308, 378–387, 391, 395, 538; great-niece of, 565
Innocent IV (Sinibaldo Fieschi), pope 1243-1254: 352, 373, 488, 560 note, 561, 566, 613, 623, 627, 722, 761; and Latin empire, 224–228; and Frederick II, 224, 225, 354–359, 441, 490, 613; and Sicily, 358–362
Inquisition, 277 note, 279, 324, 466
Ioannitsa ("Kaloyan"), brother of Asen and Peter; Vlach tsar of Bulgaria 1197–1204, king 1204–1207: 149, 201–205, 217, 760; wife of, 205
Ionian Islands, 13, 14 note, 15, 191, 235, 272
Ionian Sea, 13, 255
Iqṭāʿ (Arabic, land-grant), 686, 688, 731, 755
Iran, 662, 663, 667, 668, 670, 672, 676, 680, 686, 687, 691, 719, 720, 723–726, 730, 732; culture of, 665, 685, 689, 690, 724, 725, 729, 731; Mongols in, 717, 719, 720, 731, 761, 762, *and see* Īl-khans; religion of, 663; *see also* Persia
Iraq, 449, 571, 663, 665, 666, 672, 674, 739, 748; Ottomans in, 693 note; *see also* Mesopotamia

Irbil, lord of, 673, 700
Ireland, 352; lord of, 48
Irene Angelina, daughter of Alexius III, 179
Irene Angelina, daughter of Isaac II; wife of Roger (son of Tancred of Lecce) to 1193, wife of Philip of Swabia 1195–1208: 119, 149, 166, 171
Irene Angelina Comnena, daughter of Theodore of Epirus; 2nd wife of John Asen of Bulgaria 1240–1241: 222, 226
Irene Ducaena, wife of Alexius I Comnenus 1077–1118 (d. 1133?), 128
Irene Lascaris, daughter of Theodore I; 1st wife of John III Vatatzes (d. 1241), 214
Isaac II Angelus, Byzantine emperor 1185–1195: 37, 38, 46, 62, 88, 118, 119, 146–149, 162, 164, 600, 644, 759; and third crusade, 47, 91, 92, 94–109, 116, 117, 147, 148; and fourth crusade, 166, 169, 170, 173, 174; co-emperor 1203–1204: 150, 151, 179, 181, 182, 760; daughter of, 119, 166; sons of, 166, 168, 190; wife of, *see* Margaret (of Hungary)
Isaac Comnenus, great-nephew of Manuel I; ruler of Cyprus 1184–1191 (d. 1195), 37, 62–64, 146, 148, 600–602, 621, 643, 759; daughter of, 64; wife of, *see* Anna Angelina
Isabel, countess of Gloucester, 1st wife of John of England 1189–1199 (d. 1217), 66
Isabel, daughter of Amalric of Jerusalem and Maria Comnena; wife of Humphrey IV of Toron 1183–1190: 66, 165; 3rd wife of Conrad of Montferrat 1190–1192: 66, 80, 165, 523, 759; wife of Henry II of Champagne 1192–1197: 81, 474, 523, 547, 605, 759; 2nd wife of Aimery of Lusignan 1197–1205: 82, 530, 543, 559, 604, 611, 759; queen of Jerusalem 1190–*c.* 1206: 529, 532, 579, 580; son of, 532
Isabel, daughter of Baldwin V of Hainault; 1st wife of Philip II of France 1180–1190: 70
Isabel, daughter of Humphrey III of Toron; wife of Ṛoupen III of Armenia 1181–1187 (d. after 1198), 643
Isabel, daughter of James I of Aragon; 1st wife of Philip III of France 1262–1271: 517
Isabel (Plantagenet), daughter of John of England; 3rd wife of emperor Frederick II 1235–1241: 483
Isabel (Ṛoupenid), daughter of Leon II of Armenia; wife of Philip of Antioch 1222–1225, wife of Heṭoum I 1226–1251: 393, 540, 541, 634, 651, 659, 760
Isabel (Zabēl; Heṭoumid), daughter of Leon III of Armenia; wife of Amalric "of Lusignan" 1295–1310 (d. 1323), 656
Isabel (de Ray), wife of Othon de la Roche of Athens, 242
Isabel de la Roche, daughter of Guy I of Athens; wife of Geoffrey of Briel to 1275, 1st wife of Hugh of Brienne 1277–1279: 246, 269, 579
Isabel (Yolanda) of Brienne, daughter of John and Mary; 2nd wife of emperor Frederick II 1225–1228; princess of Jerusalem 1212–1225: 438, 442, 537, 541; queen 1225–1228: 442, 443, 451, 464, 544, 559, 611, 760
Isabel of Gibelcar ('Akkār), wife of Renart of Nephin (after 1203), 534
Isabel of Ibelin, daughter of Guy; wife of Hugh III of Cyprus (d. 1324), 580
Isabel of Ibelin, daughter of John II; wife of Hugh II of Cyprus 1264?–1267, wife of Hamo the Stranger 1272–1273; lady of Beirut 1264–1282: 580, 584, 586
Isabel of Lusignan, daughter of Hugh I of Cyprus; wife of Henry of Antioch 1233–1264, regent of Jerusalem 1263–1264: 571, 580, 606, 607
Isabel of Villehardouin, daughter of William II of Achaea and Anna; wife of Philip of Anjou 1271–1277, wife of Florent of Hainault 1289–1297, 1st wife of Philip of Savoy 1301–1311; princess of Achaea 1289–1306: 255, 256, 259, 261–269, 273, 762
Isabel Pallavicini, daughter of Guy; lady of Bodonitsa *c.* 1278–*c.* 1286: 259
Isauria, 645, 650, 726
Isenric, abbot of Admont, 92
Islam; *al-Islām* (Arabic, the submission, to God), xx; religion, 17, 397, 416, 461, 667, 689, 690, 718–720, 758; converts to, 506, 658, 720, 721, 729, 748, 751, 758
Islam; *dār al-Islām* (Arabic, abode of Islam), community of Moslems, before 1189: 4, 6, 18, 21, 28, 664, 668, 669; after 1189: 301, 506, 568, 666, 672, 721, 732, 747, 749
Ismā'īlites, Shī'ite Moslem sect, 559, 581, 665, 666, 698; *see also* Assassins
Istria: coast of, 116, 173; margrave of, 92
Italy, 58, 61, 64, 89, 160, 164, 167, 168, 170, 175, 195, 206, 214, 271, 272, 279, 334, 335, 347, 349, 373, 375, 570, 608, 610 note, 625, 760; Byzantines and, 5, 9, 25, 29, 125, 132, 136–138, 227; Normans and, 7–12, 21, 104, 125–127; Hohenstaufens and, 12, 59, 88, 90, 117–120, 137, 216, 221, 232, 256, 346–366, 435, 454, 456, 460, 468, 472, 483, 490, 530, 541, 542, 544, 546, 548, 549, 553, 611, 612; Angevins and, 255, 258, 261, 262, 268–270, 366–372, 509, 584, 588; bankers of, 492, 493, 504; crusaders from, 150, 166, 238, 396, 407, 409, 410, 412–415, 420, 421, 427, 594, 617; merchants from, 560, 569, 571, 592, 723, 730; ships from, 52, 53, 67, 109, 161, 434, 517, 592; trade with, 14, 36, 185, 273, 524, 694, 697
Ithaca, 239
Ivas, Turkoman tribe, 662, 674
Ivry (-sur-Seine), *see* Galeran

'Izz-ad-Dīn Mas'ūd, nephew of Nūr-ad-Dīn; Zengid ruler of Mosul 1180–1193: 694

Jabal Anṣārīyah, *see* Nuṣairī mountains
Jabal Nūr, 635
Jabala, 39, 423, 535, 547, 558, 703
Jacob, bishop of Patti *c.* 1220–1225: 442
Jacob Barozzi, lord of Thera 1207–after 1244: 238
Jacob di Levanto, Genoese admiral, 492
Jacob Tiepolo, Venetian podestà at Constantinople, doge of Venice 1229–1249: 213, 466
Jacob Viaro, marquis of Cerigotto 1207–1249?: 239
Jacob's Ford, 391
Jacobites (or Monophysites), Christian sect, 566, 623, 638, 685; patriarchs of, 529, 578, 648
Jaffa, 71; under Moslems 1187–1191: 73, 759; under Franks 1191–1197: 75–78, 82–85, 523–525, 529, 623, 695; under Moslems 1197–1204: 529, 530, 532, 697; under Franks 1204–1268: 448, 454, 459, 463, 472, 473, 475, 477, 479, 480, 483, 506–508, 542, 546, 552, 558, 560, 562, 564, 567, 568, 577, 707, 749; counts of, *see* Geoffrey of Lusignan 1191–1193, Aimery of Lusignan 1193–1194, Walter IV of Brienne *c.* 1221–1250, John of Ibelin 1250–1266, Guy of Ibelin 1266–1268; treaty of (1229), 455–457, 544–546, 548, 551, 558, 612, 702
Jahān-Shāh, Rukn-ad-Dīn, son of Tughrul-Shāh; Selchükid emir of Erzerum 1225–1230: 673, 683
Jalāl-ad-Dīn al-Ḥasan, Assassin master in Persia (in 1211), 666
Jalāl-ad-Dīn Mangubertī (Mengübirdi), son of Muḥammad; Khorezm-Shāh 1220–1231: 449, 561, 672, 673, 683, 701, 703, 704, 717, 761
Jalāl-ad-Dīn Rūmī, Persian mystic poet (d. *c.* 1230), 689, 732
James I, son of Peter II; king of Aragon 1213–1276: 290, 303, 304, 312, 318 note, 323, 510, 580, 722; sons of, 580, 581
James II, son of Peter III; king of Aragon and Sicily 1291–1327: 264, 593
James de la Roche, son of William of Veligosti; baron of Veligosti 1264?–1302: 259
James I of Avesnes, commander from Hainault (d. 1191), 50, 51, 65, 75, 115, 160 note
James II of Avesnes, son of James I; lord of Negroponte 1204–1209: 160, 238, 262
James of Ibelin, great-grandson of seneschal Baldwin; legal authority, 616, 619
James of Vitry, crusade preacher, 326, 380, 381; bishop of Acre 1216–1228: 381, 382, 385, 389, 392, 396, 400, 402, 405, 419, 538; cardinal-bishop (of Tusculum) 1228–1240
James Pantaléon, patriarch of Jerusalem 1255–1261: 569, 570, *and see* Urban IV
al-Jāmūs, Moslem warrior (d. 1217), 393
Janina, 263
al-Jauwād Yūnus, Muẓaffar-ad-Dīn, grandson of al-'Ādil I Saif-ad-Dīn; Aiyūbid ruler of Damascus 1238–1238 (d. *c.* 1240), 705, 706; wife of, 705
Jazira, 561, 673, 679, 684, 695, 701–704, 706, 708, 729, 737; rulers of, *see* Aiyūbids (1185–1260)
Jemri ("poor fellow"; false Siyāwush), Selchükid pretender 1276–1277: 728
Jerba, 22
Jeremiah Ghisi, brother of Andrew; co-lord of Tenos 1207–1251: 238
Jericho, 421
Jerusalem, city: under Franks 1099–1187: 37, 38, 325, 394, 578, 619, 634, 640, 643, 759; under Moslems 1187–1229: 70, 73, 75–78, 82, 83, 85, 91, 154, 155, 163, 174, 326, 332, 333, 390, 391, 396, 409, 410, 415, 422, 423, 430, 437, 444, 448, 449, 452–462, 496, 497, 523, 526, 539, 543, 697–699, 701, 705; under Franks 1229–1239: 395, 464, 469, 472, 473, 477, 545, 546, 548, 550, 702, 703, 706, 760; under Moslems 1239–1240: 478–480, 552, 761; under Franks 1240–1244: 481, 489, 558, 561, 614, 674, 709; under Moslems after 1244: 502, 505–507, 562, 564, 568, 710, 713, 743, 761; Greek patriarch of, *see* Dositheus 1669–1707; Latin patriarchs of, *see* Ralph 1191–1194, Aymar "the Monk" 1194–1202, Albert (Avogadro) 1205–1213, Ralph of Mérencourt 1214–1225, Gerald (of Lausanne) 1225–1239, Robert 1240–1254, James Pantaléon (Urban IV) 1255–1261, William 1262–1270, Thomas Agni 1272–1277, Elias (Peleti) 1279–*c.* 1287, Nicholas of Hannapes 1288–1291
Jerusalem, kingdom, before 1189: 7, 12, 18, 37, 45–47, 88, 126, 133, 344, 640, 759; 1189–1225: 42, 49–52, 63, 65, 66, 70, 71, 76, 79–81, 85, 100, 117, 121, 156, 161, 379, 388, 403, 409, 415, 417, 438, 439, 522–542, 602–605, 608, 621, 624, 625, 697, 759, 760; 1225–1243: 448, 452, 459, 463, 465, 471, 475, 481, 483–485, 542–554, 610–614, 618, 761; 1243–1291: 354, 363, 368, 369, 497, 503–505, 557–598, 614–619, 629, 762; bailies of, *see* John I of Ibelin, Odo of Montbéliard, Thomas of Acerra, Balian Grenier, Warner the German, Richard Filangieri, Ralph of Nesle, Balian of Ibelin (2), John of Ibelin (2), Geoffrey of Sargines, Henry of Antioch, Roger of San Severino, Odo Poilechien, Philip of Ibelin, Amalric of Lusignan; high court of, 195, 532, 543, 544, 546–548, 550, 551, 554, 559, 560, 570, 571, 573, 580, 582–586, 604, 606, 607, 611–613,

620; kings of, *see* Baldwin I 1100–1118, Baldwin II 1118–1131, Fulk 1131–1143, Baldwin III 1143–1163, Amalric 1163–1174, Baldwin IV 1174–1185, Baldwin V 1185–1186, Guy of Lusignan 1186–1190, Henry 1192–1197, Aimery of Lusignan 1197–1205, John of Brienne 1210–1212, Frederick (II) 1225–1228, Conrad (IV) 1228–1254, Conradin 1254–1268, Hugh (III) of Lusignan 1269–1284, John 1284–1285, Henry II 1286–1291; pretenders to, *see* Conrad of Montferrat 1190–1192, Charles I of Anjou 1277–1285; queens of, *see* Adelaide, Morfia, Maria Comnena, Sibyl 1186–1190, Isabel 1190–*c.* 1206, Mary (*c.* 1206) 1210–1212, Isabel of Brienne (1212) 1225–1228, Isabel of Ibelin; regents of, *see* John of Brienne 1212–1225, Frederick (II) 1228–1243, Alice 1243–1246, Henry (I) of Lusignan 1246–1253, Plaisance of Antioch 1253–1261, Isabel of Lusignan 1263–1264, Hugh (III) of Lusignan 1264–1269

Jews, religious community, 14 note, 180, 286, 383, 411, 466, 482, 511, 621 note; individuals, 589, 720, 721

al-Jibāl, 671, 672, 772

Jihād (Arabic, holy war), 667, 678, 679, 754

Jisr al-Majāmiʿ, 390

Jīzat Dimyāṭ, 397

Jizyah (Arabic, head tax), 26

Joachim, metropolitan of Tirnovo, Orthodox patriarch of Bulgaria 1235–1237: 219

Joan (Plantagenet), daughter of Henry II of England and Eleanor; wife of William II of Sicily 1174–1189, 4th wife of Raymond VI of Toulouse 1195–1199: 41, 58, 59, 61–64, 77, 78, 322, 600, 601

Joan, daughter of Raymond VII of Toulouse; wife of Alphonse of Poitiers 1237–1271, countess of Toulouse 1249–1271: 316, 320

Joan (of Châtillon), wife of Walter V of Brienne 1306–1311 (d. 1354), 272

John (Bossan), archbishop of Arles 1234–1258: 483

John (of Meran), archbishop of Gran 1205–1223: 387

John (Yohannēs), grandson of Ōshin II; Armenian archbishop of Sis (before 1197–1203), catholicus 1203–1206, 1208–1229: 647

John, bishop of Évreux 1180–1192: 58, 63

John (of Veirac), bishop of Limoges *c.* 1215–1218: 386

John, bishop of Lydda (before 1267–after 1271), 580

John, bishop of Sutri 1179–*c.* 1197: 118

John I ("the Red"), son of Peter of Dreux and Alice; count of Brittany and earl of Richmond 1237–1286: 470, 510

John, son of Robert II of Dreux; count of Mâcon 1224–*c.* 1240: 466, 469

John, son of Louis IX of France; count of Nevers 1265–1270, of Valois 1268–1270: 503, 516

John I, count of Ponthieu 1147–1191: 53

John, count of Sées (in 1189), 50

John ("le Scot"), nephew of Ranulf; earl of Huntingdon 1219–1237, of Chester 1232–1237: 482

John (of Antioch), son of William; lord of Botron, 570

John, son of Walter and Margaret; lord of Caesarea 1229–1241: 548, 560

John, lord of Joinville, biographer (d. 1319), 606; and crusade of 1249: 449, 491–494, 497, 498, 500, 502, 504, 505, 615 note; and Tunisian crusade, 509

John, marshal of the Hospital, 383

John ("Lackland"), son of Henry II and Eleanor: 48, 49, 53, 54, 66, 79, 82, 523; Plantagenet king of England 1199–1216: 55, 155, 157, 159, 289 note, 346 note, 384, 415, 533; and Albigensian crusade, 284, 285, 294, 297, 303, 306; and fifth crusade, 378, 382; bastard of, 402; wife of, *see* Isabel (of Gloucester)

John XXI (Peter Juliani), pope 1276–1277: 585, 616, 762

John XXII (James Duèse), pope 1316–1334: 722

John Angelus Comnenus, son of Theodore of Epirus; despot of Thessalonica 1236–1244: 222, 223, 225

John I Angelus Comnenus, illegitimate son of Michael II of Epirus; duke of Neopatras 1271–1295 (d. 1296), 247, 257, 259, 261

John II Angelus Comnenus, grandson of John I; duke of Neopatras 1303–1318: 266, 271

John Asen, son of Asen; Vlach king of Bulgaria 1218–1241: 205, 209, 210, 213–222, 226, 760, 761; wives of, *see* Maria (of Hungary), Irene Angelina Comnena

John VI Cantacuzenus, Byzantine emperor 1347–1354 (d. 1383), 270

John Chauderon, nephew of William II of Achaea; constable of Achaea, bailie 1278–1278: 258, 259

John Colonna, cardinal-priest 1212–1245, papal legate to Constantinople, 198, 213, 214

John II Comnenus, son of Alexius I: 127; Byzantine emperor 1118–1143: 10, 11, 124, 130–135, 138–141, 146, 162, 637, 677; wife of, *see* Piriska (of Hungary)

John "Comnenus", son of Alexius Axouch; Byzantine rebel (in 1201), 182 note

John Contostephanus, Byzantine general, 640

John de Catavas, Frankish commander, 253

John de la Roche, son of Guy I; duke of Athens 1263–1280: 257, 259

John Ducas, Byzantine chancellor, 91, 95, 97–99, 101, 103

John III Ducas Vatatzes, Byzantine emperor

at Nicaea 1222–1254: 214, 215, 217–228, 243, 760, 761; wives of, *see* Irene Lascaris, Constance (Hohenstaufen)
John Embriaco, son of Henry (d. 1282), 587; wife of, 587
John Ferro, Venetian merchant, 225
John Italus, Byzantine philosopher (*c.* 1080), 128
John l'Aleman, son of Warner the German; lord of Caesarea 1241–1265: 560 note
John of Alençon, archdeacon of Lisieux, 82
John of Arcis, French crusader, 415
John II of Avesnes, great-grandson of Baldwin VI; count of Hainault 1279–1304, of Holland 1299–1304: 262
John of Béthune, Frankish commander (d. 1238), 221
John of Botron, brother of William (d. 1244), 563
John of Brienne, son of Erard II: xviii, 443, 454, 544, 546, 651 note, 761; king of Jerusalem 1210–1212: 532, 536, 537, 605, 760; regent of Jerusalem 1212–1225: 438–440, 442, 537–542, 650; and fifth crusade, xvii, 383, 384, 388, 389, 392, 394, 396–398, 401, 403, 404, 406–409, 414, 415, 417–422, 424–428, 437, 496, 609, 610; Latin co-emperor of Romania 1231–1237: 216–221, 243, 466, 761; daughter of, 464; nephew of, 472; son of, 540, 651 note; wives of, *see* Mary (of Montferrat-Jerusalem), Rita (Ṛoupenid), Berengaria (of Castile)
John of Grailly, French commander, marshal of the Temple (d. after 1301), 592–594, 596, 597
John I of Ibelin, son of Balian II and Maria Comnena; constable of Jerusalem 1194–*c.* 1205, lord of Beirut *c.* 1198–1236: 460, 464, 543, 546–551, 606, 611–613; bailie of Jerusalem 1205–1210: 532, 534, 536; bailie of Cyprus 1227–1228, 1230–1236: 451, 464, 543, 549, 605, 611–613, 761; mayor of Acre 1232–1236: 464, 549–551, 613, 761; nephews of, 553, 560; sons of, 560
John of Ibelin, son of John I; lord of Arsuf 1236–1258, bailie of Jerusalem 1247–1248, 1249–1254, 1256–1258, constable 1251–1258: 472, 475, 476, 560, 567, 568, 570, 580, 585
John of Ibelin, son of Philip: 548, 560; count of Jaffa 1250–1266: 568, 574, 577, 580, 605, 619, 652 note; bailie of Jerusalem 1254–1256: 567, 713; wife of, *see* Maria (Heṭoumid)
John II of Ibelin, son of Balian III; lord of Beirut 1247–1264: 269, 573, 574, 580; wife of, *see* Alice de la Roche
John of Lügde, deacon at Hameln, 341
John I "of Lusignan", son of Hugh III; king of Cyprus and Jerusalem 1284–1285: 589, 607, 762
John I of Montfort, son of Amalric VI; count of Montfort 1241–1248: 493
John of Montfort, son of Philip; lord of Tyre 1270–1283: 580, 582, 586, 588, 589; wife of, *see* Margaret (of Antioch)
John II of Nesle, son of Ralph; count of Soissons 1237–1270: 474
John of Parma, Franciscan minister-general, 226
John of Pian del Carpine, Franciscan missionary (d. 1252), 722
John of Procida, Sicilian leader, 260
John of Ronay, vice-master of the Hospital, 614
John of Villiers, master of the Hospital 1285–1293: 590, 591, 595, 597
John V Palaeologus, grandson of Andronicus II; Byzantine emperor 1341–1347, 1354–1376, 1379–1390, 1390–1391: 232
John VIII Palaeologus, grandson of John V; Byzantine emperor 1425–1448: 233
John Palaeologus, brother of Michael VIII; ruler of Rhodes 1261–1275: 230, 247, 257
John Palaeologus, son of Andronicus II (d. 1308), 265
John Phylax, Greek turncoat, 231
John I Querini, lord of Astypalaea 1207–1231: 238
John Turco (of Ancona), Latin archbishop of Nicosia 1288–1295 (d. *c.* 1298), 596
Joigny, count of, 469
Joinville, 772; lord of, *see* John
Jordan river, 391, 743; crossings of, 390, 391, 393, 539, 698; region east of, *see* Transjordania; region west of, 77, 479, 506, 537, 552, 564
Joscelin (of Courtenay) I, cousin of Baldwin II of Jerusalem; count of Edessa 1119–1131: 635
Joscelin (of Courtenay) II, son of Joscelin I and sister of Leon I; count of Edessa 1131–1150 (titular 1150–1159), 637, 638, 641; wife of, *see* Beatrice
Joscelin (of Courtenay) III, son of Joscelin II; titular count of Edessa 1159–1200: 642
Joscius, archbishop of Tyre (before 1187–1200), chancellor of Jerusalem, 38, 40, 47, 526
Joseph de Cancy, treasurer of the Hospital 1248–1271, prior of the English Hospitallers 1273–1280 (d. after 1282), 586 note
Jubail, 529, 530, 558, 587, 588, 593; lords of, *see* Embriacos
Julian Grenier, son of Balian I; lord of Sidon 1247–1260 (titular 1260–1275), 560 note, 573, 574, 584, 652 note; wife of, *see* Euphemia (Heṭoumid)
Jumièges, 330
Jund (Arabic, salaried warrior class), 17
Justingen, *see* Anselm
Juvainī, Shams-ad-Dīn, vizir of Mongols 1263–1284: 731

Ka'bah, shrine at Mecca, 749
Kai-Kā'ūs I, 'Izz-ad-Dīn, son of Kai-Khusrau I; Selchükid sultan of Rūm 1211–1220: 393, 682, 683, 698, 699
Kai-Kā'ūs II, 'Izz-ad-Dīn, son of Kai-Khusrau II; Selchükid sultan of Rūm 1245–1249, co-sultan 1249–1261 (d. *c.* 1279), 726
Kai-Khusrau I, Ghiyāth-ad-Dīn, son of Kïlïj Arslan II; Selchükid sultan of Rūm 1192–1196, 1204–1211: 202, 649, 681–683, 696; mother of (Greek), 681
Kai-Khusrau II, Ghiyāth-ad-Dīn, son of Kai-Qobād I and Māh-Perī Khātūn; Selchükid sultan of Rūm 1237–1245: 223, 652, 673, 684, 690–692, 704, 705, 708, 725; daughter of, 652, 692 note; mother of, 223, 692; sons of, 726; wife of, 652, 692 note
Kai-Khusrau III, Ghiyāth-ad-Dīn, son of Kïlïj Arslan IV; Selchükid sultan of Rūm 1265–1283: 727
Kai-Qobād I, 'Alā'-ad-Dīn, son of Kai-Khusrau I; Selchükid sultan of Rūm 1220–1237: 541, 651 note, 652, 673, 682–684, 689, 691, 701, 703, 704; wife of (d. *c.* 1247), 113 note
Kairawan, 17, 18, 25, 27 note
Kakig (son of Kourkēn), Armenian governor of Tarsus, 633
Kalamata, 240, 244, 249, 258, 264, 265, *and see* Benjamin; barony of, 250
Kalavun, al-Manṣūr Saif-ad-Dīn, Mamluk sultan of Egypt and Syria 1279–1290: 576, 586, 588–595, 616, 617, 655, 750–756, 762; wife of, *see* Aslun Khātūn
Kalavryta, 252, 258, 264, 272; baron of, *see* Geoffrey of Tournai; barony of, 250, 258
Kalden, *see* Henry
Kalocsa, archbishop of, 387, 389
al-Kāmil Muḥammad, Nāṣir-ad-Dīn, son of al-'Ādil I Saif-ad-Dīn: 695; Aiyūbid governor of Egypt 1202–1218: 398, 539, 696, 698; sultan 1218–1238: 465, 471, 547, 550, 551, 683, 684, 700–707, 737, 761; and fifth crusade, 402, 404, 405, 408–410, 413–418, 422–428, 497, 540, 699, 700, 760; and Frederick II, 448–450, 452–459, 462, 464, 467, 543–545, 612, 614, 701, 702, 709; ruler of Damascus 1237–1238: 704, 705; brother of, 478; grandson of, 712; son of, 742 note
Kāmilī mamluks, 707, 737
Kangurlan, 719; *see also* Sultaniyeh
Kantara, 601, 612; monastery of, 626
Kara Arslan, Turkish lord of Ḥiṣn Kaifā 1144–1167?: 638
Kara-Khanids, Turkic people, 668, 669, 671
Kara-Kitai, Mongol people, 668–671, 716, 718, 721; Gur-Khan of, *see* Ye-liu Tashi
Kara-Tai, vizir of Selchükids 1249–1256: 725
Karakorum, 572, 652, 718, 744
Karaman, Karīm-ad-Dīn, Karamanid chieftain 1223–1263: 653, 727
Karamanids, Turkoman dynasty at Laranda 1223–1471: 728, 729, *and see* Karaman 1223–1263
Karpassia, 625
Kars, 664; king of, 630
Karytaina, 272; baron of, 245, 246, 258; barony of, 250, 262
Kastamonu, 133, 677, 727
Katzenellenbogen, count of, 238
Kelibia, 25
Kerak, 409, 415, 417, 423, 477, 539, 643, 674, 693, 694, 704, 706, 710–712, 714, 745, 747, 750–752; lords of, *see* Aiyūbids (of Transjordania); troops from, 563, 709
Kerman, 669, 671, 672
Kesoun, lord of, 632
Khabur river, 706, 708
Khac̱hadour, Armenian commander, 632
Khalij, 637 note
Khalīl, son of aṣ-Ṣāliḥ Aiyūb and Shajar-ad-Durr (d. before 1249), 738, 740
Khārijites, Moslem sect, 17
Kharput, 684, 704, 708
al-Kharrūbah, 52
al-Khawābī, 698
al-Khiḍr, Artukid ruler of Kharput (in 1233), 684
Khiḍr, Najm-ad-Dīn, son of Baybars; lord of Kerak 1280–1287: 750–752
Khoi, 701
Khorezm, 669, 674; troops from, 489, 561–564, 614, 662, 663, 665, 667, 670–674, 683, 684, 689–691, 701, 703–710, 761
Khorezm-Shāhs, Turkish dynasty in Persia and Transoxiana 1138–1231: 422, 669–673, 717, *and see* Anushtigin, Tököush 1172–1200, Muḥammad 1200–1220, Jalāl-ad-Dīn Manguberti 1220–1231; *see also* Rukn-ad-Dīn Ghūrshānchī
Khoul Khac̱hig, prince of Ṭornavan, 633
Khurasan, 662, 665, 669, 670, 689, 717, 721
Khuzistan, 662
Kïlïj Arslan I, Dā'ūd, son of Sulaimān; Selchükid sultan of Rūm 1092–1107: 636, 676
Kïlïj Arslan II, 'Izz-ad-Dīn, son of Mas'ūd; Selchükid sultan of Rūm 1155–1192: 140, 141, 144, 639, 640, 643, 645, 677–681, 759; and third crusade, 91, 111–113, 147, 680
Kïlïj Arslan IV, Rukn-ad-Dīn, son of Kai-Khusrau II; Selchükid co-sultan of Rūm 1249–1261, sultan 1261–1265: 653, 726, 727
Kin (or Chin), Tungus dynasty in China 1122–1234: 717
Kinānah, Arab tribe, 495
Kïpchaks, Turkic people, 575, 664, 670–672, 748, 755; *see also* Kumans, Golden Horde
Kirakos, Armenian historian (d. after 1270), 647, 648 note

Kitbogha, al-ʿĀdil Zain-ad-Dīn, Mamluk sultan of Egypt and Syria 1294–1296: 656
Kitbogha, Mongol general (d. 1260), 572–574, 653, 714, 718, 745, 761; nephew of, 573
Kiti, 612
Klokotnitsa, 761; battle (1230): 217
Knights Hospitaller, military order, 55, 439; in Syria, 46, 65, 74, 75, 392, 394, 443, 451, 454, 464, 476, 477, 479, 480, 483, 489, 530, 531, 533–536, 538, 540, 541, 544, 547, 548, 550, 552, 553, 560, 562–565, 568–570, 574, 580, 582, 585, 589–592, 594–597, 601, 615, 697, 703, 709; in Egypt, 399, 409, 414, 415, 417, 418, 420, 427, 493, 541; in Cyprus, 624; in Cilicia, 536, 650, 651 note; in Frankish Greece, 237, 251; in Rhodes, 762; fortresses, 456, 545, 576, 581, 752; houses, 458, 569, 587; individual knights, 296, 383, 387, 593, 614; masters, *see under* Hospital
Knights Templar, military order, 55, 378 note, 388, 439, 504, 762; in Syria, 46, 65, 74, 75, 392, 394, 395, 443, 444, 451, 452, 454, 457–460, 464, 476, 477, 479–481, 483–485, 489, 506, 530, 531, 533–539, 544–548, 550, 552, 553, 560, 561, 568–570, 574, 580, 582, 585, 587, 588, 590–598, 615, 649, 698, 703, 707, 708 note, 709; in Egypt, 405, 408, 409, 413–415, 417, 420, 422, 427, 493, 499; in Cyprus, 81, 148, 602, 603, 624, 759; in Cilicia, 526–528, 536, 537, 550, 639, 640, 642, 646, 654; in Frankish Greece, 237, 251, 252; fortresses, 456, 479, 545, 574–578, 581, 598; houses, 69, 459, 545, 546, 587; individual knights, 296, 383, 387, 458, 479, 563, 570, 573, 593, 597; masters, *see under* Temple; "of Islam", 739
Kogh Vasil (Basil "the Robber"), Armenian lord of Kesoun (d. 1112), 632, 638, 653
Korea, 715, 717
Köse Dagh, battle (1243): 223, 691, 708 note, 717, 725, 761
Krak de Montréal, 409, 415, 417, 423, 701, 750
Krak des Chevaliers: under Franks to 1271: 393, 456, 558, 576, 697, 698; Hospitallers of, 532, 534, 547, 550, 697; capture (1271): 581, 582, 749, 762; under Moslems after 1271: 595
Krum, Bulgarian chieftain 808–814: 204
Kubilai, brother of Möngke; Great Khan of the Mongols 1260–1294: 717
Kulin, ban of Bosnia 1180–1204: 149
Kumans (or Polovtsy), Turkic people, 125, 147, 200, 203, 220, 222, 247; mercenaries, 102, 105, 107; individuals, 205; *see also* Kîpchaks
Kuno, count of Falkenstein (and Neuburg am Inn, in 1189), 92, 93
al-Kūrānī, Shīʿite rebel (d. 1261), 746
Kurds, mountain tribes of Kurdistan, 663, 664, 668, 671, 726; troops, 84, 408, 655, 706, 707, 712, 714, 737, 740, 741, 756; individuals, 37, 408, 529, 673, 699, 739
Kutuz, al-Muẓaffar Saif-ad-Dīn, Mamluk deputy-sultan of Egypt 1252–1259, sultan 1259–1260: 573, 574, 714, 743–745, 761
Kyburg, count of, *see* Ulrich
Kyrenia, 601, 612, 613, 761

L'Erminet, 773; lord of, 527
La Clisura, 257
La Cuppa, 257
La Fauconnerie, farm, 585
La Ferté-Alais, lord of, 469, 472
La Garnache, lord of, 469
La Roche (sur Ognon), *see* De la Roches
La Roche de Russole, 578
Lacedaemon, 244, 253; bishopric of, 252; *see also* Sparta
Laconia, 237, 240, 253, 258, 264, 272
Laconia, Gulf of, 13
Ladder of Tyre, 588
Lagonesse, *see* Gonesse; *see also* Philip
Lairon, *see* Aymar
al-Lajjūn, 575
Lambert of Thury, lord of Limoux, 294 note, 309
Lampron, 633, 634, 642, 644, 650; bishops of, 645, 648 note, 649; lords of, *see* Heṭoumids
Lampsacus, 217, 219
Lancaster, count of, 360, 582; honor of, 54
Lando, archbishop of Reggio di Calabria 1217–1234, of Messina 1234–*c.* 1255: 446
Landsberg, margrave of, *see* Conrad
Langres, bishop of, 12
Languedoc, 277–324, 330, 491, 514, 760; map of, 276
Laodicea (ad Lycum), 681
Laon, 16; bishop of, *see* Anselm; district of, 238
Lapithos, lady of, 269
Laranda, 113
Larissa, 207, 238
Larmena, 257, 272
Las Navas de Tolosa, battle (1212), 297, 301, 302, 327, 760
Lascaris (Lascarids), Byzantine imperial dynasty at Nicaea 1208–1261: 688, *and see* Theodore I 1208–1222, John III (Ducas Vatatzes) 1222–1254, Theodore II 1254–1258; *see also* Constantine, Eudocia, Irene, Maria (2)
Latakia: under Moslems 1188–1260: 423, 526, 531, 535, 550, 558, 698; under Franks 1260–1287: 572, 578, 585, 590, 617; archdeacon of, 624
Lateran councils, third (1179), 282, 327 note; fourth (1215), 196, 287, 306–308, 311, 380, 382, 385, 431, 538, 760
Latin church, 87–89, 344–364, 368–375, 378, 379, 443, 457, 461, 462, 470, 656 note; and Albigensians, 281, 282, 291, 308, 317, 319, 322, 344–347; in North Africa, 27, 28; in Latin empire, 195–197; in Frankish

Greece, 241, 242 note, 251; in Cyprus, 618, 623–629; in Egypt, 403, 420, 435; in Syria, 535, 572; in Persia, 722; in China, 723; union with Armenian church, 529, 647; union with Greek church, *see under* Greek church; *see also* Papacy
Latin empire of Constantinople, 169, 187–233, 240, 242–244, 367, 377, 466, 509, 531, 532, 570, 603, 625, 628, 682, 761, *and see* Romania, Frankish; emperors of, *see* Baldwin I 1204–1205, Henry 1206–1216, Peter of Courtenay 1217–1218, Robert of Courtenay 1221–1228, Baldwin II 1228–1231, 1237–1261, John of Brienne 1231–1237; empresses of, *see* Agnes of Montferrat, Maria, Yolanda, Mary of Brienne; regents of, *see* (emperor) Henry 1205–1206, Conon of Béthune 1216–1217, 1219–1221, Yolanda 1217–1219, Mary of Courtenay 1228–1228, Narjot I of Toucy 1228–1231, 1238–1241, Philip of Toucy 1241–1251; titular emperors of, *see* Baldwin II 1261–1273, Philip of Courtenay 1273–1285; titular empress of, *see* Catherine of Courtenay 1273–1308
Latin states (in Syria), maps of, 86, 556
Latins, xv, xvii, 16, 110, 124–126, 130, 133, 140, 146–151, 176, 179–185, 189, 192–205, 208–233, 608, 635, 640, 642, 651; under Greek rule, 108, 109, 135, 143–145, 162, 165, 181, 209, 622; in Moslem service, 209, 223, 683, 691; *see also* Franks
Latrun, 77
Laurac, 294 note
Lavaur, 288, 290, 292, 293; council of (1213), 296, 298, 299, 307
Lawrence, Franciscan legate, 627
Le Bourg, *see* Baldwin (II, of Jerusalem)
Le Mans, 47, 63
Le Puiset, *see* Hugh de Puiset
Le Puy, 304, *and see* Durand
Lebadea, 241; lord of, *see* William de la Roche
Lebanon, Mount, 600
Lecce, 346; counts of, *see* Tancred, Walter of Brienne
Lefkara, 625
Leicester, earls of, 289, 482, 552; wood of, 483
Lemnos, 191, 229
Lentiana, 209
Lentini, *see* Thomas Agni
Leo (Brancaleone), cardinal-deacon 1200–1202, cardinal-priest 1202–*c.* 1230, papal legate to Bulgaria, 149, 201
Leo IX (Bruno of Egisheim), pope 1049–1054: 345
Leo, Syrian renegade, 576
Leo Gabalas, ruler of Rhodes (after 1233), 217
Leo Sgourus, lord of Corinth (d. *c.* 1208), 182 note, 202, 237, 240; wife of, *see* Eudocia Angelina
Leon (Levon) I, son of Constantine; Ṛoupenid prince of Cilician Armenia 1129–1137 (d. 1139), 133, 636–638, 640; wife of (sister of Baldwin II), 637
Leon II, son of Stephen; Ṛoupenid prince of Cilician Armenia 1187–1198: 42, 114, 119, 121, 149, 527, 529, 644, 647–649; king 1198–1219: 384, 528, 531–540, 649–651, 653, 658, 683, 697, 698, 759; daughter of, 393, 541, 634, 651; wife of, *see* Sibyl of Lusignan
Leon III, son of Heṭoum I; Heṭoumid king of Cilician Armenia 1269–1289: 576, 584, 654, 752
Leon IV, son of Ṭoros III; Heṭoumid king of Cilician Armenia 1305–1307: 658
Leonard Foscolo, lord of Anaphe 1207–1228: 239
Leopold V of Babenberg, duke of Austria 1177–1194: 91, 116
Leopold VI of Babenberg, son of Leopold V; duke of Styria 1194–1230, of Austria 1198–1230: 327 note; and third crusade, 386–389, 394, 397, 399–401, 407, 411, 539, 609
Les Barres, *see* William
Les Vaux-de-Cernay, abbot of, 174, 277 note; *and see* Peter
Lesbos, 191
Letts, Baltic people, 122
Lévis (-Saint Nom), *see* Guy
Licario, knight from Vicenza, 256, 257, 259, 272; wife of, *see* Felicia (dalle Carceri)
Liebenau, count of, *see* Siegfried
Liedekerke, *see* Walter
Liége, 331, 333 note, 401; archdeacon of, 583; bishops of, *see* Rudolph, Hugh; diocese of, 510
Liegnitz, battle (1241), 717
Lille, *see* Guy de Charpigny
Limassol, 62–64, 447, 451, 582, 599–601, 610, 612, 614, 615 note, 622–625
Limburg, dukes of, *see* Henry III, Walram IV, Henry IV
Limoges, *see* Aimery; bishop of, 386
Limoux, 294 note, 319
Lisbon, 56, 395, 396; bishop of, 395
Lisieux, archdeacon of, 82
Lithuanians, Baltic people, 121
Little Prespa Lake, 192
Livs, Baltic people, 121
Lluria, *see* Loria; *see also* Roger de
Locedio, abbot of, 173, 536
Loches, lord of, 469
Loire river, 56, 337, 341
Lombard League, 137, 348, 355, 445
Lombardy, 350–352, 354–356, 358, 362–364, 366, 469; children's crusade in, 333, 334; communes of, 166, 359, 435, 445, 549; crusaders from, 167, 232, 257, 349, 350, 412, 594; rebel barons from, 206–208, 210, 212, 239
Lombers, 294 note
London, 49, 221; Tower of, 55
Lopadium, 192

Loria, *see* Roger de Lluria
Lorraine, 331; crusaders from, 490; duke of, 385, 431
Lot river, 287 note, 295, 303
Lothair II, emperor of Germany 1125 (crowned 1133)–1137: 9, 132
Lothair Filangieri, brother of Richard (d. after 1243), 547, 548, 550, 553, 554, 557, 565
Louge river, 300
Louis VI, Capetian king of France 1108–1137: 212
Louis VII, son of Louis VI; Capetian king of France 1137–1180: 48, 137, 141; and second crusade, 8 note, 12, 15, 16, 40, 135, 185, 282; daughter of, 134; wives of, *see* Eleanor of Aquitaine, Adela (of Champagne)
Louis VIII, son of Philip II and Isabel, 54, 70; Capetian king of France 1223–1226: 287, 300, 305, 306, 314–319, 321, 440, 760; wife of, *see* Blanche of Castile
Louis IX, son of Louis VIII; Capetian king of France 1226–1270: xviii, 354, 470, 483, 760; and Languedoc, 319–322; and Latin empire, 220–222, 224–226, 246, 466–468; and crusade of 1249: 244, 245, 341, 356, 357, 426, 487–508, 566, 567, 614, 615, 627, 674, 712, 713, 735, 739–742, 761; and Tunisian crusade, 368, 508–518, 579–582, 749, 762; wife of, *see* Margaret of Provence
Louis I, son of Theobald V; count of Blois 1191–1205, "duke of Nicaea" 1204–1205: 155, 158–160, 164, 174, 182, 192, 203
Louis I, grandson of Stephen I; count of Sancerre 1218–1268: 469
Louis I (of Kelheim), nephew of Conrad of Wittelsbach; duke of Bavaria 1183–1231: 423, 435
Louis III, landgrave of Thuringia 1172–1190: 50, 65, 115
Louis IV, son of Hermann I; landgrave of Thuringia 1218–1227: 444, 446
Louis of Burgundy, grandson of duke Hugh IV; prince of Achaea (and titular king of Thessalonica) 1313–1316: 270 note; wife of, *see* Mahaut of Hainault
Loulon, 645
Louvain, count of, 173 note
Low Countries, Lowlands, 327, 330, 332; crusaders from, 326, 337, 356, 510; *see also* Netherlands, Flanders, Frisia
Lower Lorraine, duke of, 93
Lubban, 390
Lübeck, 444, *and see* Arnold; burghers from, 115, 120
Lucca, *see* Ptolemy
Lucienne of Segni, great-niece of Innocent III; 2nd wife of Bohemond V of Antioch 1235–1252, regent of Antioch and Tripoli 1252–1252: 507, 565–567, 570, 585
Lucius III (Ubaldo Allucingoli), pope 1181–1185: 282, 646 note
Lucy (-le-Bocage), *see* Guy
Lucy, daughter of Bohemond VI of Antioch; wife of Narjot of Toucy, countess of Tripoli 1288–1289: 584, 591, 592
Ludolph (of Kroppenstedt), archbishop of Magdeburg 1192–1205: 156 note, *and see* 172 note
Lügde, *see* John
Lu'lu', Badr-ad-Dīn, regent of Mosul *c.* 1210–1234, ruler 1234–1259: 662, 673, 706, 708, 711, 744; daughter of, 744
Lurs, Iranic people, 663
Lusignan, family, 63, 524, 525, 602, 614, 622–624, 759, *and see* Aimery, Amalric, Bohemond, Burgundia, Geoffrey, Guy (2), Henry I, Henry II, Hugh VIII, Hugh X, Hugh XI, Hugh I, Hugh II, Hugh III, Hugh IV, Isabel, John, Mary, Melisend, Sibyl
Lycaonia, 113
Lydda, 523, 532; archdeacon of, 624; bishops of, 563, 580
Lydia, 192
Lyons, 57, 224, 316, 317, 354, 364, 466, 468, 469; archbishop of, 348; archdeacon of, 307; councils of, (1245): 224, 357, 490, 566, 761; (1274): 583, 584, 587, 722, 762

Ma'arrat-an-Nu'mān, 700, 705
Macedonia, 191, 192, 212, 225, 228, 236, 238, 242, 246, 247, 270, 275; heresy in, 144; imperial dynasty from, 124; third crusade in, 102, 105, 108
Mâcon, bishop of, 467; count of, 466, 469
Madrasah (Arabic, school or college), 689, 738, 747, 757
Maeander river, 726; valley of, 140, 201, 681
Magdeburg, 433; archbishop of, 156 note, 172 note; burggrave of, 93, 115
Maguelonne, archdeacon of, 283
Magyars, Ugric people, 131
Māh-Perī Khātūn, concubine of Kai-Qobād I, 692 note
al-Maḥallah, 425, 426
Mahaut of Hainault, daughter of Florent of Achaea and Isabel; wife of Guy II of Athens 1305–1308, wife of Louis of Burgundy 1313–1316; princess of Achaea 1313–1318 (d. 1331), 265, 268–270
Mahdia, 18–27, 30–32, *and see* Philip; bishops of, 27, 31 note
Maḥmūd Khan, nephew of Sanjar; Kara-Khanid ruler of Khurasan 1156–1162: 669
Maina, 244, 248, 253
Maine, lord of, 48
Mainz, 89, 333, 430, 759; archbishops of, *see* Conrad of Wittelsbach, Siegfried; scholasticus of, 434
Maio of Bari, Sicilian official (d. 1160), 29–32
Maio Orsini, grandson of Margarit of

Brindisi; count of Cephalonia 1194–1238: 239, 243, 265
Maiyafariqin, 684, 693; lords of, *see* Aiyūbids (of the Jazira)
al-Majdal, 708
Majorca, 36, 270
Makhairas, Leontios, Greek chronicler, 618
Makryplagi, pass, 254, 270
Malea, Cape, 13
Malik-Ghāzī, Dānishmendid ruler 1097–1105?: 677 note
Malik-Shāh (II), Quṭb-ad-Dīn, son of Kilij Arslan II; Selchükid prince at Iconium 1188–1192: 111, 113, 680, 681
Malik-Shāh, Selchükid sultan 1072–1092: 663, 669
Malta, 17, 21; counts of, 37, 427, 436, 451, 454
Mamistra, 134, 632, 635–644, 654, 657, 762
Mamlūk (Arabic, slave; fem. *mamlūkah*), 83, 668, 735, 736, 738, 743
Mamluks, slave soldiers, of 'Abbāsids and Selchükids, 736; of Aiyūbids, 83, 84, 489, 503, 563, 705–708, 709 note, 711, 712, 736–740; of Mamluk sultans, 584, 615, 713, 714, 741, 745, 750, 755–757, 761
Mamluks, "Baḥrī", slave dynasty in Egypt and Syria 1250–1390: xviii, 363, 368, 505, 567, 573, 582, 586, 668, 694, 712, 719–722, 735, 740, 743–758, 762, *and see* Aybeg (1250) 1252–1257, 'Alī 1257–1259, Kutuz 1259–1260, Baybars 1260–1277, Berke Khan 1277–1279, Salamish 1279–1279, Kalavun 1279–1290, al-Ashraf Khalīl 1290–1293, Muḥammad 1293–1294, 1299–1309, 1310–1341, Kitbogha 1294–1296; *see also* Khiḍr, Shajar-ad-Durr; army of, 514, 573, 574, 576, 577, 581, 585, 589, 592, 593, 597, 598, 653, 657, 718, 745, 747–750, 753, 756, 761, 762, *and see* Egypt, troops from; fleet of, 723; map, 734
Manbij, 696, 708
Mandalē, sons of (at Kybistra), 635
Manfred, illegitimate son of emperor Frederick II; Hohenstaufen governor of Sicily 1250–1258: 227, 228, 359, 361, 362; king 1258–1266: 42, 232, 246, 247, 255, 257, 343, 362–367, 370, 373, 508, 579, 748, 762; wife of, *see* Helena Angelina Comnena
al-Manṣūr Ibrāhīm, Nāṣir-ad-Dīn, son of al-Mujāhid Shīrkūh; Aiyūbid ruler of Homs 1240–1246: 561–564, 708–710
al-Manṣūr Muḥammad, Nāṣir-ad-Dīn, son of al-'Azīz 'Uthmān; Aiyūbid sultan of Egypt 1198–1200: 695, 696
al-Manṣūr Muḥammad I, Nāṣir-ad-Dīn, son of al-Muẓaffar 'Uthmān; Aiyūbid governor of Hamah 1191–1193, ruler 1193–1221: 411, 534, 535, 693, 696, 697
al-Manṣūr Muḥammad II, Saif-ad-Dīn, son of al-Muzaffar Maḥmūd; Aiyūbid ruler of Hamah 1243–1284: 576, 581, 654, 711, 714; wife of, *see* 'Ā'ishah Khātūn
Mansurah, 418, 422, 424, 425, 448, 496–502, 516, 615, 700, 711, 738, 739
Mantua, 363; "bard of", 114
Manuel Angelus Comnenus, brother of Michael I of Epirus; despot of Thessalonica 1230–1236 (d. 1241), 215, 217–219, 222; wife of, *see* Maria (of Bulgaria)
Manuel Camytzes, Byzantine official, rebel (in 1201), 171
Manuel I Comnenus, son of John II and Piriska: 10; Byzantine emperor 1143–1180: 11–15, 16 note, 25, 29, 36, 90, 124, 130, 133–146, 148, 162, 165, 185, 622, 637, 639–641, 677–679; daughter of, 164; great-nephew of, 600; wives of, *see* Bertha of Sulzbach, Maria of Antioch
Manuel I Sarantenus, Orthodox patriarch at Nicaea 1217–1222: 214
Manzalah, Lake, 414, 419
Manzikert, battle (1071), 631, 679
al-Maqrīzī, Arabic historian (d. 1442), 410, 426, 453, 455, 515
Mar Athanasius, Jacobite priest, 638
Mar Yabhalāhā III, Nestorian patriarch (in 1294), 656, 722
Maraclea, 39, 581, 752; lord of, *see* Bartholomew
Maragha, 656, 721
Marash, 632, 635, 641, 656, 657, 687, 755; governor of, 632; lord of, 636
Marbach, monastery, 332, 333
Marche, counts of La, 316, 319, 607
Marco Giustiniani, Venetian consul at Acre, 568
Marco Gradenigo, Venetian podestà at Constantinople (in 1261), 231
Marco Polo, Italian traveler (d. 1324), 655, 669, 723
Marco I Sanudo, nephew of Enrico Dandolo; duke of the Archipelago 1207–*c.* 1227: 202, 238, 239, 242, 272
Marco II Sanudo, son of Angelo; duke of the Archipelago 1262–1303: 272
Marco Venier, marquis of Cerigo 1207–1238: 239
Mardin, 704; lords of, *see* Artukids
Margaret ("Maria"), daughter of Bela III of Hungary and Agnes; 2nd wife of Isaac II Angelus 1185–1204, 2nd wife of Boniface of Thessalonica 1204–1207: 147, 189, 190, 206, 207, 212
Margaret, daughter of Henry of Antioch; wife of John of Montfort 1269–1283, lady of Tyre 1284–1291 (d. 1308), 580, 593, 752
Margaret II, daughter of Latin emperor Baldwin I; countess of Flanders and Hainault 1244–1279: 360
Margaret, daughter of Louis VII of France; 2nd wife of Bela III of Hungary 1185–1196: 94
Margaret of Alsace, sister of Philip I; wife

of Baldwin V of Hainault 1169–1194; countess of Flanders 1191–1194: 70
Margaret of Ibelin, daughter of Balian II; wife of Hugh of Tiberias (to 1205), wife of Walter of Caesarea, 560
Margaret of Montaigu, 2nd wife of Peter of Dreux 1235–1241: 470
Margaret of Provence, wife of Louis IX of France 1234–1270 (d. 1296), 503, 741
Margarit of Brindisi, Sicilian admiral, count of Malta (d. 1195), 37–40, 47, 62
Maria, daughter of Andrew II of Hungary and Gertrude; 1st wife of John Asen of Bulgaria 1220–1237: 213, 220
Maria, daughter of Boril of Bulgaria; 2nd wife of Latin emperor Henry 1211–1216: 210
Maria (Heṭoumid), daughter of Constantine of Lampron; wife of John of Ibelin, of Jaffa, 652 note
Maria, daughter of Heṭoum I; wife of Guy of Ibelin, 652 note
Maria, illegitimate daughter of John Asen of Bulgaria; wife of Manuel of Thessalonica (after 1230), 215
Maria Comnena, daughter of Manuel I and Bertha; wife of Renier of Montferrat 1180–1182: 137–139, 164
Maria Comnena, great-granddaughter of John II; 2nd wife of Amalric of Jerusalem 1167–1174, wife of Balian II of Ibelin *c.* 1176–1193 (d. 1217), 66
Maria Lascaris, daughter of Theodore I; wife of Bela IV of Hungary (after 1224), 226, 393
Maria Lascaris, daughter of Theodore II; 1st wife of Nicephorus of Epirus (after 1257), 227
Maria of Antioch, daughter of Raymond of Poitiers and Constance; 2nd wife of Manuel I Comnenus 1161–1180 (d. 1182), 134, 144, 145
Marino Dandolo, lord of Andros 1207–1233: 238
Marino Filangieri, brother of Richard; archbishop of Bari 1226–1251: 359, 446, 451
Marino Sanudo, Venetian historian (d. 1533), 162, 657
Marino Zeno, Venetian podestà at Constantinople 1205–1207: 193–195
Maritsa river, 107, 191, 192, 205, 217; valley of, 101
Marj aṣ-Ṣuffar, 390, 398
Markward of Anweiler, imperial steward (d. 1202), 108, 346, 347, 349, 759
Markward of Neuenburg, chamberlain to Frederick I, 92, 95, 108
Marly (-le-Roi), lord of, 468
Marmande, 303, 315
Marmara, Sea of, 146, 171, 177, 230, 231; coast of, 191, 209, 217
Maronites, Christian sect, 621 note
al-Marqab, 393, 456, 535, 547, 553, 601, 703; Hospitallers of, 534, 586; fall of (1285), 589, 752
Marseilles, 57, 58, 64, 167, 175, 309, 335–339, 471, 472, 483, 511, 515; merchants from, 623; ships from, 57, 492; viscount of, *see* Roncelin
Marsiglio Giorgio, Venetian bailie at Tyre 1240–1244: 553, 559 note
Martin, abbot of Pairis, 164
Martin, bishop of Meissen 1170–1190: 92, 93, 115
Martin, chamberlain of the Temple, 383
Martin IV (Simon of Brie), pope 1281–1285: 369–371
Martoni (Nicholas of), Italian traveler (in 1394), 618
Mary, daughter of Conrad of Montferrat and Isabel of Jerusalem; 1st wife of John of Brienne 1210–1212; princess of Jerusalem *c.* 1206–1210, queen 1210–1212: 81 note, 442, 464, 532, 536, 537
Mary, daughter of Henry I of Champagne; wife of Latin emperor Baldwin I 1185–1204: 159, 535
Mary, daughter of Louis VII of France and Eleanor; wife of Henry I of Champagne *c.* 1149–1181 (d. 1198), 53, 159
Mary, daughter of Raymond Roupen of Antioch; wife of Philip of Montfort 1240–1268: 553, 554, 559
Mary of Antioch, daughter of Bohemond IV and Melisend; claimant to throne of Jerusalem 1269–1277 (d. after 1307), 579, 580, 583–585, 617
Mary of Antioch, daughter of Bohemond VI; 1st wife of Nicholas II of St. Omer, 261
Mary of Brienne, daughter of Latin emperor John and Rita; wife of Latin emperor Baldwin II 1231–1273 (d. *c.* 1275), 216, 217, 221, 223, 225, 229, 232, 615, 761
Mary of Courtenay, daughter of Latin emperor Peter and Yolanda; 3rd wife of Theodore I Lascaris 1218–1228, regent of Romania (in 1228), 213, 214, 216
Mary of Lusignan, daughter of Hugh I of Cyprus; wife of Walter IV of Brienne 1233–1250 (d. before 1261), 571, 606
Mary of Oignies, mystic from Brabant (d. 1213), 381
Marzano (di Nola), *see* Thomas
"Mascemuch" (?), unidentified emir at Alexandria, 337
Mashgharah, 393
al-Mashṭūb, Kurdish emir, 699; son of, *see* ʿImād-ad-Dīn Aḥmad
Massalian heresy, heretics, 144
Masʿūd I, Rukn-ad-Dīn, son of Kïlïj Arslan I; Selchükid sultan of Rūm 1116–1155: 136, 636–639, 641, 676–678
Masʿūd III, Ghiyāth-ad-Dīn, great-grandson of Kai-Kāʾūs II; last Selchükid of Rūm (after 1307), 728
al-Masʿūd Yūsuf, Ṣalāḥ-ad-Dīn, son of

al-Kāmil; Aiyūbid ruler of Yemen 1215–1229: 408, 742 note
Mas'ūd-Beg, vizir of Chaghatai Mongols, 723
Matagrifon: baron of, 258; barony of, 250
Matapan, Cape, 244
Mathesep (from Arabic *muḥtasib*, inspector of weights and measures), 620
Matthew, abbot of St. Denis, 375
Matthew II, baron of Montmorency 1189–1230: 159
Matthew, Latin patriarch of Constantinople 1221–1226: 198, 214
Matthew (Madṭēos) of Edessa, Armenian historian (d. *c.* 1136), 633
Matthew of Salerno, Sicilian official (d. 1153), 41
Matthew Paris, English chronicler (d. 1259), 157, 341, 342, 373, 468, 481–484, *and see* plates 2A, 2B
Maudūd, Rukn-ad-Dīn al-Mas'ūd, Artukid ruler of Ḥiṣn Kaifā 1219–1232: 683, 684
Maugastel, *see* Philip; *see also* Simon (archbishop of Tyre)
Mauléon, *see* Savary
Mauthausen, 93
Mazyadids, Arab dynasty at Hilla 1012–1150: 663, *and see* Dubais 1107–1134
Mecca, 23, 524, 708, 749
Mediterranean Sea, 8, 9, 17, 25, 29, 42, 135, 161, 327, 331, 370, 375, 382, 396, 397, 405, 472, 482, 508, 511, 655, 668, 715, 723, 726, 730; islands in, 21; region of eastern, 5, 26, 33, 118, 122, 126, 134, 148, 161, 264, 273, 279, 508, 661, 662, 674; region of southern, 26; region of western, 372, 512; map of central, 2; map of western, 44
Megara, 236
Meillor III of Ravendel (Ravendan), 752 note
Meissen: bishop of, 92, 93, 115; margrave of, *see* Dietrich
Melfi, bishop of, 542, 612
Melgueil, 284, 286
Melisend of Lusignan, daughter of Aimery and Isabel of Jerusalem; 2nd wife of Bohemond IV 1218–1233: 393, 540, 559, 560 note, 579, 580, 609
Melissena, —, daughter of governor of Arta; wife of Michael I of Epirus (after 1204), 201
Melitene, 132, 632, 637, 677–679; governor of, 632
Melk, advocate of, 93
Melkites, Christian Arabs, 411
Mello, *see* Dreux (2)
Melnik, 205
Melos, 239
Melun, council of (1216), 381
Menas, 105, *and see* Enos
Mengü-Timur, son of Hulagu (d. after 1281), 751
Mengüchekids (or Mengüjükids), Turkish dynasty at Erzinjan 1072–1228: 682, *and see* Bahrām-Shāh
Meran, *see* Croatia; dukes of, 92, 387, 431; *see also* Agnes, Gertrude
Mérencourt, *see* Ralph
Merseburg, 9, 22
Mesopotamia, 693–696, 699–701, 703, 705–708, 723, 730; as seat of caliphate, 662, 665, 667; Mongols in, 714, 717–719, 726; Nestorians in, 668; officials from, 712; princes of, 673; Turkomans in, 680, 684; *see also* Iraq, Jazira
Messenia, 237, 240, 246, 248, 252, 254, 258, 261, 265, 272
Messina, 40 note, 41, 58–61, 120, 382, 600, 759; treaty of (1190), 79
Messina, Strait of, 7, 59
Meteorium, 232
Metz, *see* Aubrey Clement, Conrad; burghers of, 93; diocese of, 510
Meuse river, 490
Michael (of Murèze), archbishop of Arles 1202–1217: 309
Michael V, Byzantine co-emperor 1041–1042: 633
Michael VII, Byzantine emperor 1071–1078: 633
Michael I ("Ducas") Angelus Comnenus, cousin of Isaac II Angelus; despot of Epirus 1204–1214: 151, 201, 206, 208–210, 226, 236, 237, 240, 242; wife of, *see* — Melissena
Michael II Angelus Comnenus, illegitimate son of Michael I; despot of Epirus 1236–1271: 226–228, 230, 246, 247, 257, 260, 261
Michael IV Autorianus, Orthodox patriarch at Nicaea 1208–1214: 197, 201
Michael Cantacuzenus, Byzantine official (d. 1264), 253, 254, 270
Michael Choniates, brother of Nicetas; Orthodox metropolitan of Athens 1182–1215 (d. before 1220), 252
Michael VIII Palaeologus, great-grandson of Alexius III Angelus; Byzantine co-emperor at Nicaea 1258–1261: 228–232, 246, 247, 761; emperor at Constantinople 1261–1282: 232, 248, 253–261, 367–370, 509, 584, 628, 726, 748, 761, 762
Michael IX Palaeologus, son of Andronicus II; Byzantine co-emperor 1295–1320: 657; wife of, *see* Rita (Heṭoumid)
Michael Stryphnus, Byzantine admiral, 176
Michael Tarchaniotes, Byzantine official, 260
Michael the Syrian, Jacobite historian and patriarch (d. 1199), 529, 638, 643 note, 648
Midi, 279, 283, 285, 287, 289, 294, 296, 297, 325
Mignano, peace of (1139), 9, 11 note, 22
Milan, 221, 352, 353, 445, 450; archbishop of, *see* Henry
Milly, *see* Stephanie

Milo (of Châtillon-sur-Marne and Nanteuil), bishop of Beauvais 1217–1234: 349, 403
Milo, papal secretary and legate in Languedoc (d. 1209), 286, 287, 291
al-Minā', 592
Minden, diocese of, 340
Minerve, 288, 290
Minūchihr, Shirvān-Shāh 1027–1034: 664
Mirepoix, 294 note
Mistra: under Franks 1249–1262: 244, 248; under Greeks after 1262: 253, 254, 261, 262, 264, 267, 270, 272
Mkhiṭar of Ayrivanḳ (Erivan), Armenian historian, 632
Mleh, son of Leon I; Ṛoupenid ruler of Cilician Armenia 1170–1175: 641–643
Modon, 202, 208, 237–239; bishop of, 252
Mohammed (Arabic, Muḥammad), founder of Islamic religion and community (d. 632), xx, 144, 461, 671
Moissac, 295; abbot of, 295 note
Monemvasia, 13 240, 244, 246, 248, 253; bishopric of, 252
Möngke (Turkish, Mänggü), grandson of Genghis Khan; Great Khan of the Mongols 1251–1259: 568, 572, 573, 652, 653, 717, 718
Mongolia, 573, 718, 722
Mongols, Altaic people, xviii, 230, 507, 572, 581, 615, 665, 747, 754; in Central Asia, 652, 653, 668, 669, 671, 672, 674, 715–719; in Persia, 421, 422, 509, 568, 575, 576, 656, 662, 671–673, 703, 704, 717–726, 761; in Mesopotamia, 489, 571, 573, 578, 579, 662, 667, 684, 708, 726, 742, 744, 748, 749, 761; in Anatolia, 220, 223–225, 652, 683, 687–692, 709, 717, 725–732, 750, 751, 761, 762; in Cilicia, 655, 657, 658; in Syria, 508, 571–575, 582, 586, 589, 653–655, 657, 674, 694, 714, 717–719, 721, 726, 735, 744, 745, 751, 752, 755, 761, 762; in Europe, 220, 221; Great Khans of, *see* Genghis Khan 1206–1227, Ögödai 1227–1242, Göyük 1246–1248, Möngke 1251–1259, Kubilai 1260–1294; *see also* Chaghatai, Golden Horde, Il-khans; map, 734
Monophysites, *see* Jacobites
Montaigu, *see* Margaret; lord of, 469
Montaigu (-sur-Champeix), *see* Eustorgue, Garin, Peter
Montauban, 295
Montbéliard, *see* Eschiva, Odo, Walter
Monte Cassino, abbey, 446
Monte Cristo, 353
Monte Croce, *see* Ricold
Montelongo, *see* Gregory
Montferrat, 166, 208; house of, 164, 165, 212, 215; marquis of, *see* William III, Conrad, Boniface II, William IV, Boniface III, *and also* Adelaide, Agnes, Alice, Demetrius, Mary, Renier, William "Longsword", Yolanda; marquisate of, 164, 207
Montfort (in Palestine), 448, 460, 542; *see also* Starkenburg
Montfort (-l'Amaury): baron of, *see* Simon IV; counts of, 289, *and see* Amalric VI, John I; house of, 312, 319, 582, 586, *and see* Amicie, Guy (2), Humphrey, John, Philip, Simon
Montgey, 293
Montjoie, hill, 568
Montmirail, *see* Reginald
Montmorency, *see* Alice; baron of, 159
Montmusart, 596, 597
Montpellier, 288 note, 290, 291, 304, 305, 777; conference at (1211), 291, 292
Montpensier, 319
Montréal, 294 note, 315; lord of, 293
Moors, *see* Moslems
Moravia, duke of, 93
Morea: under Greeks to 1205: 13, 135, 177, 190, 191, 235, 237; under Franks after 1205: 202, 206, 208, 229, 237–240, 243–274, 760; clergy of, 221; crusaders from, 493; primate of, 252; *see also* Achaea
Morfia, daughter of Gabriel of Melitene; wife of Baldwin II of Jerusalem (after *c.* 1101), 632
Morocco, 20, 23, 28; shaikh from, 711
Moscow, 233
Moslems (Arabic, al-Muslimūn; Saracens, Moors), members of Islamic community, xx, 85, 124, 144, 336, 348, 355, 396, 453, 457, 461, 462, 664, 665, 671, 675, 685, 686, 690, 702, 741, 747, 755, 758; in North Africa, 6 note, 21, 23, 25–28, 31, 515; in Sicily, 6, 8 note, 19, 22, 26, 28, 32–34, 337, 347, 361, 436, 439; in Spain, 21, 297, 386, 439, 466, 760; in Portugal, 50, 56, 395, 759; and Mongols, 715–721, 724, 726, 731; *see also* Islam
Mosul, 663, 699, 701, 738; merchants from, 585; rulers of, *see* Zengids (1127–1234), Lu'lu' (1234–1259)
Mosynopolis, 151, 179
al-Muʿaẓẓam ʿĪsâ, Sharaf-ad-Dīn, son of al-ʿĀdil I Saif-ad-Dīn; Aiyūbid governor of Transjordania 1186–1193: 693; ruler 1193–1227: 695; governor of Damascus 1202–1218: 389–392, 395, 398, 531, 537, 539, 696, 698, 699; ruler 1218–1227: 401, 402, 408–411, 422, 424–426, 448–450, 452, 453, 462, 543, 673, 699–701, 705
al-Mughīth ʿUmar, Fakhr-ad-Dīn, son of aṣ-Ṣāliḥ Aiyūb; Aiyūbid governor of Damascus 1238–1239 (d. 1245), 706, 709
al-Mughīth ʿUmar, Fakhr-ad-Dīn, son of al-ʿĀdil II Abū-Bakr; Aiyūbid ruler of Transjordania 1250–1263: 712, 714, 742, 747
Mughuls, Timurid dynasty in India 1526–1761 (1857): 668
Muhadhdhib-ad-Dīn, vizir of Kai-Khusrau II (d. *c.* 1245), 692

Muḥammad, ʿAlāʾ-ad-Dīn, son of Tökūsh; Khorezm-Shāh 1200–1220: 670–672, 723
Muḥammad, an-Nāṣir Nāṣir-ad-Dīn, son of Kalavun and Aslun Khātūn; Mamluk sultan of Egypt and Syria 1293–1294, 1299–1309, 1310–1341: 753
Muḥammad I, Ḥafṣid emir of Tunisia 1249–1277: 513–517, 795
Muḥammad, Nāṣir-ad-Dīn, son of Gümüshtigin Ghāzī; Dānishmendid emir c. 1134–1140: 637, 676, 677
Muḥammad, son of Rāfiʿ; nominal ruler of Gabes (in 1147), 24
Muḥammad ibn-Maimūn, governor of the Baleares (in 1122), 20 21
Muḥammad ibn-Tūmart, founder of the Muwaḥḥid sect (d. 1128), 28
Muʿīn-ad-Dīn ibn-ash-Shaikh; Egyptian general, 710
Muʿīn-ad-Dīn Sulaimān, Pervānch, son of Muhadhdhib-ad-Dīn; Selchükid chancellor 1261–1277: 727, 728
al-Muʿizz, Fāṭimid caliph at Mahdia 953–972, at Cairo 972–975: 17
al-Muʿizz, Zīrid emir in Tunisia 1016–1062: 17, 18
al-Mujāhid Shīrkūh, Ṣalāḥ-ad-Dīn, grandson of (al-Manṣūr) Shīrkūh; Aiyūbid governor of Homs 1186–1193, ruler 1193–1240: 391, 478, 693, 696, 697, 701, 706, 708
Münster, bishops of, *see* Hermann, Otto
Muntaner, Raymond, Catalan chronicler (d. 1336?), 271
Murābiṭs, Berber sect and dynasty in Morocco and Spain 1056–1147: 20, 28, *and see* ʿAlī ibn-Yūsuf; in the Baleares, 20, 33; in Tripoli, 23
Muret, battle (1213), 287, 300–304, 760
al-Mustaḍī, ʿAbbāsid caliph at Baghdad 1170–1180: 679
al-Mustanṣir, grandson of an-Nāṣir; ʿAbbāsid "caliph" at Cairo 1261–1261: 747
al-Mustanṣir, Fāṭimid caliph at Cairo 1036–1094: 18
al-Mustarshid, ʿAbbāsid caliph of Baghdad 1118–1135: 663, 677
al-Mustaʿṣim, great-grandson of an-Nāṣir; ʿAbbāsid caliph at Baghdad 1242–1258: 506, 568, 674, 711, 738, 741, 744, 747, 761
Muwaḥḥids, Berber sect and dynasty in North Africa and Spain 1130–1269: xxii, 28, 30–32, 327, 378, 379, *and see* Muḥammad ibn-Tūmart, ʿAbd-al-Muʾmin 1130–1163, Yūsuf 1163–1184
al-Muẓaffar Ghāzī, Shihāb-ad-Dīn, son of al-ʿĀdil I Saif-ad-Dīn, Aiyūbid ruler of the Jazira 1229–1244: 674, 700, 708
al-Muẓaffar Maḥmūd, Taqī-ad-Dīn, son of al-Manṣūr Muḥammad; Aiyūbid ruler of Hamah 1229–1243: 411, 478, 550, 703–705, 707, 709, 711, 712
al-Muẓaffar ʿUmar, Taqī-ad-Dīn, nephew of Saladin; Aiyūbid governor of Hamah, 1179–1191: 67, 693, 714
Myconos, 238
Myriokephalon, pass, 111; battle (1176), 137, 140, 141, 679

Nablus, 389, 390, 454, 552, 698, 701, 702, 706, 710, 713 note; attacks on, 553, 561, 709, 714; emir of, 408
Nahr Naʿmān, stream, 390
Nain, 390
Najm-ad-Dīn, Assassin master in Syria (to 1270, d. 1274), 749
Namur: count of, 213; marquisate of, 221, 222
Nangis, *see* William
Nanteuil (-le-Haudoin), *see* Andrew, Milo, Philip
Naples, 58, 61, 117, 256, 359, 361, 366; archbishop of, *see* Philip; court of, 259, 261, 269, 274; honor of, 8 note; kingdom of, 261, 262, 269, 372, 591; kings of, *see* Charles I of Anjou 1268–1285, Charles II 1285–1309; *see also* Two Sicilies
Narbonne, 291, 303–305, 307, 308; archbishops of, *see* Arnold Amalric, Peter, William; duke of, 308; viscount of, 303
Narjot I of Toucy, regent of Romania 1228–1231, 1238–1241: 216; daughter of, 244, 245, 255
Narjot II of Toucy, son of Philip; grand admiral of Naples (d. after 1288), 591; wife of, *see* Lucy (of Antioch)
Narzotto dalle Carceri, triarch of southern Euboea 1247–1264: 245; wife of, *see* Felicia (dalle Carceri)
an-Nasawī, secretary to Jalāl-ad-Dīn Mangubertī (d. after 1241), 672
an-Nāṣir, son of al-Mustaḍī; ʿAbbāsid caliph at Baghdad 1180–1225: 336, 410, 421, 422, 529, 665–667, 670–672, 688, 696, 700, 760
an-Nāṣir Dāʾūd, Ṣalāḥ-ad-Dīn, son of al-Muʿaẓẓam ʿĪsâ; Aiyūbid ruler of Damascus 1227–1229: 453, 459, 701, 702; of Transjordania 1227–1249 (d. 1259): 471, 477–480, 483, 546, 547, 553, 561–564, 674, 704–707, 709–711, 741 note
an-Nāṣir Kilij Arslan, Ṣalāḥ-ad-Dīn, son of al-Manṣūr Muḥammad; Aiyūbid ruler of Hamah 1221–1229: 701, 703
an-Nāṣir Yūsuf, Ṣalāḥ-ad-Dīn, son of al-ʿAzīz Muḥammad; Aiyūbid ruler of Aleppo 1236–1260: 493, 505, 550, 553, 564, 704, 710–712; of Damascus and Baalbek 1250–1260 (d. 1261): 505, 507, 567, 712–714, 741–743, 745–747
Nāṣir-ad-Dīn Ṭūsī, Persian scholar (d. 1274), 721
Naṣr, Assassin master in Syria (in 1194), 528
Naṣr-ad-Dīn Khoja, semi-legendary folk hero (d. c. 1285), 732
Nassau, count of, 92, 94, *and see* Walram

Naumburg (an der Saale), 777; and Zeitz, bishops of, *see* Berthold, Engelhard
Naupactus, 273
Nauplia, 202, 237, 240, 241, 259, 263
Navarino, 239, 261
Navarre, 270, 470; kings of, *see* Sancho VI 1150–1194, Theobald IV 1234–1253, Theobald V 1253–1270; princess of, *see* Berengaria
Navarre (of Acqs), bishop of Couserans 1208 ?–1211 ?, papal legate in Languedoc, 285
Naxos, 192, 202, 238, 239, 272; duke of, 271, *and see* Archipelago, dukes of
Nazareth, 745; under Moslems 1187–1229: 532, 697; under Franks 1229–1263: 455, 464, 574; under Moslems after 1263: 583, 583, 588, 616; archbishop of, 389
Negroes, 134, 736
Negroponte, island, *see* Euboea
Negroponte, town, 210, 229, 232, 238 note, 245, 251, 257; bishopric of, 252; lordship of, 239, 240; Venetians at, 240, 242, 245, 259, 272
Neo-Manichean, 329 note, *and see* Albigensian heresy
Neocastro, *see* Bartholomew
Neopatras, 213, 257; dukes of, *see* Angelus "Comnenus"
Neophytus, hermit (d. 1220), 601, 602, 624, 626
Neophytus, Orthodox archbishop of Cyprus *c.* 1220–1222: 626
Nephin, 534, 544, 587, 591, 593; lord of, 534
Nersēs ("the Gracious"), brother of Gregory III; Armenian catholicus 1166–1173: 641
Nersēs of Lampron, son of Ōshin II; Armenian archbishop of Tarsus (d. 1198), 645, 646 note, 648 note, 649
Nesle, *see* John, Ralph (2)
Nestorians, Christian sect, 507, 572, 623, 668, 715, 720–722, 745; patriarch of, 656
Netherlands, crusaders from, 115; *see also* Low Countries
Neuenburg, *see* Markward
Neuilly (-sur-Marne), *see* Fulk
Nevers, counts of, 54, 60, 212, 287, 289, 417, 469, 481, 516
Nicaea, city, 151, 197, 201, 209, 218, 760; "duchy" of, 192; patriarchs of, *see* Michael IV Autorianus 1208–1214, Manuel I Sarantenus 1217–1222, Germanus 1222–1240, Arsenius (of Apollonia) 1255–1259
Nicaea, empire, 151, 209, 211, 214, 216, 217, 223–228, 230, 244, 466, 570, 682–684, 688, 726, 760, 761; emperors of, *see* Byzantine emperors, at Nicaea 1208–1261
Nicephorus I, Byzantine emperor 802–811: 204
Nicephorus Angelus Comnenus, son of Michael II; despot of Epirus 1271–1296: 227, 260, 261, 263, 266, 267; wives of, *see* Maria Lascaris, Anna Cantacuzena
Nicephorus Melissenus, Byzantine caesar (in 1081, d. 1104), 165
Nicetas Choniates, Byzantine historian (d. *c.* 1215), 13, 139, 141–143, 150, 171, 185, 192, 204
Nicetas II Muntanes, Orthodox patriarch of Constantinople 1186–1189: 96, 103, 109
Nicholas (Maltraversi), bishop of Reggio (nell' Emilia) 1211–1243: 421
Nicholas (of Claromonte), cardinal-bishop of Tusculum 1219–1227: 438
Nicholas, chaplain to Richard I (in 1191), bishop of Le Mans 1214–1216: 63
Nicholas (of Castro Arquato), Latin patriarch of Constantinople *c.* 1234–1251: 225, 466
Nicholas III (John Gaetano Orsini), pope 1277–1280: 368, 369, 762
Nicholas IV (Jerome Masci), pope 1288–1292: 593, 594, 617, 722, 762
Nicholas Canabus, Byzantine pretender (d. 1204), 181, 182
Nicholas Falier, Venetian bailie at Negroponte 1280–1282: 259
Nicholas Lorgne, master of the Hospital 1277–1284: 587
Nicholas of Choisy, French sergeant, 614
Nicholas of Cologne, leader of Children's Crusade, 331, 333–335, 760; father of, 335
Nicholas of Hannapes, patriarch of Jerusalem 1288–1291: 597
Nicholas II of St. Omer, son of Bela, lord of half of Thebes 1258–1294, bailie of Achaea 1287–1289: 259, 261, 265; wives of, *see* Mary of Antioch, Anna Angelina Comnena
Nicholas III of St. Omer, nephew of Nicholas II; lord of Thebes 1299–1311, bailie of Achaea 1300–1302, 1304–1307 (d. 1314), 265–268
Nicholas Querini, Venetian banker, 222
Nicholas I Sanudo, son of William I; duke of the Archipelago 1323–1241: 271
Nicholas Tiepolo, Venetian naval commander, 593
Nicomedia, 205, 209, 215, 216
Nicosia, 64, 589, 602 note, 604, 606, 611, 612, 623 note, 625; archbishops of, 389, 413 note, 596, 609, 621, 624, 625, 628; cathedral of, 628; high court of, *see under* Cyprus; viscount of, 620
Nicotera, 20
Nikiz, 106, *and see* Hafsa
Nikli, 246, 254, 258, 272; barony of, 250
Nile river, 738, 747, 778; and fifth crusade: 397–402, 404–415, 423–426, 539, 609; and crusade of 1249: 492, 493, 495–502; delta of, 35, 36, 410, 411, 425, 444, 493, 496–498, 531, 537, 593
Nimburg, 778; count of, 92, 93
Nîmes, bishop of, 307
Niphon, Bogomil monk (in 1143), 144
Nish, 91, 93, 99, 100, 210

Nisi, 265
Nisibin, 706
Niẓām-al-Mulk, vizir of Selchükids in Iran (d. 1092), 736
Niẓām-al-Mulk Muḥammad, al-Harawī, vizir of Khorezm-Shāh Muḥammad, 671
Niẓāmī of Ganja, Persian poet (d. *c.* 1202), 663
Nonancourt, 49
Normandy, 47, 48, 61, 70, 79, 155, 491; crusaders from, 65, 74; duke of, 54; seneschal of, *see* William fitz Ralph
Normans, in Egypt, 35; in England, 621; in Germany, 11; in Greece, 11, 14, 15, 37, 125, 127, 136, 138, 146, 149; in Italy, 5, 6, 8, 117, 125, 132, 345; in Normandy, 53; in North Africa, 9, 16, 18–33; in Sicily, *see under* Sicily; in Syria, 5, 10, 126, 133
Norpert, 650
North Africa, 42, 339, 514; Sicilians in, 4, *and see* Normans; *see also* Tunisia
Norway, 120; king of, *see* Haakon V 1217–1263
Novara, 610, *and see* Philip
Novgorod, chronicle of, 153 note
Noyers, *see* Hugh
Nubia, 22, 749, 750, 752
Numidia, 16, 22
Nuño Sancho, count of Roussillon 1222?–1241: 318 note
Nūr-ad-Dīn Maḥmūd, son of Zengi; Zengid ruler of Syria 1146–1174: 34, 39, 140, 638–643, 678, 679, 694
Nuremberg, 91, 434; treaty of (1188), 91, 92, 95, 97, 101, 104, 107, 108
Nuṣairī mountains, 559, *and see* Jabal Anṣārīyah
Nymphaeum, 209, 218, 230

Oberto of Biandrate, regent of Thessalonica 1207–1209: 206–208, 210, 212, 214
Oberto Pallavicini, nephew of Guy; tyrant of Cremona (1250–1266), of Piacenza (1254–1257, 1260–1266), etc. (d. 1269), 363
Ochrida, 212; archbishop of, 214
Ochrida, Lake, 247
Octavian (Conti), cardinal-deacon 1182–1189, cardinal-bishop of Ostia 1189–1206, papal legate in France, 58, 157
Octavian (Ubaldini), cardinal-deacon 1244–1273, papal legate in Italy, 362
Octavian Querini, Venetian elector (in 1204), 189 note
Odo (Rigaud), archbishop of Rouen 1248–1275: 341
Odo (of Sully), bishop of Paris 1196–1208: 284
Odo III, son of Hugh III; duke of Burgundy 1192–1218: 287, 289, 290, 385
Odo (le Queux), seneschal of Carcassonne, 323
Odo of Champlitte, son of Hugh I of Champagne; viscount of Dijon (in 1202), 158 note
Odo of Châteauroux, cardinal-bishop of Tusculum 1244–1273: 490, 560 note, 627, 628
Odo of Montbéliard, nephew (or son) of Walter; constable of Jerusalem 1218–1244: 447, 452, 472, 475–477, 545; bailie 1222–1226: 444, 541, 542; co-bailie 1228–1228, 1229–1231: 546, 548; baronial co-bailie 1233–1243: 550, 551, 559, 560; lord of Tiberias 1240–1244: 564
Odo Poilechien, nephew of Martin IV; Angevin bailie at Acre 1282–1286: 588, 590
Oenoë, 200
Oghuz, Turkoman tribe, 662, 669, 670; *see also* Selchükids
Ögödai, son of Genghis Khan; Great Khan of the Mongols 1227–1242: 717
Oignies, *see* Mary
Oldenburg, *see* Wilbrand; count of, *see* Christian
Olena, bishop of, 252
Oliver (Plantagenet), illegitimate son of John of England (d. 1219), 402
Oliver (Saxo), scholasticus of Cologne, bishop of Paderborn 1224–1225, cardinal-bishop (of Sabina) 1225–1227: 381, 389, 392, 394, 396, 399–402, 407, 411, 414–416, 418, 420, 422, 424, 425, 444
Öljaitu (Khodābanda "Muḥammad"), son of Arghun; Īl-khan of Persia 1304–1316: 719
Olympia, 254
Opizon (Fieschi), nephew of Innocent IV; Latin patriarch of Antioch 1247–1268 (titular 1268–1292), 566, 575
Oreus, 235, 239, 245, 257
Orlando Pescia, Italian knight, 238
Orléans, 341
Orontes river, 533, 577, 649, 696
Orsinis, Apulian dynasty at Cephalonia 1194–1324: *see* Maio 1194–1238, Richard 1238–1304
Orthodox Christians ("Greeks"), sect, xviii, 87; in Byzantine empire, 15, 96, 97, 196, 217, 218, 232, 233, 369; in Latin empire, 196, 211; in Frankish Greece, 241, 252; in Cyprus, 608, 623–628; in Anatolia, 632, 683, 726; *see also* Greek church
Orvieto, bishop of, 228; treaty of (1281), 260
Ōshin I, Heṭoumid lord of Lampron 1073–1110: 633, 634
Ōshin II, grandson of Ōshin I; Heṭoumid lord of Lampron (d. 1168), 639, 641
Osma, bishop of, 283
Osnabrück, bishop of, *see* Arnold
Ostia, cardinal-bishops of, *see* Peter Damian, Octavian, Ugolino
Ostrovo, 226, 227
Othon de Cicon, nephew of Othon de la Roche; lord of Carystus 1250–1278: 246

Othon de la Roche, lord of Athens 1250–1225 (d. 1234), 238–242, 248; wife of, *see* Isabel (de Ray)
Otranto, 446, 447, 451
Otranto, Strait of, 255
Öttingen, count of, *see* Conrad
Otto, archbishop of Genoa 1203–1239: 609
Otto, half-brother of Conrad III of Germany; bishop of Freising 1138–1158: 11
Otto (of Oldenburg), bishop of Münster 1204–1218: 389
Otto (of Henneberg), bishop of Speyer 1188–1200: 93
Otto (of Vaudemont), bishop of Toul 1192–1197: 120
Otto (of Lippe), bishop of Utrecht 1215–1228: 389
Otto I, count of Guelders 1182–1207: 50, 51, 65, 115
Otto VII (of Andechs), son of Berthold IV; duke of Meran 1204–1234, count of (upper) Burgundy 1208–1234, margrave of Istria 1215–1230: 387, 388 note, 389, 431
Otto IV of Brunswick, son of Henry "the Lion"; Welf emperor of Germany 1201 (crowned 1209)–1211 (d. 1218), 171, 291, 297, 378, 382, 384, 431, 432
Otto of Grandison, Swiss commander (d. 1328), 595–597
Ottomans (Osmanli), Turkish people, 233, 270, 621 note, 628, 721, 725, 731, 732; sultans, *see* Sulaimān I
Outremer, 5, 34, 38, 41, 156, 161, 168, 559, 560, 562, 564, 566–569, 571, 598, 611, 738; *see also* Palestine, Syria
Oxus river, 568

Pachymeres, George, Byzantine historian (d. *c.* 1310), 231, 252
Paderborn, 381
Padua, 363
Pagan II, lord of Haifa (d. *c.* 1198), 524
Pagouran, son of Sempad; Heṭoumid lord of Babaṛon (after 1152, d. after 1198), 643, 644
Pairis, abbot of, 164
Pakrad, brother of Kogh Vasil; Armenian lord of Cyrrhus (to 1117), 636
Palaeologus, Byzantine imperial dynasty at Nicaea 1258–1261 and Constantinople 1261–1453: 143, 146, *and see* Michael VIII 1258–1282, Andronicus II 1282–1328, Michael IX (1295–1320), John V 1341–1391 (interrupted), John VIII 1425–1448; *see also* Constantine, John (2)
Palear, *see* Walter
Palermo: before 1189: 7, 8 note, 13, 19, 21, 24, 27, 28, 30, 31 note, 32, 35, 38; after 1189: 41, 119, 339; archbishop of, 449
Palestine, or the Holy Land, 675; before 1189: 15, 37; 1189–1243: 52, 60, 62, 64, 76, 82, 85, 87, 119, 147, 158 note, 383–386, 394, 396, 402, 410, 432, 434, 441, 443, 449, 455, 457, 458, 464, 484, 539, 552, 603, 604, 608, 696, 699, 701, 702, 706, 707; 1243–1291: 226, 363, 369, 373, 490, 492, 504–509, 518, 567, 573, 709, 710, 713, 717, 718, 735, 742, 743, 745, 756, 761; as goal of crusades, 4, 284, 285, 292, 298, 325, 326, 345–350, 352, 357, 362, 653, 654; of first, 126; of third, 46, 47, 50, 54, 55, 61, 63, 148; of 1197: 118, 122, 149; of fourth, 154, 155, 163, 169, 172 note, 174, 175, 177, 180, 290, 377, 531; of children's, 335; of fifth, 300, 308, 315, 378, 380, 395, 428, 430, 433, 437; of Frederick II's, 438, 461, 462, 611; of 1239: 465–473, 480, 483; of Louis IX's, 341, 497, 512, 513, 515, 581; of prince Edward's, 517, 583, 762; as goal of pilgrims, 6, 33, 38, 331, 334, 379, 600; map of, 520
Pallavicini, *see* Albert, Guy, Isabel, Oberto
Pamiers, 295, 318; statutes of (1212), 296
Pantelleria, 21, 24
Papacy (or "Rome"), 149, 371–375, 494, 518, 565, 683; and Normans, 5, 8, 33; and early Hohenstaufens, 88, 104, 117, 345–347; and fourth crusade, 154, 155, 161, 180; and Latin empire, 213, 215, 227, 232; and Frankish Greece, 239, 243, 252; and Frederick II, xviii, 348–358, 431; and later Hohenstaufens, 358–367, 509; and Angevins, 363–371, 509, 584; and Cyprus, 613, 621, 623; and Cilicia, 647, 650; and Mongols, 722; *see also* Latin church *and individual* Popes
Paphlagonia, 133
Paphos, 610, 615 note, 625; bishop of, 624
Paris, 76, 221, 224, 308, 321, 330, 336, 337, 467, 492, 512; archdeacon of, 304, 326; bishops of, 284, 292, 348, 403; doctors of, 385; livres of, 222, 491 note, 504; mark of, 56; peace of, (1229): 287, 296, 319, 323, 324, 761; (1259): 322; region around, 158, 290, 296, *and see* Île de France; Temple in, 383, 386
Parma, 355, *and see* Albert, John
Parnon, 240, 244
Paroikoi (Greek, peasant tenants), 129, 142, 143, 241, 251, 622
Paros, 192, 239
Parthenon, at Athens, 208, 241
Partzapert, lord of, 639
Passau, advocate of, 93; bishops of, *see* Dietpold, Wolfger, Ulrich
Passavant, barony of, 250, 253, 258
Patmos, 128
Patras, 237, 252; archbishopric of, 252; barony of, 250
Patras, Gulf of, 236, 237
Patriarchs, patriarchate, *see under* Antioch, Constantinople, Jerusalem, *and* Jacobites, Nestorians
Patti, 21; bishop of, 442
Paul Gradenigo, Venetian bailie at Negroponte 1254–1256: 245

Paul of Segni, brother of Lucienne; bishop of Tripoli 1261–before 1285: 585, 587
Paulician heresy, heretics, 144, 203, 204
Pazouni, brother of Ōshin I (d. after 1098), 634
Pechenegs, Turkic people, 125, 131
Pegae, 205, 209, 217
Péguilhan, *see* Aimery
Peking, 716, 718, 719, 723
Pelagius (Galvani), cardinal-deacon 1205–1210, cardinal-priest 1210–1213, cardinal-bishop of Albano 1213–1230: 211, 438, 442, 625, 627 note; papal legate on fifth crusade, xvii, 380, 402, 403, 405–407, 409–426, 430, 435–437, 462, 539–541, 609
Pelagonia, 209, 217; battle (1259), 228, 229, 247, 761
Peloponnesus, *see* Morea
Pembroke, earl of, 482
Penne-d'Agenais, 295
Pera, 178, 180
Perche, 159, *and see* Stephen; counts of, 49, 159, 164
Pergamum, 209
Périgord, 303, 306, *and see* Armand
Pernis, 102, *and see* Petrich
Perpignan, 372
Perpyriarii (Greek, freedmen) 622
Persia, 192, 421, 509, 671, 689, 703, 719, 721, 724, 731, 732, 761; Mongols of, *see* Il-khans; *see also* Iran; map of, 660
Persian language, transliteration and nomenclature, xxii
Pertous, 639, 650
Perugia, 384
Pervāneh (Persian, chancellor), 686, 727, 728
Peter ("the Venerable"), abbot of Cluny 1122–1156: 12 note, 16
Peter, abbot of Locedio, Latin patriarch of Antioch 1209–1217: 173, 536, 538
Peter, archbishop of Brindisi 1182–1196?: 119
Peter (of Limoges), archbishop of Caesarea (before 1217–after 1229), 389, 457, 458, 545
Peter (of Ameil), archbishop of Narbonne 1226–1245: 323
Peter (of Corbeil), archbishop of Sens 1200–1222: 287
Peter (of Nemours), bishop of Paris 1208–1219: 292, 403
Peter, bishop of Raab (before 1206–1218), 389
Peter (of Barisey), bishop of Toul 1165–1192: 92, 104
Peter (des Roches), bishop of Winchester 1205–1238: 445, 542
Peter, count of Vendôme 1239–1249: 493
Peter II, king of Aragon 1196–1213: 287–292, 296–302, 304, 760
Peter III, son of James I; king of Aragon 1276–1285, of Sicily 1282–1285: 260, 343, 370–372, 375, 751; wife of, *see* Constance (Hohenstaufen)
Peter, brother of Asen; Vlach tsar of Bulgaria 1196–1197: 100, 102, 107, 109, 146, 148, 201
Peter Barbo, Venetian bailie at Negroponte (in 1216), 242, 245
Peter Capocci, cardinal-deacon 1244–1259, papal legate in Calabria, 356, 359
Peter Capuano (of Amalfi), cardinal-deacon 1192–1201, cardinal-priest 1201–1214, papal legate in France and Syria, 155–157, 173, 175, 196, 534, 535
Peter Chappe, Cypriote knight, 610
Peter Damian, cardinal-bishop (of Ostia) 1058–*c.* 1066 (d. 1072), 347
Peter Embriaco, son of Guy II; lord of Jubail 1282–*c.* 1298 (d. after 1307), 593
Peter Flotte, French chancellor 1300–1302: 266
Peter of Amiens, French baron, 160
Peter of Angoulême, Latin patriarch of Antioch 1201–1208: 533, 535, 536
Peter of Benevento, papal legate in Languedoc (d. 1216?), 303–306
Peter of Bracieux, French baron, ruler of Lopadium 1204–1209: 160, 192, 209
Peter of Castelnau, archdeacon of Maguelonne, papal legate in Languedoc (d. 1208), 277, 283–286, 291, 760
Peter of Courtenay, grandson of Louis VI of France; count of Nevers and Auxerre 1184–1192, Latin emperor of Romania 1217–1218 (d. 1219?), 54, 60, 212, 213, 242, 760; wife of, *see* Yolanda (of Hainault)
Peter I of Dreux, son of Robert II; count of Brittany 1213–1237, earl of Richmond 1219–1237, lord of La Garnache and Montaigu 1235–1241? (d. 1250), 219, 319, 466–470, 474, 475, 477, 481, 483, 484; wives of, *see* Alice (of Brittany), Margaret of Montaigu
Peter of Les Vaux-de-Cernay, nephew of abbot Guy; French chronicler (d. 1219?), 277 note, 291, 292, 299, 304, 305, 327
Peter of Montaigu (-sur-Champeix), brother of Garin; master of the Temple 1219–1229: 413, 422, 424, 425, 427, 438, 452, 454, 546, 625
Peter of Pola, doge of Venice 1130–1148: 10
Peter of Sargines, archbishop of Tyre 1235–1244: 563
Peter of Vieille Bride (Brioude), master of the Hospital 1239–1242: 463, 472, 475, 484, 553
Peter Roger, lord of Cabaret (to 1211), 292
Peter Vidal, Provençal troubadour (d. 1215?), 166
Peter Ziani, doge of Venice 1205–1229: 193, 208, 239, 240, 387
Peterborough, abbot of, 45 note
Petrich, 102
Philadelphia, 98, 110; "duchy" of, 192

Philaretus (Filardos, or Vahram), Armenian lord in Anatolia (d. 1085), 632
Philip (of Heinsberg), archbishop of Cologne 1167–1191: 90
Philip (Capece Minutolo), archbishop of Naples 1288–1301: 262
Philip II ("Augustus"), son of Louis VII and Adela; Capetian king of France 1180–1223: 116, 330, 439, 459, 523, 536; and third crusade, xvii, 40, 41, 47–49, 53–61, 63, 65–71, 76, 79–82, 85, 88, 89, 91, 93, 148, 488, 522, 601, 792; and fourth crusade, 154, 155, 157, 158 note, 165, 171; and Albigensian crusade, 283–287, 291, 295 note, 297, 300, 305, 308, 312–316; and fifth crusade, 378, 380, 382; nephews of, 159; wives of, *see* Isabel (of Hainault), Agnes (of Andechs)
Philip III ("the Bold"), son of Louis IX; Capetian king of France 1270–1285: 371, 372, 375, 516–518, 751, 762; wife of, *see* Isabel (of Aragon)
Philip IV ("the Fair"), son of Philip III; Capetian king of France 1285–1314: 266, 270, 372, 374, 375, 590, 722, 723, 762
Philip, son of Frederick I; Hohenstaufen duke of Swabia and Alsace 1196–1208, king in Germany 1197–1208: 119, 149, 166, 168–174, 185, 378; wife of, *see* Irene Angelina
Philip Fontana, archbishop of Ravenna 1251–*c.* 1272, papal legate in Lombardy, 363
Philip Mouskes, Flemish chronicler (d. 1283), 219
Philip I of Alsace, count of Flanders 1168–1191: 47, 54, 55, 61, 68, 70, 93
Philip of Anjou, son of Charles I (d. 1277), 256, 258, 259; wife of, *see* Isabel of Villehardouin
Philip of Antioch, son of Bohemond IV; prince of Cilician Armenia 1222–1224 (d. 1225), 541, 550, 565, 651; wife of, *see* Isabel (Roupenid)
Philip of Courtenay, son of Latin emperor Peter and Yolanda; count of Namur 1218–1226: 213
Philip of Courtenay, son of Latin emperor Baldwin II; titular emperor of Romania 1273–1285: 225, 229, 243
Philip of Dreux, brother of count Robert II; bishop of Beauvais 1175–1217: 50, 66, 80
Philip of Ibelin, son of Balian II; bailie of Cyprus 1218–1227: 605, 610, 611, 619, 623
Philip of Ibelin, son of Guy; bailie of Jerusalem 1286–1289: 590
Philip of Lagonesse (Gonesse), marshal of Sicily, bailie of Achaea 1280–1282: 259, 260
Philip of Mahdia, Sicilian admiral (d. 1153), 29
Philip of Maugastel, imperialist baron, 550
Philip of Montfort, son of Guy and Helvis; lord of La Ferté-Alais (to 1240), 469, 472; of Toron 1240–1266: 477, 485, 551, 553, 554, 559, 574; of Tyre 1243–1270: 554, 559, 560, 562, 563, 568, 569, 576, 580–582; wife of, *see* Mary (of Antioch)
Philip of Nanteuil, French crusader, 474
Philip of Novara, Lombard chronicler and crusader, 477, 553, 559, 610, 613, 618, 619
Philip of Savoy, nephew of Amadeo V; count of Piedmont (d. 1334), prince of Achaea 1301–1306: 265–269, 273, 762; wives of, 268, *and see* Isabel of Villehardouin
Philip I of Taranto, son of Charles II; Angevin prince of Taranto 1294–1332, of Achaea 1306–1313: 263, 264, 266–270, 273; wife of, *see* Thamar (of Epirus)
Philip of Toucy, brother of Narjot I; regent of Romania 1241–1251: 226
Philippa (Filibe), daughter of Roupen III; 2nd wife of Theodore I Lascaris, 650
Philippopolis, 192, 202–204, 206; third crusade at, 94–97, 101, 102, 104–107, 110, 148
Philomelium, 111
Photius, Greek merchant, 264
Piacenza, 334
Pian del Carpine, *see* John
Picardy, 159, 341; knight from, 270
Piedmont, 266, 268; count of, 265
Pilgrim Mountain, 478, 592
Pinarhisar, 215
Piriska (of Hungary, "Irene"), wife of John II Comnenus 1104–1134: 127, 131, 134
Pisa, 334; archbishop of, 66; crusaders from, 65, 68, 69, 409, 412, 503, 596; government of, 8, 9, 30, 104, 109, 125, 132, 138, 155, 161, 338 note, 549; merchants from, in Africa: 27 note; in Byzantine empire: 132, 162; in Cyprus: 623; in Sicily, 436; in Syria: 381, 452, 524, 525, 538, 547, 560, 568–570, 590; ships from, 51, 53, 96, 109, 161, 171, 218, 219, 230, 243, 353, 759; trade with, 30, 524, 697
Plaisance of Antioch, daughter of Bohemond V and Lucienne; 3rd wife of Henry I 1250–1253, regent of Cyprus and Jerusalem 1253–1261, 1st wife of Balian of Ibelin 1254–1258: 567, 569, 570, 580, 606
Plantagenets, Angevin dynasty in England 1154–1485: 59, 67, 155, 279, *and see* Henry II 1154–1189, Richard I 1189–1199, John 1199–1216, Henry III 1216–1272, Edward I 1272–1307; *see also* Alice, Arthur, Edmund, Geoffrey, Isabel, Joan, Oliver, Richard of Cornwall
Platamon, 213, 238
Po river, valley of, 334
Podandus, 634
Poemanenum, 209, 215
Poitiers, 268, *and see* Raymond; count of, *see* Alphonse; diocese of, 466
Poitou, 48, 63, 470, 779; count of, 48; crusaders from, 52, 56, 60, 74

Pola, *see* Peter
Poland, 715, 717; clergy of, 357
Political crusades, xvii, 343–348, 358, 369, 370, 372–375; against Languedoc, 282 note, 345, *and see* Albigensian crusade; against Markward, 346, 347, 349, 759; against Frederick II, 348–358, 761; against Conrad IV, 359, 360, 761; against Manfred, 255, 343, 361–366, 373, 762; against Ezzelino, 363; against Byzantines, 365; against Conradin, 366, 762; against Peter III, 343, 371, 372, 375, 763; against the Colonnas, 374
Pondikos, 237, 249
Pons of Capdolh (Chapdeuil), troubadour (d. *c.* 1190), 382
Pons "of the Cross", master of Hungarian Templars, 387
Ponthieu, count of, 53
Pontus, *see* Pontic Heraclea
Popes, *see* Papacy, *and* Leo IX 1049–1054, Gregory VII 1073–1085, Urban II 1088–1099, Gelasius II 1118–1119, Calixtus II 1119–1124, Honorius II 1124–1130, Innocent II 1130–1143, Eugenius III 1145–1153, Hadrian IV 1154–1159, Alexander III 1159–1181, Lucius III 1181–1185, Urban III 1185–1187, Gregory VIII 1187–1187, Clement III 1187–1191, Celestine III 1191–1198, Innocent III 1198–1216, Honorius III 1216–1227, Gregory IX 1227–1241, Celestine IV 1241–1241, Innocent IV 1243–1254, Alexander IV 1254–1261, Urban IV 1261–1264, Clement IV 1265–1268, Gregory X 1271–1276, John XXI 1276–1277, Nicholas III 1277–1280, Martin IV 1281–1285, Honorius IV 1285–1287, Nicholas IV 1288–1292, Celestine V 1294–1294, Boniface VIII 1294–1303, Benedict XI 1303–1304, Clement V 1305–1314, John XXII 1316–1334; *see also* Anti-popes
Poppo VI, nephew of bishop Otto of Speyer; count of Henneberg 1157–1190: 92, 115
Port-de-Jonc, 261
Porto, cardinal-bishops of, *see* Benedict, Conrad, Romanus
Portugal, 16, 120, 395; infante of, 348; king of, *see* Sancho I 1185–1211; third crusade in, 50, 56, 58, 115, 759
Posquères, *see* William
Potenza, 15
Pozzuoli, 30, 447
Prague, bishop of, *see* Henry
Premonstratensians, order, 156, 252, 383, 384, 628
Prespa, Lake, 192, 247
Pressburg, 93, 94
Prester John, legendary Christian ruler, 669, 721
Prilep, 217
Principate, *see* Salerno; *see also* Richard
Prinitsa, 254
Probaton, 105
Procida, *see* John
Pronoia (Greek), 129, 131, 141–143, 145, 150, 165, 192
Prosek, 205, 208, 210, 213
Protovestiarios (Greek, chamberlain), 190, 249, 266
Provence, 311, 313 note, 318, 369, 508, *and see* Margaret; counts of, 259, 318; crusaders from, 167, 238, 409; marquisate of, 279, 303, 307, 309, 311, 315, 318, 320, 322, 323; merchants from, 560, 568, 569, 623 note; troubadours from, 166
Prussians, Baltic people, 121, 466
Ptolemy of Lucca, Italian chronicler (d. after 1312), 583 note
Puylaurens, 294 note, 333, *and see* William
Pyramus river, 635, 638
Pyrenees mountains, 300, 304, 309, 311, 372; region north of, 48, 288, 301, 303, 323

Qāḍī (Arabic, magistrate), 26, 456, 458, 594, 656, 702, 730
al-Qā'im, 'Abbāsid caliph 1031–1075: 18
Qaimarīyah, Kurdish regiments, 740, 741
Qal'at al-Baḥr, 448, 542, 598
Qal'at ar-Rūm, *see* Hromgla
Qal'at Ja'bar, 696
Qal'at Najm, 696
Qāqūn, 582
Quercy, 287 note, 293, 303, 304, 312, 315, 318, 320
Querfurt, *see* Conrad
Querini, *see* John, Nicholas, Octavian
al-Qulai'ah, 576, 697, 780
Quṣair, 578; lord of, *see* William

Raab, bishop of, 389
Raban, 637, 698; lords of, 632, 638
Rabban Ṣaumā, Nestorian ambassador (d. 1294), 656
Radulf (Ralph) of Caen, French chronicler (d. after 1108), 633
Rāfi', Hilālī ruler of Gabes (in 1117), 20, 24
Ragusa, archbishop of, *see* Bernard
Raiy, 670
Ralph, bishop of Lydda and Ramla (d. 1244), 563
Ralph I, count of Clermont (de l'Oise) 1162–1191: 53
Ralph (of Domfront), Latin patriarch of Antioch 1135–1139: 10
Ralph, lord of Fougères, 469
Ralph, brother of Hugh; titular lord of Tiberias 1197–1220: 529, 530, 534, 610
Ralph, patriarch of Jerusalem 1191–1194: 525
Ralph de Diceto, English chronicler (d. *c.* 1202), 65, 157
Ralph fitz Godfrey, chamberlain to Richard I (d. 1191), 64
Ralph of Coggeshall, English chronicler (d. after 1227), 157
Ralph of Mérencourt, patriarch of Jerusalem

1214–1225: 438, 440, 541; and fifth crusade, 383, 388–390, 392–394, 400, 414, 609
Ralph of Nesle, count of Soissons 1180–1237: 313
Ralph of Nesle (or "of Soissons"), son of count Ralph; bailie of Jerusalem 1243–1243: 474, 475, 485, 553, 554, 559; wife of, *see* Alice (of Champagne-Jerusalem)
Rambald (Flotta), bishop of Vaison 1193–*c.* 1210: 286
Rambald of Vacqueyras, Provençal troubadour (d. 1207?), 166
Ramerupt, 780; lord of, 50, 52
Ramla, 77, 83, 523, 532, 699; bishop of, 563
Ranulf (of Blundeville), earl of Chester 1181–1232: 402, 414, 417
Ranulf de Glanville, justiciar to Henry II 1180–1189 (d. 1190), 64
Raphael (or Ranulf), Latin archbishop of Nicosia 1278–1286: 628
Ra'š al-Mā', 390
Rascia, 127, 131, 139; rulers of, *see* Uroš II, Stephen Nemanya, *and also* Helena
Rāshid-ad-Dīn Sinān, Assassin master in Syria *c.* 1169–1193: 80
Rashīd-ad-Dīn Ṭabīb, Persian historian and official (d. 1318), 721, 724
Ravano dalle Carceri, lord of Negroponte 1209–1216: 208, 238, 239, 242, 245
Ravendan, 636, *and see* Meillor III of Ravendel
Ravenna, 450; archbishop of, 551
Ravennika, 207, 239, 242 note
Raymond, abbot of Moissac, 295 note
Raymond (of Felgar), bishop of Toulouse 1232–1270: 277 note
Raymond (of Mas d'André), bishop of Uzès 1212–*c.* 1227, papal legate in Languedoc, 297
Raymond III, count of Tripoli 1152–1187: 46, 526, 533
Raymond II, viscount of Turenne 1143–1190: 50
Raymond Berengar, count (III) of Barcelona 1082–1131, count (I) of Provence 1112–1131: 21
Raymond Berengar III, count of Provence 1209–1245: 318
Raymond of Antioch, son of Bohemond III (d. 1197), 63, 526, 527, 533, 646, 648; wife of, *see* Alice (Ṛoupenid)
Raymond of Antioch, son of Bohemond IV (d. 1213), 698
Raymond of Poitiers, prince of Antioch 1136–1149: 10, 12, 133, 134, 636, 637; wife of, *see* Constance of Antioch
Raymond V of St. Gilles, count of Toulouse 1148–1194: 48, 54, 279, 282
Raymond VI of St. Gilles, son of Raymond V; count of Toulouse 1194–1222, of Rodez 1209–1214: 155, 279, 282, 760; and Albigensian crusade: 284–288, 290–313, 315, 316, 320, 322, 327; wives of, *see* Joan (Plantagenet), Eleanor (of Aragon)
Raymond VII of St. Gilles, son of Raymond VI; count of Toulouse 1222–1249: 290, 296, 298, 300 note, 303, 306, 307, 309–323, 440, 760; wife of, *see* Sancia (of Navarre)
Raymond Roger, count of Foix 1188–1223: 293, 294, 297–304, 306, 307, 311–313, 315
Raymond Roger, nephew of Raymond VI of Toulouse; viscount of Béziers and Carcassonne 1194–1209: 286–289, 292, 294
Raymond Roupen, son of Raymond and Alice: 527, 533, 535, 537, 538, 649; prince of Antioch 1216–1219: 538, 540, 547, 649, 760; pretender in Cilicia (d. 1222), 540, 541, 651; daughter of, 355
Raymond Trencavel II, son of Raymond Roger; viscount of Carcassonne 1209–1247 (d. *c.* 1263), 292, 319
Razès, lord of, 288, 290
Recordane, 390, 453
Reddecoeur, Templar commander, 587
Reformation, 373
Regensburg, 49, 92, 114, 759; bishop of, 92, 93, 105, 120
Reggio (di Calabria), 61; archbishop of, *see* Lando
Reggio (nell' Emilia), bishop of, *see* Nicholas
Reginald (of Urslingen), duke of Spoleto 1228–1228: 441, 446, 451, 452 note, 460 note
Reginald de la Roche, son of James; baron of Damala 1302–1311: 271
Reginald fitz Jocelyn, bishop of Bath 1174–1191: 58
Reginald Grenier, lord of Sidon *c.* 1170–1187 (d. after 1200), 46, 524; wife of, *see* Helvis of Ibelin
Reginald of Châtillon, regent of Antioch 1153–1160 (d. 1187), 140, 600, 640; wives of, *see* Constance of Antioch, Stephanie of Milly
Reginald I of Dammartin, count of Boulogne 1191–1214: 155, 287
Reginald of Dampierre (-le-Château), French baron (d. 1203), 159, 531
Reginald of Haifa, son of Pagan; governor of Jerusalem, 545, 546
Reginald of Montmirail, French baron, 159
Reiner, Benedictine monk, 331
Reinerius Sacconi, Dominican inquisitor, 281
Remy, *see* Gerard
Renart, lord of Nephin, 534; wife of, *see* Isabel of Gibelcar
Renier, bishop of Bethlehem 1218?–1227?: 404
Renier, Cistercian monk, papal legate in Languedoc, 283
Renier Dandolo, son of Enrico; vice-doge of Venice 1202–1205 (d. 1208?), 168, 193
Renier of Montferrat, son of William III;

Byzantine caesar 1180–1182: 143, 164, 165, 185; wife of, *see* Maria Comnena
Renier of Trit (Trith-St. Léger), knight from Hainault, "duke of Philippopolis" 1204–1205: 192, 202–204
Renier Zeno, doge of Venice 1252–1268: 229
Reviers, *see* Baldwin de Redvers
Rheims, 373, 510; archbishops of, *see* Samson, William, Aubrey, Henry of Dreux; council of (1148), 328
Rhine river, 329, 331, 333; count-palatine of the, 120; valley of, 327, 332, 337, 760
Rhinelands, 89; crusaders from, 120
Rhodes, 62, 226, 451, 601, 681, 726, 759, 762; ruler of, 217
Rhodope mountains, 205, 225, 238
Rhone river, 284, 303, 305, 312, 317; region of, 286; region east of, 279, 322, 490; region west of, 309, 311, 315, 318, 320; valley of, 57, 287, 335, 337
Ribaldi (Latin, rogues), 327, 336
Ricaut Bonomel, Templar poet, 575 note
Richard, son of Matthew of Salerno; count of Ajello (Aiello; d. *c.* 1195), 41 note
Richard (or Richer), lord of L'Erminet, 527
Richard I ("the Lionhearted"), son of Henry II and Eleanor; Plantagenet king of England 1189–1199: 48, 49, 117, 154, 155; and third crusade, xvii, 49, 53–85, 116, 488, 522–525, 759; and Sicily, 40 note, 41, 58–61, 759; and Cyprus, 61–64, 81, 148, 523, 525, 599–603, 608, 621, 622, 646, 759; nephews of, 159, 484; sisters of, 159, 322, 600; wife of, *see* Berengaria (of Navarre)
Richard, viscount of Beaumont (-sur-Sarthe), 469, 475, 476
Richard de Camville, English knight (d. 1191), 56, 64, 601
Richard Filangieri, imperial marshal, 450–452, 543, 547, 612; bailie of Jerusalem 1231–1233: 548–550, 613; imperial bailie at Tyre 1233–1243: 469, 477, 481, 550, 551, 553, 554, 557, 559, 560, 613
Richard of Argentan, English knight, 472, 473 note
Richard of the Principate (of Salerno), regent of Edessa 1104–1108: 635
Richard Orsini, son of Maio; count of Cephalonia 1238–1304, bailie of Achaea 1297–1300: 259, 265, 267
Richard Plantagenet, son of John of England; earl of Cornwall, co-emperor (Holy Roman) 1257–1272: 360; crusade of, 463, 481–485, 489, 551, 552, 558, 614, 708, 761
Richer, bishop of Melfi 1213–after 1231: 542, 612
Richmond, earl of, 469
Ricold of Monte Croce, Dominican missionary (d. 1320), 722
Rieti, 440, 441, 450
Riez, bishop of, 285, 297
Rigord, French chronicler (d. *c.* 1209), 80
Rita, daughter of Heṭoum I; wife of Sempad or Constantine of Sarvantikar, 652 note
Rita ("Stephanie", Ṛoupenid), daughter of Leon II of Armenia; 2nd wife of John of Brienne 1214–1219: 537, 539, 540, 650, 651
Rita ("Maria" or "Xenia", Heṭoumid), daughter of Leon III of Armenia; wife of Michael IX Palaeologus (after 1296), 657
Rita (Riṭa, Heṭoumid), daughter of Sempad of Babaṛon; wife of Stephen (Ṛoupenid; to 1162, d. after 1182), 644
Robert (of Auvergne), archbishop of Lyons 1227–1234: 348
Robert, archbishop of Nazareth (before 1217–after 1220), 389
Robert (Poulain), archbishop of Rouen 1208–1221: 287
Robert (of Ableiges), bishop of Bayeux 1206–1231: 386, 389
Robert I, son of Louis VIII of France; count of Artois (d. 1250), 497–501
Robert II, son of Robert I; count of Artois 1250–1302, regent of Naples 1285–1289: 261, 262
Robert II, grandson of Louis VI of France; count of Dreux 1184–1218: 50, 51, 54, 71
Robert III (fitz Parnel), earl of Leicester 1191–1204: 289 note
Robert, patriarch of Jerusalem 1240–1254: 559, 561–563
Robert, prior of Hereford, 79
Robert Guiscard, son of Tancred of Hauteville; duke of Apulia 1059–1085: 5–7, 37, 119, 125–127, 162, 185
Robert Malet, lord of Graville, 469
Robert Mauvoisin, lord of Fanjeaux, 294 note, 295
Robert of Clari (Cléry), French crusader and chronicler (d. after 1216), 160, 172
Robert of Courçon (Curzon), cardinal-priest 1216–1219, papal legate in France, 300, 303, 304, 379, 380, 402, 406
Robert of Courtenay, butler of France (d. *c.* 1240), 469
Robert of Courtenay, son of Peter and Yolanda; Latin emperor of Romania 1221–1228: 213–216, 226, 242, 760; wife of, 215, 216
Robert of Sablé, Angevin baron, master of the Temple 1191–1193: 56
Robert of Torigny, French chronicler (d. 1186), 31
Robert of Turnham, English commander, 64, 601
Roda, 707, 738
Rodez, 303; count of, 303
Roger (of Wavrin), bishop of Cambrai 1179–1191: 93
Roger I, son of Tancred of Hauteville; count of Sicily 1072–1101: 6, 7, 18. 19; wife of, *see* Adelaide of Montferrat

Roger II, son of Roger I and Adelaide; count of Sicily 1101–1130: 5–8, 18–22, 132; king 1130–1154: 5, 8–16, 22–33, 40, 41, 132, 135, 136, 138, 141
Roger, son of Roger II of Sicily; duke of Apulia 1127–1149: 11, 135
Roger, son of Tancred of Lecce (d. 1193), 119, 166; wife of, *see* Irene Angelina
Roger Bernard II, son of Raymond Roger; count of Foix 1223–1241: 311, 315, 318–320
Roger Borsa, son of Robert Guiscard; duke of Apulia 1085–1111: 6, 7
Roger de Flor, Templar, leader of Catalans (d. 1306), 597
Roger de Lluria (of Loria), Italian admiral in Aragonese service (d. 1305), 264, 273
Roger de Mowbray, lord of Thirsk, 46
Roger of Hoveden (Howden), English chronicler (d. *c.* 1201), 55
Roger of Les Moulins, master of the Hospital 1177–1187: 45
Roger of Salerno, son of Richard of the Principate; regent of Antioch 1112–1119: 636
Roger of San Severino, Angevin bailie at Acre 1277–1282: 585, 586, 588, 616, 617
Roger of Wendover, English chronicler (d. 1236), 444
Roland, bishop of Faenza 1210–1221: 421
Rolandino of Canossa, brother of Albertino; co-lord of Thebes, 238, 241
Romagna, 366
Roman Catholic church, *see* Church, Latin
Romania, Assises of, 274; Byzantine, 96, 513; "despot" of, 268; "despotate" of, 269, 273; Frankish, 193, 202, 206, 760, *and see* Latin empire of Constantinople; Turkish, *see* Rūm
Romano (d'Ezzelino), *see* Ezzelino III
Romanus (Bonaventura), cardinal-deacon 1216–1234, cardinal-bishop (of Porto) 1234–1243, papal legate in Languedoc 1225–1229: 315–317, 319, 323
Romanus I Lecapenus, Byzantine co-emperor 919–944 (d. 948), 130, 216
Romanus IV Diogenes, Byzantine emperor 1068–1071: 632
Rome, 30, 212, 266, 434, 435, 450; as papal see, 11, 15, 27, 157, 163, 164 note, 171, 173, 175, 196, 219, 227, 241, 265, 283, 299, 306, 309, 334, 346, 351, 366, 380, 432, 437, 443, 451, 535, 542, 566, 580, 584, 722 note, *and see* Papacy; clergy of, 156, 354, 383; councils at, 353, *and see* Lateran councils; crusaders from, 383, 402, 409; people of, 350, 351, 353, 450; persons from, 566, 570, 585, 587; senators of, 364, 366
Romuald Guarna, archbishop of Salerno 1153–1181, chronicler: 25, 33 note, 137
Ronay, *see* John
Roncelin, viscount of Marseilles 1192–1215: 338
Rosetta, 30, 697, 747
Rosières (-sur-Mance), *see* Walter
Rota, 395
Rotrou III, count of Perche 1144–1191: 49
Roucy, *see* Alan
Rouen, 341; archbishop of, *see* Walter of Coutances, Robert, Odo
Rouergue, 303, 304, 315, 318, 320
Ṛoupen I, Armenian lord of Gobidaṛa (d. *c.* 1071), 633
Ṛoupen II, son of Ṭoros II; Ṛoupenid prince of Cilician Armenia 1168–1170: 642
Ṛoupen III, son of Stephen and Rita; Ṛoupenid prince of Cilician Armenia 1175–1187: 643, 644, 646; wife of, *see* Isabel (of Toron)
Ṛoupen, son of Leon I of Armenia (d. 1140), 637, 638
Ṛoupenids, Armenian dynasty in Cilicia 1080–1375: 132, 133, 633–635, 652, *and see* Ṛoupen I, Constantine, Ṭoros I 1100–1129, Leon I 1129–1137, Ṭoros II 1148–1168, Ṛoupen II 1168–1170, Mleh 1170–1175, Ṛoupen III 1175–1187, Leon II 1187–1219 (king 1198); *see also* Alice, Isabel, Philippa, Rita, Ṛoupen, Stephanie, Stephen
Roussillon, 288; count of, 318 note
Routiers (French, mercenaries), 282, 286, 294, 295, 296 note, 307, 308, 318, 319, 327
Roye, 492 note
Ruad, 598
Rubrouck, *see* William
Rudolph (of Zähringen), bishop of Liége 1167–1191: 92, 93, 104
Rudolph, bishop of Verden 1189–1205: 120
Rudolph I (of Hapsburg), Holy Roman emperor (uncrowned) 1273–1291: 593, 751
Rukn-ad-Dīn al-Hījāwī, Egyptian general, 476, 706
Rukn-ad-Dīn Baybars, Egyptian general (d. 1245), 563, 709, 710
Rukn-ad-Dīn Ghūrshānchī, son of Khorezm-Shāh Muḥammad (d. 1231), 672
Rūm ("Rome"), *see* Anatolia; *see also* Selchükids of Rūm
Rupert II, count of Nassau 1160–1192: 92, 94, 95, 109
Russia, 205, 210, 233, 601, 687, 717, 719, 720, 722
Russians, Slavic people, 122
Rustam, Turkoman leader (d. 1187), 644, 680

Saarbrücken, *see* Henry; count of, 397
Sabina, cardinal-bishops of, *see* Conrad of Wittelsbach, Oliver (Saxo)
Sablé (-sur-Sarthe), *see* Robert
Sa'd-ad-Dīn, vizir of Arghun, 720
Sa'dī, Persian poet (d. 1292), 663, 724

Safad: under Moslems to 1240: 410, 415, 479, 539; under Franks 1240–1266: 481, 508, 576, 707, 748; under Moslems after 1266: 749
Saif-ad-Dīn, *see* al-'Ādil I
Saint Basil, pass, 101
Saint Cyprien, town, 312, 313
Saint Denis, town, 330, 336 note; abbey of, 57; abbot of, 375
Saint George, castle, 264, 265, 272
Saint Gilles, village, 277, 284, 286, 291; house of, 279, 299, 307, 310, 312, 316, 320, 322, *and see* Raymond V, Raymond VI, Raymond VII
Saint Gotthard, pass, 334
Saint Helena, castle, 267, 272
Saint Hilarion, castle, 601; *see also* Dieu-damour
Saint Livrade, village, 304
Saint Omer (in France), town, castellans of, 244
Saint Omer (in Greece), castle, *see* Bela, Nicholas II, Nicholas III
Saint Peter, island, 336, 338
Saint Pol (-sur-Ternoise), counts of, *see* Hugh, Walter of Châtillon
Saint Quentin, town, *see* Simon
Saint Ruf, canons regular of, 252
Saint Sabas, monastery, 568, 569
Saint Simeon, port, 10, 559, 575, 577
Saint Thibéry, abbot of, 307
Saint Thomas, islet, 593
Saint-Sauveur, abbey, 252
Saissac, 294 note
Saladin (an-Nāṣir Ṣalāḥ-ad-Dīn Yūsuf ibn-Aiyūb), xx; Aiyūbid governor of Egypt 1169–1174: 34, 35, 140; sultan of Egypt and Syria 1174–1193: 117, 508, 523, 564, 600, 697, 699, 736, 737, 756; before Hattin (1187), 37, 146, 148, 643, 644; conquests (1187–1189), 38–40, 45, 46, 50, 82, 87–89, 91, 165, 325, 396, 423, 452, 526, 527, 529, 545, 572, 581, 598, 603, 645, 646, 759; and third crusade (1189–1192), 51–53, 67–69, 71–80, 82–85, 97, 101–103, 114, 148, 149, 417, 602, 680, 759; death of (1193), 85, 524, 528, 693, 759; heirs of, 117, 489, 567, 608, 683, 694–696, 704, 708, 713; niece of, 113
Saladin tithe, 47, 55
Ṣalāḥī mamluks, 737
Salamis, 191
Salamish, al-'Ādil Badr-ad-Dīn, son of Baybars; Mamluk sultan of Egypt and Syria 1279–1279 (d. after 1287), 750–752
Salamyah, 700
Saleph river, *see* Calycadnus
Salerno, 58, 435, *and see* Matthew, Richard of the Principate, Roger; archbishop of, 25, 137
Salgurs, Turkoman tribe, 662, 663
aṣ-Ṣāliḥ Aiyūb, Najm-ad-Dīn, son of al-Kāmil Muḥammad: 428; Aiyūbid ruler of Ḥiṣn Kaifā 1232–1239: 673, 684, 703–706; of Damascus 1238–1239, 1245–1249: 465, 471, 478, 674, 706; sultan of Egypt 1240–1249: 479–481, 483–485, 489, 493, 495–498, 503, 515, 551, 552, 561, 564, 565, 674, 707–712, 737–740, 761; ruler of Baalbek 1246–1249: 710; wife of, *see* Shajar-ad-Durr
aṣ-Ṣāliḥ Ismā'īl, 'Imād-ad-Dīn, son of al-'Ādil I Saif-ad-Dīn; Aiyūbid ruler of Damascus 1237–1237, 1239–1245, of Baalbek 1237–1246 (d. 1251), 473, 474, 478–483, 485, 552, 560, 561, 564, 704, 706, 707, 709, 710, 713
Ṣāliḥī mamluks, 707, 737, 738, 740
aṣ-Ṣāliḥīyah, town, 742
Salisbury: bishop of, *see* Hubert Walter; "earl of", 482, 499
Salm, count of (Upper), *see* Henry
Salona, 13, 238; bishopric of, 252; lord of, 244, 271
as-Salṭ, 710
Saltukids, Turkoman dynasty at Erzerum 1080-1201: 681
Salza, *see* Hermann
Salzburg, 334
Samaria, 479
Samarus, archbishop of Trani 1194–1195: 119, 622
Samos, 191
Samosata, 636, 683, 696
Samothrace, 191
Samson (de Mauvoisin), archbishop of Rheims 1140–1161: 328
Samsun, 681
Samuel (Samouēl) of Ani, Armenian chronicler (d. after 1179), 633
San Germano (Vercellese), 440, 447, 454; agreement of (1225), 440–443, 446, 447; treaty of (1230), 465, 548, 612
San Severino (Marche), *see* Roger
Sancerre, 56; count of, 53, 469, 642
Sancho, bishop of Couserans 1213–*c.* 1215: 296
Sancho VI, king of Navarre 1150–1194: 61
Sancho I, king of Portugal 1185–1211: 50, 115
Sancia, sister of Peter II of Aragon; wife of Raymond VII of Toulouse 1211–1241 (d. 1261), 290, 300 note
Sangerhausen, *see* Anno
Sanjar, son of Malik-Shāh; Selchükid ruler of Khurasan 1097–1156: 668, 669
Santa Maria do Algarve, 395
Sanudos, Venetian dynasty at Naxos 1207–1371 (1383): *see* Marco I 1207–*c.* 1227, Angelo *c.* 1227–1262, Marco II 1262–1303, William I 1303–1323, Nicholas I 1323–1341; *see also* Marino
Sapientsa, 239
Saracens, *see* Moslems
Sardinia, 350, 365, 369, 472, 512, 515
Sarepta, 393, 524
Sargines, *see* Geoffrey, Peter
Sarmīn, 708, *and see* Acharie of Sermin

Sarrasin, John, chamberlain to Louis IX, 493
Sarus river, 635
Sarvantikar, 576, 636, 644; lords of, 652 note
Sasoun, 632, *and see* Heṭoum
Savary of Mauléon, seneschal of Aquitaine (d. 1236), 294, 415
Savona, 21, 22
Savoy, *see* Philip; count of, 265
Saxony, 89, 330; crusaders from, 51, 92, 115, 120
Sayn, count of, *see* Henry
Scandinavia, clergy of, 349; crusaders from, *see under* Denmark; mercenaries from, 179, 200
Schaumburg, count of, 92
Schlettstadt, 333
Scotland, 352, 518
Scribention, 102, *and see* Sopot
Scutari, 177, 178
Scyros, 191, 236
Sebastia, 679, 680, 687, 690–692, 724, 730
Second crusade (1147–1149), 5, 8 note, 9, 11–16, 23, 40, 90, 121, 134–136, 164, 677
Sées: bishop of, 467, 468; count of, 50
Segni, *see* Lucienne, Paul; *see also* Innocent III, Gregory IX, Alexander IV
Segusio, *see* Henry
Seine river, 329, 330, 332
Selchükids, Oghuz Turkish people and dynasty in Persia and Mesopotamia 1038–1194: xxi, 662, 663, 665, 669–671, 686, 688, 736, *and see* Tughrul I 1038–1063, Malik-Shāh 1072–1092, Tughrul III 1177–1194, Sanjar; in Anatolia, *see* Selchükids of Rūm
Selchükids of Rūm, Oghuz Turkish people and dynasty in Anatolia 1077–1302: 550, 673–692, 705, 706, 708, 748, 750; and Byzantines, 97, 110, 116, 125, 132, 140, 142, 640; and Nicaeans, 200, 201, 209, 210, 213, 223, 224, 230, 232; and Armenians, 536, 540, 541, 572, 631, 639, 645, 650, 652, 653, 697; and Franks, 110–113, 127; and Mongols, 223, 673, 683, 687–692, 717, 725–732; *and see* Sulaiman I 1077–1085, Kîlîj Arslan I 1092–1107, Mas'ūd I 1116–1155, Kîlîj Arslan II 1155–1192, Kai-Khusrau I 1192–1196, 1204–1211, Sulaiman II 1196–1204, Kai-Kā'ūs I 1211–1220, Kai-Qobād I 1220–1237, Kai-Khusrau II 1237–1245, Kai-Kā'ūs II 1245–1249 (1261), Kîlîj Arslan IV (1249) 1261–1265, Kai-Khrusrau III 1265–1283; *see also* Arab, Jahān-Shāh, Jemri, Malik-Shāh (II), Mas'ūd (III), Shāhan-Shāh (2), Tughrul Arslan, Tughrul-Shāh
Seleucia, 635, 637, 645, 650, 651 note, 653
Sempad, son of Constantine of Lampron; Heṭoumid constable of Armenia (d. 1276), 648 note, 651, 652, 654, 659
Sempad, son of Leon III; Heṭoumid king of Cilician Armenia 1296–1298: 657
Sempad (Smbat), brother of Ōshin II; Heṭoumid lord of Babaṛon (d. 1152), 639
Sempad, grandson of Sempad of Babaṛon; Heṭoumid lord of Sarvantikar, 652 note; wife of, *see* Rita?
Sens, 333 note; archbishop of, *see* Peter, Walter
Serai, 723
Serbia, 91, 97, 99, 119, 127, 136, 147, 149, 367, 368; grand župans of, *see* Stephen Nemanya 1186–1196, Stephen I 1196–1217; kings of, *see* Stephen I 1217–1227, Stephen Uroš II Milutin 1281–1321
Serbs, Slavic people, 15, 116, 131, 142, 148, 210, 228, 261; and third crusade, 98–100, 107, 109
Sergiana, 254, 270
Seriphos, 257
Sermin, *see* Sarmīn; *see also* Acharie
Serres, 207, 214, 215, 217, 225, 228, 238, 242
Sestus, 103, 108
Setif, 28
Sévérac (-le-Château), 303
Sfax, 25, 27, 31
Sgouromallis, archon of Laconia, 264
Shabānkārah, Kurdish tribe, 663
Shaddādids, Kurdish dynasty at Ani, 664
Shāhan-Shāh, Bahā'-ad-Dīn, Selchükid pretender (d. 1104?), 677
Shāhan-Shāh, son of Mas'ūd; Selchükid emir at Ankara 1155–1164: 677, 678
Shahnshah, son of Ōshin II (d. after 1198), 645
Shaiyād Ḥamzah, Turkish poet (*c.* 1350), 732
Shaizar, 637, 640, 708
Shajar-ad-Durr, wife of aṣ-Ṣāliḥ Aiyūb (to 1249), regent of Egypt 1249–1250, sultanah 1250–1250, wife of Aybeg 1250–1257: 498, 503, 711, 712, 738–742, 744, 761
Shams-ad-Dīn, qadi at Jerusalem, 458
Shams-ad-Dīn al-Iṣfahānī, vizir of Selchükids 1246–1249: 725
Shams-ad-Dīn Marwān, Mamluk governor at Mecca (after 1269), 749
Sharamsāḥ, 424
Shihāb-ad-Dīn Tughrul, atabeg of Aleppo (in 1216), 698, 699
Shī'ites, legitimist 'Alid Moslem sect, 17, 34, 35, 665, 671, 721, 746
Shiloh, 390
Shīrkūh, Asad-ad-Dīn al-Manṣūr, uncle of Saladin (d. 1169), 737
Shirvān-Shāhs, *see* Minūchihr 1027–1034
Shoṭa Rusṭveli, Georgian poet (d. after 1190), 665
Shumlah, 662
Sibṭ Ibn-al-Jauzī, Arabic chronicler (d. 1257), 705
Sibyl, daughter of Amalric of Jerusalem; wife of William "Longsword" 1176–1177, wife of Guy of Lusignan 1180–1190;

queen of Jerusalem 1186–1190: 65, 66, 81, 164
Sibyl (Sibil), daughter of Heṭoum I of Armenia; wife of Bohemond VI of Antioch 1254–1275, regent of Tripoli 1275–1277 (d. after 1287), 567, 584, 591, 652 note
Sibyl, 3rd wife of Bohemond III of Antioch *c.* 1180–*c.* 1194: 644
Sibyl of Lusignan, daughter of Aimery and Isabel; 2nd wife of Leon II of Armenia (after 1210), 540
Sicard, bishop of Cremona 1185–1215: 334
Sicilian Vespers, 260, 367, 370, 588, 589, 762
Sicily, 58-60, 65, 79, 120, 166, 270, 334 note, 346, 347, 382, 427, 435, 447, 448, 450, 452 note, 469, 472, 510, 513, 516, 517, 582, 588, 748 note, 762; counts of, *see* Roger I 1072–1101, Roger II 1101–1130; crusaders from, 446, 450, 452, 456; kingdom of, 3–42, 47, 88, 104, 117, 118, 130, 132, 135–139, 141, 149, 247, 439, 444, 455, 459–461, 508, 512, 514, 579, 762, *and see* Naples, Two Sicilies; kings of, *see* Roger II 1130–1154, William I 1154–1166, William II 1166–1189, Tancred 1190–1194, Henry VI 1194–1197, Frederick II 1212–1250, Conrad IV 1250–1254, Manfred 1258–1266, Charles of Anjou 1268–1282, Peter III 1282–1285, James II 1291–1327; princess of, *see* Constance; ships from, 52, 53, 516
Sidon, district, under Moslems 1187–1192: 71; divided 1192–1240: 423, 455, 479, 524, 707; under Franks 1240–1291: 707; lords of, *see* Grenier
Sidon, port: under Moslems 1187–1197: 530; divided 1197–1227: 121, 381, 392, 393, 423, 448, 530–532, 542; under Franks 1227–1260: 448, 507, 542, 548, 702, 711; Mongols at (1260): 573; under Templars 1260–1291: 574, 587, 588, 598; *see also* Qal'at al-Baḥr
Siebenbürgen, *see* Transylvania; *see also* Alexander
Siegfried (of Eppstein), archbishop of Mainz 1202–1230: 172 note, 431
Siegfried (of Rechberg), bishop of Augsburg 1208–1227: 446
Siegfried II, count of Liebenau (in 1189), 92, 93
Siena, bankers from, 273, 366
Signoria, *see* Venice, government of
Silesia, 717
Silpius, Mount, 577
Silves, 50, 759
Simanagla, 638
Simon (of Maugastel), brother of Philip; archbishop of Tyre 1216–1227, Latin patriarch of Constantinople 1227–1232: 381, 385, 389
Simon II, count of Saarbrücken 1211–1233: 397
Simon, lord of Raban, daughter of, 638
Simon Mansel, constable of Antioch, 577
Simon II of Clermont (de l'Oise), great-nephew of count Ralph; lord of Ailly and Nesle 1214–1280: 469
Simon of Montfort, grandson of Robert II of Leicester; baron (IV) of Montfort 1181–1218: 159, 174, 175; earl of Leicester 1206–1218: 287, 289–309, 326, 327 note, 333, 344, 760; duke of Narbonne 1216–1218: 308–315, 318, 320–322, 470; brother of, 472; son of, 470; wife of, *see* Alice of Montmorency
Simon of Montfort, son of Simon IV; earl of Leicester 1239–1265: 482, 483, 552
Simon of St. Quentin, Dominican missionary and traveler (d. after 1247), 684, 687
Sinjar, 696, 706; lords of, 694, 699; qadi of, 706
Sinope, 200, 682, 687, 726, 727
Siphnos, 239, 257
Siponto, 359
Sirmium, 139, 146
Sis, 527, 541, 635, 643, 644, 646, 650, 656; archbishop of, 647; mint of, 652 note; province east of, 637 note; sacked by Mamluks (1266), 576, 654, 749; (1275), 749
Siyāwush, son of Kai-Khusrau II, *see* Jemri
Skorta, 266, 272
Skripou, 271
Slav, Alexius, cousin of Boril; Vlach chieftain at Melnik (in 1208), 205, 206, 210, 216; wives of, 206, 210
Slavs, Indo-European people, in Germany, 121; in Greece, 244, 264; in the Balkans, 124, 144, 146
Smyrna, 230
Soffredo (of Pisa), cardinal-deacon 1182–1184, cardinal-priest 1184–1208 (d. 1210), papal legate on fourth crusade, 154, 533, 534
Sofia, 99–101
Soissons, 159, 164, 166; counts of, 313, 474
Soli, 625
Somerset, 54
Sonnac, *see* William
Sopot, 102
Sozopolis, 681
Spain, 16, 21, 28, 34 note, 298, 327, 378, 384, 386, 396, 439, 490, 542, 703; clergy of, 365; crusaders from, 416
Spalato, 387, 388; archdeacon of, 388, 393
Sparta, 240, 253, 254; *see also* Lacedaemon
Spercheus river, 242
Speyer, 333; bishop of, *see* Otto
Splügen, pass, 334
Spoleto: duchy of, 355; duke of, 441, 446, 451
Sponheim, count of, *see* Henry
Sporades, 238
Starkenburg, 448, 460, 543, 576, 581; *see also* Montfort
Stavrovouni, mountain, 600

Stenimaka, 203, 204
Stephanie (Sdefania; Heṭoumid), daughter of Constantine of Lampron; 2nd wife of Henry I of Cyprus 1237–1249: 565, 652 note
Stephanie of Milly, wife of Humphrey III of Toron (to 1173), 2nd wife of Reginald of Châtillon 1176–1187, wife of Hugh III Embriaco (to 1196, d. after 1197), 529
Stephen, abbot of Eaunes (d. 1209), 296 note
Stephen IV, Armenian catholicus 1290–1292: 656
Stephen, grandson of Hugh I of Champagne; count of Chartres and Blois 1089–1102: 159
Stephen I, brother of Henry I of Champagne; count of Sancerre 1152–1191: 53, 642
Stephen I, son of Stephen Nemanya; grand župan of Serbia 1196–1217, king 1217–1227: 148, 149, 182 note, 205, 210; wife of, *see* Eudocia Angelina
Stephen III, grandson of Bela II; king of Hungary 1162–1173: 139
Stephen (Sdefanē), son of Leon I of Armenia; Ṛoupenid prince (d. 1162), 638, 639, 641, 643; wife of, *see* Rita (Heṭoumid)
Stephen Langton, cardinal-priest 1205–1228, archbishop of Canterbury 1207–1228: 346 note
Stephen Nemanya, son of Uroš II; župan of Rascia 1166?–1186, grand župan of Serbia 1186–1196 (d. 1200), 91, 99, 102, 107, 139, 146–148
Stephen of Cloyes, shepherd and visionary, 330–332, 336 note, 337, 340, 760
Stephen of Perche, son of Rotrou III; French knight, "duke of Philadelphia" (in 1204), 159, 192
Stephen of Turnham, English commander, 62
Stephen Uroš II Milutin, grandson of Stephen I; Nemanyid king of Serbia 1281–1321: 260
Stirione, Calabrese pirate, 205
Straits, *see* Bosporus, Dardanelles; map of, 152
Strassburg: bishop of, 90; diet at (1287), 90
Strategos (Greek, tax-collector), 19
Stratiotes (Greek, soldier), 129
Strez, Dobromir, brother of Boril; Vlach chieftain at Prosek (d. *c.* 1213), 205, 208–210, 216
Strymon river, 36, 37
Stymphalus, Lake, 252
Sudan, 735
Suez, isthmus, 564
Suez, port, 708
Suger, abbot of St. Denis (d. 1151), 15 note
Suger (Viegas), bishop of Lisbon *c.* 1210–before 1231: 395
Suhrawardī, Shihāb-ad-Dīn ʿUmar, Persian mystic (d. 1234), 667
Sulaimān I ("the Magnificent"), Ottoman sultan 1520–1566: 693 note
Sulaimān I, Selchükid sultan of Rūm 1077–1085: 125, 126, 676
Sulaimān II, Rukn-ad-Dīn, son of Kïlïj Arslan II; Selchükid sultan of Rūm 1196–1204: 649, 681
Sully, *see* Hugh
Sulṭān Veled, son of Jalāl-ad-Dīn Rūmī; poet and dervish master (d. 1312), 732
Sultaniyeh, archbishop of, 722; *see also* Kangurlan
Sulzbach, *see* Bertha
Sungur, Shams-ad-Dīn al-Ashkar, Egyptian emir (d. after 1287), 654, 751, 752
Sunnites, orthodox Moslem sect, 17, 18, 34, 665, 688, 721
Susa, 23, 25
Sussex, earl of, 417
Sutri, bishop of, 118
Swabia: crusaders from, 92, 93, 109, 450, 454; dukes of, *see* Frederick, Philip
Sweden: clergy of, 349; king of, *see* Eric Läspe 1223–1250
Symeon II, Orthodox patriarch of Antioch *c.* 1207–*c.* 1240: 535–537, 566
Symeon, tsar of Bulgaria 893–927: 216
Syracuse, 21, 396
Syria: church of, *see* Monophysites; Greeks in, 133, 140, 141, 174, 677, 678; Mongols in, 571–575, 582, 586, 653–655, 657, 714, 717–719, 721, 726, 744, 751; Turks in, 39, 67, 87, 489, 561, 578 note, 662, 674, 678, 680, 683, 725, 727; map of northern, 521
Syrian Gates, pass, 527, 639, 654
Syros, 239
Syvota, port, 258, 260

Tabor, Mount, 379, 391, 392, 395, 410, 537, 539, 564, 574, 697, 698
Tabriz, 653, 703, 718, 719, 724
Tafurs, 326
Tagliacozzo, battle (1268), 256, 366, 513, 762
Tagus river, 56
Ṭālib, Ḥiṣn-ad-Dīn, Arab rebel in Egypt (in 1253), 743
Tall al-ʿAjūl, 701
Tall Ḥamdūn, 541, 637–639, 644, 656, 657
Tamar, queen of Georgia 1184–1212: 200, 664, 665
Tamerlane, *see* Timur
Tamīm, son of al-Muʿizz; Zīrid emir at Mahdia 1062–1108: 18, 19
Tancred, illegitimate son of Roger, duke of Apulia; count of Lecce, king of Sicily 1190–1194: 37, 39–41, 58–60, 119, 166, 759; daughter of, 59
Tancred, nephew of Bohemond I; regent of Antioch 1101–1103, 1104–1112: 5, 127
Tancred of Hauteville, Norman knight, 26
Ṭannāḥ, 498, 499, 502

Taranto, 138, 346, 435; principality of, 359, 361, *and see* Charles, Philip
Tarbes, 295
Tarentaise, 364; archbishop of, *see* Haimo
Tarn river, 288, 315, 320; region of, 295
Tarsus: before 1189: 632–637, 642, 644; after 1189: 115, 529, 540, 541, 627, 645, 648, 651 note, 654; archbishops of, Armenian: *see* Nersēs of Lampron; Orthodox: 529, 648; governor of, 641
Tatars, *see* Mongols
Ṭaṭoul, Armenian governor at Marash (to 1104), 632, 635
Taurus mountains, 114, 133, 600, 631–634, 682, 704, 726, 728
Taygetus range, 240, 244, 248, 264
Tegüder ("Aḥmad"), son of Hulagu; Il-khan of Persia 1282–1284: 720, 751
Tell Bashir, 698, 711
Tempe, Vale of, 236
Temple (Latin, Templum Domini), at Jerusalem, 504, 545, 561; *see also* Aqṣâ mosque; knights of, *see* Knights Templar; masters of, *see* Gerard of Ridefort 1185–1189, Robert of Sablé 1191–1193, Gilbert Horal 1193–*c.* 1198, Theodat of Bersiac 1202–1204, William of Chartres 1210–1219, Peter of Montaigu 1219–1229, Armand of Périgord 1232–1244, William of Sonnac 1247–1250, William of Beaujeu 1273–1291; other masters were Walter (count) of Spelten 1189–1191, Terricus *c.* 1198–1201, Philip of Le Plessis 1204–1210?, Reginald of Vichiers 1250–1255, Thomas Berard 1256–1273
Tenos, 191, 236, 238; lord of, *see* George Ghisi
Termes, 288, 290, 294 note
Terra di Lavoro, 359
Teutonic Knights, military order, 122; in Syria, 116, 443, 448, 452, 459, 460, 476, 536, 538, 541, 544, 545, 547, 560, 562, 563, 568, 569, 582, 585, 590, 591, 594–596; in Egypt, 413, 415; in Cilicia, 650; in Frankish Greece, 237, 251; fortresses, 542, 576, 581; masters of, *see* Hermann of Salza *c.* 1210–1239, Conrad of Thuringia 1239–1240, Gerard of Malberg 1241–1244, Anno of Sangerhausen 1257–1274, Burkhard of Schwanden 1283–1290, Conrad of Feuchtwangen 1290–1296; other masters were Henry of Hohenlohe, Günther, Poppo of Osterna, Hartmann of Heldrungen, Godfrey of Hohenlohe, Siegfried of Feuchtwangen
Thamar ("Catherine"), daughter of Nicephorus of Epirus and Anna; 1st wife of Philip I of Taranto 1294–(div.) 1309: 263, 267, 270, 273
Thebes: under Greeks to 1204: 13, 14 note; under Franks after 1204: 192, 202, 208, 210, 237, 238, 241–247, 261, 272, 273; archbishopric of, 252
Thedisius, secretary to Milo, 291, 297
Thelematarioi (Greek, volunteers), 231
Theobald I, brother of Henry I; count of Bar 1191–1214, of Luxemburg 1196–1214: 293
Theobald V, brother of Henry I of Champagne; count of Blois 1152–1191: 53, 159
Theobald III, son of Henry I; count of Champagne 1197–1201: 158–160, 164, 470
Theobald IV, son of Theobald III; count of Champagne 1201–1253: 319; king of Navarre 1234–1253: 466; crusade of, 243, 463, 469–481, 483–485, 489, 551–553, 614, 706, 707, 761
Theobald V, son of Theobald IV; count of Champagne and king of Navarre 1253–1270: 510, 517
Theobald I, duke of Lorraine 1213–1220: 385, 431
Theobald of Cépoy (Chepoix), Picard knight (d. *c.* 1311), 270
Theobald Visconti, archdeacon of Liége, 583, *and see* Gregory X
Theodat of Bersiac, master of the Temple 1202–1204: 533
Theodora Angelina, sister of Isaac II; 2nd wife of Conrad of Montferrat 1185–1187 (d. before 1190), 164
Theodore, Orthodox bishop of Negroponte (*c.* 1205), 251
Theodore Angelus Comnenus, brother of Michael I, 240; despot of Epirus 1214–1230: 210, 212–214, 242; "emperor" at Thessalonica 1224–1230: 214–217, 242, 243, 760, 761; after 1230 (d. 1254), 217, 222, 226, 227
Theodore Branas, Byzantine ruler of Adrianople (after 1206), 203, 204, 210; wife of, *see* Agnes of France
Theodore Ducas, Byzantine leader, 201
Theodore I Lascaris, Byzantine emperor at Nicaea 1208–1222: 150, 151, 197, 201, 202, 204–206, 209–211, 213, 214, 393, 535, 650, 760; niece of, 210; wives of, *see* Anna Angelina, Philippa (Ṛoupenid), Mary of Courtenay
Theodore II "Lascaris", son of John III Ducas Vatatzes; Byzantine emperor at Nicaea 1254–1258: 219, 220, 228, 246, 761; wife of, *see* Helena (of Bulgaria)
Theodore Mancaphas, Byzantine rebel at Philadelphia (d. *c.* 1189), 98
Theodoric, archbishop of Ravenna 1228–1249, papal legate to Syria, 551
Thera, 238
Thermopylae, 237, 238; bishopric of, 252
Thessalonica, city: under Greeks to 1204: 4, 36, 37, 106, 118, 142, 146, 148, 165, 170, 190; under Franks 1204–1224: 165, 196, 202, 206, 207, 210, 211, 213, 214, 238, 242; under Greeks after 1224: 214, 215, 217, 222, 225, 226, 228, 266, 270, 271, 760; archbishop of, *see* Garin; metro-

politan of, 214; patron saint of, 205; treaty of (1148), 136
Thessalonica, kingdom, 190–192, 203, 205–208, 212, 236, 238–243, 252, 760; despots of, *see* Angelus "Comnenus"; kings of, *see* Boniface (II) 1204–1207, Demetrius 1209–1224
Thessaly: 1204–1261: 192, 202, 207, 212, 213, 215, 217, 236, 238, 242, 247, 252; after 1261: 257, 258, 261, 265–267, 270, 271, 273, 367
Thessy, *see* Bertrand
Thierry d'Orcques, lord of Arsuf *c.* 1192–*c.* 1205: 524
Third crusade (1189–1192), 5, 40, 41, 47, 147, 155, 159, 160 note, 560, 562, 602, 646, 759; Anglo-French phase, preparations: 47–57; in Sicily: 41, 58–61; in Cyprus: 62–64, 601, 646; in Syria: 53, 64–85, 148, 339, 522–524, 697; German phase, preparations: 88–92; in Europe, 49, 92–109, 146–148; in Anatolia: 49, 110–114, 645, 680, 682; in Syria: 49, 50, 114–116; map, 86
Thirsk, lord of, 46
Thomas, archdeacon (1230–1243) and archbishop (1243–1244) of Spalato (d. 1268), 388, 393
Thomas, bishop of Erlau 1217–1224: 389
Thomas (of Ham), constable of Tripoli (d. after 1255), 563
Thomas, governor of Mamistra, 638
Thomas, lord of Marly, 468
Thomas (Ṭoumas), grandson of Leon I; regent of Cilician Armenia 1168–1170: 642
Thomas Agni of Lentini, bishop of Bethlehem 1255–1267, archbishop of Cosenza 1267–1272, patriarch of Jerusalem 1272–1277: 570, 585
Thomas Angelus Comnenus, son of Nicephorus and Anna; despot of Epirus 1296–1318: 267
Thomas Aquinas, Italian theologian (d. 1274), 606
Thomas Morosini, Latin patriarch of Constantinople 1205–1211: 195–199, 204
Thomas of Aquino, count of Acerra, bailie of Jerusalem 1226–1228: 444, 449, 452–454, 459, 542; imperial agent in 1243: 559, 565
Thomas I of Autremencourt ("de Stromoncourt"), lord of Salona 1205–1212: 238
Thomas II of Autremencourt ("de Stromoncourt"), son of Thomas I; lord of Salona 1212–after 1258: 244
Thomas III of Autremencourt ("de Stromoncourt"), grandson of Thomas II; lord of Salona 1294–1311: 271
Thomas of Marzano, marshal of Naples, bailie of Achaea 1309–1313: 270
Thrace: before 1204: 97, 99, 104, 108, 179; 1204–1261: 190–192, 202, 203, 215, 217, 219, 220, 236, 246; after 1261: 270
Thuringia: crusaders from, 444; landgraves of, *see* Louis III, Hermann I, Louis IV, Henry Raspe IV, *and also* Conrad
Thury (-en-Valois), *see* Lambert
Tiber river, 58
Tiberias, 45, 423, 479, 561, 564, 702, 707, 710; lord of, 529, 534
Tiberias, Lake, 390, 391
Tickhill, honor of, 54
Tiflis, 664
Tigris river, xxi, 684
Timur ("Lenk", the Lame; Tamerlane), Timurid Gur-Khan 1369–1404: 724, 729
Timurids, Turkish dynasty in Transoxiana and Persia 1369–1500: 724, *and see* Timur (Tamerlane) 1369–1404
at-Tīnah, 593
Tinnis, 30, 36, 419
Tirnovo, 205, 213, 215, 760; archbishops of, 147, 219
Tökish (Takash), Khorezm-Shāh 1172–1200, sultan 1194–1200: 670, 759; wife of, *see* Turkan Khātūn
Tonkin, 715, 717
Tonnerre, count of, 259
Toqūz Khātūn (Persian; Mongol, Toghus Qatun: peacock queen), wife of Hulagu (d. 1265), 572, 720
Torigny (-sur-Vire), *see* Robert
Ṭornavan, prince of, 633
Toron: under Moslems to 1229: 120, 121, 410, 415, 530, 539, 695; under Franks 1229–1266: 455, 553, 554; under Moslems after 1266: 576, 580; lords of, 559, 560, *and see* Humphrey III, Humphrey IV, Isabel
Ṭoros, son-in-law of Gabriel of Melitene; Armenian lord of Edessa (d. 1098), 632, 634, 635
Ṭoros I, son of Constantine; Ṛoupenid prince of Cilician Armenia 1100–1129: 635, 636
Ṭoros II, son of Leon I; Ṛoupenid prince of Cilician Armenia 1148–1168: 140, 637–642; wife of, 638
Ṭoros III, son of Leon III; Heṭoumid king of Cilician Armenia 1292–1294 (d. 1296), 656, 657, 755
Ṭoros, son of Heṭoum I (d. 1266), 576, 654
Tortosa (in Spain), 396
Tortosa (in Syria), 39, 456, 547, 577, 581, 589, 598, 698; bishop of, 584, 587, 591
Toucy, *see* Narjot (2), Philip
Toul: bishops of, *see* Peter, Otto; diocese of, 510
Toulousain, 287, 294, 306, 309, 311, 315
Toulouse, city, 291 note, 292, 293, 295–300, 303–305, 308–315, 318–321, 323, 760; bishops of, 277 note, 296, 299, 306, 312; council of (1229), 323, 324; diocese of, 320
Toulouse, county, 48, 321, 470, *and see* Toulousain; countess of, *see* Joan; counts of, 279, 321, 470, 472, *and see* Raymond V, VI, *and* VII of St. Gilles

Touraine, lord of, 48
Tours, 56, 341; archbishop of, 56; livres of, 225, 349, 491–494, 504, 508, 510, 511, 517
Tower of David, fortification at Jerusalem, 472, 473, 477, 478, 545, 546, 558, 561, 562, 706
Trani, 256; archbishop of, *see* Samarus; merchants from, 622
Transcaucasia, 703
Transjordania or Transjordan, 417, 552, 693, 702, 714, 750; rulers of, *see* Aiyūbids (1188–1263); *see also* Kerak
Transoxiana, 668, 669, 671, 689, 717
Transylvania, *see* Alexander of Siebenbürgen; Germans from, 388
Trapani, 368, 370, 517
Trazarg, monastery, 644
Treaties, *see* Devol (1108), Mignano (peace of, 1139), Thessalonica (1148), Venice (1177), Constance (1183), Nuremberg (1188), Messina (1190), Jaffa (1229), Paris (peace of, 1229), San Germano (1230), Paris (peace of, 1259), Viterbo (1267), Orvieto (1281), Caltabellotta (peace of, 1302)
Trebizond, city, 200, 677, 681, 723, 730, 760
Trebizond, empire, 200, 205, 681–684, 726; emperor of, *see* Alexius Comnenus 1204–1222
Trencavel, family, 287, 288, 290, 298, 315, 760, *and see* Raymond
Treviso, 334
Trier, 331, 335
Triphylia, 248, 272
Tripoli (in Africa), 22, 23, 25–28, 30, 31
Tripoli (in Syria), city: under Franks 1109–1189: 38, 39, 46, 47, 50, 52, 645; under Franks 1189–1289: 64, 115, 393, 478, 527, 530, 534, 538, 569, 570, 577, 581, 584, 587, 591–593, 605, 609, 617, 655, 697, 752, 762; under Moslems after 1289: 754; bishops of, 585, 587, 594; burgesses of, 602; mayor of, 591
Tripoli, county, before 1189: 45; 1189–1243: 121, 456, 524, 526, 529, 532–534, 540, 544, 545, 547, 549, 550, 603; 1243–1289: 558, 566, 570, 576, 581, 584, 587, 590, 593, 752; bailie of, *see* Bartholomew; countess of, *see* Lucy 1288–1289; counts of, *see* Raymond III 1152–1187, Bohemond IV 1187–1233, Bohemond V 1233–1252, Bohemond VI 1252–1275, Bohemond VII 1275–1287; regents of, *see* Lucienne 1252–1252, Sibyl 1275–1277
Tripotamos, 269
Trith (-St. Léger), *see* Renier of Trit
Troad, 200, 202
Troina, 6
Trois-Fontaines, *see* Aubrey
Troyes, 333 note; count-palatine of, 53, 81, 523
True Cross, 46, 69, 71, 72, 77, 330, 390, 392, 407, 415, 417, 424, 428
Tsakhoud, 637 note
Tubania, 390
Tudela, *see* Benjamin, William
Tughrul I (Tughrul-Beg), Selchükid ruler 1038–1063: 670
Tughrul III, Selchükid sultan 1177–1194: 665, 670, 759
Tughrul Arslan, son of Kilij Arslan I; Selchükid emir at Melitene 1107–1124: 677
Tughrul-Shāh, Mughīth-ad-Dīn, son of Kilij Arslan II; Selchükid emir at Erzerum *c.* 1201–1225: 682
Tughtigin, atabeg of Damascus 1104–1128: 662
Tunis, 25, 30, 42, 368, 512, 515–517, 581, 582, 615
Tunisia, 4, 17, 18, 22–24, 26–28, 30–32, 511–517, 749, 762; Christians of, *see* Afāriqah; "king" of, 33, *and see* Ḥafṣids
Tunisian crusade (1270), 256, 368, 509–517, 581, 615, 749, 762
Tūrān-Shāh, al-Mu'aẓẓam Fakhr-ad-Dīn, son of Saladin; Aiyūbid prince (d. 1260), 708, 713, 714
Tūrān-Shāh, al-Mu'aẓẓam, son of aṣ-Ṣāliḥ Aiyūb: 489, 496, 498, 708, 738; Aiyūbid sultan of Egypt and ruler of Damascus and Baalbek 1249–1250: 502, 503, 505, 615, 711, 712, 739–741, 761
Turcopoles, eastern light cavalry, 35, 388, 424, 603, 620
Turenne, viscount of, *see* Raymond
Turkān Khātūn, wife of Tökush (d. *c.* 1232), 671
Turkestan, 690, 719; *see also* Central Asia
Turkey, xxi, 675, 676, 684, 685
Turkish language, transliteration and nomenclature, xxi
Turkomans, Turkic people, 712, 718, 720, 740; in Central Asia, 669; in Persia, 662, 720; in Mesopotamia, 665, 680; in Syria, 705, 710, 756; in Cilicia, 643, 653, 655; in Anatolia, 643, 644, 662, 674, 676, 678, 680, 681, 684–691, 725–732; in Georgia, 664
Turks, Altaic people, xviii, 10, 127, 390, 661–692, 716, 724, 732; and third crusade, 51, 52, 73–79, 102, 110–113; mercenaries, 102, 247, 253, 254; mamluks, 706, 712, 736, 738, 740, 757; in Cilicia, 632, 634, 636, 638, 641, 658; *and see* Ottomans, Selchükids, Turkomans
Turnham, *see* Robert, Stephen
Turun-Tai, Egyptian emir (d. 1290), 753, 754; son of, 754
Tuscany, 355, 362, 364, 435, 627, 628; bankers in, 365, 371; communes of, 549; count of, 108; crusaders from, 350, 366, 594
Tusculum, cardinal-bishops of, *see* Nicholas, James of Vitry, Odo of Châteauroux

Two Sicilies, kingdom, 8, 33; *see also* Sicily, Naples
Tyre: under Franks 1124–1189: 38, 39, 46, 47, 51, 52, 55, 96, 165, 645, 759; 1189–1225: 65–68, 71, 78, 80–82, 85, 115, 120, 121, 158 note, 161, 381, 523–525, 530, 536, 759; 1225–1243: 442, 477, 489, 542, 548–551, 553, 554, 557, 613, 761; 1243–1291: 554, 559, 560, 568–571, 577, 580, 581, 585, 588–590, 598, 607 note, 617, 762; archbishops of, *see* William, Joscius, Simon, Giles, Peter of Sargines, Bonnacorso; lady of, *see* Margaret 1284–1291; lords of, *see* Philip of Montfort 1243–1270, John 1270–1283, Humphrey 1283–1284
Tzacones, Greek people, 253
Tzurulum, 220, 222, 226

Ubald (Lanfranchi), archbishop of Pisa 1176–1208, papal legate on third crusade, 66, 69
Ugolino (de' Conti de Segni), cardinal-deacon 1198–1206, cardinal-bishop of Ostia 1206–1227: 435, *and see* Gregory IX
Uj (Turkish, marchland), 676, 680, 681, 687, 729
Ukraine, 717
Ulrich (of Andechs-Diessen), bishop of Passau 1215–1221: 423
Ulrich, cousin of Adalbert of Dillingen; count of Kyburg 1180–1231: 92, 93
Ulrich II, duke of Carinthia 1181–1202: 120
al-'Umarī, Egyptian official and traveler (d. 1348), 732
'Uqailids, Arab dynasty at Mosul 990–1096: 663
Urban II (Odo of Lagery), pope 1088–1099: 6, 126, 154, 344
Urban III (Hubert Crivelli), pope 1185–1187: 759
Urban IV (James Pantaléon, patriarch of Jerusalem 1255–1261), pope 1261–1264: 253–255, 358, 363–365, 371, 569, 570, 761
Uroš II, Primislav, župan of Rascia 1140–1151, 1152–1156: 131
Ursinus (possibly Ōshin I), Armenian lord of Adana, 633
Usāmah, 'Izz-ad-Dīn, emir of Beirut (to 1197), 530, 531, 695
Utrecht: bishop of, 389; diocese of, 381
Uzbeg, Muẓaffar-ad-Dīn, brother of Abū-Bakr; atabeg of Azerbaijan 1210–1225: 672
Uzès, bishop of, 297

Vacqueyras, *see* Rambald
Vahka, 633, 634, 637, 638, 641
Ṿahram, castellan of Corycus, 540, 651 note; wife of, *see* Alice (Ṛoupenid)
Vaison (-la-Romaine), bishop of, *see* Rambald
Valania, 558, 589, 703
Valence, 287, 305, *and see* Bernard
Valenciennes, 268
Valois, count of, 270, 371, 372
Van, Lake, 663, 672, 683
Varangian guard, 179
Vardar river, 191, 192, 205, 206, 213
Varennes (-sur-Allier), *see* Florent
Váres, Cape, 395
Ṿasil, Armenian lord of Partzapert, 639
Ṿasil, son of constable Sempad; Heṭoumid commander (in 1266), 654
Vaspurkan, 633; king of, 630
Vatatzes, *see* John III Ducas
Vatonda, 257
Velestinon, 238
Veligosti: barons of, *see* William de la Roche, James de la Roche, Reginald de la Roche; barony of, 250
Venaissin, 309
Vendôme, 330, 336; count of, 493
Venice, 38, 132, 150, 155, 159–170, 173, 175, 194, 206, 208, 221, 225, 229, 231, 235, 238, 334, 387; crusaders from, 88, 150, 168, 173–176, 179–184, 187, 232, 363, 412, 427, 596, 760; doges of, *see* Peter of Pola 1130–1148, Vitale Michiele II 1156–1173, Enrico Dandolo *c.* 1193–1205, Peter Ziani 1205–1229, Jacob Tiepolo 1229–1249, Renier Zeno 1252–1268; government (signoria) of, 8, 10, 14, 22, 104, 131, 136–139, 146, 157 note, 163, 164, 166, 168, 172, 173, 182–184, 190, 191, 193, 204, 208, 212, 217, 230, 239, 240, 245, 246, 249, 253–255, 260, 369, 511, 512, 549, 568, 570, 591, 621 note, 760; in Latin empire, 189–191, 193–199, 203, 204, 213, 214, 220, 222, 227, 229–232; merchants from, 225, 582; in Byzantine empire: 132, 138, 139, 144, 162, 185, 622; in Cilicia: 650, 655; in Cyprus: 622; in Frankish Greece: 243, 251; in Syria: 381, 548, 553, 559, 560, 568–570, 572, 579, 582, 585, 588, 590, 592, 593, 615, 698; ships from, 9, 53, 96, 109, 125, 142, 161–163, 178, 179, 181, 184, 208, 218, 219, 221, 222, 231, 238, 243, 254, 257, 260, 368, 387, 569, 592, 597, 760; trade with, 14, 697; treaty of (1177), 33, 137; vassals of, 239, 243
Verden, bishop of, *see* Rudolph
Verdun, diocese of, 510
Verissa, 215, *and see* Pinarhisar
Veroli, 438, 447
Verona, 168, 438, 450; *and see* Boniface, Felicia, Gilbert, Grapella, William (2); council of (1184), 282; crusaders from, 208, 238
Vervaena, 264
Vexin, 48
Vézelay, 12, 49, 56–58, 60, 759
Via Egnatia, road, 3

Vicenza, 256
Victor IV (Octavian, count of Tusculum), anti-pope 1159–1164: 137, 346
Vienna, 93
Vienne, 305, 335, 364
Vieste, 29
Villani, John, Italian chronicler (d. 1348), 273
Villehardouin, *see* Geoffrey (3), Isabel, William
Villiers (-le-Bel), *see* John
Vitale Michiele II, doge of Venice 1156–1173: 139
Viterbo, 11, 255, 450; treaty of (1267), 255, 256, 258–263, 367
Vitré, lord of, 469
Vitry (-en-Artois), *see* James
Vizya, 215, 226
Vlachia, 106, 147, 219; *see also* Wallachia
Vlachs, Italic people, 147, 204, 206, 219; and third crusade, 97, 98, 100, 102, 105, 107, 109; king of, 213, 218
Voden, 102
Vogt (German, advocate), 93
Vohburg, margrave of, 92, 93
Vöhringen, count of, *see* Henry
Voleron, 228
Volga river, 717, 723; valley of, 748
Volos, Gulf of, 192, 257
Vostitsa: baron of, 259, 261, 264; barony of, 250
Vukan, son of Stephen Nemanya; pretender in Montenegro 1204–1205: 149

Waldensian heresy, heretics, 279, 327 note
Wallachia, *see* Vlachia
Walram IV, son of Henry III; duke of Limburg 1221–1226: 444
Walram I of Nassau, cousin of Rupert; count 1167–1198: 92
Walter (Cornuti), archbishop of Sens 1222–1241: 467
Walter (Gray), archbishop of York 1216–1255: 483
Walter, stepson of Aymar of Lairon; constable of Cyprus, lord of Caesarea 1213–1229: 409, 609; wife of, *see* Margaret of Ibelin
Walter III, son of Erard II; count of Brienne 1189–1205: 346, 347
Walter IV, son of Walter III; count of Brienne 1205–1250, count of Jaffa *c.* 1221–1250: 472, 473, 475, 476, 484, 552, 562–564; son of, 571, 606; wife of, *see* Mary of Lusignan
Walter V, son of Hugh and Isabel; count of Brienne and Lecce 1296–1311, duke of Athens 1309–1311: 269, 271, 274, 762; wife of, *see* Joan (of Châtillon)
Walter Map, English official and chronicler (d. *c.* 1208), 327 note
Walter of Avesnes, crusader from Hainault, 389, 394, 471
Walter of Châtillon, son-in-law of Hugh IV; count of St. Pol 1205–1219: 287, 289
Walter of Coutances, archbishop of Rouen 1184–1207: 54, 58, 61, 79
Walter of Florence, bishop of Acre 1208–1216: 536
Walter of Liedekerke, Frankish captain, 264
Walter of Montbéliard, regent of Cyprus 1205–1210 (d. *c.* 1212), 537, 605; wife of, *see* Burgundia of Lusignan
Walter of Palear (Pagliara), chancellor of Sicily, bishop of Catania 1207–1232: 427, 436
Walter II of Rosières, baron of Matagrifon 1259?–1276?: 258
Walter "Pennenpié", imperial governor of Jerusalem (d. 1244), 484, 552
Waqf (Arabic, endowment), 731
Warner "the German" (of Egisheim), co-bailie of Jerusalem 1229–1229: 460, 546
Waverley, annals of, 402 note
Wazīr (Arabic, vizir), 26
Welf VI of Bavaria, duke of Spoleto (d. 1191), 10
Welfs, German dynasty, 136, 432, 450, *and see* Henry XII (of Saxony), Henry IV (of Brunswick), Otto, Welf; *see also* Guelfs
Wendover, *see* Roger
Weser river, 340
Westphalia, 330, 381
Wied, counts of, *see* Dietrich, George
Wierich of Daun, German knight, 238
Wiesenbach, *see* Godfrey
Wilbrand II, count of Hallermund 1163–1190: 92, 115
Wilbrand of Oldenburg, German traveler, bishop of Paderborn 1225–1228, of Utrecht 1228–1234: 621, 650
William, abbot of Cluny (*c.* 1212), 295 note
William (Amanieu, of Geniès), archbishop of Bordeaux 1207–1227: 287 note, 403
William (of Broue), archbishop of Narbonne 1245–1257: 490 note
William, brother of Henry I of Champagne; archbishop of Rheims 1176–1202, regent of France 1190–1191: 54, 57, 70
William, archbishop of Tyre 1174–*c.* 1187, historian, 21, 47
William, archdeacon of Paris, 304, 326
William, Benedictine monk, 331
William (of Beaumont), bishop of Angers 1202–1240: 403
William (of Carvaillon), bishop of Cahors 1208–1234: 293
William (Brewer), bishop of Exeter 1224–1244: 445, 542
William (of Auvergne), bishop of Paris 1228–1248: 348
William II, count of Chalon 1166–1203: 53
William I, son of Florent III; count of Holland 1204–1222: 395
William II, grandson of William I; count of

Holland 1234–1256, king in Germany 1247–1256: 355–360
William II, count of Joigny (d. 1255), 469
William, son of Roger Borsa; duke of Apulia 1111–1127: 7, 10 note
William (de Albini, III), earl of Arundel and Sussex 1196–1221: 417
William ("Longsword"), nephew of Richard I of England; heir to earldom of Salisbury 1226–1250: 482, 483, 499
William I, son of Roger II; king of Sicily 1154–1166: 9 note, 29–32, 136, 137
William II, son of William I; king of Sicily 1166–1189: 32–42, 58, 59, 759; and Byzantium, 36, 37, 104, 118, 119, 137, 138, 141, 149; and the third crusade, 5, 38–41, 47; wife of, *see* Joan (Plantagenet)
William (of Antioch), grandson of Bohemond III; lord of Botron (d. 1244), 563
William, lord of Chantilly, 469
William, lord of Quṣair (d. *c.* 1275), 578
William III ("the Old"), marquis of Montferrat 1135–1188: 46, 164
William IV, son of Boniface II; marquis of Montferrat 1207–1225: 206–208, 212, 214, 215, 382
William, patriarch of Jerusalem 1262–1270: 580
William (of Champagne), Tripolitan clerk, 478
William (of Rochefoucauld), viscount of Châtellerault, 50
William de Ferrers, earl of Derby (d. 1190), 50, 51
William de la Roche, brother of Guy I of Athens; baron of Veligosti 1256–1264?: 246
William de la Roche, son of Guy I; duke of Athens 1280–1287, bailie of Achaea 1285–1287: 252, 259, 261, 263, 265; wife of, *see* Helena Angelina Comnena
William II de Mandeville, earl of Essex and count of Aumale 1180–1189: 49
William Embriaco, son of Bertrand (d. 1282), 587, 591
William Farabel (of Le Puy), Antiochene knight, 540
William fitz Ralph, seneschal of Normandy, 79
William Jordan, archdeacon of Conflans, 307
William Longchamp, bishop of Ely 1189–1197, justiciar to Richard I, 54, 79
William "Longsword", son of William III of Montferrat; count of Jaffa and Ascalon 1176–1177: 164; wife of, *see* Sibyl (of Jerusalem)
William of Beaujeu, master of the Temple 1273–1291: 585, 587, 588, 590–592, 594, 595, 597, 655; secretary of, 598 note
William I of Champlitte, son of Odo; viscount of Dijon, prince of Achaea 1205–1209: 237, 239, 760
William (of Le Puiset, vicegerent) of Chartres, master of the Temple 1210–1219: 383, 389, 397, 537, 609
William of Châteauneuf, master of the Hospital 1243–1258: 561–563
William of Fors (or "of Oléron"), Poitevin lord, 56, 58
William of Gibelet (Jubail), second cousin of Guy I Embriaco; crusaders (d. before 1243), 426
William of Les Barres, Poitevin knight, 60, 61, 74
William of Nangis, French historian (d. 1300), 369
William of Posquères, merchant at Marseilles, 339
William of Puylaurens, notary to bishops of Toulouse, chronicler (d. after 1272), 277 note, 310, 313, 317 note, 320, 321
William of Rubrouck, Dominican missionary (d. 1270), 722
William of Sonnac, master of the Temple 1247–1250: 614
William of Tudela, Spanish chronicler (d. after 1213), 277 note, 285, 286, 292, 293, 300 note
William I (dalle Carceri) of Verona, hexarch, then triarch of central Euboea 1216–1263, titular king of Thessalonica 1243–1263: 245
William II (dalle Carceri) of Verona, son of William I; triarch of central Euboea 1263–1275: 256, 257
William II of Villehardouin, son of Geoffrey I: 240; prince of Achaea 1246–1278: 226–228, 243–249, 252–259, 261, 262, 272–274, 761, 762; wives of, 244, *and see* Carintana dalle Carceri, Anna Angelina Comnena
William Porcus, Genoese admiral, 336–339
William I Sanudo, son of Marco II; duke of the Archipelago 1303–1323: 271, 272
William the Breton, French chronicler (d. 1226), 380
Winchester, bishop of, 445, 542
Wittelsbach, *see* Conrad
Wolfger (of Ellenbrechtskirchen), bishop of Passau 1191–1204 (d. 1218), 120
Wöltingerode, count of, *see* Burkhard
Worms, 119, 444
Würzburg: bishop of, 90–93, 105, 115; diet at (1196), 119

Yaghi-Basan, Niẓām-ad-Dīn, son of Gümüshtigin Ghāzī; Dānishmendid emir at Sebastia 1140–1164: 677, 678
Yaḥyâ, son of al-'Azīz; Ḥammādid emir at Bougie 1121–1152: 22
Yaḥyâ, son of Tamīm; Zīrid emir at Mahdia 1108–1116: 18–20
Ya'qūb, Selchükid general (d. 1154), 639
Yasak (Turkish, law), 716
Yāzūr, 77

Ye-liu Ta-shi, Gur-Khan of the Kara-Kitai (d. 1142), prototype of "Prester John", 669
Yellow Sea, 508
Yemen, 449, 693 note, 708; rulers of, *see* Aiyūbids (1174–1229)
Yolanda, daughter of Baldwin V of Hainault; 2nd wife of Latin emperor Peter 1193–1219, empress of Romania 1217–1219: 212–214
Yolanda of Courtenay, daughter of Latin emperor Peter and Yolanda; 2nd wife of Andrew II of Hungary 1215–1233: 213
Yolanda of Montferrat ("Irene"), granddaughter of Boniface III; 2nd wife of Andronicus II Palaeologus 1285–1316: 266
York, archbishops of, 79, 483
Yorkshire, 46
Yūnus Emre, Turkish poet (d. after 1300), 732
Yūsuf, governor of Gabes (d. 1147), 24
Yūsuf, son of ʿAbd-al-Muʾmin; Muwaḥḥid caliph 1163–1184: 32

Zaccaria, Benedict, Genoese admiral, 591, 592
Zagros mountains, 663, 668
az-Ẓāhir Ghāzī, Ghiyāth-ad-Dīn, son of Saladin; Aiyūbid governor of Aleppo 1186–1193, ruler 1193–1216: 526, 528, 533, 534, 536, 537, 540, 649, 683, 693–698; wife of, *see* Ḍaifah Khātūn
Zante, 239; count of, 265, 272
Zara, 168, 172–176, 180, 289, 387, 760
Zaraca, 252
Zaratovo, bishop of, 252
Zawila, 26, 31; archbishop (?) of, 31
Zeitounion, 259, 271
Zeitz, bishops of, 120, 389
Zengi, Imād-ad-Dīn, Turkish ruler in Mosul and Syria 1127–1146: 11, 133, 134, 662
Zengids, Turkish dynasty at Aleppo 1128–1183 and Mosul 1127–1234: 662, 674, 694–696, 700, 759, *and see* Zengi 1127–1146, Nūr-ad-Dīn Maḥmūd 1146–1174, ʿIzz-ad-Dīn Masʿūd 1180–1193, ʿImād-ad-Dīn Zengi II
Zeno, *see* Marino, Renier
Zeta, 127, 131
Zīrī, Berber chieftain (d. 972?), 17
Zīrids, Berber dynasty in Tunisia 972–1148: 17–20, 23–25, 27 note, *and see* Zīrī, al-Muʿizz 1016–1062, Tamīm 1062–1108, Yaḥyâ 1108–1116, ʿAlī 1116–1121, al-Ḥasan 1121–1148
Zirʿīn, 574